American Government and Politics in the New Millennium

Eleventh Edition

American Government and Politics in the New Millennium

Eleventh Edition

Virginia Stowitts Traina
Palo Alto College
San Antonio, Texas

Christine Schultz
Santa Monica College
Santa Monica, California

Abigail Press   **Wheaton, IL 60189**

Design and Production: Abigail Press
Typesetting: Abigail Press
Typeface: AGaramond
Cover Art: Sam Tolia

**American Government and Politics
in the New Millennium**

Eleventh Edition, 2021
Printed in the United States of America
Translation rights reserved by the authors
ISBN 1-890919-09-8
      978-1-890919-09-2

Contents in Brief

Chapter One
    Constitutional Government   1

Chapter Two
    Federalism   30

Chapter Three
    Political Socialization and Public Opinion   60

Chapter Four
    Political Parties   92

Chapter Five
    Campaigns and Elections   126

Chapter Six
    The Media   168

Chapter Seven
    Interest Groups   200

Chapter Eight
    The Congress   230

Chapter Nine
    The Bureaucracy   262

Chapter Ten
    The Presidency and Leadership   290

Chapter Eleven
    The Federal Court System   332

Chapter Twelve
    Civil Liberties   366

Chapter Thirteen
    Civil Rights   408

Chapter Fourteen
    Public Policy   468

Chapter Fifteen
    Social Services   508

Chapter Sixteen
    The Environment   544

Chapter Seventeen
    Foreign Policy   584

Appendix   625
Glossary   649
Index   675

Table of Contents

Chapter One
Constitutional Government   1

  Theories of Government and Constitutionalism   2
    Is Government Necessary?   2
    Is Government a Social Contract?   4
    Democracy   5
    Constitutionalism   7
  The Framer's Challenge—Creating a Constitutional Government   9
    The Seeds of Discontent   9
    The Articles of Confederation   12
    The Gathering at Philadelphia—The Convention Setting   15
    The Gathering at Philadelphia—The Convention Charge   16
    The Gathering at Philadelphia—Designing a New Government   19
    Titles of Nobility   24
    Amending the Document   25
  Ratification and Adoption   26
    The Ratification Process   26
    Federalists versus Anti-Federalists   26
    Conclusions   27
  Chapter Notes   27
  Suggested Readings   29

Chapter Two
Federalism   30

  Types of Intergovernmental Relationships   36
    Why a Federal System?   37
    Constitutionally Mandated Intergovernmental Relationships—Vertical
      Federalism   38
    Constitutionally Mandated Intergovernmental Relationships—Horizontal
      Federalism   42

Federalism and the Federal Courts   43
States' Rights v National Power   47
The Changing Faces of Federalism   50
Federal Grant Programs   53
    Rising Interstate Conflicts   56
The Future of Federalism   56
Chapter Notes   57
Suggested Readings   59

Chapter Three
Political Socialization and Public Opinion   60

Public Culture   63
    Political Sub-Cultures   65
The Political Socialization Process   68
The Agents of Political Socialization   70
    The Family Environment   70
    Religious Affiliations   71
    Education   71
    Race/Ethnic Orientation   73
    Peer Groups   74
    Social Class/Income Level   74
    Direct Contact   75
    The Media   76
    Major Events   77
    Trust in Government   78
Public Opinion   78
Measuring Public Opinion—A Scientific Approach   80
    Selecting the Sampling Pool   81
    Formulating the Questions   82
Types of Survey Instruments   83
    Predicting Election Results—Bellwether Districts 83
    The Straw Poll   84
    The Phone or Personal Interview   84
    The Mail-in Questionnaire   85
    Internet Surveys   86
    Conclusion   86
Chapter Notes   88
Suggested Readings   91

Chapter Four
Political Parties   92

   The Anatomy of a Political Party   95
      Historical Development of Political Parties   96
      Party Systems   97
   The Political Spectrum   99
      Conservatism—The Right of the Spectrum   99
      Moderates—The Center of the Spectrum   101
      Liberalism—The Left of the Spectrum   101
      Ideological Versus Issue Base Parties   104
   American Political Parties   105
      Historical Development   105
      The Modern Republican Party   108
      The Modern Democratic Party   109
      American Third Party Movements   110
      Factions Within the American Party Organizations   110
      Organizational Structure of American Political Parties   114
      The National Party Organization   115
      The State Party Organization   120
      County/District Organization   121
      Precincts   121
      Conclusion   121
   Chapter Notes   123
   Suggested Readings   125

Chapter Five
Campaigns and Elections   126

   Nominating the Candidates   128
      Historical Background   128
      The Caucus System   129
      The Primary System   129
      The Entitlement Revolution   130
      Special Interests and the Nominating Conventions   132
      Independent and Third-Party Nominees   133
      Nominations for Congress and State Offices   133
   The General Elections   135
      House Elections   135
         Single-Member Plurality Elections   135
         Criticisms of the Single-Member System   137
      Senate Elections   138
   Presidential Elections   138
      The Electoral College   138
      Abolish the Electoral College?   141
   Campaigning in the General Election   142

The Political Context 142
Financing Campaigns 142
    How Much Campaigns Cost 142
    Where Does the Money Come From? 143
    Regulating Campaign Finance 143
    The Bipartisan Campaign Reform Act of 2002 144
    Legal Challenges to BCRA 145
Loopholes in the 2002 Campaign Finance Reform 145
    Soft Money to State Political Parties 145
    The 527 and 501c Organizations and Independent Expenditures 146
    Issue-Related Advertisements 147
    Bundling 148
Effects of the American Campaign Finance System 149
    The Incumbency Advantage 149
    Selling Access and Influence 149
    Weakening the Role of the Political Parties 150
    A Weakening of the Public Finance System 150
    Increased Number of Personally Wealthy Candidates 151
    Raising Campaign Money: A Distraction 151
    Abuse and Scandals: The Case of the Big Pharma 152
Money and Campaigns: Prognosis for the Future 152
Campaign Strategies and Tactics 153
    Polling 153
    Making the News 153
    The Tabloids 154
    Advertising 154
    Internet, Social Media, and High Tech Campaigning 155
    The Mechanics of Elections 156
        Hacking in the 2016 Election 156
        The Pandemic and the 2020 Election Mechanics 156
Political Participation in Elections: The Waxing and Waning of the
American Electorate 157
    The Waxing of the American Electorate 157
    The Waning of the American Electorate 158
    The 2020 Election Turnout 159
    Explaining Turnout 159
    Increasing Turnout 160
The Voters: Explaining Vote Choice 161
    Long-Term Forces: Group and Party Identification 161
    Short-Term Forces: Issues and Candidate Image 162
        Issues 162
        Candidate Image 163
The 2020 Presidential Election 163
    Conclusion 163
Chapter Notes 164
Suggested Readings 166

Chapter Six
The Media   168

Democracy and the Mass Media   170
   The Structure of the Mass Media   170
      Books   170
      Magazines   171
      Newspapers   171
      Television   171
      Radio   172
      Records   172
      Motion Pictures   172
      The Internet   172
      Social Media   173
   Government Regulation of the Media   173
      Technical and Ownership Regulation   174
      Regulation of Content   175
   Political Functions of the Mass Media   176
      Entertainment   177
      Surveillance   177
      Interpretation   177
      Watchdog   177
      Socialization   178
      Persuasion and Propaganda   178
      Agenda Setting   178
The Increased Importance of the Modern Mass Media   178
   A Pervasive News Media   179
   An Autonomous Press   179
      Phase I: The Early Partisan Press   179
      Phase II: The Penny Press and Yellow Journalism   180
      Phase III: Investigative Journalism   182
      Phase IV: Conglomerate Ownership of the Press   182
      Phase V: Atomization of the Media   183
      Phase VI: Citizen Journalism, Robot Journalism   183
The News Gathering Process   184
   Personal Background and Values   184
   Professional Values   185
   Organizational Factors   186
The Content of the News: Informational Biases   186
   The Bias Debate   186
   Informational Biases   187
      Infotainment   187
      Negativity   187
Coverage of Campaigns   188
   The Horserace   188
   Gaffes   188

Coverage of the Incumbent 188
Coverage of the President 189
Coverage of Congress 189
The Politicians Respond: The Management of News Coverage 190
Shorter Campaign Speeches 190
Spin Control 190
Debates 191
Political Advertisements 191
The Effects of the Mass Media 193
What People Remember and Know 193
Influencing Public Opinion 193
Setting the Political Agenda 193
Cynicism, Alienation, and Declining Efficacy 194
Behavior 194
Conclusion 194
Chapter Notes 195
Suggested Readings 198

Chapter Seven
Interest Groups 200

Defining Interest Groups 202
Interest Groups versus Political Parties 202
The Roles of Interest Groups 203
Representation 203
Political Participation 203
Education 203
Agenda Building 203
Program Monitoring 203
Who is Organized? 204
Economic Interest Groups 204
Business Groups 204
Organized Labor 205
Agriculture 206
Professional Associations 206
Citizen Groups 206
Women's Groups 206
Religious Groups 207
LBGQT 207
The Elderly 208
Environmental Groups 208
Single-Issue Groups 209
Foreign Governments 209
The Internet 209
Government Interest Groups 210

Common Features of Interest Groups   210
Biases in Interest Group Formation and Maintenance   211
   Obstacles to Interest Group Formation   211
   Overcoming the Obstacles Through Interest Group Maintenance   212
   Interest Group Bias   213
The Proliferation of Interest Groups   214
   Sources of Interest Group Proliferation   215
      Increased Government Regulation   215
      Postindustrial Changes and Public Interest Groups   216
      Interest Group Friendly Laws and Actions   216
      Cheaper Forms of Communication   217
      The Rise of Single-Issue Groups   217
Interest Group Methods and Strategies   217
   Electioneering and Political Action Committees   217
      The Creation of Political Action Committees   218
      Super PACs   218
      The Effects of PACs and Campaign Contributions   219
   Direct, or Inside, Lobbying   220
      Providing Information   220
      The Effects of Direct Lobbying   221
      Regulating Lobbying   223
   The Newest Trend in Lobbying: Supreme Court Nominations   223
   Grassroots, or Outside, Lobbying: Going Public   224
   Litigating   224
   Bribery   225
   Prospects for Reform   226
   Conclusion   226
Chapter Notes   226
Suggested Readings   229

Chapter Eight
The Congress   230

The Origin and Powers of Congress   232
   The Constitution and the Great Compromise   232
   The Powers of the House and Senate   233
      The Expressed Powers   233
      The Implicit Power   234
   The Ebb and Flow of Congressional Powers   234
   The Era of Divided Government   235
Representation in Congress   236
   Theories of Representation   236
      The Instructed-Delegate View of Representation   236
      The Trustee View of Representation   236
      The Politico View of Representation   236

The Quality of Congressional Representation 237
 Descriptive Representation 237
 Constituent Ties 238
Congressional Elections 240
 Congressional Reapportionment 240
 Redistricting and Gerrymandering 240
 Racial Gerrymandering and "Minority-Majority" Districts 241
 Candidates for Congress 241
 The Costs of Congressional Campaigns 242
 The Real but Declining Advantages of Incumbency 242
Campaign Finance and Incumbency 243
The Issue of Term Limits 243

The Organizational Structures of Congress 244
The Formal Leadership of Congress: The Political Parties 244
 Leadership in the House 244
 Leadership in the Senate 245
The Role of Money in Choosing Congressional Leadership 245
Party Discipline 245

The Committee and Subcommittee System 246
The Work of Committees: Legislation and Oversight 246
The Committee System in the Era of Divided Government 247
Types of Congressional Committees 248
 Standing Committees 248
 Select Committees 248
 Joint Committees 249
 Conference Committees 249
 The House Rules Committee 249
Committee Membership 249
Committee and Subcommittee Chairs 249
The Staff System 250
The Caucuses 251

The Legislative Process 251
Step One: The Bill is Introduced 251
Step Two: The Bill is Assigned to Committee 252
Step Three: Floor Action 253
Step Four: The Conference Committee 254
Step Five: The President 254
Step Six: Oversight 255
Conclusion 257

Chapter Notes 258
Suggested Readings 260

Chapter Nine
The Bureaucracy   262

The Development of the Bureaucratic State   265
Constitutional Beginnings   265
The Progressive Movement   265
The New Deal and Social Welfare Legislation   266
World War II   266
The Great Society and the Entitlements Revolution   267
Lobbying by Administrators   267
Ronald Reagan and Deregulation   267
Privatization of the Bureaucracy   269
Recent Changes in Size of the Bureaucracy   270
The Functions of the Bureaucratic State   272
National Maintenance   272
Clientele Services   272
Regulation   272
Redistribution of Resources   272
The Organization of the Federal Bureaucracy   273
Cabinet Departments   273
Independent Agencies   273
Regulatory Agencies or Commissions   274
Government Corporations   275
Who are the Bureaucrats?   275
A Bureaucracy of Gentlemen   275
The Spoils System   275
The Civil Service   275
Changes in the Demographic Composition of the Bureaucracy   276
Presidential Appointees   276
Where are the Bureaucrats?   276
What Bureaucracies Do   277
Policy Development   277
Rule Administration   277
Rule Making and Regulation   278
Rule Adjudication   278
Litigation   278
Program Evaluation   279
The Political Resources of the Federal Bureaucracy   279
Authority   279
Administrative Discretion   279
Expertise   279
Clientele Support   280
How Bureaucracies Make Decisions   281
The Rational-Comprehensive Model   281
The Incremental Model of Bureaucratic Decision-Making   281
Bureaucratic Accountability   282

Presidential Control over the Bureaucracy   282
Congressional Control over the Bureaucracy   283
Judicial Oversight of the Bureaucracy   284
Iron Triangles and Issue Networks   284
Reform and Reorganization   285
Benefits of Bureaucracy   286
Managing Complexity   286
Stability and Predictability   286
Conclusion   286
Chapter Notes   287
Suggested Readings   289

Chapter Ten
The Presidency and Leadership   290
Qualifications For the Presidency   293
Terms of Office   294
The Powers of the Presidency   295
The Executive/Legislative Relationship   295
Enumerated Constitutional Duties   298
Appointments   298
Commander in Chief and Warmaking   303
Pardons and Reprieves   305
Addressing Congress   306
Calling Special Sessions of Congress   307
The Creative Tools of the Presidency   307
Veto Authority   308
Executive Agreements versus Treaties   309
Executive Orders   312
Signing Statements   314
Executive Privilege   315
Presidential Immunity   315
Political Persuasion   316
Removal From Office   317
Temporary Removal   317
Impeachment   318
Threats Against the President   321
The Secret Service   324
The Vice President   324
Conclusions—Do We Have an Imperial Presidency   327
Chapter Notes   328
Suggested Readings   331

Chapter Eleven
The Federal Court System   332

Law—The Guiding Principle of Justice   334
    Codification of Law   335
The Terminology and Process of the Justice System   337
The Federal Justice System   342
    The United States Attorney General   342
    The Investigative Arm of the Department of Justice   343
    The Litigation Arm of the Department of Justice   345
The Federal Court System   346
    Constitutional Courts   346
    Selection of Judges   346
    Impeachment of Federal Judges   350
    Jurisdiction   351
    Federal District Courts   351
    Federal Appellate Courts   352
    The Supreme Court   353
    The Power of Judicial Review   354
    Federal Courts—Territorial Courts   360
    Federal Courts—United States Court of Appeals for Veterans Claims   360
    Federal Courts—Court of International Trade   360
    Federal Courts—The Court of Federal Claims   361
    Federal Courts—Court of Appeals for the Federal Circuit   361
    Federal Courts—United States Court of Appeals for the Armed Forces   361
The Final Arm of Justice—The Federal Prison System   362
    Conclusion   362
Chapter Notes   363
Suggested Readings   365

Chapter Twelve
Civil Liberties   366

The Concept of Civil Liberties   368
    Due Process   373
    The Importance of the First Amendment   374
       Freedom of Religion   374
       Freedom of Speech   379
       Obscenity   385
       Freedom of the Press   386
       Assembly and Association   388
    The Right to Bear Arms   392
    Protecting the Rights of the Accused   393
    Protection of Property and Privacy   401
    Conclusion   404

Chapter Notes   404
Suggested Readings   407

Chapter Thirteen
Civil Rights   408

    Civil Rights and Racism   412
    Theories of Racism   414
    Racism in America   418
    Native Americans   420
    African Americans   426
    The Hispanic Experience   440
    Gender Issues   453
    The LGBT Community   461
    Disabled Americans   462
    Conclusion   463
Chapter Notes   464
Suggested Readings   467

Chapter Fourteen
Public Policy   468

Public Policy Development   475
    Who Makes Public Policy?   478
    What is the Purpose of Public Policy?   484
    The Public Policy Process   488
        Problem Identification   488
        Agenda Building   492
        Formulation of Policy   493
        Budgeting   497
        Political Implications   500
        Adoption/selling   501
        Implementation   503
        Evaluation   504
    Conclusion   504
Chapter Notes   505
Suggested Readings   507

Chapter Fifteen
Social Services   508

    The Vocabulary of Poverty   512
      A Profile of America's Poor   516
      The Philosophy and Politics of Poverty   522
      The Historical Development of the Welfare State   526
      The Programs of the Welfare State Entitlements:
          Social Security and Unemployment Compensation   530
      Public Assistance Programs   532
      The Reform Bandwagon   534
      Welfare Reform—Is It Working?   535
      Health-care Reform   535
      Conclusion   540
    Chapter Notes   540
    Suggested Readings   543

Chapter Sixteen
The Environment   544

    Federal and State Roles in Environmental Policies   548
      The Air We Breathe   554
      Global Warming   564
      The Water We Drink   565
      Oil Spills and Toxic Wastes   569
      Superfund Programs   572
      Forest and Wetland Conservation   572
      Endangered Species   574
    Policy Options and the Political Climate   575
      Conclusion   580
    Chapter Notes   580
    Suggested Readings   583

Chapter Seventeen
Foreign Policy   584

    Foreign Policy Terminology   588
    Foreign Policy Options   591
    Foreign Policy Process   595
      The State of War   599
    Securing the Economy   602
    The Development of American Foreign Policy   603
      Constitutional Authority   603
         Commander-in-Chief and Warmaking   604

The Power to Make Treaties...608
The President's Foreign Policy Team...........................610
Brief Overview of American Foreign Policy................612
Current Foreign Policy Issues and Challenges Ahead.....615
The Far East: North Korea...616
Far East: China..617
Central and Latin America—Mexico and Cuba.........618
The Middle East..619
International Terrorism and Afghanistan......................620
Conclusion..621
Chapter Notes...621
Suggested Readings..624

Appendix
  Appendix A: Declaration of Independence.................625
  Appendix B: Constitution of the United States of America......628
  Appendix C: Presidential Elections.............................642
  Appendix D: Supreme Court Justices.........................646
Glossary...649
Index..675

Chapter One

CONSTITUTIONAL GOVERNMENT

In a 1794 speech delivered in the House of Commons, British lawmaker Edmund Burke reminded his fellow lawmakers of the reverence and awe he held for his nation's supreme law of the land—its constitution:

> Our Constitution is like our island, which uses and restrains its subject sea, in vain the waves roar. In that Constitution, I know and exultingly I feel, both that I am free; and that I am not free dangerously to myself or to others. I know that no power on earth, acting as I ought to do, can touch my life, my liberty or my property. I have that inward and dignified consciousness of my own security and independence which constitutes, and it's the only thing which does constitute, the proud and comfortable sentiment of freedom in the human beast.[1]

Burke's message is simple. A constitution protects one's freedom while at the same time provides the parameters within which members of a social structure can legally exercise their own individual freedoms without impeding upon the rights of others. A constitution, guided by the principles of democracy, guarantees one's rights to own and use one's property without undo interference from government as long as one follows the legal limits detailed in the document. Yet, a constitution is more than just a piece of paper. It is the one document that guides the governing arms of the nation state while at the same time, limits the power those governing arms exercise over those they govern. In particular, the United States Constitution is unique among her sister documents in that it definitively provides the means to prevent the usurpation of and the abuse of governing power through its application of the separation of powers doctrine coupled with a detailed system of checks and balances. This chapter analyzes the concept of constitutionalism and the impact the document has on all who govern as well as those who are governed.

As so eloquently articulated by Jean Jacques Rousseau, Charles de Montesquieu, David Hume, and, of course, John Locke, constitutions are social contracts negotiated among the members of a society or nation state to form a governing structure. They are unique documents giving one an insight into the guiding political philosophy, social structure, economic orientation, historical development, cultural perspectives, mores, folkways, and, in some instances, the religious perspectives of those who gathered at their respective tables to debate the issues and ultimately, to embody them into a constitution. Understanding the background of those who write the document gives one an insight as to how they addressed the issues they were tasked to handle. Constitutions are themselves fragile documents that oftentimes do not survive the test of time. They are not etched on stone tablets. Consequently, many nation states and in the United States, state constitutions must be revised or even completely rewritten to address changing perspectives. Thomas Jefferson once wrote that:

> Some men look at constitutions with sanctimonious reverence, and deem them like the ark of the covenant, too sacred to be touched. They ascribe to the men of the preceding age a wisdom more than human, and suppose what they did to be beyond amendment. . . . I am certainly not an advocate for frequent and untried changes in laws and constitutions. . . . But I know also, that laws and institutions must go hand and hand with the progress of the human mind. . . We might as well require a man to wear still the coat which fitted him when a boy, as civilized society to remain ever under the regimen of their barbarous ancestors.[2]

As discussed in Chapter 2, the Framers of the United States government discovered that their original design for their governing institutions simply did not work. They boldly opted to void the existing document and write a totally new constitution that they believed would stand the test of time. Before casting his vote for the new constitution, Benjamin Franklin commented to his fellow Framers that:

> when you assemble a number of men to have the advantage of their joint wisdom, you inevitably assemble with those men, all their prejudices, their passions, their errors of opinion, their local interests and their selfish views. From such an assembly, can a perfect production be expected? It therefore astonishes me, Sir, to find this system approaching so near to perfect as it does; and I think it will astonish our enemies, who are waiting with confidence to hear that our councils are confounded like those of the Builders of Babel. Thus I consent, Sir, to this Constitution, because I expect no better, and because I am not sure that it is not the best."[3]

This chapter examines both the concepts of constitutionalism as well as the development and implementation of the governing principles outlined in the United States Constitution. In addition, this chapter analyzes the ability of the current constitution to survive the test of time that for at least over two hundred years, it has remained intact with only twenty-seven major changes, ten of which were adopted and added to the document in 1791.

THEORIES OF GOVERNMENT AND CONSTITUTIONALISM

Is Government Necessary?

The question of the necessity of government has plagued political philosophers since Plato and Aristotle. In particular, Aristotle believed "that the state is a creation of nature, and that man is by nature a political animal. And he who by nature and not by mere accident, is without a state, is either a bad man or above humanity; he is like the tribeless, lawless and hearthless one."[4] By his use of the phrase "political animal," Aristotle was referring to man's innate survival instincts to take care of his wants and needs first regardless of the consequences to others. Just like the lion or the tiger, man's predatory nature seeks what he needs to survive, i.e., food, shelter, and clothing. What separates man from the beast is rational thinking and the need for emotional companionship with his fellow mankind. In his epic *The Politics*, Aristotle concluded that while beasts can live and survive in isolation from each other, man could not. Therefore,

> a social instinct is implanted on all men by nature. . . . For man, when perfected, is the best of animals, but, when separated from law and justice, he is the worst of all; since armed injustice is the more dangerous, and he is equipped at birth with arms, meant to be used by intelligence and virtue, which he may use for the worst ends. Wherefore, if he have not virtue, he is the most unholy and the most savage of animals, and the most full of lust and gluttony. But justice is the bond of men in states, for the administration of justice, which is the determination of what is just, is the principle order in a political society.[5]

Consequently, both Aristotle and Plato agreed that once men left their nomadic individualist lifestyles behind and bounded together into a society, they would out of necessity develop rules and regulations to protect themselves from each other. In turn, the society would create a higher authority to implement and enforce those rules upon the citizenry. Thus, the evolution of **government** defined as "the formal institutional structure and processes of a society by which policies are developed and implemented in the form of law binding on all."[6] Some form of government is a universal feature of any society whether it be a clan, tribe, city, nation state, or empire. Even the most rudimentary social structure had its own rules, regulations, codes, and laws enforced by some form of authority carried out either by a chieftain, a monarch, or a tribal council. The ancient civilizations of the Maya, Inca, Aztec, Egyptian, and Babylonian all had very sophisticated governing and religious institutions as well as structured social classes. A governing structure was necessary for they all realized that without it, there would be no means of providing for the common defense against internal and external attacks and no mechanism to maintain domestic order. Life would be chaotic.

Few, however, agreed that there was one preferred form or a single guiding political philosophy suitable for all. Both Plato and Aristotle wrestled with this dilemma. In *The Politics*, Aristotle employed a comparative study of different governing systems. He rationalized that while "every state is a community of some kind, and every community is established with a view to some good," it would be a mistake to conclude that there is only one accepted form of government since by necessity "governments differ in kind."[7] He subsequently classified different governing formats as either good or bad. Aristotle determined that a monarchy or rule of one was a sound-governing format as long as the monarch ruled for the benefit of his/her people. But once the monarch began to initiate laws for the benefit of himself or herself, the government flipped to its bad form—tyranny. Likewise, he believed that the rule of the few, an aristocracy, was a good government that if left unchecked, could well develop into a corrupt oligarchy. For governing structures centered on the rule of many, Aristotle envisioned the good form as a polity but he concluded that democracy was a bad form of government.

After studying various forms of governing formats, Jean Jacques Rousseau wrote in his *Confessions*: "I had seen that everything is rooted in politics and that, whatever might be attempted, no people would ever be other than the nature of their government made them. So the great question of the best possible government seemed to me to reduce itself to this: 'What is the nature of the government best fitted to create the most virtuous, the most enlightened, the wisest, and in fact, the best people, taking the word 'best' in its highest sense?'"[8] Consequently, Rousseau entertained the concept of **self-determination**, that is, "the aspiration of some group—grounded in some existing sentiment of national or racial identity associated with common territory, language or religion—to form its own sovereign state and to govern itself."[9] It was, therefore, left up to the people of a given state to determine for themselves both the rules they wished to follow and the format of their governing institutions.

Plato focused more on the person or persons heading a government rather than on the form of the governing system. As a young man, he was disillusioned by Athens's defeat in the Peloponnesian War to their archenemies the Spartans. Consequently, Athenian democracy was replaced by a Spartan oligarchical government that was eventually overthrown and replaced by, once again, a democratic form. However, both the ruling oligarchy and the re-emergent democratic government failed the Athenian people. A frustrated Plato lamented, "I kept waiting for favorable moments, and finally saw clearly in regard to all states now existing that without exception their system of government is bad. Their constitutions are almost beyond redemption except through some miraculous plan accompanied by good luck."[10] He concluded that the problem with the Athenian government was not its format but the people running it. In *The Republic*, Plato wrote, "existing cities are hopelessly corrupt and must remain so unless they can be rescued from their plight by philosophic rulers, i.e., if their kings become philosophers, or philosophers became kings."[11] He concluded that "the human race will not see better days until either the stock of those who rightly and genuinely follow philosophy acquire political authority, or else the class who have political control be led by some dispensation of providence to become real philosophers."[12] However, Plato would echo the same distrust that James Madison and his contemporaries expressed in Philadelphia about the fear that if left unchecked, the statesman no matter how virtuous he may be, could be easily swayed towards corruption. Plato's solution was to populate his "Just City" with three distinct classes—the rulers or philosopher kings, the auxiliaries or the military, and everyone else known as the productive class. Together, the philosopher kings and the auxiliaries would form the guardians who would watch over the people, but more importantly watch over each other. Perhaps, Plato should be renamed as the Father of Checks and Balances!

Is Government a Social Contract?

The Enlightenment philosophers including Charles de Montesquieu, John Locke, and Jean Jacques Rousseau collectively went a step further. They rationalized that in the state of nature, man had the absolute and fundamental right to life, liberty, and property. However, when men decided to collectively form a society, they had to give up their absolute natural rights in order to form a governing body that would indeed protect their rights to life, liberty and property for the benefit of the entire society, not just for the lone individual. "Thus in spite of the great advantage of living free under the law of nature, people will see that they would be better off in a civil society under government.

The main impediment to peace and safety in the state of nature is an absence of clear standards of conduct, which can be applied impartially, and effectively enforced. Each person will accordingly agree to surrender the right to enforce the law of nature. Though this is a renunciation, it actually increases everyone's rights. Without this renunciation, no rights are secure in a conflict-ridden, precarious state of nature."[13] The collectivity of the bond was a **social contract**. The contract of-tentimes known as a constitution should not be taken lightly because it is the cement that holds a citizenry together to both each other and to their governing institutions. In his *Reflections on the Revolution in France*, Edmund Burke emphasized the importance of this relationship:

> Society is indeed a contract. Subordinate contracts for objects of mere occasional interest may be dissolved at pleasure—but the state ought not to be considered as nothing better than a partnership agreement in a trade of pepper and coffee, calico, or tobacco, or some other such low concern, to be taken up for a temporary interest, and to be dissolved by the fancy of the parties. It is to be looked on with other reverence, because it is not a partner-ship in things subservient only to the gross animal existence of a temporary and perishable nature. It is a partnership in all science; a partnership in all art; a partnership in every virtue and in all perfection. As the ends of such a partnership cannot be obtained in many generations, it becomes a partnership not only between those who are living, but between those who are living, those who are dead, and those who are to be born. Each contract of each particular state is but a clause in the great primeval contract of eternal society, linking the lower with the higher natures, connecting the visible and invisible world, according to a fixed compact sanctioned by the inviolable oath which holds all physical and all moral natures, each in their appointed place.[14]

Experiencing the wrath of absolute monarchies, Locke advocated that a social contract has two purposes. The contract would specify the philosophy guiding the governing institutions as well as the structure and functions of those institutions. But most importantly, the contract had to demand limited government. "People surrender only some of their rights, and do so in order to protect the rest. In addition, the relationship between individuals and government is to enforce the law of nature and are obligated to obey government has long as it fulfills its function. For its part, government claims obedience only as long as it fulfills its function. If it violates people's rights, it loses it power and its claim to be obeyed."[15] Locke called the relationship between the governed and the governing a **fiduciary trust**. Thus, "[t]he Legislative being only a Fiduciary Power to act for certain ends, there remains still in the People a Supreme Power to remove or alter the Legislative, when they find the Legislative act contrary to the trust reposed in them."[16] The same notion was expressed by John Locke. A contract is only a binding document when all of the signees fulfill their obligations. If one or more signees fail to abide by this contractual agreement, then the aggrieved parties have the right to end the relationship.

Democracy

As a political ideology, **democracy** is basically "a system of government in which the ultimate po-litical authority is vested in the people."[17] The initial experiment with democracy occurred in the

Greek city-states with the development of the polis in approximately 8th Century B.C.E. A polis was "a small but autonomous political unit in which all major political, social and religious activities were carried out at one central location."[18] In Athens, the whole body of male citizens over twenty years of age would meet at least ten times a year as the Assembly of Ecclesia. The task of the Assembly was to pass laws governing the city-state as well as to make important foreign policy decisions including war making. Although the body was limited to only native born male Athenians, this Assembly is the best example of **pure democracy** whereby everyone had a voice in the policy making process. Leading Athens into its Golden Age, Pericles (495 BC to 429 BC) was an early advocate of democracy. In explaining the concept of the democratic ideal, Pericles emphasized that:

> our constitution is called a democracy because power is in the hands not of a minority but of the whole people. When it is a question of settling private disputes, everyone is equal before the law; when it is a question of putting oneself before another in positions of public responsibility, what counts is not membership of a particular class, but actual ability which the man possesses. No one, so long as he has it in him to be of service to the state, is kept in political obscurity because of poverty."[19]

Full participatory or pure democracy worked as long as the membership of the governing assembly was manageable. Once deemed unmanageable, the format shifted from a pure participatory body to a representative one. **Representative** or **indirect democracy** is "a form of governance in which the citizens rule through representatives, who are periodically elected in order to keep them accountable."[20] The success of any representative democratic government rests on one word—accountability. It is a shared responsibility for the governors are accountable to the people who elected them in the first place to adequately turn their issues and concerns into corrective legislative acts. In turn, the governed accomplish their responsibilities by ensuring that their elective representatives are fulfilling their responsibilities to them. The governed have options for rewarding those who are faithfully fulfilling their responsibilities by re-electing them or if they are deemed unrepresentative, then the governed can vote them out of office.

A democratic form of government is preferred for several reasons. First, the selection of the governing is determined by the people through mandated periodic election cycles. This assures that offices will become vacant at a specific time and subsequently filled by a specified process on a specific date. Under a constitutional monarchy such as Great Britain, the monarchy is a hereditary position. However, the monarch does not have any input to the crafting and implementation of legislation for that function belongs to an elected House of Commons with the hereditary House of Lords playing little or no role in the actual governing process. Second, a basic premise to a democratic government is the principle of seeking consultation from and the consent of the ruled. The democratic doctrine underscores the premise that people should get what they want regardless of how wrong it may be! The leadership of any successful democratic government must take into account the ever-changing fickle mood swings of the governed that can be supportive of their governors on one day but switch their allegiance the next day. In a democratic government, it is a wise ruler who knows that although the people do not govern themselves, they surely will create a commotion if they dislike the way they are being governed. Third, the personal freedoms granted under a democracy give people the unique opportunity to voice their concerns without the fear of retaliation from their government. Today, Americans see the news footage coming from countries of the discontented forming mass demonstrations in protest of their governments. Unable, or perhaps unwilling, to meet their demands, their respective government leadership sends in their military with the orders to use whatever it takes to disperse the mob. These governments are not true democracies for if they were, the people would have the absolute right to question the actions of their governments without fear of reprisal. Non-violent protest is a tenet of democratic governments. Lastly, democratic governments incorporate the mechanisms to prevent abuse of the governing authority. In his *Spirit of the Laws*, Charles Montesquieu stressed that "all would be lost if the same man or the same body of principal men, either of nobles or of the people, exercised these three powers: that of making the laws, that of executing public resolutions, and that of judging the crimes or the disputes of individuals."[21] Therefore, the governing authority must be divided or separated between the governing institutions.

Constitutionalism

In 1215, the concept of holding one's rulers accountable to those they ruled was conceived by a group of disgruntled nobles who demanded an audience with their king in a field called Runnymede. Throughout England and most of Europe, the nobility were bound to their king under **feudalism**, a contractual agreement between a vassal and his lord and, in turn, between the lords and their king. Each member of the nobility dutifully pledged their homage and loyalty to their king by taking a public oath to "become your man by mouth and hands, and I swear and promise to keep faith and loyalty to you against all others, and to guard your rights with all my strength."[22] The relationship was one of mutual dependency as the lords were dependent upon their king to protect their rights to hold their lands while the nobility, in turn, would perform services for the king. The relationship, however, turned sour when John assumed the throne upon the death of his brother, King Richard I. Constantly either quarreling or at war with France, John called upon his nobility to fight his wars and collect his taxes. The nobility finally decided to reign in John's misuse of power by forcing him to sign the **Magna Carta**. The agreement was basically a list of grievances against the King with the mild threat that if John did not comply, grave consequences would follow. Although John adhered to the agreement for only two weeks and his ally Pope Innocent III declared it null and void, the Magna Carta serves as the first legal document questioning a divine right of the monarch's authority over his/her people. Its importance to the development of the American constitution cannot be overlooked. This one document "eventually came to inspire the children of subsequent eras to stand up for some of the important rights contained within it. Over time, the Great Charter (Magna Carta) also took on a life and culture of its own, spawning numerous other legal documents and doctrines in the common law. Its cultural relevance in the twentieth and twenty-first centuries has solidified its importance."[23] In many respects, the Magna Carta or the Great Charter introduced a new 'ism' to political science. **Constitutionalism** is "the political principle of limited government under a written contract."[24] Today, the underlying principles of the Magna Carta still serve as a blueprint for subsequent documents commonly known as constitutions.

By definition, a **constitution** is "a fundamental or 'organic' law that establishes the framework of government of a state, assigns the powers and duties of governmental agencies, and establishes the relationship between the people and their government."[25] Whether a single document or several documents collectively known as a constitution, all constitutions have the exalted status as the organic law or supreme law over there established jurisdictions. In *The Rights of Man* (1792), Thomas Paine drew a direct connection between a constitution, a government, and the concept of the social contract by pointing out "a constitution is a thing antecedent to a government, and a government is only the creature of a constitution. The constitution of a country is not the act of its government, but of the people constituting a government."[26] Basically, a constitution has "four main purposes. First, it must provide the structure of the governmental system, the organs and institutions of public authority. Second, it must authorize the powers that the government is to possess, and allocate them among the various branches and organs. Third, it must state the limitations on governmental power, for the essence of constitutionalism is the maintenance of a balance between authority and liberty, between governmental power and individual rights. Fourth, it must provide for some means other than violent revolution by which the constitutional design can be adopted to future necessities."[27]

Embedded in the various provisions of a constitution is the state's ideological approach to its governing principles, the structure of its governing bodies, and the responsibilities placed on both the governing and the governed. An **ideology** is "the 'way of life' of a people, reflected in their collectively held ideas and beliefs concerning the nature of the ideal political system, economic order, social goals, and moral values."[28] For example, after securing their independence from the British, there was little debate that the appropriate political ideology for the United States would be a democratic one that would vest ultimate political authority with the people. **Democratic ideology** is based on the principles of:

- Individualism with the primary task of government enabling each individual to achieve his/her highest potential of development;
- Liberty that allows each individual the greatest degree of freedom consistent with societal order;
- Equality that maintains that all persons are created equal and have equal rights and opportunities; and
- Fraternity that underscores the belief those individuals will not misuse their freedom but will cooperate in creating a wholesome society.[29]

The only occupant of the White House with a Ph.D. in political science, President Woodrow Wilson held to the principle that "democracy is more than a form of government. It is a form of character. It follows upon the long discipline which gives a people self-possession, self-mastery, the habit of order, and peace and common counsel and a reverence for law."[30]

In order to be a meaningful and viable document, a constitution must be regarded as the organic law of its state. No ordinance from a city hall, no law issued by a legislative house, no decree issued by a president, and no decision issued by a court can run counter to the provisions detailed in that document. Both those who rule and those being ruled must respect the legitimacy of their state's constitution. Far too often nation states have adopted constitutions with the intention of selectively abiding by their dictates. For example, the majority of the constitutions governing the world's states call for periodic elections. While the United States conducts its election cycle according to the dictates of its constitution, many nations do not. Far too often, the frequency of the election cycle is determined by the political fortunes of the incumbent leadership who will hold elections when they know they will win and postpone them when they know they will probably lose. Constitutionally guaranteed civil rights and liberties must be consistently enforced, not selectively applied to those who favor the incumbent regime.

Envious of the respect Americans revere for their Constitution, Alexis de Tocqueville decried his own French government's inability to follow the democratic principles they detailed in the numerous constitutions and governments formed after a very violent and bloody revolution in 1789. After the defeat and exile of Napoleon, the French government installed Louis XVIII to the throne in 1814 only to be followed by Charles X in 1824, who was disposed six years later in another bloody revolution. France had a constitution but the governing bodies opted not to follow it. Instead the governing bodies wanted to change the constitution to fit their own needs. A frustrated de Tocqueville wrote:

> From what does the king derive his powers? From the Constitution. And the Peers? From the Constitution. The deputies? From the Constitution. How, then, can a king, peers, and deputies combine to change something in a law which is the sole source of their right to rule? They are nothing outside the Constitution, so on what ground could they stand in order to change the Constitution? There are just two alternatives: either their efforts are impotent against a charter which continues to be valid in spite of them, in which case they can continue to rule in its name; or they may succeed in changing the character, in which case the law from which their existence derives is gone, and they are nothing. By destroying the charter they have destroyed themselves.[31]

THE FRAMERS' CHALLENGE—CREATING A CONSTITUTIONAL GOVERNMENT

The Seeds of Discontent

Similar to her contemporaries, Great Britain's quest for colonial possessions fulfilled its objectives of providing the newly emerging British industrial machine with essential raw materials and natural resources as well as captured markets for the purchase of its finished products. After its initial colonization failure in Raleigh in 1585, the British launched a full-scale effort with the founding of Jamestown in 1607. As colony after colony was founded, the British government soon realized that governing such a vast territory would prove troublesome. Colonial governors were appointed by the Crown with the London-based Privy Council overseeing the majority of colonial affairs. The real day-to-day governing of the colonies was basically left up to the colonials themselves through their own legislative assemblies. Opening its doors in 1619, Virginia's House of Burgess was the first colonial assembly in the American colonies. As long as the colonists followed British laws, they exercised considerable local control over their affairs. However, the tide turned toward a more repressive presence from the British during the Seven Years' War or as Americans called it, the French and Indian War. The British military was tied up in a two-front war—one in Europe and the other in the colonies against the French. Lacking the full force of its military, the British government called upon local militiamen to join the war front. Faced with an ever-growing national debt, the British government then decided to impose a series of revenue generating taxes upon the American colonists. In 1764, the **Revenue Act** or as the colonials referred to it, the **Sugar Act,** placed a duty or tax on molasses and required American shippers to post bonds to guarantee compliance with British trade regulations. The **Currency Act** of 1751 prohibited colonials from issuing their own paper money as legal tender. The most objectionable law was the **Stamp Act** of 1765, requiring the purchase of a stamp for all commercial and legal documents, liquor licenses, all print media, playing cards, and dice. In addition, the British imposed the **Quartering Act** upon the colonists. This legislation mandated that colonials were to offer-up their houses to provide quarters for British soldiers. Although promised reimbursement, the act required the colonists to furnish everything from fuel, beer, rum and food to the soldiers, as well as to pay for their transportation costs. After protest riots broke out, the British retaliated by arresting the participants, confiscating firearms, and randomly searching homes and businesses at will without benefit of a warrant. Colonial discontent was widespread.

Yet, the question of what action the colonialists should take fell into three broad groups. Those who benefited from British rule really did not want to take part in any action that would jeopardize their cozy relationship with the British government. The middle-of-the-road group realized that there were serious complaints against Britain. Yet, they also believed the advantages to British rule far outweighed the disadvantages. They wanted a negotiated settlement that would enable the British government to appropriately address colonial grievances without ending British rule. The final group had had enough with the overbearing tactics of the British government. They truly believed that the door to compromise had closed and the only option left was complete separation from Britain. Those favoring continuing British rule were branded as the Loyalists or Tories while the Patriot contention wanted a complete end to British colonial rule. Tensions between the two camps grew from combative debates and heated arguments to violent acts of street violence, torture, tar-and-feathering, roaming lynch mobs, and destruction of personal and private property. Both sides were equally guilty. Fearing for their lives, many of the Loyalists fled to the safety of Canada in hopes that once the British regained control over the colonies, they could return. Unfortunately for them, several Patriot-dominated colonial governments branded them as traitors and confiscated their businesses and landholdings. An ardent Patriot, Thomas Paine lambasted the middle-of-the-road crowd by pointing out that "absolute governments have this advantage with them, they are simple; if the people suffer, they know the head from which their suffering springs; know likewise the remedy; and are not bewildered by a variety of causes and cures. But the constitution of England is so exceedingly complex, that the nation may suffer for years together without being able to discover in which part the fault lies . . . many strong and striking reasons may be given to show that nothing can settle our affairs so expeditiously as an open and determined declaration of independence."[32]

Not everyone in Parliament was supportive of their government's colonial policies. As a sitting member of the House of Commons, Edmund Burke expressed his views in speeches entitled *On American Taxation* delivered in 1774, and *On Conciliation with America* delivered in 1775, followed by a commentary entitled *A Letter to the Sheriffs in Bristol.* Burke argued that Parliament and King George should use restraint with the colonials simply because their issues were not radical or even revolutionary. All they wanted was to receive the rights and privileges guaranteed to all Englishmen for themselves. Rather than leveling an accusatory finger at the colonists, Burke viewed Parliament as allowing an incompetent home government to enact misguided and ill-conceived acts upon the colonials. In his *On American Taxation* speech he plainly posed the question:

Will they [the colonies] be content in such a state of slavery? Reflect how you are to govern a people who think they ought to be free, and think they are not. Your scheme yields no revenue, it yields nothing but discontent, disorder, disobedience; and such is the state of America, that, after wading up to your eyes in blood, you could only end just where you begun . . .[33]

As Paine predicted, the British government opted to ignore colonial complaints. Realizing there was no other option available to them, fifty-six men met as the Continental Congress in 1775 in Philadelphia to consider their options. Writing the **Declaration of Independence** was a simple task. The Declaration enumerated the various grievances the colonials had against their mother country and leveled an accusatory finger at King George for his abuse of governing authority. Thomas Jefferson felt that "with respect to our rights, and the acts of the British government contravening those rights, there was but one opinion on this side of the water. . . . When forced, therefore, to resort to arms for redress, an appeal to the tribunal of the world was deemed proper for our justification. This was the object of the Declaration of Independence."[34] However, actually signing the document was for many a very difficult personal decision. A signee, Benjamin Rush, noted that a "'pensive and awful silence pervaded the house as we were called up, one after another, to the table of the President of Congress' to sign 'what was believed by many at that time to be our own death warrants.'"[35] The document was written by John Adams, Roger Sherman, Robert Livingston, Thomas Jefferson and Benjamin Franklin. By signing this document, each man knew that if caught, they would be charged with the hanging offense of treason. After affixing his signature to the document, John Adams commented that "the die was now cast. I had passed the Rubicon. Sink or swim, live or die, survive or perish with my country, was my unalterable determination."[36] Every now and then the sober atmosphere was peppered by humor. Overweight himself, Benjamin Harrison told a skinny Elbridge Gerry that "I shall have a great advantage over you, Mr. Gerry, when we are all hung for what we are now doing. From the size and weight of my body I shall die in a few minutes, but from the lightness of your body you will dance in the air an hour or two before you are dead."[37] Of course, the most notable signature on the document is John Hancock's who commented that he wanted his signature to be so large and bold that "fat King George can read it without his spectacles."[38]

The signees had every right to fear repercussions from the British government. Many saw their fortunes and their properties confiscated. "For William Floyd of New York, it became a painful reality almost immediately. Even as Floyd sat through the final debate on independence in Philadelphia, the British armada was arriving in New York Harbor. On July 19, 1776, the British army arrived at Floyd's estate on Long Island, confiscated his house and farm and used the property as a cavalry barracks for the next seven years. The occupying troops lived by slaughtering Floyd's livestock and harvesting his produce."[39] Another signee, John Hart's property was seized by the British. Charged with treason, Hart "hid out in the Sourland Mountains, sleeping in caves and outhouses, and once in a dog kennel."[40] Richard Stockton suffered a far more dangerous fate as he was "dragged from his bed by New Jersey Loyalists, marched to Perth Amboy, handed over to the British army and put in irons. . . . Meanwhile his estate was ransacked, his livestock killed, his library burned, [and] his house was used as headquarters by British General Cornwallis."[41]

The Declaration of Independence is the embodiment of Locke, Montesquieu, Rousseau, Plato, and Aristotle. The document clearly states their case. "A government which fails to serve the ends for which it was set up has breached the contract under which it was established and forfeited the loyalty of its citizens. . . Whenever any form of government becomes destructive of these ends, it is the right of the people to alter or to abolish it, and to institute new government, laying its foundation on such principles and organizing its power in such forms, as to them shall seem most likely to effect their safety and happiness."[42]

The first shots of the inevitable revolution were fired in Massachusetts in 1775. On the 4th of July, Americans gather to celebrate America's independence from the British. As the fireworks explode over our heads and we clap gleefully to patriot music, we tend to forget that any revolution whether it be the collapse of the Roman Empire, the Bolshevik revolution over the Romanoff rule in Russia, and, of course, the America Revolution is a tragically bloody and deadly conflict. In many respects, the American Revolutionary War was both a civil war between die-hard Loyalists to the British government and the Patriots, the staunch supporters of independence from British rule, and an all-out revolutionary revolt between a marginally trained colonial army of sharpshooters against a well-trained and seasoned British military force with a proven successful war record of engagements fought both on land and at sea.

> It is easy for us to forget that with an estimated 6,800 to 8,000 Patriot battle deaths, 10,000 killed by disease in camps, and up to 16,000 or even 19,000 who perished in captivity, the number of Patriot soldiers killed in the Revolutionary War would be well over 3 million in terms of today's population and significantly more than that if we consider Patriot deaths as a proportion of only the Patriot population in 1775 or 1783. More than ten times as many Americans died, per capita, in the Revolutionary War as in World War I, and nearly five times as many as in World War II. The death rate among Revolutionary-era prisoners of war was the highest in American history. In addition, at least 20,000 British and thousands more American Loyalists, Native American, German, and French lives were lost. The Revolution extracted further human sacrifice when at war's end approximately 1 in 40 Americans went into permanent exile, the equivalent of some 7.5 million today.[43]

Six years later, the war ended with the surrender of General Cornwallis at Yorktown.

The Articles of Confederation

As the war effort began, the same men who signed the Declaration gathered once again to plan a government just in case they happened to win the war. On June 20, 1776, shortly after they declared their independence from Britain, a special committee chaired by John Dickinson met to plan a government for their future country. By November 1777, the delegates sent the final draft of the **Article of Confederation** for ratification. It was not an easy process for "each of the ex-colonies had strong objections, but amid the pressures of wartime, they all swallowed their misgivings—except Maryland, holding out for four years, until March 1781. Meanwhile, the Continental Congress was forced to carry on the war effort without any constitutional authority."[44]

The Articles established a confederative form of government hoping to serve two purposes for the newly formed nation. First, it gave to the former colonies a sense of nationalism. Instead of being thirteen different entities taking action independent of each other, they were now the United States of America, one governing body on their own shores. It was their hope that this document would bring an end to the internal strife caused by both the Loyalists and the Patriots. Second, it enabled the former colonies, now states, to retain their sovereignty and independence to govern the residents of their particular states. Life under a constitutional government was not new to them for the majority of the states had their own legislative houses and had already drafted and adopted constitutions. So, the confederative system seemed to be the best option available to them.

Under the Articles, the traditional executive and legislative functions were merged into the National Congress, composed of representatives from each state. The elimination of a strong executive was a consequence of British colonial rule. "The royal governors had been the symbol of tyranny, and so the executive office in the new [state] constitutions was deliberately weakened, while the legislature, a symbol of resistance to foreign rule, was strengthened. In eight states, the governor was chosen by the legislature, he had only a one-year term in ten states, his appointing power was generally limited, and he had the veto power in only three states. The one-year rule was common for all officials, not only for governors, as John Adams said, 'Where annual elections end, there tyranny begins.'"[45] Collectively, each state had one vote in the Congress regardless of the number of delegates selected to represent their state. Once a legislative act passed through Congress, the sovereignty of each state was preserved through the provision that nine of the thirteen state legislative bodies had to approve it before it could be implemented in any state. The National Congress was empowered to declare war, conduct foreign policy and make treaties. However, the National Congress did not have the powers to levy and collect taxes or regulate trade and commerce between the states. The Articles created a true confederative form of government whereby the member states controlled the national government, not the other way around.

It did not take long for the inherent weaknesses of the confederative system to surface. No sooner were the signatures affixed to the document, state legislative houses began arguing among themselves about boundary lines and tariffs. Without a nationally backed currency, states began to issue their own currencies and charged excessive tolls to merchants trying to haul their goods across state boundary lines. A powerless Congress could not stop a Pennsylvanian militia group from firing upon Connecticut settlers or could it address the concerns of settlers moving into the Western territories of Kentucky and Tennessee. These settlers had a long list of complaints against the national government including the "absence of congressional help in fending off constant attacks by marauding Indians, often instigated by the British and Spaniards. Nor could the state governments, they argued, effectively govern distant territories."[46] More problematic was the inability of the Congress to actually expel the British and, in particular, Spain from interfering into American affairs. "Spain and Great Britain were poised to take advantage of the frontier's 'anarchy.' To the north, British troops still garrisoned forts along the Great Lakes, a violation of the Treaty of Paris. To the South, the Spaniards who held New Orleans and claimed all the lands west of the Mississippi had closed the great river to American shipping below Natchez. King Charles III's officers were actively encouraging American settlers in Kentucky to break away from the Union and establish commercial relations with Spain."[47] Tensions between the northern and southern states were already brewing. Specifically, "many northern traders and politicians were angered by British laws that banned American merchantmen from the lucrative trade with the British West Indies, involving the exchange of southern tobacco and rice for Caribbean sugar, molasses, and rum. But Southerners feared a northern monopoly on that traffic more than they did the relatively benign British one."[48]

Unfortunately, the confederative format succeeded only to divide rather than to unite the American people. Basically, the counter-productive actions taken by the individual states against each other coupled with the inability of the National Congress to exert effective leadership to quell the growing controversies between the various states caused grave alarm. If the National Congress could not stop the states of Virginia and North Carolina from clashing with each other over a trade route, how could it stop a possible invasion from the British or some other hostile enemy? The economic viability and the security of the nation were in peril. A bearer of things to come, John Jay wrote in *Federalist #5*:

> Instead of their being "joined in affection" and free from all apprehension of different "interests," envy and jealously would soon extinguish confidence and affection, and the partial interests of each confederacy, instead of the general interests of all America, would be the only objects of their policy and pursuits. Hence, like most other bordering nations, they would always be either involved in disputes and war, or live in constant apprehension of them. . . . They who well consider the history of similar divisions and confederacies will find abundant reason to apprehend that those in contemplation would in no sense be neighbors than as they would be borderers; that they would neither love nor trust one another; but on the contrary would be prey to discord, jealousy, and mutual injuries; in short, that they would place us exactly in the situations in which some nations doubtless wish to see us, viz., formidable only to each other.[49]

As early as 1785, George Washington hosted a meeting of key political leaders from Virginia and Maryland at Mount Vernon. The discussion centered on their joint concerns over the navigation of commerce on both the Chesapeake Bay and the Potomac River. The disputing parties purposively ignored a provision in the Articles requiring the prior consent of the National Congress for all interstate agreements. They instead developed their own plan calling for uniform import duties and standardized commercial regulations. When Maryland's legislature adopted the proposals, Pennsylvania and Delaware expressed their interests in a similar joint agreement. James Madison saw this as a prime opportunity to gather people together to meet in Annapolis in September 1786, for the sole purpose of discussing the problems with the Articles and to propose possible solutions. Although nine states were invited, only five sent a delegation. However, the meeting proved fruitful as their report was distributed to all thirteen state legislatures and the National Congress suggesting that another conference be held in Philadelphia in May 1787, for the sole purpose "to take into consideration the situation of the United States, to devise further provisions as shall appear to them necessary to render the Constitution of the Federal Government adequate to the exigencies of the Union."[50]

It was not just the economic and political elites that were disenchanted with their government. In 1783, a group of disgruntled former Revolutionary War soldiers surrounded the Pennsylvania State House where the National Congress was in session, holding its membership captive for a day. These war heroes had valid concerns. Troops in the Continental Army did not receive monthly paychecks. Once the war ended, they assumed that the National Congress would give them back pay. Instead, former soldiers returned to their farms with empty pockets only to find demolished unproductive fields, no farm animals, burned out homes and barns, and overdue high property tax bills. "What payment they did collect was typically made in so-called Continental notes, which were of such little value that the phrase 'not worth a Continental' entered popular speech. Even the

Shays led a band of farmers in revolt against tax creditors attempting to repossess their farms.

states that had approved the issue of these notes now refused to accept them in payment for taxes."[51] The delegates were further insulted when the governor of Pennsylvania refused to call out its state militia to rescue them. Consequently, the National Congress became a mobile group moving their sessions from Princeton, New Jersey, to Annapolis, Maryland and finally to New York City. "The *Boston Evening Post* mocked the politicians for not being stars of the first magnitude, but rather partaking of the nature of *inferior* luminaries, or *wandering* comets."[52] Attention was then drawn to Massachusetts in 1786, when a group of approximately 1,200 angry farmers and shopkeepers under the leadership of their former Revolutionary War commander Daniel Shays launched an ill-fated insurrection against the state government. Their complaints were similar to those heard across the country. With no national or even state banking system, people had to borrow from each other to pay their taxes and even plant their crops. Cities and towns defaulted on their tax obligations. Violent protests erupted in six other states. Few if any other state militias went to the aid of their sister states to quell the violence. Meanwhile, an inept National Congress left the door wide open for state legislative houses to fill the void by enacting their own commercial agreements, treaties with foreign countries, etc. "Like most other Federalists, Madison thought that the [state] legislatures were dominated by demagogues who sought office for reasons of 'ambition' and 'personal interest' rather than 'public good.'"[53] For Madison, Washington, Alexander Hamilton, and many other concerned individuals, enough was enough.

The Gathering at Philadelphia—The Convention Setting

Although every state was encouraged to send a delegation, only fifty-five delegates actually made the journey to Philadelphia to meet in Independence Hall. Of the group, six had signed the Declaration of Independence, fourteen were either landowners or property speculators, twenty-one were veterans of the Revolutionary War, fifteen were slave owners, twenty-four were either current members of or had served in the National Congress, and thirty-four were lawyers.[54] The notables were the "whose who" of the American political scene—Benjamin Franklin, George Washington, Alexander Hamilton, John Adams, and George Mason. This gathering was the intelligentsia of their time. All were well educated and well versed on the political perspectives held by Aristotle, Plato and the Enlightenment thinkers including Locke, Rousseau, Montesquieu, John Mill, and John Stuart Mill. Those invited but not in attendance were equally among the notables—Thomas Jefferson, John Adams, Samuel Adams, Thomas Paine, and Patrick Henry. Jefferson and John Adams were absent due to their respective assignments as American ministers to France and England. Rhode Island's legislature opted not to attend while the delegation from New Hampshire was two months late due to a lack of traveling funds. Although the session was to begin on May 14, 1787, it actually kicked off on May 25. To no surprise, George Washington was elected as the president of the Convention with James Madison serving as its secretary. Meeting six days a week, the session ended on September 17, 1787.

The ensuing debates were held in secret. Guards were posted at every door, and the windows were closed so no words could escape from the room. There were no nightly press conferences and no newspaper headlines capturing the key events of the day. "Madison was convinced to the end that secrecy had given delegates freedom to speak with nearly complete candor, and even to change their minds, often several times, as they never would have done if each word had been shared with the press or with the volatile constituencies. 'If the debates had been public,' Madison later wrote, 'no constitution would ever have been adopted.'"[55] Secrecy was maintained from the first call to order to when the last man to sign the document walked out the door. "As a result of what was essentially a gentleman's agreement about tight security, no one but the delegates really knew what was said in the hall until 53 years later when Madison's widow released the meticulous notes he [Madison] had copied out each night."[56]

The Gathering at Philadelphia—The Convention's Charge

For Madison, the convention's charge was three-fold. The first item of business was to create a strong national government that would according to Madison provide:
1. Security against foreign danger;
2. Regulation of the intercourse with foreign nations;
3. Maintenance among the States;
4. Certain miscellaneous objects of general utility;
5. Restraint of the States from certain injurious acts; and
6. Provisions for giving due efficacy to all these powers."[57]

Furthermore, Madison firmly held that "an individual independence of the state is utterly irreconcilable. [Madison stated] 'let the National Government be armed with positive and complete authority.' He wanted to extend this 'national supremacy' to the judiciary as well, and noted that in order 'to give the new system its proper energy,' all this executive power should be 'ratified by the authority of the people.'"[58]

His was not the only voice advocating a stronger national government with enough teeth to keep the union together and end the strife between the various states. The Framers believed that "this country and this people seem to have been made for each other, and it appears as if it was the design of Providence, that an inheritance so proper and convenient for a band of brethren, united to each other by the strongest ties, should never split into a number of unsocial, jealous and alien sovereignties."[59] But they also did not want a national government so strong that the individual states would be stripped of their governing authority, and, ultimately, the people would become

the victims of a repressive regime. Therefore, they wanted a document that specifically listed or enumerated what powers the government could exercise. This was to be a **limited** government. After a careful assessment of the Articles, the delegates believed the document no longer suited the nation's need and unanimously voted to declare it null and void and to begin anew.

Second, Madison wanted a document that would both clearly delineate the duties of the governing and legally bind them to their charge so that they would not have any avenue to abuse their authority. In *Federalist No. 51* entitled "*Internal Checks of the New Constitution*," Madison wrote:

> Ambition must be made to counteract ambition. The interest of the man must be connected with the constitutional rights of the place. It may be a reflection on human nature, that such devices should be necessary to control the abuses of government. But what is government itself, but the greatest of all reflections on human nature? If men were angels, no government would be necessary. If angels were to govern men, neither external nor internal controls on government would be necessary. In framing a government that is to be administered by men over men, the great difficulty lies in this: you must first enable the government to control the governed; and in the next place, oblige it to control itself. A dependence on the people is, no doubt, the primary control on the government; but experience has taught mankind the necessity of auxiliary precautions.[60]

Madison's solution was to borrow from Plato the concept of checks and balances and from Montesquieu the separation of powers doctrine. Madison gained an important ally in Alexander Hamilton from New York. Hamilton aided Madison's unsuccessful efforts to strengthen the Articles of Confederation, wrote a large portion of the *Federalist Papers*, and would later play an essential role in securing ratification of the Constitution in both Virginia and New York. For Hamilton, the only way to fix the growing problems of the new nation was to implement a strong national government designed "to protect property and civil liberties from the state governments, to direct economic activities into the channels most conductive to the national welfare, and to re-establish public credit."[61] What emerged from the Convention was "the assumption that the greatest dangers to republican government are those of divisive power of faction and the threat of tyranny resulting from too great a concentration of political power. Madison's solution to those problems was to establish a powerful national government that could balance state and local units and maintain its own checks and balances to ensure moderation in the exercise of power."[62]

Third, Madison truly believed that the appropriate format for governing this nation had to be a republican government guided by the principles of democracy. A **republic** is "a form of government in which sovereign power resides in the electorate and is exercised by elected representatives who are responsible to the people."[63] In *Federalist #10*, Madison drew a distinction between a democracy and a republic:

> It is that in a democracy, the people meet and exercise the government in person; in a republic, they assemble and administer it by their representatives and agents. A democracy, consequently, will be confined to a small spot. A republic may be extended over a large region. . . . Under the confusion of names, it has been an easy task to transfer to a republic observations applicable to a democracy only; and among others, the observation that it can never be established but among a small number of people, living within a small compass of territory. Such a fallacy may have been the less perceived, as most of the popular governments of antiquity were of democratic species; and even in modern Europe, to which we own the great principle of representation, no example is seen of a government wholly popular, and founded at the same time, wholly on that principle. If Europe has the merit of discovering this great mechanical power in government . . . American can claim the merit of making the discovery the basis of unmixed and extensive republics.[64]

Peppered throughout Madison's desire for a republican government was also the fear many of the delegates held about the uncontrollable nature of democracy. When Aristotle classified his governments, he placed democracy as the bad form of the rule of the many. So the task before the Convention was how to craft a republican government capable of controlling the empowerment and zeal of democracy. The fear was that the masses, if left unchecked, would elect the wrong people to public office. Alexis de Tocqueville actually drew a distinction between the political knowledge of an aristocracy over the uneducated or ill-informed masses:

> An aristocracy is infinitely more skillful in the science of legislation than democracy can ever be. Being master of itself, it is not subject to transitory impulses; it has far-sighted plans and knows how to let them mature until the favorable opportunity offers. An aristocracy moves forward intelligently; it knows how to make the collective force of all its laws converge on one point at a time. A democracy is not like that; its laws are almost always defective or untimely. Therefore the measures of democracy are more imperfect than those of an aristocracy; it often unintentionally works against itself; but its aim is more beneficial.[65]

Consequently, the delegates on purpose did not mention in the body of the Constitution the guarantees to universal suffrage or even specify the qualifications for casting a ballot. They left those details up to the individual state legislative houses. Initially, the majority of the states required some form of property ownership as a pre-requisite for voting privileges thus eliminating a large number of people from casting a ballot. Only members of the House of Representatives would be directly elected by the people, all others indirectly. It took subsequent amendments to the Constitution to broaden the scope of voting rights and truly move this nation to a republican government.

The Gathering at Philadelphia—Designing a New Government

The next order of business was to determine the format of the new government. The Framers decided upon a federal system to replace the confederative format. Whereas the confederative format places the states in charge with the national government playing a subservient role, the federal system reverses the relationship by elevating the national government's powers above those of the states.

   One of the main problems with the Articles was that all governing authority was concentrated in just one body—the National Congress. The Framers did not want to duplicate the British system whereby a constitutionally weak monarch was totally beholden to his/her Parliament. "The draftees of the Constitution were very familiar with Sr. William Blackstone's *Commentaries on the Law of England* (1765) which asserted that: 'In all tyrannical governments the supreme magistracy, or the right both of making and of enforcing the laws, is vested in one and the same man, or one and the same body of men; and wherever these two powers are united together, there can be no public liberty.'"[66] Madison pointed out "the accumulation of all powers, legislative, executive, and judiciary, in the same hands, whether of one, a few, or many, and whether hereditary, self-appointed, or elective, may justly be pronounced the very definition of tyranny."[67] Consequently, the Framers opted to divide or separate governing authority by creating three distinct branches of government and giving them specific duties and responsibilities. The **doctrine of separation of powers** is "a major principle of American government whereby power is distributed among three branches of government—the legislative, the executive and the judicial. The officials of each branch are selected by different procedures, have different terms of office, and are independent of one another. The separation is not complete, in that each branch participates in the functions of the other through a **system of checks and balances**. The separation, however, serves to ensure that the same person or group will not make the law, enforce the law, and interpret and apply the law."[68] Thus, the legislative branch would make the laws (**Article I**) while the executive branch would be charged with the implementation of those laws (**Article II**), and if deemed necessary and as later detailed in the Judiciary Act of 1789, the judicial branch would interpret both the meaning and application of the law (**Article III**). In 1816, Founding Father and now a former president Thomas Jefferson had first-hand experience governing under the separation of powers doctrine. He pointed out that "the way to have a good and safe government is not to trust it all to one, but to divide it among the many, distributing to every one exactly the functions he is competent to [perform]. . . It is by . . . placing under every one what its own eye may superintend, that all will be done for the best."[69] The separation of powers doctrine was indeed challenged before the Supreme Court. In ***Myers v United States*** (1926), Justice Louis D. Brandies wrote in his official opinion document "the doctrine of separation of powers was adopted by the Convention of 1787, not to promote efficiency but to preclude the exercise of arbitrary power. The purpose was not to avoid friction, but, by means of the inevitable friction incident to the distribution of the governmental powers among three departments, to save the people from autocracy."[70]

Two plans emerged for the creation of a legislative body. Written by James Madison, Edmund Randolph introduced the **Virginia Plan**. This proposal called for a bicameral or two-house legislative congressional body. Representatives to the lower house (House of Representatives) would be selected by the direct vote of the people in their respective states while the membership of the upper house (Senate) would be selected by the lower house from nominees proposed from state legislative houses. The plan also called upon the Congress to select the executive or president as well as to select members of the national judiciary and a special group called the Council of Revision whose main task would be to review the constitutionality of congressional acts. The contentious part of this plan was that the number of representatives from each state would be based on the population of that state, meaning that the most populated states would have the upper hand over the less populated states. If adopted, the Virginia Plan would put one of the nation's most populous states in the driver's seat with the less populated states taking the back seat. For example, "Virginia had 16 times the population of Delaware. A plan that gave Virginia 16 times the representation in a lower house, which would in turn choose the upper house and the chief executive, would reduce Delaware to irrelevance."[71] Not pleased by that alternative, William Patterson introduced the **New Jersey Plan,** representing the interests of the smaller states. This plan called for revising the Articles simply because under the Articles, every state had the same number of representatives regardless of the population of their states. The plan addressed some of the major concerns levied against the Articles in that it called for giving the national government the power to tax, regulate interstate commerce, and oversee foreign relations. Although the delegates voted to accept the Virginia Plan, the protests from the smaller states cast a cloud about the future of both the convention and a new constitution. After months of protracted arguments, Robert Sherman proposed a compromise. The **Connecticut Plan** or as it is commonly known as the **Great Compromise**, combined the two proposals. From the Virginia Plan, the number of representatives from each state elected to the House of Representatives would be based on a state's population. The larger populated states would have more representatives in that chamber than the lesser-populated states. From the New Jersey Plan, each state would have an equal number of senators—two from each state, regardless of the population of that state. The membership of the lower house would be directly elected from the representatives' respective states while senators would be selected from their respective state legislative houses. (The Seventeenth Amendment adopted in 1913 mandates direct popular election of senators.) The executive or president would be selected from a body separate from Congress—the Electoral College.

Before the ink was dry on the Great Compromise, another issue arose that nearly caused the demise of the convention. The southern states of Virginia, North Carolina, and South Carolina included in their calculation of state population their African-American slaves, which in many instances outnumbered Anglos three or four times to one. In 1790, slaves accounted for 43 percent of South Carolina's population, followed by Georgia with 35 percent, North Carolina 25 percent, Virginia 39 percent, and Maryland 32 percent.[72] The idea of counting slaves in population tallies was not a new one. The idea first emerged in 1783 during the drafting of the Articles of Confederation. "Congress wanted to find a formula for how much money each state needed to contribute to the common treasury. Should slaves be counted in that calculation? Of course not, Southerners explained. If we count slaves, who are property, why not count horses in the North?"[73] Now in this current proposal before the Convention delegates, if slaves were to be counted as population for representational purposes, then the larger populated northern states of Pennsylvania and New York who had very few slaves would lose some of its power in the House to the southern states. The northern states simply did not want slaves to be counted at all. The southern states balked at the notion that since slaves were the private property of their owners, then the owners should pay taxes on that property just as they did for their real estate holdings. "Southerners offered to count one-half (50 percent) of the enslaved population, but Northerners insisted on two-thirds (67 percent)."[74] Once again, a compromise was reached. The **Three-fifths Compromise** called for 3/5's (60 percent) of a state's African-American slave population to count towards the population base for House representation districts and 3/5's of that same population would count in direct tax calculations.

It is interesting to note that the Framers did not believe that previous political or elective experience should be a pre-requisite for seeking elective office. The qualifications to hold the office of the president are age (thirty-five or older), native born, and a fourteen-year residency requirement prior to seeking the office. The native born and residency requirements were to prevent someone outside of the United States from seeking the office. There were no educational requirements or any mention of prior governing experience attached to qualifications for office. In an annual message to Congress, President Ulysses S. Grant commented on the lack of attaching job experience to the qualifications for the presidency: "It was my fortune or misfortune to be called to the Chief Magistracy without any prior political training. Under the circumstances, it is but reasonable to suppose that errors of judgment must have occurred."[75] The same holds true for Congress. To be a member of the Congress, the only requirements are age (twenty-five or older for the House, thirty or older for the Senate), citizenship, and residency in the state one is representing. One could speculate that the Framers did not want "professional" politicians but instead desired to see individuals from different walks of life, backgrounds, and credentials to seek public office.

The delegates did have some difficulty in assigning the various duties to the separate branches of government. Taking from their knowledge of the British Parliament, they were able to clearly see what duties should be assigned to the legislative branch. However, creating the executive branch proved to be problematic. Their only role model, if you can call him one, was George III, an hereditary monarch with a proven track record of abusing his royal powers. From the very beginning they agreed that the head of the executive branch would be elected not for life, but for a four-year term of office. If successful in his job, then it would be up to the voters through the Electoral College to grant him additional terms. In *Federalist No. 69*, "Powers of the President," Alexander Hamilton justified his support of a limited term for the president:

> In these circumstances [four-year term of office], there is a total dissimilitude between him and a King of Great Britain, who is an hereditary monarch. . . . If we consider how much less time would be requisite for establishing a dangerous influence in a single State, than for establishing a like influence throughout the United States, we must conclude that a duration of four years for the Chief Magistrate of the Union is a degree of permanency far less to be dreaded in that office."[76]

Throughout Article II, whatever power or duty is assigned to the president, there is a check upon that power in Article I. The Framers were skeptical about the office and the potential office holders.

The lack of details for the presidency would be filled in by the person who first held the office—George Washington. He pondered whether he should be called His Excellency or Mr. President, how he should greet foreign dignities, and so forth. Even he was unsure if he fit the bill for the presidency: "my movements to the chair of government will be accompanied by feelings not unlike those of a culprit, who is going to the place of his execution; so unwilling am I, in the evening of a life nearly consumed in public cares, to quit a peaceful abode for an ocean of difficulties, with that competency of political skill, abilities, and inclination which are necessary to manage the helm."[77] It was Washington who decided he needed a Cabinet of appointed experts to assist him. He subsequently formed his first Cabinet with Thomas Jefferson as Secretary of State, Alexander Hamilton as Secretary of the Treasury, Edmund Randolph as Attorney General and Henry Knox to serve as Secretary of War. Washington then formed the nation's bureaucratic structure of civil servants to run the executive branch of this government.

The Framers were sure that they needed to include in the document the provisions for a smooth transition of power if the president should die or leave office before the four-year term expired. Thus, the vice president would be the second most important person in the executive branch. The Framers simply did not know what a vice president should be doing while waiting, if necessary, to assume the vacated office of the presidency. The Framers opted to make the vice president the presiding officer of the Senate. However, his only official duty is to cast the deciding vote needed to break a tie vote in the Senate. Himself a delegate and ultimately casting his vote to approve the Constitution, John Adams served as the nation's first vice president. He lamented "my country has, in its wisdom, contrived for me the most insignificant office [the vice presidency] that ever the invention of man contrived or his imagination conceived."[78] Thomas Jefferson complained that his stint in the vice presidency was "honorable and easy, the first is but a splendid misery."[79] The role a vice president plays is perhaps defined by the president he/she serves. For many a vice president, the primary duty was indeed to sit and wait to see whether they would become a president "by accident."

The shortest of the first three articles is Article III, providing for a national judiciary. The Articles of Confederation did not provide for a national court system. The Framers believed they needed one to act as a mediator or higher authority to decide disputes between the states. The Court's original jurisdiction was limited to cases involving ambassadors and other public ministers, cases of admiralty and maritime, controversies in which the United States was a party, controversies between states, impeachment, and treason. The Article did not specify the number of judges needed to sit on the Supreme Court or any of the inferior courts. The creation of additional federal courts was left up to Congress. There were no official qualifications for a federal judgeship. The only provision in Article III is that judges would hold their offices "during good behavior," meaning that these were lifetime appointments.

The next item of business was to merge the concept of separation of powers with a system of checks and balances that would provide an internal mechanism against any branch of the government or any person within a specific branch of government from abusing power. **Checks and balances** is "the notion that constitutional devises can prevent any power within a nation from becoming absolute by being balanced against, or checked by, another source of power within that same nation."[80] Each House of Congress was given specific duties. The House of Representative has the power of the purse as specified in Article I, Section 7: "all bills for raising revenue shall originate in the House of Representatives." However, the Senate can propose amendments to the legislation and must give its stamp of approval on House revenue bills. Both houses of Congress can propose legislation but both chambers must approve the bills before they are sent to the executive branch for the president's approval. If the president vetoes the legislation, both houses must cast a 2/3's vote to overturn the veto. Neither house of Congress can adjourn without the consent of the other. The impeachment of elected officers, in particular the president, is a shared responsibility. The House of Representatives draws up the Articles of Impeachment or charges against the president. The Senate has the sole power to try impeachments with the Chief Justice of the Supreme Court acting as the presiding judge. The only exclusive powers given to the Senate are to ratify treaties and approve presidential appointments.

Each assigned task or duty given to one branch is also checked by a provision given to one or both of the other branches. The bulk of the legislative duties assigned to Congress are detailed in Article I, Section 8 of the Constitution. Although the president is designated as the commander-in-chief of the nation's military forces, only Congress can declare war. A president can send troops into a combat situation but Congress with its "power of the purse" can deny the funding for the military action. Presidents are empowered by Article II to make treaties with foreign nations. However, the Senate must consent or approve the treaty or it is not a binding agreement. As many presidents have discovered, they only have the authority to nominate to the Senate individuals to serve in their Cabinets and key government positions. It is the Senate that has the final approval over those nominations. Although presidents may appoint an individual when Congress is not in session, even his/her recess appointments are subject to Senate confirmation when the legislature reconvenes. Of course, the federal courts can declare a legislative act unconstitutional but Congress can ultimately retool that act into a constitutional amendment that once approved becomes a part of the Supreme Law of the Land. Congress can impeach a president; however, a president cannot impeach a member of Congress. The system of checks and balances, as well as the doctrine of separation of powers, has been frustrating for both members of Congress and occupants of the White House. But the system designed by the Framers forces the executive and legislative branch to work together. If not, nothing gets done.

Although the subject of slavery was discussed, many of the delegates were themselves southern slave owners. "For Madison, slavery had to be a source of appalling political irony. At the Constitutional Convention he had minced words with fellow delegates about what issue really divided them—it was not shipping versus agriculture, nor North versus South, or even the federal government versus states' rights—it was slavery."[81] Delegate Gouverneur Morris called out slavery as a 'nefarious institution.' But, as John Rutledge of South Carolina quickly reminded the delegates, 'the true question at present is whether the Southern states shall or shall not be parties to the union."[82] Therefore, the topic of completely abolishing slavery was off the table. Attempting to seek a reasonable compromise, it was pointed out to the delegates that "traffic in imported African slaves was outlawed everywhere except in Georgia and the Carolinas, yet only Massachusetts had banned slave ownership. Many delegates, Northerners and Southerners alike, disliked slavery, some also believed as Connecticut's Oliver Ellsworth said, that the arrival of cheap labor from Europe would ultimately, 'render slaves useless.'"[83] The delegates reached the consensus that the importation of slaves would end by 1808! During the ratification process, questions arose as to why the delegates opted just to end the importation of slaves but not abolish slavery altogether. Madison addressed this concern in his *Federalist Paper No. 42*: *Powers Over Foreign and Interstate Affairs*:

It was doubtless to be wished, that the power of prohibiting the importation of slaves had not been postponed until the year 1808, or rather that it had been suffered to have immediate operation. But it is not difficult to account, either for this restriction on the general government, or for the manner in which the whole clause is expressed. It ought to be considered as a great point gained in favor of humanity, that a period of twenty years may terminate forever, within these States, a traffic which has so long and so loudly upbraided the barbarism of modern policy; that within that period, it will receive a considerable discouragement from the federal government, and may be totally abolished, by a concurrent of the few States which continue the unnatural traffic, in the prohibitory example which has been given by so great a majority of the Union. Happy would it be for the unfortunate Africans, if an equal prospect lay before them of being redeemed from oppressions of their European brethren![84]

Titles of Nobility

Article I, Section 9 of the Constitution states: "No title of nobility shall be granted by the United States; and no person holding any office of profit or trust under them, shall without the consent of Congress, accept any present, emolument, office or title, of any kind whatever, from any king, prince, or foreign state." Initially, the debate centered on ending the traditional monarchial practice of granting titles of nobility to those who dutifully served their monarch. While the title alone elevated a person in prestige above others, usually nobility titles granted large estates and monetary advantages to the title holder that would be passed on from generation to generation. It was Alexander Hamilton, the son of a shopkeeper, that adamantly opposed any notion of this government granting a title to anyone. "So long as titles were excluded from American life," Hamilton argued, "there can never be serious danger that the government will be any other than that of the people."[85] Thomas Jefferson drew a "distinction between artificial aristocracy founded on wealth and birth and natural aristocracy based on a man's virtue and talents."[86] Jefferson's concept of natural aristocracy aligns with the economic concepts of capitalism and free enterprise. Section 9, also known as the **emolument clause**, means that officeholders can not use their position to enhance their own economic viability while serving in an elective position. Presidents receive gifts from foreign heads-of-state however, these gifts belong to the American people. When a president leaves office, the gifts remain behind! Yet, there have been situations where the emolument clause has been compromised. For example, in 2020, there have been several lawsuits filed by watchdog groups against a handful of Congress members and President Trump charging them with violations of the emolument clause. In the case of the Congress members, the allegation is that these individuals knew in advance that the stock market was going to take a dramatic dip due the coronavirus pandemic. They quickly sold their personal stocks before the public announcement of the nose-drive of the stock market and the declining trading value of those stocks. A lawsuit against President Trump was filed charging him with an emolument violation over his use of his personal hotel in Washington, D.C., to house foreign dignitaries and their staff during official visits and attendance at international conferences.

Amending the Document

The Framers wanted to ensure that if their document were amended, it would be a meaningful and arduous process. Article V specifies that for an amendment to be attached to the Constitution, the following steps must be followed:

1. A 2/3's vote in both the House of Representatives and the Senate or a 2/3's vote from the legislatures of "the several states" for Congress to call a national convention to even begin the amending process.
2. If the amendment passes the first step, then it must be ratified or approved by 3/4ths of the state legislative houses.

Although numerous constitutional amendments are introduced in Congress each legislative session, very few have survived step one. For step 2, usually Congress will set a specified period of approximately seven to ten years for state legislative houses to initiate their ratification processes. As in the case of the failed Equal Rights Amendment, Congress set a seven-year time frame for clearance through state legislative houses only to extend it for an additional three years to get the required 3/4's approval. To date, only seventeen amendments have made it through the entire process. The Framers understood that the document was not perfect and that changes would have to be made. But, they envisioned that any changes would be absolutely necessary and driven by sound reasoning. As Madison pointed out, "the mode preferred by the convention seems to be stamped with every mark of propriety. It guards equally against that extreme facility, which would render the Constitution too mutable; and that extreme difficulty, which might perpetuate its discovered faults. It, moreover, equally enables the general and the State governments to originate the amendment of errors, as they may be pointed out by the experience on one side, or the other."[87] President Andrew Johnson underscored the sentiments of the Framers by pointing out that "amendments to the Constitution ought not too frequently be made. . . . If continually tinkered with it will lose all its prestige and dignity, and the old instrument will be lost sight of altogether in a short time."[88]

RATIFICATION AND ADOPTION

The Ratification Process

Article VII of the proposed Constitution outlines the process by which the document would receive final ratification. Final approval would be secured by a positive vote from nine of the thirteen states. Why only nine and not thirteen states? The Framers understood that the document was a radical one in which they abolished one government and replaced it with a totally new one based on concepts of governance that had never been tried before in this nation. So, they knew that not every state would be on board. While they would have liked to require a unanimous vote of approval, they agreed that nine affirmatives constituted a majority. They did, however, want the people of each state rather than their elected state assemblymen to cast the vote. Therefore, each state was required to convene an elected convention to consider whether to adopt the document.

Federalists versus Anti-Federalists

Supporters of the Constitution, or the Federalists, gathered their forces together to battle state by state for the ratification of the document. James Madison was their primary political strategist. "He kept up a steady correspondence with allies around the country, gathering intelligence, coordinating campaigns, and offering advice on such crucial matters as the precise timing of the state conventions."[89] The opposition, now known as the Anti-Federalists, used the local media to air their complaints of virtually everything contained in the document. As a rebuttal, Madison called upon two of his closest allies—Alexander Hamilton and John Jay—to respond to the opposition's claims. The resulting *Federalist Papers* are eighty-five articles written primarily by Madison with some responses from Hamilton and Jay. As soon as an article criticizing the Constitution was published, these three had an immediate response. The Anti-Federalist faction oftentimes resorted to near violence and obstructionism to block ratification of the document. For example, "in September, Antifederalist legislators boycotted the Pennsylvania Assembly, denying it the quorum needed to authorize a convention. The tactic worked until a Federalist mob descended on the homes of two Anti-Federalist legislators and hustled them off to the State House. A quorum thus secured, the Assembly voted to call a convention."[90]

The major issue for the Anti-Federalists was that the Constitution did bind the national government to the civil rights and liberties provisions state constitutions guaranteed to its citizens. They wanted a Bill of Rights attached to the document prior to the ratification process. Hamilton came to the rescue by pointing out that "the truth is, after all the declamations we have heard, that the Constitution is itself, in every rational sense, and to every useful purpose, a bill of rights. . . And the purposed Constitution, if adopted, will be the bill of rights of the Union."[91] He went a step further by delineating portions of the Constitution guaranteeing protected rights to include the guarantee of the writ of habeas corpus, prohibitions against bill of attainder and ex-post facto laws. To finally silence the Anti-Federalist criticisms, the Federalists guaranteed that if the Constitution were ratified, the first step of the newly installed government would be to draft and adopt a Bill of Rights guaranteeing to protect civil rights and civil liberties.

The first state to ratify the document was Delaware followed by Pennsylvania, New Jersey, Georgia, and Connecticut. Massachusetts resulted in a close vote to approve the Constitution followed by Maryland, South Carolina and Rhode Island. The biggest battles were in New York with Anti-Federalists and the state's governor, George Clinton, leading the charge and in Virginia where Patrick Henry warned his fellow Virginians that if this document was approved, the national government would impose harsh taxes and strip away protected civil liberties. Henry truly thought that their state alone would sink the Constitution. However, four days before Virginians voted to approve the document, New Hampshire's approval sealed the deal as the ninth state to ratify the document. Eventually, New York approved the document and the stragglers followed suit. This was indeed what the Framers hoped for—a unanimous vote of approval.

CONCLUSIONS

As Ben Franklin so eloquently put it, the Constitution is not perfect, but it is the best to date for this nation. There is a direct connection between the Declaration of Independence and the Constitution. A close examination of both documents reveals that many of grievances lodged against the British monarchy and the Parliament were addressed through provisions in the Constitution and, in particular, the first ten amendments collectively known as the Bill of Rights. As one progresses through the text, the rights and privileges guaranteed in the Bill of Rights and subsequent amendments have an impact on the nation's judicial system (see Chapter 11), civil liberties (see Chapter 12) and civil rights (see Chapter 13), and the involvement of interest groups (see Chapter 7) and political parties (see Chapter 4) as well as citizens in the election process. Articles IV and VI of the Constitution lay down the concept of federalism and seal the relationship between national and state governments as well as the relationship state governments have with their county, local and special district governments (see Chapter 2). Of course, Articles I, II, and III firmly outline the roles of the legislative, executive, and judicial branches of the government as specifically assigned to them in the Preamble of the Constitution—promote the general welfare and provide for the common defense. This document is the appropriate application of both the separation of powers doctrine and the system of checks and balances. This is a living document, the organic law of the state, and, of course, the Supreme Law of the Land.

This document is held in reverence by all—the governed and the governing. After taking his oath of office, President John Tyler vowed that he was "determined to uphold the Constitution . . . to the upmost of my ability and in defiance of all personal consequences. What may happen to an individual is of little importance, but the Constitution of the country, or any of its great and clear principles and provisions, is too sacred to be surrendered under any circumstances whatever by those who are charged with its protection and defense."[92]

CHAPTER NOTES

[1]George Klosko, *History of Political Theory: An Introduction*, Vol. 2: Modern Political Theory, (New York, New York: Thomson/Wadsworth, 1995), 274.

[2]*Treasury of Presidential Quotations*, Caroline Thomas Harnsberger, ed., (Chicago, IL: Follett Publishing Company, 1964), 42.

[3]Jack C. Rakove, "Philadelphia Story," *The Wilson Quarterly*, Vol. 11, No. 2, Spring, 1987, 120.

[4]William Ebenstein, *Great Political Thinkers: Plato to the Present*, (New York, New York: Rinehart & Company, Inc., 1951), 76.

[5]Ibid., 77.

[6]*The American Political Dictionary*, Jack C. Plano and Milton Greenberg, eds., 10th ed., (Orlando, Florida: Harcourt Brace and Company, 1997), 12.

[7]Ebenstein, 75.

[8]Klosko, *History of Political Theory*, Vol. 2, 230.

[9]Roger Scruton, *A Dictionary of Political Thought*, (New York, New York: Harper & Row Publishers, 1982), 421.

[10]George Klosko, *History of Political Theory: An Introduction*, Vol. 1: Ancient and Medieval Political Theory, (Mason, Ohio: Cengage Learning, 2002), 49.

[11]Ibid.

[12]Ibid.

[13]Klosko, *History of Political Theory*, Vol. 2, 107.

[14]Ibid., 296.

[15]Ibid., 106.

[16]Ibid., 108.

[17]*The American Political Dictionary*, 9.

[18]William J. Duiker and Jackson J. Spievogel, *World History*, 3rd ed., (Belmont, California: Wadsworth/Thomson Learning, 2001), 99.

[19]Klosko, *History of Political Theory*, Vol. 1, 4.

[20]*The HarperCollins Dictionary of American Government and Politics*, Jay M. Shafritz, ed., (New York, New York: HarperCollins Publishers, Inc., 1992), 174.

[21]Klosko, *History of Political Theory*, Vol. 2, 202.

[22]Duiker and Spievogel, 327.

[23]Eric T. Kasper, "The Influence of Magna Carta in Limiting Executive Power in the War on Terror," *Political Science Quarterly*, Vol. 126, No. 4, Winter, 2011-2012, 547.

[24]*The American Political Dictionary*, 2.

[25]Ibid., 34.

[26]*The HarperCollins Dictionary of American Government and Politics*, 141.

[27]C. Herman Pritchett, *The American Constitutional System*, 2nd ed., (New York, New York: McGraw-Hill Book Company, 1976), 3.

[28]*The American Political Dictionary*, 13.

[29]Ibid.

[30]*Treasury of Presidential Quotes*, 61.

[31]Alexis de Tocqueville, *Democracy in America*, George Lawrence translator and J. P. Mayer, ed., (Garden City, New York: Doubleday and Company ,Inc. 1969), 724.

[32]"Thomas Paine Calls for a Break With England, 1776," *Major Problems in American Constitutional History*, Vol. 1: The Colonial Era Through Reconstruction, Kermit L. Hall, ed., (Lexington, Massachusetts: D. C. Heath and Company, 1992), 71-74.

[33]Klosko, *History of Political Theory*, Vol. 2, 285.

[34]*Treasury of Presidential Quotes*, 55.

[35]William Hogeland, "Suicide Pact: 56 Men Put Their Lives on the Line by Signing the Declaration of Independence," *American History*, Vol. 48, No. 3, August, 2013, 32.

[36]*Treasury of Presidential Quotes*, 54.

[37]Hogeland, "Suicide Pact: 56 Men Put Their Lives on the Line by Signing the Declaration of Independence," 32.

[38]Ibid., 37.

[39]Hogeland, "Suicide Pact: 565 Men Put Their Lives on the Line by Signing the Declaration of Independence," 36.

[40]Ibid.

[41]Ibid., 37.

[42]Pritchett, 8.

[43]Holger Hoock, *Scars of Independence: America's Violent Birth*, (New York, New York: Crown Publishing Group, 2017), 17.

[44]Peter Onuf, "It Is Not A Union," *The Wilson Quarterly*, Vol. 11, No. 2, Spring, 1977, 101.

[45]Pritchett, 8-9.

[46]Onuf, "It Is Not A Union," 103.

[47]Ibid., 99.

[48]Ibid., 100.

[49]John Jay, "No. 5: Perils of American Discord," *The Enduring Federalist*, Charles Beard, ed., 2nd ed., (New York, New York: Frederick Ungar Publishing Co., 1964), 50-51.

[50]Pritchett, 5.

[51]Charles Phillips, "A Day to Remember: January 25, 1787: Shays' Rebellion Gets Bloody," *American History*, Vol. 41, No. 6, February, 2007, 17.

[52]Onuf, 101.

[53]Rakove, 109.

[54]Ibid., 105.

[55]Erza Bowen, "Constitutional Convention, Philadelphia, 1787: "Something Must Be Done Or We Shall Disappoint Not Only America, But the Whole World," *Smithsonian*, Vol. 18, No. 4, July, 1987, 37.

[56]Richard Brookhiser, "Correcting the Constitution: Was the Bill of Rights Necessary?," *American History*, Vol. 50, No. 5, December, 2015, 41.

[57]Steven A. Peterson and Thomas Rasmussen, *State and Local Politics*, (New York, New York: McGraw-Hill, 1994), 24.

[58]Bowen, "Constitutional Convention, Philadelphia, 1787: "Something Must Be Done Or We Shall Disappoint Not Only America, But the Whole World", 36.

[59]John Jay, "No. 2: The True Basis of a Federal Union," *The Enduring Federalist*, Charles Beard, ed, 2nd ed., (New York, New York: Frederick Ungar Publishing Co, 1964), 39.

[60]James Madison, "No. 51: Internal Checks of the New Constitution," *The Enduring Federalist*, Charles Beard, ed., 2nd ed., (New York, New York: Frederick Ungar Publishing Co., 1964), 225.

[61]John C. Miller, *The Federalist Era: 1789-1801*, (New York, New York: Harper and Row Publishers, 1960), 35.

[62]*The American Political Dictionary*, 18.

[63]Ibid., 24.

[64]James Madison, "No. 14: The New Form of Government Adapted to Large Country," *The Enduring Federalist*, Charles Beard, ed., 2nd ed., (New York, New York: Frederick Ungar Publishing Co., 1964), 86.

[65]Alexis de Tocqueville, *Democracy in America*, 232.

[66]*The HarperCollins Dictionary of American Government and Politics*, 519-520.

[67]James Madison, "No. 47: Separation of Powers Within the Federal Government," *The Enduring Federalist*, Charles Beard, ed., 2nd ed., (New York, New York: Frederick Ungar Publishing Co., 1964), 211.

[68]*The American Political Dictionary*, 50.

[69]*Treasury of Presidential Quotes*, 122.

[70]*The HarperCollins Dictionary of American Government and Politics*, 519-520.

[71]Mark Bernstein, "The Necessity of Refusing My Signature," *American History*, Vol. 41, No. 4, October, 2006, 53.

[72]Ray Raphael, "Let's Make A Deal," *American History*, Vol. 48, No. 5, December, 2013, 52-53.

[73]Ibid., 52.

[74]Ibid., 54.

[75]*Treasury of Presidential Quotations*, 259.

[76]Alexander Hamilton, "No. 69: Powers of the President," *The Enduring Federalist*, Charles Beard, ed., 2nd ed., (New York, New York: Frederick Ungar Publishing Co, 1964), 290.

[77]*Treasury of Presidential Quotations*, 255.

[78]Ibid., 350.

[79]Ibid., 351.

[80]*The HarperCollins Dictionary of American Government and Politics*, 102.

[81]Timothy Foote, "After More Than Two Centuries, This May Be Madison's Year," *Smithsonian*, Vol. 18, No. 6, September, 1987, 84.

[82]Rakove, "Philadelphia Story," 112.

[83]Ibid.

[84]James Madison, "No. 42: Powers Over Foreign and Interstate Affairs," *The Enduring Federalist*, Charles Beard, ed., 2nd ed., (New York, New York: Frederick Ungar Publishing Co., 1964), 182-183.

[85]Richard Brookhiser, "No Kings Needed," *American History*, Vol. 51, No. 1, April, 2016, 32.

[86]Ibid.

[87]James Madison, "No. 43: Miscellaneous Powers," *The Enduring Federalist*, Charles Beard, ex., 2nd ed., (New York, New York: Frederick Ungar Publishing Co., 1964), 191.

[88]*Treasury of Presidential Quotes*, 44.

[89]A. E. Dick Howard, "Making It Work," *The Wilson Quarterly*, Vol. 111, No. 2, Spring, 1987, 122.

[90]Ibid.

[91]Alexander Hamilton, "No. 84: Why The Constitution Needs No Bill of Rights," *The Enduring Federalist*, Charles Beard, ed., 2nd ed., (New York, New York: Frederick Ungar Publishing Co., 1964), 364.

[92]*Treasury of Presidential Quotes*, 43.

SUGGESTED READINGS

Beard, Charles, H. *The Enduring Federalist*. Garden City, N.Y.: Doubleday and Co., Inc., 1948.

Collier, Christopher, and Collier, James Lincoln. *Decision in Philadelphia*. New York: Random House, 1986.

Klosko, George, *History of Political Theory: An Introduction, Vol. 1, Ancient and Medieval Political Theory*, Mason, Ohio: Cengage Learning, 2002.

—, *History of Political Theory: An Introduction, Vol. 2: Modern Political Theory*, New York, New York: Thomson/Wadsworth, 1995. 975.

CHARLESTON
MERCURY
EXTRA:

Passed unanimously at 1.15 o'clock, P. M., December 20th, 1860.

AN ORDINANCE

To dissolve the Union between the State of South Carolina and other States united with her under the compact entitled "The Constitution of the United States of America."

We, the People of the State of South Carolina, in Convention assembled, do declare and ordain, and it is hereby declared and ordained,

That the Ordinance adopted by us in Convention, on the twenty-third day of May, in the year of our Lord one thousand seven hundred and eighty-eight, whereby the Constitution of the United States of America was ratified, and also, all Acts and parts of Acts of the General Assembly of this State, ratifying amendments of the said Constitution, are hereby repealed; and that the union now subsisting between South Carolina and other States, under the name of "The United States of America," is hereby dissolved.

THE
UNION
IS
DISSOLVED!

Chapter Two

FEDERALISM

Intergovernmental relations (**IGR**) are "the complex network of interrelationships among governments, i.e., political, fiscal, programmatic, and administrative processes by which higher units of government share revenues and other resources with lower units of government, generally accompanied by special conditions that lower units must satisfy as prerequisites to receiving the assistance."[1] All nation states have levels of government from national to local communities, and each level is interrelated and interdependent upon each other, regardless of the formally outlined structure. For the United States, the structure is called federalism, a unique relationship between all levels of government that gives each some degree of independence from each other but definitely binds them together through the United States Constitution. The relationship has never been a smooth one. Even the Framers wondered whether this hybrid combination of the unitary and confederative systems coined federalism would actually work. In *Federalist #46* titled "Relative Strength of the Federal and State Governments," James Madison wrote:

> I proceed to inquire whether the federal government or the State governments will have the advantage with regard to the predilection and support of the people. Not-withstanding the different modes in which they are appointed, we must consider both of them as substantially dependent on the great body of citizens of the United States. . . . . The federal and state governments are in fact but different agents and trustees of the people, constituted with different powers, and designed for different purposes.[2]

Alexis de Tocqueville expressed the same sentiments in his *Democracy in America*:

> Among the inherent defects of every federal system, the most obvious of all is the complication of the means it employs. This system necessarily brings two sovereignties face to face. The lawgiver may succeed in making the operations of these two sovereignties as simple and balanced as possible and may enclose them both within precisely defined spheres of action, but he cannot contrive that they shall be but one or prevent their touching somewhere.[3]

Under the day-to-day grind of governing, each part of the federal system does its job from the White House to the mayor's house. However, the inherent weaknesses in the system are tragically apparent whenever a national disaster or a usually violent weather episode hits the American shores. For example, the wrath and aftermath of Katrina brought undo hardships upon the people of the Gulf Coast, particularly, New Orleans. Historically, residents along the Gulf Coast area are well aware of the typical hurricane season—the beginning of June to usually the end of September. Every year, the National Hurricane Center announces the predicted number of storms, the category levels, and a list of alternative male and female names for each storm. Hurricanes can range from the least potentially dangerous Category 1 to the extremely damaging Category 5 with its 175 plus mile per hour winds—"the big one." Despite a cadre of sophisticated weather equipment and well-trained meteorologists, predicting the path of where a hurricane will strike is extremely difficult. Far too often, Mother Nature has the final say on where a hurricane will eventually make landfall. The 2005 hurricane season was anything but typical. The number of hurricanes exceeded the chosen names from A to Z. Officials resorted to using the Greek alphabet of Alpha, Beta, Gamma, etc. And on August 29, 2005, the rare "big one" named Katrina headed, as predicted it would, straight for the approximately 455,000 residents of New Orleans, Louisiana. When Katrina hit, New Orleans was already 10 feet below sea level surrounded by its well-known levee system. Frankly, "Katrina knocked one of the nation's largest cities back to the Stone Age—no electricity, no phone system, no water, no sanitation, no commerce," no way out, and no immediate substantial help on the way from any level of government.[4]

As Katrina's high winds and storm surges tore apart New Orleans and it levees, as well as areas stretching from Louisiana to Mississippi, it also severely and painfully exposed the inability of government at all levels from city hall to the White House to alleviate the suffering of the victims of Katrina's wrath. Those who had the time, the personal transportation, and the financial means did leave the area before the storm hit. However, the majority of the area's poor, sick, and elderly simply did not have a way out without some form of public assistance. Like the majority of our nation's cities, city leaders in New Orleans did not have a full-scale evacuation plan in place. For days on end, Americans across the country watched the tragedy of the Gulf Coast unfold with report after report of starving and thirsty residents of New Orleans sitting on expressway overpasses in stifling heat waiting for someone to rescue them. Thousands of people were sitting on top of their roofs waving white pieces of cloth and holding signs hoping to attract the attention of an occasional helicopter hovering overhead to take them to safety. News footage showed stranded people using makeshift boats to ferry themselves and those they could rescue to the Superdome. Eventually, the high winds tore a hole in the Superdome's roof, rendering an already unbearable situation impossible. "In the local hospitals, doctors and nurses trapped with thousands of patients had to decide who got medicine and who got hooked up to life-saving ventilators in hot, dark wards as supplies of water, food and medicine dwindled. By the end of the first week, doctors were forced to decide between intravenously feeding themselves or their patients."[5] To add insult to injury, another major hurricane Rita would tear into the same area and coastline areas of East Texas approximately one month later.

As those 2005 Katrina winds and rain tore apart the Gulf Coast, the façade of a competent federal system crumbled before our very eyes as city leaders were at odds with state and federal officials and agencies. This is not the first and, unfortunately, will not be the last episode of federalism at its worst. November 22, 2013, marked the 50th anniversary of the assassination of President John F. Kennedy. As the Americans were glued to their television sets watching the tragic events in Dallas, behind the scenes were the on-going struggles between the federal agencies of the Secret Service, the Central Intelligence Agency (CIA), the Federal Bureau of Investigation (FBI), Texas state law enforcement agencies including the Texas Rangers, and the local Dallas police department over which level of government had jurisdiction over the investigation and the capture of Lee Harvey Oswald. On January 28, 2014, the city of Atlanta, Georgia was hit with an unusually fierce snowstorm. It is not that the South never sees snow but it only comes once and awhile, bringing just enough of the "white stuff" to close down schools and businesses, shut down all highway overpasses, build a lope-sided snowman, and have a few snowball fights. However, this snowstorm resulted in "tens of thousands of people, including children on school buses, stranded on icy, wreck-strewn roads."[6] While stranded, people slept in their cars, tried to walk home or go wherever they could find shelter. Georgia's Governor Nathan Deal blamed Atlanta Mayor Kasim Reed for not taking the looming snow storm seriously. The mayor blamed the governor's office for not supplying the metropolitan and outlying areas with heavy snow moving equipment, failing to spray the deicing chemicals on the city's highways and interstates before the snow began to fall, and for not closing down the icy overpasses before commuters were struck in traffic, sliding off the roads, or becoming victims of automobile accidents. The local media pointed the finger at the school districts who early released their students at the same time resulting in both parents trying to get to schools to pick up their children and buses trying to get students home, being stuck in the traffic congestion lasting hours into the next day. Both the mayor and the governor tried to blame the National Weather Service for underestimating the fury of the storm and its location. The Weather Service, in turn, blamed city and state officials for not taking their forecasts seriously. While elected officials were pointing countless fingers and accusations at each other, the city of Atlanta was at a standstill!

By February 2020, it became apparently clear that the American way of life was dramatically changing due to a virtually unknown spreading deadly air-born virus called corona. Originally, most Americans held to the belief that since it originated in China, it would remain in China. But the virus spread quickly across the globe much like the Bubonic Plague or Black Death that originated in Asia in 1347 and gradually spread its deadly path throughout Asia to Europe until 1351. Periodic outbreaks of the plague resurfaced until the end of the Fifteenth Century. The 2020 coronavirus has killed hundreds of thousands of people from across the globe with no end in sight. Both the United States and the rest of the international community were caught off guard by the rapid tragic impact of this virus. Across the globe, there has not been enough of anything—testing for potential virus victims, hospital beds, masks and protective gear for medical staff, ventilators, and a vaccine that could either slow the progress of the disease or cure it. For Americans, it has meant a life of sheltering in one's home and if venturing out, wearing a protective mask, and practicing new trends—social distancing and curbside deliveries. The economy has come to an abrupt halt, erasing all the favorable economic advances made since the 2008 recession. The Stock Market plunged to depths akin to the Great Depression of the 1930s. Businesses and factories were forced to close their doors leaving their workforce either furloughed or laid off. The unemployment rate has soared as millions have applied for unemployment compensation. Unfortunately, state unemployment offices cannot process the claims fast enough to starve off soaring personal and business bankruptcies. Without a paycheck, Americans are now lining up in groves for charitable food donations. Food banks are running out of food. Meanwhile, grocery stores have become the targets of hoarders of everything from meat to toilet paper. Laid off workers also lost their employee insurance benefits leaving them without the funds to even afford coronavirus tests much less several weeks of intensive care hospital-stays. Public and private schools, colleges and universities are closed for the Spring, Summer, and perhaps the fall, 2020 semesters, opting instead for online instruction. There will be no 2020 high school proms and no opportunities to walk across the stage to receive one's high school or college diplomas. Every crowd gathering activity from a sandlot baseball game to the Olympics has either been postponed or cancelled. Initially, the federal government did not take the potential devastation of this virus seriously. As more and more became infected, mayors and governors were turning their eyes towards the federal government for direction and assistance. However, the federal government was unable to provide what they needed the most—equipment, protective gear, financial assistance and, more importantly, a comprehensive federal plan to address this crisis, now called the coronavirus pandemic. Frustrated with the inability to receive viable assistance from the federal government, the governors of New York, New Jersey, Connecticut, Pennsylvania, Delaware, Rhode Island, and Massachusetts have formed their own cooperative agreement. When one state begins to see a decline in deaths and patients, that governor will give some of its medical equipment to the states that need it the most. Once again, the political finger pointing between the White House, Congress, state legislative houses and mayoral city halls have left the American people questioning the ability of their government at any level to help them survive this crisis.

At least on paper, the concept of federalism gives the national government the superior or upper hand over state and local governing authorities and, of course, the people. The **Supremacy Clause** of Article VI of the United States Constitution clearly states "this Constitution, and the laws of the United States which shall be made in pursuance thereof; . . . shall be the supreme law of the land; and the judges in every State shall be bound thereby, anything in the Constitution or laws of any State to the contrary notwithstanding." In practice, however, the relationships between the national, state and local governments have never been a solid one. The history of this nation sees far too often periods of close cooperation between them followed by episodes of clashes pitting them against each other in their struggles for control and power. Unfortunately, in the middle of their struggles are the American people who as a whole have always been fickle about the role government should play in their daily lives. Under normal circumstances, they fear the intrusion of the "big brother" muscle of the national government having a say on what they can and cannot do. Yet, whenever a natural disaster, such as a hurricane, a snow storm, a threat to national security like the destruction of the Twin Towers at the World Trade Center, the bombing at the Boston Marathon, or a coronavirus pandemic, they demand federal attention and assistance particularly when they see that their state and local governments are incapable of meeting their needs.

Before a joint session of Congress, newly inaugurated President Barack Obama delivered his first State-of-the-Union message delivered on February 24, 2009. After the speech, Louisiana's Republican Governor Bobby Jindal delivered his party's official response to Obama's speech. Jindal criticized the president's proposed stimulus package of federal funds to states, local communities, and businesses designed to jumpstart the slumping economy. He drew upon traditional Republican positions of less government, less regulatory oversight from Washington, and the fear of the big muscle of the federal government becoming too intrusive into the lives of Americans. He told the audience "there has never been a challenge that the American people, with as little interference as possible by the federal government, cannot handle."[7] Jindal perhaps regretted those words when in April 2010, an offshore deep drilling platform owned by British Petroleum (BP) exploded, the pipe line stretching miles below sea level broke, and billions of barrels of thick crude oil seeped quickly into the Gulf of Mexico off the coast of Louisiana. Jindal placed the blame for not quickly stopping the mass of black crude heading for Louisiana's shoreline directly on the federal government and, in particular, the Environmental Protection Agency (EPA). During a public press conference, the Governor said "the administration [Obama] has not provided enough equipment, including booms, skinners, vacuums and barges, and that it stood in the way of his proposal to erect artificial barrier islands" that would have prevented the oil from reaching the shoreline.[8] Jindal's remarks before and after the oil spill illustrate the re-occurring frustrations many have voiced about the federal system. No governor has been more critically vocal about President Trump's coronavirus responses than Andrew Cuomo of New York. The initial epicenter of the coronavirus was New York City. At the daily White House press conferences, President Trump enumerated the items the federal government was providing to the states. After the daily White House press briefings, the cameras shifted to Cuomo who contradicted much of what the president said. The president's order that states "reopen for business" has been met with resistance from many governors who favor a more gradual staged approach designed to marginalize the spread of the virus. Should the federal government have the power to force state governments to follow its dictates? Does the constitutional responsibility of government to promote the general welfare of the American people fall upon just the national government, the state governments, or is this a shared responsibility placed upon the backs of all levels of government? Is this the relationship the Framers envisioned for this nation? Just who is in charge, the individual state governments or the national government? Should the role of the national government be proactive and take charge of a natural disaster or a crisis or should the national government initially stand aside and allow state governments to be the first responders with the national government serving only as a backup plan?

This relationship we commonly call federalism is indeed a fragile one that is not clearly defined in the Constitution that mandates its existence. Not even the collective wisdom of the Framers could clearly delineate under all conceivable situations what actually belongs exclusively to the national government or to the states or to be shared by both. In *Federalist #45*, James Madison attempted to clarify the confusion:

> the powers delegated by the proposed Constitution to the federal government are few and defined. Those which are to remain in the State governments are numerous and indefinite. The former will be exercised principally on external objects, as war, peace, negotiation and foreign commerce; with which last the power of taxation will, for the most part, be connected. The powers reserved to the several States will extend to all objects which, in the ordinary course of affairs; concern the lives, liberties and properties of the people, and the internal order, improvement and prosperity of the state.[9]

In theory, Madison envisioned a national government that would be more focused on the external affairs and the day-to-day operations of running a nation while the state governments would be in charge of meeting the local or regional needs of the residents within their boundaries. Idealistically, Thomas Jefferson believed that "in time all the State governments as well as their central government, like the planets revolving round their common sun, acting and acted upon according to their respective weights and distances, will produce that beautiful equilibrium on which our Constitution is founded, and which I believe it will exhibit to the world in a degree of perfection, unexampled but in the planetary system itself."[10] However, the lines of responsibility have become intertwined with each other, making it almost impossible to separate them. This chapter explores and analyzes the concept of federalism and its impact upon both the national and fifty state governments.

TYPES OF INTERGOVERNMENTAL RELATIONSHIPS

In the majority of the world's nation states, the interrelationship enjoyed between national governments and their states usually conform to either a unitary or confederative relationship. In both configurations one level of government has complete authority over the other. The **unitary system** is "one in which principal power within the political system lies at the level of a national or central government rather than at the level of some smaller unit, such as a state or province."[11] Usually, the national government possesses the authority to create and, if necessary, abolish sub-government units. States and other sub-government units basically serve as administrative agents to their national governments. Under this format, power and governing authority flows from top to bottom. More than 90 percent of all modern nation states use this format. The advantages of the unitary system are (1) uniformity of public policy enforcement and (2) a centralized government. The primary disadvantage to this system is that sub-governments lack both the authority and the resources to adequately address immediate emergencies and regional demands.

In contrast, power flows from bottom to top under a confederative format. A **confederation** is "a loose collection of states in which principal power lies at the level of the individual states rather than at the level of the central or national government."[12] Created by its own sub-governing units, the national government has very narrowly defined governing authority and functions as assigned to it by the sub-governing entities. Although the national government may be empowered to create legislative acts, the individual sub-governing units must decide whether to implement those acts upon those within their boundaries. Usually, the national government is denied the power to tax and must rely upon funding from their sub–governing units. The national government may have the authority to declare war, but the national government does not have its own standing army. Therefore, it is dependent upon the sub-governing units to supply the needed manpower and weaponry. The individual units or states have the option of whether to participate with the understanding that the national government does not have the authoritarian muscle to force compliance. The relationship is indeed a very loose one. According to the enabling documents, a state or sub-governing unit may opt at any time to withdraw from the confederacy. And, the national government simply lacks the authority and the military power to force that state to remain a member. The United Nations is basically a confederative association of nation states. As evidenced by several international crises, the official response by the United Nations is oftentimes a weak one since the organization does not have the authority to compel compliance, cooperation, or even obedience from its member nations.

The **federal system** is a combination of the best features of both the unitary and confederative formats. In this configuration, governing authority and power flows simultaneously from top to

Not all citizens are treated fairly in a federated system. The distribution of goods and services required by families for a healthy and meaningful existence usually comes from the state. But what happens if the state either refuses to provide such services or, worse yet, decides to distribute them unequally? Does this occur in America? Can you cite some examples?

bottom. **Federalism** is "the mode of political organization that unites separate polities within an overarching political system by distributing power among general and constituent governments in a manner designed to protect the existence and authority of both."[13] It is a system of shared governance. Whether it is a school district, water or utility district, a city council, a county government or a state government, all levels of government have the legitimate authority to actually govern the people within respective jurisdictions.

Why A Federal System?

After winning a long fight for their independence from Britain, the former colonies initially selected a confederative governing system under the **Articles of Confederation**. Unfortunately, the weaknesses of confederative system doomed its longevity. The Framers opted to change their governing structure. Through the Constitution, the Framers basically dismantled a confederative government and replaced it with the federal model. As adopted in 1789, the Constitution "created a national government with sovereign powers of its own—powers that once belong exclusively to state governments. The proud sovereignty of the states was radically undermined; the 'state's rights' which remained, although robust in the Founding Period, bore scant resemblance to the autonomy enjoyed by the states under the Articles."[14] As detailed in Chapter 1, the Framers desired to create a government based on the concepts of separation of powers and checks and balances as well as establishing a workable and viable governing relationship between the national government and the individual states. This task was not an easy one:

> The constitutional place of the states in the federal system is determined by four elements: the provisions in the federal and state constitutions that either limit or guarantee the powers of the states vis-a-vis the federal government; the provisions in the federal constitution that give the states a role in the composition of the national government; the subsequent inter-

pretations of both sets of provisions by the courts (particularly the United States Supreme Court); and the unwritten constitutional traditions that evolved informally and only later become formally recognized through the first three, directly or indirectly.[15]

However, the Framers saw several benefits to a federal system including:

> the prevention of abuse of power because no single group is likely to gain control of government at the state and local levels; the encouragement of innovation by testing new ideas at the local level; the creation of many centers of power to resolve conflict and to handle administrative burdens; the stimulation of competition among levels of government that encourages policy innovation; and as James Madison predicted, the prevention of abuse of power because it is nearly impossible for a single group to gain control of government at all levels.[16]

Actually, there are two distinct levels of federalism in the United States. The relationship and lines of authority between the national government and her individual state governments were cemented through vertical federalism whereas horizontal federalism establishes a constitutionally mandated mutual and, hopefully, beneficial harmonious relationship between the states.

Constitutionally Mandated Intergovernmental Relationships—Vertical Federalism

Vertical federalism is the governing authority that flows up and down between the national and state governments. Vertical intergovernmental relations "take place when the national government interacts with the states or localities or when the states interact with localities."[17] This is the concept of shared governance whereby all levels of government have some governing authority, including the authority to make laws or in the case of local government, ordinances, implement them, enforce them through the application of appropriate sanctions, and govern under the watchful eye of the Constitution. "In the American federal system, sharing of functions by all planes of government is and always has been the norm."[18] The essential piece of vertical federalism, **Article VI** of the Constitution, cements the relationship between the states and the national government, and mandates without any doubt that all levels of government must comply with the spirit and meaning of the Constitution.

    Enumerated powers also referred to as **delegated powers** are "those rights and responsibilities of the U.S. government specifically provided for and listed in the Constitution."[19] To address weaknesses in the Articles of Confederation, the Framers took those specific powers originally given to the states and reassigned them to the national government. In **Article I,** the United States Congress is granted the exclusive authority to levy and collect taxes for the national government, borrow money, regulate interstate commerce, coin and establish the value of money, raise an army, establish post offices, establish the laws of naturalization, issue patents and copyrights, and declare war. These enumerated powers give the national government its muscle to exercise considerable control over all levels of government. The enumerated power to regulate interstate commerce, for example, has been used quite frequently to force state governments, business owners, and citizens to obey congressional enactments. In ***Gibbons v Ogden*** (1824), the United States Supreme Court "first put forth a broad interpretation of the commerce clause by defining interstate commerce to include all navigable waters even those within a state."[20] Subsequent Court decisions have liberally expanded the national government's interstate commerce jurisdiction as anything that has crossed or will eventually cross a state boundary line. The federal courts, Congress and the executive branch have used their power over interstate commerce to compel state compliance of congressional acts ranging from civil rights, desegregation, environmental regulations, welfare programs, work safety regulations, minimum wage laws, and highway speed limits.

The Framers also realized that they could not enumerate or list all of powers the national government would need to adjust to changing circumstances. Consequently, they added to Article I, Section 8 of the Constitution the statement that Congress can "make all Laws which shall be **necessary and proper** for carrying into execution the foregoing powers vested by this Constitution in the government of the United States, or in any department or office thereof." This clause is the **implied powers doctrine,** commonly referred to as the **necessary and proper clause** or the **elastic clause**. The implied powers doctrine gives considerable leverage to the national government to enact legislation addressing the concerns that oftentimes should be the privy of state governments. Once again, the U.S. Supreme Court has historically upheld the national government's use of its implied powers. From the beginning, the **Anti-Federalists** expressed their displeasure of the implied powers doctrine emphasizing that this clause along with the Supremacy Clause (Article VI) gave the national government far too much power over the states:

How far the clause in the 8th section of the 1st article may operate to do away all idea of confederated states, and to effect an entire consolidation of the whole into one general government, it is impossible to say. . . . But what is meant is, that the legislature of the United States are vested with the great and uncontroulable [uncontrollable] powers, of laying and collecting taxes, duties, imposts, and excises; of regulating trade, raising and supporting armies, organizing, arming, and disciplining the militia, instituting courts, and other general powers. And are by this clause invested with the power of making all laws proper and necessary, for carrying all these into execution; and they may so exercise this power as entirely to annihilate all state governments, and reduce this country to one single government. And if they may do it, it is pretty certain they will; for it will be found that the power retained by the individual states, small as it is, will be a clog upon the wheels of government of the United States; the latter therefore will be naturally included to remove it out of the way. Besides, it is a truth confirmed by the unerring experience of the ages, that every man, every body of men, invested with power, are ever disposed to increase it, and to acquire a superiority over every thing that stands in their way. This disposition, which is implanted in human nature, will operate in the federal legislature to lessen and ultimately to subvert the state authority, and having such advantages, will most certainly succeed, if the federal government succeeds at all. It must be very evident then, that what this constitution wants of being a complete consolidation of the several parts of the union into one complete government, possessed of perfect legislative, judicial, and executive powers, to all intents and purposes, it will be necessarily acquire in its exercise and operation.[21]

Although the national government has never taken any steps to "annihilate all state governments," it has from time to time interjected itself into policy areas that constitutionally and traditionally belong to the states. However, the Constitution does charge the national government with the task "to promote the general welfare" of the American people. The national government's involvement into matters such as education, transportation, civil rights, environment, etc., have taken place when state governments have demonstrated over a considerable period of time their inability to address these concerns.

Several enumerated powers are held **concurrently** by both national and all sub-government levels. For example, all governing authorities have the power to levy and collect taxes. However, each level of government must tax a different commodity and/or tax only a specified portion of the tax item such as state and federal income tax programs. Traditionally, the primary tax revenue stream for the national government is individual and corporate incomes. The majority of the states have a state income tax program combined with other sources of revenue. A state without a state income tax, Texas, relies heavily upon sales taxes and other regressive tax programs. Counties and cities have concurrent jurisdiction to tax property. Without the power to generate revenue from its residents, sub-government units would not be able to provide essential basic services. Also, the national and state governments concurrently have the power to establish judicial courts, make and enforce laws, and exercise eminent domain.

The Constitution would not have been ratified without granting some authority to the states. The Anti-Federalist camp contended that the newly written document was designed to give the national government the means to gradually strip from the states their governing authority. Specifically, the **9th Amendment** was written by James Madison "to address Anti-Federalist's concerns of 'federal intrusion upon respectively, peoples' rights and states' rights.'"[22] Furthermore, "had there been no 9th Amendment, 'Madison and his colleagues feared that it could be assumed that the people retained only the rights contained in the first eight amendments.'"[23] Both the 9th and 10th amendments compliment each other. The wording of the 9th Amendment is rather nebulous— "The enumeration in the Constitution, of certain rights, shall not be construed to deny or disparage others retained by the people." The **10th Amendment**, however, specifically grants to the states their **reserved powers**: "Those powers not delegated to the United States by the Constitution, nor prohibited by it to the States, are reserved to the States, respectively, or to the People." However, the amendment does not enumerate those powers nor does it clearly define the boundaries for the execution of those powers. Recently the intent of the 10th Amendment was openly challenged by President Trump when he was asked if the executive branch of the federal government had the authority over the individual states to lift coronavirus restrictions imposed by state governors. Trump stated that "when somebody's president of the United States, the authority is total."[24] Both the 9th and 10 Amendments were specially designed to prevent the national government from overpowering state authority. Ultimately, the Trump administration opted to leave the timing of each state's reentry into the economy up to their governors!

State authority has evolved over time to encompass four broad areas: policing, taxing, propriety authority, and eminent domain. **Police power** is "the authority to promote and safeguard the health, morals, safety and welfare of the people."[25] Consequently, all state and local authorities have their own law enforcement agencies operating under state laws and local ordinances to keep the peace. For example, the city council of San Antonio, Texas, passed a curfew ordinance in 1991, prohibiting children between the ages of 10 and 17 from any public place between the hours of 11:00 p.m. and 6:00 a.m. Exceptions were made for children accompanied by a parent and for those youths who are attending school, a government or religious sponsored activity, or lawfully employed. Parents of a child violating the ordinance are charged with a misdemeanor punishable by a fine of not less than $50 and no more than $100. Under the umbrella of police powers, state and local officials have the constitutional authority to establish their own laws and ordinances that meet the unique needs of their residents. There are no national speed limits, traffic laws, building codes, health guidelines, etc. Oftentimes, political and religious considerations impact legislative responses from state and local lawmakers. One of the major issues surrounding the coronavirus is the development of a vaccine. Many states require that all school-age children must be vaccinated against certain diseases before they attend school. In Texas, college-age students must show proof of a spinal meningitis vaccination before they can register for classes. Yet, some state legislative houses have granted vaccinated exemptions due to the parent's religious affiliations. With the coronavirus outbreak, each state and, in turn, locality is setting their own rules and timeframes for reopening their businesses and determining whether individuals must obey social distancing or even wearing a protective mask in public.

However, national law enforcement agencies such as the Federal Bureau of Investigation (FBI) do have jurisdiction when the criminal activity violates a federal law or involves crossing state boundary lines to commit a crime. State laws and local ordinances are subjected to judicial review by the federal courts when challenged on grounds of constitutionality. Actions taken by law enforcement officers also can be challenged before federal courts if their methods of enforcement violate protected constitutional rights. The **proprietary function** is "a governmental activity involving business-type operations ordinarily carried on by private companies . . . to include such activities as supplying electricity and gas, recreational facilities, garbage collection, transportation, etc."[26] This delegated power gives states and local governments the authority to provide necessary infrastructure and essential services to their citizens.

Granted to all levels of government, the power of **eminent domain** enables government to take private lands for public use as long as the property owner is justifiably compensated for loss of the property. Eminent domain has been used by all levels of government to secure private property for public use for a variety of projects from lucrative business development expansion projects, expressway and highway expansions and rights-of-way, sports venues, dams, drainage projects, high-rise apartment buildings and lately, the wall separating Mexico from the United States. The Supreme Court has been divided on the validity of eminent domain acquisitions. In 2005, the Court issued a 5-4 decision in ***Kelo v New London***. In this situation, a Connecticut city development plan included the acquisition of several residential properties to build a manufacturing plant for Pfizer, a major pharmaceutical company. Homeowners filed a suit alleging that they were denied the constitutional requirement of just compensation. The justices disagreed. Writing the majority opinion, Justice John Paul Stevens emphasized that "the government's pursuit of a public purpose will often benefit private parties." But Justice Sandra Day O'Connor dissented: "The fallout from this decision will not be random. The beneficiaries are likely those citizens who have disproportionate influence and power in the political process. . . The government has now license to transfer property from those with fewer resources to those with more."[27]

Section 9, of **Article I** of the Constitution places certain restrictions on both the national and state governments. The ***Writ of Habeas Corpus*** cannot be suspended except in cases of rebellion and insurrection. President Abraham Lincoln did suspend *habeas corpus* throughout the Civil War. All levels of government are constitutionally forbidden to issue bills of attainder, enact ex post facto laws, grant titles of nobility, and tax exports. **Section 10** of **Article I** specifically prohibits state governments from entering into treaties, granting Letters of Marque (documents issued by a nation allowing a private citizen to seize the citizens or goods of another nation), coining money, levying taxes on imports without prior congressional approval, maintaining an army or navy, forming interstate compacts with each other without prior congressional approval, and declaring war.

Constitutionally Mandated Intergovernmental Relationships—Horizontal Federalism

Horizontal federalism is "state-to-state interactions and relations."[28] The Framers were concerned about the ability of the states to cooperate with each other since the Articles of Confederation encouraged rivalry rather than cooperation. The Framers inserted **Article IV** or the **Full Faith and Credit Clause** to insure that the states would indeed work together. According to Section 1 of Article IV, "Full Faith and Credit shall be given in each State to the Public Acts, Records, and Judicial Proceedings of every other state." Furthermore, the Framers stressed the need for uniform acceptance by adding "and the Congress may by general Law prescribe the Manner in which such Acts, Records and Proceedings shall be proved, and the Effect thereof." Consequently, the majority of legal documents, including property deeds and birth and death certificates, are legal in all of the states regardless of the state originating the documents.

As stated in Section 2, "the Citizen of each State shall be entitled to all the Privileges and Immunities of Citizens of the Several States." This provision clearly places the individual as a citizen of his/her country above residency in a state. Citizens are guaranteed freedom of movement from state to state and residency in any state under the jurisdiction of the United States government. Individual states cannot put any additional requirements, such as educational attainment or income level for a person, to move to another state. Also, the requirement that states recognize and uphold individual rights and privileges as detailed in the Bill of Rights was strengthened with the passage of the Fourteenth Amendment's guarantee of equal protection and due process of the law for all citizens. The federal courts, in particular the Supreme Court, has dealt with numerous cases involving a state law or local ordinance that failed to provide equal protection and due process. In ***Fullilove v Klutznik*** (1980) the Supreme Court ruled "Congress has the authority to use quotas to remedy past discrimination in government public works programs, reasoning that the 14th Amendment's requirement of equal protection means that groups historically denied this right may be given special treatment."[29] Also, in ***Goesaert v Cleary*** (1948), the Court ruled any state laws denying women the right to practice certain occupations usually held by men to be an unconstitutional violation of the Fourteenth Amendment's equal protection clause. States, however, do exercise limited authority to treat newcomers differently. For example, state agencies are not required to honor professional and occupational licenses issued by other states. A licensed attorney in New Jersey cannot practice law in California until he/she has successfully passed the California Bar Exam. The same standards apply to teachers, hairdressers, plumbers, electricians, etc. Also, public colleges and universities can charge a higher out-of-state tuition fee to those students who do not meet local residency requirements. States can set different residency requirements for voting, filing for public office, qualifications for public office, etc. Section 2 also states that "A Person charged in any State with Treason, Felony, or other Crime, who shall flee from Justice, and found in another State, shall on Demand of the executive Authority of the State from which he fled, to be delivered up, to be removed to the State having Jurisdiction of the Crime." Therefore, the Constitution mandates that states actively participate in **interstate rendition** that is, "the return of a fugitive from justice by a state upon the demand of the executive authority of the state in which the crime was committed."[30]

The Framers addressed the practice of states arguing with each other over state boundary lines and the ownership of unsettled territories such as the Northwest Territories with a provision in Article III. This Article gives original jurisdiction to the federal courts in all cases involving "controversies between two or more States, between a State and Citizens of another state; between Citizens of different states; between Citizens of the same State claiming lands under Grants of different States." Obviously, the Framers had little faith that the individual states would successfully settle or judge fairly in disputes between each other.

FEDERALISM AND THE FEDERAL COURTS

As detailed in Chapter 11, the Judiciary Act of 1789 granted judicial review to the federal courts. Although all levels of government can pass laws, statutes or ordinances, those legislative acts that do not conform to the spirit and meaning of the United States Constitution can be judged by a panel of federal judges as unconstitutional acts. The United States Supreme Court is the court of last resort, meaning no subsequent appeal is possible. In exercising this authority, it is the federal courts that play a vitally crucial role in defining the appropriate relationship between the national and state governments.

The United States Supreme Court, however, has had periods of advocating a strong national government or **nation-centered federalism** offset by decisions that favored state laws. Immediately following the adoption of the Constitution, the newly formed Supreme Court rendered decisions in favor of a strong national government over state matters. In ***McCullough v Maryland*** (1819), the questions before the justices involved whether the national government had the authority to use eminent domain over the state of Maryland to construct a branch office of the National Bank as part of the implementation of a national banking law; and secondly, whether the state of Maryland had the right to levy and collect a property tax on the now-held federal property. This case challenged the necessary and proper clause of Article I, Section 8. Issuing a ruling that strengthened the national government's power over the states, the Supreme Court under the guidance of Chief Justice John Marshall ruled "after the most deliberate consideration, it is the unanimous and decided opinion of this Court, that the act to incorporate the Bank of the United States, is a law made in pursuance of the Constitution and is part of the supreme law of the land."[31] Additionally, Marshall stressed the power of the national government over the states by noting that their decision was based on a firm "conviction that the states have no power, by taxation or otherwise, to retard, impede, burden, or in any manner control, the operations of the constitutional laws enacted by Congress to carry into execution the powers vested in the general government. This is, we think, the unavoidable consequence of that supremacy which the Constitution has declared."[32]

Once again, Chief Justice Marshall's Court favored the national government over the states in *Cohen v Virginia* (1821) by defending the federal court's right to review judicial decisions issued by state courts. *Cohen* centered on the arrest and subsequent conviction of Cohen for illegally selling Washington, D.C., issued lottery tickets in Virginia. The Virginia state legislature had recently passed a law prohibiting the sale of any lottery tickets within the state. After losing his case at the state level, Cohen decided to file his complaint with the U.S. Supreme Court. Unfortunately for Cohen, the Supreme Court upheld the lower court ruling. Yet, just by hearing the case the Supreme Court opened the door for the federal courts to review the judgments issued by state courts. In writing the majority opinion, Marshall addressed this issue:

> The American States, as well as the American people, have believed a close and firm Union to be essential to their liberty and to their happiness. They have been taught by experience, that this Union cannot exist without a government for the whole; and they have been taught by the same experience that this government would be a mere shadow, that must disappoint all their hopes, unless invested with large portions of that sovereignty, which belongs to independent States. Under the influence of this opinion, and thus instructed by experience, the American people, in the conventions of their respective States adopted the present Constitution. If it could be doubted, whether from its nature, it was not supreme in all cases where it is empowered to act, that doubt would be removed by the declaration, that 'this constitution, and the laws of the United States, . . shall be the supreme law of the land, and the judges in every State shall be bound thereby; anything in the constitution or laws of any state to the contrary notwithstanding.' This is the authoritative language of the American people; and . . . of the American States. It marks, with lines too strong to be mistaken, the characteristic distinction between the government of the Union, and those of the States. The general government, through limited as to its objects, is supreme with respect to those objects. This principle is part of the Constitution; and if there be any who can deny its necessity, none can deny its authority.[33]

**Integration at Ole Mississippi University
James Meredith walking on the campus
of the University of Mississippi
accompanied by U. S. marshals.
October 1, 1962.**

In ***Gibbons v Ogden*** (1824), the Supreme Court tackled the question of whether the states or the national government had the authority to control shipping on the Hudson River. In 1807, the *North River Steamboat of Clermont* owned by Aaron Ogden made its maiden voyage from Albany, New York down the Hudson River, carrying raw materials to factories in New York and New Jersey. Ogden received a license to run his steamboats up and down the Hudson from Robert Livingston and Robert Fulton who had an exclusive shipping contract on the Hudson with the state of New York. A rival steamboat owner Thomas Gibson protested the state-issued exclusive contract since he had obtained a federally issued license under the Coasting Act of 1793. The question before the Court was which level government had the right to control shipping interests on the Hudson River. The Court's final decision dealt a blow to the states by once again favoring the national government over the states. The Marshall Court ruled that "this power [regulation of interstate commerce], like all others vested in Congress, is complete in itself, may be exercised to its upmost extent, and acknowledges no limitations other than are prescribed in the Constitution."[34] Chief Justice Marshall used this case to define the Court's interpretation of "interstate" commerce:

> The words are 'congress shall have the power to regulate commerce with foreign Nations, and among the several states, and with the Indian tribes' . . . The subject to be regulated is commerce; and our Constitution [is] . . . one of *enumeration, and not of definition*, to ascertain the extent of the power, it becomes necessary to settle the meaning of the word . . . Commerce, undoubtedly, is traffic, but it [is] something more—it is intercourse. It describes the commercial intercourse between nations, and parts of nations, in all its branches, and is regulated by prescribing rules for carrying on that intercourse . . . The power over commerce including navigation, was one of the primary objects for which the people of America adopted their government, and must have been contemplated in forming it. . . . The word used in this Constitution, then, comprehends, and have been always understood to comprehend, navigation within its meaning; and a power to regulate navigation is expressly granted, as if that term had been added to the word 'commerce'. To what commerce does then power extend? The Constitution informs us, to commerce 'with foreign nations, and among the several states and with the Indian tribes'. It has, we believe, been universally admitted, that these words comprehend every species of commercial intercourse between the United States and foreign nations . . . The subject to which the power is next applied, is to commerce 'among the several states.' The word 'among' means intermingled with . . . Commerce among the states cannot stop at the external boundary line of each state . . . The grant of this power carries with it the whole subject, leaving nothing for the state to act upon.[35]

Therefore, the Court's ruling gave the national government the constitutional authority to oversee all commercial activity that crosses any state boundary line, leaving the states with just the authority over commerce traveling within their state boundary lines, commonly known as **intrastate commerce**. In 1887, Congress created the **Interstate Commerce Commission (ICC)** to provide federal regulatory oversight for all surface transportation systems including trains, trucks, buses, freight forwarders and express companies as well as all in-land waterway and coastal shipping with the primary goal of eliminating rate discrimination by mandating fair rates. In 1906, the ICC's authority was expanded to include automobile transportation. The ICC was abolished in 1995 but its regulatory functions were reassigned to the Surface Transportation Board.

The Supreme Court shifted its strong national government position to a more pro-state position in the early nineteenth century. However, the Court shifted back to a pro-national government stance during the Great Depression as the national government expanded its authority over the states with the implementation of New Deal legislation. Consequently from the 1930s to the mid-1990s, "the expansion of the federal role has been greatest, for example, in matters involving individual rights, civil rights, voting rights, and legislative apportionment. It has not been as extensive in programmatic areas that affect state and local finances or directly, such as welfare and education."[36] The shifting between pro-national and pro-state positions is illustrated in three Supreme Court decisions. In 1917, the Supreme Court heard arguments in ***Bunting v Oregon*** concerning whether a state government could mandate a ten-hour workday. The Oregon state legislature passed a law mandating the employers could not work their employees over ten-hours per day. Furthermore, the company had to pay that employee time-and-a-half for those three hours. The owner of the company refused to pay the wage differential. Filing a lawsuit, Bunting claimed that the state of Oregon did not have the authority to regulate working hours of a privately held company. Supreme Court justices "for the first time made clear that states had authority to regulate working conditions in all businesses for all workers."[37] Yet, their decision centered on working conditions, not state-mandated salary scales. Basically, "the Supreme Court refused to let stand state laws setting minimum wages until 1937 . . . which paved the way for the 1938 **Federal Fair Labor Standards Act**, a national standard work week of 44 hours, and a 15-cent hourly minimum wage."[38] Initially in ***National League of Cities v Usery*** (1976), the Court ruled that the Tenth Amendment prohibited the national government from setting wages and maximum working hour requirements for state employees. However, in ***Garcia v San Antonio Metropolitan Transit Authority*** (1985), the Court reversed its *Usery* decision by ruling that a federal mandate requiring that state public employees must be paid at least the minimum wage and be granted overtime as detailed in the Fair Labor Standards Act did not violate any constitutional provision. In ***South Carolina v Baker*** (1988), the Court ruled that Congress could tax interest earned from individual savings accounts and dividends on state and locally issued bonds.

An advocate of returning more governing authority to the states, President Ronald Reagan established in 1987 a thirteen-person commission to study whether services traditionally provided by the federal government could be either privatized or reassigned to the states. He also appointed jurists to federal benches who supported his position. In particular, his appointment of Antonin Scalia in 1986 followed by George H. W. Bush's selection of Clarence Thomas to Supreme Court moved the Court to a more conservative panel favorable to a less intrusive role for the national government into matters traditionally reserved to the states. Consequently "not since before the New Deal-era constitution revolution in 1937, have the states received such protection in the U.S. Supreme Court from allegedly burdensome federal statutes."[39] A pro-state decision was handed down by the Court in ***United States v Lopez*** (1995) when the justices "struck down as exceeding congressional authority under the commerce clause, a federal law that made it a crime to carry a gun within 1,000 feet of a school. The Court declared that the law had nothing to do with commerce and intruded upon the police power of the states."[40] In ***Plintz v United States*** (1997), the Court once again backed state governments by declaring unconstitutional a provision of the Brady Bill requiring local law enforcement officials to conduct background checks before issuing handguns as an unfunded mandate and an unconstitutional intrusion upon state governing bodies. The current Court under the guidance of Chief Justice John Roberts has taken a case-by-case approach in determining whether the national government has overstepped its authority with state and local governing bodies.

STATES' RIGHTS V NATIONAL POWER

The nagging question of how much authority the national government can exercise over state and other governing authorities was debated from the very founding of this country and was a hot topic of debate during the Constitutional Convention in Philadelphia. However, the brewing and contentious political battle over the abolition of slavery drew the battle lines between the North and South over the national government's attempt to politically and economically control the southern states. Slavery was indeed abolished, but the arguments of states' rights over the national government persist today. Whenever the muscle of the national government is feared to be too instructive, state governors fight back. In the 1960s, it was Governor Ross Barnett of Mississippi that openly defied his own National Guard units who under the direct order of President John Kennedy were charged with protecting James Meredith, as he became the first African- American student admitted to the University of Mississippi. It was Lester Maddox of Georgia who hailed an ax in the air to symbolically cut the state's ties with the national government over mandated desegregation of the state's public schools. In 1994, an angry group of Texas ranchers and landowners openly challenged the Environmental Protection Agency's (EPA) mandate to protect the breeding grounds of the Golden Warbler over individual property rights. Several state governors unsuccessfully sued the national government over the Affordable Care Act as the majority of the nation's Republican governors openly defied the Obama administration by not accepting increased Medicaid funding and supporting Obamacare registration efforts. A former governor himself, President George W. Bush faced criticism from a multitude of state governors over his mandated federal education program, No Child Left Behind. The term **states' rights** is defined as the "opposition to increasing the national government's power at the expense of the states."[41] Historically, those who have advocated states' rights over national authority include Thomas Jefferson, John C. Calhoun, the Supreme Court from 1920-1937, and Presidents Ronald Reagan and George W. Bush.

John C. Calhoun (1782-1850) was undoubtedly the most ardent advocate of states' rights. A former vice president and renowned senator from South Carolina, Calhoun believed in the **compact theory** of government whereby governments were created by and existed for the benefit of the people. If that government failed to provide for its people, then the people had the right to abolish that government and begin anew. In his *Discourses of the American Constitution*, Calhoun argued that the American government was "federal and not national because it is a government of a community of States, not the government of a single State or nation."[42] Seeing the Constitution as merely an intergovernmental agreement, Calhoun wrote that "the sovereignty of the States, in the fullest sense of the term, is declared to be the essential principle of the Union; and it is not only asserted as a incontestable right, but also claimed as an absolute political necessity in order to protect the minority against the majority."[43] Accordingly, these sovereign states envisioned creating a national government with limited power over the states. States' rights advocates see the national government as merely an agent serving the needs of the state governments similar to the confederative system created under the Articles of Confederation. They stress that those powers not enumerated specifically to the national government are exclusively reserved to the states. Also, the national government has absolutely no right to use any of its enumerated and implied powers to interfere in state governance.

Calhoun developed three options that both states and the American people could take to halt the intrusive nature of the national government into state affairs. First, Calhoun shifted the placement of people in their relationship with the national government. Those advocating a strong national government, see both the national and state governments having direct authority over people with each level of government enacting and enforcing legislation independently of each other. Calhoun on the other hand, believed in the concept of **interposition** whereby "a state may place itself between its citizens and the national government so as to prevent the enforcement of national law upon its citizens."[44] He placed the states as the middlemen or buffer zones to shield the people living in their states from, as he perceived, harmful national mandates. Calhoun believed that "the states have the right 'to interpose' when the Federal government is guilty of a usurpation, because, as there is not common judge over them, they, as the parties to the compact, have to determine for themselves whether it has been violated."[45] Basically, he argued that Congress could pass any law it wanted, including the abolition of slavery; however, it was up to each state's legislative house to approve any congressional act before it could be implemented and enforced within their states. Second, Calhoun's concept of **concurrent majority** was based on the belief that "democratic decisions should be made only with the concurrence of all major segments of society."[46] Subsequently, national laws are binding only if a majority of the nation's citizens concurred with these enactments. Calhoun wrote that "government of the concurrent majority . . . excludes the possibility of oppression by giving to each interest or portion, or order—where there are established classes—the means of protecting itself by its negative against the measures calculated to advance the peculiar interests of others at its expense."[47] Once again, if Congress voted to abolish slavery, it could do so only after a national referendum election indicated that a majority of the American people agreed to it. He also had measures to protect American citizens living in frontier areas not under the protection of statehood. Calhoun believed that "each sectional majority or large interest that was not territorially based has the constitutional power to an absolute veto over any action of the federal government that, while representing the national majority, threatened the welfare of the minority."[48] Third, the last option available to the states would be **nullification** whereby a state or states could see no other avenue available but to declare the relationship between themselves and the national government null and void. This would free the states from their contractual obligation to the Constitution and allow them to establish their own sovereignty as independent nations absolutely separated from the union of the United States. Calhoun's arguments of an over intrusive national government into state affairs would prove to be one of the justifications the southern states used to secede from the union and set the stage for the American Civil War.

The issue of whether a state could successfully secede from the union was settled with the Supreme Court's ruling in ***Texas v White*** (1869). The Court's decision reinforced the sentiments of a strong national government advocated by Alexander Hamilton, George Washington and James Madison:

Signing of the Voting Rights Act by President Lyndon B. Johnson. Dr. Martin Luther King and others look on. LBJ Library photo by Yoichi Okamoto, 08/06/1965.

The Union of the States never was a purely artificial and arbitrary relation. It began among the Colonies and grew out of common origin, mutual sympathies, kindred principles, similar interests, and geographical relations. It was confirmed and strengthened by the necessities of war, and received definite form, character, and sanction, from the Articles of Confederation. By these the Union was solemnly declared to 'be perpetual.' And, when these Articles were found to be inadequate to the exigencies of the country, the Constitution was ordained 'to form a more perfect union.' But the perpetuity and indissolubility of the Union by no means implies the loss of distinct and individual existence, or of the right of self-government by the States. On the contrary, it may be not unreasonably said, that the preservation of the States, and the maintenance of their governments, are as much within the design and care of the Constitution, as the preservation of the Union and the maintenance of the National Government. *The Constitution, in all of its provisions, looks to be an indestructible Union composed of indestructible States.*[49]

In a subsequent ruling in ***Coyle v Smith*** (1911), the Court reinforced the equality of the states in the eyes of the national government. The ruling "established the principle that all states are admitted to the union on an equal footing. Congress may not enforce conditions that would undermine the equality of the states."[50] However, the Court has yet to rule that states cannot decide to split into separate states such as West Virginia from Virginia.

States' rights arguments are essential to gaining an understanding of the fragile relationship between the states and the national government. The Tea Party movement was to a degree founded on the principle of state supremacy over the national government particularly on issues such as health care, welfare programs, gun control, etc. In Texas, there is the Republic of Texas group that believes that Texas was imperialistically taken into the United States. They advocate that Texas is still an independent nation under the Republic of Texas established in 1836 after gaining its independence from Mexico. Throughout the South, southern conservative Democrats and many Republicans preach the same tune—the fear of an overly intrusive national government—Big Brother—meddling into matters that by constitutional decree should be addressed in state legislative houses, not the Capitol on Hill.

THE CHANGING FACES OF FEDERALISM

Whether state interests overshadow national interests or vice versa, the course of federalism swings back and forth. It does not, however, change in precise cycles where, for example, every fifty years the states are in the driver's seat only to see the national government turn the swing to its side for another fifty years, and so forth. Oftentimes the change is driven by the political ideology on Capitol Hill, in the White House, or both. The pattern shows that "in conservative periods, the roles of state governments have been enhanced, whereas in liberal or pro-government periods, the role of the national government has grown."[51] The gridlock in Washington, particularly in 2013, involved a Republican/conservative majority in the House of Representatives against a Democratic/liberal Senate and a Democratic/liberal president. The 2016 election of Donald Trump to the presidency brought Republican Party majorities to both houses of Congress. The 2018 midterm elections resulted in the Democrats seizing control of the House while the Republicans retained the majority in the Senate. However, the divide between liberal and conservative political philosophy is still the same as the Republicans want less government control from Washington while the Democrats want a strong presence for the federal government into state affairs. One of the historically guiding factors opening the door for the might of the national government is when the states have failed to manage their own affairs; or have demonstrated their inability to handle their own problems; or they simply ask for federal assistance. In its preamble, the United States Constitution tasks the national government with the responsibility to promote the general welfare of the people of the United States. To accomplish this, the national government has been from time to time motivated to take the upper hand over the states, not in response to period cycles or political shifts in power, but in response to particular problems and crises threatening the general welfare of the American people.

From the inception of the Constitution to 1932, the relationship between the states and the national government was one of **dual federalism** whereby "autonomous national, subnational, and local governments all pursued their own interests independently" of each other.[52] Dual federalism is also known as **layered cake federalism** since its approach to intergovernmental relationships resembles a traditional layer cake with the national government as the top tier and subsequent tiers belonging to sub-government units ranging from the states to the lowest possible governing unit. The layers are separated and protected from interference from each other by thick layers of icing. The United States Supreme Court respected this relationship with only rare occasions when the Court extended the role of the national government over the states. For example, the need for a national banking system was evidenced by the individual states' inability to control their own evolving banking industries, thus crippling national business development. In most states, banks were operating without the guidelines of state charters, charging inconsistent interest rates, and operating under unfair practices detrimental to the nation's economy. In *McCullough v Maryland* (1819), the Supreme Court upheld the national government's authority to create a national banking system. The prevailing belief of the time was that the national government had no constitutional right to intervene into a function "reserved" to the individual states. Even during the height of the Progressive Era with its cadre of social reforms, the states remained in the preeminent role. It was state governments, not the national government, that were "left to take action regarding such problems as care of dependent children. Federal domestic programs in the late 1920s were so limited that state spending was double federal spending. States also were dominant over cities as policy makers, spending about three times as much money as local governments."[53]

The 1929 collapse of the Stock Market and the tragedy of the Great Depression of the 1930s changed the relationship from dual to cooperative federalism. The states were totally unprepared to handle Depression-era problems particularly in dealing with millions of unemployed, widespread hunger, and homelessness. **Cooperative federalism** is "the notion that the national, state and local governments are interacting agents, jointly working to solve common problems, rather than being conflicting, sometimes hostile competitors pursuing similar or more likely conflicting ends.[54] The New Deal programs created by President Franklin Roosevelt were dependent upon cooperation between the national government and state and local governments to provide much needed employment opportunities, food, housing and economic development, in hopes of preventing another catastrophic economic downturn similar to the Great Depression. Cooperative federalism is also known as **marble cake federalism** since there is no distinct separation between the layers of government but rather, they are blended together just like a marble cake. Cooperative federalism brought billions of federal dollars to state and local governments for much needed infrastructure improvements, economic development, job creation programs and incentives, and social service programs. Cooperative federalism ended in 1964.

The hallmarks of Lyndon Johnson's presidency were the Great Society programs and his declared War on Poverty. He believed that with the adoption of his programs he could improve the quality of life for all Americans. The Johnson era ushered in a reconfiguration of federalism known as **creative federalism**, that is "characterized by joint planning and decision making among all levels of government (as well as the private sector), in the management of intergovernmental programs."[55] Particularly for social programs, the success of creative federalism was dependent upon "relationships between Washington and many other independent centers of decision in state and local governments, in new public bodies, in universities, in professional organizations and in business. Creative federalism includes a deliberate policy of encouraging the growth of institutions that will be independent of and, in part, antagonistic to federal government power. Almost every part of every new program transfers federal funds to some outside agency."[56] Johnson was convinced that the only way to address this nation's problems was to use the talents of a multi-leveled think tank of experts from all walks of life. During the 1960s, landmark legislation dealing with civil rights, equality of accommodations, voting rights, affirmative action, desegregation, abolition of restrictive covenants, equal employment opportunities, etc., were passed and signed into law. The implementation and enforcement phases of these new laws were legislatively given to the individual states. Initially, state governments particularly in the southern states were unwilling and very uncooperative. It was creative federalism that gave the national government its leverage to encourage and, oftentimes, force states into compliance by cementing the flow of ample and much needed federal grant money to fund the new federal mandates. To continue receiving money for low-income housing (Section 8), highway and roadway projects, public education, and so on, the states had to enforce the federal laws. Non-compliance would mean either a reduction in federal monetary allocations or, at worst, elimination of federal dollars. Creative federalism dealt another severe blow to the states. Under numerous programs, any agency, city or county government could apply and receive a federal grant without prior approval from their governor's office. And if awarded, the money went directly to the grant recipient. "As a result, by 1980 about 30 percent of all federal aid bypassed state governments, compared to 8 percent in 1960."[57]   Consequently, governors and state legislative houses lost some of their control over their own sub-government units. Governors wanted to assume the role of "gatekeeper" over federal monies. For example, a city's mayor wanted to apply for a federal grant for a low-income housing project. City leaders would have to have the permission from their state governor to even begin the application process.   If granted permission to proceed, the grant application would have to be filed with the state governor's office, which could either approve or disapprove sending it to Washington for consideration. And if the grant was awarded, the federal money would come to the governor's desk first for subsequent allocation to the local governing body. The fear in Washington was that any state governor could either keep the money for the state treasury or use if for something else.

A former governor, Ronald Reagan, entered the White House with firm the resolve to reverse the direction of intergovernmental relationships. Once again, the essence of federalism shifted back to the states. He was particularly critical of the numerous federal mandates attached to federal grants viewing them as intrusions upon the ability of states and local governments to govern for themselves and as a blatant violation of the Constitution's Tenth Amendment. Sounding like John C. Calhoun, Reagan told a national audience "it is my intention to curb the size and influence of the Federal establishment and to demand recognition of the distinction between the powers granted to the Federal Government and those reserved to the states or to the people. All of us need to be reminded that the Federal Government did not create the states; the states created the Federal Government."[58] Coined **New Federalism**, Reagan's primary goal of his reconfigured brand of federalism was "to make states' rights the effective policy of the land by reducing the role of the national government in state and local affairs by slowing the flow of federal dollars to states and municipalities as part of a national strategy to discourage their dependency on the federal government, and by returning to state and local officers more control over how money should be spent."[59] Reagan, however, had an ulterior motive. For him, New Federalism was also a tool to reduce the national deficit by shifting the financial burden for state/local infrastructure projects from the federal purse to state/local pocketbooks.

The credit for New Federalism actually belongs to President Richard Nixon. In a radio message delivered on Labor Day in 1972, Nixon warned workers "when Government tampers too much with the lives of individuals, when it unnecessarily butts into the free collective bargaining process, it cripples the private enterprise system on which the welfare of the worker depends."[60] During his tenure in the White House, Nixon consolidated numerous federal agencies overseeing state/local grant programs into ten regional councils. Federal regulations were simplified and streamlined to allow state and local governments more autonomy in the decision-making process. Reagan went a step further by consolidating fifty-seven categorical grant programs into nine broad block grants. Another sixty categorical grants were eliminated in 1981.

Once again, to reduce the federal deficit, Reagan planned to give state governments full administrative and financial responsibility for two of the nation's costliest federal programs—food stamps and Aid to Families with Dependent Children plus another forty-one smaller programs. In return, the federal government would assume control over the Medicaid program. This creative swap was stalled in Congress when state governors complained about their lack of funds to run the programs. With pressure from discontented Democrats and minority groups, Reagan abandoned New Federalism by the start of his second term of office. However, he did accomplish the easing of federal intrusion into state business by issuing **Executive Order 12612,** which eliminated and/or relaxed numerous federal regulations dealing with social service programs. However, New Federalism was only marginally successful as Congress gradually reinstated and added new federal regulations and mandates.

The course of federalism shifted once again with the election of Bill Clinton. Serving as a governor during the Reagan presidency, Clinton understood a governor's frustration of trying to solve poverty, crime, and unemployment without ample financial assistance from the national government. Yet, like Reagan, Clinton was unprepared to give states and local governing bodies a federal blank check. He created a new brand of federalism—**Constrained Empathetic Federalism** based on the creation of **empowerment zones** whereby non-federal resources are combined with modest federal-cash outlays. Clinton requested congressional funding for six urban and three rural zones. Initially, the federal government would fund the majority of the costs with the understanding that once a zone achieved its targeted economic development, the financial burden would shift to the empowerment zone, alleviating the federal government's financial commitment.

The pendulum swung again when George W. Bush entered the presidency with his intention of reconfiguring Reagan's New Federalism into his **pragmatic federalism**. Initially, he formed a special committee to evaluate which federal programs would fare better under federal or state/local control. However, pragmatic federalism never really took root. After the attacks on the World Trade Center, the Bush administration's focus was more on firming up national security and the war on terrorism. Although he was not yet ready to coin a new term for federalism, President Obama adopted Franklin Roosevelt's New Deal policies to address the nation's economic upheaval. Initially, Obama agreed to Bush's federal rescue of the automobile industry and continued fueling money into major businesses and financial institutions to reverse declining economic trends. In another package closely akin to Roosevelt's Works Progress Administration, Obama allocated federal dollars to state and local governments to address needed infrastructure projects but, at the same time, put the unemployed back to work. On the campaign trail, candidate Donald Trump hinted that he would opt for a return to a Reagan-styled federalism by eliminating and/or easing federal regulations imposed on business and industry. Regardless of what direction the federal/state pendulum swings, it is a truism that states and local communities do not have the financial resources needed to stand alone in addressing their state's problems. The federal government has and will always be called upon to provide financial assistance to sub-government units.

FEDERAL GRANT PROGRAMS

The federal government's adventure into providing financial assistance to the states actually began in 1785 with the passage of the **Northwest Land Ordinance Act** that gave federal lands for public education in the Western territories. A **grant** is "a form of gift that entails certain obligations on the part of the grantee and expectations on the part of the grantor."[61] The "gift" has strings attached to it that the recipient must fulfill or the recipient will be subjected to a sanction, fine, or denied the privilege of receiving another "gift." Federal dollars have helped to build the nation's interstate and intrastate highway systems, the Intercontinental Railroad, canals, etc. Sporadic in the beginning, the flow of federal funds via grants began to significantly increase in the 1950s. Federal grant programs are designed to give much needed federal dollars to state and local governments to offset the costs of providing for the "general welfare" of the American people. The relationship between the national and state/local governments reminds one of the tales of Robin Hood and his men of Sherwood Forest of taking from the rich and giving to the poor. Giving state and local governments federal money enables these governing bodies to provide better services to their residents, as well as to experiment with new approaches to solve decades-old urban problems. The generosity of the federal government is staggering. In 1990, the federal government gave $135,325,000,000 in federal grants-in-aid to state and local governments. By 2019, state and local governments received an estimated $749,554,000,000 from the federal government, an increase of 7.6 percent over 2018 allocations.[62] As of 2018, there are currently 1,274 funded federal grants of which 1,253 are categorical and 21 block grant programs.[63]

Collectively, **grants-in-aid** are "federal payments to states or federal or state payments to local governments for specified purposes and are usually subject to supervision and review by the granting government or agency in accordance with prescribed standards and requirements."[64] There are several types of grant programs including categorical, project, formula, and block. A **categorical grant** is a federal payment to a state or local government for a specific purpose. These grants are awarded for social service programs, educational projects, highway construction, building airports, etc. Interested parties applied and competed with each other for the federal funds. Usually categorical grants had a matching requirement whereby the recipient was required to contribute some its own money towards the project. Matching agreements could range from 10 to 50 percent of the total costs, insuring that the recipient would be anxious to complete the project since its own money was now committed to it. The two basic types of categorical grants are project and formula. Favored in the 1960s, **project grants** were used to build the majority of the nation's public housing projects. The money was allocated to state and local governments on an as-need-basis, as demonstrated through the application process. Under the **formula grant program**, Congress allocates money to states and local governments based on a predetermined formula. Constituting approximately 80 percent of all federal grants, categorical grants are preferred by Congress since they had an influential role in determining how the money would be spent. In ensure compliance to grant specifications, the federal government reserves the right to conduct periodic on-site inspections and audits. Perhaps the only major weakness in the program is the confusion over which agency to apply with and the overwhelming number of duplicated projects. Whereas categorical grants were designed for specific projects, block grants are given for prescribed broader activities ranging from health care to education. These grants have fewer federal guidelines and regulations over other grant programs, giving the recipient more flexibility in using the money. Presidents George H.W. Bush, George W. Bush and Barack Obama and most state governors prefer block grants.

Introduced by President Nixon in 1972, the cornerstone of the Robin Hood approach was the **General Revenue Fund** whereby through **revenue sharing** federal money would be provided without a cadre of burdensome strings and mandates from the federal government. Funding allocations were based on a formula that took into account an area's population, income level, tax effort, etc. Urban areas with a high percentage of below poverty-level residents would receive a larger allocation over a predominately higher income area. Revenue sharing was gradually phased out beginning in 1980 when President Carter eliminated state governments from the program. In 1986, the entire program was eliminated since the Reagan administration believed that "legislators and bureaucrats should not collect taxpayers' money from each state only to turn around and send that same money back to the states."[65]

Federal grants have always been controversial. On the positive side, the ample flow of federal dollars to resource-starved sub-government units has enabled the federal government to force grant recipients to implement federally mandated nondiscriminatory laws and workforce regulations. Grants have strengthened the relationship between the national governments and sub-government units. The national government provides the funding, overall regulations, and program goals and objectives as determined through congressional legislation. In turn, the states and/or sub-government units administer the programs, deliver the services, and implement federal mandates. However, federal grant programs have their drawbacks. A list of complaints from attendees at a National Governor's Conference held in the 1970s still ring true today:

- There is a lack of coordination among federal departments or agencies limiting the effectiveness of programs in addressing problems that the programs were designed to solve.
- The increased administrative burden on the states is oftentimes overwhelming.
- The federal executive branch has exceeded its proper authority in some areas, encroaching on matters which are in the proper jurisdiction of the states.
- Federal regulations are prescriptive in methodology rather than oriented toward end results.
- Excess reporting and paperwork requirements must be met by state/local governments participating in federal programs.
- Funding and program implementation can be held up by lengthy approval processes, absence of program guidelines, and other administrative practices that lead to serious dislocations and inequities at the state/local level.
- Lack of federal coordination and consistency in implementing direct cost determination procedures creates continuing administrative confusion for the states.[66]

A lingering complaint about all federal grant programs is the practice of the national government forcing recipients to comply with a laundry list of federal laws and regulations by attaching strings or mandates to the grants. Noncompliance can be disastrous. There are four major categories of mandates. First a **direct order** is a congressional law or regulation that must be enforced or grant recipients can be held accountable to civil or criminal penalties. For example, all federal grant recipients must comply with all of the provisions of the Equal Employment Opportunity Act, the Occupational Safety and Health Act, the Americans with Disabilities Act, Title VII of the Civil Rights Act, all subsequent civil rights laws, the Fair Labor Standards Act, and the Environmental Protection Act. Failure to comply carries a very stiff price. Second, **crossing cutting regulations** apply to every grant program including, if necessary, an environmental impact statement. Many grants contain **crossover sanctions** whereby state and local governments will lose their federal funding for noncompliance. Finally, a **partial and out-right pre-emption mandate** occurs when a state or local government fails to establish its own requirements thereby leaving the door open for the federal agency overseeing the project to have partial or complete jurisdiction over the project. Congress supports mandates as the only means of forcing state and local governments to follow its dictates or face losing billions of dollars in federal funding.

Both Congress and state legislative houses are guilty of applying unfunded mandates to their sub-governing units. An **unfunded mandate** is "one level of government requiring another to offer and pay for a program as a matter of law or as a prerequisite to partial or full funding for either the program in question or other programs."[67] For example, a state legislative house passes a law requiring that all public school districts reduce their average classroom size in the elementary and pre-school levels to ensure more quality time between teachers and students. However, the legislature does not give the school districts the additional revenue to build additional classrooms or to hire more teachers. In 1994, the Republican Party under the leadership of Speaker of the House Newt Gingrich issued its "Contract with America" that included a push for Congress to eliminate all federal unfunded mandates. In 1995, President Clinton signed into law a bill requiring the Congressional Budget Office to provide at least the cost of the proposed legislative mandate prior to the bill's approval. However, very few state legislative houses have follow suit.

While the pros and cons of federal grants programs are being continuously debated, the reality is state and local governments are dependent upon federal funding. They cannot shrink from their responsibilities to their citizens. Local governments cannot simply delegate this burden to the next lowest governing unit because there is no level below them. Emergency situations such as a hurricane in the Gulf Coast, wildfires in California, an oil spell heading for Louisiana, a snow storm in Atlanta, Georgia, or a deadly coronavirus pandemic must be properly handled. Once again, the states and definitely local governments simply do not have the funds or the resources to handle these situations by themselves.

Rising Interstate Conflicts

As evidence by the Articles of Confederation, states had numerous conflicts with each other over everything from the route of canals to state boundary lines. To correct this, the Framers envisioned that the **interstate compact**, defined as an agreement between two or more states requiring congressional approval, would fix the problem. These agreements over the years have been used to settle transportation disputes, river boundary changes, and interstate commerce issues. However, the Framers certainly did not anticipate the commercial and business rivalries of today. States openly compete with each other over sports franchises, sites for national political conventions, and business relocations. States market themselves by emphasizing their positives and downplaying their negatives. The best known sectional rivalries are between East versus West, and "sunbelt" versus "frost belt" or "rustbelt" states.

THE FUTURE OF FEDERALISM

The concepts of vertical and horizontal federalism are based on shared governance between the various levels of governing units. The Framers wanted a balanced government with national and state governments working side by side to address the nation's problems. Basically, "federalism has been praised because:

(1) it permits a flexible policy that can be adopted to individual circumstances, and therefore, reduces conflict between levels of government;

(2) it disperses power widely and thus, in its pluralism it minimizes the risk of tyranny;

(3) it encourages public participation in governance, and hence, makes office holders more accountable and more responsive to the needs of the people;

(4) likewise, a more decentralized system tends to be a more equitable distribution of benefits and burdens;

(5) it improves efficiency (by reducing the delays and red tape usually associated with a central bureaucracy), and encourages experimentation and innovation at subnational levels of government."[68]

On the other hand, critics of federalism point out that:

(1) "it protects the interests of a local majority, often at the expense of racial and other minorities;

(2) it permits states to thwart the efforts of the national government to achieve uniform standards and equal treatment across all states and this leads to inequalities;

(3) in asking states and localities to rely more on themselves it gives advantages to rich states and disadvantages to poor states."[69]

Unfortunately, no model of government is perfect nor is the relationship between governing units going to be smooth and efficient. Despite its flaws, the American brand of federalism has proven over time to be the best plan to include all levels of government into the decision-making and public policy processes. By themselves, each level of government is limited in its ability to meet even the day-to-day needs of the American people. A disaster like a hurricane, a wildfire, or a coronavirus pandemic awakens us to the realization that government is indeed limited. However, when all levels of government from the White House to City Hall put their heads together, dismiss their jealousies towards each other, stop pointing accusatory fingers at each other, and pool their resources, they can fulfill the Framers charge in the preamble to the Constitution to "promote the general welfare" of the American people.

CHAPTER NOTES

[1] *The HarperCollins Dictionary of America Government and Politics*, Jay M. Shafritz, ed., (New York, New York: HarperCollins Publishers, Inc., 1992), 301.

[2] James Madison, "No. 46: Relative Strength of the Federal and State Governments," *The Enduring Federalist*, Charles Beard, ed., 2nd ed., (New York, New York: Frederick Ungar Publishing Co., 1964), 203.

[3] Alexis de Tocqueville, *Democracy in America*, Translated by George Lawrence, J. P. Mayer, ed., (Garden City, New York: Doubleday & Company, Inc., 1969), 164.

[4] Ray Bragg, "Storm of the Century," *San Antonio Express-News* (Sunday, September 11, 2005), 4N.

[5] Ibid.

[6] "Blame Game Delicately Played in Georgia By Governor, Mayor," *San Antonio Express-News* (Friday, January 31, 2014), A8.

[7] Leonard Pitts, "Big, Bad Government? Sure, Until They Need It," *San Antonio Express-News* (Saturday, May 29, 2010), 9B.

[8]Karen Tumulty and Steven Mufson, "Officials Fueling Over Oil Cleanup," *San Antonio Express-News* (Tuesday, May 25, 2010), 1A.

[9]James Madison, "No. 45: Federal Powers Not Dangerous to the States," *The Enduring Federalist*, Charles Beard, ed., 2nd ed., (New York, New York: Frederick Ungar Publishing Company, 1964), 202.

[10]*Treasury of Presidential Quotations*, Caroline Harnsberger, ed., (Chicago, Illinois: Follett Publishing Company, 1964), 323.

[11]D. Grier Stephenson, Jr., Robert J. Bresler, Robert J. Frederich, and Joseph J. Karlesky, *American Government*, 2nd ed., (New York, New York: HarperCollins, 1992), 59.

[12]Ibid.

[13]Daniel J. Elazar, *American Federalism: A View from the States*, 3rd ed., (New York, New York: Harper & Row Publishers, 1984), 2.

[14]Russell L. Hanson, "Intergovernmental Relations," *Politics in America States: A Comparative Analysis*, Virginia Gray, Herbert Jacob, and Robert A. Albritton eds., 5th ed., (Illinois: Scott, Foresman/Little Brown, 1990), 41.

[15]Elazar, 41-42.

[16]David C. Saffell and Hary Basehart, *State and Local Government: Politics and Public Policies*, 8th ed., (New York, New York: McGraw Hill, 2005), 63.

[17]Richard Bingham and David Hedge, *State and Local Government in a Changing Society*, 2nd ed., (New York, New York: Harper and Row Publishers, 1984), 31.

[18]Elazar, 31.

[19]*The HarperCollins Dictionary of American Government and Politics*, 206.

[20]Ibid., 254.

[21]Michael Kammen, *The Origins of the America Constitution: A Documentary History*, (New York, New York: Viking Penguin, Inc., 1986), 306-308.

[22]Wallace Mendelson, "Ninth Amendment Rights and Wrongs," *Political Science Quarterly*, Vol. 110, No. 3, Fall, 1995, 410.

[23]James H. Huston, "A Nauseous Project," *The Wilson Quarterly*, Vol. XV, No. 1, Winter, 1991, 69.

[24]William Cummings, "Here's What the Constitution's 10th Amendment Says About Trump's Claim to Have Total Authority Over the States," *USAToday*, April, 14, 2020 *https://www.usatoday.com*

[25]Jack C. Plano and Milton Greenberg, *The American Political Dictionary*, 10th ed., (Orlando, Florida: Harcourt Brace & Company, 1997), 47.

[26]Ibid., 453.

[27]Allison Torres Burka, "In Pursuit of Justice: 10 Supreme Court Decisions That Defined Civil Rights," *American History*, Vol. 50, No. 5, Dec., 2015, 62.

[28]*The HarperCollins Dictionary of America Government and Politics*, 226.

[29]Ibid., 245.

[30]Plano and Greenberg, 44.

[31]Ralph A. Rossum and G. Alan Tarr, *American Constitutional Law: Cases and Interpretation*, (New York, New York: St. Martin's Press, Inc., 1983), 120.

[32]Ibid., 122.

[33]Ibid., 215.

[34]Saffell and Basehart, 42.

[35]Rossum and Tarr, 261 and 264.

[36]Richard P. Nathan, "The Role of States in American Federalism," *The State of Stats*, Carl E. Van Horn, ed., (Washington, D.C.: Congressional Quarterly, 1989), 23.

[37]Daniel B. Moskowitz, "Arguing Over Time," *American History*, Vol. 57, No. 5, Dec., 3027, 24.

[38]Ibid., 25.

[39]Steven G. Calabresi, "Federalism and the Rehnquist Court: A Normative Defense," *The Annals Of the American Academy of Political and Social Science*, Vol. 574, March, 2001, 25.

[40]Plano and Greenberg, 57.

[41]Ibid., 51.

[42]*John C. Calhoun: A Disquisition on Government and Selections from the Discourses*, C. Gordon Post, ed., (New York, New York: Bobbs-Merrill, 1953), 86.

[43]Hermann E. von Hoist, *John C. Calhoun: American Statesman Series*, Arthur M. Schlesinger, Jr., ed., (New York, New York: Chelsea House, 1980), 78-79.

[44]Plano and Greenberg, 44.

[45]von Holst, 79.

[46]Plano and Greenberg, 6.

[47]*John C. Calhoun: A Disquisition on Government and Selections from the Discourses*, 30.

[48]Steven A. Peterson and Thomas H. Rasmussen, *State and Local Politics*, (New York, New York: McGraw-Hill, 1994), 28.

[49]"*Texas v White*: The Constitutionality of Reconstruction-1869," *Documents of Texas History*, 2nd ed., Ernest Wallace, David M. Vigness and George B. Ward, eds., (Austin, Texas: State House Press, 1994), 208-209.

[50]Plano and Greenberg, 55.

[51]Nathan, 17.

[52]Malcom L. Goggin, "Federal-State Relations: New Federalism in Theory and Practice," *Perspectives on American and Texas Politics: A Collection of Essays*, Donald S. Lutz and Kent L. Tedin, eds., (Dubuque, Iowa: Kendall/Hunt, 1989), 187.

[53]Saffell and Basehart, 43.

[54]*The HarperCollins Dictionary of American Government and Politics*, 226.

[55]Ibid., 226.

[56]David B. Robertson and Dennis R. Judd, *The Development of American Public Policy: The Structure of Public Restraint*, (Glenview, Illinois: Scott, Foresman and Company, 1989), 145.

[57]Saffell and Basehart, 45.

[58]Goggin, 194.

[59]Ibid., 183-184.

[60]"Richard Nixon: Labor Day Radio Address-1972," *The Rise of Conservative America: 1945-2000: A Brief History With Document*s, Ronald Story and Bruce Laurie, eds., (Boston, Massachusetts: Bedford/St. Martins, 2008), 91.

[61]*The HarperCollins Dictionary of American Government and Politics*, 226.

[62]*ProQuest Statistical Abstract of the United States: 2020*, 8th ed., (Bethesda, Maryland: ProQuest LLC, (2019), Table 473, 298.

[63]*Federal Grants to State and Local Governments: A Historical Perspective on Contemporary Issues*, May 22, 2019, Congressional Research Service *https://crsreports.congress.gov*

[64]*The HarperCollins Dictionary of American Government and Politics*, 262.

[65]Peterson and Rasmussen, 39.

[66]Bingham and Hedge, 45.

[67]*The HarperCollins Dictionary of America Government and Politics*, 352.

[68]Goggin, 186.

[69]Ibid.

SUGGESTED READINGS

Daniel J. Elazar, *American Federalism: A View from the States*, New York, New York: Harper and Row Publishers, 1984.

David C. Saffell and Harry Basehart, *State and Local Government: Politics and Public Policies*, 8th ed., New York, New York: McGraw-Hill, 2005.

John C. Calhoun: A Disquisition on Government and Selections from the Discourses, C. Gordon Post, ed., New York, New York: Bobbs-Merrill, 1953.

Politics in the American States: A Comparative Analysis, Virginia Gray and Russell L. Hanson, eds., Illinois: Scott, Foresman/Little Brown, 1990

Chapter Three

POLITICAL SOCIALIZATION AND PUBLIC OPINION

Regardless of the form of the governing structure and the philosophical tenants guiding it, all civilizations from the ancient Greeks and Romans to today's modern nation states realize that the survival of their governments is dependent upon addressing the needs of its citizens. Yet, the governors themselves have stressed over and over that they must rely upon those they govern to tell them what those needs are. Noted Scottish political philosopher David Hume noted that "as force is always on the side of the governed, the governors have nothing to support them but opinion. It is, therefore, on opinion only that government is founded; and this maxim extends to the most despotic and most military governments, as well as to the most free and popular."[1] In *Representative Government, in Utilitarianism, Liberty and Representative Government*, John Stuart Mill emphasized the overwhelming importance of participatory democracy as a key component to creating a strong enduring government:

> There is no difficulty in showing that the ideally best form of government is that in which the sovereignty, or supreme controlling power in the last resort, is vested in the entire aggregate of the community; every citizen not only having a voice in the exercise of that ultimate sovereignty, but being, at least occasionally, called on to take actual part in the government, by the personal discharge of some public function, local or general.[2]

Defined, as "the direct involvement of individuals and groups in the decision-making processes of government" **participatory democracy** is a key component of democratic governments.[3] The ultimate survival of any democratic government is based on the premise that "not only must government retain the support of mass opinion, but [that] mass public opinion must determine basic public policy. Democracy, after all, is rule by *demos*, the common people. . . The people's elected representatives meet face to face in lieu of the people themselves, and in the end, the representatives' acts are supposed to reflect the best opinions and interests of the people."[4] In the United States, the importance of soliciting the opinion of "John Q Public" extends to everything from one's choice of who will reside in the White House to the type of foods one eats, the car one drives, the choice of one's everyday products, and so on. In the political arena, public opinion dominates a lawmaker's career beginning with one's choice of issue positions during the campaign season to their rationale behind a key vote in a legislative house. Lawmakers understand the impact public opinion has on their legislative agendas and their political futures. In 1791, James Madison strongly pointed out that "public opinion sets bonds to every government and is the real sovereign in every free one."[5] During his tenure in the White House, President Lincoln noted that "public opinion in this country is everything. . . . No policy that does not rest upon some philosophical public opinion can be permanently maintained."[6] President Franklin Roosevelt plainly stated that "the whole structure of democracy rests upon public opinion."[7]

Soliciting one's opinion on any issue appears to be a simple process. A questionnaire is mailed to a household or a phone call is made to the resident asking them a series of questions pertaining to the subject matter. Yet, one's response is far from simple. Contrary to what some think, Americans do not speak with one voice nor do they all share the same opinions or hold the same perspectives or any given issue. How anyone responds to a query is based on one's individual cultural values, their individual preferences, and their unique exposure to the facts that determine what their response will be on that question posed through a questionnaire or a phone call. This chapter focuses on the development of one's political perspectives through the political socialization process.

In 1936, incumbent President Franklin Roosevelt was up for re-election. Seven years after the Stock Market crashed, the Great Depression was still taking its toll on the American people. Although his New Deal legislation was beginning to reverse dismal economic trends, Roosevelt was confronted with a staggering 16.9 percent unemployment rate and a dismal economic outlook. His Republican opponent was Alf Landon, the former governor of Kansas. The *Literary Digest* conducted a sweeping straw poll by mailing out "10 million ballots to people whose names the publication had drawn from telephone directories and car registrations. Almost one-fourth of the ballots were returned."[8] Consequently reporters from *The Digest* proudly published a poll predicting a landslide win for Landon. According to their straw poll results, Roosevelt's chances were dismal. Election night results were an embarrassment for *The Digest* as President Roosevelt won with approximately 27.8 million votes while Landon only captured 16.7 million votes. Landon only got eight electoral votes while Roosevelt's tally was 523.[9] A similar polling embarrassment occurred in the 1948 presidential contest between Democratic incumbent President Harry S. Truman against his Republican opponent Thomas Dewey. Once again, polling results indicated a landslide win for Thomas Dewey. The *Chicago Daily Tribune* ran a banner headline for its morning after the election day edition proclaiming Dewey the winner. However, Dewey placed a dismal second place with only 189 electoral votes as Truman secured his residency in the White House with 303 electoral votes.[10] Both of these predictions were based on straw polling.

President Truman holding the infamous issue of the *Chicago Daily Tribune*

After the 1948 debacle, polling changed from a haphazard unreliable straw poll to a scientific method ushered in by Dr. George Gallup. Today the majority of office seekers and news media outlets alike employ a cadre of professional pollsters who use a variety of scientifically proven methods to determine voter preferences. Still accurately predicting a winner is problematic. Throughout the 2020 presidential election cycle, numerous polls showed a tightening race between Trump and Biden. But, few of them actually published their results or made a correct election eve prediction of the winner. The *Cook Political Report* was one of the few that weeks before the election correctly called election results for all fifty states.

With all of the scientific tools available to them, why is it so difficult for political scientists and pollsters alike to accurately obtain, analyze and subsequently use their results to correctly predict what direction the American public wants its governing officials to take in addressing the nation's pressing issues? This chapter explores the complexities of developing public opinion. An individual's unique political perspectives are not acquired in a vacuum. From infancy, one acquires their knowledge of politics by the influence of the agents of political socialization. It is a lifelong process. Oftentimes, an individual does not really realize that their opinions may not be of their own design nor are they unique to positions held by others. This chapter examines the development of one's political culture and the agents that either directly or indirectly influence the development of one's political leanings. This chapter also delves into the various avenues available to pollsters and researchers to solicit one's opinions about the politics of today from their individual opinions on the issues to their preferred choice of political parties and candidates for public office.

POLITICAL CULTURE

In *Comparative Politics: A Developmental Approach*, renowned political scientists Gabriel Almond and G. Bingham Powell define **political culture** as "the pattern of individual attitudes and orientations towards politics among members of a political system."[11] Furthermore, a political culture is "the product of both the collective history of a political system and the life histories of the individuals who currently make up the system; and this is rooted equally in public events and private experiences."[12] A nation's political culture guides its citizens in their choice of their governing structure, the political leanings of its leadership and the political positions held by its individual citizens. The importance of a nation's political culture cannot be underestimated "because these cultural factors influence how citizens act, how the political process functions, and what policy goals the government pursues."[13]

> The concept of political culture thus suggests that the traditions of a society, the spirit of its public institutions, the passions and the collective reasoning of its citizenry, and the style and operation codes of its leaders are not just random products of historical experiences, but fit together as a part of a meaningful whole and constitute an intelligible web of relations. For the individual, the political culture provides controlling guidelines for effective political behavior, and for the collectivity it gives a systematic structure of values and rational considerations which ensures coherence in the performance of institutions and organizations. In essence, thus, the political culture . . .consists of the system of empirical beliefs, expressive symbols, and values which defines the situation in which political action takes place.[14]

A nation's political culture is formed around its core values. Beginning with the Declaration of Independence, America's core values were determined by the Founding Fathers. Many of those noted statesmen were guided by the influence of the Enlightenment philosophies of John Locke, Charles Montesquieu and Jean Jacques Rousseau, and John Stuart Mill. The core values are:

Liberty—The concept that all are endowed with the inalienable rights to life, liberty, property, and the pursuit of happiness.

Equality—As stated in the Declaration of Independence by Thomas Jefferson: "We hold these truths to be self-evident, that all men are created equal."

Individualism—Within legal limits, an individual has the right to pursue his/her individual freedoms and desires without undo interference from government.

Democracy—The belief that the legitimacy of the government rests with the consent of the governed.

Rule of Law—The concept that all laws must be applied equally, impartially, and justly without giving special privileges to one group over another.

Civic Duty—The belief that all citizens have an obligation to support their country and their communities. Civic duty can range from voting, serving in the military, community service, etc.

The core values of liberty and rule of law guided the thoughts of the Founding Fathers when they wrote the Bill of Rights. The First Amendment embraces the concepts of liberty and individualism by guaranteeing religious freedom and the separation of church from state as well as protecting one's individual rights to assembly, association, and the freedom of expression. Furthermore, citizens are protected from unreasonable searches and seizures (Fourth Amendment) and guaranteed a fair judicial process if accused of committing a criminal act (Fifth through Eighth Amendments). Subsequent amendments underscore the concept of equality by abolishing slavery (Thirteenth Amendment), extending the principle of rule of law by guaranteeing equal protection and due process (Fourteenth Amendment) and extending the scope of the basic exercise of the civic responsibility of voting with the passage of the Fifteenth, Seventeenth, Nineteenth and Twenty-sixth Amendments.

With the start of the Industrial Revolution in the United States, Americans incorporated the concepts of capitalism and free enterprise into their core values. Capitalism was first introduced by Scottish economist Adam Smith in his 1776 publication *The Wealth of Nations*. **Capitalism** is "an economic system where there is a combination of private property, a generally unrestricted marketplace of goods and services, and a general assumption that the bulk of the workforce will be engaged in producing goods to sell at a profit."[15] **Free enterprise** is "the freedom of private businesses to operate competitively for profit, with minimal government regulation."[16] The two concepts go hand-in-hand. The officer seeker who promotes economic growth with the promises of lower business taxes, strong protection of private property, less government regulation, and removal of trade barriers will garner the bulk of the voters' support over those who advocate stronger government regulations over business and industry, higher taxes and strict government regulation and oversight into their business operations. During the 2020 election cycle, it was a common theme for candidates to accuse their opponents of promoting socialism over capitalism. The mere mention of socialism is the red flag buzz word for a government takeover of business and industry, the curtailment of personal rights and freedoms, the collapse of capitalism and the destruction of the free market system.

While most Americans agree in principle to the nation's core values, there are wide disparities as to the meaning, interpretation, and application these values have upon their individual political leanings. "Political culture is particularly important as the historical source of differences in habits, perspectives, and attitudes that influence political life in the various states. **Sectionalism** is particularly important as a major source of geographically rooted variations that influence state-by-state differences in responses to nationwide political, economic, and social developments."[17] Traditionally, one could divide United States into six distinct political culture zones: New England (Connecticut, Maine, Massachusetts, New Hampshire, Rhode Island and Vermont), Mid-Atlantic (Delaware, Maryland, New Jersey, Pennsylvania, and Washington, D.C.), the South (Alabama, Florida, Georgia, Kentucky, Louisiana, Mississippi, North and South Carolina, Tennessee, Virginia, and West Virginia), the Mid-West (Illinois, Indiana, Iowa, Kansas, Michigan, Minnesota, Nebraska, Ohio, North and South Dakota, and Wisconsin), the Southwest (Arizona, New Mexico, Oklahoma and Texas), and the West (Alaska, Colorado, California, Hawaii, Idaho, Montana, Nevada, Oregon, Utah, Washington, and Wyoming). Each political culture zone was unique in its economic, political, and social and cultural development. The issues confronting the South were far different from those of the Mid-Atlantic and Southwest political culture zones. The southern agricultural economy based on cotton and slavery was far different from the agricultural economy of the Mid-west. With the exception of the opening of the West, an individual's migration from one state to another was a rarity. Once they arrived on American soil, immigrant population groups established permanent residency in a particular state. Immigrants settled this country in **cluster zones** whereby the first to come would become a "safe haven" community for their fellow countrymen. In Massachusetts, for example, the Boston area was the Irish zone. In Texas, the immigrants from Germany established a German zone in New Braunfels. Therefore, for the office seeker the political positions they took were uniquely representative of their constituents' views in that designated political culture zone. For years, those positions basically remained the same. A Republican party dominated "red" state remained predictably red just as a "blue" state was reliably blue. There were very few if any "purple" states or states that flipped from red to blue and vis versa.

Permanent residency became more migratory with each economic upheaval forcing one to move from one state to another. The closing of a primary manufacturing plant in a mid-west state oftentimes forced the displaced worker to find employment in another state. During World War I, the military built numerous bases across the United States. Active military personnel and their families are subjected to periodic relocations from base to base. Just as they pack up their belongings for the move, they also take their personal political cultures and political affiliations with them. A recent article published in *Forbes* magazine analyzed the recent migratory patterns of Americans moving from one state to another. Categorized as 'outbound states,' Pennsylvania, North Dakota, Wisconsin, Utah, Kentucky, Ohio, Massachusetts, Kansas, Connecticut, New York, New Jersey and Illinois are losing population while the 'inbound states' of Alabama, Colorado, North and South Carolina, Washington, South Dakota, Nevada, Idaho, Oregon and Vermont are increasing their populations through migratory population shifts. Furthermore, job opportunities are drawing people to California, Georgia, Virginia, Rhode Island, Iowa, West Virginia, Oklahoma, Louisiana, and Nebraska.[18] Migration patterns from one state to another have created new distinctive political sub-cultural divisions that exist within each state. A comparison of state-by-state presidential election results from 2016 to 2020 will definitely indicate the influence these migratory relocations had on those election voting patterns.

Political Sub-Cultures

In *American Federalism: A View from the States*, Daniel Elazar contends that there are three political subcultures—**individualistic, moralistic** and **traditionalistic**. They "jointly inhabit the country, existing side by side or even overlapping. All three are of nationwide proportions, having spread in the course of time from coast to coast. At the same time, each subculture is strongly tied to specific sections of the country, reflecting the streams and currents of migration that have carried people of different origins and backgrounds across the continent in more or less orderly patterns."[19]

Adhering to a commonwealth ideal, the **moralistic** perspective underscores the belief that "good government is measured by the degree to which it promotes the public good and in terms of the honesty, selflessness and commitment to the public welfare of those who govern."[20] Elected officials serve for the betterment of their community rather than for their personal gain. The moralistic perspective sees government service as a short-term volunteer commitment, rather than a full-time profession. Several state constitutions have provisions limiting the terms of elective office for both their legislators and governors. Many city charters also have term limits for their council members, mayors and even city managers. As a public servant, one's monetary compensation should be at best, minimal. For example, the current Texas state constitution sets the salary of its state legislators and lieutenant governor at $7,200 per year. For decades, the city charter of San Antonio, Texas provided only a per diem of $20 a week to cover costs to attend city council meetings for both its council members and the mayor. "In the moralistic political culture, individualism is tempered by a general commitment to utilizing communal-preferably nongovernmental, but government if necessary-power to intervene into the sphere of private activities when it is considered necessary to do so for the public good or the well-being of the community. . . . Government is considered a positive instrument with a responsibility to promote the general welfare."[21]

The average citizen also bears a heightened responsibility to his/her community and civic duty beyond merely casting an election ballot. The moralistic perspective "embraces the notion that politics is ideally a matter of concern for every citizen, not just for those who are professionally committed to political careers. Indeed it is the duty of every citizen to participate in the political affairs of his commonwealth."[22] Initially, this perspective was developed by descendants of Scandinavian immigrants who settled in the Great Lakes region, Minnesota, Iowa, Oregon and Washington state.

The **individualistic** approach sees government as a marketplace run by professionals in a business-like environment. This perspective is based on a strong belief in limited government, to the extent that government only responds and becomes active when the citizenry demands action. Therefore, the only role government has over individuals is to perform strictly limited and essential functions without exerting any interference into the private lives of its citizens. "In general, government action is to be restricted to those areas primarily in the economic realm, that encourage private initiative and widespread access to the marketplace."[23] This approach sees politicians as seeking office only "as a means of controlling the distribution of favors or rewards of government rather than as a means of exercising governmental power for programmatic ends."[24] Political office is seen as a profession only for specialists who want to gain something in return for their public service. The individualistic perspective holds politics in low esteem, viewing it as a "dirty business." "In practice, then, where the individualistic political culture is dominant, there is likely to be an easy attitude toward the limits of the professionals' perquisites. Since a fair amount of corruption is expected in the normal course of things, there is relatively little popular excitement when any is found, unless it is of extraordinary character."[25]

Mass participation on the part of the average citizen is discouraged. The struggle for political control is seen as a competition between two cohesive and strong political parties, with policy issues taking a back seat. This political sub-culture developed among the Germanic and non-Puritan English settlements in the middle Atlantic states. Eventual migration from this area brought the individualistic perspective to the mid-west and western states and the plantation-based agricultural system of the Old South. This perspective "reflects an older precommercial attitude that accepts a substantially hierarchical society as part of the ordered nature of things, authorizing and expecting those at the top of the social structure to take a special and dominate role in government."[26] The "ruling elite" desires to reserve their own social, economic and political positions by actually controlling the political arena. If the elite does not seek political office on their own, they opt to openly recruit candidates whose philosophies complement their political leanings.

On the other hand, the **traditionalistic** sub-culture rests on the premise that political parties, bureaucratic agencies, and mass participation are necessary evils. This approach is "coupled with a paternalistic and elitist conception of the commonwealth. It reflects an older, precommercial attitude that accepts a substantially hierarchical society as part of the ordered nature of things, authorizing and expecting those at the top of the social structure to take a special and dominant role in government."[27] Elites seek to control the decision-making process. Any potential threat to their power structure is treated with suspicion. "Political parties are of minimal importance in traditionalistic political cultures because they encourage a degree of openness that goes against the fundamental grain of an elite-oriented political order."[28] Political parties serve the elite by recruiting candidates favorable to elitist perspectives. Bureaucratic agencies are welcomed when they complement the needs of the elites. Usually, the traditionalistic perspective would discourage expanded participation on the part of the citizenry. From the Reconstruction period to the passage of civil rights legislation in the 1960s, elites throughout the South enacted measures such as Jim Crow laws, poll taxes, literacy tests, etc., to exercise control over the masses. The maintenance of the status quo is paramount to the traditionalistic approach. Control over the legislative decision-making process must be firmly held and retained by the elite group. "When the traditionalistic political culture is dominate in the United States today, political leaders play a conservative and custodial rather than initiatory roles unless they are passed strongly from the outside."[29]

To varying degrees, all three of these political sub-cultures have an impact on the response government takes on any given issue whether it be climate change, poverty, and so forth. For example, since its founding, lawmakers at the national and state level have wrestled with the appropriate societal and governmental response to poverty. The moralistic approach views poverty as a societal concern that simply cannot be addressed by government alone. It recognizes that poverty is caused by a multiplicity of factors such an economic crisis, the adverse impact of a pandemic, etc. The individual living in poverty did not directly cause their economic reversal rather it was caused by factors beyond their control. The ability of food banks to meet the needs of the hungry rely on public funding from federal, state and local governments as well as individual monetary and food item contributions solicited from the community at large. It is a civic responsibility for the food secure public to help those who are food insecure. The individualistic approach recognizes that poverty exists. However, poverty is oftentimes viewed as a self-inflicted problem. It was the individual's lack of self-sufficiency that caused his/her poverty. It is the responsibility of the individual, not society or the community, to find the solution to his/her economic deprivation. Although recognizing the suffering, an advocate of the individualistic approach would want to provide short-term assistance to only those deserving of the assistance while at the same time, imposing restrictions on continuing access to that assistance. The traditionalistic approach also recognizes the adverse impact of poverty. The traditionalist approach provides needed assistance only if it brings a tangible benefit to the ruling elite. For example, the food stamp program provides financial assistance to those who cannot afford to purchase food. However, the list of qualifying items is controlled by the producers (farmers and ranchers) and the suppliers (grocery stores) of those items. It is a win-win program since the needy now have the means to purchase food and the producers and suppliers have a guaranteed market to profitably sell those food items.

After the dust has settled on the 2020 presidential election, political analysts will begin the arduous process of studying the voting patterns and issue positions taken by those who cast their ballots. All of us adhere to our own political philosophies and issue positions. It would be simple just to calculate who voted for Democrats over Republican candidates and vice versa. How our unique personal political culture is dependent upon several factors. In *Comparative Politics: A Developmental Approach*, Gabriel Almond and G. Bingham Powell contend that one's political culture is based on three basic factors: "(a) **cognitive orientations**, knowledge, accurate or otherwise, of political objects and beliefs; (b) **affective orientations**, feelings of attachment, involvement, rejection, and life about political objects; (c) **evaluative orientations**, judgements and opinions about political objects which usually involve applying the value standards to political objects and events.[30] For example, an individual has knowledge of a political issue such as funding for improvements to his/her city's public transportation system (cognitive orientation). This issue directly impacts this person since he/she is dependent upon the bus system for his/her daily commute to and from work (affective orientation). Consequently, this individual develops his/her own opinions about the pros and cons of the city's transportation system and articulates what improvements he/she envisions are needed to improve it (evaluative orientation).

THE POLITICAL SOCIALIZATION PROCESS

Political socialization is the "transition from generation to generation of the ethos of a political system by the conscious and unconscious instilling of the values of a political culture."[31] Political socialization is a life-time generational process. It may take

> the form of either manifest or latent transmission. It is manifest when it involves the explicit communication of information, values, or feelings toward political objects. . . Latent political socialization is the transmission of non-political attitudes which affect attitudes toward analogous roles and objects in the political system. . . . For example, the child acquires certain general attitudes of accommodation or of aggression toward other individuals. Such orientation will affect his attitudes toward political leaders and his fellow citizens. They will shape his view of politics as a process of struggle for dominance or as a means of attaining legitimate goals. Latent political socialization involves many of the most fundamental characteristics of the general culture, which may, in turn, have great effect on the political sphere.[32]

The acquisition of one's political perspectives and level of participation is an informal process. It gives us our sense of identity within our community and our nation. Nationalism and patriotism are essential for the survival of any nation state. While citizens may not always agree with the actions of their government, they must respect the right of the government to govern. If not, then that nation will never achieve internal sovereignty and legitimacy. Citizens show their loyalty and patriotism to their government by standing when their national anthem is played, saluting their nation's flag, etc. Across the nation, community-sponsored parades, memorials honoring fallen veterans, fireworks on the Fourth of July, monuments in the town squares and public parks, etc., reinforce the guiding principles and values of our nation and remind us of the sacrifices many have made to preserve those principles and values. Patriotism means that whenever one's nation is under attack, citizens put their differences aside and collectively defend their country at all costs. The aftermath of tragic attacks on the World Trade Center on September 11, 2001, brought a spirit of patriotism and unity among the American people not seen since the tragic bombing of Pearl Harbor in 1941. Americans put aside their differences and focused their attentions toward those accused of guiding those planes into the Twin Towers.

The socialization process also reinforces the ideological framework guiding one's nation state. For example, the underlying foundation of the American governing system is a firm belief in representative democracy merged with the economic concepts of capitalism and free enterprise. Beginning with the first grade in a public or private school, children are introduced to the fundamental concepts of a democratic government: protection of civil liberties and civil rights, limited government, popular sovereignty, free elections, patriotism, nationalism, and so on. Students learn the essential elements of the free enterprise system: individualism, capitalism, free-markets, and the American dream of economic success. The political socialization process teaches one how to be a "good" citizen. The model "good" citizen may not always support what their presidents or governors do, but he/she will respect the right for the governing to make laws and rules. The code of behavior for the "good" citizen drives home the point that petitioning your government

Dressed in the garb of early patriots, these marchers remind their fellow citizens of our nation's struggle for freedom and liberty.

is a valued protected right under a democratic government but participation in violent civil disobedience is the mark of a "bad" citizen.

The outcome of the socialization process determines one's level of political efficacy. **Political efficacy** is "a citizen's belief (1) that he or she can understand and participate in political affairs and (2) that the political system will be responsive."[33] Efficacy underscores the need for citizens to make informed choices at the polls. In other words, those with high levels of efficacy gather information on policy issues from varied reliable sources, attend candidate forums, vote on a regular basis, actively participate in their political party, and often seek elective office. Studies reveal that "those who lobby, demonstrate, write letters, or otherwise communicate their opinions to political decision makers usually feel more intensely about these opinions than do those who merely reply to a poll. Moreover, those who hold their opinions intensely may also be better informed."[34] However, the majority of Americans opt to limit their political participation to just casting a ballot on election day. Voting "generally requires little expenditure of money, time, or effort, and except for voting in referenda, it generally represents little in the way of direct expression of opinions on policies concerning gun control, abortion, civil rights, nuclear freezes, inflation, unemployment, taxation, bureaucracy, education, investment, armament, energy, environmental pollution, street crime, and the like and subsequent political behavior."[35] Those with low levels of political efficacy believe that their participation in the political process will have little to no impact on their current economic or societal status. Their plight will be the same regardless of who wins an election. These individuals rarely vote, if at all.

The acquisition of one's political culture is dependent upon the influence of the various agents of socialization. The primary agents of socialization are the family, educational institutions, religious affiliations, association for peer groups and interest groups, social class, the media, and career choice. Oftentimes, one's direct contact with a government agency or an elected official can influence one's level of political participation. One's trust in their government can either by reinforced or seriously impaired by a major event such as an economic upheaval, health crisis, war, terrorist attack, etc. To one degree or another, one or more of these agents will directly impact one's belief and level of participation in the political process.

THE AGENTS OF POLITICAL SOCIALIZATION

The Family Environment

The most influential and important agent of political socialization is the family environment.

> The family influences opinions in several ways. First, parents share their opinions directly with children, who may adopt them. Second, parents say or do things that children imitate. Third, children may transfer or generalize opinions from parents to other objects. When children are less positive towards parents, they are also less positive toward the president and other authority figures. Fourth, the family shapes the personality of the child. . . Individuals who are self-confident are more likely to participate in politics than others. Fifth, the family places children in a network of social and economic relationships that influences how they view the world and how the world views them.[36]

The influence of one's parents begins from infancy and carries one throughout their lifetime. Over the years, friendships once made will change. Few, if any, hold the same job throughout their working years. Habits will change. One's political or religious affiliations will change. Yet, the one strong influencing agent that stays with us throughout our lives is the family. Years later, family gatherings can be pleasant experiences if one's opinions mirror those of other family members. Yet, these events can be confrontational if a family member expresses viewpoints not embraced by others. We cannot overlook that it is the family that directly "shapes future political attitudes by defining a social position for the child: establishing ethnic, linguistic, class, and religious ties; affirming cultural values; and influencing job aspirations."[37] Initially, children adopt their parent's attitudes towards racism, politics, religion, etc. These influences can have a positive and negative impact on a child's development. For example, studies show that child and spousal abuse can be a learned trait. A child abused by their parents may become an abuser of their own children. A child who sees his father being abusive to his mother and his mother does not complain about it, is more apt to see this as acceptable behavior that he can use in the future. A young adult's drug dependency and alcoholism can be traced back to his/her parents who used drugs and abused alcohol in the home environment. Racism is also a learned trait directly tied to the family environment. If children hear their parents say racially insensitive words about minorities, then, they oftentimes feel that it is acceptable for them to say the same things. Membership in racial organizations such as the KKK are generational, passed on from father to son.

The level of one's initial participation is based on his/her parents' attitudes towards the political process. Discussions at the family dinner table encourage children to be more aware of events and issues. Usually, young adults will adopt their parents' political party affiliations and cast their first votes in line with the parents' choices. If a child sees their parents actively campaigning for a candidate, serving as precinct chairpersons, working the polls, attending candidate fund raisers, or volunteering as an election judge, they too will have an elevated level of political participation. Historically, in some families such as the Bushes, Kennedys, Rockefellers, etc., political participation is not an option, but a family obligation. The issue is not if one will run for office in the future. The question is when will they decide to enter the political arena. The opposite holds true if one's parents do not vote, express negative opinions about politicians and vocalize opposition to government-initiated policies.

Religious Affiliations

One's religious affiliation does play a key role in the political socialization process. "The religions of the world are carriers of cultural and moral values, which often have political implications. The great religious leaders have seen themselves as teachers, and their followers have usually attempted to shape the socialization of children through schooling, preaching, and religious services."[38] Baptists, Mormons, Catholics, Muslims, the Jewish, etc., all hold different views on issues such as abortion, school prayer, gambling, alcohol consumption, etc.

Although the Constitution guarantees separation of church from state, it is indeed a very fine line that oftentimes influences legislative acts. In particular, the traditional Southern Baptist/Methodist Bible Belt pushed legislative houses in twenty-eight states to enact a series of laws collectively known as **Blue Laws**, effectively "banning commercial and related activities on particular days, usually Sunday, for religious reasons or a law against anything a community considers immoral."[39] One of the nation's oldest blue laws was passed in 1677 by the New Jersey state legislature banning the singing of "immoral" songs on the Sabbath. Although repealed, Texas Blue Laws prohibited the sale of alcohol products on Sunday, prohibited shopping centers from opening before noon, and banned the sale of products deemed as "labor intensive" on Sundays. Repealed in 1961, other Texas blue laws banned the sale of air conditions, bed linens, china, footwear, home appliances, furniture, jewelry, kitchen utensils, lawn mowers, etc., on Sunday. Several other state legislative houses controlled the sale and consumption of alcohol by creating "wet" and "dry" counties. The Illinois state legislature once enacted legislation banning horse racing and the selling automobiles on Sundays. In 1990, Maine's state legislative house repealed its ban against department stores opening on Sundays. In 1987, religious broadcaster and one-time presidential candidate Pat Robertson brought a coalition of Baptists, Protestants, Roman Catholics, and Pentecostals under the umbrella of the **Christian Coalition**. A conservative pro-family organization, the Christian Coalition's agenda is pro-life and pro-traditional family values. The coalition's leadership primarily endorses conservative Republican party candidates, in particular, Ronald Reagan's and George W. Bush's candidacy for the White House.

"Where churches teach values that may be at odds with the controlling political system, the struggle over socialization can be intense."[40] John Kerry (D) from Massachusetts ran for the presidency as a pro-choice candidate. A practicing Catholic, Kerry was admonished by a Catholic Bishop and threatened with ex-communication because of his pro-choice abortion position ran against the Church's decades old position on pro-life. President Joe Biden (D) from Delaware, is also a practicing pro-choice Catholic. He too faced criticism from the hierarchy of the Catholic Church. Members of the LBGT community have been confronted with the possibility of being expelled from their houses of worship because their chosen life-style conflicts with traditional religious doctrines and practices.

Education

When the bell rings on the opening day of first grade, children have their initial experience with an authority figure other than their parents. "As in the case of the family, the school contains a particular pattern of authoritative decision making to which all students are exposed. Participation in decision making at school can do something to make up for a lack of it at home or can reinforce the previous pattern."[41] Whether it be private or public, a school is a self-contained political system that introduces children to relationships with other students, levels of authority with their teachers, principles and counselors, and a series of rules that reward compliance but punish violations. "The major impact of schooling is that it helps create "good" citizens. Citizens are taught to accept political authority and the institutions of government to channel political activity in legitimate and supportive ways. Thus, the schools provide a valuable function for the

The pledge of allegiance is a typical scene in most schools across the nation. In this way children learn the political values of the country and develop pride in their heritage. Such values and commitment are a necessary ingredient to an orderly and just society.

state."[42] At the start of each day's lessons, students stand to pledge their allegiance to the Stars and Stripes. Beginning in the elementary grades, students learn about the free enterprise system and the value of capitalism. School-sponsored events highlight national holidays such as Thanksgiving with a pageant of children portraying the pilgrims at their first Thanksgiving feast or the school choir signing patriot songs for Veterans Day, the 4th of July, etc. "Curricula and textbooks also foster commitment to government. . . Textbooks, particularly those used in elementary grades, emphasize compliance with authority and the need to be a "good" citizen. Even textbooks in advance grades often present idealized versions of the way government works and exaggerated views of the responsiveness of government to citizen participation."[43]

Group socialization outside of the classroom usually begins in middle school as students join sports teams, student councils, and clubs and organizations. Students actively participate in the democratic processes of voting and majority rule as they elect their officers, create rules and regulations, debate issues and propose group activities. They are introduced to parliamentary procedure and *Roberts Rules of Order*. By joining these groups, students develop self-confidence and leadership skills. "Schools can also play an important role in shaping attitudes about the unwritten 'rules of the political game'. . . . They can bring an awareness of other values and circumstances, providing a basis for new political aspirations. They can reinforce affection for the political system and can provide common symbols for the expressive response to the system."[44]

The college/university experience is totally different from the rote learning environment of the public/private school environment. Basically, "college leads to a broadened perspective of the world. Individuals begin to look beyond their immediate environment and see themselves as part of a larger community."[45] Culturally, the public school is in one's immediate neighborhood. It is a localized and, in some respects, a segregated environment. The college experience exposes one to different cultures and, of course, different political, social, and economic perspectives. It also opens the door to individual independent research and enables the student to seek their own answers. Oftentimes, what one learned in the public-school system is totally different from what one is exposed to on a college campus. For the entering eighteen-year-old freshman, this is the first time he/she registers to vote, attends a political rally, participates in a student protest, and casts a ballot. Studies indicate that "college students are more liberal than the population as a whole, and the longer they stay in college, the more liberal they become."[46]

The value of the years of education in developing an informed public cannot be underestimated or undervalued. One's educational experience imparts information about politics and cognate fields about a variety of skills, some of which facilitate political learning. . . Schooling increases one's capacity for understanding and working with complex, abstract, and intangible subjects, that is, subjects like politics. Skills in research, writing and speaking, developed through education, help citizens to negotiate the maze of demands that participation places on them. To cast a ballot, citizens must make sense of the candidates and issues; they must locate polling places. To write a letter to a senator, citizens must compose a persuasive message once they have identified the senator and looked up his/her address. For the grade-school educated, these are daunting tasks; for the college educated, they are easy. . . Those with many years of formal schooling are substantially more likely to read newspapers, follow the news and be politically informed, all of which makes them more aware of the opportunities to participate and more likely to possess information with which to do so.[47]

Race/Ethnic Orientation

Regardless of the issue, one's ethnic and racial orientation does have an impact on how an individual develops their political learnings and issue positions. For example, the tragic death of George Floyd and other African Americans at the hands of local law enforcement officers awakened historical racial tensions across the nation. Peaceful and, unfortunately, violent protests reignited the awareness that equal justice and due process of the law is not equally applied to all. Few would disagree that law and order are essential to the preservation of individual freedoms guaranteed by the First Amendment to the United States Constitution. The argument, therefore, is how different racial groups see the value of law enforcement in their communities. These differing viewpoints have an impact on their choice of political parties and candidates. In the 2020 presidential election, many members of the Anglo community embraced the law and order rhetoric of political candidates. Yet, other groups questioned the validity of giving law enforcement more authority over the American people.

In Fort Worth, Texas, there is a museum honoring the Texas Rangers, a group formed in 1823 by Stephen F. Austin to protect the frontier settlers from hostile Indian raids. Throughout its history, the Rangers are, at times, hailed for their bravery and condemned for their brutal tactics. For the Anglo community, the Rangers are indeed revered for their actions. For the Hispanic and Native American communities, it is a far different story. They view the Rangers as the ones who hunted down their ancestors, accused them of cattle wrestling and other crimes, and either hung or shot them to death without virtue of a fair trial.

For the African American community, law enforcement is feared rather than revered. An academy award winning movie, *The Green Book* is about a book written in 1936 by a Harlem, New York postal worker named Victor Hugo Green. Faced with continuous racial discrimination, Green wanted to warn other African Americans about what they would face if they did not stay within their boundaries. Updated in 1948, the introduction carried the warning to "carry your Green Book with you—you may need it," while the text provided a list of "hotels, guest houses, service stations, drug stores, taverns, barber shops and restaurants that were known to be safe ports of call for African American travelers. The "Green Book" listed establishments in segregationist strongholds such as Alabama and Mississippi, but its reach also extended from Connecticut to California—any place where its readers might face prejudice or danger because of their skin color."[48] The "talk" in the African American community prepares a young African American youth with guidance on how to safely deal with law enforcement and the possibility of facing discrimination from others.

The Girls Scouts learn skills to make them better citizens.

Peer Groups

Peer pressure plays a significant role in shaping one's political culture and issue positions. The sense of belonging and forming friendships outside of the immediate family begins at an early age. Organizations such as the Boys and Girls Scouts brings youngsters together as they learn skills and habits that will help them in their adult lives. Belonging to the youth choir at church or attending summer camp brings together children of different backgrounds and ethnic cultures. "A peer group socializes its members by motivating or pressuring them to conform to the attitudes or behavior accepted by the group. Individuals often adopt the views of their peers because they like or respect them or because they want to be like them."[49] Peer group conformity can uniquely define a generation such as the hippies of the 60s, women-libbers, and so on.

However, the desire to belong oftentimes compels one to change their traditional habits and beliefs just to "fit in." Conformity begins at the public school when the dance team or the band members all wear the same uniforms, or the girls all have the same hair style, etc. In college, conformity surfaces with fraternities and sororities. As members of the workforce, individuals are now confronted with a new set of peer pressures as they settle into their chosen career fields. For example, one's attire changes as one moves up the corporate ladder. Unfortunately, conformity does not openly welcome non-conformists. Far too often, individuals may totally switch their political party affiliations, change their perceived unacceptable habits or opt to remain silent when the conversation turns to a topic one does not want to discuss simply because to do so, goes against the views of the group.

Social Class/Income Level

"Most societies have significant social division based on class or occupation. Individuals live in different social worlds defined by their class position. Often, the social class divisions are politically relevant: identifying yourself as a member of the working class or the peasantry leads to distinct political views about what issues are important and which political groups best represent your interest."[50] For working class Americans, they want to hear a candidate speak about increasing the minimum wage, expanding health care benefits, preserving Social Security, guaranteeing work safety oversight, and so forth. Those employed in management positions or own a business, however, want to hear about tax reductions, less government regulation over business and industry, easing trade barriers, cutting back on required employee benefits, etc.

One's personal wealth oftentimes determines one's ability to participate in the political arena. "Participation in politics puts demands on people's scare resources. Working on a political campaign requires time; writing a letter requires verbal acuity; making a donation to a candidate requires money; signing a petition requires a sense of personal competence. Participation in politics, that is, has a price, a price that is some combination of money, time, skill, knowledge, and self-confidence. . . In short, for people whose resources are limited, politics is a luxury they often cannot afford, particularly when political outcomes may have only a modest impact on their own economic situations."[51] The average 8 to 5 American worker does not have the luxury of attending a local political debate much less to afford the time and income to be a state or national delegate to their political party's convention. Few workers feel comfortable using their lunch hour to stand in a voting line on election day. Consequently, state legislative houses and Congress have passed laws extending early voting times and days to include weekends. Unless a person has the time, money, and desire to participate, they are less likely to vote on a regular basis, or even register to vote!

There is a definite disconnection based on wealth about the value of one's level of participation in the political process. In conducting a voter registration drive, the deputize volunteer knocked on a door. The person answering the door was asked if he wanted to register to vote. The person's response was no followed by the comment that he was poor today and regardless of who won the election, he would still be poor tomorrow. "Compared with more other Western democracies, the United States has a more pronounced skew in voter turnout and other forms of political participation, with the affluent much more politically active than those who are less well off."[52]

Direct Contact

The United States Constitution's First Amendment guarantees a citizen's right to redress their government. Whether it be a city council meeting or a hearing at the state capitol, citizens are encouraged to attend these events. "These personal experiences are powerful agents of socialization, strengthening or undercutting the images presented by other agents. Does the government send retirement checks on time? Do city officials respond to citizen complaints? Are the schools teaching children? Do unemployment offices help people find jobs? Are the highways well maintained? These are very direct sources of information on how well government functions."[53] Across the nation, school board members are tackling the value of remote learning during a pandemic. City councils are pondering if they should increase property taxes, revitalize the downtown area, initiate programs to help struggling small businesses, provide adequate housing and services to their homeless population, etc. By just listening to the conversations, one can gain a valuable understanding to the complexity of these issues. Attending a state highway presentation gives one insight to complexities of right-of-way access, eminent domain issues, highway construction materials, and, of course, the timing of completing the project.

By just being a member of the audience or speaking during a citizens-to-be-heard moment gives one a valuable insight to how your elected representatives are receptive to your presence and comments. Oftentimes, elective officials are clueless on how they are perceived by their own constituents. For concerned on-looking citizens, "no matter how positive the view of the political system which has been inculcated by family and school, when a citizen is ignored by his party, cheated by his police, starved in the bread line, and finally conscripted into the army, his views of the political realm are likely to be altered."[54] Several years ago, citizens were loudly voicing their complaints about how they were being treated during the citizens-to-be-heard segment of council meetings in San Antonio, Texas. The mayor formed a special committee to investigate the concerns. Through a course of public hearings, the mayor got an earful of complaints. The concerned citizen who gathered enough courage to speak before a city council faced council members who were yawning, talking on their cell phones, conversing with their staff members, talking with each other, rolling their eyeballs in disgust, and simply not paying attention to what this individual had to say. Based upon his findings, the city council changed how it conducted its meetings.

The Media

The importance of the media as an agent of political socialization cannot be overlooked. In 1795, presidential contender John Adams praised the fourth estate:

> None of the means of information are most sacred, or have been cherished with more tenderness and care by the settlers of America, than the press. . . And you, Messieurs printers, whatever the tyrants of the earth may say of your paper, have done important service to your country. . . Be not intimidated, therefore, by any terrors from publishing with the utmost freedom whatever can be warranted by the laws of your country; nor suffer yourselves to the wheeled out of your liberty by any pretenses of politeness, delicacy, or decency. These, as they are often used, are but three different names of hypocrisy, chicanery, and cowardice.[55]

The majority of Americans rely upon their televisions or computer screens as their sole source of information. The credibility of a candidate, political party or issue is directly tied to the degree of positive or negative televised coverage the candidate or issue receives. During the "political season" campaign commercial after commercial highlights the candidate's favorable issue positions while criticizing their opponent's positions.

The following sight is sure to bring a smile to the face of any protestor or candidate running for public office. Media attention is the one indispensable ingredient to success. The media can make or break candidates and causes.

Photograph showing Vietnamese children, including Kim Phúc, running and crying after napalm was dropped from South Vietnamese Skyraider airplanes on their village of Trang Bang. June 8, 1972.

Over-reliance on these media sources does have it drawbacks. Communication networks whether it be a newspaper, television or radio station or internet source are operated as profit-making businesses. The market share or even the scope of the ban-width can dictate the programming of news broadcasts. The nightly televised news broadcast is limited to the "top stories" of the day and does not present in-depth analysis of those stories much less pressing political, social, and economic issues. Television, in particular, does a poor job of explaining complex political issues opting instead for brief overviews.

Yet, the media does impact one's political leanings and perceptions of the issues. During the early stages of the Civil Rights Movement of the 1960s, viewers saw the footage of the violent attacks against civil rights workers. Yet, the commentators rarely explained why the marches were organized in the first place. Daily television programming of the Vietnam War drove home in vivid details the horrors and reality of war from the comfort of one's living room. This is a far cry from the coverage of World War II. Americans crowded around their radios to hear descriptive commentary about the war. Newsreel footage was shown at the movie theaters. The coverage usually showed the troops preparing for battle. Rarely did one see American troops actively engaged in combat. In comparison, coverage of the Vietnam War was a nightly seven days a week visual footage of both the Vietcong and American troops firing at each other and launching air raids and bombs at one another. One of the most telling photos was a young Vietnamese girl suffering from severe burns running naked away from an American chemical attack. Televised footage was a definitive contributing factor to the anti-war protest movements of the 1970s.

Major Events

"Certain events and experiences may leave their mark on a whole society. A great war or a depression can constitute a severe political trauma for millions of individuals who may be involved."[56] The Great Depression of the 1930s changed public opinion about the role of government. Before the Depression, public opinion held that economic deprivation was self-inflicted and recovering from an economic reversal fell upon the individual, not the government. The Depression put millions out of work who had worked hard all their lives. Obviously, they were not to blame for their plight. Public opinion shifted, placing the blame for the economic disaster squarely on the shoulders of the government and demanded that the government must alleviate the suffering and reverse the economic decline. The Great Depression ushered in the modern welfare state. Initially, Covid-19 was not taken seriously by the American public. However, dramatic increases in the numbers of infected and, unfortunately, the deceased persons have shifted public opinion to demand that the government provide the necessary protective gear to health care providers and push for vaccines to cure Covid-19.

Trust in Government

A potentially potent agent is one's confidence that their government is indeed meeting the needs of its citizens. The pandemic caused by the corona-virus, the upheaval of the 2020 presidential election, the Black Lives Matter Movement and a seemingly irreversible economic decline have awakened the fears that democracy, as we know it, is in peril and our government is incapable of governing. Unfortunately, "the confidence of the American public in its political institutions is substantially lower today than it was in the 1960s."[57] In the 1960s, Americans were dealing the emerging civil rights era of peaceful demonstrations, sit-ins, boycotts, violent riots, and urban unrest. The unpopularity of the Vietnam War lead to nationwide student protests and outright anger over Watergate, the Pentagon Papers, etc. Since the 60s, we have witnessed "the media's steady preoccupation with negative news, such as policies that go awry, and with skewering politicians, especially the president, have played a crucial if unintended role in maintaining the public's negative feelings about Washington and politics in general."[58] Rather than focusing on issues, each election cycle has seen candidates tearing each other apart with personal attacks and unsubstantiated claims of malfeasance, corruption, misuse of power, etc. Few candidates stand before potential voters and articulate the programs and policies that if elected, they would implement to address the nation's overgrowing problems with unemployment, poverty, health care, infrastructure, and so forth. "These negative feelings about government are pervasive. For the last three decades, more than sixty percent of people have said, for example, that 'government is pretty much run by a few big interests looking out for themselves.'"[59] The level of one's trust in government can determine one's level of political participation. A voting public can soon turn into a non-voting public if they believe that their government has turned a blind eye to their concerns and needs.

All of these agents help to develop our political perspectives and levels of participation. No one agent at any given time is the sole influence to acquiring one's political perspectives. These agents act in conjunction with each other.

PUBLIC OPINION

Public opinion is "the aggregate of the individual feelings of a political community on a given issue; a force of such intangible power that it sets limits on what a government can do."[60] Unfortunately, the aggregate feelings of a political community changes from day to day depending upon the impact that issue has upon the individual members of that political community. Whether or not an individual participates in that telephone straw poll or the survey received in the mailbox is directly dependent upon the current impact the issue has on the recipient of that phone call or printed survey instrument. The importance or **saliency** of the issue to the respondent will determine if he/she answers the questions in the first place, and secondly, provides meaningful information through their responses. Case in point, in early February 2020, few Americans knew of the existence of Covid-19 nor did they even believe that the virus would adversely impact them. If asked what Americans believed to be the most dangerous threat facing the United States, few, if any, would have rated Covid-19 as a problem much less a life-threatening illness. However, if that same group would be asked that same question in December 2020, the majority would indeed place the threat of Covid-19 as the major problem confronting the American people. They have now been exposed to the seriousness of the illness. They have friends or relatives who have been stricken by the illness or they have had experience with the illness themselves. The economic downturn of Covid-19 has placed many Americans for the first time in their lives in unemployment and food bank distribution lines. Many are facing foreclosures and evictions from their homes and apartments. These individuals would express opinions on this economic downturn because they are being adversely impacted by it. On the other hand, those Americans who have job security, food security and are not facing possible job loss or the threat of losing their home may be sympathetic to those in need, but they may not wish to participate in a public opinion poll on these issues because they are not directly impacted by this economic downturn. An opinion poll taken before the Covid economic downturn would have found many expressing disdain for federally funded programs such as food stamps, rent subsidies, and unemployment insurance. Unfortunately, many of those who originally did not support these initiatives are now recipients of those various services that they once thought were frivolous government expenditures. They now support increasing the funding for those programs.

The mere mention of increasing taxes draws sharp criticism from those who are or will be paying the tax. From its founding, Americans subjected to property and income taxes have usually aligned themselves with candidates supporting tax reductions, not increases. Few income tax paying Americans look forward to filling those forms and unfortunately writing that check to the Internal Revenue Service. However, there are many Americans who are not positively or negatively impacted by the taxation actions of the president or Congress. The current tax laws exempt single individuals under the age of sixty-five earning less than $12,200 per year and married couples under sixty-five earning less than $24,000 from even filing an income tax form. Consequently, they would have different opinions about those menacing tax programs. In 2001, an overwhelming majority of Americans supported President George W. Bush sending military troops to Afghanistan in search of Bin Laden. However, public opinion shifted by the time of the 2016 presidential election as more Americans supported the total withdrawal of American forces from the region. When to ask the question is a quandary for researchers. "If a question is asked too soon after an event, it may result in measuring an initial, or top-of-the-head, or knee-jerk reaction, not the more-considered opinion that would be reflected were the reading delayed a week."[61]

The validity of the research is questionable when the pool of potential respondents is not directly connected to the issue or do the respondents understand the issue itself.

> Surveys that tap basic beliefs or subjects that people have thought a lot about–"Do you believe in God?" "Would you rather live in the United States or Russia?" are apt to be a good deal more accurate than surveys about subjects people have given little thought to or have little knowledge of—"Do you think our government should give military aid to the rebels fighting the Sandinista government in Nicaragua? Or "Do you think the United States should sell Alaskan oil to Japan in order to offset the U.S. Japanese trade deficit?"[62]

Consequently, researchers must dismiss the **illusion of saliency** defined as the "impressions conveyed by polls that something is important to the public when actually it is not."[63] For example, the San Antonio Chamber of Commerce Research Department once conducted a random survey several years ago about the public's potential support of building a major mall over the Edwards Recharge Zone. The results indicated that an overwhelming majority supported it. However, the results moved the Chamber to change the question simply because they realized that few knew that the Edwards Rechange Zone was the main conduit for water entering into the Edwards Aquifer, San Antonio's sole source of water. Once the question was changed to building mall over the city's sole source of water, the responses changed dramatically. Few wanted major construction to adversely impact the city's water source.

The **illusion of central tendency** is "the assumption that opinions are 'normally distributed'—that response to opinion questions are heavily distributed toward the center, as in a bell-shaped curve."[64] Central tendency usually holds true for polls addressing one's political leanings. Few Americans are ultra-liberals or ultra-conservatives. The majority of Americans fall into the middle of the spectrum or the moderate category. History shows candidates espousing far left or far right political perspectives usually lose to their more moderate political rivals. Yet, central tendency does not hold true for all issue positions. For many respondents, there are only two sets of answers—yes and no or for and against. There are no "gray areas" where one could ride the middle of the fence. Results of an opinion poll on abortion rights would show a large percentage of the respondents supporting abortion rights only to be offset with a large percentage advocating pro-life positions. Very few respondents would be placed in the middle or moderate range. The same would hold true for numerous issues such as environmental protection, civil rights, school prayer, etc. In this situation the bell curve collapses or is inverted. For a political candidate, this means that the position he/she takes on that issue will garner support only from those whose responses match the candidate's position. Very few on the opposing side would moderate their stance or even switch their position on that issue.

MEASURING PUBLIC OPINION—A SCIENTIFIC APPROACH

Political science research is indeed a science based on measurable and verifiable data. If conducted in the appropriate manner, few findings would bear the taint of "fake news." **Empirical research** is "research based on actual, 'objective' observation of phenomena."[65] What the researcher is seeking is **empirical verification** that is "characteristic of scientific knowledge, [a] demonstration by means of objective observation that a statement is true."[66] **Public opinion polls** are the "scientific instruments for measuring public opinion."[67] The results of a public opinion poll are an empirical analysis driven by the information obtained through an analysis of the data. Invalid research occurs when the researcher has a preconceived conclusion and constructs the data gathering towards that conclusion. The validity of any analysis is very dependent upon the importance of the data determining the eventual results or conclusions, not the reverse.

The crux of the research is the formulation of a **hypothesis**, defined as "a tentative or provisional or unconfirmed statement that can in principle be verified."[68] In deciding whether to run for the presidency, Joe Biden's team conducted numerous public opinion polls based on the hypothesis that Biden's credentials and issue positions would garner enough public support to win the White House. Their analysis was based on **deduction**, "a type of reasoning in which if the premises of an argument are true, the conclusion is necessarily true."[69] In other words, if the data revealed that a majority of the American voting public was aligned with Biden's issue positions, then Biden would have their support and, of course, their votes for his presidential candidacy.

Public opinion polls are usually measured as either a mean or median distribution. A **mean** distribution is "a measure of central tendency found by summing the values of the variable and dividing the total by the number of observations."[70] For example, 100 individuals responded to a public opinion poll. The researcher would add up all the tallies for the 100 respondents and divided the total by 100. This would yield the average or the mean. The results of the pre-candidate polls for Joe Biden would indicate that on an average X number of individuals would support his White House bid. Or the researcher could report the median of the results. The **median** is "the category or value above or below which one-half of the observations lie."[71] In this situation, the pollsters would report that X number of respondents supported Biden and an offsetting percentage did not. The reliability of the data is dependent upon the error margin. The **measurement error** is the "failure to identify the true distribution of opinion within a population because of errors or poorly worded questions."[72] Unfortunately no public opinion poll is perfect. Researchers do not know in advance that their questions are easily understood by the respondents or that the questions themselves generate the reliable information that they are seeking. The error margin is usually printed at the bottom of the poll results as a plus or minus. Usually, the Biden poll as an example, the results margin of error could have been plus or minus five percent, meaning that the results showing 60 percent in support of Biden were either plus five or 65 percent or minus five or 55 percent. The smaller the margin of error means that the researcher is confident that the information obtained is indeed reliable and valid.

Selecting the Sampling Pool

Polling the entire population is an impossible task. Researchers opt instead to focus on a pre-determined population group called a **sample**. The sample is a "small group selected by researchers to represent the most important characteristics of an entire population."[73] The notion of using a sample to measure public opinion was used by Jacko Bernoulli in 1713. He noted that "when a population is large, a relatively small sample randomly drawn from that population will contain, within a small and calculable margin of error, the same proportions of a given characteristic as are contained in the total population."[74] The validity of the research data is very dependent upon the accurate selection of the sample group. There are several types of sample groups. A **random sampling** is "one in which respondents are chosen mathematically, at random, with every effort made to avoid bias in the construction of the sample."[75] Usually, a computer-generate program selects a certain number of persons from a larger population group. For example, the program selects every tenth person from a list of 100,000. In this case, there are no other variables to the composition of the group other than being the tenth person on the list. On the other hand, a **selective polling** sample is one "drawn deliberately to reconstruct meaningful distributions of an entire consistency."[76] In this case, the researcher is focusing on a particular group. For example, the survey is asking parents about quality and availability of day care services in their neighborhood. Consequently, the sample group needs to be a pool of parents with young children. With the Covid-19 pandemic, education offerings have shifted from face-to-face to remote. A valid survey of the impact of remote learning versus the traditional face-to-face course offerings depends upon a sample group of respondents who have experienced both learning methods. Perhaps the most frequently used sampling selection process is the **probability sampling**. This is "a method used by pollsters to select a sample in which every individual in the population has an equal probability of being selected as a respondent so that the correct weight can be given to all segments of the population."[77] Surveys are mailed to every resident within a designated area. Everyone has the equal opportunity to answer the questions and mail the survey back. The results are calculated from the responses returned to the pollster.

The potential location of a major retail store or commercial company such as a grocery store hinges on the results of a **quota sampling** survey. In this situation, "respondents are selected whose characteristics closely match those of the general population along several significant dimensions, such as geographic region, sex, age, and race." For example, a retail store chain is seeking various locations within a urban area. It sells both high-end expensive items such as clothing, jewelry, furniture, etc. as well as less expensive similar items. Survey results focusing on one's income levels will determine both the location of a store and its product lines. Retail outlets also consider the age, race, and sex of an area's residents. Surveys will indicate that both the convenience of a store's location coupled with the attractiveness and affordability of its products will determine its potential profitability. Results from product surveys can determine the marketability of any product.

Any issue with the sampling group can lead to invalid results. "The sampling problems may be divided into those that affect

> (1) the definition of the population, (2) the size of the sample, and (3) the representativeness of the sample. In regards to the definition of the population the important problem is to decide the group about which the researcher wishes to generalize his findings. In regard to size of sample, consideration must be given to the persistent disappearance of cases in a breakdown analysis. . . . The third and perhaps most intricate sampling problem arises in connection with the method of securing a representative sample. The essential requirement of any sample is that it is as representative as possible of the population or universe from which it is taken."[79]

Researchers must also avoid sampling bias which can lead to a sampling error. A **sampling bias** "occurs whenever some elements of a population are systematically excluded from a sample."[80] For example, the researcher is conducting a survey on voter preferences on candidates running for judgeships in Sagebush. The sample should include those with differing political perspectives since voters oftentimes split ticket their voting choices opting to select candidates from both or more political parties. However, this sample only surveys registered Republicans. The resulting findings will be skewed towards Republican candidates running for those judgeships. Conducting a survey from a sample of just African Americans who have been victims of racial discrimination excludes other racial/ethnic groups who also were confronted with racial discrimination. These surveys are prime examples of a sampling error since only a portion of the impacted population was surveyed.

Formulating the Questions

Regardless of the instrument, the selection and sequencing of the questions is extremely important. Poorly written questions will yield poor responses and invalid results. "If pollsters wish to understand the true meaning of opinions, they should be warned to be especially careful to examine the implied context of the questions they ask, and they should be alert to the way that opinions are embedded in larger belief structures."[81] It is the questions that guide the respondent towards expressing their opinions. The questions prompt the respondent to think about what their answer should be and, oftentimes, particularly with a mail-in survey instrument, compels the respondent to do further research before they answer the questions.

The instrument should "(1) start with the easy questions that the respondent will enjoy answering and (2) go from the general to the specific; from the easy to hard" questions.[82] To ensure reliable feedback, the creator of the questions should:

(1)   Keep the language pitched to the level of the respondent.
(2)   Try to pick words that have the same meaning for everyone.
(3)   Avoid long questions.
(4)   Not assume that your respondent possesses factual information or first-hand options.
(5)   Protect your respondent's ego.
(6)   If you're after unpleasant orientations, give your respondent the chance to express his/her positive feelings first so that he/she is not put in an unfavorable light.
(7)   Decide on what type of question you wish to use.
(8)   Avoid ambiguous wording and bias or leading questions.[83]

The general rule of thumb is that the "questions have to be standardized and asked in precisely the same way each time, just as measuring distance one must use a standardized yardstick, or in weighing things, one must place the standard weights on the scales."[84]

There are several sets of questions a researcher can use to solicit reliable responses. A **closed-end question** provides a respondent with alternative answers. The respondent merely selects the one answer that best reflects their opinion. For example, the survey question asks the respondent of he/she supports Democrats over Republican candidates for state legislative house seats. The choices could be a) yes, b) sometimes or c) no. This leads the respondent to give either a definitive yes or no response with the understanding that a sometimes answer means that they could support members of both political parties. Yes or no or agree or disagree questions can be problematic since "there is a predisposition on the part of people to agree with a statement particularly if the statement deals with something they have little knowledge of or have not thought about."[85] To avoid this, a series of questions seeking the respondent's knowledge or expertise on the survey issue would aid the researcher in determining the validity of the respondent's choice.

Launched in 1932, survey instruments can incorporate the **Likert Scale**. This is a "five-point scale that uses both words and numbers which respondents are asked to rate an issue, person, or concept, for example, (1) strong disapprove, (2) disapprove, (3) neither approve or disapprove, (4) approve, and (5) strongly approve."[86] The intent was to give individuals several options to choose from. However, giving the respondent too many variables can result in unreliable data. For example, a question asking respondents if they use a certain product. The choices could include six or more choices from always to never using the product. Respondents are now caught in a quandary. Few would select the always or never responses to answer every question, opting instead to pick from other options.

A **leading question** also known as a **reactive question** "encourages the respondent to choose a particular response" as a means of narrowing down the pool of usable responses.[87] If conducting research on environmental issues, the leading question could be "Do you think that air pollution is hazardous to one's health? Most would select yes as the usual answer. The responses of those who did not feel that air pollution was detrimental to one's health would be excluded.

The **open-ended question** is asking the respondent to give their own opinion without prompting them to a particular anticipated response. The statement would be "I support Democrats over Republicans for state legislative house seats because _____." Or "I use this particular product because _____." The problem with using these questions is that it leaves it wide-open for lengthy replies. To avoid it, a word limit needs to be assigned for each response.

Another survey tactic is to use a **branching question** that "sorts respondents into subgroups and directs those subgroups to different parts of the questionnaire."[88] This option enables the researcher to gather data from two or more distinct groups of responses. For example, the survey instrument is asking individuals about their experiences with a health care provider. The first or branch question would ask them to select what kind of health care provider they use. Individuals who visit their primary care physician will have a different experiences and opinions about the quality of their health care provider from those who sought medical care at a drop-in medical center or the emergency room of a major hospital.

On the other hand, the researcher can use a **filter question** "to screen respondents so that the subsequent questions will be asked of only certain respondents for whom the questions are appropriate."[89] For example, the survey instrument is addressing the need for day care services. Obviously, the survey's intent is to gather information from parents of young non-school age children who require outside child-care. A series of filter questions would eliminate those who either have no children or whose children are too old for day care from those who have young children needing day care services. Filtering questions would be necessary for surveys assessing the validity of services offered by the food bank, the unemployment office, etc. Only those who need and use those services can provide the information needed to properly assess the effectiveness of those services.

TYPES OF SURVEY INSTRUMENTS

Predicting Election Results—Bellwether Districts

In watching the 2020 presidential election returns, all the major broadcasting networks projected a winner of a state with only less than one to two percent of the tallied vote. One wonders how an election result can be called with only a scant percentage of the total vote. The commentors' prediction is based on the findings gathered from a **bellwether district** defined as "a town or district that is a microcosm of the whole population of that has been found to be a good predictor of electoral outcomes."[90] The challenge for pollsters is to correctly select a small percentage of the area's voters that is totally representative of the entire population of a state, town or district. For example, the city of Sagebrush has a diverse population of 50,000 residents of which 50 percent are Anglo, 30 percent Hispanic and 20 percent African American. In building the bellwether district of 100 persons, 50 would be Anglo, 30 Hispanic and 20 African Americans. The bellwether district is further reflective of the city's gender breakdown, income levels, employment status, homeowners versus renters, education levels, etc. All these factors must be taken into account in order to develop a microcosm of 100 that is totally representative of 50,000 individuals. If it is done correctly, then the viewpoints and candidate selections of that 100 will be a solid indicator of predicting the voting preferences of 50,000.

The Straw Poll

A **straw poll** is basically an unscientific attempt to measure public sentiment or opinions on a given issue or political candidate. It was first used by the *Harrisburg Pennsylvanian* and the *Raleigh Star* newspapers in 1824 to predict the outcome of the 1824 presidential race between Andrew Jackson, Henry Clay, William H. Crawford and John Quincy Adams. Their reporters just randomly asked people on the street what candidate they would vote for in the upcoming election. Both papers published results favoring Andrew Jackson. Yet, this election went to John Quincy Adams since none of the candidates received the required number of electoral votes to outright win the White House. The choice fell to Congress who subsequently selected John Quincy Adams for the presidency. Straw polls are still used today. Their validity is highly suspect since "there is no way to ensure that the sample of individuals giving opinions is representative of the larger population."[91]

The Phone or Personal Interview

Whether soliciting information about product preferences or political candidates, polling and consulting firms hire a cadre of individuals to conduct interviews over the phone or in-person at a popular location such as a shopping mall. Valid information is dependent upon how the interviewer asks the questions. It is imperative that the interviewer receives the appropriate training before they make their first phone call or approach an individual at the mall. What needs to be avoided is **interviewer bias** that can influence the respondent's answers to the questions. The interviewer cannot interject their own personal opinions about the questions nor can they embellish the wording of the question. For example, the question being asked is "if the presidential election were held today, would you vote for Joe Biden." It should be delivered in a non-committal voice with no change in the tone of the voice. The interviewer cannot change the question—"if the presidential election were held today, would you vote for the well-qualified and talented Joe Biden." By adding words to the question, the interviewer is leading the respondent to say yes, rather than no.

Any survey conducted through phone calls is problematic. "The average political survey may require calling 15,000 numbers to identify 5,000 working telephone numbers of which about 1,000 will produce a person who agrees to be interviewed. Altogether, this effort will require 30,000 to 40,000 phone number calls. It is difficult to provide an average cost, but a typical telephone survey response of 20 to 25 percent and good quality control (including extensive interview training, questionnaire testing, and close supervision of the interviewing process) can cost $40 to $50 per interview or more. Rising costs may have serious consequences, since they increase the temptation to cut corners."[92] The response rate for phone surveys is higher than the response rate from mail-in questionnaires. Yet, phone surveys have an inherent bias. "While possession of telephones is pervasive, something like 1 out of 10 do not have a phone and the characteristics of this 1 out of 10 do not closely resemble the characteristics of the other 9 out of ten. . . . Bias in telephone surveys is partly due to who has phones and who does not, but partly also to who will agree to be interviewed and who will not."[93] The frequency of phone surveys or interviews oftentimes "turns people off" from participating. Particularly during election time, every candidate has their volunteer staff making campaign-related calls to potential voters. The basic leading question usually asks the respondent if they have heard about their candidate or if they have already voted. Far too often, the respondent will tell the interviewer that they do know about the candidate and they have already cast their ballot when they have done neither simply because they do not want to hear what the caller has to say. "Another problem facing polling is that a growing number of people are out of reach because they have a cell phone and no landline. Cell-only Americans tend to be much younger than the average and more likely to be members of a minority racial or ethnic group, and less likely to be married, or own a home."[94]

On the other hand, the personal interview has several advantages to guaranteeing a high rate of return of reliable information. Basically, "the information secured is likely to be more correct than that secured by other techniques since the interviewer can clear up seemingly inaccurate answers by explaining the questions to the informant. If the latter deliberately falsified replies, the interviewer may be trained to spot such cases and use special devices to get the truth."[95] Furthermore,

> The interviewer can collect supplementary information about the informant's personal characteristics and environment which is valuable in interpreting results and evaluating the representatives of the persons interviewed. The interviewer may catch the informant off guard and thus secure more spontaneous reactions that would be the case if a written form were mailed out for the informant to mull over. The interview can usually control which person or persons answer the questions, whereas in the mail survey, several members of the household may confer before the questions are answered. The personal interview may take long enough to allow the informant to become oriented to the topic under investigation. Questions about which the informant is like to be sensitive to can be carefully sandwiched in by the interviewer.[96]

The Mail-in Questionnaire

Researchers can obtain valuable information by using a mail-in questionnaire. This is a less expensive survey instrument since the major cost is printing and mailing the survey instrument. Usually, the survey includes a stamped self-addressed return envelope and even a meager cash incentive such as a dollar bill to encourage recipients to fill out the questionnaire and mail it back. A mail-in questionnaire can reach a wider audience that oftentimes cannot be reached by a phone, personal interview or through the internet. Unlike the phone or personal interview, there is no pressure for an immediate response to the questions. Recipients can complete it in the privacy of their home at a time convenient to them.

However, there are several disadvantages to using this research tool. First, there is a considerable low rate of return. "Mail surveys tend to have the greatest nonresponse rates and, hence, potential nonresponse bias."[97] The researcher is dependent upon the recipient to have the time, the interest in the subject of the survey itself, and the willingness to fill it out and mail it back. Not providing a postage stamp and self-address return envelope is a contributing factor of the low return rate. This is a significant problem with the mail-in questionnaire. In 1780s, Scottish laird Sr. John Sinclair decided to poll the clergy on pressing issues adversely impacting the Catholic Church. He believed that members of the Church would be more than willing to express their opinions. He mailed out 881 questionnaires with more than 120 questions.[98] However, he initially received very few returned questionnaires. Frustrated, "he introduced yet a third state-of-the-art technique—the follow up letter" and then "sent statistical missionaries to help fill out the questionnaires when his follow-up letters provide inadequate."[99]

Second, there is a possibility that the respondent may not understand the questions. The survey instructions normally do not give the respondent a resource they can contact if they need additional information to complete the survey. The more complicated the questions, the less likely a person is to complete the questionnaire. Third, the construction and sequence of the questions is essential to capturing valuable information. Fourth, a major impediment to one completing the survey is the length of the survey itself. A short survey of one or two pages in length has a better chance of being completed and mailed back versus a multiple page instrument that asks too many questions. For example, a mail-in survey asked recipients to rate what type of detergent they use on a regular basis. The survey was twenty pages in length. The questions were so repetitive that by the time one finished it, they were confused as to what detergent they actually favored.

Internet Surveys

The convenience of using the internet has provided researchers and pollsters with a ready tool to assess public opinion on everything from political candidates to food products. All the researcher needs to do is formulate the question and download them onto a website. It seems so simple, but the validity of data obtain via the internet is questionable for several reasons. First, the respondent has the option of submitting his responses multiple times. There are few mechanisms that can limit the number of respondent's replies. Second, these survey instruments either follow the Likert Scale or ask for yes or no responses with limited opportunities to offer explanations concerning their response choices. Third, the sample size is limited to only those who have internet accessibility. As evidenced by the transition from face-to-face teaching to remote learning, it is a failed assumption that everyone has internet connectivity.

Conclusions

In his State of the Union message delivered on December 19, 1859, President James Buchanan drove home the point that "public opinion in this country is all-powerful, and when its reaches a dangerous excess upon any question the good sense of the people will furnish the corrective and bring it back within safe limits."[100] Those same sentiments were expressed by President Harrison in 1888. His statement that "public opinion is the most potent monarch this world knows" underscores the value of and the need to properly solicit the opinions of the citizenry.[101] Unless elected officials have a clear understanding of what their constituents want, lawmakers are left to their own devices to assume what needs to be done. Far too often what lawmakers *assume* what their task is, is not what the public wants!

Yet, the value of public opinion rests with the public, not the pollsters or the researchers. The job of the pollster is to acquire it, measure it, and report it. The task of the public is to gain the knowledge necessary to form their own valid opinions. Pollsters stress that "the ability to link mass opinion to public policy decisions nonetheless raise[s] three serious questions. First, were the masses equipped to consider complex problems, however carefully posed by public opinion pollsters? Second, even if the masses were able to understand the problems, would they be willing to give their true opinions, those which would be predictive of subsequent political behavior? Finally, even if the first two conditions were satisfied, would representatives have the obligation to enact policies in accordance with popular opinion?"[102] After multiple decades of conducting public opinion polls and election-related research that produce meaningful and reliable data, "if political scientists knew one thing for certain, it was that citizens generally neither knew nor cared about most governmental institutions, political leaders, current issues, or public policies. For most people the day-to-day concerns of family and work were far more salient than the concerns of politics."[103] Unfortunately, elected officials realize the limitations of John Q. Public since "ordinary citizens are inevitably outsiders; they cannot be expected to appreciate the complexities seen by political decision makers."[104] For example, right before they adjourned for the 2020 Christmas holiday break, Congress passed an additional stimulus package to ease the financial burdens caused by the Covid pandemic. It is a lengthy piece of legislation allocating federal dollars to individuals below $75,000 in annual income, extending unemployment benefits, and providing funding for small businesses, and financial incentives and tax breaks for a long laundry list of lobbyists, businesses owners, etc. Few, if any, will spend the time and effort to read the over 5,000 paged bill. On the whole, the majority looks at this piece of legislation from a personal perspective, in other words, what benefits will they receive from it and when will they receive it.

One is reminded of Plato's *Allegory of the Cave*, from *The Republic*. Plato describes a dark dank cave where three prisoners since birth have had their hands, feet and necks chained to a wall in the cave. They have never seen the outside world. Unable to move about, the prisoners must stare day in and day out at the back wall of the cave. On the wall behind them, a fire is burning and illuminates images on the wall facing the prisoners. They see people carrying out their daily routines as they walk on a road running behind the wall. The setting is similar to what one would see in a puppet show as the puppeteer operates the puppets from behind a screen. For the prisoners, this is the world that they see. Eventually, one of the prisoners breaks free from his chains. He now has movement and can turn away from the wall and eventually leaves the confines of the cave. He is shocked at what he sees for he now realizes that the world he came to know in the cave is not the real world. He returns to the cave to inform his fellow prisoners of the world outside and offers to free them so they too can see "the light" of knowledge and wisdom. Afraid and apprehensive, his fellow prisoners threaten to kill him if he attempts to free them. For Plato, the cave "represents people who believe that knowledge comes from what we see and hear in the world—empirical evidence. The cave shows that believers of empirical knowledge are trapped in a 'cave' of misunderstanding."[105] Free from his bondage, "the escaped prisoner represents the Philosopher, who seeks knowledge outside of the cave and outside of the senses."[106]

The lesson learned is that one cannot seek true knowledge from one source. It is the responsibility of the individual to seek knowledge from multiple sources and to base his/her opinions from different points of view. "Political philosophers John Locke and Jean-Jacques Rousseau argued that the will of the majority in a society should be considered the general will—or what some today might refer to as public opinion."[107]

CHAPTER NOTES

[1]Michael Margolis, "Public Opinion, Polling, and Political Behavior," *The Annals*, Vol. 472, March, 1984, 62.

[2]Donald G. Tannenbaum, *Inventors of Ideas: An Introduction to Western Political Philosophy*, 3rd ed., (Boston: Massachusetts: Wadsworth Cengage Learning, 2004), 254.

[3]*The HarperCollins Dictionary of American Government and Politics*, Jay M. Shafritz, ed., (New York, New York: HarperCollins, 1992), 174.

[4]Margolis, 62.

[5]*Treasury of Presidential Quotations*, Caroline Harnsberger, ed., (Chicago, Illinois: Follett Publishing Co., 1964), 284.

[6]Ibid.

[7]Ibid., 285.

[8]J. John Martin, "The Genealogy of Public Polling," *The Annals*, Vol. 472, March, 1984, 21.

[9]*https://uselectionatlas.org.*

[10]Ibid.

[11]Gabriel Almond and G. Bingham Powell, Jr., *Comparative Politics: A Developmental Approach*, 1st ed., (Boston: Massachusetts: Little, Brown, 1966), 50.

[12]Lucian W. Pye, "Chapter 1: Introduction: Political Culture and Political Development, *Political Culture and Political Development*, Lucian W. Pye and Sidney Verba, eds., Princeton, New Jersey: Princeton University Press, 1969), 8.

[13]Almond and Powell, Jr. 57.

[14]Pye, 7-8.

[15]*The HarperCollins Dictionary of American Government and Politics*, 93.

[16]*The American Dictionary of the English Language*, William Morris, ed., 16th ed., (Boston, Massachusetts: Houghton Mifflin Company, 1982), 524.

[17]Daniel J. Elazar, *American Federalism: A View from the States*, 3rd ed., (New York, New York: Harper & Row Publishers, 1984), 110.

[18]Susan Adams and Karsten Strauss, "The U.S. States People Are Fleeing and The Ones They Are Moving To," *Forbes, https:www3forbes.com*

[19]Elazar, 114-115.

[20]Ibid., 117.

[21]Ibid.

[22]Ibid.

[23]Ibid., 116.

[24]Ibid.

[25]Ibid.

[26]Ibid., 118.

[27]Ibid.

[28]Ibid., 119.

[29]Ibid.

[30]Almond and Powell, Jr., 56.

[31]*The HarperCollins Dictionary of American Government and Politics*, 442.

[32]Almond and Powell, Jr., 65-66.

[33]*The HarperCollins Dictionary of American Government and Politics*, 439.

[34]Margolis, 64.

[35]Ibid., 65.

[36]Susan Welch, John Gruhl, Michael Steinman, John Comer and Susan Rigdon, *American Government*, 5th ed., (Minneapolis/St. Paul, Wisconsin: West Publishing Co.), 1994) 82-83.

[37]Gabriel Almond, G. Bingham Powell, Jr., Russell J. Dalton, and Kaare Storm, *Comparative Politics Today: A World* View, 9th ed., (New York, New York: Pearson, 2010), 52.

[38]Ibid., 53.

[39]*The HarperCollins Dictionary of American Government and Politics*, 65.

[40]Almond, Powell, Jr., Dalton and Storm, 53.

[41]Almond and Powell, Jr., 67-68.

[42]Welch, Gruhl, Steinman, Comer and Rigdon, 83.

[43]Ibid.

[44]Almond and Powell, Jr., 67.

[45]Welch, Gruhl, Steinman, Comer and Rigdon, 83.

[46]Ibid., 85.

[47]Steven J. Rosenstone and John Mark Hansen, *Mobilization, Participation, and Democracy In America*, 1st ed., (New York, New York: MacMillan Publishing Company, 1993), 14.

[48]*The Green Book: The Black Travelers' Guide to Jim Crow America*, https://www.history.com

[49]Almond, Powell, Jr., Dalton and Storm, 53.

[50]Ibid., 54.

[51]Rosenstone and Hansen. 14.

[52]Scott Keeter, "Poll Power," *The Wilson Quarterly*, Vol. 32, No. 4, Autumn, 2008, 56-57.

[53]Almond, Powell, Jr., Dalton and Storm, 56.

[54]Almond and Powell, Jr., 69.

[55]*A Treasury of Presidential Quotations*, 266.

[56]Almond and Powell, Jr., 65.

[57]William Keefe and Marc Hethering, *Parties, Politics and Public Policy in America*, 9th ed. (Washington, D.C.: CQ Press, 2003), 230.

[58]Ibid.

[59]Ibid.

[60]*The HarperCollins Dictionary of American Government and Politics*, 475.

[61]Burns W. Roper, "Are Polls Accurate?", *The Annals*, Vol. 472, March, 1984, 25.

[62]Ibid.

[63]Theodore Lowi and Benjamin Ginsburg, *American Government: Freedom and Power*, 4th ed., (New York, New York: W. W. Norton and Company, 1966), A42.

[64]Ibid.

[65]Janet Buttolph Johnson, and H. T. Reynolds with Jason D. Mycoff, *Political Science Research Methods*, 6th ed., (Washington, D.C.: CQ Press, 2008), 584.

[66]Ibid.

[67]Benjamin Ginsburg, Theodore J. Lowi, Margaret Weir and Robert Spitzer, *We The People: An Introduction to American Politics*, 7th ed., (New York, New York: W. W. Norton and Company, 2009), A54.

[68]Johnson and Reynolds, 584.

[69]Ibid., 583.

[70]Ibid., 587.

[71]Ibid.

[72]Ginsburg, Lowi, Weir and Spitzer, A52.

[73]Ibid., A55.

[74]Martin, 20.

[75]Lowi and Ginsburg, A47.

[76]Ibid.

[77]Ginsburg, Lowi, Weir and Spitzer, A54.

[78]Lowi and Ginsburg, A47.

[79]Delbert C. Miller, *Handbook of Research Design and Social Measurement*, 2nd ed. (New York, New York: David McKay Company, Inc. 1970), 55.

[80]Johnson and Reynolds, 583.

[81]Lester M. Milbrath, "The Context of Public Opinion: How Our Belief System Can Affect Poll Results," *The Annals*, Vol. 472, March, 1984, 36.

[82]Miller, 79-80.

[83]Ibid.
[84]Martin, 19.
[85]Roper, 33.
[86]Martim, 19.
[87]Johnson and Reynolds, 587.
[88]Ibid., 581.
[89]Ibid., 585.
[90]Lowi and Ginsburg, A38.
[91]Welch, Gruhl, Steinman, Comer and Rigdon, 88.
[92]Keeter, 60.
[93]Roper, 30.
[94]Keeter, 60.
[95]Miller, 86-88.
[96]Ibid.
[97]Roper, 30.
[98]Martin, 17.
[99]Ibid.
[100]*Treasury of Presidential Quotations*, 284.
[101]Ibid.
[102]Margolis, 63.
[103]Ibid.
[104]Ibid.
[105]*Allegory of the Cave by Plato-Summary and Meanin*g, *https://www.philosophyzer.com*
[106]Ibid.
[107]Martin, 14-15.

SUGGESTED READINGS

Asher, Herbert. *Polling and the Public: What Every Citizen Should Know*. Washington, D.C.: CQPress, 2011.

Dennis, Jack, ed. *Socialization to Politics: A Reader*. New York: John Wiley & Sons, 1973.

Doherty, Carroll, "A Public Opinion Trend that Matters: Priority for Gun Policy." Pew Research Center, 2015, htpp://www.pewresearch.org/fact-tank/2015/01/09/a-public-opinion-trend-that-matters-prioities-for-gun-policy/

Erikson, Robert S., and Kent L. Tedin. *American Public Opinion: Its Origins, Content and Impact*. 6th ed. New York: Pearson, 2016.

Greenstein, Fred I. *Children and Politics*. New Haven, Conn.: Yale University Press, 1985.

Jacobson, Gary C., *A Divider, Not a Uniter: George W. Bush and the American People*. New York: Pearson Longman, 2007.

Milburn, Michael A. *Persuasion and Politics: The Social Psychology of Public Opinion*. Belmont, Calif.: Wadsworth, Inc., 1991.

Renshon, Stanley Allen, ed. *Handbook of Political Socialization: Theory and Research*. New York: The Free Press, 1977.

Sigel, Roberta S., and Marily B. Hoskin. *The Political Involvement of Adolescents*. New Brunswick, New Jersey: Rutgers University Press, 1981.

Will, George F. *The Leveling Wind: Politics, the Culture and Other News*, 1990-1994. New York: Viking, 1994.

Woshinsky, Oliver H. *Culture and Politics: An Introduction to Mass and Elite Political Behavior*. Englewood Cliffs, New Jersey: 1995.

Chapter Four

POLITICAL PARTIES

The value of political parties in the American political process has been debated since George Washington assumed the presidency. In his famous farewell address, Washington emphasized that by their very nature political parties divide rather than unite people. He pointed out that "the spirit of party serves always to distract the public councils, and enfeeble the public administration. It agitates the community with ill-founded jealousies and false alarms; kindles the animosity of one part against another; foments occasional riot and insurrection."[1] Washington had a valid point as witnessed time and time again at both the Republican and Democratic national conventions as speaker after speaker criticizes and defiles the opposition party while at the same time highlighting the virtues and accomplishments of their own political party. John Adams lamented about the inability of political parties to work with each other with the spirit of harmony and compromise needed to address the nation's problems. "I have always called our Constitution a game of leap frog. . . . neither party will ever be strong, while they adhere to their austere, exclusive maxims. Neither party will ever be able to pursue the true interest, honor, and dignity of the nation. I lament the narrow, selfish spirit of the leaders of both parties, but can do no good to either. They are incorrigible."[2] Adams's comments ring true today as Americans witness the daily battles between Congressional Democrats and Republicans over every single piece of legislation. With congressional approval ratings at an all-time low, the interparty gridlock between Democrats and Republicans coupled with the heated bickering within the rank and file of Congressional Republicans is a daily topic of the evening news. Thomas Jefferson went a step further: "If I could not go to heaven but with a party, I would not go there at all."[3]

On the other hand, there are those who support the party system and believe that without it, our nation's pursuit of democratic principles and values would be seriously jeopardized. In a speech delivered in 1923, President Warren G. Harding underscored the value and importance of political parties:

I believe in political parties. These were the essential agencies of the popular government which made us what we are. We were never perfect, but under our party system, we wrought a development under representative democracy unmatched in all proclaimed liberty and attending human advancement. We achieve under the party system where parties were committed to policies, and party loyalty was a mark of honor and an inspiration toward accomplishment.[4]

Both interest groups and political parties bring together under their respective umbrellas those possessing similar ideological persuasions and issue positions. As a whole, interest groups have a narrower prospective than their political party counterparts. For example, the Sierra Club's agenda is advocacy for the protection and preservation of the environment. Labor unions promote the interests of the nation's workers with emphasis on wages, benefits, and working conditions. The various Chambers of Commerce actively support business development and advocate legislative actions favorable to a profitable business climate. On the other hand, political parties place as many diverse groups as possible under their broader umbrellas. The Democratic Party's base supports the majority of the nation's blue-collar workers, Hispanics, African Americans, women, lower- to lower-middle income Americans and those carrying the liberal banner. Under the Republican umbrella are business-owners, upper-middle and upper-income groups, and those who uphold to more conservative viewpoints. There are growing numbers of individuals who simply do not want to carry the Democrat or Republican label. They prefer to be called independents. The fabric that binds the majority of the American electorate to either of the two major political parties is tied to each party's unique political philosophy that molds their issue positions. The issues will be the same—poverty, national security, the economy, taxes, government regulation, etc. However, the Democratic and the Republican Party, as well as the occasional third party movements, will take different positions on those issues. While the majority of the American electorate rarely watches a party's national convention or read their party's platforms, they generally recognize the liberal camp as affiliating themselves with the Democratic Party and conservatives with the Republican Party. This chapter examines the broad political philosophies that guide each party's issue positions.

The political scene can involve one or more major parties with numerous minor or third parties. Regardless of the number of political parties, these organizations play essential roles in the election process from the recruitment of candidates for public office to turning out the vote on Election Day. It is these organizations that galvanize their supporters behind their candidates and also bind the candidates to the party label. In the American party system, it is the state and local organizations that register the voters, stage and, oftentimes, fund their party's primary elections, assistant in candidate fund raising, etc. While candidates use their party to get themselves on a general election ballot, these candidates overlook the important bond one must have with his/her party and the work party members from top to bottom do to help that candidate win on election night. Once elected, one cannot successfully drive any piece of legislation through a legislative house nor can any president be successful without the support of his/her political party. It is a team effort! This chapter delves into the organizational structure of American political parties and the roles each level plays not only in the election process but also in the development and implementation of public policy.

THE ANATOMY OF A POLITICAL PARTY

British political philosopher and himself a member of the House of Commons, Edmund Burke described a political party as "a body of men united, for promoting by their joint endeavors the national interest, upon some particular principle in which they all agreed."[5] Therefore, a **political party** is "an organization whose members are sufficiently homogeneous to band together for the overt purpose of winning elections which entitles them to exercise government power, in order to enjoy the influence, prerequisites, and advantages of authority."[6] Basically, political parties "consist of three inter-related components: the **party in the electorate**, those who identify with the party; the **party in government**, those who are appointed or elected to office as members of a political party; and the formal **party organization**, the party 'professionals' who run the party at the national, state, and local levels."[7] Each function is vital to a party's survival. For example, the influence of any political party will be short lived if the party's candidates do not win their elections since the ultimate goal of any political party is to have a meaningful if not commanding role in the formulation and implementation of public policy initiatives.

In fulfilling its **party in the electorate role**, political parties must:

- Develop a solid political philosophy that attracts individuals to affiliate themselves to the party for hopefully, the long rather than the short-term.
- Constantly recruit and support their candidates for public office.
- Oversee the internal selection process of candidates to represent their party in the general election.
- Analyze, develop and articulate the issues and the party's position on addressing them.
- Provide a venue for its members to criticize government and the officials in charge of operating that government in a non-violent and legal atmosphere.
- Develop and maintain intraparty loyalty among their rank and file membership.

Once elected to office as the **party in government**, the number one priority is to actually assume control of the government. Basically,

> in the efforts to secure control of the machinery of government, American political parties have assumed the responsibility for organizing the governments, for recruiting leaders and staffing the bureaucracies, for getting out the voters, and for welding together alliances of disparate interests in support of party tickets and programs. Although these functions are not directly concerned with public policy, they do have a rather substantial impact on policy outcomes in the government. Through their officeholders the parties become major participants in conflict resolution, policy leadership, and policy adoption and administration. Though the control and discipline of their members of the legislatures is limited, the parties are a major influence on voting in these policymaking bodies. Thus party outputs in the areas of recruiting and staffing the policymaking machinery have significant bearing on policy outcomes.[8]

After securing their respective party nominations, both the Joe Biden and Donald Trump election teams formed committees to start the screening process of individuals to fill their Cabinet, White House staff, bureaucratic chiefs and judicial positions. It is imperative that an in-coming president has as many key positions as possible filled and ready to go to work as he/she is taking the official oath of office. The party in government is effective if its leadership maintains the loyalty and the commitment of its elected officials to design and implement policy directives along the philosophical positions of his/her party. This oftentimes, places the lawmaker in an uneasy position as his/her party's policy preferences may well conflict with the needs of his/her constituents. The Trump victory in the 2016 presidential election was a sweep for Republican candidates who gained majorities in both the House and the Senate. Once the hoopla of the inauguration was over, implementing the Trump agenda proved problematic for some Republican lawmakers. Trump's request for federal funding for several hundreds of miles of wall separating Mexico from the United States resulted in congressional budget showdowns and finally, a painful partial shutdown of the federal government. While many in America favor reforming the nation's immigration system, Trump's plan on retaining adults, separating children from their parents, and eventually deporting as many as possible immigrants from Central and Latin America caused significant cleavage between Democrats and Republicans. The mid-term elections of 2018 cost the Republicans the majority in the House and significantly narrowed their majority margin in the Senate. President Abraham Lincoln once commented that "the ballot is stronger than the bullet."[9] For example, while many Republican members of Congress agreed with Trump's crackdown on illegal immigration, their constituents at home were not totally behind Trump's policy initiatives. Farmers across this nation are dependent upon migrant farm workers to pick their crops. The legal status of his/her migrant farm workers matters little to the farmer whose yearly crop yield is his/her sole source of income. The crops still need to be harvested. Obviously, in this case, a Republican representative from a rural district or farming community has a very tough decision to make. Should he/she support his/her president's position and anger the people back home or should he/she side with the people back home at the expense of the support and political displeasure of his/her party's leadership?

Cohesive **party organization** can only be achieved if a political party has a strong talented and committed staff of professionals at every level of the party's organizational structure. Among the rank and file, membership in any political party is voluntary. Those who align themselves with one party may very well switch their allegiances if they believe their party has strayed from the course or adopted a position that they simply cannot support. Internal fighting within a political party deters it from achieving its goals and objectives. It is the responsibility of the leadership to keep the party on its course. The Republican Party leadership in the House has been and probably will continue to be at loggerheads with a faction within their own ranks—the Tea Party. Regardless of the issue at hand, it is the inner core leadership of a party's organization that must keep the party together.

Historical Development of Political Parties

The concept of the modern political party actually emerged during the English Civil War between the cavaliers who supported the ill-fated Charles I and the Puritans (later known as the Round-heads) under Oliver Cromwell. Thomas Osborne, the Earl of Danbury, founded the Tory Party (the pro-king faction) while Anthony Ashley-Cooper, the Earl of Shaftesbury, founded the opposition faction known as the Whig Party (the anti-king faction). By 1675, both had drawn their political ideological lines with the Tories opting for a conservative approach and the Whigs the liberal side of the political spectrum. The Whigs are credited with the development of the first political party platform. Their stated issue positions included a strong stand for Protestantism over Catholicism, religious toleration, guarantees of personal liberties, promotion of commerce and business development, and the supremacy of Parliament over the monarchy. The rise of political parties in England was directly tied to the changing tide of the political fortunes of the entrenched enfranchised privileged few members of the aristocracy who were ruled under the absolutism of the **divine right theory of kings** against the rise of democratic governments that enabled the rising middle-class urbanites to finally enjoy the same political and personal freedoms that for so long belonged only to the aristocracy. Once only available to the privileged few, the invention of the printing press coupled with an increased emphasis on universal education, enabled the "common man" to read the writings of John Lock, Jean Jacques Rousseau, and Charles de Montesquieu. In particular, these three political philosophers stressed that governments were created by the people and empowered by the people to protect the people's natural or inalienable rights. Kings were not the sons of God; but the servants of the people who entrusted their kings to rule for the people under the people's directives.

> As democratic ideas corroded the old foundations of authority, members of the old governing elite reached out to legitimize their positions under the new notions by appealing for popular support. That appeal compelled deference to popular views but it also required the development of organization to communicate with and to manage the electorate. Thus members of a parliamentary body, who earlier occupied their seats as an incident to the ownership of property or as a prerequisite of class position, had to defer to the people—or to those who had the suffrage—and to create electoral organizations to rally voters to their support.[10]

It was the political party that drew the masses together under one umbrella and gave them the leadership they needed to pursue their common issue positions guided and crafted by their cohesive bond to a particular political philosophy, a lesson soon to be known in newly formed United States.

Party Systems

The strong two-party system in the United States is unique since the majority of nation states use the **multiparty system** defined as "an electoral system based on proportional representation that often requires a coalition of several parties to form a majority to run the government."[11] The political landscape in Norway and Sweden involves at least four to five political parties embracing the entire political spectrum from socialists and communists to middle-of-the-road agrarian and centrists to the traditional dichotomy of liberals versus conservatives. There are at least six major political parties in France while German politics is dominated by two major and three minor political parties. Lacking even one major political party, Italian politics revolves around a multiplicity of minor political parties. Consequently, in France, Germany and Italy, the leadership of these various political parties must form coalitions among each other in hopes of winning an election. Once in office, the leadership of the winning coalition stays in power only as long as they are able to fulfill the promises and concessions made to their coalition partners. In Italy, the strength of the coalition usually falls apart within a few months, meaning that the prime minister has lost "the confidence" of his parliament and must call for new elections, leading to the development of another fragile coalition government. These countries have a **conflictual party system** whereby "the legislature is dominated by parties that are far apart on issues or highly antagonistic toward each other and the political system."[12] Although they have a multitude of political parties, both Norway and Sweden follow a **consensual party system** in which "the parties commanding most of the legislative seats are not too far apart on policies and have a reasonable amount of trust in each other and in the political system."[13] In a multiparty system, citizens have a wide range of party alternatives and issue positions to determine their voting preferences. Nations such as North Korea, Cuba, China, and Vietnam use the one-party or **exclusive governing party** format. With a tight top-down structure, the party leadership "recognizes no legitimate interest aggregation by groups within the party nor does it permit any free activity by social groups, citizens or other government agencies."[14] The one-party system was used in the former Soviet Union before 1985, and the majority of the Eastern European nations before 1989.

The American political party system is basically a two-party system with minor or third parties surfacing from time to time. The two-party system fits nicely into the dichotomous relationship of the American political landscape. Beginning with the emergence of the Federalist and Jefferson-Republican Parties, the pattern follow that whatever position one party takes on an issue, the other party will take the opposite viewpoint. Since the election of Franklin Roosevelt to the presidency in 1936, the Republican Party holds to conservative viewpoints while the Democrats favor the liberal side of the political spectrum. For example, on the environment, Republicans support less government regulation while Democrats favor stronger federal regulatory oversight. The Republican Party supports legislation favorable to the business community while Democrats pursue legislation

American women had to campaign for the right to vote in the early 1900s.

addressing worker issues such as increasing the minimum wage, work safety laws, etc. For voters, it is a simple choice. The two-party system is essential to the organizational structure of legislative houses at both the national and state level. The party that wins the majority of the seats in the House of Representatives controls of the leadership of that body. The Speaker of the House is a member of the majority party. Although the vice president is the presiding officer of the United States Senate, the actual operation of the Senate's business is controlled by the Senate Majority Leader, a member of the majority party. Committee assignments are based on the majority/minority concept. The chairperson and vice chairperson of a committee are usually the members of the majority party that have served on that committee the longest among the majority party's membership. If the election results in the once minority party becoming the majority party, the chair and vice chair positions shift to those individuals from that party who have served the longest and second longest on that particular committee. The composition of the committee membership also falls under the majority/minority concept. For example, in the 2020 Congress, a committee composed of fifteen members in the House of Representatives had at least eight Democrats and seven Republicans because the Democrats held the majority of the total House seats. The opposite occurred in the Senate since the Republicans held a slim majority in that legislative body.

THE POLITICAL SPECTRUM

The guiding principles behind a political party are the philosophical approaches taken in both the selection of and the positions taken on the issues. Political scientists have developed a straight-line **political spectrum** on which they place the political philosophical positions or the ideological perspectives group follows. An **ideology** is "a comprehensive system of political beliefs about the nature of people and society."[15] The right of the line is reserved for conservative ideological positions while the left is for the more liberal approaches. The middle position is reserved for those ideological positions that are not staunchly conservative or liberal but more middle-of-the-road or moderate. A brief overview or the prevailing political philosophies indicates the underlying principles behind these positions.

Conservatism—The Right of the Spectrum

Conservatism is "the political outlook which springs from a desire to conserve existing things, held to be either good in themselves, are at least safe, familiar and the objects of trust and affection."[16] Basically, a true conservative is the defender of the status quo against any major changes to existing policies. Conservatives adhere to **incrementalism** defined as "a doctrine holding that change in a political system occurs only by small steps, each of which should be carefully evaluated before proceeding to the next step."[17] President Woodrow Wilson, a Democrat, defined conservatism as "the policy of 'make no change and consult your grandmother when in doubt.'"[18] In his *History of Political Theory*, George Klosko states that conservatism rests on six major positions:

- First, conservatives generally have a religious bent. They believe a "divine intent rules society, as well as conscience."

- Second, there is an attachment to traditional life, in spite of its variety and apparent disorder.

- Third, conservatives believe "civilized society requires orders and classes." Thus society cannot be leveled. Though all people are equal morally, they must be unequal in social terms.

- Fourth, there is a close relationship between freedom and private property. The former is made possible only by the existence of the latter, and so conservatives support the existing distribution of property, even with its inequalities.

- Fifth, conservatives have a belief in **prescription** (the action of laying down authoritative rules or directions) and distrust of reason. Consequently, reason is not an adequate guide to human conduct.

- Six, though conservatives are willing to countenance a measure of reform, they distrust more substantial change subscribing to the belief that "innovation is a devouring conflagration more often than it is a touch of progress."[19]

Basically, a true conservative supports upholding the existing social and political order. While acknowledging society's inherent inequalities based on wealth, political power, etc., conservatives embrace a class system based on wealth and, in some societies, lineage. Considered to be the father of conservative political thought, Edmund Burke based his beliefs on "a few simple generalizations: that the present state of things is the sum total of all past developments; that is too complex to understand; that meddling with it is therefore dangerous; and that arrangements that work well enough are best left alone."[20]

Just right of conservatism, **cultural conservatism** is based on "support for traditional western Judeo-Christian values not just as a matter of comfort and faith, but out of a firm belief that the secular, the economic, and the political success of the western world is rooted in this value."[21] Further to the right, the **New Right** or the **Religious Right**, places its emphasis more on religious rather than cultural values. The agenda of the Religious Right sees an extremely limited role for government across the board particularly in policy areas involving the economy, welfare programs, the environment, etc. Its membership takes very strong anti-communist and anti-socialist positions. The Religious Right upholds traditional moral values including strong pro-life positions and advocacy for prayer in the public schools. The farthest right position is held by members of the **Radical Right**. Oftentimes known as **ultraconservatives**, they hold to the belief that "those who advocate policies that differ from their own are motivated by treason. The radical right is just as intolerant of differing political opinions as is the radical left."[22] Founded by John Welch, Jr., in 1959, the **John Birch Society** is an ultraconservative organization named after John Birch, a U.S. army captain killed by Chinese Communists in 1945. With the ultimate goal of defeating communism and erasing any communist influences in America, the group advocated for the impeachment of Chief Justice Earl Warren for his perceived liberal Supreme Court rulings. Today, the group's bottom line issues focus on the United States withdrawing from both the United Nations and the North Atlantic Treaty Organization (NATO) and abolishing all federally funded welfare programs. A person adhering to the conservative position on the spectrum would uphold the free enterprise system, capitalism, a strong military, less government regulation, private property ownership and rights, cultural conservatism, and a strong sense of moral and religious values.

Moderates—The Center of the Spectrum

A **moderate** or **centrist** is "an individual or political group advocating a moderate approach to the political decision making and to the solution of social problems."[23] A moderate upholds:

- A desire for conciliation or compromise rather than confrontation.
- A preference for reform over revolution. Moderates want policy options that correctly assess a problem and offer timely and reasonable responses to fix it.
- Political transformations gradually occurring without violence against existing governing institutions.
- Tolerance towards views which do not match the consensus, but are voiced in a non-violent manner.[24]

The majority of the American electorate shares political viewpoints that place them in the middle. In many respects, the **mainstream** or the middle of the spectrum is more advantageous simply because it does not attract those whose political positions align themselves with the extremes of the traditional left (liberal) or right (conservative).

Liberalism—The Left of the Spectrum

While conservatives dread change, liberals embrace it. Initially, **liberalism** was "a political doctrine that espouses freedom of the individual from interference by the state, toleration by the state in matters of morality and religion, laissez-faire economic policies, and a belief in natural rights that exist independent of government."[25] As a political perspective, liberalism is a by-product of the Enlightenment through the writings of John Locke, Charles de Montesquieu, Jean Jacques Rousseau, Jeremy Bentham, John Mill, John Stuart Mill, Baruch Spinoza and Immanuel Kant. In his *Spirit of the Laws*, Montesquieu defines **liberty** as "in a state, that is, in a society where there are laws, liberty can consist only in having the power to do what one should want to do and in no way being constrained to do what one should not want to do."[26] Furthermore, he differentiates between **positive liberty** whereby one is forced to be free and **negative liberty** which is "that tranquility of spirit which comes from the opinion each one has of his security, and in order for him to have this liberty, the government must be such that one citizen cannot fear another citizen."[27] Basically, no government can force someone to vote (positive liberty), however, government must provide unstrained accessibility to the voting process so someone can make an individual choice whether or not to vote (negative liberty). Liberalism is based on the following concepts:

- The belief in the supreme value of the individual, his freedoms and his rights. Liberals embrace the concept of **individualism** defined as "the political, economic and social concept that places primary emphasis on the worth, freedom and well-being of the individual rather than on the group, society or nation."[28]
- The belief that every individual has natural rights, i.e., life, liberty and property, which exists independently of government. It is the responsibility of government to protect every-

one's individual rights from interference from others (**civil rights**) and from the arbitrary actions of government (**civil liberties**).

• The belief of the supreme value of freedom by limiting the power of government and preventing it from inhibiting one from exercising his/her freedoms. John Locke wrote in his *Second Treatise of Government*, that "the liberty of man in society is to be under no other legislative power but that established by consent in the commonwealth, nor under the domination of any will, or restraint of any law, but what the legislative shall enact, according to the trust put in it."[29]

• Tacit consent and the social contract. According to John Locke, **tacit consent** means that an individual who enjoys some benefit from living in a certain nation consents to obey the law of that country, therefore, giving his/her consent for the existence of that government. "Locke emphasizes that possessing property in a country constitutes consent to its government. Because it is impossible to remove one's land from a country, accepting ownership of land requires membership in a society and so consent to obey its laws."[30] The **social contract theory** underscores that once absolutely free individuals living in isolation from each other come together to form a community that out of necessity for public order, they subsequently create a governing body that establishes the rules for the exercise of certain basic fundamental rights. If the government, in turn, fails to protect those rights, then the people have the right to abolish the governing contract and begin anew.

Located slightly left of the liberal position on the spectrum, the **New Left** movement in the United States during the 1960s and 70s initially began on college campuses across the nation as students staged angry protests against the established political, social and economic order throughout the nation. The New Left was fueled by the convergence of three major political and social movements—the unpopularity of the Vietnam War, and both the civil rights and woman's liberation movements. Although there was no meaningful cohesive massive convergence of the three camps, what emerged was an agenda of common themes, i.e., anti-Vietnam War, advocacy against racial and gender discrimination, promotion of women's issues to include equal pay and abortion rights, and a sincere empathy towards the economic deprivation of the nation's poor.

Sandwiched between liberals and the far left, **libertarians** believe "in freeing people not merely from the constraints of traditional political institutions, but also from the inner constraints imposed by their mistaken attribution of power to ineffectual things."[31] Falling into the category of classical liberalism, libertarians believe that the only function of government is to provide when needed, law enforcement and military protection. Beyond that, the government has no authority over its citizens. In *Capitalism: The Unknown Ideal*, Ayn Rand, the architect of libertarianism, wrote that "the only proper function of the government of a free country is to act as an agency which protects the individual's rights, i.e., which protects the individual from physical violence."[32] Written in 1974, the Statement of Principles from the American Libertarian Party states that:

We, the members of the Libertarian Party, challenge the cult of the omnipotent state, and defend the rights of the individual. We hold that each individual has the right to exercise sole dominion over his own life, and has the right to live his life in whatever manner he chooses so long as he does not forcibly interfere with the equal right of others to live their lives in whatever manner they choose. . . We . . . hold that the sole function of government is the protection of the rights of each individual: namely, (1) the right to life—and accordingly we support laws prohibiting the initiation of physical force against others; (2) the right to liberty of speech and action—and accordingly we oppose all attempts by government to abridge the freedom of speech and press, as well as government censorship in any form; and (3) the right to property—and accordingly we oppose all government interference with private property, such as confiscation, nationalization, and eminent domain, and support laws which prohibit robbery, trespass, fraud and misrepresentation. Since government has only one legitimate function, the protection of individual rights, we opposed all interference by government in the areas of voluntary and contractual relations among individuals. Men should not be forced to sacrifice their lives and property for the benefit of others. They should be left free by government to deal with one another as free traders in a free market; and the resultant economic system, the only one compatible with the protection of man's rights, is laissez-faire capitalism.[33]

The architect of laissez-faire capitalism, Adam Smith defined it in his *The Wealth of Nations*, as "a hands-off style of governance that emphasizes freedom so capitalism's invisible hand can work its will."[35]

The bottom-line issue for Libertarians is that government must step aside to allow citizens to make their own individual choices with the understanding that each person must accept full responsibility for the consequences of his/her decisions. They advocate complete individual choice concerning one's sexual orientation and gender identity. Libertarians strongly uphold individual rights to economic liberty, abortion rights, the abolition of both the death penalty and federal income taxes, and removal of all barriers to free trade. The party's foreign policy position emphasizes that the United States government should actively participate in all international organizations that promote world peace without the use of military force.

Those under the far left umbrella include democratic socialists, Marxist socialists, communists, and anarchists. Evolving into both a social and economic movement in Europe in the middle of the nineteenth century, **socialism** is "a doctrine that advocates economic collectivism through governmental or industrial group ownership of the means of production and distribution of goods."[34] Running for the Democratic presidential nomination in 2016 and 2020, Vermont Senator Bernie Sanders declares himself to be a socialist. His issue positions are more aligned with **social liberalism** or **democratic socialism**. Democratic socialists strive to "use the political machinery of the state to achieve their goals by democratically winning power and peacefully modifying the existing system."[36] For example, his plan for Medicare-for-all would have the federal government fund and manage the entire program. The Socialist Movement in America took root around 1900 when the nationwide push for industrialization inadvertently created vast disparities in wealth. The underpaid American industrial workforce embraced socialist concepts of economic fairness and shared or collective ownership of property. In 1912, union organizer and well-known pacifist **Eugene V. Debs** ran as Socialist Party's presidential candidate. In 1893, Debs founded the American Railway Union and was frequently arrested for his strike-related activities. In 1905, he founded the International Workers of the World Union and soon became a founding member of the Social Democratic Party of the United States. Unique at that time for a third party candidate, Debs got six percent of the popular vote. As a pacifist, Debs actively organized protests against the United States involvement in World War I. In 1919, Debs was arrested, tried, convicted and sentenced to ten years for violating a federal Sedition Act prohibiting anyone from saying "disloyal, profane, scurrilous, and abusive remarks about the form of government, flag or uniform of the United States."[36] From his prison cell, Debs launched his last bid for the presidency in 1920. He was subsequently pardoned by President Warren Harding in 1921. Among the ranks of declared Socialists were artist and writer John Dos Passos (1869-1970), leading Socialist editor of *The Masses and The Liberator* Max Eastman (1883-1969), author *Looking Back Edward Bellamy* (1850-1898) and Helen Keller (1880-1968). A friend of Fredrich Engels, Florence Kelly (1859-1932) founded the National Consumers League. A founding member of the National Association for the Advancement of Colored People (NAACP), she joined authors Upton Sinclair and Jack London in organizing the Intercollegiate Socialist Society. Her primary issues were establishing a federally mandated minimum wage and an eight-hour workday and banning child labor. She worked closely with President Franklin Roosevelt's Secretary of Labor Frances Perkins to pass through Congress the **Fair Labor Standards Act** in 1938 that officially banned child labor.[38]

Communism also known as **Marxism-Leninism** envisions an end to formalized structured government by the developed of collectivistic societies. "Communism, in theory, espouses the doctrines of historical inevitability, economic determinism, labor value, and the 'inner contradictions' of capitalism, class conflict, capitalist colonialism and imperialism, world wars resulting from competition for markets, and the destruction of the bourgeoisie, the dictatorship of the proletariat, the socialist revolution, and the final 'withering away' of the state."[39] The primary advocates of both socialist and communist doctrines are Karl Marx and Friedrich Engles who collectively wrote *The Communist Manifest*. Furthermore, Marx detailed his concept of socialism in *Capital*. A Russian revolutionary, Vladimir Lenin laid out his plan for the 1917 Bolshevik Revolution and the plans for a new Russia through a series of essays entitled collectively as *The Little Lenin Library*. An **anarchist** holds that "government is an unnecessary evil and should be replaced by voluntary cooperation among individuals and groups."[40] Several anarchist groups advocate violent revolution as the only means of eliminating "the state as an instrument used by the propertied classes to dominate and exploit the people."[41]

Ideological Versus Issue Base Parties

As evidenced primarily in European politics, it is the particular political ideological prospective articulated by the party leadership that draws one to affiliate with either a conservative- or liberal-oriented party. From the voter's perspective, the candidate and/or the candidate's personal issue positions are overshadowed by the party's guiding philosophical positions. The term *Weltanschauung* oftentimes is used to describe the overall embracing power of ideologically based political parties that permeates "virtually all social relationships and thus a politics of limitless scope and total involvement."[42] However, in American politics, the focus of the voter's attention is more on the candidate than his/her political party. While many Americans label themselves as either liberals or conservatives, few can actually articulate the overriding political philosophies associated with liberalism or conservatism. Philosophically, one is apt to say that there is very little difference between a mainstream Republican and a moderate Democrat. American political parties, therefore, are more pragmatic and less ideological. "The American parties are relatively non-ideological parties of the political center. Since their mission is the organization of majorities, they cannot be deflected by the wishes of small ideological minorities. To organize the stable majorities that undergird the American polity, the parties must often compromise, soften, or smooth over the issues that divide Americans. As competitive parties in the heterogeneous American society, they must be pragmatic, brokerage parties, appealing for votes wherever those votes may be and regardless of the ultimate inconsistency of the appeal."[43] In a 1939 radio address, President Franklin Roosevelt commented "a radical is a man with both feet firmly planted in the air. A conservative is a man with two perfectly good legs, who, however, has never learned to walk forward. A reactionary is a somnambulist walking backwards. A liberal is a man who uses his legs and his hands at the behest . . . of his head."[44]

AMERICAN POLITICAL PARTIES

Historical Development

Winning the support of every elector, George Washington assumed the presidency in 1789. He was the first and only person to win the presidency without a political party nomination, endorsement, or label. "Because of his Olympian status, Washington had been able to levitate above the partisan factions. But no one else would even be able to repeat that bipartisan performance. No subsequent president would credibly claim to be above the fray."[45] Serving in his cabinet were two of his closest allies and personal friends—Thomas Jefferson as Secretary of State and Alexander Hamilton as Secretary of the Treasury. The friendship between the two quickly deteriorated as Hamilton launched his plan for a centralized banking system and the national government's assumption of the debts owned by the states from the Revolutionary War. A member of Congress, James Madison was so irked by the Hamilton's debt proposal that he resigned from Congress. Jefferson was definitely opposed to the centralized banking plan. Consequently, Hamilton and Jefferson were at loggerheads and "engaged in such fierce controversies over the proper course to pursue that Washington could not mollify them, hard though he tried."[46] Washington favored Hamilton's plans but lacked the means to secure support even among his own supposed supporters in Congress. For Hamilton, the only way for a president to ensure continual support for a president's policies was to have some form of collective leverage, like a political party. As the leader of a political party, Washington could remind other party members that his successes or failures were their successes or failures.

Consequently, Hamilton and his supporters formed the Federalist Party while Jefferson's group gathered under the banner of the Jeffersonian Republicans also known as the Democratic/Republicans. "Jefferson did not call his political party the Democrats because the 'hallowed term of the day was Republican which was the label Jefferson adopted and the press used to describe the Jeffersonian camp."[47] Historians credit Jefferson with developing the two party system and in particular, being the founding father of the modern Democratic Party. The base support for the Federalist Party came from the northern industrial and shipping business community. They favored Hamilton's pro-business positions particularly on low taxes, a strong central government, and opposition to the French Revolution. "In effect the Federalist party could lay claim to representing 'the wealth and talents' of the conservative classes in the United States. . . . He [Hamilton] and Washington resented popular agitations at home, as they abhorred such agitation in France and they thought that the 'democratic societies' springing up in towns and country districts ought to be suppressed before they got out of bounds."[48] Jefferson's party gathered their support base from agricultural interests particularly in the South. Jefferson supported the democratic zeal of the French Revolution, openly opposed any notion of a strong central government, and basically became the standard bearer of the common man. The two emerging political parties took the traditional route of today's parties. While the issues were the same, each party's position on those issues was different. Thus, one only had to choose between the two. For John Marshall, his alliance was with the Federalist Party since they believed that "the Constitution had authorized the formation of a federal government able to pay the country's debts and provide for its defense. They cited the Preamble to the Constitution as well as Article I, Section 8, which both asserted that the document's purpose was to 'provide for the common Defense and the general Welfare.' For the Federalists, that seemed to cover all sorts of federal initiatives."[49] For the Jefferson/Republicans or Anti-Federalists, "the states were sovereign. It was thus up to any individual state to determine the extent of its powers in settling disputes between the federal and state governments."[50]

In the 1792 presidential election, the clear choice for the presidency was George Washington. However, the political bickering between Jefferson and Hamilton emerge over the battle for the vice presidency. Members of the Jefferson/Republicans wanted to deny John Adams a second term as vice president "because Adams's writings on government included positive statements about the British monarchy."[51] A long-time friend of Adams, Jefferson intervened. However, the leader of the Federalist faction, Alexander Hamilton, was "so worried that he urged Adams to cut short a vacation and campaign openly against those who were—as he said—'ill disposed' toward him."[52] Opting not to "campaign" for the office, Adams was reelected to the vice presidency.

The role political parties would play in American politics took hold with the presidential election of 1796. Having served two terms of office, President Washington decided not to run for a third term. It was during his second term that Washington began to "experience the kinds of problems that plague any government. Relations with the former 'mother country' deteriorated until it seemed that another war with Great Britain might be inevitable. And on the domestic front, groups of farmers, especially those in the westernmost counties of Pennsylvania, protested and rebelled against the Washington administration's excise tax on the whiskey that they distilled from their grain, eventually rioting in the summer of 1794."[53] Washington was also hit with personal attacks and the rumors that "he was given to 'gambling, reveling, horseracing and horse whipping; and that he had even taken British bribes while he was commanding American troops."[54] However Washington's appeal to the Electors was strong enough that he could have been elected to a third term. Yet, he decided to retire from politics and return to Mount Vernon. After two terms as vice president, John Adams saw himself as the "heir apparent" to succeed Washington. The Federalists, however, decided to support two candidates—Adams and Thomas Pinckney of South Carolina. The Jefferson/Republicans endorsed both Thomas Jefferson and Aaron Burr. Of the four candidates, only Burr actively campaigned for the job. "Adams, Jefferson, and Pinckney never left home. While their parties took stands on the major issues of the day, these men embraced the classical model of politics—refusing to campaign. They believed that a man should not pursue an office; rather, the office should seek out the man. They agreed that the most talented men—what some called an aristocracy of merit—should govern, but also that ultimate power rested with the people. . . . [who would select] candidates on the basis of what Adams called the 'pure Principles of Merit,

Virtue and Public Spirit.'"[55] The election was a nasty one with the Federalists labeling Jefferson as an atheist and an ardent supporter of France. They feared that if elected, Jefferson would push the United States to ally itself with France in war with Great Britain. The Jefferson/Republicans charged Adams with being too friendly with Great Britain. Behind the scenes, both groups were trying to influence the Electors to support their candidates. Of course, the Electors had the final say. John Adams, the Federalist, won the presidency and Thomas Jefferson, the Jefferson/Republican came in second and became Adams's vice president!

The political bickering and animosity between the two parties came to blows during the 1800 presidential election. It was a nasty campaign pitting incumbent President John Adams against Thomas Jefferson, Aaron Burr, Charles Pinckney, Jr, and John Jay. "Adams desperately wanted to be re-elected. He was eager to see the French crisis through to a satisfactory resolution and, at age sixty-five, believed that a defeat would mean he would be sent home to Quincy, Massachusetts, to die in obscurity."[56] However, Adams lost public support with the passage of the Alien and Sedition Acts, which allowed the president to deport any immigrant suspected of disloyalty to the United States and provided for the suppression of any printed or verbal criticisms of his administration. Basically, Adams "demanded deference to hierarchy and class, and was continuous of new forms of political democracy."[57] Fearful of Hamilton's political power, Adams systematically dismissed any pro-Hamilton supporters from his cabinet. As anticipated, Hamilton struck back by calling Adams a "president possessed by vanity without bounds, and a jealousy capable of discoloring every object . . . a man destitute of every moral principle."[58] Hamilton also started the rumor that Adams was wheeling and dealing with King George a marriage between Adams's daughter and the king's son. Hamilton also went after Jefferson, accusing him of being a coward for avoiding military service during the Revolutionary War as well as being a hypocrite for speaking against slavery when he himself owned over 200 slaves to work his fields at Monticello. Meanwhile, Jefferson "secretly arranged to retain the services of James Callender, a talented but notorious scandalmonger who had recently become famous for his exposure of Alexander Hamilton's adulterous affair with the beautiful Maria Reynolds. Callender produced *The Prospect Before Us*, a pamphlet that described Adams as a mentally unstable monarchist who, if re-elected, intended to declare himself king and his son, John Quincy, his royal successor."[59] Denying he even hired him, Jefferson refused to pay Callender for his services. In turn, it was Callender who exposed Jefferson's sexual relationship with Sally Hemings, one of Jefferson's slaves. Jefferson picked Aaron Burr to be his vice-presidential mate simply because Burr was a leading political boss in New York. Burr promised to deliver New York votes to Jefferson on a silver platter. Jefferson and Burr both garnered seventy-three electoral votes with Adams finishing in third place. The tie was broken when one of Hamilton's pledged electors switched his vote to Jefferson. Thus, Jefferson won the presidency with Burr as his vice president. Adams lost this race in part because of the 3/5's Compromise. "Had slaves, who had no vote, not been counted, Adams would have edged Jefferson by a vote of 63 to 61."[60]

Although the Federalist Party will meet its demise by 1815, the impact of its twelve years in power was significant. "They organized a new government, set precedents that have never been broken, established a sound financial system, obtained the withdrawal of the British from the Northwest, eliminated the Spanish threat to the Southwest, and prevented the United States from becoming involved in a general European war."[61] Meanwhile, Jefferson's party successfully elected him to two presidential terms under a cohesive party platform of "frugal government, reduced national debt, smaller national defense, 'free commerce with all nations' but 'political connections with none,' freedom of religion, press, and speech."[62] Jefferson also introduced a new campaign technique—the grassroots approach of taking the candidate's message directly to the people. By 1828, the Jeffersonian-Republicans would split into two separate political parties, namely, the National Republicans and the Jacksonian Democrats. The National Republicans would regroup by 1832 as the Whigs. The Whig Party met its demise by 1848. With the election of Jackson in 1828, the Democratic Party dominated American politics until 1860 by holding the White House for all but eight years, controlling the Senate for twenty-six years and the House for twenty-four years.

The Democratic Party dramatically lost its political domination in 1860 as the party's membership was severely divided over slavery. While Abraham Lincoln had the solid support of the Republican Party behind him, the Democrats split into two factions. The northern faction nominated Senator Stephen A. Douglas, Lincoln's perennial political foe while the southern Democrats nominated incumbent vice president, John C. Breckenridge, a pro-slavery advocate from Kentucky. Former Whig Party members joined forces with the remnants of the Know-Nothing Party to form the Constitutional Union Party. This group nominated John Bell of Tennessee for the presidency. On election night, Lincoln took advantage of the split in the Democratic Party's base and won the election by losing the popular vote but carrying a large number of electoral votes primarily from the northern states. Beginning with this election, the Republicans became the dominant political force in Washington until 1932 by occupying the White House for fifty-six years and controlling the House for fifty years and the Senate for sixty years. But Republican domination began to decline with the 1929 Stock Market Crash. Its hold on Washington politics ended with the election of Franklin Roosevelt in 1932. The Democrats would hold onto the White House consecutively until the election of Republican Dwight Eisenhower in 1952. Since then control of both the White House and Congress has had periodic spurts of power holds between the two parties.

The Modern Republican Party

Emerging as a third party movement, the Republican Party's base was a mixture of supporters from failed third parties—the Whigs, Know-Nothings, Free Soilers and disgruntled anti-slavery Democrats. The party's first run at the White House was in 1856 with John C. Frémont as its presidential candidate. Although he lost the race, Frémont was able to garner approximately one-third of the popular vote and carried eleven states. Initially, the party favored the trans-continental railroad and other infrastructure improvements, homestead protection laws, protective tariffs, and took a strong anti-slavery position. Many credit Woodrow Wilson for changing the philosophical positions of both political parties. A Democrat, Wilson believed that the words in the Preamble to the United States Constitution definitively charged the federal government with the tasks to "insure domestic tranquility, provide for the common defense, and promote the general welfare." Therefore, in times of a national emergency, a threat to the nation's security, and a decline in the general welfare of the American people, it was the responsibility of the federal government to come to the aid of its people. Consequently, the Democrats endorsed a more liberal approach and the Republicans choose the more conservative roadway to address the nation's problems. The dichotomy was firmly established with the Republicans taking the conservative positions and the Democrats the liberal route.

Beginning in 1945, the Republican Party began to solidify its conservative base on the domestic front by denouncing the continuation of New Deal policies that ushered in the welfare state and in particular "to dismantle liberalism's social programs and the progressive tax policies that paid for them."[63] On foreign policy, "the advent of the cold war between the United States and the Soviet Union, moreover, led to the end of conservatism's traditional association with isolationism and suspicion of a strong military establishment. Fear of Soviet-style communism—atheistic, totalitarian, socialist, and heavily armed—turned conservatism into a force for an aggressive foreign policy aimed at collapsing communism on a worldwide scale."[64]

Every Republican Party platform since adheres to the following positions:

a) Recognition of American exceptionalism due to the nation's historical role as first as refuge, then as a defender, and exemplar of liberty

b) A firm belief in the Constitution as both the founding document and an enduring covenant

c) Rebuild the American economy through job growth by providing incentives for business and industry to create more employment opportunities by reducing business and corporate related tax programs, negotiating open-market free trade agreements, and reducing punitive government regulations

d) Reduce the federal deficit by imposing caps on future debt

e) Appoint federal judges who follow judicial restraint

f) Upholding the commitment to traditional marriage of one man and one woman

g) Support of pro-life initiatives

h) Support of a strong military

The Modern Democratic Party

In a speech delivered in 1936, President Herbert Hoover emphasized that "true liberalism seeks all legitimate freedom first, in the confident belief that without such freedom the pursuit of other blessings is in vain. Liberalism is force true of the spirit, proceeding from the deep realization that economic freedom cannot be sacrificed if political freedom is to be preserved."[65] In its various party platforms, the Democratic Party underscores its commitment to inclusion whether it be voting rights, civil rights, economic opportunities, etc.. Therefore, the primary issue positions in the party's platforms of the Democratic Party are:

a) Protection of civil liberties and the guarantee of civil rights for all to include women, workers, members of the LGBT community, minority populations, immigrants, and the disabled

b) Support for the American worker to include raising the minimum wage, providing paid medical/family leave and health care, and demanding safer working conditions

c) Advocacy for affordable housing and efforts to rehabilitate declining neighborhoods

d) Support for a sound retirement system for all Americans to include preventing any attempt to weaken the Social Security program

e) Ending systematic racism

f) Reaffirmation of the Dream Act and immigration reform leading to citizenship

g) Support for pro-choice positions

h) Strong positions on the protection of the environment

American Third Party Movements

By definition, a **third party** is "usually composed of independents and dissidents from the major parties in a two-party system that typically is based on a protest movement and that may rally sufficient voter support to affect the outcome of a state or national election."[66] The entrenched two-party system does not openly embrace the existence of third parties. The American political scene has seen these movements spring up from time to time, but they simply do not survive in the long term for several reasons. First, state legislative houses are controlled by one or both of the two major parties. These bodies have enacted state laws that make it extremely difficult for third party and independent candidates to even secure a place on the ballot. For example, Carole Keeton Strayhorn, a Republican officeholder in Texas, wanted to run against incumbent Republican governor Rick Perry. As an independent candidate, she had to obtain thousands of signatures of registered voters who did not already have a party affiliation. Second, third party movements oftentimes are formed around a specific individual who lacks the political clout within one of the two parties to even secure a nomination for an elective office. For example, Ross Perot, a billionaire businessman decided to make a run for the White House. He did not have any political experience, never held an elective office, nor did he have any long-lasting ties to either the Democratic or Republican Party. He opted to form his own political party—the Reform Party. He placed on all fifty state ballots but, obviously, did not win the election. Consequently, the Reform Party no longer exists. Third, the positions taken by third party movements are usually incorporated into either the Republican or Democratic Party. In its formative years, Ralph Nader was the perennial candidate of the Green Party, a pro-environment group. Yet, the Democratic Party already has strong positions and a proven track record of advocacy for environmental issues. The Democratic Party definitely has more clout and more presence at the ballot box than the Green Party. Fourth, third party candidates simply cannot raise the money needed to launch a competitive election for any national office. Federal campaign finance laws give campaign funds to candidates from the two major parties after they have secured their party's nomination. Third party candidates must secure a certain percentage of the popular vote to even qualify for funding. They receive their public money after the election. Table I lists the various third party movements that have arisen on the national scene.

Factions Within the American Party Organization

The success and longevity of any major political party depends on how the party leadership handles various factions under the party's wide umbrella. A **faction** is "a political group or clique that functions within a larger group, such as a government, party or organization."[67] In *Federalist #109*, James Madison defined factions as "a number of citizens, whether amounting to a majority or a minority of the whole, who are united and actuated by some common impulse of passion or of interest, adverse to the rights of other citizens, or to the permanent and aggregated interests of the community."[68] In *Federalist #14*, Madison soundly voiced his opposition to factions by pointing out that diverse factions could eventually destroy national unity since their main objective was to divide rather than to unite people. Both the Democratic and Republican Parties have encountered factional interests who challenge the party's leadership. Factions within these parties are oftentimes sanctioned groups known as caucuses. For example, the Hispanic Caucus of the Democratic Party helps the party leadership tackle such issues as immigration reform and voter registration to ensure that these issues are included into the party's platform and issue positions. Factions can be beneficial by keeping the party in touch with all of its various diverse members. However, a faction can prove just as Madison stressed, detrimental to survival of the political party. In determining the course of action to take with internal factions, party leadership members must:

> Consider the element of discontinuity in factionalism. . . . The groups lack continuity in name—as exists under a party system—and they also lack continuity in the make-up of their inner core of professional politicians or leaders. Naturally, they also lack continuity in voter support that, under the two-party conditions, provides a relatively stable following of voters for each party's candidates whoever they may be. . . . Loose factions lack the collective spirit of party organization, which at its best imposes a sense of duty and imparts a spirit of responsibility to the inner core of leaders of the organization.[69]

Currently, the Tea Party Movement is a faction operating within the Republican Party. The Tea Party could not survive on its own as a viable and long lasting third party movement. Consequently, the membership believes that their issue positions fit under the conservative umbrella of the Republican Party. Although not an official political party, the Tea Party membership did hold a convention and drafted a party platform for the 2016 election cycle. The preamble stated that "the Tea Party is an all-inclusive American grassroots movement with the belief that everyone is created equal and deserves an equal opportunity to thrive in these United States where they may 'pursue life, liberty and happiness' as stated in the **Declaration of Independence** and guaranteed by the **Constitution of the United States**."[70] Tea Party issue positions center around ten core beliefs: elimination of excessive taxes, elimination of the national debt, elimination of deficit spending, protection of free markets, strict adherence to the Constitution, promotion of civic responsibility, reducing the size of government, belief in the American people, avoiding the pitfalls of politics, and maintaining local independence.[71] Several Tea Party members have been elected under the Republican banner to both the House and Senate, as well as to several state legislative positions. Tea Party members are adamant about their issues in drastically eliminating and hopefully abolishing tax programs such as the income tax and reducing the federal budget by eliminating all government-sponsored social programs such as food stamps, Medicaid, etc. They simply do not want to compromise on their issue positions. Members of each respective political party in these legislative houses agree to disagree with each other but ultimately when they do reach a consensus on any political directive it is through discussion, debate, and compromise.

The unwillingness of the Tea Party faction to accept compromise has led to very public displays of frustrating confrontations within the Republican Party. Led primarily by Tea Party advocate Ted Cruz (R-Texas), the Republican members of both houses of Congress successfully shut down the federal government for several weeks in 2013. Every time a budget deadline lurks, Tea Party associated Republicans vow to shut down the government. Former Speaker of the House John Boehner (R-Ohio) on more than one occasion publically voiced his displeasure with the group.

Table I   **Third Parties in American Politics**

Name of the Party	Year	Major Issue Positions and Outcome
American Independent Party	1968	Strict adherence to Constitution; opposed liberalism; supported free trade and pro-life positions; strong support of 2nd Amendment; founded by George Wallace; ran Wallace for president in 1968; national presence ended with attempted assassination of Wallace.
Anti-Mason Party	1830s	Nation's original third party. Promoted abolition of secret organizations such as the Masons. Ran William Wirt for president. Party dissolved.
Constitutional Union	1860	Defended Constitution and unity of the federal government. Unsuccessfully ran John Bell for presidency.
Free Soil Party	1848	Opposed extension of slavery into the territories; supported national internal improvement programs, moderate tariffs and enactment of homestead laws. Unsuccessfully ran Martin Van Buren for president. Party dissolved. Party Issues incorporated into Republican Party.
Know-Nothing Party	1840s	Anti-immigration; prohibition against Catholics and foreign-born persons from holding elective offices and supported English as the nation's official language. Changed its name to the American Party. Its platform issues were adopted by the Republican Party. Party dissolved.
Libertarian Party	1972	Promote laws protecting individual rights; anticensorship; protection of privacy; support for the right to bear arms, the creation of an all-voluntary military, advocacy for anti-government involvement in the economy, abolition of all tariffs, abolition of all social/welfare programs; support the repeal of all compulsory education programs. Party active in state and local elections. In 2016, the Libertarian Party ran Gary Johnson as its presidential candidate and Bill Weld as the vice presidential candidate.
Populist Party	1891	Supported positions for a silver than a gold standard for American currency, denial of property ownership to aliens, confiscation of public lands given to railroad companies, balanced budgets, free public education, reforms for the prison system; Promoted worker protection laws to include the eight-hour work day; supported the abolition of the Electoral college. Ran James Weaver for president in 1892 and Terry Roosevelt in 1912. Issues adopted by the Democrats and Roosevelt returned to the Republican Party. Party dissolved.

Progressive Party	**1912**	Founded by Theodore Roosevelt. Promoted direct primaries for nomination of state and national offices; Advocated the abolishment of the Electoral College; Promoted anti-child labor laws, provisions for worker benefits to include higher wages and workers' compensation plans; supported tariffs against foreign-made products; advocated a pro-environment effort. Unsuccessfully ran Roosevelt for president. Party dissolved. Roosevelt returned to Republican Party.
Socialist Party	**1912**	Support for collective ownership of all transportation, communication, and all other large industries, the abolition of monopoly ownership, and legislation shortening the workday for all workers; advocacy for absolute right to freedom of speech; promote equal suffrage for men and women; support abolition of the Electoral College; desire to abolish judicial review and all federal-level courts; call for a national convention to revise the Constitution.
Southern Democratic Party	**1860**	Supported right of states to withdraw from the union, the institution of slavery, and the implementation and enforcement of state fugitive slave laws. Unsuccessfully ran John C. Breckinridge for president. Party dissolved.
States Rights Democratic Party	**1948**	Founded by Sen. Strom Thurmond; promote states' rights; anti-civil rights and anti-segregation position. Ran Strom Thurmond for president. Party dissolved.
The Constitution Party	**1991**	Founded in 1991 on the principle that the federal government's authority is limited to the duties and functions detailed in the United States Constitution. Unsuccessfully ran one of its founding members Darrell Castle as its 2016 presidential candidate. Party has forty-four state party organizations and has limited success in wining local city council positions. The party is aligned with the Tea Party.
The Grange	**1867**	Advocated for farmers and ranchers for regulatory action against railroads, banks and insurance companies. Declined in the 1890s as the Farmers Alliance adopted their issues. The Alliance in turn also advocated for the poor, improvements in education, and prohibition of alcoholic beverages. Its platform issues were adopted by the Democratic Party. Party dissolved.
The Green Party	**1996**	Predominately pro-environment; support peace and disarmament of nuclear weapons; support independence for Puerto Rico; support expansion and protection of civil rights; support single-payer health care, reforms of prison and justice system. Jill Stein and Ajamu Baraka ran respectively for president and vice president in

		2016; more successful at winning state elections in selective states. Platform issues similar to those of the Democratic Party.
The Reform Party	1995	Supports fiscal responsibility and accountability, fair taxation politics, "American first" position, affordable and accessible healthcare based on decisions between doctor and patient, energy independence. Founded by Ross Perot. Ran Perot for president. Active in state elections in selective states.
Veterans Party of America	2013	Headquartered in Moses Lake, Washington, the party has approximately 50,000 members with fifty state party affiliates. Not associated with either the Republican or Democratic Parties, this centralist organization's primary objective is for political leaders to adhere to the Constitution. Ran Chris Keniston and Deacon Taylor as their presidential and vice presidential candidates in the 2016 election.
Whig Party	1834	Opposed Andrew Jackson's policies; promoted industrial and business interests in Northeast; promoted higher tariffs and subsidies for shipping, and establishing relations with China and Japan. Party dissolved. 1848 Millard Fillmore elected vice president as Whig candidate who became president with death of Taylor but lost White House in 1856. Issues incorporated into Republican Party.

Organizational Structure of American Political Parties

Usually one thinks that political parties are structured like the modern corporation with the top of hierarchy controlling the entire structure. The top of the structure is supposedly controlled by the national party organization with the national chairperson and the national committee charged with overseeing the day-to-day operation of the national organization and establishing policy and procedures for state, county and local party units. The lowest rung of the party ladder is reserved for the local precincts also known in several states as the wards. Local precincts or wards are managed through a chairperson elected by their own precinct party members. This top to down structure implies that the parties operate under a centralized structure with the national committee controlling all party activities with state and local organizations having little or no autonomy. In practice, however, the pyramid is inverted because the most important and essential component of any political party is the local precinct, the lowest rung of the party ladder. In practice, American political parties are decentralized organizations. "Decentralization of power is by all odds the most important single characteristic of the American major party; more than anything else this trait distinguishes it from all others. Indeed once this truth is understood, nearly everything else about American parties is greatly illuminated. . . . The American major party is, to repeat the definition, a loose confederation of state and local bosses for limited purposes."[72] Basically, the national party organization focuses once every four years on the presidential election and rarely gets directly involved in congressional races and even less so in state gubernatorial and legislative contests. The lack of a tight cohesive organizational relationship between the various levels of the nation's two major political parties can best be described as **stratarchy**, whereby each level acts independently of each other.[73] A closer look at the duties and responsibilities assigned to each level within the party pyramid gives an insight into its internal operations.

The National Party Organization

Perhaps the most prestigious assignment for any local party member is a seat on the Democratic National Committee (DNC) or the Republican National Committee (RNC). Initially the membership of each party's core leadership team consisted of just the national chairperson elected from the entire party membership, and one man and one woman from each of the fifty states. Today, the membership of the RNC National Committee is approximately 150 while the DNC has over 300 committee members. The DNC places two (one man and one woman from each state) as well as "two hundred additional members allocated to the states on the same basis as delegates are apportioned to the national convention; and a number of delegates representing such organizations as the Democratic Governors' Conference, the U.S. Congress, the National Finance Council, the Conference of Democratic Mayors, the National Federation of Democratic Women, the Democratic County Officials Conference, the State Legislative Leader's Caucus, and the Young Democrats of America."[74] Obviously, both political parties use these plum positions on their national committees to recognize those who have either devoted a considerable amount of personal time to the party's activities or have donated considerable campaign contributions to both the parties and their candidates. Although the national committees officially elect their respective chairpersons, the selection is actually made by the president whose party controls the White House. The 2016 Democratic National Convention was to a large extent controlled by President Obama's team, even though Obama could not seek a third term. For the party out of power, the national committee does indeed select its national chairperson. Although the primary duty of the national chairperson is to be the chief fundraiser, other responsibilities include recruiting candidates, conducting campaign strategy

Organizational Chart

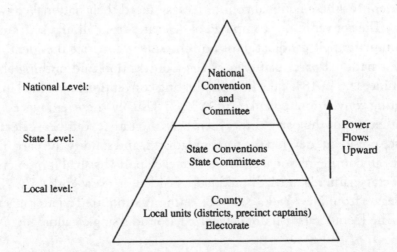

training programs for candidates and their campaign staffers, conducting issue and voter research, and when called upon, assisting their respective party's presidential candidate's campaign efforts.

Increasing the membership of the national committee oftentimes compromises the effectiveness of the body. Meeting infrequently, the primary responsibilities of these committees are confined to policy making, selecting the site of their respective national conventions, and establishing the criteria for the selection of convention delegates. While both political parties have millions of either direct card-carrying members and/or those who periodically attach themselves to one of the parties, it is ironic that the internal operations of these large organizations are actually run by a few high ranking party members. As seen in interest groups as well as political parties, the **Iron Law of Oligarchy** underscores that "in every organization, whether it be a political party, a professional union, or any other association of the kind, the aristocratic tendency manifests itself very clearly. The mechanism of the organization, while conferring a solidity of structure, induces serious changes in the organized mass, completely inverting the respective position of the leaders and the led. As a result of organization, every party or professional union becomes divided into a minority of directors and a majority of the directed."[75]

Furthermore, there is a serious "disconnect" between the national committee and the party membership as well as a lack of coordination and cooperation between the national organization and state and local party units. National organizations rarely get involved in state and local elections unless the candidate's election fortune has or could have national implications. For example, in 2006, a special election was held for the redrawn 23rd U.S. Congressional district. This election pitted incumbent Congressman Henry Bonilla (R-Texas) against former Congressman Ciro Rodriguez (D-Texas). Initially, Bonilla had a large lead over six other candidates including Rodriguez. As the polls tightened, the DNC took an interest in the election. The DNC contributed funds to the Rodriguez campaign and Former President Bill Clinton made campaign appearances on behalf of Rodriguez. On election night, Rodriguez won! National party organizations have taken a back seat as the election campaign itself has shifted elections from party-centered to candidate-centered events. Initially political parties took the center stage in planning the campaign strategy from start to finish. Today, the primary responsibility of the campaign falls upon each individual candidate who must now raise his/her own money, hire their own campaign staff, and plot for themselves the course of their campaigns from the primaries to the general elections.

The major event for these national committees is indeed their national conventions held once every four years. The convention is composed of delegates from all fifty states and U.S. territories who meet to nominate their candidates for both president and vice president, as well as to draft and approve their national party platform. "The Constitution said nothing about how to select presidential nominees. . . In 1812, the first nominating conventions were held in several states; and the first nominating convention took place in 1832."[76] Usually, these national conventions are non-controversial gatherings of the party elite. Their tasks are rather routine—select the nominees for president and vice president, develop the party's platform, and solidify the party faithful around the candidates for the upcoming national election. Yet, each party has had it moments of suspense. In 1868, the Democrats gathered at Madison Square Garden, in New York City. The infamous Boss Tweed was a delegate from New York. Susan B. Anthony submitted a letter in support of woman's suffrage rights. The Democrats had not galvanized around a single candidate. After twenty-seven presidential nomination ballots, the delegates selected Horatio Seymour, a former governor of New York as its presidential candidate. He lost in a landslide election to the Republican candidate Ulysses S. Grant. In 1921, it was the Republican National Convention that drew nationwide attention as the then former President Theodore Roosevelt wanted to run again for the Oval Office. During his successful White House bid in 1904, Roosevelt announced during a campaign tour, that he would be a one term president. Although taken aback, the Republican Party's national committee respected his decision and nominated William Howard Taft for the presidency at its 1908 national convention. Taft won the election, and in 1912, sought his party's nomination for a second term. However, Roosevelt decided that he too wanted to run for president. Meeting in Chicago, Illinois, Taft and Roosevelt battled each other for the nomination. Through the primary season, Taft had acquired more delegates than Roosevelt and felt he should be given the nod for the White House. The Taft contention were adamant that Roosevelt was out of the picture. "Taft forces wrapped the [convention] rostrum in barbed wire camouflaged with bunting, lest Roosevelt supports stormed the stage. Taft won on the first ballot; Roosevelt bolted to form a new Progressive Party."[77] The 1912 election was a disaster for the Republican Party as its base split their votes between Taft and Roosevelt, and the Democratic nominee Woodrow Wilson won with only 42.1 percent of the total popular vote.

The Democrats assembled in Chicago, Illinois, in 1968 for their national convention. Held at the height of the Vietnam and civil rights protests of the 60s, the party's leadership was on edge about potential violence erupting during their convention. They were assured by Chicago's mayor Richard Daley that he would guarantee a peaceful setting for the convention. The 1968 Democratic National Convention was anything but peaceful. While inside the convention hall speakers were talking about peace and goodwill, outside on the sidewalks and nearby streets, demonstrators were being beaten by the mayor's security forces. The media had a field day in covering the daily street violence. "For a week the police skirmished with demonstrators: police clubs, riot gear, and tear gas versus the demonstrators' eggs, rocks, and balloons filled with paint and urine. . . In one pitched battle, many officers took off their badges and waded into the crowd, nightsticks swinging and chanting, 'kill, kill, kill.' Reporters, medics, and other innocent bystanders were injured; at 3:30 a.m., police invaded candidate Eugene McCarthy's hotel headquarters and pulled some of his assistants from their beds."[78] The heightened violence prevented President Lyndon Johnson from attending his own party's national convention. Hubert Humphrey, Johnson's vice president, won the nomination but lost the election to Richard Nixon. The aftermath of the convention violence led to the Democratic National Committee forming the **McGovern-Fraser Commission** to reform the internal operations of the Democratic Party. The party adopted recommendations to increase the number of convention delegates to allow for more minorities and women to join key party committees and expanded the number of primaries to encourage wider participation for Democrats to select their party's candidates.

One of the most important committees, the **platform committee**'s job is to craft a document that embraces the overall political philosophy of the party while at the same time, incorporates into the document the important issue positions and concerns gathered during each state's party convention, which, in turn, originated in part at the district convention attended by representatives from each precinct. A **platform** is "a statement of principles and objectives espoused by a party or a candidate that is used during a campaign to win support from voters."[79] Once officially nominated, it is the responsibility of the party's candidates to incorporate party platform issues into his/her campaign effort. Once elected, it is the responsibility of the party's candidates, especially the president, to ensure his/her policy choices and decisions mirror in part the positions articulated in the party platform. President Dwight D. Eisenhower once commented that "there may be some cynics who think that a Platform is just a list of platitudes to lure the naïve voter—a sort of façade behind which candidates sneak into power and then do as they please. I am not one of those."[80] Once officially adopted at the national convention, state party organizations will blend their own issue concerns into the nation party's overall philosophy. Resolutions made at state conventions held in off-presidential years are entertained at the next national convention.

A major event for both national conventions is the highly anticipated **keynote address** delivered by each party's presidential nominee. While not covering these conventions from gavel to gavel, all of the media networks televise or record this speech. The pre-speech media hype focuses on the verbiage of the speech, how well it is anticipated that the nominee will deliver the speech, and how well the audience will react to it. Both the Republican and Democratic parties select one of their own "rising stars" to deliver the speech. A successfully delivered nationally delivered speech propels a locally known politician into the national limelight, placing his/her name as potential presidential and vice-presidential candidates. At the 1984 National Democratic Convention held in San Francisco, California, Mario Cuomo, governor of New York, delivered perhaps the most memorable keynote speech ever delivered by a Republican or a Democrat. Cuomo based his speech on then President Reagan's astonishment that many Americans were questioning the success of America since to him, "this country is a shining city on a hill."[81] Cuomo's words resonated throughout the convention center:

> But the hard truth is that not everyone is sharing in this city's splendor and glory. A shining city is perhaps all the president sees from the portico of the White House and the veranda of his ranch where everyone seems to be doing well. But there's another part of the city, that part where some people can't pay their mortgages and most young people can't afford one, where students can't afford the education they need and middle-class parents watch the dreams they hold for their children evaporate. In this part of the city there are more poor than ever, more families in trouble. More and more people who need help but can't find it. Even worse: There are elderly people who tremble in the basements of the houses there. There are people who sleep in the city's streets, in the gutter, where the glitter doesn't show. . . . We must make the American people hear our 'tale of the two cities.' We must convince them that they do not have to settle for two cities, that we can have one city, indivisible, shining for all of its people."[82]

Cuomo so impressed the leadership of the Democratic Party that evening that he was asked but declined to be a presidential candidate in 1988 and 1992. At the 2012 Democratic National Convention held in Charlotte, North Carolina, San Antonio, Texas mayor Julian Castro became the first Hispanic and the youngest person to date to deliver a keynote address. In 2014, President Obama nominated Castro to be his secretary of Housing and Urban Development. By 2016, Castro was on a short list of Hillary Clinton's potential vice president nominees. His presence with her on the campaign trail gave him the valuable experience and media exposure needed to aspire to higher national office. In 2020, Castro lunched his own bid for president.

The final night of the national convention is centered on the nominated candidates. In the text of the speeches, the nominees officially accept their party's nomination and layouts his/her own agenda for the upcoming general election. The speech will be interrupted numerous times with clapping and cheering. At the end of speech, the candidate, his/her family members, elected officials and key members of the national committee gather together to watch the balloons drop, the posters wave, the confetti fall, and the convention members cheer on their candidate for the November election. This is prime time television exposure for both the party and its candidates.

However, the media usually devotes no coverage to the internal wheeling and dealing between the national committee members, state party leadership and the candidates. For example, the official seating of the convention's delegates falls upon the shoulders of the **credentials committee** who prior to the convention sets the process for certifying a state's official delegation. Each state's party organization sends both officially elected pledged and unpledged delegates. **Pledged delegates** are chosen specifically to cast their vote for a particular candidate. Each state party organization has different criteria as to whether a delegate is pledged throughout the presidential and vice presidential selection process or released to vote their own preferences after a certain number of ballots. **Unpledged** or **independent delegates** are not required to cast their votes as their state parties wish, regardless of the number of ballots. Every national party convention has had its credentialing issues. During the 2008 presidential election convention cycle, the DNC debated whether to credential delegates from several states whose state organizations refused to follow the DNC's primary election timeline and subsequently moved their own state primaries from Super Tuesday to another date. If not credentialed, these state delegates would not have been officially admitted into the convention nor would they have been able to cast votes for the presidential and vice presidential nominees. In the end, the questionable state delegations were properly credentialed and did vote. At times, the United States Supreme Court has been tasked with negotiating party credentialing issues. In 1891, for example, the Court ruled in *Democratic Party v La Follette* that a state's party leadership could not force the DNC's credentials committee to accept a delegation that was selected in clear violation of DNC rules. In *Cousins v Wigoda* (**1975**), the Court ruled that only the credentials committee of a national political party has the authority to settle credential disputes between rival state delegations.

Both the DNC and RNC have faced criticisms that their traditional ways of "doing business" are more exclusive than inclusive and not in touch with their voting bases. In other words, the 'good ole boy" wheeling and dealing between a few well-entrenched elites actually controling the party organization from top to bottom, leaving the rank-and-file party membership to believe that their parties only needed them to cast their votes on election day for the party's slate of candidates. Particularly for the Democrats, the 1968 national convention was a tragic eye-opening internationally covered event. Amid the anti-war protests against Vietnam and the rising civil rights and feminist movements, the DNC selected Chicago, Illinois, as the site for the national convention. The convention was anything but peaceful, and many left with ill feelings about the future of the Democratic Party. DNC Chairperson Fred Harris responded to the outcries by appointing Senator

George McGovern to head a special investigation into DNC practices. Filed in 1971, the **McGovern Commission** recommended a return to grassroots politics to broaden the delegate pool, with the inclusion of minorities and women. The report recommended that state party officials could no longer demand that their delegates nominate and actually vote for their "favorite son or daughter" candidates who in the end would not even have a chance to win the prized presidential or vice presidential nomination. Also, the report recommended that at least 75 percent of a state's delegation had to be chosen at their state conventions specifically from their congressional districts or even smaller units such as districts or precincts. The RNC also reexamined their convention format and delegate selection processes. Since then both parties have continued efforts to ensure that their delegation selection process does include a broad representation reflective of the entire party membership with particular emphasis on minorities, women, and younger party supporters.

In 2016, DNC was in the headlines once again as e-mails sent by DNC chairperson Debbie Wasserman Schultz (D-Florida) were hacked and released by various news affiliates. The e-mails exposed internal concerns about the rising popularity of Bernie Sanders and whether he would be able to take the nomination from front-runner Hillary Clinton. Although Sanders was unsuccessful in denying Clinton the nomination, the fallout over the hacked e-mails resulted in Wasserman Schultz resigning her position. The possibility of future inter-party e-mail hacking has both political parties revamping their internal communication formats.

The State Party Organizations

The U.S. Constitution makes no mention of either interest groups or political parties and no subsequent amendments recognize their existence, nor detail any responsibilities and operational procedures that could guide them. The Framers did not ignore that sooner or later both interest groups and political parties would develop. They simply left it up to the states through their individual legislative houses to set the overall ground rules for the establishment and operation of both interest groups and political parties as well as establishing election procedures and rules pertinent to their individual states. Consequently, each state has its own election code, methods of selecting their slates of electors for the Electoral College, types of ballots, candidate qualifications, election certification, criteria for third party or independent candidates to gain a position on the ballot, etc. For example, in Texas the elections for statewide offices are held in non-presidential election years. Many states, however, use the presidential election cycle to select all statewide, county and local officeholders.

Usually, both political parties have elected or appointed state executive committees composed of a chairperson, vice chairperson, and other members. For the party in power of the governorship, the state chairperson is basically a ceremonial position since the governor serves as the official head or his/her political party. The basic functions of any state executive committee include canvassing state-wide election results, certifying a candidate's qualifications for office in primary and general elections, receiving candidate filing forms, in some states collecting candidate filing fees, overseeing the site location and coordinating the upcoming state convention, establishing the selection process for the state credentials and platform committees, and setting the guidelines for the selection of delegates to the national party conventions. The state chairperson is the party's "cheerleader" in that he or she promotes party unity and party platform issues at both the county and precinct levels and encourages all party leadership to continue their grassroots efforts by encouraging people to register and vote on election day, raising money for candidates, and working within the framework of both the state and national party organizations. Many state legislative houses have given state party organizations the authority to oversee and, in some instances, to take punitive sanctions against local party units who violate party rules and practices.

County/District Organizations

The county party leadership is vested in an executive committee composed of all the precinct chairs for that particular county. In larger counties, state laws may divide it into proportionately equal districts. Usually, the county chairpersons are popularly elected to either two- or four-year terms of office. County/district organizations are primarily responsible for preparing the election ballot, receiving filing forms for countywide elective positions, collecting the appropriate filing fees, and determining the ballot order for the candidates. The ballot order can be an alphabetical listing by office or a random drawing of numbers with the lowest number getting the top of the ballot position. The county/district is also responsible for canvassing the returns for the primary elections and arranging for the county/district conventions.

Precincts

The workhorse of these two major political parties is the **election precinct** or **precinct**. In some states, precincts are called **wards**. The chairperson for precincts is either selected by placement on the primary ballot or nominated and elected from the floor at the precinct convention. Normally held the evening of the party primary elections, precinct conventions are open to all individuals who voted in their party's primary elections. The primary duties of the precinct chair include mobilization of voter turnout, selecting election judges and poll watchers for the primary and general elections, arranging for the precinct convention, and serving on the county executive team.

In every way, the precinct is the core of a party's grassroots political presence. It is the primary duty of the precinct chairperson to canvass the residents within his/her precinct or ward and to separate the party die-hards from those vacillating between party loyalties and those who are not even registered to vote. It is the chairperson who coordinates voter registration drives, assists voters who need mail-in ballots and arranges rides to the polls on election days. Chairpersons may host coffees in their homes for candidates running on the lower-end of the ballot so the candidates can establish a physical presence within the community and, hopefully, encourage the attendees to drop a campaign contribution into the jar. Chairpersons oftentimes arrange for candidate forums and debates. It is also the chairperson who gathers the volunteers to distribute campaign literature, post signs, etc. One could call the precinct or ward chairperson the cheerleader-in-chief for the party.

CONCLUSIONS

In *Democracy in America,* Alexis de Tocqueville concluded that the primary goal of American political parties is to gather once every four years to elect a president. During the election, political parties take center stage. However, once the election is over, the parties fade into the shadows only to reemerge four-years later. De Tocqueville commented that:

> Moreover, in the United States as elsewhere, parties feel the need to rally around one man in order more easily to make themselves understood by the crowd. Generally, therefore, they use the presidential candidate's name as a symbol; in him they personify their theories. Hence the parties have a great interest in winning the election, not so much in order to make their doctrines triumph by the President-elect's help, as to show, by his election, that their doctrines have gained a majority.
>
> Long before the appointed day arrives, the election becomes the greatest, and one might say the only, affair occupying men's minds. At this time, the factions redouble their ardor; then every forced passion that imagination can create in a happy and peaceful country spreads excitement in broad daylight.
>
> The President, for his part, is absorbed in the task of defending himself. He no longer rules in the interest of the state, but in that of his own reelection; he prostrates himself before the majority, and often, instead of resisting their passions as duty requires, he hastens to anticipate their caprices.
>
> As the election draw near, intrigues grow more active and agitation is more lively and widespread. The citizens divide up into several camps, each of which takes its name from its candidate. The whole nation gets into a feverish state, the election is the daily theme of comment in the newspapers and private conversation, the object is every action and the subject of every thought, and the sole interest for the moment.
>
> It is true that as soon as fortune has pronounced, the ardor is dissipated, everything calms down, and the river which momentarily overflowed its banks falls back to its bed. But was it not astonishing that such a storm could have arisen?[83]

De Tocqueville's observations of American political parties in action in the 1800s are quite similar to what we witness every four years. The media covers the highlights of the national convention. The cameras are focused on the candidates making their speeches, the confetti and the balloons falling from the ceilings, etc. Once the convention lights are turned off, the candidates abandon their respective parties as they hit the campaign road. Candidates speak about what they would do if elected. Both the candidates and the media have marginalized the importance of political parties in the American electoral and governing process. Nightly news reports center on what the candidate did today, who he/she spoke to, and what they said. Rarely are the activities of the political parties mentioned. But, political parties wield their powerful influence on the public policy process behind "closed doors" for they are the driving force behind the advocacy of issues, the development of the responses, and the electability of candidates to public office. The candidates need their respective political parties to help them get elected, and once in office, they need the party to remind their fellow elected officials that one's legislative successes or failures are everyone's successes or failures! As James K. Polk lamented "we have a country as well as party to obey."[84]

CHAPTER NOTES

[1] *Treasury of Presidential Quotations*, Caroline Thomas Harnsberger, ed., (Chicago, Illinois: Follett Publishing Company, 1964), 235.

[2] Ibid., 235-236.

[3] Ibid., 236.

[4] Ibid., 238.

[5] George Sabine, *A History of Political Theory*, 3rd ed., (New York, New York: Holt, Reinhart,Winston, Inc., 1961), 611.

[6] William Goodman, *The Two-Party System in the United States*, 3rd ed., (Princeton, New Jersey: D. Van Nostrand Company, Inc., 1964), 6.

[7] Susan Welch, John Gruhl, Michael Steinman, John Comer and Susan M. Rigdon, *American Government*, 5th ed., (Minneapolis/St. Paul, Wisconsin: West Publishing Company, 1994), 146.

[8] Thomas W. Madron and Carl P. Chelf, *Political Parties in the United States*, (Boston, Massachusetts: Holbrook Press, 1974), 302-303.

[9] *Treasury of Presidential Quotations*, 18.

[10] V. O. Key, Jr., *Politics, Parties, and Pressure Groups*, 4th ed., (New York, New York: Thomas Y. Crowell Company, 1958), 220.

[11] Jack C. Plano and Milton Greenberg, *The American Political Dictionary*, 10th ed., (Orlando, Florida: Harcourt Brace and Company, 1997), 88.

[12] Gabriel A. Almond, G. Bingham Powell, Jr., Kaare Strom and Russell Dalton, *Comparative Politics Today: A World View*, 8th ed., (New York, New York: Pearson Longman, 2004), 90.

[13] Ibid.

[14] Ibid., 92.

[15] *The HarperCollins Dictionary of American Government and Politics*, Jay M. Shafritz, ed., (New York, New York: HarperCollins Publishers, 1992), 286.

[16] Roger Scruton, *A Dictionary of Political Thought*, (New York, New York: Harper & Row Publishers, 1982), 90.

[17] Plano and Greenberg, 13.

[18] *A Treasury of Presidential Quotations*, 42.

[19] George Klosko, *History of Political Theory: An Introduction*, Vol. 2: Modern Political Theory, (Belmont, California: Wadsworth Group/Thomson Learning, 1995), 266-267.

[20] Ian Adams and R. W. Dyson, *Fifty Major Political Thinkers*, (New York, New York: Routledge, 2003), 90-91.

[21] *The HarperCollins Dictionary of American Government and Politics*, 139.

[22] *The HarperCollins Dictionary of American Government and Politics*, 499

[23] Plano and Greenberg, 5.

[24] Scruton, 302.

[25] *The HarperCollins Dictionary of American Government and Politics*, 335.

[26] Klosko, 200.

[27] Ibid.

[28] Plano and Greenberg, 14.

[29] Adams and Dyson, 63.

[30] Klosko, 111.

[31] Scruton, 271.

[32] *HarperCollins Dictionary of American Government and Politics*, page 335.

[33] http://www/presidency.ucsb.edu

[34] Plano and Greenberg, 26.

[35] *The HarperCollins Dictionary of American Government and Politics*, 325.

[36] *The International Relations Dictionary*, Jack C. Plano and Roy Olton, eds., (New York, New York: Holt, Rinehart and Winston, Inc., 1969), 111.

[37] Gary B. Nash and Julie Roy Jeffrey, *The American People: Creating a Nation and a Society*, 5th ed., (New York, New York: Addison-Wesley Education Publishers, Inc., 2001), 712.

[38] Sarah Richardson, "Before Bernie," *American History*, Vol. 52, No. 1, April, 2017, 35.

[39]Plano and Greenburg, 5.

[40]Ibid., 2

[41]Ibid.

[42]Frank J. Sorauf, *Political Parties in America*, (Boston, Massachusetts: Little Brown and Company, 1968), 381.

[43]Ibid., 380.

[44]*A Treasury of Presidential Quotations*, 239.

[45]Joseph P. Ellis, "The First Democrats," *US News & World Report*, August 21, 2000, 37.

[46]Charles A. Beard and Mary R. Beard, *A Basic History of the United States*, 1st ed., (Philadelphia, Pennsylvania: The Blakeston Company, 1944), 165.

[47]Ellis, "The First Democrats," 37.

[48]Beard, 166.

[49]Robert Warnick, "Chief Justice Marshall Takes the Law in Hand," *Smithsonian*, Vol. 29, No. 8, Nov. 1998, 160.

[50]Ibid.

[51]John Ferling, "1796: The First Real Election," *American History*, Vol. 31, No. 5, December, 1996, 27.

[52]Ibid.

[53]Ibid., 24.

[54]Ibid.

[55]Ibid., 28.

[56]John Ferling, "Cliffhanger: The Electionof 1800," *Smithsonian*, Vol. 35, No. 8, November, 2004, 46.

[57]Sidney Blumenthal, "National Treasure: Banner Session," *Smithsonian*, Vol. 47, No. 6, Oct. 2016, 38.

[58]Ibid., 39.

[59]Ellis, "The First Democrats," 38.

[60]Ferling, "Cliffhanger: The Election of 1800," 50.

[61]Harry K. Carman, Harold C. Syrett and Bernard W. Wishy, *A History of the American People*, Vol. 1 to 1877, 3rd ed., (New York, New York: Alfred A. Knopf, 1967), 271.

[62]James MacGregor Burns, *The Deadlock of Democracy: Four Party Politics in America*, 2nd ed., (Englewood Cliffs, New Jersey: Prentice-Hall, Inc., 1967), 32-33.

[63]*The Rise of Conservatism in American, 1945-2000: A Brief History with Documents*, Ronald Story and Bruce Laurie, ed., (Boston, Massachusetts: Bedford/St. Martin's: 2008), 1.

[64]Ibid.

[65]*Treasury of Presidential Quotations*, 174-175.

[66]*The HarperCollins Dictionary of America Government and Politics*, 417.

[67]Plano and Greenberg, 88.

[68]Sorauf, 18-19.

[69]Ibid.

[70]http://www.teaparty-platform.com/

[71]Ibid.

[72]Sorauf, 108

[73]L. Sandy Maisel, *Parties and Elections in America: The Electoral Process*, 2nd ed., (New York, New York: McGraw-Hill, Inc., 1993), 54.

[74]William J. Keefe and Marc K. Hetherington, *Parties, Politics and Public Policy in America*, 9th ed., (Washington, D.C.: CQ Press, 2003), 16.

[75]*The HarperCollins Dictionary of America Government and Politics*, 305.

[76]Ferling, "1796: The First Real Election," 27.

[77]Richard Brookhiser, "Unconventional Wisdom," *American History*, Vol. 51, No. 4, October, 2016, 19.

[78]James Davidson, William E. Gienapp, Christine Heyrman, Mark Lytle and Michael Stoff, *Nation of Nations: A Narrative History of the American Republic*, (New York, New York: McGraw-Hill Publishing Company, 1990), 1212.

[79]Plano and Greenberg, 95.

[80]*A Treasury of Presidential Quotations*, 244.

[81]"Cuomo Wows Democrats, Blasts GOP," *San Antoni Light*, Tuesday, July 17, 1984, B5.

[82]Ibid., 9

[83]Alexis de Tocqueville, *Democracy in America*, translated by Gorge Lawrence, J. P. Mayer, eds., (Garden City, New York: Doubleday & Company, Inc., 1969), 135.

[84]*Treasury of Presidential Quotations*, 236.

SUGGESTED READINGS

Key, V.O., Jr., *Politics, Parties and Pressure Groups*, 4th ed., New York, New York: Thomas Y. Crowell, Company, 1958.

Klosko, George, *History of Political Theory: An Introduction*, Vol. 2: Modern Political Theory, Belmont, California: Wadsworth Group/Thomson Learning, 1995.

Maisel, L. Sandy, *Parties and Elections in America: The Electoral Process*, 2nd, ed., New York, New York: McGraw-Hill, Inc., 1993.

Sorauf, Frank J., *Political Parties in America*, Boston, Mass.: Little Brown and Company, 1968.

Chapter Five

CAMPAIGNS AND ELECTIONS

The global pandemic of 2020 came just as the presidential primary process got underway, changing the nature of the traditional face-to-face, hand-to-hand campaigning of the last two centuries: Rallies were canceled, primaries postponed, fund-raisers shelved, door-knocking deferred. The 2020 Democratic campaigns operated largely online, with all in-person events canceled and campaign staff instructed to work entirely from home. On March 16, 2020, the Sanders' campaign held the first-ever digital rally with musical guests, all delivered via livestream. He also broadcast a digital fireside chat. Biden similarly hosted a tele-town hall on the 16th of March. The March 15 presidential debate was moved from Phoenix to the CNN studios in Washington, and the two podiums were placed far enough apart to comply with the social distancing guidelines. There was no audience and Biden and Sanders bumped elbows rather than shake each other's hands. The Trump campaign also canceled all rallies and moved to a robust digital operation. The 2020 congressional campaigns were also forced to navigate the unchartered water of the coronavirus-altered world. The National Congressional Campaign Committee cautioned against fundraising and urged sensitivity in communications. Fund-raisers were canceled and phone calls were made instead.

Three states—Arizona, Florida and Illinois—held elections on March 17, as the coronavirus crisis was beginning to mount in the United States, but other states across the country postponed primary elections and expanded vote by mail options, citing the difficulty of holding elections during the outbreak. Sixteen states and one territory—Alaska, Connecticut, Delaware, Georgia, Hawaii, Indiana, Kentucky, Louisiana, Maryland, New Jersey, New York, Ohio, Pennsylvania, Rhode Island, West Virginia, Wyoming and Puerto Rico—either pushed back their presidential primaries or switched to voting by mail with extended deadlines. Some states even postponed their primaries multiple times, as the pandemic continued. Wisconsin was forced to hold its primary on April 7 after state Republicans blocked efforts to postpone voting there. The remaining presidential primaries were rendered largely irrelevant when Senator Bernie Sanders dropped out of the race on April 8, establishing Joseph R. Biden Jr. as the presumptive nominee. But some states also had local elections on the calendar. Tom Perez, the Democratic National Committee chairman, urged those states with upcoming contests to expand their use of voting by mail, no-excuse absentee voting, curbside ballot drop-offs and early voting. The committee also postponed its National Convention from mid-July to mid-August.

The most important, characterizing event of democracies, the act of voting itself, has been upended by the virus. The pandemic threatened in-person voting, prompting several states, for example Ohio, Louisiana and Kentucky, to postpone their primaries over health concerns. Other states like Florida, Illinois, and Arizona moved ahead with their primaries as scheduled, but made various changes, like moving polling locations out of senior living facilities and offering sanitizing materials. Officials and campaigns alike advocated for absentee or mail-in voting, where available. There were also concerns about having enough election judges and volunteers.

The 2020 campaign consisted of complicated days, for candidates, for voters, for the country as a whole. It became acutely obvious in 2020 what the world loses when campaigns move to a no-contact, no-travel form of campaigning. Politics happens in person, even in the age of social media and smartphones. Selfies are taken in person. Candidates meet Americans in real life ways, at local restaurant stops and shopping centers. Political advertisements film real-life happening—until the coronavirus crisis of 2020.

There are, however, silver linings emerging from this crisis. States looked carefully at new ways of voting that expanded early and absentee voting, reaching people online and thereby reaching more people and increasing voter turnout. The virus has, for many voters, put politics in an entirely new light, increasing the stakes of election and making it personally important to most Americans. What used to appear banal campaign rhetoric now seems vitally important as voters look for competent leaders. For many, the election of 2020 was the most important election in their lifetime.

NOMINATING THE CANDIDATES

Historical Background

When the Constitution was being written, it was assumed by the framers that George Washington would be selected to be the first president of the new United States. In addition, it was largely assumed that the supporters of the new Constitution, the Federalists as they were called, would win most of the seats in the House and Senate, for to be anything other than Federalist was to be a traitor to the new government. Beyond these minimal assumptions, little else was known. The Constitution is completely silent on the subject of elections, choosing to leave it to each state to organize and control the elections. There was little thought given to how the nomination of future candidates would be conducted.

George Washington, upon becoming president, appointed Alexander Hamilton as Secretary of the Treasury and Thomas Jefferson as Secretary of State. Because Hamilton and Jefferson held divergent views on everything from foreign policy to a national bank to internal improvements, Jefferson soon quit the cabinet and began to organize the first political party, the Jeffersonian Republicans. Jefferson based his party in Congress, drawing together members who shared his political viewpoint. Hamilton, similarly, had his group of devotees in the House and Senate.

With the differences in political ideas apparent, the beginnings of party organization underway, democratic forces running strong, and Washington expressing no desire to seek a third term, the question soon arose how each party would nominate a candidate for the highest office of the presidency. By 1800, both the Federalists under Hamilton and the Republicans under Jefferson had established congressional caucuses that would nominate their party's candidate. These congressional caucuses were made up of men in the House and Senate sharing either the Federalist or Republican views.

The Caucus System

As the early 1800s progressed and party organization grew stronger and more complex, state party organizations began to develop state caucuses. These state party caucuses chose delegates that would participate in a national party convention, which would then nominate the party's presidential candidate. These national conventions quickly replaced the congressional caucuses as vehicles for nominating candidates. By 1830, the nomination process had become extremely complex with candidates having to be nominated at a variety of geographical levels, from the smallest electoral unit up to the national convention itself. The process began with local meetings, or caucuses, of party supporters to choose delegates to attend a larger subsequent meeting, usually at the county level. Most of the delegates selected in these local caucuses openly supported one of the presidential candidates seeking the party nomination. The process finally culminated in a state party convention with delegates selecting other delegates to the national party convention that will formally nominate the party's presidential candidate.

The number of states that hold caucuses has been declining for years. Today, one or both parties in five states employ caucuses to select delegates to attend presidential nominating conventions. The Iowa caucuses, which are the first held, are similar to those in other states. The campaign in Iowa starts several months before the caucuses are actually held. In 2020, eleven candidates seeking the Democratic nomination campaigned in Iowa. The Iowa caucuses are then held in early February in private homes, schools, and churches. All who consider themselves party members can attend. They debate and vote on the candidates. The candidates receiving the most votes win delegates to later county and then state conventions. The number of delegates is proportional to the vote that the candidate received at the caucuses. The candidate must get at least 15 percent of the caucus vote in order to receive any delegates.

While Iowa is a small state and chooses only a handful of delegates to the party conventions, it is important as a bell weather of public opinion. The media widely cover these caucuses, looking to identify frontrunners in each of the two major parties. The winners of the Iowa caucuses attract not only media coverage but also the large donations that will allow them to continue to successfully campaign in the other state caucuses and primaries. Iowa, even though it is a very small state, not very representative of the rest of the country, is largely viewed as the state that can jump-start a presidential nomination. This was not the case, however, in either 2016 when Senator Ted Cruz won the Republican Iowa Caucus or in 2020 when Pete Buttigieg won the Iowa Democratic Caucus. In both of those years, the winner in Iowa did not go on to get their party's nomination.

The Primary System

Because there is no national legislation governing the selection of delegates to a national party convention, and because pressures for greater democracy and participation continued to grow throughout the early twentieth century, some states began to develop an alternative to the state caucus. In 1903, in response to reform movements seeking to end party controlled selection processes, the state of Wisconsin passed the first statewide primary law. Within only ten years, many states followed Wisconsin's lead.

In a presidential primary election, every presidential candidate who chooses to enter the state primary lists a slate of convention delegates who may, at least in some states, have promised to support his candidacy at the party's national nominating convention. Voters in that state then can choose between competing slates of national party convention delegates. In the presidential preferential primary, voters choose delegates who have not agreed to support any particular candidate.

A state primary may be either **open** or **closed**. A primary is considered closed when each voter must declare a choice of party before voting, either when registering or actually at the voting place itself. Party members in these closed primaries may only choose among those candidates on their party's ballot. The primary election is closed, then, to members of other parties. In the open primary, on the other hand, the voter receives ballots for all the parties and chooses which party election they want to vote in, right there in the voting booth on election day. A few states even have **blanket** primaries in which voters may choose candidates for various offices off different party ballots.

Whether their delegates are chosen in state **caucuses** as in Iowa or in primaries as in California, the convention system quickly worked to extend the number of people involved in the electoral process. In addition, the democratic forces that encouraged the creation of the primary system also led to more intense party competition along with efforts to extend the franchise, dropping the property qualifications for voting by 1840. Campaigns became festive affairs. For example, tens of thousands of men and women attended the Whig Party festival in Nashville in 1840. They carried torches, donned uniforms, chanted party slogans, and whipped themselves into a virtual frenzy of party sympathy.

The Entitlement Revolution

In the 1960s, new groups emerged on the scene, seeking greater representation in the American party system. In particular, the Civil Rights Movement began to make demands on the Democratic Party organization for greater representation and recognition. At the 1964 Democratic national convention, the Mississippi Freedom Democratic Party filed a challenge against an all white Mississippi delegation that had been selected through the Mississippi caucus system. The Mississippi Freedom Democratic Party charged that the Mississippi caucus system had systematically excluded blacks from registering to vote and from participating in the state party meetings.

The conflict at the 1964 Democratic national convention resulted in the 1968 Democratic convention requiring state parties to ensure that voters in each state, regardless of race, color, creed, or national origin, be given the fullest opportunity to participate in party affairs. Furthermore, in July 1967, a Special Equal Rights Committee established by the Democratic National Committee adopted unanimously a resolution urging the 1968 convention to replace any state delegation "not broadly representative of the Democrats of the state with a rival representative delegation."[1] This resolution led to the seating of the Mississippi Freedom Democratic Party delegates at the 1968 Democratic national convention held in Chicago.

The call for equal opportunity for black participation was matched by an even wider call for fuller participation on the part of all rank and file voters. It was not only the caucus system that was challenged; reformers began to look at the primary system as well. Before 1968, the primaries were nothing more than what Harry Truman called "eye wash." In fact, the election of 1952 proved Truman right. In that election year, Democratic Senator Kefauver sought to be the Democratic nominee. Kefauver, however, had angered and alienated the Democratic party organization with his Senate investigation of organized crime and subsequent embarrassment of Democrats in Illinois and Florida. Kefauver's standing was much higher with the American public who had watched the televised hearings. It was estimated that an average of 69.7 percent of American television sets in New York were watching the hearings, twice the number who watched the World Series game in October 1950.[2] The hearings were carried by television stations in twenty states.

At least in part because of this media attention, Senator Kefauver was able to win large victories in the primaries. He received over 257 delegates chosen in the various state primary elections; he needed 616 delegates to win the Democratic nomination. At the Democratic convention, after four ballots, Kefauver lost the nomination to Adlai Stevenson who was the choice of the Democratic party organization but who had entered no primaries. Stevenson went on to be solidly defeated by Eisenhower in the general election, suggesting to many that primary voters might be better judges of candidates than those in the party organization.

In 1960, another Democrat, John F. Kennedy, used the primary system to challenge party leaders and secure the nomination. Kennedy was viewed by his party as a weak presidential hopeful. He was Catholic, and never had voters elected a non-Protestant to the White House. Kennedy was also seen as young and fairly inexperienced. It was not until he won the primary of West Virginia, a largely Protestant state, that Kennedy was seen as potentially electable.

Then came 1968. On November 30, 1967, a little-known Senator from Minnesota, Eugene McCarthy, announced his intention to challenge the incumbent president, Lyndon Johnson, for the Democratic party nomination. In the state of New Hampshire, the White House made an all-out effort to mobilize public support behind the incumbent president. The effort was not very successful with Johnson receiving less than 50 percent of the vote and McCarthy garnering 41.9 percent. Then on March 16, another insurgent candidate, Robert Kennedy, entered the race for the Democratic nomination. On March 31, Lyndon Johnson announced that he was pulling out of the race. His vice president and heir apparent, Hubert Humphrey, delayed his formal declaration of intent to seek the nomination until April 27, after all the final deadlines for the primaries had passed.

At the Democratic convention that year in Chicago, Humphrey won the nomination on the first ballot with 67 percent of the delegate vote. Even in fifteen primary states, 53 percent of the delegates voted for Humphrey abandoning the wishes of the voters in their state. In 1968, most states used some form of appointment in delegate selection. Either the Governor, the state party committee, or other state committees appointed all or some of the state's delegates to the party's national convention.

As in 1952, the candidate chosen by the Democratic national convention went on to be defeated in the general election. In the aftermath of defeat, the McGovern-Fraser Commission was organized by the Democratic Party to reform the delegate selection process to make it more representative of the rank-and-file voters in the party. The results were the extended use of the primary system and a more open and inclusive process in the states that continued to use the caucus system. The

Republican Party has moved in a similar direction although less emphasis has been placed on making the delegate population demographically representative of the Republican voters.

Once selected, by either state caucus or state primary, the delegates attend their party's national nominating convention in the summer before the November general election. Originally, the party conventions actually determined the nominee of the party. Today, the conventions merely ratify the decisions made in the state caucuses and primaries. The conventions have become extravagant media events that are used by the parties to whip up enthusiasm for the nominee and the party platform.

The most widely watched part of the convention is the last night when the keynote speaker gives an address reviewing the history of the party and promising a bright future for it. A party spokesperson who reviews the candidate's background and experience then places each candidate in nomination. The roll call of the states follows, formally nominating the party's presidential nominee. The presidential and vice presidential candidates give their acceptance speeches to much cheering. Those who fought for the nomination are often welcomed on stage in a show of party unity.

Special Interests and the Nominating Conventions

While the delegate selection process has become more open to the rank-and-file members of the parties, the party conventions themselves provide special privileges to the party leadership and the interest groups that support them. For example, one tradition at the national party conventions is the parties thrown for Members of Congress by special interest groups and corporations with business pending before Congress. Special interests sponsor these events to honor Members, who in many cases have direct influence over legislation affecting their industries.

Members of Congress take special advantage of the rules surrounding conventions, which exempt them from the federal ban on gift taking. A 1995 law forbids Members of Congress from taking gifts worth more than $50 from interest group lobbyists. However, Congress left the door open during the conventions by exempting themselves from the rule during special events. Members are not even required to disclose sponsors of their events and how much the sponsors gave.

Additionally, in the wake of the new ban on "soft money" enacted as part of the 2002 McCain-Feingold law (to be discussed later in this chapter), which prevents the national political parties from accepting unlimited contributions from special interests, corporate cash has instead been pouring into the coffers of the nonprofit host committees for the Democratic and Republican conventions. Despite McCain-Feingold, these donations are still completely unlimited.

As a candidate in 2008, Barack Obama vowed to squelch the role of special interests in financing the party conventions. So, he barred corporations and lobbyists from contributing money to the Democrats 2012 national convention in Charlotte, North Carolina. Organizers, however, found ways to skirt the rules and give corporations and lobbyists a presence at the nominating convention. Despite the ban on corporate money, convention officials encouraged corporate executives to write personal checks and suggested that corporations could participate by donating goods and services to the convention, and by giving up to $100,000 through a corporate foundation. They also quietly explained to lobbyists that while they could not make contributions, they could help raise money from their clients by soliciting personal checks from executives or in-kind contributions from corporations. Lobbyists who complied then received perks like premium credentials and hotel rooms.[3]

The 2016 Republican Convention in Cleveland was the first convention to be almost totally underwritten by private money coming primarily from corporate lobbyists and Super PACs that candidate Trump had railed against. The Republican National Committee's near total dependence on private money is the direct result of a series of recent federal rule changes that eliminated public funding for conventions and made it easier for parties to rake in unlimited sums of private cash, with no extra oversight. The new rules, which passed with little fanfare in 2014, allow individual mega donors to give ten times more to national parties than they could in 2012. They also failed to close a loophole allowing corporations, lobbying firms, Super PACs, and special interest groups, which are formally prohibited from giving to the parties' conventions, to give unlimited amounts through special, non-profit committees, which are not bound by normal disclosure rules.[4]

Independent and Third-Party Nominees

Recent elections have seen strong independent candidates emerge: Ross Perot in 1992 and 1996 and Ralph Nader in 2000, 2004, and 2008. It is not easy for independent and third-party candidates to get on the ballot. State laws control access to the ballot, and Democratic and Republican legislators and governors make those laws. Unsurprisingly, the candidates of the Democratic and Republican Parties are automatically placed on the ballot in all fifty states. Independent candidates, on the other hand, must demonstrate significant support to get on the ballot through petitions signed by voters. In 2020, Senator Bernie Sanders, a self-described socialist who ran for the Senate as an Independent, was able to run as a candidate for the Democratic nomination because he, as mandated by the rules of the Democratic National Committee, signed an affidavit affirming that he is a member of the Democratic Party, would run as a Democrat, and if elected, serve as a Democrat.

Nominations for Congress and State Offices

Today, most candidates for major national and state offices are nominated through the primary election system. Thirty-seven states use primary elections to nominate candidates for all state and national offices. Primaries play at least some role in the nomination process in several other states.

Ross Perot, May 2, 1980
Photo credit: UTSA's Institute of Texan Cultures

Because partisan redistricting (discussed later in this chapter) has ensured that fewer general elections for the U.S. House of Representatives are meaningfully competitive, the primary election of the dominant party is often the most important race in many districts and money is now a key factor in determining primary election outcomes. In 2020, the party committees, alone, raised a combined $947 million for congressional and state campaigns.[5] A recent study has found that only about 5 percent of Americans donate to national political candidates and 12 percent donate across all campaigns, federal, state, and local. The study also found that a tiny share of Americans makes donations of more than $200.[6]

Many powerful incumbents have accumulated large war chests of campaign money which then further hinders electoral competition in the primary elections. Many of the 2020 congressional primary races featured only one candidate seeking his or her party's nomination, providing voters with no real choice on primary election day.[7] One reason for this is that large financial advantages of incumbents discourage meaningful competition. Normally, incumbents in Congress have an enormous financial advantage over their challengers. This is one of the reasons why congressmen's re-election rates are so high. During the 2020 election cycle, on average, incumbents in the U.S. House of Representatives enjoyed a fund-raising advantage of over one million dollars more than their challengers.

Voting turnout in primary elections tends to be relatively low, usually with less than one quarter of eligible voters participating. While the 2018 congressional midterm elections saw the highest turnout in 40 years, the 2020 primary elections did not bring a tidal wave of voters to the polls. Part of this was due, no doubt, the fact that many of the primaries took place during the height of the pandemic. Even if turnout is low, the nomination process almost certainly requires candidates to reach millions of voters across the fifty states. This has certain consequences for campaigning. First, the process takes time. Technically the selection process begins in February with the Iowa state caucuses. These are followed by the New Hampshire primaries. Even though only a very few delegates are selected in the small states of Iowa and New Hampshire, an exorbitant amount of media coverage and public attention attaches to them. The candidates victorious in these states will gain momentum from the early recognition as "winners."

In truth, the selection process begins way before February. Competitive candidates must raise huge sums of money to establish themselves as serious contenders. In 2016, Hillary Clinton was viewed as the likely Democratic candidate way before Iowa and New Hampshire because she had financial reserves unmatched by the other Democratic hopefuls.

The second upshot of this lengthy, complex nomination process is that candidates win the nomination largely on the basis of the resources they can bring, on their own, to the campaign. The national party organization will usually refrain from backing one of their party's hopefuls over the others. There is little incentive for the party to play favorites so early in the game when so much is still uncertain. In 2020, sixty-three House candidates cumulatively chipped in more than $7 million of their own money in only six months. Many of the candidates who rely on self-funding tend to be wealthy outsiders, who run against the Washington establishment.[8]

THE GENERAL ELECTIONS

By national law all 435 seats in the House of Representatives and one-third of the seats in the United States Senate must be filled every two years in the general election, held the first Tuesday after the first Monday in November of an even numbered year. In the years when a president is elected as well, the election is called a presidential election. In the years when no president is to be elected, the elections are called off-year congressional, or midterm, elections.

House Elections

Single-Member Plurality Elections

There is a series of steps involved in electing the House of Representatives that begins long before the November election of an even numbered year. The first step actually occurs every ten years: the United States Census. As mandated by the United States Constitution, every ten years an attempt is made to get an accurate count of every person residing in this country, legal and illegal (at least according to 1992 court decisions). Since 1911, the number of seats in the House has been set at 435; so, after the census, the total number of people living in the U.S. is divided by the number of seats, 435. Following the 2010 census, this will yield a number, 710,767, which is the number of people to be represented by each member of the House. The 435 seats are then apportioned to each of the states on the basis of its state population. For example, a state with the population of 1.4 million would be given two seats in the House. After the 2010 census, California was allotted 53 and Alaska 1. Washington D.C. has no seats in the House because it is not a state. After the state is told how many seats it has in the House, it must divide its state population into that number of congressional districts, each with approximately 711,000 people. This reshuffling that occurs every ten years is known as **reapportionment**.

In November, the nation votes as 435 separate congressional districts. Each district chooses one single member on the basis of which candidate gets the most votes, a plurality (not necessarily a majority). These elections are called **single-member plurality elections**.

The Framers of the American Constitution chose the single-member system to ensure that the pluralist nature of American society would be represented at the national level. Rather than adopting the European system of multi-member proportional representation in which the national popular vote is represented proportionally in a national legislature, the American system allows each small district to produce a leader to represent the dominant interest in that district. The result of such a system is that the members of the House of Representatives are usually selected because they are perceived as serving *that* district. A House member is not intended nor expected to represent the interests of the nation as a whole. As a result, voters may decide to vote for one party for the House and a different party for the presidency. In the twenty-one elections between 1952-2020, voters opted for unified control only nine times. For the past 50 years, not too long after one party achieves unified control, Americans almost reflexively put the other in charge of at least one branch of government. Such was the case in 2018, when voters returned the House of Representatives to Democratic control, leaving the presidency and the Senate in the hands of the Republicans.

An additional upshot of the single-member plurality system is that a party's share of the popular vote need not necessarily be reflected in the number of seats that party has in the House. In fact, Republicans have won a smaller percentage of seats than votes in every House election since 1954. Why? One reason is that in single-member plurality elections, the candidate who gets even one more vote than the other candidate or candidates wins the election. So, if in 275 districts the Democrats win by a small margin of 51 percent to the Republicans 49 percent and in the remaining 160 districts the Republican candidates each win with 90 percent to the Democratic candidates' 10 percent, more votes across all 435 districts will have been cast for the various Republicans but the final House delegation will consist of 275 Democrats and only 160 Republicans.

A second reason why party representation in the House may not mirror the popular vote is that some of the congressional districts have been gerrymandered by some of the state legislatures that are responsible for the drawing of district lines. **Gerrymandering** is the drawing of state district lines to benefit the political chances of one party's candidates over the other party's. Using lists of registered voters, which include the voter's party affiliation and place of residence, the political party that controls a state legislature could be tempted to draw the district lines so that their registered voters are a plurality in as many districts as possible, while the opposing party's registered voters are lumped in the remaining few districts.

The result of such gerrymandering is that the opposition party will carry only the few districts where they have been isolated. Gerrymandering effectively wastes the opposition party's votes, since the party only needs a plurality. Today, North Carolina, Maryland, Pennsylvania, West Virginia, Kentucky, Louisiana, Utah, Texas, Arkansas, and Ohio have all been gerrymandered. In

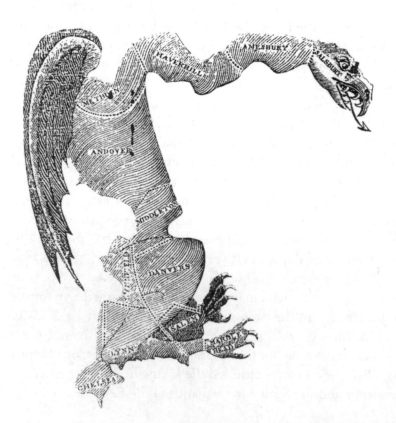

An early depiction of Governor Gerry's "Gerrymander." Gerry had this Massachusetts district drawn to ensure the election of a Democrat. The original drawing was created by cartoonist Elkanah Tinsdale in 1812.

June 2019, the Supreme Court, in a 5 to 4 decision, ruled that federal courts are powerless to hear challenges to such partisan gerrymandering. The drafters of the Constitution, Chief Justice John G. Roberts Jr. wrote for the majority, understood that politics would play a role in drawing election districts when they gave the task to state legislatures. Judges, the Chief Justice said, are not entitled to second-guess lawmakers' judgments.[9]

Criticisms of the Single-Member System

Many say that the American system is the worst ever invented.[10] Mathematicians first began to take the problems with plurality seriously in the years leading up to the French Revolution. In the 1770s, Jean-Charles Borda showed that pluralities pick the most popular candidate only in two-person races. In elections involving three or more candidates, the one with the plurality might easily lose when matched up against each of the other candidates one on one.[11]

Plurality systems, used in most U.S. elections, hand victory to the candidate with the most votes even if that candidate falls short of a majority and even if the candidate is the person the majority likes least. The current system, then, can fail to reflect the wishes of most of the people much of the time.

Various alternative systems have been suggested. One alternative is the approval voting system. **Approval voting** allows voters to choose any number of candidates. The candidate with the most total votes then wins. Approval voting has its own problems, however. It tends to produce bland, mediocre winners who lack the sharp edges that tend to turn voters off. Another alternative solution would be **cumulative voting,** in which voters can pile up several votes for a single candidate they feel strongly about. Each voter would have as many votes as candidates running and distribute those votes among the candidates or give them all to one candidate. Many feel that this would give minorities more say in American elections, without creating race-based districts. Any group that has sufficient cohesion to vote as a bloc could greatly affect the outcome of an election. Cumulative voting has been around for over one hundred years and is widely used in the private sector to elect corporate boards of directors.

The problem with all of these alternative plans is that since 1967, federal law has required that all states use single-member congressional districts. The law, passed in 1967, was designed to prevent minority votes from being diluted in at-large elections in Southern states. Ironically, scholars like Lani Guinier now argue the rule actually works to impede minority representation.[12] New legislation would be needed if change is to be made. A Washington based activist group, the Center for Voting and Democracy, helped draft legislation introduced in Congress by former Democratic Representative Cynthia McKinney of Georgia, an African American whose district prompted the Supreme Court ruling rejecting the use of race in drawing district lines. Her bill, which did not pass, would have permitted states to experiment with alternative voting schemes.

Many who study the American system see it as the worst of all worlds. Indeed, the United States is the only democracy that gives the plurality winner all the power. And the system does so not just at the House level but at the Electoral College level as well (discussed below). Robert Richie, the director of the Center for Voting and Democracy, says that "the current system is just a disaster for most voters and it's getting worse and worse."[13]

Senate Elections

Even though senators are elected by a statewide popular vote, their elections are just as likely to produce a split government, with one party in control of the Senate and another in control of the White House. One reason is that, similar to the House, a voter may perceive his or her state's two senators to be representatives of his or her state, not the entire nation. Voters are less likely to think about national issues like foreign affairs and international trade than they are to think foremost of what a candidate can do for their state.

As in the House, incumbent members seeking re-election enjoy a significant advantage. Incumbents are known to use their office to deliver valuable goods and services to their districts, in the case of House members, and states, in the case of senators. Incumbents are prone to support pork-barrel legislation, laws that deliver the *bacon* to the district or state. Challengers have a much more difficult time of it. They can make promises, but they lack a record of delivery.

A second reason that Senate elections may produce a majority party different from that which controls the presidency is that Senate elections are staggered. Only one-third of the United States Senate is up for election in any two-year election. This results in exactly what the framers of the Constitution intended: a Senate that does not reflect the temporary passions of the moment. While the framers expected the House to be the repository of majority opinion, they designed the Senate to be a bastion to preserve the rights of minority viewpoints. While the majority may sweep the House and presidency, the Senate resists such popular tides. The result has often been divided government.

PRESIDENTIAL ELECTIONS

In contrast to both the House and Senate, the election of the president entails a two-step process.

The Electoral College

The Framers of the Constitution agreed that the president, being so singularly important, should be indirectly selected rather than directly elected by the voters. They further agreed that there would be a national body, the Electoral College, that would select the president every four years. Agreement broke down, however, on the question of exactly how the states would be represented in this Electoral College. Would small states have less representation or the same level of representation as the more populous states?

The final compromise created a formula for establishing representation in the Electoral College. Each state gets a number of Electoral College delegates, and, therefore, votes for president, equal to the number of representatives that state has in the House plus an additional two for its two Senators. This formula pleases the large states because they will have a greater number of seats in the College. But it also pleases the smaller states in that a state, no matter how small its population, will have three Electoral College delegates. Because the Twenty-third Amendment awards Washington, D.C. three Electoral College votes, the total number in the Electoral College comes to 538.

Each state legislature is designated by the Constitution to select the method of selection for electors to the Electoral College. All states have written laws designating the political parties as the institutions that will in some way select the electors. The most common ways are party convention or state party committee. For example, in Kentucky, state statute says that each political party shall choose the method by which they select electors. Both the Democrats and Republicans have selected the party convention. At the party convention, each party selects the number of electors each state is constitutionally guaranteed. Only party faithful will be chosen, and they will only vote for the presidential candidate from their party. In Florida, the governor officially chooses the electors. However, he must choose only those electors selected by the parties' state executive committee.

Then on election day in November of a presidential year, state populations vote. Although the names of the presidential candidates appear on the ballot, voters are actually not casting a vote for a candidate. Rather, the voter is casting his or her ballot for the candidate's slate of electors. Each state's popular vote is then counted. The candidate that wins the plurality of the popular votes "carries" the state and wins all of its electoral votes. This means that all of that candidate's slate is elected to the Electoral College. (There are two exceptions. In Maine two and in Nebraska three of the electoral votes are awarded by congressional district. The presidential candidate who carries each district wins a single electoral vote, and the statewide winner gets two additional electoral votes.)

In short, on the first Tuesday in November, all that has transpired is the election of the 538 members of the Electoral College. While the assumption is that these delegates will keep faith with the popular vote in their state, the Electoral College delegates do not actually cast their ballots for president until December. At that time, the winning state slates travel to their various state capitals and cast their votes. Occasionally electors have broken from the popular vote. While no elector has ever changed the outcome of an election by voting against his or her party's designated candidate, there have been, since the founding of the Electoral College, 167 faithless electors. Seventy-one of these votes were changed because the original candidate died before the day on which the Electoral College cast its votes. Three electors chose to abstain rather than vote for their party's nominee. The other 93 electoral votes were changed on the personal initiative of the elector.

Although it did not impact the outcome of the election, the 2016 election did have an abnormally high number of electors breaking with their political party. Ten "faithless electors" voted contrary to the candidate who had won their state. There were eight faithless electors among Democrats and two for Republicans. Four Washington state delegates opted not to vote for Hillary Clinton with three voting for former Secretary of State Colin Powell and one for Faith Spotted Eagle who had been fighting the Dakota Access Pipeline in North Dakota. Hawaii elector David Mulinix, a Democrat, cast a ballot for Bernie Sanders over Clinton.

A candidate must receive a majority vote of the Electoral College to become president. If none of the candidates receive these 270 votes, the presidential election is thrown to the House of Representatives. There each state delegation casts one vote, choosing between the top three candidates with the most Electoral College votes. This has only happened twice, once in 1800 and again in 1824, both before the establishment of a stable two-party system.

Table 6.1: Projected Electoral Votes based on the 2020 Census

Total: 538;   Majority Needed to Elect: 270

ALABAMA - 9	MONTANA - 4
ALASKA - 3	NEBRASKA - 5
ARIZONA - 12	NEVADA - 6
ARKANSAS - 6	NEW HAMPSHIRE - 4
CALIFORNIA - 54	NEW JERSEY - 14
COLORADO - 10	NEW MEXICO - 5
CONNECTICUT - 7	NEW YORK - 28
DELAWARE - 3	NORTH CAROLINA - 16
DISTRICT OF COLUMBIA - 3	NORTH DAKOTA - 3
FLORIDA - 30	OHIO - 18
GEORGIA - 16	OKLAHOMA - 7
HAWAII - 4	OREGON - 8
IDAHO - 4	PENNSYLVANIA - 19
ILLINOIS - 19	RHODE ISLAND - 3
INDIANA - 11	SOUTH CAROLINA - 9
IOWA - 6	SOUTH DAKOTA - 3
KANSAS - 6	TENNESSEE - 11
KENTUCKY - 8	TEXAS - 40
LOUISIANA - 8	UTAH - 6
MAINE - 4	VERMONT - 3
MARYLAND - 10	VIRGINIA - 13
MASSACHUSETTS - 11	WASHINGTON - 12
MICHIGAN - 15	WEST VIRGINIA - 4
MINNESOTA - 9	WISCONSIN - 10
MISSISSIPPI - 6	WYOMING - 3
MISSOURI - 10	

Source: National Archives and Records Administration—U.S. Federal Election Commission
Last Update: 2/23/10

The Electoral College has several troubling aspects. The most worrisome is the possibility that the candidate who wins the most popular votes may not be elected president. This could happen if a candidate wins some states by a very large margin and loses by very narrow margins in the others. For example, if a candidate wins in the thirteen largest states with 51 percent of the vote and loses in the remaining states with only 10 percent of the vote, that candidate will become president although the other candidate would have received a greater number of popular votes. This has happened in four elections. In 1824, John Quincy Adams received fewer popular votes than Andrew Jackson. In that election, no candidate received a majority vote in the Electoral College, and the House went on to choose Adams over Jackson. In 1876, Rutherford Hayes received fewer popular votes than his opponent, Samuel Tildon, but still won the presidency with 50.1 percent of the Electoral College. In 1888, Grover Cleveland received 48.6 percent of the popular vote to Benjamin Harrison's 47.8 percent. Cleveland nevertheless lost to Harrison in the Electoral College by a vote of 168 to 233. In the election of 2000, George W. Bush won the presidency with 271 votes in the Electoral College even though he had fewer popular votes than his opponent Al Gore. Then this happened again in 2016. Donald Trump won the presidency despite the fact that his opponent, Hillary Clinton, received 3 million more popular votes, winning the popular vote by a margin of 2 percent.

A second undemocratic feature of the Electoral College is that not all states require their electors to cast their votes for the candidate who won the state's popular vote. The **faithless elector** (discussed above) is one who casts his or her vote for a personal choice, even a candidate who was not on the ballot. While the Framers of the American Constitution wanted the Electoral College delegates to be independent, from today's perspective the faithless elector is problematic.

Another troublesome aspect of the Electoral College is that it punishes third parties and their candidates. It is very difficult for a new, fledgling party to get more votes in any state than either of the two, well-established parties. It is not enough for a candidate to get votes; he has to get the most votes to get any representation in the Electoral College. The winner-take-all aspect of the Electoral College creates a psychology among voters that they are throwing away their votes in voting for a third party candidate. Even more disturbing is that third parties with wide support across the nation, say Ross Perot's candidacy in 1992, are the most punished. Parties that have a strong regional base, being concentrated in only certain states, like George Wallace's candidacy in 1968, have a much better chance of at least carrying a state or two and thereby receiving Electoral College representation. Some might argue that in choosing a president for the *nation*, regional parties might be better discouraged than those that have a fairly wide national appeal.

Abolish the Electoral College?

Given these significant issues, some have called for the abolishment of the Electoral College. There have been numerous proposals to revert to a direct, majoritarian popular vote. That none of these proposals has ever come close to adoption suggests that the Electoral College does have its advantages.

To begin with, the original intent of the framers was to design a strong national government but one that allowed for state representation at the national level. In fact, there is very little evidence that the Constitution was concerned with the representation of individuals; rather, the Constitution is concerned with the representation of the dominant interest in each congressional district, in the case of the House of Representatives, and each state, in the case of the Senate and Electoral College. Placed in this light, the Electoral College today continues to function effectively just as the framers intended.

Another advantage of the Electoral College is that it strengthens the mandate of the president. In our two-party system, most presidents have won with a fairly narrow margin of victory in the popular vote. Even in *landslides* like 1984, the president may win with only about 57 percent of the vote. The Electoral College takes very narrow state margins of victory and turns them into state unanimity in the Electoral College. Such amplification of the popular vote is especially important in elections like 1992 and 2016 when the winning candidate did not have even won a majority of the popular vote. In 1992, Clinton received only 43 percent of the popular vote and in 2016 Donald Trump received only 46 percent. The Electoral College system, however, allowed both Clinton and Trump to say they had received a majority because, at least at the Electoral College level, that was the case.

Finally, the Electoral College, as noted above, strengthens the two-party system by punishing third parties. A change in the Electoral College would require a constitutional amendment. Because every existing amendment to the Constitution has been proposed by two-thirds of the House and two-thirds of the Senate, the Democrats and Republicans in Congress would have to vote to break their own lock on the presidency. This is not likely.

CAMPAIGNING IN THE GENERAL ELECTION

The Political Context

The most important structural feature of a general election is whether an incumbent is seeking re-election or whether it is an open election in which there is no incumbent running. Incumbents enjoy an enormous advantage at all levels but especially in House and Senate elections. House incumbents have historically been almost impossible to defeat. The average rate of re-election for members of the House since 1964 has been 93.3 percent, and, over the last decade, it has been 96 percent. In the Senate, the average since 1964 has been 81.6 percent. Even in 2016, when anti-government sentiment hit a fever pitch, incumbents still did well with a re-election rate over 98 percent. Though the percentage was relatively low compared to previous years, there was no massive anti-incumbent movement ready to kick the establishment out of Congress. The median percent of the vote won by incumbents (65 percent) was in line with the historical average (68 percent). Even in the 2018 "Blue Wave" election, retirements were only 13 percent of the House and in 2020, only thirty-six House incumbents retired. This refutes the notion that many incumbents decided not to run or lost in the primaries. Incumbents enjoy such an advantage, at least in part, because of their ability to attract greater campaign contributions. Money is extremely important in modern campaigns.

Financing Campaigns

How Much Campaigns Cost

The 2018 election was the most expensive midterm congressional election in American history, by far, with total spending surpassing $5.7 billion.[14] Two years later, the total cost of the 2020 presidential election reached nearly $14 billion, making it the costliest election in history and surpassing the $7 billion spent in 2016.[15] The Democratic nominee, Joe Biden, is the first candidate in history to raise $1 billion from donors.

The huge campaign contributions were largely driven by rapidly increased spending among "super PACs" and outside groups that can raise unlimited amounts of money from donors. Spending by outside groups reached to more than $1.1 billion for the 2016 cycle and then more than doubled in 2020.[16] These estimates could substantially understate the total amount of money spent in 2020 for hundreds of millions of additional dollars were spent below the radar by groups that do not register with the Federal Election Commission and purport to focus on educational, not political, activities. Such groups spent at least another $500 million in the last two months of the campaign, a window during which federal law requires formal disclosure of any expenditures that mention a candidate, and they spent even more earlier in the campaign cycle on "issue ads" that are not subject to disclosure. The biggest expansion of outside spending was in the battle for the House and Senate. In 2020, almost $16 million was donated to elect one candidate for the House of Representatives.

In the wake of the Supreme Court's *Citizens United* case, individual megadonors have been playing an increasingly important role in funding campaigns. Large, individual contributions, defined by the Federal Election Commission as $200 or more, accounted for $2.9 billion of the $4 billion in individual contributions to candidates and part committees in 2018. The ten biggest megadonors combined poured $436 million into that election. For example, Sheldon and Miriam Adelson gave more than $123 million to help Republicans while Michael Bloomberg gave $90 million to help Democrats. Only 15.84 percent of all donations come from small donations from individuals while 47.09 percent comes from these megadonors.[17] These figures do not take into account issue ad spending that will be discussed below.

Where Does the Money Come From?

As of 2020, for presidential and congressional elections, donors may contribute up to $2,800 per candidate for each of the primary and general elections, or $5,600 during an election cycle. In order for a contribution to count towards the primary election limit, it must be made prior to the date of the primary election. For presidential candidates, the primary election ends on the date the candidate accepts their party's nomination. Donors may contribute up to $35,500 per calendar year to the general account of a national party committee. They may contribute up to an additional $106,500 per calendar year to each of (1) a national party's account specifically set up to fund legal proceedings and recounts; and (2) a national party's account specifically set up to defray certain office and building expenses. Contributions up to $5,000 per calendar year to a federal PAC are permissible and an unlimited amount may be made to super PACs. The collective maximum amount donors can contribute to state, district, and local parties for a federal election is $10,000 per calendar year. There are many ways, however, around these laws as the history and current state of American campaign finance suggest.

Regulating Campaign Finance

The way in which campaigns are financed in this country has changed dramatically over the last thirty-five years primarily because of changes in national campaign finance laws. Congress began to regulate campaign finance as early as the 1920s through a variety of federal corrupt practices acts. The first, passed in 1925, limited primary and general election expenses for congressional candidates. Then in the 1930s, Congress prohibited, by law, corporate and bank contributions. Then the Hatch Act (Political Activities Act) was passed in 1939 in another attempt to control political influence buying. The Hatch Act forbade contributions by government employees and individuals and companies receiving government funds, for example in the form of government contracts. In 1943, Congress went on to outlaw labor union contributions.

These early laws provided no avenue for enforcement. How could Congress know whether its laws had been violated? There was no effective way to make candidates fully disclose where they got their money or where they were spending it for that matter. The Watergate scandal of 1972 and the investigations that followed made it clear that abuse of the campaign finance system was rampant. It was discovered that large amounts of money had been illegally funneled to Nixon's committee to re-elect the president (CREEP). Congress acted quickly to prevent continued abuse of the system.

The Federal Election Campaign Act (FECA) of 1971 essentially replaced all past laws and instituted major reform. The law requires all candidates to fully disclose all contributions and expenditures in excess of $100. The effectiveness of this law was soon apparent. In 1968 before disclosure was strictly demanded, candidates reported spending $8.5 million. Only four years later, in 1972, the candidates reported to the FECA that they had spent $88.9 million.[18] The 1971 law also tried to limit the amount that each individual could spend of his own money in running for office. In *Buckley v. Valeo* the Supreme Court declared that provision of the law unconstitutional.[19]

In closing one loophole, that having to do with disclosing campaign finance information, the 1971 law opened another. The FECA said that it was permissible for corporations and labor unions to set up "separate, segregated funds . . . that could be used for a political purpose." This led to the creation of a large number of **PACs (political action committees)** that could now channel corporate, labor, and other interest group money to candidates. For a PAC to be legal, the money must be raised from at least fifty volunteer donors and must be contributed to at least five candidates in the federal election. Each corporation or each union is limited to one PAC.

In 1974, Congress amended the Federal Election Campaign Act. These amendments created the Federal Election Commission (FEC) to enforce compliance with the requirements of the act. Presidential candidates would be provided with public financing for the primaries and general elections if they agreed to limit their campaign expenditures to the amount prescribed by the law. In addition, the law limited individuals to campaign contributions of no more than $1,000 per candidate (since lifted to $2,800), $5000 per PAC, $10,000 to a state party committee, and $32,400 to a national party committee. Groups and PACs could contribute up to $5,000 per candidate in any election, primary and general.

The FECA was again amended in 1976 in response to the provisions ruled unconstitutional by *Buckley v. Valeo* and again in 1979 to allow parties to spend unlimited amounts of hard money on activities like increasing voter turnout and registration. In 1979, the Federal Election Commission ruled that political parties could spend unregulated or "soft" money for non-federal administrative and party building activities. Later, this money was used for candidate related issue ads, which led to a substantial increase in soft money contributions and expenditures in elections. This in turn created pressures leading to passage of the Bipartisan Campaign Reform Act ("BCRA").

The Bipartisan Campaign Reform Act of 2002

In 2002, Congress approved the first major overhaul of the nation's campaign finance system in a quarter century, breaking a nearly decade-long impasse that thwarted efforts to reduce the influence of big money in American politics. The Bipartisan Campaign Reform Act (also known as McCain-Feingold) bans unrestricted soft money to the political parties, restricts end-of-the-campaign advertising by outside groups, and raises limits on direct cash contributions to $2000 to a candidate, $5000 to a PAC, and $25,000 to a political party. Corporations, unions, and other groups would still be allowed to pay for issue advertisements but not within 60 days before a general election and 30 days before a primary election.

Legal Challenges to BCRA

In January 2010, in *Citizens United vs. Federal Election Commission,* the U.S. Supreme Court struck down a major portion of the McCain-Feingold campaign finance law that prevented union and corporate paid issue ads in the final 30 days of election campaigns. The Court also ruled that corporations can spend as much as they want to support candidates running for Congress or president. The High Court based its opinion on its previously stated position (*Buckley v. Valeo*) that the First Amendment protects political speech and money spent in furtherance of promoting and disseminating political speech. The Court noted that historically and legally, corporations do enjoy First Amendment rights to free speech; and that the federal campaign law criminalizing the corporate act of simply using its lawful monies to disseminate lawful political speech, is in fact an unlawful restraint of protected speech.

The decade that has followed *Citizens United* has proven to be by far the most expensive in the history of U.S. elections. Independent groups have spent billions to influence crucial races, supplanting political parties as the principal campaign fundraisers. Wealthy donors have expanded their political power by injecting unprecedented sums into elections. Secret spending has skyrocketed as "dark money" groups have found new ways to make donations without transparency.

This explosion of secret spending is not due to *Citizens United* alone. It has been enabled by a number of subsequent court decisions that have removed several restrictions in campaign finance law, by inaction from Congressional and Federal Election Commission failure to place limits on such donations. Because Congress and the FEC remain deeply divided, the crazy quilt of campaign finance rules remained in place in 2020 and are very likely to remain well into the future.

Loopholes in Campaign Finance Reform

Despite some attempts to limit the flow of money into politics, campaign spending continues to skyrocket. The money is coming in through a variety of loopholes, some tried and true and some more newly minted.

Soft Money to State Political Parties

The McCain-Feingold reforms permit state party committees to continue to raise soft money and on June 22, 2002, the Federal Election Commission amended the Bipartisan Campaign Reform Act with a series of regulations that permit broader activities by state committees. Additionally, on November 13, 2008, the national Republican Party sued the Federal Election Commission, seeking to overturn prohibitions on unregulated corporate and labor contributions and to make it easier to coordinate spending with federal candidates. The lawsuits came after the defeat of Republican presidential candidate John McCain, a fierce opponent of soft money and one of the authors of the 2002 legislation that banned the parties from raising unlimited money from corporations, unions and wealthy individuals. The RNC lawsuit said the total ban on soft money amounts to a violation of the First Amendment's guarantees of free speech and association.[20]

The 527 and 501c Organizations and Independent Expenditures

When the Supreme Court upheld the McCain-Feingold ban on unlimited donations to political parties and other groups, so-called "soft money," it had no illusions about the difficulties faced in trying to reduce the role of money in politics. "Money, like water, will always find an outlet," wrote Justices John Paul Stevens and Sandra Day O'Connor.[21] For despite passage of the new campaign finance law in 2002, soft money is still finding a niche in elections. While the McCain-Feingold legislation approved in 2002 banned the parties from receiving unlimited contributions from unions, corporations, and individuals, the Democratic and Republican national committees together raised over $250 million by May 2004, more than what they collected during the same period in 2000 when soft money was allowed. In 2020, there were 2,197 super PACs which together raised almost $3 billion dollars and spent over $2 billion.

Table 6.2

**Top Ten
2020 Super PACs**

PAC	Total Expenditures
Senate Leadership Fund	$308,903,019
Senate Majority PAC	$254,078,491
Congressional Leadership Fund	$143,102,553
America First Action	$128,740,060
Preserve America PAC	$84,827,061
Club for Growth Action	$63,538,204
Independence US PAC	$30,613,510
American Bridge 21st Century	$73,320,492
The Lincoln Project	$67,378,750
LCV Victory Fund	$55,956,948

These data are based on records released by the OpenSecrets.org on November 8, 2020.

The soft money is now also coming in through donations by two other types of independent groups. The 527s are political organizations as identified in their tax filings with the Internal Revenue Service. The number "527" refers to the section of the tax code that governs such entities. These groups are typically parties, candidates, committees or associations organized for the purpose of influencing an issue, policy, appointment or election, be it federal, state or local. Such organizations can raise unlimited funds from individuals, corporations or labor unions, but they must register with the IRS and disclose their contributions and expenditures. In 2020, 527 groups spent over $750 million during the 2020 election cycle.[22]

A second type of advocacy group is the 501c groups which are nonprofit, tax-exempt groups organized under section 501(c) of the Internal Revenue Code that can engage in varying amounts of political activity, depending on the type of group. For example, 501(c)(3) groups operate for religious, charitable, scientific or educational purposes. These groups are not supposed to engage in any political activities, though some voter registration activities are permitted. 501(c)(4) groups are commonly called "social welfare" organizations that may engage in political activities, as long as these activities do not become their primary purpose. Similar restrictions apply to Section 501(c)(5) labor and agricultural groups, and to Section 501(c)(6) business leagues, chambers of commerce, real estate boards and boards of trade.

State regulations on the independent expenditures of these groups are now likely to fall as well. The *Citizens United* case overturned the Supreme Court's earlier decision in the 1990 case, *Austin v. Michigan Chamber of Commerce,* which held that the Michigan Campaign Finance Act, which prohibited corporations from using treasury money to support or oppose candidates in elections, did not violate the First and Fourteenth Amendments. States are left little room to try and control the independent expenditures of these groups.

Many states do not even have laws that effectively regulate independent expenditures. In 2015 and 2016, $404.1 million was spent independently on state elections in 30 states tracked by the National Institute on Money in State Politics, surpassing the record set in 2013 and 2014 by $32 million.[23] The bulk of the spending continues to be devoted to a handful of races financed by a handful of spenders. For example, only 15 percent of the spenders accounted for 91 percent of the money independently spent. In only 20 states, legislative candidates received $175.2 million, up 63 percent from 2014 and up 105 percent from 2012.[24]

Issue-Related Advertisements

The most controversial provisions of the 2002 campaign finance reform had to do with the law's prohibition of issue-related advertisements that refer to a federal politician within 30 days of a primary election and 60 days of a general election. In June 2007, the Supreme Court, in a 5 to 4 decision, ruled that issue ads immediately before federal elections are not banned by the campaign finance reform law. Then in its 2010 landmark *Citizens United* ruling, the Supreme Court held that the federal government could not limit corporations, unions, associations, or individuals from spending money to influence the outcome of elections. This ruling led to the creation of super PACs which cannot make contributions directly to a candidate or campaign but can engage in unlimited spending independently of campaigns. The Center for Public Integrity estimates that the *Citizens* ruling allowed nearly one billion dollars to enter campaign coffers with $933 million coming directly from the companies, unions and individuals who took advantage of *Citizens United* to funnel money into super PACs.[25]

The FEC records show that about two-thirds of all the *Citizens United*-fueled money went to ten super PACs or political nonprofits, nine of which focused exclusively on buying media spots and ads for candidates. The proliferation of controversial political advertisements in the past de-

At the CPAC 2011, former Mass. Gov. Mitt Romney, seeking to build on his momentum as a leading candidate from the 2008 GOP nomination process, took more direct aim at Obama, delivering a speech loaded with stinging criticisms of the administration.
Credit: RTTNews

cade is a direct result of the Supreme Court's 2010 *Citizens United v. Federal Election Commission* ruling, which helped pump billions of dollars into politics from outside sources that are supposed to be untethered from candidates or political parties. Sheila Krumholz, executive director of the Center for Responsive Politics has said, "In our 35 years of following the money, we've never seen a court decision transform the campaign finance system as drastically as *Citizens United*. We have a decade of evidence, demonstrated by nearly one billion dark money dollars, that the Supreme Court got it wrong when they said political spending from independent groups would be coupled with necessary disclosure.[26]

Analysis of 2020 campaign spending also demonstrates the truth of the widely-held suspicion that little if any firewall separates super PACs from the candidates' actual campaigns. While the Federal Election Commission bans coordination between the super PAC and the actual campaign, these rules were easily skirted through the 2020 contest. In some cases, super PACs even shared mailing addresses and offices with the chosen candidate's own election campaign.[27]

Bundling

Another consequence of the Bipartisan Campaign Reform Act of 2002 limitation upon personal contributions from any one individual ($2700 for each election, with a total of $4800 for a primary and general election) and its prohibition of soft money contributions to political parties is that campaigns have shifted gears into "hard money" contributions. Instead of handing over one $100,000 check to a candidate's party (soft money), the influence peddler now hands a candidate 50 checks from different contributors of $2,700 each (hard money). This is all perfectly legal, and has an enormous effect on buying influence with the candidate or officeholder. This method is called "bundling." Bundling is the fundraising practice of pooling together a large number of contributions from PACs and individuals in order to maximize the political influence of the bundler and the interests they represent. Most often, the bundler is a corporate executive or lobbyist, with expectations of something in return. While there are disclosure requirements for bundling, they only go into effect when a bundler personally hands over checks. Most campaigns get around the disclosure provision by not having the bundler ever touch the checks. Bundling has always existed in various forms, but became organized in a more structured way in the 2000s, spearheaded by the

"Bush Pioneers" for George W. Bush's 2000 and 2004 presidential campaigns. In 2020, President Trump's re-election campaign focused on the 2014 legal changes that allow campaigns to collect six-figure donations by committees working with the national party organization. Thanks to joint fund-raising agreements between the campaign, the national committee and 22 state parties, the Trump political operation increased the maximum contribution it could accept to $580,600 per person, giving wealthy donors the ability to bundle even more of their money.[28]

Effects of the American Campaign Finance System

The Incumbency Advantage

While the COVID-19 pandemic continued to spread across the country, congressional incumbent's seeking re-election were re-elected at a staggering rate, in most cases, expanding their vote shares beyond their previous election's. Incumbents benefitted from a huge fundraising advantage over their challengers. House incumbents had a more than 7-to-1 financial advantage over their challengers. Incumbents have an even greater advantage in special-interest PAC fundraising, raising eight times the amount given to challengers. As Table 6.3 reveals, incumbents continued to enjoy a financial advantage in 2020.

Table 6.3

Incumbent Advantage
Average Raised for Campaign
2020 Election Cycle

	Senate	House
Incumbent	$20,233,173	$2,476,601
Challenger	$3,716,781	$376,562
Open Seat	$1,674,405	$568,618
Total	$5,169,322	$844,358

Based on data released by the FEC on November 3, 2020.

Selling Access and Influence

Americans have long worried that campaign contributions are a way for powerful individuals and groups to buy access to policy makers and to influence the policy making process. Concern with such influence peddling reached a crescendo immediately following the 2016 presidential election. In the 2020 race, Super Pacs raised nearly $2.5 billion, including $689 million for Biden and $367 million for Trump. In 2016, these donations paid off and are likely to similarly pay off in the aftermath of the 2020 election. Ten mega-donors, including casino magnate Sheldon Adelson and his wife Miriam, former New York mayor and media tycoon Michael Bloomberg, and billionaire George Soros, accounted for much of the Super PAC money. And as in past elections, big campaign contributions got rewarded. President Trump nominated six of his biggest donors and fundraisers to serve in his administration, lining up an unprecedented concentration of wealthy backers for top posts. The six nominees donated $11.6 million to his presidential campaign, allied Super PACs and the Republican National Committee. One single appointee, WWE co-founder Linda McMahon contributed $7.5 million and was then selected by Trump to run the Small Business Administration. Betsy DeVos, Michigan billionaire whose family co-founded Amway, contributed $1.8 million and was nominated Education Secretary, and Todd Ricketts' contribution of $1.3 million landed him the position of Deputy Commerce Secretary. While it is not unusual for top presidential donors to land plum assignments like ambassadorships in sough-after locales such as London and Paris, no president in recent history has filled a Cabinet with so many major donors.[29]

There is also evidence that campaign contributions allow powerful groups to influence public policy making. For example, both the coal and oil industries have mobilized vast resources to influence energy policy in the United States. Even though it has become very clear in recent years that American energy policy is at a crossroads, with experts agreeing that a shift in our energy and consumption is necessary to avert catastrophe brought on by global warming, there has been strong resistance to a major move away from a coal-fired electricity and oil-based economy to one based on alternative sources of renewable energy. In 2020, even in the middle of a pandemic when few were driving or flying, the estimated spending on television ads promoting coal and more oil and gas drilling or criticizing clean energy exceeded $70 million between January 2019 and June 2020.[30]

Weakening the Role of the Political Parties

As noted above, after the passage of the Bipartisan Campaign Reform Act, many of the soft money-funded activities previously undertaken by political parties were taken over by various groups. The *Citizens* decision then further fueled the rise of these nonprofit political action groups, such as Republican strategist Karl Rove's Crossroads GPS that has poured millions into campaigns. Business groups, unions, and interest groups spent upwards of $1.7 billion in 2016, including at least $180 million by groups that are not required to publicly disclose their donors. Anonymous outside interests have gone from being a relatively minor source of funding for campaign-season television ads to being the dominant player in 2020.[31]

A Weakening of the Public Finance System

As campaign money flows in from individuals, corporations, and interest groups, the public financing system is faltering. The public financing program offers presidential candidates a monthly taxpayer-financed match of up to $250 for each private contribution they raise during the primary season, up to total grants of approximately $18.6 million. To qualify, candidates must raise at least $5,000 in each of twenty states and abide by other requirements, including overall, state-by-state, and personal spending limits. Under current rules, candidates who accept matching funds in the primaries must also agree to limit their campaign spending for all of the primaries to $10 million (plus a cost-of-living adjustment). Within that, they must limit spending in each state to a dollar amount based on the state's population, and they cannot use more than $50,000 of their personal funds. What is more, candidates who take this money for the general election portion of the race must agree to limit spending to the level of the available public grant, $20 million, and not to accept private contributions at all.

Public financing of campaigns remains the least-used method of regulating money in elections, partly due to the result of the U.S. Supreme Court decision in *Buckley v. Valeo*. In that decision, the Court struck down a provision of the Federal Election Commission mandating public financing for presidential elections. States cannot require candidates to use public financing programs, and the financial advantages of private fundraising frequently prompt candidates to opt out of public financing programs, which often include expenditure limits for participants. Candidates who opt not to use public funds can solicit contributions from individuals, PACs, unions, parties, and corporations, without having to abide by state expenditure limits. No major party candidate has used public financing since Republican John McCain took $84 million in public funds in 2008. That year, Democrat Barack Obama rejected public funding and instead raised $368 million after securing the nomination, giving him a huge financial advantage over McCain, whom he defeated.

Increased Number of Personally Wealthy Candidates

The faltering of the public finance system is related to another effect of campaign finance laws: candidates who are either personally wealthy or who can appeal to many small donors by mass mailings and television will have an advantage. A candidate with only modest means and little television appeal will find it much more difficult to raise the money needed to finance a campaign. Recent campaigns have seen very wealthy candidates spend considerable amounts of their own money running for office. In 2016, presidential candidate Donald Trump's fortune was estimated by the media to be upwards of $3.7 billion. In 2020, the nominee of the Democratic Party, Joseph Biden, has an estimated net worth above $9 million. He has reported bringing in more than $15 million in the years since he left the Obama White House due to a vice presidential pension and a lucrative book deal.

Raising Campaign Money: A Distraction

Candidates are now forced to spend considerably greater amounts of time raising money. Particularly in congressional campaigns, which have no public funding, candidates must meet with many groups and many individuals to raise the money for a campaign. Insofar as many candidates for Congress are incumbent members of Congress themselves, these fund-raising activities constitute a significant distraction from legislative duties. Additionally, because fund raising activities are so demanding on a politician's time and energy, candidates are increasingly finding it more efficient to stay in the nation's capital, working the fund-raising party circuit. This means that trips home to their districts or states are made less frequently and constituents have, as a result, fewer opportunities to see their representatives. Such a focus on fund raising inside the belt of Washington, D.C., may work to insulate the politicians from the very constituents they seek to serve.

Abuse and Scandals: The Case of the Big Pharma

The phrase "Big Pharma" evokes notions of a modern-day villain, referring to an industry that many view as too powerful and too profitable to keep in check. America's disdain for the pharmaceutical industry reached fever pitch in 2015, after Turing Pharmaceuticals raised the price of its HIV treatment medication from $13.50 to a shocking $750 per pill. One observational study, which analyzed publicly available data on campaign contributions and lobbying in the US from 1999 to 2018, found that the pharmaceutical and health product industry spent $4.7 billion, an average of $233 million per year, on lobbying the U.S. federal government; $414 million on contributions to presidential and congressional electoral candidates, national party committees, and outside spending groups; and $877 million on contributions to state candidates and committees. Contributions were targeted at senior legislators in Congress involved in drafting health care laws and state committees that opposed or supported key referenda on drug pricing and regulation.[32]

Big Pharma's abuses have been widely documented. However, when it comes to eliminating unfair practices, little action has been taken. While likely reasons include the influence of lobbyists, revolving-door politics with former members of Congress becoming industry lobbyists, free-market ideologies, and government regulators' financial dependence on the pharmaceutical industry, campaign contributions are seen as laying the foundation of what is increasingly seen as the undue influence of Big Pharma.

Money and Campaigns: Prognosis for the Future

Two features of the American political landscape virtually ensure that money will play an ever-growing role in U.S. campaigns and elections. The first is the Supreme Court's heightened commitment in recent years to the Buckley V. Valeo finding that campaign money, both the giving and spending of, is a form of speech and, therefore, protected by the First Amendment to the Constitution. Former President Trump nominated three new members to the Supreme Court, bringing the number of conservatives likely to block government attempts to restrict campaign contributions to six.

While the current make-up of the Supreme Court suggests that new attempts to limit money in elections are not likely to pass muster with the Court, a second feature undermines the enforcement of the already existing laws. At present, there is no agency to provide effective oversight of campaign contributions. The Federal Election Commission (FEC) is the regulatory body established by the Federal Election Campaign Act of 1974 that is responsible for enforcing campaign finance laws. Common Cause and other citizen groups have long been critical of its effectiveness and willingness to perform the job it was created to do. Rather than providing swift rulings and forcefully policing the campaign finance system, they argue, the FEC is a failing agency that is built for gridlock and often held captive by the very elected officials that it is meant to police.

Under normal circumstances, the commission would have at least four members, the minimum required to meet, issue advisory opinions and approve enforcement action. Circumstances at the FEC, however, have been anything but normal. In 2020 the FEC had only three members, rendering it nearly powerless and the president's last nominee waited nearly three years for a Senate vote. Even if President Biden should get a new commissioner confirmed, campaign finance reform advocates lament that the agency has been hampered by structural issues, a lack of resources and partisanship that have weakened its ability to enforce the law and deter illegal election spending. They say the problem has been exacerbated by Republican leaders opposed to limits on campaign spending, who have sought to weaken the agency.[33]

CAMPAIGN STRATEGIES AND TACTICS

Polling

A good place for any candidate to begin his campaign is with an identification of the electorate's concerns. To do this, candidates have in modern times increasingly turned to pollsters and political consultants. According to year-end research tabulated by the Center for Responsive Politics, presidential candidates today spend almost $50 million on polling, surveys, and research.[34]

Well-funded candidates may begin with focus groups. These groups usually consist of ten to twenty people selected because they are representative of certain groups that a candidate particularly wants to target in his campaign. These small focus groups, questioned at great length and depth, provide a way to identify the values and issue preferences of likely voters. In 2020, for example, the Engagious Swing Voter Project conducted a large number of focus groups in key battleground counties. Each county had a disproportionately high number of swing voters who shifted their support from the nominee of one party to the other between the presidential elections of 2012 and 2016. Voters selected to participate in the groups consisted, then, of those who voted for Barack Obama in the 2012 election and then voted for Donald Trump in 2016, and those who voted for Mitt Romney in 2012 and then voted for Hillary Clinton in 2016. Engagious concluded that the 2020 election was about "Donald Trump, up or down."[35]

While focus groups are most useful in the early stages of the campaign, helping candidates identify issues of concern, other types of polls become more important as the campaign moves forward. A trend poll, for example, may be used to determine how well the candidate is doing and in what parts of the nation or state or district. In early October, tracking polls, using quick phone interviews of people on a daily basis, are used to make critical decisions about where the candidate should go and what he should try to convey.

Making the News

While polling helps the candidate tailor his message to the interests of the public, the candidate must also tailor his message to the needs of the news organizations. News values emphasize the dramatic, the conflict-laden, and the brief. Television, in particular, sees no value in airing long-winded statements by the candidates. Furthermore, most Americans have little interest in hearing them. Even newspaper readers are unlikely to read beyond the first paragraph of a story. As a result, candidates need to learn to speak in soundbites which are easily understood. They should be no longer than thirty seconds and preferably as short as ten seconds in length. For example, the 2016 Trump campaign was organized around "Making America Great Again" and in 2020 Biden called his campaign a "Fight for America's Soul."

Candidates also need to be concerned with news deadlines. It does little good for a candidate to make a major policy statement at 8:00 in the evening, too late for the national evening news, too stale for the next morning's breaking news. In fact, it may not be worth the candidate's trouble to make a policy statement at all. Given the media's preoccupation with image and the horserace aspects of a campaign, the candidate might be better to talk in generalities with good visuals running in the background.

The Tabloids

In 1992, the Twentieth Century Fund studied television coverage of that year's presidential campaign. They discovered the ascension of what they called the "new news." The new news consists of network morning shows, call-in talk shows, often with studio audiences, and other shows like *2020, Dateline, and TMZ*. These tabloid shows allow the candidates to bypass the established press.[36]

Perhaps nowhere has the sensationalizing of politics been more marked than on talk radio. In the late 1980s, AM radio was desperate for new content as listeners had migrated to FM, taking advertising dollars with them, and so on August 1, 1988, Rush Limbaugh debuted nationally on AM radio. While Limbaugh has said that he never intended to be a force in American politics, his radio show soon became exactly that offering up something Americans had never heard before. Trump's presidency is the ultimate testament to the power of talk-radio conservatism. In the winter of 2018, the president went directly to Rush Limbaugh to pledge that he would shut the government down if he did not get enough funds for his border wall. The power of radio hosts would have been unthinkable when Limbaugh first took the national airwaves in 1988, but over three decades, hosts have used the special bond forged with their audiences to largely reshape the Republican Party in their image.[37]

Advertising

In 2020, the spread of the coronavirus halted live campaign rallies, door-to-door organizing, and traditional sit-down interviews with candidates. Not surprisingly, advertising then took on an increased importance with a record $6.7 billion spent on television, radio, and digital advertising. This is nearly two times that spent in any other election cycle.[38] In addition, Michael Bloomberg himself spent over $1 billion in advertising![39]

Party strategists have begun to look beyond television and radio audiences to a whole new generation of Web surfers. While TV is still the dominant destination for political ad spending, spending on digital channels is increasing the fastest year over year. Political ad spending online topped $1 billion for the first time in 2016 up from only $22 million in 2008.[40] The digital ads serve as a quick and relatively cheap way for candidates to test out campaign messages, and the feedback from voters online from those digital ads can then be used to craft the television campaigns and even help presidential hopefuls figure out where they need to spend more time with voters.

Arguably, the online channel is more efficient than other forms of media, primarily television. There is as much, if not more, video inventory available online, and at much lower cost, including in-banner and in-stream video impressions that can be geo-targeted as well as targeted to specific demographic audiences. An additional advantage of online advertising is that political advertising online will not sell out, and candidates' ads do not run back-to-back against each other like they do on television. Furthermore, viewers cannot skip ads online, and if they are interested in learning more, they have only to click to the candidate's website where the candidate has an opportunity to immediately engage them.

The Internet, Social Media, and High-Tech Campaigning

In addition to online ads, campaigns are increasingly using e-mail to communicate with activists and raise money. Starting in 2004, blogs, which are personal, frequently updated Web pages that typically contain short essays on a particular topic, played a significant role. During the 2004 presidential campaign, Howard Dean blazed the trail of electronic campaigning through his use of these Web blogs and aggressive use of online fundraising helped transform the obscure former Vermont governor into a frontrunner for the Democratic nomination.

The importance of the Internet in American campaigns is likely to grow in the future. More than 312 million American adults, almost 90 percent of the population, now use the Internet Additionally, Web users are more likely to vote and to show an interest in politics.[41] Today, every candidate has a blog and new blogs are being added daily. They are becoming an alternative news universe, giving everyone with a PC and a Web connection access to the sorts of political gossip that was once available only to reporters on the campaign press bus.

By 2008 it became apparent that political information and political advertisements could now be made available on mobile phones. Broadband video was in 80-million phones and You Tube went mobile by the end of the 2009. In 2010, congressional candidates tried out these new virtual ways to reach voters. Then in 2016, two new technologies transformed campaign politics: Twitter and e-mail. It is safe to say that without Twitter Donald Trump would not be president, and without e-mail Hillary Clinton might have been president!

Donald Trump,
45th President of the United States of America

Currently, 72 percent of U.S. citizens of voting age actively use some form of social media, while 69 percent of Americans in the same group use Facebook alone.[42] While President Donald Trump's use of Twitter has been widely acknowledged, and certainly had a tremendous impact on the outcome of the 2016 elections, candidate Joseph Biden actually surpassed the President in many key engagement metrics. While President Trump has some 87 million followers on Twitter to Vice President Biden's 11 million followers, both candidates saw a massive and continuous increase in engagement during the 2020 election cycle.

The Mechanics of Elections

The presidential election of 2020 will no doubt go down in history as one of the strangest. While it was the most expensive campaign in history, costing an almost unimaginable $14 billion, it took four days to produce a victor and even then, with no concession from the opponent, and spawning almost forty lawsuits challenging the result. The oddity of the 2020 pandemic campaign and election, however, is in reality another in a fairly long chain of modern mechanically-challenged elections.

Hacking in the 2016 Election

On June 14, 2016, *The Washington Post* reported that hackers working for the Russian government accessed the Democratic National Committee's computer system, viewing staffers' e-mails. The Democratic National Committee has alleged that two Russian-backed groups called "Cozy Bear" and "Fancy Bear" tunneled into the committee's computer system. Then on July 25, WikiLeaks posted nearly 20,000 of these hacked e-mails. The e-mails included insults against Hillary Clinton's Democratic opponent, Bernie Sanders.

In December 2016, the FBI, the Department of Homeland Security and the Director of National Intelligence issued a joint statement accusing Russia of a decade-long cyber campaign targeting American government, infrastructure and citizens in general. President Obama then responded to this evidence by expelling 35 Russian diplomats suspected of spying, shutting down two Russian facilities in the United States, and signing an executive order outlining economic penalties for individuals and organizations involved in "tampering with, altering, or causing a misappropriation of information with the purpose or effect of interfering with or undermining election processes or institutions."[43]

The Pandemic and the 2020 Election Mechanics

The deadly pandemic of 2020 turned the act of voting upside down. Many voters expressed deep anxiety about casting their ballots in person. Many poll workers, often at high risk for infection because they are older adults, were also afraid to show up. The best alternative appeared to be early voting, using mail-in ballots, drop box ballots, even drive-through voting, but the use of these alternatives became engulfed in partisan politics with then President Donald Trump arguing that such early voting could be subject to widespread fraud. He urged his voters to vote on ground, on Election Day, and election officials worked to set up elaborate polling places that had socially distanced voting booths and hand sanitizers.

On Election Day 2020, high turnout, a massive number of mail-in ballots and slim margins between the two candidates all contributed to the delay in naming a winner. There was intense focus on Pennsylvania, where Biden led Trump by more than 27,000 votes, and Nevada, where the Democrat led by about 22,000. The prolonged wait added to the anxiety of a nation facing historic challenges, including the surging pandemic and deep political polarization. The former President Donald Trump stayed in the White House and out of sight, as more results trickled in and expanded Biden's lead in must-win Pennsylvania.

Meanwhile, Trump supporters rallied around a "Stop the Steal" campaign with lawsuits challenging the vote count spreading across several states. On November 4, the Trump campaign filed a lawsuit alleging a lack of access for poll watchers, people who observe the counting of votes, in the state of Pennsylvania. On the same day, the Trump campaign accused election officials of violating a judge's order to allow the poll watchers to be within six feet of the vote counters. Election officials insisted they behaved properly and appealed to the state's Supreme Court. There was also a legal challenge in Pennsylvania centering on the state's decision to count ballots that were postmarked by election day but arrived up to three days later. On November 6, Republicans appealed a lower court ruling to the United States Supreme Court, wanting all postal ballots received after election day to be disqualified. Another ongoing case disputed how long voters should be given to provide proof of identification if it was missing or unclear on their postal ballots. While voters are currently allowed to do this up to November 12, the Trump campaign filed a lawsuit on November 5 seeking to reduce this deadline by three days. And on November 9, the Trump campaign filed a further lawsuit to stop the certifying of results, arguing the state subjected in-person voting—which favored Donald Trump—to greater scrutiny than postal votes.

There were similar lawsuits in several other states. The Trump campaign requested a recount in Wisconsin based on what they alleged were abnormalities seen on election day, and in Michigan the Trump campaign filed a lawsuit to stop the count over claims of a lack of access to observe the process. Another lawsuit was filed on November 9, seeking to block the certification of results in Wayne County, citing further complaints from poll watchers. In Nevada, a lawsuit filed on November 5, alleged lax procedures for authenticating mail-in ballots and over 3,000 instances of ineligible individuals casting ballots. In Georgia, a lawsuit filed on November 5, alleged lax procedures for authenticating mail-in ballots and over 3,000 instances of ineligible individuals casting ballots. In Arizona, the Trump campaign filed a lawsuit on November 7, claiming some legal votes were rejected. The case cites declarations by some poll watchers and two voters who claim they had problems with voting machines.[44] To say that the 2020 election was unusual is to take it lightly!

POLITICAL PARTICIPATION IN ELECTIONS: THE WAXING AND WANING OF THE AMERICAN ELECTORATE

The Waxing of the American Electorate

At the time the Constitution was ratified, the right to vote was limited to taxpayers or property owners. By the administration of President Andrew Jackson (1829-1837), almost all of the states had extended the right to vote to all white males. Then after the Civil War and the Fifteenth Amendment, African Americans were given the constitutional right to vote. The Southern states, however, continued to find ways to disenfranchise Southern African Americans. Between 1915 and 1944, the Supreme Court overturned some of the most discriminatory of the rules: the poll tax (requiring payment to vote) and the grandfather clause (you could vote if your grandfather had had the right to vote). Still, a small proportion of Southern African Americans actually registered and voted.

It was not until the passage of the Voting Rights Act in 1965 that African-American participation in Southern elections would increase dramatically. This law suspended literacy tests and authorized the appointment of federal examiners who could order the registration of African Americans in states and counties where fewer than 50 percent of the voting-age population registered or had voted in the previous presidential election. The law also included criminal penalties for interfering with the right to vote. Additional efforts by Jesse Jackson have helped increase the voter registration among African Americans.

Though women were allowed to vote in some state elections, it was not until the Nineteenth Amendment in 1920 that women's suffrage was extended across the entire nation, doubling the size of the electorate. Then, the Twenty-sixth Amendment, ratified in 1971, gave the right to vote to eighteen-year-olds. Given these changes, the United States now has the widest voting rights of any country in the world.

The Waning of the American Electorate

Given this history of safeguarding and extending the right to vote, one would think that participation in elections would have risen over time. In fact, voting turnout has often been very low in the United States. Some argue that this decline is more apparent than real. Until the early twentieth century, voter fraud, for example, ballot-box stuffing, was common. Also, the Australian ballot was introduced at the turn of the century. This ballot was to be cast in secret in private booths. This change also helped to reduce fraudulent voting.

Voter fraud, however, cannot explain the decline in voting turnout in some recent elections. General election voter turnout for the 2014 midterms, for example, was the lowest it has been in any election cycle since World War II. Just 36.4 percent of the voting-eligible population cast ballots in 2014, continuing a steady decline in midterm voter participation that has spanned several decades. While the results are dismal, they are not surprising since participation had been dropping since the 1960 election, when voter turnout was at nearly 63.8 percent. The last time voter turnout was so low during a midterm cycle was in 1942, when only 33.9 percent of eligible voters cast ballots.

This decline in voter turnout is at least partly due to the 2013 Supreme Court ruling *Shelby County v. Holder*. In this case, the Court invalidated a decades-old rule which said that jurisdictions with a history of discrimination in voting had to pass federal scrutiny under the Voting Rights Act, referred to as "preclearance," in order to pass any new elections or voting laws. In practice, the *Shelby County* decision means that communities facing new discriminatory voting laws have had to file suits themselves or rely on Justice Department suits or challenges from outside advocates—sometimes after the discriminatory laws have already taken effect. During the Trump Administration, the Department of Justice was not interested in filing such suits on behalf of the disenfranchised voters, meaning that citizens have been on their own.

The results have been predictable. Voter-identification laws, which experts suggest will make voting harder especially for poor people, people of color, and elderly people have been passed in several states, and some voting laws that make it easier to register and cast ballots have been destroyed. For many of the jurisdictions formerly under preclearance, voting became rapidly more difficult after the *Shelby County* decision, particularly for poor and elderly black people and Latinos.[45]

The 2020 Election Turnout

Many believed that there would be an increase in voter turnout in the presidential election of 2016 given how hotly it was contested. Still, voter turnout in 2016 dipped to nearly its lowest point in two decades. Only about 55 percent of voting age citizens cast ballots, making this the lowest turnout in a presidential election since 2008, when 61.6 percent of voting-age citizens turned out. A recent study by the Institute for Democracy and Electoral Assistance found that overall in national elections since World War II, the United States ranks 103rd in voter participation out of 131 democracies.[46]

Election Day 2020 served as the culmination of an unprecedented election cycle shaped by the COVID-19 pandemic, a nationwide movement for racial justice sparked by the death of George Floyd while in police custody, and the mobilization of young people who made their voices heard in the streets and at the ballot box. Young voters increased their turnout in 2020 and made the difference in key battleground states, and the participation and overwhelming support for President-elect Joe Biden from youth of color was one of the defining elements of the election.[47] Voting turnout greatly increased in 2020 with more Americans voting than in any other in more than 100 years. Nearly 65 percent of the voting-eligible population cast a ballot.

Explaining Turnout

While there are many reasons for not voting, one that appears common to all nonvoters is that politics offers few rewards and may exact some hardships. One must register to vote, read a long ballot and make sense of it, leave work to go vote, and even wait in lines to vote. All of this to cast a ballot that will surely not, in and of itself, affect the outcome of an election.

The people most likely to vote, then, tend to be people who have ways to reduce the costs of participating and/or increase the perceived benefits. Clear party differences, education, and family socialization of civic duty are all factors that can work to reduce the burden of voting. In countries with strong parties with clear ideological differences, voters may have an easier time making sense of the choices offered to them. The American parties are weak in comparison, often expressing similar policy positions. In such a weak party system environment, it is little wonder that many voters fail to perceive the significance of casting a ballot for one candidate over the other. While strong parties are one way to reduce the costs of voting, education is certainly another. People who are educated are in a much better position to process the ballot and understand the relevance of the choices being offered. Finally, coming from a family that has instilled a strong sense of civic duty is important as a motivating force.

Family socialization experiences may also work to clarify the rewards of voting. Some children grow up in an environment that stresses the importance of voting and the significance of the right to vote. Additionally, wealth and property ownership are tied to a person's ability to perceive that they have an immediate stake in the outcome of elections. People who own homes, have children in the school system, and who are paying income taxes are more likely to see that elections are important to their lifestyle and well being.

An additional reason for low voter turnout may be the lack of competition in congressional elections. The average victory margin in U.S. House races is 40 percent, meaning winners on average won more than 70 percent of the votes cast in their race. Fewer than 1 in 10 races are won by competitive margins of less than 10 percent. Second, 77 percent of House races are won in a landslide, defined as winning by at least 20 percent. Third, on the average 97 percent of incumbents are re-elected, and two-thirds of them won their last two elections in landslides.

The non-competitiveness of congressional elections has contributed to an ongoing decline in voter participation. The states with the least competitive elections, heavily centered in the South, also have the lowest voter turnout. Obviously when powerful incumbents are faced with little or no challenge, they will not conduct the kind of energetic campaigns that might get voters to the polls.

The non-competitiveness of American electoral politics is due to several of the electoral features discussed in this chapter. The winner-take-all quality of single-member plurality elections amplifies the electoral power of the winner while discouraging voters of the opposition party in the district. Additionally, partisan methods of redistricting after every census allow state legislators to draw safe districts. The manner in which legislative districts are drawn is the single most powerful factor in who wins and loses legislative elections. In essence, the state legislators are choosing their constituents before the constituents choose them.

Increasing Turnout

From the above discussion it should be clear that turnout can be increased by reducing the cost, or the burden, of voting. In the United States the entire burden of registering to vote falls on the citizens. In most European nations, on the other hand, registration is done for you automatically by the government. Some states have moved to make registration easier. In some, people may register on the same day and at the same time as they vote. In 1993, Congress also took steps to simplify registration. The motor-voter bill requires states to allow people to register to vote when applying for a driver's license, at various state offices, and by mail.

Of course, easing registration will not necessarily increase turnout. Voting itself may impose burdens. Elections, for example, are held on Tuesdays, a work day for most. In recent elections, a greater number of Americans used absentee ballots, which allowed the voter to fill out the ballot and mail it in by a certain date. Most states are now also trying to reduce the "costs" of voting by providing an early voting period that includes the weekend. In 2016, 47 million Americans cast ballots before Election Day. By Oct. 22 of 2020, that record was broken, and by Nov. 3 it was shattered. In several states, early ballots exceeded the total number of votes cast in 2016.[48]

In 2020, motivated Americans turned out in person and by mail to ensure their ballots were counted amid a pandemic. Turnout will also increase if more people see the benefits that flow from their participation. People who perceive an immediate stake in the outcome of an election are more likely to vote. Such a perception is more likely to develop as people increase their level of political literacy. Advertising campaigns to get out the vote, for example MTV's *Rock the Vote* campaign, may increase the perception that elections are important. Revitalized political parties, with clear platforms and re-invigorated methods to mobilize voters, could certainly also contribute to a renewed voter enthusiasm with the electoral process.

THE VOTERS: EXPLAINING VOTE CHOICE

In casting their ballots, voters are influenced by both long and short-term factors. A particular election does not exist in a vacuum. Voters bring with them a set of personal characteristics and a history of experiences with past candidates and issues. The current campaign then plays upon the stage of pre-existing ties. These predispositions, for many voters, are summarized by their partisan identification, a long-term attachment to one of the political parties. This party identification may be thought of as an anchor sunk in the past. A current campaign with its short-term forces of candidates and current issues may produce waves and swells that either may or may not be able to dislodge the partisan anchor.

Long-Term Forces: Group and Party Identification

Party identification is a general, long-term, psychological attachment to a political party. Early studies in the 1940s and 1950s found that most people expressed a long-term attachment to one or the other of the two political parties. Researchers found, furthermore, that these attachments were very stable over time, so stable that one could actually describe a social group profile for each party.[49] What this means is that each of the parties was a coalition of groups that had, for relatively long periods, been tied to it. For example, upper-middle class Protestant voters have tended to call themselves Republican since the late 1800s, while Catholics, Jews, and other newer immigrant groups have disproportionately been tied to the Democratic Party. Loyalty to a party was, then, cemented by a larger group tie to the party, a tie passed down from one generation to another.

The early studies of voting behavior also found that this group identification with a party was an important determinant of the vote. About 40 percent of voters, in these early polls, would say that they had made up their mind for whom they would vote before the election campaign even began; and this intention was usually consistent with their party identification. Furthermore, on election day voters in the 1950s tended to cast a vote consistent with their long-term partisan identification, and over 60 percent even voted a straight ticket, remaining loyal to their party across national, state, and local offices.[50]

Beginning in the mid 1960s the long-term ties to the political parties seemed to weaken in with only 30 percent saying that they had made up their minds before the campaign began and 44 percent saying they would not decide until after the debates. Voters also exhibited greater volatility, often defecting from partisanship when casting their ballots. From the middle of the 1960s through the 1990s, over 60 percent split their ticket, switching their votes from party to party.[51] Today, however, partisanship is on the rise.

The 2018 mid-term election evidenced a trend with fewer Americans splitting their ballots, instead opting to vote straight party tickets. This election had the smallest number of people splitting their ballots between the parties going back to at least 1990.[52] In 2020, in an era of increasing partisanship, split-ticket voting continued to be rare, with only 4 percent of registered voters in states with a Senate contest saying they would support Donald Trump or Joe Biden and a Senate candidate from the opposing party. And in 2020, voting for both the House and Senate, partisanship prevailed. A recent analysis of U.S. Senate elections since 2012 shows how rare it is for a Senate race to go a different way from a state's votes in presidential elections. In 139 regular and special elections for the Senate since 2012, 8 8 percent have been won by candidates from the same party that won that state's most recent presidential contest.[53] Similarly, only 4 percent of registered voters said they planned to vote for Biden and the Republican candidate for House in their district or Donald Trump and the Democratic House candidate. This is little changed from 2016. The increased partisanship in recent elections is also evidenced by how few voters choose to cast their ballots for a third-party candidate. In 2020, only 6 percent of voters said they planned to cast their ballots this way.[54]

Party identification is still an important determinant of vote choice for many individuals and groups in the electorate. In recent elections, the pattern of votes, along with other evidence about the political leanings of young voters, suggests that a significant generational shift in political allegiance is occurring. This pattern has been building for several years and is underscored among voters in 2008. Among voters ages 18-29, a 19-point gap now separates Democratic Party affiliation (45 percent) and Republican affiliation (26 percent). In 2000, party affiliation was split nearly evenly among the young. The party gap among young voters has expanded over the last four years. Since 2004, Democratic identification among voters under age 30 has increased 8 points, while Republican identification has fallen by 9 points. The percentage of young voters declining to identify with either of the two major parties remained stable at 29 percent.[55]

While party identification is a strong determinant of the vote, there is always some defection from this partisan identification. These defections, together with the vote decision of those who express no partisan predisposition (about 25 percent of the population) can be explained by short-term forces associated with a current campaign, its candidates, and issues.

Short-Term Forces: Issues and Candidate Image

Issues

Issues can be important determinants of vote choice. Some people may make a prospective vote decision, identifying the candidates' positions and determining which candidate is likely to serve the interests of the voters. Other members of the electorate may vote retrospectively, evaluating the current office holders and voting to reward or punish that office holder on the basis of his/her record in office. In general, studies have found that retrospective voting is much less demanding and, therefore, more likely to be the way in which voters use issues in voting.

Of all the issues that are likely to drive short-term electoral forces as well as defections from partisanship, the state of the economy is by far the most important. Studies have shown, however, that the voter's *perception* of the economy as a whole may be more important than the *actual* state of the voter's own pocketbook or for that matter the *actual* state of the economy itself.

The most important campaign issue in 2020 was the troubled economy. With the country in the midst of a recession, nearly eight-in-ten registered voters (79 percent) said the economy would be very important to them in making their decision, and as the country continued to grapple with the coronavirus pandemic, 62 percent of voters said the outbreak would be a very important factor in their decision about who to support in the fall of 2020.[56]

Candidate Image

Studies have consistently found that candidate image is more important than the issue positions of the candidates. While character issues have always been important in American campaigns, they seem to be becoming more central to the vote decision. In recent elections, character issues have been extremely important: Clinton's alleged extramarital affairs, his avoidance, while a college student, of the draft during the Vietnam War, his visit to the Soviet Union, and use of marijuana. Character issues need not always be negative. Leadership, honesty, and decisiveness are also characteristics that voters consider in selecting a candidate. Arthur Miller, in fact, found that along with concern about the deficit, the candidate's level of *caring* were the two strongest predictors of the vote.[57]

THE 2020 PRESIDENTIAL ELECTION

CONCLUSION

Democracies rest on elections and popular participation in them. This is because true and peaceful competition that takes place in the electoral arena is a way for a society to reach decisions. At the same time such participation works to channel support for the democratically elected institutions of government. In the end, the stability of democratic regimes rests on mass support.

Some are coming to question the health and vitality of American electoral politics and, therefore, of the American form of government itself. As we saw at the beginning of this chapter, campaigns are increasingly expensive, and driven by advertising and poll technology. Yet substantive media coverage of campaigns and elections is declining, and congressional races are almost completely dominated by the incumbents who can use the vast resources of their office to discourage meaningful opposition. True competition is disappearing at a rapid rate.

As competition in the electoral arena declines, political conflict spills over to other arenas. Lowi and Ginsberg argue that unelected institutions are now at the epicenter of political conflict: the criminal justice system and courts and the mass media.[43] Between the early 1970s and the present, there has been a tenfold increase in the number of indictments brought by federal prosecutors against national, state, and local officials. In addition, there have been numerous investigations that have not resulted in indictments. The prominence of the courts has also been heightened by the great number of major policy issues that are being fought out in the courts. Abortion, women's rights, civil rights, and a host of environmental issues are currently being debated by judges and juries. The media, as well, have become prominent players in this nonelectoral politics. Today, investigative reporters are eager to publicize and expose official misconduct and Tweeting and Retweeting are now major forms of political communication..

Not only has conflict spilled outside the electoral arena, the conflict has also intensified. We have had almost three decades of divided government marked by intense battles between the legislative and executive branches. Perhaps because the partisan battles of today are not being fully decided through the elections that enjoy either low voter turnout or allegations of vote fraud, conflict continues to be fought out in acrimonious struggles between the branches of government. Neither Congress nor the president will concede defeat, both claiming to be the majority party. In the end, however, the question is whether democratic politics can remain robust in an atmosphere of weak political parties, candidate-centered media campaigns, and special interest group financing of campaigns.

CHAPTER NOTES

[1] Pablo Boczkowski, "Has Election 2016 Been a Turning Point for the Influence of the News Media," NiemanLab, November 8, 2016, *http://www.niemanlab.org/2016/11/has-election-2016-been-a-turning-point-for-the-influence-of-the-news-media/*

[2] William Crotty, *Party Reform* (New York Longman, 1983), 13-25.

[3] Matea Gold, "Democrats Give Special Interests a Role at Convention," *Los Angeles Times*, April 5, 2012, *http://articles.latimes.com/2012/apr/05/nation/la-na-convention-money-20120406.*

[4] Haley Sweetland Edwards and Chris Wilson, "Why We Don't Know Who's Funding the Republican Convention," *Time*, July 17, 2016, *https://time.com/4401622/republican-convention-donations-transparency/*

[5] BallotPedia, "Party Committee Fundraising 2019–2020," April 2020, *https://ballotpedia.org/Party_committee_fundraising,_2019-2020*

[6] Amy Sherman, "How Many Americans Actually Donate to Political Candidates?" *POLITIFACT*, January 24, 2020, *https://www.politifact.com/factchecks/2020/jan/24/andrew-yang/what-percent-americans-donate-political-candidates/*

[7] Kyle Kondik, "House 2020: Incumbents Hardly Ever Lose Primaries," *Rasmussen Reports*, May 30, 2020, *https://www.rasmussenreports.com/public_content/political_commentary/commentary_by_kyle_kondik/house_2020_incumbents_hardly_ever_lose_primaries*

[8] Jessica Piper, "Wealthy Candidates Pay Their Own Way, but It's Not an Easy Path to Victory," *Center for Responsive Politics OpenSecrets.org*, July 24, 2019, *https://www.opensecrets.org/news/2019/07/wealthy-candidates-pay-their-own-way/*

[9] Adam Liptak, "Supreme Court Bars Challenges to Partisan Gerrymandering," *The New York Times*, June 27, 2019, *https://www.nytimes.com/2019/06/27/us/politics/supreme-court-gerrymandering.html*

[10] Donald Saari, "Vetoing the Way We Vote," *Los Angeles Times*, 16 August 1995, A1.

[11] Andrew Colman and Ian Pountney, "Borda's Voting Paradox," *Behavioral Science* 23 1978), 15–20.

[12] Lani Guinier, *Tyranny of the Majority* (New York: Free Press, 1995).

[13] Ibid.

[14] Center for Responsive Politics, "Most Expensive Midterm Ever: Cost of 2018 Election Surpasses $5.7 Billion," OpenSecrets.org, October 25, 2016, *https://www.opensecrets.org/news/2019/02/cost-of-2018-election-5pnt7bil/*

[15] Center for Responsive Politics, "2020 Election to Cost $14 Billion, Blowing Away Spending Records," Open Secrets.org, October 28, 2020, *https://www.opensecrets.org/news/2020/10/cost-of-2020-election-14billion-update/*

[16] Ibid.

[17] Ibid.

[18] *Federal Election Commission*, "The First Ten Years: 1975-1985," Washington, D.C. Federal Election Commission, 14 April 1985, 1.

[19] *The Associated Press, "Republican Party Challenges 'Soft Money' Laws," http://msnbc.msn.com/id/27699900, November 13, 2008*

[20] CLC Advancing Democracy Through Law, "Spike in Campaign Finance Lawsuits Nationwide Following Citizens United," September 15, 2010, *https://campaignlegal.org/update/spike-campaign-finance-lawsuits-nationwide-following-citizens-united-court-cases-interest*

[21] Charles Lane, "Supreme Court Upholds McCain-Feingold Campaign Law," *The Washington Post*, December 11, 2003.

[22] Center for Responsive Politics, "527s: Advocacy Group Spending," *OpenSecrets.org*, *https://www.opensecrets.org/527s/index.php, June 2020.*

[23] T. J. Stepleton, "Independent Spending Overview, 2015 and 2016," *FollowTheMoney.org*, February 14, 2018, *https://www.followthemoney.org/research/institute-reports/independent-spending-overview-2015-and-2016*

[24]Ibid.

[25]Laura Gottesdiener, "The Top 10 Biggest Beneficiaries of 'Citizens United' in the 2012 Election," AlterNet, *http://www.huffingtonpost.com/2013/01/21/citizens-united_n_2519178.html?utm_hp_ref=politics*

[26]Center for Responsive Politics, "More Money, Less Transparency: A Decade Under Citizens United," *OpenSecrets.org*, June 2020.

[27]Center for Responsive Politics, "2020 Outside Spending by Super PAC," *OpenSectrets.org*, 2020.

[28]Maggie Haberman, "Trump Campaign Plans Greater Focus on 'Bundlers,'" *The New York Times*, January 17, 2020, *https://www.nytimes.com/2020/01/17/us/politics/trump-campaign-bundling.html*

[29]Jonathan Berr, "Election 2016's Price Tage: $6.8 Billion," *CBS Money Watch*, November 8, 2016, *http://www.cbsnews.com/news/election-2016s-price-tag-6-8-billion/)*

[30]Dino Grandoni, "The Energy 202: The Oil Sector's Political Spending is Down During the Pandemic," *PowerPost*, October 6, 2020, *https://www.washingtonpost.com/politics/2020/10/06/energy-202-oil-sector-political-spending-is-down-during-pandemic/*

[31]Center for Responsive Politics, "2020 Outside Spending," *OpenSecrets.org*, November 9, 2020, *https://www.opensecrets.org/outsidespending/*

[32]Olivier J. Wouters, "Lobbying Expenditures and Campaign Contributions by the Pharmaceutical and Health Product Industry in the United States, 1999–2018," *JAMA Internal Medicine*, May 2020, *https://www.ncbi.nlm.nih.gov/pmc/articles/PMC7054854/#:~:text=This%20observational%20study%2C%20which%20analyzed,%24414%20million%20on%20contributions%20to*

[33]Eric Lightblau, "F.E.C. Can't Curb 2016 Election Abuse, Commission Chief Says," *The New York Times*, May 2, 2015, Politics.

[34]Center for Responsive Politics, "Cost of Election," *OpenSecrets.org*, *https://www.opensecrets.org/elections-overview/cost-of-election?cycle=2020&display=T&infl=N*

[35]Engagious, Swing Voter Project, 2020, *https://engagious.com/swingvoters*

[36]The Twentieth Century Fund, 1-800-President (New York Twentieth Century Fund Press, 1993), 31.

[37]Brian Rosenwald, "They Just Wanted to Entertain," *The Atlantic*, August 21, 2019, *https://www.theatlantic.com/ideas/archive/2019/08/talk-radio-made-todays-republican-party/596380/*

[38]Mark Murray, "Projection: $6.7 Billion Could be Spent on Advertising in 2020 Election," *Meet the Press Blog*, November 11, 2020, *https://www.nbcnews.com/politics/meet-the-press/blog/meet-press-blog-latest-news-analysis-data-driving-political-discussion-n988541/ncrd1207951#blogHeader*

[39]Alexander Burns, "Bloomberg Funds Late-Minute Advertising Blitz in Texas and Ohio," *The New York Times*, October 27, 2020, *https://www.nbcnews.com/politics/meet-the-press/blog/meet-press-blog-latest-news-analysis-data-driving-political-discussion-n988541/ncrd1207951#blogHeader*

[40]Kristina Monllos, " Digital is the Testbed: Why the 2020 Election is Focused on Online Advertising," *Digiday*, October 25, 2019, *https://digiday.com/marketing/digital-testbed-2020-election-focused-online-advertising/*

[41]PewResearchCenter, "Politics Fact Sheet", November 14, 2012, *http://www.pewinternet.org/fact-sheets/politics-fact-sheet/*

[42]Peter Suciu, "Social Media Could Determine the Outcome of the 2020 Election," *Forbes*, October 26, 2020, *https://www.forbes.com/sites/petersuciu/2020/10/26/social-media-could-determin41the-outcome-of-the-2020-election/?sh=4519200e26f6*

[43]Steven Rosenfeld, "Machine Problems Worsened 2008 Voting Woes," *www.alternet.org?democracy/107034/machine_problems_worsened_2008_voting_woes, November 13, 2008.*

[44]Reality Check Team, "U.S. Election 2020: What Legal Challenges is Trump Planning?", BBC News, November11, 2020, *https://www.bbc.com/news/election-us-2020-54724960*

[45]Vann Newkirk, "How Shelby County v. Holder Broke America," *The Atlantic*, July 10, 2018, *https://www.theatlantic.com/politics/archive/2018/07/how-shelby-county-broke-america/564707/In this case,*

[46]Drew Desilver, "In Past Elections, U.S. Trailed Most Developed Countries in Voter Turnout," *Pew Research Center: FACTANK News in Numbers*, November 3, 2020, *https://www.pewresearch.org/fact-tank/2020/11/03/in-past-elections-u-s-trailed-most-developed-countries-in-voter-turnout/*

[47]Kevin Schaul, Kate Rabinowitz, and Ted Mellnik, "2020 Turnout is the Highest in Over a Century," *The Washington Post*, November 5, 2020, *https://www.washingtonpost.com/graphics/2020/elections/voter-turnout/*

[48]Brittany Renee Mayes and Kate Rabinowitz, "The U.S. Hit 73% of 2016 Voting Before Election Day," *The Washington Post*, November 3, 2020, *https://www.washingtonpost.com/graphics/2020/elections/early-voting-numbers-so-far/*

[49]Norman H. Nie, Sidney Verba, and John R. Petrocik, *The Changing American Voter* (Cambridge, MA: Harvard University Press, 1976), 29.

[50]Ibid.

[51]Amy Burke, "Party Decline," *The American Prospect*, April 30, 2001, *https://prospect.org/power/partyecline/*

[52]Geoffrey Skelley, "Split-Ticket Voting Hit a New Low in 2018 Senate and Governor Races," *FiveThirtyEight*, November 19, 2018, *https://fivethirtyeight.com/features/split-ticket-voting-hit-a-new-low-in-2018-senate-and-governor-races/*

[53]Drew Desilver, "Most Senate Elections Reflect States' Presidential Votes," *Pew Research Center FACTANK*, September 1, 2020, *https://www.pewresearch.org/fact-tank/2020/09/01/most-senate-elections-reflect-states-presidential-votes/*

[54]Pew Research Center, "Large Shares of Voters Plan to Vote a Straight Party Ticket for President, Senate, and House, October 21, 2020, *https://www.pewresearch.org/politics/2020/10/21/large-shares-of-voters-plan-to-vote-a-straight-party-ticket-for-president-senate-and-house/*

[55]Scott Keeter, "Young Voters in the 2008 Election," Pew Center Research Publications, *http://pewresearch.org, November 13, 2008.*

[56]Pew Research Center, Important Issues in the 2020 Election, August 13, 2020, *https://www.pewresearch.org/politics/2020/08/13/important-issues-in-the-2020-election/*

[57]Arthur Miller, "Arthur Miller Lecture on Politics and the Art of Acting," *National Endowment for the Humanities*, March 26, 2001, *https://www.neh.gov/about/awards/jefferson-lecture/arthur-miller-lecture.*

SUGGESTED READINGS

Ackerman, Brice and Ian Avers. *Voting and Dollars*. New Haven, CT: Yale University Press, 2004.

Browning, Graeme. *Electronic Democracy*. New York: Cyberage, 2002.

Cahn, David and Jack Cahn. *When Millenials Rule*. New York: Simon and Schuster, 2016.

Campbell, Angus, and Converse, Philip E., Miller, Warren E., and Stokes, Donald E. *The American Voter*. New York: John Wiley, 1960.

Feltus, William, Kenneth Goldstein, and Matthew Dallek. *Inside Campaigns*. Washington, D.C.: CQ Press, 2016.

Ginsberg, Benjamin and Martin Shefter, *Politics by Other Means: Institutional Conflict and the Declining Significance of Elections in America*. New York: Norton, 1999.

Herrick, Rebekah. *Minorities and Representation in American Politics*. Washington, D.C.: CQ Press, 2016.

Hochschild, Arlie Russell. *Strangers in Their Own Land*. New York: The New Press, 2016.

Nelson, Michael. *The Elections of 2016*. Washington: CQ Press, 2017.

Overton, Spencer, *Stealing Democracy: The New Politics of Voter Suppression*. New York: W.W. Norton, 2007.

Packer, George. *The Unwinding: An Inner History of the New America*. New York: Farrar, Straus and Giroux, 2016.

Raymond, Allen and Ian Spiegelman. *How to Rig an Election*. New York: Simon and Schuster, 2008.

Schaffner, Brian and John A. Clark. *Making Sense of the 2016 Elections*. Washington, D.C.: CQ Press, 2017.

Sides, John, Daron Shaw, Matt Grossmna, Et Al. *Campaigns and Elections*. New York: W.W. Norton, 2015.

Web Sites

Center for Voting and Democracy, www.fairvote.org.
The Color of Money, www.colorofmoney.org.
Common Cause. www.commoncause.org.
CQ Moneyline. www.moneyline.cq.com/pml/home.do.
Federal Election Commission Webpage. www.fec.gov.
JibJab, www.jibjab.com.
OpenSecrets. *www.opensecrets.org.*
Presidential Campaign Websites www.4president.us/
Voter Information Services, *www.vis.org.*

Chapter Six

THE MEDIA

The coronavirus pandemic has posed a serious challenge to the economics of journalism at the very time it has also made accurate news reporting more important than ever. Newspaper, television, and social media publishers have all had to deal with the economic fallout of the coronavirus outbreak. The economic hardship is coming primarily from the loss of advertising revenue as companies are slashing their marketing budgets in the atmosphere of great economic insecurity. Estimates are that the virus will end up costing the United States advertising industry billions of dollars in lost revenue.[1]

There is little doubt that news media will be changed by this crisis and the news is both good and bad. National news organizations are seeing a resurgence in their popularity with readership and viewership increasing to levels unseen in recent years. However, while the coronavirus inspired an unprecedented surge in news consumption, it did not result in a concurrent surge in advertising revenues. Companies, that would in better times, be advertising, are pulling back as they have suffered enormous economic consequences of social distancing and isolation policies. Advertisers also pulled ads fearing that the ads would run adjacent to the extremely negative stories about the virus. In total, more than two million ads were pulled in the single month of March 2020, due to advertisers not wanting their ads to appear next to stories about the pandemic.[2]

The coronavirus also speeded the collapse of local news organizations. With local sports and events canceled and restaurants and bars shuttered, local newsrooms have little to cover and have also lost the places where they used to distribute their papers and big screen TVs. In response, local news organizations have laid off staff, ceased print publishing, or temporarily shut down. The local newspaper conglomerate Gannett's stock plummeted. On November 19, 2020, when it merged with GateHouse, the stock opened at $6.70. On March 22, it had dropped to $1.61. The hope is that the layoffs and losses will be temporary but many fear that this may be the death knell of local news.

While news organizations are bleeding money and laying off journalists, high-quality and accurate reporting have never been more important because misinformation spreads as quickly as the virus. In the spring of 2020, coronavirus information became a toxic blend of truths and lies with memes, doctored screenshots, and fraudulent links spreading like wildfire. WhatsApp quickly became a breeding ground for unsourced claims, and WhatsApp groups had member counts stretching into the hundreds, receiving forwarded messages from sources that could not be checked. Fact-checking organization Snopes was forced to cut back its own content production in order to keep up with checking all the misinformation. This fact-checking took on a new importance as people spent long periods in self-isolation, dependent on media news. Usage of Facebook and other social media services including private messaging and video chatting surged during the epidemic and left people open to being influenced by less than factually accurate news.

Misinformation did find its way into the American public. While 51 percent of the public said that they were following the news about the virus closely, with another 38 percent following it fairly closely, almost half the public said that they had been exposed to some made-up news related to the virus.[3] To meet the challenge, Facebook pledged to invest $100 million in the news industry, $25 million of which would be provided in grant funding for the local news and the other $75 million would be directed to worldwide news organizations. This may not, however, be enough to ensure the public has accurate information. A pandemic makes all of us targets for misinformation mainly because the pace of scientific discovery cannot keep pace with information technology and the result is often reckless information that is partly true but politically skewed.[4]

While the physical analog world of hotels, restaurants, and airplanes was being decimated by the virus, the digital world took on a whole new importance. In the post pandemic world, technology, including digital news, is likely to be more powerful and dominant. In early 2020, people were expressing a deep cynicism and criticism of technology but that has largely dissipated as people have become increasingly dependent on that very technology for their very existence, as well as their news.

DEMOCRACY AND THE MASS MEDIA

In a democracy, communications must move in two directions: from government to citizens and from citizens to their government. In the United States, a technologically complex nation of over 300 million people, communication in either of these directions would be virtually impossible without mass forms of communication.

The Structure of the Mass Media

The term **mass media** covers the seven major channels of communication that carry messages to a mass audience.

Books

Between 600,000 and one million books are published each year in the United States. While most of them are designed for entertainment, many others focus on public policy and government. Even before he became President, Barack Obama made $8.8 million from his bestseller *Audacity of Hope* and children's book *Of Thee I Sing: A Letter to My Daughters*. Then once in office, Obama earned another $15.6 million as an author.[5] In 2019, The Mueller Report sold 375,000 copies in the first weeks of its release.

Magazines

Close to ten thousand magazines are published each year in the United States, and the average American reads at least two a week. Again, many of these are solely for entertainment. Still, many others are specifically designed to address matters of political interest. *Time*, *Newsweek*, and *U.S. News and World Report* have a combined circulation of over 10 million readers. In addition, there are numerous magazines targeted at readers with particular ideological perspectives, for example, *Nation*, *New Republic*, and *The National Review*. Finally, there are many professional journals like the *American Political Science Review*.

Newspapers

According to the most recently available data, there are 1,279 daily newspapers in the United States with a circulation of 28.6 million for weekday and 30.8 million for Sunday, down 8 percent and 9 percent respectively from the previous year.[6] Both newspaper circulation and readership have recently declined dramatically as more people are turning to online sources for their news. Back in 1970, newspapers sold roughly one newspaper per household every day in America. By 2008, daily newspaper sales equaled only half the households and today only 9 percent of Americans say newspapers are their main news source.[7]

Television

At one time, the three networks—ABC, NBC, and CBS—and their affiliates controlled the medium of television. Today, however, the networks are part of a much larger and more competitive market. The arrival of cable and satellite television has greatly increased the number of stations available to many in the United States. During the economic recession the number of homes that had cable declined to the 1990 level. But alternative delivery systems' (ADS) penetration grew markedly in 2010, reaching 28.7 percent of TV households, an all-time high. In 2020 the direct broadcast satellite, the largest component of ADS, is at 30.3 percent, up from 27.6 percent in Nov. 2007. Whether broadcast, cable, or satellite, television remains the medium most used and relied upon by the American public. The average household spends seven hours a day in front of the television set, and the average individual spends three hours a day watching TV. Americans say that they are most likely to get the news from television, and they tend to feel that television news is the most credible. A new survey has shown that 53 percent of registered voters across the United States named television as their primary source for news. Only 21 percent said they prefer to get their news from the Internet and 9 percent said that they would rather turn to social media for the latest news.[8]

Radio

There are over fifteen thousand radio stations, divided between the AM and FM bands. The average American listens to the radio two-and-a-half hours a day. Today, talk radio programs like that of conservative Rush Limbaugh have become potent forces in the world of politics. Politicians and candidates use talk radio to interact with the American public. Ideologues on the left and the right compete for talk radio time to disseminate their particular views on the issues of the day.

Records

Each year more than seven million records, tapes, and compact discs are sold in the United States. While CDs are primarily produced and consumed for enjoyment, many of the most popular songs have overtly political themes and messages. Rock concerts and rock artists often raise funds for politically charged causes such as AIDs, environment, world hunger, to name a few. For example, in March 2020, during the COVID crisis, Elton John hosted the Fox Presents The iHeart Living Room Concert for America. Recording stars Billie Eilish, Camila Cabello, Sam Smith, Alicia Keys, and Billie Joe Armstrong paid tribute to health care professionals and first responders and encouraged viewers to support and donate to organizations Feeding America and First Responders Children's Foundation.

Motion Pictures

Twelve thousand theaters across the country show approximately 250 films a year. Many of these movies deal with political subjects, for example, the 1941 classic *Citizen Kane*, Al Gore's *An Inconvenient Truth*, and the 2008 Oscar-winning films *Milk* and *Lincoln* in 2012. More recently, *Vice*, *The Ides of March*, and *The Dictator* were considered some of the best movies of 2020.

The Internet

Before the COVID-19 pandemic of 2020, the traditional news outlets were failing to expand their audiences despite the high level of interest in the war on terrorism and the financial crisis of 2008-2009, which had led to an increase in the amount of time Americans spent on the news. With traditional media trends flat, there was a steady growth in the audience for online news. As of 2016, there are over 287 million Internet users in the United States, and Internet news, once largely the province of young, white males, now attracts a growing number of minorities. The percentage of African Americans who regularly go online for news has grown from 16 percent in 2000 to over 80 percent in 2016. The Internet population has also broadened to include more older Americans. Nearly three-quarters of Americans in their 50s and early 60s say they go online, up from 45 percent in 2000. Education continues to be the biggest single factor driving online news use, largely due to the continuing gap in Internet access. Fully 91 percent of college graduates regularly use the web for news, compared with just 36 percent of those who do not finish high school. Both men and women over age 40 without a degree are the least likely to go online for news with any regularity.[9] The year 2020 did see a resurgence in the public's attention to traditional news sources. For example, newspaper readership, with the biggest beneficiaries being local news sites, saw huge jumps in traffic as people tried to learn how the pandemic was affecting their local hometowns.[10]

Social Media

The political landscape has been radically altered by the social media's pervasive influence on public discourse. It was only twenty years ago that people thought Vice President Al Gore was weird for texting his wife, Tipper. By 2016, every politician was checking e-mail on a Smartphone and monitoring what the media and voters were saying on social media platforms. While social media had played a major role in the 2012 election, it was 2016 that saw Americans become comfortable interacting on platforms like *Facebook*, *Twitter*, *Snapchat*, and *Instagram*.

Social media, like *Facebook* and *Twitter*, empower one-on-one local engagement. A political campaign relying on social networks can decentralize its message and reach individual voters directly. While tweets and updates may not sway voters in of themselves, building strong online communities of supporters can translate into electoral success. By 2016, technology had created an unprecedented level of transparency among the candidates, for example Hillary Clinton's emails and Donald Trump's tweeting. Social media, in particular, are now driving conversations, clarifying facts, and adding another layer of complexity to the campaign process.

The social media are mostly the domain of younger Internet users and while young adults (18-24) are, as a group, less interested in political activities, they are far more likely than any other group to use blogs and social networking sites to engage in political discussions. A new report by Pew Internet and American Life Project has found that 34 percent of young adults make political use of social networking sites and 34 percent post political material on the Internet. What will be interesting to watch, the Pew study points out, is how these younger users will use these existing networks as they get older. It will also be interesting to see if these developments will mean that socio-economic status will become less of an indicator of civic engagement, or if these new technologies will create new barriers of entry for those with a lower income and education level.[11]

Government Regulation of the Media

Thomas Jefferson wrote that "Our liberty depends on freedom of the press, and that cannot be limited without being lost."[12] Jefferson would be pleased with the amount of freedom enjoyed by the press today. Unlike journalists in many European and most African and Asian countries, journalists in the United States do not need a license to practice their trade. Stories do not have to be cleared with the government before publication and, in fact, the courts of this country have consistently ruled that there can be no prior restraint of the media.

The First Amendment does indeed give the media considerable freedom from governmental interference. Still, this freedom is not complete. There are very real constraints on the content of mass communications. One of the most important of these constraints takes the form of government regulation of three aspects of media operation.

Technical and Ownership Regulation

In the early years of radio, there was chaos. Stations would often broadcast on similar frequencies, thereby jamming each others signals. The broadcasters petitioned the government to make some sense out of the cacophony. The result was that Congress passed the Federal Radio Act of 1927, which declared public ownership of the airwaves. The argument was that there was only a scarce number of airwaves, and these needed to be regulated in the interest of the American public. Accordingly, the law requires that private broadcasters obtain a license in order to use these airwaves.

Later, in 1934, Congress passed the Federal Communications Act, which created the Federal Communications Commission (FCC). The FCC has seven members, chosen by the president, with no more than four members being from the same political party. The members of the FCC serve a fixed term of seven years. They may not be removed by the president and can only be removed through impeachment by the House and conviction by the Senate. This makes the FCC an independent regulatory agency.

The FCC regulates all interstate and international communication by radio, television, cable, and satellite. The FCC is also charged by Congress to regulate the ownership of the mass media. From its beginning, the FCC has been charged by Congress with a broad mandate to enforce an even broader standard: regulating the country's communications networks according to "the public interest." In addition to regulating broadcast media, the FCC allocates wireless spectrum worth hundreds of billions of dollars, approves consumer technologies like Wi-Fi and smartphones, dispenses tens of billions of dollars of subsidies, and much more. Today, the FCC has substantial power over the country's technology and media companies, including Google, Comcast-NBCUniversal, Verizon, and DirecTV.

In the 1950s the FCC loosened its ownership rules somewhat to allow a single owner to own up to seven AM, seven FM, and seven television stations across the nation. By the 1980s the number of television stations had more than quadrupled, and the number of radio stations had tripled. The

The following sight is sure to bring a smile to the face of any protestor or candidate running for public office. Media attention is the one indispensable ingredient to success. The media can make or break candidates and causes.

FCC responded by further relaxing its ownership limits, allowing an owner to control up to twelve of each type of broadcast medium. The technological developments of the 1990s continued to make the 1930s structure of communications regulation obsolete. In 1996, Congress overwhelmingly approved a major telecommunications act that sought to replace government regulation with competition. The act removed the long-standing barriers between sectors of the telecommunications industry. For example, the new legislation abolished the local phone monopolies and allowed local companies to compete in offering long distance services.

On June 2, 2003, the Federal Communications commission relaxed decades-old restraints on the broadcast industry. The new rules repealed a 28-year-old ban on cross-ownership of TV stations and newspapers in all but the smallest media markets and one person or company would be able to own three TV stations up from two. This broad revision of ownership rules would clear the way for further consolidation by the biggest media conglomerates, enhancing the economic prospects of companies such as News Corp., Viacom Inc., and Tribune Co., parent of the *Los Angeles Times*. Also under the new rules, broadcasters would be permitted to own stations reaching 45 percent of the nation's viewers, up from 35 percent. Taken together, the new rules would allow a single company to own the following media outlets in Los Angeles: the *Los Angeles Times*, KTLA, KCBS Channel 2, KCOP Channel 13, Time Warner Cable, KIIS-FM, KROQ-FM, KNX-AM, KFWB-AM, and KABC-AM. Then in late 2007, despite staunch opposition from both Congress and media watchdog groups, the FCC voted 3-2 to further relax its rules against businesses consolidating ownership of media outlets in a given region.

In January 2009, the FCC took up the issue of Internet regulation, and in December 2010, a divided Federal Communications Commission approved new "net neutrality" rules. **Net neutrality** is the concept that as providers of this ever-important public resource, they must maintain a neutral, hands-off policy of allowing that information to flow unmolested. The 2009 rules prohibited Internet providers such as telephone and cable companies from discriminating against Internet services, such as those that come from their rivals. Then in 2015, the administration of Barack Obama prohibited internet providers from charging more for certain content or from giving preferential treatment to certain websites over others. These rules were short-lived because on June 11, 2018, the FCC's Restoring Internet Freedom Order took effect. The FCC said that it repealed the net neutrality rues because they restrained broadband providers like Verizon and Comcast from experimenting with new business models and investing in technology. The issue of net neutrality, however, is not dead. Several states have taken measures to ensure that the riles stay in effect. As of 2020, twenty-nine state legislatures had introduced bills meant to ensure net neutrality.

Regulation of Content

The First Amendment bars congressional interference with the press. But because broadcast channels are scarce, or at least were scarce until the arrival of cable and satellite technology, Congress has argued a right and need to regulate the content of the broadcast media. This congressional duty to regulate does not extend to the theoretically unlimited world of news print.

There are two principal restraints on broadcast content in effect today. First, the FCC requires a station that gives or sells air time to a candidate for any public office make an equal amount of time, under the same conditions, available to other candidates for that same office. This is called the **equal time provision**. Congress passed the law requiring the FCC to monitor compliance with this provision because it wanted to ensure a level and fair playing field for political debate in the United States. The idea of equal time came out of the regulation that has to do with political advertising. The idea, simply put, is if a broadcast station sells advertising time or offers free time to a candidate for public office, it has to offer similar access to other candidates Congress, however, has never extended the equal opportunities rule to news coverage.

In 1949 the FCC created a second rule, the **fairness doctrine**, which required that stations provide opportunities for the expression of conflicting views on issues. Like the equal-time provision, the fairness doctrine was never applied to news coverage. In 1987, the FCC repealed the fairness doctrine because the growth of cable television made it unnecessary. Recent efforts on the part of Congress to enact the fairness doctrine into law have failed.

There are three other legal restraints that place limitations on the content of both the print and broadcast media. Libel laws preclude the media's printing or airing of a story that unjustly and falsely damages a person's reputation. Obscenity laws limit the media's right to show obscene materials. Finally, there are laws limiting the media's access to classified information about intelligence operations.

In addition to the legal restraints, media content, especially in regard to the coverage of war, is also constrained by government pressure. During the Spanish-American War of 1898 and throughout World Wars I and II, journalists considered themselves part of the war effort. Beginning with the Korean and then Vietnam Wars, the press took an increasingly independent and critical view of the military. When the Vietnam War ended, many in the military blamed the press for "losing Vietnam." In 1983, the Pentagon barred all journalists from the initial invasion of Grenada. During this same period, the Reagan administration threatened to prosecute reporters for violating espionage laws.[13] Then in 1989, the Pentagon selected a dozen reporters to cover the invasion of Panama but restricted them to an airport until nearly all the fighting was over. During the first Persian Gulf War, the Pentagon accredited pools of journalists who had to first pass a military security review and who could then only interview military personnel with an escort present. News organizations filed suit charging the military with violating the First Amendment. Before the lawsuit against Gulf War press restrictions could come before a judge, however, Desert Storm ended. For the war in Iraq in 2003, the U.S. military devised new press rules. About 500 reporters (one-fifth of them from foreign countries) were placed, or "embedded," in military units. Since then embedded journalists have been given greater access to operational combat missions.[14]

Political Functions of the Mass Media

Entertainment

The news media in the United States are different from the media in other countries in that they are almost all private, for-profit corporate enterprises. This means that one of their principal functions is to make money for those who own them. These profits are tied to the media's ability to sell off their space, in the case of newspapers, or time, in the case of radio and television, and the Internet to corporate advertisers called sponsors. Advertising revenues are directly related to the size of the audience, usually measured in terms of newspaper circulation or reader/viewer ratings. The ratings

Roosevelt was an outstanding media president.

game, the need to attract large audiences, will even affect the content of the news and public affairs programs. The dramatic and sensational, the conflicted and the sordid, are more likely to attract large audiences.

Surveillance

Surveillance involves the press's role in the definition of what constitutes "news." The media are the gatekeepers, determining what the public sees, reads, and hears. It is the job of a journalist to sort through the enormous number of stories that might be considered as news and winnow them down, giving the audience a distilled, condensed version of reality.

Interpretation

But the news is nothing as simple as reality, or even parts of reality. The news is a story about reality told by a storyteller, a journalist. The media place events and people in a context, probing motives, causes, and effects. It is quite common for a newspaper or TV news program to run a segment that offers analysis and interpretation. In addition, there are whole programs devoted to such interpretative news reporting, for example, *60 Minutes*, *Nightline*, and *20/20*.

Watchdog

Traditionally, the American press has accepted responsibility for protecting the public from corrupt, incompetent, or deceitful politicians. In 2004, for example, the press reported the abuses of prisoners by U.S. soldiers in Iraq. Graphic photos of naked Iraqi prisoners forced into humiliating sexual poses were aired on national television news. Congress, forced by the airing of these photos to respond, launched hearings to discover why U.S. troops had behaved in such an illegal and horrible manner.

Socialization

The media are the principal purveyors of American culture, influencing particularly the young and recent immigrants. Studies have shown that children pick up most of their political information and many of their most basic values from the mass media.[15] Children who have the most exposure to mass communications tend to be better informed and have more political opinions than those who have less exposure.[16]

Persuasion and Propaganda

The mass media have long been looked at as vehicles to be used to persuade and mobilize mass publics. Governments, public officials, candidates, and interest groups have all, at one time or another, attempted to turn media coverage to their advantage. Advertisements and public information programs are examples of modern forms of propaganda. But all political campaigns involve propaganda designed to persuade and mobilize support.

Agenda Setting

Many believe that the media's power to persuade and change opinions is greatly overrated. They suggest instead that the media's primary power is the power to influence what the public thinks about rather than what they think. Issues prominently featured in the media, for example, become the issues that citizens think are most important. In 1990, on the twentieth anniversary of Earth Day, the television news featured many stories on the environment. Studies have shown that such coverage led many in the public to focus on environmental issues as a top priority. Certainly the media's coverage of Donald Trump's 2016 campaign for the presidency helped to jettison the issue of immigration onto the national political agenda.

THE INCREASED IMPORTANCE OF THE MODERN MASS MEDIA

The media have become the political intermediary in the American political system. This role has grown out of two modern, parallel developments. The first is the pervasiveness of the American media that has in turn led to the public's and politicians' increased reliance upon the press. The second is the movement of the press into an increasingly autonomous position, largely free from political controls.[17]

A Pervasive News Media

The media are more pervasive today than ever before. The types of media, however, that Americans use on a regular basis have changed radically in the last two decades. Newspaper circulation has been in decline for many years, but the drop accelerated during the Great Recession that lasted from 2007 through 2009. The aptly named NewsPaperDeathWatch.com has documented the hard times that have hit newspapers with giants like *The New York Times*, *The Wall Street Journal*, and Reuters laying off staff and consolidating sections. Most of the remaining papers are switching to a hybrid print/online format. In some cases, they have gone online-only. In 2009, CNN listed digital publishing as one of the Top 10 Tech Trends. The article also mentioned Twitter and other micro-blogs as a huge threat to the newspaper business. The article noted, "[Twitter] lets authors post short bursts of information, which become searchable the moment someone clicks 'send.'"[18] When it comes to news, a daily paper simply cannot compete with the up-to-the-second Internet. And of course, there is the added incentive that the Internet is free.

The audience for the three television-based news sectors—network news, cable television, and local news—continues to be strong. Large portions of the public, and so too advertisers, are still drawn to the television as a source of news. In 2015, network television news programs grew advertising revenues by 6 percent in the evening and 14 percent in the morning. Cable news also increased advertising revenues and subscriber revenues for a total growth of 10 percent. Local news advertising revenues similarly saw an increase in advertising revenues.[19]

Despite current financial strength, though, TV-based news cannot ignore the public's, particularly the young public's, pull toward digital. Today those under thirty are far less likely than those over thirty to watch any news on television.[20] More Americans are getting their news today from the Internet than from newspapers or radio, and three-fourths say they hear of news via e-mail or updates on social media sites, according to a new report. Sixty-one percent of Americans said they get at least some of their news online, according to a survey by the Pew Internet and American Life Project. That is compared with 54 percent who said they listen to a radio news program and 50 percent who said they read a national or local print newspaper. Almost all respondents, 92 percent, said they get their news from more than one platform. "In the digital era, news has become omnipresent. Americans access it in multiple formats on multiple platforms on myriad devices," reads the report, based on a survey conducted in 2010. "The days of loyalty to a particular news organization on a particular piece of technology in a particular form are gone."[21]

An Autonomous Press

The American press had its early beginnings as a partisan tool first of the American revolutionaries and then of the first political parties. Over the course of two centuries, however, the press has been transformed into a fiercely independent, autonomous profession, or as some call it, a "fourth estate."

Phase I: The Early Partisan Press

The first continuous newspaper in the United States was published in Boston by two brothers, John and Duncan Campbell.[22] The single-sheet Boston *Newsletter* began publication on April 24, 1704.

By 1750, there were thirteen regular newspapers being printed in the colonies and gradually four-page papers replaced the single sheet.

The spread of the colonial press was actively encouraged by the government. In fact, these early papers were under the control of the British colonial government. Most papers carried on their mastheads "By Authority" and received a subsidy for publishing the proceedings of the colonial governments. Besides these subsidies, the papers were also sustained through lucrative government printing contracts. A final aspect of government control was to be found in the fact that the papers could be prosecuted for seditious libel if they included content seen as offensive to the colonial authorities.

During the Revolutionary War, the newspapers actively distanced themselves from the British colonial governments. The Stamp Act that had placed a tax on newspapers greatly angered the press, and as their anger made its way onto the pages of the papers, the press became the engine that would drive opinion against the British.

The press became further politicized during the fight over ratification of the new Constitution of 1787. The supporters of the Constitution sought to mobilize opinion through *The Federalist Papers* while the opponents of the new Constitution argued their case in the *Letters of a Federal Farmer*. This period of history is early evidence of the critical role the press plays in linking government and public opinion.

After the Constitution was ratified, the press remained partisan and politicized. Alexander Hamilton encouraged John Fenno, an ardent Federalist, to come to the nation's capital and establish a newspaper to serve as a voice for the administration of President Washington. Hamilton's encouragement of Fenno came primarily through the promise of government printing jobs. In response, the Jeffersonian Republicans cultivated Philip Freneau, urging him to publish a Republican journal, luring him with the promise of a government position, personal loans, and government printing contracts.

During the Jacksonian period, increased and intensified competition within and between the political parties led to an even greater party reliance on the press to mobilize electoral support. As the parties continued to subsidize and support the press through government printing contracts and patronage appointments, the number of newspapers burgeoned to over 12,000, with one copy for every fifteen people. Largely because of their financial dependence on the parties, the press remained intensely partisan during this period. The U.S. Census listed only 5 percent of all newspapers as "neutral" or "independent."

Phase II: The Penny Press and Yellow Journalism

After the Civil War, rapid breakthroughs in printing and communication technologies worked to give the press greater financial independence, thereby freeing it from its earlier partisan control. The high-speed rotary press meant lower costs and lower subscription rates. In addition, the invention of the telegraph carried with it the ability to disseminate information between cities at low cost. Growing numbers of people in the urban centers of the country provided a ready audience for the cheaper newspapers. When the suffrage was extended in the 1800s to nonproperty owning white males, this audience was not only ready but eager as well for political news. Finally, the commercialization and industrialization of America created a merchant class eager to reach mass audiences by way of advertising. The press was no longer dependent on the political parties. In the end, politicians themselves began to relinquish their partisan hold on the press as they found other ways to communicate with the public, in particular, strong party organizations geared to mass mobilization.

Together these developments worked to create a penny press with mass readership and much greater independence from partisan control. The editors of these newspapers often engaged in **yellow journalism,** focusing on sensationalism and scandal. Also during this period, an elite set of newspapers, including for example the *New York Times*, was developing. These newspapers were beginning to define their work as a profession, and the journalists working for these papers adopted a libertarian theory of the press.

The libertarian theory argued that journalists must print "the truth." It is not, according to libertarian theory, the job of the journalist to express his own viewpoint. Rather, the journalist is merely a conduit for the views of others. For example, it was not uncommon in the first half of the eighteenth century to find newspapers expounding the political philosophy of the owner of the newspaper. The press moguls of the nineteenth century, men like William Randolph Hearst and Joseph Pulitzer, had great influence on American government and society.

The libertarian theory of the press worked to the advantage of sitting presidents as well. During the period from 1870 through the middle of the 1960s, presidents in particular had greater access to press coverage and used the press as a bully pulpit to shape public opinion. It was generally accepted that in exchange for press access to politicians, certain topics would be off limits to the press corps. The private behavior of politicians and behind-the-scenes partisan machinations, for example, were taboo. Even John F. Kennedy's Addison's disease, for example, was left undiscussed in the press.[23]

Ronald Reagan was one of the best with the media.

Phase III: Investigative Journalism

In the middle of the 1960s, people began to see that big business was dominating many of the economic markets in the United States. It was little wonder that journalists soon began to look at the marketplace of ideas and recognize that this market too was dominated by established politicians often at the expense of other views. By the 1960s the prohibitive cost of starting a newspaper meant that the only way to get into the newspaper business was to buy out an existing one. Broadcasting further challenged the libertarian theory's assumption of an unlimited number of outlets for the expression of ideas. The technology of broadcasting made unlimited access impossible at the same time that it called for government regulation.

The Vietnam War, Watergate, and the Kerner Commission's criticism of media coverage of race relations worked to further call into question just how open a marketplace the press had ever been to any views other than those of the political establishment of public officials and established leaders. As a result, journalists began to articulate a new professional code of social responsibility. The professional press corps began to argue that the American public has a right to know the full story. If the full story does not spring from the mouth of officials, journalists have the responsibility to go behind the scenes and unearth the full story.

The result was the advocacy journalism of the late 1960s. Reporters felt justified in using journalism for what they perceived to be morally just causes: fighting corruption in government, disclosing environmental degradation, and unearthing examples of racial inequity. By the 1970s, advocacy journalism had given way to a new stage of adversarial journalism with the journalists actively challenging statements made by officials. The press acts as the opposition. The press's tradition of yellow journalism muckraking, the new technology of television, and the press's increasing access to alternative sources of information allowed the press to assume this role. In addition, the investigative, inside story made good sense economically; such stories filled with conflict and titillation built audiences that could then be sold to corporate advertisers.

Phase IV: Conglomerate Ownership of the Press

Today the news media are big business. In 1983, fifty companies controlled over 90 percent of all the media in the United States. When President Bill Clinton signed the Telecommunications Act of 1996 into law, it eased restrictions on media cross-ownership so that one company—or person—could own multiple media businesses (like broadcast stations, cable stations, newspapers, and websites). Though the law was intended to increase competition by reducing regulation, it instead allowed large corporations to strengthen their dominance through mergers and buyouts. Consequently, by 2011, six companies controlled over 90 percent: General Electric, News Corporation, Disney, Viacom, Time Warner, and CBS. Put another way, 232 media executives control the information diet of 300 million Americans. Even 70 percent of cable news is owned by these same 6 corporations.

Ownership of social media is similarly concentrated in a few corporate hands. The platforms owned by *Facebook* (*Instagram*), Google (*YouTube*, *Google+*), LinkedIn, and Yahoo (Tumblr) are collectively used by billions of people around the world, and these companies have a combined market value of hundreds of billions of dollars. These giants are actively buying up competitors.

Google has acquired over 160 companies, Yahoo over 100, Twitter over 30, Facebook over 45, and LinkedIn over 10.[24]

Phase V: Atomization of the Media

Despite the growing concentration of media ownership, a contrary trend, an atomization of the media, has also developed in recent years. Whereas concentration has led to a national media, atomization has fragmented the influence of this national media. The major newspapers and networks have lost their dominance, while other media, some not even considered news organizations, have started to play a greater role in American politics.

This trend is partly the result of technological changes. First, the national networks began to lose viewers to the local news stations. The local stations are now linked together via satellite and can thereby share coverage of national and international affairs. Next, the traditional stations lost viewers to the cable television, which because of their number can offer more, specialized programming. The offerings of cable television have become more focused. This "narrow casting" appeals to small segments of the audience in contrast to the networks' more generalized attempts to appeal to a mass audience. For example, C-SPAN provides live coverage of Congress and allows viewers to see and hear Congress at work.

There are other cable stations that cater to various racial and ethnic groups. A cable system in Los Angeles and New York is targeted to the Jewish population. A cable channel in California broadcasts in Chinese, one in Hawaii broadcasts in Japanese, and one in Connecticut and Massachusetts broadcasts in Portuguese. Stations in New York provide programs in Greek, Hindi, Korean, and Russian.

The Internet has led to additional news sites. Major newspapers can now be read on-line, as can several political magazines. Often these on-line services are at the forefront of the news. During the 2010 campaign, Web logs, or "blogs," played a critical role. Free Republic and the DailyKos are two of the ideologically driven Web logs that managed to attract hundreds of thousands of readers and helped shape the presidential campaign and contributed to a powerful grassroots mobilization of voters.

The trend toward atomization of the media is also a reflection of the increasing partisan polarization of the American electorate following the 2000, 2004, 2008, 2012, 2016, and 2020 elections. This polarization is clearly reflected in the viewing habits of Americans. Since 2000, the number of people who regularly watch the Fox News Channel has increased by nearly half from 17 percent to 25 percent and the gains have been greatest among political conservatives. At the same time, CNN, Fox's principal rival, has a more Democrat-leaning audience than in the past. Audiences for Rush Limbaugh's radio show are overwhelmingly conservative and Republican. By contrast, audiences for some other news sources notable NPR, the NewsHour, and magazines like the *New Yorker*, the *Atlantic*, and *Harper's* tilt liberal and Democratic.[25]

Phase VI: Citizen Journalism, Robot Journalism

Journalists and reporters no longer control political discourse. Increasingly, individuals are doing what only professional reporters used to do, reporting information. The emergence of the Internet and social media, with blogs, podcasts, streaming video and other Web-related innovations, has made citizen journalism possible. The Internet now gives average people the ability to transmit information globally. This was a power once reserved for only the very largest media corporations and news agencies.

In the early 2000s, citizen journalism was hailed as a revolution that would make newsgathering a more democratic process, one that would no longer solely be the province of professional reporters. But citizen journalism remains a work in progress that has yet to fulfill such hopes. One problem is that citizen journalism has been marred by inaccurate reporting, such as reports during Superstorm Sandy that the New York Stock Exchange had been flooded. And with most citizen journalists not being paid for their work, it seems unrealistic to expect them to have the same commitment to their work that the paid professionals do. During the 2016 campaign, misinformation spread within seconds of being posted on social media. False Tweets were re-Tweeted also within seconds. That's a problem that doesn't seem likely to disappear any time soon.

Intensifying the problem is that some of these new journalists are not even human; they are robots. In 2016, a surprisingly high percentage of the political discussion taking place on Twitter was created by pro-Donald Trump and pro-Hillary Clinton software robots, or social bots, with the express purpose of distorting the online discussion regarding the election. Researchers analyzed 20 million election-related tweets created between Sept. 16 and Oct. 21, 2016. They found that robots, rather than people, produced 3.8 million tweets, or 19 percent. Social bots also accounted for 400,000 of the 2.8 million individual users, or nearly 15 percent of the population.[26] Another study has found that automated pro-Trump activity outnumbered automated pro-Hillary Clinton activity by a 5:1 ratio by Election Day. And many of the automated Trump messages were not truthful. For example, a widely disseminated Trump robo-tweet said that Democrats could vote on a different day than Republicans; that Clinton had a stroke during the final week of the election; and that an FBI agent associated with her email investigation was involved in a murder-suicide.[27]

THE NEWS GATHERING PROCESS

There are three main sets of factors that affect news decisions.

Personal Background and Values

Many years ago sociologist Herbert Gans found that media personnel tend to be drawn disproportionately from middle and upper middle class backgrounds.[28] Even today there are still very few minorities in the journalistic professions. It is perhaps not surprising that reporters tend to have values that correspond to their socioeconomic backgrounds. Studies have found that journalists tend to have a positive orientation to private business, emphasize individualism, and take moderate positions on political and social matters.[29] While some have suggested that journalists tend to be liberal, no such consistent ideological bias has ever been documented. For example, a recent analysis looked to see if there is a relationship between the accounts journalists follow on Twitter and the partisanship of their work. The researchers identified 644 political journalists from 25 news outlets, including the *New York Times, Washington Post, Wall Street Journal, Dallas Morning News,*

Arizona Republic, *Huffington Post*, and *Breitbart News*. They analyzed the Twitter accounts these journalists were following and then their published work. They found the publications tended to produce ideologically neutral even slightly conservative, pro-business content despite accusations that these media outlets had a partisan bias.[30]

It may be more difficult for the voices of women and minority groups to be heard because the ownership of mass media by only a handful of huge conglomerates has worked to reduce ownership by women and minorities. In the landmark 2003 decision *Prometheus v. FCC*, the Third Circuit chastised the FCC for ignoring the issue of female and minority ownership of mass media outlets. Following the decision, however, the FCC has done almost nothing to address the issue. Consequently, from October 2006 to October 2007, the number of minority-owned commercial TV stations decreased by 8.5 percent. In the same time period, the number of African-American-owned stations decreased by nearly 70 percent. Finally, it should be noted that there has been no improvement in the level of minority broadcast television ownership since 1998, even as the total universe of stations has increased by approximately 13 percent.

The state of female and minority ownership in the broadcast sector is even more shocking when compared to other industries. Women own 28 percent of all non-farm businesses but currently own less than 6 percent of commercial broadcast television stations. Minorities own 18 percent of all non-farm businesses, but own approximately 3 percent of commercial broadcast television stations. While female and minority ownership has been advancing slowly in other sectors since the late 1990s, it has gotten progressively worse in the broadcast industry. The level of minority ownership in the general non-farm sector rose 23 percent from 1997 to 2002. However, from 1998 to 2007, the level of minority broadcast TV ownership dropped.[31] The under representation of women and minorities affects content. One study of 2012 election-year coverage found that major American newspapers and TV news programs featured up to seven times as many quotes from men than women. This held true even when "women's issues" were the subject.[32] Additionally, even though women today comprise two-thirds of graduates with degrees in journalism or mass communications, the media industry is less than one-third women.[33]

Professional Values

Since the beginning of the 1900s, journalists have increasingly taken themselves seriously as professionals. The result has been the creation of journalistic societies, trade journals, and even a code of ethics to be followed. Reporters today follow certain standards of decency, refusing, for example, to print, say, or quote racial epithets. In addition, reporters depend on documentary practices such as reliance on reliable sources. Finally, since Watergate, journalists see themselves as social critics, crusaders for justice, ombudsmen for the disadvantaged. The post-Watergate generation of journalists takes a participatory stance. In Carl Bernstein's words: "The job of the press is not to follow Ronald Reagan's or George Bush's agenda, but to make its *own* decisions about what's important for the country."[34]

The new citizen journalism discussed above is challenging the professional values of journalists. There are now content farms that produce news by using cheap networks of freelancers. For example, Yahoo has bought such a farm, *Associated Content*, for about $100 million. Demand Media uses freelancers to deliver information for online sections of traditional media such as *USA Today* and

San Francisco Chronicle. *Examiner.com* has over 40,000 freelance workers and its *BleacherReport* boasts more than 3,600 unpaid authors. *The Huffington Post*, which employs 53 staff to edit and produce original content, uses the unpaid services of 6,000 bloggers. The spread of content farms presents a challenge to the profession of journalism.[35]

Organizational Factors

Perhaps more important than either personal background or professional considerations are the economic imperatives of the modern mass media. The news media, as noted above, are now part of larger conglomerates. These conglomerates often include non-media companies, and they are usually run by business executives who have little or no background in the media. The governing imperative of such conglomerates is to make a profit. To make a profit both newspapers and broadcasting must build an audience. This audience can then be sold to corporate advertisers, or sponsors.

Advertising is big business. Despite its lowest ratings in history, the broadcast industry experienced a banner year in 2016. Advertisers paid $74.7 billion to the networks and broadcast stations and an additional $59.6 billion to cable networks. Social network advertising revenues have also grown enormously in recent years. In 2016, mobile social networking alone reached revenues of $23.68 billion. Advertising on social network sites broke the $25 billion revenue mark by 2015.[36] Between 2018 and 2019, social media advertising grew 3.6 percent to $28.9 billion and digital ad revenue overall increased 21.8 percent from 2017 with a total internet ad revenue of $107.5 billion by the beginning of 2019.[37]

THE CONTENT OF THE NEWS: INFORMATIONAL BIASES

The Bias Debate

The media's growing importance has led to an increased concern over possible bias in media coverage of current events and people in the news. Left-wing critics claim that the press is simply a tool of "the establishment." Michael Parenti, for example, sees corporate ownership of the mass media as inevitably leading journalists in a pro-capitalist, pro-corporate posture.[38] These critics see all forms of mass communication as bolstering the establishment line. Even films are viewed as reinforcing capitalist dogma. There is an equal number of media critics on the right. They see the media as the tool of anti-government, anti-American "liberals." Journalists are viewed as advocates of a pro-welfare spending, anti-business, liberal agenda.

What critics on the left and right have failed to realize is the overriding influence of the economic pressures on the increasingly competitive mass media. A continually biased program is unlikely to attract a large audience. To ensure profits, the media must entertain the audience. The pressure to entertain and make money is far more determinant of media content than ideological purity. Both the networks and newspapers are experiencing stiffer competition—the networks from cable and Internet and the newspapers from social media and human-interest tabloids. This increased competition in a field already driven by the profit motive works to produce a number of informational, rather than partisan, biases in media content.

Informational Biases

Infotainment

As discussed above, the first priority of the media is to build an audience. This means that even political matters will be played as "stories." The news tends to personalize, concentrating on individuals rather than institutions or process. For example, stories on the president commonly focus on some personal habit or trait of the person holding the office. Similarly, statistical data is often glossed over in favor of an illustration using an individual's story. For example, a jump in unemployment may be illustrated by an interview with someone standing in an unemployment line.

The media also attempt to build audiences through a focus on the dramatic, the visual, the exceptional. Violence is a central element of the news because it tends to be so visual. Change is emphasized over continuity, and news stories often follow certain intuitively understandable schema: good versus bad, rich versus poor.

Several authors have recently noted that audiences for news programs are built and maintained when the content of the news is brought to the lowest common denominator. Responding to the merger of Capital Cities/ABC with Disney, author Brian Stonehill, director of the Media Studies Program at Pomona College, argues that "the juvenile sets the tone for the culture, and the escapism of fun and games wins a shutout over the business of information."[39]

Negativity

An outgrowth of the media's need to entertain as well as its professional adherence to a watch-dog role, is a tendency to accentuate the negative aspects of American life. Journalists are intent upon publicizing the missteps of political leaders. The media's preference for "bad news" can be seen, for example, in the fact that the negative coverage of presidential candidates has risen steadily in recent decades and now exceeds the positive coverage.

Much of today's political discourse starts on social media, and the medium often amplifies vitriol and slants information. Social media give people the power to organize and inform, but social media are also frequently used to exhibit narcissism and ignorance. Such behavior reflects the uglier side of political discourse. Political analyst Brian Solis argues that many people simply have not learned how to be civil on social sites and instead use these channels as a way of imposing their own perspective, thrusting it upon the community in ways that are divisive.[40]

In 2016, social media made politics more combative than ever before, in terms of both agenda and slant. For example, a recent study from the Anti-Defamation League found that a total of 2.6 million tweets containing language frequently found in anti-Semitic speech were posted across Twitter between August 2015 and July 2016.[41] As noted above, the combative quality of social media discourse is heightened by the fact that much of this discourse does not come from human beings.

COVERAGE OF CAMPAIGNS

The informational biases built into the mass media can all be seen in the media's coverage of political campaigns. An agenda dominated by problems, divisive issues, and the "negative" dominates campaign coverage. Reporters seek to find the story behind the official story. A former editor of *The Washington Post* has said of reporters: "[They] want to be important players in the political process, not passive bystanders. They want to mix it up with the candidates, join the debate and defend the Republic as surrogates of the masses."[42] As a result, campaign coverage tends to follow a fairly set formula.

The Horserace

The media's proclivity toward the personal, the dramatic, and the divisive has led campaigns to be covered primarily as horseraces between competing sets of candidates. In 2020, election news coverage was dominated by the competitive game, and coverage was devoted overwhelmingly to the question of winning and losing. In recent elections, poll results, election returns, delegate counts, electoral projections, fundraising success, and the like, along with the candidates' tactical and strategic maneuvering, accounted for more than half of the reporting.[43]

This fixation on the horserace may stem from the fact that many journalists were once campaign insiders. For example, ABC's Jeff Greenfield, George Stephanopoules, and George Will, NBC's Ken Bode, CBS's Diane Sawyer, PBS's Bill Moyer and David Gergen, and *The New York Times's* William Safire were all campaign insiders before they were journalists. It is little wonder that these journalists see campaigns in terms of strategy and winning.[44]

Gaffes

In Washington, an off-the-cuff remark is referred to as a gaffe. A gaffe has been defined as the trouble a politician gets into when he or she says what is actually being thought. The media often amplify the initial gaffe by repeatedly covering it, and the politician unwittingly further amplifies it by repeatedly apologizing over it. The end result is that such mistakes trap candidates in a spiral of controversy, getting them in ever-deeper trouble.

Presidential candidate, Joseph Biden had some widely covered gaffes during the coronavirus pandemic. For example, in March 2020, candidate Biden called the coronavirus the "conavirus" and shorty after that got the number of grandchildren he has wrong.[45] President Trump, running for reelection, tweeted these Biden gaffes but that quickly backfired as Twitter users replied with examples of the president's own flubs and falsehoods. Apparently, there were plenty of gaffes to go around.[46]

Coverage of the Incumbent

Incumbents running for re-election enjoy a number of advantages over their challengers, including a greater amount of media attention. Because the incumbent is in a position of power, the press corps is more likely to cover his or her actions. It is not unusual, for example, for the press to become almost fixated on a president's eating habits, holiday travels, and golf game, in addition to his discharge of the affairs of state. A recent study has found, however, that such abundant coverage is not always a good thing. Apparently journalists believe that because incumbents enjoy an advantage in terms of the amount of coverage, the press corps must balance this advantage by scrutinizing more carefully his or her actions. Such intense scrutiny leads to more negative coverage. Media coverage of the incumbents running in the 2016 congressional races was overwhelmingly negative. The Republicans received 23 percent positive coverage and 77 percent negative. For the Democrats, the comments were 22 percent positive and 78 percent negative.[47]

COVERAGE OF THE PRESIDENT

All the informational biases discussed above lead the news media to fixate on the presidency. The president is one individual while the Congress is made up of 535 individuals. The presidency is dramatic; the Supreme Court is less so. In foreign affairs, the president is virtually the sole actor, and foreign affairs often involve a crisis likely to dominate the news agenda. Finally, that the president has sole responsibility for nuclear weapons, together with assassinations and assassination attempts, has heightened the press's interest in the health and well-being of the president.

This focus on the presidency is also stimulated by the White House itself. White House correspondents, numbering close to seventy-five, cover the White House as a regular beat and rely on information they receive from the president's own staff, information carefully crafted by the staff to control the direction of the story. The most frequent form such control takes is the press release, a prepared text distributed to reporters in the hopes that they will use it verbatim. A daily news briefing at 11:30 A.M. enables reporters to question the president's press secretary about these news releases and get film footage for the nightly television news. To no small extent, the correspondents are the captives of the White House press releases.

Such intense scrutiny may set the president up for eventual negative coverage as his performance falls short of heightened expectations. While news coverage of presidents has always tended to be fairly negative, broadcast news of President Trump's first term in office was even more so, with 90 percent of the coverage being negative.[48]

COVERAGE OF CONGRESS

Most reporters in Washington are accredited to sit in the House and Senate press galleries, but only about four hundred cover Congress exclusively. Most news about Congress comes from the numerous press releases issued by the members of Congress. In addition, C-Span now covers Congress live.

In general, Congress tends to receive less coverage than does the president, because of the informational biases of the media discussed above. Congress does not walk. Congress does not talk. Consequently, it is difficult to personalize the institution in the same way that the office of the presidency can be personalized. When the Congress can be made more personal and dramatic, it is more likely to get on the news. After the Republicans in the House censured President Obama for not being open and transparent enough, particularly regarding healthcare reform, C-SPAN proposed to the then-presumptive House Speaker John Boehner an increase in the number and scope of press cameras in the House chamber.[49] A study by the Pew Research Center's Project for Excellence in Journalism, however, has found that 27 states now have no Washington reporters, and the number of papers with bureaus in the capital has dropped by "about half since the mid-1980s. An online news website in Maine, a state which now has no Washington reporters, describes the implications well: "In place of having someone on the scene, Maine news organizations rely on interviews with delegation members to determine what they're up to. This method has several obvious drawbacks, the most glaring being that our elected officials in the nation's capital aren't likely to tell us anything they don't want us to know."[50] Not only does the demise of print journalism impact what we know about what our representatives are doing on our behalf in Washington, it also means citizens are flying more or less blind when it is time for them to vote.

THE POLITICIANS RESPOND: THE MANAGEMENT OF NEWS COVERAGE

Shorter Campaign Speeches

Candidates' and politicians' speeches are getting shorter and shorter. In the nineteenth century, hour-long speeches were the norm. Today, candidates deliver stump speeches in less than seventeen minutes. Politicians know that whatever they say is likely to be reduced to only a few seconds on the evening news. To control these few seconds of air time, candidates speak in soundbites, tricky little statements that are most likely to fill the media's need for drama and brevity. In 2008, Barack Obama's "Yes we can" was so often repeated that a song was made out of it and made available on iTunes. Donald Trump, first as a candidate and then as president, communicated primarily through very short Tweets. From his official declaration of his candidacy in June 2015 through the first two and a half years as president, he tweeted over 17,000 times. His tweets are considered official statements by the president of the United States.

Spin Control

Politicians have not been willing to sit by idly, leaving journalists in control of the news agenda. A group of political consultants, "spin doctors," have begun to play a central role in determining strategy, first at the presidential campaign level and then in more and more state and local races. These consultants attempt to tailor the politician's message to the needs of the news organizations for drama, personalization, and brevity. Increasingly, these consultants stage media events, situations that are simply too newsworthy for the media to pass up. For example, during the 2020 pandemic, the Trump administration tried to control the news about when they knew the pandemic was a global threat.

Debates

Candidates ideally would like to get as much free media coverage that they can control as possible. The presidential debates that have been regular features of presidential campaigns since 1960 offer the perfect setting for a candidate to warehouse his ideas with fairly little intervention on the part of journalists. In general, the political challenger has the most to gain from a debate. The challenger needs the attention, has little to lose, and gains the appearance of being presidential because of being on the same stage with the president himself. The incumbent president, on the other hand, has little to gain and may lose by making a mistake or appearing unprepared.

The debates are usually only an hour and a half in length, and usually no more than three debates are televised. The candidates can, however, extend the reach and importance of the debates by getting the news media to continue to discuss what occurred in the debates and perhaps show film footage from the debates repeatedly. Presidential debates have, therefore, also begun to turn on the production of effective, catchy soundbites. Today, in a ninety minute debate each candidate will actually speak for less than thirty minutes.

One of the most important features of presidential debates is exclusivity. For the nation's scores of third-party presidential candidates, the debates are the political equivalent of not getting asked to the high school prom. While Pat Buchanan, Ralph Nader, and other third-party candidates sought to fight back through lawsuits and the Internet, they should not have taken their exclusion personally. Third-party candidates have been getting the debate brush-off since 1960, when Congress modified a 1934 law that required any broadcast station staging a debate to welcome all candidates. Congress suspended that rule to let Richard Nixon and John F. Kennedy square off by themselves in the first televised debates.

A special nonprofit commission selected by the Republican and Democratic hierarchy now controls the task of selecting who appears in the presidential debates. Not surprisingly, the bipartisan Commission on Presidential Debates, established in 1987, has set the bar higher than the current third-party candidates can jump, mandating they score at least 15 percent in nationwide polls. Only Ralph Nader came close in 2000 with 5 percent.

Political Advertisements

While politicians can never hope to control completely either the content or slant of their *free* news coverage, they can turn to paid political advertisements over which they can exert complete control over the message. Political advertisements have a long history in this country, but they have become increasingly central components of modern campaigns.

The new importance of political advertising has six sources. First, the primary election system used to choose nominees for public office require candidates to appeal directly to thousands, even millions, of voters. In the case of presidential primaries, candidates must reach voters in each of the thirty-eight separate states that employ primary elections. Second, advertisements now represent the biggest campaign expenditure in most campaigns. In 1952, only 30 percent of overall funds were so spent. In 2012, candidates bought over $1 billion in air time; that is eight times as much, after inflation, as was spent in 1972.[43] In 2016, the candidates for the presidency aired more than

210,000 television commercials. Hillary Clinton spent $141.7 million in ads and Donald Trump spent only $58.8 million on ads, instead depending more heavily on Tweets and other social media.[51]

A third factor working to increase the importance of advertisements is that there are legal limits on how much candidates for certain public offices can spend on their campaigns. Such limits lead candidates to place a premium on reaching the most voters at the lowest possible cost. A fourth source of the centrality of advertisements in modern campaigns is found in the legal limits placed on how much money the Democratic and Republican National Committees and interest groups can donate to a candidate's campaign. However, one way around these limits is for interest groups and political parties to make and air an advertisement on behalf of the candidate. Such independent spending is not limited by federal campaign finance laws, and the Supreme Court in July 1996 ruled that parties and groups may spend unlimited amounts on behalf of candidates. The Bipartisan Campaign Reform Act (BCRA) of 2002 prohibited any corporate expenditure on issue ads mentioning the names of candidates during the period 30 days before a Federal primary and 60 days before a Federal general election. The FEC then ruled that any ad mentioning a candidate in the pre-election period was prohibited by BCRA. In 2007, however, the Supreme Court ruled the prohibition unconstitutional as applied to a Wisconsin Right to Life group. The group had aired ads in 2004 urging voters to contact Wisconsin Senators Feingold and Kohl to oppose a Senate filibuster. The ads did not specifically support or oppose the election of Senator Feingold, who was up for reelection that year, but it clearly stated a candidate's name. The decision in the case, *Federal Election Commission v. Wisconsin Right to Life, Inc.* led to an increase in issue advertising during elections.

The changing structure of the advertisements themselves may account for their increased importance. Today's television advertisements employ the rich multimodal properties of television. These advertisements use montage, music, and symbolism to create an entire mood. The soft focus, long shots, and slow music are the grammar of this mood. In addition, the increasing negativity built into modern advertisements has made them more powerful campaign tools. Not only have studies shown that people tend to remember negative messages better than positive ones, but also negative ads are dramatic, personal, conflict-laden, in short, newsworthy. The news media often pick up soundbites taken from the advertisements and replay them on the evening news. The news media thereby amplify and legitimize the negativity of the original advertisement, and they do so for free!

Negative political ads hit a new low during the election of 2020. In 2020, there were numerous political advertisements attacking the government's response to the coronavirus pandemic and numerous other ads firing shots at the Democrats. Up to a third of all ads aired could be considered attack ads, pointing out the negative qualities of the opponent. Studies consistently show that people remember negative ads more than they remember positive ones. Anyone looking to pore through those ads and more can go to the Political TV Ad Archive. The archive, a project of the nonprofit Internet Archive, provides a searchable, viewable and shareable online archive of election political TV ads.[52]

Political advertisements may also carry subliminal messages that covertly influence viewers' attitudes. In 2008, an anti-Obama video produced by the McCain campaign contained an eight-minute montage of sometimes-contradictory statements about the Iraq war made by Senator Barack

Obama. At the very beginning, the title, "The Obama Iraq Documentary," flashes into place in a blaze of orange. For a single frame, a tiny fraction of a second, Obama's face is framed by the following prominent letters: "a l q D." While many editing programs do allow randomized letter placement, for a brief moment, letters that the brain may want to play with and try and spell something that makes sense with, frame Obama's face. If you type "al qD" into Google, you get this response: "Did you mean: al qaeda."

Finally, political advertisements may have become more important because they may be more informative than the news itself. While most of the news coverage of elections on early and late-evening broadcasts is devoted to campaign strategy and polling, outpacing reporting on policy issues by a margin of more than three to one (65 percent to 17 percent) political advertisements often carry a good amount about the candidates positions.[53]

THE EFFECTS OF THE MASS MEDIA

What People Remember and Know

Since the late 1980s, the emergence of 24-hour cable news as a dominant news source and the explosive growth of the Internet have led to major changes in the American public's news habits. But a new nationwide survey finds that the digital revolution and attendant changes in news audience behaviors have had little impact on how much Americans know about national and international affairs. On average, today's citizens are about as able to name their leaders, and are about as aware of major news events, as was the public nearly 20 years ago. In 1989, for example, 74 percent could come up with the name of the vice president; today, it is somewhat fewer who can do so (69 percent). Recent surveys find bipartisan voter ignorance about basic facts about government and policy, with only 36 percent of Americans being able to pass the relatively simple civics test administered to people seeking to become citizens. Today, 52 percent of Americans cannot name even one member of the United States Supreme Court.[54]

Influencing Public Opinion

Documenting the effects of mass media on specific attitudes is difficult. Studies have found that prolonged, sustained media coverage on a single topic, especially in a crisis like war, can significantly influence mass opinions.[55] The same study found that of all the people expressing opinions on the news, for example the president, members of Congress, network commentators had the greatest influence on the audience. Other studies have found that even a single story can influence attitude change.[56]

Setting the Political Agenda

Evidence suggests that media coverage does heighten the audience's concern with certain topics over others. Social media tend to favor the brief over the deep, the cutting over the carefully considered, emotionalism over reason, the outrageous over the truthful. The more visceral and outlandish the message, the faster it travels and the longer it holds the fickle eye of social media. In both 2016 and 2020, it was the fiery "Feel the Bern" Bernie Sanders and the often bellicose and crude Donald Trump that got followed, friended, liked, hearted, and hashtagged. Studies have found that for the most part, voters in 2016 were less concerned with policy than with everything else. Talkwalker, a social media analytics company, found that the top three political themes across social media platforms during the campaign year were Donald Trump's comments about women, Hillary Clinton's ongoing email scandal, and Donald Trump's refusal to release his tax returns. "Social media may have played a role in creating a kind of scandal-driven, as opposed to issue-driven, campaign," said Todd Grossman, CEO of Talkwalker Americas, "where topics such as Trump's attitude towards women, Trump's tax returns and Clinton's emails have tended to dominate discussion as opposed to actual policy issues."[57]

Cynicism, Alienation, and Declining Efficacy

The press's role in setting the political agenda also means that the increasingly sensational and negative topics covered in the news will dominate the public's agenda as well. Years ago, Michael J. Robinson attempted to document that the CBS documentary "The Selling of the Pentagon" produced antimilitary attitudes in the program's audience.[58] A more recent study has shown that the media attentive are more likely to pick up negative views of the economy.[59]

Other studies have found that those most attentive to the news experience reduced levels of political efficacy with feelings of political powerlessness and mistrust. One study concluded that "the presentation of news in a manner that conveys a high degree of political conflict or criticism leads to a sense of distrust and inefficacy among newspaper readers."[60]

Behavior

There is little consistent evidence that mass forms of communication can alter behavior. For example, recent studies attempting to link violence on television with violence in young adults have failed to find a clear causal relationship. What the mass media appear to be able to do is channel the behavior of people already predisposed to behave in a particular way. For example, news coverage and political advertisements may work to reinforce an individual's pre-existing partisan views, thereby further encouraging that individual to vote for the favored candidate. Another study has found a relationship between teenage suicide rates in already troubled youths and media coverage of teenage suicide.[61]

CONCLUSION

This chapter has focused primarily on the role of the mass media in transmitting images and information to the citizenry of this country. The media are equally important transmitters of the citizens' views to those in government. Throughout history, journalists have suggested policy concerns and offered solutions to pressing problems. In doing so, the mass media have worked to bring issues of public concern to those in government. Today, the media have developed sophisticated methods to tap mass sentiments. Beginning in the 1800s, newspapers conducted straw polls to measure public opinion. These polls usually questioned subscribers but made no scientific attempt to get a random sample. By the middle of the twentieth century, the media began to conduct scientific polls and develop their own survey research divisions. Newspapers and broadcasters even team up to do extensive polling together. Virtually every day, the results of one major poll or another are published. During the 2020 campaign, CNN and *USA Today* reported a fresh poll daily from September 30 through the November election.

Recent developments suggest that the media link between governed and government will only become a more direct one in the future. The 2020 campaign organized supporters and reached voters who no longer rely primarily on information from newspapers and television. YouTube now provides people a continual stream of political information, and cell phone text messages remind them to vote.

Not all consequences of the new technology are likely to be benign, for while American elections have always included a certain amount of deceptive practices, the advent of Internet technology allows for a more widespread and effective dissemination of misinformation. In 2016, for example, robo calls told people their polling places had been changed. According to the National Network for Election Reform, registered voters in Virginia, Colorado, and New Mexico reported receiving phone calls in the days before the election claiming that their registrations were cancelled and that if they tried to vote they would be arrested. Domain names with prospective and actual vice-presidential nominees' names also popped up on the Internet, leading to sites with unexpected information.

At the moment, most states do not have adequate or any legislation that addresses the concerns inherent in such deceptive practices, and candidates have not done a good job of protecting themselves by proactively registering typo domains.[62] What remains to be seen is whether the new forms of media will work to create an electronic democracy with fully informed and participating citizens. Today's audience is now at once better informed, more skeptical and, from reading blogs and other social media, sometimes trafficking in rumors or suspect information.

CHAPTER NOTES

[1]Jon Porter, "Facebook Invests $100 Million in Journalism as COVID-19 Makes It More Vital Than Ever," *The Verge*, March 30, 2020, *https://www.theverge.com/2020/3/30/21199358/facebook-investment-journalism-grants-100-Jon Porter, million-dollars-advertising-spend*

[2]Crag Silverman,, "Coronavirus Ad Blocking Is Starving Some News Sires of Revenue," *BuzzFeed News*, March 27, 2020, *https://www.buzzfeednews.com/article/craigsilverman/news-sites-need-ads-to-survive-the-coronavirus-more-than-35)*

[3]Amy Mitchell and J. Oliphant Baxter, "Americans Immersed in COVUD-19 News," *Pew Research Center*, March 18, 2020, *https://www.journalism.org/2020/03/18/americans-immersed-in-covid-19-news-most-think-media-are-doing-fairly-well-covering-it/*

[4]Charlie Warzel, "What We Pretend to Know About Coronavirus Could Kill Us," The *New York Times*, April 5, 2020, *https://www.nytimes.com/2020/04/03/opinion/sunday/coronavirus-fake-news.html*

[5]Dan Alexander, "How Barack Obama Has Made $20 Million Since Arriving in Washington," *Forbes*, January 20, 2017, *https://www.forbes.com/sites/danalexander/2017/01/20/how-barack-obama-has-made-20-million-since-arriving-in-washington/#644f711e5bf0*

[6]Statista, "Number of Daily Newspapers in the United States from 1970 to 2018," *Statista*, March 3, 2020, *https://www.statista.com/statistics/183408/number-of-us-daily-newspapers-since-1975/*

[7] Lydia Saad, "TV Is Americans' Main Source of News," *Gallup*, July 8, 2013, *http://www.gallup.com/poll/163412/americans-main-source-news.aspx.*

[8]The Hill, "Poll: Majority of Voters Name TV as Primary News Source," *The Hill*, December 5, 2019, *https://thehill.com/hilltv/rising/473301-poll-majority-of-voters-name-tv-as-primary-news-source*

[9]The Pew Research Center, "News Audiences Increasingly Politicize," *http://people-press.org, June 8, 2004, p.4.*

[10]Ella Koeze and Nathaniel Popper, "The Virus Changed the Way We Internet," *The New Your Times*, April 7, 2020, *https://www.nytimes.com/interactive/2020/04/07/technology/coronavirus-internet-use.html*

[11]Frederic Lardinois, "Social Media is Slowly Changing the Demographics of Political Engagement," *ReadWriteWeb,*September1,2009, *http://www.readwriteweb.com/archives/social_media_is_slowly_changing_the_demographics_0.php*

[12]Quoted in Robert Kurz, "Congress and the Media: Forces in the Struggle Over Foreign Policy," in *The Media in Foreign Policy*, ed. Simon Serfaty (New York: St. Martin's, 1990), 77.

[13]Phil Gailey, "U.S. Bars Coverage of Grenada Action; News Groups Protest," *The New York Times*, October 27, 1983, *https://www.nytimes.com/1983/10/27/world/us-bars-coverage-of-grenada-action-news-groups-protest.html*

[14]Jay Peterzell, "Can the CIA Spook the Press?" *Columbia Journalism Review* (July/ August 1986): 18-19.

[15]Sara Prot, et al, "Media as Agents of Socialization," *APA PsycNET*, April 2020, *https://psycnet.apa.org/record/2015-05080-012*

[16]Doris Graber, *Mass Media and American Politics* (Washington, D.C.: Congressional Quarterly Press, 1980), 127.

[17]Richard Davis, *The Press and American Politics* (New York: Longman, 1992), 6.

[18]Alexander Moschina, "The 'Must Own' Tech Stock for 2011," *Investment U*, January 8, 2011, *http://www.investmentu.com/2011/January/the-mcclatchy-company-newspaper-publishing-company.html.*

[19]Amy Mitchell and Jesse Holcomb, "State of the News Media 2016," *Pew Research Center,* June 15, 2016, *http://www.journalism.org/2016/06/15/state-of-the-news-media-2016/.*

[20] Antonis Kalogeropoulos, "How Younger Generations Consume News Differently," *University of Oxford Digital News Report*, April 2020, *http://www.digitalnewsreport.org/survey/2019/how-younger-generations-consume-news-differently/*

[21]Doug Gross, "Survey: More Americans Get News from Internet than Newspapers or Radio," *CNN Tech*, March 1, 2010, *http://articles.cnn.com/2010-03-01/tech/social.network.news_1_social-networking-sites-social-media-social-experience?_s=PM:TECH.*

[22]Alfred McLung Lee, *The Daily Newspaper in America* (New York: Macmillan, 1937), 17.

[23]James MacGregor Burns, *John Kennedy: A Political Profile* (New York: Harcourt, Brace, 1960).

[24]Free Press, "Who Owns the media," *Free Press*, March 2020, *https://www.freepress.net/issues/media-control/media-consolidation/who-owns-media*

[25]The Pew Research Center, "News Audiences Increasingly Politicized," p.2.

[26]University of Southern California, "Fake Tweets, Real Consequences for the Election," *Phys.Org*, November 4, 2016, *http://phys.org/news/2016-11-fake-tweets-real-consequences-election.html.*

[27]Gideon Resnick, "How Pro-Trump Twitter Bots Spread Fake News," *The Daily Beast*, November 16, 2016, *http://www.thedailybeast.com/articles/2016/11/17/how-pro-trump-twitter-bots-spread-fake-news.html.*

[28]Herbert J. Gans, *Deciding What's News* (New York: Pantheon, 1979).

[29]Michael Parenti, *Inventing Reality* (1985).

[30]Denise-Marie Ordway, "Partisanship of Journalists' Twitter Networks," *Journalist's Resource*, November 9, 2018, *https://journalistsresource.org/studies/society/news-media/twitter-partisanship-journalist-bias-research/*

[31]Out of the Picture 2007: Minority & Female TV Station Ownership in the United States," *http://www.freepress.net/files/otp2007.pdf, October, 2007.*

[32]"Diversity in Media Ownership," *freepress.net*, 2016, *http://www.freepress.net/diversity-media-ownership.*

[33]Catherine York, "Women Dominate Journalism Schools, but Newsrooms are Still a Different Story," *Poynter*, September 18, 2017, *https://www.poynter.org/business-work/2017/women-dominate-journalism-schools-but-newsrooms-are-still-a-different-story/*

[34]Carl Bernstein quoted in *Vanity Fair*, March, 1989, 106.

[35]Roumen Dimitrov, "Do Social Media Spell the End of Journalism as a Profession," *Global Media Journal*, volume 10 issue 1, 2016, *http://www.hca.westernsydney.edu.au/gmjau/?p=799.*

[36]"Social Network Ad Spending to Hit $23.68 Billion Worldwide in 2015," *eMarketer,* April 15, 2015, *https://www.emarketer.com/Article/Social-Network-Ad-Spending-Hit-2368-Billion-Worldwide-2015/1012357.*

[37]Megan Graham, "Digital Ad Revenue in the US Surpassed $100 Billion for the First Time in 2018," *Tech Drovers,* May 7, 2019, *https://www.cnbc.com/2019/05/07/digital-ad-revenue-in-the-us-topped-100-billion-for-the-first-time.html*

[38]Parenti, *Inventing Reality.*

[39]"The Mickey Moused Media," *Los Angeles Times*, 1 August 1995, B9.

[40]Matt Kapko, "How Social Media is Shaping the 2016 Presidential Election," *CIO*, September 29, 2016, *www.cio.com/article/3125120/social-networking/how-social-media-is-shaping-the-2016-presidential-electionhtml.*

[41]Sanders, "Instagram: The New Political War Room?" *NPR*, September 3, 2015, *http://www.npr.org/sections/itsallpolitics/2015/09/03/436923997/instagram-the-new-political-war-room)*

[42]Richard Harwood, "The Press Should Set The Agenda," *Washington Post*, 26 September 1988, sec. 4, 3.

[43]Thomas Patterson, "News Coverage of the 2016 Presidential Primaries: Horse race Reporting and Its Consequences," Harvard Kennedy School Shorenstein Center on Media, Politics and Public Policy, July 11, 2016, *https://shorensteincenter.org/news-coverage-2016-presidential-primaries/.*

[44]Kathleen Jamieson, *Dirty Politics* (New York: Oxford University Press, 1992), 181-2.

[45]Tim Hains, "Sky News Host Marvels at Biden Gaffe Montage," *Real Clear Politics*, March 8, 2020, *https://www.realclearpolitics.com/video/2020/03/08/sky_news_host_marvels_at_joe_biden_gaffe_montage_not_enough_popcorn_in_the_world_for_biden-trump_debate.html*

[46]Ed Mazza, "Trump Mocks Biden's Gaffes and It Goes About as Well as You'd Expect," *Politics*, March 3, 2020, *https://www.huffpost.com/entry/donald-trump-joe-biden-gaffes_n_5e0045c5b67ed38b37bf04*

[47]Seth Masket, "The Real Bias in the Media Coverage of the Presidential Camapigns," *PacificStandard*, September 12, 2016, *https://psmag.com/the-real-bias-in-the-media-coverage-of-presidential-campaigns-e69ff2391b6f#.ewp3ba3ci.*

[48]Jennifer Harper, "Broadcast Tradition: 90% of Trump Coverage Remains Negative," *The Washington Times*, January 15, 2019, *https://www.washingtontimes.com/news/2019/jan/15/a-broadcast-tradition-90-of-trump-coverage-remains/*

[49]Kelly Born, "What Happened to Coverage of Congress?" Hewlett Foundation, May 28, 2014, *http://www.hewlett.org/what-happened-to-coverage-of-congress/.*

[50]Meredith Jessup, "Obama Paid $18K to Monitor "Negative' Coverage of Oil Spill," *The Blaze*, September 13, 2010, *http://www.theblaze.com/stories/obama-administration-hired-media-guru-to-monitor-negative-coverage-of-oil-spill-response.*

[51]Jacob Pramuk, "Trump Spent About Half of What Clinton Did on his Way to the Presidency," *CNBC*, November 9, 2016, *http://www.cnbc.com/2016/11/09/trump-spent-about-half-of-what-clinton-did-on-his-way-to-the-presidency.html.*

[52]William La Jeunesse, "Negative Ads Blanketing Airwaves in 2016," *Fox News Politics*, February 4, 2016, *http://www.foxnews.com/politics/2016/02/04/negative-ads-blanketing-airwaves-in-2016-campaign.html*

[53]The PEW Research Center for the People and the Press, "Public Knowledge of Current Affairs Changed by News and Information Revolution," *http://people-press.org/report/319, April 15, 2007.*

[54]Ilya Somin, "Political Ignorance and the Midterm Elections," *Reason*, November 5, 2018, *https://reason.com/2018/11/05/political-ignorance-and-the-midterm-elec/*

[55]Benjamin Page, Robert Y. Shapiro, and Glen R. Dempsey, "What Moves Public Opinion?" *American Political Science Review* 81 (March 1987): 31.

[56]David L. Jordan, "Newspaper Effects on Policy Preferences," *Public Opinion Quarterly* 57 (Summer 1993): 191-204.

[57]Sam Sanders, "Did Social Media Ruin Election of 2016?", *NPR*, November 8, 2016, *http://www.npr.org/2016/11/08/500686320/did-social-media-ruin-election-2016*

[58]Michael J. Robinson, "Public Affairs Television and the Growth of Video Malaise," *American Political Science Review* 70 (1976): 425-30.

[59]David E. Harrington, "Economic News on Television: the Determinants of Coverage," *Public Opinion Quarterly* 53 (Spring 1989): 17-40.

[60]Arthur Miller, Edie Goldenberg, and Lutz Ebring, "Type-Set Politics," *American Political Science Review* 73 (1979): 77.

[61]Madelyn Gould and David Shaffer "The Impact of Suicide in TV Movies," *New England Journal of Medicine* 315 (11 September 1986): 685-94.

[62]Common Cause, "Deceptive Practices 2.0," *http://www.commoncause.org/deceptive_practices_report.pdf)*

SUGGESTED READINGS

Alterman, Eric. *What Liberal Media? The Truth About Bias and the News.* New York: Basic Books, 2004.

Anderson, David M. and Michael Cornfield, eds. *The Civic Web: Online Politics And Democratic Values.* Lanham, MD,: Rowman & Littlefield, 2003.

Bagdikian, Ben. *The New Media Monopoly.* Boston: Beacon Press, 2004.

Campbell, Richard, Christopher Martin, and Bettina Fabos. *Media and Culture.* New York: St. Martin's Press, 2009.

Chester, Jeff. *Digital Destiny: New Media and the Future of Democracy.* New York: New Press, 2008.

Fenton, Tom. *Bad News: The Decline of Reporting, the Business of News, and the Danger to Us All.* New York: Harper Collins, 2005.

Flew, Terry. *New Media.* Oxford: Oxford University Press, 2014.

Graber, Doris A. *Mass Media and American Politics.* 9th Ed Washington, D.C.: CQ Press, 2002.

Hamilton, James T. *All the News That's Fit to Sell.* Princeton, NJ: Princeton University Press, 2004.

Herman, Edward S. and Chomsky, Noam. *Manufacturing Consent: The Political Economy of the Mass Media.* New York: Pantheon Books, 1988.

Iyengar, Shanto. *Media Politics: A Citizen's Guide.* New York: W.W. Norton, 2015.

Jenkins, Henry. *Convergence Culture: Where Old and New Media Collide.* New York: New York University Press, 2008.

Leigh, David and Luke Harding. *WikiLeaks: Inside Julian Assange's War on Secrecy.* London: Guardian Books, 2011

Schaeffer, Todd and Thomas Birkland. *Encyclopedia of Media and Politics.* Washington, D.C.: CQ Press, 2007.

Weaver, David, et al. *The American Journalist in the 21st Century: U.S. News People at the Dawn of a New Millennium.* New York: Eribaum, 2006.

West, Darrell M. *Air Wars: Television Advertising in Election Campaigns, 1952-2008,* 5th ed. Washington, D.C.: CQ Press, 2009.

Web Sites

Accuracy in the Media, www.aim.org.
Claremont Institute. www.townhall.com
The Drudge Report http://www.drudgereport.com/
Federal Communications Commission, www.fcc.gov.
Huffington Post http://www.huffingtonpost.com/
Journalism.org, www.journalism.org.
Newseum, www.newseum.org.
Pew Research Center for the People and Press https://digitalliteracy.gov/pew-research-center-
    people-and-press
Politico http://www.politico.com/
TotalNEWS. www.totalnews.com.

Chapter Seven

INTEREST GROUPS

The year 2019 saw federal lobbying spending surpassing $3.47 billion, a nine-year high, as industries sought to influence Congress and the Trump administration on trade policy and tariffs, drug prices, and the healthcare system. The health sector alone spent a record $594 million on lobbying in 2019, up nearly 5 percent from 2018. Within the health sector, the pharmaceuticals/health products industry spent $295 million to stop legislation to regulate drug prices and to fight drug price controls proposed by the Trump administration. Other interest groups, such as health professionals and health services and HMOs, spent more on lobbying in 2019 than any previous year. Private equity firms that control physician staffing companies launched a massive ad campaign, spending nearly $54 million on ads to pressure lawmakers. Other groups also spent record amounts of money to influence government in 2019 and 2020. The Trump administration's proposed trade agreements with China and other countries attracted huge interest group lobbying with a record 1,430 clients reported lobbying on the issue of trade in 2019. Amazon and General Motors hired Washington lobbyists to secure exemptions from tariffs. The transportation sector spent $259 million, the air transport industry spent $104 million, and the communications/electronics interest groups spent a record $435 million lobbying Washington.

One might think, or at least hope, that a pandemic crisis would motivate people and groups to rise above their self-interests. The coronavirus of 2020, however, reveals that interest group politics remain strong and well even in a pandemic. In March 2020, Congress passed, and the president signed, a $2.2 trillion relief bill that established a $450 billion lending program to support struggling businesses and provide $350 billion in loans to small businesses. The stimulus bill launched a lobbying bonanza in Washington as companies frantically tried to influence the bill and its effects on their sectors. Powerful companies and trade groups that had a long history of lobbying Congress immediately asked for more than $2.7 trillion in grants, loans and other assistance. Airlines and airports ended up being big winners, garnering $29 million in direct grants and up to another

$29 billion in loans. The health care industry lobbyists also succeeded in securing government assistance. A Super PAC funded by New York hospitals and closely tied to Senate Minority Leader Chuck Schumer pushed to secure a portion of the $100 billion allocated in the law for health care. Other health industry groups including the American Hospital Association asked for an additional $100 billion, while for-profit hospitals asked for $225 billion.

In the end, the massive coronavirus stimulus package included a grab bag of home-state favors and rewards for special interests, often completely unrelated to the pandemic. For example, one provision in the law speeds up the Food and Drug Administration's ability to approve sunscreen products. Not coincidentally, the sunscreen company, L'Oréal, is headquartered in Kentucky, home state of the Senate Majority Leader Mitch McConnell. The bill also gave $25 million for the Kennedy Center for the Performing Arts in Washington, $13 million for Howard University, $75 million for the National Endowment for the Humanities, and another $50 million to the Institute of Museum and Library Services.

Apparently, even in crises, self-interest is hard to contain. Even though gyms and fitness centers were closed due to the pandemic, Adidas lobbied for use of pretax dollars to pay for gym memberships and fitness equipment. Drone makers urged the Trump administration to grant waivers that would allow them to be used more widely. Pig farmers, citing coronavirus, lobbied to expedite foreign worker visas. It appears that when a crisis hits, concerns about government spending and looming deficits get moved aside and, in the rush, to meet the crisis head on, both political parties are open to intense pressure from their key constituencies. The conditions for a blitzkrieg of lobbying in such a situation are ideal.[1]

DEFINING INTEREST GROUPS

An **interest group** is an organization of people and or companies with specific policy goals, entering the policy process at several points. The key here is that an interest group is an *organization*. There are many people with many interests throughout the United States; but many, if not most, fail to organize with others to pursue their goals. In addition, many of the groups that do go on to get organized pursue private or social purposes. Groups only become political interest groups when they try to affect policies of local, state, and federal governments.

Interest Groups versus Political Parties

Political parties and interest groups are often easily confused because they both seek to influence policy; they are, however, distinct. Political parties nominate candidates for office and seek to gain office by aggregating groups into a coalition. In doing this, political parties often try to mute their policy positions to appeal to as many differing groups as possible. Interest groups, on the other hand, seek to articulate the specific viewpoint of the group. While it is true that some groups have a wider set of concerns than others, every interest group is concerned with representing the position or positions of the group. Usually, the interest group stands little to win from muting its position.

The Roles of Interest Groups

While political parties do mainly one thing, nominate candidates and run them for office, interest groups play several roles.

Representation

Perhaps the most important role performed by an interest group is representing the interests of its members. The Tobacco Institute promotes the interests of cigarette companies, and the Human Rights Campaign Fund works to advance the cause of gay and lesbian rights.

Political Participation

Interest groups provide people with an avenue to participate in politics. Many people feel that their vote is not very important. Still, these people may see strength in numbers and interest groups as the vehicle to express this strength.

Education

Interest groups expend a great deal of effort on educating their members, the general public, and government officials. It is quite common to see spokespersons for interest groups interviewed on television news programs or talk shows. Groups may also advertise both on television and in the newspapers. Interest groups may even try direct-mail campaigns to explain their viewpoints and mobilize support.

Agenda Building

By educating their members, the general public, and public officials, interest groups are seeking to set the agenda of issues that are to be actively debated by policy makers. In 2016, messages of no more than 140 characters were used to influence the agenda of that year's political campaign. Issues emphasized in tweets often are subsequently discussed in blogs, talk radio, and news stories. To increase how many Twitter users see political tweets, interest groups often include hashtags. For example, those on the political left tend to use hashtags such as #p2, which stands for Progressive 2.0. Those on the political right often use #tcot, which means Top Conservatives on Twitter.

Program Monitoring

Interest groups are not only concerned about what laws are passed; they are also concerned with the implementation of policy. Interest groups monitor how the government administers the programs that affect them. Sometimes the law may even require federal agencies to work with interest groups to ensure that their interests are taken into account. Clearly interest groups play several important roles in American politics. They shape policy outcomes through representation of their members, providing an avenue of participation, education, agenda setting, and the monitoring of government programs. Still, some groups may be more effective at fulfilling these roles than other groups. Some citizens may never see their interests represented. Some groups may mislead rather than educate officials and the public. Other groups may work to distort national priorities and programs to benefit their interests at the expense of the nation as a whole. To understand the inequities and inefficiencies of interest group politics, it is necessary to understand that some groups simply get better organized than others.

WHO IS ORGANIZED?

There is an astounding number of interest groups in the United States. *The Encyclopedia of Associations*, a voluntary government publication of national interest groups, lists over twenty-five thousand organizations working to affect public policy. The number of groups is matched by their incredible diversity. Everyone from the National Cricket Growers to the Flying Physicians is listed in the numerous volumes of the *Encyclopedia*. The multiplicity and obscurity of the groups disguise, however, some typical membership patterns.

Economic Interest Groups

Business Groups

Business groups are the most common type of interest group. Business groups account for approximately 20 percent of the organized interest groups in Washington. If one adds in lobbyists and law firms hired to represent business interests, business interests constitute up to 70 percent of all groups housed in the national capital.[2]

There are three distinct types of business organizations. The organization with the broadest membership is the peak business association. Peak associations attempt to speak for the entire business community. The Chamber of Commerce, for example, represents an assortment of local chambers of commerce and other groups. The National Association of Manufacturers (NAM) represents more than ten thousand manufacturing firms, and the Business Roundtable represents the country's two hundred largest corporations.

Businesses may also attempt to advance their interests through trade associations. These organizations represent companies in the same line of business. Mobil, Shell, and Texaco, for example, belong to the U.S. Petroleum Association.

Finally, many businesses try to influence public policy on an individual basis. Most large companies have offices in Washington or hire Washington lobbying firms to work with government officials in the making and implementation of policy.

While the Republican Party has traditionally favored business, in recent years the Democrats have also worked in the interests of the business community. The pro-business stance of the two parties reflects business's increasing financial contributions to both parties. For example, in 2016, Renaissance Technologies donated a total of $54,415,635 to candidates running for national public office. Fifty-four percent of these dollars went to Democrats and 46 percent to Republicans.[3]

Organized Labor

Union membership has declined steadily since 1983, the earliest year for which strictly comparable data are available. Even private-sector industries with a relatively high concentration of union members, such as transportation and manufacturing, have experienced declining membership rates. In contrast, union membership rates in the public sector, which are much higher than in private industries, have held fairly steady since the early 1980s. The union membership rate is the proportion of employed wage and salary workers who are union members. In 2020, the percent of wage and salary workers who were members of unions was 10.3 percent, down by .2 percentage points from the previous year. The union membership rate of public-sector workers (33.6 percent) continued to be more than five times higher than the rate of private-sector workers (6.2 percent).[4]

The public's perception of these public sector unions has become very negative in recent years as overgenerous contracts, lavish pensions, and benefits and early retirement have put states in dire fiscal straits. It is predicted that the pension funds of eight states—California, Connecticut, Indiana, New Jersey, Hawaii, Louisiana, Oklahoma, and Illinois—will go broke by the end of fiscal year 2020. At the national level, the Obama administration was even more generous with unions. Amid savage private-sector job cuts, one-third of the funds from the 2009 stimulus bill went to state and local governments, mainly to rescue public-sector employees. An executive order strongly encouraged government agencies to use construction companies with unionized workforces for any federal construction project over $25 million. Additionally, when the Obama administration bailed out Chrysler and GM, their unions won special favors, and he imposed tariffs on imports of Chinese tires at a union's request.

The approval of labor unions has decreased across a very wide demographic cross section of America, including in union-oriented households. According to the Gallup organization, today, 32 percent of respondents currently have an unfavorable opinion of labor unions. From 1939 to the present, the percent expressing an unfavorable opinion of unions has always been between 20 and 40 percent of the American public.[5]

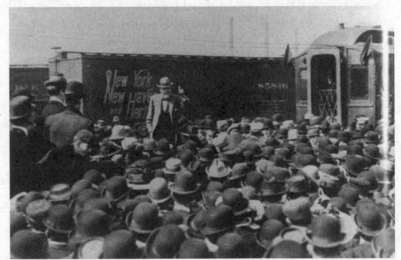

Unionism in America grew out of the strife between low-paid workers and the greed of capitalism. The struggle for unionization was long and bitter but was eventually won when the government recognized the right of workers to organize. Eugene Debbs is shown here addressing railroad workers. He and other union officials were jailed for disobeying a court injunction against the Pullman Strike of 1894.

Agriculture

There are two types of organizations representing agricultural groups. General farm interest groups, the biggest of which is the American Farm Bureau Federation, seek to represent the interests shared by most farmers. For example, the American Farm Bureau speaks for the interests of large farms while the National Farmers Organization and the National Farmers Union represent the interests of the smaller farmer.

A newer type of agricultural group is found in those that have organized around specific commodities. Today, almost every crop and type of livestock has a corresponding group. Pigs have the National Swine Improvement Federation. Lettuce greens have the National Leafy Greens Council.

Professional Associations

Professional associations represent occupations that usually involve extensive education and formal training and perhaps government licensing. The American Medical Association (AMA) and the American Bar Association (ABA) are two prominent examples of professional associations.

Citizen Groups

Unlike economic interest groups, citizen groups, often called **public interest groups**, work to promote their vision of the public good. Citizen groups exist for almost every issue but the most visible have been in the area of consumer protection and environmental policy making. Some groups advance broad agendas. For example, People for the American Way is a liberal interest group that pushes its position on issues from school prayer to abortion to censorship of the arts. Other citizen groups are single-issue groups that are organized around one specific issue, like abortion, saving the whales, or drunk driving.

Women's Groups

There are many groups organized to advocate women's equality. The National Organization for Women (NOW) is the largest of these groups with 500,000 members and chapters in all of the fifty states. In recent years the women's movement has divided between groups pushing an ideological agenda, such as NOW, which continues to focus on the issue of abortion, and more pragmatic groups, such as the National Women's Political Caucus, which seeks to elect women to public office regardless of their stands on specific issues. Another group, EMILY's List, an acronym (Early Money is Like Yeast), is a national political action committee that works to elect pro-choice female Democrats. The group has turned the bundling of campaign contributions into an art form, enlisting thousands of members nationwide to direct their money to key races. In the 2020 election cycle, EMILY's List contributed a total of almost $5 million in campaign contributions and outside spending on behalf of candidates.[6]

Religious Groups

Religious groups have become increasingly well organized and politicized. Evangelical Protestants, for example, today play an important role in the Republican Party. Not only do they heavily vote for Republican candidates, they were also the most consistently supportive of the Trump presidency. For example, at the height of the COVID-19 pandemic crisis, 77 percent of evangelicals said they were at least somewhat confident that President Trump was doing a good job responding to the outbreak, including half who said they were very confident. By comparison, only about half of Americans overall (52 percent) said that Trump underplayed the risks, including majorities who say this among the religiously unaffiliated (64 percent), African American Protestants (67 percent), and Jews (73 percent).[7] At the other end of the spectrum, an overwhelming majority of members of the African Methodist Episcopal Church (AME) (92 percent) identify with or lean toward the Democratic Party, while just 4 percent say they favor the Republican Party (an 88-point gap). Similarly, 87 percent of members of the National Baptist Convention and 75 percent of members of the Church of God in Christ (another historically black denomination) identify as Democrats.[8]

LBGQT

After World War II, the first gay rights groups organized to share information and fight police repression. During the 1960s, the gay rights movement became better organized and more visible. By 1972, gay rights issues were being addressed by politicians, and by 1973 the American Psychiatric Association removed homosexuality from its list of mental disorders. The election of Bill Clinton in 1992 was a crucial turning point for gay rights. He ended the federal policy treating homosexuals as security risks and invited gay activists to the White House for the first time.

Lesbian, gay, bisexual, and transgender (LGBT) groups actively organized in 2010 to work for the repeal of the Defense of Marriage Act and laws barring discrimination in employment and easing the path toward gay adoption. These groups are largely credited with the historic repeal of the military's "Don't Ask, Don't Tell" Policy in December 2010. In 2013, President Obama in his second inaugural address made history by referring to "our gay brothers and sisters."

In 2016 the North Carolina HB2 law, which prevents transgender people from using bathrooms corresponding to the gender with which they identify propelled LBGQT issues to the forefront of the campaign agenda and both Hillary Clinton and Donald Trump voiced support for the LBGQT community. Trump made history during his speech at the Republican National Convention, becoming the first GOP nominee to pledge support to the LGBT community in a nomination speech. He pledged to protect LGBT people from terrorism after a shooting that killed dozens of people at a gay club in Orlando.

In 2020, the LGBTQ Victory Fund, the only national organization dedicated to electing LGBTQ leaders to public office, endorsed 32 openly LBGTQ candidates for 2020 races. More openly LBGTQ candidates ran for public office in 2020 than in any previous election year, surpassing the 72 who ran in the "Rainbow Wave" of 2018. The Victory Fund endorsed 122 LGBTQ candidates for 2020.[9]

The Elderly

Today, 16.1 percent of the nation's population is over sixty-five. Several groups, sometimes called the "gray lobby," represent their interests. Founded in 1958 to provide insurance for the elderly, the American Association of Retired Persons (AARP), with thirty-eight million members, is the largest and of its most powerful interest groups. The AARP, through an active mail drive, attracts eight thousand new members every day. For only $16, anyone over fifty can join and gain access to the bounty of benefits provided by the organization, everything from auto and home insurance to car rentals.

With 1,800 employees and eighteen lobbyists, the AARP has become a potent political force. The goals of the AARP are primarily to preserve and expand government benefits to the elderly, which total about $14 billion each month. Most recently, the AARP actively supported the Affordable Care Act (ACA). The ACA provides health coverage protections that go beyond the ability of individuals to buy affordable insurance on the Health Insurance Marketplace. The law includes free preventive services and helps lower prescription drug costs for millions of Medicare beneficiaries, allows people under 26 to remain on their parents' health insurance and allows states to expand Medicaid so more low-income Americans can have access to affordable health care. The AARP filed an *amicus* brief in the U.S. Court of Appeals for the Fifth Circuit supporting the ACA.[10]

Several groups have formed to try to stem the power of the gray lobby. Groups such as Americans for Generational Equity and Children's Defense Fund are, however, smaller and less influential than AARP.

Environmental Groups

In the United States, a wide range of organizations sometimes called non-governmental organizations or NGOs represents the organized environmental movement. The largest and most influential environmental organizations are the so called Group of Ten: Environmental Defense Fund, National Wildlife Federation, National Audubon Society, Defenders of Wildlife, The Wilderness Society, Natural Resources Defense Council, World Wide Fund for Nature, Friends of the Earth, Sierra Club, and Izaak Walton League.

According to research conducted by the Urban Institute, an economic and social policy research group, the number of nonprofit organizations dedicated to conservation and the environment rose faster than the number of nonprofit groups overall since 1995, growing by 4.6 percent per year compared to 2.8 percent per year for all nonprofits. In fact, the environmental movement has expanded in the number of organizations, members, and total revenue almost every year since 1960. The study further shows that while there is a core group of prominent national organizations, more interestingly, there is a larger, more rapidly growing group of regional, local and other specialized groups fighting for environmental causes.[11]

As public awareness and the environmental sciences have improved in recent years, environmental issues have broadened to include key concepts such as "sustainability" and also new emerging concerns such as ozone depletion, acid rain, global warming, and biogenetic pollution. Today, environmental movements often interact or are linked with other social movements such as the animal rights, anti-nuclear weapons and/or nuclear power, peace, poverty, hunger, and human rights movements.

Single-Issue Groups

Single-issue groups are distinguished by their concern for a single issue and their reluctance to compromise. The abortion issue has generated a number of single-issue groups. The National Right to Life Committee is supporting a constitutional amendment to ban all abortions. The committee works to elect candidates that favor such an amendment and defeat those who do not. The same-sex marriage issue has also generated single-issue groups. Today, the largest single-issue group, and arguably the most powerful, is the National Rifle Association. In the 2018 election cycle, the NRA contributed over $11 million to candidates running for office and spent over $5 million in lobbying efforts.[12]

Foreign Governments

Foreign governments, foreign corporations, and citizens of foreign countries are also represented in Washington. Governments of the largest U.S. trading partners, such as Japan, South Korea, Canada, and the European Union (EU) countries, maintain large research and lobbying staffs. Even smaller nations, such as those in Central America, engage lobbyists when legislation affecting their interests is under consideration by Congress. Based on what is publicly reported, foreign governments spent $530 million in 2018 to develop relationships within the United States with members of Congress, federal agencies and even the media. In 2018, a diplomatic crisis tearing at the Middle East ignited a multimillion-dollar battle for influence in Washington between bitter rivals Qatar and the United Arab Emirates (UAE). Both countries spent heavily on lawyers, lobbyists, public relations and advertising to seek better trade and security relationships with the United States. Qatar paid a $2.5 million retainer to the law firm of former U.S. Attorney General John Ashcroft while the UAE had an arrangement with The Harbour Group, a public relations and public affairs firm, for up to $5 million annually.[13]

The Internet

Web activism is perhaps the newest addition to organizational efforts to influence government and policy making. A group called TechFreedom has actively worked to build bipartisan support for protections against government snooping in Americans' private communications and location information. It recruited other organizations to join the Digital Due process coalition to oppose a sweeping "digital dragnet" that would allow law enforcement to track the Internet use of every American. There are now numerous other interest groups, for example the Center for Democracy and Technology, fighting to ensure that the Internet is open, innovative, and free of government control.[14]

Perhaps no issue has so incited interest group activity more than the issue of Net Neutrality. Net neutrality is a set of rules in place aimed at giving internet users equal access to all web content while preventing internet providers from favoring certain sites over others. For example, the worry has been that if Comcast, an internet service provider and parent company of NBC, wanted to stream NBC shows faster than ABC shows, it could do so. To make sure this does not happen, a number of groups have organized in support of net neutrality including the Electronic Frontier

Foundation, Free Press, and Fight for the Future. Telecom and internet service companies, however, have strongly opposed net neutrality and have contributed heavily to political war chests.[15]

Government Interest Groups

Because the federal government in Washington controls most of the financial resources of the country and because the federal government gives grants of money to states and localities, state and local governments organize to lobby for these funds. In addition, the National Governors' Association, the National Association of Counties, and the National League of Cities all work to influence national policy on a wide array of issues affecting their levels of government.

Since the beginning of online shopping, states have missed out on billions of dollars in revenue from online sales that are exempt from taxation by federal law. With that much money at stake, it is no surprise that collection of online sales taxes has become a high priority for state and local government lobbying groups in Washington, D.C. Not only have bipartisan groups like the National Governors Association, National Association of Counties, and U.S. Conference of Mayors backed legislation to tax online sales, but even antitax governors such as Wisconsin's Scott Walker have lent their support. Yet multiple proposals over the last decade—including the current Marketplace Fairness Act first introduced in 2013—stalled in Congress. Some states, including New York, California, Rhode Island, Georgia among several others, have found ways to tax online sales. New York, for example, collects sales tax from online retailers and Amazon, among other online retailers, collects sales tax in those states.

COMMON FEATURES OF INTEREST GROUPS

While there are thousands of interest groups in the United States and while they come in all types and sizes, they share certain organizational features. First, every group must have a leadership and decision-making structure. The complexity of this structure will differ by group, but at a fundamental level, the group will need a staff including a public relations office, or a lobbying office, preferably in Washington, D.C. Second, the group must build a financial structure capable of sustaining the organization and funding group activities. Most groups require members to pay dues, and they often solicit additional funds through mailings and fundraising activities. Third, all groups must attract members to pay the dues and engage in group activities.

To attract such a membership, groups can offer three kinds of incentives. **Solidary incentives** involve the pleasure that members get from joining the group. Such incentives may include companionship and status. Parent-Teacher Associations and the Rotary Club are good examples of groups based principally on the provision of solidary incentives. **Material incentives** include anything that might make the group financially attractive to a member. The American Association of Retired Persons, for example, offers a grocery list of low-cost insurance, low-cost travel, and discounts in a variety of stores. These material incentives can only be obtained by people who join the group. The third type of incentive is the **purposive incentive**, the goals of the group. Some groups can attract members on the basis of passionate feelings about the group cause. Groups that rely primarily on their goals to attract members tend to be smaller groups where the purpose of the group involves a

Unfortunately, some issues are not easily resolved. To dramatize their cause against "acid rain," members of Green Peace, an environmental group, hung banners from smokestacks in four different European countries to protest factory emissions.

clear economic self interest. Groups with more amorphous purposes, for example, peace or solving world hunger, may have more difficulty arousing passion in their members for reasons discussed in the next section.

BIASES IN INTEREST GROUP FORMATION AND MAINTENANCE

The tremendous number and diversity of interest groups in the United States may disguise some inherent biases in the universe of interest group politics. The fact is that not all interests get organized and represented by groups. Neither are all groups that are organized equal in strength and influence. There are serious obstacles in the way of both interest group formation and interest group maintenance.

Obstacles to Interest Group Formation

The main obstacle to interest group organization is the problem of getting people to actually join the group, pay the dues, go to meetings and, in short, do the work. Many people may share a particular concern or interest; few will actually join the group. The reason that so few join the group is that all interest groups provide what economists call *collective goods*, benefits that will go not only to members of the group but nonmembers as well. Why go the full nine yards and work for the group when one can receive the benefits without expending the effort? In other words, interest groups are plagued by the age-old problem of free-riders, people who take the collective good without paying for it or working for it.

Some groups are faced with a greater free-rider problem than others. In 1965, in his book *The Logic of Collective Action,* Mancur Olson argued that interests shared by a larger number of people have a harder time getting organized than those shared by only a few people.[16] The reason, according to Olson, is that the larger the number of people sharing an interest the more likely each individual is to make the rational calculation that his or her effort is not needed and that someone will do the work of obtaining the collective good. For example, many people are concerned with a cleaner environment; yet, many refuse to donate time or money to the cause, not because they do not care but rather because they figure with so many other people out there concerned with the environment, there must surely be others who will do the work. Everyone will receive the benefits from a cleaner environment, but only a few will do the work. In a small group, however, members are more likely to see that if they fail to do the work, maybe no one will do the work. Consequently, maybe the collective good will not be obtained at all.

Additionally, when an interest is shared by a large number of people, it may often be the case that each individual member's share of the collective good is quite small. For example, a group called Heal the Bay works to clean up the Santa Monica Bay in southern California. While everyone would like a cleaner bay, each person's share of the bay is quite small, with many not living right on the coast or swimming in the bay regularly. On the other hand, in a small group the benefits may be very large. Say that one hundred people allegedly harmed by breast implants sue the manufacturer and receive thirty million dollars in damages. Quite obviously, the incentive to organize becomes stronger as the member's share of the collective good becomes larger.

The result of this collective good, free-rider problem is that many groups, particularly the larger ones, have a hard time tapping their potential membership. In the end, once organized, the groups may appear illegitimate and unrepresentative in that they have tapped such a small percentage of the population that should be concerned with the issue. Politicians tend to address issues only when they perceive the public to be fully aroused about and organized to pursue that issue. If a group has managed to organize only a bare fraction of those who should be sympathetic to the cause, politicians are likely to take a wait-and-see attitude.

What is important is that groups have a large *market share*, the number of members actually in the group compared to its potential membership. For years the American Medical Association (AMA) enrolled a very large percentage (more than 70 percent) of the nation's doctors as members. As its membership declined, however, so did the influence of the AMA.

Overcoming the Obstacles Through Interest Group Maintenance

After the publication of Olson's book, groups began to make serious efforts to attract and maintain their membership. One of the best ways for groups to attract members and keep them active in the group is to offer selective benefits, or one might think of them as noncollective goods, to only those who actually join the group. Such selective benefits can take any or all of three forms: material, solidary, and expressive benefits.

Material benefits are goods and services that come from belonging to a group. For example, the very well organized American Association for Retired Persons offers members a cornucopia of cheap travel rates, insurance benefits, and a monthly magazine. Similarly, the National Rifle Association's $45 annual membership fee entitles one to a magazine subscription, a shooter's cap, and eligibility to apply for a low-interest credit card. Fundraisers for public television often offer coffee mugs to those who make a contribution of a certain amount. Of course, selective benefits need not be material. Groups may also entice members with the **solidary benefits** of fun, camaraderie, and status. Other groups may offer **expressive benefits**, those derived from working for an interest group whose cause they see as just and right.

Selective goods are, however, expensive to provide. In each of the next 15 years, another 3 million Americans will reach age 50. Each one will get an invitation to join perhaps the most muscular political organization in the country, the American Association of Retired People (AARP). The AARP currently has a whole *Membership Benefit Guide* that is a treasure trove of selective benefits. The glossary lists benefits in all of the following: Travel, Health and Wellness, Entertainment, Restaurants, Shopping and Groceries, Insurance, Finances, Work and Jobs, Family and Caregiving, Auto Services, Advocacy, Magazines and Resources, Community, and contacts. The provision of all these selective goods is expensive.

This provision siphons off money that the group might have otherwise used for political purposes like lobbying or campaign funding. Smaller groups, with less of a free-rider problem, are, therefore, at an advantage in that they do not have to spend money on these selective goods. In addition, business and trade groups, which often tend to be small, have the additional advantage in that their members have a clear economic self-interest. Such a clear self-interest may work to get the group organized making the provision of selective goods unnecessary.

Interest Group Bias

Although there are tens of thousands of interest groups organized in the United States, the interests of all the people are not equally represented. Studies have consistently shown that the affluent, the better educated, those with a clear self-interest, are far more likely to join groups, participate at high levels, and remain with the group. There are, of course, significant examples of poor, uneducated people getting organized. Cesar Chavez successfully organized farm workers into the United Farm Workers Union. Still, such cases are more the exception than the rule. As this chapter has discussed, groups with a large potential membership and groups that are organized around issues that may not be clearly related to the members' economic self-interest may face additional problems both in organization formation and maintenance. These groups are quite often those that attempt to speak for the poor, the consumers, the environment, and the disenfranchised.

While donations are still crucial (and are often abused, as the recent revelations about "soft money" excesses in recent presidential elections show), they are not the only keys to the kingdom. These days, interest organizations are valued more for the votes they can deliver. Most powerful groups have large numbers of geographically dispersed and politically active members who focus their energies on a narrow range of issues. In other words, they know their convictions and vote them. In this era of low voter turnout, that kind of commitment can mean the difference between victory and defeat in close elections, which translates into real heft on the legislative front. Few things are more important to a Congressman than getting reelected.

Many powerful groups were propelled there on the strength of their long-established grassroots networks. Kings of the town hall meeting are the American Association of Retired Persons; the National Federation of Independent Business, better known as the small-business lobby; the National Rifle Association; the Christian Coalition; and the National Right to Life Committee. This is not to say that money does not talk at all anymore. The AFL-CIO garnered great grades for both its grassroots and its campaign fundraising.

In contrast, groups with huge memberships that also have an intense self-interest in government payouts are the National Education Association and AFSCME, the American Federation of State, County, and Municipal Employees, whose members rely on government for their paychecks. More to the point are the Veterans of Foreign Wars and the American Legion, whose members not only get veterans' benefits but also have a patriotic pull on politicians. The lesson: It takes both time and more than a modicum of support from politicians in both political parties for an interest group to gain any real standing in the hidebound world of Washington.[17]

THE PROLIFERATION OF INTEREST GROUPS

Americans have long worried about this bias in interest group organization and activity. Even at the time of the writing of the Constitution, it was clear that divisions among the citizenry were inevitable, sown into the very fabric of a free society. Writing in 1787, James Madison warned that these "factions" could prove dangerous to the larger public interest as they attempted to control policy making on their own behalf. For Madison, tyranny by either a majority or minority was problematic.

According to Madison, only two solutions exist to cure the "mischief of faction." One is to do away with the very freedom that spawns the conflict between groups. This solution Madison rejected because it would destroy the foundation of the American experiment in self-government. The other solution would be to encourage and nurture the factious nature of American society. Madison's vision was of a large, diverse nation with so many differences of opinion that domination by any one group would be unlikely. A group that might form on the basis of agreement on one issue would probably be internally divided by differences of opinion on other issues.

> Take in a greater variety of parties and interest [and] you will make it less probable that a majority of the whole will have a common motive to invade the rights of other citizens . . . [Hence the advantage] enjoyed by a large over a small republic.[18]

Madison's constitutional theory was that a government must actually encourage the proliferation of interest groups to prevent tyranny by any one group. This theory is today called **pluralism**. The theory suggests that all interests are and should be free to pursue their goals through bargaining and compromising, accommodating the interests of other groups. Madison's solution may be seen at work today. Since the founding of this nation, groups have proliferated at a phenomenal rate. Today, the bias in favor of the wealthy, the educated, and the professional is somewhat mitigated by the recent expansion in the number of interest groups found in this country. Tyranny by any one group is made less likely in such an environment rich with interest group organization and activity. While this proliferation is partly a result of what Madison called a large republic, the seeds of the proliferation are also to be found in more modern developments.

Sources of Interest Group Proliferation

Increased Government Regulation

Before the Second World War, the national government played a relatively limited role in American life. After the war, the federal government began to regulate various sectors of the economy and society. In the 1970s, the reach of government regulation had extended to almost every nook and cranny of the country's life. In the 1940s and 1950s, laws were passed regulating the eight-hour work day, child labor, and minimum wages. In the 1960s, with President Lyndon Johnson's War on Poverty, additional laws were passed to regulate race relations. Such government regulations have a powerful politicizing effect, often igniting interest group organization and activity.

The greatest expansion in government regulation came in the 1970s when the national government moved into the areas of automobiles, oil, gas, education, and health care. A *New York Times* report notes that these regulations spawned increased interest group activity in all the regulated areas.[19] The first groups to organize were usually the affected industries, organizing to fight the regulations. But just as a pebble tossed into a pond sets off concentric circles, so did government regulation spawn growing interest group activity. New groups, often called **clientele groups**, soon sprang up to encourage the regulation and to influence the distribution of the benefits of regulation. A clientele group is a group or segment of society whose interests are directly affected or promoted by a government agency. The first clientele department was the Department of Agriculture established by Congress in 1862 to promote the interests of farmers.

Recently, despite serious concerns that U.S. chemical plants could be targets for terrorists, the chemical industry has successfully blocked legislation that would mandate more stringent security rules for chemical manufacturers and others. Following the September 11 attacks, the Environmental Protection Agency warned that 123 chemical plants across the country each contained enough toxic chemicals to kill or injure one million people, if terrorists attacked the facility, and that another 750 facilities could threaten more than 100,000 people. Due in part to the generous campaign donations from the chemical plants, neither Congress nor the White House, nor any federal agency, has been successful in closing this large hole in homeland security.

Court decisions and presidential actions may also stimulate interest group organizations. For example, when the Supreme Court stepped into the abortion controversy in 1973 with *Roe v. Wade*, pro-life groups were quick to organize. Then, the *Webster* case set off the pro-choice groups. Other issues, such as school prayer, flag burning, and the death penalty, have set off a similar pattern of group proliferation. Perhaps no issue has spawned more interest group activity than the battle over health care and when it comes to lobbying Washington, no single industry can match the lobbying power of the health-care industry.

The influence of the health sector on the U.S. government is not a new one—the industry spent $552 million in 2009, significantly influencing the conversation while Congress and the president debated the Affordable Care Act. Spending has remained high ever since, with almost $231 million of the $488 million spent on health-care lobbying in 2014 coming just from the pharmaceutical industry. The health-care industry even outspends defense and oil and gas in lobbying efforts, and individual organizations like the American Medical Association are some of the biggest spenders in

Washington. Unlike the oil and gas industry, spending is more evenly divided between Republicans and Democrats. The Center for Public Integrity documented 4,525 Washington lobbyists influencing health-care legislation; this works out to eight lobbyists for every member of Congress.[20]

Postindustrial Changes and Public Interest Groups

The spread of affluence and education in the United States has led to a society that is capable of thinking of more than mere subsistence issues, a society that some have called **postindustrial**. On the other hand, countries plagued with constant poverty and endless wars are societies that may not spawn interest groups concerned with saving whales. In addition, agrarian, preindustrial nations are not faced with the technological complexities that would breed groups such as Mothers Against Drunk Drivers and consumer safety groups concerned with breast implants.

Postindustrial changes in the United States have generated a large number of interests, particularly among occupational and professional groups in the areas of science and technology. For example, genetic engineering associations have sprung up in the wake of recent DNA discoveries. The excesses and errors of technology have also increased the number of groups in American society. Today there are dozens of groups organized to protect animal rights, including People for Ethical Treatment of Animals (PETA), Progressive Animal Welfare Society (PAWS), Committee to Abolish Sport Hunting (CASH), and the Animal Rights Network (ARN). Postindustrial affluence has freed discretionary income and channeled it towards these new causes.

Great numbers of new groups that have sprung up particularly in the affluent, professional, and college-educated sector of American society have led some to label this a "New Politics" movement.[21] The members fueling this New Politics had formative experiences rooted in the civil rights movement and the Vietnam War. Today, new politics issues include environmental protection, women's rights, nuclear disarmament, and gay and transgender rights.

A major result of the New Politics movement is the creation of "public interest" groups. These groups are not based on the economic self-interest of the members. Rather, the benefits to their members are largely ideological. Today, many public interest groups are important players in Washington politics. Most are environmental and consumer groups, but there are other groups that work on corporate accountability, good government, and poverty issues. Common Cause, the Sierra Club, the Environmental Defense Fund, and Greenpeace are all examples of public interest groups.[22]

Interest Group Friendly Laws and Actions

An additional stimulus to the New Politics groups, and group proliferation in general, has been the wide array of environmental and consumer laws that has opened up avenues for group participation in the policy-making process. Such legislative invitations to group participation have not always been the norm. Early in the twentieth century workers often found it hard to organize because business and industry used government-backed injunctions to prevent labor strikes. By the 1930s, prohibition of such injunctions in private labor disputes and the rights of collective bargaining were established and union formation flourished with government approval and protection. Recent campaign finance laws (discussed below) have also contributed to group proliferation.[23]

Government often intervenes directly in group creation. Since the 1960s, for example, the federal government has been especially active in providing start-up funds for groups. Interest group scholar Jack Walker found that nine citizens' groups out of ten received some outside funding in the initial stages of development.[24] For example, the Center for Substance Abuse and Prevention (CSAP), which is part of the Department of Health and Human Services, gives grants to hundreds of nonprofit groups, financing after-school and summer youth programs, counseling for pregnant women, drug-free work place programs, and good nutrition workshops.

Cheaper Forms of Communication

After World War II great technological changes produced a variety of communication forms that would allow groups to reach their members more easily and facilitate their communication with government officials. Bulk mail rates and special phone rates reduced the costs of communication. These were followed by the FAX machine and the personal computer. Today, individuals and groups can communicate directly with public officials through the Internet and E-mail. Not only is such communication direct, it is immediate.

There are now also numerous computer mailing list companies that allow groups to target potential members. These companies assemble a bank of information about people including subscription lists, information put on warranty cards, and membership lists of other groups. A group trying to get laws to censor sex and violence in rock lyrics and videos, for example, might buy from such a company a subscription list of conservative readers of the magazine *National Review*. These people then can be contacted through the mail. These letters are personally addressed and the group message specifically tailored to the individual receiving the letter.

The Rise of Single-Issue Groups

The recent proliferation of interest groups has been fueled largely by a new type of group that first began to emerge in the 1970s: single-issue groups. These groups have three characteristics. First, they are concerned with only one issue. Second, their members are people new to politics. Finally, the group either will not or cannot compromise on the issue. The pro-life and pro-choice groups, Mothers Against Drunk Drivers, and the anti-nuclear proliferation groups are all examples of single-issue groups.

INTEREST GROUP METHODS AND STRATEGIES

Interest groups use four principal methods in their effort to influence policymaking: electioneering, lobbying, mobilizing public opinion, and litigating.

Electioneering and Political Action Committees

Whenever and wherever people seek to influence decision making, the following is always good advice: get friends in the right places. Interest groups work very hard at doing exactly that. Given that in the United States 450,000 government officials get into office through elections, interest groups must affect election outcomes. There are many ways for groups and individuals to affect elections. They can man the phone banks on election eve; they can go door-to-door with campaign literature; they can vote. But the principal way in which interest groups affect elections today is through money. And the candidates are more than willing to play the game by taking it.

The Creation of Political Action Committees

The United States is the only country that expects its candidates for public office to raise virtually all the money necessary to run for office. Even in presidential elections, where there is public financing available, the candidates still work to raise additional millions of dollars. As campaign costs have escalated, candidates have had to mine as many sources of money as possible. Interest groups are one of those sources, and a lucrative one at that.

Before the early 1970s, national laws made it illegal for banks, corporations, labor unions, and businesses with government contracts to make campaign donations. While one result of these laws was to keep these groups at bay, the other result was that the laws allowed wealthy individuals to be the primary, if not sole, source of campaign money. So, in the 1970s Congress passed several laws to prevent "fat cat" donors from "buying" the loyalty of elected officials through the financing of their campaigns. The 1971 Federal Election Campaign Act limited individuals to $1,000 (today it is $2,800 per candidate in an election cycle) cash contribution per candidate. The law, however, allowed interest groups, including corporations, businesses, and labor unions, to set up **political action committees** (PACs), organizations that solicit campaign contributions from group members and channel those funds to candidates' campaigns. PACs are now the primary avenue by which interest groups contribute to federal election campaigns.

Federal campaign finance law limits PACs to cash contributions of no more than $5,000 per election, per candidate for national office. Under the law, primary, general, run-off, and special elections are all considered to be separate elections. As a result, a PAC may contribute $5,000 to each. In addition, the Supreme Court in the 1976 case of *Buckley v. Valeo* struck down as unconstitutional any attempt to deny individuals or groups the right to spend "on behalf of" a candidate. The Court argued that such spending was a form of "speech" and therefore protected by the First Amendment. The result is that PACs can spend unlimited amounts of money on in-kind services.

The number of PACs exploded in the 1970s. Today, nearly 5,000 PACs are active in the electoral process.[25] Corporate PACs give the most money, followed in order by PACs representing trade, health associations, and labor. In 2018, the National Association of Realtors contributed the most with donations totaling $3.5 million, followed by the National Beer Wholesalers Association, AT&T, and Northrop.[26]

Super PACS

In 2002, Congress tried to limit the growing influence of Political Action Committees in the McCain-Feingold Bipartisan Campaign Reform Act. But a Supreme Court decision of January 21, 2010, *Citizens United v. Federal Election Commission*, overturned a portion of the law that prohibited corporations and unions from funding, through their general fund, any "electioneering communications" for 30 days before a primary or 60 days before a general election. They also overruled a 1990 decision that limited corporate spending in support or opposition of a candidate.

The *Citizens* case has led to the creation of super PACs. Technically known as independent expenditure-only committees, Super PACs may raise unlimited sums of money from corporations, unions, associations, and individuals and then spend unlimited sums to overtly advocate for or against political candidates. As is the case for traditional PACS, Super PACs must report their donors to the Federal Election Commission on either a monthly or quarterly basis (their choice). Unlike traditional PACs, however, Super PACs are prohibited from donating money directly to political candidates. As of January 2017, 2,408 groups organized as Super PACs have reported total receipts of $1,797,385,051 and total independent expenditures of $1,120,411,097 in the 2016 election cycle. Priorities USA Action, which supported Hillary Clinton, was the biggest donor, spending $132,438,801 on her behalf.[27]

The Effects of PACs and Campaign Contributions

PAC contributions benefit some candidates over others. Interest groups are pragmatic organizations. Given the high re-election rates in Congress, PACs favor the incumbents running for re-election. House incumbents collect nearly 13 times more money from PACs than the challengers receive.[28] Furthermore, more than half of the money raised by House incumbents comes from PACs.[29]

Incumbents feel the effects of PACs in other ways as well. A second effect of the privately financed campaign system in the United States is that politicians are distracted from their job of governing, with their energies siphoned off by having to raise the inordinate amounts of money needed to run an effective campaign. Candidates become entrepreneurs raising, in some cases, tens of thousands of dollars in a day's round of PAC cocktail parties, lunches, and dinners. A related problem is that incumbents running for re-election can raise money more efficiently by staying in Washington and working the PAC circuit of fundraisers. As a result, incumbents are spending less time at home with their constituents.

It might be expected that a third effect of PACs is that influence is being bought. While there is little evidence that PAC contributions actually buy the votes of politicians, there is evidence that PAC money can, and does, buy access. A member of Congress or one of the congressional staff is not likely to turn a deaf ear to a representative of an interest group that has donated generously to his or her campaign. The so-called Keating Five is a case in point. In this case, five senators, Alan Cranston (D-Calif.), Dennis DeConcini (D-Ariz.), John Glenn (D-Ohio), John McCain (R-Ariz.), and Donald Riegle (D-Mich.), came under the scrutiny of the Senate Ethics Committee. There were charges that these senators had sought to pressure the Federal Home Loan Bank Board to give lenient regulatory treatment to Lincoln Savings and Loan Association, headed by Charles Keating, a wealthy political contributor. The bank later failed, at a cost to government of more than $2 billion.[30] Buying access to politicians seems to be the main point of electioneering. Senator Edward Kennedy once remarked that we "have the best Congress money can buy."[31]

Direct, or Inside, Lobbying

Once an interest group has access through campaign donations, the group will try to influence what those elected politicians do. Interest groups do this through **lobbying**, pressuring through the provision of information, often highly technical in nature. Most politicians are inexpert in many of the policy areas they govern. They come to rely on the expert advice provided by interest groups.

The phrase *to lobby* originated in seventeenth-century England where people seeking to influence the government stopped members of the Parliament in a large lobby off the floor of the House of Commons. Perhaps because of this, lobbying is usually associated even in this country with Congress. But interest groups also lobby the executive branch of government. Executive branch lobbying focuses on senior staff aides in the White House and the various federal agencies. Even the president is lobbied and encourages lobbying activities through the Office of Public Liaison, an office whose express purpose is to communicate with interest groups.

The Federal Regulation of Lobbying Act defines a **lobbyist** as "any person who shall engage himself or pay any consideration for the purpose of attempting to influence the passage or defeat of any legislation of the Congress of the United States." In 2020, there were almost 12,500 lobbyists, and they spent a total of $3.47 billion on their lobbying efforts.[32]

There are different types of lobbyists. Some groups send one of their own members to Washington to lobby on the group's behalf. Such amateur lobbyists are often unfamiliar with the intricate workings of the Washington establishment and may find it difficult to gain access to the critical centers of power. A second type of lobbyist, the staff lobbyist, is a paid professional who works full time for a particular interest group.

Groups may hire a third type of lobbyist who has Washington experience, particularly lawyers, former members of Congress, or former employees of executive branch agencies and departments. Government officials often leave office and become lobbyists. Federal law does prohibit members of Congress and executive branch officials from lobbying on matters they worked on while in government for one year after leaving office. Even so, today there are more than 11,000 registered federal lobbyists and 430 of them are former members of Congress. Since 1996, 43 percent of members of Congress who left office since 1998 have become lobbyists.[33]

There is a revolving door in Washington, with former members of Congress and executive branch officials becoming lobbyists but also lobbyists going into government. Donald Trump campaigned as an outsider who vowed to "drain the swamp" in Washington. The president-elect's transition team, however, was packed with lobbyists for the fossil fuel, chemical, pharmaceutical, and tobacco industries: energy adviser Michael Catanzaro, a lobbyist for Koch Industries and the Walt Disney Company; adviser Eric Ueland, a Senate Republican staffer who previously lobbied for Goldman Sachs; and Transition General Counsel William Palatucci, an attorney in New Jersey whose lobbying firm represents Aetna and Verizon. Rick Holt, Christine Ciccone, Rich Bagger, and Mike Ferguson were among the other corporate lobbyists who helped manage the transition effort.

Providing Information

Interest groups spend a considerable amount of time engaged in what is called **direct lobbying**. One study of Washington lobbyists found that 98 percent use direct contact with government of-

A PAC for the NRA sends letters to its constituents to update them on the voting behavior of their legislators. Notice the letter identifying which legislators supported NRA's position on a critical piece of legislation. Members are urged to write to their House and Senate legislators.

ficials to express their group's views.[34] Information is the key to direct lobbying. A lobbyist will, of course, try to present information that supports the interest group's position on an issue. Still, over the long term, lobbyists cannot afford to be perceived by policy makers as biased or untrustworthy. A lobbyist's access to a politician is only as good as the expert information he or she can provide. Lobbyists must maintain daily contact with politicians, providing them with information and data. Corporate groups, in particular, often have hundreds, even thousands, of personnel all equipped to provide mounds of information on a minute's notice.[35]

Recently, interest groups have taken to virtual lobbying through use of the Internet and other social networking sites. During the pandemic of 2020, with capitols closed to the public, the mechanics of lobbying had to change. Most legislatures were not in session and those that were still meeting were only allowing in legislators, staff and members media. Legislators themselves were trying to keep their distance from one another. Software companies like Dr. Gooder have created software that empowers online lobbying activities such as petition building and emailing government representatives. Dr. Gooder can even match interest group supporters with their local representatives through an embeddable online email form.[36]

The Effects of Direct Lobbying

Lobbying often leads to the development of a close relationship between the interest group, the congressional committee involved in the policy area important to the group, and members of a bureaucratic department or agency responsible for the implementation of those policies. Such a tight relationship is referred to as an **iron triangle**, with three points: the interest group, the congressional committee, and the bureaucratic department or agency. These three points are mutually supporting. A committee member takes campaign donations from an interest group and is then lobbied by that group. The interest group also seeks out the bureaucracy as an ally who then can bring additional pressure on the congressional committee members. Remember also that there is often an exchange of personnel among the three points of the triangle. Many defeated or retired members of Congress join or form Washington law firms that are filled with lobbyists. A study has

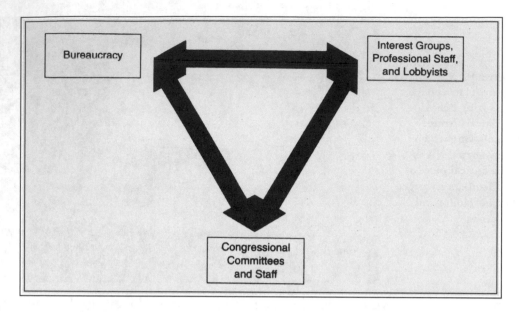

found that 43 percent of the House and Senate members who left government to join private life since 1998 have registered to lobby.[37] According to a 2010 report by the *New York Times*, more than 125 former congressional personnel, from aides on the banking committees to elected officials, are now working on behalf of financial companies, using their expertise and connections to influence legislation that is meant to regulate the financial industry. Visa has the most lobbyists with ties to Washington, 37, followed by Goldman Sachs, Prudential Financial, and Citigroup.[38]

The point is that the interest of the interest group becomes the interest of the congressional committee members and bureaucrats. The relationship is referred to as *iron* because other than the three major players, everyone else is left out. The unorganized, those without lobbyists on Capitol Hill, those who lack expertise, are largely on the list of uninvited. In addition, presidents who come in with their own agenda for change may soon be faced with recalcitrant iron triangles. The president, in such cases, is usually the new boy in town, whereas the incumbent members of Congress, lobbyists, and career bureaucrats may have been part of the Washington establishment for twenty years or more. There is little reason to think that they will be willing to see or do things the president's way.

An example of an iron triangle is federal policy toward veterans, which is dominated by the "Big Six" interest groups: American Legion, Veterans of Foreign Affairs, Paralyzed Veterans of America, Disabled American Veterans, American Veterans, and Vietnam Veterans of America. These powerful lobbies have made it extremely difficult for the government to pursue the modernization and innovation of services to veterans. These groups, working with the Department of Veterans Affairs and the congressional committees that deal with veterans, act as an Iron Triangle, closing policy off from change that would disrupt the status quo. The veto power of the "Big Six" is exacerbated by a lack of any alternative centers of expertise and power. Philanthropists, businesses, academics, and think tanks are all frozen out.[s]

Regulating Lobbying

Lobbying is a form of speech and, therefore, protected by the First Amendment to the Constitution. In 1946, Congress passed the Federal Regulation of Lobbying Act, which requires groups and individuals seeking to influence legislation to register with the secretary of the Senate and the clerk of the House and to file quarterly financial reports. In 1954, in the case of *United States v. Harriss*, the Supreme Court upheld the 1946 law but limited its application to only lobbying involving direct contacts with members of Congress.[39] Not only was the 1946 law limited in its application, it was also very difficult to enforce.

In 2007, Congress passed the Lobbying Transparency and Accountability Act that requires registered lobbyists to report lobbying activities quarterly, as opposed to semiannually. These reports must include the disclosure of funds that lobbyists donate to candidates personally, as well as funds raised from clients, which are then "bundled" and given to politicians as larger contributions. Disclosure reports must be submitted to the Secretary of the Senate no later than 20 days after the end of the quarterly period. The reports must be made available electronically with free access to the public over the Internet, as well.

The regulations discussed above are limited in several respects. The registration and reporting requirements do not extend to grassroots organizations. Nor is there any enforcement organization to make sure there is compliance with the law. Congressional officials who suspect violations may refer them to the Justice Department for action. Fines for breaking the law may be as high as $50,000.

The Newest Trend in Lobbying: Supreme Court Nominations

A recent consensus exists among judicial scholars that judicial power is expanding and this expansion of judicial power has, in turn, politicized the process through which judicial appointments are made. Interest groups now actively seek to influence the Senate's confirmation of nominees to the U.S. Supreme Court. A new analysis of the role of interest groups and their television advertising campaigns by the Brennan Center for Justice at the NYU School of Law concludes that while the spending levels have not as yet reached the stratosphere, interest group spending on television ads and other lobbying tools can have a potent effect on who becomes a judge in America.[40] Recently, business groups with interests before the U.S. Supreme Court orchestrated a multi-faceted campaign to pressure the Senate to quickly confirm Judge Brett Kavanaugh to the Supreme Court.

Attempts to influence judicial appointments are likely to increase in the future. Under the Internal Revenue Code, tax-exempt organizations such as social welfare organizations under section 501(c)(4), labor, agricultural, or horticultural organizations under section 501(c)(5), and business leagues under section 501(c)(6) may engage in unlimited lobbying and are allowed to try to influence the nomination or confirmation of a potential justice to the federal court, including the Supreme Court. As discussed earlier in this Chapter, these groups now play a significant role in politics.

Grassroots, or Outside, Lobbying: Going Public

Going public is a strategy that attempts to mobilize the widest and most favorable climate of public opinion. Whereas direct lobbying involves contact between a lobbyist and a politician, this grassroots lobbying uses rank-and-file members and other supporters to bring pressure on government. Such an outside strategy may include education campaigns, demonstrations, letter writing, and any other strategy that attempts to mobilize a large number of people to bring pressure on policy makers.

One way interest groups try to mobilize public opinion is by educating the public about issues. A group may send speakers armed with pamphlets to address gatherings of policy makers and other groups. A media campaign may prove even more effective. The pro-life groups have made considerable inroads into mass public opinion on abortion through their emotionally charged advertisements. In general, the great expense of media campaigns limits their widespread use to only those interest groups that have significant financial resources. The corporate sector appears to have the advantage here. Even as early as the 1930s, some were identifying a *new lobby* of public relations professionals.[41] The 1970s, however, saw a rapid rise in the sophisticated use of advertising to sway public opinion. The oil companies, particular Mobil and Chevron, began airing advertisements that were directed at soothing the sentiment of the American public. These advertisements were not designed to sell gasoline but rather to create a more sympathetic picture of corporations. Microsoft is another corporation that has always seen public and media relations as an integral part of their success. Over the years, their need to communicate has increased with their size and the controversy surrounding their dominant position in software markets.

Interest groups may try to obtain free media coverage. Protests, sit-ins, and demonstrations are often specifically tailored for the evening news. After the 2016 election of Donald Trump, women organized marches across the nation. The first march was held on January 21, 2017 with five million women and allies marching. Anniversary marches were held in following years and evolved into Women's March Foundation, a powerful new group spanning the entire nation.[42] The civil rights movement, women's movement, and environmental movement all show, however, that such movements can be kept alive, but it takes enormous organizational skills and charismatic leadership.

Litigating

Interest groups can also pursue the method of legal advocacy, trying to achieve goals through litigation. Interest groups can use the courts to affect public policy in any of three ways. First, the group may bring a suit on behalf of the group itself. Second, the group can finance suits brought by other individuals. In fact, groups sometimes actively seek test cases where they can challenge the constitutionality of existing laws or the ways in which they have been implemented. For example, in the 1950s, the National Association for the Advancement of Colored People was looking for a test case to challenge the racially segregated southern school system. Thurgood Marshall, a young attorney working for the NAACP, successfully litigated the case on behalf of the Browns. Finally, a group may also participate in the litigation process by petitioning the court for the right to file an *amicus curiae* ("friend of the court") brief that lays out arguments why the court should rule in favor of one of the parties to the case. A 1989 abortion case drew a record 78 such briefs. They were evenly divided between those who favored or opposed the right to abortion. In February 2003, however, that previous record was broken when over sixty groups filed friend-of-the-court briefs in defense of the University of Michigan's use of race-based affirmative action in their admissions policy.

The public interest groups spawned by the New Politics movement have been particularly active in the litigation process. The controversy over the completion of a dam being built by the Tennessee Valley Authority (TVA) is an example of New Politics litigation. The dam would have ruined the habitat for a small fish known as the snail darter. The Endangered Species Act at that time prohibited federal agencies from engaging in any actions that would "jeopardize the continued existence of an endangered or threatened species or . . . result in the adverse modification or destruction of [the species'] critical habitat." In *TVA v. Hill*, the Supreme Court held that the act made it an unqualified duty for agencies to refrain from taking actions that would harm the threatened or endangered species.[43]

Businesses and corporations have responded to the strong public interest movement by mobilizing their own forces. The period since 1970 has seen a massive increase in the number of businesses lobbying offices in Washington, and many trade associations headquartered elsewhere moved to Washington or opened branch offices there. Corporations now spend about $2.6 billion a year on reported lobbying expenditures, more than the $2 billion we spend to fund the House of Representatives ($1.18 billion) and Senate ($860 million). Today, the biggest companies have upwards of 100 lobbyists representing them, allowing them to be everywhere, all the time. For every dollar spent on lobbying by labor unions and public-interest groups together, large corporations and their associations now spend $34. Of the 100 organizations that spend the most on lobbying, 95 consistently represent business.[44] The result has been that many of the early victories of public interest groups have been overturned or muted by Congress or other court decisions.

Bribery

While there may be only a fine line between campaign donations and bribery, the line is nonetheless drawn by the legal code. Bribery involves the giving of cash gifts, worth over a certain amount, in exchange for a politician's promise to act in a certain way. The history of the United States has been punctuated with scandals involving interest groups bribing politicians. On July 29, 2008, Senator Ted Stevens was indicted by a federal grand jury on seven counts of failing to report gifts received from VECO Corporation and its CEO Bill Allen on his Senate financial disclosure forms and was formally charged with violation of provisions of the Ethics in Government Act. Stevens, seeking to clear his name before the November election, pleaded not guilty and asserted his right to a speedy trial. The trial began on September 25, 2008 in Washington, D.C., and on October 27, 2008, barely a week before the election, Stevens was found guilty on all seven counts. He went on to lose his re-election bid on November 4, 2008.

Bribery is probably not as widespread as many fear. It is a risky strategy for an interest group to pursue. As a result, it is mostly used to sustain a friendship rather than convert an enemy. In addition, bribery works best when the issue involved is fairly narrow, for example, involving a government contract. The bigger the issue, the more participants are likely to be involved and the more media coverage devoted to it. Bribery fares poorly in such an open arena of policy making.

Prospects for Reform

Even if the problem of illegal bribery is not overwhelming, when coupled with the legal system of campaign finance and PACs, perhaps some reform is needed. Some sectors of the interest group community do enjoy advantages over others. Such advantages may impede the equal opportunity of all groups to be heard in the political system. The Madisonian design, in other words, has not worked perfectly.

Allowing those who have the clearest self-interest and the resources to communicate and amplify their message may lead to inefficient and even bad policy-making. For example, environmental economists have attempted to quantify the toll anti-climate lobbying efforts take on society. Between 2000 and 2016, 14 percent of all recorded lobbying was directed against the Waxman-Markey legislation, which would have limited the amount of greenhouse gases produced nationally. The legislation was never passed. The authors calculate that power firms curtailing government action on climate change reduced social benefits to the cost of $60 billion even after costs such as reduction in farming yields and lower GDP were taken into account.[45]

CONCLUSION

James Madison recognized that in a free and diverse nation, groups would inevitably form and attempt to impress their will on others. He called what we now know as interest groups, factions, and defined them as groups "whether amounting to a majority or minority of the whole, who are united and actuated by some common impulse of passion, or interest, adverse to the rights of other citizens, or to the permanent and aggregate interest of the community."[46] Madison believed that the only solution to the tendency of factions to impose their will on the greater society is a large republic that encourages a greater diversity of opinion thereby making despotism at the hands of any one group difficult if not impossible.

Madison's idea of forming a republic to keep interest groups from becoming too powerful has not turned out exactly as planned. The reality of the American political landscape is that interest groups have always better represented those with the greatest resources, and the least wealthy have suffered because of their failure to organize. The challenge of democracy is to provide the freedom that will allow all members of the society to participate in policy making and to find new ways to harness the power of interest groups for the greater national interest.

CHAPTER NOTES

[1]Hillstrom Evers, "Lobbying Spending in 2019 Nears All-Time High as Health Sector Smashes Records," *OpenSecrets.org*, January 24, 2020, *https://www.opensecrets.org/news/2020/01/lobbying-spending-in-2019-near-all-time-high/*

[2]John T. Tierney and Kay Lehman Scholzman, "Congress and Organized Interests," in *Congressional Politics*, ed. Christopher J. Deering (Chicago: Dorsey Press, 1989), 198.

[3] Center for Responsive Politics, "Top Organizational Contributors," *OpenSecrets.org*, *https://www.opensecrets.org/orgs/list.php*.

[4]*Bureau of Labor, Bureau of Labor Statistics News Release, January 22, 2020,*
https://www.bls.gov/news.release/pdf/union2.pdf

[5]*Gallup Organization, Gallup News: Labor Unions, August 28, 2019,*
https://news.gallup.com/poll/12751/labor-unions.aspx

[6]*Open Secrets.Org,* "Emily's List," 2020, *https://www.opensecrets.org/orgs//summary?id=d000000113*

[7]Pew Research Center, "Most White Evangelicals Satisfied with Trump's Initial Response to the
COVID-19 Outbreak," March 19, 2020, *https://www.pewresearch.org/fact-tank/2020/03/19/most-*
white-evangelicals-satisfied-with-trumps-initial-response-to-the-covid-19-outbreak/

[8]Michael Lipka, "U.S. Religious Groups and Their Political Leanings," *Pew Research Center,* February 23,
2016, *http://www.pewresearch.org/fact-tank/2016/02/23/u-s-religious-groups-and-their-political-leanings/.*

[9]*Victory Fund,* "Victory Fund Endorses 32 New LGBTQ Candidates for 2020," January 22, 2020,
https://victoryfund.org/news/victory-fund-endorses-32-new-lgbtq-candidates-for-2020-historic-
opportunities-in-state-legislatures/

[10]AARP, ""AARP Urges Federal Appeals Court to Preserve the ACA," in *Politics and Society Advocacy,*
April 1, 2019, *https://www.aarp.org/politics-society/advocacy/info-2019/affordable-care-act-brief.html*

[11]Kenny Luna, "Number of Environmental NGO's Growing By Leaps and Bounds," *Treehugger,* December 5,
2008, *http://www.treehugger.com/files/2008/12/number-of-environmental-groups-growing-rapidly.php*

[12]*OpenSecrets.org,* "National Rifle Association," April 11, 2020, *https://www.opensecrets.org/orgs//summary?*
topnumcycle=2020&toprecipcycle=All%20cycles&contribcycle=All%20cycles&lobcycle=
All%20cycles&outspendcycle=All%20cycles&id=d000000082

[13]Richard Lardner, "Qatar, UAE Spend Heavily on Lobbysists Amid a War of Words," *AP News,*
March 30, 2018*, https://apnews.com/b2d5003280e343a88985d784e9060586/Qatar,-UAE-spend-*
heavily-on-lobbyists-amid-a-war-of-word

[14]*Center for Democracy and Technology,* "Our Work Has Never Been More Important," 2018 Annual Report,
https://cdt.org/

[15]*Electronic Frontier Foundation,* "Net Neutrality," April, 2020, *https://www.eff.org/issues/net-neutrality*

[16]Mancur Olson, *The Logic of Collective Action* (Cambridge: Harvard University Press, 1965).

[17]Jeffrey H. Birnbaum, "Washington's Power 25," http://money.cnn.com Dec. 8, 2006.

[18]James Madison, *Federalist Paper No. 10* in *The Federalist Papers,* ed. Clinton Rossiter (New York:
New American Library, 1961), 83.

[19]John Herbers, "Special Interests Gaining Power as Voter Disillusionment Grows," *New York Times,*
14 Nov. 1978, 1.

[20]Mint Press News Desk, "Why Don't We Have a Single Payer Health Care Ask Medical lobbyists,"
MintPress News, June 17, 2015, *http://www.mintpressnews.com/why-dont-we-have-single-payer-*
healthcare-ask-medical-lobbyists/206642/

[21]Theodore J. Lowi and Benjamin Ginsberg, *American Government,* 3d ed. (New York: W.W. Norton, 1994).

[22]Andrew McFarland, *Common Cause* (Chatham, N.J.: Chatham House, 1984).

[23]Allan J. Cigler and Burdett A. Loomis, *Interest Group Politics* (Washington, D.C.: Congressional
Quarterly Press, 1991).

[24]Jack L. Walker, "The Origins and Maintenance of Interest Groups in America," *American Political
Science Review* 77 (June 1983): 390-406..

[25]Federal Election Commission, *FEC Releases 1992 Year-End Pac Count,* 23 January 1993, 1.

[26]*OpenSecrets.org,* "Top PACs," 2018, *https://www.opensecrets.org/overview/toppacs.php?cycle=2020*

[27]Center for Responsive Politics, "2016 Outside Spending, by Super PAC," *Open Secrets.org,* 2016,
https://www.opensecrets.org/outsidespending/summ.php?chrt=V&type=S.

[28]"Political Action Committees," http://ap.grolier.com,2005.

[29]Center for Responsive Politics, "Incumbent Advantage," *Open Sectets.org*, 2016, *https://www.opensecrets.org/overview/incumbs.php*

[30]Nathaniel C. Nash, "Savings Unit Donations Criticized," *New York Times*, 29 June 29 1990, D4.

[31]Theodore J. Lowi and Benjamin Ginsberg, *American Politics*, 4th ed. (New York: W.W. Norton, 1996), 497.

[32]*Statista*, "Total Lobbying Spending in the United States from 1998 to 2019," March 4, 2020, *https://www.statista.com/statistics/257337/total-lobbying-spending-in-the-us/*

[33]Congressman David Cicilline, "Cicilline, Loebsack Re-Introduce Lifetime Lobbying Ban for Former Members of Congress." June 15, 2019, *https://cicilline.house.gov/press-release/cicilline-loebsack-re-introduce-lifetime-lobbying-ban-former-members-congress.*

[34]Key Lehman Schlozman, and John T. Tierney, *Organized Interest and American Democracy* (New York: Harper and Row, 1986), 50.

[35]John E. Chubb, *Interest Groups and the Bureaucracy* (Stanford, Ca.: Stanford University Press, 1983), 144.

[36]*https://dogooder.co/why-dogooder/lobbying-software-that-helps-you-influence-lawmakers*

[37]Jeffrey H. Bimbaum, "Hill a Steppingstone to K Street for Some," *The Washington Post*, July 27, 2005, *http://www.washingtonpost.com/wp-dyn/content/article/2005/07/26/AR2005072601562.html*

[38]*OpenSecrets.org*, "Top Industries," April 2020, *https://www.opensecrets.org/revolving/top.php?display=I*

[39]*United States v. Harriss*, 347 U.S. 612 (1954).

[40]Brennan Center, "Three Nominations Reveal Contrasting Influence of Interest Groups in High Court Nomination Process," *http://www.bennancenter.org/content/resource/three_nominations_reveal_contrast*

[41]*Pendelton-Herring, Group Representation Before Congress* (New York: McGraw Hill, 1936).

[42]Women's March Los Angeles, "Voter Action: Women's March Foundation," March 2020, *https://www.womensmarchla.org/*

[43]*TVA v. Hill*, 437 U.S. 153 (1978).

[44]Jeffrey Bimbaum, "The Road to Riches is Called K Street," *The Washington Post*, June 22, 2005, *http://www.washingtonpost.com/wp-dyn/content/article/2005/06/21/AR2005062101632.html*

[45]Josh Gabbatiss, "Lobbying Against Key U.S. Climate Regulation Cost Society $60 Billion, Study Finds," *CarbonBrief*, May 25, 2019, *https://www.carbonbrief.org/lobbying-against-key-us-climate-regulation-cost-society-60bn-study-finds.*

[46]James Madison, *Federalist #10* in *The Federalist Papers*, ed. Clinton Rossiter (New York: New American Library, 1961).

SUGGESTED READINGS

Ainesworth, Scott H. and Kenneth A. Shepsle. *Analyzing Interest Groups.* New York: W. W. Norton, 2003.

Baumgartner, Frank, Jeffrey Berry, Beth L. Leech, David C. Kimball, and Mary Hojnacki. *Lobbying and Policy Change: Who Wins, Who Loses and Why.* Chicago: University of Chicago Press, 2009.

Berry, Jeffrey M. *The Interest Group Society*, 6th ed. New York: Longman, 2016.

Birnbaum, Jeffrey. *The Lobbyists: How Influence Peddlers Work Their Way in Washington.* New York: Random House, 1992.

Cigler, Alan J. and Burdett A. Loomis, eds. *Interest Group Politics,* 9th ed. Washington. D.C.: CQ Press, 2015.

Godwin, Kenneth, Scott Ainsworth, and Erik Godwin. *Lobbying and Policymaking.* Washington. D.C.: Sage Publishing, 2012

Grossman, Matt. *The Not-So-Special Interests: Interest Groups, Public Representation, and American Governance*, Palo Alto: Stanford University Press, 2012.

Olson, Mancur. *The Logic of Collective Action.* Cambridge, MA: Harvard University Press, 1965.

Paxton, Pamela. *Women, Politics, and Power*. Washington, D.C.: CQ Press, 2016.

Rozell, Mark J., Clyde Wilcox, and David Madland. *Interest Groups in American Campaigns: The New Face of Electioneering*. Washington, D.C.: CQ Press, 2005.

Strolovitch, Dara. *Affirmative Advocacy: Race, Class and Gender in Interest Group Politics.* Chicago: University of Chicago Press, 2007.

Truman, David B. *The Governmental Process: Political Interests and Public Opinion*, 2nd ed. New York: Knopf, 1971.

Web Sites

Center for Responsive Politics. www.opensecrets.org.

Federal Election Commission. www.fec.gov.

Institute for Global Communications. www.igc.apc.org

Internet Public Library Association. www.ipl.org/ref/AON.

Political Advocacy Groups: A Directory of U.S. Lobbyists. www.vancouver.wsu.edu/fac/kfountain/.

MoveOn, www.moveon.org.

Senate Office of Public Records. http://sopr.senate.gov.

U.S. Public Interest Research Group (PIRG). www.uspirg.org.

Chapter Eight

THE CONGRESS

To listen to the news, one would think that partisan gridlock in Congress is a new phenomenon. Such is hardly the case! While the term **gridlock** appears to have first been used in the aftermath of the 1980 election, the early authors of the American Constitution in the 1700s lamented the deadlock that gripped the Continental Congress and was rooted in its very design, which made the national government a repository of state interests. While Hamilton hoped to avoid such gridlock in the new Constitution of 1787, James Madison succeeded in giving the United States a national government that was, to no small extent, a political system designed not to work, a government of sharply limited and separated powers. Still, the creation of gridlock for gridlock's sake was not what the Framers of the Constitution intended.

Having first suffered as colonists at the hands of Great Britain and then upon independence, further suffering from the conflicts at the state level between the in-debt farmers and the rising national creditor class, the Framers sought a strong national government that could govern—deliberately and efficiently, albeit insulated from the passions of popular majorities. Even though the Framers may not have preferred it, gridlock may be a frequent consequence of the Constitution, and in many ways, gridlock is endemic to our national politics, the natural consequence of separated institutions sharing and competing for power. In many ways, the United States government runs on Blackstone's ratio: It is better that ten guilty persons escape than that one innocent suffer. Better for the national government to do nothing, then to do something quickly, lackadaisically, and without consensus.

Despite the basic constitutional design that favors slow and careful over bold and quick, gridlock has not always plagued the United States Congress. The Great Society Congress under Lyndon Johnson, for example, enacted landmark health care, environment, civil rights, transportation, and education legislation. At other times, gridlock has prevailed, as when, in 1992, congressional efforts to cut the capital gains tax and to reform lobbying, campaign finance, banking, parental leave, and voter registration laws all ended in deadlock. Similarly, in January 2019, a divided Congress started its new session with House Democrats implementing a series of changes to the standing rules that would make it harder for Congress and President Trump to agree on major legislation. Not surprisingly, Congress soon became gridlocked over a partial government shutdown, kicking off what appeared to all to be another two years of inactivity and partisan confrontation. It was this divided session of Congress that led to the 2020 impeachment of the president and his trial in the Senate.

It is nothing short of amazing, then, that it was this session of Congress that, only three months after the impeachment and trial, turned around in March 2020 and passed the Coronavirus Aid, Relief, and Economic Security Act, a $2 trillion stimulus bill that is the largest in modern history, more than doubling the stimulus act passed in 2009 during that financial crisis. The act affects individuals, big businesses, small businesses, state and local governments, and public services. Passing the act was not easy. There were days of intense, rapid, and on-and-off negotiations that pitted the Republican and Democratic leadership against each other. While global markets reeled and the American economy convulsed, at the thirteenth hour, Congress approved in an extraordinary 96-0 vote a package that was nothing more than awe-inspiring to a nation and a world caught in a pandemic.

The coronavirus consensus of March 2020, however, was soon upended in April. The backbone of the $2 trillion bill, the Paycheck Protection Program, ran out of money and while everyone agreed that the program deserved to be injected with more cash, negotiations were stalled in an impasse. Democrats pushed for more money for local and state governments, and the Republicans saw this as the red line they could not cross. In the end, the Senate adjourned with no agreement reached.

The lesson to be learned from this is that Congress can act quickly and effectively but Congress can also reach impasses that are difficult, sometimes impossible, to break. Crises have always given policymakers powers to bypass legislative gridlock and entrenched interests. The coronavirus crisis of March 2020 allowed the implementation of ideas that would have been considered very radical only months prior. The speed with which U.S. legislators embraced government intervention in the economy, such as direct cash transfers, freezes on mortgage foreclosures, and government nationalization of distressed firms was a major feat of bipartisanship, would only a month before have been impossible. Such resourcefulness holds an important lesson for the present. The United States certainly has the material and financial means to overcome the virus and the social and economic dislocation it has caused. Congress also has the will and the procedural rules to create gridlock. While many wish for normalcy to return, it is impossible to believe that the post-pandemic world will not change the United States and its institutions of government with it. Congressional policymaking and collective action are not likely to ever be the same again. The key now will be to draw on the lessons that moments of congressional solidarity and inventiveness during the coronavirus pandemic of 2020 taught us.

THE ORIGIN AND POWERS OF CONGRESS

The Constitution and the Great Compromise

Perhaps because the framers of the Constitution believed that Congress would be the most powerful branch of the national government, the most contentious issue at the constitutional convention concerned the question of how the states would be represented in this national legislature. The small states, which had the most to fear from union, wanted equal representation in a one-chamber legislature; this was put forth as the New Jersey Plan. The more populous states, on the other hand, supported the Virginia Plan that proposed a two-chamber legislature. One of its chambers, the lower chamber, would have state representation on the basis of state population; this chamber would then select an upper chamber.

The final Connecticut Compromise created a **bicameral**, meaning two chamber, national legislature. The House of Representatives, the lower chamber, is apportioned to the states on the basis of state population. The United States Senate, the upper chamber, has equal state representation with each state having two senators, originally to be selected by their various state legislatures. While the House members serve only a two-year term and all seats are elected in every two-year election, the senators serve a six-year term, and only one third of the Senate is selected in any two-year election.

The Powers of the House and Senate

The Expressed Powers

The first seventeen clauses of Article I, section 8, specify most of the **enumerated powers** of Congress, powers expressly given to the national legislature by the Constitution. The most important of the domestic powers listed are the rights of Congress to collect taxes, to spend money, and to regulate commerce. The most important foreign policy power is the power to declare war. Other sections of the Constitution give Congress a wide range of additional powers. Article 1, section 5 gives Congress the power to establish rules for its own members. Article 1, section 7 gives it the power to override a presidential veto. Congress is also given the power to define the appellate jurisdiction of the Supreme Court (Article III, section 1), regulate relations between the states (Article I, section 10 and Article IV), and propose amendments to the Constitution (Article V). In addition, amendments to the Constitution have provided additional congressional power. The Twelfth Amendment, for example, requires Congress to certify the election of the president and vice president or to choose these officers if no candidate has received a majority of the electoral college vote. Congress may levy an income tax under the Sixteenth Amendment.

The House and Senate do have some responsibilities that they discharge on their own. Only the House of Representatives can originate revenue bills. Early colonial Americans had been sensitive about the issue of taxation without representation. As a result, the framers believed that money matters should be passed first by the House, the chamber that has representation on the basis of population, and only after that would the Senate address the issue. According to Article I, section 2 the House has the power to impeach a federal judge, the president, or vice president. To **impeach** means to bring up on charges, calling for a trial in the Senate. If two-thirds of the senators vote to convict, the federal official is then removed from office.

The Senate has the power to advise the president when he is appointing federal judges, ambassadors, and cabinet positions. In addition, the Senate can either vote to confirm or reject these appointments. The Senate also has the power to ratify or reject treaties negotiated by a president with a foreign nation.

The impeachment trial of President Andrew Johnson, who became president with the assassination of Abraham Lincoln, took place in the Senate.

The Implicit Power

Under Article I, section 8, the **elastic clause**, Congress has the power "to make all Laws which shall be necessary and proper to carrying into Execution the foregoing powers [of Article I], and all other Powers vested by this Constitution in the Government of the United States, or in any Department or Officer thereof." The open-ended quality of the elastic clause has allowed Congress to define and redefine its powers over time and thereby alter the balance of power Congress shares with the president.

The Ebb and Flow of Congressional Powers

Because the framers of the Constitution feared tyranny emanating from any source, executive or legislative, they pitted Congress and the president against each other. For the first one hundred years, Congress clearly was the more dominant institution. Congress chose to use the powers outlined in Article I, section 8 and further extended its power by defining other activities as within its scope under the elastic clause. Even in foreign affairs, Congress exercised its muscle. The War of 1812 was planned and directed by Congress. After the Civil War, when President Andrew Johnson tried to interfere with congressional plans for Reconstruction, he was summarily impeached, though missed conviction in the Senate by one vote.

By the 1960s, however, congressional dominance was declining. The presidency became the stronger of the two branches. Franklin Roosevelt's "New Deal," Harry Truman's "Fair Deal," John

F. Kennedy's "New Frontier," and Lyndon Johnson's "Great Society" had transformed American politics, placing the president in the center of the legislative process. Similarly, in foreign affairs, presidential initiative and direction took the country into both World Wars and then later wars in Korea and Vietnam.

The strength of either the presidency or the Congress as an institution is at least partly the result of the institution's ties to important groups in the American electorate. Until the administration of Franklin Roosevelt, people were more likely to see Congress as their representative institution. But Roosevelt's New Deal mobilized organized labor, farmers, African Americans, and key sectors of American industry and tied their loyalty to the executive branch of government. Such electoral support was and continues to be empowering to the branch that can best mobilize it.

Events of the later 1960s and 1970s set the stage for a reassertion of congressional power. Groups that had not found the executive branch hospitable to their claims, now turned to the legislative branch to defend their interests. Environmental and consumer groups, along with civil rights and women's groups, pressed their claims upon Congress and, in doing so, provided a base for the reassertion of congressional power. It was inevitable that conflict would grow between the executive and legislative branches of government; and grow it did beginning during the Johnson administration.[1]

The most dramatic illustration of this growing tension was the congressional Watergate investigation that eventually led to the resignation of President Richard Nixon. But the tension between the branches has evidenced itself in other ways as well. Increasingly, Congress passed legislation mandating clear and specific action by the president, for example, the Wars Powers Act and the Endangered Species Act. Congress has also moved to increase its budgetary powers through the Budget and Impoundment Control Act of 1974 and the creation of the Congressional Budget Office (CBO).

Congress has asserted its power through the Iran-Contra investigation of President Reagan and the Whitewater investigation of President Clinton, and, of course, the impeachment of President Trump. In 2019, the Democratic majority in the House of Representatives approved more subpoenas than they have written laws. Fifty-six subpoenas were issued during the Ukraine investigation, ten more than the 46 House bills that became law in 2019.[2]

The Era of Divided Government

By the end of the 1980s, divided government had become the norm in American politics, certainly at the national level and often in the state governments as well. In the six decades since 1955, the national government—presidency, House, and Senate—have been controlled by the same party for only 18 years. In such a state of divided government, it is hard to see either the president or Congress as the more powerful. A better understanding of the workings of the national government would be to see that any policy making, in the absence of a terrible world crisis like the coronavirus epidemic, is likely to be incremental, as Congress and the president inch their way toward common ground. Such common ground is largely to be found in symbolic politics.[3] For example, control of the deficit through budgetary ceilings and caps on spending is a way for both branches of government to appear to be doing something without really making substantive policy decisions. From 2011 through December 2019, Congress was singularly unproductive, shutting down most government functions and passing very few bills, lurching from crisis to crisis, and angering the American electorate.

REPRESENTATION IN CONGRESS

Theories of Representation

While Article I, section 8, outlines the specific powers of Congress, the essence of all congressional powers is the quality of congressional representation. The United States Congress was created by the framers to be the branch of the federal government that represented the population. The question is what does *representation* mean? There are different theories as to what constitutes representation.

The Instructed-Delegate View of Representation

Some believe that legislators are duty bound to mirror the views of a majority of their constituents. The argument is that members of Congress are delegates with specific instructions from their voters at home on how to vote on critical issues. Delegates are not supposed to vote the party-line; nor are they to vote their conscience. For a member of Congress to be a delegate of his constituents, the constituents would have to hold well-formed views on the issues. In addition, they would have to have a clear-cut policy preference. Neither condition is likely to be found in reality. On many issues voters may not have enough information to formulate an opinion. On many other issues, there may be no majority opinion.

The Trustee View of Representation

Edmund Burke argued that legislators must be free to vote as they see best.[4] Burke saw the legislator as a **trustee**, to do what he/she believed to be in the best interest of the society. Members, according to this theory, are expected to pursue the broad interests of the larger society and vote against the narrow interests of the constituents if these are in conflict with the needs of the greater society.

The Politico View of Representation

Studies have found that most members of Congress are neither pure delegates nor pure trustees.[5] Members of Congress try to combine both the delegate and trustee perspectives into a pragmatic mix, the so-called **politico** approach. Members from marginal districts, those in which the election was close, may tend to see themselves as obligated to vote as their constituents intend. Legislators from safer districts may feel freer to express their conscience. In addition, there may be times when the wishes of the voters are unclear or contradictory or cases in which constituents have no opinion; in such areas, the member may feel the need to act more as a trustee than a delegate. In any district, however, there are likely to be some issues on which constituents have pronounced opinions on which representatives feel they enjoy little latitude in supporting their constituents' preferences. For example, representatives from wheat, cotton, or tobacco districts will not be able to exercise great discretion on farm issues. Likewise, members from oil rich states can hardly risk being anything other than the advocates of the oil industries.

The Quality of Congressional Representation

When acting as either a delegate or a trustee, a member's ability to represent his or her district or state largely depends on two factors: descriptive representation and ties to a constituency.

Descriptive Representation

There are some who believe that the quality of representation in the United States Congress is dependent upon how descriptively representative the Congress is. The argument is that a legislature should be demographically similar to the general population.[6] If a high quality of representation really does hinge on descriptive representation, the Congress of the United States faces serious problems. The people we elect to Congress are not a cross section of American society. While nearly one-third of all workers in the United States are employed in blue collar jobs, most members are professionals, drawn primarily from business and legal backgrounds.[7] Seventeen percent of U.S. families earn less than $50,000 a year and only 49.8 percent of American families earn over $100,000 a year, yet 100 percent of the members of Congress earn over that amount. In 2020, annual congressional salaries were $174,000.00. Seventy-six richest members of Congress have an estimated net worth of over $3 million each.[8]

Over the years Congress has become more diverse and the 116th session of Congress elected in November 2018, was the most diverse in our country's history, including more minorities, women,

Several southern states elected African-American senators and representatives to Congress after African Americans gained voting rights in 1870.

religions, sexual orientations, and backgrounds than ever. The 116th Congress had a total of 105 women, 101 in the U.S. House of Representatives and 4 in the Senate. There were also 4 female territorial delegates in the House. More than one-in-five members (22 percent) of the 116th Congress were racial or ethnic minorities. Overall, 116 lawmakers were nonwhite. This represents an 84 percent increase over the 107th Congress of 2001-2003, which had only 63 minority members. With the congressional elections of November 2018, the number of openly LGBTQ members of Congress rose to an all-time high of 10—eight in the House and two in the Senate—up from seven.

Although recent Congresses have continued to set new highs for racial and ethnic diversity, they have still been disproportionately white when compared with the overall U.S. population. Nonwhites make up 39 percent of the nation's population, according to U.S. Census Bureau and only 22 percent of Congress. African Americans currently make up 13 percent of the United States population but only 9.5 percent of the House and the share of Hispanics in the U.S. population (18 percent) is twice as high as it is in the House (9 percent). Asians account for 6 percent of the national population but 3 percent of House members. In the Senate, only 9 are a racial or ethnic minority, with 4 senators being Hispanic, 3 Asian, and 3 African Americans. No nonwhite Senators were elected in the election of 2018. Non-Hispanic whites are 61 percent of the U.S. population but are 78 percent of the Congress. In fact, this discrepancy has widened over time. Way back in 1981, 94 percent of the Congress was white, compared with 80 percent of the U.S. population.

There is reason to believe that the descriptive characteristics of the members of Congress may affect the legislative process. The Congressional Black Caucus was formed in 1969 when the thirteen black members of the U.S. House of Representatives joined together to strengthen their efforts to address the legislative concerns of black and minority citizens. Today, the fifty-five members of the Congressional Black Caucus represent many of the largest and most populated urban centers in the country, together with some of the most expansive and rural congressional districts in the nation. These members, now as in the past, have been called upon to work as advocates for America's varied constituent interests and the CBC has been involved in legislative initiatives ranging from full employment to welfare reform, international human rights, from minority business development to expanded educational opportunities. Most noteworthy is the CBC alternative budget, which the Caucus has produced continually for over 20 years. Historically, the CBC alternative budget policies depart significantly from administration budget recommendations as the Caucus seeks to preserve a national commitment to fair treatment for urban and rural America, the elderly, students, small businessmen and women, middle- and low-income wage earners, the economically disadvantaged and a new world order. There is also a more informal Congressional Hispanic Caucus that includes members of Congress of Hispanic descent. The Caucus is dedicated to voicing and advancing issues affecting Hispanic Americans in the United States.

Constituent Ties

Evidence suggests that members of Congress do not need to look like their constituents to feel the pressure to serve those who live in their state or district. Members claim that they spend significant amounts of time and energy on addressing the individual level and state or district level needs of their constituents. When a member of Congress works on the statewide or district wide needs, it is often called **pork barrel or earmarks**. When a member of Congress attempts to serve individual needs of a particular constituent it is commonly called **casework**.

Pork Barrel Legislation and Earmarks. Members of Congress cannot afford to systematically neglect constituency pressure emanating from groups within their district or state. Representatives from districts with defense industries, and perhaps thousands of jobs tied to those industries, are likely to feel the pressure to support defense spending that may end up funding a lucrative contract with one or more of these firms. A Senator from Florida knows that a vote for an increase in social security payments is a vote for the elderly, so many of whom live in his state.

Pork barrel legislation used to be very common in the United States Congress. Some have argued that pork barrel bills are the only ones that members of Congress take seriously because they are seen as so important to the members' chances for re-election. Often, controversial bills could only achieve passage by being filled with pet projects that mobilize the support of members of Congress and maybe even the president himself.

In 2006, for example, Congress passed the $16 billion Foreign Operations Bill, which pays for everything from the Peace Corps to the aerial fumigation of Colombian coca. The 3,320-page bill includes $100,000 for goat-meat research in Texas, $549,000 for "Future Foods" development in Illinois, $569,000 for "Cool Season Legume Research" in Idaho and Washington, $63,000 for a program to combat noxious weeds in the desert Southwest, and $175,000 for obesity research in Texas. It was the biggest single piece of pork-barrel legislation in American history.[9]

On January 5, 2007, in the first one hundred hours of the 110th session of Congress, the new Democratic majority in the House of Representative imposed substantial new restrictions on earmarking. The new rules do not end the practice of packing legislation with pork, but they do force legislators to attach their names to the pet items they slip into spending or tax bills and to certify that they have no personal financial stake in their earmarks. Then in December of 2010, Congress announced a moratorium on earmarks. In January 2017, at the beginning of the new session of Congress, the Republican majority began to push for a return of the earmark, and in 2019, there was a record increase in pork spending, costing the American taxpayer $15.3 billion. Among the notable examples from this year's book: $9 million for a fruit fly quarantine program, $12 million for aquatic plant control, nearly $8 million for the purchase of new fish screens, and nearly $14 million for wild horse and burro management.[10]

Casework. There is fairly consistent communication between constituents and congressional offices. Even in the 1970s, the House and Senate post office handled nearly 100 million pieces of incoming mail.[11] Today, with the Internet, members are even more accessible to the mass public. House members claim that over a quarter of their time and nearly two-thirds of their staff members' time is devoted to working on the needs of individual constituents.[12]

Casework can take several forms. **Patronage** is a direct form of casework in which the member of Congress runs interference with a federal administrative agency seeking favorable treatment for a constituent or constituents. Patronage may even take the form of securing a government job for a constituent.

Casework can also take the form of a **private bill**, a proposal to grant some kind of relief or special privilege to the person named in the bill. Approximately 75 percent of the private bills introduced into Congress are concerned with helping foreign nationals who are unable to get permanent visas in this country.[13]

Congressional Elections

The process of electing members of Congress is decentralized. Congressional elections are controlled by individual state governments, which must, however, conform to the U. S. Constitution and national statute. The Constitution states that representatives are to be elected every second year by popular ballot, and the number of seats awarded to each state be established by a decennial census. Each state has at least one representative, with most congressional districts having slightly more than seven hundred thousand residents. Today, each state's two senators are elected by their state's voters for a six-year term. Only one-third of the senators are elected in any two-year election.

Congressional Reapportionment

By far the most complicated aspects of congressional elections are the issues of **reapportionment** (the allocation of seats in the House to each state after each census) and **redistricting** (the redrawing of the boundaries of the districts within each state).

Congress sets the number of seats in the House, and the number of seats in the House has grown with the country. The Constitution set the number of representatives at 65 from 1787 until the first Census of 1790, when it was increased to 105. The House has had 435 seats since 1913. Reapportionment is the process of dividing these 435 memberships, or seats, in the House of Representatives among the 50 states based on the state population figures collected during the census that is conducted every ten years on the decade.

The first decennial census was conducted in 1790 and has been taken every ten years as mandated by Article I, Section 2 of the U.S. Constitution. Since the first census, conducted by Thomas Jefferson, the decennial count has been the basis for our representative form of government as envisioned by our nation's Founding Fathers. In 1790, each member of the House of Representatives represented about 34,000 residents. Today, the House has more than quadrupled in size, and each member represents about 20 times as many constituents.

In 1962, in the case *Baker v Carr*, the Supreme Court held that reapportionment must not violate the Fourteenth Amendment principle that no state can deny to any person "the equal protection of the laws." Then in the 1964 case of *Wesberry v Sanders* the Court held that reapportionment must not violate the "one person, one vote" principle embodied in Article I, Section 2, of the Constitution, which requires that members of Congress be chosen "by the People of the several States." Prior to *Wesberry*, severe malapportionment had resulted in some districts containing two or three times the populations of other districts in the same state, thereby diluting the vote in the more populous districts. After the Census is completed, states must redistrict, divide their state populations into congressional districts. Each state decides for itself who will draw its district lines, which has led to a few different models: state legislature, political commissions and independent commissions. This is called **redistricting**.

Redistricting and Gerrymandering

While the one person, one vote principle has dealt with the issue of district size successfully, the issue of how to draw the district boundaries has not yet been completely resolved. It is usually the job of each state legislature to divide its state's population into the number of congressional districts apportioned to it following the census. Many districts have been gerrymandered. A district is said to be gerrymandered when the dominant party in the state legislature alters the shape of the state's districts substantially in order to maximize its party's electoral strength at the expense of the legislature's minority party. The dominant party in the state legislature can do this by concentrating the opposition party's voters in as few districts as possible while carefully dispersing its own party members thinly across many districts, keeping them in the plurality in as many districts as possible.

The Supreme Court has declined to outlaw partisan gerrymandering—saying only states can police the drawing of districts. In 2013, the Court also removed a key safeguard against the practice by gutting the Voting Rights Act of 1965. The Voting Rights Act ended literacy tests, poll taxes, and voting restrictions that had disenfranchised millions of minority voters for decades. It also required areas of the country with a history of using these discriminatory tactics to get federal approval before making any changes to voting. In 2013 in the case of *Shelby County v. Holder*, the Court allowed these areas of the country free reign over voting rules once again. For the first time since 1965, local officials could now close polls or change voting laws without the permission of the federal government. In the 5-4 ruling, Chief Justice John Roberts implied that the problems of systemic racism and voter discrimination no longer existed.

The Court ruling means states with a history of racial discrimination, including Texas, Florida and North Carolina, no longer have to clear their redistricting maps with the Department of Justice before putting them in place. That ruling, along with the growing populations, changing demographics and mostly single-party control, create a situation in which the southern states are likely to engage in partisan gerrymandering.[14]

Racial Gerrymandering and "Minority-Majority" Districts

In the early 1990s, the Supreme Court actually began to encourage a type of gerrymandering that made possible the election of a minority representative from what is termed a "minority-majority" area. Under the mandate of the Voting Rights Act of 1965, the Justice Department issued directives to states after the 1990 census instructing them to create congressional districts that would maximize the voting power of minority groups, that is, create districts in which the minority voters were the majority. In the 2017 Supreme Court case, *Cooper v. Harris*, the Court concluded that North Carolina violated the Equal Protections Clause of the 14th Amendment by separating voters in different districts on the basis of race without "sufficient justification" for doing so. It is important to understand that a state can use race when drawing its legislative maps. Race, however, can only be used as the predominant factor if the state has a compelling, but not personal or partisan, interest in doing so. Experts think that the *Cooper* case opens the door for the Supreme Court to reconsider the constitutionality of partisan gerrymandering.[15]

Candidates for Congress

Candidates for congressional seats are largely self-selected. They are likely to be people who have been active in local politics. Because congressional campaigns are expensive, candidates also must have access to substantial resources.

Most candidates for Congress must win the nomination of their party through a direct primary, in which voters identified with their party choose among their party's candidates, picking the one they would like to see run against the opposing party in the general election. Because voter turnout tends to be very low in primary elections, those who do vote tend to be more ideological than those who stay home. As a result, Democratic candidates often take more liberal positions and Republican candidates more conservative positions, trying to appeal to the ideologues in their party. Later, in the general election when turnout is higher, these same candidates may have to moderate their views to attract the votes of independents, voters from the other party, and moderate voters in their own party.

The Costs of Congressional Campaigns

United States House and Senate candidates running in the 2018 election cycle reported raising a total of $5.7 billion, making it the most expensive midterm election ever. While a record 793 women ran and raised money in the 2018 congressional races, female donors also contributed to campaigns in record amounts and accounted for $514 million of donations larger than $200 to major party candidates. About three-quarters of the money contributed by women went to Democrats. The Florida U.S. Senate race in which the Republican Rick Scott defeated the Democratic incumbent Bill Nelson was the most expensive contest of the midterms. Candidates and groups spent $209 million to shape that race, with Scott pouring more than $63 million of his personal fortune into the contest.[16] In 2018, the candidate who spent the most money tended to win, though this trend is stronger in the House than in the Senate. In the House 88.8 percent of the big spenders won and in the Senate 82.9 percent did.[17]

The Real but Declining Advantages of Incumbency

The re-election rate for members of Congress is exceptionally high, especially considering how unpopular the institution is in the eyes of the American public. The re-election rate among all the 435 members of the House has been as high as 98 percent in modern history, and it's rarely dipped below 90 percent. There are several reasons why incumbents have a fairly certain lock on re-election. First, many House districts have been gerrymandered and are today safe seats. Second, incumbents have very high name recognition. Third, incumbents have the ability to regularly mail self-congratulatory newsletters to constituents at taxpayer expense and to earmark money for pet projects in their districts. Finally, members of Congress who raise money for their colleagues are also rewarded with large amounts of campaign money for their own campaigns, making it even more difficult to unseat incumbents.

The incumbency re-election rate for the House has gone as high as 98 percent in 2014 and 97 percent in 2016. In 2018, however, the incumbency effect fell to 91 percent and in this century, the incumbency advantage has significantly diminished, especially for the Senate, with the electoral benefit of already being a member of Congress down to less than 3 percentage points.[18] In 2018, 17 percent of U.S. Senate incumbents seeking re-election were defeated. This was the highest percentage since the 2014 midterm election when 21 percent of Senate incumbents were defeated. Thirty-four House incumbents, 9 percent, were defeated in 2018, and this was the highest percentage of incumbents defeated since 2012, when 10.2 percent were not re-elected.[19]

Campaign Finance and Incumbency

For many years, researchers overlooked the role of campaign contributions in the re-election of incumbents. This was because incumbents win even when they spend less than their challengers. Because so many incumbents will win re-election, they usually win whether they spend more or less than their opponent.

The problem with such studies is that they have focused on campaign *spending*. What they should look at is the relationship between money *raised* and winning, not money *spent* and winning. Incumbents enjoy an enormous advantage not enjoyed by their challengers: PAC money. Political action committees gave almost 90 percent of their donations to congressional incumbents during the 2016-2018 election cycle. For example, Agribusiness gave 93.5 percent to incumbents, Communications/Electronics 95.6 percent, Defense 96.6 percent, and Finance 94 percent.[20]

Even though incumbents raise more money than challengers, they do not necessarily spend all the money. Any unused campaign money goes into a **war chest**; this money can then be used for the following campaign or given to the incumbent's political party upon his retirement from Congress. Many incumbents have amassed significant war chests, so significant, in fact, that they may scare an opponent off. A significant number of congressional incumbents run unopposed, at least partly because their war chests are so daunting to a challenger. Obviously, if one runs unopposed, one will win. It is the money raised and amassed in huge war chests, but not necessarily spent, that may scare potential challengers out of the arena.

A certain number of House races every year are non-competitive. In 2018, 42 races—9.7 percent of all House elections—had only one major-party candidate. A full 39 of those seats lacked a Republican candidate, while just three did not have a Democratic running, a vast improvement for the Democrats, who had no candidate in 27 races in 2016, and in 36 races in 2014. There have been 125 districts in 28 states that had just one major-party candidate running at some point in the last three election cycles.[21]

The Issue of Term Limits

The enormous advantages enjoyed by incumbents have led many to call for mandatory term limits. Term limits are popular. Today, 82 percent of Americans are in favor of a constitutional amendment that would place term limits on members of Congress.[22] Twenty-three states tried to limit the terms of their delegation to Congress, with the general formula being three terms [six years] in the U.S. House and two terms [twelve years] in the U.S. Senate. As they pertain to Congress, however, these laws are no longer enforceable because of lawsuits filed by term limits foes. In *U.S. Term Limits Inc. vs. Thornton*, the Supreme Court, by a vote of 5 to 4, declared that a state has no power to impose limits on the number of terms for which its members of the U. S. Congress are eligible either by amending its own constitution or state law. Because the Constitution explicitly addresses qualifications for both the House and Senate, the Court reasoned that the only way to change terms of office would be through the amendment process.

THE ORGANIZATIONAL STRUCTURES OF CONGRESS

Power in Congress is heavily decentralized. What limited leadership there is, comes in four forms: the party system, the committee system, the staff, and the caucuses.

The Formal Leadership of Congress: The Political Parties

Leadership in the House

Every two years, at the beginning of a new Congress, the members of each party gather to elect their House leaders. This gathering is usually referred to as the caucus, or conference. The elected leader of the majority party becomes the **Speaker of the House**. House leadership is primarily exercised by the speaker. He presides over meetings in the House. He appoints members to joint committees and conference committees. He schedules legislation for floor action. He decides points of order and interprets the rules with the aid of the House parliamentarian. He refers bills and resolutions to the appropriate standing committees in the House. In 1975, the speaker's powers were enlarged by the House Democratic caucus, which gave its party's speaker the power to appoint the Democratic Steering Committee, which determines new committee assignments for House Democrats. A speaker may fully participate in floor debate, and he may vote, although in recent years, the speaker has only voted to break a tie. The Speaker also is second-in-line to the presidency under the Presidential Succession Act of 1947 after the vice president, and the Speaker plays a role in the 25th Amendment's process to deal with the event of a presidential disability.

After the speaker is selected, the House majority caucus then elects a **majority leader**. The majority leader is the spokesperson for the majority party in the House and generally acts as the speaker's first lieutenant. The majority leader also conducts most of the substantive and procedural floor debate.

The minority party goes through roughly the same process, selecting a **minority leader**. Like the majority leader, the minority leader is primarily responsible for maintaining party cohesion and acting as the party's spokesperson. The minority leader also speaks on behalf of the president if the president is of that party.

The formal leadership of each party also includes assistants known as **whips**. The whips assist the party leaders by transmitting information from the leaders to party members and by getting party members onto the floor when a vote is being called. Even before the vote is taken, the whips will have conducted polls of their party's members and communicated members' intentions to the leaders. Today, both the Republican and Democratic whips are elected by their party's caucus.

Next in line in importance for each party is its **Committee on Committees** whose tasks are to assign newly elected legislators to committees and deal with the requests of incumbent members for transfers from one committee to another. Members usually receive the assignments they want; and they usually request assignment on a committee related to the dominant interests in their districts.

Finally, a member of the majority party chairs every committee and subcommittee. In general, the most senior member, the one with the longest continuous service on that committee, is the chair. This is also true in the Senate.

Leadership in the Senate

The two highest-ranking leaders in the Senate are defined by the Constitution and are largely ceremonial. Under the Constitution, the vice president is the president of the Senate but rarely attends meetings of the Senate and may vote only to break a tie. The Constitution also allows the Senate to elect a **president pro tempore** to preside over the Senate in the vice president's absence. The president pro tem is a member of the majority party and usually is the member with the longest continuous service in the Senate.

The real leadership power in the Senate is exercised, as in the House, by the **majority floor leader**, the **minority floor leader**, and the whips, all elected by party caucus. These leaders have powers similar to their counterparts in the House. They schedule debate, make committee assignments, select members to the conference committees, mobilize the party vote, and act as their party's spokesperson. The Democratic leaders are more powerful than the Republican leaders in the Senate. This is because the Democratic floor leader is also the chairperson of all the following: The Democratic Conference (caucus), the Steering Committee (makes committee assignments), and the Policy Committee (schedules legislation for floor action).

The Role of Money in Choosing Congressional Leadership

The leadership positions in Congress are often determined primarily by the ability to raise campaign money. For example, the Speaker of the House, Nancy Pelosi, earned the job at least in part because she is known to be a very savvy fundraiser. In the 2018 electoral cycle, Speaker Pelosi distributed campaign money through the Nancy Pelosi Victory Fund and PAC to the Future. Additionally, the Democratic Congressional Campaign Committee received hefty contributions directly from the Speaker and her joint fundraising committee totaling $4 million.[23]

Party Discipline

A vote on which 90 percent or more of the members of one party take a particular position while at least 90 percent of the members of the other party take the opposing position is called a **party vote**. In the early 1900s, party votes accounted for nearly one-half of all votes in Congress. Today, they are very rare. Much more common is a weaker form of party voting in which the majority of a party votes one way, and the majority of the other party votes the other way. Such voting has increased in recent years.

Party voting reached record highs in 2017 but then took a dramatic nose-dive in 2018 as lawmakers worked across the aisle on high-profile legislation like the rewriting of the Dodd-Frank financial law, a legislative package to deal with the opioid crisis, and an overhaul of the country's criminal justice laws. The total number of party unity votes in the House fell from 76 percent of the total votes taken in the House in 2017, a record, to 59 percent in 2018, the lowest since 2010. In the Senate, the decline was even more dramatic with the total number of unity votes dropping 19 points from the year before—from 68.9 percent of all votes taken in 2017 down to just under half of all votes—49.6 percent in 2018. That marks the second-lowest figure since 2002.

The 2018 midterm election saw the defeat of a large number of moderates in both parties, those who had been the most likely to cross party lines. In 2019 and 2020, party unity scores, consequently, started to climb, returning to their earlier 2017 levels. Carlos Curbelo, a moderate Republican from Florida who lost his bid for re-election in 2018, said, "The two-party system is yielding a lot of leaders who don't see the incentive to compromise, don't see the incentive to negotiate and actually solve the nation's problems," he said. "On the contrary, they like to leave the challenges unsolved. That way they can exploit them come campaign season."[24]

THE COMMITTEE AND SUBCOMMITTEE SYSTEM

The Work of Committees: Legislation and Oversight

In any institution as large as the United States Congress, a division of labor is necessary. Because most members of Congress have backgrounds in law or business, they cannot be expected to be experts on all the wide variety of issues on which they are asked to vote. Every year, thousands of bills are introduced into Congress. As a result, members must specialize in one or two issue areas of particular importance to their districts or states. They will then sit on committees and subcommittees dealing with these issue areas.

Most of the actual work of legislating is done by the committees and subcommittees within Congress. Committees usually control the fate of bills, particularly in three ways. First, the committee controls the scheduling of hearings and formal action on a bill and decides which of its subcommittees will act on the bill. A committee can hold up action on the bill and thereby virtually kill its chances to be considered by the entire chamber and passed into law. The only way to remove a bill from a House committee is through a **discharge petition**, signed by 218 members of the House. While such petitions are rare, they were used multiple times during this mid-20th-century era to force movement on civil rights bills, as the Rules Committee was chaired by Howard "Judge" Smith, infamous for his inaction on such legislation. Sometimes the threat of a discharge petition is enough as the sight of a growing number of signatures on a discharge petition at the end of the year in 1963 successfully pressured Smith to move a version of what would become known as the Civil Rights Act of 1964 out of committee. In 1970, a discharge petition forced the Equal Rights Amendment (ERA) out of the Judiciary Committee (though the amendment was never ratified).[25]

Committees control the fate of a bill in a second way: they mark-up the bill. To mark-up means to alter the bill, essentially rewriting it. It is this marked-up version of the bill that will be submitted for consideration to the entire chamber, either House or Senate.

Committees exercise a third form of control over legislation: the committee vote, while not binding on the chamber, almost always determines the chamber's final vote. Committees and subcommittees make a formal report on proposed legislation. These reports are available from the Government Printing Office. The committee's decisions can be reversed on the floor of the chamber, but this is highly unlikely. The whole point of a committee system is to allow for specialization and the effective division of labor.

The work of committees does not end when the bill goes to the entire chamber for consideration. Members of the committee act as floor managers of the bill, offering advice to other members and lining up support. Finally if there are any differences between the version of the bill passed by the House and the version passed by the Senate, it is the committee members who will be asked to serve on a conference committee whose duty it is to adjust the legislation into a compromise that, if the bill is to be passed, must be acceptable to a majority in both chambers.

Even after the legislation is passed into law, the work of the committees and subcommittees is not finished. Committee members remain active in their role of oversight, the process of monitoring the bureaucracy in its administration of policy. Oversight is accomplished primarily through committee hearings. At these hearings, agency heads, even cabinet secretaries, testify concerning their progress, or lack thereof, in administering the law and carrying out the will of Congress. Committee members and their staff question agency officials, probing particular areas that may seem problematic. If the committee feels the agency is not complying with either the letter or the spirit of the law, it may seek to cut the agency's budget to secure compliance with congressional intent.

The Committee System in the Era of Divided Government

Congress's oversight function has become especially visible in the modern era of divided government. In the four decades since the Watergate scandal erupted, the same party has simultaneously controlled the White House and both Houses of Congress for only 14 years: during Jimmy Carter's one-term presidency, during the first 2 years of Clinton's first term, from 2002-2006, from 2009-2010, and 2017-2018.

The result has been to set off what amounts to guerrilla warfare between the executive and legislative branches. In 1973, the Senate established the Select Committee on Campaign Activities to investigate the misdeeds of the 1972 presidential campaign, otherwise known as the Watergate scandal. This was followed the next year by the House Judiciary Committee's hearings on the impeachment of President Nixon for his attempt to cover up the scandal. Shortly after the Judiciary Committee recommended these articles of impeachment, the president resigned.

After the Republicans lost control of Congress following the midterm elections of 2006, there was a flurry of congressional investigations of George W. Bush's executive branch. In their first two months on the job, Democrats held an astounding 81 hearings on the war in Iraq. Foremost among these hearings were the inquiries into conditions at Walter Reed Army Medical Center. Apart from the war, questions concerning FBI domestic surveillance under the Patriot Act also provoked a string of hearings and demands on Capitol Hill for revising the law to protect civil liberties. There was also an investigation into the firing of eight federal prosecutors, allegedly for partisan political purposes, which prompted widespread calls for the resignation of Attorney General Alberto Gonzales and subpoena threats for presidential advisors Harriet Miers and Karl Rove.

Not surprisingly, when the Republicans regained control of the House in 2011, many began to call for investigations of the Obama administration. On January 3, the first day of the new session of Congress, Rep. Darrell Issa, Chairman of the House Oversight Committee, launched investigations on everything from WikiLeaks to Fannie Mae to corruption in Afghanistan. The outline of the Committee's hearing topics also included investigation of how regulation impacts job creation, recalls at the Food and Drug Administration and the failure of the Financial Crisis Inquiry Commission to agree on the causes of the market meltdown.[26]

More recently, when the Democrats regained control of the House in 2018, there was a spate of congressional investigations of President Trump. The House Permanent Select Committee on Intelligence reopened the investigation into Russian interference in the 2016 election, the House Oversight and Reform Committee looked into the potential malpractice in how security clearances were issued in the White House and probed President Trump's finances by investigating the president's accounting firm, and the House Financial Services Committee investigated President Trump's connections with Deutsche Bank.

Types of Congressional Committees

Standing Committees

The standing committee is the most important type of committee in Congress. These are permanent committees that specialize in a particular policy area. For example, the Banking, Finance, and Urban Affairs Committee in the House and the Banking, Housing, and Urban Affairs Committee in the Senate specialize in legislation dealing primarily with the banking industry.

Party leaders determine which members serve on each committee. The majority party always has a majority of members on each committee. The majority party names the chair of each committee based on seniority, power, loyalty, and other criteria. Committee chairs have substantial power: they schedule hearings and votes and can easily kill a bill if they choose. The senior committee member from the minority party is called the ranking member. Members of Congress try to get good committee assignments. Most members want to be on powerful committees, such as the Ways and Means Committee (which deals with taxes and revenue), or on a committee that covers issues important to their constituents. Getting a good committee assignment can make reelection easier for members. Typically, seventeen to twenty House members sit on each of these committees, with members sitting on an average of two standing committees. Members who serve on either the Appropriations, Rules, or Ways and Means Committee, however, can only serve on that one committee. Senators sit on two standing committees and one minor committee (either the Rules and Administration Committee or the Veterans Affairs Committee).

Select Committees

A select committee is a temporary committee created by Congress to fill a certain purpose. After they report to their chamber, they are disbanded. Select committees are often investigative committees, for example, those dealing with Watergate, Iran-Contra, and Whitewater, and most recently, the Trump-Ukraine Impeachment inquiry. On April 2, 2020, Speaker of the House Pelosi announced the formation of a bipartisan select committee to oversee the Trump administration's distribution of more that $2 trillion in coronavirus relief funds.

Joint Committees

A joint committee is *joint* in several respects. It is created by the House and Senate, and it is made up of members from both chambers and from both political parties. Joint committees may be either temporary or permanent, but they always deal with very specific policy areas, such as economic policy or taxation.

Conference Committees

The conference committee is both a joint committee and a temporary committee. It is created by the House and Senate to work out a compromise in the case in which the House and Senate pass different versions of a bill. While only about 15 to 25 percent of all bills go to conference committee, almost all the most important and controversial ones will.

The House Rules Committee

The House Rules Committee is a uniquely powerful committee. It serves as a gatekeeper, structuring floor action. The Rules Committee sets the time limit on debate and decides whether and in what ways the bill can be amended from the floor.

Committee Membership

One of the first things newly elected members of Congress do upon arriving in Washington is to write to their parties' congressional leadership and the other members of their state delegation, indicating their committee preferences. Members seek to get on committees that will achieve three goals: re-election, influence in Congress, and the opportunity to make policy in areas they think are important.[27] Party leaders generally honor these requests because they want their party members to serve their constituents and thereby win re-election.

Each party in each chamber has its own particular way of making committee assignments. In the House, for example, the Democrats and Republicans have their Steering and Policy Committees. While these committees do have the authority to assign their party members to the committees and subcommittees, every committee must reflect the party balance of the entire chamber and every chair of every committee will be from the majority party in that chamber. In other words, if the Senate has, say, 60 Republicans and 40 Democrats, every committee and subcommittee in the Senate will have approximately 60 percent Republicans and 40 percent Democrats, and every chair will be a Republican.

Committee and Subcommittee Chairs

Until the 1970s, there was a simple rule for picking committee chairs: the seniority system. This system assigned the chair position to the committee member of the majority party who had the longest continued service on that committee. In the early 1970s, in the wake of the Watergate scandal, Congress faced a revolt staged by younger, newly elected members. Both parties moved to permit their party members to vote on committee chairs.

Members of Congress still tend to favor the seniority system because it is seen as a nonpartisan method for selecting committee chairmen, as opposed to a system that employs patronage, cronyism, and favoritism. The seniority system also enhances the power of the committee chairs (limited to six years since 1995) because they are no longer beholden to the interests of party leaders. Because of the nature of the terms of office, seniority is more important in the Senate (where the terms are for six years), than in the House of Representatives (where the terms are for only two years).[28]

There have been a series of reforms to somewhat reduce the power of the chairs. Chairs of a generation ago could bully members and bottle up legislation and succeed in killing it all together. Today's chairs are less able to control their committees decision-making processes.[29] They still are primarily responsible for scheduling their committees' hearings, hiring staff, appointing subcommittees, and managing committee bills once they are brought to the floor of the chamber. During the 2019 investigations of President Trump, ten new powerful Democratic House committee chairs launched subpoena-powered investigations into the president's finances, Russian interference, and administration ethics scandals. These committee chairs held the important power to decide where to expend their committee's investigative resources.[30]

The Staff System

More than 38,660 people are employed by the United States Congress. The average Senate office employs about thirty staff members but twice that number work for senators from the more populous states. House members employ about fifteen staff members.[31] These staffers handle constituent communications and deal with the details of legislative and administrative actions. Increasingly, staffers are responsible for formulating proposals, organizing hearings, dealing with interest group lobbyists, and advising the members for whom they work.

Besides their personal staff, Congress employs more than three thousand committee staffers. These employees are permanent and stay from one session of Congress to the next. Key pieces of important legislation have been proposed or altered by these committee staff members. Senator Robert Morgan (D-N.C.) has said, "this country is basically run by the legislative staffs of the Senate and House of Representatives."[32]

Congress has also created three different support institutions to enable Congress to oversee the actions of the executive branch, its administrative agencies, and the president himself. The Congressional Research Service does research on policy proposals. The General Accountability Office is Congress' financial watchdog over the bureaucracy, checking the departments and agencies to make sure they are spending the money appropriated by Congress in the way in which Congress meant it to be spent. The Congressional Budget Office assesses the economic implications and probable costs of proposed federal programs. Finally, a section of the Library of Congress acts as an information and fact-finding center for legislators and their staff members. It provides a computer based record of the content and status of major bills that can be accessed by members and their staff.

The Caucuses

Caucuses, which fall under the broader label of "congressional member organizations," are groups of senators or representatives who share certain opinions, interests, or social characteristics. Some of the most important caucuses are the Congressional Black Caucus, the Congressional Caucus for Women's Issues, and the Hispanic Caucus. These three have actively sought to advance the interests of the groups they represent through the promotion of legislation and lobbying administrative agencies for favorable treatment. The Congressional Black Caucus now includes over forty members and has dramatically increased its role in the policy-making process.

The number of congressional caucuses and CMOs (which are not necessarily registered with the House Administration Committee or its Senate counterpart) has exploded over the last few decades. In 1993, there were just over 100. In the last Congress, there were 694, according to the Congressional Research Service. That's more than one caucus for every member of Congress. The proliferation of caucus groups in recent years has led to the formation of some groups that one might not think of as typically associated with legislative work. In 2013, Representatives Aaron Schock and Tulsi Gabbard formed the Congressional Future Caucus, dedicated to all things millennial. There are also a Congressional Soccer Caucus, the Bourbon Caucus, the Congressional Kidney Caucus, the Congressional Bike Caucus, and the Civility Caucus. On average, members of the House belong to 34 of these caucuses, according to Congressional Research Service data, while senators typically belong to about 18 of them. (There are far fewer caucuses in the Senate than in the House.)[33]

THE LEGISLATIVE PROCESS

For a bill to become law, it must pass through a series of steps in both the House and the Senate and be passed by a majority of both chambers in identical form. While flow charts may make the legislative process appear to be neat and tidy, the reality is far more complex and far messier. A bill may be introduced in one chamber, work its way through that chamber and then be taken up by the other chamber of Congress. Or a bill might be working its way through the two chambers simultaneously, though not necessarily at exactly the same stage in both. It is also not necessarily the case that the version of the bill in the Senate will be the same as the version in the House. In general, however, the steps discussed below must be completed within one two-year session of Congress. All sessions run from January of an odd year through December of the following even year.

Step One: The Bill is Introduced

The formal legislative process begins when a member of Congress introduces a bill. But before a bill can be introduced, a problem must be identified, and a solution formulated. In short, the issue must get on the congressional agenda. An issue can exist for a time without becoming a *political* issue.

Issues get on the legislative agenda in a variety of ways. Certainly, a sudden crisis can propel an issue to the forefront, for example, the terrorist attacks on September 11, 2001 or the coronavirus of 2020. Sustained media coverage of an issue can also work the issue into the collective congressional consciousness. Presidents can also bring an issue to the fore, as President Trump did with the issue of immigration. Interest groups are quite often instrumental in politicizing an issue, for example, Mothers Against Drunk Driving.

Of course, members of Congress themselves may be instrumental in advancing an issue to the legislative agenda, particularly in two situations. When the president is of one party and the other party controls both or even just one of the chambers of Congress, initiation of legislation is very likely to come from Congress itself. When the Democrats took control of the House after the 2018 elections, they quickly unveiled their ambitious "A Better Deal for Our Democracy," with proposals to protect and improve voting rights, new ethics laws, and campaign finance reforms, including policies that would make lobbyists' activities more transparent and tighten rules around bribery and fraud convictions. The other situation that tends to encourage congressional initiation of legislation is when one or more members of Congress are seeking to be nominated as a candidate for the presidency. This was the case in 2020 when Senators Klobuchar, Sanders, Harris, Warren, Bennet, Gillibrand, and Booker and House members Gabbard, Ryan, Moulton, and Swalwell all sought the Democratic nomination.

Step Two: The Bill is Assigned to Committee

After a bill is introduced, in the House by a House member and in the Senate by a senator, it will be assigned to a committee that has jurisdiction over that policy area. The Speaker of the House and the majority leader in the Senate are responsible for this assignation. While it is often very clear which committee should receive the bill, there are some cases when it is less than clear. In these situations, the leaders can use their discretion to send the bill to a committee that will be friendly to it or to a committee that may be more hostile to the bill.

Once assigned to committee, the bill then will be further assigned to one of the committee's appropriate subcommittees. The subcommittee will do three things with the bill. First, the staffers of the committee members will conduct research on the issue, and the subcommittee may choose to hold hearings on the issue. The committee members will want to hear from people with expertise in the issue area. This group will likely include interest group lobbyists and bureaucrats from the executive branch department or agency involved in the issue area. These people will be asked to testify at the hearing.

When the subcommittee feels that it has sufficient information, it will hold meetings called **mark-up sessions**. The original bill will be marked-up, altered to reflect the information Congress gleaned from the hearing process. Finally, the subcommittee will vote on the bill. If passed, the bill will be sent by the subcommittee to its full committee. The full committee may accept the recommendation of its subcommittee or choose to hold its own hearings and prepare its own bill. It should be noted, however, that many bills will *die* in committee, with little or no consideration given to them. Many pieces of the legislation may be symbolic in that members of Congress introduce them to please some group in their constituency but expect nothing to be done on the final bill. In a typical session of Congress, 95 percent of the roughly eight thousand bills introduced die in committee. In those cases when the committee has acted on the bill, the bill is ready to go to the floor of the chamber.

In the House, before the bill goes to the floor, it must go the House Rules Committee. The Rules Committee attaches a rule to the bill that will govern the floor debate in the House. The Rules Committee specifies the length of debate and decides whether amendments can be added from the floor and, if so, of what type.

Before the bill can go to the floor, in both the House and Senate, it must be placed on the calendar. The majority and minority leaders, after consultation with committee chairs, the White House, and the leaders from the other chamber, place the bill on the calendar. Some bills are given an early date while others stay on the calendar from one session to the next.

Step Three: Floor Action

Debate in the House of Representatives is structured by the Rules Committee and the Speaker of the House. The Speaker can decide whether to grant recognition to a member. The time allotted by the Rules Committee for debate is usually controlled by the bill's sponsor and by its leading opponent. These two are usually the chairman of the committee to which the bill was assigned and the ranking minority member on that committee.

Debate on the floor of the Senate can only be structured by unanimous consent agreements to set the starting time and length of debate and if a senator wants to stop a bill from being passed, he or she may start a **filibuster**, speaking for as long as the member wants. To end a filibuster requires a vote of cloture. Sixteen senators must propose closing off debate. Then, after a two-day waiting period, sixty senators must vote for cloture for the debate to be ended. After cloture, each senator may speak for a maximum of one hour on a bill before a vote is taken. Breaking each of these filibusters adds days, even weeks, to every bill.

The number of Senate filibusters has increased in recent years. Not all modern filibusters can be easily identified because even the mere threat of a filibuster can be enough to prevent consideration of a bill, and there is no easy source of data on threatened filibusters. However, the Senate does publicly report the number of cloture votes held, votes to break a filibuster in progress. Those numbers have skyrocketed. From 1917, when the cloture rule was put in place, to 1970, there were fewer than 60 cloture motions; the most notable filibusters where those blocking civil rights legislation. Between 1970 and 2000, cloture votes increased to an average of about 17 per year. Finally, starting in the 2000s, minority parties in the Senate began to routinely filibuster substantive legislation proposed by the other party. During this period, from 2000 to 2018, an average of 53 cloture votes were held every year, with a continuing trend upward.[34]

While the filibuster can no longer be used to block executive and judicial branch nominees, many recent important pieces of legislation have died at the hands of the Senate filibuster. The list of filibustered bills includes efforts to strengthen labor unions, protect the environment, create high-paying jobs, reduce pay discrimination, improve campaign and lobbying disclosures, provide a pathway to citizenship for Dreamers, and reduce taxes. Perhaps most notably, gun safety legislation, even though supported by majorities in both the Hose and Senate, have never survived because they lacked a filibuster-proof supermajority in the Senate. Americans overwhelmingly support universal background checks, regardless of political party. Moreover, 64 percent of Americans support stricter gun laws in general, and yet, Congress has not passed a significant gun violence prevention bill since the early 1990s, when Congress passed a temporary ban on assault weapons; measures to prevent some domestic abusers from possessing guns; and the Brady Handgun Violence Prevention Act, which required background checks for some gun purchases. In fact, the only significant gun-related legislation that passed during the past 25 years was to protect gun retailers and manufacturers from liability.[35]

The Senate of the United States is purposefully structured to allow intense minorities to block legislation. Whereas the House is the repository of majoritarianism, the Senate is the protector of the minority. The filibuster is only one of several techniques that allow for this minority veto. Under Senate rules, members are able to propose unlimited amendments to a bill. Each amendment must be voted on before the bill can come to a final vote. The introduction of new amendments can only be blocked by unanimous consent.

When debate is finished, a vote may be called. If a majority of the House votes for a bill, it is passed by the House. A majority vote in the Senate similarly passes the bill in that chamber. If there are any differences between the version passed by the House and the version passed by the Senate, then the bill is sent to a conference committee.

Step Four: The Conference Committee

It is often the case that a bill passed by the House will differ in significant ways from that passed by the Senate. In such cases, a conference committee is composed of the senior members of the committees and subcommittees that had had responsibility for the bills. The job of the conference committee is to work out a compromise version of the bill. When the bill gets out of conference, the House-Senate conference report must be approved on the floor of each chamber. Usually such approval is given readily. The bill can then be voted on. If it is passed by a majority of the House and a majority of the Senate, the bill then goes to the president.

It should be noted that the members of a conference committee are often chosen because they have strong ties to the interest groups impacted by the proposed bill. For example, in 2017 when the largest tax rewrite in decades was powering through Congress, the 11,000 registered interest group lobbyists working on tax-related issues focused their attention on the fourteen members of the Conference Committee. Fund-raisers held by members of the conference committee during the tax reform debate were hot tickets for tax lobbyists, who paid thousands of dollars for face time with lawmakers who controlled the fate of valued tax loopholes.[36]

Step Five: The President

When a president receives the bill, he may do any of three things with it. In most situation, he will sign the bill, in which case it becomes law. He may, on the other hand, choose to let the bill sit for ten days, excluding Sunday. On the tenth day, the bill becomes law without his signature. A president may choose to follow this course when he is presented with a bill that he does not approve of but for political purposes is willing to go along with Congress.

The third thing the president can do is **veto** the bill. The veto is the president's constitutional right to reject a piece of legislation passed by Congress. To veto a bill, the president must return it to the chamber in which it originated within ten days with his objections to the bill. Congress can try to override the president's veto, but such an override requires a two-thirds vote in both chambers. Overrides are very rare.

If Congress adjourns during this ten-day period in which the president may act, and the president has taken no action, the bill is considered **pocket vetoed**. A pocket veto cannot be overridden by Congress for the simple reason that Congress has adjourned.

For a brief period, the president also enjoyed the power of the **line item veto**. In 1996 President Clinton signed into law a bill passed by Congress authorizing the item veto that allows a president five calendar days following Congress' passage of a bill to notify Congress of his decision to "rescind" an item in the bill. President Clinton used the power 82 times on 11 laws before the Supreme Court in 1998 in *Clinton v. City of New York* declared that the line-item veto is unconstitutional because it would give unilateral power to the president to amend the text of laws, a power given to the Congress in the Constitution. Presidents Bush and Obama both sought ways to get a line-item veto, and in March 2018, President Trump again called upon Congress to give him the line-item veto, all to no avail.[37]

Step Six: Oversight

Once Congress has passed a bill and the president has either signed it or allowed it to become law, the law must be put into effect. In the executive branch there are departments and agencies specifically responsible for executing the laws of the land. Members of Congress and their committees must oversee how these departments and agencies carry out the policies passed into law by Congress. This is the **oversight** function of Congress.

Congressional supervision of the executive branch bureaucracy takes several forms. First, no agency or department may exist (except for a few presidential offices and special commissions) without congressional approval. It is Congress that passes the **enabling legislation** that creates these agencies and empowers them. During the presidency of George Washington, Congress created three departments: Treasury, State, and War. Today, the bureaucracy has grown to over eighteen hundred departments, agencies, commissions, and government corporations, with a budget of over one and a half trillion dollars, and employing over five million people. While Congress cannot control all aspects of personnel selection, the Senate does have the constitutional power to advise and to consent to (or refuse to consent to) presidential nominations of top agency and department personnel.

The vast size of the bureaucracy does make oversight difficult. In addition, the legislative process itself complicates effective oversight. Congress tends to pass laws that are general outlines for policy development. Congress cannot anticipate all the possible applications of the law and so leaves much for the bureaucracy to fill in. On a typical weekday, agencies issue more than a hundred pages of new regulations. Determining how good a job a particular agency is doing will not be an easy job.

Congress also exercises oversight through its control of the budget. No money may be spent unless it has first been authorized and appropriated by Congress. **Authorization legislation** originates in a legislative committee and states the maximum amount of money an agency may spend on a given program. This authorization may be permanent, it may be fixed for a number of years, or it may be annual. Once funds have been authorized by Congress, they also must be appropriated.

HOW A BILL BECOMES A LAW

It is much easier to kill a bill than to pass one. Opponents of a bill must only defeat the bill once to kill it; in order to pass it, its proponents must continually secure passage at all different stages of the legislative process. A typical piece of legislation must pass both houses of Congress in the same language before it is sent to the President.

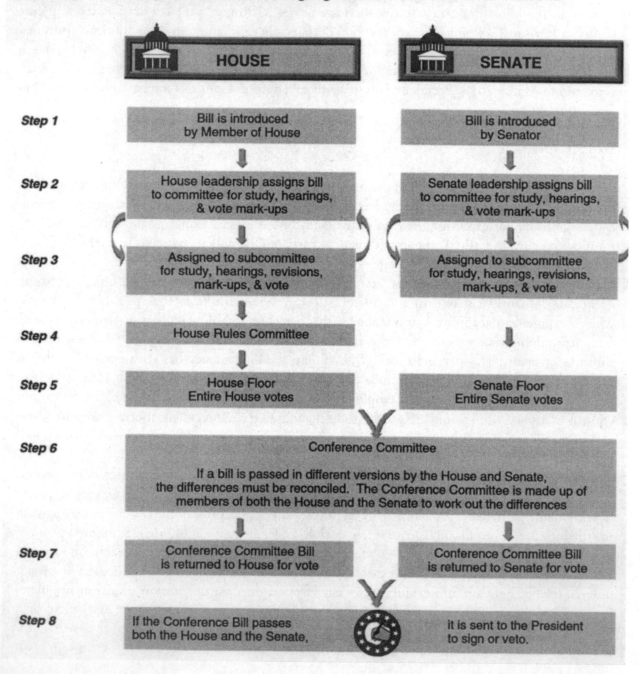

HOUSE

SENATE

Step 1 — Bill is introduced by Member of House / Bill is introduced by Senator

Step 2 — House leadership assigns bill to committee for study, hearings, & vote mark-ups / Senate leadership assigns bill to committee for study, hearings, & vote mark-ups

Step 3 — Assigned to subcommittee for study, hearings, revisions, mark-ups, & vote / Assigned to subcommittee for study, hearings, revisions, mark-ups, & vote

Step 4 — House Rules Committee

Step 5 — House Floor Entire House votes / Senate Floor Entire Senate votes

Step 6 — Conference Committee

If a bill is passed in different versions by the House and Senate, the differences must be reconciled. The Conference Committee is made up of members of both the House and the Senate to work out the differences

Step 7 — Conference Committee Bill is returned to House for vote / Conference Committee Bill is returned to Senate for vote

Step 8 — If the Conference Bill passes both the House and the Senate, it is sent to the President to sign or veto.

Appropriations are usually made annually and originate from the House Appropriations Committee and its various subcommittees. The Appropriations Committee may, and often does, appropriate less than was authorized.

Congress' oversight function does not stop once the money has been appropriated to the department or agency. In fact, Congress can actively participate in the activities of the bureaucracy. A congressional committee may obtain the right to pass on certain agency decisions. This is called **committee clearance**, and though the agency is not legally bound by the committee's decision, few agencies would risk angering the committee that largely controls its budget.

Perhaps the most visible and dramatic form of congressional oversight of the bureaucracy is the **investigation**. This investigative power of Congress is not mentioned in the Constitution but has been seen as implicit in the legislative powers of Congress. The Supreme Court has consistently upheld wide investigative powers.[38] As part of this investigative power, Congress may also hold committee hearings and investigations and give these committees the power to subpoena witnesses, take oaths, cross-examine, compel testimony, and bring criminal charges for contempt and perjury. The most formal oversight methods include conducting a hearing or requesting a report on specific agency practices.

The March 2020 $2 trillion economic stimulus law passed during the coronavirus pandemic, created a Congressional Oversight Committee that required that the Federal Reserve Board publicly release information about every company that received taxpayer-backed lending and would motor what those companies would do after receiving the taxpayer support. The Oversight Committee asked the Fed to provide details about the identity of borrowers, the terms of the loans and the intended use of the proceeds, and it sought documents and information about the equity supporting the deals, and proof that the money would not go to foreign businesses or companies controlled by White House officials or members of Congress and their families.[39]

Oversight may also be done more informally, through day-to-day contact between committee members and administrators in the executive branch. Congress has a large number of staff members working on oversight issues, as well as several specialized oversight offices, the congressional Budget Office, the Office of Technology Assessment, the Government Accounting Office, and the congressional Research Service of the Library of Congress.

CONCLUSIONS

The authors of the American Constitution created a national government with multiple centers of power. The idea was to represent many factions and provide incentives for them to bargain and compromise in the national interest. The authors' concern, however, was so primarily concerned with checking power with power, that they gave little consideration to how government would then effectively function at all. To some extent, this neglect has been corrected over time with the creation of political parties to unify policy choices, congressional committees to organize the legislative process., and a congressional seniority system that rewarded teamwork. But there have been other forces at work that have undermined the ability of Congress to act at all.

Candidates for Congress now ascend through a primary process dominated by extremist candidates and powerful, well-funded interest groups from which they gain electoral and campaign finance support. Low voter turnout in the primary elections leaves large swaths of the moderate American electorate unrepresented. Campaign finance reform has not taken money out of politics but rather diverted it to private, less accountable channels that spend millions on political advertising on both traditional and social media. The parties, once largely responsible for funding their party's candidates for Congress, have seen their role replaced by super PACs that are less transparent, harder to regulate, and less accountable to the people. Congressional decision making is now more open and transparent and the use of pork to get legislation through is looked down upon. Together, the candidates, those who vote in low-turnout primaries, and the PACs that support them have been driving Congress toward greater polarization.

Then came the pandemic coronavirus crisis of 2020. For a moment, the nation sheltered in place while its Congress passed a series of laws providing trillions of dollars in emergency governmental aid. In normal times, these measures could only have been passed methodically, grindingly, through a series of congressional hearings taking months and months. The year 2020, however, was not normal times. The question now is whether Americans have the collective will to tackle current and future problems like global climate change. The biggest obstacle is a deep-rooted public antipathy for politics and politicians that dates back to the founding of this country. With a 74 percent disapproval rate and a 22 percent approval rate, Congress remains, a challenged institution.[40]

CHAPTER NOTES

[1] Theodore J. Lowi and Benjamin Ginsberg, *American Government*, 4th ed. (New York: W. W. Norton, 1996), 198.

[2] Stephen Dinan and Gabriella Munoz, "Former House Lawyer Says Pelosi's Impeachment Inquiry 'Is Illegal,'" *Washington Post*, October 22, 2019, *https://www.washingtontimes.com/news/2019/oct/22/nancy-pelosi-democrats-produce-more-subpoenas-laws/*

[3] Lowi and Ginsberg, *American Government*, 749.

[4] Edmund Burke, *Burke's Politics*, ed. Ross J. H. Hoffman and Paul Levick (New York: A.A. Knopf, 1949).

[5] Roger Davidson, *The Role of Congressmen* (New York: Pegasus, 1977), 117.

[6] Hanna Fenichel Pitkin, *The Concept of Representation* (Berkeley: University of California Press, 1967), 60-91.

[7] Norman J. Ornstein, Thomas E. Mann, and Michael J. Malbin, eds., *Vital Statistics on Congress, 1993-94* (Washington, D.C.: Congressional Quarterly Press, 1994), 58-61.

[8] Samuel Stebbins and John Harrington, "Here Are the Members of Congress with the Highest Net Worth," *USA Today*, October 25, 2019, *https://www.usatoday.com/story/money/2019/10/25/richest-members-of-congress-by-net-worth/40290533/*

[9]"Highway Bill Larded with Hometown Projects," *Champaign-Urbana News-Gazette*, March 30, 1999, p.A5.

[10]Cavan Hagerty, "2019 Pig Book Shows Record Increase in Pork Barrel Spending," *Americans for Tax Reform*, June 18, 2019, *https://www.atr.org/2019-pig-book-shows-record-increase-pork-barrel-spending*

[11]*Congressional Quarterly, Guide to the Congress of the United States*, 2d ed. (Washington, D.C.: Congressional Quarterly Press, 1976), 588.

[12]John S. Saloma, *Congress and the New Politics* (Boston: Little, Brown, 1969), 184-85.

[13]*Congressional Quarterly Guide*, 229-310.

[14]Rob Arthur and Allison McCann, "How the Gutting of the Voting Rights Act Led to Hundreds of Closed Polls," *Vice News*, October 16, 2018, *https://news.vice.com/en_us/article/kz58qx/how-the-gutting-of-the-voting-rights-act-led-to-closed-polls*

[15]German Lopez, "The Supreme Court's Big Racial Gerrymandering Decision, Explained," *Vox*, May 22, 2017, *https://www.vox.com/policy-and-politics/2017/5/22/15676250/supreme-court-racial-gerrymandering-north-carolina*

[16]Fredreka Schouten, "A Record $5.7 Billion Was Spent on the 2018 Elections for Congress," *CNN Politics*, February 7, 2019, *https://www.cnn.com/2019/02/07/politics/midterm-election-costs-topped-5-7-billion/index.html*

[17]*OpenSecrets.org*, "Did Money Win?" *OpenSecrets.org*, March, 2020, *https://www.opensecrets.org/elections-overview/did-money-win*

[18]Nathaniel Rakick, "How Much Was Incumbency Worth in 2018?" *Five Thirty Eight*, December 6, 2018, *https://fivethirtyeight.com/features/how-much-was-incumbency-worth-in-2018/*

[19]Noah Rudnick, "Exploring the Incumbency Advantage," *Sabato's Crystal Ball: UVA Center for Politics*, August 23, 2018, *http://centerforpolitics.org/crystalball/articles/exploring-the-incumbency-advantage/*

[20]*OpenSecrets.org*, "PAC Dollars to Incumbents, Challengers, and Open Seat Candidates," *OpenSecret.org*, March 2010, *https://www.opensecrets.org/overview/pac2cands.php?cycle=2020*

[21]Matt Taibbi, "Far Too Many House Seats Have Been Uncontested for Too Long," *Rolling Stone*, November 6, 2018, *https://www.rollingstone.com/politics/politics-features/uncontested-house-seats-history-752658/*

[22]*The Hill*, "Americans Tend to be in Favor of Term Limits for Most Institutions, Says Pollster," September 27,2018, *https://thehill.com/hilltv/what-americas-thinking/408781-americans-tend-to-be-in-favor-of-term-limits-for-most*

[23]Will Lennon, "Pelosi's Prowess as a Fundraiser Helps Her Secure Speakership," *OpenSecret.org*, November 28, 2018, *https://www.opensecrets.org/news/2018/11/nancy-pelosi-returns-to-speakership/*

[24]Jonathan Miller, "Party Unity on Congressional Votes Takes a Dive: CQ Vote Studies," *Roll Call*, February 28, 2019, *https://www.rollcall.com/2019/02/28/party-unity-on-congressional-votes-takes-a-dive-cq-vote-studies/*

[25]Olivia B. Waxman, "The Old-School Trick That Finally Pushed the House to Move on Immigration," *Time*, June 13, 2018, *https://time.com/5308755/discharge-petitions-definition-purpose-history/*

[26]Jake Sherman, "Democrats Tap Top Obama Lawyer to Counter Darrell Issa," *Politico*, January 3, 2011, *http://www.politico.com/news/stories/0111/46981.html*

[27]Richard F. Fenno, Jr., *Congressmen in Committees* (Boston: Little, Brown, 1973), 1.

[28]Kathy Gill, "The Effects of the Seniority System on How Congress Works," *ThoughtCo.*, May 30, 2019, *https://www.thoughtco.com/what-is-the-seniority-system-3368073*

[29]Christopher J. Deering and Steven S. Smith, *Committees in Congress*, 3rd ed. (Washington, D.C.: Congressional Quarterly Press, 1997).

[30]Andrew Prokop, et al., "The 10 New Democratic House Committee Chairs Who Are About to Make Trump's Life Hell," *Vox*, January 3, 2019, *https://www.vox.com/2019/1/3/18134919/congress-house-2019-committee-investigations-trump-impeachment*

[31]Congtessional Research Service, *Federal Workforce Statistics Sources*, October 24, 2019, *https://fas.org/sgp/crs/misc/R43590.pdf*

[32]Benjamin Ginsberg and Theodore Lowi, *We the People: An Introduction to American Politics*, 5th ed., New York: W.W. Norton, 2020, 180.

[33]Sarah Mimms, "Congress Has a Caucus for Everything," *The Atlantic*, April 18, 2014, *https://www.theatlantic.com/politics/archive/2014/04/congress-caucus-for-everything/360894/*

[34]Alex Tausanovitch and Sam Berger, "The Impact of the Filibuster on Federal Policymaking," *Center for American Progress*, December 5, 2019, *https://www.americanprogress.org/issues/democracy/reports/2019/12/05/478199/*

impact-filibuster-federal-policymaking/

[35] Ibid.

[36] Kenneth P. Vogel and Jim Tankersley, "With Billions at Stake in Tax Debate, Lobbyists Played Hardball," *The New York Times*, December 15, 2017,
https://www.nytimes.com/2017/12/15/us/politics/lobbyists-tax-overhaul-congress.html

[37] Jen Kirby, "Trump Wants a Line-Item Veto. One Problem: It's Unconstitutional," *Vox*, March 23, 2018,
https://www.vox.com/2018/3/23/17157130/trump-omnibus-spending-line-item-veto-clinton

[38] Edward S. Corwin, *The Constitution and What It Means Today*, 13th ed. (Princeton, N.J.: Princeton University Press, 1973), 151.

[39] Alan Rappeport, "One Person is Overseeing Congress's Bailout Loans. He Wants Answers," *The New York Times*, April 15, 2020, *https://www.nytimes.com/2020/04/15/us/politics/bailout-oversight-ramamurti-coronavirus.html*

[40] Statista, "Do You Approve of the Way Congress Is Handling Its Job?" *Statista*, March 31, 2010,
https://www.statista.com/statistics/207579/public-approval-rating-of-the-us-congress/

SUGGESTED READINGS

Bell, Lauren Cohen. *Master the U.S. Congress: A Simulation for Students.* Belmont, CA: Wadsworth, 2004.

Congressional Quarterly, *CQ's Politics in America.* Washington, D.C.: CQ Press, 2014.

Daley, David. *Ratf**ked: The True Story Behind the Secret Plan to Steal America's Democracy.* New York: W.W. Norton, 2016.

Davidson, Roger, Walter Olesvek, and Frances Lee. *Congress and Its Members*, 12th ed. Washington D.C.: CQ Press, 2015.

Dodd, Larewnce C. and Bruce Oppenheimer, eds. *Congress Reconsidered,* 10th ed. Washington, D.C.: CQ Press, 2016.

Dodson, Debra L. *The Impact of Women in Congress.* New York: Oxford University Press, 2006.

Jacobson, Gary C. T*he Politics of Congressional Elections*, 8th ed. New York: Longman, 2012.

Koger, Gregory. *Filibustering: A Political Hsitory of Obstruction in the House and Senate.* Chicago: University of Chicago Press, 2010.

Palmer, Barbara, and Denise Simon. *Breaking the Political Glass Ceiling: Women and Congressional Elections.* 2nd ed. New York: Routledge, 2008.

Sinclair, Barbara. *Unorthodox Lawmaking: New Legislative Processes in the U.S. Congress*, 3rd ed. Washington, D.C.: CQ Press, 2008.

Smith, Stephen S., Jason M. Roberts, and Ryan V. Vander Wielen. *The American Congress.* New York: Cambridge University Press, 2007.

Web Sites

Congress. <u>www.congress.org.</u>

Cook Political Report. <u>www.cookpolitical.com.</u>

CQ's Politics <u>www.rollcall.com/politics</u>

Federal Register. <u>www.access.gpo.gov.</u>

Federal World. <u>www.fedworld.gov.</u>

General Services Administration. <u>www.gsa.gov.</u>

The Sunlight Foundation and Taxpayers for Common Sense. <u>http://earmarkwatch.org.</u>

U.S. Government Gateway Site. <u>www.usa.gov.</u>

U.S. House of Representatives. <u>www.house.gov.</u>

U.S. Office of Management and Budget. <u>www.omb.gov.</u>

U.S. Senate. <u>www.senate.gov.</u>

The U.S. Government Printing Office Access on the Web. <u>www.gpoaccess.go</u>v

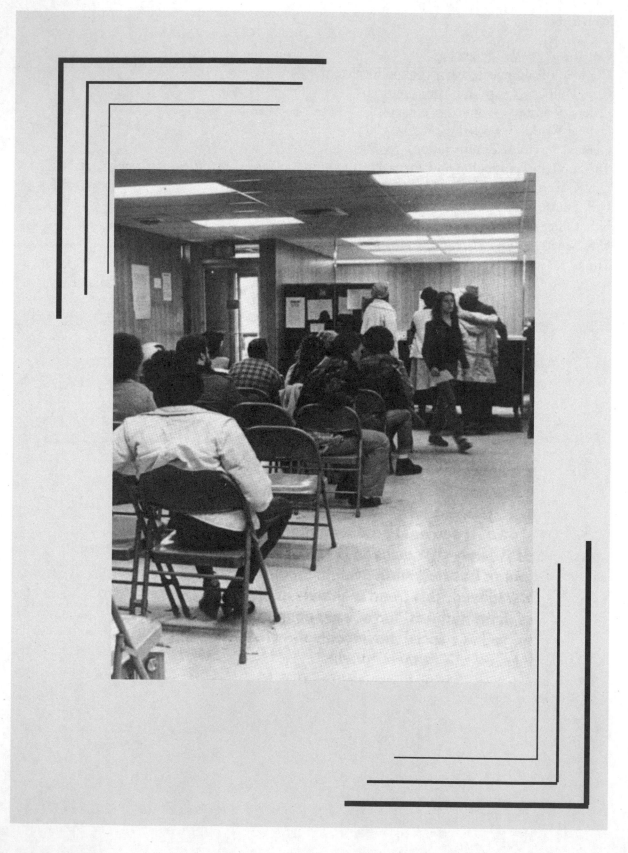

Chapter Nine

THE BUREAUCRACY

The executive branch bureaucracy is caught in the wider tension in the United States between private enterprise and government power and red tape and between ideological commitments to reduce the size of government and the overarching need for regulation to protect public safety. Recent years have seen an increasing call to reduce the size of the federal bureaucracy and yet, we live in the age of recurrent crises. We want and need the government to identify problems before they become huge problems and then act quickly with a coordinated and effective response. There is a fundamental tension, however, between streamlining government, reducing bureaucrat red tape, and having a government that acts effectively. The recent 2020 coronavirus pandemic brought these tensions between private and government power and between deregulation and regulation into sharp focus. In the end, the coronavirus pandemic of 2020 is a case study of both too little bureaucracy and too much bureaucracy, and the tension between private enterprise and government bureaucracy.

When President Trump took office, he attempted to streamline the National Security Council by disbanding the National Security Council's office for pandemics. In March 2020, when the virus hit with ferocity, the effort to contain it was sluggish and confused because there was an absence of effective structures within the bureaucracy itself. A pandemics office might have filled a vital role from the first moments of the crisis—coordination. Additionally, much of the needed expertise had also been lost and was slow to regroup. The National Institutes of Health leader, Dr. Anthony Fauci, stepped into the vacuum, but he acknowledged the loss of the pandemics team that had been cut.

While the Trump administration reduced the role of the National Security Council office for pandemics, there was still plenty of bureaucratic red tape to slow the United States's response to the crisis. Most of the country was unprepared for a pandemic and pre-crisis regulations slowed responses to a crawl. For example, many companies, idled or slowed by the virus, were willing and able to retool their factories to manufacture goods desperately needed to fight the pandemic. They could not do so, however, because of bureaucratic regulations that take months to approve such a factory retooling. Even when bureaucratic regulations were lifted, they were lifted very late in the game. For example, the Food and Drug Administration waived some restrictions on the production and sale of surgical masks but that was over two months after the first coronavirus case in the United States was confirmed in Washington state on January 20.

Perhaps the single most important failure of the U.S. response to COVID-19 has been the very slow provision of testing. This was a failure of bureaucracy. For more than a month, the Centers for Disease Control and Prevention only allowed the use of its test, which was highly inaccurate, and eventually had to be retracted, even as companies were willing and able to produce better and faster kits. Federal health agencies initially declined to certify tests produced by these private companies, even though the head of the FDA was publicly recommending that they do so as early as February 2, 2020. South Korea, on the other hand, was able to control the virus because of its widespread testing. The utter failure of the United States government to get good, sound tests into the hands of medical practitioners is a case study in top-down, centrally managed government bureaucracy, bound by outdated rules and practices, and unable to nimbly meet rising emergencies. The same over-regulation plagued the production of the N95 respirator masks. These masks are produced for medical use and construction industry use but because the masks have been classified by the federal government as "medical," manufacturers were required to jump through numerous hoops, such as special tests of flammability and strength.

Given the woefully inadequate bureaucratic response, it is not surprising that there have been cries for more deregulation and more outsourcing to the private sector. But outsourcing projects with critical public-health implications to private companies that focus on maximizing profits is not always consistent with the government's goal of emergency preparedness. Take the case of ventilators. In the wake of SARS, MERS, the bird flu, and swine flu, the Centers for Disease Control and Prevention saw that the federal bureaucracy needed to re-evaluate their strategy for the next public health emergency. They saw a real shortage of ventilators and created a project code—named Aura. The federal government's Strategic National Stockpile had ventilators in its warehouses, but not in the quantities that would be necessary to combat a major pandemic. So, in 2006, The Department of Health and Human Services established a new bureaucratic division, the Biomedical Advanced Research and Development Authority, with a mandate to prepare medical responses to chemical, biological, and nuclear attacks, as well as infectious diseases. They estimated that 70,000 machines would be required in a moderate influenza pandemic. The government hired a small California company to design the new ventilators, but they were never able to do the design. As a result, the development of ventilators was delayed by five years. In 2014, the government tried again to outsource the production of ventilators. It took five years for the ventilators built by this company to get final government approval. As of April 2020, at the apex of the crisis, none of these ventilators were yet to be deployed.[1]

What the COVID-19 crises has laid bare is that America was "rudderless, blind-sided, lethargic, and uncoordinated" largely because of both too much and too little bureaucratic control.[2] To meet this pandemic, as well as future ones, it will take bureaucratic reorganization and streamlining along with a sound working relationship between these government bureaucracies and private enterprise. There is some sign that this is happening. The Food and Drug Administration in April 2020 moved quickly to approve tests that can deliver results in less than an hour developed by private labs. The real success of controlling the coronavirus will depend on the national bureaucracy working with private enterprise to deploy an effective vaccine. The first steps have been impressive with the creation of a possible vaccine by two corporations Moderna Therapeutics and the National Institutes of Health. Actual use of the vaccine will require at least a year as the Food and Drug Administration will oversee the animal testing, large-scale human trials, dosage studies, and mass manufacturing of the vaccine. The bureaucracy and private enterprise joint work will take 12 to 18 months. One thing is for sure: The United States will need to rethink the organization of its bureaucracies to better deal with future emergencies and reconfigure government-private enterprise relationships.

THE DEVELOPMENT OF THE BUREAUCRATIC STATE

Constitutional Beginnings

The Constitution does not specify the structure of the federal bureaucracy. The seeds of the modern administrative state, however, can be found in Article II, section 2, paragraph 2. The president is told that he may appoint, with the advice and consent of the Senate, "ambassadors, other public ministers and consuls, judges of the Supreme Court, and all other officers of the United States whose appointments are not herein otherwise provided for, and which shall be established by law." The Constitution, then, gave both Congress and the president authority to devise and operate a bureaucracy. Congress has the power by law to create new agencies, and the president has the power to appoint (subject to Senate confirmation) the heads of the agencies.

The first Congress that met in 1789 created a simple bureaucratic structure consisting of three executive departments: the Department of State, the Department of War, and the Department of the Treasury. The first Congress also established the positions of the attorney general and postmaster general. The attorney general is the government's chief legal official, and in 1870 when Congress created the Department of Justice, the attorney general became the head of that department. The postmaster general is in charge of the Post Office.

All in all, the early bureaucracy was quite small. The original Department of State had only nine employees. Even by 1816, the federal bureaucracy employed fewer than five thousand people. The federal bureaucracy, however, grew rapidly thereafter. For the most part, the growth of the bureaucracy stems from the deep-rooted American belief that problems have solutions and progress can be made.

The Progressive Movement

In the early 1900s, a philosophy of political reform, Progressivism, began to call into question the dominant economic theory of the nineteenth century, laissez-faire. The theory of **laissez-faire** dictated a minimal role for the government in economic management. Business was viewed as largely autonomous, and government action was to be discouraged as obtrusive and unnecessary.

By the end of the nineteenth century it had become apparent that the laissez-faire, hands-off approach had allowed the emergence of huge oligopolies, dominating whole fields such as railroads. Gradually, people began to see the need for government involvement in at least parts of the economy. The question was which of the institutions of government would be responsible for protecting the marketplace from its own oligopolistic tendencies.

President Lyndon Johnson took on new commitments with programs of the Great Society.

The answer given by the Progressives of the early twentieth century was the creation of the modern administrative state. Congress moved to create new bureaucratic agencies enabled to regulate specific industries. The Federal Trade Commission (FTC) was created in 1914 to protect consumers from unfair business practices especially in advertising and labeling. The Food and Drug Administration (FDA) was created in 1906 to regulate the purity and safety of foods and pharmaceuticals.

The New Deal and Social Welfare Legislation

The economic depression of the 1930s reaffirmed the nation's belief that government action was essential to economic stability and the financial security of individuals. The enormous effects of economic cycles on the population of the United States convinced most that any needed government intervention would have to come from the federal level of government. State governments were simply not equipped to deal with national economic cycles. As a result, it fell to Franklin Roosevelt and his New Deal legislative program to expand the scope of government action into areas of unemployment, electrical production, housing, and bank regulation. The Railroad Retirement Act of 1934 was the first federal attempt at an extensive security program. In 1935, the Social Security Act created a fund into which workers pay so that they will have income upon retirement. Today, Social Security pays over 69 million Americans every month with the average person receiving about $18,036 per year.[3]

World War II

By the 1940s, the federal government's role in regulating the economy was largely accepted as necessary. What was less clearly established was a permanent infrastructure of an administrative state. The New Deal involved many emergency boards and did not work to create a more permanent set of regulatory bodies.

World War II would lead to the creation of a permanent administrative state. During the war, the national government hired thousands of people. When the war ended, many of these people were absorbed into the civilian bureaucracy.

The Great Society and the Entitlements Revolution

By the end of the administration of President Lyndon Johnson, the size of the bureaucracy would reach its postwar peak, with 2.9 million civilian employees and an additional 3.6 million military personnel. In the 1950s, new problems had spawned new agencies to solve them. For example, in 1953, Congress created the Department of Health, Education, and Welfare (renamed the Department of Health and Human Services in 1979) to administer the nation's health, education, and assistance programs. Other departments and agencies were spawned in the 1960s when new interest groups began to press their claims on government. For example, Ralph Nader, a consumer activist, drew the public's attention to faulty automobile designs that posed a threat to the consumer. Congress responded in 1966 with the creation of the National Safety Agency (later renamed the Highway Traffic Safety Administration).

The programs of Lyndon Johnson's Great Society were a natural outgrowth of the public's growing sense that the government was responsible for the social welfare of the people. The government took on new commitments in the areas of aid to minorities and the poor. As a result, more and more groups began to see themselves as entitled to government protection. As the programs and their clientele groups grew in number, so did the bureaucratic agencies of the federal government.

Lobbying by Administrators

The budgets and staffs of bureaucratic departments and agencies have continued to grow as a result of activist bureaucrats seeking to defend their budgets and expand their authority. These administrators have often reinvented themselves to assure their continued existence. For example, after the collapse of the Soviet Union, the Department of Defense began to pressure Congress for budgets to do research on worldwide environmental degradation.[4] Similarly the Central Intelligence Agency (CIA) has recently defended their continued existence as necessary to the fight against the international drug trade. As a result, the national bureaucracy and federal spending have kept pace with the growth of the economy and society.

Ronald Reagan and Deregulation

America's acceptance of bureaucratic regulation developed slowly and never fully eclipsed a basic American dislike of government. Laissez-faire is deeply embedded in the very capitalist fabric of the American economy. Perhaps, then, it is not surprising that as the bureaucratic state grew, uneasiness with it grew as well. By 1980, the American public was expressing disgust with the bureaucracy and government intervention. This disgust coalesced in support of Ronald Reagan in 1980 and then again in 1984.

President Reagan became the spokesperson for the belief that the national government was too involved in regulation, interfering in what should be the natural working of the business markets.

Conservatives championed deregulation as a way to return unhampered efficiency to the market-place.

Considerable deregulation was accomplished in the late 1970s and 1980s, most notably in the airline, trucking, financial services, and telecommunications industries.[5] In each of these areas, the government began to loosen the regulatory ties that were now seen as placing American industries in a less competitive posture in the now global economy. Some deregulation did lead to greater benefits for consumers. For example, in the case of the airlines, the Civil Aeronautics Board (CAB) had been determining fares and controlling access to routes. Some argued that such regulations actually reduced competition between airlines, thereby adversely affecting consumers.

Not all the deregulatory efforts, however, have proved so beneficial to the American economy or to American consumers. Some deregulation has led to horrific results. Savings and loans had been regulated by the national government up through 1988. The reasoning behind such regulation was that money is deposited in a savings and loan on the depositor's full faith that the money will be safe and will be returned on demand with interest. Many depositors come from the population of fixed income elderly retirees, seeking a secure investment.

The economic depression of the 1930s made it amply clear that such security may require some government regulation. As a result, the savings and loans came to be regulated in three ways. First, the savings and loans were told that they must keep a certain amount of the depositors' money "on deposit" in case depositors wish to withdraw funds. Second, the savings and loans were limited with the types of investments they could make with the depositors' money. Specifically, they were limited to making home loans, seen as the most secure because the home acts as collateral for the loan, can be repossessed and resold through foreclosure proceedings, and the depositors' money thereby recouped. Finally, the government insured the deposits just in case the savings and loans did lose the depositors' money in bad home loans.

The savings and loans ran profitably under such regulations until the 1970s when a number of competitors for depositors' money entered the picture. These new investment banking houses, free from government regulation, could promise the depositors greater interest on their money. As the financial market became more competitive, the savings and loans asked the government to ease the regulations and thereby allow them to compete more effectively with the investment banking houses.

Between 1980 and 1983, Congress approved a number of changes that significantly deregulated the savings and loans industry. In brief, Congress allowed the savings and loans to keep less of the depositors' money on reserve and to make riskier investments with depositors' money, and then increased the insurance on deposits from $40,000 to $100,000.

While these changes began to reshape the savings and loans industry, the Reagan administration refused to allow the Federal Home Loan Bank Board, which was in charge of supervising the system, to hire the bank examiners it believed it needed to monitor the health of the system. As the real estate market began to slide, the savings and loans began to have trouble. Eventually, they were plunged into insolvency, and taxpayers had to cover the insured deposits to the tune of hundreds of billions of dollars.

More recently, energy companies were deregulated, and again disaster followed. When energy companies were deregulated, the belief was that a deregulated market would send cheaper and more reliable supplies of electricity coursing into homes and offices across the nation. What happened instead was that Enron Corporation, the vast energy trader at the center of the new freewheeling U.S. power markets, collapsed amid a blizzard of questionable financial deals. California, the first big state to deregulate its electricity market, watched its experiment in deregulation turn into a disaster, with intermittent blackouts and retail power rates as much as 40 percent higher than they were the year before. For the consumer, energy deregulation has been anything but good news. Unlike the deregulated telecommunications market, where fierce competition brought down prices while guaranteeing a reasonable level of reliability, the deregulated power market provided no real benefits and many costs. Consumers have been at the mercy of wholesale forces they often cannot understand and have few real options to switch service providers.

Many blame the catastrophic deregulation of energy companies on the campaign finance system. In the 2000 election cycle, the oil and gas sector contributed $15.4 million in contributions to the national party committees; electric utilities contributed $10.1 million more. Enron, alone, gave more the $1.4 million. Many believe that the Enron contributions exempted the company from oversight by the government agencies charged with protecting the interests of the employees, retirees, and shareholders. In other words, some say, the company paid the cop on the beat to take a nap.

Such debacles have fueled support of government regulations. Farmers continue to pressure for government subsidies administered by the Department of Agriculture. Labor unions want the protection offered to workers by the Occupational Safety and Health Administration. Defense contractors lobby for the lucrative government contracts of the Defense Department. In short, many Americans very much want the protections provided by the modern bureaucratic state. In light of such support, it is unlikely that any significant reduction in the size of the bureaucracy is likely in the near future.

Privatization of the Bureaucracy

As noted above, Congress, for over three decades, has been engaged in a bipartisan effort to shrink the size of government. But today, although fewer people appear on federal payrolls, more people than ever work for the U.S. government.

This seeming paradox has been achieved by hiring private contractors to perform many of the tasks previously performed by federal employees. According to the Congressional Budget Office, the U.S. government spent $4.79 trillion in 2020. While the budget's largest portions go toward benefit programs such as Social Security and Medicaid, hundreds of billions of federal dollars also end up going to just a handful of companies in the private sector.

Through its various agencies and departments, the federal government has millions of contractual obligations with private companies, both domestic and foreign. While most of the companies receiving lucrative government contracts are military contractors, several are health insurance providers, including TriWest Healthcare Alliance Corp. which was given sole control of the Department of Veterans Affairs primary community care programs. Other federal dollars go to universities like California Institute of Technology that was paid a total of $2.4 billion from NASA to fund the Jet Propulsion Laboratory, a center located near the university campus that carries out robotic exploration of space. All total, the government paid 30 companies at least $2.3 billion each in fiscal 2020. Four companies were each awarded federal contracts worth over $14 billion—more than the entire budget for the Environmental Protection Agency or the Department of the Interior.[6] While nobody knows exactly how many contractors the government employs, Paul Light of the Brookings Institution estimates that the federal budget funds a "shadow government" of nearly 6 million contractors, about half of them in defense. That means contractors outnumber civil servants and military personnel by a ratio of 2 to 1.[7]

How did this privatization of the federal bureaucracy occur? President Ronald Reagan who sought to downsize what he saw as a bloated federal workforce launched the privatization. His mission has been embraced by every subsequent administration and, in 1998, was codified by Congress with the Federal Activities Inventory Reform Act. This law requires government agencies and departments to publish an annual accounting of which tasks under their auspices "are not inherently governmental functions" and could, therefore, be put out to private bid. The coronavirus pandemic of 2020 increased the calls for further privatization.[8]

There are several concerns about the privatization of the federal workforce. First, these private contractors are driven solely by profit not the pursuance of the public good. Second, private contractors are not necessarily more efficient. In Iraq much of the $21 billion spent on reconstruction went to high-priced foreign contractors rather than low-cost local labor. For example, non-Iraqi contractors charged $25 million to repaint 20 police stations, a job the government of Basra claims could have been done by local forms for $5 million. Finally, how should this growing army of workers be managed? Most of the contracts are not subject to competitive bidding and once they get the contract, the government is so dependent on them that it is virtually impossible to end the contract. These and other concerns will continue to fuel the debate about a privatized bureaucracy.

Recent Changes in Size of the Bureaucracy

The terrorist attack on September 11, 2001, resulted in the creation of a new department in the executive branch, the Department of Homeland Security. Formed in 2002 from the combination of 22 departments and agencies, the Department of Homeland Security works to improve the security of the United States. The Department's work includes customs, border, and immigration enforcement; emergency response to natural and manmade disasters; antiterrorism work; and cybersecurity. Today it has more than 240,000 employees and is the third largest department, after the Departments of Defense and Veterans' Affairs. Its annual budget is close to $50 billion.

A second increase in the bureaucracy came with the passage of the 11,588,500 word long Affordable Care Act in 2009, which greatly enlarged the role of the Department of Health and Human Services and the IRS in health care. In 2008, prior to the Obama Administration, the Department of Health and Human Services employed 75,400 workers. Only two years after the passage of the Affordable Care Act, that Department had grown to over 100,000 employees. The IRS spent over $1 million dollars to implement Obamacare in its first two years.[9]

Ever since President Barack Obama signed the Affordable Care Act ten years ago, it has faced legislative, legal, and political assaults. It has withstood more than 60 votes to repeal it from Republican-controlled Congresses, two Supreme Court decisions, the gutting of one of its main provisions (the tax penalty for not having insurance) and a president who campaigned on promises to get rid of it. While the act still stands, the uninsured rate has started back up. In 2018, 8.5 percent of the population did not have health insurance, up from 7.9 percent the year before. It was the first increase since the Affordable Care Act passed and came even as the economy was doing well. The elimination of the mandate requiring most people to have coverage, as well as the steep budget cuts for marketing and programs that helped people learn about new insurance options, appear to have reduced the number of people covered by the act.

The Trump administration's attempt to rein in the role of the federal government in the provision of health care is part of a larger intention to curtail the size and role of the entire federal bureaucracy. During the 2016 campaign, candidate Trump promised to downsize the federal government through attrition, suggesting three bureaucrats retire for each new hire, and he proposed that agencies be required to sunset two rules for every new regulation they promulgate. Most shrinkage in the size of the bureaucracy, however, has stemmed from budget cuts. In March 2020, President Trump released a $4.8 trillion budget proposal that included deep cuts to student loan assistance, affordable housing efforts, food stamps and Medicaid, reflecting the president's election-year effort to continue shrinking the federal safety net. The White House budget, however, is largely a messaging document that reflects the administration's spending priorities. The House of Representatives, controlled by Democrats, proposed large tax increases on the rich and expansions of government efforts to provide health care, education, affordable housing and aid for the poor. In the end, the final budget was not as Draconian as the president wanted.

Still, the size of the federal bureaucracy shrank for the first time in decades under President Trump. The bureaucracy grew during the presidency of Barack Obama. In the first nine months of 2009, Obama's first year in office, the government added 188,000 permanent employees, growing to 1.84 million. During the first term of the Trump presidency, however, there was a fairly steep decline in the number of people working in the bureaucracy, and by 2017, President Trump had already begun to reverse the growth seen during the Obama administration when the government added a total of 188,000 bureaucrats. By the end of September 2017, the federal government had 1.94 million permanent workers, down nearly 16,000 overall since the beginning of the year. The last time federal employment dropped was during President Clinton's first year in the White House. Much of the decrease in employment during the Trump years has been due to voluntary departures that have contributed to the shrinking workforce. During the first six months of the administration, 71,285 career employees quit or retired.

The decline in the number of federal bureaucrats has been matched by an apparent decline in the number of bureaucratic regulations. There is no question that while the number of federal regulations grew under President Obama, the number declined greatly during the first term of the Trump presidency. Scholars look at the page count of the *Federal Register*, which is a list of government regulations, to get a sense of the number of regulations. In his last year in office, 2016, President Obama set the all-time *Federal Register* page record with 95,894 pages. President Trump's *Federal Register* page count is 61,950 which is a 35 percent drop from Obama's record.[10]

Even at the height of the 2020 pandemic, the Trump administration continued to push legislation that would rollback health and environmental regulations. For example, the administration sought to end a rule that requires disclosure of data behind any scientific study, including confidential medical record, even though fourteen state attorney generals, the National Governors Association, the National League of Cities and dozens of other government, public health and environmental groups and officials supported the disclosure to make it possible for regulators to draw on findings of public health studies, particularly in emergency situations like the COVID-19 pandemic.[11]

THE FUNCTIONS OF THE BUREAUCRATIC STATE

Today, the functions of the federal bureaucracy fall into four main categories. It is not uncommon for a federal department or agency to perform more than one of these functions, or even all of these functions.

National Maintenance

After the Constitution was ratified, Congress moved to create the beginnings of a bureaucratic state that could perform the basic functions essential to maintaining the country. Originally, three departments were created: the Treasury Department to collect tax revenue, the State Department to conduct relations with other countries, and the Department of War to defend the country militarily. Congress also created the Post Office to allow for communication across a fairly vast expanse of land. As long as the functions of the federal government were linked to national maintenance, the bureaucracy's growth occurred when the nation grew. So as new western territories were settled, Congress was moved to create the Interior Department in 1849 to manage these new territories.

Clientele Services

Toward the middle of the nineteenth century, particular groups began to seek government services. Farmers, labor, and business were the first to press their claims. They were soon followed, however, by the poor, racial minorities, women, and veterans, to name only a few. Today, many of the departments at the federal level are specifically designed to serve the clientele needs of these groups: the Departments of Agriculture, Labor, Health and Human Services, Housing and Urban Development, Education, and Veterans Affairs.

Regulation

The federal government early on moved to regulate the economy. Prices of goods and services, the amount of competition in the marketplace, and the kinds of information that must be disclosed to consumers were all regulated by the national bureaucracy. In the 1960s, government regulation was extended into other areas. Congress has created agencies to regulate the quality of our air and water, our workplaces, and the safety of the goods we buy.

Redistribution of Resources

The fourth function of the federal bureaucracy is its most recent: the government's attempt to redistribute resources between groups in our society. Most redistributive efforts involve direct payments to individuals and groups. For example, Aid to Families with Dependent Children for many years involved cash subsidies paid to needy families. Similarly, the Social Security system makes cash payments to the elderly.

While many people think of these redistributive efforts as primarily going to the less privileged members of society, redistribution often goes to the wealthy as well. For example, the Department of Agriculture subsidizes farmers, many of whom are large corporate farmers. The Department of Defense gives lucrative government contracts to large corporations. Finally, Social Security payments go to the wealthy elderly as well as the poor elderly.

THE ORGANIZATION OF THE FEDERAL BUREAUCRACY

The federal bureaucracy includes four types of organizations: cabinet departments, independent agencies, regulatory agencies or commissions, and government corporations.

Cabinet Departments

Executive departments were the first bureaucratic organizations created by Congress, and they are now the biggest units of the executive branch bureaucracy. Today, there are fifteen departments, and they meet most of the federal government's responsibilities. These departments are headed by a single individual who, while appointed by the president with the "advice and consent" of the Senate, may be removed by the president acting alone.

The fourteen secretaries and the attorney general, who heads the Department of Justice, make up what has become known as the **cabinet**. In theory, the cabinet is meant to be the president's closest set of advisers. Historically, however, presidents have made little use of their cabinets, preferring instead to rely on the White House staff. Such a preference for the White House staff stems from the fact that the departments are created by Congress, funded by Congress, and overseen by Congress. The White House staff is more under the control of the president himself.

Each of the executive departments is quite large. As a result, the departments are further divided into many agencies, bureaus, and offices. For example, the Department of the Treasury oversees the U.S. Mint, the Bureau of Alcohol, Tobacco, and Firearms, the Secret Service, and the Internal Revenue Service.

The creation of the fifteenth department, the Department of Homeland Security, is the most significant transformation of the U.S. government in over a half-century. The mission of the department is to prevent terrorist attacks from within and without the United States, reduce America's vulnerability to terrorism, and minimize the damage and recover from attacks that do occur. The department has a clear organizational structure with four divisions: border and transportation security, emergency preparedness and response, chemical, biological, radiological, and nuclear countermeasures, and information analysis and infrastructure protection.

Independent Agencies

Independent agencies are not part of any executive department and their heads lack cabinet status. Independent agencies may be headed by a single individual or by a commission. These agencies have been created by Congress to perform a particular function. Some, like the Small Business Administration, provide a service; others (discussed in the next section), like the Environmental Protection Agency, perform a regulatory function. These agencies also vary in how closely they are tied to the president. Some, like the Central Intelligence Agency, are very directly under the influence of the president. Others, like NASA (National Aeronautics and Space Administration), are much less so.

A disappointed office seeker assassinated President Garfield. Civil service positions began to replace the "spoils system."

Regulatory Agencies or Commissions

Even though the **regulatory agencies** are the second most important type of organization within the federal bureaucracy, after the cabinet departments, they are fairly recent creations of Congress. As noted earlier in this chapter, the national government did not begin to regulate economic and social affairs until the Progressive period of the late nineteenth century. The first independent regulatory commission, the Interstate Commerce Commission, was established in 1887.

All regulatory agencies perform the same basic function: they try to promote the public interest by writing and enforcing rules that regulate a sector of the economy or specific type of activity. The rules made by these agencies have the force of law.

Regulatory agencies may be either of two kinds. Some are actually bureaus housed within one of the 15 departments. For example, the Food and Drug Administration is part of the Department of Health and Human Services. The Occupational Safety and Health Administration (OSHA) is housed within the Department of Labor. On the other hand, there are regulatory agencies that are independent of any department. The Federal Communications Commission (FCC), the Federal Aviation Agency (FAA), and the International Trade Commission (ITC) are all independent regulatory bodies.

Regulatory agencies and commissions tend to be much smaller than the fifteen departments. Also, the regulatory bodies are headed by a small number of commissioners (usually an odd number) appointed for a fixed term by the president with the consent of the Senate. The heads of the regulatory agencies are more removed from presidential control than are the heads of the departments because they serve staggered fixed terms. When a president comes into office, he will have to deal with commissioners appointed by a previous president. He will be able to appoint new commissioners only as vacancies open up.

While the regulatory agencies tend to be largely beyond the purview of the president, they are not independent of all types of political pressure. Client groups actively lobby the regulatory agencies to issue rules that are in their favor. For example, for most of its history, the Interstate Commerce Commission was closely tied to the interests of the railroad and trucking industries.

Government Corporations

Finally, Congress has created a small number of **government corporations** that provide public services that could be provided by the private sector. Government corporations are government-owned businesses that sell a service or a product to the public and thereby generate their own revenues. For example, the Postal Service, the Tennessee Valley Authority (TVA), and the Federal Deposit Insurance Corporation (FDIC) all charge for the service they provide whether it be stamps, electricity, or depositors' insurance. Some government corporations are headed by an individual; others have a plural leadership.

WHO ARE THE BUREAUCRATS?

The national bureaucracy employs about 2.1 million civilian employees, accounting for close to 2 percent of the entire United States work force.[12] Most of these workers are today hired through the civil service process. Such was not always the case.

A Bureaucracy of Gentlemen

In the early years of the nation's history, service in the bureaucracy was considered the special purview of an elite class. Government office was seen as a prize to be awarded to men of experience, education, and wisdom. Presidents from the two major political parties, the Federalists and the Democratic-Republicans, appointed men drawn largely from these elite ranks.

The Spoils System

The **spoils system**, the practice of hiring and firing federal workers on the basis of party loyalty, was introduced in 1829 by Andrew Jackson. Under the spoils system, the "spoils" of government jobs were doled out by the victorious candidate to loyal campaign workers, friends, and even relatives. Such patronage following an election resulted in almost a complete turnover in government jobs.

By the early 1880s, the public was fairly cynical about the integrity and efficiency of a bureaucracy built upon party loyalty and nepotism. Public office was seen as the path to self-enrichment and corruption flourished. Finally, when President James Garfield was assassinated by a disgruntled campaign worker who was not awarded a job by Garfield, it became clear that a system based on merit was preferable to the spoils system.

The Civil Service

In 1883 Congress passed the **Pendleton Act**, which created the Civil Service Commission (now called the Office of Personnel Management). This commission makes sure that bureaucratic positions are filled on the basis of merit, not partisanship or cronyism.

In the beginning, only 10 percent of federal jobs were covered by the civil service system. Today, over 80 percent of federal employees fall within the purview of the civil service. Of these, approximately 60 percent are hired through the General Classification System, and another 25 percent are covered by the Postal Service System. Federal positions not covered by the civil service, those at the highest level of the bureaucracy, are appointed by the president with the advice and consent of the Senate.[13]

The line between civil servants and presidential appointees has been somewhat muted by the Civil Service Reform Act of 1978. This act creates the Senior Executive Service (SES), consisting of civil servants, today numbering about eight thousand, who have reached the highest level in their particular career path. The purpose of the SES is to allow these career bureaucrats to move into other positions that are usually reserved for appointees of the president. Individuals who join the ranks of the SES can be moved from one job to another by the sitting president.

Changes in the Demographic Composition of the Bureaucracy

Beginning as a "government by gentlemen," the bureaucracy has been slow to reflect the diversity of the expanding nation.[14] In the early 1970s, Congress moved to require the federal government to follow affirmative action guidelines in hiring. As a result of such guidelines, women now make up 50 percent of the federal work force and racial minorities make up an additional 26 percent. Still, at the highest level of the civil service, minorities are underrepresented.[15]

Presidential Appointees

While most of the bureaucratic positions are filled through the civil service, presidents may nominate a second category of bureaucrats called political appointees. To fill these positions, the president and his advisers solicit suggestions from politicians, businesspeople, and interest groups. Appointments to these positions offer the president a way to pay off political debts, reward campaign contributors, or reward voting blocs, for example women or African Americans, within his party. Often, the appointee may have strong ties to the interest groups whose interests he or she may be in charge of overseeing. Many of President Trump's appointees have deep ties to major industries. For example, his nominee for Secretary of State, Rex Tillerson, had been the CEO of ExxonMobil, which began drilling operations in Russia despite U.S. sanctions that prohibited doing business with that country. Trump's pick for Secretary of Energy was Rick Perry who sits on the board of Sunoco Logistics Partners, which is the company behind the controversial Dakota Access pipeline. Other industries represented among Trump's administration include manufacturing, and entertainment and media.[16]

WHERE ARE THE BUREAUCRATS?

Most of the national government's workers are employed outside Washington. Fewer than 350,000 (or about 12 percent) of career civilian employees work in the Washington area. The vast majority are scattered throughout the country and the world. In fact, nearly 20,000 federal civilian employees work in territories belonging to the United States, and another 100,000 in foreign nations. California, Texas, Florida, and several other states each house more than 100,000 civilian employees. Congress has every incentive to try to spread the jobs around. These jobs are "pork" for the members districts and states, "pork" that might help gain them reelection.

Many people believe that the welfare state now employs the greatest number of civilian employees. In reality, less than 15 percent of bureaucrats work in welfare agencies such as the Social Security Administration. The Department of Veterans Affairs employs twice the number of workers than these welfare agencies and nearly one-third of the civilian bureaucrats work for the army, the navy, the air force, or some other defense related agency.

WHAT BUREAUCRACIES DO

Bureaucracies implement policy. They take congressional, presidential, and sometimes even judicial pronouncements and develop procedures and rules to implement the policy goals outlined, often vaguely, in these pronouncements. In implementing policy, the bureaucracy comes to manage the day-to-day routines of government: training the armed services, delivering the mail, and building the country's roads. The sections that follow discuss the many ways in which the bureaucracy implements policy.

Policy Development

Members of the executive branch are often very involved in the development and drafting of legislation. Sometimes the initiative for such involvement may come from the bureaucracy, at other times from Congress. For example, Congress routinely asks agencies to respond to countless official and unofficial inquiries, some of which may lead to new legislation. Furthermore, congressional hearings on proposed legislation usually include members of the bureaucracy. Such expert testimony from the bureaucrats has considerable influence on congressional decision-making.

All government agencies devote a considerable amount of their time and resources to research, and collecting and analyzing mounds of data. Some agencies, in fact, have such data collection as their principal task. The Bureau of Labor Statistics, for example, collects and publishes information about the economy while the Centers for Disease Control compile public health statistics.

Rule Administration

Cabinet departments, regulatory agencies, and government corporations are all creatures of Congress. Because the Constitution is silent as to the question of how the president shall faithfully execute the laws of the land, Congress has had to fill in the gaps. It is Congress that creates the different agencies and departments through enabling legislation that directly empowers the bureaucracy. Such enabling legislation cannot possibly describe every specific situation or contingency. As a result, Congress often leaves the bureaucracy with significant administrative discretion. Particularly in the areas of domestic and international security, Congress has afforded agencies enormous latitude.

Rule administration is the core function of the national bureaucracy. Departments and agencies carry out the policies of the Congress, the president, and even the courts. For example, the Environmental Protection Agency (EPA) is responsible for administering the multitude of laws passed by Congress to clean up the nation's air and water.

Rule Making and Regulation

The bureaucracy has a number of ways to carry out policy. The most common is through rule making. The bureaucracy issues regulations that are simply rules that govern the operation of government programs. These rules are the way in which the bureaucracy fleshes out the more general guidelines laid down by Congress in laws.

Regulations have the effect of law. For example, Congress passed the Nutrition Labeling and Education Act. The Food and Drug Administration (FDA) then needed to formulate rules to implement the law. The FDA has mandated that labels specifically list the nutritional content of food products. Because bureaucratic rules have the force of law, an agency must follow very detailed procedures in issuing these rules. For example, the agency must propose the rule by publishing it and giving all interested parties an opportunity to comment on the regulation.

Rule Adjudication

Many federal agencies are responsible for determining if the rules they administer have been broken, a process known as **rule adjudication**. Acting like a court, the agency provides the affected parties the opportunity to present arguments and evidence in a more-or-less formal hearing. In addition, more than twenty-five federal agencies employ administrative law judges to help them determine whether defendants have violated any relevant rules. Today, more than twenty-five federal agencies employ a combined total of nearly 2000 administrative law judges. As a greater number of federal agencies have gained responsibility for regulating economic activity, rule adjudication has grown in importance.[17]

Litigation

The most serious disputes between an agency and those affected by its decisions may end up in federal court. The courts have the authority to review all agency rules and decisions brought before them. In general, any party adversely affected by an agency decision has standing to bring suit. The 1970 Clean Air Act, for example, authorized three different types of suits: challenges to environmental protection agency rules and regulations, citizen suits seeking the performance of duties by the EPA, and enforcement suits against polluters.[18]

The 2010 health-care bill created over a hundred new commissions and boards. By creating new federally enforceable rights and obligations, layers of complex federal regulations, and dozens of new programs and agencies, the Health Care Reform Law generated a flood of litigation. To implement the legislation, federal bureaucrats necessarily generated thousands of pages of regulations. Under the Administrative Procedure Act, trial lawyers—as well as attorneys for industry, the medical profession, and countless interest groups—challenged not only the substance of the regulations, but also the procedures used to generate them. Twenty-eight states filed joint or individual lawsuits to strike down the mandate that individuals buy health insurance and the Attorneys General for several states indicated their primary basis for the challenge was a violation of state sovereignty.[19]

Program Evaluation

Congress, the civil service, and the president usually all require agencies to keep fairly detailed records of their various programs and to evaluate them on an ongoing basis. Both Congress and the president may also rely on outside consultants, analysts, and scholars for program evaluation. For example, the Department of Education spends upwards of $100 million per year on program evaluation and program data collection.[20]

THE POLITICAL RESOURCES OF THE FEDERAL BUREAUCRACY

Authority

The bureaucracy possesses authority because Congress passes legislation granting it and because other players recognize it by obeying its decisions.

Administrative Discretion

The power of a department or agency does not simply hinge on congressional delegations of power. Congress gives agencies great latitude to make policy; this is called **administrative discretion**. For example, Congress charges agencies with protecting the "public interest" but leaves them free to determine what specific policies will best serve the public. At times, Congress may be able to define the problem but may not be able to define a particular solution. Congress, then, leaves it to the bureaucracy to fill in the specifics. The Internal Revenue Service, for example, exercises enormous discretion in administering the tax law. It oversees a vast system that affects nearly everyone. The IRS must make choices about how to allocate its limited resources when interpreting, applying, and enforcing the law, and it exercises discretion informally in myriad ways. For example, it decides in which areas of tax law to issue regulations or other guidance, how to allocate enforcement efforts among various activities or groups, and whether to litigate or appeal specific issues. The exercise of discretion in these informal ways is subject to oversight by congressionally created bodies such as the U.S. Treasury Inspector General for Tax Administration (TIGTA), the Taxpayer Advocate Service and the U.S. Treasury IRS Oversight Board, and congressional committees such as the House Committee on Government Oversight and Reform, and the House Ways and Means Subcommittee on Oversight.[21]

Expertise

When Congress grants power to a particular bureau or agency, it usually does so by way of a fairly broad and general grant of authority. Congress expects that bureaucrats, specialists in a particular area, will use their expertise in applying the laws in specific cases. Agencies gain considerable power, then, from the expertise of their employees. This expertise also allows the bureaucrats to be a considerable source for the development of policy proposals and the lobbying for them. Studies have found that many of the bills introduced into Congress have actually been drafted by members of the bureaucracy.

The fact that bureaucrats are hired, and can only be fired, through the civil service process contributes to their level of expertise. Most civil servants spend their entire career within one agency, gaining considerable expertise over the course of many years. Few members of Congress will ever develop this level of knowledge in one particular policy area. This gives the members of the federal bureaucracy a significant advantage in pressing their claims upon the legislative branch of government.

The expertise of the bureaucrats gives them a significant amount of independence from the political appointees who are their superiors. After all, the typical career bureaucrat will remain in the agency long after political superiors have been replaced. Their job security may allow the bureaucrats to resist the dictates of their bosses. Such bureaucratic resistance tends to frustrate not only the political appointee technically at the helm of the department but also the president who appointed him.

Clientele Support

The groups and organizations affected by an agency's actions form its **clientele**. Many of the departments and agencies in the executive branch are specifically what political scientists call **clientele agencies**. These are agencies specifically designed by law to foster and promote the interests of certain groups. For example, the Department of Labor and Commerce was created by Congress in 1903 "to foster, promote, and develop the foreign and domestic commerce, the mining, the manufacturing, the shipping, and fishing industries, and the transportation facilities of the United States."[22]

The power of an agency depends heavily on the power of its clientele. An agency that is actively supported by large, well-organized, and well-funded groups is much more likely to achieve its goals than is an agency with little or weak support. Interest groups can help the agency by bringing pressure on Congress and the president, for bigger budgets, greater powers, or new duties. As a result, congressional committees and subcommittees may become very important parts of an agency's clientele.

There tends to be regular communication between the agency, the clientele groups, and committee members in Congress. This routinized communication makes the agency a lobbyist on the group's behalf and the group a lobbyist on the agency's behalf. The result is the development of very close relationships between congressional committee members, clientele groups, and agencies. Such cozy relationships are often referred to as **iron triangles**.[23] These relationships tend to work to reinforce a particular program against drastic change or abolition at the hands of a hostile president.[24] Iron triangles make clientele agencies the hardest to change or coordinate. Generally, these agencies are able to resist external demands by vigorously defending their own prerogatives. Because of this resistance to change, Congress and the president have frequently been forced to create a new clientele agency rather than to try to convince an existing one to implement programs that the agency opposes.

HOW BUREAUCRACIES MAKE DECISIONS

Political scientists have offered two alternative models to describe bureaucratic decision-making.

The Rational-Comprehensive Model

The rational-comprehensive model of bureaucratic decision making suggests that bureaucrats follow a sequence of four steps:

1. Clear specification and prioritization of the goals to achieve along with their underlying values.
2. Identification of all alternative methods for achieving those goals.
3. Identification and evaluation, according to formal rules, of all the various outcomes likely to result from each method.
4. In each step, reliance upon information and analysis.

Bureaucratic policy implementation often does not conform to an ideal, rational process in which a problem is identified, various solutions weighed in terms of their costs and benefits, and the most effective, cheapest solution settled upon. Indeed, studies of how policy actually gets made in the federal bureaucracy suggest that the rational-comprehensive model may be far from reality.

The Incremental Model of Bureaucratic Decision-Making

In his classic article "The Science of Muddling Through," Charles Lindblom argues that a more prevalent model of bureaucratic decision making is the incremental model.[25] Bureaucrats work under the constraints of time and limited resources. Under such conditions, it may not be possible to research all the possible solutions to a problem. In the end, Lindblom suggests bureaucrats seek a solution in the modification of an already existing policy. In incrementally altering the status quo, policy making inches along one step at a time.

Incrementalism exhibits the following characteristics:

1. The problem itself may not be clearly defined. For example, take the problem of poverty. What is the problem to be solved: feeding and housing people, preparing them for a job, or actually getting them a job? Often a problem is multi-faceted, and solving one aspect may make another aspect all the worse. For example, the provision of housing and food may work to discourage a poor person from seeking to get a job.

2. For a variety of reasons, only certain solutions are identified for serious consideration. First, policymakers may not know what to do about a particular problem. Second, it is often difficult to imagine doing things differently than the way you are currently doing them. As a result, radically different approaches to a problem are rarely considered. Finally, limited time and resources may make identification and analysis of all possible solutions unfeasible.

3. The values needed to assess the various solutions are unclear and unranked.

4. Policymakers tend to stop their analysis of solutions when they find one that is "good enough."

Incrementalism leads to a form of decision-making best described as just "muddling through." Rational, comprehensive, scientific analysis of a wide assortment of alternative policies is either not feasible or impossible. As a result, decision-makers make do with "good enough" as they make incremental changes to the status quo.

BUREAUCRATIC ACCOUNTABILITY

Big government, at least in the abstract, is unpopular with the public. The size of the federal bureaucracy is often equated with waste, remoteness, and incompetence. Even during the last thirty years, a period of "deregulation," the government holds title to 400,000 buildings and rents 50,000 additional buildings. Many people believe that the national government has become an octopus, uncontrolled, uncontrollable, and largely unaccountable.

Presidential Control over the Bureaucracy

Presidents have never found it easy to exercise control over the bureaucracy, and civil service and other reforms have further insulated most government workers from the partisan politics inherent in both Congress and the presidency. An incoming president can appoint fewer than 1 percent of all executive branch employees, that is approximately four thousand people out of a bureaucracy that numbers in the millions.[26]

While it is true that the president nominates those who will fill the top policy-making positions in government, these appointments must be made with the advice and consent of the Senate. Additionally, most of these appointees are not personal friends of the president, nor do they tend to be drawn from the ranks of loyal campaign workers. Instead, most come from the sectors for which they will be responsible. For example, the top officials in the Department of Defense tend to have military backgrounds or experience in the defense industries. The Federal Communications Commission (FCC) has often included people from the communications industry.

The American system of separated powers and checks and balances further exacerbates a president's ability to control the direction of the bureaucracy. The party winning a presidential election does not necessarily gain control of the national government. The president has limited time, limited political resources, and limited influence over the millions of decisions made by thousands of bureaucrats each day.

A president with a very clear agenda and a loyal White House staff may still be able to influence the direction of bureaucratic policymaking. The Trump administration, for example, has tried to increase the transparency of the federal bureaucracy. On October 9, 2019, President Trump issued Executive Order 13891, Promoting the Rule of Law Through Improved Agency Guidance Documents, to promote transparency by ensuring that all active guidance documents are made available to the public. The new guidance portal provides an indexed database that allows the public to search for documents based on a range of criteria that include date of issuance, general subject matter, and summary of contents.[27] Oversight by a staff of about thirty analysts, however, has always been selective, and indeed the process has been formally confined to "significant regulations" since the

Clinton administration. Presidents simply lack the organizational capacity to monitor and influence what agencies do in more than a selective way.

Frustration with bureaucratic independence and leaks caused the Trump administration to charge that there was a bureaucratic *Deep State* in Washington. The reports of the Ukraine affair and a secret whistleblower inside the deepest reaches of the intelligence community caused the president to charge that career officials inside the government were working at cross-purposes to the president, disclosing information that fueled his political opponents and eventually led to his impeachment. Questions arose as to whether there was a resistance in the executive branch to the Trump presidency, and if there was, what power do bureaucrats actually have to defy a president's agenda.

A recent study has found that the bureaucracy is involved in conflict on an almost daily basis, but not with the president. Rather, bureaucrats tend to be hemmed in by longstanding relationships with the many other bureaucrats in the executive branch. The practical power of bureaucrats to steer the ship is heavily circumscribed by the fact that the very actions of bureaucrats are authorized and overseen by an elected Congress.[28]

Congressional Control over the Bureaucracy

Congress, with an institutional staff of more than forty thousand, is more readily equipped to oversee the federal bureaucracy. It is Congress that creates the agencies, determines their organization and duties, and funds the budgets. In addition, Congress oversees the activities of the bureaucrats in appropriations hearings, special investigations, and congressional hearings. It is the Senate that confirms presidential appointments of high, cabinet-level officials. In fact, Congress has a whole committee dedicated to being the watchdog over the federal bureaucracy. The House Oversight Committee's mission is to ensure the efficiency, effectiveness, and accountability of the federal government and all its agencies

Congress can significantly influence agency behavior by the statutes that it enacts. In the past, Congress has passed broad statutes that left much to the bureaucrats' discretions. Since the 1960s, however, Congress has attempted to restrict such agency discretion. Until 1983, Congress made increasing use of the **legislative veto**, a law that grants broad power to the executive branch but reserves for Congress the power to block the exercise of power in particular cases.

In 1983, in the *Chadha* case, the Supreme Court declared the legislative veto unconstitutional, ruling that the legislative veto violated the constitutional requirement of separation of powers among the branches of the federal government.[29] Even after the *Chadha* decision, Congress has continued to pass laws containing legislative vetoes. Congress has also rewritten some of the laws so as to require both Houses of Congress and a signature by the president.

Congress has also recently moved to tighten the financial reins on the bureaucracy. No money may be spent by the bureaucracy unless it has first been authorized and appropriated by Congress. In the past, many programs enjoyed permanent authorization. Today, most programs are permanently funded, for example Social Security and the hiring of military personnel. Increasingly, however, there has been a trend toward annual authorizations that enable Congress to strengthen its oversight of executive agencies and their spending. After the military procurement abuses of the 1980s, for example, Congress made Defense Department budgets for military equipment subject to annual authorizations.

Even after the funds have been authorized by Congress, they cannot be spent unless they are also appropriated by Congress. The House Appropriations Committee and its various subcommittees control appropriations. Because appropriations may be, and often are, for less than the amount authorized, Congress can at this second stage further control the budgets of the various bureaucratic departments and agencies.

The most visible and dramatic form of congressional oversight is the investigation. While the power to investigate is not mentioned in the Constitution, it is implicit in Congress' power to legislate. Congress may subpoena a person, compelling that person to come testify before Congress. If the person refuses, Congress may charge him or her with contempt and either vote to send the person to jail or refer the matter to a court for further action.

While it is apparent that Congress does exercise oversight over the executive bureaucracy, none of this is to say that Congress exerts significant control, only that it exerts more control than the president. Many charge that members of Congress actually benefit from the red tape associated with the national bureaucracy, gaining popularity and prestige from running interference with the bureaucracy and interceding on behalf of their constituents. In addition, many point to the fact that members of Congress, ever eager for re-election, avoid conflict by delegating sweeping authority to the agencies and bureaus.

Judicial Oversight of the Bureaucracy

History suggests that Congress has often been unwilling to take responsibility to check the bureaucratic state. And while the Trump administration has tried to slow the trend toward greater regulation, there are still some 222,000 federal regulators and volumes of the regulations they promulgate. The judicial branch, however, can also impose constraints on the bureaucracy. This occurs when the federal court system becomes involved in a lawsuit that is filed against an agency. Such cases often end up in legislative courts such as the Tax Court, Court of Claims, or other specialized courts.

Two precedents that have shaped judicial opinions for decade are described as the "Auer deference" and "Chevron deference," where the Court directed lower courts to defer to an agency's interpretations of laws passed by Congress if those interpretations are deemed "reasonable." With the elevation of Justice Brett Kavanaugh to the Supreme Court in 2019, judicial scrutiny of bureaucratic discretion in executing the laws of Congress may now increase. There is now a fifth member on the nine-member Court who has expressed skepticism toward judicial deference to bureaucratic claims of authority. In the June 26, 2019 case, *Kisor v. Wilkie*, a 5–4 Court upheld the Auer doctrine and judicial deference to an agency's interpretation of its own regulation but only four justices actually validated the Auer doctrine. Chief Justice Roberts provided the fifth vote solely out of respect for precedent. The majority decision imposes stringent conditions on the applicability of Auer and future court decisions are likely to reject other cases of bureaucratic agency discretion.[30]

Iron Triangles and Issue Networks

The legislative, congressional, executive, and judicial constraints all serve as checks on the bureaucracy, but agencies can still establish powerful alliances. In fact, one reason that presidents, Congress, and the courts often find it difficult to control bureaucracies is that the agencies have strong ties to interest groups, on the one hand, and to particular committees and subcommittees in Congress, on the other. As discussed in Chapter Eight, when agencies, groups, and committees come to depend on each other for support and information, they form what political scientists refer to as **iron triangles** or **subgovernments**.

The decisions reached by members of the iron triangle may not be easily controlled, or interfered with, by the president or Congress as a whole. As pointed out in Chapter Nine, Congress often defers to the decisions reached at the committee or subcommittee stage. Especially when an issue has little press coverage and, therefore, low visibility, decisions reached by the members of the iron triangle are likely to be final.

There is mounting evidence that the concept of iron triangles is overly simplistic, especially when applied to issue areas of higher visibility and greater conflict. In the modern period, as the number of interest groups and policy experts has expanded, congressional committees and bureaucratic agencies may be bombarded with competing demands from multiple sides of an issue. These relationships may be better characterized as fluid **issue networks** in areas like the environment, abortion, gun ownership, and drug laws. Whether these relationships are iron or fluid, they still work to make congressional or presidential oversight over the bureaucracy difficult.[31]

REFORM AND REORGANIZATION

Some are calling for a complete overhaul of the civil service system. In an era in which term limits for elected government officials are gaining in popularity, perhaps it is not surprising that some are calling for term limits for career civil servants. Limiting their tenure is seen as a way to break up the iron triangles and bring new blood and breathe new life into the system.

These calls for reform are only the latest in a long string of efforts to rein in the federal bureaucracy. In 1946, Congress passed the **Administrative Procedures Act (APA),** which requires that citizens have the opportunity to be heard concerning proposed rules or regulations to be issued by the executive branch bureaucracy. The APA also allows citizens to appeal adverse decisions by the bureaucracy to the federal courts.

The increasing power of the federal executive branch also has led to concerns about the public's access to information. The **Freedom of Information Act** (FOIA), passed in 1967 and strengthened in 1974, was designed to address these problems. FOIA requires that government agencies make information "promptly available" to any person who asks for it. Some types of information are exempt: information that would compromise national security, law enforcement, personal privacy, or trade secrets.

Congress has also moved to open government meetings to the public. The **Sunshine Act** requires government agencies headed by commissions or boards to be open to the public. A similar law, the **Federal Advisory Committee Act**, applies this openness requirement to meetings involving executive officials and private citizens. Congress has also tried to make it easier for the bureaucracy to be held accountable through the 1989 **Whistle-Blower Protection Act**. This law says that agencies may not punish an employee who reports fraud, waste, corruption, or abuse on the part of their agency. This law also creates the Office of Special Counsel to help enforce the act. Up until 2019, very few employees have chosen to exercise their right to "blow the whistle" on their employer.

Recently, however, there were several high-profile whistleblowers that received an enormous amount of coverage in the media. During the House investigation of the Trump administration's delay of Ukrainian aid, multiple whistleblowers provided information.

As noted earlier in this chapter, presidents have tried to reform the bureaucracy. Most recently, immediately upon being elected in November 2016, Donald Trump and the Republicans in Congress began drawing up plans to take on the bureaucracy by eroding job protections, reducing benefits that federal workers have received for generations, hiring freezes, an end to automatic pay raises, and a green light to fire poor performers. Trump's election as an outsider promised to shake up a bureaucratic system that many voters think is awash with "waste, fraud, and abuse."[32]

BENEFITS OF BUREAUCRACY

For all the complaining about big government, there are real and clear benefits of bureaucracy.

Managing Complexity

Life in modern America is complex. Government programs are increasingly sophisticated. Members of Congress are generalists usually not well equipped to deal with all the subtleties that new situations can entail. The tax code of the United States, for example, is nearly three thousand pages long. Only a well-staffed office of accountants can cope with such legal complexity.

Stability and Predictability

The stability and predictability of the federal bureaucracy allow citizens to more effectively grapple with their government. In addition, some communities, like the business community, rely on a certain amount of consistency in government rules, regulations, and programs. Constant reform would leave many in confusion.

CONCLUSION

While campaigning for the presidency in 2016, Donald Trump promised to "drain the swamp," to get rid of the members of Congress, bureaucrats, and interest group lobbyists that he argued are working together to serve themselves and special interests at the expense of the American public. He promised to replace these career politicians with the new voices of those previously outside of government, ending corruption and graft. To accomplish this, the new president argued for term limits on Congress, a hiring freeze on bureaucrats, and a five-year ban on lobbying after working in his administration and a promise that no lobbyists would work in his administration.

While all this sounds good on paper, it is no easy task. In fact, policy making requires difficult choices and trade-offs among countless competing interests, many with legitimate arguments that their needs are real and need to be served. Policymaking involves resolving significant complexities that arise in a nation of 320 million people with an $18 trillion economy and thousands and thousands of pages of existing rules and regulations.

To function efficiently, the federal workforce needs to attract and retain top talent. Hiring freezes for federal agencies would lead to a brain drain in the executive branch of government as the most talented leave to seek more secure jobs elsewhere. Those who remain in the agencies are the ones who cannot find employment elsewhere. Then, as government bureaucrats leave, agencies become even more dependent on private lobbyists for policy expertise. There will be fewer bureaucrats doing more work leaving them less time to challenge an experienced industry lobbyist who knows all the ins and outs of an issue. A blanket-hiring freeze intended to shrink the workforce by attrition will only make the federal government more dependent on lobbyists.

The reality of democracy in the world's largest economy and third most populous country is that national policymaking is complicated. It requires considerable knowledge and experience to understand the rules, forge compromises, and resolve trade-offs. Democracy is a system for making hard trade-offs among competing interests. And to make those trade-offs fairly and intelligently requires knowledge and experience. The surest way to empower special interests is to make government dumber.[33]

CHAPTER NOTES

[1]Nicholas Kulish, Sarah Kliff, and Jessica Silver-Greenberg, "The US. Tried to Build a New Fleet of Ventilators. The Mission Failed," *The New York Times*, March 29, 2020. *https://www.nytimes.com/2020/03/29/business/coronavirus-us-ventilator-shortage.html)*

[2]Ed Yong, "How the Pandemic Will End," *The Atlantic*, March 25, 2020. *https://www.theatlantic.com/health/archive/2020/03/how-will-coronavirus-end/608719/)*

[3]Robert Powell, "4 Changes that Could Affect Social Security in 2020," *USA Today*, January 17, 2020, *https://www.usatoday.com/story/money/2020/01/17/social-security-2020-6-changes-you-should-expect-year/2827098001/*

[4]Philip Shabecoff, "Senator Urges Military Resources Be Turned to Environmental Battle," *New York Times*, 29 June 1990, A1.

[5]Martha Derthwick, and Paul J. Quirk, *The Politics of Deregulation* (Washington, D.C.: Congressional Quarterly Press, 1985).

[6]Samuel Stebbins and Michael B. Sauter, "These 30 companies, including Boeing, Get the Most Money from the Federal Government," *USA Today*, January 17, 2020, *https://www.usatoday.com/story/money/business/2019/03/27/lockheed-martin-boeing-get-most-money-federal-government/39232293/*

[7]Paul C. Light, "Fact Sheet on the New True Size of Government," Center for Public Service, Sept. 5, 2003, *http://www.brookings.edu.*

[8]Jon Hartley, "Deregulate to Help the Private Sector Fight Coronavirus," *National Review*, March 20, 2020, *https://www.nationalreview.com/2020/03/deregulate-to-help-the-private-sector-fight-coronavirus-2/*

[9]"Obamacare is Building a Massive Bureaucracy," *Crossroads GPS, http://www.crossroadsgps.org/obamacare-is-building-a-massive-bureaucracy/*

[10]Clyde Wayne Crews, "Trump Regulations: Federal Register Page Count Is Lowest In Quarter Century," *Competitive Enterprise Institute*, December 29, 2017, *https://cei.org/blog/trump-regulations-federal-register-page-count-lowest-quarter-century*

[11]Ellen Knickmeyer, "Trump Administration is Still Rolling Back Environmental Protections as Nation Wrestles with Coronavirus," *Time*, March 24, 2020, *https://time.com/5808726/trump-administration-epa-rollbacks-coronavirus/*

[12]U.S. Bureau of the Census, Statistical Abstract of the United States, 1992 (Washington, D.C.: U.S. Government Printing Office, 1992), 331-381.

[13]U.S. Bureau of the Census, Statistical Abstract of the United States, 1995, 115th ed. (Washington, D.C.: Bureau of the Census, 1995), 350.

[14]Frederick C. Mosher, *Democracy and the Public Service*, 2d ed. (New York: Oxford University Press, 1982) 58-60.

[15]U.S. Bureau of the Census, Statistical Abstract, 1992, 332-33.

[16]Donna Tam, "The Major Industry Ties of Trump's Cabinet Picks," *Thomson Reuters*, December 23, 2016, *http://www.marketplace.org/2016/12/20/economy/major-industry-ties-trump-s-cabinet-picks*

[17]Ann Crittenden, "Quotas for Good Old Boys," *Wall Street Journal*, 14 June 1995, 1.

[18]R. Shep Melnick, *Regulation and the Courts* (Washington, D.C.: Brookings Institute, 1989), 55.

[19]Curt Levey, "Health-Care Reform Could Create a Litigation Explosion," *The Wall Street Journal. Opinion Journal*, February 10, 2010, *http://online.wsj.com/article/SB10001424052748704541004575011390617073222.html*

[20]U.S. Department of Education, "New Directions for Program Evaluation at the U.S. Department of Education," *ED.gov*, 2004, *http://www2.ed.gov/news/pressreleases/2002/04/evaluation.htm.*

[21]Lily Kahng, "The IRS Tea Party Controversy and Administrative Discretion," *Cornell Law Review*, Vol.99:41

[22]U.S. Department of Labor, *https://www.dol.gov/*

[23]Theodore Lowi, *The End of Liberalism*, New York: W.W. Norton and Company, 1979, page 276.

[24]Martin Shapiro, "The Presidency and the Federal Courts," in *Politics and the Oval Office*, ed. Arnold Meltser (San Francisco: Institute for Contemporary Studies, 1981), Chapter 8.

[25]Charles Lindblom, "The Science of Muddling Through," *Public Administration Review* 19 (Spring 1959): 19.

[26]*EPA Press Office,* "EPA Meets President Trump's Deadline, Making Agency Guidance Available to the Public," *https://www.epa.gov/newsreleases/epa-meets-president-trumps-deadline-makes-agency-guidance-available-public*

[27]Rebecca Ingber, "Bureaucratic Resistance and the Deep State Myth," *Just Security,* October 18, 2019, *https://www.justsecurity.org/66643/bureaucratic-resistance-and-the-deep-state-myth/*

[28]*Immigration and Naturalization Service v. Chadha*, 462 U. S. 919 (1983).

[29]Paul W. Hughes and Michael B. Kimberly, "SCOTUS Creates Opportunities to Challenge Administrative Regulation: Implications of *Kisor v. Wilkie*," *McDermott Partners*, June 28, 2019, https://www.mwe.com /insights/scotus-creates-opportunities-to-challenge-administrative-regulation-implications-of-kisor-v-wilkie/

[30]Hugh Heclo, "Issues Networks and the Executive Establishment," in *The New American Political System* ed. Anthony King (Washington, D. C.: American Enterprise Institute, 1978), 87-124.3

[31]Robert Brodsky, "Obama Calls for End of '20th Century Bureaucracy,'" *Government executive.com*, August 29, 2008, *http://www.govexec.com/dailyfed/0808/082908ts1.htm.*

[32]Lee Drutman, "Why 'Draining the Swamp' makes America Dumber," *CNN Opinion*, December 12, 2016, *http://www.cnn.com/2016/12/12/opinions/drain-the-swamp-drutman/*

[33]Lisa Rein, "Trump Has a Plan for Government Workers. They're Not Going to Like It," *The Washington Post*, November 21, 2016, *https://www.washingtonpost.com/news/powerpost/wp/2016/11/21/trump-republicans-plan-to-target-government-workers-benefits-and-job-security/?utm_term=.cd4002f196f7*

SUGGESTED READINGS

Aberbach, Joel D., and Mark A. Peterson, eds. *Institutions of American Democracy: The Executive Branch* (Institutions of American Democracy Series). New York: Oxford University Press, 2006.

Downs, Anthony. *Inside Bureaucracy.* Boston: Little, Brown, 1967.

Goodsell, Charles T. *The New Case for Bureaucracy: A Public Administration Polemic,* 4th ed. Washington, D.C.: CQ Press, 2014.

Gormlcy, William T. and Steven J Balla. *Bureaucracy and Democracy: Accountability and Performance,* 2nd ed. Washington, D.C.: CQ Press, 2004.

Heclo, Hugh. *A Government of Strangers: Executive Politics in Washington.* Washington, D.C.: Brookings Institution, 1977.

Howard, Philip K. *The Rule of Nobody: Saving America from Dead Laws and Broken Government.* New York: W.W. Norton, 2015.

Johnson, Ronald N. and Gary D. Libecap. *The Federal Civil Service and the Problem of Bureaucracy.* Chicago: University of Chicago Press, 1994.

Kettl, Donald F. and James W. Fesler. *The Politics of the Administrative Process,* 4th ed. Washington, D.C.: CQ Press, 2009.

Light, Paul C. *A Government Ill Executed: The Decline of the Federal Service and How to Reverse it.* Cambridge, MA: Harvard University Press, 2008.

Maxwell, Bruce. *Insider's Guide to Finding a Job in Washington.* Washington, D.C.:CQ Press, 2000.

Meier, Kenneth. *Politics and the Bureaucracy: Policy-Making in the Fourth Branch of Government,* 5th ed. Fort Worth, Texas: Harcourt-Brace, 2006.

Nelson, William. *The Roots of the American Bureaucracy, 1830 – 1900.* Washington, D.C.: Beard Books, 2006.

Pressman, Jeffrey L and Aaron Wildavsky. *Implementation*, 3rd ed. Berkeley: University of California Press, 1984.

Reich, Robert. *Locked in the Cabinet.* New York: Knopf, 1997.

Stivers, Camilla, ed. *Democracy, Bureaucracy, and the Study of Administration.* Boulder, CO: Westview Press, 2001.

Verkuil, Paul. *Outsourcing Sovereignty: Why Privatization of Government Functions Threatens Democracy and What We Can Do About It.* New York: Cambridge University Press, 2007.

Wood, Dan B. *Bureaucratic Dynamics: The Role of Bureaucracy in a Democracy.* Boulder, CO: Westview, 1994.

Web Sites

Department of Homeland Security, www.dhs.gov.

Fed World Information Network. www.fedworld.gov.

FirstGov. www.firstgov.gov.

Library of Congress, www.loc.gov.

National Archives and Records Administration. www.nara.gov.

Project on Government Oversight, www.pogo.org

The Reason Foundation, www.reason.org/areas/topic/privatization.

Chapter Ten

THE PRESIDENCY AND LEADERSHIP

On January 20, 2021, President-elect Joseph R. Biden walked down the long-hallowed halls of the Capitol building towards the doors opening to the West front of the building leading towards the elaborately decorated platform to publicly take his oath of office as the nation's 46th president. With few exceptions, the pomp and traditions of the inauguration were established in 1789 when the nation's first President George Washington took his constitutionally mandated oath of office standing on the balcony of Federal Hall in New York City. He placed his hand on a Bible to take his oath of office and gave the nation's first presidential inaugural address. The evening closed with public gatherings, parties and, of course, fireworks!

As Washington took his oath, the reality of the job he was just elected to settled in. Even though he presided over the Constitutional Convention that wrote the document that detailed the duties and responsibilities of the presidency, Washington was awestruck at the tasks ahead of him. He doubted he could do the job even before he stood on that balcony. He feared that "he lacked the requisite skills for the presidency, the 'ocean of difficulties' facing the country—all gave him pause on the eve of his momentous trip to New York. In a letter to his friend Edward Rutledge, he made it seem as if the presidency was little short of a death sentence and that, in accepting it, he had given up all expectations of private happiness in this world."[1] As the nation's first chief executive officer, he realized that he would be the model for all who would follow him. He lamented to Rutledge that he knew "that my countrymen will except too much from me. I fear, if the issue of public measures should not correspond with their sanguine expectations, they will turn the extravagant . . . praises which they are heaping upon me at this moment into equally extravagant . . .censures."[2] The man who molded a ragtag group of frontiersmen into a revolutionary army, survived the harsh winter of Valley Forge, forced the military-might of the British army to surrender at Yorktown, served as president of the Constitutional Convention and was, and still is, the only person unanimously elected to the presidency by the Electoral College, dreaded the office he was about to assume. In

1789, just before he took that oath, Washington commented that "my movements to the chair of government will be accompanied by the feelings not unlike those of a culprit, who is going to the place of his execution; so unwilling am I, in the evening of a life nearly consumed in public cares, to quit a peaceful abode for an ocean of difficulties, without that competency of political skill, abilities, and inclination, which are necessary to manage the helm."[3] At one time or more during their presidency, the forty-five men who have followed President Washington shared the same doubts he had about their ability to "faithfully execute the office of the President of the United States."

For an incoming president, the easiest part seems to be winning the election. The hardest part is what happens after one takes that oath of office. This chapter examines both the constitutionally mandated duties of the presidency as well as the unwritten demands the American citizenry place upon their presidents. Every president from Washington to Biden have been mindful of their legacies and how their actions will be viewed for generations to come. Presidents want to be known for their successes, not their failures. The nation's youngest president, Theodore Roosevelt, echoed those sentiments shared by all presidents. He pointed out that "it isn't how long you are President that counts, but what you accomplished as President. I've had my chance; I did fairly well with it. I made some kind of place in history for myself. Someone else might have done better than I, but I could not, for I did my best."[4]

This chapter also explores the growing power of the presidency. The Framers envisioned the executive and legislative branches sharing power, with the legislative houses making laws and the executive branch merely implementing them. "Over the course of two hundred [plus] years, the presidency has been continuously shaped and reshaped by the forty[six] leaders—some strong and decisive, some weak or passive—who have served in that role; by the demands forced upon the office; by the challenges of a growing, increasingly complex industrial civilization and a series of national and international crises; by the thousands of statutes passed by Congress; and by the changing mandates and expectations of the American people at whose pleasure the President serves."[5] The growth in presidential power offset by the decline of Congressional authority reached a pinnacle in the 1970's beginning with "the imperial presidency" of the Nixon Administration. The perceived balance between the two branches shifted dramatically in favor of the executive branch. Congress has yet to successfully reign in the growing power of the presidency. Whether we like it or not, the American presidency has evolved from its initial task of overseeing the governance of thirteen states to becoming the preeminent leader of the free world!

Basically, the American presidency is a daunting task. President John Adams once commented that "no man who ever held the office of the President would congratulate a friend on obtaining it."[6] The question remains as to whether or not the American electorate puts too much pressure on our presidents to successfully solve all of the nation's problems within a four-year, or if they are lucky enough to win re-election, eight years.

Whatever else a President newly come to the White House may look forward to, he will, if he be wise, realize from the first moment that he is certain to disappoint the hopes of many of the members of his constituency who collectively compose the nation. There are at least two reasons in support of this expectation. In the first place, as the President exercises the duties of his high office he will be compelled to make choices, and every choice he makes, whether in respect of measures or of men, will displease or disillusion those who do not agree with him. In the second place—and in the number of citizens affected this is the more important category—the nation expects more of the President than he can possibly do; more than we give him either the authority or the means to do. Thus, expecting from him the impossible, inevitably we shall be disappointed in his performance.[7]

QUALIFICATIONS FOR THE PRESIDENCY

Article II, Section 2 of the Constitution sets the qualifications of any person seeking the presidency:

No person except a natural-born citizen, or a citizen of the United States at the time of the adoption of the Constitution, shall be eligible to the office of the president; neither shall any person be eligible to that office who shall not have obtained to the age of thirty-five years, and been fourteen years a resident within the United States.

Basically, there are only three qualifications: natural born citizenship, age, and residency. Both the presidential and vice-presidential candidates must be natural-born citizens. Yet, the constitution does not define the term "natural-born." Can a person who was not born in the United States claim to be a natural born citizen and thus, be a viable candidate for the presidency? The Framers addressed this with the phrase "at the time of the adoption of the Constitution." Several members of the Constitutional Convention were born outside of the United States but were now citizens of the United States and, of course, eligible to run for the presidency. This was of particular importance to Alexander Hamilton. He was born in Charlestown, a city of Saint Kitts and Nevis, an island in the West Indies. Also, the question was answered by the United States Supreme Court in its 1898 decision in *United States v Wong Kim Ark*. The Court ruled that "anyone born on U.S. soil and subject to its jurisdiction is a natural born citizen, regardless of parental citizenship."[8] Questioning the natural born status of a presidential candidate virtually dominated the 2008 presidential election. A group called the Birthers openly questioned Barack Obama's natural born status. They claimed that Obama was born in Africa and smuggled into the country to run for the presidency. A key spokesperson for the group was Donald Trump who publicly challenged Obama's citizenship and repeatedly asked Obama to provide a copy of his birth certificate. However, Obama was indeed born in a hospital in Hawaii. Senator from Texas and a former presidential contender, Ted Cruz, was born in Canada. Although his father was born in Cuba, his mother is a natural born citizen of the United States. Thus, Cruz is indeed a natural born citizen. The same situation applied to President Chester Arthur. While his critics claimed he was born in Canada to non-American citizens, Arthur's birth certificate clearly showed that he was born in Vermont. Former governor of Louisiana, Bobby Jindal's birthright was questioned since his parents were both born in India. But Jindal's birth certificate confirms that he was born in Baton Rouge. Senator Marc Rubio's parents fled Cuba, but Rubio was born in the United States. When Kamala Harris was selected for the vice presidency, the same Birther questions arose as they questioned her birthright. Yes, her parents hail from foreign soils, but she was born in the United States. The only state-residency requirement is that both the president and vice president cannot be from the same state. For example, when

George W. Bush selected Dick Chaney as his vice-presidential candidate, both Chaney and Bush declared Texas as their home state. Chaney had to change his official residence to Wyoming.

What is interesting is that there are no constitutional qualifications for the presidency requiring previous governing experience or a level of educational attainment. Only a handful of presidents have entered the highest political office of the nation without holding at least one elective governing position. Several of the nation's first presidents had served at least as members of their colonial assemblies. Presidents Franklin Roosevelt, Jimmy Carter, Bill Clinton and Ronald Reagan, Lyndon Johnson, Gerald Ford, Barack Obama, Joseph Biden and others were either governors or members of Congress representing their respective states. Ulysses S. Grant came to Oval Office as one of the few presidents lacking any governing experience whatsoever. Throughout his tenure in the White House, his administration was known more for its corruption than for its accomplishments. Grant woefully pointed out that "it was my fortune or misfortune to be called to the Chief Magistracy without any prior political training. Under the circumstances, it is but reasonable to suppose that errors of judgment must have occurred."[9] Both George Washington and Andrew Johnson had little formal education. Although he had some political experience under his belt, Johnson was basically homeschooled by his wife.

Although one's religious affiliation is not an official qualification for the presidency, it certainly has had an impact on the electability of a presidential candidate. In 1948, Al Smith launched his bid for the White House. After serving three terms as the governor of New York, Smith possessed the political expertise needed to seek the White House. But the issue of the campaign was not his resume, it was his religion—Catholic. Al Smith was the nation's first Catholic presidential candidate. He was beaten in a landslide election by his opponent Republican Herbert Hoover. John F. Kennedy did become the nation's first Irish Catholic president. But his religious affiliation was a major issue. The Nixon campaign ran a campaign advertisement portraying the President of the United States asleep in the White House when a telephone rang in his bedroom. Next to the bed was a table with three phones—a red one for national security, a black one for the White House and a gold and white phone symbolizing the Vatican. The commercial stops as the president's hand rests upon the gold and white phone followed by the caption that the American people needed a president who answered to the American people, not the Pope. Both practicing Catholics, John Kerry and Joe Biden garnered mixed support from their fellow Catholics since they advocate pro-choice positions on abortion. As the nation's second Catholic president, "Biden opposes abortion as a personal matter, but wrote in his 2007 memoir that he doesn't 'have a right to impose my view on the rest of society.'"[10]

Terms of Office

Article II does not specify the number of terms a president can serve. Washington set the practice of serving only two terms. "He resisted efforts to make him a king and established the precedent that no one should serve more than two terms as president. He voluntarily yielded power. His enemy George III, remarked in 1796, as Washington's second term was coming to an end, 'If George Washington goes back to his farm, he will be the greatest character of his age.' As George Will wrote, 'the final component of Washington's indispensability was the imperishable example he gave by proclaiming himself dispensable.'"[11] In 1805, President Thomas Jefferson was pressured to run for a third term of office. Jefferson declined saying that "George Washington set the example of voluntary retirement after eight years. I shall follow it."[12] While the majority honored the tradition, a few presidents did offer their opinions about the length of a president's term of office while others contemplated seeking a third term. In 1877, President Rutherford B. Hayes "recommended an amendment to the Constitution prescribing a term of six years for the presidential office and forbidding a re-election."[13] President William Henry Harrison echoed the same sentiments. He believed that "it is part of wisdom for a republic to limit the service of that officer at least to whom she has instructed the management of her foreign relations, the execution of her laws, and the command of her armies and navies to a period so short as to prevent his forgetting that he is the accountable agent, not the principal; the servant, not the master."[14]

In 1880, President Grant wanted to run for a third term, but he did not have the backing of the Republican Party to win the nomination. President Theodore Roosevelt made an unsuccessful bid for a third term in 1912. The question of limiting the terms arose when President Franklin Roosevelt did break the tradition by being the elected to both a third and fourth term. His opponent Republican Thomas Dewey voiced his support for limiting a president to only two terms. "In a speech in Buffalo [New York] on October 31, 1944, Dewey said, 'four terms or sixteen years is the most dangerous threat to our freedom ever proposed. That is one reason why I believe that two terms must be established as the limit by constitutional amendment.'"[15] Roosevelt died shortly after taking the oath of office for the fourth time. If he had completed that term of office, Roosevelt would have been president for sixteen years. And if he opted to and public support was behind him, he would have had the option to run for a fifth term.

In 1947, the Republican controlled House and Senate passed the **22nd Amendment** limiting the president to only two terms of office. Ratified in 1951, the amendment would have allowed the incumbent president to seek a third term. But President Truman declined. Furthermore, the amendment restricts the number of terms a vice president who assumes the unfinished term of the presidency can serve in the oval office. According to the Amendment, "no person who has held the office of President, or acted as President, for more than two years of a term to which some other person was elected President shall be elected to the office of the President more than once." This limits the vice president to serve only ten years as president. Lyndon Johnson assumed the presidency with the assassination of John Kennedy in 1963. Johnson served only one year as president in the Kennedy administration, making him eligible to run for two terms. Gerald Ford, however, assumed the presidency after Nixon's resignation in August 1974, making him eligible for only one term of office.

THE POWERS OF THE PRESIDENCY

The Executive/Legislative Relationship

The Constitution grants the president sweeping enumerated and implied powers. However, those powers were extended to the executive branch with the understanding that the relationship between the legislative and executive branches is indeed a partnership guided under the principles of separation of powers and checks and balances. The legislative branch has a constitutional role in every action a president takes and vice versa. In *Federalist #48*, James Madison addressed the concerns of the Anti-Federalists that constitutional provisions did not give Congress enough control over the executive branch. Madison firmly believed that the legislative branch did indeed have the upper hand:

> The legislative department derives a superiority in our government from other circumstances. Its constitutional powers being at once more extensive, and less susceptible of precise limits, it can, with the great facility, mask, under complicated and indirect measures, the encroachments which it makes on the coordinate departments. It is not unfrequently a question of real nicety in legislative bodies, whether the opportunity of a particular measure will, or will not, extend beyond the legislative sphere. On the other side, the executive power being restrained within a narrower compass, and being more simple in its nature, and the judiciary being described by landmarks still uncertain, projects of usurpation by either of these departments would immediately betray and defeat themselves. Nor is this all: as the legislative department alone has access to the pockets of the people, and has in some constitutions full discretion, and in all a prevailing influence, over the pecuniary rewards of those who fill the other departments, a dependence is thus created in the latter, which gives still greater facility to encroachments of the former.[16]

While on paper the relationship seems to be clearly defined, the relationship between the two branches is indeed a fragile one. Although Washington truly believed in the concepts of separation of powers and checks and balances, he too was, at times, frustrated by the inability of Congress to act quickly to address pressing issues and problems. Congress is by its very nature a deliberative body. It is impractical to assume that a body of 435 members of the House and 100 members of the Senate can deliver the immediate responses the public demands. Whenever the United States is faced with a crisis, the public turns to their president for answers.

> "Americans have come to expect a lot of their presidents, most perhaps than any man can deliver. We say that the president runs the country, but in practice, presidents have trouble running large parts of the government. We hold the president responsible for the economy, even though he has few economic levers at his command. We expect the commander in chief to lead us to victory in war, and then we complain when we think he is micro-managing the military. And we tend to think of the president as the personification of the nation he leads. Few other democracies combine the position of head of government and head of state. We do."[17]

Consequently, the success or failure of a president's administration to be all things to all of the people is tied directly to his/her relationship with the legislative branch of government. Each president must determine for themselves their leadership style in fulfilling their constitutional duties as well as their dealings with Congress. Traditionally, there are three styles of leadership. The **Taftian** or **Contractual Theory** is "a view of presidential power that holds that the president is limited by specific grants of power authorized in the Constitution and by statute."[18] In particular,

President Taft took a strict constructionist approach to the presidency. He held to the belief that "the president can exercise no power which cannot be fairly and reasonably traced to some specific grant of power or justly implied and included within such express grant as proper and necessary to its exercise."[19] This does not mean that Taft just waited for the legislative branch to direct him nor that he only adhered to the enumerated powers in Article II. Whatever Taft initiated as president he wanted to be sure his actions did not violate his constitutionally mandated authority. Presidents Rutherford B. Hayes, Chester A. Arthur, Warren G. Harding and Calvin Coolidge adhered to the Contractual Theory.

The exact opposite to the Contractual Theory is the **Stewardship Theory**, the "view of presidential powers that holds that the president has not only the right but also the duty to do anything needed to safeguard the nation and to protect the American people, unless such action is specifically forbidden by the Constitution."[20] Cartoons during the Theodore Roosevelt administration showed the president actually steering a ship! Both Presidents Woodrow Wilson, and Franklin Roosevelt used this leadership style. This leadership theory gives a president more "wiggle room" in his decision-making process but the catchall phrase is "unless such action is specifically forbidden by the Constitution."

Finally, the **Prerogative Theory** "holds that the chief executive can exercise extraordinary power if needed to protect and preserve the nation."[21] In particular, Abraham Lincoln embraced this theory by "arguing that the oath of office required him to both preserve the Constitution and to take otherwise unconstitutional measures to ensure that the Constitution itself was well preserved."[22] During the course of the American Civil War, Lincoln violated his constitutional duties more than once. Franklin Roosevelt actually by-passed Congress and violated several laws when "he took the initiative in the exchange with Great Britain of 50 American destroyers for bases in the Western Hemisphere."[23] Rightfully Congress could have initiated impeachment charges against Roosevelt. Richard Nixon overstepped his boundaries in conducting illegal bombing raids in Cambodia. Congress had repealed the Gulf of Tokin Resolution allowing for air attacks against nations such as Cambodia that were either initiating or aiding and abetting North Vietnamese airstrikes in South Vietnam aimed at South Vietnamese and American forces. President Ronald Reagan could have been charged with impeachable offensives for his impoundment of monies allocated by Congress for domestic expenditures that he used to purchase weaponry for the Iran-Contra episode. Of course, Thomas Jefferson drew the ire of Congress when he purchased the Louisiana Territory from the French without first asking permission from Congress.

From Washington to Biden, all presidents have been confronted with the necessity of using all three of these leadership models during their presidencies. The intensity and immediacy of the situation at hand forces a president to act with expediency. In 1864, faced with the brutality of the American Civil War, a war-torn President Lincoln asked "what is the presidency worth to men if I have no country?"[24] Lincoln believed that the only way to save the nation that he was elected to govern and to protect, was to do whatever was necessary to preserve it. And he was going to do this with or without a favorable nod from Congress. Far too often waiting for Congress to react is not a viable option. At best, Congress is a reactionary body, not a pro-active one.

The President confers with senior advisors in the Oval Office.
Feb. 4, 2009. White House Photo by Pete Souza

ENUMERATED CONSTITUTIONAL DUTIES

Article II, Sections **2** and **3** of the Constitution details the duties and responsibilities assigned to the president.

Appointments

As specified in Section 2, the president has the authority to "appoint all other officers of the United States, whose appointments are not herein otherwise provided for which shall be established by law" and to "fill up vacancies that may happen during the recess of the Senate, by granting commissions which shall expire at the end of the next session." The Framers realized that president would need to establish his own team. The **appointment powers** of the presidency extend to wide range of officeholders to include Cabinet secretaries, deputy secretaries, undersecretaries, assistant secretaries, general counsels of various agencies, judicial appointments to the Supreme Court and all federal benches, and ambassadors to head foreign delegations. Furthermore, Section 3 gives the president the authority to appoint officers to **inferior** offices, that is those not specifically listed in Section 2. These appointees are not subject to the Senate confirmation process.

In *Federalist #66*, Alexander Hamilton clarified the role of the Senate in the presidential appointment process:

It will be the office of the President to nominate, and with the advice and consent of the Senate, to appoint. There will, of course, be no exertion of choice on the part of the Senate. They may defeat one choice of the Executive, and oblige him to make another; but they can not themselves choose–they can only ratify or reject the choice of the President. They might even entertain a preference to some other person, at the very moment they were asserting to the new proposed, because there might be no positive ground of opposition to him; and they could not be sure, if they withheld their assent, that the subsequent nomination would fall upon their own favorite, or upon any other person in their estimation more meritorious than the one rejected. Thus it could hardly happen, that the majority of the Senate would feel any other complacency toward the object of an appointment than such as the appearances of merit might inspire, and the proofs of want of it destroy.[25]

The Constitution also restricts the ability of sitting congresspersons to obtain presidential appointments for themselves within the executive branch. The document specifically "prohibits Senators and Representatives from being appointed to any federal office created—or to any federal office increased in salary–during their terms of office (the **Ineligibility Clause**). Furthermore, no officer of the United States 'shall be a Member of Either House during his Continuance in Office' (the **Incompatibility Clause**)."[26] For example, Kamala Harris had to resign her Senate seat before she took the oath of office as vice president. She could not hold two government positions at the same time.

The appointment process is riddled with politics. Once a presidential contender gains the nomination of his/her political party, his/her team is inundated with resumes of aspirants seeking a prime high-ranking government job. In 1861, Abraham Lincoln lamented that "these office-seekers are a curse to the country; no sooner was my election certain, than I became the prey of hundreds of hungry persistent applicants for office, whose highest ambition is to feed at the Government's crib. . . This human struggle and scramble for office, for a way to live without work, will finally test the strength of our institutions."[27] Presidential elections are expensive. While candidates bragged about the number of one-dollar donations they receive, they are very dependent upon generosity of the wealthy. In return, these donors are expecting some sort of recognition or reward for supporting their candidate. A high-level government appointment is a powerful feather in one's cap! Yet, the success of any president's tenure in the White House is dependent upon the experience an appointee brings to his/her office. It is the task of the transition team to pick the right person for the right job. All presidents have had to face the turmoil of pleasing some but disappointing many. The reality is your friend today could quickly become your enemy tomorrow. President Rutherford B. Hayes lamented that "appointments and removals [should] be made on business principles and fixed rules. Let no man be put out or in merely because he is our friend."[28] President Polk was simply amazed about the number of resumes he received from individuals who simply did not have any qualifications for any government position. He wrote that:

In the midst of the annoyances of the herd of lazy, worthless people who come to Washington for office instead of going to work . . . I am sometimes amused at their applications. . . . One of these office seekers placed his papers of recommendation . . . No particular office was specified . . . but he answered that he thought he would be a good hand at making Treaties . . . and would like to be a minister abroad. This is about as reasonable as many other applications which were made to me.[29]

Approximately 1,200 presidential nominees to executive-level positions must pass the scrutiny of the Senate by a simple majority vote. It is the responsibility of the in-coming president's transition team to vet candidates before the president forwards his/her recommendation for Senate consideration. Beginning in 1953, all candidates for executive office positions must undergo an extensive Federal Bureau of Investigation (FBI) background check. The FBI will interview the applicant's family members, co-workers, neighbors, etc. They will scrutinize the applicant's financial records, personnel files and even confirm their academic credentials. The **Ethics Act** of 1978 requires applicants to fill out numerous financial disclosure and conflict-of-interest forms as well as provide a list "of every foreign trip and every foreigner met, every speech given over the past several years, and every investment and income item" over their lifetime."[30] In 2013, President Obama nominated Chuck Hagel a long-time serving Republican lawmaker, as his secretary of defense. Even though the Democrats held the majority in the Senate, Obama felt certain Hagel's confirmation would be smooth sailing. Hagel's reputation was unquestionable. Yet the Senate Judiciary Committee gave Hagel anything but smooth sailing. One Senator from Hagel's Republic Party continued to question why Hagel omitted a handful of speeches from his nomination forms. Hagel eventually won confirmation. "One cabinet officer estimated it cost about $20,000 in legal and accountants' fees to ensure the forms were completed and accurate."[31]

A candidate for a federal judicial bench must provide a detail account of all of the cases they handled either as a lawyer or a judge. That can prove to be a very arduous task. For example, President George W. Bush nominated Harriet Miers to replace the retiring Associate Justice to the Supreme Court Sandra Day O'Connor. Miers had served as Bush's attorney during his tenure as the governor of Texas and was currently his White House Counsel. Miers' nomination ran into trouble simply because she did not submit the detailed paperwork required by the Senate Judiciary Committee. Bush had to withdraw her nomination and replaced her with Samuel Alito who did successfully pass the scrutiny of the Senate Judiciary Committee. Many potential nominees respectfully turn down the president's offer simply because they do not want to fill out the stack of required forms or undergo the oftentimes perceived overly intrusive background checks.

Even before the nominee is officially announced, the president must be mindful of **senatorial courtesy** by informing and hopefully gaining approval of the appointee's senator(s). Overlooking senatorial courtesy can seriously jeopardize the confirmation process. Once the paperwork is submitted, the next hurdle is just getting a hearing before the appropriate Senate committee. In 2016, President Obama nominated Merrick Garland as an Associate Justice to the Supreme Court to replace the late Associate Justice Antonin Scalia. Unfortunately, the Republican Majority Leader Mitch McConnell continued to stall Garland's hearing before the Senate Judiciary Committee. McConnell wanted the position to remain vacant until after the 2016 presidential election in hopes that a Republican would win the race and ultimately select Scalia's replacement. In 2021, President Joe Biden nominated Garland as his Attorney General. Once again, Garland's scheduled committee hearing is in limbo. This stalling of confirmation hearings is not new. During the first Clinton administration "the 786 top-level Clinton nominees requiring Senate confirmation took an average of almost nine months after inauguration to assume their posts—meaning that they missed more than a sixth of the presidential term! Thanks to a President [Clinton] who moved slowly to name top officials, a glacial presidential vetting process, slow FBI background checks for nominees, and a balky Senate confirmation process, securing a top appointed position was like running a marathon in molasses."[32]

Presidents are saddled with the reality that a presidential appointee can sit in Senate limbo for over a year or more. "The lag in getting people into office seriously impedes good government. A new president's first year—clearly the most important year for accomplishments and the most vulnerable to mistakes—is now routinely impaired by the lack of supporting staff. For executive agencies, leaderless periods mean decisions not made, initiatives not launched, and accountability not upheld."[33] The departments under a Cabinet-level office simply cannot effectively function without a boss any more than a federal bench can sit idle for months on end without a judge presiding over it. Presidents have opted to use an end-round tacit—the recess appointment. A **recess appointment** is "an appointment of a federal official made by the president to fill a vacancy while the Senate is not in session."[34] However, a congressional act denies the appointee his/her salary if the appointee's application was submitted for confirmation before the Senate adjourned but the Senate did not move on the nomination. Also, the temporary appointment will expire at the end of the next congressional session if the Senate still has not completed the confirmation process. A recess appointment enables the executive branch operations to continue. However, the nominee's future employment is still in limbo. It is not usual for a presidential appointee faced with this uncertainty to withdraw their nomination or decline to even accept the nomination in the first place. Presidents also have the option of using **temporary** or **interim appointments** to cover the death or resignation of an incumbent. Yet, these individuals can only be employed for 210 days. Efforts to "reform" the appointment process began in 1998 with the passage of the **Vacancies Reform Act**. This legislation aimed to reassert the Senate's advise and consent power by placing strict limitations on the service of acting appointees, in particular interim U.S. attorneys assigned to the Justice Department.

Unfortunately, rarely does an appointee to an executive office remain in his/her position for the duration of a president's term of office. They usually serve two years or less. During the administration of both George H.W. Bush, George W. Bush and Bill Clinton, the average tenure of their appointees was only 2.5 years. A quarter of their appointees served more than three years. The Nixon administrative staff was a revolving door with appointees leaving within less than two years. Even after the turmoil of winning confirmation, Chuck Hagel resigned his position as secretary defense in November 2014. The constant turnover is worrisome since these individuals oversee crucial departments and agencies in the federal bureaucracy.

No president can know for certain that they have selected the right person to serve in his/her administration. Oftentimes, a casual or friendly personal relationship changes dramatically when your friend is now your employee. Presidents are also under intense pressure from their own party leadership to select certain individuals for key administration positions. For example, in 1808, Democrat/Republican candidate James Madison won the presidential election. It seemed that almost everyone who had supported his campaign came knocking on the door for a presidential appointment. A prominent member of the inner circle of the Democratic/Republican Party, U.S. Senator Samuel Smith pushed the Madison team to elevate his brother from his position as President Jefferson's Secretary of the Navy to Secretary of State. Madison, however, wanted to nominate Albert Gallatin instead. Pressured by Senator Smith, Madison caved in and nominated Smith. As Madison's Secretary of State, Smith had the habit of conducting the affairs of state without first consulting with Madison. "In March 1811, Madison finally had a sit-down with his Secretary of State. He told Smith he had been not only disloyal but incompetent. Smith wrote diplomatic letters 'so crude and inadequate' that Madison had to 'write them anew myself;' repeatedly, State Department business had been 'thrown . . . into my hands.'"[35] Madison wanted to fire him. But Smith's brother once again pressured Madison to retain him. Consequently, Madison opted to offer Smith other jobs to include becoming the minister to Russia. Smith refused, resigned, and publicly criticized Madison. Madison replaced him with James Monroe.

Abraham Lincoln initially appointed William Seward as Secretary of State, Salmon P. Chase as Secretary of the Treasury, Simon Cameron as Secretary of War and Edward Bates as attorney general. "Cameron was loyal, but incompetent and crooked—less than a year later Lincoln canned him, offering to send him to Russia."[36] Oftentimes, individuals use their appointed positions to boost their own political ambitions. Chase was so politically ambitious that he desired to run for the presidency. Chase decided to ruin the careers of both Lincoln and Steward by spreading the rumors that Lincoln was so incompetent that he left the day-to-day operations of the White House to Steward. Chase launched an ill-conceived smear campaign that backfired, resulting in his registration from Lincoln's cabinet. Andrew Johnson inherited Seward when he assumed the presidency after Lincoln's assassination. His attempt to fire Seward led to Johnson's impeachment trial.

The 1881 assassination of President James Garfield was at the hands of Charles J. Guiteau. Mentally unbalanced, Guiteau believed that he was instrumental in Garfield's election to the presidency. He believed that Garfield would indeed reward him for his support by appointing him as the ambassador to Austria. Guiteau was an unsuccessful lawyer with absolutely no diplomatic experience. Yet he was aggressively persistent in pursuing the appointment. However, the Garfield transition team passed on his application and did not forward his name for Garfield's consideration. Garfield did not interview him. Totally dejected and down on his luck, "Guiteau moved to Washington, where he stayed in hotels and skipped out without paying. He spent most of his days in Lafayette Park, across from the White House. He had already decided to kill the president."[37] He stalked Garfield for months and followed him to the Baltimore and Potomac Railroad Station, where he fatally shot Garfield in the back. Guiteau was tried, convicted, and executed.

The process of removing a Senate-confirmed presidential nominee is a publicly dicey situation. What the Senate confirms, only the Senate can unconfirm. A president can only recommend the dismissal of an appointee. The president in writing must submit to the Senate the reasons behind his/her decision to remove the individual from his/her position. To avoid this, presidents will ask the appointee to officially submit a letter of resignation. This saves a potentially embarrassing situation for both the appointee and the president.

At all costs, presidents want to avoid the public scrutiny leveled against them such as when President Truman in 1951, he relieved General Douglas MacArthur from his command of United Nations' forces in Korea. Serving as the Supreme Commander of the Allied Powers in Japan, MacArthur was hailed as an American hero for negotiating Japan's surrender to end World War II. He was given a warm welcome home with a ticker tape parade. MacArthur's familiarity with the Far East made him the likely choice to command American forces in the Korean conflict. The North Korean army had crossed the 38th parallel and attacked the South Korean army. The General, however, soon drew the ire of President Truman. "Time and again MacArthur and the administration seemed to be at cross-purposes. On July 31, 1950, barely six weeks after the start of the fighting in Korea, MacArthur flew to the island of Formosa for a two-day visit with General Chiang Kai-shek, the Chinese Nationalist leader. Chiang Kai-shek was an ardent supporter of democracy for China. In the aftermath of the visit, MacArthur waited almost a week to present a report of the meeting to Washington; moreover, Chiang Kai-shek made a vague statement implying that he and the American general had made secret agreements."[38] "In a speech he delivered to a veterans group, MacArthur praised his own expertise while at the same time attacking his boss for not understanding 'the Orient.' They do not grasp that it is the pattern of Oriental psychology to respect and follow aggressive, resolute and dynamic leadership—to turn quickly from leadership characterized by timidity or vacillation—and they underestimate the Oriental mentality."[39] MacArthur wanted to bomb not only cities in North Korea but Communist-held cities in China with the hopes of installing Chiang Kai-shek as the president of China. Desiring a bid for the White House himself, MacArthur continued to publicly criticize Truman's approach to the Korean Conflict, hoping to put himself in a more favorable light as a defender of the nation's growing international role and of impressing the American electorate. Before his Secretary of State George C. Marshall could tell MacArthur in private that he was being relieved of his duties, a radio report leaked the information. MacArthur learned of his firing through a radio broadcast announcement that "General MacArthur has been a perverse subordinate, complaining about the Truman administration's policies and going so far as to suggest that they were responsible for military setbacks in Korea."[40] An enraged MacArthur decided to challenge his dismissal before the Senate. The Senate, however, supported Truman's decision but did allow MacArthur to address a highly publicized joint session of Congress where he delivered his famous speech "that old soldiers never die."

Commander-in-Chief and Warmaking

As specified in Section 2, the "President shall be the commander in chief of the army and navy of the United States, and the military of the several States, when called into the actual service of the United States. . ." The intent of the Framers was never to give the executive branch the right to declare war. The **war clause** of the Constitution clearly states "the Congress shall have to power . . . to declare war." The role of the president as commander-in-chief is a limited one. It is the president's responsibility to act as the first general of the army and first admiral of the navy in conducting the action of warfare as determined by Congress. It is Congress that appropriates the money for the nation's military forces. For example, presidents can recommend to Congress that the air force needs a new missile detection system. But, it is Congress that approves and appropriates the money for that initiative. It was the intentions of the Framers that the president's authority extends only to **defensive** actions.

> The need to trust in executive judgement and secretion for defensive actions more accurately represents the understanding of the Framers. At the Philadelphia Convention they recognized an implied power of the president to "**repel sudden attacks.**" When it was proposed that Congress be empowered to "make war," Charles Pinckney objected that legislative proceedings "were too slow" for the safety of the country in an emergency. . . Madison and Elbridge Gerry moved to insert "declare" for "make," thereby "leaving to the Executive the power to repel sudden attacks." Their motion carried. This trust in executive

judgement applies to **defense actions** at a time of an emergency, not to **general** or **offensive** military actions.[41] (Emphasis added by author)

Therefore, the political authority and policy directive rests with Congress, not the president. The distinction is that presidents command the nation's military forces in the execution of the directives dictated by Congress. If a president views the military commitment as a long-term rather than a short-term response, the president must ask or wait for Congress to issue an official declaration of war. A staunch defender of separation of powers, Madison strongly warned against giving a President the right to declare war:

> Those who are to *conduct a war* cannot in the nature of things, be proper or safe judges, whether *a war ought* to be *commenced, continued*, or *concluded*. They are barred from the latter functions by a great principle in free government, analogous to that which separates the sword from the purse, or the power of executing from the power of exacting laws.[42]

Although the Framers envisioned that Congress would have the upper hand over the executive in war making, presidents have found ways to circumvent Congress' authority. George Washington personally led state militias from Pennsylvania, Virginia, Maryland and New Jersey to end the Whiskey Rebellion. He justified his actions in his annual speech delivered to a joint session of Congress on November 19, 1794, emphasizing that "some of the citizens of the United States have been found capable of insurrection. . . I put in motion . . . an army, which . . . might perhaps, be rendering resistance desperate, prevent the effusion of blood."[43] President James Monroe bypassed congressional approval when he sent General Andrew Jackson to cross into Spanish-held Florida to attack the Seminoles. James K. Polk did not seek prior congressional approval when he declared war with Mexico over the United States' annexation of Texas. Oftentimes, Congress will

Then Vice President Joe Biden speaks at the welcome home ceremony for members of the 3rd Brigade 101st Airborne Division who returned from Afghanistan at Fort Campbell, Kentucky, February 11, 2011. White House Photo by David Lienemann

**President Ford announcing his pardon of Richard Nixon from the Oval Office.
September 8, 1974 Photo credit: Gerald R. Ford Library**

grant extraordinary war-related powers to the president. In 1917, the **National Defense Act** gave President Wilson authority to purchase, borrow, or use any other means possible to properly arm American forces in Europe fighting World War I. Wilson creatively used his new powers to control the production, storage and transportation of all military artillery, fix production costs, etc. By 1920, Congress stripped Wilson of his extraordinary war time powers. Since its passage, the 1973 War Powers Act has created problems in the relationship between Congress and the president. The intent of the legislation was to force the president to notify Congress within 48 hours of any troop commitments to foreign soils, unless there is a viable threat to national security. But presidents have opted to use the national security threat clause to bypass prudent notification of congressional leadership.

Pardons and Reprieves

The president has the constitutional authority to grant "reprieves and pardons for offenses against the United States, except in cases of impeachment." A **pardon** is "an executive grant of a release from the punishment or legal consequences of a crime before or after conviction."[44] "The power belongs to the president alone. Congress cannot limit the pardon authority, and the courts cannot review exercises of the pardon power."[45] Receiving a presidential pardon, however, addresses only federal offenses as specified in the pardon documents. It does not exempt an individual from future federal or state criminal charges or civil litigation. During the final days of a presidential term, numerous requests for pardons and reprieves pile up on the president's desk. Washington pardoned the two leaders of the Whiskey Rebellion. Lincoln pardoned several hundred Union Army deserters. Andrew Johnson drew the ire of the Radical Republicans when "on May 29, 1865, . . . Johnson pardoned all former military personnel below the rank of colonel in the Confederate Army or lieutenant in its navy. Johnson stipulated that higher-ranking former Confederate military officers and West Point or Annapolis graduates who had turned their coats had to apply individually for pardons, along with all civil and diplomatic officers of the 'pretended Confederate government.'"[46] Leader of the Confederate forces, General Robert E. Lee, applied for a pardon and took the required loyalty oath to the federal government. During his twelve years in the White House, President Franklin Roosevelt holds the record of issuing 2,819 pardons while President George W. Bush granted only 74.[47]

The most publicized and criticized pardon was issued by President Gerald Ford to President Richard Nixon. The impeachment charges against Nixon were damaging. There was the real possibility that Nixon would be the first president impeached, removed from office, and denied the right to run for office again. He also could have faced federal criminal charges. The options for Nixon were limited—resign from office and hope for a presidential pardon. Nixon even pondered pardoning himself. Yet, that was not a viable option. Instead, "Nixon implored Gerald Ford for a guarantee that upon taking office, he would pardon Nixon. Ford refused. Nixon resigned on August 9, 1974. . . . On September 8, 1974, Ford granted his predecessor a 'full, free, and absolute pardon' for any crimes Nixon committed as president."[48] Without the full pardon, Nixon could have faced a long list of criminal charges to include bribery of judges, destroying evidence, obstruction of justice, and so forth. In return, Nixon issued a public acknowledgement of his guilt stating that his "regret and pain at the anguish of my mistakes over Watergate have caused the nation and the presidency."[49] In retrospect, Ford's pardon of Nixon saved the nation and the Republican Party from the embarrassment of having an impeached president facing federal criminal charges. But the outcry from the public over that pardon dearly ruined Ford's potential political fortunes and any chance he would have had of a future successful run for the White House.

Addressing Congress

Article II, Section 3 requires the president to deliver a yearly State of the Union address to a joint session of Congress and to articulate his recommendations to Congress "such measures he shall judge necessary and expedient." On the surface, the State of the Union speech given by the president is a ceremonial constitutional requirement of the presidency. Yet, overtime the president's annual message has become a "media event." The pomp and circumstance of the federal government is on parade from the official announcement of the president's entrance to the chamber. By tradition, the president hands a copy of his speech to both the Speaker of the House and the vice president who are seated behind the president. The media focuses on who the First Lady is sitting next to and, of course, what she is wearing. Commentators report whether the president's speech is well received by the members of the House and Senate. Throughout the speech, they note if the president receives spontaneous interruptions of applause or polite silence. The cameras will pan the audience, highlighting the president's supporters and, of course, those of the opposition party who sit in silence. At Trump's last State of the Union message, the media noted that Congresswomen regardless of party lines, were sitting together. All were wearing white in honor of the 100th anniversary of the passing of the 19th Amendment giving women voting rights. Beginning with President Reagan, the placement of individuals sitting by the First Lady have become focal points of the president's speech. The president makes references to those individuals during the course of delivering the speech by recognizing their accomplishments or using them as examples of the key policy initia-

President Barack Obama shakes hands with Speaker of the House John Boehner before delivering the State of the Union address at the U.S. Capitol in Washington, D.C.
Jan. 25, 2011. White House Photo by Pete Souza

tives the president is placing before Congress. The speech itself outlines the president's legislative message to Congress of what legislative priorities he/she would like for Congress to consider during its upcoming session. After the speech, both the Republicans and Democrats select one of their members to address the nation about the context of the speech. Obviously, the president's political party will praise the speech as one of the best speeches ever delivered, and the other party will criticize almost every word of it. On February 5, 2020, President Trump delivered his final State of the Union speech. What caught the attention of the viewing audience was Speaker of the House Nancy Pelosi tearing up President Trump's speech four times while he was delivering it.

Calling Special Sessions of Congress

Section 3 of Article II of the Constitution grants the president the authority to "convene both Houses, or either of them, and in the case of disagreement between them, with respect to the time of adjournment, he may adjourn them to such time as he shall think proper." Usually, presidents will call special sessions only in times of extreme emergencies or threats confronting the nation. President Roosevelt called a special session after the Japanese attack on Pearl Harbor asking Congress for a declaration of war against Japan and Germany.

THE CREATIVE TOOLS OF THE PRESIDENCY

The Constitution specifically charges the president with the duty of "faithfully" executing all laws passed by Congress. Yet, far too often the wishes of Congress collide with the preferences of the president. The Framers understood that there would be times when both the legislative and executive branches would collide. So, they gave the president both constitutional provisions and by omission of details, wiggle room for presidents to use creative tools to either block congressional actions or to bend them to the president's advantage.

Veto Authority

A president's veto authority is detailed in **Article I, Section** 7 of the Constitution:

> Every bill which shall have passed the House of Representatives and the Senate, shall, before it becomes a law, be presented to the President of the United States; if he approve he shall sign it, but if not he shall return it with objections to that House in which it originated, who shall enter the objections at large on their journal, and proceed to reconsider it. If after such reconsideration two-thirds of that House shall agree to pass the bill, it shall be sent, together with the objections, to the other House, by which likewise be reconsidered, and if approved by two-thirds of that House, it shall become a law. But in all cases the votes of both Houses shall be determined by yeas and nays, and the names of the persons voting for and against the bill shall be entered in the journal of each House respectively. If any bill shall not be returned by the President within ten days (Sundays excepted) after it shall have been presented to him, the same shall be law, in like manner as if he had signed it, unless the Congress by their adjournment prevent its return, in which case it shall not be law."

A Latin word for "I forbid," a **veto** is "a legislative power vested in a chief executive to return a bill unsigned to the legislative body with the reasons for his objections."[50] Whenever a bill is sent to the president for his/her approval, the Constitution gives the chief executive ten days to render his/her decision. If the bill meets the president's needs, the president will sign the bill and return it to Congress. If the president decides to veto the bill, the president must send it back to the House it originated in with stated objections. However, the president's objections must be pertinent to the bill. The president simply cannot say that he/she does not like the legislation. The objections are necessary for Congress to a) understand why the president rejected it and b) if the objections are reasonable, enable Congress to "fix it" with some assurance that if Congress addresses the president's objections by creating a new bill, that the president would approve it. If Congress adjourns before the ten days have expired, the president can use a **pocket veto**, "a special veto power exercised at the end of a legislative session whereby bills not signed by a chief executive die after a specified time."[51]

The Constitution checks a president's veto authority by giving Congress the opportunity to override the veto. It takes a 2/3's vote in both Houses of Congress to initiate an override. The propensity of an override depends upon which political party holds the majority of the seats in each House. For example, if the president's party holds the majority of the seats in both the Senate and the House, a 2/3's majority for an override is possible but not likely. Congressional overrides occur more frequently when the majority of the seats in both or either one of legislative houses is held by the opposition party.

President Andrew Johnson noted that "the veto power enables the people to resist and repeal encroachments in their rights. It had its origin in old Rome and before Christ 497 which would make, since its origin, 2,345 years . . . [The Framers] were in favor of the veto power, as established in the Constitution. James Madison 'the great Apostle of Liberty', exercised this power six times during his eight years' administration. . . . Thus, it will be seen, that from the origin of the government, the veto, as exercised by the executive, is conservative. If it is tyranny to exercise this power, I am willing to abide by it."[52] Johnson used his veto authority twenty-nine times but Congress overrode him fifteen times. The presidents with the most vetoes are Harrison, Grant and the lending vetoing contender is Franklin Roosevelt with 635 vetoes and only nine of them were overridden.[53]

The key to avoiding a veto is to threaten to veto. Advance warning of a potential presidential veto may well move Congress to address the president's concerns in hopes of avoiding a veto! President Taft thought that was a viable option. He noted that "it's an old maxim that there are other ways of killing a cat than by chocking it with butter, and it is a great deal easier . . . to use one's influence with the legislators to prevent objectionable bills passing than it is to wait until they do pass and then veto them."[54] Taft's congressional negotiation skills paid off since he had thirty-nine vetoes with only one overridden by Congress.[55] President George W. Bush was extremely successful in his veto strategy. "He has the smartest, most successful veto strategy of any president in recent history and is rewriting the book on presidential relations with Congress. . . Bush has surprised even his own advisors by vetoing twelve bills so far without Congress overriding him a single time. . . . What sets Bush apart from recent GOP presidents, though, is his success in using the veto—or the threat of one—as a negotiating tool to get concessions from Democrats on bills he is anxious to approve. . . For Bush the veto should not always be considered at the end of a bill's evolution but only part of an ongoing process of compromise."[56] President Cleveland did not agree with Taft's approach. He noted that "the unpleasant incidents which accompany the use of the veto power would tempt its avoidance if such a course did not involve an abandonment of constitutional duty and an assent to legislation for which the Executive is not willing to share the responsibility."[57] In his eight years in the White House, Cleveland voted 684 bills with only seven overridden by Congress.

What the majority of the nation's governors have, and presidents do not, is a **line-item veto**. This veto enables the executive to line out an appropriated budget amount in a bill without actually vetoing the bill. Beginning with President Grant, every president since has pushed Congress to grant the president a line-item veto option. Sponsored by Senators Bob Dole and John McCain, the **Line-Item Veto Act** was passed in 1996. President Clinton was the first president to use it. Hailing it as a plus for the executive branch, Clinton remarked that "from now on, presidents will be able to say 'no' to wasteful spending or tax loopholes, even as they say 'yes' to vital legislation."[58] Clinton's use of the line-item veto was short lived. In a 6-3 ruling the Supreme Court ruled in *Clinton v City of New York* (1998) that the presidential line-item veto was unconstitutional.

Executive Agreements versus Treaties

According to **Article II, Section 2** of the Constitution, the president "shall have power, by and with the consent of the Senate, to make treaties, provided two-thirds of the Senate concur." Beginning with George Washington, the Senate has established the tradition of saving its consent role until after a president's staff have undergone the arduous negotiation process with foreign dignitaries, written

Jimmy Carter and Omar Torrijos signing the Panama Canal Treaty.
June 16, 1978   Photo Credit: Jimmy Carter Library

the document, and publicly witnessed the president affixing his/her signature to the document. The signed document is then presented to the Senate for its 2/3's vote of approval. However, the Senate has taken upon itself to now offer "advice and consent" by changing the wording, amending the document, or completely rejecting it. Woodrow Wilson personally went to France to negotiate the **Treaty of Versailles,** marking the end of World War I. Embedded in the document were his **Fourteen Points.** Wilson truly believed that the best way to avoid war is to bring the warring parties together to meet with arbitrators to reach a peaceful settlement to their grievances. Wilson called for the creation of the **League of Nations**, the model for the United Nations. When he brought back the treaty for Senate approval, he was met with opposition from both sides of the aisle. The Senate refused to ratify the document. Jimmy Carter negotiated with the government of Panama to turn the canal over to the Panamanian government. Built by and operated by the United States for over one hundred years, the canal had lost its usefulness to American shipping interests. The ships simply could no longer carry a heavy cargo through the canal. The Carter administration felt the United States government should no longer manage a canal they could no longer use. The Senate rejected that treaty. His **Strategic Arms Limitation Treaty (SALT II)** failed to win Senate approval. The Senate's refusal to ratify treaties made by its own president, places the president in an embarrassing position. To avoid this from happening, presidents have found a way to bypass the Senate by using an **executive agreement**. As detailed in Chapter 17, these agreements are not subjected to scrutiny of the Senate nor do they require senatorial approval. Does a president have the constitutional authority to bypass Senate ratification of treaties by conducting foreign policy through executive agreements?

Yes, "the executive branch claims four sources of constitutional authority under which the president may enter into executive agreements: (1) the president's duty as chief executive to represent the nation in foreign affairs; (2) the president's authority to receive ambassadors and other public ministers, and to recognize foreign governments; (3) the president's authority as Commander in Chief; and (4) the president's authority to "take care that the laws be faithfully executed."[59] With the passage of the **Logan Act** in 1799, Congress protected the president's authority in conducting foreign affairs by banning private citizens from negotiating their own trade agreements with foreign governments.

The legality of the executive agreement has been upheld in a series of Supreme Court rulings. In *Altman and Company v United States* (1912), the Court ruled that an agreement signed by the president with the French government was a legal document. The right of the president to use executive agreements was confirm by the Court's ruling in *Monaco v Mississippi* (1934). In *United States v Curtiss-Wright Export Corp.* (1936), the Court upheld President Roosevelt's right to ban Curtiss-Wright from selling arms and ammunition directly to the Bolivian and Paraguayan government without consulting the president. Justice Sutherland's opinion stressed that "'the president alone has the power to speak or listen as a representative of the nation.' Congress may provide the president with a special degree of discretion in external matters which would not be afforded domestically. Roosevelt thus had the discretion to determine what impact a certain policy might have on foreign affairs and make decisions accordingly, even had Congress not authorized him."[60] In *United States v Pink* (1942), the Supreme Court's ruling elevated the executive agreement to same status as a treaty under Article VI of the Constitution. In other words, the executive agreement was like a treaty, the supreme law of the land.

Congress has tried with little success to reign in the propensity of presidents to use executive agreements without Congressional approval. In 1950, Senator Bricker of Ohio introduced a proposed constitutional amendment severely limiting a president's use of executive agreements. The amendment stated that "a provision of a treaty which conflicts with this Constitution shall not be of any force or effect; a treaty shall become effective as an internal law in the United States only through legislation which would be valid in the absence of a treaty; [and] Congress shall have power to regulate all executive agreements."[61] The Eisenhower administration contended that this amendment would seriously jeopardize the president's power to conduct foreign affairs and decided to confront Congress over this amendment. "Secretary [of State John Foster] Dulles and other Eisenhower officials rode up to Capitol Hill to appear before a Senate Judiciary subcommittee."[62] Bricker's amendment failed to pass in the Senate by only one vote. In 1969, the Senate Foreign Relations Committee discovered numerous executive agreements signed during several presidential administrations to include a) 1964 agreement promising American military assistance to Thailand in case of an external attack; b) 1964 agreements initiating a secret war in Laos; c) an agreement guaranteeing military supplies and technical assistance to Ethiopia; and d) agreements initiating the installation of 7,000 nuclear warheads in Europe. Congress did pass the **Case-Zablocki Act** limiting the president's use of pure executive agreements along with the requirement that the president must submit to Congress after sixty days any executive agreement not deemed a threat to national security. With its power of the purse, Congress can refuse to appropriate funds for any executive agreement. Furthermore, future presidents do have the authority to nullify executive agreements executed by a previous administration. However, the president still has the upper hand in using executive agreements simply because presidents can bypass Congress by transferring money between allocated funds in his/her foreign policy budget and use unexpended money not returned to Congress for reallocation. In his/her role as Commander in Chief, presidents can declare military armaments obsolete. Now, the president can supply weapons and military supplies to foreign governments without congressional approval.

The first executive agreement was the **Rush-Bagot Agreement** signed by President James Monroe and British authorities calling for the withdrawal of both American and British naval forces from the Great Lakes. Thomas Jefferson did submit an executive agreement after he negotiated the purchase of the Louisiana territory from the French government. In 1940, President Roosevelt used an executive agreement to give the British mothball U.S. destroyers in exchange for strategic British naval stations in the Caribbean. President Kennedy signed a mutual alliance executive agreement with Francis Franco of Spain. This agreement reinforced the spirit of the North Atlantic Treaty Organization by pledging that an attack from a foreign aggressor against Spain constituted an attack against the United States. Because of Franco's support of Nazi Germany during World War II, Spain had been denied NATO membership. All presidents have used executive agreements more frequently than they have used the treaty option.

Executive Orders

An **executive order** is "a rule or regulation, issued by the president, a governor or some administrative authority, that has the effect of a law."[63] Presidents justify their use of executive orders from their constitutional charge to "take care that the laws be faithfully executed" for domestic-related items, the Commander in Chief clause for defense-related items, and their expressed powers granted through congressional statutes. Beginning with George Washington, all presidents have used executive orders far too often to bypass Congress. Presidents believe that the duties assigned to their office demands immediate action as opposed to the more deliberative legislative bodies of the House and Senate whose formal procedures and practices prohibit prompt action. Beginning in 1907, all executive orders are assigned a number and with the passage of the **Federal Register Act** of 1936, executive orders are published in the *Federal Register*, with the exception of those that have "no general applicability and legal effect."[64]

Immediately after the formalities of the inauguration, President Biden signed into law more than two dozen executive orders. His orders regarding the Covid-19 pandemic require that anyone on federal property must wear a mask, follow required physical distancing guidelines and other health measures. He issued an executive order establishing a position of a Covid-19 response coordinator reporting to the executive office. He also rejoined the World Health Organization (WHO), and placed Covid-19 restrictions to include wearing masks for anyone using domestic or foreign transportation systems to include inter-city buses, airplanes, etc. He also issued an executive order providing federal assistance to local school districts to coordinate the timing when schools could return to face-to-face learning. Other executive orders mandated allocation of federal funding to help struggling businesses, especially locally owned ones. The list of executive orders is extensive and far-reaching. Since then, President Biden has had numerous public signings of additional executive orders. Can presidents govern through executive orders? With few legal restrictions, the answer is yes!

During his tenure in the White House, President Franklin Roosevelt signed approximately 3,210 executive orders to include several to seize primary military-related manufacturing plants such as the North American Aviation plant in California, navy contracted shipbuilding companies, and over 4,000 coal companies. Roosevelt justified his actions as the nation's commander in chief. His actions moved Congress to pass the **War Labor Disputes Act** in 1943, giving the president extra legal standing to nationalize these key war-related industries. His Executive Order 8802 established a Committee on Fair Employment Practices to ensure that all federal contractors followed non-discriminatory practices in hiring, firing and promotion of employees. Roosevelt also used an executive order to place Japanese Americans residing on the West Coast into internment camps for the duration of World War II. It was Harry Truman who issued Executive Order 9981 in 1948 that mandated racial integration of the military, opened the doors for minority military personnel to seek promotions to higher ranking positions, and ended racial discrimination in federal employment. President Kennedy created the Peace Corp through his Executive Order 10924. President Johnson issued Executive Order 11246 requiring all federal government contractors to adhere to the nation's affirmative action programs. President Nixon used executive orders to give federal employees the right to join labor unions and created the Federal Labor Relations Council to expand bargaining rights for federal employees.

However, presidents can draw the ire of both Congress and the Supreme Court over the legality of their executive orders. At the height of the Korean War, the nation's major steel mills were on the verge of a nationwide union workers' strike. Obviously, those steel mills were extremely important to the war effort. Without them fully operating, the production of much needed military equipment would come to a grinding halt, placing American troops in grave danger. President Truman issued an executive order demanding that his Secretary of Commerce not only seize but place military personnel in charge of running those steel mills. He justified his actions as commander in chief. He left the door open for Congress to either reverse or endorse his order. Congress opted not to respond. The steel companies immediately obtained an injunction to halt the president's actions. Granted by a federal court, a federal appeals court stayed the injunction. The issue now laid on the shoulders of the Supreme Court. In **Youngstown Sheet and Tube Company v Sawyer** (1952), Justice Black delivered the majority opinion in favor of the Steel Mills, thus rendering Truman's executive order unconstitutional:

> We are asked to decide whether the president was acting within his constitutional power when he issued an order directing the Secretary of Commerce to take possession of and operate most of the Nation's steel mills. . . . The Founders of this Nation entrusted the lawmaking power to the Congress alone in both good and bad times. It would do no good to recall the historical events, the fears of power and the hopes for freedom that lay behind their choice. Such a review would not but confirm our holding that this seizure order cannot stand. The judgment of the District Court is affirmed.[65]

Congress put its own restrictions upon presidents frequently using executive orders to circumvent Congress by reigning in the president's purse strings. "Congress invoked its power of the purse in 1944 by passing the '**Russell Amendment**' to prevent presidents from using appropriated funds to finance agencies created by executive order unless Congress had specifically appropriated for the agency or specifically authorized the expenditure of funds by it."[66] Yet, presidents still find creative ways to bypass Congress. For example, President Ronald Reagan substituted the traditional executive order for national security decision directives which are not required by legislative decree to be published in the *Federal Register*.

Signing Statements

"Presidential **signing statements** are "the official pronouncements issued by the president contemporaneously to the signing of a bill into law that, in addition to commenting on the law generally, have been used to forward the president's interpretation of the statutory language; to assert constitutional objections to the provisions contained therein; and concordantly, to announce that the provisions of the law will be administered in a manner that comports with the administration's conception of the president's constitutional prerogatives."[67] The constitutional basis for this option is questionable. The Constitution itself does not afford the president the authority to use signing statements. Article I states that the

> president "shall sign" a bill of which he approves, while in vetoing a measure the president is required [constitutionally] to return the measure "with his Objections to that House in which It shall have originated." However, presidents have issued such statements since the Monroe Administration, and there is little evidence constitutional or legal support for the provision that the president may be constrained from issuing a statement regarding a provision of the law.[68]

Presidents are constitutionally bound to execute laws passed by Congress. Yet, the wording of the law and the operational definitions of the measure's terms are oftentimes nebulous or omitted from the text. Without proper direction as to the **intent** and **meaning** of a Congressional act, it is up to the implementor, in this case the president, to determine for him/herself the meaning and intent of that law. While other presidents have infrequently used them, the Reagan administration "issued 250 signing statements, 86 of which objected to one or more of the statutory provisions signed into law. George H. W. Bush continued to employ signing statements to further presidential prerogatives, issuing 228 signing statements, 107 of which raise constitutional or legal objections."[69] The Obama administration, however, used them infrequently by issuing 20 signing statements, of which 10 (50 percent) contain constitutional challenges to an enacted statutory provision."[70]

Signing statements are a powerful tool of the presidency. The president oversees all executive branch bureaucratic agencies. It is the president who directs his/her Cabinet officers on how the president wishes a legislative act to be enforced. In turn, directives from those Cabinet officers filter down to the bureaucrats who are now charged with implementing legislative acts. If Congress views that the president's intent on the implementation of a law is flawed, the only action Congress can take is to either pass corrective legislation or to rely upon the federal courts to render the president's interpretation and implementation of that law as an unconstitutional breach of presidential authority.

Executive Privilege

Executive privilege is "the right of executive officials to refuse to appear before or to withhold information from a legislative committee or a court."[71] Although not specifically addressed in the Constitution, executive privilege is an implied power of the presidency. The very nature of the job exposes the president to extremely sensitive information. The very conversations within the Oval Office are very sensitive within themselves and should be granted the protection of remaining behind close doors. Confidential conversations within the walls of the Oval Office should not be the topic of the evening news.

Presidents will complain about Congress's investigative tactics, but they begrudgingly comply. The question becomes as to what documents Congress can reasonably request from the president. In *Barenblatt v United States* (1959), the Supreme Court ruled against Barenblatt's contention that the First Amendment guarantees protection against government inquiries of one's political beliefs. In this case, Barenblatt refused to answer questions about his political affiliation (Communist Party) before the House Un-American Activities Committee (HUAC). This ruling in this case is problematic whenever an employee or any officer of a government agency under the executive branch is confronted with testifying before a congressional investigative committee. The only exception is that "Congress cannot inquire into matters which are within the exclusive province of one of the other branches of government."[72]

However, Congress does have the authority to investigate the executive branch for malfeasance. Congress can and does conduct both public and private hearings and request documents from the executive branch. Executive privilege, however, is not absolute. An ardent supporter of executive privilege, President Andrew Jackson "told Congress that if it could point to any case where there is the slightest reason to suspect corruption or abuse of trust, no obstacle which I can remove shall be interposed to prevent the fullest scrutiny by all legal means. The offices of all departments will be opened to you, and every proper facility furnished for this purpose."[73]

President Nixon, however, thought otherwise. The Congressional investigation into Watergate became a legal battle between Congress and the executive branch over the reach of executive privilege. Not only did Nixon withhold key evidence, he tried to prevent any member of his inner circle from testifying before Congress. He claimed that executive privilege extended not only to the president but to the staff of the White House Office. In *U.S. v Nixon* (1974), the Supreme Court ruled against Nixon. Faced with the inevitability of Congress conducting a widespread investigation, Nixon opted to resigned.

Presidential Immunity

Although the Senate acquitted President Trump from charges in inciting the insurrection and the mob attack of the Capitol on January 6, 2021, the question remains as to whether or not he will be subjected to potential civil and criminal litigation. "Presidential immunity was singled out for special protection in *Nixon v Fitzgerald* (1982) when the Supreme Court held that the president is entitled to absolute immunity in civil suits regarding all his official acts. This immunity is 'rooted in the constitutional tradition of the separation of power.' Personal vulnerability to suits for civil damages, said the Court, 'could distract a president from his public duties.'"[74] Yet, for President

Trump several questions remain about the extent of his immunity. Was the speech he delivered on January 6, an "official act"? Secondly, as the individuals arrested for their actions in the Capitol go to trial, their defense may be that the president's words before and during the event led them to their violent acts. Can the president be called upon to give a deposition? And can the victims of the attack file a civil suit against him?

These questions were partially answered by the Supreme Court's ruling in ***Mississippi v Johnson*** (1857). The issue before the Court involved President Andrew Johnson's order placing the former confederate states under federal authority. The Radical Republican Congress passed a bill calling for the southern states to be divided into five military districts. Johnson vetoed the bill, but Congress overrode his veto. The governor of Mississippi filed the suit challenging the federal government's actions. He charged that the Constitution's charge was to govern over people, not states. Although the Supreme Court passed on this case by declaring it a political question, Justice Salmon Chase noted that the Court's decision "made clear that not only did the president not enjoy absolute immunity from lawsuits but that the decision did not cut off the avenue to the court for those convinced a law is unconstitutional. Chase's assurance: Aggrieved citizens cannot ask judges to stop the president from enforcing the law, but if *after the fact* that enforcement causes a party injury, that party can go to court to challenge its constitutionality."[75]

Political Persuasion

Presidents can indirectly persuade Congress to abide by their wishes by encouraging the public to voice their displeasure with Congress. While early presidents opted not to use that tactic, Theodore Roosevelt and Woodrow Wilson sought public support whenever Congress strayed from their agendas. Wilson not only made numerous public speeches, "he also invented the press conference so that he could exercise similar influence without leaving Washington" or his own office.[76] Wilson commented that "publicity is one of the purifying elements of politics. . . Nothing checks all the bad practices of politics like public exposure. . . . An Irishman, seen digging around the wall of a house, was asked what he was doing. He answered, 'Faith, I am letting the dark out of the cellar.' Now, that is exactly what we want to do."[77] For Wilson, the "dark of the cellar" was aimed at those members of the House and the Senate who stood in his way. Franklin Roosevelt used his famous "fireside chats" to pull the public into supporting his New Deal legislation and his lead-lease program to aid the British prior to the United States' entry into World War II. Harry Truman compared going public to a military mission:

> The maneuvers in a battle are like the man in politics. In the military they have . . . a five-paragraph order. In the first paragraph—You make an estimate of the enemy, his condition and what he can do. In the second . . . —You make an estimate of your condition and what you can do. In the third . . . —You decide what you are going to do. In the fourth . . . —You set up your logistics and supply sources to *carry* out what you are going to do. In the fifth, —You tell *where* you are going to be so that everybody can reach you. That is all there is to politics.[78]

President Biden has signaled that he wants to have periodic televised "chats" with the American people to keep them in-the-loop of his legislative agenda and policy proposals. Presidents want to drive home the point that it is them and not Congress that have your best interests at heart. Whenever this nation faces a crisis, the public turns to the president for comfort, assurance of safety, and answers. They rarely, if at all, call their congressperson.

Behind closed doors, presidents will hold sessions with both those whose votes he/she can count on and, most importantly, those congresspersons who need to be reminded that they need to support their president. No president was better at twisting arms of the reluctant than Lyndon Baines Johnson. He adhered to the principle that "if you're in politics and you can't tell when you walk into a room who's for you and who's against you, then you're in the wrong line of work."[79] Presidents remind lawmakers that come election time, a friendly visit from the resident of the White House will draw crowds. A few supporting words from a president can definitely help their re-election chances. And conversely, a president's words aimed that those who opt not to support him/her can seriously jeopardize one's political future.

REMOVAL FROM OFFICE

Temporary Removal

On October 1919, newspapers across the country ran bold headlines that President Wilson was seriously ill and unable to make public appearances. The seriousness of the president's illness was kept under wraps by his wife Edith Wilson and his personal physical Dr. Cary T. Grayson for several days until Grayson finally announced that Wilson had suffered a paralyzing stroke. Logically, his Vice President Thomas Marshall should have immediately assumed the presidency. Yet, Wilson was physically unable to write or to even sign his registration letter. Marshall insisted that "the only way he would step in would be if Congress were to declare Wilson incapacitated and then only if Edith Wilson and Grayson went along. . . . The Constitution prescribed no method for removing a disabled president. The decision rested with the incumbent, and the incumbent Wilson showed no desire to step aside."[80] Without consulting Congress, Edith Wilson "made two fateful choices following the onset of her husband's illness. She refused to disclose the true nature of the President's condition to the public, and she restricted access to visitors and information."[81] It was business as usual with the vice president doing his job while Mrs. Wilson was dutifully acting as president upon supposedly, her husband's directives. She was also the 'gatekeeper' since she "withheld anything even the daily papers, that she feared might trouble him."[82]

Franklin Roosevelt suffered from the crippling effects of polio long before he assumed the presidency. Yet, he too suffered from periodic illnesses. The picture of Roosevelt at the Yalta Conference clearly shows his declining health. President Kennedy had severe back-related ailments. Yet, there was still no provision to cover presidential disability until 1967, when Congress adopted the **25th Amendment** to the Constitution. It calls for the vice president to assume the office of the presidency upon the removal of the president upon his/her death or resignation. The amendment addresses the temporary removal of a president. The president in writing will indicate when he/she in unable to execute their duties. The vice president will be the acting president until the president indicates that he/she is able to resume their duties. President Reagan turned over his presidential duties to his vice president during his recovery from injuries suffered from Charles Hinckley's attempted presidential assassination. The tradition holds that whenever the president undergoes a medical procedure, he/she officially assigns their duties to the vice president.

Section 4 of the Amendment addresses the Wilson problem. If the president refuses to resign due to a physical or mental incapacitation, the vice president or a majority of the "principal officers of the executive departments" can send a written request to both the President Pro Tempore of the Senate and the Speaker of the House recommending the removal of the president. The vice president will assume the presidential duties until the president notifies both the President Pro Tempore of the Senate and the Speaker of the House that he/she can reassume their duties. Yet, if the vice president and the executive officers believe that the president is still unable to perform his/her duties, then Congress makes the decision. The amendment clearly states that "if the Congress, within twenty-one days after receipt of the latter written declaration, or if Congress is not in session, within twenty-one days after Congress is required to assemble, determines that by two-thirds vote of both Houses that the president is unable to discharge the powers and duties of his office, the Vice President shall continue to discharge the same as Acting President." To date, no president has been removed from office under the 25th Amendment. However, Don Regan, Reagan's White House Chief of Staff from 1985-87, revealed that there was concern among Reagan's cabinet members that the president was suffering from the early signs of Alzheimer's disease and was too mentally incapacitated to remain in office. There was also pressure put upon Vice President Mike Pence to consider invoking the 25th Amendment to remove President Trump from the Oval Office.

Impeachment

Impeachment is "a formal accusation, rendered by the lower house of a legislative body, that commits an accused civil official for trial in the upper house."[83] **Article II, Section 4** of the Constitution states that "the President, Vice President and all civil officers of the United States shall be removed from office on impeachment for, and on conviction of, treason, bribery, or other high crimes and misdemeanors." While the attention is focused on the presidency, all federal judges and civil officials of the United States government can be impeached from their respective benches and offices. "In the national government, constitutional authority to *impeach* is vested in the House and the power to *try* impeachment cases rests with the Senate."[84] **Article I, Section 3** of the Constitution details the impeachment process. The House conducts the initial investigation of an official's perceived illegal and/or unacceptable behavior or actions. The articles of impeachment are drawn up by a House committee. If the committee approves the charges, the articles are then presented to the full House. With a majority vote, the officeholder is impeached, and the articles of impeachment are forward to the Senate for trial. The Constitution stipulates that the Chief Justice of the Supreme Court will be the presiding judge over Senate impeachment trials. A two-thirds majority of members present is required for a conviction. Once convicted, the Senate will vote on the actions to be taken. The options are limited to removing the individual from their office and secondly, prohibiting that individual from seeking public office. According to the Constitution, impeach-

Prime Minister of Israel, Yitzhak Rabin, President Clinton, and Yasser Arafat, chairman of the Palestine Liberation Organization, shaking hands in an electrifying ceremony. September 1993. Photo credits: Clinton Presidential Materials Project

ment does not exempt the convicted individual from facing indictment, trial, possible conviction, and punishment in a court of law. To date, the House of Representatives have impeached three presidents—Andrew Johnson, William Jefferson Clinton, and Donald Trump. All of them have been acquitted by the Senate.

On February 24, 1868, the House of Representatives voted for the first time to impeach a sitting president—**Andrew Johnson**. In his 1860 bid for the White House, Lincoln selected Hannibal Hamlin as his running mate. But in his re-election bid, Lincoln selected Johnson, a southern Democrat as his vice president. Born in North Carolina in 1808, Johnson was raised in poverty. Both of his parents were illiterate. At a young age, Johnson was apprenticed and indentured to a tailor. He subsequently moved to Tennessee and opened his own tailor business. Despite these obstacles, Johnson's political career is impressive—elected to both the House of Representatives and the United States Senate in the 1840s and 50s. When Tennessee opted to succeed from the Union, Johnson remained in the Senate. In 1862 President Lincoln appointed Johnson as the Military Governor of Tennessee. In 1864, the Republicans of the National Union Party nominated the Lincoln/Johnson ticket for the White House. With the assassination of Lincoln in 1865, Johnson became president. The Congressional Radical Republicans led by Thaddeus Stevens and Benjamin Butler pushed for the passage of the **Reconstruction Acts** that granted voting rights to former slaves and prohibited former Confederates from public office. Johnson, however, favored Lincoln's reconstruction plan of bringing the Confederate states back into the union as quickly and as humanely possible. As the Radical Republican Congress passed a cadre of harsh Reconstruction Acts, Johnson tried his best to block their implementation. Johnson and the Radical Republicans were at loggerheads with each other. With every punitive law, Johnson opted to stall the implementation or to out right veto the laws, only to have Congress override his vetoes. In 1866, Congress passed a civil rights act granting citizenship to former slaves. Johnson once again vetoed the bill but Congress overrode his veto.

Johnson also had clashes with Lincoln's Secretary of War—Edwin M. Stanton. In 1867, Congress passed the **Tenure of Office Act**, prohibiting the president from removing any civil officer without the Senate's consent. Johnson, of course, vetoed the act but Congress overrode his veto. While Congress was on recess, Johnson fired Stanton and replaced him with Ulysses Grant, a direct violation of the Tenure of Office Act. Once back in session, Congress reinstated Stanton, and Grant resigned. Johnson retaliated and, once again, fired Stanton who locked himself in his office and refused to leave. Congress had had enough. On February 24, 1868, the House of Representatives formally charged Johnson of violating the Tenure of Office Act, citing Johnson for "bringing into disgrace, ridicule, hatred, contempt, and reproach the Congress of the United States."[86] By a vote of 126 to 47, Johnson was impeached. The Senate trial began on March 4, 1868. Johnson opted to try to save his presidency. The Senators were "impressed with Johnson's good behavior during the trial. . . He promised to enforce the Reconstruction Acts and to give no more speeches attacking Congress. He also appointed a man well-liked by most Republicans, General John M. Schofield, as the new Secretary of War."[87] Only one vote in the Senate saved Johnson from being convicted and removed from office. However, for the rest of his tenure in the White House, the Radical Republicans continued to pass Reconstruction legislation that Johnson vetoed but Congress overrode.

In 1998, the news media was having a field day covering the extra martial affair President **Bill Clinton** had with Monica Lewinsky, a White House intern. Kenneth Starr had been tasked with investigating the Clintons' involvement in Whitewater, an unsuccessful Arkansas land development project. Starr began to hear rumors about the Clinton affair and decided to investigate it. On August 17, 1998, Clinton faced a grand jury investigation of his affair. Monica Lewinsky provided detailed facts about her sexual affair with the president. Clinton, however, downplayed the affairs and basically lied to the grand jury. Starr responded to Clinton's testimony by sending a detailed report to the House of Representatives alleging "grounds for impeaching Clinton for lying under oath [to a federal grand jury], obstruction of justice, abuse of power and other offenses."[87] On a partisan vote, the House Judiciary Committee sent to the House floor two articles of impeachment, "charging the president with perjury in his grand jury testimony and obstructing justice in his dealings with various potential witnesses."[88] The House voted to impeach him. In January 1999, the Senate began its phase of the impeachment process. Since the Democrats held the majority in the Senate, a conviction was not likely. Clinton was acquitted but "those voting against impeachment argued that the president's actions constituted 'low' and tawdry actions involving private matters, not 'high crimes and misdemeanors' amounting to offenses against the state."[89]

President Donald Trump will bear the dubious distinction of being impeached twice by the House of Representatives. On December 18, 2019, the House adopted two impeachment articles against Trump: abuse of power and obstruction of Congress. The articles were based on the allegations that Trump illegally solicited the Ukrainian government's support of his 2016 election bid. Furthermore, Trump was accused of pressuring the Ukrainian government by withholding much needed military aid and refusing to host the Ukrainian president for the White House visit into investigating Hunter Biden's business dealings with the Ukrainian government. The obstruction of Congress charge centered on the Trump administration's ignoring subpoenas by the House Judiciary Committee for documents and refusing to testify during hearings. The House voted to impeach him on both charges. However, the Senate voted to acquit him on both charges. The second House impeachment charge was incitement of insurrection for the January 6, 2021, riot and break-in into the Capitol building causing extensive property damage and the death of five individuals to include a Capitol police officer. The article of impeachment was sent to the Senate. The Senate voted to acquit him.

Saved by a presidential pardon, President **Richard Nixon** faced impeachment and possible criminal charges for his administration's involvement in the **Watergate** scandal. The Watergate Hotel was the headquarters for the Democratic National Committee (DNC). Although denying that he ordered it, on June 17, 1970, five men were caught in the act of breaking into the DNC offices with the intent of stealing documents and planting bugging devices throughout the offices. Nixon's paranoia led him to believe that key government agencies and interest groups were conspiring against him to ruin his presidency. The downfall of Nixon was that his paranoia drove him to tape almost every conversation that occurred in the Oval Office. Nicknamed the Watergate tapes, the recordings revealed that "in the summer of 1971, Nixon was convinced that classified documents had been spirited out of the State Department and locked up at the Brookings Institution, a liberal think tank."[90] The tapes revealed that Nixon ordered a break-in to retrieve those documents. When issued a subpoena for the tapes, Nixon refused claiming executive privilege. In *U.S. v Nixon*, the Supreme Court ruled against Nixon's claim of executive privilege. The House Judiciary Committee charged Nixon with three impeachable offenses: obstruction of justice into the Watergate burglary investigation, abuse of power by using federal law enforcement and intelligence agencies for his own political purposes, and contempt of Congress for his refusal to comply with the Judiciary Committee's subpoenas. Nixon resigned before the House could impeach him. Years later Nixon's legal counsel John Dean pointed out that "the lesson of Watergate is don't get caught if you abuse power, and if you cannot, your abuses, as several Nixon successors have shown, simply tell the world you are using your power for the good of America, and act like you mean it. That will sound cynical, but it is the sad truth."[91]

THREATS AGAINST THE PRESIDENT

Unfortunately, every elected official whether it be a mayor or the President of the United States is confronted with the reality that he/she will please some but disappoint many. These are high-profile jobs that can place the officeholder in a precarious position. Death threats are more common than we would like to think. Ironically, President Abraham Lincoln did not want an overly protective security force following him around. "I cannot be shut up in an iron cage and guarded. A president must go among the people," Lincoln explained. "One man's life is as dear to him as another's, and if a man takes my life, he may be reasonably sure that he will lose his own." The president thought about assassination, yes, "but I do not believe it is my fate to die in this way!"[92] Even before he took his oath of office, Lincoln received death threats. Samuel Mores Felton, president of the Philadelphia, Wilmington and Baltimore railroad, hired Pinkerton detectives to protect Lincoln as he traveled from Illinois to Washington, D.C. Going undercover, Pinkerton himself discovered a viable plot from a group tied to anti-union and anti-abolitionist causes. The unsuccessful plan was to create a disturbance drawing Lincoln's protection guards away from him, allowing a gunman to kill the president-elect. In 1864, a shot from a long rifle missed Lincoln's head by mere inches as the bullet went through his tall stove-pipe hat. He received a constant barrage of threatening letters. He had an aide go through the mail to remove any disturbing letters from the stack before giving the mail to Mrs. Lincoln. As he was beginning his second term of office, Lincoln was assassinated by John Wilkes Booth at Ford's Theater on April 14, 1865. After Lincoln died, there was an unsuccessful attempt by an anti-union group to kidnap his body and hold it for ransom in exchange for the release of several of the group's incarcerated compatriots.

President James Garfield was assassinated in 1881. On September 6, 1901, President William McKinley paid an official visit to the Pan-American Exposition in Buffalo, New York. Standing in the reception line was Leon Czolgosz, a victim of the nation's recent economic crisis. "President McKinley greeted each person with a warm smile and a handshake. . . One man in line had his hand wrapped in a hankerchief. . . McKinley saw the man's apparent disability and he reached to shake his left hand. Suddenly Leon Czolgosz thrust his bandaged right hand into the president's chest. Onlookers heard two sharp popping sounds, like small firecrackers, and a thin veil of gray smoke rose up in front of the president."[93] McKinley suffered two gunshot wounds—one to his shoulder and the other pierced his stomach. Czolgosz was arrested at the scene. Despite efforts to save him,

Swearing in of Lyndon B. Johnson as president, Air Force One, Love Field, Dallas, Texas. November 22, 1963
Photo credit: LBJ Library

McKinley died on September 14, 1901. At his trial, Czolgosz entered a guilty plea and proclaimed that he was an anarchist inspired by Emma Goldman, an outspoken advocate of socialism. He was convicted and executed.

As the television cameras followed the motorcade through the streets of Dallas, millions of Americans watched in horror as shots fired from the Book Depository building fatally struck President John F. Kennedy and seriously wounded Texas Governor John Connally. Equally shocking, television cameras once again provided live coverage of the killing of Kennedy's accused assassin Lee Harvey Oswald by Jack Ruby as Oswald was being transferred to another jail facility.

While four presidents have been assassinated, others have been the targets of attempted assassinations. In 1835, Richard Lawrence, a house painter, attempted to assassinate President Andrew Jackson. His pistols, however, misfired. Jackson beat him with his cane. Lawrence was found not guilty by reason of insanity. In 1912, former President Theodore Roosevelt was seeking a third presidential term as a candidate of the Progressive Party. While on a campaign stop in Milwaukee, Wisconsin, John Flammang Schrank shot Roosevelt in the chest. Schrank, a New York saloon-keeper, stalked Roosevelt for weeks. Roosevelt's life was saved by his folded speech tucked in his suit pocket. "X-rays determined that the bullet had lodged in a rib. It would remain there for the rest of his life."[94] Schrank was declared insane and institutionalized. March 30, 1981, President Ronald Reagan was shot by John Hinckley Jr. Reagan was returning to his motorcade after delivering a speech at the Washington Hilton Hotel. Reagan was seriously wounded along with three other members of his party. Arrested, Hinckley was declared insane and institutionalized until his release in 2016.

Secret service agents subdue John Hinkley after he had shot President Reagan. Press Secretary James Brady and patrolman Thomas Delahanty lie on the ground after being hit by the gunfire. In all, Hinkley fired six shots before being subdued.

In November 1948, President Harry Truman and the first lady had to relocate to the Blair House while the White House residency was undergoing renovations. On November 1, 1950, Griselio Torresola and Oscar Collazo approached the Blair House from two different directions, opening fire on the Secret Service agents and the White House police guarding the residence. Both men were members of a volatile Puerto Rican Nationalist Party. Collazo had left Puerto Rico and moved to New York. Torresola was a felon released from a federal prison. Both men entered the House, killing one of the guards. Torresola was killed and Collazo was arrested. Given the death penalty, Truman commuted his sentence to life in prison. He was released from prison in 1979 by President Carter. On September 5, 1975, President Gerald Ford was approached by Lynette "Squeaky" Fromme, a follower of mass-murderer Charles Manson. She attempted to shoot Ford with an unloaded gun. Restrained by Secret Service, she was sentence to life in prison. Just seventeen days later, Sara Jane Moore actually fired a revolver at Ford. A bystander grabbed the gun as she was firing it. The bullet hit a building, not the president. She was sentence to life in prison.

President Nixon was the target of at least three serious attempts on his life. In one situation, the gunman hijacked a DC-9 from the Baltimore-Washington International Airport after he killed a FAA police officer and both pilots. The gunman killed himself. Bill Clinton received five major threats and Obama received numerous death threats to include a lone gunman firing several rounds at the White House with a semi-automatic rifle, a letter laced with ricin, and a package containing a fabricated pipe bomb. President Trump received several letters with ricin and crushed castor beans.

The Secret Service

Founded in 1865, the Secret Service of today began as an agency under the Department of the Treasury tasked with investigating counterfeiting. By 1867, their responsibilities centered on investigating fraud schemes against the government, the Ku Klux Klan, smugglers, mail robbers and other infractions against the federal government. By 1894, the Secret Service provided part-time protection for President Grover Cleveland. With the assassination of President William McKinley in 1901, Congress gave the Secret Service the responsibility of providing full-time security details for the president. By 1908, protection was extended to the president-elect. After the failed assassination attempt against President Truman, the Secret Service was charged with protecting not only the president but members of his immediate family and the vice president. Today, Secret Service protection is provided to the president and his immediate family members, the vice president and his/her immediate family members, the president and vice-president elect, and life-time protection to former presidents and their wives. Minor children of a former president are granted protection until they reach 16 years of age. Secret Service protection is automatically provided to the candidate and spouse of a major presidential or vice-presidential candidate.

THE VICE PRESIDENT

Article II, Section 2 of the Constitution details the job description of the "number two" top executive position—the vice president. The Article states "in case of the removal of the President from office or his death, resignation, or inability to discharge the power and duties of the said office, the same shall devolve on the Vice President . . ." Other than meeting the same qualifications as a presidential candidate, Article II provides no duties for the vice president other than be in waiting to assume the office if something tragic should befall the president. The only official legislative duty of the vice president is in **Article I, Section 3**: "the Vice President of the United States shall be President of the Senate, but shall have no vote, unless they be equally divided." At the Constitutional Convention, "Ben Franklin thought the appropriate name for the vice president might be 'His Superfluous Excellency.'" President Woodrow Wilson said of the office: 'There is very little to be said about the Vice President . . . his importance consists in the fact that he may cease to be vice president. . . And the chief embarrassment in discussing his office is, that in explaining how little there is to be said about it, one has evidently said all there is to say.'"[95]

The nation's first vice president, John Adams, publicly complained about his salary. He was "offended by his paltry $5,000-a-year salary, which compared miserably with Washington's $25,000."[96] Serving as John Adams' vice president, Thomas Jefferson remarked that the job "will give me philosophical evenings in winter, and rural days in summer."[97] The vice president did not have a office in the White House or an official residence until Jimmy Carter's presidency. Walter Mondale became the first vice president to take up residence in the Blair House. Most vice presidents opted to reside in "their own homes or pursuits to an inconsequential role in Washington, where most VPs lived in boarding houses. Thomas Jefferson regarded his vice presidency as a "tranquil and unoffending station," and spent much of it at Monticello. George Dallas [James Polk's vice president] maintained a lucrative law practice, writing of his official post: "Where is he to go? What has he to do?—No where, nothing." Daniel Tompkins [James Monroe's vice president] a drunken embezzler described as a "degraded sot," paid so little heed to his duties that Congress docked his salary."[98] President Wilson's vice president Thomas Marshall had a guard accompany him on a visit to Colorado. Marshall told his audience that he asked the guard "what he was doing. He said he was guarding my person. I said 'You labor in vain. Nobody was ever crazy enough to shoot at a vice president.'"[99]

Selecting the right person to be "number two" can be a dicey situation. A presidential candidate needs to balance the ticket with someone who he/she believes will be a productive partner respectful of the position they hold. They want a vice presidential candidate who will contribute to his/her presidency, not detract from it. During the Democratic Convention in 1972, presidential candidate George McGovern announced his selection of Thomas Eagleton of Missouri as his running mate. However, reporters leaked Eagleton's mental issues that were so serious that Eagleton had to receive electric shock treatments. McGovern withdrew his name and nominated Sargent Shriver, a Kennedy brother-in-law, as his new running mate. President Richard Nixon thought he had selected the best candidate as his running mate. However, his choice, Spiro Agnew had to resign the vice presidency over allegations that he received kickbacks when he was governor of Maryland. A president needs to pick a vice president who will not embarrass him/her. A well-known politician, Adlai Stevenson was selected by Grover Cleveland as his vice president. Stevenson publicly insulted Cleveland when a reporter asked "if President Cleveland had consulted him about anything of even minor consequence. 'Not yet,' he said. 'But there are still a few weeks of my term remaining.'"[100] Republican presidential contender John McCain selected Sarah Palin as his running mate. The rationale was that by putting a woman on the ticket, the Republican Party would bring more women into their party. Yet, Palin proved to be detriment to McCain's election possibilities.

Once inaugurated, the vice president is oftentimes ignored by the White House inner circle or becomes the victim of public ridicule. "Lyndon Johnson feuded with the Kennedys and their aids, who called him 'Uncle Cornpone.' . . . Nelson Rockefeller, given little but ceremonial duties by President Ford, said of his job: 'I go to funerals. I go to earthquakes.' Dick Cheney shot a friend in the face during a hunting outing."[101] Perhaps the one vice president who was the bashing target of evening news commentators and late night TV hosts more so than his fellow vice presidents was Dan Quayle, George H. W. Bush's vice president. One of his malapropisms entered *Bartlett's Familiar Quotations*: "What a waste it is to lose one's mind. Or not to have a mind is being very wasteful."[102] Quayle was noted for his misspelling of potato and his failed attempts at humor.

Perhaps the worst part of the job is the lack of playing an active role in the day-to-day operations of the presidency. Imagine the fate of John Tyler. He was elected as William Henry Harrison's vice president. Harrison died one month after taking the oath of office. Members of Harrison's Whig Party did not want Tyler to become president. They wanted the office to remain vacant with the Cabinet governing the country. Tyler instead "took matters into his own hands. He ordered a judge to administer the presidential oath to him. There was nothing in the Constitution to argue either for or against this maneuver."[103] Until 1974, a vice president was usually excluded from daily presidential briefings, Cabinet meetings, and matters of national security. They were not required to attend those briefings. They had to be invited to attend! During the Cuban Missile Crisis, President Kennedy turned to his brother Attorney General Robert Kennedy, his secretaries of State, and Defense, not Vice President Lyndon Johnson. Equally left out of the loop, Harry

Kamala Harris is an American politician and attorney serving as the 49th vice president of the United States. She is the United States' first female vice president, the highest-ranking female official in U.S. history, and the first African American and first Asian American vice president.

Truman became president only eighty-three days after he took the oath of the office for the vice presidency. When he walked into the Oval Office as president, Truman said that he "felt like the moon, stars and all the planets had fallen on me. It felt as if I had lived five lifetimes in my first five days as President. . . I was beginning to realize how little the Founding Fathers had been able to anticipate the preparations necessary for a man to become president so suddenly. It's a mighty leap from the vice presidency to the presidency when one is forced to make it without warning."[104] Truman remedied this problem when he was elected to his own term as president. He had his vice president Albert Barkley assigned a seat on National Security Council, a place at regularly scheduled Cabinet meetings, raised Barkley's salary, and commissioned an official seal and flag for the vice presidency.

Once a vice president becomes president, there is no constitutional requirement to replace the vice president's position until the passage of the **25th Amendment** in 1967. When he assumed the presidency, President Gerald Ford appointed former New York Governor Nelson Rockefeller as his vice president.

The focus is on the president, not the vice president. Like Prince Philip, the Queen of England is his wife, but she is his monarch. Officially, he always walks behind her. The same holds true for a vice president—one step or more behind the president he/she serves. Vice presidents do not assume the limelight unless their president allows them to. The relationship is, however, a two-way street. Presidents need the respect of their vice presidents. For example, Herbert Hoover selected Charles Curtis as his running mate. His political credentials were impressive: elected to the Senate from Kansas he was the current Senate Majority Leader. Curtis was a member of the Kaw Nation, raised on the reservation. Interesting to note, Native Americans were given voting rights in 1925, just in time to cast their ballots in the upcoming 1928 election. Hoover won the election. But in his inaugural address, he never mentioned Curtis, who became the nation's first vice president of color.

It is incumbent for a president to train his/her vice president to assume the presidency on a moment's notice. The transition of power between an incumbent president and his/her vice president is tragic and sad. A nation will mourn the loss of a sitting president. But they do expect that the vice president is readily available, knowledgeable about the job, and capable of carrying out the responsibilities of the presidency.

CONCLUSIONS—DO WE HAVE AN IMPERIAL PRESIDENCY?

The answer is no! Every president has tried at times to circumvent the legislative branch. It is the nature of the power struggle between the executive and legislative branches. Yet, the Nixon administration's attempt to flex its muscle went beyond the usual wrangling for power between the two branches. "The loss in Vietnam and the crime of Watergate gave a bad name to 'national security' and 'executive privilege,' noble phrases Nixon frequently invoked to justify his illegal acts. The scandals had the effect of undermining executive authority—of dismantling what the historian and JFK advisor Arthur Schlesinger Jr., called 'the Imperial Presidency.' Power was, in effect, turned over from its traditional and most forceful executors—the White House, the Pentagon, the intelligence agencies to the people and organizations that are supposed to function as a check on power: the courts, the press, congressional watchdog committees. . . But pendulums do swing, especially when they get a hard shove."[105]

"There are cycles in American history—periods of enhanced presidential authority followed by epochs of exalted congressional powers."[106] As the Framers envisioned, the power pendulum will swing back and forth between the legislative and executive branches. But the Framers knew that their concepts of separation of powers and checks and balances would eventually moderate the intensity of the swing. When the presidency oversteps his constitutional authority, it falls upon the Congress to reign it in just as when Congress oversteps into the authority of the presidency, it is the president's responsibility to reign it in.

CHAPTER NOTES

[1]Ron Chernow, "The Reluctant President," *Smithsonian*, Vol. 41, No. 10, February, 2011, 45.

[2]Ibid.

[3]*Treasury of Presidential Quotations*, Caroline Thomas Harnsberger, ed., (Chicago, Illinois: Follette Publishing Company, 1964), 255.

[4]Ibid.

[5]John E. Ferling, "The Evolving Presidency," *American History Illustrated*, Vol. XXIV, No. 2, April, 1989, 13.

[6]*Treasury of Presidential Quotations*, 255.

[7]Louis Brownlow, "What We Expect the President To Do," *The Presidency*, Aaron Wildavsky, ed., (Boston, Massachusetts: Little, Brown and Company, 1969), 35.

[8]*https://www.law.cornell.edu*

[9]*Treasury of Presidential Quotations*, 259.

[10]"As Biden Prays for Healing, Catholics Clash Over President's Faith, *https://www.msn.com*

[11]Stephen E. Ambreose, "Flawed Founders," *Smithsonian*, Vol. 33, No. 8, November, 2002, 131.

[12]*Treasury of Presidential Quotations*, 255.

[13]Ibid., 259.

[14]Ibid., 257.

[15]"FDR's Third-Term Election and the 22nd Amendment," *https://constitutioncenter.org*

[16]Alexander Hamilton, John Jay, James Madison, *The Federalist*, (New York, New York: The Modern Library), 323.

[17]Michael Barone, "Shaping An Office," *US News and World Report*, (December 13, 2004), 42.

[18]*The American Political Dictionary*, Jack C. Plano and Milton Greenburg, eds., (New York, New York: Harcourt, Brace College Publishers, 1957), 203.

[19]*"Approaching the Presidency: Roosevelt & Taft,"* *https://ethnicsunwrapped*

[20]*The American Political Dictionary*, 203.

[21]Ibid., 202.

[22]Jon R. Bond and Keven B. Smith, *The Promise and Performance of American Democracy*, 10th ed., (Belmont, California: Thomson Wadsworth, 2008), 430.

[23]*The American Political Dictionary*, 202.

[24]*Treasury of Presidential Quotations*, 259.

[25]*The Enduring Federalist*, Charles A. Beard, ed., (New York, New York: Frederick Ungar Publishing Company, 1964), 282-283.

[26]Louis Fisher, *Constitutional Conflicts Between Congress and the President*, 5th ed., (Lawrence, Kansas: University of Kansas Press, 2007), 23.

[27]*Treasury of Presidential Quotations*, 206.

[28]Ibid., 13.

[29]Ibid., 206.

[30]Norman Ornstein and Thomas Donilon, "The Confirmation Clog," *Foreign Affairs*, Vol. 79, No. 6, November/December, 2000), 90.

[31]Ibid.

[32]Ibid., 88.

[33]Ibid., 89.

[34]*The American Political Dictionary*, 205.

[35]Richard Brookhiser, "Bucking the Boss," *American History*, Vol. 53, No. 6, February, 2019, 16.

[36]Ibid.

[37]Gilbert King, "The Stalking of the President," *Smithsonian*, Vol. 42, No. 10, January 12, 2012, 1.

[38]Harry J. Maihafer, "Message to MacArthur," *American History*, Vol. 33, No. 2, May/June, 1996, 30.

[39]Ibid.

[40]Ibid., 28.

[41]Fisher, 250.

[42]Ibid.

[43]Anthony Brandt, "Rye Whiskey, Rye Whiskey," *American History*, Vol. 49, No. 3, August, 2014, 46.

[44]*The American Political Dictionary*, 195.

[45]Joseph Connor, "Power of the Pardon," *American History*, Vol. 53, No. 1, April, 2018, 43.

[46]Ibid., 47.

[47]"Number of Pardons by President," *https://www.thoughco.com*

[48]Joseph Connor, 43.

[49]Ibid.

[50]*The American Political Dictionary*, 195.

[51]Ibid., 196.

[52]*Treasury of Presidential Quotations*, 349.

[53]"U.S. Senate: Vetoes 1789 to Present," *https://www.senate.gov*

[54]*Treasury of Presidential Quotations*, 350.

[55]"U.S. Senate: Vetoes 1789 to Present" *https://www.senate.gov*

[56]"Bush's Veto Strategy," *US News and World Report*, (July 2, 1990), 18.

[57]*Treasury of Presidential Quotations*, 350.

[58]"Line-Item Veto: Why the U.S. President Does Not Have This Power," *https://www.thoughtco.com*

[59]Fisher, 242-243.

[60]"*United States v Curtiss-Wright Export Corporation*," *oyez.www.oyez.org/cases*

[61]"National Affairs: The Bricker Amendment: A Cure Worse than the Disease," *https://content/time.com*

[62]Ibid.

[63]*The American Political Dictionary*, 190.

[64]"Executive Orders: The American President Project" *https://www.presidency*

[65]Ralph A. Rossum and G., Alan Tarr, *American Constitutional Law: Cases and Interpretation*, (New York, New York: St. Martin's Press, 1983), 161.

[66]Fisher, 106.

[67]"Presidential Signing Statements: Constitutional and Institutional Implications," *Congressional Research Service*, January 4, 2012, 1. *www.crs.gov*

[68]Ibid.

[69]Ibid.

[70]Ibid.

[71]*The American Political Dictionary*, 191.

[72]Fisher, 178-179.

[73]Ibid., 178.

[74]Ibid., 170.

[75]Daniel B. Moskowitz, "Courting Controversy," *American History*, Vol. 54, No. 6, February, 2020, 23.

[76]Matthew Crenson and Benjamin Ginsberg, "'Because I Said So,'" *American History*, Vol. 41, No. 2, June, 2007, 46.

[77]*Treasury of Presidential Quotations*, 243.

[78]Ibid., 244.

[79]Ibid., 245.

[80]Joseph Connor, "Big Lie," *American History*, Vol. 52, No. 2, June, 2017, 36-37.

[81]Colleen Roche, "American Biography: Edith Gault Wilson," *American History*, Vol. 39, No. 5, December, 2004, 70.

[82]Ibid.

[83]*The American Political Dictionary*, 150.

[84]Ibid.

[85]"The Impeachment of Andrew Johnson," *https://www.pbs.org*

[86]Ibid.

[87]Russell Riley, "The Clinton Impeachment and Its Fallout," *https://www.millercenter.org*

[88]Ibid.

[89]Ibid.

[90]Chris Whipple, "Nixon's SOB," *American History*, Vol.5 2, No. 4, October, 2017, 51.

[91]Richard Ernsberger, Jr., "Interview; John W. Dean, Counsel to President Nixon," *American History*, Vol. 48, No. 4, October, 2013, 20

[92]Terry Alford, "The Psychic Connection," *Smithsonian*, Vol. 45, No. 11, March, 2016, 40.

[93]Wyatt Kingseed, "The Assassination of William McKinley," *American History Illustrated*, Vol. XXXVI, No. 4, October, 2001, 25.

[94]Patricia O'Toole, "Assassination Foiled," *Smithsonian*, Vol. 45, No. 11, March, 2016, 40.

[95]Richard Bauman, "'The Worse' Best Job in the United States," *American History*, Vol. 39, No. 3, August, 2004, 52.

[96]Michael Kernan, "In 1789, A Farmer Went to New York to Become President," *Smithsonian*, Vol. 41, No. 10, February, 2011, 51.

[97]Richard Bauman, 52.

[98]Tony Hortwiz, "We're Number 2!," *Smithsonian*, Vol. 43, No. 4, July/August., 2012, 28.

[99]Bauman, 52.

[100]Ibid., 28.

[101]Ibid., 30.

[102]Ibid.

[103]Marty Jones, "The Thirty-One Day Presidency," *American History*, Vol. 41, No. 1, April, 2006, 55.

[104]Bauman, 52.

[105]Evan Thomas, "A Long Shadow," *Newsweek*, (June 13, 2005), 25.

[106]Ferling, 54.

SUGGESTED READINGS

Barber, James David. *The Presidential Character: Predicting Performance in the White House,* 4th ed. Englewood Cliffs, N.J.: Prentice Hall, 1992.

Burns, James MacGregor. *Leadership.* New York: Harpers Perennial, 2010.

Cronin, Thomas E., Michael A. Genovese, and Meenekshi Bose. *The Paradoxes of the American Presidency.* 5th ed. New York: Oxford University Press, 2012.

Greenstein, Fred I. *The Presidential Difference: Leadership Style From F.D.R. to Obama.* Princeton, N.J.: Princeton University Press, 3rd ed., 2009

Hinckley, Barbara. *The Symbolic Presidency: How Presidents Portray Themselves.* New York: Rutledge, 1990.

Kranish Michael, and Marc Fisher. *Trump Revealed: An American Journey of Ambition, Ego, Money and Power.* New York: Scribner, 2016.

Pious, Richard M. *The Presidency.* Boston, Mass.: Allyn and Bacon, 1996.

Schier, Steven., Ed. *Debating The Obama Presidency.* Lanham, MD.: Rowman & Littlefield, 2016.

Schlesinger, Arthur M. Jr. *The Imperial Presidency.* Boston, Mass.: Houghton Mifflin Company, 1973.

Wayne, Stephen J. *Personality and Politics: Obama for and against Himself.* Washington, D.C.: CQPress, 2011.

Chapter Eleven

THE FEDERAL COURT SYSTEM

The necessity of a body of rules and regulations to govern the day-to-day operations of a village, city, town, empire or nation state as well as to set the standards for appropriate behavior of any society is as old as civilization itself. A nation without law is a lawless one, riddled with injustices whereby no one can ever feel secure in their surroundings. It is a truism that governments cannot exist without laws; and laws cannot exist without government to implement and enforce them upon the citizenry.   As Theodore Roosevelt once commented:

> No nation ever yet retained its freedom for any length of time after losing its respect for the law, after losing the law-abiding spirit, the spirit that really makes orderly liberty. . . . No man is above the law and no man is below it; nor do we ask any man's permission when we require him to obey it. Obedience to the law is demanded as a right; not asked as a favor.[1]

This chapter examines the development of law and the impact law has on the American judicial system.

As its 2020 term came to a close, all eyes were focused on the nine justices of the Supreme Court hearing arguments from both sides of issues regarding the future of the "faithless elector" voting in the Electoral College and the Deferred Action for Childhood Arrivals (DACA); the constitutionality of states mandating that physicians performing abortions have admitting privileges to hospitals; whether or not an employer can fire a person based on their gender identity; and the right of a New York grand jury and the United States House of Representatives to demand the release of tax filings and financial records of a sitting president, namely, Donald J. Trump. Most Americans view the Supreme Court as the definitive arm of the federal judiciary system. The media only covers the most controversial cases heard by the Court. This overlooks that at the end of the Court's 2018 term, their caseload increased from 6,315 filings in the 2017 term to 6,442, of which

73 were formally argued before the bench.[2] Yet, this body of justices is just one of the many federal courts that decide both original and appellate jurisdiction cases. In turn, the caseload before these courts is staggering. The 2019 docket revealed that 48,486 cases were filed with the thirteen federal appellate courts, 297,877 civil cases and 92,678 criminal cases with the U.S. District Courts, and 776,674 in the U.S. Bankruptcy Courts.[3] Behind the scenes are the numerous individuals employed in the investigation of federal criminal and civil offenses. Comprised of forty separate organizations under its umbrella, the United States Department of Justice employs over 113,000 employees operating under a $39.8 billion budget for fiscal year 2019.[4] This chapter examines the federal justice system beginning with the investigation and gathering of evidence phase to the final decision rendered by the juries and judges.

LAW—THE GUIDING PRINCIPLE OF JUSTICE

Law is simply "a body of rules enacted by public officials in a legitimate manner and backed by the force of the state."[5] The importance of law cannot be underestimated. A Roman jurist and noted statesman, Cicero (106-43 B.C.) wrote that:

> law is the highest reason, implanted in Nature, which commands what ought to be done and forbids the opposite . . . the origin of justice is to be found in law, for law is it's natural force; it is the mind and reason of the intelligent man, the standards by which justice and injustice are measured.[6]

However, there is no universal or standard body of law applicable to all of mankind. Each society has had to develop its own body of laws. A nation's set of laws is unique to that nation, perhaps the ultimate embodiment of that particular nation's history, social mores and folkways, cultural perspectives, moral values, religious perspectives, and political viewpoints. Throughout many nations in the Middle East, the development of their laws and legal systems is directly tied to Islam for there is no separation of church and state. In the United States, separation of church and state means that while religious values and morals are important to the American people, they are not the driving force in the creation of the laws that rule over them. In addition, the degree of enforcement of law varies from nation state to nation state. For example, the United States imposes the death penalty for heinous criminal acts while many other nations have either abolished the death penalty or never imposed it in the first place.

Laws are only meaningful if all members subject to the laws have a clear understanding of the nature of the laws, the criteria for obedience of those laws, and the penalties for one's disobedience. "Law comprises three basic elements—force, official authority, regularity—the combination which differentiates law from mere custom or morals in a society."[7] The legitimacy of any government, regardless of the political philosophy underlying it, must have the ability to both make and enforce laws. In 1923, President Warren G. Harding told a crowded audience that "laws, of course, represent restrictions upon individual liberty, and in these very restrictions make liberty more secure."[8] People respect their nation's right to make laws if that government, in turn, makes sure their laws are both necessary and reasonable. President Calvin Coolidge reminded members of the Massachusetts state assembly that "men do not make laws. They do but discover them. Laws must be justified by something more than the will of the majority. They must rest on the eternal foundation of righteousness."[9] In 1912, President Woodrow Wilson reemphasized that the purpose of laws was "not to guide the strong, but to protect the weak. Law is meant more for the beginners in every enterprise than for those who have achieved. Law is beckoning on the future generations, heartening them, cheering them."[10]

Of equal importance, governments must enforce those laws in an equitable, fair, and consistent manner. As evidenced in Chapters 12 and 13, the United States Supreme Court's docket is filled with cases focusing on laws that are claimed to be procedurally and substantially questionable. Justice is not served when laws are vaguely written and enforced unfairly and unequally. The statute in front of the United States Supreme Court building in Washington, D.C., depicts Lady Justice. She wears a blindfold over her eyes to remind everyone that in the eyes of the law, everyone is equal regardless of who you are and what status you hold in society.

Codification of Law

In the ancient world, the growth of villages, towns and cities mandated a higher authority to make and enforce rules upon the citizenry. The Sumerians developed a rudimentary code of laws. The credit for the initial codification of those laws belongs to Babylonian King Hammurabi who compiled a concise listing of over 282 laws. The Babylonian empire had a strict system of justice, oftentimes not equally applied. "A crime against a member of the upper class (a noble) by a member of the lower class (a commoner) was punished more severely than the same offense against a member of the lower class."[11] Well known for its emphasis of "an eye for an eye," the Code's punishments were harsh. For example, according to No. 25: "if fire broke out in a free man's house and a free man, who went to extinguish it, cast his eye on the goods of the owner of the house and has appropriated the goods of the owner of the house, that free man shall be thrown into that fire."[12] Justinian (527-565), Emperor of the Eastern Roman Empire, codified Roman law into the *Corpus Luris Civilis* (Latin for *The Body of Civil Law*).

In 1066, William the Conqueror of Normandy successfully invaded and conquered Great Britain. He soon discovered that British laws were haphazardly applied for the same crime depending upon the shire in which the crime was committed. He codified these laws and standardized the penalties. Kings Henry I and Henry II continued the codification process. Consequently, "the term 'common' law was used for the law developed in the King's Courts and was generally employed in order to distinguish between it and that of the ecclesiastical courts," commonly known as **canon law**.[13] Henry II went a step further requiring judges to put in writing the details of the cases they heard and the rational for their decisions. Thus, the judges began to use **precedents** whereby they would find "a case previously decided that serves as a legal guide for the resolution of subsequent cases" similar to the one currently under their consideration.[14] This practice gives legitimacy to the body of the law, underscores the necessity of laws and, if found guilty, the punishments are equally, fairly and consistently applied. Judicial precedents are based on the Latin term ***stare decisis***, meaning "'let the decision stand'; the legal principle that once a precedent is established, all similar cases should be decided the same way."[15] Henry II also required that his judges travel throughout the countryside trying cases in remote areas rather than holding court in major cities. Thus, Henry is credited with the practice of using traveling or **circuit judges**. A cornerstone of the American judicial system, precedents gives a judge the confidence that the decisions rendered in his/her court are validated by previous court rulings. Judges are less likely to stray from *stare decisis* since an errant or unsubstantiated ruling that clearly violates the protected constitutional rights of the accused can be appealed to a higher state or federal court for review with the possibility of the judge's ruling being overturned.

The application of precedents was vital to the codification of **common law** defined as "law developed in England by judges who made legal decisions in absence of written law. Such decisions served as precedents and became 'common' to all in England. Common law is judge-made, it uses precedent, and it is found in multiple sources."[16] Underscoring the importance of common law to the legitimacy of any judicial system, Associate Justice of the U. S. Supreme Court from 1902 to 1932 Oliver Wendell Homes wrote in his *The Common Law* (1881):

> The life of the law has not been logic; it has been experience. The felt necessities of the time, the prevalent moral and political theories, institutions of public policy, avowed or unconscious, even the prejudices which judges share with their fellow men, have had a good deal more to do than syllogism in determining the rules by which men should be governed. The law embodies the story of a nation's development through the many centuries, and it cannot be dealt with as if it contained only axioms and corollaries of a book of mathematics. In order to know what it is, we must know what is has been, and what it tends to become . . . the very considerations which judges rarely mention, and always with an apology, are the secret roots from which the law draws all the juices of life. I mean, of course, considerations of what is expedient for the community concerned.[17]

Closely akin to common law, **equity law** begins where the law ends. Basically, "equity leaves the judge reasonably free to order *preventive* measures—and under some circumstances even *remedial* ones—usually in the form of a writ, such as an *injunction*, or restraining order, designed to afford a remedy not otherwise obtainable, and traditionally given upon a showing of peril."[18] A **writ** is "an order in writing issued by a court ordering the performance of an act or prohibiting some act."[19] For example, judges can order that children be removed from a home pending the conclusion of a divorce and child custody hearings or issue protective orders to prevent alleged spousal abusers from having any contact with the abused party. Judges can also issue an **injunction** defined as "an order issued by a court in an equity proceeding to compel or restrain the performance of an act by an individual or government official. Violation of an injunction constitutes contempt of court, punishable by fine or imprisonment."[20] Federal judges frequently use injunctions to halt a state law or ordinance from taking effect while it is under the Court's review.

Additional bodies of law include **constitutional law** that is the compilation of all court rulings on the meaning of the various words, phrases, and clauses in the United States Constitution."[21] Bureaucratic agencies are tasked with the implementation of congressional acts. Usually the law empowers the agencies to implement new laws but leaves the details of how to administer these laws up to the agencies. Thus, **administrative law** is "that branch of law that creates administrative agencies, establishes their methods of procedures, and determines the scope of judicial review of agency practices and actions."[22] The majority of the nation's federal and, to some degree, state government agencies are empowered with quasi-legislative and quasi-judicial authority over the implementation of their assigned legislative responsibilities. **Quasi-judicial** authority is the power "exercised by administrative agencies that have the characteristics of a judicial act."[23] These agencies can include conduct investigations, hold hearings, and subsequently render decisions that have the force of law. Of equal importance, **quasi-legislative** authority gives these agencies the power to make the rules necessary to both implement and enforce legislative acts assigned to them.

THE TERMINOLOGY AND PROCESS OF THE JUSTICE SYSTEM

The primary charge of the federal justice system is to enforce laws as prescribed by the United States Congress. These laws fall into two broad categories. **Civil law** "deals with the disagreements between individuals, for example, a dispute over ownership of private property."[24] The parties involved in a civil suit are the **plaintiff** who initiates the grievance and the **defendant**, the person accused of causing harm to either the person or to the property of the plaintiff. Civil litigation usually involves disputes over contracts, domestic and business relations, destruction of property, medical malpractice, and fraud. In the American judicial system, a conviction in a civil case is based upon the **preponderance of the evidence** defined as "the standard of proof required to prevail at trial. To win, the plaintiff must show that the greater weight or preponderance of the evidence supports his/her version of the facts."[25] The focus of a civil suit is to determine whether the defendant's actions were negligent towards the plaintiff. **Negligence** is "carelessness or the failure to use ordinary care, under the particular circumstances revealed by the evidence in the lawsuit."[26] The plaintiff is seeking a remedy that is the "vindication of a claim of right; a legal procedure by which a right is enforced or the violation of a right is prevented or compensated."[27] The remedies are usually a monetary settlement or a **tort** granted to the injured party (the plaintiff), a fine paid to the courts by the defendant, or, in some instances, a prison term plus a fine. **Tort law** is "the law of civil wrongs. It concerns conduct that causes injury and fails to measure up to some standard set by society."[28] If negligence is established, the question arises as to the monetary value of the remedy. Usually, this involves two steps. For example, in January 2014, a plant in West Virginia owned by Freedman Industries suffered a major chemical spill that poured toxic substances into the Elk River, the sole source of water for that area, resulting in over 300,000 residents unable to drink, bathe, or even wash dishes and clothes for several days. The Environmental Protection Agency (EPA) surely wanted to hold the company liable for the damages. The question is not whether the company was responsible for it was their company that polluted that river. The hardest task before the jury is to determine the monetary damage caused to the affected parties by the company's actions as well as the monetary and legal sanctions to be lodged against the company for its violation of both federal water pollution laws and standards set by the Environmental Protect Agency (EPA). The first step would involve reimbursing the residents for the current damage caused by the chemical spill. What is more difficult to determine is future monetary loss. The adverse impact of a chemical spill could take years or decades to determine. On both the national and state political level, Republican candidates have pushed for the enactment of tort reform citing that companies simply cannot afford to pay large monetary settlements. The Civil Rights Division of the Justice Department can charge and try a person for violations of another's civil rights. Here again, the initial remedy addresses current damage (i.e., physical injuries, identifiable mental issues); however, the hardest question is how much should the defendant pay to the plaintiff for future physical impairment related to the initial injury and/or the possibility of reoccurring or to be discovered issues.

Criminal law is the embodiment of "offenses against the state itself—actions that may be directed against a person but that are deemed to be offensive to society as a whole."[29] A conviction of criminal charges is based on guilt **beyond a reasonable doubt**. In other words, a member of a jury or the judge cannot render a guilty verdict if he/she has any doubt of the person's guilt. A criminal violation is categorized according to the severity of the action. A **felony** is "a serious crime punishable by death or by imprisonment in a penitentiary for a year or more."[30] According to Section 3559, United States Code, Title 18, there are five levels of federal felony offenses:

- Class A felony—life imprisonment, or if the maximum penalty is death.
- Class B felony—25 years or more.
- Class C felony—less than 25 years but more than 10 years.
- Class D felony—less than 10 years but more than 5 years.
- Class E felony—less than 5 years but more than 1 year.
- All classes carry a maximum fine of $250,000.[31]

A **misdemeanor** is "a minor criminal offense."[32] The U.S. Department of Justice has four levels of misdemeanor offenses:

- Class A misdemeanor—1 year or less but more than 6 months and a maximum fine of $100,000.
- Class B misdemeanor—6 months or less but more than 30 days and a possible fine of $5,000.
- Class C misdemeanor—30 days or less but more than 5 days and a possible fine of $5,000.
- Infraction—5 days or less, or if no imprisonment is authorized, a possible fine of $5,000.[33]

A more detailed overview of the protected constitutional rights of the accused is addressed in Chapter 11—Civil Liberties. However, the proper execution of the investigation of any criminal activity is vital to securing a conviction whether the case is tried in a federal or state court. The most vital component part to the judicial process is the initial investigation of the crime scene to include the gathering of evidence, apprehending and interrogating the suspect(s), and building a solid case against the accused. By the time a case does go to trial, federal agents could have the best of the nation's federal prosecutors, but if the evidence gathered by the investigative teams was flawed or compromised, then the prosecution will lose the case. Unlike a city or state police force, federal investigative agents have the best equipment, the most advanced forensics laboratories in the nation, and the best trained personnel. The likelihood of federal prosecutors not winning a case is marginal in comparison to state legal systems. But occasionally, they do indeed lose a case due to flawed investigative techniques and compromised evidence.

The majority of the problems for any level of law enforcement have centered on both the investigative and pre-trail actions from illegal search warrants, improper wiretapping, illegal interrogation techniques, and coerced confessions. In particular, the legalities of the search warrant and the interrogation process can be problematic. A **search warrant** is "a written document signed by a judge or magistrate, authorizing a law enforcement officer to conduct a search."[34] Under normal circumstances, a search must be conducted with the 4th Amendment to the Constitution in mind, which clearly states that there must be a **probable cause**, that is a "set of facts and circumstances that would induce a reasonably intelligent prudent person to believe a particular person had committed a specific crime or reasonable grounds to make or to believe an accusation."[35] In addition, the evidence recovered through the search should be directly tied to the specific criminal action detailed in the warrant. If evidence has been improperly seized or it is not tied to the charge at hand, then the judge will evoke the **exclusionary rule**, meaning "evidence which is otherwise admissible may not be used in a criminal trial if it is a product of illegal police conduct."[36] To avoid this possibility from happening, the officer seeking a warrant should under normal circumstances prepare an application for a warrant that indicates the reason for the search, the location of the search, and the items sought through the search. Once signed by a federal magistrate, the federal officer can now use the warrant to conduct the search.

But what if the officer believes that by the time he/she obtains the warrant, the evidence sought will have disappeared or been destroyed? In this situation, law enforcement can conduct an on the spot **warrantless search**. If the owner of the property grants permission, the search can take place without an official warrant. With or without warrant, evidence seized during a search is legal if it is in **plain view**. For example, a Drug Enforcement Agent (DEA) is conducting a search for illegal drugs. In plain view of his sight is an operating Meth Lab. This agent can seize the equipment and charge the defendant with an additional violation since the object in question was indeed in plain sight of the agent. However, if in the course of the search, the agent finds Meth Lab equipment hidden in the back of a closet, then it is questionable whether the additional charges will be upheld in court. Also, there are situations that occur when in the process of a search, an agent will seize items directly linked to the criminal act but were not listed on the warrant. This constitutes a **good faith exception** to seize the evidence. In *Illinois v Krull* (1967), the Supreme Court did rule that the good faith exception did apply to warrantless searches. However, agents must be careful to ensure that the evidence seized is definitely tied to a criminal act or the defendant's legal team will attempt to rule the evidence as inadmissible during pre-trial and trial proceedings.

Another area of concern is the interrogation of the suspect. **Investigative** questioning can continue without legal representative present. Yet, when the investigative questioning shifts to **accusatory** questioning, the process must stop immediately if the accused evokes his/her right to legal counsel (***Minnick v Mississippi,*** 1990). Any confession obtained through physical or psychological coercion is inadmissible in court. Oftentimes, the accused will agree to confess to the criminal charge before him/her as part of a plea agreement. **Plea bargaining** is "the process through which a defendant pleads guilty to a criminal charge with the expectation of receiving some consideration from the state."[37] While critics charge that plea bargaining is used by defendants as a convenient way to avoid trial or a lengthy prison term by just promising to provide law enforcement with additional information, law enforcement sees numerous advantages to it. First, agents have gotten what they wanted in the first place—a confession that taken voluntarily will hold up in court. Second, it surely saves the federal government the time and money of a trial. More importantly, the agreement can lead to the apprehension of an individual that committed a more serious crime. Federal law enforcement has used the **witness protection program** as an effective bargaining chip to gain evidence leading towards the arrest and conviction of leaders of organized crime such as the Mafia and drug cartels. At any time during the interrogation process, federal agents can issue an **arrest warrant**, "a document issued by a judicial officer directing a law enforcement officer to arrest an identified person who has been accused of a specific crime. For an arrest warrant to be issued there must be either a sworn complaint or evidence of probable cause that the person being arrested committed a crime.[38]

The Constitution does mandate that anyone accused of a crime must be informed of the charges against him/her within a reasonable period of time. The initial **appearance** of the accused occurs within a few hours or days following the initial arrest. Usually for misdemeanor offenses, the accused merely enters a plea and the magistrate disposes of the case. A federal magistrate is "a minor judicial officer who holds preliminary hearings in federal criminal cases, issues arrest warrants, sets bail, and, if the parties consent, holds jury and nonjury trials in civil cases or in criminal misdemeanor cases and supervises the selection of jurors in felony cases."[39] For felony charges, a plea at this stage is not allowed. Once the **charging document** detailing the particulars of the charges has been presented, the accused is presented at the **arraignment**, a "hearing before a court having jurisdiction in a criminal case, in which the identity of the defendant is established, the defendant is informed of his/her rights, and the defendant is required to enter a plea."[40] A defendant can avoid a trial by entering in a *nolo contendere plea*, a "Latin phrase meaning 'I will not contest it.' A plea of 'no contest' in a criminal case means that the defendant does not directly admit guilt but submits to sentencing or other punishment."[41] It is up to the discretion of the judge to either sentence the defendant at that moment or opt to hold a sentencing hearing at a later date. If the defendant enters a not guilty plea, then the judge will determine the disposition of the defendant pending trial by either granting **bail** (a cash payment for release), releasing the defendant on **personal recognizance** based on the lack of a prior criminal record, employment, ties to the community, and not deemed at a flight risk, or **remand** in jail until after the preliminary hearing whereby a judge will determine whether to grant bail or to continue to remand the defendant until and during trial. At this juncture of the process, the defendant is asked whether or not he/she has obtained legal counsel. If the defendant indicates he/she cannot afford to hire a personal attorney, the federal courts will use the **assigned counsel system** whereby the judge will provide an attorney selected from a list of qualified attorneys paid at public cost to represent the defendant. Attorneys whether privately acquired or court appointed, can opt to take the case on *pro bono public*, a Latin phrase meaning for the public good. Often abbreviated to *pro bono*, it usually stands for work done by lawyers without pay for some charitable or public purpose."[42] With the exception of providing testimony at trial, the role of federal investigative agents has ended.

An intermediate step, a **federal grand jury** is tasked with the chore of reviewing the prosecution's evidence before the trial begins. The notion of a grand jury is a product of English law under King Henry II. The 5th Amendment to the Constitution states that "no person shall be held to answer for a capital, otherwise infamous crime, unless on a presentment or indictment of a grand jury." While states have the option to use a grand jury, the federal judicial system does not have an option. Grand juries are impaneled for a specified period of time, usually three to six months. Composed of at least six members, panelists are drawn from different walks of life. They do not meet daily but will convene periodically or on an as needs basis. The functions of a grand jury have been described as the shield and sword of the judicial system. "Shield refers to the protections the grand jury offers, serving as a buffer between the state and its citizens, preventing the government from using the criminal process against its enemies. Sword refers to the investigatory powers of this body."[43] Grand juries have considerable investigative authority in that they can issue a **subpoena**, "an order of a court, grand jury, legislative body or committee, or any duly authorized administrative agency, compelling the attendance of a person."[44] Furthermore, a *subpoena duces tecum* could be issued requiring the individual to produce specific documents pertinent to the case under consideration. A witness failing to appear can be charged with contempt, resulting in a fine, imprisonment, or both. Grand juries can also grant witnesses **immunity** from further prosecution if their testimony will lead to possible criminal charges against them. The most generous is **transitional immunity** that provides "absolute protection against prosecution for any event or transaction about which a witness is compelled to give testimony or furnish evidence."[45] After its investigation, the grand jury will render a decision. A **true bill** is "an indictment made and endorsed by a grand jury when it finds that there is sufficient evidence to bring a person to trial."[46] However, if the grand jury determines that the evidence presented is not sufficient enough for a jury trial, they will issue a **no bill** decision. With a no bill decision, the prosecution has the opportunity to gather additional evidence to secure a true bill or release the defendant.

If a trial does take place, the defendant has the opportunity to ask for a non-jury trial, whereby the evidence against him/her is presented to a judge who then renders his/her decision or proceed to a jury trial. A federal trial jury pool is impaneled for a month with prospective jurors checking usually every Sunday evening to determine whether they need to report the next morning. Since federal court districts can extend over several counties, the federal court system reimburses jurors for the commute and, if selected for jury service, their hotel/motel, and meal expenses if the commute is a certain distance from the federal courthouse. The selection process of a federal trial jury is the same used for state jury service. The jury pool is narrowed by a series of **peremptory challenges** from both the defense and prosecution attorneys to eliminate jurors without stating a specific reason. Additional questions from both sides will continue to eliminate jurors to the required number of usually twelve. Once the jury has been selected, the presiding judge will issue the official charge to the jury members. To ensure a fair and impartial trial, judges may issue a **gag order**, "a judge's order that lawyers and witnesses not discuss the trial with outsiders."[47] A juror that compromises the order will be removed from the panel, which can lead to the defense ordering the judge to declare a mistrial. For high profile cases, federal judges can grant a **change of venue**, which is "the movement of a case from the jurisdiction of one court to that of another court that has the same subject-matter jurisdiction but is in a different geographical location."[48]

After the presentation of the evidence from both the defense and prosecution, the state will rest its case, allowing the judge to charge the jury with the instructions of deliberation. Usually, the judge informs the jury of its sentencing options, if indeed, they find the defendant guilty. The sentence should match the severity of the crime, if not the case could very well be appealed to a higher court. Judges oftentimes will issue a **determinate sentence** that carries "a term of imprisonment that has a specific number of years."[49]

THE FEDERAL JUSTICE SYSTEM

Like state judicial systems, the federal justice system is composed of four primary entities. Unlike state judicial systems, three of the four parts fall under the direction of the U.S. Department of Justice headed by one person—the United States Attorney General. The investigative arm is charged with the apprehension, investigation, and charging of individuals suspected of committing a federal felony or misdemeanor offense. The prosecuting arm of the department involves the U.S. District Attorneys presenting the state's case in court against the accused. The Bureau of Prisons oversees the incarceration and possible parole of those convicted of a criminal offense. The advantage to the federal system is that three of the component parts are all under one umbrella controlled by just one person. As stated in its FY 2019 Agency Financial Report, the mission of the Department of Justice is:

> To enforce the law and defend the interests of the United States according to the law; to ensure public safety against threats foreign and domestic; to provide federal leadership in preventing and controlling crime; and to seek just punishment for those guilty of unlawful behavior; and to ensure fair and impartial administration of justice for all Americans.[50]

The department's strategic goals for 2018-2022 are "1) enhance national security and counter the threat of terrorism; 2) secure the borders and enhance immigration enforcement and adjudication; 3) reduce violent crime and promote public safety; and 4) promote rule of law, integrity, and good government."[51]

The fourth part is, of course, the federal court system.

The United States Attorney General

Heading the Department of Justice is the United States Attorney General who in addition to administering the department serves as the nation's chief law enforcement officer and lawyer. The position was originally established with the passage of the Judiciary Act of 1789. The duties of the office are to prosecute and conduct all suits filed in the Supreme Court in which the United States government is a party, i.e., constitutionality of congressional laws and executive acts and treaties, and provide legal advice to the President of the United States or to any head of a federal department. The position is filled by a presidential appointment with confirmation by the Senate. Edmund Randolph, a noted statesman and Constitutional Framer from Virginia, first held the position. Other notables include William Pinkney appointed by James Madison; Edwin Stanton appointed by James Buchanan; Harlan Stone appointed by Grover Cleveland; Robert F. Kennedy appointed by his brother John F. Kennedy; John Mitchell of Watergate fame appointed by Richard Nixon; Janet Reno, the first woman to hold the position, appointed by Bill Clinton; and Alberto Gonzales, the first Hispanic attorney general, appointed by George W. Bush. The first African American to hold the position, Eric Holder, was named acting attorney general by George W. Bush but the Senate approved him for the permanent position upon nomination by President Barack Obama. Upon Holder's resignation, Obama appointed Loretta E. Lynch, making her the first African-American woman to hold this position. The attorney general can be dismissed by the president at any time and is subject to impeachment by the House of Representative on charges as specified in the Constitution for "treason, bribery, and other high crimes and misdemeanors." Elected to the U.S. Senate in 1996, Jeff Sessions was nominated by President Trump in 2017 as his attorney general. Their relationship proved to be a rocky one as Trump was openly critical of Sessions' management of the Justice Department. Rather than being fired, Sessions officially resigned from his position in 2018. Subsequently, William Barr was nominated by the president and confirmed by the Senate to assume the vacated attorney general position. Table 1 is an organizational chart of the Department of Justice. All of these agencies report directly to the attorney general.

The Investigative Arm of the Department of Justice

Although there are several agencies falling under the investigative arm of the Department of Justice, the major ones are the Federal Bureau of Investigation, the U.S. Marshals Service, the United States Drug Enforcement Administration, and the Bureau of Alcohol, Tobacco, Firearms and Explosives. Each agency is assigned specific tasks in enforcing federal laws.

The mention of federal criminal investigations brings to mind only one agency—the **Federal Bureau of Investigation (FBI)**. The agency was created in 1908 by then Attorney General Charles Bonaparte during the Theodore Roosevelt administration. Initially, the agency investigated violations of national banking laws, naturalization issues, antitrust laws, bankruptcy filings, and land fraud schemes. The notoriety of the FBI soared during the 'lawless years" of 1921-1933 with prohibition and the rise of gangsters such as Bonnie and Clyde and Al Capone, and the appointment of J. Edgar Hoover as its director, a position he held for forty-eight years. The FBI investigates criminal violations involving over two hundred various categories of federal criminal laws and also serves as the nation's primary internal security agency. One of its major duties is to investigate all criminal activities on Native American Reservations.

The nation's oldest investigative federal agency is **United States Marshals Service** created with the passage of the Federal Judiciary Act of 1789. Appointed by the president or the attorney general, there are ninety-four U.S. Marshals assigned to ninety-four district offices across the nation as well as the U.S. territories of Guam, the Mariana Islands, Puerto Rico and the Virgin Islands. Deputy U.S. Marshals are assigned to all federal courts to escort defendants to and from trial, protect judges, prosecutors and witnesses, and conduct courtroom and courthouse security. Outside of the courtroom, U.S. Marshals also conduct domestic and international fugitive investigations. Some are assigned to the federal prison system to secure prisoners and defendants in custody, transport prisoners and defendants to and from the jail to the courthouse, receive prisoners from other federal law enforcement agencies, conduct jail inspections, and protect government witnesses.

Founded in 1973 by the Nixon administration, the **United States Drug Enforcement Administration (DEA)** is charged with enforcement of the Controlled Substance Act to include the growing, manufacturing, and distribution of controlled substances. Its agents combat drug smuggling into and within the nation by apprehending the traffickers, sellers, and users of controlled substances. It shares some of its duties with both the FBI and Immigration and Customs Enforcement.

Table 1

The United States Department of Justice

Established July 1, 1870, the Department of Justice is headed by the Attorney General of the United States. Forty separate component organizations are under the direction of the Attorney General.

Office of the Attorney General

Deputy Attorney General

Associate Attorney General

Solicitor General	Investigative Agencies:	Litigating Divisions:
U.S. Attorneys	Federal Bureau of Investigation	Antitrust
	Drug Enforcement Administration	Civil Rights
	Bureau of Alcohol, Tobacco, Firearms	Criminal and Civil
	and Explosives	Environment and Natural Resources
		Tax

Offices:	Other Agencies:	Special Programs:
Office of Legal Policy	U.S. Marshals Service	Office of Justice Programs
Office of Legislative Affairs	Bureau of Prisons	Office on Violence Against Women
Office of Public Affairs	National Security Division	Office of Community Oriented
		Policing Services
Office of Legal Counsel	Executive Office for U.S. Trustees	Office of Policy Information
Office of Tribal Justice	Justice Management Division	Office of Professional Responsibility
		Advisory Office
Office of the Solicitor	Executive Office for Immigration	Office of Professional Responsibility
General	Review	
	Community Relations Service	
	Office of the Inspector General	
	Community Oriented Policing Services	
	Foreign Claims Settlement	
	Interpol Washington	
	Office of the Pardon Attorney	
	U.S Parole Commission	
	Executive Office for Organized Crime Drug	
	Enforcement Taskforce	

It is the sole agency responsible for conducting all drug-related investigations abroad. The agency also manages a national drug intelligence program in cooperation with state, local and foreign governments. The agency serves as the nation's liaison with the United States and Interpol on issues related to international drug control programs.

Created in 1972, the Bureau of Alcohol, Tobacco, Firearms and Explosives (ATF) is tasked with the responsibilities of investigating and preventing the unlawful use, manufacturing, and possession of illegal firearms and explosives, as well as acts of arson and bombings. It regulates through federal licensing requirements, the sale, possession and transportation of firearms, ammunition, and explosives via interstate commerce. The agency also investigates illegal trafficking of alcohol and tobacco products. ATF works closely with other federal agencies, state and local law enforcement agencies, and promotes local community awareness programs such as the Project Safe Neighborhoods.

The Litigation Arm of the Department of Justice

The litigation divisions falling under the direction of the Department of Justice include the Antitrust, Civil, Civil Rights, Criminal, Environmental and Natural Resources, and Tax divisions. These cases are prosecuted by the **United States Attorneys**. They also defend the United States government when it is sued in a federal trial court. Each federal judicial court has at least one U.S. Attorney assigned to its district as well as several federal assistant attorneys. Currently, there are ninety-four U.S. Attorneys in all fifty states, the District of Columbia, Guam, the Mariana Islands, Puerto Rico, and the U.S. Virgin Islands. All U.S. attorneys are presidential appointees serving a four-year term. They too are subject to Senate confirmation. At the end of the president's term, all of these attorneys submit their resignations when the opposition party wins the White House. The president, in turn, may re-appoint them or opt to appoint others to the positions. Regardless, nominees for a U.S. attorney position must reside in the federal district court he/she will prosecute in and, of course, they all must be licensed attorneys. While one would expect that these attorneys follow the letter of the law, one cannot overlook that these are political appointees that sometimes can fall victim to Washington political intrigue. For example, George W. Bush's administration ran into considerable controversy when his legal team in the White House decided mid-way into Bush's first term of office to fire several of these attorneys for poor job performance, even though they did not have any indication that they were not performing their jobs. It was revealed later that their firings were due to the lack of enthusiasm of prosecuting cases akin to the political agenda of the Bush administration.

The **Solicitor General of the United States** represents the federal government in all litigation presented before the Supreme Court. Approximately two-thirds of the Supreme Court's yearly docket involves the federal government. All such litigation is channeled through this office. The solicitor general reviews to determine which cases the government will take action on as well as the official positions the government will present to the Court. Along with his/her staff, the solicitor general prepares the appropriate positions briefs and other required papers filed on behalf of the government to the Supreme Court. The solicitor general presents the majority of the oral arguments in support of the government's position in cases before the Court or can assign cases to the assistant to the solicitor general or to another federal attorney. In addition, it is the solicitor general's office that reviews all cases decided against the government by lower federal courts to determine whether to initiate the appeal process and, if so, what positions the government will pursue. Also, he/she is responsible for determining whether the government will participate as ***amicus curiae*** (Latin for "friend of the court").

THE FEDERAL COURT SYSTEM

Constitutional Courts

There are two types of federal courts. The Framers of the Constitution created Article I, legislative courts, and Article III, judicial courts. Legislative courts have administrative, quasi-legislative, as well as traditional judicial duties. Justices of legislative courts are appointed by the president with Senate confirmation and serve for specified terms. Courts falling under Article III are trial courts. Judges for Article III courts are also appointed by the president with Senate confirmation but serve under "good behavior," that is, for life terms.

Selection of Judges

Article III, Section 1 of the United States Constitution states that "the judicial power of the United States shall be vested in one Supreme Court, and in such inferior courts as the Congress may from time to time ordain and establish. The judges, both of the Supreme and inferior courts, shall hold their offices during good behavior, and shall, at stated times, receive for their services a compensation which shall not be diminished during the continuance in office." **Article II, Section 2** gives the president the power to appoint judges to federal benches; however, the United States Senate is empowered to conduct the necessary confirmation hearings and to confirm or not confirm the president's nominee.

It seems like such a simple process. The president nominates and the Senate confirms. Some nominees have sailed through the Senate process while others have had an arduous task of receiving a favorable vote. In general, presidents have been very selective in choosing their nominees to the nation's highest judicial bench. In 1801, President John Adams nominated his Secretary of State John Marshall to be the nation's fourth Chief Justice. Marshall's resume was extremely impressive—veteran of the American Revolution, elected to both the Virginia state house and the U.S. Congress, and a cabinet member in the Adams administration. Serving as Chief Justice from 1801 to 1835, Marshall presided over the Court's landmark decision in *Marbury v Madison*. He guided the Supreme Court through a "series of decisions involving the balance of power between the federal government and the states that laid the legal foundation for the young republic."[52] Oliver Wendell Holmes was nominated by President Theodore Roosevelt and served as an associate justice from 1902 to 1932. At the time of his appointment, Holmes was a well-known legal scholar, author of *The Common Law*, and had served for two decades as a justice of the Massachusetts state supreme court. He was famously known in legal circles for "his articulation of 'clear and present danger' exception to the right of free speech in the unanimous ruling in **Schneck v United States** (1919) of which he famously declared that First Amendment protections do not apply to any individual 'falsely shouting fire in a crowded theater and causing a panic.'"[53] President Lyndon Johnson nominated Thurgood Marshall, the first African-American jurist to the Supreme Court. The grandson of a slave, Marshall was an icon of the 1960s civil rights movement and a preeminent lawyer who successfully argued for the plaintiffs before the Supreme Court in the *Brown v Board of Education* case. President Ronald Reagan nominated the first woman to the bench—Sandra Day O'Connor.

Nominated by President Obama, Sonia Sotomayor became the first Hispanic woman to serve on the Supreme Court. He also won confirmation of Elena Kagan. President Trump's nominee Neil Gorsuch sailed through the confirmation process.

However, nominees by Presidents Woodrow Wilson, Franklin Roosevelt, George H. W. Bush, Ronald Reagan and Donald Trump had uphill battles during their Senate confirmation sessions. In 1916, Woodrow Wilson nominated Louis Brandeis. With a proven track record of advocacy for social justice and individual rights, Wilson believed that Brandeis's nomination would sail through the Senate without much controversy. However, it was the nominee's religion that was the stumbling block. A Jew, Brandeis faced stiff questioning but eventually won confirmation, serving as an associate justice from 1916 to 1939. Placed in nomination by President Roosevelt, Hugo Black had been a United States senator from Alabama. Yet, his confirmation was nearly blocked by senators questioning Black's affiliation with the KKK. The cameras were rolling during the Senate confirmation of George H.W. Bush's nomination of Clarence Thomas to replace retiring jurist Thurgood Marshall. Thomas was accused by a former employee, Anita Hill, of sexual harassment. Fearful of reprisals from Thomas, Hill waited years until she secured a "safe" job before leveling accusations against Thomas. The media had a field day with each word of her testimony before the Senate Judiciary Committee making headlines on the evening news networks. She could not file an official EEOC (Equal Employment Opportunity Commission) compliant because the statute of limitations had expired. However, she did go into in-depth detail about the incident during the confirmation hearings. Thomas narrowly won confirmation to the Supreme Court. A worst fate awaited Robert Bork a sitting federal judge nominated by Reagan for a seat on the Supreme Court. The grilling Bork took from the Senate panel was at times extremely hostile. Bork was his

President Ronald Reagan nominated the first woman to the bench.

**Sandra Day O'Connor.
Library of Congress**

own worst enemy since he had the habit of being disrespectful, rude, and very condescending to members of the panel. While the cameras were rolling, Bork presented himself as the definitive legal expert, oftentimes verbally challenging the legal expertise of panel members, especially Senator Ted Kennedy. Despite a public advertising campaign from the Reagan camp, Bork did not win Senate confirmation. Faced with a Republican majority in the Senate, President Obama officially nominated Merrick B. Garland, a federal appeals court judge to fill the vacancy caused by the sudden death of Justice Antonio Scalia in 2016. Garland was viewed as a favorite candidate to both sides of the aisle. Yet, the Republican Senate majority dug in their heels and refused to even grant Garland a chance to be questioned by the Senate Judiciary Committee. The Supreme Court was forced to conduct their judicial duties with only eight members, leading to several 4 to 4 decisions. The ninth spot of the Supreme Court bench was filled with President Trump's successful Senate confirmation of Neil Gorsuch. Yet, another confirmation battle erupted with Trump's nomination of Brett Kavanaugh. Appointed in 2006 to a judgeship on the U.S. Court of Appeals, Kavanaugh was accused of sexual assault by Christine Ford. The alleged assault happened decades earlier when both attended a high school party. Ford testified in vivid detail about the assault, basically accusing Kavanaugh and others of gang rape. Meanwhile, two other women accused Kavanaugh of inappropriate sexual behavior. Receiving full media coverage, Ford's testimony nearly cost Kavanaugh his chance to sit on the Supreme Court. In his emotionally charged testimony, Kavanaugh denied all the allegations. Media networks preempted their daily soap opera programming to cover the confirmation hearings. Experts were canvassing senators to determine how they would cast their votes when the nomination reached the Senate floor. Particularly, Senator Susan Collins (R-Maine) was basically harassed by reporters after the conclusion of the daily hearings about her views on Kavanaugh and how she would eventually cast her vote. President Trump issued statements favoring his nominee and openly criticized Ford's testimony. With a very narrow margin, Kavanaugh won confirmation. Why is securing a federal bench so difficult?

Part of the blame can be levied at the Framers. The Constitution lists no specific qualifications for the job. There is absolutely no requirement that a judge to a federal bench have a law degree, legal experience, or prior bench experience. Yet with few exceptions, presidents usually nominate individuals who do have law degrees and have decades of either legal or bench experience. "The most notable trend in recent decades has been for presidents to put forward nominees who have empty files; impressive academic and judicial resumes combined with a sparse history of controversial speeches or writings that might be turned against them during the confirmation process. Such formulaic selections reflect the vagaries of our political system, but also our discomfort with people who are creative thinkers and can't be easily pigeonholed as either judicial activists or strict constructionists."[54] George H.W. Bush surely followed this pattern with his 1990 Supreme Court nomination of David Souter. Bush opted "play-it-safe-politics—especially on the abortion issue—dictated who was not chosen. The maneuver left many activists uncertainly combing Souter's personal and professional background for clues about the bright but unknown nominee."[55] When a bench becomes available, the president's staff shifts through the mounds of applications to find the right person to fit the job. Sometimes, an excellent candidate will withdraw from consideration in anticipation of a rough time in front of the Senate Judiciary Committee.

A presidential nominee can run into immediate trouble if the president bypasses the time-honored tradition of **senatorial courtesy.** Presidents need the support of every senator they can muster. So the tradition holds that before the nominee is formally announced, the president makes a courtesy call to the senator of his party from the nominee's state to gage whether the senator will back the appointee. Of course, the confirmation process is supposedly an easier one for both the president and his/her nominee if the president's party holds a clear majority of the seats in the Senate.

In 1912, President Woodrow stressed his rather idealistic belief that Americans "have a right to expect that our judges will have their eyes open, even though the law which they administer hasn't awakened. What this country needs above everything else is a body of laws which will look after the men who are on the make rather than men who are already made. Because the men who are already made are not going to live indefinitely, and they are not always kind enough to leave sons as able and as honest as they are."[56] Basically, Wilson envisioned that judges could put their individual political perspectives aside and make their judgements based on the merits of the laws before them. However, today, the judicial philosophy of the nominee is more of a consideration than the judicial expertise of the candidate. For conservatives, the appropriate approach is **judicial self-restraint,** defined as "a self-imposed limitation on judicial decision making. [It is] the tendency of judges to favor a narrow interpretation of the laws and to defer to the policy judgment of the legislative and executive branches."[57] Conservatives hold that "when a strict interpretation of the Constitution, according to the fixed rules which govern the interpretation of laws, is abandoned, and theoretical opinions of individuals are allowed to control its meaning, we have no longer a Constitution; we are under the government of individual men, who for the time being have power to declare what the Constitution is, according to their own views of what it ought to mean."[58] On the other hand, liberals or Democrats prefer federal judges to follow **judicial activism,** whereby "the making of new public policies [is] through the decision of judges. This may take the form of a reversal or modification of a prior court decision, the nullification of a law passed by the legislature, or the overturning of some action of the executive branch."[59] For example, in rendering the decision in **Brown v the Board of Education** (1954), the arguments centered on whether the lack of an equal education was a violation of the Fourteenth Amendment's guarantee of equal protection of the law. Using judicial activism, the Court would have heard and ruled on the case even though the word education is not directly tied to the equal protection clause of that amendment. On the other hand, a judicial self-restraint Court would not have even heard the case because the Fourteenth Amendment does not specifically mention educational equality under the equal protection of the laws clause. Therefore, this Court would call the issue a **political question**, that is, "a doctrine enunciated by the Supreme Court holding that certain constitutional issues cannot be decided by the courts but are to be decided by the executive or legislative branches."[60] Members of the Senate Judiciary Committee comb through the nominee's legal background. Every case the nominee may have defended or prosecuted as a lawyer or rendered a decision on as a judge is carefully reviewed for any sign of the nominee's personal approach to judicial decision-making. The activism versus self-restraint argument is the prevailing "two approaches to the judicial decision making in the American political system. Activists hold that a judge should use his/her position to promote desirable social ends. Proponents of self-restraint counter than in deciding cases, a judge should defer to the legislative and executive branches, which are politically responsible to the voters, and not indulge his/her personal philosophy" when making a decision.[61]

However, once confirmed there is no guarantee that the nominee will stick to the same judicial philosophical position that won him/her Senate confirmation. For example, Republican President

Dwight Eisenhower appointed two people to the Supreme Court who he believed were conservative and strict or self-restraining judges. Yet, both William Brennan and Earl Warren turned out to be far more on the liberal or activist side than Eisenhower could have ever envisioned. Bryon White, a Democrat, was selected to the bench by John Kennedy. Yet, White voted more frequently on the conservative side of the Court than with his more liberal jurists.

Both presidents and members of Congress have not always been enamored by the decisions of the Supreme Court and lower federal courts. While usually turning to the media to express their displeasure, no president besides Franklin Roosevelt has tried to "stack" the Court with jurists favorable to the president's political perspectives. In 1936, President Roosevelt had just won his second term of office. During his first administration, he persuaded Congress to enact his New Deal measures designed to reverse the economic upheaval caused by the Great Depression. Congress gave approval for the creation of the National Recovery Administration (NRA) and the Agricultural Adjustment Administration (AAA) as well as the Securities and Exchange Commission (SEC), the Rural Electrification Administration, and the Works Progress Administration (WPA). Roosevelt felt confident that he had at least five justices of the Supreme Court who would not overturn any of his legislative acts. However, he soon became worried when the newest member of the bench, Owen Roberts, began to lean towards the four justices against Roosevelt's programs. To counter this turn of events, Roosevelt decided to marginalize the power of the anti-Roosevelt or commonly known as the gang of four now five jurists by just adding more judges to both the Supreme Court and the lower level federal court benches. He rationalized that since Article III of the Constitution did not specify the number of seats on the Supreme Court or any other federal court, then the number of justices could be increased or decreased by Congress at any given time. "On February 5, 1937, Roosevelt asked Congress to empower him to appoint an additional justice for any member of the Court over the age of 70 who did not retire. He sought to name as many as six additional Supreme Court justices, as well as up to 44 judges to the lower federal courts."[62] While Congress pondered Roosevelt's request, Justice Roberts suddenly had a change of heart and switched his position from judicial restraint to judicial activism. He began to cast his vote in favor of Roosevelt's legislative agenda. Justice Roberts did save the day since both President Roosevelt and Congress abandoned the court packing scheme and no president since has ever suggested increasing the number of Supreme Court judges.

Impeachment of Federal Judges

Although these are life-time appointments, federal judges can be removed from the bench through the constitutionally mandated impeachment process. In keeping with the adage that "no man is above the law," the Framers rationalized that any appointed or elected person could well abuse their authority. Therefore, the Framers expanded their list of officials subject to impeachment to include all civil officers of the federal government. The first federal judge to be impeached was John Pickering who was removed in 1803 on charges of on-the-job intoxication and improperly handling property claims. The most notable jurist to face impeachment was Associate Supreme Court Justice Samuel Chase. In 1804, he was charged with a nebulous accusation of being overly aggressive in his questioning of attorneys presenting arguments before the Court. Of the eight charges against him, one concerned "Chase's 'mobocracy' remarks, the others old business ('nauseating littleness,' one Senator called them)."[63] After exhaustive debate, Chase was cleared of all charges. In 1831, District Judge James Peck was acquitted of several charges of abuse of power. District Judge West Humphreys was impeached and removed from office in 1862 over his refusal to hear certain cases before his bench. In 1873, District Judge Mark Delahay was formally impeached by the House of Representatives on charges of on-the-job intoxication but resigned from office before the Senate had its opportunity to remove him from office. Over the years, several other federal judges have been formally impeached and removed from office to include Charles Swayne (1904) for abuse of his office; Richard Archbald (1912) for not recusing himself from cases he was involved with prior to his federal bench appointment; Halsted Ritter (1936) accused of not recusing himself from cases he was previously involved with; Harry Claiborne (1986) for income tax evasion; Alecee Hastings (1988) for accepting bribes; Walter Nixon (1989) for committing perjury before a federal grand jury; Samuel Kent (2009) for sexual assault, perjury, and obstruction of justice; and Thomas Porteous, Jr., (2010) for accepting bribes and committing perjury.[64]

Jurisdiction

Jurisdiction is the "authority vested in a court to hear and decide a case."[65] Each of the three levels of the federal court system has a prescribed list of judicial issues under **original jurisdiction**, defined as "the authority of a court to hear a case in the first instance."[66] All federal district courts have original jurisdiction over any criminal or civil violations of federal laws. **Appellate jurisdiction** is the "authority of a court to review decisions of an inferior court."[67] Both the federal appellate courts and the Supreme Court basically hear appeals from lower court decisions or on challenges to state or federal legislative acts. As specified in the Constitution, the Supreme Court has original jurisdiction to settle suits between two or more states. It does share original jurisdiction with federal district courts in cases involving charges against foreign ambassadors or counsels, in cases involving the federal government against a state, and in cases levied by a state against citizens of another state or against aliens.

Federal District Courts

Currently, there are 860 federal district judges including those assigned to the territorial courts. There are ninety-four federal judicial districts with at least one district in each state, as well as a courts assigned to the District of Columbia and Puerto Rico. The president nominates these judges to these courts with Senate confirmation for lifetime terms. The caseload before these courts is staggering. In 2018, there were 277,010 civil cases filed in federal district courts with 286,969 terminated, meaning a decision was reached, and 339,313 cases pending, meaning that these cases had not been put on the courts' dockets. During the same period, there were 81,533 criminal cases filed with 76,589 determinations and 97,411 cases pending. In 2018, U.S. Bankruptcy Courts had 779,828 cases filed, 838,148 determinations and 1,035,967 cases pending.[68] The cases before the justices included contract issues, real estate property actions including foreclosures, tort actions such as personal injury and medical malpractice, personal property damage, actions under statutes, bankruptcy suits, civil rights litigation, environmental concerns, prisoner petitions, labor law, immigration issues, securities-related issues, social security laws, tax suits, and freedom of information petitions for the release and/or use of government documents.

Federal Appellate Courts

There are twelve Federal Appellate Court geographical districts in the United States plus one circuit court—the Court of Appeals for the Federal Circuit. Each court has three to fifteen permanent or lifetime appointed judges assigned to it. The president with Senate confirmation appoints these positions. The judges can hear cases either in a group of three or **en banc**, defined as a "French term referring to a session of an appellate court in which all the judges of the court participate."[69]

By definition, an **appeal** is "a formal request to a higher court that it review the actions of a lower court."[70] The term **appellant** refers to "the party usually the losing one, that seeks to overturn the decision of a lower court by appealing to a higher court."[71] Not every case heard as original jurisdiction in a state or federal court is appealed. For a case to even to be heard by the federal appeals courts, the question before the jurists must a constitutional one, in that, the defendant or the losing party in a lawsuit has to tie their concern directly to a violation of a provision in the U.S. Constitution. For example, an individual accused of robbing a bank, a federal crime, has been tried and convicted in a federal district court. In the process of interrogation, the defendant requested a lawyer, but the request was denied and the questioning continued. This situation is directly tied to the rights and privileges within the Constitution. The defendant's denied request for an attorney to be present during interrogation is a constitutional violation of his/her right to legal representation. The appellate court would definitely entertain hearing this case. A defendant tried in a state court can seek a federal appeal without first going through the state appellate process if the issue at hand is seen as a violation of the U.S. Constitution. If it were a violation of the state constitution, then this case would begin the appeals process at the state appellate level. As previously stated, if a decision rendered by the federal appellate court is appealed to the Supreme Court, the Supreme Court can refuse to hear the case, thus making the Federal Appeals Court the court of last resort.

There is no real trial on the appellate level. The convicted individual or, as in the case of a civil matter, the aggrieved party and any of the witnesses that testified at the trial court do not testify or even appear before the appellate court. Each side of the issue has their legal team address the court. On legislative matters, both Federal Appellate Courts and the Supreme Court have the power of judicial review. Appellate judges are only interested in the constitutional question laid before them. They are not concerned, for example, about the particulars of a murder trial or how brutal the offense may have been, the name of the victim, etc. For them, it is the constitutional basis for the appeal that is the one and only issue before the panel. Oftentimes, the same issue is presented before two or more appellate courts. For example, several federal appellate judges have issued rulings on state laws pertaining to same-sex marriage prohibitions. One judge ruled in favor of the laws while another ruled the state laws unconstitutional. Since the appellate judges cannot come to one decision, ultimately, it was the Supreme Court that decided the matter when it ruled in ***Obergefell v Hodges*** (2015) that the U.S. Constitution does guarantee a right to same-sex marriage.

If the appellate court upholds the lower court's decision, then the aggrieved party can either accept the outcome or try an appeal to the Supreme Court. If the appeals court rules in favor of the aggrieved party then, in the case of a criminal conviction, the decision of the lower court is overturned. The resolution of the case then falls upon the original prosecuting agency such as the U.S. Attorney or in a state matter the District Attorney who now must decide whether to retry the individual or allow the appellate ruling to stand. A new trial probably will not take place especially if the evidence used against the defendant has been either ruled unconstitutional or has been compromised.

The Supreme Court

It is an arduous process for a judicial issue to make it through the appeals process and wind up on the Supreme Court's docket. To file an appeal at the appellate or Supreme Court level, the aggrieved party must submit a **brief**, "a document prepared by an attorney for presentation to the court containing arguments and data in support of a case. The brief will embody points of law, precedents, and in a case involving a major social issue, relevant economic, sociological and other scientific evidence."[72] The Court issues a manual that guides one in the preparation of the brief. It cannot be handwritten. In fact, the Supreme Court has accepted only a handful of written briefs with the most famous being for *Gideon v Wainwright*. The briefs are presented to the justices who in turn, depend upon their assigned law clerks to read them. If a law clerk believes this is indeed a case the Court should hear, he/she presents it to their assigned judge. The majority of the Court's seasonal docket is filed through the ***writ of certiorari***, "an order or writ from a higher court demanding that a lower court send up the record of a case for review."[73] This usually happens after four of the nine justices invoked the **rule of four**, meaning that four of the justices want to consider this case for the Court's review.

Once the case is on the Court's docket, legal experts from both sides of the issue prepare their **oral arguments** to be delivered at a precise date for a designated time period. During the oral arguments, the justices will ask questions of the presenters, interrupt them with their own comments, or even consult with each other. For cases argued before the appellate courts or the Supreme Court, no decision is rendered immediately after oral arguments have been presented. A final decision could take months or years. Usually during their annual session, which begins in October, the justices reserve either a Wednesday or Friday of each week to discuss the cases that have been presented to them. The Chief Justice presides over the session with each of the justices speaking in order of seniority. This is a closed-door secret meeting. Each justice will cast a vote. If a majority is not reached then the justices may ask for additional information to affirm their decisions. It could take several conferences and several rounds of voting before a final decision is reached.

Table 2

The Justices of the United States Supreme Court		
Justice	**Appointed by**	**Date Confirmed**
Chief Justice John Roberts	George W. Bush	Sept. 29, 2005
Associate Justice Clarence Thomas	George H.W. Bush	Oct. 23, 1991
Associate Justice Stephen G. Breyer	Bill Clinton	Aug. 3, 1994
Associate Justice Samuel Alito, Jr.	George W. Bush	Jan. 31, 2006
Associate Justice Sonia Sotomayor	Barack Obama	Aug. 8, 2009
Associate Justice Elena Kagan	Barack Obama	Aug. 7, 2010
Associate Justice Neil Gorsuch	Donald Trump	April 10, 2017
Associate Justice Brett Kavanaugh	Donald Trump	October 6, 2018
Associate Justice Amy Coney Barrett	Donald Trump	October 27, 2020

The Power of Judicial Review

In was the intention of the Framers to make the judicial branch an equal partner with the legislative and executive branches. In a 1788 speech, Oliver Ellsworth explained the role of the judicial branch:

> This constitution defines the extent of the powers of the general government. If the general legislative should at any time overleap their limits, the judicial department is a constitutional check. If the United States go beyond their powers, if they make a law which the Constitution does not authorize, it is void; and the judicial power, the national judges, who, to secure their impartiality, are to be made independent, will declare it void.[74]

With the passage of the **Judiciary Act of 1789**, the federal courts at all levels were granted the right of judicial review. Section 25 of the law empowers, in particular, the United States Supreme Court to render:

> a final judgment or decree in any suit, in the highest court of law or equity of a state in which a decision in the suit could be had, where is drawn in question the validity of a treaty or statute of, or an authority exercised, under the United States, and the decision is against their validity; or where is drawn in question the validity of a statute of, or an authority exercised under, any State, on the ground of their being repugnant to the constitution, treaties, or laws of the United States, and the decision is in favour of such their validity, or where is drawn in question the construction of any clause of the constitution, or of a treaty, or statute of, or commission held under, the United States, and the decision is against the title, right, privilege or exemption, specially set up or claimed by either party, under such clause of said Constitution, treaty, statute, or commission, may be re-examined, and reversed or affirmed in the Supreme Court of the United States, in the same manner and under the same regulations, and the writ shall have the same effect as if the judgment or decree complained of had been rendered or passed in a circuit court, and the proceedings

upon the reversal shall also be the same, except the Supreme Court, instead of remanding the cause for a final decision as before provided, may, at their discretion, if the cause shall have been once remanded before, proceed to a final decision of the same, and award execution. **But no other error shall be assigned or regarded as a ground of reversal in any such as aforesaid**, than such as appears on the face of the record, and immediately respects the before-mentioned questions of validity or construction of said constitution, treaties, statutes, commissions, or authorities in dispute . . .[75]

Many congressional and state legislative acts initially have been declared unconstitutional by lower federal courts on the grounds that these laws do indeed conflict with the spirit and meaning of the United States Constitution. Any challenges to these rulings are heard at the federal appellate court level with the possibility of eventually being heard by the Supreme Court. As the court of last resort for constitutional challenges, the Supreme Court can opt to hear the merits of the constitutional issue and render its own decision or merely pass on it, thus making the lower federal court's ruling the final decision on the matter. Table 3 lists a selective number of Supreme Court decisions that have impacted both federal and state criminal and court proceedings in matters ranging from confessions to victims' rights.

Table 3

Selective List of Supreme Court Cases

Subject Area	Case	Decision
Confessions	*Arizona v Fulminate* (1991)	Coerced confessions do not automatically turnover a conviction.
	Ashcraft v Tennessee (1944)	A confession obtained through psychological coercion is not a voluntary one; inadmissible in court.
	Brown v Mississippi (1936)	A confession obtained by physical coercion is an unconstitutional violation of 14th Amendment's due process clause.
	Harris v New York (1971)	Voluntary statements made prior to a defendant being apprised of constitutional rights can be used at trial to impeach the defendant's credibility.
Constitutional Rights	*Chavez v Martinez* (2003)	Failure of a police officer to apprise suspect of Miranda cannot be used against the officer in civil suit.
	Dickerson v U.S. (2000)	Upheld *Miranda v Arizona*.
	Illinois v Perkins (1990)	A law enforcement officer can pose as a inmate to obtain a confession without apprising inmate of Miranda rights.
Court Proceedings	*Press Enterprises v Superior Court* (1986)	All preliminary hearings must be open to the public.
	Miranda v Arizona (1966)	See under Right to Counsel
	New York v Quarles (1984)	Issues of public safety can justify an officer's failure to provide Miranda Warnings before questioning begins.
Cruel/Unusual Punishment	*Payne v Tennessee* (1991)	The introduction of victim's impact statements during sentencing is not a violation of 8th Amendment.
Death Penalty	*Atkins v Virginia* (2002)	Death penalty cannot be used for defendants with IQ under 70 or less.

	K Edmund v Florida (1982)	Court ruled that the death penalty is not allowed for a defendant who was a minor participant in a felony since he/she did not kill, attempted to kill or intended to kill.
	Furman v Georgia (1972)	Death penalty ruled unconstitutional.
	Glossip v Gross (2015)	The use of a particular drug in the combination of drugs used in the legal injection is not a violation of the 8th Amendment's prohibition against cruel and unusual punishment.
	Godfrey v Georgia (1980)	The death penalty is not a viable sentencing option for ordinary murder.
	Gregg v Georgia (1976)	Death penalty laws do not necessarily constitute "cruel and unusual" punishment.
	Hall v Florida (2014)	Supreme Court rejected Florida's IQ mentally disabled cutoff score by declaring it too rigid in determining the death penalty for mentally disabled individuals.
	Hurst v Florida (2016)	Court ruled that Florida's capital sentencing format violated the 6th Amendment by permitting the judge and not the jury to impose the death sentence.
	Roper v Simmons (2005)	Court declared the execution of juvenile offenders an unconstitutional violation of the 8th Amendment.
	Thompson v Oklahoma (1988)	The death penalty cannot be given to defendants under the age of fifteen.
	Wilkerson v Utah (1879)	Court upheld that executions detailed in state statues are constitutional and do not violate the 8th Amendment's prohibition against cruel and unusual punishment.
Due Process	Brady v Maryland (1963)	Due process is violated when prosecutors withhold evidence from the defense that might be favorable to the defendant.
	Duncan v Louisiana (1968)	The due process clause of 14th Amendment binds 6th Amendment's right to jury trial to the states.
	Williams v Pennsylvania (2016)	Supreme Court ruled that the state of Pennsylvania violated Williams's right to due process when a state supreme court justice who, in his former job as a district attorney in the defendant's original trial, later participated as a judge in an appeal of the same case.
Evidence	Jencks v U.S. (1957)	Prior inconsistent statements made by a witness must be made available to the defense.
	Pennsylvania v Muniz (1990)	Police officers can ask routine questions and video tape responses to those suspected of DWI violations.
	U.S. v Scheffer (1998)	Polygraphs cannot be used in court as evidence.
Exclusionary Rule	Mapp v Ohio (1961)	Exclusionary rule applies to both federal and state law enforcement agencies.
Grand Jury	Hurtado v California (1884)	States are not required to use the grand jury system for felony charges.
Guilty Pleas	Boykin v Alabama (1969)	It is up to the judge to determine if a plea of guilty was knowingly entered and absolutely voluntary.
Independent Counsels	Morrison v Olson (1988)	Use of independent counsels is constitutional.
Jury Selection	Georgia v McCullum (1992)	The defense cannot exclude jurors based on race.
	Taylor v Louisiana (1972)	Women cannot be excluded from jury duty.
	Witherspoon v Illinois (1968)	Prospective jurors cannot be eliminated due to their views on the death penalty.

Jury Trial	*Baldwin v New York* (1970)	Individuals accused of petty offenses do not have right to a jury trial.
	Ballew v Georgia (1978)	Six is the minimum number for a jury panel.
	Foster v Chatman (2016)	Justices granted a new trial to Foster, an African-American defendant, who was initially sentenced to death by an all-white jury after Georgia prosecutors struck all African-American prospective jurors from the jury panel.
	Morgan v Illinois (1992)	A defendant can challenge for cause a prospective juror who would automatically opt for the death penalty in every capital case.
	Ring v Arizona (2002)	Only juries can decide the critical sentencing issues in a death penalty case.
	Spaziano v Florida (1984)	Court ruled that it is constitutional for a judge to over ride a jury's recommendation of life imprisonment and impose the death penalty; overturned *Ring v Arizona*.
Prison Conditions	*Ruiz v Estelle* (1980)	Prison overcrowding unconstitutional under 8th Amendment.
Prisoner Rights	*Holt v Hobbs* (2015)	Prison officials must allow Muslim inmates their protected religious freedom to grow beards in observation of a traditional religious practice of Islam.
Privacy	*Bond v U.S.* (2000)	Passengers on a bus or train have an expectation of privacy when they place their luggage in overhead storage.
Prosecutors	*Berger v U.S.* (1935)	The primary task of a prosecutor's job is the pursuit of justice, not just winning cases.
	Buckley v Fitzsimmons (1993)	Prosecutors have qualified immunity from civil law suits for their actions during criminal investigations.
	Burns v Reed (1993)	Prosecutors have qualified immunity from lawsuits concerning their advice to the police.
	Imbler v Pachtman (1976)	Prosecutors have absolute immunity from civil liability during a criminal prosecution.
	Kalina v Fletcher (1997)	Prosecutors can be sued for making false statements in affidavits.
Rape/Sexual Assault	*Coker v Georgia* (1977)	Rape is not a capital death penalty offense.
Right to Counsel	*Alabama v Shelton* (2002)	Court-appointed counsel must be granted to a defendant facing suspended jail term for a minor charge.
	Argersinger v Hamlim (1972)	Non-felony defendants have right to a court-appointed counsel.
	Betts v Brady (1942)	Indigent defendants accused of a noncapital crime are not guaranteed court-appointed counsel.
	Douglas v California (1963)	Indigents have right to court-appointed counsel for their first appeal.
	Hamilton v Alabama (1961)	Counsel is required during arraignment.
	In re Gault (1967)	Juveniles have right to counsel under 6th Amendment.
	Johnson v Zerbst (1938)	Indigent defendants in federal court are guaranteed court-appointed counsel.
	Missick v Mississippi (1990)	Once the defendant has asked for legal representation, interrogation cannot resume until attorney present.

	Miranda v Arizona (1966)	Counsel must be guaranteed when requested by the accused during interrogation; defendant must be apprised of constitutional rights prior to waiving those rights.
	Powell v Alabama (1932)	Court-appointed counsel guaranteed to indigent defendants accused in capital cases.
	Roe v Flores-Ortega (2000)	A lawyer's failure to file an appeal does not constitute ineffective counsel.
	Strickland v Washington (1984)	One's defense attorney can be judged as ineffective only if the court proceedings were unfair and the judgment would have been different.
	Wiggins v Smith (2003)	Lawyer's inability to conduct a complete investigation into client's background does not constitute ineffcctive defense.
Searches	*Bingham City v Stuart* (2006)	Police can enter a home without a warrant if they have an objectively reasonable assumption that the occupant has been seriously injured or is in imminent danger of being injured.
	Chinnel v California (1969)	During a search, police can only search the person and the immediate area.
	Florida v J.L. (2000)	Police cannot stop a motorist and conduct a search based solely on an anonymous tip.
	Florida v Jardines (2013)	Ruled using a drug-sniffing dog on a porch to detect drugs in the house an unconstitutional violation of 4th Amendment.
	Illinois v Rodriguez (1990)	Good faith exception search is constitutional even though victim allowed entry into an apartment she no longer resided in.
	Illinois v Wardlow (2000)	A suspect running from police can be subjected to a stop-and-frisk search.
	Knowles v Iowa (1998)	Just issuing a speeding ticket does not give police right to search the vehicle.
	Maryland v King (2013)	Not a violation of 4th Amendment to use cotton swab to collect DNA from arrested suspected.
	Missouri v McNeely (2013)	Warrant may be required to draw blood by needle to check alcohol levels.
	Payton v Tennessee (1980)	Arrest warrant is required to enter a suspect's private residence with the exception of the suspect's consent or an emergency situation.
	Riley v California (2014)	Police are required to have a warrant to search the cellphones of individuals they arrest. Overturned a long standing practice of allowing warrantless searches in connection with arrests.
	Samson v California (2006)	Court ruled that the 4th Amendment does not prohibit the right of law enforcement to conduct a suspicion-less search of a parolee.
	U.S. v Leon (1984)	Upheld a limited use of good faith exception for search warrents.
Self-Defense	*Faretta v California* (1975)	Defendants have the constitutional right to self-defense.
Self-Incrimination	*Kastigar v U.S.* (1972)	Use immunity is not a violation of the 5th Amendment's guarantee of protection from self-incrimination.

Sources	*Brazburg v Hayes* (1972)	Journalists cannot claim confidentiality to sources when subpoenaed before grand juries.
Substantive Due Process	*Lanzetta v New Jersey* (1938)	A law is unconstitutional if the meaning of the law is so vague that "men of common intelligence must necessarily guess as to its meaning."
Victims' Rights	*Booth v Maryland* (1963)	Victim impact statements are unconstitutional in capital cases because statements can result in a arbitrary and capricious application of death penalty.

While the public eagerly awaits an appellate or a Supreme Court's final decision, legal experts are more anxious to read the written opinions of the justices related to the decision. These opinions are a part of the precedents judges and lawyers use to render a judgment for cases in the future that mirror the same issues addressed by the higher courts. Legislators and legal experts look towards these opinions to guide them in crafting future legislation to ensure that these bills will not conflict with the Court's rulings. The only way to really overturn a decision made by a federal appellate or Supreme Court is for Congress to pass and the voters to approve an amendment to the Constitution.

These opinions fall into several different categories. For example, in 1947 the Supreme Court ruled 5 to 4 in ***Everson v Board of Education of the Township of Ewing***, that the township's practice of using public tax money to offset the costs of public transportation to both public and private schools for children from low-income families was constitutional. The five justices represent the majority while the four are in the minority. If the Chief Justice of the Supreme Court voted with the majority, the writing of the **majority opinion** falls upon his/her shoulders or he/she may assign it to another justice of the majority group.

If the Chief Justice's vote puts him/her into the minority pool, the most senior justice in the majority group selects the justice to write the majority opinion. Once completed, the opinion is reviewed by the justices in their respective groups. The body of the opinion details the constitutional issue before the Court and why in this case the five justices were the majority in upholding the constitutionality of the laws allowing the use of public money for bus fare for students attending private schools. The justice would point out that this was a legal and thus a constitutional application of the child benefit theory (see Chapter 12). The minority justice would choose one of their group to write the **dissenting** or **minority opinion** citing why they did not uphold the constitutionality of the Ewing initiative. Both groups can have a jurist who may have voted either yea or nay but did so for different reasons. This constitutes a **concurring opinion**. An **extended opinion** is "a separate opinion that partly concurs and party dissents from an opinion of the court."[76] Any level of court can be called upon to issue an **advisory opinion** defined as "an opinion given by a court, though no actual case or controversy is before it, on the constitutional or legal effect of a law."[77] This may be a prudent practice for any lawmaker or legislative or executive body to get before they decide to entertain legislation that will certainly be ruled as unconstitutional by the Court when challenged before it.

Beginning with the landmark decision in ***Marbury v Madison*** (1803), members of the Supreme Court have defended their use of judicial review. For example, in one of his opinions issued in 1958, Chief Justice Earl Warren wrote:

> We are mindful of the gravity of the issue inevitable raised whenever the constitutionality of an Act of the National Legislature is challenged. . . . [But] we are oath-bound to defend the Constitution. This obligation requires that Congressional enactments be judged by the standards of the Constitution. The Judiciary has the duty of implementing the constitutional safeguards that protect individual rights. . . . The provisions of the Constitution are not time-worn adages or hollow shibboleths. They are vital, living principles that authorize and limit governmental power in our Nation. They are rules of government. When the constitutionality of an Act of Congress is challenged in this Court, we must apply those rules. If we do not, the words of the Constitution become little more than good advice. . . We do well to approach the task cautiously, as all our predecessor have counseled. But the ordeal of judgment cannot be shirked.[78]

The impact of the Court's power of judicial review cannot be understated. Their decisions have had a tremendous impact on the interpretation and extension of civil liberties (see Chapter 12), on the advancement of civil rights and voting privileges (see Chapter 13), on the relationship between federal and state governments (see Chapter 2), on the implementation of federal regulatory laws (see Chapters 9 and 16), on the conduct of elections and political campaigns (see Chapters 4 and 5) and to some extent, on foreign policy (see Chapter 17).

Federal Courts—Territorial Courts

Territorial courts were created as Article I courts by Congress to hear cases of original jurisdiction involving federal law and bankruptcy cases. Article I judgeships were established initially in the Virgin Islands in 1937 and later in Guam in 1950 and the Commonwealth of the Northern Mariana Islands in 1977. The president appoints judges to these benches with confirmation from the Senate for fixed terms of ten years.

Federal Courts—United States Court of Appeals for Veterans Claims

This court was created in 1988 when President Reagan signed into law the Veterans' Judicial Review Act. As a court of record, this court is part of the federal judiciary and does not fall under the direction of the Department of Veterans Affairs. The court is staffed with seven judges serving fifteen-year terms. Once a judge's term has expired, the judge has the option to remain as a recall-eligible senior judge. This court has exclusive jurisdiction over any decision issued by the Board of Veterans' Appeals filed by a claimant challenging the Board's decision.

Federal Courts—Court of International Trade

Originally established by Congress in 1926 as the Customs Court, its name was changed by Congress to the Court of International Trade. The primary duty of the court is to settle disputes arising over the federal government's tariff laws and any duties levied on imported goods. The court is composed of nine judges appointed to lifetime terms by the president with Senate confirmation. Although its main office is in New York City, there are courts established throughout the nation's principal ports of entry. Although initially an Article I court, it was changed to an Article III court in 1956.

Federal Courts—The Court of Federal Claims

Originally established in 1855, the Article I Court of Federal Claims hears cases filed by private individuals against the federal government involving breaches of contract, injuries caused by the negligent behavior of government employees, claims involving the recovery of other claims such as back pay, tax refunds, eminent domain claims against the federal government, dismissal issues from federal civilian and active military personnel, disputes over patents and copyrights, and land claims brought by Native Americans against the federal government. It also handles claims referred to them by Congress and executive branch departments. The court has sixteen judges appointed for fixed fifteen-year terms by the president with Senate confirmation.

Federal Courts—Court of Appeals for the Federal Circuit

Established by Congress in 1982, the court has the same judicial standing as the federal Courts of Appeals with the exception that its jurisdiction is national rather than geographical. This appellate court was created to consolidate the caseloads from both the former Court of Customers and Patent Appeals with the appellate function of the Court of Claims. The court's appellate jurisdiction extends to issues involving disputes over patents, copyrights and trademarks; appeals from district courts involving contractual matters and Internal Revenue cases in which the United States is the defendant; appeals from the Federal Court of Claims, Court of International Trade, and Court of Veterans Appeals, and any issues involving a review of administrative rulings issued by the Patent and Trademark Office, the International Trade Commission, the Secretary of Commerce, Department of Veterans Affairs, etc. The court is composed of twelve judges nominated by the president with Senate confirmation for life terms. Panels of three judges or en banc can hear their cases.

Federal Courts—United States Court of Appeals for the Armed Forces

As an Article I body, this court was established in 1950 to review military court martial decisions. The primary responsibilities of the court are to review decisions affecting top military personnel and all military court decisions resulting in death penalty sentences. It also is empowered to review other cases upon petition to include bad conduct discharges or military code violations resulting in a lengthy prison term. The court operates under military laws and rules established by Congress. The court is composed of five non-military judges appointed by the president with Senate confirmation for fifteen-year terms.

THE FINAL ARM OF JUSTICE—THE FEDERAL PRISON SYSTEM

If convicted of a federal crime, one will serve their imprisonment in a federal prison overseen by the Bureau of Prisons, a federal agency under the direction of the Attorney General's Office. The number of individuals either incarcerated in a federal minimum or maximum prison or under some form of supervision is staggering. As of April 2020, there were 174,837 convicted federal felons with 145,613 in Bureau of Prisons custody, 17,885 federal inmates held in privately managed facilities and 11,339 held in other types of facilities.[79] A profile of this prison population reveals that 50 percent are in the age group of 31 to 45. Approximately 73,824 or 45.4 percent of the 2020 prison population were convicted of drug offenses with the second highest federal criminal offense being possession of weapons, explosives and arson, accounting for 19.4 percent of the total incarcerated prison population. A racial profile reveals that 68.1 percent are non-Hispanic (White and African American) and 31.1 percent are Hispanic. Of the total incarcerated federal prison population, 92.9 percent are male with only 7.1 percent female inmates. The majority of the prison population is serving sentences ranging from five to fifteen years with only 4,450 with life sentences and 62 death sentenced inmates.[80]

These statistics point to the on-growing debate about what direction the nation's criminal justice system should take regarding its sentencing options and growing prison populations. One side believes in the **just desserts** concept whereby the "punishment for criminal-wrong doing should be proportionate to the severity of the offense."[81] Supporters of this option want both state and national legislative houses to enact strong criminal sanctions for a wide range of offenses. The other side promotes the concept of **rehabilitation**, "the notion that punishment is intended to restore offenders to a constructive role in society; based on the assumption that criminal behavior is a treatable disorder caused by social or psychological ailments."[82] Perhaps the resolution to the prison population is not philosophical but monetary. The cost to maintain both the federal and state prison population, as well as providing the appropriate supervision of those released, is depleting both federal and state budgets. Many states are contemplating de-criminalizing certain offenses from felony to misdemeanor or even eliminating them from the criminal list. During his final days in the White House, President Obama pardoned hundreds of prisoners convicted for drug possession violations because he believed that their sentences were initially too harsh for the crimes they had committed.

CONCLUSIONS

Initially, the Framers envisioned that the legislative branch would be predominant over the executive and that the judiciary would fulfill a supportive role for both. However, once the Framers granted judicial review to the federal courts and mandated life-time terms for federal judges, the federal judiciary now had the muscle to exert itself as a co-equal to both the legislative and executive branches. Today, Americans pay just as much attention to an impending key Supreme Court decision as they do to a presidential speech or policy move. Under the guidance of a series of very capable legal experts, the United States Department of Justice has expanded its jurisdiction and exerts itself as a powerful force in the apprehension and conviction of criminals, protecting of the nation's borders, and stamping out terrorist threats to national security. When called upon, this federal department provides legal expertise and forensic support to state and local law enforcement agencies.

Whether you advocate for an activist or strict constructionist jurist, the judges sitting on an appellate or Supreme Court bench do make and influence the course of this nation's laws. One could credit the Supreme Court with lighting the spark to the Civil Rights Movement of the 1960s. It was the Court's decision in *Brown v the Board of Education of Topeka, Kansas* that began the erosion and eventual demise of the separate but equal doctrine. It has been the courts and not Congress or state legislative houses that have taken the "bull by the horns" in securing voting rights for the American people. No longer in a supportive role, the federal judiciary is indeed an equal partner and, at times, the dominant voice in the federal government.

CHAPTER NOTES

[1] *Treasury of Presidential Quotations*, Caroline Thomas Harnsburger, ed., (Chicago, Illinois: Follett Publishing Company, 1964), 167-168.

[2] *https://www.supremecourt.gov/public-info-year-end/2019-endreport*

[3] Ibid.

[4] Department of Justice, FY 2019 Agency Financial Report, November, 2019, I 3-9.

[5] David W. Neubauer, *America's Courts and the Criminal Justice System*, 8th ed., (Belmont, California: Wadsworth Thomson Learning, 2005), 479.

[6] Henry J. Abraham, *The Judicial Process*, 2nd ed., (New York, New York: Oxford University Press, 1968), 7.

[7] Robert A. Carp, Ronald Stidham and Kenneth L. Manning, *Judicial Process in America*, 6th ed., (Washington, D.C.: CQ press, 2004), 3.

[8] *Treasury of Presidential Quotations*, 169.

[9] Ibid.

[10] Ibid., 168.

[11] William J. Duiker and Jackson J. Spielvogel, *World History*, 3rd ed., (Belmont, California: Wadsworth Thomson Learning, 2005), 11.

[12] Ibid., 12.

[13] Abraham, 10.

[14] Neubauer, 480.

[15] *The American Political Dictionary*, Jack C. Plano and Milton Greenberg, eds., 10th ed., (Harcourt Brace College Publishers, 1997), 278.

[16] Neubauer, 477.

[17] Abraham, 15.

[18] Ibid., 17.

[19] *The American Political Dictionary*, 284.

[20] Ibid., 265.

[21] Carp, Stidham, and Manning, 8-9.

[22] *The American Political Dictionary*, 248.

[23] *The American Political Dictionary*, 232.

[24] Carp, Stidham, and Manning, 7.

[25] Neubauer, 480.

[26] Carp, Stidham, and Manning, 258.

[27] Neubauer, 481.

[28] Carp, Stidham, and Manning, 258.

[29] Ibid., 7.

[30] *The American Political Dictionary*, 263.

[31] U.S. Code 3571-Sentence of Fine 2020, *https://www.law.cornell.edu/uscode/text/18/3571*

[32] *The American Political Dictionary*, 271.

[33] U.S. Code 3571-Sentence of Fine 2020

[34] Neubauer, 270.

[35] *The HarperCollins Dictionary of American Government and Politics*, Jay M. Shafritz, ed., (New York, New York: HarperCollins Publishers, 1992), 468.

[36] John C. Domino, *Civil Rights and Liberties: Toward the 21st Century*, (New York, New York: Harper Collins Publishers, 1994), 140.

[37] Neubauer, 285.

[38] *The HarperCollins Dictionary of American Government and Politics*, 38-39.

[39] *The American Political Dictionary*, 263.

[40] *The HarperCollins Dictionary of American Government and Politics*, 38.

[41] Ibid., 480.

[42] Ibid., 467.

[43] Neubauer, 277.

[44] *The American Political Dictionary*, 279.

[45] Neubauer, 482.

[46] *The HarperCollins Dictionary of American Government and Politics*, 62.

[47] Neubauer, 478.

[48] *The HarperCollins Dictionary of American Government and Politics*, 100.

[49] Neubauer, 477.

[50] U.S. Department of Justice, FY 2019 Agency Financial Report, I-1.

[51] Ibid.

[52] Jonathan Turley, "The 9 Incredibles," *American History*, Vol. 44, No. 4, October, 2009, 32.

[53] Ibid.

[54] Ibid., 31.

[55] _____, "In Search of Souter," *U.S. News & World Report*, August, 6, 1990, 20.

[56] *Treasury of Presidential Quotations*, 168.

[57] *The HarperCollins Dictionary of American Government and Politics*, 313.

[58] Gary L. McDowell, "Rights Without Roots," *The Wilson Quarterly*, Vol. XV, No. 1, Winter, 1991, 78.

[59] *The HarperCollins Dictionary of American Government and Politics*, 312.

[60] *The American Political Dictionary*, 274.

[61] Ibid.

[62] William E. Leuchtenburg, "Showdown on the Court," *Smithsonian*, Vol. 36, No. 2, May, 2005, 109.

[63] Richard Brookhiser, "The Supreme Court Has Never Risen Completely Above the Political Fray," *American History*, Vol. 47, No. 5, December 2012, 23.

[64] Joseph Connor, "High Crimes: The Perils of Impeachment-What We've Learned in 200-Plus Years of Pulling the Pin," *American History*, Vol. 53, No. 6, February 2019, 32-39.

[65] Ibid., 267.

[66] Ibid., 272.

[67] Ibid., 250.

[68] *https://www.uscourts.gov/judicial-caseload-indicators-federal*

[69] Neubauer, 478.

[70] *The HarperCollins Dictionary of American Government and Politics*, 30.

[71] Neubauer, 476.

[72] *The American Political Dictionary*, 272.

[73] *The HarperCollins Dictionary of American Government and Politics*, 99.

[74] Charles A. Beard, *The Supreme Court and the Constitution*, (Englecliffs, New Jersey: Prentice-Hall, Inc., 1962), 82.

[75] Michael Kammen, *The Origins of the American Constitution: A Documentary History*, (New York, New York: Viking Penguin, Inc., 1986), 382.

[76] *The American Political Dictionary*, 406.

[77] Ibid., 149.

[78] Beard, 10.

[79] *https://www/bop.gov/about/statistics/population*

[80] Ibid.

[81] Neubauer, 479.

[82] Ibid., 481.

SUGGESTED READINGS

Abraham, Henry J. and Barbara A. Perry, *Freedom and the Court: Civil Rights and Liberties in the United States*, 8th ed., Lawrence, Kansas: University of Kansas, 2003.

Carp, Robert A., Ronald Stidham, and Kenneth L. Manning, *Judicial Process in America*, 6th ed., Washington, D.C.:CQ Press, 2004.

Hensley, Thomas R., Christopher E. Smith and Joyce A. Baugh, *The Changing Supreme Court: Constitutional Rights and Liberties*, Minneapolis/St. Paul , Minnesota: West Publishing, 1997.

Neubauer, David W. *America's Courts and the American Judicial System*, 8th ed., Belmont, California: Thomson Wadsworth, 2005.

O'Brien, David. *Storm Center: The Supreme Court in American Politics*, 3rd ed., New York, New York: W. W. Norton and Company, 1993.

Chapter Twelve

CIVIL LIBERTIES

While the debate over the context of the new constitution was brewing in Philadelphia, Thomas Jefferson wrote to his dear friend James Madison that "while there were many things about the proposed Constitution that please him, first among the things he did not like was 'the omission of a bill of rights, providing clearly, and without the aid of sophism, for freedom of religion, freedom of the press, . . . and trials by jury in all matters of fact triable by the laws of the land. . . .'"[1] At the end of his letter, Jefferson stressed that a bill of rights was absolutely necessary because "it is what the people are entitled to against every government on earth, ... and what no just government should refuse. . . ."[2] Our rights to speak freely, to practice our religious beliefs, to gather with others, to redress our government without fear of imprisonment, to have a fair public trial, and so on are embodied in the Bill of Rights. The Framers guaranteed these rights to **all** citizens by attaching the Bill of Rights to the supreme law of the land—the United States Constitution. "Our nation was founded on the idea that all men are created equal, that they are endowed by their Creator with certain inalienable rights, and that governments are instituted among men to secure the rights nature gives. From the beginning, Americans have believed that if their country was about anything, it was about personal freedom and the rights that helped secure it."[3]

The Framers went a step further to ensure that no level of government could strip citizens of their protected rights. In 1789, the United States Congress passed the **Judiciary Act**, which among many provisions gave the newly created Supreme Court the power of judicial review. The key to understanding the longevity of those inalienable rights called civil liberties rests in part with the Supreme Court's use of judicial review. This chapter focuses on the creation, interpretation, and subsequent preservation of the civil liberties enumerated in the Bill of Rights.

However, the preservation of our civil liberties does not and should not rest wholly upon the shoulders of the nine justices of the Supreme Court. The governed, or citizens, bear an equal burden. The constraints placed upon the governing emphasize that laws are man-made. "Americans are much given to saying with pride—with more pride, perhaps, than understanding—that they live under a government of laws and not a government of men. But laws, of course, are man-made. The Constitution of the United States, the supreme law of the land, was framed by mortal men. Ordinary mortals legislate in Congress, administer the laws in the executive branch of the government, and interpret the laws in the judicial branch. These laws were not delivered to us on tablets from Mount Sinai; they are not self-executing; and there are inevitable conflicts about the application and construction of them."[4] Consequently, this chapter also explores the roles played by ordinary citizens such as Ernesto Miranda, Steven Engle, Dollree Mapp, and Clarence Gideon in reminding the governing of their responsibility to preserve, protect, promote, and defend those precious civil liberties.

The continuing quest to preserve and, in some circumstances, to expand the scope of civil liberties has been oftentimes derailed by events that have seriously threatened the viability of the United States. At the beginning of the Civil War, President Abraham Lincoln issued orders curtailing certain civil liberties such as the *writ of habeas corpus*. President Franklin Roosevelt signed the order that placed American citizens of Japanese extraction into detention camps for the duration of World War II. President George W. Bush was confronted with the same challenge that these two presidents had to face. The tragic international terrorists' attacks of September 11, 2001, placed this nation into a perilous threatened state of emergency. Prompted by the Bush administration, Congress enacted legislature granting more police powers to federal law enforcement agencies that do, to some degree, seriously challenge the scope of American civil liberties. The Preamble of the United States Constitution charges the national government with the tasks to "provide for the common defense" and to "promote the general welfare" of the American people. When the future of the nation is challenged, it is the responsibility of the nation's leaders to do whatever is necessary to protect the American people from threats to their survival, while at the same time trying to avoid the erosion of those precious individual freedoms and civil liberties the Framers gave to us in the Bill of Rights.

THE CONCEPT OF CIVIL LIBERTIES

In 1215, English noblemen gathered in Runnymede to force their king to sign a pledge guaranteeing the preservation of certain privileges and rights to all Englishmen, regardless of rank and bloodline. The **Magna Carta** was the initial quest of Englishmen to end the arbitrary rule of their monarchs who governed under the **divine right theory** of kings. This concept of kingship rested on "the notion that monarchs rule by the will of, indeed in place of God. Since God created this situation, any effort to change it would be considered sinful, because it is through kings that God works his will on men."[5] Subsequently, the writings of John Locke, Jean Jacques Rousseau, and Charles de Montesquieu drew a distinction between alienable and inalienable rights. "Alienable natural rights were those that individuals could have ceded to society, if they wished; inalienable natural rights were so fundamental to human welfare that they were not considered to be in the power of individuals to surrender."[6] Accordingly, Locke's concept of the social contract rested on the belief that men gladly gave up their individual alienable natural rights as a tradeoff for a governing structure that would provide and protect everyone's inalienable rights. In his *Two Treaties on Government*, John Locke joined the ranks of John Stuart Mill and Jean J. Rousseau, who firmly believed that **civil liberties** were indeed **inalienable rights** "that belong to individuals by the nature of humanity, and which cannot be taken away without violating that humanity."[7] For Locke, those fundamental rights were life, liberty and property. Retaining the rights to life and liberty, the Framers opted to borrow from Locke a more expansive notion of property to include more than physical possessions such as land by using the term "pursuit of happiness" to encompass artistic and intellectual expressions. In his *Essay Concerning Human Understanding* (1690), Locke stressed that "as therefore the highest perfection of intellectual nature lies in a careful and constant pursuit of true and solid happiness, so the care of ourselves that we mistake not imaginary for real happiness is the necessary foundation of our liberty."[8]

Although concerned about the protection of individual freedoms, the Framers did not include a bill of rights into the original document. "James Madison, for example, argued that since the Constitution was one of strictly enumerated powers, the federal government was necessarily prevented from passing legislation that would trample individual rights."[9] Besides, the newly formed thirteen states had already written constitutions containing protections of individual rights and freedoms. However, there was no consistency of guaranteed rights in those documents. They were at best "a jarring but exciting combination of ringing declarations of universal principles of a motley collection of common law procedures."[10] Case in point, "two states passed over a free press guarantee; four neglected to ban excessive fines, excessive bail, compulsory self-incrimination, and general search warrants. Five ignored protections for the rights of assemble, petition, counsel, and trial by jury in civil cases. Seven omitted a prohibition of *ex post facto* laws. Nine failed to . . . condemn bills of attainder. Ten said nothing about freedom of speech, while eleven were silent on double jeopardy."[11] It was the Anti-Federalists who used the inconsistencies of rights detailed in individual state constitutions and the obvious omission of a separate bill of rights in the federal document as their main argument against the ratification of the Constitution. "Within hours of the delegates signing the Constitution, George Mason published a pamphlet entitled *Objections to This Constitution of Government*, the central theme of which was that the absence of a 'declaration of rights' made the Constitution unacceptable. Without limitations, Mason believed, the federal government would infringe the basic rights of the citizenry. '[T]he laws of the general government,' Mason warned, 'being paramount to the law and constitution of the several States, the Declaration of Rights in the separate States are no security.'"[12]

Once the Congress convened under the newly adopted Constitution, James Madison led the charge to adopt a Bill of Rights. It is interesting to note that "the first ten amendments to the federal Constitution contain twenty-seven separate rights. Six of these rights, or about 20 percent, first appeared in the Magna Carta. Twenty-one or about 75 percent had their initial formulation in colonial documents written before the 1689 English Bill of Rights. Even more impressive, all but the Ninth Amendment could be found in several of the state constitutions written between 1776 and 1787."[13] Essentially, the Bill of Rights corrected many of the abuses levied by the British government over its own citizens. Throughout its history, England has a blemished record of denying speedy trials, jury trials, reasonable bail, *writ of Habeas Corpus*, protections from cruel punishment, freedom of religious practices and beliefs, freedom of speech, and so on. The Framers were quick to recognize how important protecting these basic rights were to the successfulness of a democratic government. The permanency of these rights was assured with the adoption of **Article VI (Supremacy Clause)** that declared the Constitution and all subsequent amendments to the document as the supreme law of the land. Any state law or local ordinance deemed in conflict with the spirit and meaning of the Constitution would be declared an unconstitutional act. Therefore, the Framers guaranteed to the governed that the governing would not undo what they had created.

However, the Framers were concerned that the absolute and unrestrained individual pursuit of inalienable rights would severely jeopardize the concept of a unified civil society. It was a question of **individual liberty** defined as "the condition of being free from restrictions or constraints" versus the creation of government restraints on the pursuit of those rights for the protection of society as a whole.[14] The Framers rationalized that "if we were to live in a truly 'civil' society, we must agree to respect the rights of others and subject our activities to reasonable restrictions enacted for the good of society."[15] **Reasonable restrictions** are the logical and rational curtailments enacted by government upon the absolute unrestrained pursuit of inalienable rights in order to guarantee the protection of those rights to all members of a civil society. Subsequently, religious freedom is not an absolute right. One cannot be arrested because his/her religious beliefs are socially unacceptable. However, one can be arrested when his/her pursuit of their religious beliefs breaks a law or causes damage to another's property or harm to another person. Also, freedom of speech is not an absolute right to say whatever an individual wishes to say. Freedom of speech ceases to be a protected right when one's words shifts to fighting words that create a clear and present danger to others.

The phrase "reasonable restrictions" is essential to understanding the relationship of government at all levels to the United States Supreme Court. The Framers never provided a clear-cut guideline for legislating reasonable restrictions on civil liberties. For example, the Second Amendment guarantees the right to bear arms. However, the Framers did not define what constitutes an acceptable weapon or did they explain under what conditions weapons could be legally used. What is reasonable bail? What constitutes a fair trial? Under what conditions can a witness declare protection from prosecution under the Fifth Amendment? Or was the lack of specific definitions and parameters purposeful with the intent of leaving the "details" for future generations of lawmakers and jurists seeking to meet the changing needs of the American people:

> [S]hould we not pay the authors [the Framers] the compliment of believing that they meant no more than they said? What they left unsaid, they left open for us to decide. What then are the judges looking for, if it is not the intent of those who made the Constitution? . . . The Constitution has become something in its own right. It is an integral part of what men do with it. It has long ceased to be more than what other men hoped they would do or intended them to do. The Constitution, together with the Court's work, is not so much pushed by the plans of the past as pulled by the hopes of the future. It is not stuffed, but pregnant with meaning. The intent of the Framers when it is not expressed is only that we, the Congress, the President, and the Court, should be allowed to make good on their best hopes and cash in on their boldest bets. What our forefathers said they said. What they didn't say, they meant to leave to us, and what they said ambiguously, indefinitely, equivocally, or indistinctly, is in so far not said.[16]

Table 12.1

The Bill of Rights

Amendment I - Congress shall make no law respecting an establishment of religion, or prohibiting the free exercise thereof; or abridging the freedom of speech, or of the press; or the right of the people peaceable to assemble, and to petition the Government for a redress of grievances.

Amendment II - A well-regulated militia, being necessary to the security of a free State, the right of the people to keep and bear arms, shall not be infringed.

Amendment III - No soldier shall, in time of peace be quartered in any house, without the consent of the owner, nor in time of war, but in a manner to be prescribed by law.

Amendment IV - The right of the people to be secure in their persons, houses, papers, and effects, against unreasonable searches and seizures, shall not be violated, and no warrants shall issue, but upon probable cause, supported by oath or affirmation, and particularly describing the place to be searched, and the persons or things to be seized.

Amendment V - No person shall be held to answer for a capital, or otherwise infamous crime, unless on a presentment or indictment of a Grand Jury, except in cases arising in the land or naval forces, or in the militia, when in actual service in time of war or public danger; nor shall any person be subject for the same offense to be twice put in jeopardy of life or limb; nor shall be compelled in any criminal case to be a witness against himself, nor be deprived of life, liberty, or property, without due process of law; nor shall private property be taken for public use without just compensation.

Amendment VI - In criminal prosecutions, the accused shall enjoy the right to a speedy and public trial, by an impartial jury of the State and district wherein the crime shall have been committed, which district shall have been previously ascertained by law, and to be informed of the nature and cause of the accusation; to be confronted with the witnesses against him; to have compulsory process for obtaining witnesses in his favor, and to have the assistance of counsel for his defense.

Amendment VII - In Suits at common law, where the value in controversy shall exceed twenty dollars, the right of trial by jury shall be preserved, and no fact tried by a jury, shall be otherwise reexamined in any Court of the United States, than according to the rules of the common law.

Amendment VIII - Excessive bail shall not be required, nor excessive fines imposed, nor cruel and unusual punishments inflicted.

Amendment XI - The enumeration in the Constitution, of certain rights, shall not be construed to deny or disparage others retained by the people.

Amendment X - The powers not delegated to the United States by the Constitution, nor prohibited by it to the States, are reserved to the States respectively, or to the people.

Amendment Pertaining to Application of Civil Liberties:

Amendment XIV - All persons born or naturalized in the United States, and subject to the jurisdiction thereof, are citizens of the United States and of the State wherein they reside. No state shall make or enforce any laws which shall abridge the privileges or immunities of citizens of the United States; nor shall any State deprive any person of life, liberty, or property, without due process of law; nor deny to any person within its jurisdiction the equal protection of the laws.

In 1789, the United States Congress passed the **Judiciary Act**, the enabling legislation establishing the court system outlined in Article III of the Constitution. Among its provisions was the concept of **judicial review**. Basically, judicial review "authorizes the Supreme Court to hold unconstitutional, and hence, unenforceable any law, any official action based upon a law, any other action by a public official it deems-upon careful reflection and in line with the inherent tradition of the law and judicial restraint-to be in conflict with the Constitution."[17] Far too often, the lack of specifics in the Bill of Rights has produced problems for lawmakers. Too often Congress and state legislative houses have passed what they considered to be reasonable laws only to have the federal courts and the court of last resort, the Supreme Court, declare their legislative actions as unreasonable restraints upon protected civil rights and liberties, and thus unconstitutional. The Framers correctly anticipated that as the composition of the Supreme Court membership changes, so can their decisions. For example, the death penalty was ruled in 1972 as an unconstitutional violation of the Eighth Amendment only to be reinstated as constitutional by the Court in 1976.

The initial question confronting the Supreme Court was whether certain provisions of the Bill of Rights were enforceable upon just the national government or applicable to all levels of government. In *Barron v Baltimore* (1833), Chief Justice John Marshall ruled that the first ten amendments to the United States Constitution were enforceable only on the actions of the national government. Marshall believed that "the Constitution was ordained and established by the people of the United States for themselves, for their own government, and not for the government of the individual states . . . . The powers they conferred on this government were to be exercised by itself; and the limitations on power, if expressed in general terms are . . . necessarily applicable to the government created by the instrument. They are limitations of power granted in the instrument itself: not of distinct governments framed by different persons and for different reasons."[18]

The passage of the **Fourteenth Amendment** with its provisions of equal protection and due process paved the path for the Supreme Court to reverse its original decision outlined in *Barron*. In *Gitlow v New York* (1925), Gitlow challenged the ruling of the New York State Supreme Court that declared his use of the *Communist Manifesto* in classroom lectures as subversive and unconstitutionally protected speech. The Supreme Court's ruling in this case is significant for two reasons. First, the Court applied the phrase "**clear and present danger**" used initially in its ruling in *Schenck v United States* (1919), as its litmus test for determining the fine line between protected and unprotected speech. Second, and most importantly, the Court clearly expressed its desire to apply the Bill of Rights to the states through the Fourteenth Amendment. The justices rationalized that "for present purposes we may and do assume that freedom of speech and of the press which are protected by the First Amendment from abridgment by Congress are among the fundamental personal rights and liberties protected by the due process clause of the Fourteenth Amendment from impairment by the states."[19] The Supreme Court upheld Gitlow's lower court conviction. After serving nearly five years of his ten-year sentence, Gitlow was pardoned by New York Governor Al Smith.

However, the Supreme Court did not and has not yet ruled that the entire Bill of Rights is applicable to all levels of government, particularly the states. Since the *Gitlow* case, the Supreme Court has used a piece-meal and often confusing practice of **selective incorporation**. In other words, justices *selectively* apply the due process clause of the Fourteenth Amendment to the states when the constitutional issue tied to the Bill of Rights appeals to the Court's interests. The Court has incorporated the First Amendment's establishment clause (usually referred to as the separation of church and state doctrine) to the states as well as issues involving cruel and unusual punishment, right to counsel, and double jeopardy, among others. "Those provisions that remain unincorporated are: 1) grand jury indictments (Fifth Amendment), 2) trial by jury in civil cases (Seventh Amendment), 3) the excessive bail and fines prohibitions (Eighth Amendment), 4) the right to bear arms (Second Amendment), and 5) the safeguard against involuntary quartering of troops in private homes (Third Amendment)."[20] Historically, liberal jurists favor expanding incorporation whereas conservative jurists, including the current Chief Justice of the Supreme Court John Roberts, reframe from expanding the scope of the Court's jurisdiction into state affairs.

Although the Bill of Rights guarantees sweeping civil liberties and rights, one must remember that initially these rights were granted to a small segment of the population. Voting privileges were granted to only white male property owners until the election of Andrew Jackson to the presidency. According to the Constitution, Native Americans are citizens of foreign nations. They were finally granted American citizenship in 1924 and, therefore, were only then granted protected civil rights and liberties. Until the passage of the Thirteenth Amendment to the United States Constitution, African Americans were not citizens with protected rights, they were slaves or indentured servants. Even though recognized as American citizens, women did not have the rights to own property or to vote until the passage of the Nineteenth Amendment. In has taken years of political battles and corrective legislation to provide to all of this nation's citizens the rights and privileges stated in the Constitution and its Bill of Rights.

Due Process

The application of **due process** is a particularly important consideration in any issue concerning civil liberties and civil rights. Due process involves "the procedural safeguards guaranteed to those who would be deprived of life, liberty, or property because they are accused of criminal wrongdoing."[21] The Fifth and Fourteenth Amendments forbid both the national and state governments from denying to any person life, liberty, and property without due process of the law. Today the application of due process extends beyond the criminal court room to issues involving employment and termination processes, voting rights, and so on. "The concept of due process of law and its application to our federal and state governments is based on an extensive reservoir of *constitutionally expressed and implied limitations upon governmental authority*, ultimately determined by the judicial process, and upon those basic notions of fairness and decency which govern, or ought to govern, the relationships between rulers and ruled."[22] An ardent advocate for due process, Thomas Jefferson noted that "freedom of religion, freedom of the press, freedom of person under the protection of *habeas corpus*; and trial by juries impartially selected—these principles form the bright constellation which has gone before us."[23]

The law involves the concepts of procedural and substantive due process. **Substantive due process** refers "to the *content or subject matter* of a law or ordinance; that is, whether what it deals with what it is trying to accomplish, *contextually* conforms to due process of the law. The ***Dred Scott v Sandford*** case heard by the Supreme Court in 1857 "marks the first suggestion of what would become the legal doctrine of Substantive Due Process. This doctrine asserted that the constitutional guarantee of due process of law did not only require the just administration of legal *procedures*; it also allowed the courts to scrutinize the *substance of laws* for infringements of, say, the right to own private property—in the case of *Dred Scott*, slaves. Thus, the Court ruled that the Constitution barred Congress from tampering with the noxious institution of slavery."[24]   On the other hand, **procedural due process**—as the most litigated of the two—refers to the manner in which a law, an ordinance, administrative practice, or judicial task is carried out; that is, whether the procedures employed by those who are charged with the application of the law or ordinance violate *procedural* due process, regardless of the substance of the former."[25]   Laws must be equally enacted and enforced. Yet, some enactments are so vague in content that people of common intelligence must guess as to their meaning and application. Government cannot hold citizens accountable for obeying laws that provide nebulous enforcement guidelines to law enforcement personnel, judges, juries, and, of course, the citizens themselves. Second, laws must be clearly written whereby all parties understand what the law means. For example, in 1971 the Supreme Court heard arguments in *Coates v Cincinnati* that posed both procedural and substantive issues involving a Cincinnati city ordinance. Dennis Coates and several companions were arrested for violating a city ordinance that made it illegal for three or more persons who assembled on any street corner, sidewalk, or vacant lot to display any behavior that was deemed annoying to persons passing by. The Supreme Court ruled this ordinance as an unconstitutional act for several reasons. First, the ordinance was both procedurally unenforceable and too vague in content and substance. Without properly defining what constituted "annoying behavior," both citizens and law enforcement personnel were confused as to the differences between acceptable and unacceptable behavior. Like the appreciation of art, the definition of annoying behavior is a subjective one. Individual interpretation of annoying behavior leads to a discriminatory application of the ordinance. Second, the ordinance was a direct violation of the right to assemble as guaranteed by the First Amendment to the United States Constitution. Again, the power of judicial review rescued the citizen from unfair and unconstitutional treatment.

The Importance of the First Amendment

The **First Amendment** to the United States Constitution addresses the fundamental civil liberties granted to the American people. This amendment states that "Congress shall make no law respecting an establishment of religion, or prohibiting the free exercise thereof; or abridging the freedom of speech, or of the press; or the right of the people peaceably to assemble and to petition the Government for a redress of grievances." An analysis of the interpretation and application of reasonable restrictions clearly illustrates the roles the federal court system, legislative houses, interest groups, and the people have in establishing acceptable limits for exercising these freedoms.

Freedom of Religion

The phrase "Congress shall make no laws respecting the establishment of religion" is called the **establishment clause**. The Framers did not want government to sponsor one religion over others nor to advocate one religious practice over other practices. The Framers justified their actions by emphasizing century old problems the English government had when it sponsored one religion over other religions and the horrible loss of life and property resulting from religious conflicts. The tendency for one religious group to believe that their teachings and practices should take the preeminent position over other beliefs and practices has led to religious conflicts and a breakdown of religious tolerance for centuries. "The bitter memories of religious intolerance suffered by American colonists before coming to America can be seen in a statement in 1774 by the First Continental Congress declaring that the Church of England [Anglicanism] was '. . . a religion that has deluged [England] in blood, and dispersed bigotry, persecution, murder, and rebellion through every part of the world.'"[26]

Banished from the Massachusetts colony for his religious beliefs, Roger Williams "steadfastly maintained that religion was something personal, something defined by an individual's relationship with his or her god. It could not—should not be—coerced by anyone, especially kings, magistrates, or the decree of governments. Forcing someone to worship according to the Christian faith was antithetical to Christ's own teachings."[27] Subsequently, the choice of one's religious beliefs and practices would rest with the individual, not government. The Framers opted to separate church or religious issues from government by incorporating the **separation of church and state doctrine** into the First Amendment. In particular, George Washington and Thomas Jefferson stressed that religious tolerance and diversification of religious beliefs in this country were to be encouraged, not discouraged. In his capacity as the nation's first president, Washington negotiated a treaty primarily written by John Adams and ratified by the United States Senate in 1797 that assured the Muslim-dominated nation of Tripoli that "the Government of the United States is not, in any sense, founded on the Christian religion."[28] After introducing a bill stressing religious tolerance, Jefferson emphasized that the purpose of the legislation was "meant to comprehend, within the mantle of its protection, the Jew and the Gentile, the Christian and the Mahometan, the Hindoo [Hindu] and infidel of every domination" would be free to exercise their religious beliefs without prejudice from the nation's governing bodies.[29] Supreme Court Justice Hugo Black once wrote that the First Amendment's Establishment Clause meant:

> neither a state nor the Federal Government can set up a church. Neither can pass laws which aid one religion, aid all religions, or prefer one religion over another. Neither can force nor influence a person to go to or to remain away from church against his will or force him to profess a belief or disbelief in any religion. No person can be punished for entertaining or professing religious beliefs or disbeliefs, for church attendance or nonattendance. No tax in any amount, large or small, can be levied to support any religious activities or institutions, whatever they may be called, or whatever form they may adopt to teach or practice religion. Neither a state or the Federal Government can, openly or secretly, participate in the affairs of any religious organizations or groups and vice versa. In the words of Jefferson, the clause was intended to erect a wall of separation between Church and State.[30]

The Supreme Court has become the champion for ensuring that this fragile wall separating church from state remains intact by steadfastly preserving the right of individuals to hold diverse religious beliefs and practices without recrimination. Consequently, "the balance between the promise of the Declaration of Independence, with its evocation of divine origins and destiny, and the practicalities of the Constitution, with its checks on extremism, remains the most brilliant of American successes."[31] The primary religious-based issues addressed by the Supreme Court clearly indicate its historical effort to uphold that balance.

One of the initial questions concerned the use of public funds derived from tax dollars to promote education in public, private, and parochial schools. In 1947, the Supreme Court heard arguments in ***Everson v Board of Education of the Township of Ewing***, questioning the constitutionality of a New Jersey state law that providing public funding to qualifying parents to offset the costs of public transportation for their children to and from both public and private schools. Everson filed a suit challenging the use of public funds to send children to parochial schools as a violation of the Establishment Clause. In rendering their 5 to 4 decision in favor of funding the program, the justices applied the **child benefit theory** whereby public funding can be provided to students who attend public, private and parochial schools as long as it is the child, rather than the school, that benefits from the funding. Justice Black argued that the New Jersey law "does no more than provide a general program to help parents get their children, regardless of their religion, safely and expeditiously to and from accredited schools."[32] President Lyndon Johnson applied the same argument when he signed into law the Elementary and Secondary Education Act of 1965. This legislation was the first major infusion of federal money into the nation's private and public schools. The Court's ruling in ***Lemon v Kurtzman*** (1971) established the guidelines for subsequent religious-based issues. The *Lemon* case addressed two state programs that provided state funding to private schools. Pennsylvania's plan allocated state funds to private schools for instructional salaries, textbooks, and instructional materials used for nonreligious classes. The Rhode Island state legislature provided a 15 percent pay increase to teachers in private schools teaching nonreligious classes. In both cases, the Court ruled 8-1 that these programs were unconstitutional violations of separation of church and state. Writing for the majority of the Court, Chief Justice Warren Burger emphasized that "we need not decide whether these legislative precautions restrict the principal or primary effort of the programs to the point where they do not offend the Religious Clauses, for we conclude that the cumulative impact of the entire relationship arising under the statutes in each State involves excessive government entanglement between government and religion."[33] The resulting **Lemon Test** is a three-part test that determines whether the law's purpose is basically secular; whether the law's primary effect neither advances nor inhibits religion; and whether the law excessively entangles church and state. For example, in ***Mitchell v Helms*** (2000) the Supreme Court upheld a Louisiana law providing public funding for instructional equipment to include computers, maps, books, etc., to both public and private schools as long as it is "in a secular neutral non-ideological way."[34] The Supreme Court also upheld a lower court's ruling in favor of a 1997 Arizona law granting a tax credit up to $500 for donations to parochial and private school scholarship and tuition assistance programs. Once again, the money is donated to a program benefiting students and is not directed to any particular school.

In response to the declining quality of the nation's public school systems, the Republican Party, guided by members of its conservative wing, advocated voucher programs whereby parents could choose to transfer their children from low performing public schools to higher rated public, private, and parochial schools. To offset additional tuition, textbook and transportation costs, parents would receive taxpayer-funded vouchers. For example, the Ohio state legislature adopted a pilot program for children attending public schools in Cleveland. "The program gave parents $2,250 per child in tuition vouchers to be used in about 50 schools."[35] Declaring that the "Ohio program is entirely neutral with respect to religion," the Supreme Court ruled in its 2002 session that the

Students in public schools have always prayed, especially around test time. But, the Court objects to sponsorship or encouragement of prayer by public-school authorities. The Court has ruled that prayer can not be an attempt on the part of the government to promote religion.

Cleveland voucher program is constitutional.[36] "Justice Sandra Day O'Connor; writing a concurring opinion with the majority of the Supreme Court, said she was 'persuaded that the Cleveland voucher program affords parents of eligible children genuine non-religious options consistent with separation of church and state protections."[37] Since this ruling, state legislative houses across the nation have either initiated or entertained legislation sponsoring school voucher programs.

Perhaps the most controversial religious issue addressed by the Supreme Court is prayer in the public school systems. In 1962 and 1963, the Supreme Court heard two cases challenging government-sponsored prayer in the classroom. In *Engle v Vitale* (1962), Steven Engle challenged a 1951 decision of the New York State Board of Regents to approve a brief prayer for recital in the public schools. In 1958, the New Hyde Park School District required their students to recite the prayer each day in every class. Engle protested on the grounds that his two children were required to recite the prayer. Engle charged that an official prayer mandated to be recited in the public schools violated both the First Amendment's guarantees of freedom of religion and the separation of church and state doctrine. The Supreme Court ruled 8 to 1 in favor of Engle. Justice Black wrote "that by using its public school system to encourage recitation of the Regents' prayer, the State of New York has adopted a practice wholly inconsistent with the Establishment Clause. *There can, of course, be no doubt* that New York's program of daily classroom invocation of God's blessing as prescribed in the Regents' prayer is a religious activity. It is a solemn avowal of divine faith and supplication for the blessing of the Almighty. . . [T]he constitutional prohibition against laws respecting an establishment of religion must at least mean that in this country it is no part of the business of government to compose official prayers for any group of the American people to recite as part of a religious program carried on by government."[38]

The companion case was the *School District of Abington Township v Schempp* (1963). In this case, a Pennsylvania law required the verbal reading of ten verses from the Bible at the beginning of each school day in all public schools. Children could be excused from this exercise with parental consent. The Schempp family objected to the readings because their Unitarian faith did not interpret the meaning of the Bible in the same manner as other religions. They also felt that their children were the subjects of ridicule because they were sent out into the hallway during the readings. Ruling 8 to 1 in favor of Schempp, the Supreme Court decided that mandated Biblical readings conducted in a public school setting were indeed an unconstitutional violation of the doctrine of separation of church and state.

In both cases, the Supreme Court never ruled that prayer in the public schools was unconstitutional. Since the *Engle* and *Schempp* rulings, the Supreme Court has addressed several cases concerning prayer in the nation's public schools. In 1985, for example, the Court heard arguments in **Wallace v Jaffree**. The primary issue focused on the implementation of an 1981 law passed by the Alabama state legislature which stated that "at the commencement of the first class of each day in all grades in all public schools the teacher in charge of the room in which each class is held, may announce that a period of silence not to exceed one minute in duration shall be observed for meditation or voluntary prayer, and during any such period no other activities shall be engaged in."[39] On behalf of his three children, Ishmael Jaffree charged that the Alabama law was an unconstitutional act in violation of the First Amendment's guarantee of religious freedom. Initially, a federal district court judge upheld the Alabama law. However, a federal appellant court overturned the lower court's ruling. In a 6 to 3 decision, the Supreme Court upheld the appellant court's decision. Justice Paul Stevens stressed that "the legislation [was] enacted for the sole purpose of expressing the State's endorsement of prayer activities for one minute at the beginning of each school day. The addition of 'or voluntary prayer' indicates that the State intended to characterize prayer as a favored practice. Such an endorsement is not consistent with the establishment principle that the government must pursue a course of complete neutrality toward religion."[40]

In 1992, the Supreme Court ruled in **Lee v Weisman** that clergy-led prayer at public school graduation ceremonies is a violation of the separation of church and state doctrine. "That ruling allowed prayer at school graduation ceremonies only if school officials instructed students to keep them non-sectarian and non-proselytizing."[41] The Supreme Court also addressed the issue of student-led prayers at high school football games. Students attending the Santa Fe School District in Texas decided to continue the tradition of a pre-game prayer conducted by a member of the student body over the stadium's public address system. Two parents sought legal action to end public pre-game prayers. The 5th United States Circuit Court of Appeals ruled that student-led prayers were an unconstitutional violation of the First Amendment's Establishment Clause. The Supreme Court has consistently upheld the belief that *voluntary* prayer in the nation's public schools is legal; however, *involuntary* prayer is not!

The current trend is to allow "a moment of silence" or "a moment for self-reflection" to be used in the public school systems. This policy underscores voluntary self reflection without mentioning the word prayer. The constitutionality of "a moment of silence" was upheld by the Supreme Court during its 2001 session when the justices declined to address a challenge to a lower court's affirmation of Virginia's moment of silence law. "For nearly 25 years, Virginia law allowed school districts the choice of holding a moment of silence for 60 seconds. . . But in 2000, the state's legislature and governor changed the law to require that all schools take part in the moment."[42] The Virginia law clearly met the Supreme Court's litmus test since it is "a moment of silence law that is clearly drafted and implemented so as to permit prayer, meditation, and reflection within the prescribed period, without endorsing one alternative over the others . . .[because it does] not favor the child who chooses to pray over the child who chooses to meditate or reflect."[43]

Traditionally, the Supreme Court has held that religious practices are constitutional as long as the activity is lawful and does not violate the personal rights or the property of others. The Supreme

Court upheld the use of animal sacrifices as a bona fide religious ceremony in its ruling in *Church of the Lukumi Babbalu Aye v Hialeah* (1993). In *West Virginia State Board of Education v Barnette* (1943), the Supreme Court ruled that the state's law requiring all teachers and pupils in the public schools to participate in a daily flag salute ceremony or face expulsion from school clearly violated the religious rights of members of the Jehovah Witnesses. Writing for the majority, Justice Jackson stated that "to sustain the compulsory flag salute, we are required to say that a Bill of Rights which guards the individual's right to speak his own mind, left it open to public authorities to compel him to utter what is not in his mind."[44] During its 2014 term, the Supreme Court ruled in *Town of Greece v Galloway* that the use of a sectarian prayer at the beginning of a city council or town hall meeting was constitutional. The Court also addressed if an employer can deny their employees certain benefits based upon the employer's religious beliefs. The issue concerned a provision under the Affordable Care Act requiring employers to provide insurance coverage to their female employees for contraception. In 2014, the Court ruled in *Burwell v Hobby Lobby* that the First Amendment's protection of religious freedom did allow the employer to deny this coverage since it conflicted with his/her own personal religious beliefs. The Court, however, has always required employers to provide **reasonable** religious accommodations to their employees, such as honoring one's religious holidays and practices. For example, in *Equal Employment Opportunity Commission v Abercrombie and Fitch* (2015), the Court ruled that the employer's actions of firing a female employee for wearing her hijab at work as a violation of the company's dress code was an unconstitutional act of religious discrimination. In a wide variety of rulings on complex issues ranging from school prayer to state-funded public/private education voucher programs, the Supreme Court has consistently upheld that the "**exercise clause** protects our right to believe or not to believe in any religious doctrine, prohibits all government regulation of religious beliefs; forbids the government from compelling us to worship; prohibits the punishment of religious beliefs that the government believes to be false; and denies to the state the power to grant benefits or place burdens on the basis of religious beliefs or status."[45]

Freedom of Speech

Over the 2012 summer months, a controversial film condemning Islam and its prophet Mohammad produced by an independent American filmmaker was seen in movie theaters throughout the world, resulting in deadly riots and protests throughout the Middle East. Worldwide Islamic leaders and heads of the Arab states called upon President Obama to ban the movie and silence its producer. However, the president upheld to the belief that the right to express one's opinion is a sacred privilege to all Americans. Although we may not like what some people say and do, we do respect their right to express their viewpoints. Addressing the membership of the United Nations, Obama told the gathering that although the movie was indeed inflammatory to the Islamic faith, the filmmaker had the protected right to express his viewpoint. In America, he pointed out:

> We do so because in a diverse society, efforts to restrict speech can become a tool to silence critics, or oppress minorities. We do so because given our power of faith in our lives, and the passion that religious differences can inflame, the strongest weapon against hateful speech is not repression, it is more speech—the voices of tolerance that rally against bigotry and

blasphemy, and lift up the values of understanding and mutual respect. Americans have fought the globe to protect the right of all people to express their views.[46]

Any government action slightly resembling censorship is met with sharp criticism. Lawmakers do not want to repeat the backlash the Federalist Party received in 1798 when it ventured into the realm of censorship with the passage of four laws commonly known as the **Alien and Sedition Acts**. The Federalists' rationale for suppressing free speech was deeply rooted in the developing revolution in France. They viewed the overthrow of the French monarchy "as the degeneration of legitimate government into mob rule, particularly during the 1793 and 1794 bloody 'Reign of Terror' when counterrevolutionaries lost their lives on the guillotine. Federalist fears deepened as they watched the new French republican government encourage wars of liberation and conquest in Belgium, Switzerland, Holland, and on the Italian peninsula. In 1798 rumors spread about a possible French invasion of America, one that allegedly would be supported by American traitors and a large number of French émigrés that grew to more than 20,000."[47] The **Naturalization Act** extended the immigrant residency requirement for citizenship from five to fourteen years. The president was empowered through both the **Alien Act** and **Alien Enemies Act** to arrest and subsequently expel all aliens deemed to be a threat to the security of the nation. The most objectionable law was the **Sedition Act,** which made it "illegal to publish or utter any statements about the government that were 'false, scandalous and malicious' with the 'intent to defame' or to bring Congress or the president into 'contempt or disrepute.'"[48] Several journalists were tried and convicted of violating the Sedition Act. The legality of the Sedition Act was one of the primary issues in the presidential election of 1800 as Republican candidate Thomas Jefferson denied Federalist candidate John Adams a second presidential term of office. Jefferson subsequently repealed the Sedition Act and pardoned those convicted of violating it.

Overall, Supreme Court decisions have expanded the scope of the freedoms of speech and expression from political campaigns to video games. In 1976, the Court ruled in ***Buckley v Valeo*** that a provision of 1974 congressional act limiting how much personal money a candidate could spend on his/her election was unconstitutional. The rationale was that candidates must have every opportunity to reach out to the voting public. The same sentiment guided the Court's 2010 decision in ***Citizens United v Federal Elections Commission*** when it declared a provision in the Bipartisan Campaign Reform Act barring the airing of political advertisements days before an election day as an unconstitutional violation of free speech. It also struck down an Arizona law that gave state matching campaign funds to candidates who adhered to the state mandated personal campaign spending level as once again, a violation of free speech. In 2011, the Court ruled unconstitutional a California law banning the sale of videos deemed too violent for children. During its 2015 term, the Court heard two cases involving free speech issues. In ***Reed v Town of Gilbert, Arizona,*** the Court ruled as an unconstitutional violation of the First Amendment a town ordinance placing different limits of acceptable language for political, ideological, and direction signs. In ***Walker v Texas Division of the Sons of Confederate Veterans***, the issue involved whether the Department of Transportation (TXDOT) in Texas could prohibit the issuance of specialty license plates bearing the Confederate war flag. TXDOT officials viewed the display of this flag as a racially discriminatory action against the state's African-American community. The Court decided that the action taken by TXDOT was appropriate and, therefore, not a violation of the First Amendment's guarantee to free speech.

However, the Court has drawn the line between acceptable and unacceptable exercises of free speech. Simply, we do not have the absolute right to say or to do whatever we want to do. The Supreme Court has distinguished protected speech from unconstitutional breaches of freedom of speech. **Pure speech** is "speech without any conduct."[49] A person's words are constitutionally protected as long as those words do not pose a harm to others. The Supreme Court distinguished acceptable from unacceptable speech in its ruling in *Schenck v United States* (1919). Schenck had been convicted by a lower court for violating the Espionage Act of 1917 by distributing Socialist-inspired leaflets encouraging men to resist the draft imposed at the height of World War I. Ruling unanimously against Schenck, the Supreme Court ruled that his actions created a "clear and present danger" to others. Justice Holmes wrote:

> We admit that in many places and in *ordinary times* the defendants in saying all that was said in the circular would have been within their constitutional rights. *But the character of every act depends upon the circumstances in which it is done.* . . . The most stringent protection of free speech would not protect a man in *falsely* shouting fire in a theatre and causing a panic. It does not even protect a man from an injunction against uttering words that have all the effects of force. . . . *The question in every case is whether the words used are used in such circumstances and are of such a nature as to create* **a clear and present danger** *that they will bring about the substantive evils that Congress has a right to prevent.* When a nation is at war many things that might be said in time of peace are such a hindrance to its effort that their utterance will not be endured so long as men fight and that no Court could regard them as being protected by any constitutional right.[50]

Words that present a clear and present danger are unconstitutional. Collectively these words are called **fighting words**. The Supreme Court defines fighting words as words that by their very nature inflict injury upon those to whom they are addressed. If an individual's words incite his/her audience to violence, then that individual can be held accountable for the crowd's actions. It is the resulting actions of the words and not necessarily the words themselves that can be deemed unconstitutional. For example, in 2010, the Supreme Court heard arguments against the actions of the Westboro Baptist Church of Kansas. The congregation composed mostly of family members of its pastor, stage anti-gay protests on public property during the funerals of servicemen killed in combat. Their signs reflect their viewpoint that God is punishing America for its support of the gay community by killing its soldiers. Although the words are indeed painful to family members attending the funeral services of their fallen soldiers, the Supreme Court ruled that the words on the signs and the actions of the protestors do not by themselves lead to violence, and are therefore, protected by the First Amendment.

Symbolic speech is "the use of symbols, rather than words, to convey ideas."[51] The turmoil of Vietnam in the late 60s and early 70s filled the Supreme Court's docket with cases involving the use of symbolic speech. In 1969, the Supreme Court heard arguments in *Tinker v Des Moines School District*. The defendants were thirteen-year old Mary Beth Tinker, her fifteen-year brother

Not all areas of free speech are protected. The Court has ruled that some practices are clearly illegal. Here, Goddard C. Graves, 22, burns his selective service classification card in front of the local draft board office as a protest against the Vietnam War. Although this gesture of symbolic speech is prohibited, a ruling by the Court gave such protection to burning the American flag.

John, and fifteen-year old Christopher Eckhart. These three students decided to wear black armbands protesting the war in Vietnam to school. The high school administration had a policy prohibiting the wearing of any armbands to school. Violators would be required to remove them, be sent home, and suspended from school. The students were joined by four others who, in turn, refused to remove them and were subsequently suspended. The school district argued that the wearing of these armbands presented a clear and present danger to other students. The Supreme Court ruled differently in a 7-2 ruling supporting the students' First Amendment rights. Speaking for the majority, Justice Abe Fortas wrote that "First Amendment rights, applied in the light of special characteristics of the school environment, are available to teachers and students. It can be hardly argued that either students or teachers shed their constitutional right of freedom of speech or expression at the schoolhouse gate. Maintaining that right might spawn disagreements and disturbances, but our Constitution says that we must take that risk, and our history says that it is this sort of hazardous freedom—the kind of openness—that is the basis of our national strength and of independence and vigor of Americans."[52] Yet, the justices also recognized the role of school authorities to "bar speech given reasonable evidence that such a speech would 'materially and substantially' interfere with good scholastic order."[53] Furthermore, the Supreme Court ruled in *Cohen v California* (1971) that the wearing of a jacket bearing an inappropriate four-letter word against the draft was a protected right. However, the Supreme Court does not consider a violation of a law to be a constitutionally protected expression of free speech. In *United States v O'Brien* (1968), the Supreme Court, for example, upheld O'Brien's conviction for burning his draft card in protest against Vietnam. Although O'Brien's protest was constitutionally protected, his actions of destroying government documents (draft cards) were not afforded the same protection.

The burning of the American flag evokes the strong emotions of the American people. However, the Supreme Court has held the burning of the flag in protest as a protected expression of speech. In *Street v New York* (1969), the Supreme Court reversed a lower court's conviction of Street for

The Court stated, "We do not consecrate the flag by punishing its desecration, for in doing so we dilute the freedom that this cherished emblem represents."

defacing and burning the flag. Street's defiant actions followed the 1960 ambush shooting of James Meredith in Mississippi. Likewise, during the 1984 Republican National Convention held in Dallas, Texas, Gregory Johnson headed a political protest against President Reagan. Following their march, Johnson set fire to an American flag soaked in kerosene. No bystanders were physically injured. Johnson was arrested by the Dallas police and charged with a violation of a state law prohibiting the desecration of the American flag. He was convicted in a Texas court of a Class A misdemeanor and sentenced to one year in prison and a $2,000 fine. In a close 5 to 4 decision, the Supreme Court ruled in *Texas v Johnson* that Johnson's actions were constitutionally protected under the First Amendment. Stressing that burning the American flag is not under normal circumstances socially acceptable, Justice Brennan wrote: "Our decision is a reaffirmation of the principles of freedom and inclusiveness that the flag but reflects, and of the conviction that our toleration of criticism such as Johnson's is a sign and source of our strength. We do not consecrate the flag by punishing its desecration, for in doing so we dilute the freedom that this cherished emblem represents."[54] In 1989, Congress thought it had afforded the American flag the appropriate protection with the passage of the Federal Flag Protection Act, only to have it declared unconstitutional by the Supreme Court a year later.

The anti-Vietnam War protests of the 60s and 70s resurfaced with the George W. Bush administration's invasion of Iraq. The fear of potential terrorist acts on American soil moved the Federal Bureau of Investigation (FBI) and the Department of Homeland Security to closely monitor the formation and in particular, the tactics used by anti-war groups. In the time of war or threats to national security, the line separating protected from unprotected speech is blurred. Recalling the infiltration tactics used by the Nixon administration during the height of Vietnam, Anthony Romero, executive director of the American Civil Liberties Union, stated "the FBI is dangerously targeting Americans who are engaged in nothing more than lawful protest and dissent. The line between terrorism and legitimate civil disobedience is blurred, and I have a serious concern about whether we're going back to the days of [J. Edgar] Hoover."[55] Of course, this nation can ill-afford a repeat of events that occurred at Kent State University on May 4, 1970. Across the nation, college students were demonstrating against the Vietnam War and, in particular, President Nixon's decision to bomb Cambodia. The governor of Ohio vowed to "use 'every force possible' to maintain order and drive the protestors out of Kent. He called them 'worse than the brown shirts and the communist element, and also the nightriders and the vigilantes. They are the worse type of people we harbor in America.'"[56] The governor called in the National Guard to break up the protests and bring calm back to the campus. On that fateful day, the guardsmen were supposed to peacefully disperse the crowd from the college's Commons area. After throwing gas canisters at the students, the guardsmen retreated only to have angry students follow them. Suddenly, "28 guardsmen wheeled and fired on students. At 12:55 p.m., 61 shots from M-1 rifles rained down the hill [near the Commons] for 13 seconds . . . . Four students lay dead in the parking lot, and nine others were wounded."[57]

Freedom of speech is unconstitutionally protected when its use deliberately harms the character and reputation of another person. **Slander** is verbal malicious attacks against another person. On the other hand, **libel** is defamation of character in print or by other visual presentations. The reasonable restrictions involving slander and libel revolve around the intent of the initiating party. In 1964, the Supreme Court addressed the issue of libel in its decision in **New York Times v Sullivan**. "*Sullivan* arose over two principles in conflict: the right of the press to publish without government interference and the right of individuals to use the government—that is, the courts—to obtain recompense when defamed."[58] Sullivan, a Montgomery, Alabama police commissioner, was awarded $500,000 in damages by a lower court to settle his lawsuit against the *New York Times* for printing an advertisement containing false statements charging his police force with brutality and discrimination against African Americans. The Supreme Court reversed the lower court decision. The *New York Times* was deemed not accountable for several reasons. First, public officials are natural targets for verbal and printed attacks. Second, erroneous statements are often unavoidable. If the media were held accountable for every erroneous statement it made, the courts would be flooded with libel and slander cases. Third, and most importantly, the Supreme Court ruled that "even false statements about official conduct, therefore, enjoy constitutional protection, unless they were made with actual malice; that is with the knowledge that they were false or with a reckless disregard of whether or not they were false."[59] The mere printing of false statements is not libel unless those statements were printed with a reckless disregard for the truth for the sole purpose of maliciously harming the reputation of an individual.

In the future, the Supreme Court will be confronted in judging the constitutionality of state laws criminalizing bullying tactics that oftentimes are so severely painful that the victim commits suicide. While there is no federal law on the books condemning or criminalizing the practice of bullying, all fifty state legislative houses have passed legislation condemning and in forty-three states criminalizing incidents of bullying in their public-school systems. The questions are multi-leveled. Can school district officials and law enforcement monitor an individual's access to the internet to determine whether or not those e-mails constitute bullying? At what point does the initiator's use of the internet cease to be a protected First Amendment right? Can the initiator of these e-mails be charged with a crime if the recipient of those hurtful e-mails commits suicide?

Adult book stores, such as this one, have been the battlefield for many local communities. Although the Supreme Court has ruled that it is unconstitutional to ban them, zoning ordinances restricting them to certain areas is permissible.

Obscenity

If art is in the eyes of the beholder, the same standard applies to determining what is or is not obscene. According to the United States Constitution, we do have the freedom to express ourselves in both word and deed. Paintings, motion pictures, advertisements, dance forms, sculpture, and literature are modes of expression. One's personal judgement as to whether a painting is an art worthy piece or an obscene depiction should be a personal decision. However, too often it is left to the courts to determine what constitutes obscenity and to establish the criteria for reasonable restrictions. In *Roth v United States* (1957), Justice Brennan drew a fine line in distinguishing the difference between constitutionally and unconstitutionally protected creative expression. Writing for the majority, Brennan pointed out that "the First Amendment was not intended to protect every utterance . . . . All ideas having even the slightest redeeming social importance—unorthodox ideas, controversial ideas, even ideas hateful to the prevailing climate of opinion—have the full protection of the guaranties unless excludable because they encroach upon the limited area of more important interests. But implicit in the history of the First Amendment is the rejection of obscenity as utterly without redeeming social importance . . . It has been well observed that such utterances are no essential part of any exposition of ideas, and are of such slight social value as a step to truth that any benefit that may be derived from them is clearly outweighed by the social interest in order and morality. . . . We hold that obscenity is not within the area of constitutionally protected speech or press."[60] Chief Justice Earl Warren believed that precisely defining obscenity was "the Court's most difficult area of adjudication. What is 'obscenity' to some is mere 'realism' to others; what is 'lascivious' in the eyes of one reader is merely 'colorful' in those of another; what is 'lewd' to one parent may well be 'instructive' to another."[61] In *Miller v California* (1973), the Supreme Court ruled that actions or objects could be deemed obscene only if they meet all three of the following criteria:

1. Whether the average person, applying contemporary community standards, would find that the work taken as a whole, appeals to the prurient interest.

2.   Whether the work depicts or describes, in a patently offensive way, sexual conduct specifically defined by the applicable state law.

3.   Whether the work taken as a whole, lacks serious literary, artistic, political or scientific value.[62]

Reasonable restrictions tell us that the personal possession of obscene materials by an adult is a protected right. However, the sale and distribution of sexually explicit materials to minors are a crime. Child pornography is a crime. Erotic dancing by an adult, however, is a form of expression legally protected by the First Amendment. Basically for the majority of the obscenity cases argued in the nation's courts, the distinction between legal and illegal activities is determined primarily by the age of the participating parties.

Freedom of the Press

Owner of a printing company, James Franklin hired his twelve-year old brother Benjamin as his apprentice. Benjamin Franklin eventually published his own newspaper—*The Pennsylvanian Gazette*. In his editorial *Apology for Printers*, Franklin wrote that "'the job of printers is to allow people to express these differing opinions.' There would be very little printed, he noted, if publishers produced only things that offended nobody. 'Printers are educated in the belief that when men differ in opinion, both sides ought equally to have the advantage of being heard by the public; and that when Truth and Error have fair play, the former is always an overmatch for the latter. It is unreasonable to imagine that printers approve of everything they print. If its likewise unreasonable what some assert, that printers ought not to print anything but what they approve; since . . . an end would thereby be put to free writing, and the world would afterwards have nothing to read but what happened to be the opinion of printers."[63]

A free press is essential to democratic governments. Citizens do have the right to know what their government is or is not doing. The Supreme Court has protected the sanctity of the fourth estate, the press. In 1931, the Supreme Court established the boundary line of "**no prior restraint**" in its decision in *Near v Minnesota*. The editor of the *Saturday Press*, Jay Near, was well known for using his paper to express his "anti-Semitic, anti-Catholic, anti-labor, and anti-black viewpoints. In addition, in a series of articles, Near charged that Minneapolis police and prosecutors were in collusion with Jewish gangsters involved in gambling, bootlegging, and racketeering.[64] The county attorney decided to "stop the presses" by accusing Near of being in violation of a Minnesota public nuisance law prohibiting the publishing of materials deemed to be "malicious, scandalous and defamatory."[65] Ruling in favor of Near, the Supreme Court's decision mandated that the only time government can legally bar the press from publishing a story is when such an action poses a real and eminent threat to national security. For example, it would have been a threat to national security for the press to publish in advance the exact date and time of the dropping of nuclear bombs on Japan during World War II or to divulge the schedule for sending scud missiles into Iraq during the Gulf War. It is not a breach of national security to publish information about these activities after the fact.

The concept of no prior restraint was held to close scrutiny when the Supreme Court heard arguments in *New York Times v United States* (1971). The case centered on the actions of Daniel

Dr. Daniel Ellsberg, antiwar activist who was arrested for releasing the secret "Pentagon Papers," holds an impromptu news conference outside a federal building in Boston while his wife, Patricia, waits behind him. Daniel Ellsberg was indicted for espionage, theft, and conspiracy. His case was dismissed on the grounds of government misconduct.

Ellsberg, a temporary federal employee who discovered a cache of secret government documents detailing the cover-up by the federal government regarding the United States' initial entry into the Vietnam conflict. Ellsberg was a trusted ally to the paper's reporters since he occasionally provided background information for storylines. Ellsberg voluntarily offered the seized documents to the *New York Times* and the *Washington Post*. After publishing the first excerpts from the documents, both newspapers were placed under federal court ordered injunctions to stop the presses. The federal government claimed that publishing these sensitive documents presented a threat to national security, even though the United States was already heavily involved in the Vietnam conflict. The Supreme Court ruled against the federal government's actions. Justice Black credited the papers' bold actions to print the documents by stating, "in my view, far from deserving condemnation for their courageous reporting, the *New York Times,* the *Washington Post*, and other newspapers should be commended for serving the purpose that the Framers saw so clearly. In revealing the workings of government that led to the Vietnam War, the newspapers nobly did precisely that which the Founders [Framers] hoped and trusted they would do."[66] The Supreme Court also decided that the purported threat to national security was non-existent since the event had already happened. Ellsberg, however, still suffered the consequences of his actions. He was charged by federal authorities for violating the Espionage Act of 1917, a conviction carrying a 110-year sentence. All charges against Ellsberg were dismissed by a federal judge on the grounds that federal investigative agencies used illegal tactics in gathering evidence against him. A similar fate may wait for Eric Snowden, an employee of the National Security Agency (NSA) who leaked to the public the internal records of the NSA detailing the agency's monitoring of e-mails, internet connections, and phone calls made by American citizens. The agency justifies its actions by pointing out that preventive rather than reactive actions will halt terrorist attacks against the United States. Snowden and his supporters take the position that the agency's policies violate protected First Amendment rights. Wanted for numerous federal criminal charges including treason, Snowden fled the United States and was granted asylum in Russia.

Although the First Amendment initially extended constitutional protections to the print media, the rise of the electronic media to include television, cable, and internet accessibility has expanded the application of "freedom of the press." Established in 1934, the **Federal Communications Commission (FCC)** sets the programming and broadcasting guidelines for the majority of the nation's television and radio stations. In 1996, Congress passed the **Telecommunications Act** requiring cable stations that did not abide by the FCC's programming guidelines for airing sexually explicit programs only at late-night hours to completely block out their signal to protect children from watching these programs. In a 5 to 4 decision, the Supreme Court ruled that the Telecommunications Act was an unconstitutional infringement upon the stations' protected First Amendment rights. In 1997, the Supreme Court ruled that the **Communications Decency Act** was an unconstitutional infringement upon users of the internet. The act banned the electronic transmission of any materials deemed indecent to minors. "This was the first time that the highest court had contemplated the status of the key medium of the next century. Instead of regarding the Net with caution the court usually shows while exploring new frontiers, the justices went out of their way to assure that this most democratic of mediums would receive the highest level of protection. Internet speakers will not be shackled with the regulations that limit content on television and radio; instead, they will enjoy the freedom granted to printed matter."[67]

Assembly and Association

A basic civil liberty granted to all American citizens is the right to associate with others and to assemble or to join their ranks if we so choose to do so. The freedom of association is just as important to a free society as the freedoms of speech, redress, and religion. Our history, however, has been severely tainted by the actions of racial supremacy groups, such as the Klan, skinhead groups, the American Nazi Party, and so on. However, in times that pose a threat to national security, the federal government is empowered by federal legislation to take extraordinary steps to protect its citizens. Particularly in the aftermath of September 11, 2001, outraged citizens demanded that the White House and Congress enact measures empowering federal agencies to investigate the actions of, identify members affiliated with, and even infiltrate the ranks of international terrorist organizations as well as domestic-based interest groups hostile to the American government. However, the Framers never intended for governing authorities at any level to legislate whether citizens could affiliate with certain groups deemed in conflict with our nation's fundamental principles. The rights to protest and redress the government are fundamental constitutionally protected rights. Allowing

The price of free society! The Court has ruled that the constitutional right to free speech and assembly apply to all citizens regardless of how offensive their beliefs might be to the majority.

someone to join the local PTA but arresting a person affiliated with a white supremacist group is unconstitutional. However, individuals can be held legally accountable for their actions that violate another's rights to life and property whether their actions were guided by a group's philosophy or advocacy of violence.

In determining whether an action is constitutional, the fine line for the Supreme Court has been the difference between mere advocacy and action. In 1969, the Supreme Court heard arguments in ***Brandenburg v Ohio,*** a landmark case that set the stage for subsequent rulings in assembly-related cases. Charles Brandenburg, leader of a local Ku Klux Klan (KKK) chapter, invited a television station to film several Klan rallies. The film contained excerpts from his speech in which he stated that "if our president, our Congress, our Supreme Court, continues to suppress the white, Caucasian race, it's possible that there might have to be some revengence taken."[68] No violent action resulted from his speech. Brandenburg, however, was arrested and convicted of violating Ohio's Criminal Syndicalism Act, prohibiting the advocacy of terrorism. The Supreme Court overturned Brandenburg's conviction because the Ohio statute was designed "to punish mere advocacy and to forbid on pain of criminal punishment, assembly with others merely to advocate the described type of action. Such a statute falls within the condemnation of the First and Fourteenth Amendments."[69]

The question of assembly arose once again in 1978 with the emotionally charged case, ***Village of Skokie v National Socialist Party.*** The National Socialist Party, also known as the American Nazi Party, wanted to hold a public march through the predominately Jewish suburb of Skokie, Illinois. Since the majority of the suburb's residents were either survivors of or had lost relatives in the Nazi concentration camps of World War II, they were furious and petitioned their city council to deny the group a parade permit. Denied the permit, the Nazi Party filed a challenge on the grounds that their First Amendment rights had been violated. The Illinois state courts refused to allow the march on the grounds that it might create a clear and present danger to the residents of Skokie. The Supreme Court reversed all lower court rulings on the grounds that a mere presumption of violence is not a valid reason to deny the group's constitutional right to march. This decision was a reasonable restriction accommodating to both parties. Although the Nazi Party decided to bypass Skokie and march through downtown Chicago, they retained their constitutional right to stage a public march as long as they applied for the proper permits. For those who would have been offended by the message of the marchers, their protected rights not to watch the march were preserved!

On May 25, 2020, four Minneapolis, Wisconsin police officers used a deadly chokehold in their attempts to arrest George Floyd. Ruled a homicide, Floyd's death resulted in both international and nationwide protests against police violence and reignited the "Black Lives Matter" movement originally organized in 2013 following the killing of Trayvon Martin, an African-American youth shot by George Zimmerman in 2012. In Minneapolis and other major cities across the nation, peaceful demonstrations quickly turned to violent riots against law enforcement resulting in beatings, lootings, and the destruction of private and public properties. The scenes on the evening news of protesters wearing "I can't breathe" masks reminded many of the rioting and destruction and burning of properties in the Watts area of Los Angeles, California, following the jury verdict in the Rodney King case. With the protests and, unfortunately, the violence erupting across the country, the Trump administration wanted to declare a national emergency and activate both national guard units and the military to quell the violence. While in the United States, peaceful protests are protected constitutional rights of free speech and assembly, wanton violence against persons and property is not afforded constitutional protection. **Riot Acts** or **Anti-Riot Acts** have been on the nation's legislative books since colonial times.

In 1714, the British Parliament enacted a Riot Act making it a felony offense for "any persons to the number of 12 or more unlawfully, riotously, and tumultuously assemble together to the disturbance of the public peace" for more than one hour.[70] This law was an improvement over previous Parliamentary acts making rioting "punishable by death, often preceded by torture and degradation so harsh as to alienate citizens and encourage juries to nullify the law by refusing to find individuals guilty of rioting."[71] Enforcing the Riot Act fell upon local authorities, not the British military. The Riot Act extended to all British colonial possessions to include the American colonies. However, several of the American colonies took matters into their own hands by enacting their own versions of a riot act. "Colonial Connecticut needed only a single jailbreak to pass a riot act in 1722. New Jersey, where mobs repeatedly had broken into jails to rescue prisoners, passed a riot act in 1747 to keep the peace. Pennsylvania imposed a riot act in 1764. . . In 1770, the face-off that became the Boston Massacre occurred with no reading of the Riot Act because no civilian authority had summoned the Redcoats who did the shooting. . . North Carolina passed a riot act in 1771 which 'made it a felony for crowds of 10 or more to remain in place within an hour of the reading of the act,' allowed official use of force without investigation, exempted from prosecution deputies accused of maiming or killing rioters, and authorized the governor to raise a militia at public expense to enforce the measure."[72] The Militia Act of 1792 was passed by Congress calling upon local militias to restore peace as well as "empowering the president, upon state request, to issue a proclamation ordering 'insurgents to disperse, and retire peaceable to their respective abodes within a limited time.'"[73]

While the Civil Rights Act of 1968 is hailed as a victory for the 1960s civil rights movement, this act has its own anti-riot provision making it a federal offense to cross intentionally from one state into another state for the purpose of either personally or aiding and abetting others in inciting a riot. While most state-initiated anti-riot laws fail to pass, currently only Tennessee, Oklahoma and North and South Dakota have enacted them. SB 902 passed by the Tennessee state legislature levies a $200 fine for anyone obstructing access to a street or highway for an emergency vehicle. In Oklahoma, HB 1123 punishes protestors who trespass on "critical infrastructures" and HB 2128 makes anyone arrested for rioting liable for any property damage caused in the act of his/her trespassing on public or private property. In the 1990s, the Presidential Executive Order on Restoring State, Tribal and Local Law Enforcement's Access to Life-Saving Equipment and Resources reinstated a previous order allowing for the transfer of surplus military equipment to police departments to handle riotous situations. President Obama opted not to use federal action to end the riots prompted by the killing of Michael Brown by Ferguson, Missouri police officers on August 10, 2014. Trump restored the program when he signed Executive Order 13809 in 2017. If a state governor requests it, the federal government will send for free, weaponized vehicles, certain large-caliber ammunition, riot gear, and other military equipment to end violent protests and riots. Although no governors requested federal military assistance, the Trump administration did deploy national guard units to protect the White House and other federal buildings from potential destruction.

The rise of teenage gangs has prompted municipal governments across the country to implement curfew laws designed to restrict teenagers' accessibility to gang-related activities. These city ordinances mandate that unsupervised juveniles cannot be allowed on city streets after a predetermined time period. In 1999, the Supreme Court essentially gave municipal governments a green light to continue curfew laws. The same court, however, ruled that an anti-gang ordinance crafted by the Chicago, Illinois, city council was unconstitutional. Enacted in 1992, the ordinance allowed the Chicago police to disperse and/or arrest individuals "if they stood or sat around in one place with no apparent purpose in the presence of a suspected gang member."[74] In *Chicago v Morales*, the Supreme Court ruled 6 to 3 that this ordinance was a violation of the First Amendment's right to association and assembly. Writing in support of the majority, Justice John Paul Stevens noted that "the ordinance allowed the police to order people to move on without inquiring into their reasons for remaining in one place. . . It matters not whether the reason that a gang member and his father, for example, loiter near Wrigley Field is to rob an unsuspecting fan or just to get a glimpse of Sammy Sosa leaving the ballpark. Friends, relatives, teachers, counselors, or even total strangers might unwittingly engage in forbidden loitering if they happen to engage in idle conversation with a gang member."[75] The Supreme Court further ruled that the vagueness of the Chicago city ordinance posed both substantive and procedural due process problems by giving the police too much discretion in predetermining the intent of those individuals participating in a sidewalk gathering.

However, the threat to national security posed by September 11 was real and, unfortunately, the reality is that this country is not shielded from another act of terrorism. The Bush administration and Congress responded after September 11 by merging both foreign and domestic federal intelligence agencies under one roof—the Department of Homeland Security. Congress passed the **Patriot Act** in conjunction with several presidential executive orders and additional congressional acts narrowing the scope of protected civil liberties including freedom of speech, association, unreasonable searches, and guarantees to speedy and public trials. In particular, the Patriot Act grants law enforcement expanded rights to wiretapping, tracking e-mails and internet sources, and legalizing conduct that would be otherwise illegal such as surprise searches of suspected terrorists' property as well as the authority to increase security checks at airports and international borders.

A similar piece of legislation, the **Smith Act,** was enacted during the Cold War as a result of the Red Scare and McCarthyism. Overtime, the federal courts eventually dismantled provisions of the Smith Act. A federal judge ruled that the Patriot Act's provision of allowing the National Security Agency (NSA) to keep records of Americans' phone calls was unconstitutional. The judge ordered the agency to stop recording the calls and to destroy all records of calls made by the lawsuit's plaintiffs. Complaints levied by airline passengers have resulted in the relaxation of security rules at the nation's airports. Librarians have voiced their concerns about federal agencies monitoring the library checkout records of library users. The federal courts are now beginning to dismantle the Patriot Act in the same piecemeal fashion as they used with the Smith Act.

The Right to Bear Arms

Throughout the thirteen original colonies, local residents, particularly in isolated rural areas, had to form local militias to defend themselves from hostile Indian raids. Militia members had to supply their own weaponry. It was common for the flint-locked rifle to be visibly hung above the family fireplace so when the community bell called militia members to action, one could just grab their gun and report for duty. When the relationship between the British government and colonists soured, British colonial governing bodies decided to punish the colonists by confiscating their weapons. The colonists were outraged. Therefore, the Framers addressed this concern through the **Second · Amendment** to the Constitution that guarantees the right to bear arms.

Since its adoption in 1791, applying reasonable restrictions to the Second Amendment has always been a bone of contention. The mere mention of "gun control" is met with disdain by gun owners and those who don't own a gun but simply do not want any level of government restricting their access to potentially purchase and own a firearm. The right to bear an arm of defense is directly tied to the prevailing belief that one should be able to do whatever is necessary to defend one's life and property from harm. Founded in 1871, the **National Rifle Association** is the most powerful organization supporting gun rights and ownership. The "gun lobby" in Washington and in all fifty state legislative houses constantly monitors any legislation restricting access to firearms. However, reasonable restrictions have been applied to the Second Amendment, for example, the **National Firearms Act** of 1934 banned the sale and use of machine guns and levied a tax on both gun manufacturers and sellers. Following the assassination of President Kennedy, the **Gun Control Act** (1968) restricted gun sales across state lines and tightened license requirements for gun sellers. In 1972, the federal Bureau of Alcohol, Tobacco, Firearms and Explosives (ATF) was created to enforce federal gun and weapon laws. The most controversial legislation was the **Brady Bill** named for Jim Brady, President Reagan's press secretary who was seriously wounded during the attempted assassination of the president. This legislation mandated a five-day waiting period and a detailed background check before anyone could purchase a handgun. The law's ban on assault weapons has expired.

Whether or not to restrict the types of weapons or to impose stricter limits on gun ownership is a consistently "hot bed" political and social issue. Gun control advocates point to the tragic mass murders on the campus of Virginia Tech, at a crowded movie theater in Aurora, Colorado, the December 14, 2012, slaying of six adults and twenty children in a Newtown, Connecticut elementary school, the mass killings by a lone gunman in an Orlando, Florida nightclub, the tragic murder of church members attending a prayer meeting in South Carolina, the October 2017 slaying of 158 persons attending an outdoor music festival by a lone gunman shooting from a nearby high-rise hotel, and the nightly gun violence scenes on the local news across the nation's cities as a call to action to restrict gun ownership. Gun rights advocates take the opposite stand by pointing out that mass murders and urban street violence can be seriously diminished if ordinary citizens could just openly carry their guns as a display of potential retaliation against anyone attempting such a violent act. Several state legislative houses have enacted open carry laws. For example, the Texas law allows owners of concealed handgun licenses to carry their weapons on their person in public places to include colleges and universities. Whether or not the knowledge that someone in a crowded theater, a college campus, or a teacher in the classroom is carrying a weapon can actually prevent a tragic mass murder is still to be determined.

Protecting the Rights of the Accused

The American judicial system artfully created by the Framers is firmly based on the **adversary system** whereby the accused is innocent until proven guilty. The burden of proof is placed squarely on the shoulders of the prosecution who must establish beyond a **reasonable doubt** that the accused did indeed commit a crime. Regardless of the severity of the crime, the accused has the same protected civil liberties as any other American citizen, until the accused has been declared guilty by a jury of his/her peers. "The Constitution strongly emphasizes the protection of rights of defendants in the criminal process. The original document contains no fewer than seven provisions specifically addressed to this matter—these are in keeping with the Founder's [Framers] concern to protect minorities (in this case, unpopular defendants) from the tyrannical excesses of an aggrieved or outraged majority . . . . The Bill of Rights places an even greater stress on criminal procedure. Of the twenty-three separate rights enumerated in the first eight amendments, thirteen relate to the treatment of criminal defendants."[76] The protection of the rights of the accused was needed to reverse the historical pattern governments used to abuse its citizens. The history of Europe is tainted by arbitrary arrests, imprisonment without benefit of trial, horrific punishment methods, and so on. The Framers realized that citizens should be protected from criminals. However, even criminals, particularly those *accused* of a criminal action, should be treated in a humane and fair manner.

The initial problem was whether these amendments applied to both the federal and state governments. The states were charged with establishing their own criminal procedures. Article III of the United States Constitution gave the federal court system extremely limited original jurisdiction in both criminal and civil matters. Despite the passage of the Fourteenth Amendment's provision of due process and equal protection, the Supreme Court was extremely reluctant to require the states to incorporate protections for the accused as detailed in the Bill of Rights into their state judicial procedures. "In its earliest interpretation of the Fourteenth Amendment, the famous *Slaughterhouse Cases* of 1873, the Supreme Court reaffirmed Marshall's opinion in *Barron* that the guarantees in the Bill of Rights and the Fourteenth Amendment were not construed to apply to the states."[77] However, the Supreme Court opted for selective incorporation of pretrial rights.

The landmark case cementing the states to compliance with the "fundamental rights" guaranteed in the Bill of Rights was ***Palko v Connecticut*** (1937). Frank Palko was originally indicted and tried on a first-degree murder charge. However, the jury found Palko guilty of a second-degree murder charge and gave him a life sentence without parole possibilities. The state appealed the decision to the Connecticut Supreme Court of Errors. This court subsequently overturned the original decision and ordered a new trial. Palko was tried again on a first-degree murder charge, convicted, and handed the death sentence. Palko petitioned the Supreme Court to overturn his latest conviction as a violation of the Fifth Amendment's protection against double jeopardy and the Fourteenth Amendment's guarantee of due process. The Supreme Court ruled against Palko. However, Justice Benjamin Cardozo's "carefully crafted opinion has long been regarded as a catalyst in the nationalization of the rights of the accused, as it established categorically that the states were obligated to the fundamental imperatives of the Bill of Rights through the Fourteenth Amendment. Cardozo distinguished rights that are fundamental—the very essence of a scheme of ordered liberty—from rights that are not quite so fundamental . . . . Fundamental rights must always be applied to the states, whereas, others may be applied to the states only when state action violates the due process clause of the Fourteenth Amendment."[78] Subsequent Supreme Court rulings conform with Cardozo's position.

The Framers firmly believed that no one should be arbitrarily arrested and allowed to waste away in prison without knowing the charges against them. A guaranteed constitutional right, a ***writ of Habeas Corpus*** is "an order to an incarcerating official to bring a person held in custody before the court to determine if the person is being held lawfully."[79] Basically, the accused is brought before a judge or magistrate within a short time after arrest. The accused and the presiding court official are informed of the charges against the accused by the arresting officer. The accused is then given the opportunity to explain his/her actions. If the presiding court official finds the arresting officer's actions valid, the accused will be held for further confinement or granted bail options. If the arresting officer does not provide a valid reason for the arrest, the presiding court official will release the accused.

The question of whether accused persons can waive their constitutionally protected rights to self-incrimination even though the accused is unaware of their rights in the first place was addressed by the Supreme Court in *Miranda v Arizona* (1966). Ernesto Miranda was arrested and questioned about the kidnapping and rape of an eighteen-year-old girl. During interrogation, Miranda signed a confession with a statement waving his constitutional protection against self-incrimination. However, Miranda did not have any prior knowledge of the United States Constitution, its Bill of Rights, and his protected constitutional rights. Miranda did not even speak English fluently. The arresting officers argued that they assumed Miranda was aware of his protected right to remain silent and voluntarily waived that right. The confession was admitted as evidence during the trial. Miranda was convicted and sentenced to twenty to thirty years in prison. The Supreme Court ruled 5 to 4 that Miranda's rights had been violated. Chief Justice Earl Warren "made it clear that the prosecution may not use a statement against the accused elicited during custodial interrogation 'unless it demonstrates the use of effective safeguards to secure' his or her constitutional rights, and they must be made known to the accused. Interrogation could proceed if the accused 'voluntarily, knowingly, and intelligently' makes a waiver of the rights to which he or she is entitled."[80] The Supreme Court mandated that law enforcement personnel must verbally apprise an arrested suspect of the following rights prior to questioning:

1. He must be told he has the right to stay silent.
2. He must be told anything he says may be used against him in court.
3. He must be told he has the right to have an attorney with him before any questioning begins.
4. He must be told that, if he wants an attorney but cannot afford one, an attorney will be provided for him free.
5. If, after being told this, an arrested suspect says he does not want a lawyer and is willing to be questioned, he may be, provided he reached his decision "knowingly and intelligently."
6. If, after being told all his rights, a suspect agrees to be questioned, he can shut off the questions any time after they have started, whether or not he has an attorney with him.[81]

In addition, law enforcement officials must operate on a more than reasonable assumption that the accused understands English. If not, the arresting officers should postpone questioning until an interpreter can be present. Once these warnings are given, the accused may opt to stop answering questions at any time; halt an interrogation until legal representation is present; or voluntarily waive his rights.

The *Miranda* case was revisited by the Supreme Court in a case questioning whether a section of a federal anti-crime law, allowing voluntary confessions without benefit of *Miranda* protections, could be used as evidence during a trial. Ruling against the federal government, the Supreme Court reaffirmed the necessity of *Miranda* in a 7 to 2 decision. Chief Justice William Rehnquist commented that "*Miranda* announced a constitutional rule that Congress may not supersede legislatively. We decline to overrule *Miranda* ourselves. *Miranda* has become embedded in routine police practice to the point where the warnings have become part of our national culture."[82]

The Fourth Amendment protects citizens from unreasonable searches and seizures. The English concept that a "man's home is his castle" was first addressed in the Magna Carta. Yet, the British Parliament used the excuses of crime prevention and avoidance of paying duties and taxes on goods and services in their efforts to continue the practice of random searches and seizures. Agents of the Royal Custom House would just bust into anyone's abode and seize whatever they deemed to be illegal! The growing list of offenses included "preventing illegal imports, manufactures; poaching; counterfeiting; unlicensed printing; seditious, heretical or lewd publications; and non-payment of taxes. Taxes extended to hearths and stoves, to estates, to intoxicating drinks; to a variety of consumer goods such as salt, candles, soap, glass and paper, and to foreign goods."[83] In 1763, William Pitt declared before the British Parliament that "the poorest man may, in his cottage, bid defiance to all the forces of the Crown. It may be frail; its roof may shake; the wind may blow through it; the storm may enter, the rain may enter, but the King of England may not enter; all his force does not cross the threshold of the ruined tenement."[84] Author of *History of the Crown* published in 1736, Sr. Matthew Hale "criticized warrants that failed to name the persons sought for the crime or the places to be searched for evidence of theft. He even laid a basis for the concept of probable cause by maintaining that the person seeking a warrant should be examined judicially under oath so that the magistrate could determine whether he had grounds for his suspicions. Hale also asserted that an officer who made an illegal search and arrest was liable to a civil suit for false arrest."[85] Despite the encouraging words of Pitt and Hale,, the Crown continued to conduct invasive searches through the use of general warrants. These search documents were issued without probable cause, allowing English custom agents to seize whatever they deemed of value to compensate for delinquent taxes. In the American colonies, the **Townshend Acts** of 1767 granted colonial courts the power to use general warrants. At a 1772 Boston Town Meeting, colonists complained that:

> "Thus our houses and even our bed chambers, are exposed to be ransacked, our boxes, chests and trunks broke open, ravaged and plundered by wretches, whom no prudent man would venture to employ even as menial servants; whenever they are pleased to say they suspect there are in the house wares for which the duties have not been paid. Flagrant instances of the wanton exercise of this power have frequently happened in this and other seaport towns. By this we are cut off from that domestic security which renders the lives of the most unhappy in some measure agreeable. Those Officers may under colour of law and the cloak of a general warrant break thro' the sacred rights of the domicil, ransack mens' houses, destroy their securities, carry off their property, and with little danger to themselves commit the most horred murders."[86]

After declaring their independence from England, several of the newly formed states addressed the issue of searches and seizures in their state constitutions. These documents outlawed the use of general warrants, opting instead for courts to issue specific warrants detailing both the items subjected to the search and possible seizure, as well as the rationale for the search. For example, the tenth article of the 1776 Pennsylvania constitution states "that the people have a right to hold themselves, their houses, papers and possessions free from search and seizure, and therefore, warrants without oaths or affirmations first made, affording a sufficient foundation for them, and whereby any officer or messenger may be commanded or required to search suspected places, or to seize any person or persons, his or their property, not particularly described are contrary to that right, and ought not to be granted."[87] Consequently the Framers used the guidelines established in these early state constitutions when they penned the Fourth Amendment to the United States Constitution.

Although Americans fear rising crime and demand swift action against violators, the Supreme Court has exercised reasonable restrictions in delineating proper from improper searches and seizures, and the effects a search has on the fate of the accused. "As far back as 1886, in *Boyd v United States,* the Court in effect, tied the Fourth Amendment to the Fifth Amendment's self-incrimination provision, indicating that the two 'run almost into each other.' An unreasonable search and seizure, the Court felt, is in reality a 'compulsory extortion' of evidence that could result in compulsory self-incrimination."[88] The key to understanding the logic of the Supreme Court's rulings rests with the interpretation of probable cause and the application of the exclusionary rule.

Under normal circumstances, police officers should obtain a search warrant issued by a magistrate prior to conducting the search. Officers must demonstrate **probable cause**, that is, a reasonable assumption that a crime has or will be committed. The suspicion of the execution of a criminal act compels the search and possible seizure of evidence. A proper warrant must describe the places to be searched and the items to be seized. The **exclusionary rule** means "that evidence which is otherwise admissible may not be used in a criminal trial if it is a product of illegal police conduct."[89] One of the landmark cases tying probable cause to the exclusionary rule is *Mapp v Ohio* (1961).

In May 1957, three Cleveland police officers arrived at Dollree Mapp's residence after receiving a tip that she was harboring a wanted fugitive. After twice refusing to admit the police without a search warrant, the officers forcibly gained entry, physically assaulted her, and handcuffed her. The search did not produce the sought after fugitive. However, Mapp was arrested and subsequently convicted of possession of the obscene materials the officers seized during their search. The Supreme Court overturned Mapp's conviction. Speaking for the majority, Justice Tom C. Clark wrote that "all evidence obtained by searches and seizures in violation of the Constitution is, by that same authority [Amendment Four], inadmissible in a state court and since the **Fourth Amendment**'s right of privacy has been declared enforceable against the States through the Due Process Clause of the Fourteenth, it is enforceable against them by the same sanction of exclusion as is used against the Federal Government."[90] Since its initial ruling, the Supreme Court has revisited several of the issues raised by the *Mapp* case, particularly involving permission to enter, unannounced entries, and searches conducted without a warrant. In a 5-4 decision, in ***Hudson v Michigan*** (2006), the Court ruled that "yes, the so-called knock-and-announce rule is violated when police fail to announce their presence and wait a reasonable amount of time before entering someone's home and what they find once they're inside. But no, that violation isn't sufficiently related to what they find during a search to justify banned drugs, guns or any other evidence that's uncovered from later criminal proceedings."[91] The Court also ruled in ***Brigham City v Stuart*** (2006) that police officers after viewing a violent melee through a window did not need a warrant to enter the residence to break up the fight. Chief Justice John Roberts wrote: "the role of a peace officer includes preventing violence and restoring order, not simply rendering first aid to casualties; an officer is not like a boxing (or hockey) referee, poised to stop a bout only if it becomes too one-sided."[92] In ***Georgia v Randolph*** (2006), the Supreme Court ruled that a homeowner can prevent police from conducting a warrant-less search even if a spouse or co-owner granted permission. Justice David Souter wrote that "a warrantless search of a shared dwelling for evidence over the express refusal of consent by a physically present resident cannot be justified as reasonable."[93]

The Court has heard numerous cases involving searches and seizures conducted outside the protection of a person's home. For example, Steven Dewayne Bond was a passenger on a Grayhound Bus that was stopped at an immigration checkpoint in California. A random squeezing of his luggage convinced agents that Bond was carrying controlled substances. Upon opening the bag, the agents discovered a package of methamphetamines. Bond was subsequently convicted of drug possession. Bond's attorneys argued that the random squeezing of the luggage constituted an illegal search and seizure. The Supreme Court concurred. The Supreme Court dealt another blow to law enforcement ruling that police officers cannot search people and their vehicles after issuing a routine traffic citation. Local police officers in Iowa searched Patrick Knowles' car after he was given a traffic ticket. The search of the vehicle revealed that Knowles was carrying marijuana. Although recognizing the necessity for searching suspects after their arrests for dangerous weapons, the Supreme Court ruled that in this situation, no arrest occurred, therefore, the search was illegal. Therefore, "absent probable cause and/or a warrant, police may not conduct a full-blown search of motorists and their vehicles after pulling them over and ticketing them for speeding or other minor traffic violations."[94] The Supreme Court has oftentimes ruled on the side of law enforcement. During its 2004-2005 session, the Court ruled that during routine traffic violation stops, law enforcement could legally use drug-sniffing dogs to detect possible possession of illegal substances. In support of the Court's 6-2 decision, Justice Paul Stevens wrote that "a dog sniff conducted during a concededly lawful traffic stop that reveals no information other than the location of a substance that no individual has any right to possess does not violate the Fourth Amendment."[95]

The right to counsel is guaranteed by the **Sixth Amendment**. However, not every person accused of a criminal action can afford an attorney nor are they guaranteed that their legal representation will provide an adequate defense. The Supreme Court addressed the issue of court appointed legal representation in capital criminal cases in *Powell v Alabama* (1932). Powell and six other African-American youths were arrested, indicted, tried, and given the death penalty for the rape of two Anglo women. The trials began six days after their arrests with two tried at a time in proceedings lasting only a day. The Supreme Court ruled overwhelmingly that all of the defendants were blatantly denied their rights of due process and equal protection of the law. Lacking financial resources, the defendants were provided court-appointed attorneys on the day of their trials. Echoing the sentiments of his fellow justices, Justice Sutherland wrote that "in light of the facts—the ignorance and illiteracy of the defendants, their youth, the circumstances of public hostility, the imprisonment and close surveillance of the defendants by the military forces, the fact that their friends and families were all in other states and communication with them necessarily difficult, and above all, that they stood in deadly peril of their lives—we think the failure of the trial court to give them reasonable time and opportunity to secure counsel was a clear denial of due process."[96]

In *Escobedo v Illinois* (1964), the question before the Supreme Court was whether legal representation should be present during the interrogation of the defendant by law enforcement officials. Danny Escobedo and three others were arrested for the fatal shooting of his brother-in-law. Initially, Escobedo was released after fourteen and a half hours of questioning without the presence of legal representation. Escobedo was rearrested, and despite the requests of both the defendant and his lawyer, legal representation was not present during that interrogation period. Consequently, Escobedo did make incriminating statements that led to his indictment and conviction. Escobedo petitioned the Supreme Court to overturn his conviction on the belief that his Sixth Amendment right to counsel had been violated. "Justice Arthur Goldberg's opinion for the majority stressed the need for counsel when the police action shifts from the investigatory to the accusatory stage, that is, when the focus is directed on the accused and the purpose of interrogation is to elicit a confession."[97] The Supreme Court overturned Escobedo's conviction.

One of the most highly profile cases heard by the Supreme Court was *Gideon v Wainwright* (1963). Clarence Gideon was arrested for burglarizing a pool hall. Gideon could not afford to hire an attorney. His plea for a court appointed attorney was denied since the Florida courts granted these requests only to defendants accused of capital criminal charges. Gideon pleaded not guilty, conducted his own defense, and, of course, was found guilty. From his prison cell, Gideon submitted to the Court one of the rarely accepted hand-written briefs. In a 9-0 decision, the Supreme Court overturned Gideon's conviction. The decision in this case "extended the absolute right of indigents to have counsel assigned in all criminal cases—save those involving certain misdemeanors—by making the Sixth Amendment's requirements of the Assistance of Counsel obligatory upon the states via the due process of the law clause of the Fourteenth Amendment."[98] Gideon was retried and acquitted.

American society is still debating whether the death penalty is a violation of the **Eighth Amendment**'s prohibition against cruel and unusual punishment. After winning independence, the states created penitentiaries as viable substitutes to punish violent criminals. Michigan and Wisconsin abolished the death penalty in the 1840s while other states restricted its use and banned public executions. Today the death penalty is just as controversial as it was in the eighteenth century. The Supreme Court has vacillated over the appropriateness of the death penalty. In 1972, the Court ruled in *Furman v Georgia* that the use of the death penalty in this particular case was a violation of the Fourteenth Amendment. "Although the Court never decided that execution was necessarily cruel and unusual punishment, the justices outlawed mandatory death sentences and approved a two stage process for capital cases, with guilt determined first and punishment fixed later by predetermined standards."[99] The *Furman* decision made states reevaluate their capital punishment laws and resulted in a virtual moratorium of the death penalty. The Court reversed its decision against the use of the death penalty in 1976, giving the green light for states to reintroduce the use of capital punishment. The number of executions rose dramatically. Recent death penalty related decisions rendered by both the federal district courts and the Supreme Court indicate a change in prospective once again towards restricting the use of capital punishment. U.S. District Judge Jed Rakoff declared the 1994 Death Penalty Act unconstitutional. The judge's ruling was based on the fact "that the best available evidence indicates that on one hand, innocent people are sentenced to death with materially greater frequency than was previously supposed and that, on the other hand, convincing proof of their innocence often does not emerge until long after the convictions."[100] Although the Supreme Court has not once again declared the death penalty unconstitutional, three of its decisions placed limitations on its use. In a 6-3 decision, the Court ruled that the execution of mentally handicapped inmates was an unconstitutional violation of the Eighth Amendment's prohibition against cruel and unusual punishment. During its 2002 session, the jurists ruled that juries, not judges, must determine whether a convicted murderer should receive the death penalty. Affirming the 7-2 decision, Justice Ruth Bader Ginsburg stated that "the Constitution guarantees a trial by jury, and that right extends to weighing whether a particular killing merits death or life in prison."[101] In 2005, the Supreme Court ruled in a 5-4 decision that the execution of juveniles was indeed cruel and unusual punishment. In support of the majority opinion, Justice Anthony Kennedy wrote: "The . . . national consensus here—the rejection of the juvenile death penalty in the majority of the states; the infrequency of its use even where it remains on the books; and the consistency in the trend toward abolition of the practice—provide sufficient evidence that today our society view juveniles, in the words . . . used respecting the mentally retarded as 'categorically less culpable than the average criminal.' Once the diminished culpability of juveniles is recognized, it is evident that the penological justifications for the death penalty apply to them with lesser force than to adults. The age of 18 is the point where society draws the line for many purposes between childhood and adulthood. It is, we conclude, the age at which the line for death eligibility ought to rest."[102] In 2006, the Supreme Court opened the door for death row inmates to challenge their sentences through DNA testing. Calling for a new trial, Justice Kennedy wrote "that the DNA evidence, combined with other errors in the case, made it quite probably that [Paul Gregory] House could convince jurors of his innocence" of committing a murder that happened twenty years ago.[103]

While the debate continues over the death penalty, violent crimes continue to plague the nation's cities. Several states have opted to impose longer prison terms without the possibility of

Former Governor George Ryan (R. IL) (left) and Senator Dick Durbin (D. IL) (right) at a news conference. On Saturday, Jan. 11, 2003, Former Gov. George Ryan cleared Illinois' death row, commuting 167 condemned inmates' sentences in the broadest attack at the death penalty in decades. Ryan's decision came three years after he temporarily halted state executions to examine the system's fairness. George Ryan said, "I had to act. Our capital system is haunted by the demon of error—error in determining guilty, and error in determining who among the guilty deserves to die."

parole in hopes that the knowledge of spending years and years in prison will be an effective deterrent to committing a criminal act. President Clinton introduced the concept of "three strikes and your out" mandating that an individual convicted of a third felony would receive an automatic life prison sentence, regardless of the nature of the crime. Clinton also signed "Aimee's Law" whereby "a murderer, child molester or rapist released before serving 85 percent of his or her sentence, or before his or her jail term passes the national average for the offense, then commits the same crime in a different state, the original jailing state will have to pay for the new investigation and incarceration with its federal crime funds."[104] During its 2004-2005 session, the Supreme Court gave judges more latitude in determining sentencing options when it ruled the Sentencing Reform Act unconstitutional. Now, federal judges are able judge on their own without the influence of Congress whether or not the circumstances involved in the commission of a felony merits a stiffer sentence.

The appeals process has also been revisited with several states enacting laws limiting the accessibility of the convicted to the court system. In the past, those convicted of a crime in a state court could seek a direct appeal to a federal court if that individual received the death penalty or could demonstrate that his/her constitutionally protected rights were violated at some point from arrest to conviction. In 1999, the Supreme Court ruled 6 to 3 that those convicted of crimes in state courts must initiate their appeals at the state-court level. "Writing for the majority, Justice Sandra Day O'Connor said that as long as a state has given its supreme court the choice to review a case, federal courts should require state inmates make use of the available process to give the state court a chance to exercise its discretionary jurisdiction."[105] The inmate still has the option to begin the appeal process at the federal court level only if the state court refuses to hear the case. Supreme Court justices further restricted the appeals process to death row inmates. The issue involved a provision of the Anti-Terrorism and Effective Death Penalty Act that shorten the time between conviction and execution. In a 5 to 4 decision, Justice O'Connor stated that "the law requires a hands-off approach by federal judges unless a state court clearly is wrong about some Supreme Court precedent or unreasonably applies that principle to the facts of the prisoner's case."[106] The Supreme Court sent a clear message that defense attorneys can use the federal courts only if the state court system has clearly violated the constitutional rights of the accused. "This decision makes clear that the *writ of habeas corpus* is not to be used as a device to go judge-shopping, running the same marginal claims past multiple sets of judges."[107]

The **Sixth Amendment** to the United States Constitution entitles those accused of committing a criminal offense to be judged by a jury of one's peers. The majority of the nation's state and federal courts select nine to twelve members from a panel of potential jurors. These individuals are charged with weighing the evidence and, subsequently, rendering a verdict of guilt or innocence. The concept of the jury system emerged in England after the Norman invasion. Determining the method of proving one's guilt or innocence has taken numerous avenues. Prior to the arrival of William the Conqueror, "under Saxon law, if you could carry several pounds of glowing red-hot iron in your bare hands for nine steps or walk barefoot over nine red-hot plowshares without getting any blisters, you were not guilty. . . In Britain, Africa and parts of Asia, plunging your arm into boiling water, oil or lead without the usual results proved your innocence. Water was also knowledgeable stuff. The innocent sank; the guilty floated and could be fished and dealt with."[108] In some instances, the Saxons dismissed the hot irons and opted for a rudimentary jury composed of twelve people. The practice of the twelve-member jury is credited to Morgan of Glamorgan, Prince of Wales. In 725 A.D., he wrote: "For as Christ and his Twelve Apostles were finally to judge the world, so human tribunals should be composed of the king and twelve wise men."[109] The jury system, however, has posed serious questions as to whether a panel of nine to twelve can be a truly fair and impartial group capable of rendering a decision based solely on the evidence presented during the trial without injecting their own biases and emotions into their deliberations.

The rulings of the Supreme Court have upheld and preserved the rights of the accused. Both state and federal courts have been more inclined to grant **changes of venue** for high profile cases to ensure a fair trial for the accused. For example, the federal trial of those accused of the tragic bombing of the federal building in Oklahoma City was moved to another federal district court. The judge believed that finding a fair and impartial jury in the Oklahoma district was an impossible task.

Protection of Property and Privacy

In *Democracy in America*, Alexis de Tocqueville observed that "in no other country in the world is the love of property keener or more alert than in the United States and nowhere else does the majority display less inclination toward doctrines which in any way threaten the way property is owned."[110] Once again, the Framers desired to reverse the historical patterns of governments using arbitrary measures to seize private property for political purposes. The Articles of Confederation failed miserably to protect the rights of property owners to transact their business without undo interference from individual state governments. It was the business community and property owners that compelled the Framers to meet in Philadelphia in the first place. Consequently, the Framers created a document that specifically granted constitutional protections for the right to own, use, rent, invest, and contract for property with the minimal interjection of government. After all, the free enterprise system is based on the concept of private property ownership.

Article I, Section 10 of the United States Constitution prohibits the states from passing any laws that impair the obligation of contracts. Known as the **Contract Clause**, this provision was designed to prevent state governments from passing laws that would expand a debtor's right not to pay an obligation or to back out of a contractual agreement. However, the Constitution did not give property owners the exclusive right to do whatever they wanted to do with their property. Property ownership and property rights evoke the classic struggle of the individual or private needs against the collective good of the community or public needs. It has been the task of state and federal courts under the guidance of the Supreme Court that have selectively applied the concept of reasonable restrictions to property issues.

The Supreme Court began gradually to restrict the exclusiveness of the contract clause in the 1880s by subjecting contracts to reasonable police powers designed to protect the health, safety, welfare, and, in some instances, the morals of the public. In *Home Building and Loan Association v Blaisdell* (1934), the Supreme Court ruled that contracts between two or more parties could be modified by state laws to prevent social and economic catastrophe. Subsequent rulings have upheld federal regulations ranging from worker safety standards to the proper disposal of hazardous substances by property and business owners. City and county ordinances can determine whether a home owner can paint his residence a certain color or fix the site location of sexually explicit businesses and establishments selling liquor, and so on. These actions are constitutional as long as these restrictions are not unreasonable applications of police powers.

The Framers also recognized the necessity for government to seize or to use private property for the collective benefit of the community or the nation. The United States Constitution specifically grants the power of **eminent domain** to the federal government. However, the property owner must receive just compensation for the loss of his/her property. The states and other subgovernmental units received the right of eminent domain through the Fourteenth Amendment. The use of reasonable restrictions is key to understanding the scope of eminent domain. Governments need privately held lands to build additional government buildings, public schools and hospitals, to expand the nation's transportation systems, and so on. But, the rights of property owners must be recognized and justly compensated for their losses. During its 2006 session, the Supreme Court ruled that governments could use eminent domain to condemn lower valued residential property as blighted or a slum in order to allow a private business to develop the land into higher valued residential property such as townhouses. Not supportive of the Court's ruling, property owners across the nation pushed their state legislative houses to enact laws restricting the use of eminent domain for private gain.

Privacy issues are tied directly to the Fourth Amendment's protection from unreasonable searches and seizures particularly when law enforcement enters a private residence. In *Boyd v United States* (1886), the Supreme Court decided that "the Fourth and Fourteenth Amendments extend to all invasions on the part of the [federal] government and its employees of the sanctity of a man's home and the privacies of life. It is not the breaking of his doors and the rummaging of his drawers that constitutes the essence of the offense, but it is the invasion of his indefeasible right of personal security, personal liberty, and private property."[111] However, the Supreme Court did not address this issue seriously until technological advancements gave law enforcement the capability to use wiretapping and sophisticated surveillance tools to enhance their efforts to apprehend potential lawbreakers. In *Olmstead v United States* (1928), the Supreme Court applied reasonable restrictions to the right to privacy and gave law enforcement a boost by ruling that wiretapping was not a breach of the Fourth Amendment. At the height of the Prohibition Era, Ray Olmstead and several of his cohorts were convicted of violating the National Prohibition Act for their bootlegging activities. The federal government introduced wiretapped conversations between the defendants as their primary incriminating evidence. The Supreme Court justified its ruling against Olmstead with the rationalization that "if a person installs a telephone for the purpose of projecting his or her voice outside of the home, then the person gives up an expectation of privacy in the conversation."[112]

However, the Supreme Court did not give law enforcement the green light to spy on American citizens at will. In *Silverman v United States* (1961), the Supreme Court ruled that law enforcement eavesdropping on conversations in private residences through the pipes of a heating system was an unconstitutional violation of the Fourth Amendment. The use of electronic listening and recording devices in public telephone booths drew the ire of the Supreme Court. In *Katz v United States* (1967), Justice Potter Stewart wrote "that when a person enters such a booth, closes the door behind him, and pays a toll to make a call, he is entitled to assume that the words he utters into the mouthpiece will not be broadcasted to the world."[113] Corrective legislation was passed with the 1968 Omnibus Crime Control and Safe Streets Act, which granted limited use of wiretapping and bugging devices for investigative purposes. This legislation allowed warrantless use of listening devices for forty-eight hours for emerging investigations involving organized crime or threats to national security. Although subsequent legislation has expanded the use of listening devices, the courts do weigh the absence of a warrant when judging admissibility of evidence against the accused.

Privacy issues extend to a wide variety of subjects from drug testing, alternative lifestyles, reproductive freedom, and so on. However, the increased use of drugs has prompted businesses and insurance companies to push for drug-free working environments through random drug testing. Although the use of drugs is extremely detrimental to the survival of our society, some Americans believe that random blood sampling and supervised urination is a gross violation of one's dignity and an invasion of privacy. It's a basic question of protecting the rights of the individual to privacy or the intrusion into a person's lifestyle to preserve the safety of the public. In a series of decisions, the Supreme Court did rule that testing for drugs or alcohol by penetrating the skin is a search under the Fourth Amendment (*Terry v Ohio*, 1968), as well as the use of breathalyzer tests on suspected drunken drivers (*California v Trombetta*, 1984). Despite the cries of civil libertarians, the Rehnquist Court ruled 6-3 in favor of mandatory drug testing in *Skinner v Railway Labor Executives Association* (1989).

The Supreme Court could be confronted by extremely complicated privacy issues caused by advanced high-tech computer systems and breakthroughs in genetic testing. Computer hackers are capable now of accessing information about an individual's buying habits, credit history, and medical problems. How can the average citizen protect his privacy when potentially damaging information is only an access code away? Who do you sue? The person who accessed the data in the first place or the company that gathered it and made it so readily available? Advanced genetic testing has the capability to chart a person's medical history through generational genetic patterns. Should the right to know whether you have a defective gene that will eventually give you cancer be held in strict confidence, or should it be publicly revealed to potential insurance carriers and employers? Could this information create a new form of discrimination whereby healthy individuals will be denied employment, long-term loans, and health insurance because their medical profile indicates a generational genetic pattern of heart disease?

CONCLUSIONS

The Framers seized the moment to craft a document suitable to a democratic government by advancing the causes of freedom, individualism, and equality. "That Constitution erected a fortification for freedom. It furnishes safeguards against ourselves, against our passions and extravagances. It set forth in a Bill of Rights those 'inalienable rights,' which no Congress, no government, no majority of the people could invade or violate."[114] The Framers also created a federal court system charged with the heavy burden of defending this document from those desiring to weaken it or to deny protected rights to others. With judicial review, the Supreme Court has become the definitive authority and ultimate defender of the Constitution and the Bill of Rights. However, the preservation of freedom, individualism, and equality has not been an easy task to accomplish. "There remains intense controversy over the definition, scope, and application of these values. For one thing, in particular circumstances these values may and do collide and conflict with each other. Individualism, for example, may conflict with what many might think is necessary to safeguard the 'public interest' or to promote the 'general welfare.' Then again, suppose these values are denied by government itself (and others) to particular individuals. How and to what extent should government intervene to rectify the damage that has been done? And might such intervention itself be viewed as an encroachment upon these very values, e.g., individual freedom? These questions continue to pose a dilemma for American politics and politicians."[115]

CHAPTER NOTES

[1]"The Bill of Rights: Amendments I-X," Milton R. Konvitz, ed., *An American Primer,* Daniel J. Boorstin, ed., (Chicago, Illinois: The University of Chicago Press, 1966), 171.

[2]Ibid., 172.

[3]Gary L. McDowell, "Rights Without Roots," *The Wilson Quarterly*, Vol. XV, No. 1, Winter, 1991, 71.

[4]Alan Barth, *The Rights of Free Men: An Essential Guide to Civil Liberties*, James E. Clayton, ed., (New York: Alfred A. Knopf, 1987), 111-112.

[5] Jay M. Shafritz, *HarperCollins Dictionary of American Government and Politics*, (New York, New York: HarperCollins Publishers, Inc. 1992), 186.

[6]James H. Hutson, "A Nauseous Project," *The Wilson Quarterly*, Vol. XV, No. 1, Winter, 1991, 63.

[7]Leon W. Blevins, *Texas Government in National Perspective*, (N. J.: Prentice-Hall, 1987), 221.

[8]Robert Darton, "The Pursuit of Happiness," *The Wilson Quarterly*, Vol. XIX, No. 4, Autumn, 1995, 48.

[9]Kermit L. Hall, "Framing the Bill of Rights," *By and For the People: Constitutional Rights in American History*, Kermit L. Hall, ed., (Arlington Heights, Illinois: Harlan-Davidson, Inc., 1991), 17.

[10]Huston, "A Nauseous Project," 62.

[11]Ibid.

[12]Hall, "Framing the Bill of Rights," 18.

[13]Ibid. 17.

[14]John C. Domino, *Civil Rights and Liberties: Toward the 21st Century*, (New York, New York: HarperCollins College Publishers, Inc., 1994), 1.

[15]Ibid., 2.

[16]Paul Brest, "The Intentions of the Adopters in the Eyes of the Beholder," *The Bill of Rights: Original Meaning and Current Understanding*, Eugene W. Hickok, ed., (Charlottesville, Virginia: University Press of Virginia, 1991), 23.

[17]Henry J. Abraham and Barbara A. Perry, *Freedom & The Court: Civil Rights and Liberties in the United States*, 8th ed., (Lawrence, Kansas: The University Press of Kansas, 2003), 3-4.

[18]Lucius J. Barker and Twiley W. Barker, Jr., *Civil Liberties and the Constitution*, 6th ed., (Englewood Cliffs, New Jersey: Prentice-Hall, 1990), 13.

[19]Ibid.

[20]Kermit L. Hall, "Introduction," *By and For the People: Constitutional Rights in American History*, Kermit L. Hall, ed. (Arlington Heights, Illinois: Harlan-Davidson, Inc., 1991), 8.

[21]Domino, 132.

[22]Abraham, 109.

[23]*Treasury of Presidential Quotations*, Caroline B. Harnsberger, ed., (Chicago, Illinois: Follett Publishing Co., 1964), 106.

[24]McDowell, "Rights Without Roots," 74.

[25]Abraham, 109.

[26]Thomas R. Hensley, Christopher E. Smith and Joyce A. Baugh, *The Changing Supreme Court: Constitutional Rights and Liberties* (St. Paul, Minnesota: West Publishing, Co., 1997), 132.

[27]"Liberty for the Soul," *American History*, (Vol. 42, No. 1, April, 2007), 27.

[28]John Meacham, "God and the Founders", *Newsweek*, April 10, 2006, 54.

[29]Ibid.

[30]Hensley, 141.

[31]Meacham, 54.

[32]Hensley, 139-140.

[33]Ibid., 152.

[34]Anjetta McQueen, "Religious Schools Get Public Aid," *San Antonio Express-News* (Thursday, June 29, 2000), 12A.

[35]Gary Martin, "High Court Oks School Vouchers," *San Antonio Express-News*, (Friday, June 28, 2002), 12A.

[36]Martin, "High Court Oks School Vouchers," 1A.

[37]Ibid., 12A.

[38]Abraham, 310.

[39]Hensley, 162.

[40]Ibid., 163.

[41]J. Michael Parker and Cecilia Balli, "Justices to Tackle Football Prayers," *San Antonio Express-News* (Tuesday, November 16, 1999), 1A.

[42]Mark Helm, "Silent Nod Given to 'Silence' Law," *San Antonio Express-News*, (Tuesday, October, 30, 2001), 10A.

[43]Hensley, 164.

[44]Ibid., 206.

[45]Domino, 87-88.

[46]"Obama Defends Right to Free Speech in U.S. Talk," *San Antonio Express-News*, (Wednesday, September 26, 2012), 2A.

[47]Larry Gragg, "Order vs. Liberty," *American History* (Vol. XXIII, No. 4, October, 1998), 26.

[48]Ibid.

[49]Susan Welch, John Gruhl, Michael Steinman, John Comer, and Susan M. Rigdon, *American Government*, 5th ed., (St. Paul, Minn.: West Publishing Co., 1994), 450.

[50]Abraham, 178.

[51]Welch, 454.

[52]Daniel B. Moskowitz, "Schooled in Speech," *American History*, Vol. 54, No. 4, October 2019, 23.

[53]Ibid.

[54]Domino, 47.

[55]Eric Lichtblau, "FBI Keeps Tabs on War Protests," *San Antonio Express-News* (Sunday, November 23, 2003), 10A.

[56]Charles Phillips, "A Day To Remember: May 4, 1970," *American History*, (Vol. 39, No. 2, June, 2004), 18.

[57]Ibid.

[58]Daniel B. Moskowitz, "Drawing a Line on Libel," *American History*, Vol. 54, No. 1, April 2019, 22.

[59]Ralph A. Rossum and G. Alan Tarr, *American Constitutional Law: Cases and Interpretations*, (New York: St. Martin's Press, 1983), 383.

[60]Hensley, 381.

[61]Abraham, 231.

[62]Domino, 67.

[63]Walter Issacon, "Citizen Ben's 7 Greatest Virtues," *Time*, July 2003, 44.

[64]Hensley, 326.

[65]Ibid.

[66]Rossum, 418.

[67]Steven Levy, "On the Net Anything Goes," *Newsweek*, July 7, 1997, 28.

[68]Rossum, 397.

[69]Ibid., 398.

[70]Dennis Melamed, "Really Reading the Riot Act," *American History*, Vol. 52, No. 6, February 2018, 52.

[71]Ibid., 54.

[72]Ibid.

[73]Ibid., 56.

[74]Aaron Epstein, "Anti-Gang Loitering Ordinance Rejected," *San Antonio Express-News* (Friday, June 11, 1999), 1A.

[75]Ibid., 1A and 20A.

[76]Rossum, 469.

[77]Domino, 133-134.

[78]Ibid., 138.

[79]Hensley, 895.

[80]Barker, 263.

[81]Abraham, 142.

[82]Mark Helm, "Miranda Warning: Court Upholds 'The Right to Remain Silent,'" *San Antonio Express-News* (Tuesday, June 27, 2000), 1A.

[83]Leonard W. Levey, "The Origins of the Fourth Amendment," *Political Science Quarterly*, Vol. 114, No. 1, Spring 1999, 81-82.

[84]Ibid., 80.

[85]Ibid., 81.

[86]Ibid., 92.

[87]Ibid., 93.

[88]Barker, 249.

[89]Domino, 140.

[90]Abraham, 69.

[91]Stephen Henderson, "Court Comes Down on Cops' Side," *San Antonio Express-News*, (Friday, June 16, 2006), 1A.

[92]Gina Holland, "Justices Say Cops Can Enter Homes to Stop Violence," *San Antonio Express-News*, (Tuesday, May 23, 2006), 4A.

[93]David G. Savage, "Court Slams A Door on Cops," *San Antonio Express-News*, (Thursday, March 23, 2006), 1A.

[94]Abraham, 159.

[95]Jan Crawford Greenburg, "High Court Expands Police Right to Search," *San Antonio Express-News,* (Tuesday, January 25, 2005), 1A.

[96] Rossum, 522.

[97]Barker, 268.

[98]Abraham, 138.

[99]Domino, 98.

[100]Delvin Barrett, "Federal Death Penalty Halted," *San Antonio Express-News*, (Tuesday, July 2, 2002), 3A.

[101]Anne Gearan, "Justices Give Jury Last Say On Executions," *San Antonio Express-News*, (Tuesday, June 25, 2002), 6A.

[102]Marco Robbins, "Justices Rule Teen Killers Can't Be Put To Death," *San Antonio Express-News,* (Wednesday, March 2, 2005), 6A.

[103]Stephen Henderson, "Killers Get New Way to Avoid Needle," *San Antonio Express-News,* (Tuesday, June 13, 2006),6A.

[104]Jesse J. Holland, "Crime Package Approved; Will Turn Up Heat on States," *San Antonio Express-News* (Thursday, October 12, 2000), 6A.

[105]Linda Greenhouse, "Court Limits Inmate Appeals," *San Antonio Express-News* (June 8, 1999), 1A and 6A.

[106]Richard Carelli, "Justices Make Death Row Appeals Tougher," *San Antonio Express-News* (Wednesday, April 19, 2000), 6A.

[107]Ibid.

[108]Barbara Holland, "You Swear That You Will Well and Truly Try?" *Smithsonian,* (Vol. 25, No. 12, March 1995), 110.

[109]Ibid., 108.

[110]Alexis de Tocqueville, *Democracy in America,* J. P. Mayer, ed., (Gordon City, New York: Doubleday and Co., Inc., 1969), 638-639.

[111]Domino, 190.

[112]Ibid.

[113]Barker, 569.

[114]Barth, 122.

[115]Barker, 10.

SUGGESTED READINGS

Abraham Henry J., and Barbara A. Perry, *Freedom & the Court: Civil Rights & Liberties in the United States,* 8th ed., Lawrence, Kansas: University Press of Kansas, 2003.

Barth, Alan. *The Rights of Free Men: An Essential Guide to Civil Liberties.* James E. Clayton, ed. New York: Alfred A. Knopf, 1987.

Domino, John C. *Civil Rights and Liberties: Toward the 21st Century.* New York: Harper Collins College Publishers, Inc., 1994.

Hall, Kermit L. ed. *By and For the People: Constitutional Rights in American History.* Arlington Heights, Ill.: Harlan Davidson, Inc., 1991.

Hensley, Thomas R., Christopher E. Smith and Joyce A. Baugh, *The Changing Supreme Court: Constitutional Rights and Liberties,* St. Paul, Minnesota: West Publishing Co., 1997.

Rossum, Ralph A., and G. Alan Tarr. *American Constitutional Law: Cases and Interpretations.* New York: St. Martin's Press, 1983.

Signing of the Civil Rights Act of 1964.

Chapter Thirteen

CIVIL RIGHTS

On August 29, 2013, President Barack Obama, our nation's first African-American president, addressed the nation at the same location that Dr. Martin L. King, Jr., delivered his "I Have A Dream" speech fifty years ago. To the thousands of people gathered around the reflecting pool near the Lincoln Memorial, his words echoed the challenges still ahead. Acknowledging fifty years of progress towards racial equality, President Obama stressed that "to dismiss the magnitude of this progress, to suggest as some sometimes do that little has changed, that dishonors the courage and the sacrifice of those who paid the price to march in those years. But we would dishonor those heroes as well to suggest that the work of this nation is somehow complete. The arc of the moral universe may bend towards justice, but it doesn't bend on its own. To secure the gains this country has made requires constant vigilance, not complacency."[1] Sadly, vigilance and non-complacency alone will not end the incidents of racism, prejudice, and discrimination that have haunted this nation since its founding.

Nor can we ever forget the faces of those who have been the victims of racially motivated hatred and violence. On September 15, 1963, four young African-American girls in Birmingham, Alabama, decided to make a last minute visit to their deserted church's basement lounge after Sunday school. A dynamite bomb planted outside the church by members of the Ku Klux Klan (KKK) exploded killing 11-year-old Denise McNair, 14-year-olds Cynthia Wesley, Carole Robertson and Addie Mae Collins, and injuring twenty others. Although the Federal Bureau of Investigation (FBI) quickly identified four Klansmen as the likely suspects, it took 39 years before the final suspect was tried and convicted of the bombing. Basically, "the killers of the girls hid for decades inside a brittle silence that cracked only when they boasted among kin and people they believed held the same hatred."[2]

In the early hours of June 2, 1998, James Byrd left a family gathering to begin his walk to his home in Jasper, Texas. As he walked along a dark road, three white ex-cons with ties to an in-prison white supremacy group, stopped and offered Byrd, an African American, a ride. Accustomed to hitch hiking, Byrd willingly accepted their offer and got into the bed of their truck. Byrd never made it home that night. Instead, the three men beat him unconscious, chained him to the tailgate of the truck, and dragged him to his death. The three were captured, charged, and subsequently convicted of first-degree murder. Two received the death penalty. On Friday, April 28, 2000, an Anglo male randomly opened fire in several suburban Pittsburgh, Pennsylvania communities. "The gunman fatally shot a person of Indian descent at an Indian grocery store, two employees at a Chinese restaurant and a black [African-American] man at a martial arts school. A Jewish woman who lived next door to the suspect's parents was found dead in her home."[3] He also shot out the glass doors of a nearby synagogue and painted the outside walls with swastikas. With the exception of one of the victims, the suspect did not know these people nor did they do anything to provoke him. They were simply at the wrong place at the wrong time. On October 7, 1998, Matthew Shepard, a twenty-one-year-old student at the University of Wyoming, struck up a conversation with two young men at a local gay bar. Since he knew one of the men, Shepard felt comfortable in joining them for a night on the town. Once outside the bar, the two men attacked Shepard. The two took Shepard to a rural area where he was severely beaten, pistol-whipped, tortured, and left for dead tied to a barb-wired fence post. Shepard was murdered because he was gay! His two companions were eventually arrested, convicted, and given life sentences. They would have been charged with an upgraded offense of a hate crime, but Wyoming did not have such a law on its books. On the evening of June 17, 2015, Dylann Roof, a twenty-one year old Anglo man walked into the historical Emanuel African Methodist Episcopal Church in Charleston, South Carolina to attend a prayer meeting. The African-American parishioners included Rev. Clemanta C. Pinckney, the church's leader and a South Carolina State Senator, and members of his immediate family. Roof politely took a seat, participated in the prayer meeting, and then stood up and starting shooting the gathered parishioners. Nine of the twelve members at the prayer session including Rev. Pinckney were killed. Roof was charged with thirty-three federal counts including hate crime charges. A white supremacist, Roof readily admitted he committed these horrific crimes. Roof was convicted on all charges and given the death sentence. All of the above mentioned criminal acts were racially motivated by the killer's hatred of minorities. Although incidents of this caliber are extremely isolated tragedies, what happened at that church in Birmingham, on that dirt road in Jasper, in the prayer meeting room in the Emanuel Church, in that isolated barb-wired pasture in Wyoming, and on those streets in Pittsburgh reminded all of us that racism still haunts a nation that was founded, in part, on the sacredly revered Declaration of Independence that boldly proclaims that "all men are created equal." Yet, nothing is further from the truth. For thousands of years, the history of humanity has been continuously marred by periods of horrific and, far too often, deadly indignities leveled by individuals upon their fellow human beings. For over two hundred years, United States lawmakers have struggled to erase the blemishes of previous conditions of servitude, racial hatred, and gender discrimination only to be confronted by a new wave of racism, sexism, and intolerance.

For many Americans, the civil rights movement of the 1960's and 70's did awaken the social consciousness of this nation to the destructiveness of racism. Yet, the awakening failed to solve the problems. The obvious shortcomings and failures of the public policy process to address racial discrimination are seen in the faces of those the laws were supposed to help. Far too often minorities feel that the scales of justice move too slowly to bring those accused of civil rights violations to justice. For example, in 1966, the bullet-riddled body of Ben Chester White, an African-American farmhand, was found in Pretty Creek, near Natchez, Mississippi. Three known Klansmen were arrested with one actually confessing to the murder. All three were acquitted in state courts. In 2003, the federal government reopened the case, charging 72-year-old Ernest Avants, the only defendant still living, with the crime. The federal government discovered a loophole. "For years his [Avants] acquittal of state murder charges in the 1960s had shielded him from new prosecution. But White's body was found on federal land, in a national forest, enough to get around double jeopardy and give federal prosecutors jurisdiction."[4] Another tragic case was the 1964 slayings of James Chaney, 21, an African American from Mississippi and his two white companions from New York. They were three young men traveling through the Deep South trying to register potential African-American voters. Although more than a dozen well-known Klan members were involved in the slayings, only a few were actually charged, tried and convicted. "One of the men who was convicted, Sam Bowers—the Neshoba County Klan's Imperial Wizard—later said that he was 'quite delighted to have been the main instigator of the entire affair,' meaning the real instigator [Edgar Ray] Killen, 'walk out of the courtroom a free man.'"[5] Although Killen was never charged with the crimes in state courts, he was tried on federal-civil rights violations in 1967, but acquitted by an all-white jury. In 2005, the state of Mississippi officially charged 79-year-old Killen with three counts of murder. It took forty plus years to bring the man responsible for these murders to justice. The **Black Lives Matter Movement** began in 2012 with the tragic death of Trayvon Martin, a seventeen-year-old African-American youth at the hands of George Zimmerman. Visiting his father, Martin was walking back to his father's apartment after making a purchase at a nearby convenience store. A resident of the same apartment complex, Zimmerman and Martin clashed with Zimmerman ultimately fatally shooting Martin. Charged with murder, Zimmerman's trial made nationwide headlines. His acquittal set off weeks of protests and riots. The African-American community was outraged. The outrage resurfaced once again with the May 25, 2020, death of African-American George Floyd who died on the street of injuries caused by the actions of four Minneapolis, Minnesota, police officers. In arresting Floyd, one of the officers used a chock-hold on Floyd's neck by placing his knee on the back of the man's throat. Despite Floyd's pleas that he could not breathe, the officer continued to put pressure on Floyd's throat while the three other officers stood by and did not intervene. The four officers were fired. The officer placing the chock-hold has been charged with third degree murder and second-degree manslaughter while the other three have been charged with aiding and abetting. Reaction to Floyd's death sparked international condemnation against **systematic racism** and calls for defunding police departments. Peaceful and violent protests erupted in cities across the country and drew out into streets large crowds of protesters from London, Paris, Stockholm, and so forth. Once again, frustrations and disappointments experienced by this nation's minority groups are further fueled by the perception that their lawmakers and their government move too slowly to enact the proper corrective legislation with enough governmental muscle to end racial discrimination.

Any discussion of civil rights must also encompass the struggles of American women to gain an equitable footing with their male counterparts. Incidences of gender-based discrimination are just as offensive as racial discrimination. Charges of sexual harassment are prevalent. Women are still struggling with wage disparity issues as their male counterparts continue to earn more than they do in comparable positions. Although few dispute the need to reform the welfare state, national women's organizations are adamantly opposed to the rhetoric of welfare reform that openly attacks, belittles, and blames low income single parent women for the faults of the welfare system.

While women and minorities are seeking redress through the courts and legislative houses, some Americans believe that an over zealous government has gone too far by arbitrarily granting special treatment for minorities and women to the detriment of its Anglo male citizens. Although the majority of all Americans support the concepts and philosophy of civil rights and are themselves law-abiding citizens, a small group of white supremacists and militants have become extremely vocal and, in some cases, violent in venting their anger against politicians, lawmakers, and government. The fear that government is systematically stripping away their rights while giving preferential treatment to minorities, women, and immigrants has materialized into white backlash attacks against affirmative action, civil rights laws, and immigration policies. Both sides have valid arguments; however, the rhetoric of the debate has become hostile, laden with racial slurs and charges of racism from both sides.

The challenge before government at all levels is to protect and uphold the rights and privileges of all its citizens. On June 14, 1997, President Bill Clinton introduced his plan to end racial strife in a speech delivered at the University of California—San Diego. Entitled "One America in the 21st Century: The President's Initiative on Race," the president's plan had five goals: "to articulate the President's vision of a just, unified America; to inform the nation about the facts surrounding race in this country; to promote a constructive dialogue and work through the difficult issues of race; to encourage leadership at the federal, state, and local community levels to help bridge racial divides; and to identify policy and program recommendations and solutions to critical areas such as education and economic opportunity."[6] On paper, this seemed to be a simple charge for a country founded on the democratic principles of equality and freedom. However, racial tolerance, gender equality, and political and social acceptability have eluded this country for over 200 years. Men and women of diverse races, nationalities, and beliefs have and will in all likelihood continue to battle against racial and gender discrimination, physical and verbal abuses, and threats just to gain the right to have a job at a decent and fair wage, to hold and purchase property, to receive an equitable educational opportunity, and to participate in the full spectrum of the political process. Their struggles will continue because we as a nation have finally realized that equality is one of the most difficult public policy issues confronting this country. The inability of this nation's people to achieve racial and gender equality is deeply rooted in the historical, political, and cultural development of this nation. Of course, government has and probably will continue to pass laws mandating equality laden with sanctions to be leveled against those who choose not to comply with the laws. However, laws cannot change attitudes no matter how hard lawmakers try. This chapter focuses on the development and theories of racism and prejudice and the struggles of those targeted with the slurs and the repercussions of racism. This chapter also examines the actions government has taken to address the issues of racism and gender discrimination in this country.

Civil Rights and Racism

Civil rights are collectively known as "the acts of government intended to protect disadvantaged classes of persons or minority groups from arbitrary, unreasonable, or discriminatory treatment."[7] Government at all levels has the authority to pass laws and statutes designed to protect citizens against prejudicial and discriminatory actions caused by other citizens. Basically, these laws protect us from each other. Essentially a learned behavior, **prejudice** is "a feeling or act of any individual or any group in which a prejudgment about someone else or another group is made on the basis of emotion rather than reason."[8] **Discrimination** is an action precipitated by prejudice against an individual or group.

There are two forms of discrimination. The most obvious form is **de jure discrimination** whereby a *purposeful action* adversely impacts one group over another group. The creation of "all white" communities across this country was accomplished through a series of government ordinances backed by personal threats and reprisals to keep minority groups out of certain cities and towns. However, **de facto discrimination** is an *undeliberate action* adversely impacting one group over another group. For example, white flight to the suburbs created racially segregated neighborhoods, located primarily in economically depressed and deteriorating central business districts. No laws or deliberate actions were taken to force Anglo residents to leave their inner city neighborhoods. These individuals simply possessed the resources and the desire to relocate. The question of whether the adverse action was a result of de facto or de jure discrimination usually arises over a multiplicity of issues ranging from legislative redistricting and reapportionment issues to public school financing problems.

Before delving into the theories of racism, it is important to understand the vital role the Supreme Court has taken in promoting and protecting civil rights as the means of eradicating the damages wrought by prejudice, discrimination, and racism. "When the race controversy attained a degree of no longer an ignorable public concern at the highest governmental level in the late 1940s, it was the judicial branch of the government, with the Supreme Court at its apex, which led the other branches in tackling the problem. While it probably did not lead eagerly or joyously, a people's rightful claims could no longer be ignored merely because the political, in particular, the legislative branch refused then to become involved beyond the most cursory of levels, and in fact consistently passed the problems on to the Court. It is an intriguing question how much strife might have been spared and how much understanding might have been engendered had the elective branches of the government provided the decisive leadership with which they are charged and, as subsequent events proved, of which they are capable when pressed."[9] For example, the 1960s civil rights movement actually began when the Supreme Court completely dismantled the nearly century-old concept of separate but equal in its landmark ruling in *Brown v the Board of Education of Topeka, Kansas* (1954). The pattern appears to be that once the federal judicial bench renders a decision concerning civil rights, it then becomes the responsibility of the legislative and executive branches to enact the much needed corrective legislation.

Unfortunately, the only public policy options normally open to lawmakers are the alleviative, preventive, and punitive. (These policy options are discussed in detail in Chapter 14.) The civil rights acts were designed to prevent incidences of racial discrimination from spreading by penalizing violators with both civil and criminal sanctions. The suffering of those adversely impacted by acts of discrimination is alleviated by civil monetary determinations as well as criminal sanctions, particularly acts that violate a person's civil rights. **Affirmative actions** are the formalized efforts on the part of government to remedy previous incidences of past discrimination particularly in the employment and political processes. The purpose of affirmative action is two-fold. First, it alleviates those adversely impacted by racial discrimination by sanctioning actions to reverse previous conditions of discrimination in the workplace. Second, affirmative action like civil rights laws prevents further damage by providing punitive sanctions against violators. The curative approach is not a viable option at this point due to the deeply rooted attitudes of racism and discrimination that have been and continue to be instilled through the cultural and social development of all population groups.

Theories of Racism

For centuries, humanity has been emboiled in a great debate over whether equality is achievable in multicultural societies. Colonized by immigrants, the United States population is a mixture of people hailing from various countries who brought their cultural values, folkways, and mores to America's shores. Americans oftentimes try to convince themselves that their multicultural society is a melting pot of diversity that speaks with one voice. This nation's continual struggle to achieve racial and cultural equality reveals a country that speaks with many voices, oftentimes in conflict with each other. Europe has experienced its own struggles with multiculturalism. "Only fifty years ago, a collection of distinct nations that were mostly linguistically and culturally homogenous, Europe has become a multicultural stew, one that has grown all the faster with the collapse of the Soviet Union, the removal of trade barriers and blurring of national borders, and the desire of the poor in Asia, Africa and the Middle East to seek a better life. Increasingly, those who say they have done their best to adapt socially and culturally in their adopted countries complain they're kept at arm's length by the majority, tolerated at best, marginalized, mocked and attacked at worst."[10] Not every European openly embraces the concept of multiculturalism. Even the ancient Greeks clearly divided their societies by granting citizens a full spectrum of political, social, and economic privileges while denying those same rights to noncitizens. Slaves fared worse. An advocate of equality, Aristotle "on the other hand was sure that all men possessed reason, but thought that the distinguishing mark of slaves was that they possessed only so much of the power of reason as to enable them to understand their masters, without being able to reason for themselves; and he concluded that manual workers ought not to participate in government on the grounds that their lives denied them the opportunity to cultivate the qualities essential to wisdom."[11] Embedded in Aristotle's words are four of the prevailing rationalizations for racism: nativism, the superior/inferior concept, the economic theory of racism, and the concept of racial separation. An examination of each concept reveals the basis for racism in America.

The concept of **nativism** is based on the belief that only those born on their country's soil should reap the benefits of their birthrights. The first generation of English colonists born in America quickly established themselves as the natives of this country. The original immigrants now became the **host culture** for subsequent immigrants. For example, the United States Constitution recognizes the lofty status of the native culture by declaring that only a native-born person can be president. Alexis de Tocqueville observed this distinct separation between the native-born and others by noting that in the United States "the first that attracts attention, and the first in enlightenment, power, and happiness is the white man, the European, man 'par excellence,' below him come the Negro [African American] and the Indian."[12] When he wrote *Democracy in America* in 1835, the majority of the nation's African American and Native American population groups were not recognized as citizens. Eventually, the host or native culture becomes very protective of its superior position, seeing any intrusion of an outside culture as a threat to their livelihood and survival.

The concept of nativism surfaced in the 1790s as Americans began their quest to preserve and protect their culture by advocating English-only and pressing for anti-immigration laws. "In the flush of their newfound freedom, the Americans began to view all foreigners—even those from England—as possible carriers of anti-republican beliefs that might threaten the new nation. They tended to suspect that the Catholics might be monarchist subversives and that anyone French might attempt to ferment the kind of unrest that had led to the French Revolution."[13] The cries against increased immigration were coupled with violence, racial slurs, and harassment towards immigrants, particularly the Irish and Catholics.

Around 1850 a national organization called the Secret Order of the Star Spangled Banner was formed in New York. Renamed the Order of United Americans, lodges were formed in every state, with approximately 960 organizations in New York alone. "Only native-born male citizens of the Protestant faith, born of Protestant parents, reared under Protestant influence and not united in marriage with a Roman Catholic, could actually join a lodge."[14] The nativist movement developed into the **Know-Nothings,** a third political party movement launched in 1854. In their first campaign effort, "they elected more than a hundred Congressmen, eight governors and thousands of local officials, including the mayors of Boston, Philadelphia and Chicago. They won control of state legislatures in a half dozen states, from New Hampshire to California, and made a strong showing in a dozen more from New York to Louisiana."[15] In 1856, the party ran Millard Filmore for president. His electoral defeat was the swan song for the Know-Nothing movement. However, the party's primary anti-immigrant policy continues to play a key role in American politics. Today, the debate on immigration reform echoes the same concerns expressed in the 1790's as congressional proposals include efforts "to restrict immigration, limit the rights of immigrants, and increase the length of time needed to become a naturalized citizen."[16] In the 2010 mid-term elections, several candidates advocated amending the Constitution to remove the portion of the Fourteenth Amendment, which automatically gives citizenship rights to those born on American soil. Reforming the nation's immigration system was a key issue in the 2016 presidential elections. Both in the primaries and the general election, presidential candidates vowed to reign in illegal immigration.

On campaign trail, candidate Trump was very vocal in his disdain of immigrants from Mexico. He told audiences that "when Mexico sends its people, they're not sending their best. . . They're sending people that have lots of problems, and they're bringing those problems with us. They're bringing drugs. They're bringing crime. They're rapists. . . The Mexican government is much smarter, much sharper, much more cunning. And they send the bad ones over because they don't want to pay for them. They don't want to take care of them."[17] As president, Trump's anti-immigration policies have focused on the shared border between Mexico and the United States. Through a series of executive orders, he threatened economic sanctions against Mexico and several Central American countries for not blocking people from leaving their countries, secured funding to continue building a wall separating Mexico from the United States, strengthened the power of the federal government to deport illegal immigrants, filed lawsuits with the Supreme Court challenging the validity of the DACA program, and further punished illegals by separating children from their parents and housing adults and children in detention facilities. He banned immigration from several Middle Eastern nations. Trump also advocated ending "birth right," a provision of the 1790 congressional act granting citizenship to immigrants providing that "their children born in the United States had citizenship by 'virtue of *jus soli*,' '*right of soil*,' regardless of parental nationality."[18] Consequently, "when unauthorized immigrants have a child in the United States, that child is a citizen. Raising a child who is a citizen enhances the parents' chances of gaining permanent residence. Upon turning twenty-one, that child can sponsor his or her parents for lawful permanent residence. . . The Center for Immigration Studies says more than 300,000 American children per year are born to unauthorized immigrants."[19]

Closely related to nativism, the **superior/inferior** explanation for racism is based on the belief that one group or culture is genetically, intellectually, and culturally more superior than any other group. Thus, the superior group becomes the natural choice to rule over the inferiors. Adolph Hitler viewed the Germanic race as the genetically superior race. His desire to create an Aryan nation served as his justification for his horrific actions against Jews during the 1930s and 1940s. In *Mein Kampf*, Hitler envisioned a new world order dominated by the Aryan or Germanic race whereby races would be divided into three groups: "the culture-creating or Aryan race; the culture-bearing races which can borrow and adopt but cannot create; and the culture-destroying race, namely, the Jews."[20] The culture-creating race is destined to rule over the genetically inferior races. In addition, advocates of this theory believe that members of certain white "races" are destined to rule not only over the nonwhite races but over the other white races as well. Under this more specific version of the doctrine of white supremacy, "the tall, blond, blue-eyed peoples of northern and western Europe were the modern remnants of a talented race called the Nordics (or Teutons), who were descended from the ancient Aryans of India. The Nordics were said to have a special talent for political organization that enabled their members to form representative governments and create just laws; hence, the Nordic portion of the White race was destined to rule over all races, including the shorter 'alpine' and the darker-skinned 'Mediterranean' portion of the White race."[21]

The superior/inferior concept of racism is often justified as a benevolent action to protect a perceived inferior race from self-destruction. In 1732, prominent slaver John Barbat wrote "that the slave's conditions in his own country were so appalling that it was a kindness to ship him to the West Indies and more considerate masters, not to mention the inestimable advantage they may reap of becoming Christians, and saving their souls."[22] This is basically the same rationale used by the Spanish conquistadors and missionaries for the enslavement of Native American tribes in Central and Latin America. The white South African apartheid policies were based on the notion that black Africans were historically and genetically too inferior to survive on their own. Armed with the lofty challenge of saving souls and protecting those incapable of protecting themselves, the self-proclaimed superior races have been able to conquer and, subsequently, control the fortunes of those deemed inferior.

In his book, *Jim Crow America*, Jim Conrad states that racism is purely an economic issue, not a culturally or genetically based concept. For example, in the United States it was the overwhelming desire for land, natural resources, and gold that compelled Anglo Americans to use whatever means available to them to acquire these precious treasures. Native American tribes were the initial targets because they possessed vast rich fertile land holdings. The discovery of gold on Indian land just intensified the greed factor. In 1863, representatives from the federal government met with Nez Perces tribal leaders to negotiate the purchase of approximately 90 percent of their reservation lands located in the territory that would become the states of Washington, Oregon and Idaho. Signed by only a handful of the tribal leaders, the federal government "agreed to pay the Nez Perces $265,000 for the ceded land. In his report to the Commissioner of Indian Affairs in Washington, Superintendent Calvin Hale announced the signing of the treaty as a great victory for the government: 'The amount thus relinquished is very nearly six million of acres, and is obtained at a cost not exceeding eight cents per acre . . . In the tract of country there is much that is exceedingly valuable, by reason of its gold and silver mines, whilst many of its valleys, and much of its uplands, will be found desirable and necessary for agricultural and grazing purposes.'"[23]

Once these groups become economically depressed and totally dependent upon their benefactors, Native Americans, slaves, Hispanics, and immigrants alike were denied accessibility to the two tools that could liberate them—education and voting rights. Minorities, in particular, were constantly reminded of their inferior status by a series of laws known as **Jim Crow**, which successfully built a wall of separation between them and Anglo Americans. According to Conrad, racial explanations are overshadowed by the prevailing economic issue. "The issue comes down to pennies, then, and so it has been since the time when slave traders marched into Africa, handed out a few bottles of rum, and walked off with a hundred or so human commodities. The profit was enormous . . . . Twenty-five cents in the hands of two white men is twenty-five cents less in the hands of a African-American laundress. Magnify that in terms of the economic process intensively at work in all Southern states, and almost as sharply operative in the north, and you can put an arrow through the heart of Jim Crow.[24] The economic theory also fuels anti-immigrant sentiments. When the economy slumps and job security is questionable, some Americans see the flow of immigrants as a threat to their own economic viability. Another traditional economic argument for halting immigration is the belief that immigrants keep the wage system depressed by accepting jobs that pay at or below minimum wage levels.

Another perspective of racism is **separation**. Immigrants, for example, usually lived among members of their own culture, forming their own cities within a city such as China Town, Little Italy, and so on. Within their own neighborhoods, they felt more secure in speaking their own language and adhering to their own traditions and beliefs. Separation was further encouraged with the denial of interracial and intercultural marriages. The creation of cluster neighborhoods or zones was enforced by invisible lines and barriers backed by social, economic, and political laws, customs, and mores on the part of all parties involved. Immigrant groups themselves were just as eager to avoid intrusions into their cultures just as much as the host Anglo cultures wanted to protect their own lifestyles and livelihoods. However, separation from other cultures creates isolation and can lead to the fear of other cultures. "The minute society separates people from each other by color or class, it sets in motion diverse economic, psychological, and cultural processes. Society builds two antithetical cultures side by side. They can be different economies and different cultures separated by a railroad track or a picket fence, and one can then pit one culture against the other and make each group hate and misunderstand the other."[25] Once races and cultures have been separated from each other for generations, it is easy to see why feelings of prejudice, mistrust, and suspicion would develop. In part, the desire of lawmakers to integrate the various races has been only marginally successful in this country because of a long history of cultural and racial separations.

Oftentimes, fear of a real or potential threat to national security can result in racist policies or actions levied at a particular ethnic or cultural group that played no active role in planning or executing the threat. For example, the Japanese attack on Pearl Harbor in Hawaii in December 1941, sent shock waves throughout the United States that perhaps the Japanese government had already convinced Japanese sympathizers and/or already placed military personnel along the Pacific coastline to launch an actual invasion of the United States. Perceiving this as a viable threat to national security, federal officials decided to intern Japanese immigrants and Japanese-American-born citizens living on the West Coast into internment camps for the duration of the war against Japan. The official order dated February 19, 1942, initially ordered Japanese Americans on the West Coast to stay inside their homes from 8 p.m. to 6 a.m. By May, they were ordered to leave their homes and report to local military bases. These American-born citizens were given only a few hours to collect some personal belongings that would fit into a suitcase. Facing an uncertain future, these individuals left behind everything! American-born, Fred Korematsu was fired from his job because he was Japanese American. He tried to flee California but was later arrested and charged in violation of the relocation order. The Civil Liberties Union sued the federal government on the grounds that "treating everyone of Japanese descent as a security risk, with no hearing or avenue to prove fealty to the United States, violated the Fifth Amendment guarantee that depriving someone of his or her liberty required 'due process of the law.'"[26] In **Korematsu v United States** (1944), the Supreme Court upheld the government's relocation order. In total, 120,000 people of Japanese descent of which 65 percent were American citizens were resettled into barbed-wired detention facilities surrounded by search-lights and armed guards. Japanese-Americans did serve in the war effort with distinction, but they were not assigned to the Japanese front. The United States government finally issued an official apology for the internments, and a provision of the 1988 Civil Liberties Act paid each detainee or his/her family member $20,000 each in reparations. Asking for $148,000,000 to cover lost property, the federal government paid only $37,000,000 to the detainees.[27] Immediately following the terrorist attacks on the World Trade Center, numerous physical and property-related crimes against Muslim Americans were reported.

Racism in America

Of course, we cannot overlook the obvious. All people, regardless of their own racial and cultural identity, harbor to some extent prejudices against others. These acquired habits have become as much a part of our own roots and traditions as patriotism and nationalism are to every American. It should be clearly understood that not every Anglo American is a racist nor is every member of a minority group a victim of racial discrimination and hatred. Regardless of their individual racial backgrounds, the majority of the American people have learned to transcend past discriminatory practices by coming to terms with their own prejudices. However, there are some individuals who harbor intense hatred towards others. Their vocal and sometimes violent displays of their hatred divide rather than unite the American people.

The increase in the number of racially motivated crimes has created a new category of criminal offenses—hate crimes. In 2009, President Barack Obama signed into law the **Matthew Shepard and James Byrd, Jr., Hate Crime Prevention Act**, enabling the federal government to upgrade a criminal act as a hate crime when "(1) the crime was committed because of the actual or perceived race, color, religion, national origin of any person or (2) the crime was committed because of the actual or perceived religion, national origin, gender, sexual orientation, gender identity, or disability of any person and the crime affected interstate or foreign commerce or occurred within federal special maritime and territorial jurisdiction."[28] Shepard, a homosexual was brutally beaten, tied to a fence, and left to die while Byrd, an African American, was murdered by three white men who offered him a ride. As defined in the FBI's annual Hate Crimes Statistical Report, **hate crimes** are "crimes that manifest evidence of prejudice based on race, gender, or gender identity, religion, disability, sexual orientation, or ethnicity."[26] The Bureau's 2018 report indicates 7,120 hate crime incidents involving 8,496 reported incidences by 8,819 victims. Approximately, 6,266 victims could identify their offenders. Of the reported incidents, 57.5 percent were motivated by race, ethnicity and ancestry bias, 20.2 percent by religious bias and 17.0 percent by sexual-orientation bias.[29] The latest barrage of hate-filled rhetoric has been leveled against Chinese Americans who are wrongly accused of bringing the coronavirus to the United States. President Trump repeatedly uses the verbiage of Kung flu and Chinavirus in his attempt to the lay the blame for the spread of the virus onto the Chinese. Yet, Asian and Chinese Americans did not bring the disease to the United States. Within a three-month period, 832 incidents of assaults and verbal tirades were reported in just California.[30] Hate crimes occur across the country such as a Texas man sentenced to 15 years in prison for luring and subsequently beating a young gay man because of the victim's sexual orientation; a former member of the KKK sentenced for burning a cross in front of an interracial family's home in Tennessee; a Utah man sentenced for threatening an interracial family; in Mississippi, four men indicted for a racially-motivated crime spree; and a man from New Mexico indicted for making anti-Semitic threats against a Jewish businesswoman.[31] These figures illustrate only the reported incidents whereby an individual violated the rights and property of others purely on the grounds of hatred.

Several law enforcement units have been practicing their own form of racial discrimination known as **racial profiling**. This practice is based on the assumption that criminals possess certain common traits and characteristics that separate them from the law-abiding citizen. Armed with a profile of those most likely to commit a crime, law enforcement officers in several states have been stopping innocent drivers, subjecting them to vehicle searches, and, in some instances, harassing them simply because they possess physical characteristics associated with the criminal element. The 9th U.S. Circuit Court of Appeals overturned the United States Border Patrol's use of racial profiling against Hispanics. The justices defended their decision by pointing out that "stops based on race or ethnic appearance send the underlying message to all our citizens that those who are not white [Anglo] are judged by the color of their skin alone. Such stops also send a clear message that those who are not white [Anglo] enjoy a lesser degree of constitutional protection—that they are in effect assumed to be potential criminals first and individuals second."[32] In 2013, the Supreme Court dealt a near fatal blow to Arizona's tough immigration enforcement law by ruling it as racial profiling, and thus unconstitutional. Known as Senate Bill 1070, the Court struck down the provisions requiring that all immigrants carry on their person at all times their immigration papers, making it a criminal offense for an illegal immigrant to seek work or hold a job, and allowing law enforcement to arrest any suspected illegal immigrant without a search warrant. The Court did uphold the right of state and local law enforcement to demand proof of citizenship and/or immigration status when an individual is stopped for other matters, such as a traffic violation with the understanding that the Court would revisit this if it is being used in a discriminatory manner.

An examination of the struggles of Native Americans, Hispanics, African Americans, women, and immigrants to achieve the same civil rights granted by the Framers initially to only white male citizens reveals that this country has yet to reverse racism and discrimination. There is much left to be done. At the 1848 Seneca Falls Convention, Frederick Douglass reminded the audience of the ultimate goal of civil rights when he declared that "right is of no sex, truth is of no color."[33]

Native Americans

No racial group has suffered more humiliation, destruction, abuse, and discrimination from the "white man's" ways than the American Indian. Where once hundreds of thousands of Indians inhabited this land, today there are only "562 distinct tribes with federal recognition, and scores of others recognized only locally or not at all."[34] Basically, Native Americans fell victim to the economic theory of racism justified by the superior-inferior concept. North American Indians became a target from the very beginning of the colonial experience since they possessed what American settlers desired most—rich fertile lands. The arrival of the first English colonists to the shores of the James River in 1607 initiated this over 400-year-old relationship as the settlers carved out of the virgin forests the Jamestown colony. Predictably, Native Americans viewed the white man's encroachment into their lands as a threat to their culture, livelihood, and, ultimately, their survival. Consequently, the settlers were subjected to continuous attacks from members of the Powhatan chiefdom, a confederative alliance consisting of nearly 30 different tribes. After seven years of attacks and counterattacks, the colonists captured Pocahontas, daughter of the chief. Both sides unofficially agreed to end the warfare. However, "hostilities persisted until a peace settlement in 1632. But colonial expansion continued, gobbling up Powhatan land. Opechancanough [Pocahontas' uncle] retaliated again in 1644 in a final spasm of attacks, killing more than 500 colonists."[35] The livelihood of Native American tribes fall into two general categories. **Agriculturalist** tribes lived off the land. Through generational trial and error, they knew what type of crops would grow best on their land. Their meat supply was the animals native to their land. If those tribes were uprooted and relocated elsewhere, their survival was questionable since they had to adjust to new soils that were not suitable to their traditional foodstuffs. **Nomadic** tribes followed their meat source, usually the buffalo. Thousands of nomadic Native Americans starved to death after settlers, the military and railroad workers intentionally slaughtered massive herds of buffalo. Native American tribes initially sought to negotiate with Anglo-American settlers as they saw more and more of their lands taken

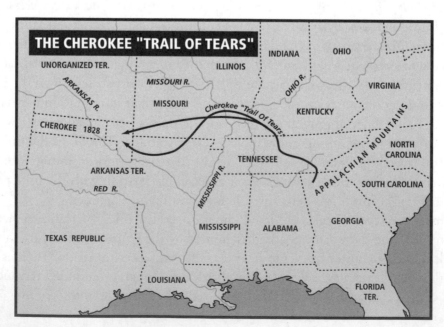

from them. Tribal leaders quickly realized that the only viable option left for Native Americans was to fight to keep what was theirs.

The initial public policy response from the British government was to relocate various tribes first west to the Mississippi and then to lands further beyond. The negotiation process began in earnest at the end of the French and Indian War, fought between 1754 and 1761. Pontiac, an Ottawa chief, convinced the tribal leaders of the Hurons, Potawatomi, Chippewas, Delawares, Kickapoos, Shawnees, and other tribes to join forces to drive the English out of America. Confronted with the might of the British military, Pontiac sued for peace by signing the Proclamation of 1763, which declared that: (1) all land west of the crest of the Appalachian Mountains was "Indian Country"; (2) any settlers west of the Appalachian who had not acquired a legal title to their land from the Indians must return to the colonies; and (3) all future land purchases from the Indians must be conducted in public meetings attended by representatives of the king.[36] As anticipated, colonists violated the treaty by establishing more settlements in "Indian Country." After winning independence, the newly formed United States government continued the practice of signing nation-to-nation treaties with tribal leaders.

The Framers, however, did not draw a distinction between treaties negotiated between Native American tribes and sovereign foreign nations when they elevated all treaties as "the supreme law of the land" in Article VI, Section 2, of the United States Constitution. The question of whether Native American tribes were separate sovereign nations was addressed by the Supreme Court under Chief Justice John Marshall. Between 1823 and 1832, the Court developed the federal trust doctrine with its decisions in *Johnson v McIntosh, Cherokee Nation v Georgia,* and *Worcester v Georgia.* These three cases are collectively known as the **Marshall Trilogy**. Basically, Marshall's rulings held that "the federal government and the Indian nations are inextricably bound together as trustee to obligee. . . .He also ruled that treaties are a granting of rights from the Indians to the federal government, not the other way around, and all rights not granted by the Indians are presumed to be reserved by the Indians."[37] In other words, expansion into lands held by Native American tribes was supposed to be a negotiated legal process whereby the fundamental rights of the tribes were to be respected. However, treaties between the United States government and the Iroquois, Delawares, Wyandots, Chippewas, Ottawas, Shawnees, Cherokees, Choctaws, Chickasaws, Seminoles, Cheyenne, and Navajo were openly violated by the zeal of **manifest destiny**, the belief that the Anglo-American's destiny was to own all of the land between the Atlantic and Pacific Oceans. Uprooting whole tribes from their sacred ancestral lands and forcing them to walk hundreds of miles to reach far western territories only served to accelerate the tension and mistrust between the United States government and Native American tribal leaders. The Jackson administration signed approximately ninety-four treaties demanding tribal relocations. The **Trail of Tears** resulted in the forced relocation of the Cherokees, Choctaws, Creeks, Chickasaws, and Seminoles from east of the Mississippi to Indian territory on the opposite side of the river simply because gold was discovered in Georgia in 1829. The Seminoles, in particular, posed serious problems for the government's relocation schemes. In retaliation of the **Indian Removal Act** (1830), the Seminoles launched their own war against the United States known as the Second Seminole War. Eventually, "the United States removed 3,800 Seminoles to Indian Territory, but at a terrible price. The war lasted for an interminable seven years, 1,500 American soldiers died, and the cost has been estimated at between $20,000,000 to $60,000,000—significantly more than the United States paid for the entire Louisiana Purchase only fifty-two years earlier.[38]

Native Americans began to fight back with violent attacks against settlers. Realizing that a peaceful settlement was impossible, the federal government gave its army the green light, in effect, to exterminate those tribes who refused to relocate. Lawmakers justified their actions by portraying Indians as savage killers bent on brutally attacking and scalping innocent settlers whose only desire was to carve out a better life for themselves and their families by moving West. In 1862, the United States Army was ordered to begin the extermination of the Mescalero Apaches. Granted leniency, approximately 400 tribal members were relocated to Bosque Redondo, a remote area in the New Mexico territory. The Navajos were next. "Well over half the estimated 12,000 Navajos eventually were rounded up. They first went to Fort Canby, near present-day Window Rock, Arizona, where many died of exposure and dysentery. Survivors were sent off in groups to march 300 miles to Bosque Redondo. . . Some who could not keep up the pace, including the elderly, children and pregnant women, were shot by soldiers. . . In all, nearly 3,000 Navajos died at Bosque Redondo."[39] The slaughter of the Plains Indians began in earnest when on January 29, 1863, the United States cavalry under the leadership of Col. Patrick O'Connor attacked a Shoshone tribe at Bear Creek, near present day Salt Lake City, Utah. Tribe after tribe saw its mighty braves, women, and children killed by bullets, diseases, and starvation. The Battle of Bear River was "much more grim than better-known Indian massacres at Sand Creek in Colorado Territory, where 133 Cheyennes were killed by troopers on Nov. 28, 1864, and at Wounded Knee, S. D., where soldiers slaughtered 153 Sioux on Dec. 28, 1890."[40]

Placed on reservations, Native Americans became the victims to the whims of lawmakers as they vacillated between policies advocating **cultural assimilation** and **separation**. Assimilation meant that reservation Indians were to become "civilized" by adopting to the white man's society and culture. "The Bureau of Indian Affairs (BIA) agents, who supervised the reservations, tried to root-out Native American ways and replace them with white dress and hairstyles, the English language, and the Christian religion."[41] For the Navajo, a 1868 treaty with the federal government designated land in New Mexico, Arizona and Utah as tribal lands. A provision in the treaty called for compulsory education for all Navajo children living on the reservation. Since there were no schools on reservation lands, the federal government decided that these children would be sent to faraway missionary schools. The intent was to teach these children how to live in the "white man's world." "Tribal leaders noted that 'our language-which retains our timeless traditions and embodies our stories, songs and prayers-eroded. Ceremonial and ritual ties weakened. The schools followed military structure and discipline: Children were divided into 'companies,' issued uniforms and marched to and from activities. Their hair was cut or shaved. Because speaking Navajo was forbidden, many children did not speak at all. . . . Nowhere in [the] lessons was there any mention of Native history."[42] A retired military officer, Richard Pratt and Sarah Mather, a school teacher at the Rosebud Reservation in South Dakota in 1879, began their roundup of recruits for his newly established boarding school in Pennsylvania. Rosebud is the reservation for the Lakota Sioux. Pratt believed that if you "dress an Indian in white man's clothes, cut his hair, and show him white man's technological achievement and creature comforts, the theory went, and he would want to embrace the white man's world."[43] Although Pratt's school closed in 1918, others similar to his remained open until the 1960s. In 1975, Congress passed the Indian Self-Determination and Education Assistance Act giving the tribes control over their children's education. In 1990, Congress passed a law preserving the Navajo language and traditions.

One of the primary issues for Native Americans is reclaiming ownership of or at least royalties from their ancestral lands. In 1887, the United States Congress passed the **Dawes Severalty Act** as a concerted effort to break up large reservation holdings that bonded Native Americans to their tribes. "Rather than allotting reservation lands to tribal groups, the act allowed the president [of the United States] to distribute these lands to individuals. Private property, the framers of the bill reasoned, would undermine communal norms and tribal identity and encourage Indians to settle down and farm as white men did."[44] However, the land redistribution scheme merely took Indian lands held supposedly in trust by the Bureau of Indian Affairs from public oversight to private ownership. "Within 20 years of the Dawes Act, Native Americans had lost 60 percent of their lands. The federal government held the profits from land sales 'in trust' and used them for 'civilizing' missions."[45]

Recent federal legislation coupled with favorable federal court rulings have given Native Americans more control over their lands and, subsequently, their own futures. In particular, the federal courts have rendered favorable decisions in cases involving treaty violations by the federal government. The Oneida Indian Nation has been battling in court since 1920 seeking compensation from the state of New York over 250,000 acres located between Utica and Syracuse, land the tribe claims that was stolen from them. "The federal government first signed a treaty reserving some 270,000 acres for the Oneidas in 1794, after tribe members fought British troops and reportedly lugged 600 bushels of corn hundreds of miles to George Washington's starving troops at Valley Forge. Congress, however, specified that all future purchases of Indian lands could proceed only with federal consent. The Oneidas signed some 27 treaties with New York State over the years, but only one of the state's treaties received federal approval. Eventually, the Oneidas' lands in the state dwindled to a single 32-acre tract."[46] In 1985, the Supreme Court ruled that the initial 1794 treaty was a binding document. The Blackfeet are also challenging the BIA's withholding of trust money from the sale or lease of Indian lands dating back to 1820. Through treaty agreements, Native American tribes were given the land that was initially deemed unfit for cultivation and settlement. Today, it is estimated that these lands hold 40 percent of the nation's coal reserves, 65 percent of the nation's uranium supply, ample veins of gold, silver, cadmium, platinum and manganese, large untapped pockets of natural gas and oil, acre after acre of uncut prime timber, and 20 percent of the nation's fresh water.[47]

According to the National Congress of American Indians, "there are 574 federally recognized Indian Nations (variously called tribes, nations, band, pueblos, communities and native villages) in the United States. Approximately 229 of these ethnically, culturally and linguistically diverse nations are located in Alaska; the other federal recognized tribes are located in thirty-five states."[48] As of 2018, the United States Census Bureau reports that 4,1487,000 persons identify themselves as either American Indian or Alaska Native, representing 1.4 percent of the nation's total population.[49] With few exceptions, the majority of the nation's Native Americans live at or below the poverty level. The lack of advanced education continues to be a perennial concern for Native Americans. For example, of the associate degrees awarded in 2017, only 9,268 or 0.9 percent of the 1,005,649 degrees conferred were awarded to Native Americans. The number of advanced degrees beyond the associates awarded to Native Americans in 2017 was only 1.7 percent of the total number of awarded degrees.[50] One's level of education is tied directly to viable employment opportunities and economic mobility. Table 13.1 illustrates some of the important events that have had both a positive and negative impact on Native Americans.

Table 13. 1

Significant Events for Native Americans

Date	Event
1778	The newly formed United States negotiates its first treaty with an Indian nation promising future statehood to the Delawares.
1787-1789	The United States Constitution gives the federal government the exclusive authority to regulate trade and commerce with Indian tribes.
1809	Treaty of Fort Wayne secures 2.5 million acres from Indians for Anglo-American settlement in Ohio and Indiana.
1813-1814	The Creek Wars end with treaty agreements relinquishing all lands held by the Creeks in the Southeast to the American government.
1817-1818	First Seminole War.
1820-1824	Kickapoos resist removal from Illinois territory.
1824	Bureau of Indian Affairs established under the War Department.
1830	Congress passes the Indian Removal Act.
1835-1842	Second Seminole War.
1853-1856	United States government obtains 174 million acres of Indian lands through treaties.
1854	United States Indian Affairs Commission ends the Indian Removal Policy.
1855-1858	Third Seminole War.
1861-1863	Mangas Colorados and Cochise lead Apache uprising.
1862	Smallpox kills 200,000 Indians in the Northwest Coast.
1863-1866	Navajo Wars in New Mexico and Arizona.
1866	United States Congress declares Indian land as right-of-way for construction of the Trans-Continental Railroad.
1876-1877	Sioux Wars waged by Sioux, Cheyenne and Arapaho under Sitting Bull and Crazy Horse.
1881-1886	Apache resistance under Geronimo.
1885	The last great herd of buffalo is exterminated.
1887	Congress passes the General Allotment Act or the Dawes Act.

1924	Congress grants citizenship to Native Americans.
1926	National Council of American Indians is formed.
1928	Charles Curtis, Kansas Indian and United States Senator, is elected vice president under Herbert Hoover.
1934	Congress passes United States Indian Reorganization Act, reversing United States practice of land allotment by establishing tribal self-government and landholding.
1946	Congress passes the Indian Claims Commission Act granting permission for tribes to place damage claims against the United States government for federal takings of tribal land.
1953	House Concurrent Resolution 108 ends the federal-tribal relationship. Public Law 280 enabled states to assume criminal and civil jurisdiction in matters involving Indians as litigants living on reservation lands. Originally, these matters were dealt with either in tribal and/or federal courts.
1965	Congress passes Voting Rights Act ensuring suffrage to all Native Americans.
1968	Passage of the American Indian Civil Rights Act extending civil liberties outlined in the Bill of Rights to Indians living on reservations.
1969-1971	Members of Red Power movement occupy Alcatraz Island to call attention to the plight of Native Americans.
1973	Members of American Indian Movement and 200 armed Oglala Sioux occupy site of Wounded Knee Massacre on Pine Ridge Reservation in South Dakota for 71 days.
1975	Congress passes the Indian Self-Determination and Education Assistance Act authorizing the Secretaries of the Interior and Health, Education and Welfare to directly make contracts and Issue grants to federally recognized Indian tribes
1978	Congress passes American Indian Freedom of Religion Act, and the Indian Civil Welfare Act delineating the rules for adoption and custody of Native American children
1987	Ben Nighthorse Campbell from Colorado was elected to U.S. House of Representatives, elected to U.S. Senate in 1992 and 1998, and served as captain of U.S. Olympic Judo team in 1964.
1988	Congress passes Indian Gaming Regulatory Act, allowing Indians to operate casinos on their reservations under guidelines established by the states.
1990	Congress passes Native American Graves Protection and Repatriation Act.
1999	President Bill Clinton becomes the first president to visit an Indian reservation since President Franklin Roosevelt included a stop at a Cherokee reservation while on vacation in North Carolina in 1936.
2004	National Museum of the American Indian opens in Washington, D.C.

African Americans

The economic prosperity of the pre-Civil War South was the result to a large degree of the back-breaking toil of African-American slaves and their descendants who worked in the fields from sun up to sun down either bent over picking cotton, wielding a machete cutting sugar cane, or standing in ankle-deep water planting and harvesting rice. Most Southerners rationalized the exploitation, brutality, injustice, and degradation of slaves with the "old assumptions of Anglo-Saxon superiority and innate African inferiority, white supremacy, and Negro [African American] subordination."[51] The institution of slavery completely controlled the fate of the slave from birth to death. Slaves were part of their owner's properties just like the house, the fields, and the furniture. "Born a slave in Maryland in 1818, Frederick Douglass secretly taught himself to read and write, and in 1838, he escaped and fled north to become the most famous Black [African American] man of his times, an eloquent abolitionist, orator, writer and newspaper publisher. He was also a radical who repeatedly criticized Lincoln for moving too slowly to free the slaves."[52] Douglass once remarked that "whatever of comfort is necessary for him [the slave] for his body or soul that is inconsistent with his being property, is carefully wrested from him, not only by public opinion but by the laws of the country . . . . He [the slave] is deprived of education. God gave him an intellect; the slaveholder declares it shall not be cultivated."[53] The denial of education, even the simplest forms of reading and writing, reinforced the concept of the superior/inferior relationship by making the slave more dependent upon his master and, thus, less likely to be disobedient or to run away.

Slavery was first introduced to the colonies in 1619 when a few Black Africans were brought to the new world to harvest Jamestown's tobacco crop. "Within a decade after South Carolina's 1691 adoption of a comprehensive slave code, other Colonies had laws defining and regulating human chattel."[54] Aided by a lucrative cross-Atlantic slave trading industry, the slave system grew rapidly. "By the eve of the [American] Revolution, slave-holding was deeply rooted in all of those Colonies, with New York City, among colonial cities, standing second only to Charleston, S.C., in its population of slaves."[55] The emerging slave system was economically attractive to both agricultural interests in the South and the developing textile industries in the North. Although many plantation owners and farmers opposed the institution of slavery on moral grounds, economic reality prevented the abolition of the system. Thomas Jefferson "not only embraced slavery as essential to maintaining his personal standard of living, . . . he was at the forefront of efforts by Virginia plantation owners to modernize and prolong the 'peculiar institution'. . . In his lifetime, Jefferson owned more than 600 slaves and sold or gave away nearly 200. At any given time he kept about 130 slaves to labor on his 5,000-acre plantation."[56] If slavery was abolished, Jefferson "proposed that freed Blacks [African Americans] be colonized in Africa. Jefferson rejected the possibility of a biracial society in America after abolition because he believed that ex-slaves could never forget the terrible injustices inflicted upon them by their former masters, but more importantly, because he was convinced himself that Blacks [African Americans] by nature were intellectually inferior to whites."[57] A plantation owner himself, James Madison had his own plan for emancipation of slavery:

Emancipation would have to involve adequate recompense to the freed slaves' owners and the consent of both slave and master. Madison's idea for purchasing their [the slaves] freedom was to sell off by an act of Congress, 200 million acres of the nation's undeveloped

Western land at $3 per acre. This would be legal, fair, and probably constitutional, he thought. He did not think for a minute that emancipated slaves would be able to settle in the states where they had once been enslaved or, for that matter anywhere in the United States. . . He joined and gave financial support to the new **American Colonization Society**, whose aim was to train freed slaves in educational camps in Maryland, and settle them on land the Society had brought on the west coast of Africa and given the hopeful name of Liberia.[58]

Both Jefferson and Madison were more concerned about the economic loss planation owners would face with the loss of their labor force than they were about the fate of former slaves. The American Colonization Society failed miserably. "By 1835, the facts were that in eighteen years the Colonization Society had succeeded in resettling just 3,000 ex-slaves as freemen in Africa, at a time when the slave population in America was growing by 60,000 per year."[59] "By as early as 1815, cotton was America's most valuable export, and the worth of the people who harvested the product grew apace with cotton's steadily growing value. 'By the eve of the Civil War, the dollar value of slaves was greater than the dollar value of all of America's banks, railroads, and manufacturing combined.'"[60] Unable to halt the spread of slavery in the traditional southern states, the **abolitionist movement** convinced Congress to limit the spread of slavery into the new territories seeking statehood with the passage of the **Missouri Compromise** in 1820.

Pennsylvania's southern border was the famous Mason-Dixon line, separating the north from the south. Ardent anti-slavery advocates, the **Society of Friends** (the Quakers) were able to convince the Pennsylvanian state legislature to abolish slavery in 1780 with the passage of the **Gradual Abolition Act**. Pennsylvania became the unofficial headquarters of the famous **underground railroad**. With the assistance of "conductors," abolitionists were able to rescue fugitive slaves and secretly move them from station to station until they reached Canada. Thaddeus Stevens, a Pennsylvanian native and member of Congress, was a very vocal advocate for the abolition movement. He led the fight against the **Fugitive Slave Laws** initiated by Senator Henry Clay. Enacted throughout the south, these laws mandated the capture and return of any escaped slave and severe punishment to anyone refusing to help capture fleeing slaves. Clay's law gave judges $10 if they decided for the slaveholder and only $5 if they ruled in favor of the former slave. Stevens and his mistress/housekeeper mulatto Lydia Smith used his home in Lancaster, Pennsylvania "as a station on the Underground Railroad, concealing runaway slaves in a hidden cistern connected to the house by a secret tunnel."[61] Records indicate that between 1820 and 1860, some 9,000 slaves were guided to freedom."[62]

The fate of the Missouri Compromise was determined by the Supreme Court's decision in *Dred Scott v Sandford* (1857). First, the Court invalidated the Missouri Compromise of 1820 as an unconstitutional intrusion into state affairs. Second, it ruled that Dred Scott, a slave, did not have the right to sue the government because he was not a citizen. Third, Scott was still considered to be a slave since the Court affirmed that slaves were the property of their owners, and only their owners could release them from their bondage.

The man who would eventually abolish slavery echoed superior/inferior sentiments against slaves in a speech delivered in 1858 at a Republican Party function. Abraham Lincoln stated: "I will say then that I am not, nor ever have been in favor of bringing about in any way the social and political equality of the white [Anglo] and black [African American] races, [applause]—that

The Supreme Court decided that Dred Scott was not a citizen of the United States.

I am not nor ever have been in favor of making voters or jurors of Negroes [African Americans], nor of qualifying them to hold office, nor to intermarry with white [Anglo] people, and I will say in addition to this that there is a physical difference between black [African American] and white [Anglo] races which I believe will forever forbid the two races living together on the terms of social and political equality. And inasmuch as they cannot so live, while they do remain together, there must be the position of superior and inferior, and I as much as any other man, am in favor of having the superior position assigned to the white [Anglo] race."[63] During the Civil War, free African Americans living in the Northern states were initially denied the right to join the military effort. "The hardest problem for black [African American] men was not in being brave, it was in getting a chance to fight at all. At every step, they were confronted with racial scorn and fear, created by the long existence of slavery itself."[64] In 1862, Congress passed the **Militia Act**, enabling African Americans to join the warfront. However, African Americans received less than half of the standard soldier pay and were denied any officer and command positions. At the end of the war, "some 180,000 black [African-American] soldiers served in the Union Army, about 10 percent of its total strength; 2,800 were killed in battle, 34,000 died of disease in the field, and twenty-one were awarded the Medal of Honor for bravery."[65]

The end of the Civil War brought limited social, economic, and political relief to former slaves. Economic viability was difficult, if not immediately impossible. Few knew how to read or write. Few had ventured far from their plantations. Once emancipated, few knew how to survive on their own. During the final months of the Civil War, General William Sherman attempted to entice southern African Americans to join the union cause by offering to each family forty-acres of prime farmland in Georgia and South Carolina. He also promised to lend them Army mules. Congress also allocated approximately 850,000 acres of southern soil to the Freedman's Bureau. In turn, the Bureau was supposed to help former slaves make the transition from slavery to freedom by giving them land. Few received any land since President Andrew Johnson used his executive muscle to allow former Confederates to quickly reclaim their properties. In 1865, the United States Congress finally outlawed slavery with the passage of the **Thirteenth Amendment**. Former slaves were granted citizenship with the passage of the **Fourteenth Amendment** and voting privileges with the **Fifteenth**

Amendment. The **Civil Rights Act of 1866** granted former slaves the rights to own property, file lawsuits, and make contractual agreements. Initially, the Republican-dominated Congress used these three constitutional amendments and the Civil Rights Act to punish defeated members of the **Confederate States of America**. Known as the **Radical Republicans**, these individuals desired to topple the Southern aristocracy by placing former slaves into policy-making roles. Across the South, former Confederate officials, soldiers, and anyone who supported the Southern cause lost their rights to vote and to run for elective office. Consequently, citizenship and voting privileges enabled former slaves to now run for public office. "Every session of the Virginia General Assembly from 1869 to 1891 contained black [African American] members. Between 1876 and 1894 North Carolinians elected fifty-two blacks [African Americans] to the lower house of their state legislature, and between 1878 and 1902, forty-seven blacks [African Americans] served in the South Carolina General Assembly . . . . Southern states elected two blacks [African Americans] to the U. S. House of Representatives after Reconstruction, the same number elected during Reconstruction. Every Congress but one between 1869 and 1901 had at least one black [African American] member from the South."[66]

"Yet despite these enactments, despite the mandates of Amendment Fourteen, and despite the language of the Fifteenth Amendment of 1870 which on its face seemed to assure to blacks [African Americans] the privilege of the ballot, neither the myth of white supremacy nor the fact of color prejudice was wiped out."[67] The southern states struck back at the federal government by enacting a series of legislative acts and city ordinances known as black codes or **Jim Crow laws** that denied freedoms and political rights to African Americans. Punitive sanctions were levied against both African Americans and whites providing assistance to freedmen. The term Jim Crow originated with Anglo actor Thomas Dartmouth Rice. Born in 1808, Rice performed in the Bowery Theater in New York City blackening his face and "wearing ragged and patched clothing, suggesting the garb a runaway slave might wear, and adopted a signature crooked posture . . . [that] was commenting on the risk of crippling injuries that workers in factories and other industrialized settings faced in the United States."[68]

National lawmakers soon realized "that you cannot change the mores of a people by law, and since the social segregation of the races is the most deep-seated and pervasive of the Southern mores, it is evident that he who attempts to change it by law runs risks of incalculable gravity."[69] Jim Crow laws began to have an impact on African-American accessibility to the ballot box, blocking full political participation. The **grandfather clause** required passing a **literacy test** for those potential voters whose grandfathers could not vote before 1867. Variations of the grandfather clause were incorporated into the state constitutions of South Carolina, Louisiana, North Carolina, Alabama, Virginia, Georgia, and Oklahoma. The **poll tax**, a state mandated voting fee, was enacted in Florida, Tennessee, Arkansas, and Texas. The Democratic Party's **white only primary** effectively eliminated African-American participation, since in most general races, the opposition party did not run a candidate. This tactic was adopted in South Carolina, Arkansas, Georgia, Florida, Tennessee, Alabama, Mississippi, Kentucky, Texas, Louisiana, Oklahoma, Virginia, and North Carolina.

Jim Crow laws also socially separated Anglos from African Americans. Immediately following the election of 1884, "the rumor, when it struck, was deemed as vile as any that had ever hit the nation's capitol. A 'colored man' [African American], people were whispering, had attended a White House function. Grover Cleveland swiftly responded. 'It so happens,' the President assured the nation, 'that I have never in my official position, either when sleeping or walking, alive or dead, on my head or my heels, dined, lunched, or supped or invited to a wedding reception any colored [African-American] man, woman, or child.'"[70] The mean-spiritedness of Jim Crow pervaded legislative houses across this nation. The Virginia state legislature passed a 1912 ordinance mandating segregated residential districts. The law made it "unlawful for any colored [African-American] person to move into a white district, or a white [Anglo] person to move into a colored [African-American] district. This act [did] not preclude persons of either race employed as servants by persons of the other race from residing on the premises of the employer."[71] In the Southern states, the segregation of the races was conducted under the **separate but equal** policy. "They [African Americans] were either excluded from railway cars, omnibuses, stage coaches, and steamboats or assigned to special 'Jim Crow' sections; they sat, when permitted, in secluded and remote corners of theaters and lecture halls; they could not enter most hotels, restaurants, and resorts, except as servants; they prayed in 'Negro [African-American] pews' in white [Anglo] churches, and if partaking of the sacrament of the Lord's supper, they waited until the whites [Anglos] had been served the bread and wine. Moreover, they were often educated in segregated schools, punished in segregated prisons, nursed in segregated hospitals, and buried in segregated cemetaries."[72] Almost all the southern states passed laws requiring railroad stations to have separate waiting rooms and segregated cars. Conditions in public transportation oftentimes put African-American passages at risk. For example, in 1935, an African-American family boarded a northbound train from Mississippi. "They were packed into the Jim Crow car, which, by custom was at the front of the train, the first to absorb the impact in the event of a collusion. They would not be permitted into the dining car, so they carried fried chicken and boiled eggs to tide them over for the journey."[73] Public facilities had separate drinking fountains, restrooms, swimming pools, and parks. "There was nothing particularly secretive about either public or private discrimination; it was simply a way of life."[74] These tactics effectively created African-American ghettos and slum areas whereby African Americans were kept economically, socially, and politically depressed. In smaller towns, an invisible line successfully separated African Americans from Anglos. The term "living on the wrong side of the tracks" indicated the societal status of the resident. Both the white and black communities felt the adverse impact of Jim Crow. Civil rights advocate James Meredith stressed that "you can't forget that whites in the South were as unfree as any black. White supremacy was official and legal—it was enforced by judges and the law people—and a white that failed to acknowledge and carry out the mandate of white supremacy was as subject to persecution as any black."[75]

Ironically, the Supreme Court upheld Jim Crow laws in hearing a case that originated in Louisiana. Originally a French colony, Louisiana was far more liberal in its treatment of African Americans than her sister states. "New Orleans began experimenting with integrated public schools—the only southern city to do so. Blacks [African Americans] served with whites [Anglos] on juries and public boards. New Orleans had an integrated police department with a color-blind municipal pay scale... Between the years 1868 and 1896, racial intermarriage was made legal, and Louisiana elected 32 black [African-American] state senators and 95 state representatives. It had the only black [African-American] governor in U.S. history before the late 1980's."[76] With the end of Reconstruction, the power of the Radical Republicans in the South began to erode as former Confederates, armed with their voting rights, reestablished the Democratic Party power base in the South. In 1890, the Louisiana legislature passed the **Separate Car Act**, mandating separate accommodations for Anglo and African-American patrons. "Under its terms any railway company that did not provide separate coaches for blacks [African Americans] and whites [Anglos] could be fined $500. Except for nurses attending children of the other race, individual whites [Anglos] and blacks [African Americans] would be forbidden to ride together or risk a $25 fine or 20 days in jail."[77] Opposition groups decided to test the validity of the law. Homer Plessy, who was one-eighth African American, was purposely selected by the East Louisiana Railroad to sit in the "white" section of the railway car headed from New Orleans to Covington. Railroad officials believed the uproar of Plessy's arrest would convince the courts that the law was unconstitutional. When ordered to give up his seat, Plessy refused and was arrested. Plessy sued, believing that the Louisiana law violated the Thirteenth and Fourteenth Amendments to the United States Constitution. The Supreme Court's 1896 ruling in *Plessy v Ferguson* resulted in a 7 to 0 vote against Plessy. In defense of its decision, the Court maintained that "a statute that made a legal distinction between the races on the basis of color did not destroy the legal equality of the races or create a condition of slavery; it merely reflected the social distinctions based on color that existed in society. Furthermore, while the object of the Fourteenth Amendment was to enforce the absolute legal and political equality of the two races, it was not intended to abolish distinctions based upon color or enforce social equality and the 'commingling' of the two races upon terms unsatisfactory to either."[78] This ruling gave state legislative houses the ability to continue passing laws separating the races, providing the segregated accommodations or services were basically in principle equal. The Supreme Court also struck down the **Civil Rights Act of 1875**, prohibiting private discrimination in accommodations, transportation, and public places of amusement. The Court's decision was based on the premise that the Fourteenth Amendment applied to state or public actions, not to private activities.

African Americans were "kept in their place" through the intimidation of the **Ku Klux Klan (KKK)**. The Klan emerged in the South during the Reconstruction era. Garbed in white robes and hoods, Klansmen used a variety of scare tactics against defiant African Americans and whites [Anglos] sympathetic to the plight of African Americans. Burning crosses, public tar and featherings, floggings, and lynchings were used throughout the South to remind African Americans of their

The Ku Klux Klan was politically strong in the South. Action was directed at African Americans and white sympathizers.

inferior status. The steadfastness of the Klan was openly challenged by President Grant with the passage of the **Enforcement Act** of 1871. Hoping to put the Klan out of business, this law "allowed persons deprived of their rights under the Constitution to bring suit in federal courts (rather than state courts). It defined conspiracy to deprive citizens of the equal protection of the laws or prevent citizens of the equal protection of the laws or prevent citizens from voting, and it permitted the prosecution of such conspiracies in federal courts."[79] It also empowered the president to suspend the *writ of habeas corpus*. By October 1871, Grant suspended *habeas corpus* in nine counties in South Carolina and sent federal marshals and troops to arrest Klan members and other marauders and hold them for federal prosecution. Subsequently, "political violence in South Carolina and across the South declined dramatically, and soon the KKK virtually disappeared from southern life, not to be seen again until the 20th century."[80] While the Klan may have been crippled, the actions of southern state legislative houses and their courts continued to level legal sanctions against African Americans. Thurgood Marshall once commented that "even in Mississippi a Negro [African American] will get a trial longer than 42 minutes, if he is fortunate enough to be brought to trial."[81] In some southern communities, African Americans could be arrested for petty offenses, such as not stepping off the sidewalk to make way for an Anglo pedestrian. Far too often, "justice" for African Americans was a lynch mob, not a jury of twelve impartial men and women. "In the past two decades of the nineteenth century more than 2,500 blacks [African Americans] were lynched in the South. Another thousand or so were murdered in this way in the first decade and a half of the new century."[82] It was the efforts of the **Association of Southern Women for the Prevention of Lynching** that finally gained public support of state laws prohibiting lynching. During its 2002 term, the Supreme Court heard arguments in a case concerning the Klan's continued practice of burning crosses as a means of intimidating African Americans. Known for his quiet demeanor on the bench, Justice Clarence Thomas, the Court's only African-American member, decried that "this [the Klan's activities] was a reign of terror, and the cross was a symbol of that reign of terror. Isn't that significantly greater than intimidation or a threat? . . . We had almost 100 years of lynching and activity in the South by the Knights of Camellia and the Ku Klux Klan. It was intended to cause fear and to terrorize a population."[83]

Jim Crow also meant that African Americans were prohibited from moving into white neighborhoods by the restrictive covenant, redlining, and steering techniques. A **restrictive covenant** was a provision in a mortgage contract that forbade the buyer from eventually selling the house to a member of a minority race. If such a sale occurred, the property could revert back to the original owner. Another ploy was to increase the selling price of the property based upon the interested party's race, placing the sale price at a prohibitive cost. **Steering** was the practice of just showing properties to minorities located in solely minority residential areas, thus keeping them away from already segregated white [Anglo] neighborhoods. **Redlining** was the tactic used by financial institutions to deny loans to individuals wanting to purchase property in a racially changing neighborhood. The loan would either be denied outright or the interest rate would be substantially increased to discourage the potential borrower.

In ***Buchanan v Warley***, the Supreme Court ruled in 1917 that city ordinances could not prevent a homeowner from selling his home to whomever he/she wanted to. Since the Court ruled against public ordinances, homeowners and developers took the private route by putting a restrictive covenant into homeowners' deeds. In the 1940s, it is estimated that the restrictive covenant "covered eighty percent of residential property in Chicago and Los Angeles."[84] In *Shelley v Kraemer* (1944), the Supreme Court finally ended the use of restrictive covenants. The case involved an African-American family (Shelley) who had just moved into their newly purchased home when they received eviction notices that evening demanding that they leave the development immediately. The original homeowners signed deeds with the provision that "people of the African-American or Mongolian race could not live there."[85]

African Americans began to challenge Jim Crow laws and acts of discrimination by forming community and nationally based organizations. In 1909 a well-known African-American scholar, W.E.B. DuBois, founded the **National Association for the Advancement of Colored Persons** (NAACP). Groups leading the charge for equality for African Americans included the Congress of Racial Equality (CORE), and the Southern Christian Leadership Conference (SCLC), founded by the late Dr. Martin L. King, Jr., in 1956. The modern civil rights movement drew national attention to the adverse discriminatory practices of Jim Crow when Mrs. Rosa Parks [an African American] was arrested for refusing to give up her seat on a Montgomery, Alabama bus to a white [Anglo] person; four African-American students at the North Carolina Agricultural and Technical College sat peacefully at a lunch counter at Woolworth's while employees refused to serve them and bystanders hurled racial insults and food at them; and Dr. Martin L. King, Jr., led protesters in peaceful, nonviolent demonstrations throughout the South. When asked why she refused to give up her seat, Rosa Parks said "my feet were hurting, and I didn't know why I refused to stand up when they told me. But the real reason of my not standing up was I felt that I had a right to be treated as any other passenger. We had endured that kind of treatment for too long."[86] Honored as the Mother of the Civil Rights Movement, Mrs. Parks continued her fight for equal treatment.

The mule-drawn wagon bearing the body of Dr. Martin Luther King, Jr. moves up Auburn Avenue toward downtown Atlanta after funeral services for the slain civil rights leader. Winner of the Nobel Peace Prize and a staunch supporter of nonviolence, Dr. Martin Luther King, Jr. was assassinated in Memphis, Tennessee, on April 4, 1968.

But, Miss Parks was not the first African-American women arrested for refusing to give up her seat on a bus. In 1946, the Supreme Court heard arguments in *Morgan v Virginia*. Irene Morgan, an African American, got on a Greyhound Bus in Virginia headed for Baltimore, Maryland. She sat three rows from the back of the bus with another African-American woman. As the bus began to fill with passengers, the bus driver asked both women to move to the back of the bus. By Virginia state law, the "bus driver was supposed to rearrange his customers along racially separate lines. If Kelly [the bus driver] could not persuade Morgan to move, he himself would be guilty of a misdemeanor."[87] While the other woman moved, Morgan refused and was dragged off the bus by sheriff's deputies. She paid a $100 fine for resisting arrest and refused to pay the fine for violating Virginia's segregation laws. Even though this was a Virginia segregation law, Morgan's case made it to the Supreme Court because the bus crossed a state boundary line and thus, participated in interstate commerce—federal jurisdiction. The Court ruled 6-1 in Morgan's favor.

A new term began to emerge from the protesters—**integration**. "One cannot be close to the problem very long without hearing that word. *Integration* is what the Negro [African American] has not got. He is on the outside, and he wants to be on the inside. He is not allowed to play or live or work as others and he wants to play, live, and work as others. He occupies a negative position, and desires the positive. The principle of integration (and its opposite, non-integration) cuts a pattern through the nation just as widespread but far more complex than the transportation system over which the trains roll, planes fly, farm wagons crawl, and people walk."[88] The demand for inclusion from a group excluded from the political, social, and cultural environment of mainstream America for over two hundred years could no longer be ignored or dismissed. One by one the repressive practices of Jim Crow began to be challenged and successfully overturned by the federal courts. The actions of the Supreme Court awakened Congress to pass a series of civil rights acts, which provided voting rights and desegregation of public accommodations and public schools to correct past abuses. The first major civil rights bill since Reconstruction, the **Civil Rights Act of 1957**, created the United States Commission on Civil Rights and the Civil Rights Section of the Justice Department. The federal government was now empowered to obtain injunctions to halt illegal voting activities. The **Civil Rights Act of 1960** authorized federal appointed voter referees to conduct voter registration drives and to monitor federal elections in areas with historical patterns of voting problems. The **Civil Rights Act of 1964** prohibited discrimination in public accommodations and employment practices. Discriminatory housing practices to include restrictive convenants, redlining and steering were prohibited with the passage of the **Civil Rights Act of 1968**.

The Supreme Court began to curtail discriminatory voting practices as early as 1927. In *Nixon v Herndon*, the Supreme Court invalidated the Texas White Primary Law of 1924, which mandated that "in no event shall a Negro [African American] be eligible to participate in a Democratic primary election in the State of Texas, and should a Negro [African American] vote in a Democratic primary election, such ballot shall be void and election officials shall not count the same."[89] Defiantly, the Texas Democratic Party continued the white-only primary by declaring the party a private club capable of establishing its own membership criteria. The Supreme Court finally dealt the fatal blow to this practice by ruling in *Smith v Allwright* (1944) that the Texas Democratic Party was not a private club but an agent of the state, subject to state and federal mandates. As a state agency, the party could no longer deny voting privileges to any qualified voter for any election.

The poll tax was outlawed with the passage of the **Twenty-fourth Amendment** to the United States Constitution. In *Guinn v United States* (1915), the Supreme Court invalidated Oklahoma's grandfather clause as a direct violation of the Fifteenth Amendment. The literacy test was dismantled in a piecemeal fashion. The **Civil Rights Act of 1964** required states to accept a sixth grade education as meeting voter literacy and testing requirements. Minor errors on the test or voter registration card, such as abbreviations, could not be used to deny voting privileges. The **Voting Rights Act of 1965** suspended the use of discriminatory literacy tests. A 1970 amendment to the Voting Rights Act completely eliminated the literacy requirement.

Jim Crow also extended to the military. Usually, African-American soldiers were assigned to kitchen duty, road construction, and menial noncombat duties. During World War II, for example, African Americans were denied officer and leadership roles. Supervised by Anglo officers, African-American soldiers were far too often segregated into their own camps, barracks, mess halls, and even latrines. "More than a million blacks [African Americans] served in that war, of the more than 16 million U.S. military personnel. Most were assigned to construction, transportation, service or support units."[90] On July 26, 1948, President Harry Truman issued **Executive Order No. 9981**, which desegregated the military by mandating "equality of treatment and opportunity for all persons in the armed forces without regard to race, color, religion or national origin."[91]

As the war effort ramped up, First Lady Eleanor Roosevelt visited Tuskegee Institute, a predominately African-American college founded in 1881 that had a well-renowned civil pilot program. One year later, the Army Air Corp decided to use nearby Moton Field as a training facility for African-American men. The first thirteen cadets became the "nation's first all-black unit, the 99th Fighter Squadron. Deployed to Africa in 1943, the 99th flew its first combat mission in June 1943. By the war's end, some 450 of the 992 airmen training at Tuskegee had served overseas, completing 1,578 missions, destroying 260 enemy planes, and sinking a German battleship. In some 200 missions, they never lost a single bomber to the enemy. They earned ninety-five Distinguished Flying Crosses, a Distinguished Unit Citation and eight Purple Hearts. . . . Sixty-six Tuskegee airmen were killed in action and thirty-two became prisoners of war."[92] The success of the Tuskegee Airmen set the stage for expanding military command positions to all minorities. After serving as the supreme commander of the European front, now President Dwight Eisenhower started the ball rolling in implementing Truman's order by desegregating Washington, D.C. "When he took office in 1953, an African-American visitor to downtown Washington could not rent a hotel room, buy a meal, attend a movie or easily find a drink of water or a restroom outside the city's black [African American] neighborhoods. . . By October 30, 1954, not a single segregated combat unit remained."[93]

The demise of the "separate but equal" doctrine began with the certainly separate but definitely unequal conditions in public schools and colleges across the nation. For example, Herman Sweatt, an African-American mail carrier from Houston, Texas, wanted to attend the University of Texas Law School. Sweatt was denied admission because of his race. His only option was to attend the Texas State University for Negroes, an academically inferior school when compared to the University of Texas. In *Sweatt v Painter* (1950), the Supreme Court ruled that Sweatt should not be forced to attend a racially separated inferior school. "By ruling that the term *equal* applied not only to tangible factors, such as university buildings, books, and faculty, but to intangible qualities such as institutional reputation and opportunity to interact with a cross-section of the legal profession, the Court made it more difficult for states to maintain and justify separate but equal or 'dual' school systems."[94] A similar ruling was made that same year in ***McLaurin v Oklahoma State Regents***. The University of Oklahoma did not have a separate graduate school for African Americans. The university would admit African Americans on a segregated basis, meaning that African Americans sat in totally segregated classes and facilities from white students. The Court ruled against the university's policy.

In 1954, the Supreme Court handed down its "separate but equal" shattering ruling in ***Brown v the Board of Education of Topeka, Kansas***. Eight-year-old Linda Brown was refused admittance to an all-white public school located just five blocks from her home because of her race. Instead, she was forced to attend an African-American school located twenty-one blocks from her home. The *Brown* suit was one of four filed by African-American families confronted with similar situations in South Carolina, Virginia, and Delaware. Basically, African-American children were forced to attend poorly equipped, inadequately staffed, and seriously underfunded African-American public schools. The question before the Court was whether the Fourteenth Amendment's equal protection clause extended to public schools. The Supreme Court ruled unanimously with Brown concluding that *"in the field of public education the doctrine of 'separate but equal' has no place. Separate educational facilities are inherently unequal . . .* The plaintiffs and others similarly situated for whom the actions have been brought are, by reason of the segregation complained of, *deprived of the equal protection of the laws guaranteed by the Fourteenth Amendment."*[95] The *Brown* decision dismantled the philosophical basis of Jim Crow. However, public schools, colleges, and universities reluctantly and defiantly opened their doors to African-American students. Orval Faubus, governor of Arkansas, openly defied desegregation of Little Rock's four high schools by closing them down for the entire 1958-59 academic year, leaving approximately 3,700 public school students to make their own arrangements. To counter the governor's actions, federal authorities decided to force desegregation by enrolling nine African-American students into Little Rock's Central High School. With the assistance of the United States Army, the nine were finally admitted into the door of the high school. Their school year, however, was not a pleasant experience. "The nine students were bombarded with racial hatred. The U.S. Department of Justice had assigned a bodyguard to each of them, but white [Anglo] students still harassed them. They were body-slammed into lockers, attacked in gym class, tripped in the hallways, and pushed down stairs. And the name calling was incessant. So were the death threats."[96] By 1960, the federal government realized that it had to assume a more forceful role in desegregating public schools and facilities. "In Louisiana, Mississippi, Alabama, Georgia, and South Carolina there has been no change at all. In Florida, Arkansas, Tennessee, North Carolina and Virginia, only an occasional school district has allowed white [Anglo] and colored [African American] children to sit in the same classrooms. Texas, Oklahoma, Missouri, Kentucky, West Virginia, Maryland, Delaware, and the District of Columbia range, however, from extensive to complete desegregation of schools."[97] Consequently, the enforcement of desegregation was accomplished through court mandated busing and federal threats of denial of federal money to schools participating in discriminatory practices. Subsequent court decisions and legislative acts mandated desegregation of all public facilities and accommodations. The now outlawed practices of separate but equal proved to be very costly to the South, both in budgetary dollars and public image as the rest of the country began to see the impact of their discriminatory practices. One observer noted that Jim Crow laws "compels the South to have to buy two of everything, two schools, two toilets, two communities, two worlds."[98]

The victories won by civil rights leaders in the 1960s should not be underestimated. Civil rights activists were murdered for their efforts to register African Americans to vote in the Deep South. Martin L. King, Jr., Malcolm X, Medgar Evers, and many others were slain because their quest for African-American equality was viewed by some as too revolutionary for mainstream America. The Civil Rights Movement of the 60s has resulted in more African Americans registering, voting, and running for public office. Although not the first African American to make a bid for the White House, electing Barack Obama to the Oval Office took the collective will-power of the "rainbow coalition" that Dr. Martin Luther King, Jr., so passionately sought. On the evening of both of his successful elections to the presidency, Obama faced a multitude of American citizens—black, brown, white—all celebrating as one. Commemorating the 50th anniversary of King's speech, speaker after speaker recalled the struggles confronted by King and his followers and the price they paid for the enactment of laws outlawing discriminatory practices, protecting voting rights, and giving African Americans accessibility to social, economic, and political mobility. However, as each speaker painfully noted that "but for all that progress, sizable gaps remain between white and black America in areas of wealth, income, poverty and economic opportunity."[99]

As a result of the tragic deaths of Trayvon Martin and Michael Brown, George Floyd, Tamir Rice, Eric Garner, Breonna Taylor, Justin Howell, James Floyd, and Ray Brooks, the emergence of the Black Lives Matter movement is more than just a protest against the tragic deaths of many African Americans by police officers, neighborhood-related criminal activities, drive-by shootings, and gang retaliations. It is a comprehensive plea to address the issues of poverty, lack of education, high unemployment rates, deteriorating neighborhoods, rising violent crime, and so forth that confront African-American communities across this country. The *Joint Economic State of Black America in 2020* produced by a Joint Economic Committee indicates that:

• Despite significant economic progress over the past decades, Black Americans experience far worse economic conditions than Whites or the population as a whole.

• The unemployment rate for Black Americans has been approximately twice the rate for Whites.

• The difference in the unemployment rates for Blacks and Whites shrink for college graduates; However, even in a strong economy, the unemployment rate is 50% higher for Black Americans.

• Black Americans are over twice as likely to live in poverty and Black children are three times as likely to live in poverty as White children.

• The typical Black household earns a fraction of White households—just 59 cents for every dollar. The gap between Black and White annual household incomes is about $29,000 per year. The median wealth of Black families ($17,000) is less than one-tenth that of White families.

• Much less than half (42%) of Black families own their homes compared to almost three-quarters (73%) of White families.

• The incarceration rate for Black Americans is falling, but is still nearly six times the rate for White Americans.[100]

The 2020 outpouring of protesters across the nation over the death of George Floyd were reminiscent of the civil rights marches and protests of the 1960s with one major difference. The composition of the 2020 protests was indeed the rainbow coalition that Dr. Martin Luther King, Jr., envisioned for his civil rights movement. Unfortunately, the issues confronting the African American population of 2020 are the same ones articulated in the 1960s. In 1963, President Lyndon Johnson addressed the nation about the true meaning of the civil rights movement:

> To strike the chains of a slave is noble. To leave him the captive of the color of his skin is hypocrisy. While we in America have freed the slave of his chains, we have not freed his heirs of their color. Until justice is blind of color, until education is unaware of race, until opportunity ceases to squint its eyes at the pigmentation of human complexions, emancipation will be a proclamation, but it will not be a fact. To that the proclamation of emancipation is not fulfilled in fact, to the extent we shall have fallen short of assuring freedom to the free. . . The counsel of the day is not the counsel of courage. A government conceived and dedicated to the purpose that all men are born free and equal cannot pervert its mission by rephrasing the purpose to suggest that men shall be free today-but shall be equal a little later.[101]

Table 13.2 is a selective listing of significant events and achievements for African Americans.

Table 13.2

Significant Events for African Americans

Date	Event
1619	The first African slaves arrive in Virginia.
1831	William Lloyd Garrison begins publishing *The Liberator*, an abolitionist newspaper. Nat Turner leads rebellion in Virginia, resulting in the deaths of 57 white men, women, and children. Turner was executed for his role.
1833	Lewis Tappan, Theodore Weld and William Garrison establish the American Anti-Slavery Society, a national organization opposing slavery.
1851	Sojourner Truth gives her "Ain't I A Woman?" speech at the women's rights convention held in Akron, Ohio. Myrtilla Miner opens the first school to train African-American women to be teachers.
1852	Harriet Beecher Stowe publishes *Uncle Tom's Cabin*.
1855	In *Missouri v Celia, a Slave,* an African-American woman is declared to be property without the right to defend herself against her master's continuous acts of rape. She was eventually executed for murdering her master. Fighting breaks out in Kansas, known as "Bloody Kansas."
1857	The U.S. Supreme Court rules in *Dred Scott v Sanford* that slaves are not citizens; therefore, they do not have the right to sue. This case nullifies the Missouri Compromise.
1862	Mary Jane Patterson is the first African-American woman to receive a full baccalaureate degree from Oberlin College.

1863	Lincoln issues his Gettysburg Address to include the Emancipation Proclamation.
1865	Congress passes the 13th Amendment abolishing slavery. Lee surrenders. Lincoln is assassinated. The Freedmen's Bureau is founded to assist newly freed slaves. Black codes enacted across the southern states.
1866	The 14th Amendment granting citizenship to former slaves is passed by Congress. The Civil Rights Bill of 1866 is passed over President Johnson's veto. The Ku Klux Klan is organized.
1870	The 15th Amendment, expanding voting rights to former male slaves, is officially ratified.
1875	Civil Rights Act of 1875, guaranteeing desegregated public facilities, passes Congress. This law will be ruled as unconstitutional by the Supreme Court in the *Civil Rights Cases*, 1883.
1896	The National Association of Colored Women, founded by Margaret Murray Washington, unites several African-American women's groups under one organization. Mary Church Terrell serves as its first president. In *Plessy v Ferguson,* the Supreme Court upholds the separate but equal doctrine.
1909	The National Association for the Advancement of Colored Persons (NAACP) is formed with W. E. B. Dubois as its first president.
1935	Mary McLeod Bethune organizes the National Council of Negro Women as a lobbying group for African-American women. Key agenda items focus on fighting job discrimination, racism & sexism.
1939	Marian Anderson gives a concert at the Lincoln Memorial.
1954	*Brown v Board of Education of Topeka, Kansas* discussion by the Supreme Court overturns *Plessy v Ferguson* by negating the separate but equal doctrine.
1955	Montgomery Bus Boycott organized in protest to Rosa Parks being arrested for refusing to give up her bus seat to a white person. The boycott is staged from December 5, 1955 to December 21, 1956. The Interstate Commerce Commission bans segregation on interstate travel. Emmett Till is killed on August 28.
1956	Tallahassee Bus Boycott begins on May 27. The boycott ends in March 1958. Autherine Lucy is admitted to the University of Alabama. The Southern Manifesto is presented. The Supreme Court upholds the use of busing for desegregation of public schools.
1957	Southern Christian Leadership Conference is formed. Protests begin at the Little Rock Central High School. The protests end in May 1959. The first civil rights bill since 1875 passes through Congress.
1960	Greensboro sit-in occurs on February 1, followed by sit-ins and boycotts all over the South and in some northern cities. Civil Rights Act of 1960 signed.
1961	Freedom Rides occur during the summer. Federal courts order Hunter and Holmes to be admitted to the University of Georgia.
1962	James Meredith enters the University of Mississippi. John Kennedy federalizes Mississippi State Troopers to protect Meredith. Los Angeles riots occur on April 27 followed by the Ole Mississippi riots in October.

1963	University of Alabama desegregation crisis occurs as George Wallace attempts to block federal troops sent by the president. John Kennedy meets with civil rights leaders for the March on Washington, August 28. Medgar Evers and John Kennedy are killed.
1964	Title VII of the Civil Rights Act barring employment discrimination by private employers, employment agencies, and unions is enacted. Martin L. King, Jr., awarded Nobel Prize. The 24th Amendment to the U.S. Constitution, banning the poll tax, is ratified. Race riots occur in New York, New Jersey, Chicago, and Philadelphia. Goodman, Schwerner, and Chaney killed on June 24.
1965	Lyndon Johnson enacts Executive Order 11246 calling for the federal government to take affirmative action in overcoming employment discrimination. Voting Rights Act signed into law. Malcolm X is killed. Race riots in Watts.
1968	Martin L. King, Jr., and Robert Kennedy are assassinated. Riots at the Democratic Convention.
1971	Shirley Chisholm (D-NY) is the first African-American woman elected to the U.S. Congress.
1972	Barbara Jordan (D-TX) becomes the first African American elected to U.S. Congress from a southern state.
1984	The nonpartisan National Political Congress of Black Women is founded by Shirley Chisholm to address women's rights issues and to encourage political participation.
1988	Rev. Barbara Harris becomes the first female African-American bishop of the Episcopal Church.
1990	The number of African-American women elected to office increased from 131 in 1970 to 1,950 in 1990.
1992	Carol Moseley-Braun (D-Ill). becomes the first African-American woman elected to the U.S. Senate.
2000	Colin S. Powell becomes the first African American to serve as the nation's Secretary of State and Condoleezza Rice becomes the first woman and African American to serve as the National Security Advisor.
2005	Condoleezza Rice becomes the first African-American woman to serve as the nation's Secretary of State.
2009	Barack Obama is inaugurated as the nation's 44th President of the United States, becoming the first African American to hold the office; Eric Holder becomes the nation's first African-American Attorney General.
2015-2017	Appointed by President Obama, Loretta Lynch becomes the nation's first African-American female Attorney General.

The Hispanic Experience

Other victims of discrimination, racial hatred, prejudice, and stereotyping are Hispanics, Americans of Mexican and Spanish descent. When most Americans voice their concerns over illegal immigration, their attention is focused on the Mexican national crossing the Rio Grande in the Southwestern states or the international border into California. Anti-immigration advocates fail to mention that other nationalities have come to this country illegally. They also fail to recognize the invaluable contributions the Hispanic community made to the cultural enrichment and economic viability of this nation. In addition, we should not forget that "the Spanish Mexicans of the Southwest are not truly an immigrant group, for they are in their traditional home.[102] Hispanics are the fastest growing minority group in the United States. "While Hispanics made up less than 15 percent of the population in 2005, the Census Bureau predicts they will be a quarter of the country by 2050. The Hispanic population is expected to jump from 42 million to over 100 million, making up nearly half of the nation's total projected growth during that time."[103] Despite their booming population, Hispanics have been victimized by the very same philosophy of Anglo superiority that is used against African Americans. The "Hispanic" community also suffers from stereotyping that fails to recognize the cultural diversity of those called "Hispanics." "The label Latino or Hispanic covers people who come from two dozen countries and who can claim mixtures of Spanish, Portuguese, Indian, African, Italian, German and Italian ancestry."[104] Basically the Hispanic community is composed of three culturally, socially, and politically diverse groups who live in different areas of the country. "Mexican-Americans, who make up almost two-thirds of the Hispanics in the United States, are concentrated in the Southwest. Cuban-Americans live primarily in South Florida. Puerto Rican Americans have settled mostly in the Northeast, particularly in New York City and New Jersey."[105] Politically, Mexican-Americans promote liberal Democratic candidates while Cuban-Americans are known to cast a bloc vote for conservative Republican candidates.

The growing distrust between Hispanics and Anglo Americans began in earnest with the colonization of Texas. Unable to settle Texas with families from Spain and Mexico, both governments opened up the region to Anglo Americans through a land grant program known as the **empresario system**. Initially welcomed into the region, Anglo Americans soon began to take advantage of their hosts by openly defying the Mexican government. The aftermath of the inevitable Texas Revolution made the already fragile relationship deteriorate further as Hispanics encountered "the wrath of Anglos, who considered them a conquered people and an alien race and who persecuted them with impunity."[106] Although there are several explanations for the racial tensions between Hispanics and Anglos, the economic theory of racism was evident in the settlement of the Southwestern states and California. Like the Native American tribes, Spanish and Mexican landowners held a precious commodity Anglo Americans wanted—vast landholdings. Anglo American settlers guided by a government bent on achieving its manifest destiny cast an envious and greedy eye upon those vast parcels of land that were granted by the Spanish monarchy to the economic elites or Creoles. Gradually, Anglo Americans used a variety of schemes to seize these lands.

Meanwhile, the non-economic elite Hispanics, known as **Mestizos,** became the primary labor force in building the nation's railroads, working in the mines extracting precious natural resources, toiling in the fields picking agricultural crops, or riding fence on cattle ranches. Relegated to a life of picking fruits and vegetables, herding cattle or laboring at unskilled or semiskilled jobs at exceptionally low wages, Hispanic workers were needed for their muscles, not their minds. Testifying before the House Immigration and Naturalization Committee in 1920, then Congressman John Nance Garner from Uvalde, Texas, stated: "I believe I am within the bounds of truth when I say that the Mexican man is the superior laborer when it comes to grubbing land. . . And I may add that the prices that they charge are much less than the same labor would be from either the

Chávez was a leader for the Hispanic farm workers.

Negro [African American] or the white man and for the same time they do . . . a third more—they produce a third more results from their labor then either the Negro [African American] or white man would do."[107] Unfortunately, Hispanics were subjected to the same Jim Crow laws and acts of wanton discrimination as those levied against African Americans. "For roughly 75 years after the end of the war between Mexico and the United States, Mexican Americans in the Southwest contended with segregation in the public schools, segregation and discrimination in public facilities such as restaurants, movie theaters, swimming pools, and barbershops; primary election procedures that prevented them from exercising their right to vote; and discrimination in housing. They also suffered discrimination in the administration of justice that prevented them from serving on juries and treated violence against them as so common as to pass almost unnoticed."[108]

The story of the farm laborer or **campesino** in the Southwest and California is a tragic one. The movement of Mexican labor into the United States picked up stream during World War I. "In California, the demand for workers in the citrus, melon, tomato, and other industries increased sharply, encouraging Mexicans to come across the border to perform these necessary tasks. The other southwestern states were similarly affected. Workers were needed in Texas to tend the cotton, spinach, and onion crops and in Arizona, New Mexico, and Colorado to raise vegetables, forage crops, and sugar beets."[109] Since these are not yearly crops, the term "seasonal" or "migratory" workers was used to describe this Mexican labor force. At the turn of the twentieth century, approximately 85 percent of Hispanics living in Texas were employed as farm workers, ranch hands, and tenant farmers. Tenant farmers worked the landowner's fields from sun up to sun down in return for extremely low wages, a one-room shack, and a small plot of land to grow their own vegetables. The future of tenant farmers rested squarely upon the shoulders of the landowner, who could at any time raise rents, restrict planting, or relocate and remove the tenant from his property. Whether stationary or migratory, the farm workers of today toil in the fields picking and harvesting crops in the same bent over position assumed by their fathers and grandfathers. Living conditions are in some instances akin to third world poverty. Job security is just as nonexistent as health care and education. Severe weather destroys both crops and jobs. In the mid 1960s, the late César Chávez began organizing campesinos into the **United Farm Workers Union (UFW)**. This organization brought national attention to the living and working conditions of farm workers in Texas and California by its series of protests and strikes over the picking of lettuce and grapes. "In the 1970s, they [the campesinos] still faced lamentable working conditions. Most fields lacked restrooms, and since modesty compelled women to delay their bodily functions for hours, they suffered from disproportionately high levels of kidney infections. Wages remained as low as $2 or $3 for a typical day of field labor. Diseases such as typhoid, typhus, dysentery, and leprosy afflicted farm workers to a degree unknown to other Texans. Infant mortality rates among the campesinos in South Texas were among the highest in the United States at that time, and the life expectancy for field hands hovered around forty-nine."[110]

The success of the United Farm Workers Union has helped to produce corrective legislation designed to improve the lifestyle of farm workers. They can apply for unemployment and workers compensation benefits. Their children can attend schools offering half day class schedules to accommodate those students who must spend a portion of their day working along side their parents. State health laws mandate that growers provide clean drinking water and field restrooms. Although the wage scale has gradually increased, farm workers still are not fairly compensated for a hard day's work. "Picking a 50-pound bag of onions earns a farm worker $1.20 (market price is $6 per bag). . . The rate for harvesting a 10-gallon bucket of jalapeno peppers is $1. When they work watermelon, cantaloupe, lettuce and cabbage fields, they can earn minimum wage. Clearing a large field of weeds might pay $500. UFW leaders say a 'respectable wage' would be $8 an hour."[111] Farm workers still do not have collective bargaining rights, life insurance, health care, or protection against hazardous pesticides and chemicals. Growing up in migrant farm labor camps, Chávez knew first hand the problems confronting Hispanic farm workers. Although he dedicated his life to organizing workers and conducting voter registration drives, Chávez strongly believed that political empowerment alone could not fully uplift Hispanics from their plight. In a 1973 interview, Chávez stated:

> But political power alone is not enough. Although I've been at it for some twenty years, all the time and the money and effort haven't brought about any significant change whatsoever. Effective political power is never going to come, particularly to minority groups unless they have economic power. And however poor they are, even the poor people can organize economic power.
>
> Political power by itself, as we've tried to fathom it and to fashion it, is like having a car that doesn't have any motor in it. It is like striking a match that goes out. Economic power is like having a generator to keep that bulb burning all the time. So we have to develop economic power to assure a continuation of political power . . . . As a continuation of our struggle, I think we can develop economic power and put it into the hands of the people so they can have more control over their own lives, and then begin to change the system. We want radical change. Nothing short of radical change is going to have an impact on our lives or our problems. We want sufficient power to control our own destinies. This is our struggle. It is a lifetime job. The work for social change and against social injustice is never ended.[112]

The untimely death of Chávez has left a leadership void in the Hispanic community. "Many Hispanics regard[ed] Chávez as akin to Mohandas Gandhi in India and Martin Luther King, Jr., in the United States because of his belief nonviolent protests lead to social change."[113] On November 28, 2000, the Hispanic community lost another hero—United States Congressman Henry B. Gonzalez. He too devoted his life's work to the Hispanic community. Although more Hispanics are being elected to state and national legislative houses, there has been no one to rise to the occasion as a viable replacement for Chávez or Gonzalez. Table 13.3 is a selective list of significant events for Hispanic Americans.

The Hispanic community has been in some respects adversely impacted by illegal immigration of Mexican nationals into the United States. In the Southwestern border states, it is still a daily task for Immigration and Naturalization Service agents to round up illegals who crossed over the border or swam across the Rio Grande and send them back home. Mexican nationals are also buying their way into the United States by hiring a coyote to smuggle them across the border. The trip can prove to be deadly. Far too often illegals are crammed into un-air conditioned vehicles, semi-tracker trailers, and railroad cars. Fearful of being captured by border guards, coyotes will often abandon the vehicle or the railroad car, leaving the illegals locked inside. If the border agents do not find them soon enough, illegal immigrants usually die of heat-related illnesses or starvation. The simple solution would be to hire more agents and seal up the border. But, the issue of illegal immigration and the exploration of possible solutions is far more complicated and more difficult to solve. In part, the number of illegals from Mexico is directly tied to the Mexican economy. Although Mexico is improving its economic footing, the wealth is still distributed to a very small percentage of Mexico's people. Mired in third and fourth world poverty, Mexican nationals see even a below minimum wage job in the United States as their only means to feed, clothe, and educate their children.

There are, however, several misnomers and misconceptions about Mexican immigration into this country. First, the advocates of anti-immigration laws always point a finger at the Hispanic community as the source of this country's immigration woes. While immigrants were entering this country in the thousands from Europe, relatively few Mexican nationals entered the country as permanent residents for nearly fifty years after the signing of the Treaty of Guadalupe Hidalgo, ending the Mexican War. "For one period, in fact, between 1886 and 1893, there are no official records of immigration from Mexico into the United States."[114] The increase flow of immigrants has been seen in periods of economic upheavals and political discords in Mexico. For example, "the latter years of the nineteen century and extending into 1910 were the distressful conditions many faced under the dictatorship of President Profirio Diaz. The rural poor were forcibly removed from their common lands by ambitious land barons and faced a dismal life of peonage on the rural estates. . . . The Mexican Revolution which broke out in 1910 and lasted until 1920 also became a catalyst for migration. Mexicans fled to the United States to escape the horrors of war or reprisals from the feuding factions."[115] Second, the United States government has not always cast a negative eye at the Mexican national worker. For example, the United States experienced a dramatic decrease in cheap farm laborers during and immediately after World War II. The United States government contracted with the Mexican government to bring agricultural workers into the United States. The **Bracero program** allowed farm workers to enter the country under the following conditions: "free transportation and food; guarantees concerning wages, working conditions, and housing; and the right of Mexican officials to make inspections and to investigate workers' complaints."[116] The program ended in 1964 as growers sought ways to bypass the program by hiring illegal Mexican nationals at wages far below those offered through the Bracero contracts. Third, not every person crossing the border is a Mexican national. Since Mexico is the only Central and Latin American country sharing a border with the United States, it has become the "pathway" to the United States for many from Central American countries such as Honduras, Guatemala, El Salvador, Costa Rica, and Nicaragua.

Fourth, illegal immigration, particularly from Mexico, has resulted in "white fear," a new concept of the economic theory of racism. **White fear** is the feeling "of becoming a member of the new minority as the existing minority becomes a majority within the social community."[117] The potential loss of economic viability, and social and political clout fuels the fires of those advocating stronger anti-immigration laws. Expressing their fears that the continuous flow of both legal and illegal Mexican immigrants crossing the Rio Grande will eventually take jobs away from American workers and depress the wage market, white fear advocates created a system of political and economic barriers against Hispanic citizens. Particularly in the Southwestern states, Hispanics were kept from developing any political muscle to flex at city, state, or national legislative houses. Redistricting plans ensured that Hispanics were grossly under-represented in legislative houses while at-large city council elections precluded the election of Hispanic candidates. While statistics do not support their claims against Mexican nationals, the cries of white fear accelerate whenever the American economy slumps or job security becomes questionable.

Basically, "as long as there was a shortage of cheap labor, the 'Mexicans' were welcomed and praised as cooperative, uncomplaining workers; but when economic times were bad, 'American' officials wanted the 'Mexicans' to go 'home.'"[118] The Mexican nationals' threat to American job security is in itself a misnomer since the majority of Mexican nationals and other Hispanic immigrants are seasonal workers toiling at jobs few Americans want to work.

Beginning with the election of Ronald Reagan, anti-immigration advocates joined forces with the conservative wing of the Republican Party and gained the upper-hand in promoting immigration reform legislation. A series of 1997 immigration laws made it more difficult for both foreigners to seek political asylum and legal immigrants to bring immediate family members into the country. Particularly after September 11, 2001, the federal government was granted more authority to deport immigrants who arrived without proper documentation. All job applicants are required to provide proof of work eligibility and citizenship status. Beginning in January 2004, the Bush administration made it more expensive to become a legal worker or a citizen by increasing the fees to apply for citizenship; to apply, replace, or renew a permanent residency card, also known as a green card; to petition to bring in a fiancé or family member into the country; and all had to be fingerprinted. A key element of the Bush administration was to discourage illegal immigration while at the same time, provide foreign nationals the opportunity to work legally in the United States under a guest worker program similar to the Bracero program.

Table 13.3

Significant Events for Hispanic Americans

Date	Event
1845	Texas is admitted into the United States.
1846	The United States declares war on Mexico.
1848	The Treaty of Guadalupe Hidalgo ends the war with Mexico. The United States purchases Mexican territories held in the Southwest for $15 million with the promise of respecting the property rights of Mexicans living now in the U. S. and allowing them to become citizens.
1897	Mexican-American Miguel A. Otero is appointed governor of New Mexico.
1910	The Mexican Revolution brings Mexican nationals to the U. S. for safety and employment. Mexican immigrants become a source of cheap farm labor in the Southwest.
1918-21	More than 50,000 Mexican nationals are recruited to combat a labor shortage in the Southwest.
1924	The Immigration Act of 1924 establishes guidelines for the admission of Mexican workers, collecting a head tax on each. More than 89,000 enter the U. S. on permanent visas while others enter illegally to avoid the fees.
1928	The *Confederacion de Uniones Obreras Mexicanas* (CUOM) is formed to organize all Mexican workers in the U. S. to fight for wage parity and an end to racial discrimination. Octaviano Larrazola (NM) is the first Mexican American elected to the U. S. Senate.
1929	The League of United Latin American Citizens (LULAC) forms in Corpus Christi, Texas, to help Mexican Americans assume their rightful places as U. S. citizens and to fight discriminatory practices.
1931	Female Mexican-American garment workers in Los Angeles, California, are unionized by labor organizer Rose Pesotta.
1939	El Congreso del Pueblo de Habla Espanola (The Spanish Speaking People's Congress) is founded by Lusia Moreno. This working-class organization aims to secure basic rights for all Spanish-speaking people in the U. S. by forming a unified labor movement to combat poverty and discrimination. Mexican Americans in Beeville, Texas, desegregate the local high school.
1942	The bracero program begins, allowing Mexican nationals to work in the Southwest as a source of cheap agriculture labor. The program ends in 1964. Approximately, 300,000 Mexican-American men served in WWII with 17 awarded the Congressional Medal of Honor.
1946	LULAC supports a class-action suit by Gonzalo Mendez against several school districts in California. The Federal District Court rules that segregation in these school districts is unconstitutional. Andres Morales becomes the first Mexican American to be elected to a city council in California since the 19th century.
1947	The Community Service Organization (CSO) is established in Los Angeles to encourage voter registration and grass-roots political support for Mexican Americans.

1953-58 The U. S. Immigration Service arrests and deports over 3.8 million persons of Mexican descent during Operation Wetback. Many U. S. citizens are deported unfairly.

1961 Henry B. Gonzalez (D-Tex) is the first Mexican American elected to the U. S. House of Representatives from Texas. He retired from the House in 1998.

1962 César Chávez organizes the National Farm Workers Association (NFWA) in Delano, California.

1965 César Chávez and the NFWA begin a grape boycott, targeting Schenley Industries and the Di Giorgio Corporation.

1967 Corky Gonzales writes the epic poem "I Am Joaquin." The Mexican-American Legal Defense and Education Fund (MALDF) is formed. The Brown Berets are established in Los Angeles, California.

1974 Willie Velasquez forms the Southwest Voter Registration and Education Project. MANA, the Mexican-American Women's National Association, is established as a feminist activist organization. By 1990, MANA chapters operate in 16 states.

1975 The 1965 Voting Rights Act is extended to the Southwest.

1981 Elected mayor of San Antonio, Texas, Henry Cisneros is first Hispanic mayor of a major city.

1992 Lucille Roybal-Allard (D-CA) becomes the first Mexican-American woman elected to the U. S. House of Representatives.

1993-97 Henry Cisneros appointed by President Clinton to Secretary of Housing and Urban Development.

1997 Bill Richardson of New Mexico becomes first Hispanic appointed as U.S. Ambassador to United Nations and appointed by President Clinton as Secretary of Energy in 1998.

2002 Bill Richardson elected as governor of New Mexico.

2005 Ken Salazar (D-Colorado) is elected to the U.S. Senate but resigns in 2009 to become the Secretary of the Interior.

2006 Bob Menendez (D-New Jersey) is elected to the U.S. Senate.

2011 Susana Martinez (R-New Mexico) is elected governor.

2013 Ted Cruz (R-Texas) is elected to the U.S. Senate.

2017 Catherine Cortez Masto (D-Nevada) is elected to the U.S. Senate.
Chris Sununu (R-New Hampshire) is elected governor.

2019 Michelle Lujan Grisham (D-New Mexico) is elected governor.

2020 Julian Castro (D-Texas) makes an unsuccessful bid for the presidency.

An ill-fated attempt introduced by Senators John McCain (R-Arizona) and Edward Kennedy (D-Massachusetts) would have allowed workers who have illegally worked in the country for six years or more, to apply for green cards and eventually gain citizenship. Anti-immigration advocates successfully got Congress to approve the building of a fence along the Mexico/United States border. However, the Obama administration canceled it due to budget deficits. As a candidate, President Trump announced his plans to build a wall separating the two nations with the vow that Mexico would pay for it. Although the wall is being built with federal money, the Mexican government has officially condemned the fence and adamantly refuses to pay for it.

Since the founding of this nation, it has been the responsibility of the federal government to enact and enforce immigration laws. Table 13.4 is a selective list of both the immigration laws passed by Congress and executive orders signed by presidents.

Table 13.4 **Selective List of Immigration Laws**

Date Legislation or Executive Order

1790 **Naturalization Act**—only Anglo (white) immigrants could be granted citizenship. This law established the nation's first citizenship guidelines: two years of residency in the country and one year of residency in the immigrant's state.

1864 **Contract Labor Law**—encouraged immigration by providing federal assistance to pay the immigrant's passage with the proviso that the money would be recovered by placing a lien in the immigrants pay. The law was repealed in 1868.

1882 **Chinese Exclusion Act**—banned citizenship for Chinese immigrants, prohibited further Chinese immigration for ten years, and prohibited entry of Chinese criminals, paupers, and the mentally ill.

1884-86 **Chinese Exclusion Acts**—collectively suspended immigration of Chinese laborers, barred all reentry of Chinese laborers who returned to China but wanted to return to the United States, and established guidelines for the expulsion of immigrants.

1891 Bureau of Immigration established under the Treasury Department.

1903 Congress added polygamists and political radicals to the exclusion list.

1906 Congress made knowledge of English a basic requirement for citizenship.

1907 Congress added people with physical and metal disabilities and tuberculosis and children unaccompanied by their parents to the exclusion list. The law also restricted immigrants from Japan.

1913, 1923& 1930 **Alien Land Laws**—Congress prohibited Asian immigrants from owning land and other forms of property in the United States.

1917 **Immigration Act of 1917**—Congress prohibited immigration of Asian Indians and individuals from South Asia. Illiterates, persons of psychopathic inferiority, men and women entering into the country for immoral purposes, alcoholics, stowaways, and vagrants were added to the exclusion list.

1921   **Emergency Immigration Act**—Congress limited European immigration to three percent of the number of each nationality present in the United States in 1890, limited immigration from Southern and Eastern Europe and banned all immigration from Asia.

1924   The Border Patrol was established. Congress passed the Immigration Act of 1924 that reduced the 1921 immigration quota to 2 percent based on the 1890 Census, barred entry of Japanese and Asian nationals and denied citizenship to approximately 47,000 Japanese aliens.

1927   **National Origin Act**—Congress placed overall limits of 150,000 per year for immigrants from European countries and excluded all immigration from East Asia.

1943   **Magnuson Act**—lifted citizenship barriers for most immigrants of Asian origin, repealed the Exclusion Act of 1882, established a quota for Chinese immigration, and granted citizenship for eligible Chinese immigrants. Separate legislation established the Bracero Program for immigrant workers from North, South and Central America.

1946   **Asian Exclusion Repeal Acts**—Congress cut Filipino immigration to only fifty persons per year, reclassified all Filipinos in the United States as aliens, and excluded immigration from China, Japan, India, and the Philippines. Procedures were established to allow immigration of foreign-born wives, finance(e)s, husbands, and children of U.S. military personnel.

1948   Congress enacted the nation's first policy to admit persons fleeing persecution up to 205,000 refugees over a two-year period.

1952   **McCarran-Walter Act**—Congress abolished the 1917 Asian Barred Zone, set quotas on the number of immigrants allowed into the United States, allowed 100 ethnic Chinese to enter annually, tightened security and screening procedures for immigrants, and mandated the rights of exclusion and deportation of any alien engaging in activities prejudicial to the public interest or subversive to national security.

1965   **Hart-Cellar Act**—revised the McCarran-Walter Act by eliminating immigration quotas. The law established seven criteria for future immigration: (1) unmarried adult sons and daughters of citizens, (2) spouses and unmarried sons and daughters of permanent residents, (3) professionals, scientists, and artists of exceptional ability; (4) siblings of adult citizens, (5) workers, skilled and unskilled in occupations experiencing labor shortages, (6) refugees from Communist-dominated countries, and (7) refugees from countries uprooted by natural catastrophes.

1968   **Immigration Reform and Control Act**—Legal status was granted to undocumented aliens who live and work in the United States for a specified time and, imposed fines on employers hiring newly arrived undocumented workers.

1975   **Indochina Migration and Refugee Assistance Act**—Legislation facilitated the immigration and resettlement of Southeast Asian refugees.

1986   **Immigration Reform and Control Act**—Congress granted legal status to aliens residing in the United States in an unlawful manner since January 1982. The law established sanctions against employers hiring or referring illegal aliens to work in the United States, created a new classification for temporary agricultural workers and established a visa waver pilot program for non-immigrants without existing visas.

1990   **Immigration Act**—Law granted citizenship to aliens admitted legally into the United States and granted immigration status to those officially certified as refugees.

1994	President Clinton enacts **Operation Gatekeeper**, an executive order for border fencing, increased federal patrols and massive deportations of illegals crossing from Mexico into the United States.
1998	**Nicaraguan Adjustment and Central American Relief Act**—Congress granted permanent residency (green cards) to certain Nicaraguans, Cubans, Salvadorans, Guatemalans, and nationals of former Soviet bloc countries and their dependents.
2002	**Homeland Security Act**—Congress created the Department of Homeland Security and assigned to it immigration enforcement and adjudication.
2006	**Secure Fence Act**—Congress authorized the construction of a border fence along 700 miles of shared border between the United States and Mexico.
2012	**Deferred Action for Childhood Arrivals (DACA)**—Presidential executive order issued by President Obama offering deferred action from deportation and eligibility for work for persons of illegal aliens brought to the United States as children.
2014	**Deferred Action for Parents of Americans and Lawful Permanent Residents (DAPA)**—Presidential executive order issued by President Obama deferring deportations of illegal aliens living in the United States since 2010 who had children who were American citizens or legal permanent residents.
2015-18	Federal District Court overturned DAPA and in 2018, a federal judge ruled that DACA was likely unconstitutional but allowed it to remain in place while awaiting further litigation.
2017	Through a series of executive orders, President Trump placed restrictions in refugee admissions, limited the number of refugees to 45,000 per year, issued travel restrictions from a list of nations, rescinded the DAPA policy, suspended immigration from six countries, approved ICE raids targeting suspected criminals, and authorized construction of a border wall between the United States and Mexico.
2018	Federal judge rules that the Trump administration must keep renewing DACA permits but upholds the continuing construction of the wall. Trump proposes ending birthright citizenship. A partial government shutdown occurs when Congress refuses to fund border wall construction.
2019	Trump declares a national state of emergency over illegal immigrants coming from Mexico, sends federal troops to secure the border, initiates child separations for parents illegally crossing the border.
2020	Supreme Court rules that the Department of Homeland Security did not properly follow guidelines when seeking to end DACA. DACA is temporarily upheld.

Between 1880 and 1908, Chinese and Japanese immigration was restricted. Passed over President Wilson's veto, a 1917 law required immigrants to pass a literacy test before they could be admitted into the country. In 1921, Congress limited European immigration in any one year to 3 percent of the number of each nationality admitted into the United States in 1910. The **National Origins Act of 1927** limited European immigration to 150,000 per year. Subsequent legislation banned Asian immigrants. The Supreme Court has consistently held that immigration-related issues rest with the federal and not state governments. "A 1986 federal law forbids states from enacting stricter criminal or civil penalties for illegal immigration than those adopted by Congress.[119] In a 2006 decision, the Supreme Court signaled that federal law, not state laws, guide the nation's immigration and deportation policies. In an 8-1 decision the Court ruled in favor of an immigrant who had violated a South Dakota law making it a deportable offense to possess illegal substances. "The issue before the Supreme Court was the interpretation of the federal Immigration and Nationality Act, which says immigrants found guilty of aggravated felonies are subject to deportation. Conduct that's a felony under state law but a misdemeanor under the Controlled Substance Act isn't a felony for purposes of immigration."[120] However, it has been the inability of Congress to pass immigration reform measures, coupled with the changing pattern of illegal immigration from the traditional border states to regions from the Midwest, Rocky Mountains to New England and the increased drug-related gang war violence in Mexico that has moved state legislative houses to enact their own versions of immigration reform only to see their legislative issues ruled unconstitutional or unenforceable by the federal courts.

A measure supported by the Obama administration, the **Dream Act** failed to win congressional approval. Introduced in 2001, this law would have provided an easier path towards citizenship for illegal immigrants who were brought into the United States as children. To qualify, the applicant had to submit to a background check from Homeland Security and have a clean criminal record. Once approved, the applicant would be granted a ten-year conditional residency permit with the understanding that during that period, they could at least complete two years of college or join the United States military. While the law would have applied to all illegal children, the Hispanic community in particular would have reaped the benefits. Although they supported Obama's reelection to the White House, the Hispanic community continued to express their displeasure with the Obama administration's failure to press Congress for immigration reform, in particular the passage of the Dream Act. Senator Marc Rubio (R-Fla.) also pledged to offer his own plan for immigration reform but failed to win over his Republican colleagues to support his effort. Obama did initiate the **Deferred Action for Childhood Arrivals (DACA)** in 2012. "Under the policy, people younger than 31 can apply for a two-year deferral of any deportation if they can prove they came to the United States before the age of 16, have lived here for the past five years, have not been convicted of select crimes and are not a threat to national security. Applicants must have a high school diploma or GED, be currently enrolled in school or have been honorably discharged from the military."[121] However, this program does not lead to permanent citizenship. Applicants must pay an application fee of approximately $465 plus be subjected to background checks and provide financial, medical and employment records. Also, there is no appeal if one's application is denied. In a tied vote, the Supreme Court upheld a lower federal court ruling in *United States v Texas* (2016) against Obama's **Deferred Action for Parents of Americans and Lawful Permanent Residents (DAPA)** and affirmed the Court's injunction blocking implementation of the president's executive order. A 2020 ruling by the Supreme Court temporarily upholds DACA, but the Trump administration vowed to take measures to end the program. DAPA allows approximately five million unauthorized immigrants who are the parents of legal citizens to remain in the country and to apply for work permits.

The key to Hispanic empowerment does begin within the political arena. In the 1970s, a small group of students from St. Mary's University in San Antonio, Texas, led by Jose Angel Gutierrez founded a third political party movement dedicated to the causes of the Hispanic community. **La Raza Unida** (LRU) began in the South Texas Rio Grande Valley, a predominately agricultural area stretching south of San Antonio to the Mexican border. The majority of the region's Hispanic population are farm workers who toil in the fields picking fruits and vegetables, earning at or below minimum wages. The party began at the lowest political level by winning positions on the Crystal City, Texas, city council and school board. La Raza ceased to be a viable third party as the organization's political agenda was adopted by the Democrats, which usually garner at least two-thirds or better of the Hispanic vote in local, state and national election efforts. Founded in 1968, the National Council of La Raza provides a cadre of lobbyists to promote Hispanic issue concerns in state and national legislative houses. Hispanic organizations such as the **League of United Latin American Citizens** (LULAC) and the **Mexican-American Legal Defense and Educational Fund** (MALDF) keep the social, economic, and political needs of the Hispanic community alive by conducting voter registration drives, recruiting and supporting Hispanic candidates, and lobbying legislative and executive houses across the country. Outdated discriminatory redistricting plans have been successfully challenged in federal courts, and the corrective legislation embodied in the Voting Rights Act and subsequent amendments have provided bilingual ballots and materials. In 1968, the late Willie Velasquez, another graduate of St. Mary's University, founded the **Southwest Voter Registration Project** (SVRP) and organized voter registration drives throughout Southwest Texas, California, Arizona, and New Mexico. However, the Supreme Court ruled in 2013 that Section 5 of the Voting Rights Act was unconstitutional. In particular, Section 5 was the backbone of the legislation since it required many state legislative houses and city/local officials to submit their electoral redistricting plans for pre-clearance by the U.S. Justice Department if there was an historical pattern of voter irregularities and gerrymandering of representational districts designed to deny minorities' equal representation. During its 2015 term, the Supreme Court rule 5-4 against the Alabama state legislature's practice of minority voting packing in its 2012 state redistricting plans.

No Hispanic had ever served in a cabinet level position until President Ronald Reagan appointed Lauro Cavazos as Secretary of Education and President Clinton appointed Henry Cisneros and Frederico Pena to his team. President George W. Bush appointed several Hispanics to high ranking positions including Alberto Gonzalez to attorney general. Hispanic empowerment is also hampered by a lack of cooperation among Hispanics. "Even activists acknowledge that Hispanic potential has been sapped by the group's overall political apathy and its inability to knit together Mexican-Americans, Cuban-Americans, Puerto Ricans, and other factions . . . . Hispanics don't have any issues they can come together on . . . . The only things they really have in common are that they tend to be Catholic, speak Spanish, have generally the same skin color, and have some of the same cultural values. Other than that they are very different and distinct groups."[122] Hispanic political clout, however, is beginning to exert its presence. Traditionally, Hispanics joined the ranks of African-American voters in their solid support of Democratic candidates. The Democratic Party continues to draw a large percentage of the Hispanic vote due to the party's positions on immigration, education, the economy, and health care. The Hispanic vote cannot be taken for granted. The increase in Hispanic voting clout "should serve as a cautionary note to anyone in political life that campaigning in this community is a lot more than speaking Spanish."[123] Hispanics have made some significant electoral advancements with the election of Republican Ted Cruz, a Cuban American from Texas to the U.S. Senate in 2013, Republican Marco Rubio to the governorship of Florida, Michelle Lujan Grisham a Democrat to the governorship of New Mexico. New York's United States House of Representatives delegation includes Nydia Velasquez (D), Alexandria Ocasio-Cortez,(D), Jose Serrano (D), Antonio Delgado (D). Both Ted Cruz and Julian Castro a Democrat from Texas have launched unsuccessful bids for the presidency. The Hispanic community, however, must begin to exert more of a solid presence in the political arena and actively recruit and, subsequently, elect more Hispanic candidates to public office to ensure that the quest so eloquently voiced by the late Cesar Chávez will not fall upon deaf ears.

Gender Issues

In 1776, Abigail Adams warned her husband John Adams to: "Remember the Ladies, and be more generous and favorable to them than your ancestors. Do not put such unlimited powers into the hands of the Husbands. Remember all Men would be tyrants if they could. If particular care and attention is not paid to the Ladies, we are determined to ferment a Rebellion, and will not hold ourselves bound by any Laws in which we have no voice, or Representation."[124] Unfortunately, the Framers chose to ignore her warnings, opting instead to deny women basic rights guaranteed to men through the United States Constitution. In 2020, women across the nation celebrated the 100th anniversary of the passage of the **Nineteenth Amendment** to the United States Constitution, granting women suffrage rights. While civil rights struggles have been focused primarily on minority groups, we cannot overlook the tremendous and arduous task women of this nation faced to not only vote but to own property, apply for credit, get an education, earn a decent wage, and even serve on a jury. These basic rights should have been guaranteed to all American citizens, male and female, when the Framers pinned both the Constitution and the Bill of Rights.

For centuries, however, gender-based discrimination fueled by paternalistic attitudes has kept women in subservient roles. It was women of all creeds and colors who worked side by side their male counterparts to build this nation. Yet, they realized from the very beginning that they had very few civil rights that fell under the protection of the Bill of Rights, no meaningful voice in the political arena, and only a marginal role in society. In 1872, ardent feminist Victoria Woodhull decided to take on incumbent President Ulysses S. Grant and Horace Greeley for the race for the White House. The first woman to run for the presidency, Woodhull's time was "a much more difficult one for women, who then had almost no rights to property or person. If a married woman worked, her wages were given directly to her husband. She could not dispose of her property upon death. If she divorced, she automatically forfeited custody of her children. Women could not enter universities, law schools or medical schools. They could not vote. Most significantly, women had no control over their own bodies. There were no laws to protect them from physical abuse at the hands of their husbands or fathers, although some states stipulated the size of the objects that might be used to inflict discipline . . . . Men were allowed all means of sexual license, but a woman who committed adultery was subject to a jail sentence."[125] As a candidate of the **Equal Rights Party**, Woodhull selected Frederick Douglass as her running mate. Although improvements have been made, women not only in the United States but across the globe are still battling against those historical and cultural barriers that continue to keep them in a subservient role, usually one step behind their male counterparts.

The **paternalistic attitude** of male superiority over women is supported by the myth that women are just too fragile mentally and physically to survive the rigors of life by themselves. Women need a "knight in shining armor" to protect them from harm and unpleasantness. The Southern plantation system went a step further by placing women on pedestals. Frail and fragile like a treasured piece of fine bone china, women became the objects of worship, requiring the constant watchful protective eye of their husbands and fathers. The frontier experience with its encouragement of rugged individualism played right into the hands of paternalism by creating the "macho" male role. In 1873, Supreme Court Justice Joseph Bradley wrote:

> Man is, or should be, woman's protector and defender. The natural and proper timidity and delicacy which belongs to the female sex evidently unfits it for many of the occupations of civil life. The constitution of the family organization, which is founded in the divine ordinance, as well as in the nature of things, indicates the domestic sphere as that which properly belongs to the domain and functions of womanhood. The harmony . . . of interests and views which belong, or should belong, to the family institution is repugnant to the idea of woman adopting a distinct and independent career from that of her husband. . . The paramount destiny and mission of woman are to fulfill the noble and benign offices of wife and mother.[126]

Paternalistic attitudes toward women resulted in repressive laws, social barriers, restrictive employment opportunities, and denial of education. Oddly, single women had more rights and freedoms than married women. "The very being of woman was suspended during marriage or at least incorporated into that of her husband, under whose wing she maintained her legal status."[127] State legislative houses passed laws prohibiting women from selling or borrowing against her own private property without their husband's permission. Women could not on their own enter into contracts, apply for loans and credit, witness a will, sue, or serve on a jury. The Texas Constitution once contained an amendment barring women from purchasing a refrigerator without prior approval from their spouses.

With very few exceptions, women did not venture forth into the world of politics until the beginning of the Abolitionist Movement in the 1830s. However, antislavery organizations did not openly embrace or offer leadership roles to women. A disgusted Sarah Grimke wrote the president of the Boston Female Anti-Slavery Society that "all history attests that man has subjugated woman to his will, used her as a means to promote his selfish gratifications, to minister to his sensual pleasure, to be instrumental in promoting his comfort; but never has he desired to promote her to the rank she was created to fill. He has done all he could to debase and enslave her mind; and now he looks triumphantly on the ruin he has wrought, and says, the being he has thus deeply injured is his inferior."[128] The plight of women prompted Lucretia Mott and Elizabeth Cady Stanton to organize the first Women's Rights Convention held at Seneca Falls, New York, in 1848. Their penning of the **Declaration of Sentiments and Resolutions** declaring women equal to men set the stage for the Woman's Suffrage Movement. Stanton was adamant about gaining the right to vote for women. She argued "to have drunkards, idiots, horse racing rum-selling rowdies, ignorant foreigners, and silly boys fully recognized [with voting privileges], while we ourselves are thrust out from all the rights that belong to citizens, is too grossly insulting to be longer quietly submitted to. The right is ours. We must have it."[129] The Supreme Court gave the emerging movement a chance to vent its frustrations when the Court ruled in *Minor v Happersat* (1875) that the Fourteenth Amendment to the United States Constitution did not give women the right to vote. The quest for a constitutional amendment to reverse the Court's decision solidified an emerging feminist movement to the cause of suffrage.

Ardent feminists, Elizabeth Cady Stanton and Susan B. Anthony, founded *The Revolution*, a weekly newspaper focusing on feminist issues. Stanton and Anthony also formed the **National American Woman Suffrage Association** while Lucy Stone organized the **American Woman Suffrage Association**. Author of the short story *The Yellow Wall-Paper*, Francis Perkins Gilman took on the economic issues confronting women. The incidents of the mistreatment of workers, particularly women, were too frequent to be ignored. "Far from gaining in personal freedom, women were increasingly the victims of the factories and workshops; competition no doubt drove their employers to exploit their defenseless positions on the labour market just as the need for subsistence, the absence of special qualifications, and the lack of alternatives drove innumerable young women into the factories and garment-making shops."[130] Women garment workers joined women of all classes in massive demonstrations as the New York Women's Trade Union League staged strikes in 1909.

Of course, women's organizations were confronted with the task of uniting the majority of nation's men and women behind "the cause." Author of *Uncle Tom's Cabin,* Harriet Beecher Stowe and her sister Catharine Beecher were the leading voices opposing woman's suffrage. In an 1869 article, they commented:

> Let us suppose that our friends have gained the ballot and the powers of office: Are there any real beneficent measures for our sex, which they would enforce by law and penalties, that fathers, brothers, and husbands would not grant to a united petition of our sex, or even to a majority of the wise and good? Would these not confer what the wives, mothers, and sisters deemed best for themselves and the children they train, very much sooner than they would give power and office to our sex to enforce these advantages by law? Would it not be a wiser thing to ask for what we need, before trying so circuitous and dangerous a method? God has given to man the physical power, so that all that woman may gain, either by petitions or by ballot, will be the gift of love or of duty; and the ballot never will be accorded till benevolent and conscientious men are the majority—a millennial point far beyond our present kin.[131]

Lacking cohesive leadership, women's organizations needed a board-base issue to draw the various factions together. The **Temperance Movement** in the 1900s helped to solidify women behind the desire to rid the nation of alcohol. Their efforts resulted in the passage of the **Eighteenth Amendment** and the Prohibition Era. Meanwhile, a new suffrage leadership was emerging under Dr. Anna Howard Shaw, Carrie Chapman Catt, and Alice Paul, founder of the Congressional Union, which later became the **Woman's Party**. Although several states allowed women to vote in statewide and local elections, women did not have voting rights in national elections. Both Paul and Chapman organized daily marches and protests in front of the White House to jar a reluctant President Woodrow Wilson to assert pressure for the passage of a woman's suffrage amendment. Women's organizations began lobbying Wilson immediately after he took office in 1913. In his 1916 re-election effort, Wilson advocated giving women the right to vote. However, once re-elected, he changed his mind. Members of the National Woman's Party met with Wilson on January 9, 1917, only to be rebuffed in their efforts. "The next morning the White House picketing began. The press described the picketers as 'Silent Sentinels.' Nearly every day, rain or shine, whenever Congress was in session, they were there. They stood essentially motionless, holding large purple, white, and gold banners. 'How long must women wait?' some banners asked. 'President Wilson, what will you do for woman suffrage?'"[132] To break the monotony of daily protests, Alice Paul had "theme days" whereby the messages on the banners would be changed on a daily basis. "Between 1915 and 1920, organized women working on social issues encompassed an estimated five to seven million. This is based on 2.5 million suffragists, another 750,000 in the Women's Temperance Union, 1.5 million in the Women's Club movement and at least another one million Black [African American] and Jewish women working in the women's trade unions."[133] Today, we see the grainy photos of the women marching through the streets of New York City and Washington, D.C. "If you look at the black-and-white photographs of suffragists, it's tempting to see the women as quaint: spectacles and undyed buns, heavy coats and long dresses, ankle boots and feathered hats. In fact, they would face fierce-braving ridicule, arrest, imprisonment and treatment that came close to torture."[134] Finally Wilson caved in. Approved by Congress in 1919, the **Nineteenth Amendment** was ratified by the required number of states by August 1920.

The suffrage movement involved a complex array of political, social, and economic issues. Women were scorned, publicly and socially humiliated, arrested, jailed and even killed in their struggle to reverse the stranglehold of paternalism. Conditions in the jails were horrible. "The cells at the workhouse in Occoquan, Virginia, were small, dark and rat-infested. Bedding hadn't been cleaned in almost a year; the staff handled it only with rubber gloves. The suffragists held contests to see who had the most mealworms in her food. For extended periods the women were allowed no visitors or legal counsel. All mail was censored . . . Dorothy Day, 20, the future founder of the Catholic Worker Movement, had her arms twisted and was violently thrown against an iron bench. Dora Lewis, 55, was knocked unconscious. Lucy Burns, identified as a Woman's Party leader, was beaten and left handcuffed to her cell bars with her hands above her head."[135] Alice Paul was arrested for protesting in front of the White House. Staging a protest hunger strike, Paul was forced-fed simply because the White House feared the repercussions her death would have on the American public and, ultimately, political careers. "Hoping to discredit her by having her diagnosed as mentally ill, the warden moved her to the psychopathic ward, where the screams of patients and a flashlight shined in her face every hour, kept her awake."[136] Once they were released from prison, the women continued their fight to gain social, economic, legal, and political equality with their male counterparts.

With the exception of the war years of the 1920s and 1940s, employment opportunities for women were limited to a few low paying positions usually available to just single women. In most states, female public school teachers had to resign their positions when they married. In the 1920s, women gained in the job market by replacing men who were fighting overseas. However, the Depression Era reversed this trend as women were deliberately fired to open up job opportunities for unemployed men. World War II again gave women a chance for employment as they replaced men in industrial and manufacturing positions. Today, the economic necessity of the two-household income has substantially increased the number of females in the workforce.

Despite countless litigations and legislative acts correcting previous adverse actions, women are still confronted by a multiplicity of job-related discriminatory practices. The **pay equity** issue addresses the problem that women earn less than their male counterparts employed in comparable positions. Women, as a whole, earn less since they hold the majority of clerical and secretarial positions, collectively known as **pink collar** jobs. Across the board, men earn more than women. The trends clearly show that within each racial/ethnic group, women are now earning the majority of college-level degrees versus their male counterparts. However, the wage disparity gap still favors men. A man with only a high school diploma will earn approximately $44,466 compared to $29,158 for a woman with that same high school diploma employed in a comparable job. A woman with a bachelors degree employed in a similar position to her male counterpart earns only $53,804 per year while he brings home $67,763. A woman with an earned masters degree will earn approximately $71,262 while her male counterpart employed in the same position earns $87,674. The professional category includes doctors, lawyers, engineers, scientists, etc. Once again, women earn on an average $111,145 per year while men in comparable positions with the same educational credentials earn an average of $138,378.[137] Whether they are Anglo, African American, or Hispanic, women in all of these categories earn less than men. Although job promotability and mobility opportunities for women have increased substantially, women are still victims of the **glass ceiling**, which prohibits them from becoming the CEO or president of the firm. A military career for women is still a controversial issue. Initially women entered the military in hopes of building a career by moving up the promotional ladder. However, the majority of them were traditionally confined to non-combat duties such as nursing and official clerical duties. The majority of the command positions were held by men, particularly those assigned to combat commanding roles. Forced through congressional acts, presidential decrees and orders by the Secretary of Defense, military academies reluctantly opened their doors to female cadets. Secretary of Defense Chuck Hagel cleared the way for women to serve in combat. Yet, these sweeping changes have been tarnished by the on-going sexual assault and sexual harassment charges made by women against their male trainers and commanders.

The woman's movement, like other social movements, has failed to maintain a consistent and cohesive battlefront. In the 1920s, "the newly political liberated womanhood of America made no move to disturb the social order; they arranged themselves instead along lines already marked out by the structure and economic interests of a society dominated by men. What was more surprising and disappointing to those who had hoped for real alterations among the roles in American society was the limping and limited manner in which women attempted to move into positions occupied by men throughout industry or the professions. Leaders of the suffrage movement did not see their duty now as that of inspiring a diffused and dispersed multitude of followers . . . ."[138] True to form, the woman's movement declined after winning the suffrage battle only to re-emerge in the 1960s under new leadership and new issues—reproductive freedom and women's liberation. The feminist movement achieved its goal when the Supreme Court upheld reproductive freedom of choice in *Roe v Wade* (1973). The women's movement began to decline in the 1980s, only to re-emerge in the 1990s with the issue of electing more women to public office. In the 1992 "Year of the Woman," women did succeed in increasing their numbers in state and national elective offices. In 2007, Senator Hillary Clinton (D-NY) made an unsuccessful bid for the presidency. At the 2016 Democratic National Convention, Hillary Clinton became the first woman to win a major political party's presidential nomination. Although she lost the electoral vote to her Republican rival, she won the popular vote by nearly three million.

The feminist movement has yet to address the problems confronting the average woman and those women who are undereducated and living in poverty. The separate sisters—"women in minority groups; women in 'traditional' women's jobs; women who stay at home to raise children; elderly, rural, some poor and younger women—acknowledge their debt to feminism's early battles. But they charge that the feminist movement has failed to broaden its base and remains made up largely of white, highly educated women who have not adequately addressed the issues that matter to them: child care rather than lesbian and abortion rights, economic survival rather than political equality, the sticky floor rather than the glass ceiling."[139] In addition, women's organizations like minority groups have not established a consistent proactive record. They join to battle an issue and then disperse. For example, their lack of cohesive vigilance has enabled state legislative houses to pass anti-abortion legislation that is successfully and legally chipping away at the provisions of *Roe v Wade*. Their success hinges on pursuing a proactive diverse array of issues that will unite women of diverse races and incomes rather than just reacting to a problem.

Table 13.5

Significant Events for American Women

Date	Event
1848	The first women's rights convention is held in Seneca Falls, New York on July 19 and 20. A *Declaration of Sentiments and Resolutions*, setting the agenda for the woman's movement, was adopted.
1850	First national woman's rights convention held in Worchester, Massachusetts. Quaker physicians establish Female Medical College of Pennsylvania in Philadelphia, Pennsylvania. Due to threats, their first graduate had to have police protection.
1851	Sojourner Truth gives her speech "Ain't I a Woman?" at the woman's rights convention in Akron, Ohio.
1855	Lucy Stone becomes the first woman on record to keep her maiden name after marriage. Supreme Court rules in *Missouri v Celia, a Slave*, that an African-American woman is property and cannot defend herself against her master's act of rape.
1866	The American Equal Rights Association is founded. This is the first organization in the United States advocating national suffrage rights for women.
1868	Sorosis, the first professional club for women, is founded. The Working Women's Protective Union in New York is founded by middle- and upper-class women to lobby for laws protecting women workers. Elizabeth Cady Stanton and Susan B. Anthony begin publishing *The Revolution*, a women's periodical.
1869	Women shoe stitchers from six states form the Daughters of St. Crispin, the first national women's labor organization. The first woman suffrage law in the United States passes in the territory of Wyoming. Susan B. Anthony and Elizabeth Cady Stanton form the National Woman Suffrage Association as Lucy Stone establishes the American Woman Suffrage Association.
1870	For the first time in the history of jurisprudence, women serve on juries in the Wyoming Territory. Iowa becomes the first state to admit a woman to the bar.

1872   Congress passes an equal pay law for women federal employees. Susan B. Anthony is arrested, tried, found guilty, and fined $100 for registering and voting in the presidential election. Victoria Woodhull runs for the presidency as a candidate of the Equal Rights Party.

1873   In *Bradwell v Illinois*, Supreme Court affirms that states can restrict women from practicing any profession when it conflicts with a woman's role to "preserve family harmony and uphold the law of the Creator."

1874   The Supreme Court rules in *Bradwell v Illinois* that states can restrict women from any professional career "to preserve family harmony and uphold the law of the Creator." The Woman's Christian Temperance Union is founded by Annie Wittenmyer.

1875   The Supreme Court rules in *Minor v Happersett* that the 14th Amendment does not give women the right to vote.

1878   The Susan B. Anthony Amendment giving women the right to vote is introduced in Congress.

1879   Belva Lockwood is the first woman to argue a case before the Supreme Court.

1884   Belva Lockwood, presidential candidate of the National Equal Rights Party, becomes the first woman to receive votes in a presidential election.

1913   Ida H. Wells-Barnett funds Alpha Suffrage Club of Chicago, first African-American woman's suffrage organization. On March 3, 5,000 suffragists march in Washington, DC. On May 10, 20,000 women and 500 men participate in a New York City suffrage march.

1917   Jeanette Rankin of Montana becomes the first woman elected to the U. S. Congress. In January, suffragists begin a silent vigil in front of the White House.

1919   The House of Representatives and the Senate pass the woman suffrage amendment.

1920   On August 26, the 19th Amendment to the Constitution is ratified, giving American women citizens the right to vote.

1924   Nellie Tayloe Ross of Wyoming becomes the first woman elected governor of a state.

1926   Bertha Knight Landes is the first woman elected mayor of a sizable U. S. city (Seattle, Washington).

1932   The National Recovery Act bars benefits for families with more than one breadwinner from receiving benefits. Hatti Wyatt Caraway from Louisiana becomes first woman elected to the United States Senate.

1933   Frances Perkins becomes the first woman to serve in a president's cabinet.

1948   Margaret Chase Smith (R-Maine) becomes the first woman elected to the U. S. Senate in her own right. In 1964, she is the first woman to run for the presidency in the primaries of a major political party.

1961   President Kennedy creates the President's Commission on the Status of Woman and appoints Eleanor Roosevelt as its chairperson.

1963   The Equal Pay Act, establishing equal pay for men and women performing the same job duties, passes Congress.

1964   Patsy Mink (D-Hawaii) becomes the first Asian-American woman elected to the U. S. Congress.

1966   The National Organization for Women (NOW) is founded as a civil rights organization for women.

1968   Nominated by the Communist Party, Charlene Mitchell becomes the first African-American woman to run for the presidency. Shirley Chisholm (D-NY) is the first African-American woman elected to United States House of Representatives.

1970   Betty Freidan organizes the first Women's Equality Day, August 26, to mark the 50th anniversary of women's right to vote. The Equal Rights Amendment is reintroduced into Congress.

1972   Patsy Mink runs in the Democratic presidential primaries. Shirley Chisholm becomes the first African-American woman to seek the presidency from a major political party.

1973   The Supreme Court rules in *Roe v Wade* that women have a right to an abortion. This overturns forty-six state laws banning the procedure.

1974   The Equal Credit Opportunity Act prohibits sex discrimination in all consumer credit practices. Ella Grasso (Connecticut) becomes the first woman to win election as governor in her own right.

1975   The Supreme Court rules in *Taylor v Louisiana* that states cannot prohibit women from serving on juries.

1976   Ellen McCormick is the first female presidential candidate to receive federal funds and Secret Service protection.

1978   Amending the Civil Rights Act of 1964, the Pregnancy Discrimination Act bans employment discrimination against pregnant workers.

1981   Sandra Day O'Connor becomes the first woman appointed to the U. S. Supreme Court. In 1993, Ruth Bader Ginsburg was appointed to the bench.

1982   The Equal Rights Amendment fails to secure ratification. Over 900 women hold positions as state legislators, compared with 344 a decade ago.

1984   Geraldine Ferraro (D-NY) becomes the first woman vice presidential candidate of a major political party. Nominated by both the U.S. Citizens Party and the Peace and Freedom Party, Sonia Johnson becomes the first third-party candidate to qualify for federal matching funds. Emily's List is founded.

1986   The U. S. Supreme Court declares sexual harassment as a form of illegal employment discrimination.

1988   Lenora Fulani becomes the first woman to have her name placed on the ballot for president in all fifty states and won the most votes of any female candidate for president to date. Patricia Schroeder runs unsuccessfully for the Democratic Party presidential nomination.

1992   The Year of the Woman results in twenty-four women elected to the House of Representatives and 6 to the Senate, including Lucille Roybal-Allard (D-CA), the first Mexican-American woman in the House; Nydia Velazquez (D-NY), the first Puerto Rican woman elected to the House; Carol Moseley-Braun (D-IL), the first African-American woman elected to the Senate; Barbara Boxer and Dianne Feinstein (D-CA), the first two women elected to the Senate from the same state. Janet Reno becomes the first U.S. woman attorney general.

1996	Supreme Court rules in *United States v Virginia* that the male-only admissions policy of the Virginia Military Institute violated the 14th Amendment to the Constitution.
1997	Madeleine Albright is appointed Secretary of State, becoming the first woman to hold that position.
2005	President Bush names Condoleezza Rice as his Secretary of State.
2007	Nancy Pelosi (D-CA) becomes the first woman Speaker of the House of Representatives.
2008	Senator Hillary Clinton (D-New York) makes an unsuccessful bid for the Democratic presidential nomination but is appointed as Secretary of State in the Obama White House.
2009	President Obama successfully appoints Sonia Sotomayor, the first Hispanic woman to the United States Supreme Court.
2010	President Obama successfully appoints Elena Kagan, a Jewish woman, to the United States Supreme Court.
2015	President Obama appoints Loretta Lynch to Attorney General making her the first African-American woman to hold that position.
2016	Hillary Clinton becomes the first woman nominated for the presidency by a major political party.

The LGBT Community

Just based upon their sexual orientation, homosexuals were denied a wide range of privileges enjoyed by the "straight" community. Homosexuals in partner relationships were faced with the reality that their relationships had no legal standing. In other words, their relationships defied the traditional definition of a couple as being one of a man with a woman. Anyone in the military suspected of or openly declaring their homosexuality was discharged, regardless of their military performance records. Many state legislative houses passed laws and constitutional amendments defining marriage as between a natural born man and a natural born woman. In 1996, Congress passed the **Defense of Marriage Act (DOMA)** that mirrored state laws. Basically, these laws simply did not recognize gay and lesbian relationships. If one partner was employed, he/she could not qualify their partners for dependent health-care coverage and other fringe benefits. If one of the partners was hospitalized, the other partner could not be considered as the legal guardian capable of making necessary and, in some instances, life-saving decisions for his/her partner. Guy and lesbian partners were denied death benefits at both the state and federal level including social security.

Gradually, public opinion has changed. During his first term of office, President Clinton addressed the issue of discriminatory practices against homosexuals in the military. Although lacking definitive evidence that one's homosexual orientation was detrimental to a successful military career, the military systematically eliminated gays and lesbians from its ranks through blatant harassment, early discharges, and threats of court-martials. President Clinton offered a compromise policy of "don't ask, don't tell" as a means of eliminating harassment and allowing gays and lesbians to successfully pursue a long-term career in the military. Candidate Barack Obama vowed to rescind the policy altogether pointing out that one's sexual orientation should not be an issue of whether an individual could fulfill their military obligations. Once in the White House, he did move Congress to overturn it.

Several state legislative houses were pressed to change their laws regarding gay and lesbian partnerships. During its 2013 session, the United States Supreme Court heard arguments against the constitutionality of DOMA. The pro-gay community argued that denial of federal survivorship benefits of a legally married gay or lesbian couple while granting the same benefits to a traditional marriage of man to woman was disparate treatment. In 2015, the Supreme Court in ***Obergefell v Hodges*** ruled DOMA unconstitutional with its 5 to 4 decision guaranteeing the right to same-sex marriage.

Disabled Americans

Unfortunately, disabled Americans have been the targets of discriminatory practices that have denied them social acceptance, personal mobility, and economic viability. Some have disabilities so severe that they cannot care for themselves, much less hold a job. Historically, care for the disabled fell upon individual family members and private charities and institutions. State and local governments provided few, if any, means of assistance. The national government did not provide substantial support for disabled Americans until 1920 with the passage of the **Vocational Rehabilitation Act**. The **Social Security Act** provides federal income-support for the disabled. It was not until 1948 that a special presidential commission was established to explore the problems confronted by the disabled.

For the disabled, normal errands can be extremely frustrating, oftentimes, impossible to achieve. Although corrective legislation has been passed at federal, state, and local levels, the laws are only marginally successful in addressing disability concerns. The United States Constitution prohibits any level of government from passing **ex post facto** laws. Once passed, legislation is enforceable for present actions, not for actions that occurred before the law was passed. For example, the **Architectural Barriers Act** (1970), the **Rehabilitation Act** (1973), and the **Americans with Disabilities Act (ADA)** (1990) require that all new public buildings must be handicapped accessible. These laws, however, cannot mandate that buildings constructed prior to the legislation must be reconfigured to accommodate the disabled. The legislation can only strongly encourage owners of existing public buildings to provide *reasonable but affordable* accommodations. Transportation issues were initially addressed with the passage of the **Urban Mass Transportation Act** in 1970. This act required that state and local governments must ensure that their transportation systems are handicapped accessible.

Title VII of the **Civil Rights Act of 1964** initially barred employment discrimination based on race, color, national origin, religion, and sex. Subsequent legislation has expanded the parameters to include age (individuals over the age of 40), Vietnam era veterans, and the handicapped. "The aim of the civil rights legislation is to prohibit any considerations of disability-related characteristics unless they can be shown to affect ability to perform the job."[140] The law prohibits employers from using any action that treats disabled employees differently from non-disabled employees. "**Disparate treatment** refers to actions in which employers treat people with disabilities differently. **Disparate impact** results when the standards for employment have the effect of excluding people with disabilities on the basis of standards or tests that are not directly related to determining the skills or experience necessary to perform the job."[141]

The major flaw of the ADA law is the legislation's inability to clearly define what constitutes a disability and to set clear-cut direction for reasonable accommodations for the disabled. "In defining the disabled population, the act not only includes anyone with a physical or mental impairment that substantially limits one or more of the major life activities but also includes anyone with a record of having such an impairment or anyone who is perceived as having such an impairment."[142] The issue of reasonable accommodations is oftentimes confusing to employers. For example, what reasonable accommodations should an employer provide to employees who suffer from mental impairments, chronic illnesses, or a bad back? How reasonable should employers be?

While lawmakers and jurists argue over what constitutes a disability, disabled Americans are earning far less than their non-disabled counterparts. In order to lead productive lives, disabled Americans must be able to earn the same paycheck as the non-disabled. Of course, no legislation can change the negative attitudes and stereotypes that are used against the disabled.

CONCLUSION

The public policy process has tried to respond to the needs of minority population groups and women by removing many of the political, economic, and social barriers that kept the doors of success locked for so long. Corrective legislation is, of course, part of the solution. However, the leadership of minority and women's organizations must fulfill their obligations by actively pursuing an all inclusive agenda in the political arena. Lawmakers favorable to minority and women's issues cannot continue to promote legislation in hostile political environments without the full support of the groups they are trying to help. Low voter turnout among minority and female population groups feeds right into the hands of those legislators seeking to hold the line and, in some instances, roll back the clock on civil rights and liberties for minorities and women. These groups cannot afford compliancy.

Frederick Douglass once wrote that the "so-called race problem cannot be solved by keeping the Negro [African American] poor, degraded, ignorant and half-starved . . . It cannot be solved by keeping the wages of the laborer back by fraud . . . It cannot be done by ballot-box stuffing . . . or by confusing Negro [African-American] voters by cunning devices. It can, however, be done, and very easily done . . . Let the white [Anglo] people of the North and the South conquer their prejudices . . . Time and strength are not equal to the task before me. But could I be heard by this great nation, I would call to mind the sublime and glorious truths with which, at its birth, it saluted a listening world . . . Put away your race prejudice. Banish the idea that one class must rule over another. Recognize... that the rights of the humblest citizen are as worthy of protection as are those of the highest, and . . . your Republic will stand and flourish forever."[143] Although speaking on behalf of the African-American community, Douglass' words apply to all who have suffered from discrimination and prejudice. The United States Constitution and the Bill of Rights protects the civil rights of all Americans, not just a few. The Framers charged the nation's leaders with the task of preserving these civil rights for generations to come. As previously mentioned, presidents and governors can compel legislative houses to pass laws ranging from banning discrimination and to outlawing hate motivated crimes. However, Douglass' challenge transcends laws. All Americans regardless of their race, gender or sexual orientation, must practice what Douglass preached—put away your prejudices.

CHAPTER NOTES

[1]"Obama Cites His Own Dream for America," *San Antonio Express-News* (Thursday, August 29, 2013), A6.

[2]Rick Bragg, "Justice At Last," *San Antonio Express-News* (Thursday, May 23, 2002), 10A.

[3]Todd Spangler, "Race Tied to Fatal Shooting," *San Antonio Express-News* (Saturday, April 29, 2000), 1A.

[4]Rick Bragg, "Klansman Faces Trial in '66 Mississippi Slaying", *San Antonio Express-News* (Sunday, January 26, 2003), 14A.

[5]Tim Pagdett, "Long Wait for Justice", *Time* (January 17, 2005), 53.

[6]Bill Clinton, *One America in the 21st Century: The President's Initiative on Race*, (Washington, D.C., March 13, 1998.

[7]Judith A. Winston, "One America in the 21st Century: The President's Initiative on Race," *The National Voter* (The League of Women Voters, March/April 1998), (6-7), 6.

[8]John C. Domino, *Civil Rights and Liberties: Toward the 21st Century*, (New York: HarperCollins Publishers, 1994), 2.

[9]Henry J. Abraham and Barbara A. Perry, *Freedom & the Court: Civil Rights & Liberties in the United States,* 8th ed., (Lawrence, Kansas: The University Press of Kansas, 2003), 367-368.

[10]Kevin Cullen, "Europe Scowls At Immigrants," *San Antonio Express-News* (Friday, December 29, 2000), 26A.

[11]J. R. Poole, *The Pursuit of Equality in American History*, (Los Angeles, Calif.: University of California Press, 1978), 6-7.

[12]Alexis de Tocqueville, *Democracy in America*, Translated by George Lawrence, J. P. Mayer, ed. (Garden City, New York: Doubleday and Company, Inc., 1969), 317.

[13]Dale McLemore and Harriet D. Romo, *Racial and Ethnic Relations in America*, 7th ed., (Boston, Massachusetts: Pearson Education, Inc., 2005), 47-48.

[14]Robert Wernick, "The Rise and Fall of a Fervid Third Party," *The Smithsonian* (November, 1996), 152.

[15]Ibid., 154.

[16]McLemore, 115.

[17]Carolina Moreno, "9 Outrageous Things Donald Trump Has Said About Latinos," *https://www.huffpost.com*

[18]Joseph Connor, "Born in the USA," *American History*, Vol. 54, No. 2, June, 2019, 31.

[19]Ibid., 39.

[20]George H. Sabine, *The History of Political Thought*, 3d ed. (New York: Holt, Reinhart and Winston, 1961), 906.

[21]McLemore, 117-118.

[22]Joseph E. Harris, *Africans and Their History*, 2nd ed. (New York: New American Library Penguin, Inc., 1987), 18.

[23] David Vachon, "Chief Joseph Refuses to Sell Tribal Lands," *Old News*, March, 2004, 1.

[24]Earl Conrad, *Jim Crow America*, 2nd ed., (New York, New York: Duell, Sloan and Pearce, 1947) 27-28.

[25]Ibid., 94.

[26]Daniel B. Moskowitz, "Call of Shame," *American History*, Vol. 54, No. 3, Aug., 2019, 23.

[27]Christine M. Keiser, "A First-Class U.S. Citizen," *American History*, Vol. 44, No. 2, June, 2009, 23.

[28]*http://www.justice.gov.crt*

[29]U.S. Department of Justice, Federal Bureau of Investigation, H*ate Crime Statistics*, 2018, Fall, 2019, *https://www.fbi.gov*

[30]Ibid.

[31]*Latest Hate Crime Statistics Report, http://www.fbi.gov*

[32]Henry Weinstein, "Court Bars Racial Profiling on Border," *San Antonio Express-News* (Wed., April 12, 2000), 19A.

[33]Richard Conniff, "Frederick Douglass Always Knew He Was Meant to be Free," *The Smithsonian*, (February, 1995), 116.

[34]Thomas Hayden, "Modern Life," *U.S. News & World Report* (October 4, 2004), 46.

[35]Bill Baskervill, "Indians Say 'No Thanks,'" *San Antonio Express-News* (Thursday November 23, 2000), 3AA.

[36]McLemore, 291.

[37]Paul VanDevelder, "What Do We Owe the Indians?" *American History,* Vol. 44, No. 2, June, 2009, 35.

[38]Floyd B. Largent, Jr., "The Florida Quadmire," *American History*, Vol. XXXIV, No. 4, October, 1999, 42.

[39]Anthony Dellafora, "Center May Preserve Story of 'Long Walk,'" *Dallas Morning News* (Sunday, March 8, 1998), 45A.

[40]"U.S. May Soon Admit Battle Was Massacre," *The San Antonio Express-News*, (Sunday, March 11, 1990), 6A.

[41]Susan B. Welch, John Gruhl, Michael Steinman, John Comer, and Susan M. Rigdon, *American Government*, 5th ed. (St. Paul, Minn.: West Publishing Co., 1994), 505.

[42]Luci Tapahonso, "Two Nations," *Smithsonian*, Vol. 47, No. 4, July/August, 2016, 73.

[43]Mary Kay Morel, "Captain Pratt's School," *American History*, Vol. 32, No. 2, June, 1997, 28.

[44]Gary B. Nash and Julie Roy Jeffrey, *The American People: Creating A Nation and A Society*, 5th ed., (New York, New York: Addison-Wesley Educational Publishers, Inc., 2001), 546.

[45]Ibid.

[46]David Whitman, "A Court Fight Truly Off the Reservation," *U.S. News & World Report* (April 5, 1999), 42.

[47]VanDevelder, "What Do We Owe the Indians?" 32.

[48]"Tribal Nations and the United States: An Introduction," National Congress of American Indians, July 6, 2020, *http://www.ncai.org*

[49]*ProQuest Statistical Abstract of the United States: 2020*, 8th ed., (Bethesda, Maryland: ProQuest, 2019), Table 20, 23.

[50]Ibid., Table 320, 207.

[51]C. Van Woodward, *The Strange Career of Jim Crow*, 3rd. ed. (New York: Oxford University Press, 1974), 11.

[52]Peter Carlson, "Abraham Lincoln Meets Frederick Douglass," *American History*, Vol. 46, No. 6, February, 2011, 28-29.

[53]Conrad, 109.

[54]Jay Tolson, "The Complex Story of Slavery", *U.S. News & World Report*, February 14, 2005, 66.

[55]Ibid., 66-67.

[56]Henry Wiencek, "Thomas Jefferson: Slave Master," *American History*, Vol. 47, No. 4, October, 2012, 28.

[57]Eugene R. Sheridan, "Apostle of Republican Liberty," *American History Illustrated*, March/April, 1993, 36.

[58]Timothy Foote, "After More Than Two Centuries, This May Be Mr. Madison's Year," *Smithsonian*, Vol. 18, No. 6, September, 1987, 86.

[59]Ibid., 88.

[60]Tolson, "The Complex Story of Slavery," 67.

[61]Peter Carlson, "Lincoln's Feisty Foil," *American History*, Vol. 48, No. 1, April, 2013, 52.

[62]William Kastatus, "The Christiana Tragedy," *American History*, Vol. 37, No 4, October, 2002, 50.

[63]Woodward, 21.

[64]Jack Fincher, "The Hard Fight Was Getting Into the Fight At All," *Smithsonian*, Vol. 21, No. 7, October, 1990, 46.

[65]Ibid.

[66]Woodward, 54.

[67]Abraham, 374.

[68]Sarah Richardson, "As American as Jim Crow," *American History*, Vol. 53, No. 1, April, 2018, 55.

[69]Woodward, 104.

[70]"A Farewell to 'Mr. Civil Rights'," *U. S. News & World Report*, (February 8, 1993), 10.

[71]onrad, 98.

[72]Woodward, 18-19.

[73]Isabel Wilkerson, "The Road to Freedom," *Smithsonian*, Vol. 47, No. 5, September, 2016, 41.

[74]Abraham, 375.

[75]Carolyn Kleiner Butler, "Down In Mississippi", *Smithsonian*, Vol. 35, No. 11, February, 2005, 24.

[76]Keith Weldon Medley, "The Sad Story Of How 'Separate But Equal' Was Born," *Smithsonian*, Vol. 24, No. 11, February, 1994, 106.

[77]Ibid., 108-109.

[78]Domino, 226.

[79]H. W. Brands, "Grant Takes On The Klan," *American History*, Vol. 47, No. 5, Dec. 2012, 46.

[80]Ibid.

[81]David Uhler, "Jim Crow Was A Loser in Korean War," *San Antonio Express-News* (Sunday, June 4, 2000), 1A.

[82]Paul Finkleman, "Race and the Constitution," *By and For the People: Constitutional Rights in American History*, Kermit L. Hall, ed., (Illinois: Harland Davidson, Inc., 1990), 155.

[83]Gregg Holland, "Quiet Justice Speaks Out on Cross Burning", *San Antonio Express-News* (Thursday, December 12, 2002), 4A.

[84]Daniel Moskowitz, "Closing Down Covenants," *American History*, Vol. 53, No. 2, June, 2018, 22-23.

[85]Ibid.

[86]Bree Fowler, "'Mother of the Civil Rights Movement' Dies", *San Antonio Express-News*, (Tuesday, October 25, 2005), 1A.

[87]Daniel Moskowitz, "No, I Will Not Move to the Back of the Bus," *American History*, Vol. 52, No. 3, August, 2017, 42.

[88]Conrad, 156.

[89]braham, 420.

[90]Uhler, 1A.

[91]Ibid.

[92]Keith Weldon Medley, "On Clipped Wings," *Smithsonian*, Vol. 35, No. 2, May, 2004, 22.

[93]David A. Nichols, "Unless We Progress, We Regress," *American History*, Vol. 50, No. 3, August, 2015, 56.

[94]Domino, 227.

[95]Abraham, 396.

[96]Scott Parks, "The Little Rock Nine: School Integration Battle Changed Lives Of Players in Central High Drama," *Dallas Morning News* (Sunday, September 21, 1997), 45A and 56A.

[97]Alan Barth, *The Rights of Free Men: An Essential Guide to Civil Liberties*, James E. Clayton, ed., (New York: Alfred A. Knopf, 1987), 172.

[98]Conrad, 207.

[99]Dan Balz, "The Agenda Remains Unfinished," *San Antonio Express-News*, (Sunday, August 25, 2013), A25.

[100]*The Economic State of Black America in 2020*, Joint Economic Committee, Congressman Don Beyer, Vice Chair, *www.jec.senate.gov*

[101]*Treasury of Presidential Quotations*, Caroline Thomas Harnsberger, ed., (Chicago, Illinois: Follett Publishing Company, 1964), 204.

[102]McLemore, 227.

[103]Will Sullivan, "A Population's Assimilation," *U.S. News & World Report*, April 23, 2007, 34.

[104]Mark Helm, "Diversity Among Hispanics Make For Political Disunity," *San Antonio Express-News* (Tuesday, October 13, 1998), 1A.

[105]Ibid.

[106]Arnold DeLeon, "Los Tejanos: An Overview of Their History," *The Texas Heritage*, Ben Procter and Archie McDonald, eds., 1st ed., (Ill.: Harlan Davidson, Inc., 1980), 134.

[107]Arnold DeLeon, *Mexican-Americans in Texas: A Brief History*, (Ill.: Harlan Davidson, Inc., 1991), 67.

[108]McLemore, 243.

[109]Ibid., 236-237.

[110]DeLeon, *Mexican-Americans in Texas: A Brief History*, 134.

[111]Hector Saldana, "United They Stand," *San Antonio Express-News* (Sunday, March, 31, 2002), 5J.

[112]"An Interview," *Voice of Diversity: Perspectives on American Political Ideals and Institutions*, Pat Andrews, ed., (Guilford, Conn.: The Dushkin Publishing Group, Inc., 1995), 164-165.

[113]Mark Helm, "Soldiers Blazed The Trail to Political Prominence," *San Antonio Express-News* (Sunday, October 11, 1998), 17A.

[114]McLemore, 223.

[115]DeLeon, *Mexican-Americans in Texas: A Brief History*, 66.

[116]McLemore, 238-239.

[117]Blevins, 259.

[118]McLemore, 238.

[119]Erick Schelzig, "States Immigration Laws May Not Pass Court Test," *San Antonio Express-News*, (Sunday, August 20, 2006) 8A.

[120]Pete Yost, "High Court Slaps Leash on Booting Immigrants," *San Antonio Express-News*, (Wednesday, December 6, 2006), 7A.

[102]"Deferred Deportation Plan to Begin," *San Antonio Express-News* (Sunday, August 12, 2012), A5.

[122]Tim Lopes, "Hispanic Muscle Going Unflexed," *The Houston Chronicle*, (Sunday, April 16, 1995), 6A.

[123]Gary Martin, "Latino Vote Bloc Hard to Pin Down," *San Antonio Express-News*, (Friday, October 4, 2002, 18A.

[124]Paula Petrek, "Women and The Bill of Rights,"*By and For the People: Constitutional Rights in American History*, Kermit L. Hall, ed., (Ill.: Harlan Davidson, Inc., 1991), 133.

[125]Barbara Goldsmith, "The Woman Who Set America on Its Ear," *Parade Magazine, The San Antonio Express-News* (Sunday, March 8, 1998), 14-15.

[126]Domino, 252.

[127]Paula Petrek, 134.

[128]Poole, 301.

[129]Rynder, 25.

[130]Ibid., 307.

[131]"Catharine Beecher and Harriet Beecher Stowe on Why Women Should Not Seek the Vote," *Major Problems in American Women's History,* Mary Beth Norton and Ruth M. Alexander, ed., 2nd ed., (Lexington, Mass.: D.C. Heath and Company, 1996), 169.

[132]"The Object at Hand," *Smithsonian*, Vol. 23, No. 12, March, 1993, 30.

[133]Peter Nye, "Moving from Parlor to Politics," T*he National Voter*, April/May, 1990, 14.

[134]Lisa Mundy, "America's Second Revolution," *Smithsonian*, Vol. 50, No. 1, April, 2009, 39.

[135]"The Object at Hand"

[136]Ibid.

[137]*ProQuest Statistical Abstract of the United States: 2020*, Table 258, 171.

[138]Poole, 309-310.

[139]"Separating the Sisters," *U. S. News & World Report*, (March 28, 1994), 49.

[140]Nancy R. Mudrick, "Employment Discrimination Laws for Disability: Utilization And Outcome," *The Annals of the American Academy of Political and Social Science*, Vol. 549, January, 1997, 55.

[141]Ibid., 56.

[142]Marjorie L. Baldwin, "Can the ADA Achieve Its Employment Goal?", *The Annals of the American Academy of Political and Social Science*, Vol. 549, January, 1997, 40-41.

[143]Coniff, 127.

SUGGESTED READINGS

Abraham, Henry J., and Barbara A. Perry, *Freedom & the Court: Civil Rights & Liberties in the United States,* 8th ed., Lawrence, Kansas: University Press of Kansas, 2003.

Barth, Alan. *The Rights of Free Men: An Essential Guide to Civil Liberties*. James E. Clayton, ed. New York: Alfred A. Knopf, 1987.

Conrad, Earl. *Jim Crow America*. 2d ed. New York: Duell, Sloan, and Peace, 1947.

Domino, John C. *Civil Rights and Liberties: Toward the 21st Century*. New York: HarperCollins Publishers, 1994.

McLemore S. Dale, and Harriet D. Romo, *Racial and Ethical Relations in America*, 7th Ed., Boston, Mass.: Pearson Education Inc. 2005.

Tocqueville, Alexis de. *Democracy in America*. Translated by George Lawrence, J. P. Mayer, eds. Garden City, N. Y.: Doubleday and Company, Inc., 1969.

Woodward, C. Van. *The Strange Career of Jim Crow*. 3rd ed. New York: Oxford University

Conrad, Earl. *Jim Crow America*. 2d ed. New York: Duell, Sloan, and Peace, 1947.

APPROVED

MAR 2 3 2010

President Barack Obama's signature on the Patient Protection and Affordable Care Act at the White House, March 23, 2010. The President signed the Act with 22 different pens.

Chapter Fourteen

PUBLIC POLICY

On December 31, 2019, government officials in Wuhan, China, announced dozens of its residents were suffering from an unidentified virus whose symptoms were akin to influenza or a mild case of pneumonia. With an estimated population of 11 million, Wuhan is the capitol city of the Hubi Providence. Initially, Chinese medical experts did not believe that the virus could be spread by humans. Instead, they thought customers were exposed to the disease through the poultry and animals sold at a wet market. By January 11, 2020, the Chinese government confirmed its first death from the virus. The victim was a regular customer at the Huanan Seafood Wholesale Market, a wet market in Wuhan. Wet markets are public markets that sell fresh meat, fish, produce and various perishable goods while dry markets sell durable goods. While not all wet markets sell live animals, they are known to slaughter animals and birds, particularly chickens, upon customer requests. Wet markets are not just found in China. Wet markets are located throughout the world to include the United States. American wet markets are in several states to include California and New York. There are approximately eighty wet markets in New York City alone that sell turtles, ducks, chickens, and goats. The wet markets in Southeast Asia, China, and Africa help to meet the needs of food insecure people by providing fresh meat at an affordable price.

The number of infected persons rose into the thousands in Wuhan as the virus acquired its own name—coronavirus. By January 23, 2020, the Chinese government officially sealed off Wuhan by cancelling all modes of public and private transportation in and out of the city. On January 30, the World Health Organization (WHO) declared the spreading virus "'a public health emergency of international concern. China's Foreign Ministry spokeswoman said that it would continue to work with the WHO and other countries to protect public health, and the U.S. State Department warned travelers to avoid China."[1] The disease had already infected persons in Taiwan, Japan, Thailand, South Korea and the United States. On January 31, the response from the Trump administration was to suspend entry into the United States to any foreign nationals who had traveled to China in the past fourteen days, exempting immediate family members of American citizens and permanent

U.S. residents. Despite the warnings of the WHO, leaders of the international community to include the Trump administration failed to recognize the potential seriousness of this mysterious virus.

Those believing that the virus was confined to only China were rudely awakened when the *Diamond Princess*, a cruise ship on a trip to Southwest Asia with more than 3,600 passengers, was quarantined in Yokohama, Japan. The passengers and crew members were tested for coronavirus. Test results revealed that abroad that ship was the largest number of coronavirus victims outside of China. On February 11, 2020, the WHO officially banded the name of the disease as coronavirus or Covid-19 as "the death toll in China had reached 1,113 and the total number of confirmed cases rose to 44,653. There were 393 cases outside China, in 24 countries."[2] The disease was spreading throughout Asia and Europe. In South Korea, the government's attempt to stop the spread of the disease included the closing of all kindergartens, nursing homes, community centers and the cancellation of all public events to include political rallies. By February 23, Italy began to see thousands infected with the virus resulting in hundreds of deaths and the closing of all schools and the cancellation of all group events. Reports of virus victims were reported in Iran by February 24 and in Brazil by February 26. By the end of February 2020, the disease had spread into Northern Ireland, Wales, Germany, France, England, Switzerland, Belarus, Estonia and Lithuania.

The first reported death in the United States from coronavirus happened on February 29, 2020. The Trump administration finally responded to the spreading virus by issuing a travel warning to those wanting to travel to Italy and South Korea. By March 3, the Center for Disease Control (CDC) lifted all federal restrictions to coronavirus testing while the number of infected rose to 90,000 globally with 3,000 fatalities.[3] On March 11, the WHO officially named the coronavirus a pandemic. The American stock exchange took a nosedive, the worst since the Great Depression as Trump put a thirty-day halt to any travelers from European countries with the exception of Great Britain. Finally, on March 13, President Trump declared the coronavirus outbreak in the United States a national emergency and offered $50 billion to states and territories to assist in their efforts to stop the spread of the disease. All major sporting events including the 2020 Summer Olympic games were either postponed or cancelled. Schools, colleges and universities were physically closing down, opting instead for remote learning. Retail stores, businesses and restaurants were closing their doors until further notice. By March 26, the United States was now leading the world in confirmed cases, and the nightly news broadcasts were reporting daily death tallies. Particularly hard hit was New York City. The pictures of health care workers carrying out the dead to refrigerated 18-wheelers brought home the point that this disease was not going to just go away any time soon. It took from December 31, 2019 to March 13, 2020, for the Trump administration to finally recognize the existence of the disease, the rate of infection in the United States, the rising death toll, and the catastrophic domino-effect this virus was having on the nation's economy. The excuse was that this was a first for the United States. But was it?

In 1918, Haskell County, Kansas, was farm country where crops were planted and livestock, especially hogs, were raised. The area was also a popular spot for seventeen different species of migratory birds. "Scientists today understand that bird influenza viruses, like human influenza viruses, can also infect hogs, and when a bird virus and a human virus infect the same pig cell, their different genes can be shuffled and exchanged like playing cards, resulting in a new, perhaps especially lethal, virus."[4] Although they did not know that they had been exposed to influenza, several men from Haskell County visited Camp Funston, in Kansas. They, of course, infected several soldiers who in turn, spread it to everyone else. Unknowing that they too had influenza, these soldiers were transferred to other bases. In turn, newly infected soldiers carried the disease to the civilian population. In the United States, the pandemic of 1918-19 resulted in 25.8 million infected with influenza, 670,000 dying from the disease with children under the age of five accounting for 20 percent of the deaths.[5] One of the victims was Frederick Trump, grandfather of President Trump. Due to the war effort, the disease traveled with American soldiers to the battlefields of Europe. It is "'strongly suggestive' that the disease started in the United States and spread to France with 'the arrival of American troops'. . . . the pandemic lasted just 15 months but was the deadliest disease outbreak in human history, killing between 50 million to 100 million people worldwide. . . the pandemic killed more people in a year than AIDS has killed in 40 years, more than the bubonic plague killed in a century."[6] While the death toll of the 2019-2020 coronavirus is still climbing, the suggested remedies offered by the medical experts in 1919 should sound familiar to us in 2020. Medical experts in 1919 called for more testing, development of a vaccine, expanded research for anti-viral drugs, hand washing, covering coughs, staying home when sick, and widespread closing of public venues such as schools!

The coronavirus of 2020 has shredded the American economy as manufacturing and industrial companies and businesses were closed for nearly two months. Employees were either fired or furloughed with no clear understanding when they would or if ever return to work. Many now former employees lost their company-paid health insurance. If they were hospitalized with the coronavirus and survived, they are faced with a bill for their hospital stay with basically no money on hand to pay the bill. The U.S. Department of Labor indicated that the unemployment rate in April 2019, was 3.6 percent or 5,850,000 American workers were without a job. By the end of April 2020, the unemployment rate was 14.7 percent, equating to 23,078,000 unemployed persons.[7] Even as businesses were reopening, many workers simply could not immediately return to work because their day care centers had not reopened, and public school summer programs were shelved. From the beginning of the shutdown of the economy in March 2020, food banks became the sole source of food for millions of the unemployed. Across the nation, the nightly news reports showed hundreds of cars lining up at food bank distribution centers. Tragically, as of May 28, 2020, there are approximately 1.7 million confirmed cases of coronavirus in the United States alone and over 104,000 Americans had perished from this disease. The fear was that a second wave of the disease would occur that would drive up both the numbers of those infected and unfortunately, coronavirus-related fatalities. In times of crisis, people turn to their government for answers and kind words of hope. In this situation, the Trump administration was too late in recognizing the seriousness of both the CDC's and the WHO's dire warnings about the adverse impact of this disease. Despite the cries from governors and mayors for federal help, the Trump administration's response was "too little, too late." There were not enough protective masks and clothing to protect physicians and health care workers from the disease. There were not enough ventilators to offset the breathing difficulties caused by this disease. Hospitals across the nation did not have enough beds to accommodate patients. Cities were converting convention centers, sports arenas, and abandoned hotels into makeshift hospitals. There was a severe shortage of testing materials and, of course, the promise a quickly discovered vaccine did not materialize. A study conducted by Columbia University sends a startling message that "if the United States had been imposing social distancing measures one week earlier than it did in March, about 36,000 fewer people would have died in the coronavirus outbreak. . . And if the country had begun locking down cities and limiting social contract on March 1, two weeks earlier than most people started staying home, the vast majority of the nation's deaths—about 83 percent—would have been avoided, the researchers estimated. Under that scenario, about 54,000 fewer people would have died by early May."[8]

While attempting to address the health-care crisis, the Trump administration opted to put its major emphasis on economic recovery. On March 27, 2020, President Trump signed a bi-partisan $2 trillion stimulus package with the hope of reversing negative economic trends. The goal was to get Americans back to work, back to spending money, and reopening businesses. The package included a one-time $1,200 payment to individual taxpayers, $2,400 for married couples filing jointly and $500 extra per qualifying child under the age of 17. Single individual tax filers with incomes above $75,000, married couples filing jointly with incomes above $150,000, and heads of households with dependents with an income of over $112,500 would not receive a stimulus payment. The bill also included an additional $600 per month for four months for those receiving unemployment benefits. State unemployment benefits were extended from the traditional 26 weeks to 39. The unemployment benefits were extended to furloughed workers.[9]

President Trump announced that the money would be forthcoming almost immediately. Taking the president at his word, many were daily checking their mailboxes for their checks while others were looking at the government's stimulus website to see if they qualified and how much they would receive. However, the problems in distributing the stimulus payments began immediately. Initially, stimulus payments were issued either through direct deposit or with a mailed check. The Treasury Department worked off the list of filed taxpayers without checking the status of the taxpayers. Unfortunately, thousands of checks were mailed to deceased persons. Once realizing this, the Treasury Department asked for the money to be returned. To qualify for a stimulus check, one had to have filed tax returns either in 2018 or 2019. Millions of Americans have incomes so low that by IRS guidelines, they do not have to file a tax return. Those individuals did not receive a check in the mail. Many taxpayers received their stimulus money as late as June 1, 2020, through a bank-issued debit card. Filing for unemployment was a nightmare. The unemployed must file through their individual state unemployment offices. One could not file in person because the unemployment offices were closed. The only option left was to file electronically. However, the onslaught of applications overloaded computer systems resulting in lengthy computer software crashes. Meanwhile, cash-strapped American workers who were either waiting for their stimulus payment, unemployment check, or a return to work were faced with the reality of not being able to pay the monthly mortgage or rent payment, utility bill or even buy groceries. And, the anticipated boast to the economy did not materialize as states were reluctant to reopen their economies, and the average American shopper was equally reluctant to venture out in fear of getting infected with coronavirus.

It would be easy to place the blame for the federal government's slow response to the rapid tragic spread of the pandemic and the rocky implementation of the stimulus plan squarely on the shoulders of the Trump administration. Yet, one must realize that this country has not been faced with a health crisis of this magnitude since 1919. Other nations have faced tragic health care crises such as the Ebola pandemic that swept over Africa. But, these tragic health-related crises happened on another continent or in another country. Americans saw these events on the evening news! Congress could have stepped forward and taken the lead. However, the tensions between a Democratic-controlled House and a Republican-controlled Senate made bipartisanship extremely difficult. One cannot overlook that the Democratic-controlled House impeached President Trump and subsequently, it was the Republican-controlled Senate that acquitted him of those impeachable charges. Numerous miscues and mistakes were made by both the legislative and executive branches of this government. Meanwhile, many Americans were suffering and dying from this disease. The economy was falling to dire levels not seen since the Great Depression. Americans wanted quick solutions from a government that simply could not deliver quickly crafted successful legislative responses. For one cannot overlook the fact that while public policy is itself a product of politics, the blame for policy failures cannot be solely contributed to "politics as usual." The primary cause of poorly written and ineffective public policies is the inability of both legislative houses and members of executive branch alike to follow the public policy process from start to finish. The majority of this nation's laws and city ordinances suffer from crippling design flaws that may ultimately result in policy failures.

Most lawmakers propose legislation with good intentions in mind. For example, the New Deal legislation of Franklin Roosevelt's administration that produced the modern welfare state was founded on the principles of government helping those in financial need. The Great Depression, caused by the 1929 crash of the stock market, put millions of hardworking Americans and their families out of work and one step away from starvation and potentially irreversible financial ruin. State and local governments, as well as private charities, simply did not have the resources to meet the needs of the destitute. Roosevelt reasoned that a compassionate government should without question address the needs of its people.

However, good intentions do not necessarily produce skillfully crafted and successfully implemented public policies. In the 1980s and 1990s, it became clearly evident that the welfare state created by President Franklin Roosevelt had deteriorated to the point that politicians from all political parties advocated reforming it with the ultimate goal of actually eliminating the bulk of its income support programs. A bureaucratic nightmare, the welfare system produced an economically disadvantaged underclass that became almost totally dependent upon the "system" for survival. The hardworking and over-tax-burdened middle class resented a welfare system that continuously needed more tax dollars to fund its programs, while failing to deliver on its lofty promise to eliminate poverty. Public opinion shifted from favoring a benevolent government intent on providing for everyone faced with adverse economic hardships to one that provided for only those who were not only truly desperate but willing to work for their share of the dole. The welfare system, as originally conceived, broke down. However, the welfare reform package finally enacted during the Clinton administration has not adequately addressed the needs of the nation's poor. Just establishing stiffer eligibility requirements and time limits for services does not mean that former recipients of government-sponsored income support programs have raised their income levels to the point that they no longer need government assistance. In some instances, the poor are in a worse situation because of welfare reform.

In the 1970s, Americans were awakened to the state of their deteriorating environment. Lawmakers responded by enacting corrective legislation covering an array of environmental concerns from cleaner air and water to protection of endangered plants and wildlife. Once again, good intentions did not produce effective policies. Business and industry see environmental laws laden with costly impact statements, threats of litigation, fines and penalties as cost prohibitive and unnecessary impediments to the economic viability of the free market system. On the other hand, environmentalists believe that the existing laws are just halfhearted attempts to address a potentially irreversible problem. They criticize the government for doing too little too late to save our planet. Public opinion is also divided. The average American citizen is concerned about the environment. All agree that something must be done to ensure a cleaner environment or the future of this planet may be in serious jeopardy. However, these same citizens are fearful that the expense of producing environmentally safe consumer products will be cost prohibitive. They are also concerned as to the extent of the personal sacrifices they may be asked to make to preserve the environment. Both sides are not pleased with the existing laws. On the campaign trail, candidate Donald Trump expressed his concern that federal and state environmental regulations were a hinderance to business development, particularly the oil and gas industries. As president, Trump has systematically weakened the power of environmental agencies to enforce the more rigid environmental restrictions implemented by the Obama administration.

After the tragic September 11, 2001, terrorists' attacks on the World Trade Center, the pressure was on the George W. Bush administration to reevaluate existing domestic and foreign security agencies to guarantee to the American public that this type of terrorist attack would not happen on American soil again. The Bush administration consolidated the domestic-oriented Federal Bureau of Investigation with the foreign-oriented Central Intelligence Agency under one roof—a cabinet-level Department of Homeland Security. Congress swiftly passed the Patriot Act giving federal agencies more authority over surveillance, including the monitoring of telephone and internet communications. A list of potential terrorists and terrorist sympathizers was drawn up to prevent these individuals from entering the country. Security at the airports was tightened to include personal body scans, x-raying of luggage, and restricting carry-on items. Just when Americans were beginning to feel "secure" again, on April 15, 2013, the Tsarnaev brothers ignited bombs during the Boston Marathon leaving three dead and approximately 264 injured. Among the questions posed by citizens and lawmakers alike was that with all of these new surveillance laws and security-empowered federal agencies, how could a terrorist attack on American soil happen again? What went wrong?

This chapter explores the public policy process from the inception of the concept to its final evaluation as a means of discovering exactly what goes wrong with the majority of the public policy initiatives created by the legislative and executive branches at all levels of government from the national to the city/county level. In actuality, the "process" of public policy is a series of steps that must be equally weighed in importance. Overlooking just one step can condemn a potentially successful legislative action to failure before it is even written. Public policy is more than a legislative act. The final product is the embodiment of the prevailing political, economic, social, and cultural philosophies of the time. The answers to who makes public policy begins with the average citizen and ends on the desk of the president to await its fate. While the wheeling and dealing between party leaders, legislators, and the president continues, the average citizen must pay close attention to lawmakers actions because the outcome of their decisions impacts everyone. "Public polices in a modern, complex society are indeed ubiquitous. They confer advantages and disadvantages, cause pleasure, irritation, and pain, and collectively have important consequences for our well-being and

Taxpayers had lofty desires for the space program. America won the race to place a man on the moon. Watching the lift-off of the first American in space. (L-R) Vice President Johnson, Arthur Schlesinger, Adm. Arleigh Burke, President Kennedy and Mrs. Kennedy, White House, Office of the President's Secretary. May 5, 1961..
Photo credit: Cecil Stoughton, White House/ JFK Library

happiness. They constitute a significant portion of our environment. This being so, we should know something about public policies, including how they are formed, budgeted, implemented and evaluated."[10] Eventually, the prudent student of government will conclude that "politics is about policy. The decisions that government makes are the end result of a complex process. Many potential issues never get discussed seriously by political leaders; and policy is not necessarily determined even for those issues on which serious debate takes place. Even after policies have been announced, the politics of the policy process continues, as efforts may be made to shape implementation of the program."[11] The creation of the policy is often more important than the policy itself. The success or failure of a policy initiative hinges more on how it was created, budgeted, implemented, and evaluated than the problem or issue the policy was intended to address. The process of creating public policy extends to all items of domestic and foreign policy issues and considerations. This chapter explores how to create a policy masterpiece while avoiding a policy disaster.

PUBLIC POLICY DEVELOPMENT

The term **policy** is defined as "a relatively stable, purposive course of action followed by an actor or set of actors in dealing with a problem or matter of concern."[12] Policy, therefore, is not just a statement concerning a problem or issue. It is a purposeful action designed to reach a defined goal or objective. Policy originates in both the private and public sectors with one major exception. Created by governmental bodies, **public policy** can be defined as "an officially expressed intention backed by a sanction, which can be a reward or punishment."[13] Governing institutions at all levels make public policy. Laws, edits, rules, and ordinances are public policy initiatives created by governing bodies in response to the demands of the citizens for authoritative action deemed necessary to address a public concern, issue, or need. Consequently, "public policy has an authoritative, legally coercive quality that the policies of private organizations do not have."[14] If citizens obey and follow the policy directives of their government, they are rewarded for their obedience. Contrary, citizens who disobey the laws of their government will be punished by a sanction, fine, imprisonment, or any combination thereof.

The development of public policy at any level of government is based upon four fundamental principles. First, public policy initiatives created in a democratic government are the products of conflict and accommodation. As evidenced by the day to day bickering between legislative and executive leaders, "all forms of political organization have a bias in favor of the exploitation of some kinds of conflicts and the suppression of others because organization is the mobilization of bias. Some issues are organized into politics while others are organized out."[15] The result, the policy directive, is a compromise between various factions and key governmental actors. Regardless of the issues before a legislative house, "there is opposition to virtually every policy proposal, and agreement is reached only after bargains have been struck and compromises have been agreed on."[16] Initially, the Framers envisioned lawmakers from both sides of the Congressional aisle putting aside their individual political perspectives to work together as a team with the executive branch to create meaningful legislative acts designed to address the needs of the American people. Yet, few presidential administrations have had a solid working relationship with their Congresses. The political differences between the elected representatives of the two political parties coupled with the in-fighting within the ranks of each political party have produced only a handful of bills crafted with a meaningful bipartisan spirit. Historians have noted over eighty physical clashes between congresspersons since the opening of the nation's first congressional session. Perhaps the most well-known brawl occurred on May 22, 1856, when a member of the House of Representatives barged into the Senate chamber and physically beat unconscious Senator Charles Sumner. A senator from Massachusetts, Sumner was a strong anti-slavery Republican who led the charge in blocking Kansas from entering the Union as a slave state. In his famous "Crimes Against Kansas" speech, Sumner targeted fellow Senators Stephen A. Douglas (D-Ill.) and Andrew Butler (D-SC). On the floor of the Senate, Sumner attacked Douglas as a "noise-some, squat, and nameless animal . . . not a proper model for an American Senator" and went after an absent Butler by accusing him of taking a pro-slavery mistress.[17] A close friend of Butler's, Representative Preston Brooks walked into the Senate chamber and "slammed his metal-topped cane onto the unsuspecting Sumner's head. . . Bleeding profusely, Sumner was carried away. Brooks walked calmly out of the chamber without being detained by the stunned onlookers."[18] Although physical violence has not resurfaced in these hallow legislative halls, the animosity between Democrats and Republicans have earned the title of "hostile Congress." The 2013 congressional session witnessed the most publicly aired political bickering in decades. Labeled as the "doing nothing" Congress, both political sides of the aisle spent more time in grudge matches then they did in passing legislation. The attacks went beyond political differences oftentimes resulting in insults hurled at each other. The battles centered on everything from the federal budget, Obamacare, and the confirmation of Obama's appointees. The budget impasse resulted in a complete shutdown of the federal government. The shutdown, of course, did very little to instill public confidence in the nation's foremost legislative body. The federal government was twice shutdown over Trump's immigration proposals and the building of the wall. Angry words and accusations were hurled by both House and Senate members at each other during the impeachment proceedings of President Trump. Regardless of the setting or the issue at hand, political bickering is a given in the creation of public policy initiatives. It is an extremely high stakes game with every interested party desiring to be a winner, and not a loser.

Second, public policy is a series of outputs and inputs. **"Policy outputs** are the things actually done by agencies in pursuance of policy decisions and statements."[19] For example, the policy establishing the income tax was supposed to create a progressive tax program whereby everyone would pay their proportionate share of taxes. Those with higher incomes would pay a higher amount of tax in comparison to those with lower incomes. However, subsequent policy initiatives and practices have resulted in a regressive income tax plan. By allowing deductions for a wide-range of expenditures and investments, taxpayers in the highest income brackets are actually paying a considerable lower percentage of their income toward their tax obligations than those whose earnings are in the lower income brackets.

Policy outcomes are" the consequences for society, intended or unintended, that stem from deliberate governmental action or inaction."[20] For example, the civil rights acts were enacted to ban discriminatory actions against minorities, particularly African Americans, in all areas including employment, voting, housing, education, and public accommodations. The implementation of these laws lead to profound and oftentimes violent upheavals to the political, social, and cultural traditions embraced by American society. Laws designed to eliminate discrimination by encouraging desegregation often resulted in sit-ins, race riots, violent protests, and race-related killings that further eroded the fragile relationship between the Anglo and African-American communities. The resulting lesson painfully learned by lawmakers and jurists alike was that legislative acts alone cannot change longstanding attitudes and beliefs.

Third, there is a distinct difference between decision-making and policy-making. **Decision-making** "involves making a discrete choice from among two or more alternatives," whereas, **policy-making** "typically encompasses a flow and pattern of action that extends over time and includes many decisions, some routine and some not so routine."[21] Decisions are made on a daily basis, often without the benefit of a deliberation process. To be effective, policy decisions must be treated as purposeful deliberative actions resulting from an intense and often lengthy planning process. Quick decisions on the part of lawmakers can have disastrous policy results.

Fourth, the taxpayer demands that lawmakers create policies that are both cost-effective and successful in achieving intended goals and objectives, subsequently, "the need is to design realistic goals that embrace a balance between efficiency and effectiveness."[22] Efficiency and effectiveness are often diametrically opposed to each other. For example, the national space program is an expensive project. Americans expect the space program to launch space shuttles, build space stations, and explore the galaxy at the cheapest cost possible. Far too often taxpayers' expectations are lofty desires that cannot be fulfilled by lawmakers. There can be a balance between efficiency, effectiveness, and cost. However, in the case of the space program and other government programs, the quality and quantity of the service is questionable when the budget alone guides the policy decision process.

Who Makes Public Policy?

There is a multiplicity of key actors in the public policy process. Each actor plays an essential role in the creation, implementation, and evaluation of a policy directive. The interplay between the actors is politics at its best and worst.

Public opinion does play a vital role in determining the scope and response of policy issues and outcomes. Basically, public opinion is collectively "those public perspectives or viewpoints on policy issues that public officials consider or take into account in making decisions."[23] Elected officials do listen to public opinion. Input from concerned citizens is essential to a democratic government. Citizens express their concerns through public opinion polls and, most importantly, the ballot box. Despite the oftentimes fickleness of public opinion, it is a truism in politics that those "elected public officials who totally ignore public opinion and do not include it among their criteria for decisions, should any be so foolish, are likely to find themselves out of luck at election time."[24] However, public opinion is hard for lawmakers to gage on a long-term basis since it is so unpredictable. Surveys reveal that public opinion can change from staunchly supporting a policy decision to hostility against it. The public unrealistically wants immediate actions from their lawmakers that miraculously address their concerns. A disappointed public can turn government on its backside without mercy. The Democrats were able to hold onto their majority status in both the House and the Senate and win the White House in 2008 due to a large extent on the unpopularity of the Bush presidency's policies in both Iraq and Afghanistan as well as the failure of his administration to successfully address an already declining economy. In 2010, the Democrats lost the majority in the House. The 2012 election cycle gave Obama a second term, but the Republicans maintained their majority in the House and the Democrats kept control of the Senate. The 2014 midterm elections shifted leadership in the Senate to the Republicans. The 2016 presidential election was a sweep for Republicans who maintained their majorities in both houses of Congress and won the top prize— the White House. The 2018 election took its toll on the Trump administration. Republicans were soundly defeated in the House, opening the door for the newly elected Speaker of the House Nancy Pelosi to ponder impeaching the president. When Trump delivered his 2020 State of the Union address to a joint session of Congress, Pelosi tore up her copy of his speech while Trump was delivering it. In the Senate, Republicans maintained their majority, but the margin was significantly narrowed with Democrat victories. Dealing with the tragic impact of the coronavirus and the rapidly declining economy, the American public needs more from their legislative bodies than media coverage of their conflicts. In particular with this crisis in mind, "the American public does not seem to feel that the government copes very well at all. Congress has been portrayed as unproductive and spineless, unwilling to tackle the tough problems that require discipline or sacrifice."[25]

Interest groups play an extremely important role in the policy process. The 1960s saw the rapid rise of liberal citizen groups advocating a wide range of issue positions from anti-war protests to voting rights, equal opportunity, and environmental concerns. Today, a wide range of citizen or social movement groups have impacted public policy decisions in "defense and foreign affairs; health care policy pertaining to AIDS and abortion; environmental protection; and the rights of various groups including women, gays, the handicapped, the homeless, and racial and ethnic minorities."[26] The Framers were concerned that interest groups would eventually fragment and destroy the collective spirit of community and nationalism. In actuality, the growth of interest groups has strengthened the democratic nature of the political system. "The rise of liberal citizen groups was largely responsible for catalyzing an explosion in the growth of all interest groups. Efforts to limit the impact of liberal citizen groups failed, and the policy-making process became more open and more participatory."[27] Openness and transparency demanded that lawmakers change their approach towards interest groups. "Policymaking moved away from the closed subgovernments, each involving a relatively stable and restricted group of lobbyists and key government officials to much broader policymaking communities. Policymaking in earlier years is typically described as a product of consensual negotiations between a small number of back-scratching participants."[28] Once confined to closed-door meetings, congressional hearings are now fully open to the public through the watchful eyes of the media. Cable television networks now offer continuous daily broadcasts of congressional committee hearings. The media has helped to keep those once closed doors wide open to the public. Currently aligned with the conservative wing of the Republican Party, the Tea Party Movement's agenda includes a provision that whenever a law is introduced into one of the legislative houses, the full text of the law is placed on the internet so citizens can read a proposed legislative act in its entirety before a congressional vote is cast. They simply want more transparency in government.

The past fifty years have also witnessed a change in the tactics traditionally used by social movement groups. The 1960s style of haphazardly organized protest movements, massive rallies, sit-ins, and, sometimes, violent displays of behavior have been replaced by well-organized "going public" media campaigns; professionally trained lobbyists sitting side by side those representing economic and business interests; well-financed and highly visible political action committees capable of raising large sums of money for candidates garnering the groups' public endorsements; a cadre of well-prepared attorneys poised to use litigation through the courts whenever the legislative side of government fails to push their causes; and a well-organized structure of locally-based chapters guided by a strong national organization capable of mobilizing its membership on a very short notice. Today, citizen or social movement interest groups resemble a corporate structure.

It has also become more difficult for lawmakers to successfully fulfill the requests of social movement groups since many of these organizations are apt to pursue narrowly defined ideological issues such as abortion, school prayer, environmental concerns, and so on. The traditional public policy approach rested on the belief that consensus is a compromised product of conflict and accommodation with each participant able to claim a partial victory. Unfortunately, lawmakers find compromise oftentimes impossible when working with groups that take an "all or nothing" approach. "Democracy requires adequate representation of interests as well as institutions capable of addressing difficult policy problems. For policy makers who must balance the demand for representation with the need for results, the key is thinking creatively about how to build coalitions and structure negotiations between large groups of actors."[29] Far too often, the agenda items of social movements are in direct conflict with the business and economic interests of this country, placing lawmakers in a perilously difficult and often impossible position of trying to broker a compromise.

There are noticeable pros and cons to interest group involvement in the public policy arena. "On the positive side, interest group politics create a dynamism, often through conflict, that draws out diversity in policy proposals, a diversity producing innovation and social change. Interest groups also provide access for the public to effect government decision-making . . . . On the negative side, interest groups fighting for their special goals can fragment the policy process. This struggle reduces the leadership's capacity to direct citizen demands toward an effective solution, promoting instead a compromise that may partially satisfy each group but not resolve the initial issue."[30]

Political parties exert their influence directly on public policy issues by electing lawmakers. It is the elected official's primary responsibility to his/her political party to actively pursue the agenda outlined in their party's platform. The leadership of legislative houses is controlled by the political parties. Loyalty to one's political party and its agenda can mean a key committee assignment for a legislator. Unlike interest groups, political parties are board-based umbrella organizations pursuing a multiplicity of diverse policy items. "Generally, parties have a broader range of policy concerns than do interest groups; hence, they act more as brokers than as advocates for particular interests in policy formation."[31] The credibility of a political party rests solely with the ability of its elected party members to enact public policy on behalf of their party.

Since both the president and members of Congress are popularly elected representatives of their respective political parties, the roles they play in the development of public policy are paramount throughout the process. As lawmakers, they must take on issues concerning the few and transform them into policies potentially benefiting the many. The Framers compounded the complexity of this task by creating a two-house (bicameral) legislature charged with different focuses. The House of Representatives was designed to serve regional needs. Members of the House are obligated to pursue issues beneficial to his/her constituents. A congressperson voting against a legislative act

President Reagan holds a National Security Council meeting on the Persian Gulf with National Security Advisor Colin Powell in the Oval Office. April 18, 1988.

potentially beneficial to his/her constituents could pay a career-ending price on election day. In contrast, senators are focused more on the needs of the nation as a whole. However, they too must ensure that what benefits the whole will to some degree benefit the state they represent. Basically, "representatives tend to be known as subject matter 'specialists' while senators tend to be 'generalists.' If the Senate has been the nation's great forum, a representative said, then the House has been its workshop."[32] Sometimes enacting what is morally and ethically correct conflicts with what is politically correct. Members of Congress are also members of their respective political parties and their ideological positions. It is a duty of congressional party leaders to constantly remind members of their party loyalties wherever a key vote is on the floor.

Since the executive is constitutionally bound to work with the legislature, the president oftentimes finds himself in the middle of the congressional fray. In 1936, President Franklin Roosevelt, a Democrat, remarked on a comment made by his Republican cousin: "Theodore Roosevelt said, 'Sometimes I wish I could be president and Congress too.' Well, I suppose if the truth be told, he is not the only president that has had that idea."[33] Franklin Roosevelt was merely echoing the frustrations all presidents have had in their dealings with the legislative branch. Executive-legislative relationships do shape the course of public policy. Legislatively successful presidents have developed a strong positive working relationship with their Congresses. Of course, the relationship is far smoother if the president's political party holds the majority of the seats in both Houses. Nevertheless, presidents do exercise influence at all levels of the legislative process to include the ultimate threat and/or use of the veto.

Beginning with George Washington, every resident of the Oval Office wants future generations to know his particular impact on American history. "It has been a habit of presidents to try to write their own history, to establish themselves as a legitimate embodiment of America's past and shaper of America's future."[34] A president's legacy is seen through the legislation passed during his administration. Therefore, it is imperative that the president and his White House staff play an important role in the development and eventual implementation of public policy. Presidents officially inform Congress about their policy agendas through their yearly delivery of the State of the Union message. Realizing they have only four, or if lucky, eight years in office, presidents are prone to promise too much in the beginning, only to see their lofty expectations reduced by Congress into piecemeal legislative victories. Richard Nixon appeared to be totally prepared for the reality of Washington, D.C. However, "for a man with a perfect resume to become president— military officer, congressman, senator, vice-president for eight years—it was surprising how much Nixon's views on policy making changed in the first two years of his administration."[35] Initially, Nixon advocated complete and expedient elimination of the Great Society programs that were the cornerstone of the Johnson administration. He quickly found himself at odds with his staff over the appropriate approach his administration should take with Congress. "Thus, the administration's initial problem was not deciding what its policies were, instead it was converting campaign policy positions to the 'bullet proof' presidential messages and detailed draft legislation that can achieve major changes in public policy."[36] Nixon quickly found out what every president has discovered, that Congress is reluctant to approve quick sweeping changes advocated by the White House. Instead, they prefer to take several small steps rather than one large leap. After pressure from congressional Republicans and the White House staff, a staff person noted that "a consensus emerged that the president [Nixon] should launch relatively few initiatives, because we could not

**President Bush signing the Americans With Disabilities Act in the Rose Garden of the White House.
July 26, 1990. Photo credit: George Bush Presidential Library**

afford many; we needed to be bold, but we needed to get results; and we needed to communicate a focused approach."[37]

However, the congressional incremental approach can be extremely frustrating for presidents. For example, in 1946, President Harry Truman was determined that he would desegregate all branches of the military's officer corps. Truman was facing pressure from civil rights organizations to fulfill his campaign promises. "Harry Truman was crude and ineloquent, but he made tough decisions and got them mostly right (a view that stands up well)."[38] Bypassing Congress and his own party's congressional leadership, Truman took the initiative by issuing an executive order. Truman's action changed the leadership core of the nation's military branches. Traditionally, African Americans and other minority military personnel were limited to non-leadership roles. Truman's desegregation plan provided the impetus for minorities to strive for officer positions. Colin Powell was able to become the first African American to be named the Chairman of the Joint Chiefs of Staff, and ultimately, Secretary of State in part because Harry Truman could not wait for Congress to drag its collective feet. With or without the blessings of Congress, presidents can and do exert a tremendous impact on the direction of this nation's domestic and foreign policy initiatives.

The **media** has a direct role in public policy by bringing sensitive issues to the public's attention, and playing a key role in shaping public opinion. The key for government agencies and elected officials is to learn how use the media to their advantage. "President Bill Clinton, for one, showed extraordinary talent at using direct televised presidential addresses and nationally televised 'town meetings' to reach citizens in the studio audience and nationwide audiences who witnessed and identified with this direct interaction. . . . some commentators have observed that part of President Clinton's skill in influencing (and some would say misleading) public opinion about his sexual affairs later aggravated his legal and constitutional problems—and as with his State of the Union address during his trial, helped him survive those challenges."[39]

Traditionally, **bureaucrats** were viewed as mere implementors of public policy with little impact on the development of policy directives. This perspective has changed dramatically. "Although it was once common doctrine in political science that administrative agencies only carried into effect, more or less automatically, policies determined by the 'political' branches of government, now it is axiomatic that politics and administration are blended, and that administrative agencies are often significantly involved in the formation of public policies. This is particularly apparent, given the concept of policy as encompassing what government actually does over time concerning a problem or situation."[40] Consequently, bureaucracies do shape public policy. Bureaucratic agencies begin their influence at the initial stages of policy development. Lawmakers are not experts on every policy issue. They rely upon bureaucratic agencies to provide research and testimony before committee hearings. Their input can determine the course of action Congress will eventually take on a policy issue. However, federal agencies will also flex their muscles to block unfavorable legislation by actively lobbying members of Congress and soliciting the support of key interest groups. In addition, bureaucracies can make or break policy initiatives simply by the manner in which agencies implement a new policy directive. Bureaucrats can control the fate of any law since the majority of the congressional legislation leaves implementation schemes totally in the hands of the responsible federal agency.

Many federal, state, and local laws have been overturned by the federal courts. The **judiciary** does make public policy whenever it declares a law unconstitutional. **Article VI** of the United States Constitution called the **Supremacy Clause** has been interpreted to allow the United States federal courts to rule any law passed at any level of government as unconstitutional when that law conflicts with the spirit and meaning of the United States Constitution. The power of **judicial review** has compelled government at all levels to reconsider its course of public policy options. A judge's gavel makes public policy!

The Supreme Court's 1954 ruling in *Brown v Board of Education of Topeka, Kansas*, began the modern civil rights movement. The United States Congress and state legislative houses began to pass laws reversing over one hundred years of discriminatory practices aimed at minorities. The *Roe v Wade* (1973) decision overturned about forty-six state laws prohibiting elective abortion procedures. In 2005, the Supreme Court handed down two significant rulings involving criminal procedures used by state courts nationwide. First, the Court declared the federal sentencing guidelines established by Congress two decades ago as unconstitutional. Basically, "the Supreme Court said making the guidelines mandatory violated a defendant's Sixth Amendment right to a jury trial because they call for judges to make factual decisions that affect prison time. Under the ruling [of the Supreme Court] the guidelines are now only advisory; federal judges are free to sentence convicted criminals as they see fit, but they may be subject to reversal if appeals courts find them 'unreasonable.'"[41] The Supreme Court also ruled that the application of the death penalty to defendants under the age of eighteen is a violation of the Eighth Amendment's prohibition against cruel and unusual punishment. As the nation's court-of-last-resort, there can be no appeals of the body's decisions.

In summary, the key actors in the public policy process are the public, interest groups, political parties, the media, the bureaucracy, the courts, and elected officials. All of these actors play a key role in shaping public policy. All public policy is a byproduct of conflict, consensus, accommodation, and compromise among these essential policy actors.

What is the Purpose of Public Policy?

Governments enact public policy in response to the public's demand to address an on-going or new concern, issue or problem. Far too often the initial approach taken by government to address the nation's on-going pressing issues failed to accomplish its stated goals and objectives. Hopefully, corrective public policy will present a new alternative or change from the traditional approach. Also, government may not have had to respond to this policy concern before. The Framers did not address such issues as the environment, air traffic, radio and television programming issues, and so on. In the early 1800s, the environment was not an issue, much less a potential threat to the survival of mankind.

Through public policy, government at any level must be able to enforce legislative acts either through sanctions, fines, or imprisonment for noncompliance. "Consequently, it must be clearly understood that all public policies are coercive, even when they are motivated by the best and most beneficent of intentions . . . . For us, the coercive element in public policy should instill not absolute opposition but a healthy respect for the risks as well as the good that may be inherent in any public policy."[42] In other words, public policy through its enforcement mechanisms, modifies our behavior and, in some cases, changes our perspectives. Few of us like to drive the posted speed limit. But we definitely modify our driving habits to the mandated speed when we see the police car in front of us since we all want to avoid a costly ticket.

The primary purpose of law enforcement is to serve as a visible deterrent to crime. Criminal statutes and civil fines and penalties are attached to each criminal activity to warn an individual of the consequences of his/her criminal actions. The problem confronting law enforcement is the same problem faced by the Environmental Protection Agency, the Immigration Service, Internal Revenue Service, and any other government agency charged with enforcing a government policy. By May 2020, state and local governments were trying to figure out how to reopen their economies with the ultimate goals of re-energizing their economies while at the same time enabling people to return to their normal lives without getting infected with the coronavirus. Medical experts, governors, and mayors alike all stressed the necessity for social distancing and for individuals to wear face masks in public. Local communities warned residents that they could be ticketed or even arrested for non-compliance. But state and local leaders soon realized that once "the flood gates were opened," enforcing compliance was going to be virtually impossible. Basically, how can government ensure that the penalties for noncompliance are severe enough to mandate compliance and deter a would be violator? As we will discover, government at all levels has failed to find the absolute deterrent penalty.

Governments can use a variety of tools besides laws to force behavior modifications. The direct approach is through contracting and licensing. **Government contracts** contain mandates that the recipient must enact or face losing the contract. A federal housing contract, for example, will specify the types of approved building materials, construction methods, inspection criteria, and so forth to include compliance with federal laws, such as the Equal Employment Opportunity Act, Occupational Safety and Health Act, Americans with Disabilities Act, and wage and labor laws. To enforce these requirements, each segment of the construction project must be open to inspection by federal agents before the next phase can begin. Noncompliance means loss of existing and, perhaps, future contracts. The contract mandates ensure that taxpayer money will produce a properly constructed product at the best possible price.

A **license** is "a privilege granted by government to do something that it otherwise considers to be illegal."[43] A license compels behavior modification by forcing the recipient to comply with industry or professional standards. Noncompliance can mean revoking the license and denying the recipient to practice his/her own profession. The threat of removing the license should ensure proper professional conduct. Teachers, doctors, lawyers, and even plumbers and hairdressers must be licensed by their state governments to practice their trades.

Particularly in the foreign policy arena, nations such as the United States, are more apt to use sanctions rather than full-scale warfare as a viable option to force weaker nations to comply with their demands. **Sanctions** are "the penalties meted out as consequences of illegal conduct."[44] Sanctions can range from economic restrictions on exports and imports, suspension of diplomatic ties, to limited military intervention. For example, the United States government severed all diplomatic ties with Cuba following Castro's rise to power in 1959. In addition, the United States issued an economic embargo prohibiting any shipments of cigars and sugar from the island nation into American ports. During his administration, President Obama wanted to re-establish diplomatic ties with Cuba particularly after the death of Fidel Castro. He ordered the re-opening of the American Embassy in Havana and the exchange of ambassadorial delegations. However, the Trump administration reversed Obama's efforts and re-imposed sanctions on Cuba. The Obama administration used sanctions against Russia after the Russian military intervened in Ukraine. Obama joined member nations of the European Union and other international organizations in condemning Russia's brutal invasion. Russia, in turn, leveled its own series of sanctions to include a total ban on food imports from the European Union, the United States, Norway, Canada and Australia. Obama went a step further in freezing American bank accounts and investments held by Russian oligarchs. One of the issues surrounding the 2016 presidential election was the charge that the Russian government through various intermediaries had directly and indirectly interfered in the election in hopes Donald Trump would win the presidency. The accusations are based on the premise that once elected, Trump would lift the sanctions imposed on Russia. Yet, the Trump administration has imposed its own series of sanctions on Middle Eastern nations, Russia, etc. The most punitive sanctions have been imposed on China, leading to a trade war adversely impacting both the American and Chinese economies. Sanctions, however, must be used with caution. "In absence of an international executive to enforce the law, the imposition of sanctions depends upon the degree of consensus in the international community and on the willingness of each member of the state system to accept responsibility to uphold the law. To be effective in specific cases, sanctions must create more hardship for the offending state than is created for the states applying the sanctions."[45] Severe sanctions can be an effective short-term plan to modify the offending nation's behavior as long as the entire international community abides by them. Gulf War I was fought by the international community against Iraq's invasion of Kuwait. Suffering a humiliating defeat, Iraq was placed under severe sanctions levied by the United Nations. The Iraqi government could only sell a predetermined amount of oil with the understanding that the generated revenues could be used only for food and medical necessities. The Iraqi government tried every conceivable way to circumvent the sanctions while at the same time, showing media coverage of the adverse impact the imposed sanctions were having on the Iraqi people. Years of economic sanctions did not produce the anticipated goal of crippling the Iraqi government. The Trump administration has leveled economically punitive sanctions on both Iran and North Korea aimed at ending both nations developing nuclear programs. The success of these sanctions is questionable since North Korea occasionally continues to test-fire what it contends to be a nuclear missile, and the Iranian government continues to promote its own nuclear program as a domestic effort to modernize its nation rather than to launch an offensive attack.

Indirectly, every citizen's spending habits are governmentally controlled through taxing, banking, and pricing policies. The on-going tensions in the oil-rich Middle East plays havoc with the price of gasoline at the pump. For example, political tensions and regional government instability throughout the Middle East heightened after Saddam Hussein's invasion of Kuwait and President George H.W. Bush's military initiative to liberate it. In the United States, the price of a gallon of regular grade gasoline quickly rose to over four dollars in some areas of the country. The rapid increase in the price of gasoline forced drivers to use their vehicles less frequently than when gasoline prices were lower. Drivers began to conserve fuel opting for either carpooling or using public transportation. Once the prices went down, drivers reverted back to their old ways.

An **economic stimulus package** is "a package of economic measures put together by a government to stimulate a foundering economy. The objective of a stimulus package is to reinvigorate the economy and prevent or reserve a recession by boosting employment and spending."[46] When the Stock Market crashed in 1929, the pressure was on President Hoover to "stop the bleeding" by using federal money to reverse the dramatic economic trends. Yet, Hoover would not budge. He held that "government borrowing . . . is a device to load our extravagance and waste on the next generation. But increasing government debts can carry immediate punishment, for that is the road to inflation. There is far more courage in reducing our gigantic national debt than increasing it. And that is a duty to our children."[47] While desiring to reduce the nation's debt is an admirable goal, it is not an appropriate option when the nation's economy is in deep peril. It was up to Hoover's successor Franklin Roosevelt to launch a massive federally backed stimulus economic plan. The argument rested on the premise that if the economy slumps and unemployment increases, it is time for the federal government to open its purse and pour money into the economy. Money from the public sector (the federal government) is placed into the hands of the private sector (businesses, industry, consumers, workers, etc.) in hopes that the private sector will now have the economic means and the confidence to spend money, buy more goods, and put the unemployed back to work. Since the Great Depression, any downturn in the nation's economy has moved presidents to do what Franklin Roosevelt did in 1932. In February 1993, President Bill Clinton launched his own stimulus package by asking Congress to spend "roughly $16 billion more in the current fiscal year—partly for grants to the states to build new highways and for an extension of unemployment insurance to the long-term jobless . . . $15 billion in new tax breaks, including an investment tax to spark businesses' spending on plants and equipment."[48] To pay for this, Clinton offered tax increases designed to stimulate the struggling economy while at the same time, reduce the nation's deficit by raising taxes on everything from personal incomes to cigarettes and alcoholic beverages. The Clinton stimulus package did enable the economy to make a marginal recovery. In 2008, newly elected President Obama was confronted with once again, a struggling economy. The Obama team pushed Congress to enact another stimulus package—the **American Recovery and Reinvestment Act**. "The approximate cost of the stimulus package was estimated to be $787 billion at the time of passage, later revised to $831 billion between 2009 and 2019."[49] The package included tax reductions for both individuals and companies, increased federal funding for Medicaid, COBRA, the Veterans Health Administration, and community and military hospitals, a boost to federal education funding to include Pell Grants and Head Start programs, additional funding for re-training programs for the unemployed, increased allocations for food banks, Meal on Wheels and free school lunch programs, increased federal spending for infrastructure projects particularly for highways and bridge construction, and approximately $27.2 billion for a wide-range of energy efficiency and renewable energy projects.[50] The first phase of the Trump administration's stimulus package was aimed at putting federal money directly into the consumer's hands to prompt them to begin buying goods and services from the private business sector. Instead recipients used the money to catch up on their mounting outstanding debts. Subsequently, the administration enacted two additional stimulus packages that once again did little to reverse declining economic trends. When asked whether the Trump administration would push for a fourth stimulus package, Kevin Hassett, chairman of the Council of Economic Advisors, remarked "I think that it's premature given that the $9 trillion of aid that passed in the last three phases, given that it is still out there and there's still a bunch of it that's going to be delivered over the next month. We think that we have a little moment . . . the luxury of a moment to learn about what's going on so that the next step that we take can be prudent."[51]

Government can modify our use of certain products and public services by charging us a fee. **User fees** or charges are "specified sums that consumers of a government service pay to receive that service."[52] The United States Park Service assesses a higher user fee for those individuals utilizing the nation's parks. The Service wanted to provide additional protection to wildlife and parklands by reducing the number of visitors and campers to these sites. Park rangers used to charge a fee for each vehicle that entered a park, regardless of the number of individuals in the vehicle. The new regulations stipulate that each person in the vehicle will pay a fee to use the parks. The per-person fee has accomplished its intended purpose of reducing the number of visitors. User fees provide governments at all levels with the mechanisms to control the use of the service while at the same time provide additional revenue for the maintenance and delivery of that service.

Unfortunately, severe legislative impasses between Congress and the president have resulted in a partial or complete shutdown of the federal government. Presidents opt for a shutdown in hopes that the ire of the American public will be intense enough to move their elected congresspersons to mend their fences with the White House and at least meet the president half-way. Even a partial government shut down adversely impacts everyone. It is very frustrating for an individual who needs to contact the Social Security office about their benefits, a taxpayer seeking assistance from the Internal Revenue Service, etc., to send that e-mail or make a phone call to only receive the message that the office is closed! A full government shut down reminds everyone just how dependent they are upon their government. In 1995-1996, President Clinton ordered a government shutdown lasting for twenty-one days over his opposition to Congress imposing what he considered to be draconian budget cuts. In 2013, President Obama shutdown the government for sixteen days over Republican congressional opposition over the implementation of his **Patient Protection and Affordable Care Act**, commonly known as Obamacare. The Trump administration bears the distinction of evoking two shutdowns with the 2018-2019, one being the longest one to date. The first shutdown was in January 2018, when Congress failed to pass a budget, opting instead for three short term budget authorizations. The major issue was House Democrats insisting that the budget had to include funding for Deferred Action for Childhood Arrivals (DECA) and assurances that children under the DREAM Act would not be deported. In 2018-2019, the thirty-five day shutdown was over Trump's dispute with Congress, particularly with House Democrats, over funding for his U.S.-Mexico border wall. While shutdowns pit a defiant president against an equally defiant Congress, they adversely harm the American economy. Government employees are furloughed, some losing their health care benefits. There is a significant downturn in economic growth. The first Trump-generated government shutdown affected all federal government agencies, furloughing approximately 692,900 federal employees while the second one furloughed approximately 380,000 employees. The cost of both shutdowns amounted to an approximate $5 billion in lost revenue.[53]

The Public Policy Process

The development of public policy is "analogous to biological natural selection. In what we have called the policy primeval soup, many ideas float around, encountering new ideas, and forming combinations and recombinations . . . . Through the imposition of criteria by which some ideas are selected out for survival while others are discarded, order is developed from chaos, pattern from randomness. These criteria include technical feasibility, congruence with values of community members, and the anticipation of culture constraints, including a budget constraint, public acceptability, and politician's receptivity."[54] The **process** of developing the policy is the key to creating effective policy initiatives. The task confronting lawmakers is a difficult one. However, "legislators and other policy formulators can go a long way toward assuring effective policy implementation if they see that a statute incorporates a sound technical theory, provides precise and clearly ranked objectives, and structures the implementation process in a wide number of ways so as to maximize the probability of target group compliance. In addition, they can take positive steps to appoint skillful and supportive implementing officials, to provide adequate appropriations and to monitor carefully the behavior of implementing agencies throughout the long implementation process, and to be aware of the effects of changing socio-economic conditions and of new legislation (even in supposedly unrelated areas) on the original statute."[55] Lawmakers can make good laws if they are totally committed to the process from the start to the finish. The process involves eight crucial steps. Each step is vital to the success of the policy initiative and must be afforded equal attention. If one step is marginally treated or overlooked, the policy initiative, no matter how necessary, will usually fail. Bad ineffective public policy is the result of poor planning. The process begins with the difficult task of identifying the problem and ends with an evaluation of the resulting policy initiative.

Problem Identification

The first step confronting lawmakers is to identify the problem. A **policy problem** is "a condition or situation that produces needs or dissatisfaction among people and for which relief or redress by

The most significant reform enacted in 1935 was the Social Security Act.

governmental action is sought."[56] Not all issues and concerns expressed by the general public will become policy problems requiring government action. Far too often, city halls are faced with the ire of one citizen who wants council to pass an ordinance addressing his one particular concern, a concern that may not be an issue for anyone else. For example, Mrs. Brown claims that her trash cans are being periodically damaged by city trash crews. She calls her councilperson demanding that city leaders pass an ordinance fining garbage workers for abusing garbage containers. Of course, she is the only one making this request. City Council members simply cannot do this because identified "public problems are those affecting a substantial number of people and having broad effects, including consequences for persons not directly involved. Such occurrences as dirty air, unwholesome food, the practice of abortion, urban traffic congestion, crowded prisons, and global warming are conditions that may become public problems if they produce sufficient anxiety, discontent, or dissatisfaction to cause many people to seek governmental remedies."[57]

Generally, public policy problems fall into one of two categories, namely foreign and domestic, however, foreign policy decisions can positively and negatively impact domestic considerations and vice versa. For example, President Jimmy Carter decided to punish the former Soviet Union over its invasion of Afghanistan by cancelling wheat shipments to the Soviets. The Soviet Union had been experiencing severe grain shortages caused by over ten years of crop failures. The United States Department of Agriculture purchased wheat from American farmers only to ship it free to the Soviets. Cash-strapped farmers were relieved that their surplus grain stored in silos had finally found a buyer. The subsequent grain embargo cost farmers dearly and created a domestic policy embarrassment for the Carter administration. This breakdown in the wall of separation between domestic and foreign policy has produced "**intermestic issues**," that is, "those issues (such as trade, finance, pollution, energy, terrorism, human rights, etc.) which overlapped the foreign and domestic policy boundaries."[58] Lawmakers are confronted with the realization that their actions on internal

**LBJ and Harry Truman
(day of Medicare Bill Signing).
July 30, 1965**

or domestic issues effect foreign policy matters and vice versa. Consequently, the public policy arena has become more complex.

There is also a noticeable difference between substantive and procedural problems. "**Procedural problems** relate to how government is organized, and how it conducts its operations and activities. **Substantive problems** are concerned with the actual consequences of human activity, whether it involves free speech, the sale of used cars or environmental pollution."[59] Each problem area demands unique policy directives to address the issues and concerns.

Too often legislation treats what the problem causes without actually solving the problem. "The effort to define a problem by identifying the causes of broad conditions rests on a certain conception of cause. In this conception, any problem has deep or primary causes that can be found if one only looks hard enough and does careful research.... Once 'the' cause is identified, policy should seek to eliminate it, modify it, reduce it, suppress it, or neutralize it, thereby eliminating or reducing the problem."[60] The contributing factors or **causal factors** should be the targets of legislative action if lawmakers want to solve the problem. The solution to crime is not just arresting more people and building more jails. Today, the United States has a record number of prisons; court dockets are teeming with new criminal cases; more people are being arrested; and convicts are serving longer sentences without parole. The crime rate is declining for some offenses. However, crime has not been eliminated. The actual criminal act is the end result stemming from a multiplicity of complex causal factors. The solution to crime rests, in part, with adequately identifying the causal factors that motivate a person to commit a crime.

Oftentimes, lawmakers believe they have identified the correct casual factors only to find out that they have wasted their energies by focusing on something that is closely associated with the problem but is not the cause of the problem in the first place. For example in the fourteenth and seventeenth centuries, the Bubonic Plague, or Black Death, killed thousands of people in Europe and England. Initially, lawmakers were convinced that the disease was being spread by rats. The public policy decision was to kill the rats and destroy the homes and personal belongings of the dead. The Plague, however, remained. Lawmakers overlooked the actual cause of the disease. True, rats and their fleas spread the disease to humans, but the real culprit was the living style of the citizens. Residents threw trash out into the streets, and personal waste was pitched into open sewers. The rats and their fleas were thriving in the debris. The solution to curing the disease was to eliminate the cause by encouraging healthier personal habits and proper sanitation procedures. Through corrective legislation backed by sanctions, personal and sanitation habits improved as the rats, their fleas, and the disease disappeared.

Another consideration is the distinct difference between a crisis situation and a problem. The policy responses are significantly different for both situations. A crisis situation demands an immediate short-term response from government. In the case of an advancing hurricane, prudent evacuation plans must be executed to remove people, their pets, and livestock from rising waters. Temporary housing, food, and clothing for the displaced, heavy equipment to clear roadways and restore public utilities, clean drinking water, medical services, and so on are the prudent and necessary responses required to address the crisis. The same short-term crisis responses would apply to any natural or man-made disaster. The long-term problem, however, involves an in-depth analysis of what caused the problem in the first place. In the case of a hurricane, the long-term solution rests with tactics to minimize property loss and eliminate loss of life when the next storm comes ashore. In the case of New Orleans, the federal Army Corps of Engineers was deemed responsible for the collapse of the levees that failed to hold back the surge of wind-swept water generated by the fury of Katrina. The Corps' task is to rebuild those levees to ensure that they will hold up against a Category 5 hurricane storm surge. Along the Gulf Coast and interior flood-prone areas, such as San Antonio, Texas, the emphasis has been on flood control projects. Although expensive undertakings, underground drainage systems take flood waters away from central business districts to rural areas, thus minimizing both loss of life and property damage. City ordinances have been passed prohibiting flooded out residents from rebuilding their homes in flood-plain areas. Turning traditionally flooding personal properties into public parklands means less costly rescues, property damage and, of course, loss of life. In the case of the wildfires that raged in California, Colorado, Texas, and Utah, part of the long-term problem is to clear-out dying bush in forest areas caused by long-term droughts. County and local governments need to revise their zoning regulations to prevent residential construction in wilderness areas. While one may want privacy and an unobstructed view of the countryside, living in a canyon or on a mountain side comes with the reality that the property is probably not easily accessible to emergency vehicles nor is there even a fire hydrant near one's property line. A prudent in-depth analysis can produce successful long-term solutions. However, when lawmakers treat problems as crises, unfortunately the problems will never be adequately addressed or solved.

Lawmakers must also avoid the trap of allowing public opinion to turn a problem into a crisis. Public outcry is not necessarily a crisis situation. The senseless tragic bombing of a federal building in Oklahoma City, Oklahoma, was caused by two individuals marginally associated with a paramilitary anti-government group. Likewise, James Byrd, an African American, was dragged to his death by three men advocating the racial hatred espoused by the Ku Klux Klan. The existence of these anti-government and racial hatred groups is a problem, but not a crisis. Although the ideological foundations of these groups are objectionable to the majority of the American people, the United States Constitution does guarantee the right of association. The document does not distinguish between acceptable and unacceptable groups. This nation's lawmakers can not overreact by passing legislation forbidding association with racially objectionable groups. The rational approach is to hold individuals legally accountable when their actions, whether they be guided by their affiliation to a racial supremacy group, caused harm to individuals or their property.

Agenda Building

Once the causal factors have been identified, an agenda, or action plan, must be developed. The agenda is the embodiment of the philosophical and technical approaches to an identified policy issue. For example, Democrat and Republican lawmakers agree that the nation's health care system is in critical condition. Americans are paying too much of their hard earned income into tax programs. The minimum wage needs to be increased. The national debt is too high. Each political party, however, has different philosophical approaches to these issues. Consequently, each party follows a different agenda.

An effective agenda should attack all the identified causal factors at the same time. Doctors have realized that bombarding one side of a cancerous tumor with heavy doses of radiation and chemotherapy will halt the growth of the tumor on just the treated side while the untreated side continues to grow. The same holds true for public policy. By treating and curing just one symptom, policy makers allow the other symptoms to grow stronger. The drug policies passed during the Reagan administration desired to end the importation of drugs into the country. Instead of focusing on all international drug sources, the agenda focused primarily on Columbia. Columbian drug trafficking was substantially slowed. However, the flow of drugs continued as other international drug operatives assumed the Columbian share of the market.

"In the issue of death and injuries resulting from drunk driving, both our laws and our cultural beliefs place responsibility with the drunk driver. There are certainly alternative ways of viewing the problem: we could blame vehicle design (for materials and structure more likely to injure or kill in a crash); highway design (for curves likely to cause accidents); lack of ambulance service or nearby hospitals; lax enforcement of drunk-driving penalties by police; or even availability of alcoholic beverages . . . Even when there is a strong statistical and logical link between substance and a problem—such as between alcohol and car accidents, handguns and homicides, tobacco and cancer deaths, or cocaine and overdose deaths—there is still a range of places to locate control and impose sanctions . . . . In the case of alcohol, we have traditionally seen drinkers as the cause and limited sanctions to them, although sellers have more recently been made to bear the costs. In lung cancer deaths, we have blamed the smoker primarily, but to the extent that people have sought to place blame elsewhere, they have gone after cigarette manufacturers, not sellers or tobacco growers. With handgun homicides, we have limited blame to the user of guns, rather than imposing sanctions on either the seller or manufacturers."[61]

Regardless of the issue, the answer to solving the problem rests with identifying all of the factors that caused the problem in the first place and holding each factor equally accountable for its actions. Again, the good intentions of lawmakers fail to achieve anticipated results when they overlook that effective public policy must attack the problem from all sides.

Action plans must contain well defined goals and objectives to ensure that all of the involved parties have a clear understanding of the intent of the policy directive. A **goal** is the end result of an action. For example, the ultimate goal of the Medicare program is to ensure that elderly and permanently disabled citizens are provided with government-sponsored health care. **Objectives**, on the other hand, are the strategies used to obtain the desired goals. Clearly defined and precise goals and objectives are an essential ingredient to the successful implementation of a policy directive just as a set of blueprints is to a homebuilder. "Statutory objectives that are precise and clearly ranked in importance serve as an indispensable aid in program evaluation, as unambiguous directives to implementing officials, and as a resource available to supporters of those objectives both inside and outside the implementing agencies."[62]

Action plans must also include measurable and attainable goals and objectives. Far too often, lawmakers attempt to sell their ideas as wondrous miracle cures. How many times have voters heard their leaders pledge that their proposed policy or program will completely eradicate a problem, only to see the policy fall disastrously short of its objectives. For example, President Lyndon Johnson's War on Poverty program was designed to eliminate poverty. Johnson's pledge was a lofty, unreasonable, and unattainable goal. Lawmakers should be honest and realistic with their constituents. An anticrime package designed to achieve a 5 percent reduction in crime each year over a five-year period has a better chance of seeing this goal achieved and/or exceeded over a policy with the lofty goal of eliminating all crime within a five-year period.

Formulation of Policy

The formulation process involves more than just designing the programs and the policy responses needed to address agenda items. Lawmakers must first determine the policy approach, and the type of policy option, as well as whether the responsibility for the resulting programs should be assigned to the public or private sector. Usually, lawmakers opt for one of four policy approaches: punitive, alleviative, preventive, and, the rarely used, curative. The selection of the policy approach will fluctuate depending upon the prevailing political philosophy of lawmakers, public opinion, the severity of the deprivation and/or damage, and the status of the nation's economy.

The **punitive approach** rests upon the premise that the problem arose from self-inflicted causal factors. For example, there is a belief that poverty is usually a self-inflicted result of an individual's failure to achieve economic viability. Guided by the concepts of Social Darwinism and the free market theory, the belief holds that poverty is "the product of moral or character deficiencies in the individual. If people were poor, it was their own fault" and, subsequently, their responsibility alone to rise above their economic deprivation.[63] The punitive approach recognizes their economic needs while, at the same time, punishing the poor for their misfortunes. For example, communities provide shelters for the homeless. A homeless person can remain in the shelter as long as he/she follows the shelter's rules. Rent subsidy programs such as Section 8 are available for those whose incomes fall below a pre-determined level. However, a subsidized resident can be denied continued housing benefits if he/she does not perform customary maintenance or deliberately destroys the property. For social service programs, the usual approach has been an attempt to distinguish the deserving from the undeserving poor. Means-tested programs require applicants to demonstrate that they are indeed deserving of the benefits of the government program. The same approach has been used in a wide range of policy issues including environmental concerns. The majority of the environmental laws are designed to identify and punish violators. Few environmental laws award businesses, industries, and individuals for not polluting. The punitive approach is a reactionary response to an existing problem. The primary objective of the punitive approach is to *punish* violators, not *solve* problems.

The **alleviative approach** seeks to relieve the suffering caused by the policy problem without adequately addressing the problem itself. For example, the New Deal programs were designed as temporary measures to relieve the suffering of economic deprivation caused by the Great Depression. The Roosevelt administration believed that temporary federally funded social programs would stop the suffering while the economy recovered on its own. "The designers of the Social Security Act in 1935 assumed that needs-tested public assistance would wither away as younger workers became fully covered by social insurance—an expectation that was shattered by changing demographics, steadily expanding welfare rolls, and more generous benefits during the postwar period."[64] Unable and, in most respects, unwilling to face the actual causes of poverty and eventually attempt to cure it, lawmakers opted for the easy way out. Relieving or alleviating the suffering of the effected parties is an excellent short-term policy alternative that should never be used as a long-term policy commitment. The same observation can be made for the majority of the social service programs enacted by the federal government. Building more prisons merely alleviates the suffering criminals inflict upon society. Providing the homeless with overnight temporary shelters and three square meals a day simply alleviates the suffering of hunger. Merely easing the pain does not cure the problem of homelessness and hunger.. In addition, the alleviative approach is extremely costly to taxpayers who demand that their dollars actually eliminate the policy problem.

The third option is the **preventive strategy**. This alternative adverts actually curing the problem by just preventing it from getting worse. The farm price subsidy programs were designed to prevent farmers and food processors from losing more money. The program was based on the assumption that by controlling the supply of the product, the price of the product would be stabilized. The Social Security program was designed to prevent retired workers from falling into poverty by creating a self-funded insurance program for workers. Medicare and medigap insurance programs were designed to prevent senior citizens from falling below the poverty level due to medical expenses. Social preventive policy schemes have successfully built a safety net from the ills of poverty for retired workers, the elderly, and disabled Americans while successfully avoiding the task of curing the potential income deprivations confronting these citizens. Again, the preventive strategy should be treated as a short-term response that realistically will not meet the long-term goal of eliminating the problem.

The most difficult and, subsequently, the least used policy option is the **curative approach**. The primary objective of this option is to eliminate or cure the problem. The bulk of today's problems can be solved eventually or, at least, dramatically reduced in scope and adverse impact. It is possible, for example, to eliminate some types of crime and to successfully protect the environment from future pollution. Yet, no government-sponsored program can effectively eliminate crime just as no legislative act or regulatory policy can eradicate current environmental damage. The ultimate success of the curative approach is dependent upon several factors. First, this approach can be used only after a deliberative assessment has been made that correctly identifies the factors that created the problem in the first place. Second, the curative approach mandates a long-term policy commitment. Long-term solutions also need non-partisan support. This is exceptionally difficult to achieve in a democratic environment whereby periodic elections can unseat incumbent administrations.

Most lawmakers opt for a combination of the punitive, alleviative, and preventive approaches. For example, the Clean Water Act is designed to prevent future pollution to our nation's water supply by mandating quality standards while using the alleviative option to relieve the suffering and damage caused by previous incidences of water pollution. The punitive approach to the Clean Water Act includes a series of criminal and civil sanctions to be levied on those who participate in pollution activities. The curative approach, however, is seldom used.

Decision-makers must also select the type of policy required to meet anticipated goals and objectives. Domestic policy alternatives include distributive, redistributive, and regulatory options. **Distributive policies** are "governmental actions that convey tangible benefits to individuals, groups or corporations."[65] The most commonly used form of distributive policy is the subsidy. **Subsidies** are "simply government grants of cash and other commodities."[66] However, subsidies must be used correctly to achieve anticipated results. Initially, the gift of the subsidy is given with few strings or conditions attached. For example, the Department of Agriculture gives farmer Brown a cash payment for not planting turnips. The recipient continues to receive the subsidy to the point that farmer Brown becomes financially dependent upon receiving the yearly payment. Once dependency is established, government can now begin to add more stringent conditions to the gift. The coercive arm of government will now threaten to reduce and/or actually revoke the gift if farmer Brown fails to meet the new conditions. The dependency factor usually results in compliance! Subsidies can range from agricultural payments to partial or full payments to low income individuals to offset rent expenses. The United States government uses a wide range of subsidies such as cash payments, military arms and equipment, and humanitarian aid in cementing its relationships with foreign countries.

On the other hand, a **redistributive policy** is "a conscious attempt by the government to manipulate the allocation of wealth, property, rights, or some other value among broad classes or groups in society."[67] Those policies are often called Robin Hood programs since the wealth of the affluent is given to the economically disadvantaged. The federal grant programs of the 1960s and 1970s were designed to reallocate federal tax revenues to the poorer states under the premise that the wealthier states could afford their own infrastructure programs. Consequently, economically strapped states, such as Arkansas, received large federal cash outlays to rebuild its highways, bridges, airports, and so on. The welfare system is another example of redistributive policy. The popularity

496 / *Chapter Fourteen*

of redistributive policies is directly tied to the economy. When the economy is in a healthy growth pattern, the wealthier states rarely balk at sharing their wealth. However, whenever the economy sours and the once wealthy states are now confronted with budget deficits, they are reluctant to share and may even get in line behind the less wealthy states who are asking for federal funding.

Finally, lawmakers may opt to use regulatory actions to address a domestic issue or problem. **Regulatory actions** are "governmental actions that extend government control over particular behavior of private individuals or businesses."[68] Initiated in 1887 with the creation of the Interstate Commerce Commission, the federal government has used regulatory actions to exert its influence into virtually every segment of the economy from banking to the environment. To insure regulatory compliance, each act is accompanied by a series of punishing civil, criminal, and monetary sanctions. As evidenced in our discussion of environmental issues, businesses, corporations, farmers, and ranchers, as well as property owners, have come to resent the federal mandates attached to federal regulatory legislation. Lawmakers should realize by now that regulatory policies laden with costly mandates followed by extremely punitive sanctions do not lead to effective public policy that is openly embraced by the regulated party.

In addressing foreign policy concerns, lawmakers generally mold their policy decisions into one of three policy options. The decision may involve a **crisis policy response**. This option is used when "the perception of a threat to national security cuts across normal channels of decisions."[69] Due to the sensitivity and the potential threat to national security, crisis issues are centered in the executive branch of the government. As evidenced by the Cuban Missile Crisis, President Kennedy involved only a few key members of his cabinet in formulating his response to the presence of Soviet missiles in Cuba. Although the executive branch has more latitude in foreign policy concerns, both the legislative and executive branches are involved in the formulation of foreign policy issues. **Strategic defense policy** is "oriented toward foreign policy and international politics, and it involves the units and uses of military force, their strength, and their deployment."[70] The initial decision to send troops rests with the president. The continual deployment of those troops will involve congressional action, particularly when the time limits under the War Powers Act have expired. The formulation of the policy response involves more than just sending troops into hostile territories. For example, the deployment of troops into Bosnia was only one piece of a complex American foreign policy initiative aimed at ending the civil war in former Yugoslavia. Congress assumes a larger role in foreign policy when the issue requires the use of a **structural defense policy**. This option is "oriented toward foreign policy and international politics, and it involves decisions about the procurement, allocation, and organization of men, money, and material that constitute the military forces."[71]

Lawmakers must consider which sector of the economy, namely, public or private, will be responsible for the implementation of the program. Traditionally, government services and policies have been the sole responsibility of government or the public sector. Each new major piece of legislation led to the creation of another federal agency and the hiring of more government employees. The outcry to cut the federal deficit, reduce spending, and balance the budget has led lawmakers to consider another option. The current move is towards privatization that reassigns some functional areas from the public or government sector to the private sector through contracting. Technically, **privatization** is "a general effort to relieve the disincentives toward efficiency in public organizations by subjecting them to the incentives of the private market."[72] Privatization has gained supporters who believe this scheme will save the government money in personnel and equipment costs, while at the same time, relieving government of the burdens of providing a service to the public. Enthusiastic proponents would like "to privatize the full gamut of public assets and services, including many forms of public provisions such as public schools, national parks, public-transport infrastructure, and prisons, whose origins and rationale fall comfortably within the gambit of the classical liberal state. In privatization they believe they have found a sovereign remedy against all ailments to the body politic, good for stimulating economic growth, improving the efficiency of services, slimming down the state, and expanding individual freedom, including the opportunities to disadvantaged minorities, too."[73] Despite lofty expectations, privatization should be used sparingly and with extreme discretion. The drawbacks of privatization include loss of control over that functional area. Government will bear the responsibility and the blame when things go wrong whether the problem is handled by the public or private sector. Second, government can not privatize all functions due to the sensitivity of the function. For example, local governments would be very foolish and irresponsible to contract to the private sector all of its law enforcement functions.

The actual formulation of public policy also involves all the key actors. Once an idea evolves into a proposed piece of legislation, all potentially effected parties are set for action. "As the formulation process moves toward the decision stage, some proposals will be rejected, others accepted, still others modified; differences will be narrowed; bargains will be struck, until ultimately, in some instances, the final policy decision will be only a formality. In other instances, the question will be in doubt until the votes are counted or the decision is announced."[74] The formulation phase is the most politically heightened step in the process of developing public policy.

Budgeting

The proper preparation of a budget is a crucial step in the development of public policy initiatives. A **budget** is a "technical document in the form of a detailed balance sheet that identifies expenditures and revenues for all government activities."[75] The budget is the embodiment of the national government's prevailing fiscal policies. Basically, **fiscal policy** is "public policy that concerns taxes, government spending, public debt, and management of government money."[76] The preparation of a budget entails the estimation of expected expenditures and calls upon the skillful talents of budget makers to find the funding sources needed to pay for these items. For example, state governments are using everything from lotteries, casino gambling, horse racing, state income taxes, and a full array of fines, fees, and special taxes to fund their activities. The budget is also a political document, indicating in dollar amounts to specified budget categories the prevailing political ideologies of lawmakers. "If politics is regarded as conflict over whose preferences are to prevail in the determination of policy, then the budget records the outcomes of this struggle."[77]

Agenda items must reflect budgetary reality. Attainable goals and objectives must be affordable. An improperly budgeted program is doomed for several reasons. First, lawmakers may grossly underestimate the cost of the program. Usually this happens on long-term projects. The cost projections for each year should be increased to adjust for increases in salaries, equipment, materials, maintenance, and customary expenses. "Financial resources are perhaps particularly problematic in labor-intensive service delivery programs and in regulatory programs with a high scientific or technological component, where implementing agencies often lack the funds to engage in the research and development necessary to examine critically the information presented by target groups and, in some cases, to develop alternative technologies."[78] A poorly funded program means that targeted service areas will shrink considerably, rendering the program a failure. Second, lawmakers are extremely skeptical of appropriating large sums of money for an unproven project. The program must look good enough on paper and promise long lasting results to garner full budgetary treatment. Third, voters can influence the budgeting process. Voters always want top quality services while at the same time demanding budgetary cuts.

A priority in the budgeting process is whether to **dedicate** or **earmark** funds to certain budgetary items. States more often than the national government use dedicated budgetary strategies to fund highways, public education, and so on. Dedicating does ensure that the money will be used for its intended purpose. However, once revenue is dedicated it cannot be transferred to another budget item or used to offset an unexpected crisis.

A sometimes ominous term associated with the budgeting process is porkbarreling. **Porkbarrel politics** is "the use of political influence by members of Congress to secure government funds and projects for their constituents."[79] A congressperson's job includes fighting for federal funds for projects and needs within his/her legislative district.

Taxation has become the traditional means for governments to acquire revenue. A **tax** is a "compulsory contribution for a public purpose rather than for the personnel benefit of an individual."[80] Tax dollars are returned to the citizens in the form of public services. Citizens constantly demand increases in services. However, the majority of Americans are weary of paying taxes and do not support too many politicians and lawmakers advocating tax increases. In developing a tax program, lawmakers must select a plan that will provide a reliable ample source of revenue with a minimal effect on the taxpayers' pocketbooks.

There are several key factors that lawmakers must consider in determining the type of tax they wish to levy on citizens. First, **elasticity** is "an economic criterion applied to a tax which refers to the tax's ability to generate increased revenue as economic growth or inflation increases."[81] A highly **elastic tax** will expand and/or contract proportionally with economic growth or stagnation. Elastic taxes are reliable and predictable sources of revenue. The income tax is the best example of an elastic tax. As a person's income increases, his/her tax burden increases. A tax is tagged as **inelastic** when it does not generate increased revenues in proportion to economic growth. Sales taxes are inelastic taxes. The sales tax rate is fixed. It does not matter what the individual's income level is, the amount of tax is fixed on the item. An individual whose income is $100,000 will pay the same amount of tax on an item of clothing as an individual earning $10,000 who purchases the same item.

Lawmakers must take into account the potential **reliability** of the tax as a source of revenue. A tax that meets its anticipated level of revenue is a better program than a tax that is highly unpredictable in revenue returns. "Sales, property and income taxes are reliable because experts can predict with only a small margin of error future economic growth and activity upon which taxes are based. Severance taxes on energy production can be unreliable because the income they generate is affected by rapidly changing and unpredictable international political forces."[82]

Tax accuracy and reliability go hand in hand. Governments must have adequate revenue sources to accurately predict income generation. Revenue may be lost if the measurement tool to assess tax values is inadequate or antiquated. Accurate tax sources are essential to economic security. The

Internal Revenue Service depends upon employers accurately submitting W-2 wage information to both the IRS and the employee. The "honor system" is an extremely unreliable revenue reporting source as some taxpayers purposefully would not report their current earnings.

How much money a tax will ultimately produce is called the **tax yield**. The cost of administering the tax program and eventually collecting the tax can effect the yield of the tax. "Taxes that return substantial sums of money at minimal costs are preferred to taxes that require large outlays for moderate revenues."[83] The easiest taxes to administer and collect are income and sales taxes. These taxes produce a higher yield over property taxes. Property taxes are costly to administer because property must be assessed for its tax value on a regular basis.

The **tax effort** is "a measure of whether, given a state's economic situation, it is taxing above or below its capacity to raise revenue."[84] In other words, states with strong track records of economic growth have the potential to raise ample revenues at average tax rates, if willing to do so.

The **visibility** of a tax is an important political consideration for lawmakers. Although very reliable revenue sources, income and property taxes are highly visible. The taypayer receives an income tax form and a property tax bill in the mail. To add salt to the wound, taxpayers are constantly reminded to pay those taxes on time or face costly late charges, fines, imprisonment, or loss of property. On the other hand, sales taxes are low visibility taxes since the majority of consumers do not keep records of sales tax expenditures. Politicians usually prefer low visibility tax programs.

The **application** of the tax program is another major consideration for budget makers. The primary categories for budget expenses are operating costs and capital expenditures. **Operating expenses** are yearly expenses needed to run government. These items would include salaries, benefits, equipment, rent, utilities, supplies, and so on. **Capital expenses** are multi-year or amortized expenses. A new mainframe computer system or a new building is an expense allocated over five, ten, or thirty year periods. It is essential that reliable revenue sources be used to fund operating expenses.

There are four types of taxes government may levy upon its citizens. A **progressive tax** is "one that increases the tax burden for upper-income people while reducing it for lower-income people."[85] Income, property, and corporate taxes are progressive tax programs. The national government relies heavily on income and corporate taxes; whereas, most state, county, and city governments rely on property taxes. In contrast, a **regressive tax** "increases the tax burden for lower-income people while reducing it for upper-income people."[86] Sales, excise, and energy taxes are regressive taxes since they place a heavier burden on individuals whose incomes are in the middle to lower brackets than those in the upper income levels. The national government uses a wide variety of regressive tax programs such as taxes on cigarettes, alcohol, and so on. Advocated by President Ronald Reagan, **proportional taxes** impose equal tax burdens regardless of one's income level. Reagan believed in a **flat tax rate** on income with no deductions. Subsequently, a 5 percent tax rate would produce the same tax burden regardless if one's income was $10,000 or $100,000 per year. Finally, the tax system can follow a **benefit principle system**. "Under this principle, those who reap more benefits from government services should shoulder more of the tax burden than people who do not avail themselves of service opportunities to the same degree."[87] Municipal governments impose a wide range of user fees to offset the costs of maintaining their roads and public transportation systems.

Tax equity or the fairness of the tax is another major consideration for lawmakers. As long as the taxpayer believes the tax is fairly applied and justifiable, he/she will pay the tax. However, this country separated itself from England in part over inequitable taxes imposed on the colonists. The principle of fairness in taxation cannot be overlooked by lawmakers seeking re-election.

The selection of the budget strategy is also vital to the planning process. There are several budgetary strategies available to budget makers. The **incremental process** has been the traditional budgetary approach. It is virtually an automatic process whereby federal agencies receive marginal budget increases or decreases with each new budget cycle. Federal agencies merely submit their budget requests with a built-in increase. Without much review, budget makers would normally accept the budget request. However, there are several potentially severe drawbacks to using the incremental system. "There is little attempt to evaluate program results or compare across different program areas in a given fiscal year. Such systematic evaluation would require a number of factors not readily available to most state (or federal) agencies: clear agreement on programmic objectives, reliable methods of measuring progress towards those objectives, and personnel skilled in methods of policy analysis."[88] Second, the incremental system encourages federal agencies to inflate their budget requests and to spend all of their allocated money during the fiscal year. "Typically, administrators ask for more money than they actually need, believing that those appropriating the money will automatically cut budgetary requests. Also they tend to spend all funds that are allocated for a specific time, such as a fiscal year, because to return funds can lead to a reduction of funds during the next budgetary period."[89] Experimental budgetary strategies include the **planning program budgeting (PPB)** concept with a cost benefit analysis feature. The focus is on programs, not line item allocations. "Agencies were obliged by PPB to define each activity's objectives and to indicate how the budget amounts related to the objectives, how to accomplish the objectives in alternative ways, and whether the objectives were being accomplished."[90] The cost benefit is a built-in feature. **Zero-based budgeting** is similar to PPB. It is a program based strategy. However, each agency's budget has to be totally rewritten with each budgetary cycle starting from zero. Agencies submit their budgetary requests every year as if they were just beginning their operations. Zero-based budgeting has lost some of its appeal since it is a very complicated process for all parties involved.

Political Implications

Regardless of the policy issue, all lawmakers must consider the potential political implications of their actions. Each legislative action will provide benefits to one group and hardships to another. One of the fundamental keys is to hurt those who cannot politically hurt you. For example, Democrats and Republicans ran their 1994 and 1996 election campaigns on the need for welfare reform. By pointing out the failure of the program plus examples of fraud and abuse, politicians scored with the middle class voter at the expense of those lower income groups most likely to be welfare recipients. Why? Voter statistics indicate that the poor usually do not vote in large enough numbers to be an electoral threat. A well-crafted public policy initiative adversely hurts those groups who are too politically weak to hurt lawmakers.

All presidents have been keenly aware that their foreign policy decisions are often more visible and potentially harmful to their political careers. Few Americans are concerned about foreign aid packages or the shipment of grains to foreign countries. However, once a president commits American forces to a foreign soil, the American public pays close attention. A failing war effort will ruin the re-election opportunities for an otherwise popular president. For example, Lyndon Johnson decided not to seek re-election based primarily on his administration's failure to bring the Vietnam War to a successful conclusion. He knew he would not win the election. Perhaps the election of 1980 would have had a different outcome if President Jimmy Carter's mission to rescue the hostages in the American embassy in Iran had been successful.

The political implications for a congressperson are long lasting since each vote becomes public record. The congressperson's opposition will not let the public forget those votes perhaps cast years ago that ran against the grain of current public opinion. Interest groups and political action committees do review congressional voting records to ensure that both endorsed candidates and individuals requesting endorsements have been true to the bottom line issues of their groups. Far too often incumbent candidates must justify their actions for voting for or against controversial legislative items such as abortion, school prayer, gun control, and so on.

Adoption/selling

A policy must be sellable to the recipient and, if required, the group targeted to fund the program. Politicians must package their programs by emphasizing the good benefits and downplaying any potential negatives. Poor salesmanship can destroy a perfectly well designed program. At a glance, the Affordable Care Act should have garnered nationwide support, particularly among the millions without any health insurance coverage. Obama explained to all Americans that once implemented, this legislation would make it "against the law for insurance companies to deny you coverage or charge you more because of pre-existing medical condition like diabetes, high blood pressure or asthma. And they could no longer drop you from coverage just because you got sick or got into an accident. What's more, insurance companies could no longer impose an annual cap on your health benefits. They could not deny you coverage simply because you made a mistake on your paperwork. Most plans must now cover preventive services like cholesterol and cancer screenings, at no out-of-pocket cost. And, being a woman is no longer a pre-existing condition."[91] However, the Obama administration severely underestimated the potency and determination of the bill's critics. As evidenced during Obama's 2012 presidential re-election bid and the 2016 presidential primary season, every Republican running for his/her party's nomination called Obamacare socialized medicine. Nothing could be further from the truth. The federal government is only providing an access to an exchange of many privately owned insurance carriers following the coverage detailed in ACA. Despite their best efforts, the Obama administration did not effectively remove the stigma of socialized medicine from the ACA. Another problem was the lag time between the signing of the legislation and the implementation of the program. It took four years before anyone could sign up for the insurance coverage. This gave the opposition four years of continuous efforts to discredit every provision of the legislation. The Obama administration spent the majority of those years responding to critics and defending its signature program. A frustrated President Obama told the American people "my main message today is we're not going back. If I've got to fight another three years to make sure this law works, that's what I'll do. . . . We need to make sure that folks refocus on what's at stake here. Go back. Take a look at what's actually going on. It can make a difference in your lives and the lives of your families. I'm going to need some help in spreading the word."[92]

Public opinion and support for public policy actions are a series of peaks and valleys. On the 2000 campaign trail, George W. Bush advocated sharing the nation's budgetary surplus with taxpayers by lowering income tax rates and providing a one time tax refund to every American taxpayer. The perceivably overtaxed American voter was elated that meaningful tax relief could become a reality. After the 2000 election, the Bush administration followed through on its promise. Yet, the Bush tax rebate did not garner the anticipated overwhelming support from the American taxpayer for several reasons. First, candidate Bush made a lofty promise of a tax rebate without revealing how much would be refunded nor which taxpayers would qualify for the rebate. After the election, the Bush administration stated that all single taxpayers would receive $300 while married couples who filed a joint return would receive a $600 rebate. In actuality, the majority of the nation's taxpayers received less than what was promised. Many taxpayers received no rebate. Individuals who owed outstanding taxes were excluded as well as the poorest Americans whose incomes fell below taxable income scales. Therefore, the tax rebate and the proposed reduction in income tax rates for all Americans was perceived as just another tax break for the nation's wealthy. Second, the Bush administration was convinced that tax rebates would be used to buy new goods and services that would generate economic growth. Unfortunately, the maximum refund amount of $300 was not enough of a stimulus to prompt Americans to buy higher-end consumer goods. The majority of individuals who received rebates used the money to pay outstanding debts. Third, the inability of the Bush administration to properly sell their tax rebate program soured many Americans against additional tax rebates and tax reductions. "In fact, four in five think cuts generally benefit someone else. . . The public also is decidedly more sympathetic to congressional candidates who place a higher priority on balancing the budget than they do on cutting taxes—with three-fourths preferring the budget-balancers and only a fourth supporting the tax-cutters."[93] It is remarkable that a policy effort designed to give tax dollars back to taxpayers actually resulted in taxpayers wanting their tax dollars to be used to balance the budget!

The selling process is an ongoing process extending throughout the life-cycle of the public policy initiative. Supporters of both foreign and domestic policy directives must not forget that "a statute, no matter how well it structures implementation, is not a sufficient condition for assuring target group compliance with its objectives. Assuring sufficient compliance to actually achieve those objectives normally takes at least three to five, and often ten to twenty, years. During this period, there are constant pressures for even supportive agency officials to lose their commitment, for supportive constituency groups and sovereigns to fail to maintain active political support, and for the entire process to be gradually undermined by changing socioeconomic forces."[94] Lawmakers must not overlook that targeted groups adversely affected by a policy directive will gain the upper hand in the battle for public opinion support if left unchecked. "There is a general tendency for organized constituency support for a wide variety of programs—including environmental and consumer protection, as well as efforts to aid the poor—to decline over time, while opposition from target groups to the costs imposed on them remains constant or actually increases. This shift in the balance of constituency support for such programs gradually becomes reflected in a shift in support among members of the legislature as a whole and the committees in the relevant subsystem(s).[95] Candidates espousing the negatives of an existing policy effort, once elected, will introduce measures to reform or dismantle that policy effort. Particularly in foreign policy, the waxing and waning of public support and subsequent congressional actions has resulted in the United States flip flopping in its relations with foreign countries. These governments are confused and, far too often, become suspicious of the everchanging policies of the United States government. Consistency in foreign policy is extremely difficult to achieve.

Implementation

Despite the well advertised policy flops, governments can and do successfully implement many of its public policy initiatives. Successful implementation ensures that policies will achieve their anticipated results well within their budgetary constraints. Paul Sabatier and David Mazmanian believe that policies can be successful if the following conditions are met:

1. The program is based on a sound theory relating changes in target group behavior to the achievement of the desired end-state (objectives).
2. The statute (or other basic policy decision) contains unambiguous policy directives and structures the implementation process so as to maximize the likelihood that target groups will perform as desired.
3. The leaders of the implementing agencies possess substantial managerial and political skill and are committed to statutory goals.
4. The program is actively supported by organized constituency groups and by a few key legislators (or the chief executive) throughout the implementation process, with the courts being neutral or supportive.
5. The relative priority of statutory objectives is not significantly undermined over time by the emergency of conflicting public policies or by changes in relevant socioeconomic conditions that undermine the statute's "technical" theory or political support.[96]

A successfully implemented policy directive is not achieved by accident or through sheer luck. It takes a staff committed to executing all the required steps according to the designated time table by using all the necessary tools including budget, personnel, and equipment. Lawmakers can certainly help the implementation process by first clearly delineating the levels of responsibility and, most importantly, the measurements of accountability to be followed by the agency designated to oversee the implementation of the policy directive. Bureaucrats can make or break a good policy simply by the manner in which they phase in the implementation process. "Any new program requires implementing officials who are not merely neutral but also sufficiently committed and persistent to develop new regulations and standard operating procedures and to enforce them in the face of resistance from target groups and from public officials reluctant to make mandated changes."[97] Far too often legislatively created programs have failed due to the lackluster and haphazard actions of bureaucratic agencies.

Second, successful programs correctly anticipate the demand for the service and adequately allocate resources to meet the demand. Resources include personnel, equipment, site location, and revenue. For example, opening a new facility to handle food distribution to a low income group with one clerk in a building located in a higher income neighborhood is missing the targeted service group. This is poor allocation of resources and a waste of money.

Third, long-term policy initiatives are multiple year phased in projects. Each phase must be implemented to produce anticipated goals and objectives. It can take as long as ten to twenty years before even a well-crafted policy can fulfill its goals and objectives. Unfortunately, "an overemphasis on pragmatism can produce a focus on immediate results rather than long term or enduring programs."[98] Impatience on the part of the average American citizen can ruin a perfectly designed long-term plan. The tendency is to implement one or two phases and use a half implemented program as the sole measurement of the success or failure of the entire program. Also, a change in administrations and party leadership could conceivably prevent a program from achieving full implementation. A newly elected Democrat president is unlikely to continue to carry out policies initiated by a Republican president and vice versa.

Evaluation

The final stage of the policy process is a complete and honest evaluation of the policy and resulting programs. Essentially, "governments cannot make rational policy choices unless they can evaluate whether programs attain their objectives. Without evaluation, they cannot know which programs are successful, which administrative practices work, and even which groups of employees are competent."[99] Every program should be effectively evaluated to determine its successes or failures. "At a minimum, policy evaluation requires that we know what we want to accomplish with a given policy (policy objectives), how we are trying to do it (programs), and what, if anything, we have accomplished toward attainment of the objectives (impacts or outcomes, and the relation of the policy thereto). And, in measuring accomplishments, we need to determine not only that some change in real-life conditions has occurred, such as a reduction in the unemployment rate, but also that it was due to policy actions and not to other factors, such as private economic decisions."[100] Government at all levels can learn from its mistakes by conducting a meaningful evaluation of the actions they took, and the steps they should have taken to properly address the issue or the problem. If a meaningful evaluation does not take place, then it will be government as usual—responding to a crisis after crisis rather than preventing the crisis from happening in the first place.

CONCLUSION

The planning process is a series of eight steps beginning with problem identification and culminating with an in-depth evaluation process. As previously stated, each step is equally vital to the development of cost effective, administratively effective, and goal achievable public policy initiatives. It takes a well thought out action plan to create good public policy. As we examine public policy issues, we should remember how the planning process was applied in addressing these concerns.

CHAPTER NOTES

[1]Derrick Bryson Taylor, "How the Coronavirus Pandemic Unfolded: A Timeline," *The New York Times*, *https://www.nytimes.com/article/coronavirus-timeline*

[2]Ibid.

[3]Ibid.

[4]John M. Barry, "Journal of the Plague Year," *Smithsonian*, Vol. 48, No. 7, November, 2017, 34.

[5]Ibid., 37.

[6]Ibid., 36.

[7]R.J. Marques, "Skyrocketing Unemployment Rates, Data Shows Hispanics Are the Hardest Hit Economically During the Coronavirus Pandemic," *KSAT News*, May 28, 2020, *https://www.ksat.com*

[8]James Glanz and Campbell Robertson, "Lockdown Delays Cost at Least 36,000 Lives, Data Shows," *https://www.msn.com/en-us/news/us*

[9]Kelly Ann Smith, "Your Guide to the Federal Stimulus Package," *https://www.forbes.com*

[10]James E. Anderson, *Public Policymaking: An Introduction*, 5th ed., (Boston: Massachusetts: Houghton Mifflin Company, 2003), 1.

[11]Steven A. Peterson and Thomas H. Rassmussen, *State and Local Politics*, (New York, N. Y.: McGraw-Hill, Inc., 1994), 199.

[12]Anderson, Public Policymaking: An Introduction, 248.

[13]Theodore Lowi and Benjamin Ginsburg, *American Government: Freedom and Power*, 4th ed., (NewYork, New York: W. W. Norton & Co., 1996), 607.

[14]Anderson, *Public Policymaking: An Introduction*, 5.

[15]Ibid., 95.

[16]David C. Saffell, *State and Local Government: Politics and Public Policies*, 4th ed., (New York, New York: McGraw-Hill, Inc., 1990), 239.

[17]"The Canning of Senator Charles Sumner," *https://www.senate.gov/artandhistory*

[18]Ibid.

[19]Anderson, *Public Policymaking: An Introduction*, 248.

[20]Ibid., 249.

[21]Ibid., 14.

[22]Gerry Riposa and Nelson Dometrius, "Studying Public Policy," *Texas Public Policy*, Gerry Riposa, ed., (Dubuque, Iowa: Kendall/Hunt Publishers, 1987), 11.

[23]Anderson, *Public Policymaking: An Introduction*, 130.

[24]Ibid., 132.

[25]Jeffrey M. Berry, "Citizen Groups and the Changing Nature of Interest Group Politics in America," *The Annals, The American Academy of Political and Social Science* (Newbury Park, California: Sage Publications, 1993), Vol. 528, July, 1993, 41.

[26]Thomas R. Rochon and Daniel A. Mazmanian, "Social Movements and the Policy Process," *The Annals, The American Academy of Political and Social Science*, (Newbury Park, California: Sage Publications, 1993), Vol. 528, July, 1993, 76.

[27]Barry, 31.

[28]Ibid., 34.

[29]Ibid., 41.

[30]Riposa, 9.

[31]Anderson, *Public Policymaking: An Introduction*, 60.

[32]Walter K. Olezek, *Congressional Procedures and the Policy Process*, 3rd. ed., (Washington, D.C.: *The Congressional Quarterly*, 1989), 25-26.

[33]*Treasury of Presidential Quotations*, Caroline Thomas Harnsberger, ed., (Chicago, Illinois: Follett Publishing Co., 1964), 263.

[34]Michael Barone, "The Politics of Negation," *U.S. News & World Report*, February 20, 2006, 40.

[35]Edward L. Harper, "Domestic Policy Making in the Nixon Administration: An Evolving Process," *Presidential Studies Quarterly*, (New York, N. Y.: The Center for the Study of the Presidency, 1996), Vol. XXVI, No. 1, Winter, 1996, 41.

[36]Ibid.

[37]Ibid., 47.

[38]Barone, "*The Politics of Negation*," 40.

[39]James L. Garnett, "Administrative Communication (Or How To Make All the Rest Work): The Concept of Its Professional Centrality," *Public Administration: Concepts and Cases*, Richard Stillman, ed., 8th ed., (Boston: Massachusetts: Houghton Mifflin Co., 2005), 260.

[40]Anderson, *Public Policymaking: An Introduction*, 52-53.

[41]Hope Yen, "Ruling on Sentences Has Judges Scratching Their Heads," *San Antonio Express-News*, (Friday, January, 28, 2005), 12A.

[42]Theodore Lowi and Benjamin Ginsburg, *American Government: Freedom and Power*, 3rd ed., (New York, New York: W. W. Norton & Co., 1994), 620.

[43]Lowi and Ginsburg, 4th ed., 611.

[44]Jack O. Plano and Roy Olton, *The International Relations Dictionary*, (New York, New York: Holt, Reinhart and Winston, Inc., 1969), 265.

[45]Ibid.

[46]Investopedia, *https://www.investopedia.com/terms*

[47]*Treasury of Presidential Quotations*, 54.

[48]"Clinton's New Budget Recipe," *U.S. News & World Report*, February 15, 1993, 36.

[49]American Recovery and Reinvestment Act of 2009, *https://www.congress.gov*

[50]Ibid.

[51]Alison Main, Betsy Klein, Nicky Robertson and Sarah Westwood, "Trump Administration Officials Say Fourth Economic Stimulus Package Is Premature," *CNN*, May 29, 2020, *https://ww.cnn.com*

[52]Jay M. Shafritz, *The HarperCollins Dictionary of American Gov and Politics*, (N. Y., N. Y.: HarperCollins, Inc., 1992), 590.

[53]"The Impact of Government Shutdowns on States," *https://www/cnn/com*

[54]Peterson, 190-91.

[55]Paul Sabatier and Daniel Mazmanian, "The Conditions of Effective Implementation: A Guide to Accomplishing Policy Objectives," *Public Administration: Concepts and Cases*, Richard Stillman, ed., 4th ed., (Princeton, New Jersey: Houghton Mifflin Co., 1998) 387.

[56]Anderson, *Public Policy Making: An Introduction*, 55-56.

[57]Ibid., 81.

[58]Richard Maidment and Anthony McGrew, *The American Political Process*, (Beverly Hills, California: Sage Publications, Inc., 1981), 135.

[59]James E. Anderson, *Public Policy Making*, (New York, New York: Prager Publishers, 1975), 57.

[60]Deborah A. Stone, *Public Paradox and Political Reason*, (New York, New York: HarperCollins College Publishers, 1988),147.

[61]Ibid., 162-163.

[62]Sabatier and Mazmanian, 380.

[63]Randall W. Bland, Alfred B. Sullivan, Robert E. Biles, Charles P. Elliott, Jr., and Beryle E. Pettus, *Texas Government Today*, 5th ed., (Pacific Grove, California: Brooks/Cole Publishing Co., 1992), 432.

[64]Sar A. Levitan, "How the Welfare System Promotes Economic Security," *Political Science Quarterly*, (New York, New York: The Academy of Political Science), Vol. 100, No. 3, Fall, 1985, 453.

[65]Randall B. Ripley and Grace A. Granklin, *Congress, the Bureaucracy and Public Policy*, (Homewood, Illinois: The Dorsey Press, 1976), 16.

[66]Lowi and Ginsburg, *American Government*, 4th ed., 610.

[67]Ripley, 18.

[68]Ibid.

[69]Ibid., 19.

[70]Ibid.

[71]Ibid.

[72]Robert W. Bailey, "Uses and Misuses of Privatization," *Prospects for Privatization*, Steve H. Hanke, ed., (New York, New York: The Academy of Political Science, 1987), *Proceedings*, Vol. 36, No. 3, 138.

[73]Paul Starr, "The Limits of Privatization," *Prospects for Privatization*, Steve H. Hanke, ed., (New York, New York: The Academy of Political Science, 1987), 124.

[74]Anderson, *Public Policy Making: An Introduction*, 119.

[75]Bland, 329.

[76]Ibid., 332.

[77]Aaron Wildansky, "Budgeting as a Political Process," *Public Administration: Concepts and Cases*, Richard J. Stillman, 4th ed., (Princeton: New Jersey: Houghton Mifflin Co., 1988), 346.

[78]Sabatier and Mazmanian, 381.

[79]Grier D. Stephenson, Jr., Robert J. Bresler, Robert J. Friedrich and Joseph J. Karlesky, *American Government*, 2nd ed., (New York, New York: HarperCollins Publishers, 1992), G15.

[80]Eugene W. Jones, Joe E. Ericson, Lyle C. Brown, and Robert S. Trotter, Jr., *Practicing Texas Politics*, 8th ed., (New York, New York: Houghton Mifflin Co., 1992), 433.

[81]Nelson C. Dometrius, "Government Revenues and Expenditure Policy," *Texas Public Policy*, (Dubuque, Iowa: Kendall/Hunt Publishing Co., 1987), 33.

[82]Ibid., 34.

[83]Ann O'M. Bowman and Richard C. Kearney, State and Local Government, (Boston, Massachusetts: Houghton Mifflin Co., 1990), 374.

[84]Susan B. Hansen, "The Politics of State Taxing and Spending," *Politics in the American States: A Comparative Analysis*, Virginia Gray, Herbert Jacob and Robert Albritton, eds., 5th ed., (New York, New York: HarperCollins Publishers, Inc., 1990), 348.

[85]John J. Harrigan and David C. Nice, *Politics and Policy in States and Communities*, 8th ed., (New York, New York: Pearson Education, 2004), 306.

[86]Ibid.

[87]Bowman, 374.

[88]Hansen, 362.

[89]Leon W. Blevins, *Texas Government in National Perspective*, (Englewood Cliffs, New Jersey: Prentice-Hall, Inc., 1987), 317.

[90]Harrigan and Nice, 257.

[91]Kathleen Sebelius, "Another View: Affordable Care Act Will Bring a Healthy New Year," *San Antonio Express-News*, (Wednesday, January 1, 2014), A15.

[92]"Obama: The Health Care Law Is Working," *San Antonio Express-News*, (December 4, 2013), A12.

[93]Will Lester, "Tax Rebates Haven't Sold 4 in 5 Americans on Cuts." *San Antonio Express-News*, (Wednesday, April 3, 2002), 12A.

[94]Sabatier and Mazmanian, 383.

[95]Ibid., 384.

[96]Ibid., 379.

[97]Ibid., 381.

[98]Nelson C. Dometrius, "The Texas Policy Environment," *Texas Public Policy,* Gerry Riposa, ed., (Dubuque, Iowa: Kendall/Hunt Publishers, 1987), 18.

[99]Harrigan and Nice, 254.

[100]Anderson, *Public Policy Making*, 134-135.

SUGGESTED READINGS

Anderson, James E., *Public Policymaking: An Introduction*, 5th edition, Boston, Mass.: Houghton Mifflin Company, 2003.

Harrigan, John B. and David C. Nice, *Politics and Policy in States and Communities,* 8th edition, New York, New York: Pearson Education, 2004.

Mainment, Richard, and Anthony McGrew. *The American Political Process*, Beverly Hills, Calif.: Sage Publications, Inc., 1981.

Peterson, Steven A., and Thomas H. Rassmussen. *State and Local Politics*. New York: McGraw-Hill, Inc., 1994.

Saffell, David C. and Harry Basehart, *State and Local Government: Politics and Public Policies,* 8th edition, Boston, Mass.: McGraw-Hill Companies, 2005.

Stillman, Richard J. II., ed., *Public Administration: Concepts and Cases*, 8th edition, Boston, Mass.: Houghton Mifflin Company, 2005.

Stone, Deborah A. *Public Policy Making*. New York: Praeger Publishers, 1975.

Chapter Fifteen

SOCIAL SERVICES

In his 1964 State of the Union Message, President Lyndon Johnson addressed a joint session of Congress emphasizing the nation's on-going dilemma of successfully alleviating poverty. Acknowledging the failures of previous administrations from Washington to himself, Johnson in his plain-spoken manner stated that:

> Very often a lack of jobs and money is not the cause of poverty, but the symptom. The cause may lie deeper in our failure to give our fellow citizens a fair chance to develop their own capacities, in a lack of education and training, in a lack of medical care and housing, in a lack of decent communities in which to live and bring up their children. But whatever the cause, our joint federal-loan effort must pursue poverty, pursue it wherever it exists . . . Our aim is not only to relieve the symptom but to cure it, and above all, prevent it.[1]

Johnson ended his speech by launching his **War on Poverty** plan, a series of legislative proposals that would not just alleviate the suffering of poverty but actually eliminate it.

Although strides have been made, the reality is that poverty still stirs deep emotions on both sides of the political spectrum and troubles the consciousness of every American. It is ironic that a nation so blessed with natural resources, ingenuity, and wealth still has millions of its citizens living below the nation's poverty level, roaming the streets during the day with absolutely no place to call home, or living in fear that they are just one step away from falling into the dismal black hole we call poverty. Increases or decreases in both unemployment and poverty rates are tied directly to ups and downs of the economy. Case in point, at the end of 2019, the nation's unemployment rate was 3.5 percent, the lowest rate since 1969.[2] The United States Census Bureau reported that the poverty rate in 2019 had declined to 10.5 percent from 11.8 percent in 2018, a decrease of 1.3 percent.[3] The rosy economic future took a nose-dive beginning March 2020 as the little known virus of Covid-19 became a world-wide pandemic. By April 2020, the nation's unemployment rate was 14.7 percent and "every state and the District of Columbia reached unemployment rates greater than their highest unemployment rates during the Great Recession" of the 1980s.[4] In just one week in May 2020, "5.2 million people filed unemployment claims, bringing the total to 22 million in four weeks since President Trump declared a national emergency. . . The United States has not seen this level of job loss since the Great Depression.[5] Despite the federal government's two rounds of stimulus packages initially giving qualified individuals $1,200 followed by $600 plus extending unemployment benefits and protections against housing foreclosures and rental evictions, the tragedy of the pandemic continues to wreck havoc on both the nation's economy and its people. The staggering number of businesses either permanently shutting their doors or filing for bankruptcy has crippled the job market. Initially, many workers were furloughed in hopes that life as we know it would return within a few months. Yet, the intensity and deadly fierceness of this virus has put far too many of the once employed into the unemployment lines with little or no hope of finding a new job in the immediate future. The nightly news programs show rows of cars lined up at food distribution centers and the food bank. While it is hopeful that the Covid-19 vaccinations will end the pandemic within a short period of time, it will take years for the economy to recover enough to see both the unemployment and the poverty rates decline significantly.

The reality is that poverty has always been with us. It has and will continue to plague this nation and baffle our elected officials from George Washington to Joe Biden as each has pondered how to marginalize it or as Lyndon Johnson hoped years ago, actually eliminate it. Despite the efforts of state legislative houses and Capitol Hill, the poor have yet to find the right road leading them to a better life and economic security. Where did we go wrong? Why does the American Dream of promised riches and success continue to elude millions of Americans? These tough questions have yet to be answered.

While few can disagree that the United States has chronic poverty-related issues, any mention of providing more assistance, reforming the existing welfare system, and, of course, implementing a national health care system draws out the philosophical differences between liberals and conservatives and Democrats versus Republicans. At the end of 2020, congressional members on both sides of the aisle did not argue that another economic stimulus package was needed to address Covid-19 related economic woes. The battle was, once again, over how much to give struggling American families and the unemployed. During the summer, House majority Democrats passed a bill granting individuals under a certain annual income a one-time $2,000 payment. The Republican-dominated Senate sat on it until December. Their plan called for a one-time $600 payment plus extending unemployment benefits and a freeze on foreclosures and evictions. President Trump, a Republican, switched party lines in support of the $2,000 stimulus plan. The resulting congressional compromise was $600. This haggling over the amount is nothing new. Congress's actions in 2020 only mirror a historical pattern of battles over welfare programs. For example, in the late 1980s, heavily overburdened state legislative houses began to question the ability of the welfare state created by Franklin Roosevelt's think tank to meet the needs of the impoverished, while at the same time pleasing taxpayers whose hard earned dollars fund the system. Politicians and lawmakers agreed that the welfare system needed major repair work simply because it was not working. The all too simple solution was to turn a blind eye to the millions of Americans in financial need by slashing billions of federal dollars from welfare programs that had been providing a safety net against the harshness of poverty since 1935. Yet, this option is not a viable solution. Governments merely washing their hands of welfare programs will not miraculously erase poverty or eliminate the suffering and deprivation.

The 2020 presidential campaign took a unique approach to poverty. Instead of emphasizing the depth of poverty and their proposals to address it, candidates from both political parties devoted the majority of their domestic agenda on jobs creation while successfully avoiding the difficult issue of poverty. The underlying message was that if the nation's businesses and industries could just create more jobs at higher pay, there would be less persons living in poverty. This is a rather simplistic approach to an extremely complicated problem.

While this nation's leaders are so critical of the failures of other countries to address their poverty-related issues, our lawmakers have failed for over two hundred years to adequately come to grips with the human side of this nation's poverty-related problems. The politics of poverty directly affects millions of faces from all races, ages, and genders that oftentimes fare worse under the new programs and funding options crafted in congressional and executive committee rooms. It is this human face of poverty that this nation cannot morally or consciously ignore. We, as citizens, must also remember that poverty involves more than just statistics on a chart or a dollar figure on a budget line. For every number on a chart, bell-curve, or bar graph there is a face of a man, woman, or child who, with few exceptions, found themselves impoverished through no direct fault of their own.

The solution to poverty lies in an extremely complex and painfully difficult re-examination of the American social and economic consciousness. The Framers of the Constitution recognized government's burdensome responsibility of meeting the needs of **all** of its citizens whether rich or poor by charging government with the task of providing for and promoting the general welfare. While liberals and conservatives continue to argue over the proper philosophical approaches to solving poverty, and congressional Democrats and Republicans hurl insults at each other, the sad reality is that the number of poverty-stricken Americans continues to increase as the gap between rich and poor widens. In addition, millions of Americans are employed at minimum or below minimum wage jobs without the benefits of life insurance, pension plans, and health-care coverage for themselves or their family members. Rock bottom poor roam the streets, seeking shelter at night in crowded shelters or the parks and alleys of our nation's streets. As it tore apart the city of New Orleans and portions of the Gulf Coast, hurricane Katrina also exposed the depth of decades-old chronic poverty. "'I hope we realize that the people of New Orleans weren't just abandoned during the hurricane,' then-Sen. Barack Obama said . . . on the floor of the Senate. 'They were abandoned long-ago—to murder and mayhem in the streets, to substandard schools, to dilapidated housing, to inadequate health care, to a pervasive sense of hopelessness.'"[6] The adverse economic impact of the pandemic had exposed a once seemingly untouchable economic class to the list of vulnerable groups—the American middle class. For many middle-class Americans, the assurance of job security is gone. These first-time initial claim filers have joined the perennially unemployed hoping they too qualify for unemployment benefits. Once the contributors to the food banks and clothing drives, they are now among the recipients who wait in their cars for hours in hopes of receiving a box of food or clothing items. Since March 2020, "1.1 million Americans filed initial claims for unemployment benefits. In total, 19.6 million Americans filed for some form of ongoing jobless benefits in the week ending December 12 [2020]."[7] In reality, the United States is a rich nation for the privileged few and a poor one for millions. Poverty does not discriminate in its choice of victims, nor is anyone completely safe from its stranglehold.

This chapter examines the depth of poverty confronting this nation as well as the difficult tasks faced by lawmakers to address the underlying causal factors that lead to poverty and economic deprivation. Basically, since the founding of this country, lawmakers have attempted to address only the **immediate** needs of the poor. The resulting legislative actions have only marginally alleviated the suffering of many, but not all of the poor, and have failed miserably to solve the problems of poverty. This chapter explores the policy actions pursued by all levels of government in their valiant but unsuccessful attempts to fulfill their obligations and challenges of promoting the general welfare. Of course, no discussion of the issue of poverty would be complete without exploring the current health-care crisis confronting not only the poor of this nation but all Americans.

THE VOCABULARY OF POVERTY

Poverty is "the state of condition of being poor by lacking the means of providing material needs or comforts."[8] One of the major problems confronting lawmakers is the actual determination

Table 15.1

Weighted Average Poverty Thresholds: 1980-2019

Size of Unit	1980	1990	2000	2010	2019
One Person (unrelated)	$4,190	$6,652	$8,794	$11,137	$13,011
Under 65 Years	4,290	6,800	8,959	11,344	13,300
65 Years and Over	3,949	6,268	8,259	11,354	12,261
Two Persons Householder	5,363	8,509	11,235	14,216	16,521
Under 65 Years	5,537	8,794	11,589	15,589	17,196
65 Years and Older	4,983	7,905	10,418	13,194	15,468
Three Persons	6,585	10,419	13,740	17,373	20,335
Four Persons	8,414	13,359	17,604	22,315	26,172
Five Persons	9,966	15,792	20,815	26,442	31,021
Six Persons	11,269	17,839	23,533	29,904	35,129
Seven Persons	12,761	20,241	26,750	34,019	40,016
Eight Persons	14,199	22,582	29,701	37,953	44,461
Nine Or More Persons	16,896	26,848	35,150	45,224	52,875

Source: U.S. Census Bureau.

of the number of people who are actually living in poverty. "The current formula was created by President Lyndon Johnson to keep score in his 'war on poverty' and has remained unchanged since 1965."[9] The number will fluctuate depending upon the measurement tool or factor used to determine economic deprivation. For years, policy makers have used a loose definition of the **poverty level** or **threshold** to determine actual numbers as well as benefit eligibility. "Based on the assumption that poor families spend one-third of their income on food, the United States Social Security Administration sets an official poverty line at three times the amount of income needed to eat according to a modest food plan."[10] This numerical figure is adjusted annually for inflation. Poverty levels are established for a wide range of variables. Table 15.1 details the poverty thresholds for an individual to nine or more family members from 1980 to 2019. In 2019, the poverty levels were $13,011 for an individual over the age of 65; $20,335 for a family of three and $26,172 for a family of four. The highest range was $52,875 for nine or more persons. Each year the income levels are only marginally increased. For example, the average poverty threshold for household of three persons increased only by $2,962 between 2010 and 2019.

Both liberals and conservatives believe that the current method of determining the poverty level needs to be changed to reflect a more realistic measurement tool of deprivation. "Conservative critics of the official definition point out that it [the poverty level] is based on cash income and does not count family assets or 'in-kind' (non-cash) benefits from government such as food stamps, medical care, and public housing. If poverty rate calculations include these factors, the 'net poverty' rate is lower than the official rate; fewer people are considered poor."[11] On the other hand, liberals contend that "taxes, work expenses, child care costs, and medical expenses paid by consumers from their own pocket should be deducted from cash income."[12] By using these factors, the number of individuals living below the poverty level would increase. "Economists have long criticized the official poverty rate as inadequate. Based on a half-century-old government formula, the official rate continues to assume the average family spends one-third of its income on food. Those costs have actually shrunk to a much smaller share, more like one-seventh."[13]

Many of the homeless manage to eke out only a miserable existence.

Poverty levels can also be determined in absolute and relative terms. **Absolute poverty** is defined as "the minimum subsistence income needed to survive deprivation."[14] This determination is based on the cost of a modest income outlay for food, shelter, and clothing. The federal government currently measures poverty in absolute terms, using food as the primary factor. **Relative poverty** compares an individual's income to the nation's overall standard of living. This elastic approach takes into account the ups and downs of the nation's economic growth and prosperity. As the standard of living increases, the gap between rich and poor widens, producing an increase in the number of persons whose incomes fall below the poverty level. An adverse economic situation would shrink the gap between rich and poor, resulting in a reduction in the total number of people living below the poverty level.

There are several subcategories of impoverishment. The **working poor** are usually undereducated high school dropouts who are either employed full time or part-time at minimum or below minimum wage positions. "In 2019, 82.3 million workers age 16 and older in the United States were paid at hourly rates, representing 58.1 percent of all wage and salary workers. Among those paid by the hour, 392,000 workers earned exactly the prevailing federal minimum wage of $7.25 per hour. About 1.2 million had wages below the federal minimum."[15] Their salaries do not generate enough income to place them above the poverty level. Some of these individuals are holding two or more part-time jobs at the same time. For the nation's working poor "every little setback is a crisis to them; unkindness or fear immobilizes them. Depression, low self-esteem and hopelessness all combine to make them exceptionally fragile. Supporting two kids on the minimum wage requires a lot of togetherness, not to mention sheer stamina. Fighting one's way through the welfare bureaucracy to get the help to which one is entitled is a challenge for someone with a college degree with a lot of self-confidence; try doing it after an eight-hour workday with no transportation, especially if your English isn't good and you are terrified of authority. (Offices open 9 to 5, with long waiting periods, endless forms and proof of income and assets required.) 'Catch-22' is not a trite phrase for poor Americans—it's a way of life."[16] The only benefits part-time workers receive is social security and worker's compensation since health-care and maybe pension benefits are mandatory only if employees work over 37.5 hours per week for a total of 2,080 hours per year. A full time minimum wage job will guarantee health care and life insurance benefits for the worker. However, the cost of dependent care is usually totally or partially the responsibility of the worker.

In the 1990s, a new subcategory of the working poor emerged under the label of **hyperpoor**. These individuals have annual incomes that total less than half of the official poverty level. Many of the nation's mentally and physically handicapped Americans fall into this category. In addition, the hyperpoor include those individuals who are not technically homeless but who must rely upon family members and friends to augment their costs for food and housing. Oftentimes, undereducated and unskilled legal and illegal immigrants fall into this category. For example, in South Texas, individuals who lack the skills to hold regular jobs, gather early every morning at a designated site whereby small building, paving, and construction contractors and farmers can seek a crew of laborers for a day's work. These individuals, known as **day laborers**, are paid a small wage in cash after their employer drops them off at the pickup site after the day's tasks are completed.

The **nonworking poor** include those individuals receiving unemployment compensation, the unemployed without benefits, the homeless, the totally disabled/mentally ill, and the elderly whose incomes fall below the poverty level. An accurate accounting of the nonworking poor is difficult to determine. The unemployment rate, for example, is supposed to indicate the total number of jobless Americans. However, the unemployment rate is an unreliable measuring tool since it only accounts for the unemployed who are currently receiving some form of unemployment compensation. It cannot account for those individuals whose benefits have been depleted even though they are still unemployed or for those who did not qualify for unemployment compensation.

The **feminization of poverty** recognizes the increase in the number of single-parent families headed by a female whose income falls below the poverty level. Since the 1960s, there has been a dramatic steady increase in the number of female-headed households. This rise in matriarchal families is attributed to the increase in the number of divorces, separations, out-of-wedlock pregnancies, and for non-traditional independent living styles. Usually these women are too undereducated and underskilled for the higher paying job market. Consequently, they are employed at the lowest ranking positions at minimum wage or slightly higher without immediate opportunity for promotion or advancement. Stereotypically, the feminization of poverty is seen as a minority out-of-wedlock teenager who drops out of high school, never to return again. This generalization overlooks that the ranks of poor women with dependent children includes those who completed high school and married shortly afterward. After years of marriage, these women now find themselves divorced without marketable job skills beyond low paying service-sector positions, struggling to support their children on a paltry sum of child support from their ex-husbands. Basically, "the U.S. labor market has always failed women who have little formal education and sporadic job experiences. Low-income women are still segregated into low-paying occupations, despite the vast improvements for college-educated women."[17] As single parents, these women must oftentimes make the difficult decision between meeting the needs of their children and their employment-related responsibilities. "Employers, especially those who employ low-wage workers, will not tolerate workers who come in late because a school bus did not show up, miss days because there was no child care or a kid was sick, or worry about their children at 3 p.m. instead of doing their work."[18] In 2019, the annual median family income for a married couple household was $102,308, compared to a median family income of $69,244 for a male householder with no spouse present, and a median family income of $48,098 for a female householder with no spouse present.[19]

Another subcategory of poverty distinguishes the permanently or persistently poor from the marginally or temporarily poor. The determination is based on an individual's income level over a ten-year span. A person is considered **permanently** or **persistently** poor when his/her income has been below the poverty level for eight years or longer within the ten-year period. Individuals whose incomes are below the poverty level for less than two years within the same ten-year span, are **temporarily** or **marginally** poor. Of course, each group has a different set of needs to overcome their financial deprivations. The persistently poor require long-term housing, extensive job training and educational programs, food, and other financial assistance. The temporarily poor need short-term assistance such as unemployment compensation, health-care benefits, and perhaps food stamps and shelter while seeking another job. However, most social programs crafted at both the national and state levels tend to be "one size fits all" plans that truly do not meet the unique needs of both groups.

A Profile of America's Poor

The concept of the American Dream is based on the belief that anyone in the United States can become a rich person if he/she gets an education, works hard and takes advantage of any and every opportunity to improve one's economic status. In reality, the rags to riches story happens to only a very few. The majority work hard and try their best to climb up that corporate ladder, only to see the American Dream happening to someone else.

Basically, lower- and middle-class Americans continue to find themselves with less and less income for basic necessities such as rent, clothing, food, transportation, day care, and health-care costs. A major contributing factor is the disparity in wage treatment. From 1997 to 2006, the minimum wage was stuck at $5.15 per hour. Corrective legislation gradually raised the rate to $7.25 by 2009. If the worker has a full-time job, his/her yearly salary before taxes and benefits are deducted is $15,080. Raising the federal minimum wage has always been a politically-charged battle between Republicans and Democrats in Congress and far too often between the White House and Congress. In his 2014 State of the Union message delivered before a joint session of Congress, President Obama asked the body to increase the minimum wage to at least $9 per hour. Congress opted not to do it! Meanwhile, state legislative houses can raise or lower their state minimum wages without congressional approval. While the federal minimum wage will remain at $7.25 per hour, twenty states will be increasing their minimum wage scales effective January 1, 2021. "In New Mexico, the minimum wage will increase to $10.50, up $1.50 from the current $9 wage. And in California, the rate for employers with 26 workers or more will rise from $13 to $14 an hour, the highest state-wide baseline in the country. In Minnesota, the gain is just 8 cents, to a $10.08 hourly rate for large employers."[20] While appreciated, these modest raises in the minimum wage scale are just cost-of-living adjustments. In other words, the increase will just about cover a marginal increase in the worker's personal financial obligations. Over the past decade the job market has shifted from the traditional hiring of primarily full time workers to a part-time workforce. As of November 2020, 124,165,000 Americans were employed as full-time workers, that is, working at between thirty-five and forty hours per week as compared to 25,879,000 Americans classified as part-time workers, working less than thirty-five hours per week. Approximately 6,690,000 or 4.5 percent of the nation's labor force simultaneously held two or more jobs.[21] Many lower-income families rely upon their teenage children to take on a parttime job to augment the family income. However, few non-minimum wage jobs are available to them. Teenagers between the ages of 16 through 19 have an unemployment rate of 14.0 percent, the highest percentage of any age group.[22]

There is the adage that the rich get richer and poor get poorer. Table 15.2 indicates the share of aggregate income held by American households. The lowest one fifth of the nation's total households have incomes ranging from zero to $40,000. They collectively hold only 3.1 percent of the nation's total household income. The highest fifth control 51.9 percent of the nation's income with the top 5 percent of that bracket holding onto 23.0 percent of the total wealth. Consequently, 4/5's of the nation's total households had only an aggregate share of 48.2 percent of the nation's wealth whereas, 1/5 controls 51.9 percent. The wealth gap between the ultra-rich and everyone else is increasing, not decreasing.

Table 15.2
Share of Aggregate Income Received by Each Fifth and Top Five Percent of Households—2019

Total Number of Households as of 2019—128,451,000

Fifth	Upper Limit of Each Fifth	Percent Distribution of Aggregate Income
Lowest Fifth	$ 40,000	3.1%
Second Fifth	69,000	8.3%
Third Fifth	105,038	14.1%
Fourth Fifth	164,930	22.7%
Highest Fifth		51.9%
Total 5% - Lower Income Limit	304,153	23.0%

Source: U.S. Census Bureau, *Current Population Survey: Annual Social and Economic Supplements* (CPS ASEC)

The gap between rich and poor is further widened by this nation's dependency upon state and federal income taxes and regressive tax programs that place a heavier tax burden upon middle and lower income groups. Sales, property, and excise taxes, as well as user fees, consume a greater chunk of the paychecks earned by the average American worker than those whose wages place them into the upper income brackets. One of the hot-bed issues of the 2012 presidential campaign was tax fairness. Democrat candidate President Barack Obama wanted to shift the tax burden from the middle to upper income class. The campaign was, in many respects, a class-based warfare with the Democrats emerging as the champion of the middle and lower income classes and the Republicans strongly supporting the lower tax rates for the wealthiest Americans while the Tea Party wing of the Republican Party wanted no tax increases whatsoever for anyone. During the 2016 race for the White House, both Democrats and Republicans pledged tax reform. The Clinton team wanted to increase taxes for the wealthy and lower taxes for the middle class. Team Trump wanted to decrease the tax rate for businesses and the wealthy. Both candidates really did not devote much attention to the nation's poor. Congress subsequently fulfilled Trump's campaign promise by lowering the top individual tax rate from 39.6 percent to 37 percent and cutting the corporate tax rate from 35 percent to 21 percent.[23] Although the measure did eliminate a laundry list of tax deductions, the tax burden fell once again upon the middle- and lower-income taxpayers. On the campaign trail, Democrat presidential candidate Joe Biden vowed to end the Trump-era tax program by shifting the majority of the tax burden back onto the wealthy while at the same time, lowering taxes for the middle- and lower-income groups.

Poor and lower-middle income Americans are confronted with the task of finding affordable housing. The majority of the nation's poor are forced to live in rental properties, relying on government subsidized housing to offset the costs. Finding affordable livable housing is becoming extremely difficult. For too many Americans, the dream of owning a new or even a pre-owned home is cost prohibitive. The nation's economic downturn faced by the Obama administration was in part fueled by the rise in the number of single-family home foreclosures. An inflated real estate market coupled with low mortgage interest rates was attractive to those seeking to purchase a home. However, as the economy soured and unemployment rose, many homeowners simply could not make the monthly mortgage payments. At the same time, home values declined, leaving the homeowner with the option of selling a house at less than what they owed on the home. In other words, the homeowner was upside down on the mortgage loan. For many the only option was to allow the mortgage loan to default resulting in a foreclosure, leaving the former homeowner with a ruined credit rating and slim chances of purchasing a home in the near future. The economic woes of the Covid-19 pandemic have placed millions of Americans in peril of losing their housing. At the end of December 2020, it is estimated that "more than 85.4 million adults, or 35.6 percent live in a household where it's been somewhat or very difficult to pay for usual household expenses. . . . Nearly 13 million adults, or 9.1 percent are not current on their rent or mortgage or have slight or no confidence that they can pay next month's housing bill on time."[24] Both federal stimulus packages provided protection against foreclosures and evictions and state and local governments have enacted short-term measures to assist with mortgage and rent payments. Yet, without these protections, too many Americans are just one step away from losing the roof over their heads.

The impoverished and homeless of this nation are further adversely affected by the stereotypical myths about poverty that far too often cloud the perceptions of lawmakers and the general public. The myth portrays the poor as shiftless, lazy, able-bodied men and women who simply refuse to fend for themselves, opting instead for a life of dependency upon the government's generosity. The homeless are seen as filthy unkept winos and bums who roam the streets panhandling for money to fund their addictive habits. The media has for the past fifty years helped to create the image of impoverishment. In the 1960s, the poor were portrayed as rural Anglos living in the mountainous isolated areas of Appalachia. Pictures documented the poor as living in one-room shacks without electricity or indoor plumbing. The stereotype changed in the 1980s as the poor were portrayed as primarily African Americans living in rundown urban areas called the ghettoes. Stereotypes help to shield Americans from the reality and complexity of poverty.

The majority of Americans are actually in denial about homelessness, impoverishment, and poverty. **Denial** is defined as "the inability to recognize a problem in the face of compelling evidence."[25] The majority of Americans are in denial as to the historical depth of our nation's poverty problem. Far too often seen as a third-world country's problem, Americans simply can not continue to ignore the fact that this nation's poverty level is "the highest in the developed world and more than twice as high as in most other industrialized countries, which all strike a more generous social contract with their weakest citizens."[26] Across the board, census statistics shatter the myths and reveal the reality that poverty strikes the very young and old of this nation in every hamlet from the East to West Coast and definitely cuts across all racial barriers. The Census Bureau tracks the total number of persons by race whose incomes fall below the poverty level. In 2019, approximately 33,984,000 persons accounting for 10.5 percent of the nation's population had incomes falling below the poverty level.[27] Historically, the percentages for poverty-stricken Anglos (Whites) has been consistently lower than percentages for Hispanics and Blacks (African Americans). However, the total number of Anglos (Whites) living in poverty continues to be higher than the tallies for Blacks (African Americans) and Hispanics. In 2019, 22,512,000 accounting for 9.1 percent of all Anglos (Whites) had incomes below the official poverty level compared to 8,073,000 or 18.8 percent of Blacks (African Americans) and 9,545,000 or 15.7 percent of Hispanics.[28]

The fate of our nation's children is directly tied to their parents' income status. In 2019, 10,165,000 or 14.1 percent of all children under the age of eighteen were living in poverty conditions. A further breakdown reveals that 6,209,000 or 12.0 percent are White (Anglo), 2,831,000 or 26.3 percent are Black (African American), 3,796,000 or 20.6 percent are Hispanic.[29] Published yearly by the Annie E. Casey Foundation, the 2020 *Kids Count* utilizing data from 2018, indicated the following:

- 12,998,000 or 18 percent of the nation's children live in poverty.
- 19,579,000 or 27 percent of children live in households where one or more parents lack secure employment.
- 22,566,000 or 41 percent of all children live in households with a high housing cost burden.
- 1,186,000 or 9 percent of all children are teenagers not in school and not working.
- 4,215,000 young children between the ages of 3 and 4 are not in school.
- 66 percent of the nation's children are not proficient in reading and 67 percent of Eighth graders are not proficient in math.
- 15 percent of the nation's children are not graduating from high school on time.
- 23,980,000 or 35 percent of all children live in single-parent families.
- 9,205,000 or 13 percent of children live in families where the household head lacks a high school diploma.
- 7,717,000 or 10 percent of children live in high-poverty designated area.[30]

The two primary keys to removing oneself from the shackles of endless poverty are education and economic viability. "Students from low socioeconomic status (SES) backgrounds or low-income families are 2.4 times more likely to drop out of high school than students in middle SES families, and 10 times more likely to drop out than high SES students."[31] Furthermore, lifetime earnings for a high school dropout are severely limited to minimum wage or less employment opportunities. The majority of the nation's employers require at least a high school diploma for even those lowest paying positions. In addition, "nearly 83 percent of incarcerated persons are also high school dropouts."[32] The two go hand and hand. Unfortunately, this nation is confronted with a consistently high number of teenagers who opt not to complete their high school educations. High dropout rates coupled with low test scores in reading, mathematics and English have resulted in state legislative houses assuming a more pro-active role in the administration of traditionally locally controlled public school districts. A former teacher, President Lyndon Johnson stressed that "education is mankind's only hope. Education is the imperative of a universal and lasting peace. Education is the key that unlocks progress in the struggle against hunger and want and injustice wherever they may exist on the earth. It is the path which now beckons us toward the planets and the stars. Above all else, it is the well-spring of freedom and peace."[33] As the governor of Texas, George W. Bush demanded more accountability from the state's public schools. A cornerstone of his presidency, Bush pledged that the reforms he implemented in Texas were well suited for all of the nation's public schools. He vowed that his plan would indeed leave "no child left behind." However, standardized testing scores in mathematics, reading and English reveal that many children are being left further and further behind the learning curve. The inability of the nation's public school system to properly educate American's youth prompted a frustrated President Kennedy to challenge education leaders to initiate much needed reforms:

It is within your power to see that schools no longer produce mathematical illiterates—or students who can identify all the wives of Henry the Eighth, but not the countries bordering Afghanistan—or scholars whose education has been so specialized as to exclude them from participation in current events—men like Lord John Russell, of whom Queen Victoria once remarked that he would be a better man if he knew a third subject, but he was interested in nothing but the Constitution of 1688 and himself. Civilization, according to the old saying 'is a race between education and catastrophe.' It is up to you to determine the winner.[34]

Poverty also affects the nation's elderly. In 2019, 4,858,000 or 8.9 percent of the nation's total population over the age of sixty-five had incomes below the poverty level despite the fact that many of them are either employed, receiving a work-related pension, social security benefits and/or an additional form of government assistance.[35] This figure would be substantially higher if senior citizens were not receiving Social Security and Medicare benefits. However, lawmakers are concerned that the present Social Security system will not be able to meet the income needs of an expanding senior population with potential life expectancies into their eighties and nineties.

A category of poverty that cannot be overlooked is this nation's homeless population. As previously stated, an accurate accounting of the homeless is virtually impossible. Usually, estimates include those who are living in the streets or in shelters and does not include those who are living with a relative or someone else simply because they cannot afford their own housing. Therefore, the numbers vary depending on how one defines the parameters of "homeless." Another factor is the nomadic lifestyle of the homeless. According to the National Alliance to End Homelessness, In 2019, 565,715 individuals accounting for 17 out of every 10,000 people in the United States were experiencing homelessness.[36] These are the individuals who are either sleeping outside or in an emergency shelter or registered into a transitional housing program. It is estimated that "seventy percent of people experiencing homelessness are individuals who are living on their own or in the company of other adults. The remainder (30 percent) are people in families with children."[37] While all racial/ethnic groups can experience homelessness, the most vulnerable groups are Pacific Islanders and Native Americans of which "160 people experience homelessness out of every 10,000."[38] The National Alliance to End Homelessness, defines **chronically homeless** as an individual or family that has "a disabling condition and has been continuously homeless for one year or more or has experienced at least four episodes of homelessness in the last three years."[39] As of January 2019, it was estimated that:

- 96,141 homeless individuals have chronic patterns of homelessness representing 24 percent of the total population of homeless individuals.

- 65 percent of chronically homeless individuals were living on the street, in a car, park, or other location not meant for human habitation.
- since 2017, the number of individuals with patterns of chronic homelessness has declined 20 percent.[40]

The rise in the number of homeless veterans prompted President Obama's Secretary of Veterans Affairs to conduct a nationwide search for homeless veterans with the goal of providing them with permanent housing and long-term veteran services. Despite his efforts, 2019 figures indicate that 37,085 or 7 percent of the nation's homeless population are veterans.[41] Of the homeless veteran population:

- 22,740 veterans were sheltered, while 14,345 were unsheltered.
- most homeless veterans are without children; only 2 percent were homeless as part of a family.
- 90.3 percent were men, while 8.9 percent (3,292) were women.[42]

Although many of the homeless would qualify for food stamps, they simply cannot use them effectively. Without shelter, they cannot carry or store a large amount of perishable food items or can goods. Only a handful of restaurants and fast-food chains will accept food stamps. In 1996, Congress attached a work requirement for food stamp recipients. According to the law, "able-bodied adults without children are required to work for at least 20 hours a week to get food stamps for more than three months out of a three-year period."[43] Far too many of the homeless are either too physically or mentally impaired to hold a job or lack employable skills. These individuals are caught in a "Catch 22" situation with no viable solution in sight.

The average American citizen is perplexed about the plight of the homeless. "On one hand, many people want to reach out and help these destitute and troubled men, women, and children; on the other, they are frustrated because, despite so many public and private efforts, nothing has eliminated or even decreased homelessness."[44] Once tolerant city councils are passing ordinances removing homeless persons from their makeshift housing in parks and under expressway underpasses; arresting panhandlers for loitering; and charging winos with public drunkenness. The city council in Asheville, North Carolina, enacted an ordinance "barring aggressive panhandling with fines of up to $500 and up to 20 days in jail for people with at least five prior misdemeanors. . . . Orlando [Florida] barred people from sitting or lying on downtown sidewalks, with violators fined $500 and sent to jail for 60 days. Panhandling was restricted to 'blue boxes' drawn on downtown sidewalks."[45] Patterned after a facility in Florida, several major cities have opted to address their homeless issues by constructing a self-contained homeless community known as Haven for Hope. These facilities provide protected separate housing for both single individuals and families. The centers include health and dental clinics, day care facilities, education and job training centers, etc. The Havens for Hope actually accomplish two major goals. First, they provide necessary services needed to alleviate the adverse impact of being homeless. Second, they provide the means of removing the homeless from the streets.

Statistics reveal that the poverty stricken are either very young or very old. The majority of the children living in poverty are being raised in single-parent female-headed households. We also know that poverty adversely affects more Anglo individuals and families than other racial groups, although a larger percentage of ethnic minorities live in impoverished conditions. Studies indicate that homelessness can strike anyone at any time, particularly those surviving from paycheck to paycheck. Nor can one overlook the possibility of being unemployed. The safety net programs of the traditional welfare system have kept millions from becoming mired in poverty. Unfortunately, safety net programs mask the depth of this nation's poverty situation. For example, in 2015 "4 million people in poor households were doubled up with family and friends, the most common prior living situation before becoming homeless."[46] The lack of decent affordable housing for low-income individuals and families is a national crisis. "In 2018, 6.5 million Americans experienced severe housing cost burden, which means they spent more than 50 percent of their income on housing. This marked the fourth straight year of decreases in the size of this group. However, the number of severely cost burdened Americans is still 13 percent higher than it was in 2007, the year the nation began monitoring homelessness data."[47] These are pre-Covid-19 figures. With the start of 2021, the number of homeowners and renters in peril of losing their homes has increased dramatically. This is the real picture of poverty. The faces of those living in poverty are not just skid row bums, hobos, and winos. They are, in reality, a cross section of American society. Traditionally, the federal government's role in addressing homelessness has been marginal. State legislative houses have also been reluctant to initiate legislative acts to aid in ending homelessness. For decades, the task of providing shelter, medical and mental care, long-term housing, food, etc., has been borne by local and county governments, religious groups, and private charities.

The Philosophy and Politics of Poverty

One of the major issues of the 1980 presidential election between Republican Ronald Reagan and Democrat incumbent President Jimmy Carter was welfare reform. Both cited problems with Johnson's War on Poverty program. Once inaugurated into the White House, President Reagan launched his plan to redo the entire welfare system. Initially, he had the backing from both Republicans and Democrats. However, their zeal for reform revealed that both political parties were, and still are, sharply divided over the philosophical nature of the concept of welfare and welfare reform. In 1996, lawmakers argued over every aspect of the welfare system from methodical approaches to funding options. The resulting package of reform measures received mixed reviews as critics on both sides of the political spectrum leveled criticisms and complaints while vowing to enact corrective legislation to address identified program weaknesses. Against the backdrop of a sagging economy, Democrats continued their traditional cry to increase government funding for social service programs as President George W. Bush advocated the traditional conservative Republican complaint that the government spends far too much money on welfare programs. During the 2008 campaign, President Barack Obama pledged he would revisit the welfare package enacted in 1996 with the intent of expanding the programs offered to the nation's poor. During his eight years in the White House, President Obama had to shift his emphasis from welfare reform to economic recovery as this nation faced its worst economic downturn since the Great Depression. The campaign rhetoric of the 2016 presidential race rarely mentioned reforming the existing welfare system, as once again the emphasis was on economic recovery and job creation. The economic adverse impact of the pandemic on both the lower and middle classes will move the incoming Biden administration to reassess and, perhaps, reform the existing welfare system.

Republican Party leaders openly advocate the traditional conservative belief that economic deprivation is the inevitable result of an individual's failure and, in some cases, laziness to avail one's self of the free market's promise of economic viability and riches. They strongly believe that the American Dream of economic success is like the brass ring at the carnival. The ring can be grabbed by anyone who possesses the talent, determination, and desire to grab it. It's the individual who makes the choice between success and failure, not the economy or any other outside factor. Conservatives concede that the competitive nature of capitalism will naturally award the brass ring to only a select few because they possess a higher level of competitive skills over others. This competitive edge is often explained by Charles Darwin's concept of the survival of the fittest. Subsequently, "life's circumstances will always put some people into poverty, but the people with initiative will overcome their poverty."[48] Most conservatives, therefore, believe that government should play an extremely limited role in aiding the impoverished with benefits limited to the deserving poor, to the physically and mentally impaired, or to those of advanced age unable to compete and survive.

Extreme conservatives uphold that all welfare programs have failed miserably because the impoverished themselves are just too culturally and intellectually deficient to use government-sponsored programs and benefits to lift themselves out of their poverty. In *The Unheavenly City*, Edward C. Banfield argued that economic deprivation is an inwardly acquired trait that eventually evolves into a culture of poverty. Therefore:

> extreme present-orientedness, not lack of income or wealth, is the principal cause of poverty in the sense of the 'culture of poverty.' Most of those caught up in this culture are unable and unwilling to plan for the future, to sacrifice immediate gratifications in favor of future ones, or to accept the disciplines that are required in order to get and to spend. Their inabilities are probably culturally given in most cases.[49]

It followed, according to this line of reasoning, that the welfare state created by Franklin Roosevelt merely sustained the culture of poverty by making benefit recipients dependent upon the government for their survival.

The election of Ronald Reagan to the White House gave anti-welfare conservative Republicans the opportunity to lay the philosophical groundwork that produced the welfare reform legislation passed by the 104th Congress. A strong advocate of the competitiveness of the free market feature of capitalism, Reagan continuously blamed the welfare system for instilling dependency by robbing benefit recipients of their dignity and self-reliancy. "At the heart of President Reagan's opposition to federal welfare initiatives lies the suspicion that the poor are morally different from the non-poor—that they do not share the values and aspirations of working Americans, that they do not respond to the incentives and opportunities of the market in the same way as the more prosperous do."[50] Republican-led legislative acts at state and national levels are designed to redirect the poor back to the conservative concept of the proper work ethic by tightening benefit eligibility requirements, limiting benefits, and requiring recipients to work, while at the same time, slashing federal budgetary dollars traditionally allocated for social service programs. In December 2020, the United States Congress debated whether to issue another stimulus package to offset the hardships of the Covid-19 pandemic. Few disagreed that another stimulus package was needed. The argument, however, focused on the amount. Democrats wanted a $2,000 payment for all non-family individuals, $4,000 for married couples and an additional amount for each minor child in the family unit. However, Senate Majority Leader Mitch McConnell stuck to the traditional Republican conservative philosophy by reducing the proposed stimulus package to only $600. This became a political battleground issue in the run-off Senate races in Georgia. Democrat President-elect Joe Biden, his Vice President-elect Kamala Harris and former President Obama campaigned for those Democrat candidates with the promise that if the Democrats gained control of the Senate, the $2,000 stimulus package would be back on the table, passed quickly and mailed to qualifying individuals.

The liberal perspective is that:

those who are living in poverty have not individually created their poverty any more than those who are prosperous have individually produced their wealth. The fine line between success and failure represents one of the most sensitive and complex unsolved phenomena of the era of space, conglomerates and megalopolises. The future . . . of this nation may well rest upon the effectiveness with which the political and economic leadership recognizes and provides for the needs of the less fortunate.[51]

The Democratic Party became the standard bearer for the liberal perspective with the election of Woodrow Wilson to the presidency. Every Democrat president since has to some degree promoted government sponsored programs to meet the needs of impoverished and lower-income Americans with programs ranging from federally insured student loans to food stamps and Medicaid.

Liberals base their position on three major premises. First, they believe that the historical pattern of economic prosperity followed by devastating recessions, high inflation, and depressions have placed the American worker in constant economic peril. It's the fickleness of the economy and the inability of government to respond to economic upheavals that cause poverty and deprivation. Second, statistics support the liberal contention that far too many hard working Americans are losing economically as the rich become richer and the poor only become poorer. Liberals believe that government has the obligation to assist workers in reversing this trend. They stress that without the intervention of government, "the gap between rich and poor would tend to widen in an advanced economy, generating more unacceptable disparities and straining the fabric of an open, free, and democratic society."[52] Third, liberals believe that economic, social, and political equality for all Americans can be realized only through the efforts of the government. Consequently, the safety net created by President Franklin Roosevelt was designed "not only to seek to prevent extreme deprivation among the most disadvantaged, but also to attempt to cushion the impact of economic misfortune and uncertainty on the more advantaged and affluent members of society. The resulting 'safety net' has been remarkably successful in shielding diverse segments of the population from the full brunt of the vagaries and hardships implicit in a free market economy."[53] Affirmative action legislation helped to open the economic doors to disadvantaged Americans, particularly minorities and women. The Voting Rights Act passed during Lyndon Johnson's term in the White House extended voting privileges to the disenfranchised. The liberal perspective underscores inclusion and equal opportunities to the have nots in their struggles to become haves.

The welfare system and the never ending quest to reform it involves a wide range of interested parties. Of course, welfare recipients are extremely concerned that the elimination of benefits will just deepen rather than help them to overcome their suffering. After all, they are the ones in the "economic bubble" whereby any hint of an economic downslide could cost them their jobs. Requiring welfare recipients to work in order to keep their benefits only works if the jobs they are qualified for are available to them. However, the poor are, in most instances, the silent voices in the public policy process simply because they really do not participate. Few vote or even voice their concerns at public meetings or congressional hearings. The poor do not have the powerful advocates and lobbyists that other interest groups use to affect the public policy process. Yet, their survival may very well hinge on the actions of others who have very little first hand knowledge of the plight of the poor beyond statistical and budgetary reports. The poor were not consulted about the direction and scope of welfare reform.

The elderly have voiced their concerns about the future of Social Security, Medicare, and health-care reform. They want assurances from the national government that the Social Security system is financially sound for themselves and for future generations. Health-care reform has seniors worried as the federal government threatens to cut billions from Medicare programs. They fear that cuts in Medicare coverage and the uncertain future of Obamacare will lead to inadequate health care. The lobbyists representing the **American Association of Retired Persons (AARP)** are constantly watching legislative actions at both the state and national level. Talks about health-care reform have disabled veterans worried that their federally funded health-care benefits will be severely cut or eliminated, thereby, leaving the majority of them without any form of health-care coverage. Women's organizations play an important role as they see welfare and health-care reform adversely affecting low-income women and children. They are fearful that any additional reform efforts will result in "a whole new world of hurt coming. A world where you scare people. You confuse them. You threaten to take their benefits and make them scared for their children. And its OK to do this because they are just lazy welfare moms anyway."[54] Far too often, lawmakers and politicians alike from both political parties have used demeaning rhetoric towards the recipients of public assistance programs, particularly women.

The providers of public welfare and health-care assistance are equally concerned whenever lawmakers threaten to reform the system. For example, extreme cuts in the food stamp program can adversely impact the nation's farmers and ranchers. It is their food products that are eventually sold in the nation's supermarkets to both cash and food stamp carrying patrons. Any discussion of health-care reform is closely watched by the owners of the nation's drug companies and health-care providers. Cuts in Medicare and Medicaid and any proposed changes to Obamacare coverage are keenly watched by the **American Medical Association (AMA)**, the **American Hospital Association (AHA)**, and other health-care-based interest groups. State and federal cost containment efforts mean less money for health-care providers. Health-care providers are worried that reform means a drastic and tragic loss of quality health care for their patients. The elderly, the impoverished, children, disabled veterans, care providers, farmers, and so on are the key players involved in the legislative battles over welfare and health-care reform. They have a vested interest either personally or professionally in any legislation involving public assistance and health-care interests. Often at odds with each other, the push for reform has the recipients and the providers of health care and social services on the same side as they desire to see that any reform measure adequately protects their interests.

The Historical Development of the Welfare State

Throughout the history of humankind, civilizations have always recognized their responsibility to address the needs of the deserving poor while at the same time holding an unpleasant distaste for those deemed to be undeserving of their charitable efforts.

> Most people in all cultures enjoy the feeling of helping others, and most cultures consider charity a community or religious duty or a measure of good character. But a distaste for freeloaders also characterizes many cultures. The violator may appear to not really need the help, or to use the help in a bad way, or to not work hard. The giver then feels taken in and may become hostile and resentful. But if the recipient is truly needy and unable to help himself or herself—a child, for example, or a handicapped person—the giver no longer feels exploited or concerned about freeloading. Those mixed feelings about giving and sharing have surrounded aid to the needy for centuries in most cultures.[55]

The distinction between the deserving and undeserving poor has pervaded every public policy initiative addressing this nation's poor since its founding. "The first American settlers understood the relationship between work, survival and dependence. The original colonists came from a broad cross section of English society that included many of England's wandering homeless, vagrants, bona fide criminals, lunatics, and misfits of all sorts."[56] Public sympathy was extended to the aged, the sick, the disabled, and the temporarily impoverished due to economic downturns and job loss. It was a community responsibility to help those in true need. The able-bodied, however, received harsh treatment. "As Cotton Mather put it, 'For those who indulge in idleness, the express command of God unto us is, that we should let them starve.'"[57] The English poor laws served as a foundation for the colonial response to poverty and homelessness. Although programs varied from colony to colony, "there were four basic responses to poverty: auctioning off the poor ('selling' them to the lowest bidder, who agreed to care for and maintain them with public funds), contracting the poor (placing them in private homes at public expense), outdoor relief (basic assistance given outside the confines of a public institution), and the poorhouse (public institutions, also known as indoor relief)."[58]

After the Revolutionary War, the newly created states usually opted for outdoor relief assistance aimed primarily to assist long-term community residents confronted with a serious injury, illness, or death of the breadwinner. Pensions were established for war widows and orphans. Local tax dollars supported relief programs as the national government played practically no major role in social service programs. To offset costs, local authorities used several options including "'**binding out**' (indenturing the poor to families needing laborers or servants), '**farming out**' (requiring men to work for wages that were in turn used for their support), and arrangements similar to modern foster care whereby indigents were placed in homes where they received care or where their children were apprenticed to craftsmen to learn trades."[59] Charges of fraud and abuse, as well as the growing belief that outdoor relief programs were undermining the fabric of American society, led to a new alternative—the poorhouse or **almshouse**.

The poorhouses took the poor, the mentally ill, and the criminal element off the streets. It was believed that "institutional life would not only protect the individual from corrupting influences but also allow the individual to reform."[60] Although popular in the 1820s and 1830s, poorhouses soon became just as distasteful as outdoor relief. Despite reform efforts, poorhouses were targeted by Progressive reformers for their deplorable conditions. Report after report revealed that "graft, corruption, and brutality were common; alcohol was smuggled in; inmates came and went; fifth and disorder prevailed; criminals, alcoholics, women, mothers, children, and infants were mixed together. Mortality rates were high."[61] There were no state regulatory laws governing the operation of orphanages and poorhouses. There were, with few exceptions, no requirements for periodic on-sight inspections. Poorhouses and orphanages received little monetary support from state treasuries. Dependent upon private donations, orphanages and poorhouses farmed out their residents as laborers for farmers, ranchers, and businessmen and as servants for private residences. Workers' earnings went directly to the orphanage or the poorhouse to help offset operational costs. The only viable options to the poorhouse were shelters provided through religious or private charity groups, outdoor relief, or an innovative form of the poorhouse called the **settlement house**.

Settlement houses were community centers located in the poor districts of major cities. These centers would provide guidance, services, and basic skills training to anyone living within the neighborhood. Settlement workers were usually recent college graduates from middle and upper class families who lived in the settlement houses. "The settlement house movement unabashedly promoted bourgeois values and habits—instructing the poor in everything from art appreciation and home economics to the importance of establishing savings accounts. To children in poverty, it offered recreation, books, clubs, as well as a sense of the history of American democratic institutions. It approached thousands of the urban poor, particularly children and teenagers, with a message

Jane Addams in Chicago working at Hull House.

of inclusion in the larger world beyond the slums."[62] Similar to those operating in London, the first American settlement house, known as the **Neighborhood Guild**, was opened by Dr. Stanton Coit in the Lower East Side of New York in 1886. By the turn of the century nearly a hundred settlement houses had been opened throughout the United States. The most notable centers were Jane Addams' **Hull House** in Chicago (1889), Robert A. Woods' South End House in Boston (1892), and Lillian Wald's Henry Street Settlement in New York (1893). Settlement houses were only marginally successful since their reliance upon private donations could not keep up with the cost of maintaining the houses much less meeting the demands of the ever increasing number of impoverished Americans.

The states were extremely ill-prepared for the economic deprivation caused by the crash of the Stock Market in 1929. Millions of hardworking Americans were suddenly unemployed. Their savings were gone since banks were not required to insure their deposits. The city streets were soon crowded with Depression Era homeless. Private charity-sponsored soup kitchens and breadlines could not feed all the hungry. As state coffers dwindled, governors began to turn toward the federal government for assistance and, most importantly, money. The United States Congress enacted the **New Deal** proposals of President Franklin Roosevelt, which included work programs under the **Civilian Conservation Corps**, the **Works Progress Administration**, the **Emergency Relief Administration**, and the **National Youth Corps**. These programs were jointly funded by national and state governments with the bulk of the funding coming from Washington, D.C.

The current welfare system began in earnest when the United States Congress passed the **Social Security Act of 1935**. This landmark piece of legislation established two major insurance programs geared towards protecting the elderly and the unemployed from slipping into poverty. The **Old**

FDR at the Grand Coulee Dam in Washington. October 2, 1937

Grand Coulee Dam on the Columbia River in Washington, which created a 150-mile long lake. Together with the Bonneville Dam (also on the Columbia), the Grand Coulee gave the Pacific Northwest the cheapest electricity in the nation and created the potential for significant economic and population growth. TheBonneville and Grand Coulee Dams made the state of Washington the largest per capita recipient of New Deal funds. The benefits of this dam building program, in terms of economic development and population growth, did not come to fruition until the post-World War II years.

Age Insurance program created a self-funded insurance plan providing pensions and benefits for the elderly and disabled; the **Unemployment Insurance** program assisted workers temporarily laid off their jobs. The Social Security Act also created several public assistance programs including **Old Age Assistance**, **Aid to the Blind**, and **Aid to Dependent Children** (later changed to **Aid to Families with Dependent Children**). The bulk of the New Deal policies were designed as alleviative and preventive actions, that is, temporary public assistance to relieve the suffering while protecting millions more from falling into poverty. These temporary fixes almost became permanent fixtures.

The nation's next major assault on poverty occurred when President Lyndon Johnson introduced his **War on Poverty** program in the 1960s. In a speech delivered on May 22, 1964 at the University of Michigan, President Johnson not only declared war on poverty but introduced his concept of the **Great Society**:

"The Great Society rests on abundance and liberty for all. It demands an end to poverty and racial injustice, to which we are totally committed to in our time. But that is just the beginning. The Great Society is a place where every child can find knowledge to enrich his mind and to enlarge his talents. It is a place where leisure is a welcome chance to build and reflect; not a feared cause of boredom and restlessness. It is a place where the city of man serves not only the needs of the body and the demands of commerce but the desire for beauty and the hunger for community. It is a place where man can renew contact with nature. It is a place which honors creation for its own sake and for what it adds to the understanding of the race. It is a place where men are more concerned with the quality of their goals than the quantity of their goods."[63]

The Johnson administration opted for a curative approach to solving poverty by retaining several of the alleviative and preventive plans created by New Deal initiatives and creating a wide variety of programs designed to address and, hopefully, eliminate poverty. The whole program was based on the belief that poverty could be eliminated by providing the poor with the essential tools needed to lift themselves out of their economic deprivation. An inadequate educational opportunity and the lack of proper job training programs were viewed as two of the primary reasons why many Americans were confronted with a lifetime of at or below minimum wage jobs with extremely limited opportunities for advancement.

The **Economic Opportunity Act of 1965** established the Office of Economic Opportunity designed to coordinate all federal initiatives with state and local governments. The War on Poverty was this nation's first major assault designed to eliminate poverty. The package of antipoverty measures also included programs to enhance the quality of life for the needy through such initiatives as the **Model Cities** program. Federal dollars were allocated for the construction of low-income housing units throughout the nation's economically depressed inner cities. Revitalization plans were encouraged as a means of revamping depressed central business districts in hopes of attracting higher paying job opportunities to inner cities.

The architects of the New Deal and the War on Poverty programs established the pattern for all subsequent social service initiatives. First, the federal government and state legislative houses realized that the complexity of poverty with its ever increasing numbers of impoverished Americans was beyond the limited abilities of the states to handle totally on their own. The horror story of states scrambling to meet immediate needs of the Depression Era unemployed could not be repeated again. Consequently, the federal government would create the policy response and target a specific service group for benefit coverage. While this provided nationally based responses to national issues and problems, the federal government's role deprived the states of their rights to create their own programs. Consequently, few state lawmakers have created innovative public assistance programs independent of the federal government.

Second, program funding was either totally or partially provided by the federal government. Leaving the states off-the-hook, the federal government allowed the states to become totally dependent upon federal funding to assist their state's impoverished. State legislatures could create budgets with the lowest allocations possible for social service programs knowing that the federal government would foot the bill.

Third, the states would continue to receive federal funding only if they complied with the minimal requirements set by the federal government. For example, each state was required to create a separate state agency to administer each federal program. The federal government assumed the majority of the responsibility for funding the program while leaving the administrative chores to the individual states. However, the creation of a multiplicity of state agencies merely complements the fragmentary and decentralized organization of state governments creating duplication of services, mounds of red tape, and little accountability on the part of state agencies.

Fourth, the federal government permitted the states to set their own eligibility requirements, benefit amounts, service delivery options, and punitive sanctions for abuse as long as the states followed the minimal eligibility and benefit standards set by the federal government. Consequently, the majority of state programs use the punitive public policy approach by just tightening the eligibility requirements every year to guarantee that only the truly deserving receive assistance. Each year, stiffer penalties are attached to each program to guard against fraud and abuse. Unfortunately, the zeal to attached punitive sanctions has cast a suspicious eye on anyone seeking government assistance. Statistics reveal a discrepancy between those in economic need and those receiving government-sponsored assistance. Many needy Americans simply do not apply for assistance because of the stigmatized image associated with "welfare."

Finally, benefit allocations vary from state to state. States can opt to pay only the minimal benefit amount, which is usually totally funded by the federal government, or they can add-on their own allocation to the minimum. "In general, programs tend to be most generous in states with wealth, strong labor unions, high voter turnout by poor people, and liberal political beliefs or cultures. The generous states are found disproportionately in the Northeast, Midwest, and Pacific regions, and the least generous states tend to be in the South, Southwest, and Rocky Mountain regions."[64]

The Programs of the Welfare State Entitlements:
Social Security and Unemployment Compensation

Initially, both **Social Security** and **unemployment compensation** were marketed as temporary programs. Today, they are viewed by some as absolute guaranteed rights for American workers. Millions of retired American citizens believe that they "toiled for years to send Uncle Sam a mountain of dollar bills. These taxes went into individual accounts with their names and Social Security numbers emblazoned on them; now, seniors are simply withdrawing what is rightfully their own."[65] Yet, "Social Security has never been an insurance program, it has never been a contract that we make with ourselves to fund our own retirement, and our tax money is not set aside in a trust fund, as advertised. Nor are our benefits tied to how much we paid in taxes. Most people get back many times what they put in, even after interest is accounted for. To be precise, Social Security is an intergenerational transfer of money from workers to non-workers. Kind of like welfare. Exactly like welfare."[66] The Supreme Court settled the issue by its 1960 ruling in *Flemming v Nestor* that Social Security is not a guaranteed right. Justice John Harlan noted that Social Security was "designed to function into the indefinite future, and its specific provisions rests on predictions as to expected economic conditions, which must inevitably prove less than wholly accurate, and on judgments and preferences as to the proper allocation of the nation's resources which evolving economic and social conditions will of necessity in some cases modify."[67]

Social Security is funded through payroll taxes paid by employees and employers. Workers are eligible to receive benefits as early as age 55 if they are deemed unemployable due to permanent disabilities. The benefit amount is based on the individual worker's work history, including length of employment as well as salary history. Those retirees that worked the majority of their adult lives at higher paying jobs will receive a higher benefit amount over those who worked just as long but at lower paying jobs. In 2018, retired workers received an average monthly benefit of $1,461, disabled workers $1,234, and non-disabled widows and widowers $1,388.[68] Usually Social Security recipients would receive a yearly cost-of-living adjustment ranging from 2 to 3 percent. The monthly benefits plus a marginal yearly adjustment simply leaves little disposable income for expenses beyond the essentials of food, shelter and clothing. Therefore, the monthly benefits for the average retired worker are not enough to maintain a comfortable lifestyle. Many elderly receive just enough in benefits to put them into the **safety net**, just one perilous step away from poverty.

Initially, seniors were subjected to an earnings penalty that required the government to deduct $1 in Social Security benefits for every $3 dollars earned by seniors under the age of 70. It was estimated that "more than 800,000 lost part or all of their benefits because of the earnings limit."[69] Once the Social Security recipient turned 70, he or she could earn as much as they could without any reductions in benefits. In 2000, President Clinton signed legislation removing the earnings penalty. Now seniors regardless of their age, can continue to work full or part-time jobs without the fear of losing their full Social Security benefits. If Social Security was a true pension program, retirees would receive benefits equal only to what they initially paid into the plan. Social Security, however, guarantees benefits for the life of the retired worker with survivor benefits for their spouses of 50 percent of the original benefit. Consequently, there is a point where Social Security ceases to be a pension and becomes an entitlement or public assistance payment. **Entitlements** are "benefits provided by government to which recipients have a legally enforceable right."[70] Social Security, Medicare, veteran's benefits, and military retirement benefits are entitlement programs.

The survival of Social Security has lawmakers searching for remedies to keep the program soluble and intact. Currently, the total amount of employee/employer contributions is sufficient to provide benefits for today's retirees. Yet, statistics do indicate an alarming increase in the number of retirees living longer with an offsetting decrease in wage earners. Proposals to save Social Security include reducing annual cost-of-living adjustments (COLAs), reducing benefits for high-income beneficiaries, increasing the Social Security payroll tax, increasing the amount of earnings subject to the payroll tax, taxing Social Security like a private pension program, establishing individual accounts, allowing workers to invest a portion of their potential Social Security benefits, and, if all else fails, reducing or actually cutting benefits.

Unemployment compensation was designed to be a temporary entitlement benefit for temporarily displaced workers. Mandated by the federal government, the states determine eligibility requirements, benefit allocations, and benefit time frames. Not every unemployed worker automatically receives unemployment benefits. In most states, individuals who have been involuntarily separated from their employment through no fault of their own will receive full benefits. However, in several states, voluntary separations and terminations by employee actions result in reduced payments or no benefits at all. Recipients are required to continue to search for work or lose their benefits. Generally, it is extremely difficult for unemployed recipients to make financial ends meet. This is particularly problematic for the higher-end of the salary scale employee who loses his/her job.

Public Assistance Programs

The bulk of state and federal public assistance programs are means-tested plans providing in-kind services or cash transfer benefits. **Means-tested eligibility** is based upon the applicant's documented inability to provide for his/herself the desired benefit because of depressed income levels. Basic welfare and Supplemental Security Income (SSI) are two of the cash-transfer programs available to the needy. Each program is available to those who meet the qualifications. For example, the federally funded **Supplemental Security Income** program was designed to provide cash payments to lower income elderly, the blind, disabled adults, and children. To qualify, recipients must have incomes below 185 percent of the poverty level. **In-kind programs** are means-tested services providing "assistance that has a cash value even though it is not received in cash."[71] Subsidized public housing and day care, Medicare, the Special Supplemental Program for Women, Infants, and Children (WIC), food stamps, and legal services are examples of in-kind assistance programs.

Originally introduced in 1964 to the American public as the Food Stamp Program, the **Supplemental Nutrition Assistance Program (SNAP)** is designed to provide an in-kind exchange of coupons for food items to offset nutritional deficiencies and hunger among America's needy. Administered by the Department of Agriculture through state and county public assistance agencies, the program is totally funded by the national government to include two-thirds of state and county administrative costs. The stamps are supposed to be used to buy staple products, not items that cannot be consumed such as paper products, household cleaners, and so on. To qualify for the program, the applicant must meet three criteria: a) his/her gross monthly income must be at or below 130 percent of the poverty line, or $2,252 a month for a three-person family with an exception granted for households with an elderly or disabled member, b) the net monthly income after deductions such as high housing costs and child care, must be less than or equal to the poverty line, and c) assets must fall below certain limits (for 2019, income of $1,150 for households without an elderly or disabled member and $3,500 for those with an elderly or disabled member).[72] In 2019, the maximum monthly benefit ranged from $192 for a one-person household to $762 for a five-member household.[73]

The Census Bureau defines **food secure** as "a household [that] had access at all times to enough food for an active healthy life for all household members, with no need for recourse to socially unacceptable food sources or extraordinary coping behaviors to meet their basic food needs. **Food**

insecure households had limited or uncertain ability to acquire acceptable foods in socially accept-able ways. Food insecure households with hunger were those with one or more household members who were hungry at least sometime during the period due to inadequate resources for food."[74] Food stamps have become for many Americans a household necessity simply because their paychecks cannot be stretched enough to cover rent, day care, utilities, and medical costs, plus monthly food costs. Unfortunately, many Americans who are in need of food stamps opt not to participate in the program either because of the complicated application process or they are too embarrassed to ask for government assistance. With the passage of the Elementary and Secondary Education Act during the Johnson administration, the federal government has funded school lunch subsidiary programs providing a free lunch to children whose parents simply cannot afford to provide them with one. Without these federally-funded meal programs, these children would probably receive only one meal per day. The Obama administration urged that both the Departments of Agricul-ture and Education push public and private schools to offer nutritious fat-free meals and restrict vending machines to selling only healthy products as a way to offset the growing number of obese children. Since the free lunch and breakfast programs are only available during the normal school year term, many community organizations, and public and private schools, as well as higher edu-cational institutions, have used federal grant money for summer school programs. These programs provide school-age children with additional educational opportunities, nutritious meals, and for their working parents, free child care services.

As with any federally-funded assistance program, critics point out that SNAP is too costly for the government to fund and is riddled with abuse and fraud. Basically, SNAP provides recipients with a coupon book. This does allow the recipient to receive cash back when the grocery bill is less than the face value of the coupons. Some have been charged with selling their stamps to someone else or exchanging the coupons for items not covered under the program. Some states like Texas have addressed this problem by using a pre-approved line-of-credit card that can be used for only approved grocery purchases. However, the majority of program recipients do not abuse the pro-gram nor do they participate in fraud. For those who simply do not participate in the program or do not meet eligibility requirements, cities and community organizations across the nation have established food banks whose shelves are stocked through private donations. Community-based voluntary food programs also include meals-on-wheels that deliver hot prepared meals to qualifying elderly and disabled individuals.

The **Special Supplemental Program for Women, Infants and Children**, commonly known as **WIC**, was created to provide nutritional food staples to pregnant women, breastfeeding mothers, mothers up to six months after giving birth, and children under the age of five. Funded by the federal government, this program is administered by the Food and Nutrition Service of the Department of Agriculture with assistance from state and county public agencies. Recipients receive vouchers for food items including milk, iron-fortified infant formula, cheese, eggs, fruit juice, cereals, peanut butter, and beans. The WIC program provides immunizations and prenatal care for free or at a nominal fee. The WIC program has been very successful in reducing health-care costs by treating infants with low birth weights. Additional funded federal programs include Head Start, Summer Food Service Program, Elderly Nutrition Program, Emergency Food Assistance Program (TEFAP), Commodity Distribution Program, Food Distribution on Indian Reservations (FDPIR), and the Hunger and Food Insecurity Program.

The Reform Bandwagon

The political climate of the 1980s and 1990s compelled state legislative houses across this country to enact their own welfare reform initiatives. With few exceptions, state lawmakers took a punitive approach by placing time limits on benefits, requiring recipients to seek work, stiffening eligibility requirements, and placing stronger punitive measures to curb abuse. Although an advocate of welfare reform, President Clinton reluctantly signed into law the **Personal Responsibility and Work Opportunity Act** on July 31, 1996. His signature ushered in the long-awaited package of welfare reform initiatives destined to revamp the system established over 50 years ago. In some respects, this legislation merely duplicated many of the punitive measures already adopted by several states. The legislation's major provisions include:

A) Limiting lifetime welfare benefits to five years.

B) Requiring the head of household to find work within two years or the entire family would lose its benefits.

C) Mandating that at least half of all single parents in any state be employed or involved in work-related activities such as school or job training. However, the new federal law prevents state governments from penalizing women on welfare who are unable to secure day care for their children under six years of age.

D) Limiting all childless adults between 18 and 50 years of age to three months of food stamps during a three-year period. Workers who have exhausted their three month supply of food stamps can apply for an additional three months if they are laid off their jobs during the three-year period.

E) Requiring unwed teenage mothers to live with their parents and attend school to receive benefits. Furthermore, the law does give the states the latitude to deny benefits to teenage mothers who do not meet the new requirements and to children born while the mother is receiving benefits.

F) Prohibiting food stamps and cash aid to anyone convicted of felony drug charges. However, pregnant women and adults in drug programs are exempt.

G) Prohibiting future legal immigrants from receiving Medicaid benefits during their first five years of residency in the United States.

The federal government did soften the punitiveness of the reform package by inserting provisions for exemptions; establishing funding requirements on the states designed to prevent states from eliminating all of their social service programs; and providing additional federal funds to offset potential economic crises such as recessions and periods of high unemployment. Each state is allowed hardship exemptions up to 20 percent of their current welfare cases. This provision ensures a continuation of benefits for the elderly and disabled citizens. The states are also prohibited from dramatically slashing their state budgetary allocations for social service programs. States must maintain their social service budgets at 80 percent of their 1994 levels or face severe reductions in their federal funding. The federal law does provide additional federal funding to states with high unemployment rates or fast-growing populations.

Welfare Reform – Is It Working?

The success of the 1996 welfare reform package is tied directly to the nation's economic ups and downs. Initially, one could declare welfare reform a success. Statistically, more poverty-level Americans were removed from the public dole. More were finding employment. But, the question of whether the poor were truly benefiting from welfare reform still plagued lawmakers. Were the income gains of the poor meaningful enough to ensure that they were, as promised, never again to seek public assistance for their daily survival? Were the job opportunities viable ones that would eventually lead to salary increases and possible promotions? Was the economy strong enough in the long run to ensure that the poor were no longer the likely victims of economic downturns?

The initial setting for welfare reform could not have occurred at a better time. The United States economy was booming. The service sector generated an ample number of positions for those with marginal and limited job skills. However, these jobs are usually at minimum or slightly above minimum wage with very little opportunities for advancement. A minimum wage salary simply will not provide enough income to cover the costs of rising rents, gasoline, food, day care, clothing and of course, health care. For welfare reform, true success meant that a former recipient of benefits was able to earn enough to safely say that they had left 'the system' behind. The economic downturn beginning in 2006 has meant a statistical reversal as more and more Americans lost their jobs, their homes, and their credit ratings. The economic reforms enacted by the Obama administration were beginning to gradually bring the economy to a healthier state. The growing economy of the Trump administration came to a grinding halt with the Covid-19 pandemic. With unemployment soaring to double digits, many Americans who once voiced opposition to welfare programs were now applying for these income support programs. Food banks needed to replenish their shelves on a daily basis. The previous cries for welfare reform have been replaced by calls for additional federal assistance to help struggling Americans through this tragic economic and health-care crisis. For many displaced workers, their jobs are gone. The incoming Biden administration will need to revisit the entire package of income assistance programs to ensure that they provide more, not less, assistance.

Health-care Reform

Vowing to revamp the nation's health-care system, candidate Barack Obama told millions of Americans about his personal experience with the existing health-care system as he watched his terminally ill mother suffer through the last stages of breast cancer while at the same time battling with insurance companies, doctors, and hospitals over whether certain procedures were covered, and working through the mounds of forms, bureaucratic red tape, and the ever-growing pile of unpaid medical and drug bills. On March 23, 2010, President Obama signed into law a highly partisan and very controversial sweeping health-care package aimed to meet his goals of a) providing insurance to nation's uninsured; b) reducing rising health-care costs; c) shifting the emphasis of health care from reactionary to preventive; and d) correcting deficiencies in the prescription drug legislation passed during the Bush administration.

Obama is not the first president to promote a national health care plan nor are the provisions of his **Affordable Care Act (ACA)** revolutionary. In 1912, President Teddy Roosevelt promised his Bull Moose Party supporters that "the protection of home life against the hazards of sickness [would be prevented] through the adoption of a system of social insurance."[75] He could not fulfill his promise since he lost the election. In 1932, his cousin President Franklin Roosevelt formed a Committee on the Costs of Medical Care composed of medical professionals and economists to design a universal health care program. Roosevelt could not get Congress to back his plan.

In 1954, President Harry Truman introduced the **National Health Act** to Congress. "Truman saw the issue as one of fairness. Wealthy Americans could afford medical care. Poor Americans get charity care. However, Americans in the middle were left out on a limb. Serious illness or injury could and did gut family finances; at some point, nearly a quarter of the population had gone into debt to pay medical bills."[76] "Citing how during World War II, pre-induction physicals found five million men medically unfit for military service," Truman told Congress that "health care would never be affordable for all 'unless government is bold enough to do something about it.'"[77] Truman's plan called for the federal government to cover all medical costs in full. The insured would not have to pay any deductibles or co-pays. Similar to Obamacare, all eligible persons would be required or mandated to enroll. "The mandate arose out of mathematical necessity . . . If the plan were voluntary, those likeliest to enroll would be people with pre-existing health conditions and those at the greatest risk for illness. . . Healthy Americans might roll the dice and opt out."[78] The survival of any health care plan whether it be public or private is dependent upon having more healthy people paying into it than the unhealthy. This is the same argument Obama made with the ACA to justify his mandate requirement! Truman's plan called for a "3 percent federal payroll tax on incomes up to $3,600 [that] would pay for medical, hospital and dental care for an estimated 100 million Americans, about 80 percent of the population" at that time.[79] Truman's plan was dead-on-arrival as his Republican congressional counterparts labeled it as socialism. "Morris Fishbein, MD, editor of the *Journal of the American Medical Association*, denounced the National Health Act as 'the kind of regimentation that led to the totalitarianism in Germany and the downfall of that nation.' The National Grange, a farmer's organization, attacked the concept of compulsory medical insurance for being as 'un-American as the Gestapo.'"[80]

The next serious attempt of reforming the nation's health care system fell to President Bill Clinton. He put the wheels into motion by creating the National Health Board, a group of health care providers, national and local business leaders, consumers, and members from pertinent government agencies. The Board recommended the creation of insurance purchasing pools funded by the federal government and overseen by the Board. Individuals could select their health care coverage from fifteen plans. Companies could continue to offer their employees health care benefits as long as their plans provided the basic services covered under Clinton's plan. The unemployed could purchase insurance through tax credits. Clinton's plan provided continuous coverage regardless of one's employment status or changes of employment. Medicare would be funded by the federal government; but Medicaid costs would be shared by both federal and state governments. As expected, the Clinton health care plan met sharp opposition in Congress and never had a chance of passing.

The official launch of the ACA also known as **Obamacare** was a rocky one. The anticipation of the approximately 48 million uninsured Americans becoming insured was "put on hold" on the first day of enrollment the October 1, 2013. The rush to get enrolled caused the software to crash. Eventually and gradually, the software was repaired and many for the first time, had health insurance. Throughout Obama's tenure in the White House, Republicans in Congress unsuccessfully tried over forty times to either under fund, un-fund or repeal the Affordable Care Act. In 2012, the Supreme Court ruled that Obama's "requirement of all Americans to have health insurance, originally enforced with a financial penalty was constitutional under Congress' taxing power."[81] All of the 2016 Republican presidential candidates called for its demise. Donald Trump made it a campaign mandate that if he won the White House, he would end Obamacare. The Trump administration filed additional court challenges to the law and closed access to the ACA exchanges, effectively denying the uninsured to purchase healthcare plans. As the cases of Covid-19 soared, elected officials from both sides of the aisle wanted the exchanges reopened. "Instead, the President said the federal government will reimburse hospitals for treating uninsured coronavirus patients by using funds from Congress' rescue package."[82] However, the average cost of hospitalization for Covid-19 is $34,662 to $45,683 per person. "For people without insurance or who went out of their network—the costs range from $45,683 for people aged 51 to 60 and $34,662 for those in 23 to 30 age bracket. The highest average allowed amount paid to the provider [the hospital, doctors, etc.] under an insurance plan was $24,012 for people aged 51 to 60 and, at its lowest, $17,094 for people above the age 70."[83] There will be a point where the federal government will not be able to cover these costs. The Trump administration finally allowed ACA enrollments. By the end of 2020, "nearly half a million Americans turned to the federal Obamacare exchanges after losing health care coverage. At least some workers who were furloughed or temporarily laid off, however, were able to maintain their job-based health coverage. And others are now returning to work. But still others are learning their layoffs are permanent or are losing their positions in new waves of downsizings."[84] During its 2020 term, the United States Supreme Court heard arguments in *Texas v California* filed by eighteen Republican-led states to completely invalidate the ACA's mandate and basically end Obamacare. The Supreme Court's decision will be issued by June 2021.

Despite Obamacare, Medicaid and Medicare, in 2019, 29,639,000 or 9.2 percent of the nation's population are uninsured.[85] Currently, the United States is the only highly industrialized nation in the world without a universal coverage national health-care plan. Currently, the United States health-care system ranks 37th among her sister nation states. France, Italy, San Marino, Andorra, Malta, Singapore and others have more efficient, effective and embracive health care systems than the United States. However, the United States spends $10,246 per capita, accounting for 17.1 percent of its gross domestic product, making its health care system the most expensive in the world![86]

In addition to the ACA, the three basic publicly funded programs are Medicaid, Medicare and the Children's Health Insurance Program. A jointly funded federal and state program, **Medicaid**, was created in 1965 as part of the War on Poverty. Medicaid was designed as a preventive health-care system whereby a child with a cold would receive the medication necessary to prevent that cold from developing into a potentially life-threatening illness mandating more costly health-care services. Medicaid is an in-kind program with the payment given directly to the provider of the service. Medicaid spending consists of direct payments issued for outpatient and inpatient care services, hospital care, nursing home services, and long-term care facilities. Since the patients receive no direct cash payments, charges of fraud, overpricing, and unnecessary medical treatments must be rightfully levied at the health-care providers. Initially, the program provided benefits to only those receiving Aid to Families with Dependent Children (AFDC) or Supplemental Security Insurance (SSI) benefits. Congress extended Medicaid coverage in 1972 by adding benefits for nursing home and intermediate care facilities for the treatment of the mentally ill. Coverage for prenatal, obstetrics, and follow up medical care for one year for pregnant women was added in 1986. By 1988, states were required to extend Medicaid coverage for one year after families became ineligible for AFDC benefits to allow time for personal economic recoveries. Congress also lowered the original eligibility requirements to include children up to age six. In 1990, Congress extended coverage to include children up to age eighteen. The 1996 welfare reform legislation officially changed the name of AFDC to the **Temporary Assistance to Needy Families (TANF)**. The costs of this program are shared between federal and state governments. To help the states ease their Medicaid burden, President George W. Bush signed into law in 2008 a Medicaid reform package that enabled the states to charge recipients premiums and higher co-payments for doctor's visits, hospital care, and prescription medications. The legislation also gave the states the latitude to drop coverage for those who opted not to pay the additional fees. States can opt not to participate in Medicaid, but the cost to the states to bear the total cost of providing health care for their needy would be staggering. In 2019, 55,851,000 are receiving Medicaid benefits.[87]

Although Medicaid provides insurance coverage to the nation's poor, it does not cover children raised in families whose incomes are too high to qualify for Medicaid coverage but are still too low to afford the premiums for dependent care coverage. Enacted by Congress in 1997 and extended in 2009 with the passage of the **Children's Health Insurance Program Reauthorization Act (CHIP)**, low-cost health insurance is provided through a federal/state partnership with the federal government bearing the financial costs of the plan.

Medicare was supposed to be the nation's health-care plan extending coverage to all Americans. The ensuing battle between conservatives against the plan and the liberal camp promoting it resulted in a program that basically provides coverage only to the nation's elderly. Liberals originally hoped that over time, coverage would be expanded in an incremental fashion with children first, followed by pregnant women and other groups until the goal of universal coverage was achieved. "All Medicare enthusiasts took for granted that the rhetoric of enactment should emphasize the expansion of access, not the regulation and overhaul of United States medicine. The clear aim was to reduce the risks of financial disaster for the elderly and their families, and the clear understanding was that Congress would demand a largely hands-off posture towards doctors and hospitals providing the care that Medicare would provide."[88] Coverage is automatically granted to all persons over 65 who have paid Social Security taxes during their working lives and to their spouses. Funded totally by the federal government, the Medicare plan is administered by the Social Security Administration. The program provides two plans of health coverage. Part A, commonly known as HI, provides mandatory hospitalization coverage. Part B permits participants to purchase through beneficiary premiums and general tax revenues coverage for doctor's fees and other medical expenses to include prescription drugs. Basically, a program that started out as a universal health-care plan has become a very limited plan geared primarily for retired workers over age sixty-five. Not all of the nation's seniors receive coverage. In 2019, 58,779,000 are receiving Medicare benefits.[89]

The Bush administration launched its health-care reform package by focusing on Plan B of the original Medicare legislation. Passed in 2003, the **Medicare Prescription Drug Improvement and Modernization Act** was hailed as "the most sweeping change to Medicare since its founding in 1965," with the primary purpose of bringing "the accelerating costs of prescription drugs under control."[90] A controversial piece of legislation, Republican leaders were able to gradually garner the support of the American Association of Retired Persons (AARP) into its camp. AARP leadership felt that although the bill had major flaws, it was a baby step in the right direction to addressing the rising costs of medical care and prescription drugs. However, many rank and file AARP members were outraged, resorting to canceling their memberships and tearing up their AARP cards. The major provisions of the legislation included increasing the premium of the Part B Medicare Plan on a sliding scale whereby those with incomes over $200,000 would pay 80 percent of their premiums; and raising the deductible to $110 as well as providing a tax shelter for those individuals with high-deductible health insurance. The plan, however, still maintained that the private sector and not the public sector would provide the insurance plans and coverage options to participants.

The most controversial section of the legislation dealt with prescription drugs. On paper, the new approach seemed to be simple. The drug portion of Medicare is known as Plan D. "In addition to a monthly premium, seniors must pay for the first $250 in annual costs for covered drugs, the standard deductible. When the year's drug costs reach $251, plan participants start paying out-of-pocket 25 percent of the cost [of the medications] until their contributions hit $2,250. Then comes the infamous '**doughnut hole**' in which Part D enrollees are responsible for the entire cost of drugs between $2,251 and $5,100. Above that, catastrophic coverage must kick in, whereby seniors shall out just a small portion (5 percent of the cost or a co-pay of a few dollars) of their annual drug costs."[91] One of the problems is that the cycle begins anew every January 1. Seniors can opt to stay with their current Medicare managed plan, their company retirement plan or opt for a private insurance carrier that offers a medical plan with prescription drug coverage. Basically, "the government is subsidizing dozens of private insurers to offer their own plans (many are offering more than one), which have to meet or exceed the federal government's drug benefit standard. The plans will either be stand-alone prescription drugs plans (PDPs) to supplement Medicare's existing medical coverage or will be part of a more comprehensive Medicare private health plan like a health maintenance or preferred provider organization."[92] Regardless of the plan they picked, seniors found out quickly that their annual drug costs fell into the doughnut hole when they went to the pharmacy to pick up their medications thinking they only had to pay a co-pay but instead had to pay the full amount. Unable to pay the full costs of the prescriptions, seniors were once again facing the choice that this reform package was supposed to fix. They were counting the number of pills they could afford, regardless of the medical necessity of taking the full dosage of pills for the prescribed period of time. This situation basically leaves the elderly with only two choices. First, they can purchase **medigap insurance** to supplement their Medicare coverage. Supplemental insurance usually pays 80 percent or better of the costs not covered by Medicare once the policyholder's expenses exceed the standard deductible amounts. Second, those unable to purchase medigap plans must just limit their health-care options to what they can afford with Medicare. The Obama health care law partially fixes the doughnut problem with an initial $150 rebate and providing a 50 percent discount on prescriptions purchased in the doughnut hole range.

Another area of concern is the claims of fraudulent use of both Medicaid and Medicare by health-care providers and drug companies. In particular, the Obama administration wanted to reign in Medicare fraud claims of over-charging for basic medical services, billing errors, billing for unnecessary equipment and procedures, or billing for services never rendered.

Supporters of the Obama health-care reform effort point out that this is the first time the federal government has enacted a comprehensive approach to addressing this nation's health-care issues. Since the New Deal legislation, health care has been reformed in a incremental fashion. The Johnson administration implemented Medicare for the qualifying elderly and Medicaid for the poor. In 1996, the Clinton administration supported the passage of legislation allowing already covered workers to obtain immediate health-care coverage after a change of jobs even if they had a pre-existing illness. It also mandated that new employees had to receive health-care coverage within twelve months of hire. Furthermore, the measure included tax-deductible medical savings accounts primarily for the self-employed and those employed by small companies unable to offer group plans.

CONCLUSION

Can the federal government and state legislative houses turn a blind eye to this nation's poor, old, disabled and sick? The answer is a resounding no. Should government and society as a whole provide the incentives and avenues for the impoverished to be less dependent upon the dole and gain self-sufficiency and economic security? Yes, of course. For too long government at all levels has taken the path of providing assistance that just attempts to ease the suffering and prevent it from becoming worse. However, the suffering has not been eased enough. The recent economic downturn has only meant that more people are poor, homeless, and jobless. The fear of becoming poor has not abated, nor has the costs of maintaining the welfare system decreased at all. We are still a frustrated nation! Morally, we cannot stand by and do nothing for starving, impoverished, elderly, and disabled citizens. Financially, we cannot afford to provide for all of their needs. The heart stretches out but the wallet cannot keep up with the pace. Politically, partisan politics levels the blame of the party in power for not fixing the problems and decries the party that tries to fix them. We simply do not have an answer to address the reasons behind chronic poverty and homelessness.

CHAPTER NOTES

[1] *Treasury of Presidential Quotations,* Caroline Thomas Harnsberger, ed., (Chicago, Illinois: Follet Publishing Company, 1964), 246.

[2] *https://www.bls.gov.mlf/2020*

[3] U.S. Census Bureau, *Current Population Survey,* 2019 and 2020 Annual Social and Economic Supplements.

[4] *Unemployment Rates During the COVID-19 Pandemic: In Brief,* Congressional Research Service, *https://crsreports/congress.gov*

[5] *https://www.washingtonpost.com*

[6] Jonathan Alter, "The Other America: An Enduring Shame," *Newsweek,* September 19, 2005, 42.

[7] Anneken Tappe, "Another 787,000 Americans Filed First-time Claims for Jobless Benefits Last Week," *CNN,* *https://www.cnn.com/2020/12/31*

[8] *The American Heritage Dictionary of the English Language: New College Edition,* (Boston, Massachusetts: Houghton Mifflin Co., 1982), 1027.

[9]Louis Uchitelle, "Census Bureau May Raise Poverty Level," *San Antonio Express-News* (Monday, October 18, 1999), 7A.

[10]John J. Harrigan and David C. Nice, *Politics and Policy in States and Communities,* 8th ed., (New York, New York: Pearson Education, Inc., 2004), 332.

[11]Randall Bland, Alfred B. Sullivan, Robert E. Biles, Charles P. Elloitt, Jr., and Beryl E. Pettus, *Texas Government Today*, 5th ed. (Pacific Grove, Calif.: Brooks/Cole Publishing Co., 1992), 431.

[12]"Committee to Recommend Broader Definition of Poverty," *The Dallas Morning News*, (Sunday, April 30, 1995), 4A.

[13]"49.7 Million Americans in Poverty, Census Bureau Says."

[14]Harrigan, 332.

[15]"U.S. Bureau of Labor Statistics, *Characteristics of Minimum Wage Workers, 2019,*" Washington, D.C., *https://www.bls.gov*

[16]Molly Ivins, "The Working Poor Have Names, Faces," *San Antonio Express-News* (Monday, January 3, 2000), 5B.

[17]Randy Albelda, "Fallacies of Welfare-To-Work Policies," *The Annals*, The American Academy of Political and Social Science, Vol. 577, September, 2001, 66-78, 72.

[18]Ibid., 72-73.

[19]U.S. Census Bureau, *Income and Poverty in the United States: 2019*, Table A1—Income Summary Measures by Selected Characteristics: 2018-2019

[20]Alicia Wallace, "These 20 States Will Raise Their Minimum Wage by January 1, *CNN*, *https://www.cnn. Com/2020/12/30/business/minimum-wage-2021*

[21]Bureau of Labor Statistics, *The Employment Situation-November, 2020*, Table A-9—Household Data- Selected Employment Indicators

[22]Ibid., Table A-10 – Selected Unemployment Indicators, Seasonally Adjusted

[23]"Trump's Tax Plan: How It Affects You," *The Balance*, *https://www.thebalance.com*

[24]Tami Luhjby, "Five Stark Measures Showing Rising American Suffering as Congress Stalls on Aid," *CNN*, *https://www.cnn.com/2020/12/18*

[25]Alter, 44.

[26]Alice S. Baum and Donald W. Burnes, *A Nation in Denial: The Truth About the Homeless*, (Boulder, Colorado: Westview Press, 1993), 3.

[27]U.S. Census Bureau, *Income and Poverty in the United States, 2019,*" Table B-1—People in Poverty By Selected Characteristics: 2018-2019

[28]Ibid.

[29]U.S. Census Bureau, *Current Population Survey, 1960-2020: Annual Social and Economic Supplements* (CPS ASEC), Table b-6—Poverty Status of People by Age, Race and Hispanic Origin: 1959-2019

[30]*2020 Kids Court Data Book Interactive*, The Annie E. Casey Foundation, *https:www.aecf.org*

[31]"High School Dropout Rate," Educationdata.org, *https://educationdata.org*

[32]Ibid.

[33]*Treasury of Presidential Quotations*, 79.

[34]Ibid., 78.

[35]*Current Population Survey, 2019-2020 Annua Social and Economic Supplements*, Table B-12—People In Poverty by Selected Characteristics, 2018-2019

[36]National Alliance to End Homelessness, *State of Homelessness: 2020*, *https://endhomelessness.org*

[37]Ibid.

[38]Ibid.

[39]National Alliance to End Homelessness, *State of Homelessness: 2016*, *https://endhomelessness.org*

[40]National Alliance to End Homelessness, *Chronically Homeless*, *https://endhomlessness.org*

[41]*State of Homelessness, 2020*, *https://endhomelessness.org*

[42]National Alliance to End Homelessness, *Veterans 2021*, *https://endhomelessness.org*

[43]Philip Brasher, "Advocates Allege Homeless Unfairly Denied Food Stamps," *San Antonio Express-News* (Wednesday, November 24, 1999) 7A.

[44]Ibid., 11.

[45]Robert Tanner, "Cities Pushing Back At Pushy Panhandlers," *San Antonio Express-News* (Sunday, December 22, 2002), 22A.

[46]National Alliance to End Homelessness, *State of Homelessness:2020 Edition*, *https://endhomelessness.org*

[47]Ibid.

[48]Harrigan, 337.

[49]Edward C. Banfield, *The Unheavenly City*, (Boston, Massachusetts: Little, Brown, and Company, 1970), 125-126.

[50]Sar A. Levitan, "How the Welfare System Promotes Economic Security," *Political Science Quarterly,* (The Academy of Political and Social Science, Vol. 26, No. 3, Fall, 1985, 449.

[51]Edward J. Harpham, "Welfare Reform in Perspective," *Texas At the Crossroads: People, Politics and Policy*, Anthony Champagne and Edward J. Harpham, eds., (College Station, Texas: Texas A & M University Press, 1987), 283.

[52]Levitan, 453.

[53]Ibid., 447-448.

[54]Helen O'Neill, "Welfare Well Drying Up," *Houston Chronicle,* (Sunday, June 9, 1996), (4A-5A), 5A.

[55]Linda Gordon, "Who Deserves Help? Who Must Provide," *The Annals*, The American Academy of Political and Social Science, Vol. 577, September 2001, 12-24, 14.

[56]Baum, 92.

[57]Joel F. Handler, *The Poverty of Welfare Reform*, (New Haven, Connecticut: Yale University Press, 1995), 12.

[58]Ibid.

[59]Baum, 92.

[60]Handler, 14.

[61]Ibid., 16.

[62]Howard Hysock, Fighting Poverty the Old-Fashioned Way," *The Wilson Quarterly*, Vol. XIV, No. 2, Spring, 1990, 78-9l, 80.

[63]"Lyndon Baines Johnson, President of the United States, 1963-1969: The Great Society," *Documents of Texas History*, Ernest Wallace, David M. Vigness and George B. Ward, eds. (Austin, Texas: State House Press, 1994), 289-290.

[64]Harrigan, 342.

[65]Susan Dentzer, "You're Not As Entitled as You Think," *U.S. News & World Report,* (March 20, 1995), 67.

[66]Joel Achenbach, "Why Poorer Classes Foot The Social Security Bill," *San Antonio Light* (Sunday, June 2, 1990) L1.

[67]Michael Barone, "Future Shock," *U.S. News & World Report*, June 13, 2005, 38.

[68]*Annual Statistical Supplement to the Social Security Bulletin, 2019, https:www.ssa.gov*

[69]"'Earnings Penalty' Removal Endorsed," *San Antonio Express-News* (Sunday, February 20, 2000) 13A.

[70]Jack C. Plano and Milton Greenburg, *The American Political Dictionary* (Orlando, Florida: Harcourt, Brace and Jananovich College Publishers, 1993), 489.

[71]Harrigan, 347.

[72]*Policy Basic: The Supplemental Assistance Program (SNAP)*, Center on Budget and Policy Priorities, 2019, *https://www.cbpp.org*

[73]Ibid.

[74]*Statistical Abstract of the United States: 2010*, 129th ed., Table 209, 135.

[75]Joseph Connor, "Give Them Healthcare, Harry," *American History*, Vol. 54, No. 4, October 4, 2019, 43.

[76]Ibid.

[77]Ibid., 42.

[78]Ibid., 44.

[79]Ibid., 43.

[80]Ibid., 43-44

[81]Devid Dwyer, "Obamacare Appears Likely to Survive Supreme Court Challenge," *https://abcnews.go.com*

[82]Ibid.

[83]"Hospitalized Care for COVID-19 Averages $34,662 to $45,683, Varying by Age," *https://www.healthcarefinancenews.com*

[84]Tami Lubhy, "Nearly Half a Million People Flocked to Obamacare After Losing Coverage This Year," *https://www.cn.com*

[85]*The World Almanac and Book of Facts: 2021*, (Brainnerd, Minnesota: Skyhorse Publishing, 2020), 181.

[86]Ibid.

[87]U.S. Census Bureau, *Current Population Survey, 2019 and 2020 Annual Social and EconomicSupplement* (CPS ASEC), Table 1—Coverage Numbers and Rates by Type of Health Insurance

[88]Ted Marmar and Julie Beglin, "Medicare and It Grew. . .and Grew. . .and Grew. . . ," *San Antonio Express-News*, (June 25, 1995), 21.

[89]*Current Population Survey, 2019 and 2020 Annual Social and Economic Supplement* (CPS ASEC), Table I—Coverage Numbers and Rates by Type of Health Insurance

[90]Travis E. Poling and Gary Martin, 'Medicare Rewrite Is Not A Cure-All," *San Antonio Express-News*, (Friday, December 26, 2003), 1A.

[91]Katherine Hobson, "How The Plan Works," *U.S. News & World Report*, (November 7, 2005), 74.
[92]Ibid., 72.

SUGGESTED READINGS

Banfield, Edward C. *The Unheavenly City*. Boston, Massachusetts: Little, Brown and Co., 1970.

Baum, Alice S., And Donald W. Burnes, *A Nation in Denial: The Truth About Homelessness*. Boulder, Colorado: Westview Press, 1993.

Handler, Joel F. *The Poverty of Welfare Reform*. New Haven, Connecticut: Yale Univ. Press, 1995.

Heidenheimer, Arnold, Hugh Helco, and Carolyn Teich Adams, *Comparative Public Policy: The Politics of Social Choice in America, Europe, and Japan*, 3d ed., New York, New Yotk: St. Martin's Press, 1990.

Web Sites:

www.medicare.gov
www.cms.hhs.gov/home/medicaid.asp
www.aarp.org/health/insurance
www.fns.usda.gov/fsp - USDA Food Stamp Program
aspe.hhs.gov/poverty/08poverty.shtml - poverty guidelines
www.census.gov
www.hud.gov/homes - HUD homes

Chapter Sixteen

THE ENVIRONMENT

When the colonists first landed in the New World, they stepped upon the shores of their new homeland awe-strucked by the sight before them. Here was a land rich beyond their expectations. Abounding with the richness of natural resources, America offered millions of acres of virgin forests and wilderness teeming with a vast array of plants and wildlife. Rivers and streams were crystal clear, revealing plentiful stocks of fish. All of this beauty was crowned by clear blue skies. To Native Americans, the earth was the center of their universe. They worshiped and praised her lands and seas. They honored her creatures, plants, mountains, forests, and rivers. They revered her moon, sun, stars, and skies. They feared her anger that was so often vented in violent storms, harsh winters, and dry summers. They treasured the land. "The Indians stressed the web of life, the interconnectedness of land and man and creature."[1] Unfortunately, the European mindset viewed natural resources quite differently from Native Americans. "Chief Luther Standing Bear of the Oglala Sioux put it this way: 'Only to the white [Anglo] man was nature a wilderness and only to him was the land 'infested' with 'wild' animals and 'savage' people. To us it was tame. Earth was bountiful and we were surrounded with the blessing of the Great Mystery."[2] The beauty of this land was soon jeopardized with the continuous flow of new settlers bringing technological advancements to the emerging agricultural and industrial sectors of the New World. "Successive generations of immigrants have come to this country in search of economic opportunity. They arrived from Ireland and Germany in 1850, from Italy and Russia in 1920, and from Haiti and Mexico in 1990. Their hard work transformed abundant natural resources into a cornucopia of material wealth but at a cost of declining environmental quality. We have depleted the fertility of our soils, cut down primeval forests, and used water supplies faster than they can be replenished. Our fields produce meat, milk, and vegetables, but the nation's streams are polluted when fertilizer, pesticide, and animal waste residues run off the land. Factories convert raw materials into appliances, plastic products, and paper, but they also dump waste materials into the air and water."[3] Today, over one hundred years of industrialization with its all too familiar smokestacks have made this country materially wealthy beyond one's expectations but environmentally damaged almost beyond the hopes of repair. The legacy of the twentieth century will include the tragic vocabulary of environmental damage: ozone alerts, smog, pollution, acid rain, deforestation, endangered species, and hazardous wastes. The challenge is to finally solve the puzzle of how man and nature can co-exist without destroying each other.

The task is even more daunting when one realizes that environmental damage is not just an American problem. It is an international concern that affects every single country, rich and poor alike. It is also an on-going political battle between those who believe that climate change is just a natural cycle of a changing earth and those who hold that mankind is the primary culprit behind the rapid deterioration of the environment. Founded in 1988 by the request of the members of the United Nations, the Intergovernmental Panel on Climate Change (IPC) is a group of highly specialized scientists in the field of environmental studies analyzing all aspects of the environment including climate change. The highly acclaimed group was awarded a Nobel Peace Prize in 2007. Their latest report entitled *Climate Change 2014: Synthesis Report* (SYR) states that the:

> human influence on the climate system is clear and growing, with impacts observed across all continents and oceans. Many of the observed changes since the 1950s are unprecedented over the decades to millennia. The IPC is now 95 percent certain that humans are the main cause of current global warming. In addition SYR finds that more human activities disrupt the climate, the greater the risks of severe, pervasive and irreversible impacts for people and ecosystems, and long-lasting changes in all components of the climate system. The SYR highlights that we have the means to limit climate change and its risks, with many solutions that allow for continued economic and human development. However, stabilizing temperature increase to below 2°C relative to pre-industrial levels will require an urgent and fundamental departure from business as usual. Moreover, the longer we wait to take action, the more it will cost and the greater the technological, economic, social and institutional challenges we will face.[4]

The human side of environmental damage is overwhelming. The World Health Organization estimates that approximately seven million people accounting for "one in eight of total global deaths" die as a direct result of illnesses tied to air pollution.[5] Furthermore, nearly half of the world's population is concentrated in very densely populated urban areas that lack adequate water sources and proper sanitation systems. "With 1.2 billion people lacking clean water, waterborne infections account for 80 percent of all infectious diseases. Increased water pollution creates breeding grounds for malaria-carrying mosquitoes, killing 12 million to 2.7 million people a year. . . Unsanitary living conditions account for more than 5 million deaths per year, of which more than half are children."[6] The world's population is continuing to grow. "The world's population is projected to grow from 7.7 billion in 2019 to 8.5 billion in 2030 (10% increase), and further to 9.7 billion to 2050 (26%) and to 10.9 billion in 2100 (42%). The largest increases in population between 2019 and 2050 will take place in: India, Nigeria, Pakistan, the Democratic Republic of the Congo, Ethiopia, the Untied Republic Tanzania, Indonesia, Egypt, and the United States of America (in descending order of the expected increase). Around 2027, India is projected to overtake China as the world's most populous country."[7]

Confronted with its own laundry list of environmental concerns, American lawmakers and citizens alike are still searching for the solution that will enable industry to provide us with the goods and services we are dependent upon without causing further damage to the air we breathe and the water we drink. To date, this quest has proven to be extremely difficult to accomplish. The desire to strike a balance between the constitutionally protected rights of property owners and the preservation of the environment evokes strong sentiments and hotly contested debates that sharply divide public opinion. On the one hand, property owners should be able to use and dispose of their property as they choose without undo interference from government. On the other hand, the desire to preserve society and its quality of life does depend upon the maintenance of an ecosystem free of pollution and contamination whereby plants and wildlife can successfully coexist with humankind. In every legislative house at *all* levels of government, there are constant battles between environmentalists and property owners over everything. The issue whether to cut trees to make way for a new mall or business park can wreck havoc at a city council meeting. Part of the problem rests with us, average American citizens. "Although Americans express a general desire to protect their environment, they are reluctant to sacrifice their standard of living to slow the rate of natural resource use and to reduce pollution. As they implement federal environmental rules, state and local governments have been careful to protect local economic interests from being harmed seriously by environmental interests."[8] Despite countless environmental laws riddled with severe sanctions against violators, the United States lags substantially behind other nations in its efforts to address environmental concerns. The 2020 Environmental Performance Index (EPI) ranks nations on their current environmental performances. The top ten nations with the most favorable environmental performance efforts are Denmark, Luxembourg, Switzerland, Great Britain, France, Austria, Finland, Sweden, Norway, and Germany. The United States was 24th.[9] Nor does it appear that the United States is making a concerted effort to improve its rating. Major environmental disasters such as the 2010 BP (British Petroleum) oil rig explosion in the Gulf of Mexico that killed over 35 rig workers, cost BP billions of dollars and brought manslaughter charges against several BP managers; a major fertilizer plant explosion in 2013 that nearly leveled the small community of West Texas; the 2014 dangerous chemical spill into the main water supply for nine counties in West Virginia adversely impacting 300,000 residents who must drink bottled water and not use any tap water for anything, including washing clothes and bathing; the tragedy of the residents of Flint, Michigan who were kept in the dark for over eighteen months by their city leaders that their household water was laden with toxic levels of lead causing dozens to be diagnosed with lead poisoning; the tragic loss of both human and wildlife caused by the continuous wildfires in California and Arizona; the explosion of a 2,000 gallon propylene tank in Houston, Texas, killing two workers and destroying hundreds of homes near the plant, only point out that this nation has a long way to go in addressing its environmental problems. This chapter examines both the policy options available to lawmakers as well as future policy choices against the backdrop of an American society struggling to face the reality of the damage their actions have done to the quality of their environment.

Environmental issues and policy considerations are still in the infancy stage when compared to centuries-old poverty-related issues. Environmental politics did not emerge in the United States until the early 1970s when the country's consciousness was awakened to accept the truth that their century-old wanton and abusive habits had produced an extensive array of severe and, in some instances, irreversible damage. All the nation's waterways were to varying degrees polluted with run-offs from pesticides, fertilizers, chemicals, and industrial and municipal wastes. Rural residents were urged to boil their drinking water to ward off the ingestion of harmful substances. Lead-based paint, which had been the only paint base available for decades, was now labeled as a contributing cause of respiratory diseases and cancer. The once clear blue skies were suddenly noticed for their grayish and brownish hues caused by the spewing of polluting byproducts from the smokestacks of the nation's major industrial areas. The nation's coastal areas were hit with severe oil spills that spoiled tourist and resort areas and killed countless numbers of animals and marine life. Forests and wetlands became the victims of progress as bulldozers and dredgers drained swamplands and chopped whole stands of trees to make way for business and residential construction projects. Ozone alerts began to warn people with chronic respiratory ailments to remain indoors due to dangerously high levels of smog and air pollution. It was discovered during the 1970s that farm workers were the victims of deadly skin cancers acquired through years of hand-harvesting fruits and vegetables heavily sprayed with pesticides. The examples are too numerous to mention within the scope of this chapter. Consequently, this chapter focuses on the extent of the environmental damage to our nation's air, water, coastal areas, wetlands, wildlife, forests, and the problems associated with the disposal of nuclear, hazardous, and solid waste materials.

This chapter also presents a balanced approach by examining both sides of the issue. Traditionally, business and industry have fought regulatory laws that pose a threat to their livelihood. Environmental laws are, with few exceptions, laden with severe punitive actions against violators. Business leaders feel that they have been unfairly targeted and unduly punished for using acceptable traditional industrial production methods that have only now been deemed harmful to the environment. They have a valid argument that cannot be ignored by lawmakers. Antipollution devices are expensive. The increased cost of producing a product is passed onto the American consumer who is always searching for the best product at the cheapest price possible. Yes, these laws are expensive to implement. Irate property owners, business leaders, and anti-big government groups are constantly lobbying Congress to relax environmental restrictions and reduce punitive fines. Environmental groups also have a vital concern. Environmental damage must be curtailed or the future of this planet is in serious jeopardy. In *The Human Home*, British writer J. A. Walker wrote: "How are Americans to restore the environment to its proper position as an essentially political issue, over which reasonable people will disagree . . . ? How can we regain the attitude of those earlier ages which saw the natural world as pointing to the divine without itself being divine? How can we cherish our environment without making a fetish of it?"[10] Thus, the mission of environmental advocates is a noble one—protect the balance between humankind and nature. This chapter explores the role that lobbyists/advocates on each side of the environmental issue play in the creation and subsequent implementation of environmental legislation.

FEDERAL AND STATE ROLES IN ENVIRONMENT POLICIES

The reserved powers clause of the Tenth Amendment delegated to the states those governing powers not specifically granted to the national government. Consequently, the states were initially responsible for addressing environmental concerns. The national government played only a marginal role. Historically, government at all levels did not involve themselves with environmental issues with the exception of a natural disaster. For example, the Johnstown Flood of 1889 gained national attention when over 2,200 residents of several small Pennsylvania towns located at the bottom of a valley were tragically swept away after the collapse of a man-made earthen dam shoring up a river located on the top of the valley's edge. The tragedy, however, did not result in any corrective legislative actions from Congress nor were actions taken against those responsible for operating the dam. The cries of the nation's earliest environmentalists fell upon deaf ears. Former United States Minister to Turkey, George Perkins Marsh, wrote *Man and Nature* in 1864, a novel depicting the destructiveness of deforestation. Marsh believed that "man is everywhere a disturbing agent. Wherever he plants his foot, the harmonies of nature are turned to discords . . . It is certain that a desolation, like that which has overwhelmed many once beautiful and fertile regions of Europe, awaits an important part of the territory of the United States . . . unless prompt measures are taken to check the action of destructive causes already in operation."[11] Marsh's words were instrumental in motivating a group of bird watchers to form the **American Forestry Association** (AFA), an interest group promoting conservation of the nation's forests. An avid naturalist, John Muir once commented that "pollution, defilement, squalor are words that never would have been created had man lived conformably to Nature. Birds, insects, bears die as cleanly and are disposed of as beautifully . . . The woods are full of dead and dying trees, yet needed for their beauty to complete the beauty of the living. . . . How beautiful is all Death!"[12] In 1892, Muir founded the Sierra Club "to lead city people into the mountains, where he hoped that they would learn to see granite peaks and glacial valleys as he did."[13] A realist, "Muir believed that the retreats where he and others felt such strong emotion were worth defending against the forces of technology and economic development."[14] Consequently, the Sierra Club would evolve into the preeminent political force devoted to the protection of the environment. It was individuals, not national, state, or local governments, that took the early steps to rein in the destruction of the environment. Whether it be George Marsh, John Muir, Al Gore, Teddy Roosevelt, Rachel Carson, Bill Clinton, or Barack Obama, it should be noted that "nearly every aspect of environmentalism since the founding of the AFA has demonstrated the same pattern:

Theodore Roosevelt meets with conservationist John Muir in the Yosemite Valley. Roosevelt succeeded in making preservation of America's natural resources an important issue.

a charismatic and influential individual who discerns a problem and formulates a public concern; a group that forms itself around him/her or around his/her ideas and exerts educational pressure on the Congress; legislation that creates some new kind of reserve—national park, national forest, national monument, national wildlife sanctuary or wilderness area; and finally, an increasingly specific body of regulatory law for the protection of what has been set aside."[15]

The first notable piece of federal legislation concerning the environment was the **Refuse Act** passed in 1899. This legislation required that potential dumpers of waste materials into navigable rivers had to obtain a permit from the Army Corps of Engineers prior to dumping. Due to sixteen years of constant pressure from the AFA, Congress finally responded with the passage of the **General Revision Act** in 1891, granting the President of the United States the authority to promote the general welfare by setting aside forest lands for preserves and parks. Presidents Benjamin Harrison, Grover Cleveland and Teddy Roosevelt did exercise this right by "putting 43 million acres of forest, mainly in the west out of reach of the loggers."[16] Another pioneer environmentalist, George Bird Grinnell, was a boyhood friend of Teddy Roosevelt. Owner of *Forest and Stream*, Grinnell "carried on an impassioned campaign against market hunters, poachers and women who wore feathers on their hats.[17] With the backing of the **Audubon Societies**, Grinnell was instrumental in moving Congress to pass the **Park Protection Act** of 1894, prohibiting hunting in national parks. As the nation's first "environmental president" Teddy Roosevelt believed that "the Nation behaves well if it treats the national resources as assets which it must turn over to the next generation increased, and not impaired in value."[18] In 1903, Roosevelt established the nation's first wildlife sanctuary, **Pelican Island**. In 1905, he founded the **United States Forestry Service**. In 1906, Roosevelt signed into law the **Antiquities Act**. The initial intent of the legislation was to protect archeological sites in the Southwest from grave robbers. This legislation, however, empowered the President of the United States to set aside for federal protection any monuments or sites, including forests, considered to be precious or threatened. When Roosevelt took office, the nation's only national park was Yellowstone. By 1916, however, there were thirteen. "The **National Park Act** [1916] gave these reserves their stated purpose, public enjoyment, public use *without impairment,* and created the National Park Service to carry it out."[19] In 1908, Roosevelt hosted an environmental conference attended by state governors, environmentalists and business leaders. He told the gathering:

Indeed, the growth of this Nation by leaps and bounds makes one of the most striking and important chapters in the history of the world. Its growth has been due to the rapid development, and alas that it should be said! to the rapid destruction of our natural resources. Nature has supplied to us in the United States, and still supplies to us, more kinds of resources in a more lavish degree than has ever been the case at any other time or with any other people. Our position in the world has been attained by the extent and thoroughness of the control we have achieved over nature. . . . The wise use of all of our natural resources, which are our national resources as well, is the great material question of today. . . . In the past we have admitted the right of the individual to injure the future of the Republic for his own present profit. In fact there has been a good deal of a demand for unrestricted individualism, for the right of the individual to injure the future of all of us for his own temporary and immediate profit. The time has come for a change. As a people we have the right and the duty, second to none other but the right and duty of obeying the moral law, of requiring and doing justice, to protect ourselves and our children against the wasteful development of our natural resources.[20]

When Teddy Roosevelt left office, the zeal for environmentalism went underground. With the exception of the New Deal's Civilian Conservation Corps and the Works Progress Administration in the 1930s, no major environmental legislation was passed until the 1960s.

The issue of environmental quality surfaced in the early 1960s as public awareness began to focus less on the economy and more on the quality of the environment. This shift in values occurred in part because a "period of sustained prosperity following World II brought about a fundamental intergenerational shift in value priorities within Western societies. Citizens became less preoccupied with basic material needs and began to place a higher priority on the quality of their lives. This value shift appears to have been most pronounced among people in white-collar and service occupations—a growing segment of all Western populations . . . . Post-materialists place particularly high value on protection of the environment and a life-style that is high-quality but simple."[21] Policymakers also realized that the states lacked the initiative and the resources to address emerging environmental concerns. "They [the states] could not afford to develop the technical expertise on pollution issues; they had no jurisdiction over pollution generated in other states upstream or upwind; and polluting industries could threaten to move their operations elsewhere to escape compliance with strict environmental rules."[22] Consequently, the individual states needed the muscle of the federal government to establish the guidelines for legislative and, if necessary, legal action to halt environmental damage.

Rachel Carson gave the emerging environmental movement a shot in the arm when her book, *Silent Spring,* was published in 1962. In her novel, the earth and all of humankind is destroyed not by an invading army from outer space but by the wanton use of synthetic chemicals such as DDT, heptachlor, aldrin, and chlordane. Carson weaves her tale of environmental doom around her thesis that:

> the unique speed of human actions, combined with the introduction of synthetic chemicals for insect control, would accelerate the occurrence of resistance mutations to such a degree that invincible insects would swagger across the Earth. Industrial alchemists would then fashion ever-stronger portions in a frantic attempt to stop the superbugs. Armed with mutated immunity the superbugs would defy the new poisons; as farmers grew desperate, pesticides would be sprayed indiscriminately. The superbugs would escape unharmed, but indiscriminate spraying would wipe out the crops, flowers, and "friendly" insects farmers hoped to encourage. The battle would end in less than a human generation, with favored species vanquished at every turn. Once the earthworm, a key friendly species, fell extinct from excess spraying of poisons, the food chain of songbirds would be destroyed forever. The next year would come a silent spring.[23]

Placing the blame for the ruin of earth squarely on the backs of all mankind, Carson declares that "the 'control of nature' is a phrase conceived in arrogance, born of the Neanderthal Age of biology and philosophy, when it was supposed that nature exists for the convenience of man."[24] *Silent Spring* did for the environmental movement what *The Jungle* did in promoting a stunned national government to move against the meat packing industry with the passage of the **Pure Food and Drug Act**. The federal government responded by passing laws placing controls and bans on DDT, other pesticides, and herbicides.

The United States Congress was jarred into action. In 1963, it passed the **Clean Air Act** giving the federal government a powerful, and to date, permanent role over state and local governments in the creation, implementation, and enforcement of environmental public policy issues. Another pioneering environmentalist, Howard Zahnister, executive director of the Wilderness Society, saw fifteen years of work finally result in the 1964 passage of the **Wilderness Act**. This legislation defined **wilderness** "as an area where the earth and its community of life are untrammeled by man, where man himself is a visitor who does not remain."[25] Congress declared approximately 9.1 million acres as wilderness now falling under the protection of the federal government.

The environmental issue became a volatile political concern in the 1970s. Both presidential candidates Edmund Muskie(D) and Richard Nixon(R) campaigned for rapid and severe federal responses to clean up environmental damage, punish violators, and protect the environment from further damage. During his tenure in the White House, President Nixon was instrumental in convincing Congress to pass "a remarkable series of acts, including the revised Clean Air Act of 1970; the sweeping National Environmental Policy Act of 1970, which created the Environmental Protection Agency and the Council on Environmental Quality and required environmental impact statements for all construction projects affecting land owned by the federal government; the Federal Water Pollution Control Act of 1972; and the Endangered Species Act of 1973."[26] Regardless of their individual political philosophies and party loyalties, only a handful of presidential candidates have opted not to take pro-environmental positions. For example, President Jimmy Carter noted that the task of addressing environmental issues should not just be left to the lawmakers. He understood that everyone had a role to play. Carter emphasized that:

> most of the environmental damage which now occurs, can be prevented. The additional cost of responsible surface mining, or preventing oil spills, or cleaning auto and power plants emissions is low, compared to the costs to society and future generations if we fail to act. . . . To maintain environmental quality, and to improve the quality of life for our people is an essential goal, and in its pursuit, we must act responsibly. . . . It makes little sense, if we are concerned about the quality of life, to talk about having to choose between employment and the environment or between enough energy and environmental quality. . . . We must have all three: employment, energy, a decent environment. I will work to achieve this goal. . . The President has a responsibility to the people who elect him. But he also has a responsibility to future generations. The President is their steward. I intend to be a worthy steward and to see that we pass on to our children, and our children's children, an environment and a country of which we can be proud.[27]

Support for preventive legislation gained public endorsement. "In a survey conducted by the *New York Times* in 1989, an astonishing 80 percent of those polled agreed with the proposition that 'Protecting the environment is so important that requirements and standards cannot be too high, and continuing environmental improvements must be made regardless of cost.'"[28]

Environmental issues were certainly a leading campaign topic during the 2000 presidential elections. Vice President Al Gore had already demonstrated his pledge to promote pro-environmental legislation if he were to be elected to the White House. Then candidate George W. Bush echoed his own commitment to a cleaner environment despite the fact that his vice presidential candidate Dick Cheney was the immediate past president of Halliburton, one of the nation's leading oil and gas producers. Bush promised that if elected he would, along with other environmental actions, seek regulations on carbon dioxide emissions from power plants. His proposal included declaring sulfur dioxide, nitrogen oxide, mercury and carbon dioxide as pollutants subject to regulation by the Environmental Protection Agency (EPA). After assuming the office, President Bush reversed his campaign promise by telling Congress that he would not require the EPA to regulate carbon dioxide emissions from power plants. In addition, the Bush administration withdrew United States participation in the **Kyoto Agreement**. Much to the ire of environmentalists, the Bush administration made a concerted effort to weaken the investigative arm of federal and state environmental agencies, relax environmental standards, and either weaken or actually eliminate legislatively mandated sanctions against polluters. Citing the cost of unnecessary and overburdening restrictions on business and industry, Bush promoted an industry-wide voluntary approach to federal regulations, particularly environmental laws. Meanwhile, Al Gore continued his efforts to promote environmental awareness to include global warming. In 2007, he testified before a joint congressional hearing about the extent of existing and future environmental damage and offered his proposals to include reducing carbon dioxide and other warming gasses by 90 percent in 2050, banning construction of coal-burning power plants that lacked the technology to both capture and store greenhouse gases, imposing stricter fuel efficiency standards for cars and trucks, imposing a tax on carbon emissions, enacting an international climate change treaty, banning incandescent light bulbs, mandating de facto compliance with the Kyoto Protocol, and creating tax breaks and other incentives for those producing or selling electricity.[29] For his efforts, Gore was awarded a Nobel Peace Prize and won an Academy Award for the short-subject film made based on his book *An Inconvenient Truth*.

In his 2008 presidential race, Barack Obama detailed his plans for the environment to include:

- A cap-and-trade system to cut carbon dioxide emissions to 80 percent below 1990 levels;
- Raising efficiency standards to 52 miles per gallon by 2026;
- Goal of renewable energy generating 25 percent of United States electricity by 2025;
- Proposing having at least 60 billion gallons of biofuels in the nation's supply by 2030;
- Advocacy of coal-to-liquid fuels if they emit 20 percent less carbon than conventional gas;
- And stressing that although nuclear power is not optimal, it can be used as an energy source.[30]

The economic recession severely hit the nation's major automobile and truck manufacturers. Auto giants to include General Motors and Chrysler sought federal assistance to keep their companies afloat. President Obama insisted that any reorganization plan and/or federal bailout request for the auto industry had to include meaningful initiatives to build more fuel efficient and environmentally friendly vehicles. In 2009, the White House issued a series of federally-backed rules covering gasoline mileage standards and additional curbs on vehicle emissions. In his re-election bid, Obama reemphasized his commitment to promote renewable energy as well as to further reduce carbon emissions. On the campaign trail, President Obama stated:

So we have a choice to make. We can remain one of the world's leading importers of foreign oil, or we can make the investments that allow us to become the world's leading exporter of renewable energy. We can let climate change continue to go unchecked, or we can help stop it. We can let the jobs of tomorrow be created abroad, or we can create those jobs right here in America and lay the foundation for lasting prosperity. . . . We've been talking about climate change in Washington for years and energy independence and efficiency for years. . . . But no matter how many scientists testified about greenhouse gases, no matter how much evidence that they're threatening our weather patterns, nothing happened with global warming until now.[31]

Confronted with a "hostile" Congress for the majority of his eight years in the Oval Office, Obama won praise even from his critics on his environmental policies. Former EPA administrator during the Clinton White House years, Carol M. Browner noted "looking at individual policy accomplishments doesn't do justice to President Obama's legacy on climate change . . . The component parts of his actions—from making cars and power plants cleaner to preserving major swaths of land and sea for future generations to leading on global ocean policy to beginning to take on industrial methane pollution—tell a story about how he and his administration addressed the problem. But the story is larger than that. I'd say the president's legacy on climate change lies in his success in making climate change a central policy obligation, getting millions of Americans to care about it. . . ."[32] During his final days in office, he did officially halt future construction of the Keystone Pipeline and used the Antiquities Act to place environmentally threatened areas under federal protection.

On the campaign trail, then Republican presidential candidate Donald Trump detailed his environmental priorities if he were to be elected to the White House. Taking the position that climate change is not a serious problem, Trump took a strong stand in support of fossil fuels by openly supporting fracking and the Keystone Pipeline project, while at the same time demeaning renewable energy initiatives such as windfarms. He strongly criticized the perceived over-reaching policies and practices of the Environmental Protection Agency, vowing that if elected, he would abolish the agency altogether. One of his first actions as president was to issue an executive order mandating the completion of the Keystone Pipeline. Trump systematically rolled back environmental regulations particularly those perceived to adversely impact non-renewable energy-based businesses and industries.

April 20 is celebrated as Earth Day to remind us of what has been done and what legislation still needs to be enacted to protect this environment. Table 16.1 details the major pieces of environmental legislation passed by Congress. The majority of the legislation passed at both the national and state levels is designed with a ten- or twenty-year life cycle, whereby the initiating governing level must decide whether to extend the legislation for another life cycle. Against this backdrop, environmentalists can never rest easy that public opinion, office seekers, and lawmakers will be on their side whenever these legislative items are before Congress.

The Air We Breathe

The survival of the earth's inhabitants is very dependent upon the quality of the air they breathe. **Air** is basically a "mixture of nitrogen (78.084 percent), oxygen (20.948 percent), argon (0.934 percent), carbon dioxide (0.032 percent), and traces of neon, helium, krypton, hydrogen, xenon, methane, and vitreous oxide."[33] Each element performs an essential function: nitrogen, oxygen, and carbon dioxide are essential for the survival of plant and animal life; oxygen is a basic element necessary for higher forms of life; carbon dioxide plays a key role in photosynthesis and food production; ozone, a byproduct of oxygen, protects life forms from dangerous ultraviolet light; and so on. Even the slightest contamination of these elements jeopardizes the quality of the air all forms of life breathe.

Air pollution is defined "as a group of chemical compounds that are in the wrong place or in the wrong concentration at the wrong time."[34] Air pollution is caused by the release of **suspended particulates** such as ash, smoke, dust, soot, and liquid droplets into the air by the burning of fuels, agricultural practices, and industrial processes. Sulfur dioxide (SO_2) is a particularly harmful substance created by the release of sulfur-based fuels from the burning of coal and oil. On the other hand, carbon monoxide (CO) is released when fuels such as gasoline are not burned completely.

Air pollution also consists of toxic air pollutants that are released into the air during the manufacturing processes used by refineries, chemical plants, and dry cleaners. Toxins are also produced by the burning of lead-based gasoline. The combination of all of these components of air pollution may form into smog, haze, or acid rain. **Smog** occurs when "nitrogen oxides (Nox) produced by burning fuel and volatile organic compounds (VOCs) escape to the atmosphere."[35] Producing a hazy dirty brown cloud, smog is the end product of the mixing of over one hundred various compounds with sunlight and heat. **Ozone** is a primary ingredient of smog. Many of the nation's major cities have ozone alert days urging residents to prevent further damage by not gassing up the car or mowing the lawn during alert hours while at the same time warning those with respiratory ailments and allergies to remain indoors. Similar to smog, **haze** refers to "wide-scale, low-level pollution that obstructs visibility."[36] In the 1970s, scientists discovered that the average American was unknowingly contributing to the nation's air pollution problems simply by using everyday products containing **chlorofluorocarbons** or **CFCs**. Now regarded as one of the worst ozone-depleting chemicals, CFCs belong to "a family of inert, nontoxic and easily liquefied chemicals used in refrigeration, air conditioning, packaging, and insulation or as solvents or aerosol propellants."[37] In particular, primary manufacturers such as DuPont used CFCs for the production of housing insulation products and Freon, the chemical used for practically every air conditioning system from home use to vehicles. A 1974 report indicated that CFCs were responsible for adding chlorine to the stratosphere, further eroding the ozone layer. Consequently, "the United States banned CFCs as aerosol propellants in all nonessential applications (ranging from hair sprays to deodorants to furniture polish). U.S. production of CFCs dropped by 95 percent."[38] However, the production of CFCs for industrial use continued. It was the response of the international community that gradually but finally ended CFC production in developed countries by 1996. It began with the Vienna Convention on the Protection of the Ozone Layer in 1985 whereby over twenty-eight nations agreed to find a reasonable CFC substitute by 1990. In 1987, the **Montreal Protocol** signed by 125 nations "froze the production of CFCs by European Community members at mid-1989 levels and called for 50 percent reductions in emissions by 1999. The treaty permitted developing countries to increase CFC use for ten more years, allowing the former USSR to continue production through 1990."[39] A 1990 amendment to the Montreal Protocol banned the complete use of CFCs by 2000 with a subsequent amendment pushing the date back to 1996. The global elimination of CFCs has been so successful that scientists now predict that "ozone levels could recover to their 1979 levels by 2050."[40]

Table 16.1

Selective List of Federal Environmental Laws

Air Pollution Control Act (1955) - Provided federal funding for air pollution control research projects.

Air Quality Act (1967) - Created nationwide federal air quality regions and set acceptable pollution levels for each region. Required that all state and local governments must develop their own standards for air quality or follow federal mandates.

Antiquities Act (1906) – Authorized the President of the United States to set aside by proclamation sites to include national monuments and parcels of land that are objects of historical and scientific interests.

Asbestos Hazard Emergency Response Act (1986) – Required the EPA to conduct inspection and removal of asbestos-containing materials from the nation's public schools.

Atomic Energy Acts (1946 and 1954) – Created the nation's civilian nuclear energy programs.

Clean Air Act (1963) - Provided federal funding and assistance to local and state governments in their efforts to establish air pollution control programs.

Clean Air Act Amendments (1965) - Set federal pollution standards for automobile exhaust emissions.

Clean Air Act Amendments (1970) - Empowered the Environmental Protection Agency to establish national air pollution standards; restricted the discharge of major pollutants into the lower atmosphere; mandated that automobile manufacturers reduce emissions of nitrogen oxide, hydrocarbon, and carbon monoxide by 90 percent.

Clean Air Act Amendments (1990) - Established formulas for the development of anti-polluting gasoline fuels for use in the nation's smoggiest cities; mandated further emissions reductions of carbon monoxide and exhaust emissions by year 2003; placed additional restrictions on toxic pollutants.

Clean Water Act (1972) – Also known as the **Federal Water Pollution Control Act Amendments of 1972**, the federal government's major program overseeing the quality of all surface water.

Clean Water Act (1974) (known as the Safe Water Drinking Act) - Set federal safe drinking water standards for all water suppliers servicing more than 25 people.

Coastal Zone Management Act (1972) – Created the Office of Ocean and Coastal Resource Management to give federal grants to states for the development of their plans to preserve coastal areas and estuarine sanctuaries.

Comprehensive Environmental Response, Compensation, and Liability Act (1980) - Established the federal-level Superfund to clean up toxic waste sites.

Emergency Planning and Community Right-to-Know Act (EPCRA) (1986) – Also known as Title III of the Superfund Amendments and Reauthorization Act of 1986, designed to provide federal assistance to local communities in protecting public health, safety and the environment from chemical hazards; responsible for providing the community with information on chemical hazards that may impact the public and the dissemination of procedures to be followed in the event of an emergency hazardous situation.

Endangered Species Act (1973) - Empowered the Departments of Interior and Commerce to purchase land and water for the sole purpose of protecting, restoring, and propagating endangered species; established an identification and listing system for endangered and threatened species.

Energy Policy and Conservation Act (1975) – Created the nation's Strategic Petroleum Reserve to offset future oil and gas shortages in emergency situations.

Federal Hazardous Liquid Pipeline Safety Act (1979) - Set federal guidelines for the transportation of hazardous liquids by pipelines.

Federal Insecticide, Fungicide and Rodenticide Act (1947) – Authorized the registration and labeling of pesticides used as agricultural chemicals.

Federal Land Policy and Management Act (1976) – Empowered the Bureau of Land Management to oversee the leasing of federally held lands for livestock grazing.

Federal Natural Gas Pipeline Safety Act - Set federal guidelines for the transportation of natural and other gases by pipelines.

Federal Water Pollution Control Act (1948) - Established federal standards for the treatment of municipal wastes prior to discharge. (Revised in 1965 and 1967)

Federal Water Pollution Control Act Amendments (1972) - Mandated national water quality standards and goals for the rehabilitation of polluted waters into safe water sources for recreational and fishing purposes.

Fish Conservation and Management Act (1976) - Restricted foreign fishing in U. S. territorial waters.

General Revision Act (1891) – Authorized the President of the United States to establish forest reserves on public land.

Lacey Act (1900) - Outlawed interstate exportation or importation of wildlife harvested or possessed in violation of federal laws.

Marine Mammal Protection Act (1972) - Prohibited the killing and importation of whales and nearly all marine mammals.

Migratory Bird Conservation Act (1929) - Empowered the federal government to purchase land for waterfowl refuges.

Migratory Bird Hunting Stamp Act (1934) - Required hunters over age 16 to purchase a stamp or license before hunting migratory waterfowl.

Migratory Bird Treaty Act (1918) - Prohibited the hunting or injury of wild birds migrating between the United States, Britain, and Mexico.

National Energy Act (1978) – Deregulated the pricing of natural gas; encouraged alternative energy sources such as solar and geothermal; granted tax credits for home insulation; and encouraged conservation efforts in home-related products and motor vehicles.

National Environmental Policy Act (1969) - Mandated the establishment of the Council for Environmental Quality, and the Environmental Protection Agency.

National Forest Management Act (1976) – Established stricter guidelines for the harvesting and selling of timber and placed limits on clear-cutting of forests.

National Park Act (1916) – Stated that the purpose of national parks was to guarantee public enjoyment and public use without impairment. This legislation established the National Park Service.

National Wildlife Refuge System Improvement Act (1997) – Underscored the need for wildlife protection and the creation of programs supporting wildlife-dependent recreation.

Nuclear Waste Policy Act (1982) – Mandated the construction of federally-supervised permanent disposal sites for nuclear waste.

Oil Pollution Act (1990) – Passed immediately after the Exxon *Valdez* oil spill; required all oil companies to create and submit oil spill contingency plans and to train their employees on containment efforts.

Park Protection Act (1894) – Prohibited hunting in national parks.

Pittman-Robertson Act (1937) - Allocated revenue for state wildlife conservation efforts from the collection of excise taxes on rifles, shotguns, ammunition, and archery equipment.

Pollution Prevention Act (1990) – Aimed at reducing the amount of pollution in the environment by mandating changes in the production, operation and use of raw materials by both private industry and the government.

Refuse Act (1899) - Mandated issuance of a permit for dumping of refuse into any navigable waterway.

Resource Conservation and Recovery Act (1976) - Granted federal control over hazardous wastes; prohibited the creation of new dumping sites without prior permission; mandated the upgrade of existing open dumps to sanitary landfills or face closure.

Safe Drinking Water Act (1974) – Addresses issues relating to the quality and safety of drinking water by authorizing the EPA to set purity standards for aboveground and underground water sources that are designated for human consumption.

Solid Waste Disposal Act (1965) - Provided federal assistance to state and local governments for the establishment of guidelines for solid waste disposal activities.

Surface Mining Control and Reclamation Act (1977) – Placed strict guidelines for strip mining projects to include the restoration of areas subject to strip mining.

Toxic Substances Control Act (1976) – Empowered the EPA to identify, register, evaluate and regulate all commercially used chemicals that posed an "unreasonable risk."

Water Quality Act (1965) - Set federal standards for the discharge of harmful substances into water sources.

Wilderness Act (1964) – Authorized a "hands-off" protection for special areas carved out of the national forest, national park and Bureau of Land Management lands.

Another type of air pollution, **acid rain**, is a "complex chemical and atmospheric phenomenon that occurs when emissions of sulfur and nitrogen compounds and other substances are transformed by chemical processes in the atmosphere, often far from the original source, and then deposited on earth in either a wet or dry form. The wet form, properly called 'acid rain,' can fall as rain, snow, or fog. The dry forms are acidic gases and particulates."[41] Acid rain was a contributing factor to a cooling of relations between the United States and Canada during the Reagan administration. The Canadian government threatened to stall a lucrative trade agreement unless the United States took measures to curtail acid rain pollution. Created in the United States, the polluting effects of acid rain were crossing into Canada destroying crops and deteriorating buildings and national monuments, as well as polluting Canadian air.

The various elements that create air pollution are harmful to human beings. Ozone pollution causes respiratory ailments including shortness of breath, premature aging of the lungs, eye irritation, nasal congestion, and asthma, as well as reduced resistance to infections. Eye and throat irritation, cancer, and bronchitis are directly linked to long-term exposure to particulate matter. Both sulfur dioxide and nitrogen dioxide cause respiratory tract infections and damage to both the lung tissue and immune system. Carbon monoxide severely impairs, often with fatal results, the blood's ability to carry oxygen. It can also cause severe damage to the nervous, cardiovascular, and pulmonary systems. Brain damage and mental retardation can be caused by exposure to lead.

Traditionally throughout the hot summer months, farmers, ranchers, and homeowners, particularly in the Southwest and Western sections of the country, cast a hopeful eye at any cloud that could bring much needed rain to rescue their crops, their livestock, and their lawns from withering and dying. State and local governments have resorted to cloud seeding as a means of jump-starting the rain making process. Weather experts usually point to the El Nino and El Nina weather cycles as the primary culprits for prolonged periods of drought conditions followed by short-lived monsoon like flooding. Scientists, however, have recently cast a suspicious eye towards air pollution as a likely contributor to drought conditions. A study "for the first time, seems to provide direct evidence that tiny particles in industrial pollution cause physical changes in clouds that prevent water from condensing into raindrops and snowflakes."[42] Although the report concedes that definitely pinpointing the source of the pollution that caused the lack of meaningful precipitation is extremely difficult due to changing wind currents, scientists strongly believe that "it is a physical, rather than a chemical process that blocks formation of rain and snow. Industrial plants spew particles formed by fuel combustion that are much smaller than the water droplets normally found in clouds. The small pollution particles inhibit the cloud's water droplets from coalescing into large drops to create rain. Smaller water droplets also are slower to freeze, reducing the ice particles in clouds. In types of clouds that are short-lived, the lack of larger droplets reduces, or even eliminates, the precipitation."[43]

Initially, the federal government believed that air pollution and its subsequent cleanup were the responsibility of the states. Opting for a marginal role, Congress passed the **Air Pollution Control Act** of 1955. This law enabled the federal government to provide funding to those states conducting research on air pollution. The **Clean Air Act** of 1963 provided a $95 million grant-in-aid program to assist state governments in setting their own air quality standards. In 1965, Congress mandated federal emissions standards for hydrocarbons and carbon monoxide for new motor vehicles. The federal regulations were issued in 1966 for the 1968 model year. Congress was still "reluctant to give any real regulatory power to federal officials, however, even though the states were doing relatively little and many air pollution problems transcended state boundaries."[44] The **Air Quality Act** of 1967 went a step further by authorizing the creation of approximately 247 metropolitan air quality regions for the sole purpose of establishing their own air quality standards and developing plans to meet their anticipated goals. For the first time, Congress used a punitive policy approach by authorizing the then Department of Health, Education, and Welfare to force noncomplying states to use federal standards or face loss of federal funds. However, this law proved to be very ineffective. "By 1970, no state had put into place a complete set of standards for any pollutant and the federal government had designated less than one-third of the metropolitan air quality regions that had been projected."[45]

In his State of the Union message delivered in 1970, President Richard Nixon decided to "get tough" with the states by proclaiming both the need for comprehensive federal air quality standards and expanded federal authority to implement the actions required to meet those standards. The **Clean Air Act** of 1970 aimed "to protect and enhance the quality of the nation's air resources so as to promote the public health and welfare and the productive capacity of its population."[46] This law empowered the newly created **Environmental Protection Agency (EPA)** to establish **national ambient air quality standards (NAAQS)** for ozone, carbon monoxide, sulfur dioxide, particulate matter, nitrogen dioxide, and lead. Areas would be designated as **attainment** if air quality met federal standards. Areas failing to meet the standards for one or more NAAQS would be designated as **nonattainment**. Once the EPA announced the standards, states had nine months to develop their implementation plans. In turn, the EPA was to ensure that each plan included monitoring requirements, emission limitations for the six elements, provisions for periodic inspection of sites, and the testing of motor vehicles, as well as a state budgetary commitment to enforce air pollution standards. In addition, motor vehicle emissions of carbon monoxide and hydrocarbons were to be reduced by 90 percent beginning with the 1975 models. Nitrogen oxide emissions were to be cut by 90 percent by 1976. The EPA was granted enforcement power to include leveling fines from up to $10,000 per day for anyone removing a pollution control device to $25,000 per day for each violation of pollution. The investigative tools given to the EPA included injunctions to halt polluting activities pending legal actions. For the first time, citizens could file suits against both the polluter and the EPA for failure to respond to reported incidences of air pollution.

Despite heated debate from all sides of the issue, it was the Nixon administration that garnered public and political support for this legislation. However, the president's aim was to oversee the enactment of legislation that accomplished the goals of both protecting the environment and shielding America's business and industry from unreasonable regulations and penalties. "Part of its motivation [the Nixon administration] was a concern that regulation in some states but not in others, put regulated industries at a competitive disadvantage. Industry representatives also lobbied for one set of federal standards rather than a variety of state provisions. They prevailed on Congress to prohibit the states from imposing more aggressive regulation than provided in the Clean Air Act of 1970."[47] This initial "get tough" policy was further compromised by subsequent amendments to the Clean Air Act that year after year granted waivers to automobile manufacturers that successfully blocked full implementation of the stronger emissions standards. Amendments passed in 1977 did threaten to deny federal funding for highway and sewage treatment projects to those states not in compliance with the Clean Air Act. However, the federal government opted to avoid taking such actions.

Although the Reagan administration sought to weaken it, the George Bush administration did enact a series of amendments to the **Clean Air Act** in 1990. This package included a mandatory production phaseout of chlorofluorocarbons, carbon-tetrachloride, methyl chloroform, and hydrochlorofluorocarbons, all major contributors to ozone pollution. Vehicle manufacturers were required to reduce harmful emissions and to improve emissions control devices. The gasoline companies were required to produce cleaner burning fuels. Industry was required to reduce emissions levels of both sulfur dioxide and nitrate oxide in an attempt to reduce acid rain levels. The 1990 amendments targeted 250 hazardous pollutants for emissions reductions of 90 percent by 2003. In 1993, diesel engine trucks were added to the list of motor vehicles subjected to emissions control standards.

The air pollution laws passed since 1970 have produced a mixed-bag of results. From 1970 to 1991, "emissions levels of many pollutants have dropped: lead by 96 percent, sulfur dioxide by 28 percent, particulates by 61 percent."[48] However, more Americans are driving personal vehicles, resulting in noticeable increases in ozone, carbon monoxide, and nitrogen oxide emissions levels thus offsetting any decreases. A well-known urban historian, the late Lewis Mumford, once commented that Americans "had adopted the cloverleaf as the national flower."[49] The invention of the automobile enabled Americans to freely travel across the country. However, the automobile's continued success is dependent upon a unique combination of fossil fuels commonly known as gasoline, rubber tires, and miles upon miles of asphalt and concrete roadways. Urban sprawl and highways go hand in hand. "Two million homes are built each year—and with them comes the proliferation of superstores, strip malls, and office parks. Badly planned and not planned, they turn up in the wrong places, allowed by the wrong building and zoning codes. Supported by the infrastructure of the automobile, from highways to sewage lines, and by subsidies for big oil and tax relief for developers, these trophies of highway-fed economic growth consume two million acres of productive farmland a year, according to the American Farmland Trust, and uncounted acres of woods and wetlands."[50] As early as 1991, congressional leaders recognized the necessity of encouraging alternative means of transportation to offset the polluting ways of the personal automobile culture. The **Intermodal Surface Transportation Efficiency Act** allocated $155 billion over a six-year period to "encourage foot power, bike power, mass transit, and other transportation alternatives. Two billion dollars from the act would support transportation-related 'enhancement' projects: fixing up a train station, for instance, or rehabilitating a bridge. . . Further the act mandated an additional billion dollars to Congestion Mitigation Air Quality funds, supporting a broad and vital array of projects ranging from buying alternative-fuel buses to laying light rail lines to organizing ridesharing."[51] Reliable and rapid mass transportation systems do help to reduce the number of commuters using personal vehicles. The majority of the nation's sophisticated mass transportation systems are concentrated in a handful of large metropolitan cities such as New York and Chicago. In most cities, the bus line with its reputation for unreliable service is the mass transportation system. Part of his plan to jump start the nation's economy, President Obama offered billions of dollars in stimulus money to the states not only for infrastructure improvements to upgrade the nation's deteriorating roads and bridges, but to develop alternative transportation options to include both high speed and light rail train systems. In addition, his package of new federally standardized emissions rules would have "required each automaker's fleet of cars and light trucks to average 35.5 mpg [miles per gallon] by 2016."[52]

In 2020, the Trump administration rolled back Obama's strict emission standards by issuing the Safer Affordable-Fuel-Efficient (SAFE) Vehicles Rule. Pressured by the auto industry to freeze existing standards without an increase, Trump opted to increase the standards by only 1.5%, far less than Obama's policy of 5%. Outraged environmentalists criticized Trump's move since "the new rule will lead to nearly a billion additional metric tons of climate warming CO2 in the atmosphere, and that consumers will end up losing money by buying about 80 billion more gallons of gas."[53]

While Obama's energy policies were designed to replace the nation's dependency on fossil fuels with alternative renewable energy sources, the Trump administration adopted policies and practices favoring traditional non-renewable fuels such as oil, coal, and natural gas. Trump supports the experts who believe that 40.5 billion barrels of oil can be recovered within the continental United States with an additional 76 billion barrels in nearby offshore sites, such as the Gulf of Mexico, the Alaskan shoreline, etc.[54] Since the Clinton presidency, Congress and environmentalists have been battling over drilling for oil in Alaska's Arctic National Wildlife Refuge. "A 1998 U.S. Geological Survey assessment still used today concluded it's almost certain there are at least 5.6 billion barrels of recoverable oil and possibly as much as 16 billion barrels (a 5 percent likelihood) beneath the refuge's 1.5 million-acre coastal plain."[55] Fearful of the encroachment of oil derricks and tanker trucks, environmentalists want to keep the pristine area preserved for endangered and protected species. Oil companies, on the other hand, believe "there is enough oil in the refuge to supply every drop needed by New Hampshire for 315 years or Maine for 299 years. It's enough oil for the nation's capitol for 1,710 years."[56]

When one thinks of the oil and natural gas business, one envisions row after row of tall oil derricks and huge drills inching their way into the earth's core in search of precious liquid gold. However, the oil derrick has virtually given way to a new extraction process—fracking. Basically, hydraulic fracturing or fracking "involves safely tapping shale and other tight-rock formations by drilling a mile or more below the surface before gradually turning horizontal and continuing several thousands of feet more. Thus, a single surface site can accommodate a number of wells. Once the well is drilled, cased, and cemented, small perforations are made in the horizontal portion of the well pipe, through which a typical mixture of water (90 percent), sand (9.5 percent) and additives (0.5 percent) is pumped at high pressure to create micro-fractures in the rock that are held open by the grains of sand" allowing for the extraction of the oil and natural gas deposits stored in these hidden rock formations.[57] Fracking enables the oilman to reach deep deposits of oil and gas that the traditional drilling methods cannot accomplish. However, fracking is controversial. Many residents of rural areas are voicing their concerns about the possible contamination of their water sources, such as wells and aquifer systems. Several areas in Oklahoma in particular have experienced an increase in the number of earthquakes that many geologists contribute to fracking. The discovery of a potential massive deposit of untapped oil and gas has led to an oil boom and bust similar to the gold rush days of old. In South Texas, residents of several small communities saw their small-town lifestyle turned upside as the geologists announced a potential fracking site that brought hundreds of oil workers to their communities. When the boom hit, the communities were ill prepared for the onslaught. Suddenly, there were no vacancy signs on all of the motels and local trailer parks. The restaurants were overcrowded. The two-lane highways were jammed with row after row of tanker trucks. Yes, the city coffers grew but only as long as the oil and gas remained in the earth. Once extracted, everyone in the oil field left only to go down the road to the next town.

Of course, once oil and natural gas are extracted from the earth, these products must be sent for processing and storage. Environmentalists and property owners are in a battle against oil producers over the construction of massive oil pipelines. The controversial **Keystone Pipeline** is a 1,179 mile-long pipeline originating in Hardisty, Canada, designed to transport approximately 830,000 barrels of oil per day across a portion of Canada only to make a dramatic turn into the United States to its final destination, Houston, Texas.[58] A proposed extension of the pipeline became a heated political issue as President Obama, on the recommendations from the EPA, halted construction of both projects. The EPA wanted guarantees that at reasonable intervals, a monitor would check the line to catch any possible leaks and if a leak did occur, TransCanada already had measures in place for a rapid response to address any possible contamination of water sources. Through an executive order, however, President Trump has given the green light to restart construction of the pipeline and the proposed extension. Another pipeline project, the **Trans Mountain Pipeline** would take oil from Edmonton, Canada to Anacortes, Washington. On the positive side, "the project would give Canada's oil industry something it desperately wants—a wide open conduit between their tar sands and the global market. Direct access to overseas customers could fetch tar sands oil a high price."[59] The **Dakota Access Pipeline** project has drawn the ire of the Standing Rock Sioux since the route will be near the Sioux Reservation. Tribal leaders and environmentalists hold that "first, the pipeline would pass under the Missouri River (at Lake Oahe) just a half a mile upstream of the Tribe's reservation boundary, where a spill would be culturally and economically catastrophic. Second, the pipeline would pass through areas of great cultural significance, such as sacred sites and burials that federal law seeks to protect."[60] Vowing to stand their ground, tribal leaders have blockaded access to the land, leading to violent clashes with law enforcement. If completed, the route of this estimated $3.8 billion pipeline will carry oil from North Dakota through South Dakota and Iowa to its final destination in Illinois.[61]

The nation's quest to find more liquid gold hit a tragically significant snag after the BP oil spill in the Gulf of Mexico. Citing safety concerns about off-shore oil drilling projects, President Obama issued a moratorium on all deep water oil projects until new safety regulations could be developed. In particular, the administration wanted offshore operators to develop emergency evacuation plans, blowout prevention measures, and oil spill containment options, etc. However, the outcry from the major oil companies and drilling firms caused the Obama administration to retreat.

A primary source for the nation's on-going problem with air pollution is industries heavily involved in chemical, oil and gas production, and refining businesses. Corpus Christi, Texas, for example, is well known for its natural beaches along the Gulf of Mexico. While tourism is big business, the city's largest employers are six refineries located all in a row on a 10-mile corridor known as Refinery Row. These six refineries employ 23,000 and pump millions of dollars per year into the local economy. Unfortunately, Refinery Row is a prime example of industry butting its head with urban development. Initially, these refineries were built outside of the city limits. Overtime, however, laxed or non-existent city and county zoning regulations allowed for the construction of single-family homes and business virtually across the street from the refineries. Although these companies have spent millions on pollution control devices and installed smokestack scrappers, residents and business-owners alike suffer the adverse impact of a continuous twenty-four hours seven days a week of billowing smoke, ash and harmful substances polluting their neighborhoods. There are days when the air smells like rotten eggs from the emission of hydrogen sulfide. Parking a car in the street overnight means that in the morning, one is dusting off the nightly accumulation of ash and soot covering the entire vehicle. Once the area's residential properties were prime real estate. Today, these neighborhoods support a dependent minority underclass that simply cannot afford to move elsewhere. Finding a buyer for one's home is not a viable option since given a choice, few would want to live right next door to a polluting oil refinery. Although the area's benzene levels are within the EPA's parameters for compliance, the levels are among the highest in Texas. Work-related accidents in chemical plants are not uncommon. The U.S. Chemical Safety and Hazard Investigation Board reports that "since 1998, an average of five plant workers have been killed every month in the United States by explosions or leaks of chemicals. . . There is at least one chemical accident somewhere in the nation everyday."[62] Far too often, the aftermath of a chemical or hazard substance explosion is a frustrating tug of war between an industrial giant and homeowners. For example, the 2020 explosion 2,000-gallon propylene tank at the Watson Grinding & Manufacturing Company in Houston was so powerful that it blew off the roofs, doors, and windows of nearby homes while burning scores of other properties. The lingering cloud of volatile chemicals forced mandatory evacuations. Initially, "the CEO of Watson made—and then rescinded—a promise to pay for all the damage the explosion caused. Lawyers who have filed hundreds of lawsuits against the company say it will not have the resources to make every victim whole. And insurance companies have responded unevenly, granting some claims while denying or challenging others."[63] To add salt to the wound, within days after the explosion, Watson filed for bankruptcy.

In some areas, the quality of the nation's air is questionable. Through the EPA, the Obama administration took a stronger stand on the enforcement of air quality standards. In 2010, the EPA established a greenhouse gas emissions compliance plan for Arizona, Arkansas, Florida, Idaho, Kansas, Oregon and Wyoming. Severe actions were taken against Texas as the EPA in 2010, "declared Texas unfit to regulate its own greenhouse gas emissions and took over carbon dioxide permitting of any new or expanding industrial facilities starting January 2 [2011]."[64]

Global Warming

"The earth's atmosphere works like a greenhouse: It traps solar radiation, making life on earth possible. **Climate change** describes a rise in the earth's temperature caused by an increase in the concentration of certain gases, especially carbon dioxide."[65] Although not alarmists, both climate experts and environmentalists have expressed serious concerns that the future of the earth's greenhouse is being severely compromised to the point that the damage may not be reversible. They warn of **global warming** or the **greenhouse effect** that occurs when "methane, carbon dioxide, and certain other air pollutants increase, trapping heat in the earth's atmosphere and gradually warming it."[66] If their predictions are correct, "the results could be devastating: rising oceans, ferocious hurricanes, and prolonged droughts."[67] So far, the evidence clearly indicates that the earth is, indeed, getting warmer. According to the Intergovernmental Panel on Climate Change, "each of the last three decades has been successively warmer at the Earth's surface than any preceding decade since 1850."[68] Higher temperatures mean that the polar ice caps are melting. It is predicted that "by the end of this century, Arctic temperatures could reach as high as 130,000 years ago, when the oceans were 13 to 20 feet higher than now."[69]   On June 19, 2020, in Verkhoyansk, a small town in Siberia, Russia, the temperature "reached 100.4 degrees Fahrenheit, 32 degrees above the normal high temperature. This is likely the hottest temperature ever recorded in Siberia and also the hottest temperature ever recorded north of the Arctic Circle."[70]   What happens in Greenland and Antarctica does have an impact elsewhere.   For example, experts believe that approximately one-third of the coral reefs in the Caribbean waters are dying due to global warming and rising sea temperatures.   "The mortality that we're seeing now is of the extremely slow-growing reef-building corals.   These are corals that are the foundation of the reef . . . We're talking colonies that were here when Columbus came by have died in the past three to four months.   Some of the devastated coral never can be replaced because it only grows the width of a dime per year."[71]   The potential demise of the coral reefs means economic ruin for the tourist industries in Puerto Rico and the Virgin Islands.

Realizing that global warming is an international problem involving all nation states, approximately 160 nations, including the United States, signed the 1997 **Kyoto Protocol** to the 1992 UN Framework Convention on Climate Change.   The agreement "set binding reduction targets and assigned emissions caps based on 1990 greenhouse gas emissions.   Nations were given a five-year window (2008-2012) in which to achieve its targets.   The United States agreed to reduce emissions to 7 percent below 1990 levels by 2010."[72]   However, in March 2001, the United States became the only industrialized nation to withdraw from the agreement.   The George W. Bush administration faulted the agreement for not placing developing nations on the same time table for emissions reductions as the more advanced or industrial nations.   The international environmental community was outraged with Bush, and during his tenure in the White House, whenever he attended an international conference he was met with angry protesters.   The Obama administration enacted tougher restrictions on the emission of greenhouse gases from power plants.   In 2014, the Supreme Court upheld the EPA's authority to both regulate and enforce the new standards with its ruling in ***Hall v Florida***.

The Water We Drink

On paper, the United States has an abundant supply of water, totaling 269,717 square miles of water consisting of 85,076 square miles of inland water, 42,390 square miles of coastal waters, 60,093 square miles of water in the Great Lakes and 82,157 square miles of water in United States territories.[73]   In reality, the United States has regions with an over abundant supply of water offset by areas that face yearly droughts and water shortages.   Since humans are composed of approximately 80 percent of water, clean and plentiful sources of water are absolutely essential to our survival.   Yet, Americans, in particular, rank as the world's largest consumers of water.   "The average American family uses more than 300 gallons of water per day at home.   Roughly 70 percent of this use occurs indoors.   Normally, outdoor water use accounts for 30 percent of household use yet it can be much higher in drier parts of the country and in more water-intensive landscapes."[74]   Of course, the demand for water increases as the population grows.   Unfortunately, Americans have wasted their water resources for far too many years.   It is extremely difficult to drive home the need for water conservation particularly when homeowners want beautiful year-round green lawns.

Unfortunately too many of the nation's rivers and lakes have been used as dumping sites for industrial and municipal wastes.   Historically, government at *all* levels was extremely reluctant to recognize the damage caused by dumping wastes into the nation's waterways.   The federal government did recognize the need for sewage treatment plants by enacting a 1948 law providing federal funds to local communities to build and operate these facilities. It was not until 1965 that Congress mandated that states applying for these federal dollars had to establish clean water standards as a criterion for grant consideration. By the 1970s, incidences of severe water pollution could no longer be ignored. For all practical purposes, Lake Erie was "dead, with garbage and rotting fish regularly washing onto beaches and runoff of fertilizer and raw sewage causing massive algae blooms that starved fish of oxygen. The Cuyahoga River [in Cleveland, Ohio], which feeds Erie, was so polluted with oil, logs, sewage and every other kind of garbage that it caught fire on June 22, 1969. The Walleye in Erie contained so much toxic mercury that the government banned its consumption. Cormorants were born horribly deformed by pesticides, local populations of peregrine falcons have been driven toward extinction by DDT, and lake trout in Michigan and Huron were wiped out by over-fishing."[75] The majority of the nation's waterways located near heavy and medium-sized industrial plants were heavily polluted. "Before 1972, at least 18,000 communities regularly dumped their untreated raw sewage into rivers and lakes. Food, textile, paper, chemical, metal, and other industries discharged 25 trillion gallons of waste water each year."[76] The federal government's response was the passage of the **Water Pollution Control Act** (also known as the **Clean Water Act**) in 1972. This legislation established guidelines for nationwide water pollution standards.

The Clean Water Act also created the **National Pollution Discharge Elimination System (NPDES)** whereby all businesses and industries must file for a permit prior to discharging and/or dumping any effluents into a waterway. Municipalities are required to install more sophisticated purification treatment processes into their sewer systems. The Clean Water Act gave the administration and enforcement duties to the EPA, which passed the bulk of the responsibilities onto the states. States were required to establish separate state agencies to handle water pollution problems. In addition, state governments were given the latitude to pass their own water pollution-related legislation as long as state-mandated standards did not undermine federal restrictions and penalties. Federal and state guidelines mandated that all surface water be tested for the presence of harmful substances to include arsenic, lead, toxaphene, and chromium. The Clean Water Act was renewed in 1977, 1987, 1997 and 2007.

One of the major problems associated with water pollution is determining the origination of the pollution and the identity of the polluting party. The Clean Water Act does draw a distinction between nonpoint and point source pollution. **Point source pollution** is defined as "a pollution source that has a precise, identifiable location, such as a pipe or smokestack."[77] Any business or industrial plant visibly dumping industrial and hazardous wastes into a waterway could be cited for point source pollution. **Non-point source pollution** is "a pollution source that is diffuse, such as urban runoff."[78] A river or stream could be heavily polluted with runoffs from fertilizers and pesticides originating from several farms and ranches located along that waterway. Determining the identity of the guilty party is extremely difficult, if not impossible.

The Clean Water Act has produced some positive results. "From 1972 to 1982, the amount of **biochemical oxygen demand (BOD)** (the amount of oxygen needed by bacteria to breakdown a specific amount of organic matter) declined by 46 percent at municipal sewage treatment plants and by at least 71 percent in industrial discharges."[79] Progress in cleaning up the nation's waterways has been met with marginal success. Rivers are classified as either good, threatened or impaired. Bodies of water are declared impaired when they cannot support aquatic life or are unsafe for fishing or swimming. According to the EPA's National Water Quality Inventory Report issued in 2017, states assessed only 1,107,002 of the nation's 3.5 million miles of rivers and streams. Their findings indicated that 614,153 were identified as impaired, 487,299 garnered good ratings but 5,500 fell into the threatened category. Only 18,513,899 of the nation's 41.7 million acres of lakes, ponds and reservoirs were assessed. The findings indicated that 13,009,273 acres are impaired and 34,621 were deemed threatened. Only 5,470,00 were rated as good. Of the nation's 87,791 square miles of bays and estuaries, only 35,094 were assessed. Assessment reports indicated that 27,483 square miles are impaired while only 7,611 miles were deemed as good. Only 1,232,559 of the nation's approximate 107,700,000 wetland acres were evaluated. The findings revealed that 657,907 acres are impaired while only 574,907 acres were rated as good.[80] The leading causes of impairment are pathogens, sediment, nutrients, organic enrichment (fertilizers) and habitat alterations.

Dams have also been identified as a contributing factor to water pollution. Damming rivers seemed to be the perfect solution to an area's drought conditions particularly in the West and Southwest regions of the United States. The Army Corps of Engineers provided a helping hand in determining the site location and size of the dam. "For nearly a century local water districts and Congress have regarded any Western rivers that flowed to the sea unimpeded as a colossal waste—a waste of water that could be captured for farming and urban development, a waste of potential hydropower, a waste of potential recreation sites that could be created by backing up the great rivers into lakes. To harness the water, federal and state agencies, as well as private developers, have built more than 600 major dams this century [20th]."[81] Damming a river does successfully prevent water from eventually spilling into the ocean. However, it also destroys natural habitat for sea creatures, animals, birds and plants. Damming also provides recreational spots for fishermen and outdoorsmen. However, it destroys the natural runoff patterns for rain. Far too often disastrous floods are caused by the inability of water to runoff naturally from properties. Now the Army Corps of Engineers is leading the charge to tear them down.

Oceans are also heavily polluted. "Throughout the world, important water bodies—especially the oceans—have become virtual waste bins for the tons of plastic products dumped daily by commercial fishermen, military vessels, merchant ships, passenger liners, pleasure boats, offshore oil and gas drilling operations, the plastics industry and sewage treatment plants."[82] While the sun is coming up over the ocean's horizon, it is tragic to realize that the first sight one has in the morning is the fleet of front end loaders making their daily sweep of the trash either thrown on the beach by people or washed up on shore by the evening tide. Because oceans usually fall under international laws, few nations have enacted legislation designed to protect their shorelines from trash and pollution. The victims are the birds and sea creatures who must wade through the piles of garbage.

In 1974, Congress passed the **Safe Water Drinking Act** with the promise of guaranteeing to all Americans a plentiful and healthy supply of drinking water. This legislation set federal standards for all suppliers of drinking water serving more than twenty-five people. The law was amended in 1986 with the provision that water suppliers test for dozens of chemicals and bacterial substances and notify their customers when water supplies did not meet federal standards. The amendments also banned the use of lead pipes in public water systems.

Despite federal and state laws, the federal government still cannot guarantee a safe drinking water supply. Far too many communities must boil their water to remove unwanted substances. The renowned **United States Center for Disease Control and Prevention (CDC)** warned those individuals with weakened immune systems, such as AIDS, and chemotherapy patients to either use bottled or boiled water.

Groundwater is still in grave jeopardy of contamination from pesticides, human, animal and industrial wastes, home cleaning products, and gasoline. In addition, municipal governments across the country are confronting costly problems with fixing and or replacing leaking and rupturing water mains and sewer systems. A ruptured sewer main can lead to the introduction of harmful substances, such as pathogens, into the drinking water system. Floods caused by a major storm system or a hurricane will ruin municipal water and sewer systems. In the aftermath of Hurricane Katrina, residents along the Gulf Coast and in Louisiana were warned not to use or come in contact with any of their water supply systems. The flood waters themselves were heavily laden with toxic substances, backed-up sewer waste, and gasoline and oil products from the ruptured underground storage tanks, etc. In January 2014, over 300,000 residents in nine counties in West Virginia were ordered not to drink, bathe, or wash clothes or dishes because their tap water was contaminated from a chemical spill in the Elk River. Owned by Freedom Industries, the chemical spill "occurred after a broken water line caused the ground to freeze beneath an aging chemical storage tank, pushing an unidentified object into the bottom of the tank. The resulting puncture allowed 7,500 gallons of 4-methylcyclohexane methanol, a chemical that washes impurities from coal to escape" into the Elk River, the primary source of drinking water in that area.[85] Facing potential lawsuits and fines from the EPA, the company filed for Chapter 11 bankruptcy.

Located in the middle of two of the nation's Great Lakes, it would be logical to assume that the city of Flint, Michigan, would provide all of its residents with an ample supply of clean drinking water. For years, city leadership used Lake Huron as its primary source of drinking water. However in 2014, the city decided to save money by switching its water source to the Flint River, "a notorious tributary that runs through town known to locals for its filth."[84] Almost immediately, residents began to notice that the once clear water coming out of their kitchen faucets was now turning brown and began to smell and taste different from what they were accustomed to drinking. For two years, city leaders continued to tell complaining users that there was no problem. But, there was a big problem. "The Flint River is highly corrosive: 19 times more so than the Lake Huron supply. . . The state Department of Environmental Quality wasn't treating the Flint River water with an anti-corrosive agent, in violation of federal law. . . but what residents couldn't see was far worse. About half of the service lines to homes in Flint are made of lead and because the water wasn't properly treated, lead began leaching into the water supply, in addition to the iron."[85] For eighteen months, city leaders knew about the condition of the drinking water supply but opted not to inform city residents. Yet within a few weeks, parents noticed that their children were becoming ill. Despite periodic trips to the doctor, the children's health was not improving, but only getting worse. Doctors were at a loss to explain the cause of their ailments. Finally, tests revealed that these children were suffering from lead poisoning, an irreversible illness. The devastating adverse impact of lead poisoning is well documented. Lead poisoning is "a well-known potent neurotoxin. There's tons of evidence on what lead does to a child, and it is one of the most damning things that you can do to a population. It drops your IQ, it affects your behavior, it's been linked to criminality, [and] it has multigenerational impacts. There is no safe level of lead in a child."[86] The public outcry has prompted the governor to finally take action by declaring a state of emergency. City leaders have switched back to Lake Huron water. Estimated costs to replace the old pipes are beyond Flint's budget, prompting city leaders to seek federal financial assistance. Residents were provided bottled water while the EPA joined state and local officials in conducting numerous lengthy investigations. Citizen groups called for a full federal criminal investigation of all parties involved to include the mayor, city department heads and the state's governor. Further outrage followed when city leaders opted to charge residents for their once free bottled water. Although improvements have been made, the costs of treatment will run into the billions for, after all, lead poisoning is an irreversible illness requiring expensive life-long treatments.

City governments can no longer ignore taking "action on the fissures spreading in the 700,000 miles of pipes that deliver water to U.S. homes and businesses. Three generations of water mains are at risk: cast-iron pipes of the 1880s, thinner conduits of the 1920s, and even less sturdy post-World War II tubes. Cost estimates range from the EPA's $151 billion figure to a $1 trillion tally by a coalition of water industry, engineering, and environmental groups. The American Water Works Association (AWWA) projects costs as high as $6,900 per household in some small towns."[87] Several municipalities are taking action to protect their drinking water supplies. Cities such as Dayton, Ohio, and San Antonio, Texas, are using restrictive and/or no-development zoning laws to protect their underground aquifer systems. In Dunedin, Florida, residents angry over the rust in their tap water, pressured city leaders to build a new water treatment plant with membrane-filtration systems.

Oil Spills and Toxic Wastes

On April 12, 2010, the nation's focus was on a deepwater drilling rig named Horizon, owned by the drilling company Trans-ocean and leased to British Petroleum (BP). Located in the Gulf of Mexico off the Louisiana coastline, "an explosion rocked the rig, igniting a massive fire. Eleven workers were killed in the inferno, and 17 more were injured. Within two days, while Coast Guard ships were still searching for survivors, the ruined Horizon sank, dragging its equipment and pipes to the bottom of the ocean, 5,000 ft. below."[88] The explosion unleashed a massive oil spill stretching over 2,000 miles that was headed directly towards Louisiana's Barataria Bay. Unable to seal the well head, the oil gushed out at the rate of over 200,000 gallons a day as Gulf Coast residents came to the rescue of oil-soaked birds, turtles, and other marine animals. Work crews used oil dispersants to break up the floating thick crude oil and booms to soak it up before it washed ashore. It took four agonizing months for BP officials and engineers to drill a relief well, plug the broken one with mud and finally seal it. The oil giant had already paid out nearly $42 billion for cleanup and related costs.[89] This spill is definitely the largest to date to hit America's coastline. After admitting culpability in dumping nearly 3.19 million barrels of oil along the Gulf shore lines of Florida, Alabama, Texas, Mississippi and Louisiana, BP launched a lengthy six-year battle over the assessment of the damages filed against it. On April 6, 2016, a federal district judge approved "the largest environmental damage settlement in United States history—$20.8 billion."[90]

In 1989, Americans were horrified as the Exxon *Valdez* went aground on Alaska's pristine Prince William Sound, spilling its cargo of crude oil over 900 square miles. The black goo spoiled shorelines, killed millions of marine animals and fish, and destroyed the fishing industry for several seasons. Three more major oil spills occurred that year. The Greek tanker, *World Prodigy*, struck a reef in Narragansett Bay, Rhode Island, dumping 420,000 of No. 2 fuel oil into the waterway. "In Delaware where the Uruguayan tanker, *Presidente Rivera*, ran aground and spilled 300,000 gallons of heavy No. 6 oil, about 70 percent had been cleaned up. The smallest of the spills, which occurred when a barge collided with a cargo ship in the Houston Ship Channel and released 250,000 gallons of heavy crude, was almost completely recovered."[91] Unfortunately, every year there are reported incidents of oil spills, tanker explosions, and offshore ruptured pipelines. For example, in 2017 alone, there were 2,472 oil spills resulting in 241,204 gallons of oil dumped into United States coastal and off-shore waters.[92]

Obviously not every oil spill is preventable, but the majority of them can be avoided. Faced with the reality that only 10 percent of oil spilled is usually recovered, one would assume that the federal government would have taken extraordinary measures to keep disastrous oil spills to the bare minimum. However, interest group politics driven by the major oil producers has successfully prevented the federal government from taking severe punitive criminal and civil actions against violators. For example, then United States Senator Lloyd Bentsen introduced in 1989 a bill requiring all domestically owned oil tankers to use a triple hull structure around the oil storage tanks. Although public opinion sided with Bentsen, particularly after the *Valdez* episode, the legislation was defeated on the grounds that it was a costly unnecessary mandate against both big and small oil firms that would ultimately result in higher prices at the pump. The major oil companies had already served notice that if the bill passed, they would simply bypass the legislation by contracting out to foreign tanker companies to ship their oil. As merely the contracting party, the oil companies could transport their oil more cheaply while at the same time avoiding costly litigation if the tanker spilled its load. Our beaches, marine life, and, in some instances, economic viability is in jeopardy every time one of these tankers enters into America's waters.

The proper identification, storage, and disposal of hazardous, nuclear, and solid and municipal wastes are problems confronting all levels of government. Nuclear energy is a cost-effective method of supplying electricity to homes. Yet, scientists have yet to develop a safe method for the disposal of radioactive materials, much less obsolete nuclear reactors. The Industrial Revolution introduced manufacturing processes that produced toxic byproducts. For over one hundred years, it was an acceptable practice to dump these hazardous substances into waterways and vacant lots. The United States government is just as guilty as the nation's industrial giants. Beginning in the mid-1980s, Congress and the White House began searching for ways to save money. They decided that with the end of the Cold War and the collapse of the Soviet Union, the United States government no longer needed a large standing army supported by thousands of civil servants. The answer was to begin closing down American military bases. However, the Pentagon and lawmakers soon realized that the money they were going to save in closing the bases was small in comparison to the money they were going to be spending to clean up the hazardous materials housed and, unfortunately, dumped on these military bases. In California, McClellan Air Force Base is still in the process of being converted from public to private hands. "Decades of dumping, leaks and spills at the base have left the heavily used aquifer contaminated with chlorinated solvents and fuels that will take more than 30 years to clean up . . . Cleanup is not expected to be finished until 2034. The projected cleanup tab for the 64-year old base is $984 million with $300 already spent."[93]

In addition to military installations, commercial nuclear power plants have their own problems disposing of their high-level radioactive wastes. As of 2020, there are 98 nuclear power plants located in 30 states. The dilemma confronting the EPA is the location of sites for the disposal of radioactive waste materials. The fear of a potential disaster evokes strong emotions from citizens as government officials seek to find dump sites. Oftentimes politics enters into the picture. Although Americans enjoy the benefits of nuclear power, they are extremely fearful of nuclear accidents, particularly when the discussion of a potential site is their neighborhood!

Today, it is known that the disposal of nuclear and industrial byproducts must be properly stored and ultimately disposed of to prevent hazardous spills and contaminations; and individuals must dispose of their solid wastes and trash in a nonpolluting and responsible manner. However, the proper disposal of these materials is extremely costly and demands sacrifices from all participating parties. The federal government took the lead by setting the guidelines for the identification, monitoring, and disposal of solid and industrial waste products in 1976 with the passage of the **Toxic Substance Control Act. Solid waste** is defined as "refuse materials composed primarily of solids at normal ambient temperatures."[94] The EPA was empowered through this legislation to establish testing procedures for new chemical substances before they could be sold. The EPA also authorized federal and state authorities to ban the sale of any harmful substances. The law specifically prohibited the sale of toxic polychlorinated biphenyls (PCB) not contained in closed systems. On January 1, 2000, the Clinton administration imposed tighter reporting rules on the use of toxic substances. The old rules required "release reports by companies that manufacture or process more than 25,000 pounds or use more than 10,000 pounds of toxic chemicals a year. The new rules require reports by companies that use 100 pounds a year, or, for some especially dangerous chemicals, 10 pounds a year."[95] The **Resource Conservation and Recovery Act** of 1976 established the process for the disposal of hazardous wastes.

Both federal and state laws prohibit the transportation of any hazardous materials through municipal areas. The risk of a derailment or traffic accident is minimized by redirecting vehicles and rail carriers carrying hazardous substances to rural routes. However, the potentiality of an accident resulting in the release of toxic and harmful substances into rivers, waterways, soil, and the air is still a tragic reality. All parties involved in the storage and disposal of toxic and hazardous materials must record the site with the appropriate county offices as well as file monthly and yearly reports.

The average American throws away tons of garbage every year. **Municipal solid waste (MSW)** is defined as "solid waste resulting from or incidental to municipal, community, commercial, institutional, and recreational activities including garbage, rubbish, ashes, street cleanings, dead animals, abandoned automobiles, and all other solid waste other than industrial waste."[96] Once it was perfectly acceptable to pile up the trash in landfills and trash dumps, pitch it out the window to the streets below, or simply burn it in the privacy of one's backyard. In 2017, "the total generation of MSW was 267.8 million tones or 4.51 pounds per person per day. Of the MSW generated, approximately 67 million tons were recycled, and 27 million tons were composted. Together, more than 94 million tons of MSW were recycled and composted, equivalent to a 35.2 percent recycling and composting rate."[97] Although federal and state laws set guidelines for the disposal of these products, the ultimate responsibility falls squarely upon the shoulders of city and county governments. The laws establish extremely strict regulations covering a wide range of municipal waste activities, including the size of the landfill and the height of the trash piles. Site location is an extremely delicate situation since no one wants a landfill in their backyard. However, the trash can be piled only as high as the federally mandated level allows. Cities can apply for a variance to buy time until a new site can be located. There is just too much trash and too little landfill space to dump it on. In addition, reclamation of landfills is virtually worthless since it is unlikely that anyone would want to build their homes or businesses on a filled-in landfill that may emit harmful vapors and odors.

Communities have adopted volunteer recycling programs for newspapers, paper products, glass, plastics, and aluminum cans. However, converting recycled products into reusable goods is still an expensive venture. Although environmentally aware, the average American consumer is reluctant to purchase higher priced items made from recycled products. Another alternative is incineration, whereby unsorted trash is burned. Although incineration does reduce the need for landfill space, the process of burning mass amounts of trash does pose potential harmful effects to air quality. Site selection proposals for incineration plants produce heated battles between angry residents vehemently opposed to having smokestacks release byproducts from burning trash over their homes and city leaders desperate to find cost effective trash disposal methods. Advanced incineration systems include mass burn combustors, modular combustion systems, refuse-driven fuel combustors, and waste-to-energy plants. Obviously, this nation's major cities are facing an uphill battle unless cost-effective and environmentally safe alternative trash disposal methods are adopted within the immediate future.

Superfund Programs

Since the cost of properly disposing and cleaning up hazardous, solid, and municipal wastes is often too expensive for the violators to bear alone, the **Comprehensive Environmental Response Compensation and Liability Act** established a federally funded Superfund in 1980. Basically, "the federal government imposed taxes on oil and chemical companies and certain other corporations that went directly into a cleanup trust fund, which reached its peak of $3.8 billion in 1996."[98] The special taxes expired in 2006 with Congress taking no action to revive the fund. The EPA, however, continued to identify sites and used the outstanding balance until the funds ran out. The EPA continues to cleanup sites with taxpayer money. The **Emergency Planning and Community Right-to-Know Act** passed in 1986 requires local businesses to notify communities about the types of hazardous substances they use and how these products were being stored, used, and disposed. The **Pollution Prevention Act** (1990) expanded reporting guidelines to include both the amount of waste recycled and the amount of waste not produced because of antipollution devices. The **Community Right-to-Know-More Act** (1991) requires public disclosure of how much of a hazardous chemical is used to produce a particular product.

Forest and Wetland Conservation

The EPA defines **wetlands** as "areas that are inundated or saturated by surface or groundwater often enough or for a long enough period to support vegetation adapted for saturated soils."[99] The wetlands play a fundamental role in maintaining the balance of nature since "among other functions, they reduce flood and storm damage, provide wildlife and fish habitat, help improve water quality by filtering run-off, protect drinking water sources, and provide recreation opportunities."[100] By contrast, **deepwater habitats** are "permanently flooded land lying below the deepwater boundary of wetlands. Deepwater habitats include environments where surface water is permanent and often deep, so that the water, rather than air, is the principal medium within which the dominant organisms live, whether or not they are attached to the substrate."[101] Unfortunately, the wetlands have become the victims of a growing population's demand for residential, recreational, and commercial construction. Initially, both the federal and state governments encouraged the dredging and filling of wetland properties to the point that "about half of the 200 million acres of wetlands in the contiguous 48 states at the time of the European colonization have been lost."[102] The desire of government to protect and preserve wetlands is a classic case of government's charge to promote the "public good" clashing head-on with the treasured rights of private property ownership since over 3/4's of all wetlands is held in private hands.

There are, however, several federal and state laws establishing guidelines for the use and disposition of wetlands property. Section 404 of the Clean Water Act requires the issuance of permits to any interested party involved in the draining and/or filling of wetlands. The U.S. Army Corps of Engineers is the primary agency charged with the issuance of these permits and with periodic inspection of the sites. A provision of the 1990 **Farm Bill** requires that farmers and ranchers receiving U.S. Department of Agriculture benefits and subsidies must protect any wetlands located on their property. In addition, the **Wetlands Reserve Program** provides cash incentives to property owners as a means of encouraging preservation efforts. These legislative enactments, however, have failed to halt the gradual erosion of these precious habitat areas.

With approximately 1.5 million acres, the Florida Everglades is the nation's third largest national park. It is the breeding grounds and habitat for countless species of animal, plant and marine life. However, Florida's booming population resulted in the dredging of Everglades swamp land for the construction of single- and multi-story dwellings, and the diversion of its water to augment depleting suburban water needs. In addition, the sugar industry has gradually taken Everglades land and converted it into farmland. The Everglades is a natural buffer zone that protects the populated areas from the havoc caused by frequent hurricanes. The erosion of the Everglades has resulted in costlier hurricane damage in both loss of life and property. Conservationists have convinced Florida's governor to launch a program to rehabilitate the Everglades. The legislature struck a deal to purchase for $1.75 billion approximately 187,000 acres of former Everglades land from U.S. Sugar Corp.[103] It is hoped that rehabilitation of the area will offer increased protection for endangered and threatened species and provide the needed buffer zone for the Florida coastline.

The nation's forests are also in peril as more and more acres of trees are cut every year. The lumber is used to build homes and businesses. The pulp is processed into the billions of reams of paper and paper products used every day. Forests play an essential role in the maintenance of a healthy clean environment, as well as provide natural habitats for a wide range of plant and animal life. "At the time of white settlement, approximately, 1.1 billion acres of forest thrived in the United States, covering 49 percent of the landscape. From the 1600s to 1920, 370 million acres of forests (34 percent) were cleared, leaving 730 million acres today. Only 10 to 15 percent of today's forests have never been cut."[104] Management of publicly owned forests falls under the jurisdiction of the United States Forest Service. These forests are used for recreation, timber harvest, wildlife habitat, watershed protection, and wilderness and range management. President Bill Clinton used his authority as outlined in the Antiquities Act of 1906 to add another 58,518,000 acres for protection by the federal government.[105] Through his executive order, these lands are now protected from future road building, private development, oil and gas exploration, drilling, and logging. The Bush administration was taken aback by Clinton's actions and called upon the federal courts to overrule Clinton's midnight hour use of the Antiquities Act. As a candidate, Bush openly advocated the exploration and possible drilling of oil from the Alaskan wilderness as a means of decreasing the nation's dependency upon foreign oil. The 9th Circuit Court of Appeals, however, ruled in favor of President Clinton. The ruling "prohibits virtually all road building in roadless parcels of 5,000 acres or more, acreage that covers a third of America's national forest or 2 percent of the nation's land mass."[106] The ruling includes Alaska's 17-million acre Tongass National Forest.

President Obama followed Clinton's ample use of the Antiquities Act by naming three new national monuments: the 704,000-acre Basin and Range National Monument in Nevada, a 100 mile stretch of land in northern California, and the Waco Mammoth National Monument in Texas. "Together, the new monuments protect over one million acres of public lands. These monuments will also provide a boost to local economies by attracting visitors and generating more revenue and jobs for local communities . . . With these designations, President Obama will have used the Antiquities Act to establish or expand 19 national monuments. Altogether, he has protected more than 260 million acres of public lands and waters—more than any other president."[107]

Endangered Species

Passed in 1973, the **Endangered Species Act (ESA)** is still one of the most controversial of the federally enacted environmental laws. The law empowers the U.S. Fish and Wildlife Service to prohibit the harassing, collection, capture, and hunting of any species determined to be threatened or in danger of extinction. The ESA defines **endangered species** as "one in danger of becoming extinct throughout all or a significant part of its natural range; whereas, a **threatened species** is "one likely to become endangered in the foreseeable future."[108] As of 2020, the U.S. Fish and Wildlife Service listed 503 species of animals, birds, reptiles, amphibians, fish, snails, clams, crustaceans, insects, and arachnids as endangered with an additional 171 listed as threatened species. The list also includes 772 plants as endangered and 171 as threatened for extinction.[109] However, environmentalists believe the law is not strong enough in protecting species from the encroachment of progress. Viewing it as a reactionary program, they believe that "ideally, the ESA should serve as an emergency room for species on the decline, but only if we also practice preventive medicine by helping healthy populations of wildlife before they get into trouble."[110] They point to the few successes such as the American Bald Eagle, the alligator, and so on and compare these to the growing list of extinct and soon-to-be extinct species.

Opponents believe the law goes too far by placing the value of one animal or bird above economic progress, jobs, and property rights. On the Gulf Coast, fishermen complained that using turtle excluder devices, or break-away nets, would severely hamper the shrimping business, placing smaller trawlers out of business. Protecting the habitat of the California gnatcatcher, a small, blue-gray bird, has land developers crying foul. In Texas, the Edwards Underground Recharge Zone is the only breeding habitat for the rare blind catfish. The Fish and Wildlife Service and other environmentally charged federal agencies and the federal court system are still debating how to protect this fish while drought-prone South Texas seeks to meet the water needs of its residents. The list of complaints goes on and on.

Despite the critics, the ESA is "the one legal mechanism in the United States that can force communities to balance conservation with development."[111] The ESA has been successful in slowing the rate of extinction. And, those shrimpers on the Gulf Coast actually improved their catch by using those nets. The logging business in the Pacific Northwest has lost more jobs due to automation and a growing timber industry in the Southeastern part of the United States than to the protection of the spotted owl.

POLICY OPTIONS AND THE POLITICAL CLIMATE

Particularly with environmental issues, policy options are limited. The curative policy approach is not a viable option since existing environmental damage cannot be substantially reversed, much less cured. The alleviative approach can be used to address property or health-related problems caused by previous incidences of environmental damage. However, this option is viable only if the source of the pollution can be identified. For example, an area's residents are experiencing high incidents of lung-related illnesses caused by bacteria in the water supply. Medical experts believe the source of the problem is the one river that runs through this community. However, the water in this river has been contaminated for years as the five to six major industries located on its banks have dumped their industrial byproducts into it. Determining who is responsible for the pollution and ultimately liable for damages is almost impossible. In addition, liability for pollution-related damage is questionable since the majority of the laws have "grandfather" clauses that protect businesses and individuals from litigation for polluting activities that happened before the laws were passed.

Consequently, lawmakers turn to the preventive and punitive approaches. Every environmental law seeks to prevent future damage by punishing those who pollute with strict penalties and with criminal sanctions to deter would-be polluters. "Interestingly, the government of the United States, whose political and legal culture is the most protective of private property rights, takes the most confrontational position towards private polluters of any nation. Its laws are the strictest, giving administrators the least discretion in their dealings with industry."[112] However, the evidence clearly indicates that this nation continues to have a serious environmental problem. It is clear that "the strictness of laws and procedures in the United States has not necessarily produced better results than in other countries that take a more conciliatory stance towards industry."[113] If the laws are strong in verbiage and punitive penalties, why does this nation continue to have an evergrowing environmental problem? The answer rests with an evaluation of (a) the effectiveness of the EPA and other federal agencies; (b) the policy approach used to produce regulations; (c) the lack of incentives to encourage nonpolluting activities; (d) the inability to enforce regulations in a timely and consistent manner; and (e) an often hostile political climate.

Created in 1970 with the passage of the **Environmental Protection Act**, the **Environmental Protection Agency (EPA)** was initially charged with overseeing air and water pollution problems. The role of the EPA has been expanded to include hazardous wastes, pesticides, noise pollution, and, in part, endangered species. The EPA monitors potential environmental damage by requiring all federal agencies to file an **impact statement** detailing any potential harm a project might cause to the environment, as well as proposing solutions to prevent undo environmental damage and potential efforts on the part of a project's sponsors to maintain and hopefully enhance the productivity of the environment. The EPA has the power to make or break a project. If irreversible harm will occur, the EPA should and will cancel a project. Usually, the EPA opts to attach additional requirements or **mandates** to a project in hopes of avoiding environmental damage. The mandates may indirectly lead to the demise of a project simply because they add to project costs. The EPA also reserves the right to inspect all aspects of the construction to ensure compliance.

The EPA has become the enemy to many construction firms, land developers, property owners, state and local governments, environmentalists, and lawmakers and politicians from both sides of the political spectrum. These groups usually have few kind words for the EPA and its impact statements, mandates, and regulations. Critics believe that the command and control approach used by the EPA is "excessively rigid and insensitive to geographical and technical differences and for being inefficient."[114] Rural areas, for example, are subjected to the same standards as heavily populated urban areas.

The EPA's command and control approach also permits the agency to set the compliance guidelines but turns enforcement over to a myriad of state and federal agencies. This strategy severely compromises the effectiveness of the EPA. First, states may and do pass their own environmental laws. "Generally, the states are not precluded from enforcing criteria more stringent than those required by federal laws, and are given considerable leeway to follow enforcement interpretations which may not be fully consistent with those applied at the federal level."[115] Some states do pass environmental laws that are considerably more strict in scope as well as laden with far more punitive measures than federal sanctions. On the other hand, some states opt for a minimalist approach by barely enforcing federal guidelines. For example, the Texas Commission on Environmental Quality (TCEQ) is charged with conducting periodic inspections, assessment of fines and penalties, and investigating reported violations of state environmental laws. The fertilizer plant that exploded in January 2013 in West, Texas, is owned by West Fertilizer. A complaint of a heavy ammonia smell was filed with the TCEQ in 2006. Although cited by the TCEQ for a permit violation, little to no follow up was conducted. A contributing factor to the 2013 explosion was heavy concentrations of ammonia! Second, the EPA is not the sole implementer of environmental laws and regulations. The agency shares its authority with a myriad of federal agencies including the Fish and Wildlife Service, the Corps of Engineers, the Interior Department, the National Park Service, and so on. The states have overlapped this fragmented approach by creating numerous state agencies with duplicated functions. A business trying to comply with the various rules often deals with too many agencies, each requiring the submission of duplicated reports, paperwork, and procedures. Although on paper the EPA did set national standards, the individual states have wreaked havoc with them, leaving everyone involved in a state of confusion.

The Science Advisory Board leveled another criticism of the EPA by calling it "a largely 'reactive' agency, insufficiently oriented toward opportunities for the greatest risk reduction . . . . The board also called upon the EPA to pursue a much broader agenda than it has in the past, and to take responsibility for protecting the environment, not just for implementing environmental law by addressing the most serious risks, whether or not agency action is required by law."[116] Basically, the EPA has done very little to prevent damage since it appears to react after the damage has been done!

The policy approach with its emphasis on punitive sanctions is a major point of disagreement to business, industry, and property owners. "The implementation process for environmental laws in the United States is by far the most formalized, rule-oriented, and adversarial—in a word, confrontational."[117] The EPA emerges not as a friend to business but as a sinister rule-laden monster fixated on complicated rules and procedures that are burdensome and often too costly for business to bear. Far too often, environmental issues are decided by judges, not the EPA or its complicated rules. "Regulations are based on collected evidence marshalled by the contending sides and interpreted according to specific procedures that are open to appeals and legal challenges at all stages. The rule-making process is typically long and contentious, often ending in litigation."[118] It can take years of legal action to adjudicate one case. Meanwhile, the accused polluters can continue their polluting ways while the attorneys battle it out in the courts.

The rules themselves are just as reactive. The United States Constitution prohibits the enactment of ex post facto laws. Consequently, laws are enforceable and penalties are binding only for future violations. For example, both federal and state laws mandate that all injection or underground wells and surface pits be plugged and/or filled upon completion of extraction activities. Yet, these laws do not apply to wells drilled before the laws were passed. Natural resource-rich states have thousands of abandoned gas, oil, and water wells left unplugged and pits left unfilled. A small town in Texas lost a whole school bus load of children who drowned when their bus was hit by a truck, pushing the bus into a water-filled abandoned gravel pit. The owner of the pit was not liable since the pit was created before the legislation requiring to fill it was passed.

Perhaps the business community would be more cooperative if the EPA and other environmental agencies would offer incentives to those who voluntarily exceed federally mandated compliance levels. "A factory might be able to reduce its emissions by 70 percent rather than the required 50 percent at little additional cost, but the factory most likely will not do the additional cleanup—its goal is to minimize the cost of product, not to provide a cleaner environment for society."[119] Could not the EPA and other federal and state agencies encourage more conservation through the development of environmentally safe production methods by offering incentives towards research and rewards for results rather than just punishing the violators?

The EPA's enforcement track-record has been described as being mired in lengthy and costly litigation that results in lenient cleanup schedules and few fines. Too often the EPA's targets are small and medium-sized businesses and industries who can not afford the daily fines much less the expensive legal fees to fight a lengthy court room battle with the federal government. Larger firms, however, can afford to tie up the EPA for years while they continue to pollute the environment. Basically, the EPA is "reluctant to enforce standards against large companies with political clout or small profit margins, especially industries crucial to the nation's economic health. To take action against a large industry requires significant political will all the way up to the White House."[120] Although the EPA would have investigated the BP oil spill, President Obama put the investigation on the fast track by taking a very active role in addressing the damage caused by the spill. He initiated a federal-level committee to ensure that those adversely impacted by that spill would be compensated for their current and future losses. He also placed a ban on deep-water drilling projects until the companies involved in off-shore drilling could implement appropriate safety measures to protect both rig workers and the environment from future catastrophic harm. The failure of environmental agencies to take on the giants has ruined their effectiveness, tarnished their reputations, and left small businesses with a justifiable charge of foul play.

The political climate is particularly important in the development and implementation of environmental policies. Public sympathy does support the cause of environmentalists. It would seem reasonable to assume that since public opinion is solidly behind protecting the environment, that lawmakers could easily address this issue. However, like so many other issues, fickle public opinion can change rapidly. The urge to clean up the environment waxes and wanes when the words "sacrifice," "cost," and "accountability" enter into the picture. In general, the American public is not committed to long-term sacrifice without seeing immediate tangible results capable of encouraging them to continue their efforts.

"We associate environmentalism with the burgeoning of grassroots citizen participation in the 1960s throughout the Western countries. As motivating issues, nuclear power and other environmental concerns were second only to the Vietnam War in their power to mobilize middle-class citizens."[121] Today, environmental groups continue to pursue their bottom-line issues. Preeminent groups include the Sierra Club, Wildlife Federation, Environmental Defense Fund, National Resources Defense Council, Greenpeace, and the radial Greens group. Their message advocating a cleaner environment is soundly backed by the visible evidence and statistical data detailing environmental damage. However, the tactics they use often adversely impact their effectiveness. The environmental movement had difficulties "incorporating itself into national politics, largely because its goals and styles did not fit that of traditional party politics."[122] Consequently, environmental groups rely upon protests, demonstrations, and mass arrests to get their point across. Doomsday predictions by environmentalists have led some to label them as extremists who are willing to sacrifice the economic viability of this country to protect the environment from the encroachment of progress. "Environmentalists' perchance for doomsaying is coming back to haunt them. By overstating evidence, by presenting hypotheses as certainties, and predictions as facts to create a sense of urgency, scientist-activists have jeopardized their own creditability."[123]

There is a growing number of individuals who simply believe that environmentalists are wrong about the dangers of global warming, air pollution, etc. Rep. Ann Marie Buerkle (R-NY) stated in a 2010 campaign debate that "'a lot of the global warming myth has been exposed' . . . she added that 'the jury's still out' on whether fossil fuel burning contributes to global warming."[124] Rep. Dan Benishek (R-Michigan) believes global warming is "all baloney. It's all baloney. I think it's just some scheme. I just don't believe it. You know, I'm a scientist, I'm a surgeon, I've done scientific research papers; there's a lot of skepticism."[125] During the 2016 Republican presidential primary candidate debates, the majority of the candidates to include Donald Trump questioned the validity of climatologists, environmentalists and scientists who claim that the current crisis of global warming is basically caused by wantonly destructive habits of mankind.

Support for or against an issue is oftentimes tied to one's income level. Environmental groups, like the majority of the nation's interest groups, attract advocates from upper- and middle-income classes who view the value of the environment differently from their lower-income counterparts. "The economically secure are more willing to close down polluting factories. They are more willing to ban logging operations in order to preserve wilderness areas and to pay extra for canned goods in order to reduce the cannery's waste emissions into a river."[126] The affluent can afford to make these sacrifices without seriously compromising their social and economic viability. The poor may be sympathetic to environmental concerns; however, they cannot afford to make personal sacrifices. To them, environmentalists and their causes mean factory and business closings and loss of jobs. To the mechanic, factory worker, oil field worker, and so on "their jobs depend upon exploiting environmental resources; their first priority is to maintain a healthy growing economy, and keep factories operating even if emissions pollute the air; feeding one's family and paying the rent are of primary importance; an unpleasant smell in the air is of relatively little concern. Smoke means jobs."[127] It is obvious why the average American factory worker does not embrace the message of environmentalists.

Although the Democratic Party has been more receptive in embracing environmental causes and the cry for stronger federal regulations, the party still must deal with political reality. Among the voting population are those who are adversely affected by strict environmental policies. The Republican Party is well known for its opposition to governmental regulation, particularly environmental laws. Their cries to end the role of big government meddling into the affairs of business, industry, and private property owners win support nationwide. Both parties are guilty of wanting "to please the voting public by jumping on the 'ecological band wagon' while not alienating the business interests so dominate in the pollution problem and yet so essential to their political successes."[128] The policy positions of the Democratic White House of the Obama administration were far different from the actions taken by the Republican White House under President Trump. Obama opted to side with environmentalists by implementing more strident emission standards for all motor vehicles, placing acres of pristine wilderness under the protection of the Antiquities Act, taking an active federal role in addressing the Deepwater Horizon disaster caused by BP, and so forth. The Trump administration, however, took the traditional pro-business positions advocated for decades by the Republican Party. Under his directives, his administration lowered the emission standards set by Obama. The oversight powers of the Environmental Protection Agency were diminished. And one by one, environmental regulations and enforcement penalty guidelines were either reduced or eliminated. For example, the Trump administration weakened the regulatory arm of the Clean Water Act by just reducing the number of waterways initially placed under the watchful eye of the federal government. "Obama's executive action, which broadened the definition of 'waters of the United States,' applied to about 60 percent of U.S. waterways."[129] Regulation of the other 40 percent now fall under guidelines set by state legislative houses. The problem is that every state has different legislatively created environmental standards that are most instances, less strident than those set by the federal government. While environmentalists aligned with the Democratic Party were supportive of Obama's policies, property owners, farmers and ranchers, and natural-resource based businesses and industries aligned with the Republican Party were very vocal in expressing their displeasure with these policies. On the campaign trail, Trump acknowledged their concerns and promised that if elected, he would ease what he referred to as 'overbearing and extremely punitive' regulations. For example, with the new revisions to the Clean Water Act, the Trump administration acknowledged that while clean water is essential for everyone's survival, environmental policies must not retard economic growth. "After taking office, Trump aggressively sought to roll back environmental regulations, particularly those seen as an obstacle to business. According to an analysis by *The New York Times*, the administration revised or eliminated more than 90 environmental rules in the past three years, although several were reinstated following legal challenges and several others are still in the courts."[130]

Environmental issues are further complicated by the inclusion of the international community. Policy-makers in the United States must work closely with other countries to ensure a steadfast commitment that protecting the environment is essential to the world's survival, not just the United States. The relationship between United States lawmakers and the international community is a fragile one. Not all nations have the resources that the United States has to deal with environmental concerns. Nor can the United States afford to "lord over" other countries by trying to dominate the policy responses. In addition, the environment, unlike other policy issues such as poverty, transportation, education, and so on, is a problem that the United States cannot address by itself. What happens in the Brazilian rain forest, for example, directly has an impact on environmental efforts in the United States. Effective international environmental policies can only become a reality with a solid and unified front from the international community.

CONCLUSION

In the United States, the collective "we," the industrialists, business people, workers, consumers, politicians, lawmakers, and so on have polluted our communities, our country, and our planet. We are to blame for polluting the air, water supply, and waterways. We have allowed our quest for progress and modernization to jeopardize plant and wildlife and to deplete the forests and wetlands. The problem is how can the collective "we" put this wanton destruction to a screeching halt. Obviously, no one is pleased with the current strategy of passing strict regulatory laws backed with costly punitive sanctions. Environmentalists view these enactments as an ineffective tool in combating environmental damage while the opposing camp is embodied in lengthy legal battles as they attempt to ward off both the regulations and the regulators. The current federal and state laws may be strong in verbiage and intent but are weak in implementation, in fair and just enforcement, and in results. No one factor, including the environment itself, is winning the war. The collective "we" can save the environment by not placing the blame on each other but by collectively beginning to make the sacrifices needed to preserve our planet.

CHAPTER NOTES

[1]Wallace Stenger, "It All Began With Conservation," *Smithsonian*, Vol. 21, No. 1, April, 1990, 35.
[2]Ibid.
[3]Steven A. Peterson and Thomas H. Rausmussen, *State and Local Politics*, (New York: McGraw-Hill, Inc., 1994), 241.
[4]Intergovernmental Panel on Climate Change, *Climate Change 2014 Synthesis Report*, April 2016, v.
[5]*https://www.who.int/mediacentre.*
[6]*https://www.news.cornell.edu.*
[7]*World Population Prospects 2019: Highlights*, United Nations: Department of Economic and Social Affairs, June, 2019, *https://wwwpopulation.un.org./wpp*
[8]Peterson, 261.
[9]*2020 EPI Results, Environmental Performance Index, https://eip.vale.edu/epi-results/2020.*
[10]Peter Borelli, "Environmental Philosophy," *Major Problems in American Environmental History*, Carolyn Merchant, ed., (Lexington, Massachusetts: D. C. Heath, 1993), 567.
[11]tenger, "It All Began With Conservation," 38.
[12]Borelli, "Environmental Philosophy," 560.
[13]Steven Stoll, *U.S. Environmentalism Since 1945: A Brief History with Documents*, (Boston, Massachusetts: Bedford/St. Martin's, 2007), 8.
[14]Ibid.
[15]Stenger, "It All Began With Conservation," 39.

[16]Ibid.

[17]Ibid.

[18]*Treasury of Presidential Quotations*, Caroline Thomas Harsberger, ed., (Chicago: Follett Publishing Co., 1964), 41.

[19]Stenger, "It All Began With Conservation," 40.

[20]"Theodore Roosevelt Publicizes Conservation, 1908," *Major Problems in American Environmental History*, 350-352.

[21]Arnold Heidenheimer, Hugh Helco, and Carolyn Teich Adams, *Comparative Public Policy: The Politics of Social Choice in America, Europe, and Japan*, 3rd ed., (New York, New York: St. Martins Press, 1990), 316.

[22]Peterson, 251.

[23]Gregg Easterbrook, *A Moment On the Earth: The Coming Age of Environmental Optimism,* (New York, New York: Penguin Books, USA, Inc., 1995), 79-80.

[24]Stephen Klaidman, "Muddling Through," *The Wilson Quarterly*, Vol. XV, No. 2, Spring, 1991, 74.

[25]Stenger, "It All Began With Conservation," 43.

[26]Stoll, 19.

[27]*The Presidential Campaign 1976: Jimmy Carter*, Vol. I, Part 1, (Washington, D.C.: United States Government Printing Office, 1978), 662 & 664.

[28]Klaidman, 73.

[29]Jeff Nesmith, "Gore Tells Congress 'The Planet Has A Fever,'" *San Antonio Express-News* (Thursday, March 22, 2007), 3A.

[30]Jerry Adler, "Just the Tree of Us," *Newsweek*, April 14, 2008, 43-48.

[31]"Obama Position On The Environment," *http://2012.presidential-candidates.org/Obama.Environment.php.*

[32]*http://nationswell.com/15-experts-obamas-environmental-legacy/.*

[33]Gary C. Bryner, *Blue Skies, Green Politics: The Clean Air Act of 1990*, 1st ed., (Washington, D.C.: CQ Press, 1993), 41.

[34]Ibid., 42.

[35]*The 1993 Information Please Environmental Handbook*, compiled by the World Resource Institute, (New York, New York: Houghton Mifflin Co., 1993), 88.

[36]Bryner, 42.

[37]Ibid.

[38]Susan L. Cutter and William H. Renwick, *Exploitation, Conservation, and Preservation: A Geographic Perspective on Natural Resource Use*, 4th ed., (Hoboken, New Jersey: John Wiley & Sons, Inc., 2004), 281.

[39]Ibid.

[40]Ibid., 282.

[41]Bryner, 187.

[42]Marla Cone, "Study Says Pollutant Suppress Rain, Snowfall," *San Antonio Express-News* (Sunday, March 12, 2000), 8A.

[43]Ibid.

[44]Klaidman, 81.

[45]Ibid.

[46]Ibid., 83.

[47]Ibid., 84.

[48]Ibid.

[49]Jane Holtz Kay, "Moving In The Right Direction," *Preservation*, Vol. 49, No. 3, May/June, 1997, 53.

[50]Ibid.

[51]Ibid.

[52]John M. Broder, "U.S. Fuel Efficient Standards Going Up," *San Antonio Express-News*, (Tuesday, May 19, 2009), 1A.

[53]Nathan Rott and Jennifer Ludden, "Trump Administration Weakens Emission Standards," *https: www.npr.org/2020/03/31.*

[54]H. Josef Herbert, "Nobody Knows How Much Oil Refuge Holds," *San Antonio Express-News*, (Tuesday, Dec. 20, 2005),5A.

[55]Ibid.

[56]Ibid.

[57]http://www.watis-is-fracking.

[58]https://www.westringfellow.com/2016.

[59] David A. Baker, "Canadians Eyeing More Access by Pipeline to U.S. West Coast, *San Antonio Express-News* (Thursday, April 25, 2013), B1.

[60]http://www.smithsonianmag.com.

[61]http://www.wowt,com/content/news.

[62]Marianne Lavelle, "Blasts, But Not From the Past," *U.S. News & World Report*, July 17, 2000, 18.

[63]Dylan McGuinness, "Victims of Houston Plant Blast Are Still Struggling to Recover," *San Antonio ExpressNews* (Sunday, June 21, 2020), A4.

[64]R. G. Ratcliffe, "Texas Loses Say Over Air Quality," *San Antonio Express-News*, (Friday, December 4, 2010), 1A.

[65]Stoll, 17.

[66]Susan Welch, John Gruhl, Michael Steinman, John Comer, and Susan M. Ridgon, *American Government*, 5th ed., (Minneapolis, Minnesota: West Publishing Co., 1994), 615.

[67]Bret Schulte, "Turning Up The Heat", *U.S. News & World Report*, April 10, 2006, 34.

[68]*Climate Change 2014 Synthesis Report*, 40.

[69]"Concern About Polar Ice Melt, Rising Seas Become More Heated," *San Antonio Express-News*, (Fri, March 24, 2006),1A.

[70]Jeff Beradelli, "Arctic Records Its Hottest Temperature Ever," *CBS News, https:www.com/em-us/weather*

[71]Seth Borenstein, "Hot Water, Disease Kills Coral Reefs That Columbus Saw," *San Antonio Express-News*, (Friday, March 31, 2006), 10A.

[72]Cutter, 202.

[73]*Proquest Statistical Abstract of the United States, 2020,* 8th ed., (Bethesda, Maryland: ProQuest, LLC, 2019), Table 399, 253.

[74]"Water Use Today," *Water Sense*, United States Environmental Protection Agency, http://www.epa.gov/watersense

[75]Peter Annin and Sharon Begley, "Great Lake Effect," *Newsweek*, July 5, 1999, 52.

[76]Welch, 615.

[77]Cutter, 377.

[78]Ibid., 376.

[79]*The 1993 Information Please Environmental Handbook*, 38 & 40.

[80]U.S. Environmental Protection Agency, *National Water Quality Inventory: Report to Congress- August, 2017*, (Washington, D.C., 2017), 6-18.

[81]Andrew Murr and Sharon Begley, "Dams Are Not Forever," *Newsweek*, November 17, 1997, 70.

[82]Michael Weisskopf, "Plastic Reaps A Grim Harvest In the Oceans of the World," *Smithsonian*, Vol. 18, No. 12, March, 1988, 59.

[83]"Company In West Virginia Spill Files For Bankruptcy," *San Antonio Express-News* (January 18, 2014), A11.

[84]Sara Ganim and Linh Tran, "How Tap Water Became Toxic in Flint, Michigan, http://www.cnn.

[85]Ibid.

[86]Ibid.

[87]Marianne Lavelle and Joshua Kurlantzick, "The Coming Water Crisis," *U.S. News & World Report*, Aug. 12, 2002, 24.

[88]Bryan Walsh, "The Meaning of the Mess," *Time*, (May 17, 2010), 30.

[89]"Analysis: BP's U.S. Gulf Oil Spill Settlement Challenges May Backfire," *Reuters*, http://www.reuters.com.artcle/2014/01/15

[90]National Oceanic and Atmosphere Administration, "Deepwater Horizon Oil Spill Settlements: Where the Money Went," *https://www.noaa.gov.*

[91]Barbara Rudolph, "Whose Mess Is It?", *Time*, July 10, 1989, 42.

[92]*Proquest Statistical Abstract of the United States*, Table 427, 265.

[93]Jerry Needham, "The McClellan Monster," *San Antonio Express-News* (Saturday, October 21, 2000), 15A.

[94]Cutter, 379.

[95]William C. Mann, "Clinton Airs Tougher Rules for Toxic Pollution," *San Antonio Express-News* (Sun., Oct. 31, 1999), 13A.

[96]Randy Lee Loftis, "Texas Environment: State of Neglect," *The Dallas Morning News* (Sunday, November 24, 1991),3N.

[97]*National Overview: Facts and Figures on Materials, Wastes and Recycling, https://www.epa.gov/facts-and-figures-about-materials waste.*

[98]Juliet Eilperin, "EPA Will Push Congress to Reestablish Superfund Tax," *San Antonio Express-News*, (Monday, June 21, 2010), 4A.

[99]Elana Cohen, "Protecting Wetlands: Creating A Sense of Stewardship," *The National Voter*, (Washington, D.C.: League of Women Voters of the United States, June/July, 1996), 15.

[100]Ibid.

[101]*Statistical Abstract of the United States: 2012,* 131st ed., Table 370, 228.

[102]Cohen, 15.

[103]Joel Achenbach, "Florida Strikes Everglades Deal," *San Antonio Express-News* (Wednesday, June 25, 2008), 1A.

[104]*The 1993 Information Please Environmental Handbook*, 176-177.

[105]John Heilpirn, "Court Again Slaps Limits on Use of National Forests," *San Antonio Express-News* (Sun., Dec. 15, 2002), 11AA.

[106]Ibid.

[107]http://www.breirbart.com.

[108]*Statistical Abstract of the United States: 2012*, 131st ed., Table 387, 236.

[109]U.S. Fish and Wildlife Service, *Listed Species Summary, https://ecos.fws.gov.*

[110]*The 1993 Information Please Environmental Handbook*, 159.

[111]Ibid.

[112]Heidenheimer, 310.

[113]Ibid.

[114]Bryner, 20.

[115]J. Gordon Arbuckle, etal., *Environmental Law Handbook*, 111th ed., (Rockville, Md.: Government Institute, Inc., 1991), 8.

[116]Bryner, 32.

[117]Heidenheimer, 323.

[118]Ibid.

[119]Peterson, 259.

[120]Welch, 614.

[121]Heidenheimer, 310.

[122]Ibid.

[123]"The Doomsday Myths," *U.S. News and World Report*, December 13, 1993, 81.

[124]"Conservation Group Targets 5 Republicans," *San Antonio Express-News* (Thursday, July 24, 2012), A5.

[125]Ibid.

[126]Peterson, 243.

[127]Ibid.

[128]"Wilbourn E. Benton, *Texas Politics: Constraints and Opportunities*, 5th ed., (Chicago, Illinois: Nelson-Hill, 1984), 375.

[129]Scott Neuman and Colin Dwyer, "Trump Administration Cuts Back on Federal Protections for Streams and Wetlands, *https://www.npr.org*

[130]Ibid.

SUGGESTED READINGS

Esterbrook, Gregg, *A Moment on the Earth: The Coming Age of Environmental Optimism*, New York, New York: Penguin Books USA, 1995.

Harrigan, John J., and David C. Nice, *Politics and Policy in States and Communities*, 8th ed., New York, New York: Pearson Education, Inc., 2004.

Heidenheimer, Arnold, Hugh Heclo, and Carolyn Teich Adams. *Comparative Public Policy: The Politics of Social Choice in America, Europe, and Japan.* 3rd ed. New York: St. Martin's Press, 1990.

Klaidman, Stephen. "Muddling Through," *The Wilson Quarterly*. Spring, 1991, Vol. XV, No. 2, pp.73-82.

Peterson, Steven A. and Thomas H. Rausmussen. *State and Local Politics.* New York: McGraw-Hill, Inc., 1994.

Web Sites:

unfccc.int/kyoto_protoco - Kyoto Treaty

environment.about.com

unfccc.int - official site for UN Climate Secretariat

Joe Biden
46th President of the United States

Chapter Seventeen

FOREIGN POLICY

In a letter written to James Monroe in 1796, President George Washington clearly expressed his position on whether the new nation should become involved in world affairs:

> I have always given it as my decided opinion that no nation had a right to intermeddle in the internal concerns of another; that every one had a right to form and adopt whatever government they like best to live under themselves; if this country could, consistently with its engagements, maintain a strict neutrality and thereby preserve peace, it was bound to do so by motives of policy, interest, and every other consideration. . . . Tis our true policy to steer clear of permanent alliances with any portion of the foreign world.[1]

Less than two hundred years later, then Senator John F. Kennedy told an audience in Madison, Wisconsin, that although the United States did not seek it or want it, this country was now the leader of the free world, a role it simply could not abandon:

> Every American is now involved in the world. "The tragic events of . . . turmoil through which we have just passed have made us citizens of the world," said Woodrow Wilson. For a time we tried to dodge this new responsibility, but the world depression, World War II, and the Cold War have finally conveyed his message: "There can be no turning back. Our own fortunes as a nation are involved – whether we would have it so or not.[2]

Whereas few voters in 1789 quizzed George Washington about his foreign policy agenda, the presidential debates focused more on foreign policy concerns with exception of the economic crisis and the human tragedy caused by the Covid-19 pandemic, than on pressing domestic issues. Voters of the twenty-first century want to know that their choice for the nation's highest office has at least knowledge of and, at best, expertise in foreign policy. Every resident of the Oval Office beginning with Franklin Roosevelt has spent countless hours on the phone, on a plane or at a conference room table in a foreign country meeting with foreign leaders in hopes of bringing a nonviolent conclusion to a volatile international problem. All nations are faced with the reality that where once one or several nations dominated over the others, today we now live in an international community that is dependent upon each other. With the helicopter carrying the Trumps' leaving the White House as president for the last time and the limo carrying the newly sworn in President Joe Biden drove into the White House driveway, the presidency changed hands but the turmoil around the world did not change. Although the Egyptian people successfully ousted their entrenched president Hosni Mubarak in 2011, his successor Muhammad Morsi was quickly ousted by a military coup. In 2021, the military is still in control as the Egyptian people now understand the fragile nature of democracy. The Syrian civil war is now entering its tenth bloody year with no end in sight. The United States is still backing the rebels opposed to the Assad regime as the Russians continue to back the Assad government. The rebel opposition, Syrian army, American forces and the Russian military are all joined together for once aiming to defeat a common enemy—ISIS. Meanwhile, refugees fleeing Syria and other Middle Eastern and African nations have found whatever conveyance possible to cross the Mediterranean to seek asylum in European nations. The sight of fleeing refugees is overwhelming and tragically, several thousands have drowned as their overcrowded boats have capsized and sank into the Mediterranean waters. Meanwhile, the Chinese government has strained its relationship with Japan over who has the territorial rights to numerous uninhabited islands in the Pacific Ocean. The Trump administration leveled a potentially crippling trade war against the Chinese government as the citizenry of Wuhan were dealing with the outbreak of the coronavirus. The North Korean leader Kim Jong-un continues his threat of all-out nuclear war. Occasionally, his government will unsuccessfully launch a "nuclear" weapon as a reminder that he is a major "player" in world affairs. Relations with Mexico continue to be seriously strained over Trump's immigration policies. During the 2016 campaign, Trump vowed to end illegal immigration of migrants from Central and Latin American countries traveling through Mexico and crossing the Rio Grande River by building a wall separating the two countries. Trump proclaimed that Mexico would pay for the wall. As he leaves office in 2021, portions of the wall have been built but Mexico certainly has not paid one dime towards its construction. To further curtail illegal immigration, the Trump administration opted for policies keeping migrants in Mexico while they await their asylum hearings, adding more strident rules for immigrants, and if immigrants did cross illegally, separating parents from their children by deporting the parents and retaining the children in the United States in detention camps. Meanwhile, accusations of international tampering into the 2016 presidential election were focused on Russia with the Trump administration attempting to deflect those accusations by casting an accusatory finger at Ukraine. The turmoil of which nation interfered in the election directly led to the House of Representatives' first impeachment of Trump. The president was accused and convicted in the House of abuse of power and obstruction of justice with Congress. The list of foreign policy concerns is never ending. Regardless of the international crisis, the reality is that the United States is indeed a vital player, if not, the dominate one in the international arena. This chapter focuses the development and execution of United States foreign policy actions. This chapter focuses on the vital role the United States plays in the international arena.

As in the domestic policy arena, the President of the United States may well be the primary spokesperson for this country in foreign affairs but he/she still has to turn to the Senate for approval of treaties and appointments of ambassadors and, of course, key cabinet posts such as the Secretary of State, and to both the House of Representatives and the Senate for the funds to conduct foreign policy initiatives and, if necessary, for approval of a formal declaration of war. Unfortunately, the working relationship between the president and Congress in foreign policy has not always been a cordial one. Far too often, presidents have been frustrated by their inability to sway Congress to their policy choices. Unfortunately over the course of time, presidents have found both constitutionally legal and, at times, potentially illegal means of bypassing Congress. And, Congress has on occasion given the president more latitude than the Constitution grants, only to be placed into the situation of legislatively bringing the presidency back into line. This chapter examines the oftentimes shaky relationship between the executive and legislative branch in foreign policy development.

The media usually shows the president or his representatives standing among the worlds' leaders in a friendly setting, shaking hands or casually speaking or joking with each other. Not allowed behind the closed doors, the media cannot show the American people the complicated negotiation process involved in addressing international problems. The development of policy options that preserve the vital interests of the United States, while at the same time meeting the needs of the other foreign leaders gathered at the table, is an extremely complicated and delicate process. Case in point, several representatives of the princely houses of the German provinces met to discuss the possibility of uniting into the nation state of Germany. One of the delegates refused to sit at the conference table because his chair was not the same distance from the other representatives. Unfortunately, the delegate was extremely overweight! The solution was to carve into the table enough room to allow his chair to be the same distance from the others. Once that was accomplished, the representative joined into the negotiations. After numerous conferences and conflicts between the various factions, Germany was finally unified in 1871. The same confrontational and hostile political environment erupted when Great Britain decided to leave the European Union. In particular, the maintenance of longstanding mutual friendships among the various nations is an extremely difficult and delicate process. Everyone at that table must be able to go home with something that benefits their people. Consequently, a focus of this chapter is on the vocabulary and "mechanics" of foreign policy initiatives, as well as a brief regional analysis of the problems confronting the Biden administration in the development of its future foreign policy initiatives.

In the Preamble to the Constitution, the Framers tasked the national government to "provide for the common defense." In other words, the Framers guaranteed the American people that their government would do whatever is necessary to protect their lives, property, and way of life. It is a very daunting and sobering task placed upon the shoulders of the president in his role as the nation's commander-in-chief. Throughout the history of this country, the American people have been very uneasy about warfare in general and in particular about sending American combat forces onto foreign soil. Every president faces the reality that among the troops he sends into combat, many will not return. During the Civil War, President Abraham Lincoln always wore black. Biographers have noted that rarely did he sleep a full eight hours. President Harry Truman had to live with the fact that ultimately it was his decision and his decision alone to drop nuclear bombs on Japanese civilians. President Kennedy was joined by his brother Robert Kennedy and key advisors as they

President Lyndon B. Johnson listens to a tape sent by Captain Charles Robb, his son-in-law, from Vietnam. Cabinet Room, White House, Washington, D.C. July 31, 1968.
Photo Credit: LBJ Library photo by Jack Kightlinger

monitored the growing hostile situation between the United States and the Soviet Union during the Cuban Missile Crisis, knowing that the nation was on the brink of a nuclear confrontation. The photograph of Lyndon Johnson slumped over a table with tears in his eyes after listening to a taped recording from his son-in-law Chuck Robb, an officer in Vietnam, detailing a combat mission shows the emotional torment of the president who sent those troops into that battle zone. Particularly in foreign policy, a president must tread carefully.

FOREIGN POLICY TERMINOLOGY

Foreign policy is "a strategy or planned course of action developed by the decision makers of a state vis-à-vis other **states** or **international entities** aimed at achieving specific goals defined in terms of **national interests**."[3] The construct of international entities evolved from the massive empires of Romans and Mongols to smaller territories commonly known as states or nation states. A **nation state** is "a state organized for the government of a nation whose territory is determined by national customs and expectations."[4] Although a group of people may well have the commonality of language and customs, the bringing together of various ethnic groups under one governing authority has proven to be a very difficult process. The last two groups to form into nation states in Europe were Italy and Germany. While the majority of the European nations had been formed during and immediately after the Middle Ages, it was not until 1871 that unification documents were officially signed in Italy and Germany. What was lacking was the spirit of **nationalism**, that is, "the spirit of belonging together or the corporate will that seeks to preserve the identity of the group by institutionalizing it in the form of a state."[5] Now that the United States combat military forces have left Iraq, the task of the Iraqi government is to convince the Kurds, Sunni, and Shiites that they can peacefully come together as Iraqis under one unified government. The "nations" of

Afghanistan and Iraq will never be viable nation states until the various tribes and factions forgo their individual interests and loyalties for the collective general will of the nation.

The ability of a nation state to hold its own over other nation states is dependent upon several factors to include: "1) size, location, climate, and topography of the national territory; 2) the natural resources, sources of energy, and foodstuffs that can be produced; 3) the population, its size, density, age and sex composition, and its per capita relationship to national income; 4) the size and efficiency of the industrial plant; 5) the extent and effectiveness of the transportation system and communications media; 6) the educational system, research facilities, and the number and quality of the scientific and technical elite; 7) the size, training, equipment, and spirit of the military forces; 8) the nature and strength of the nation's political, economic and social system; 9) the quality of its diplomats and diplomacy; and 10) the national character and morale of the people."[6] Only a select few of today's 200 nation states possess all of these factors that enable them to dominate the direction of worldwide international relations. Furthermore, political scientists and economists have developed criteria for categorizing nation states. For the sake of this discussion, let's use the relationship between industry and agriculture. In first world power nation states, industry dominates the economic growth of the nation with agriculture playing a vitally important support role. In second world power nation states, industry and agriculture are equal economic partners. In third world power nation states, agriculture dominates with industry playing a second and, in most instances, a marginal role. In fourth world power nation states, agriculture is the primary economic factor. Since the majority of these nations have been extractive colonial possessions, they have the future capacity for industrialization but need to learn how to retain and subsequently use their own natural resources. There are a few nation states that fall into the fifth world power category whereby they have a difficult time producing enough food to feed their own people and lack the natural resources and the technological skills required for industrial development. Defined as "a condition characterized by economic, social and political backwardness when measured by the standards of the advanced societies," **underdevelopment** means that those nation states falling into the third, fourth and fifth categories also have significantly high infant mortality rates, extreme poverty, a heavy dependence upon subsistence agriculture, high illiteracy rates, extensive use of child labor, a rigid social structure that severely restricts social mobility, and unstable governments.[7]

A nation's foreign policy agenda is based on the pursuit of its **national** or **vital interests**. National interests are "the fundamental objective and ultimate determinant that guides the decision makers of a state in making foreign policy."[8] Basically, all nation states want to preserve their independence to include the right to **self-determination**, that is, "the right of a group of people who consider themselves separate and distinct from others to determine for themselves the state in which they will live and the form of government it will have."[9] If the Framers gathered in Philadelphia had the right to abolish one form of government (confederate) for another (federal), then other nations should have that same right to change both the structure and the political ideology driving that change without interference from the international community. Self-determination underscores the ability to preserve one's culture, religion, customs, and traditions. Akin with self-determination, all nation states seek to exercise their right to **sovereignty**, which is "the independent legal authority over a population in a particular territory, based on the recognized right to self-determination."[10] In other words, all nation states want their governing bodies to exercise "**internal sovereignty** which means the right, without external intervention to determine matters having to do with one's own citizens" and **external sovereignty** which is "the right to conclude binding agreements (treaties) with other states" without interference from other nation states.[11] Both as president of the Constitutional Convention and of the United States, George Washington expressed the belief that every president has embraced that ". . . . every one had a right to form and adopt whatever government they like best to live under themselves."[12] In particular, many third, fourth and fifth world power nation states must oftentimes rely upon a third party to intervene internally whenever their governments are in peril of being overthrown by a military coup or a powerful group, such as the Taliban in Afghanistan. These nations are more often to be the signees to a first power nation state's treaty rather than be the primary initiator of the document. These countries simply do not have the military might or the diplomatic presence to conduct their own foreign policy.

Every nation state wants to be able to secure its borders and protect its citizens from harm. Regardless of their geographical size and the thickness of their national wallets, all nation states maintain at least a standing army and navy. The dilemma confronting the first power nations is whether every nation should have access to the ultimate weapons of mass destruction—nuclear capability. Today, the international community is closely monitoring the North Korean government's launching of short-range nuclear weapons and Iran's development of its own nuclear program.

Another common national interest is protection of one's economic viability. In part, the Cold War was a struggle over economic philosophies. The Soviet Union wanted to expand its socialist system of state ownership of the means of production throughout the Eastern bloc nations. On the other hand, the United States countered by seeking to convince other nation states that the only viable economic system was capitalism. The expansion of trade routes and the acquisition of natural resources were the driving force behind the colonial aspirations of the British, French, Spanish, Portuguese, Dutch, and other nations.

Historians will certainly view the destruction of the World Trade Center in New York City, on September 11, 2001, as a turning point in American foreign, as well as domestic policy.©Danny C. Sze Photography

Basically, the national interests of the United States fall into four board categories:

- Protect our physical security.
- Protect the physical security of our neighbors and major democratic allies.
- Protect our economic security.
- Extend our sphere of influence.[13]

All of the nation's foreign policy decisions are geared towards these four broad objectives.

Since pursuing all of the various national interests at once is virtually impossible, nation states focus their attention on a selective handful of objectives collectively known as the **vital interests**. The others are relegated to secondary considerations. The top priorities vary from nation to nation and hopefully will change to meet new challenges. For example, the United States focused its energy during the Cold War on challenging the Soviet system by encouraging other nation states to adopt democracy and capitalism. Since then the international community has witnessed the breakup of the Soviet Union, the decline of socialist doctrinaire, and the movement on the part of both China and Russia towards a free market or capitalist economic system. Consequently, the focus of United States foreign policy had to change. After September 11, 2001, the nation's focus shifted from a still viable Cold War mentality against Russia and China to international terrorism. In order to remain a player on the international scene, a nation state's foreign policy emphasis must change as events change. If not, the policy direction is stale and ineffective.

FOREIGN POLICY OPTIONS

In general terms, a nation state can opt to pursue its vital interests in three board policy options, namely, neutrality, isolationism and internationalism. All nation states want physical security, that is, the ability to ward off potential threats of invasion, attacks, or conquest from other nation states. Since gaining its independence through the Peace of Westphalia of 1648, Switzerland has pursued a policy of **neutrality**. Basically, a neutral state takes no part in a war but retains the right to defend its territory against attacks. "Neutral duties include: 1) impartiality; 2) refraining from aiding any belligerent; 3) denying to belligerents the use of neutral territory; and 4) permitting belligerents to interfere with commerce to the extent specified by international law."[14] During World War II, many Europeans fled the advancement of Hitler's army by fleeing to Switzerland and obtaining Swiss citizenship, which protected them from being extradited to Germany. To date, Switzerland has never applied to join the United Nations and only participates in non-political international organizations.

Isolationism is "the policy of curtailing as much as possible a nation's international relations so one's country can exist in peace and harmony by itself in the world."[15] From independence until the 1890's, the United States followed a policy of isolationism as the nation focused internally to expand its borders from the East to the West coast. It sporadically and selectively participated in international incidents. For centuries, both the Japanese and the Chinese were isolationists or closed-door nations until the need to expand their trade routes convinced them to open the doors and establish relations with other nations. The Trump administration embraced a semi-isolationist foreign policy with its

592 / *Chapter Seventeen*

new **sovereigntist approach** to international law. According to Trump, "international treaties give too much authority to foreign states and international organizations, taking power that should instead belong to domestic political institutions."[16] For example, in withdrawing the United States from the Global Compact on Migration, Trump's Secretary of State Rex Tillerson defended this move by pointing out that "we [the United States] simply cannot in good faith support a process that could undermine the sovereign right of the United States to enforce our immigration laws and secure our borders."[17] In other words, the United States has the sole right to initiate and enforce whatever foreign and domestic actions it wishes to take without interference from any other nation.

A middle road option, an **alliance,** is "an agreement by [nation] states to support each other militarily in the event of an attack against any member, or to advance their mutual interests."[18] These alliance agreements are based on the Three Musketeers pledge of "one for all and all for one." A nation state would become involved in an international incident or a war only when a member of the pact was attacked or threatened by a non-member. Therefore, a nation state could selectively involve itself in international affairs if called upon to fulfill its obligations as outlined in the alliance. In the fifteenth century, individual associations of merchants throughout Europe joined forces into the **Hanseatic League**. The League members were able to control their own towns and extract trade and business concessions from foreign rulers. They even successfully declared war on the Scandinavian counties, forcing their monarchs to make considerable trade concessions. After the defeat of Napoleon, Tsar Alexander I crafted a unsuccessful **Holy Alliance** agreement between Russia, Prussia, and Austria. "It was an attempt to establish an all-embracing international system on the principles of Christian justice, charity, and peace."[19] The **Quadruple Alliance** formed in 1815 between the governments of Austria, Prussia, Russia, and Great Britain was a successful effort. These rulers agreed to "preserve the territorial boundaries they had set, to insure the perpetual exclusion of [Napoleon] Bonaparte and his dynasty from the French throne, to combat the principles of the Revolution, and to prevent any future revolutionary uprising."[20] Immediately after World War II, the tension between the United States and the Soviet Union [Russia] ushered in a period commonly known as the **Cold War.** Nation states were now confronted with taking sides of either aligning with the United States or with the Soviet Union. A **bipolarity** is "a rigid balance of power system in which decisive power is polarized into two rival power-centers."[21] Consequently, American foreign policy initiatives centered on a **balance of power** focus whereby nation states "deal with the problems of national security in the context of shifting alliances and alignments."[22] The **North Atlantic Treaty Organization (NATO)** was formed in 1949 by the West for the sole purpose of "blocking the threat of Soviet military aggression in Europe through combined conventional forces and by affording Western European states the protection of the American nuclear deterrent."[23] "The signatories bound themselves: (1) to consult together whenever the territorial integrity, independence, or security of any member was threatened; and (2) to consider an armed attack on one as an attack on all, and in case of such an attack each would take such action as it deemed necessary, including the use of armed force."[24] The initial membership included Belgium, Britain, Denmark, France, Germany, Greece, Iceland, Italy, Luxembourg, the Netherlands, Norway, Portugal, Turkey, and the United States. In retaliation, the Soviet Union responded with its own collective security agreement, the **Warsaw Pact** signed by the Eastern bloc countries of Albania, Bulgaria, Czechoslovakia, East Germany, Hungary, Poland, Romania, and the Soviet Union in 1955. In 1956, the

Hungarian government launched a short-lived revolution against Soviet domination. Despite pleas for assistance, NATO decided not to send troops into Hungary because it feared Soviet retaliation and the possibility of World War III erupting in Europe. The official excuse was that Hungary was not a member of the NATO alliance, and, therefore, NATO members were obligated to only assist fellow alliance members.

At the height of the Cold War, both the United States and the Soviet Union used foreign aid and military assistance packages as a means of "winning friends" within the international community, particularly with third-, fourth- and fifth world nations. The leaders of these nations had to carefully weigh the pursuit of their vital interests and carefully choose which side they wanted to alien themselves with. Warm relationships with the United States meant lukewarm or cold relations with the Soviet Union and vice versa. Oftentimes, world leaders would try to use both sides to their advantage. For example, in the 1960s, President Nassar of Egypt wanted to build a dam on the Nile River. He did not have the money or the technology for the project. So, he negotiated between the United States and the Soviet Union for the funding and the necessary engineering expertise. Both governments contributed to the project. When the dam was officially inaugurated in 1971, Nassar invited officials from both the Soviet Union and the United States to help him "cut the ribbon."

The first American president to visit Europe, Woodrow Wilson came to Paris in 1918 determined to make the world safe for democracy by forming an alliance of the worlds' leaders under the umbrella of the **League of Nations**. The League's constitution, or Covenant, formed Part One of the Versailles Treaty and consisted of twenty-six articles. The League's "purpose, according to the Preamble, was to promote international cooperation, preserve peace, and provide security. This was to be done by accepting obligations not to resort to war, by establishing international law as the rule of conduct among governments, and by respecting treaty commitments."[25] Wilson firmly believed that international disputes could be won by words, not guns. In his 1919 address to the United States Senate, Wilson stressed that "the League of Nations was the only hope for mankind. . . Dare we reject it and break the heart of the world?"[26] Furthermore Wilson was a realist who knew the limitations of his League:

> Is the League an absolute guarantee against war? No, I do not know any absolute
> guarantee against the errors of human judgment or the violence of human passion,
> But I tell you this: with a cooling space of nine months for human passion, not much
> of it will keep hot . . . Illustrating the great by the small, that is true of the passions
> of nations. . . Give them space to cool off . . . I believe that men will see the truth.[27]

The United States Senate saw otherwise by rejecting the Treaty of Versailles and withdrawing United States membership from the League.

The League of Nations, however, was the forerunner of the world's ultimate multinational agreement—the **United Nations**. Offered by Roosevelt during the Yalta Conference, the United Nations Charter was drawn up and signed on June 26, 1945, and once ratified by fifty-one nations, became effective on October 24, 1945. Roosevelt truly believed that "the greatest need of the world today is the assurance of permanent peace—an assurance based on mutual understanding and mutual regard. . . Today, we seek a moral basis for peace if the fruit of it is oppression, or starvation, or cruelty, or human life dominated by armed camps. It cannot be a sound peace if small nations must live in fear of powerful neighbors. It cannot be a moral peace if freedom from invasion is sold to tribute. It cannot be an intelligent peace if it denies free passage to that knowledge of those ideals which permit men to find common ground. It cannot be a righteous peace if worship of God is denied."[28] The organization's purpose is "to maintain peace and security, to take collective measures for preventing war and aggression, to settle disputes among nations, to develop friendly relations based on the principle of equal rights and self determination, and to promote cooperation in handling international problems."[29]

The opposite of isolationism is **internationalism**, that is, the belief that the course of international events demands that a powerful nation state, such as the United States, must assume an active, and to a large degree, a leadership role in determining the outcome of those events. It's like being the captain of the ship. The direction the ship takes is not determined by the cabin boy but by the captain. In 1901, President William McKinley wanted to jar the United States from its isolation position. He emphasized that

> isolation is no longer possible or desirable. At the beginning of the nineteenth century there was not a mile of steam railroad on the globe. Now there are enough miles to make its circuit many times. Then there was not a line of electric telegraph; now we have a vast mileage traversing all lands and seas. God and man have linked the nations together. No nation can no longer be indifferent to any other. And as we are brought more and more in touch with each other the less occasion there is for misunderstandings and the stronger the disposition, when we have differences, to adjust them in the court of arbitration, which is the noblest form for settlement of international disputes.[30]

In 1919, President Wilson also envisioned an international leadership role for the United States. He stated that "America can not be an ostrich with its head in the sand. America can not shut itself out from the rest of the world."[31] While the majority of presidents following Wilson and McKinley saw the necessity for a predominate role for the United States in international affairs, the questions remain as to frequency and extent of manpower and costs associated with the nation's involvement into international problems and issues. In 1956, then United States Senator John F. Kennedy remarked that

> one of the most serious weaknesses that has hampered the long-range effectiveness of American foreign policy over the past several years is the overemphasis upon our role as 'volunteer fire department' for the world. . . Whenever and wherever fire breaks out . . . our firemen rush in, wheeling up their heavy equipment, and resorting to every known method of containing and extinguishing the blaze. The crowd gathers—the usually successful efforts of our able volunteers are heartily applauded—and then the firemen rush off to the next conflagration, leaving the grateful but still stunned inhabitants to clean up the rubble, pick up the pieces, and rebuild their homes with whatever resources are available. The role to be sure, is a necessary one; but it is not the only role to be played. . . A volunteer fire department halts but rarely prevents fires.[32]

Consequently, the nation state is establishing **hegemony**, defined as "the extension by one state of preponderant influence or control over another state or region."[33] Although it is advantageous for one or more nation states to assume the predominate role, they must be careful not to be accused of **ethnocentrism**, the belief that one's own culture is far superior to any other culture.

Closely akin to internationalism, **interventionism** is "the coercive interference in the affairs of a state by another group of states to affect the internal and external policies of that state."[34] According to international law, the policy of interventionism is legal under the following conditions: "1) if the intervening state has been granted such a right by treaty; 2) if a state violates an agreement for joint policy determination by acting unilaterally; 3) if intervention is necessary to protect a state's citizens; 4) if it is necessary for self-defense; or 5) if a state violates international law."[35] Since World War II, the United States government has oftentimes used the intervention option. However, there is a fine line between intervention and imperialism. **Imperialism** is "the domination of one state by another, usually for exploitative purposes."[36] Conquest of taking land away from weaker civilizations has been a trade-mark of the more militarily powerful and advanced civilizations such as the Romans, Greeks, Egyptians, Babylonians, Mongols, etc., as the means to building their large land-massed empires. By the 16th Century, empire-building acquired a new brand—colonialism. **Colonialism** is "the rule of an area and its people by an extended sovereignty that results from a policy of imperialism."[37] Colonial possessions enabled the acquirer or as in the case of the British government, the "mother country" to transport or relocate their own people to a newly acquired territory to establish a new political order and/or to superimpose rule over less-developed indigenous people. The establishment of the American colonies followed that pattern. The British government encouraged immigration to its North American territories while at the same time, imposing its form of government upon Native Americans. At the height of her reign, Queen Victoria could rightly brag that the sun never set on the British Empire. The United States extended its world-wide influence through imperialism. "In the years around 1900, the United States leaped from a continental empire to overseas empire by asserting power over Cuba, Puerto Rico, Hawaii, Guam and, amid terrible violence, the Philippines. [President] Theodore Roosevelt, the era's iconic imperialist, considered this a leap toward national greatness . . Roosevelt considered colonialism as a form of 'Christian charity.'"[38]

Particularly in third power nations, the intervention of the United States into their internal affairs may be welcomed by the incumbent government but verbally resented by its citizens who see the United States as not a benevolent friend but as an imperialistic enemy.

FOREIGN POLICY PROCESS

With few exceptions, the initial step is diplomacy with the hope of preventing a small-scale developing international incident from becoming a full-scale war. During the Nixon administration, Secretary of State Henry Kissinger was the catalyst behind **détente**, "a French word meaning 'the easing of strained relations.'"[39] And in the 1980s, Soviet leader Mikhail Gorbachev introduced **glasnost**, the Russian word for openness. Both policies were designed to ease the tension between the United States and the Soviet Union. Through cultural exchanges, mutual visits to each other's country, the Soviet Union was able to improve the standard of living for its people by gingerly moving its economic philosophy from state-ownership under socialism to the free market of capitalism.

Oftentimes, a third party representative is needed to mediate and broker a deal between the aggrieved parties. For example, the political and religious divide between Arab countries and Israel has been widening ever since the first Jewish settlers arrived in what today is known as Israel. In 1978, President Jimmy Carter invited Egyptian President Anwar Sadat and Israeli Prime Minister Menachem Begin to Camp David, Maryland, site of the presidential retreat. It marked the first time that an Arab leader directly met with and talked to an Israeli government official. Signed in March 1979, the **Camp David Accords** was a landmark agreement between the two leaders whereby Egypt would become the first Arab nation to officially recognize Israel and, in return, Israel would gradually begin withdrawing from the Sinai Peninsula, an area it had occupied since the 1967 Six-Day War. Although many serious concerns such as the creation of an independent state of Palestine were not discussed, the bringing together of these two bitter enemies and getting them to the table and agreeing on some concessions was a shot in the arm for United States relations with both Israel and the Arab countries. Carter received a Nobel Peace Prize for his efforts to bring some sense of peace to the Middle East. As a multinational peace keeping force, the United Nations has been successful in defusing external conflicts between two or more nations as well as acting as a neutral arbitrator in ending internal coups, political upheavals, and revolutions.

Agreements are oftentimes signed between world leaders to express their support of or cooperation of a particular issue. World-wide environmental conferences often yield agreements to pursue a cleaner environment, protect endangered species, and promote clean water projects to impoverished nations. There is a wide range of nuclear agreements pledging the signees to reduce their stockpiles and minimize or actually eliminate testing activities. **Bilateral agreements** are between two nation states; whereas, **multi-lateral agreements** bear the signatures of numerous world leaders. Signed in 1945, the **Yalta Agreement** set the parameters for the surrender of Germany. President Franklin Roosevelt, British Prime Minister Winston Churchill and Soviet Marshal Joseph Stalin agreed

Carter brought Menachem Begin and Anwar Sadat, leaders of Israel and Egypt, respectively, to the Camp David presidential retreat. After thirteen days of bargaining, the three leaders announced the framework for a negotiating process and a peace treaty. September 7, 1978 Photo credit: Jimmy Carter Library

Churchill, Franklin D. Roosevelt, and Stalin at the Livadia Palace in Yalta. February 9, 1945 Photo credit: FDR Presidential Library

to an unconditional surrender for Germany, swift trial for high-ranking German Nazi officers for war crimes, reparations from the German government, self-determination for the newly liberated countries in Eastern Europe, and the role Great Britain, the United States and the Soviet Union would play in the newly created United Nations. In return for the concessions he received, Stalin pledged that the Soviet Union would join the allies in the Pacific front within three months after the end of hostilities in Germany. The war with Japan ended before the Soviets could join the Pacific front. A multi-lateral and multi-national agreement can also lend validity to a unilateral decision. In the case of the Iraq War, the United States could have invaded Iraq on its own. However, the Bush administration wanted a nod of approval from the international community. He sought and got the support of approximately forty nations to include Great Britain, France, and Nicaragua. While it is doubtful that Nicaragua's contribution went beyond having its name on the list, what the Bush administration wanted was to send a clear message to Baghdad that it was not just the United States condemning the Iraqi government but the entire international community.

A **treaty** is "a formal agreement entered into between two or more countries. The treaty process includes negotiation, signing, ratification, exchange of ratifications, publishing and proclamation, and treaty execution."[40] Usually, a treaty is a negotiated settlement between the winners and losers of an armed conflict. Signed in 1783, the **Treaty of Paris** officially ended the American Revolutionary War. The British government recognized the independence of the United States and her claim to the territories west of the Mississippi, north to Canada and south to the Floridas. In 1903, President Teddy Roosevelt successfully negotiated the **Hay-Herran Treaty**, an agreement leasing to the "United States a narrow strip of land across the Central American isthmus and allowed the U.S. to purchase the right-of-way and equipment of a French-based construction consortium established in the area" that was originally rejected by the Columbian government.[41] With Senate approval in hand, this treaty gave the United States the pathway to build the Panama Canal. Treaties can also address mutual defense issues. For example, the **Japanese-American Security Treaty** of 1954 and 1960 is a bilateral defense pact pledging that both parties would respond if the security of Japan was threatened. The treaty gives the United States the authority to maintain military bases on the island with the understanding that military forces can be deployed "1) without prior consultation, to maintain peace and security in the Far East; 2) following consultation, to defend Japan against an armed attack; and 3) at the express request of the Japanese government to help suppress domestic disorders in Japan resulting from the instigation or intervention of an outside power."[42] The treaty fulfills the national interests of both nations. Japan has the assurance that the United States will help to promote the security of their nation. The United States can continue to maintain a military presence in Japan while at the same time solidifying its economic presence in the Far East.

A nation state can be supportive of another's international conflict without committing its own military forces to an armed conflict. In the late 1930s, President Franklin Roosevelt knew that war between Europe and Nazi Germany was inevitable. However, he realized that gaining American support for another European front war so close to the end of World War I was impractical. His administration also realized that the European countries, particularly Great Britain, needed help to offset Nazi Germany's intention to conquer all of Europe, including Great Britain. To avoid a declaration of war from Germany, the Roosevelt administration found a unique way to getting war material to the British. **Lend-lease** enabled the Roosevelt administration to lend much needed military equipment, airplanes, weaponry, and everything short of military personnel to the British with a gentlemen's agreement that the British would eventually reimburse the United States for its generous offer.

At the height of the Cold War, both the United States and the Soviet Union used foreign aid and military assistance packages as a means of "winning friends" within the international community, particularly with third-, fourth- and fifth world nation states. In 2016, Secretary of State John Kerry submitted his budget proposals for the upcoming 2017 fiscal year. In his State of the Union Message, President Obama advocated for a smarter approach to American foreign policy by calling for a "patient and disciplined strategy that uses every element of our nation's power" which "means a wise application of military power . . . rally the world behind causes that are right [and] seeing our foreign assistance as part of our national security, not something separate, not charity."[43] Secretary Kerry's budgetary requests underscored the primary objectives of the Obama administration's foreign policy:

> Our country's ability to influence events abroad depends on our willingness to tap into all of the resources at our disposal; combining our unquestioned military might with creative diplomacy and tangible support for democracy, development, and human rights. Our purpose in doing so is to promote the safety, prosperity, and overall well-being of the American people at a turbulent time in a complex world: to counter violent extremism; defeat terrorist organizations such as ISIL and al-Qa'ida; combat climate change; promote America's economic interests; prevent the proliferation of dangerous weapons; curb international narcotics trafficking; protect the global environment; combat hunger and epidemic disease; respond to humanitarian emergencies; advance the status of women and girls; and encourage high standards of governance in countries across the globe."[44]

However, President Trump's new sovereigntist approach was based on withdrawing the United States from treaties, international agreements, and previous executive orders that he believed were disadvantageous to the nation's economic prosperity. After his inauguration, Trump withdrew the United States from **Intermediate-Range Nuclear Forces Treaty**, an arms control agreement with Russia implemented in 1987. He also pulled the United States out of the **Paris Agreement** of 2015, an international pact to curb use of fossil fuels and the **Trans-Pacific Partnership** (2016), a trade deal negotiated by the Obama administration to counter China's growing economic power in the Far East. He also renegotiated **KORUS**, a 2012 trade agreement between the United States and South Korea and the 1994 **North American Free Trade Agreement** (**NAFTA**) between Mexico, Canada and the United States. "Trump's time in office saw the president remove the U.S. from multiple international organizations and did not hide his frustration with international trade groups and security alliances."[45] He was particularly critical of the United Nations and the World Health Organization. He also verbally admonished the European members of the NATO for not contributing their fair share of dues to the organization. Incoming President Joe Biden indicated that one of his first duties after taking the oath of office would be to rejoin the Paris Agreement.

On the other hand, embargos and economic sanctions are frequently used to punish a nation state for unacceptable behavior. Economic sanctions are effective in the short run but are not a viable long-term option. For example, the United Nations did impose an economic embargo on Iraq for its production of those mysterious weapons of mass destruction. Initially, the economic sanctions were effective. However, the Iraqi government was able to bypass the stranglehold of the sanctions by negotiating "under the table" deals with those nation states sympathetic to Iraq. Although rarely used, presidents can force nations to comply with United States policy directives by freezing that nation's international assets and investments. The Obama administration took a unique approach to Russia's military operations in the Ukraine. Instead of freezing Russian national assets, Obama opted to freeze the personal international holdings and bank accounts of several of President Vladimir Putin's closet friends and allies.

The State of War

War is defined as "the hostilities between states or within a state or territory undertaken by means of armed force.[46] An official **state of war** "exists in the legal sense when two or more states declare *officially* that a condition of hostilities exists between them."[47] When diplomatic talks are no longer a viable option, the best course of action may be to launch a military strike in hopes of defusing the growing tensions. The sophistication of defense response systems is not fool-proof. What world leaders must avoid at all-costs is an accidental war that is "unattended armed conflict touched off by incidents caused by human error or mechanical failure."[48] A **preventive war** option is a limited but powerful military maneuver designed to scare the other side away from hostile action and draw them back to the negotiation table. For example, the Israeli government oftentimes lines up its tanks and positions its heavily armed troops along the Palestinian border as a powerful reminder of what is to come if the Palestinians launch an attack. This tactic goes hand in hand with **psychological warfare** whereby pamphlets or leaflets are dropped from military planes over enemy lines warning the people of an appending attack if they do not convince their government to cease hostile actions. During the

Iraq War, the United States military drop millions of leaflets telling the Iraqi people about the virtues of a democratic government and the personal rights they would have if they only would overthrow the Hussein government. Before sending ground troops into combat, the military launched nightly missile barrages and played loud music at night hoping to keep the Iraqi army awake, on edge, and thus too tired to fight.

There are two major categories of armed conflicts. A **limited war** is "an armed conflict fought for objectives less than the total destruction of the enemy and his unconditional surrender."[49] Considering the potentially world-ending destruction caused by nuclear weapons, every military action launched by any nation state after World War II has been limited warfare. At the beginning of the early stages of the Cold War, political scientist Hans J. Morgenthau correctly predicted the pattern of modern warfare. In *Politics Among Nations: The Struggle for Power and Peace*, Morgenthau reasoned that both the United States and the Soviet Union understood fully that they could launch a nuclear attack against each other at any given time. Once one side fired a long-range nuclear warhead, the other side had **second-strike capability,** that is, the commitment to fight back. If that were to happen, the United States and the Soviet Union could destroy the entire planet. So an all-out nuclear war was off the table. However, both sides still wanted the opportunity to flex their muscles at each other. The answer was **selective limited warfare**. According to Morgenthau's model, both the Soviet Union and the United States could engage in regional limited wars. For example, the Iran/Iraq War saw the Soviets supplying military personnel, weaponry, and air support to Iran while the United States government gave military equipment and warplanes to Iraq. While the international community saw Iranian troops attacking Iraqi forces, it was the Soviet Union and the United States pulling the strings behind the scenes. The same scenario would be used in internal conflicts. For example, during the **Iran/Contra Conflict**, the United States government supported the Contras in their battle with the Sandinistas who were backed by the Soviets through the Cuban government.

World War I and World War II fall into the category of total war. A **total war** involves "1) participation of entire populations in the war effort; 2) terrorization of civilian populations to destroy their will to fight; 3) the use of modern weapons offering a vast range of destructive power; 4) participation of most nations in the war, with fighting carried on globally; 5) gross violations of the international rules of warfare; 6) intense mass emotional attachment to nationalist or ideological ideas or goals that transform the war into a morale crusade for both sides; 7) demands for unconditional surrender; 8) and the political, economic and social reconstruction of the defeated states according to the dictates of the victors."[50] Both wars involved the entire populations of the warring factions and even those who were not directly involved in the hostilities. Particularly with World War II, the advancement of Adolf Hitler into European countries caused massive panic, relocations, and a horrific lost of civilian lives. One source estimates that over six million Soviet citizens were either killed through German military operations or died in German run labor and concentration camps. The Japanese were equally brutal as their military slaughtered non-combatants throughout their acquisition of islands and territories in the Pacific. They also either killed or imprisoned countless members of Japanese resistance forces and Allied troops.

Regardless of whether a nation is involved in a limited or total war, each participating nation state must, or at least should, adhere to the established rules of warfare, that is, "the principles set forth in international law to govern the conduct of nations engaged in hostilities."[51] War is not for the faint of heart. No country places its independence and security on the line or places its citizens in potentially deadly harm with the intention of losing a war. By its very nature, war is inhumane. However, world leaders have come to realize that there is a line in the sand that no nation should violate unless there is no other alternative available to secure victory. The rules of warfare are delineated in a series of documents commonly known as the **Geneva Conventions**. The first **Geneva Conference** involved representatives of twenty-six nations gathering in 1899 in Geneva, Switzerland, to develop the appropriate guidelines for land warfare tactics. The **Declaration of Paris** signed in 1856 abolished privateering. The **Geneva Conventions of 1864 and 1906** mandate the humane treatment for military personnel wounded in battle. The **Hague Convention of 1907** outlaws the use of dumdum bullets and poisonous gas, as well as the use of balloons for bombing missions. The **Geneva Conventions of 1929 and 1949** set the guidelines for the treatment of prisoners, sick and wounded military personnel, and the protection of civilian populations held by the enemy. The **London Protocol of 1936** limits the use of submarines against non-combatant merchant ships. The body of international law with its provisions for humane treatment and prohibitions against unwarranted cruelty should also be followed by all parties involved in warfare.

To hold violators accountable for their actions, the Permanent Court of International Justice was formed in 1922. In 1946, the United Nations assumed authority over trying war crimes violators. At the end of World War II, the top command of both the Japanese and German military and key leaders from both governments were tried, convicted and, in some instances, executed for war crimes. Sixty-seven years later the Japanese government is still apologizing for the Bataan Death March where in April 1942, "78,000 prisoners of war (12,000 American and 66,000 Filipinos) [were] marched by the Japanese 65 miles over six days to a prisoner-of-war camp. As many as 11,000 prisoners died on the march."[52] The German government is still dealing with the horrors of the Holocaust and the millions of people that died in the labor and concentration camps. In 2002, the **International Criminal Court (ICC)** was sanctioned by sixty-six nations to be the official governing body over war crime trials. Currently, ninety-four nations have ratified the treaty establishing the court. With its eighteen judges, the court prosecutes crimes against humanity. **Genocide** is "acts committed with the intent to destroy, in whole or part, a national, ethnical, racial or religious group."[53] **Crimes against humanity** are those acts "committed as part of a widespread or systematic attack directed against any civilian population."[54] Crimes include murder, extermination of a population, enslavement of individuals, mass deportations, torture, rape, enforce prostitution, the crime of apartheid, ethnic cleansing, and so forth. A conviction on any one of these charges can result in a long prison sentence or death.

The use of nuclear weapons to end the Pacific front of World War II ushered in the ultimate weapon of mass destruction. Whereas nuclear power can be used for appropriate means, such as the generation of electrical power, the first world power nation states are always uneasy when a second- or third world power nation state acquires even the rudimentary components for a nuclear reactor or purchases nuclear warheads. The continued threat of a nuclear war between the United States and the Soviet Union created a **balance of terror** whereby both stock piled nuclear weapons to the point it became a quest to see who had the highest number of the most powerful warheads. Both were on constant alert for a **preemptive strike**, "a first-strike nuclear attack undertaken on the assumption that an enemy state is planning an imminent nuclear attack."[55] To prevent these weapons from getting into the wrong hands, the United States government has negotiated and signed numerous arms limitations agreements. In return for a nation state reducing or eliminating its nuclear arsenal, the United States has pledged foreign aid, non-nuclear military support, and funds for infrastructure improvements. Basically, the nuclear-holding nations are using the policy of **deterrence** designed to "discourage other states from pursuing policies unwanted by the deterring state or states."[56]

SECURING THE ECONOMY

All nation states want to preserve and expand their economies. The growth of the bourgeois, commonly known as the middle class, in Europe prompted the search for luxury goods to include silk and spices. Marco Polo's historical journey in 1245-1247 to China established a series of trade routes known collectively as the **Silk Road**. European governments eventually sent explorers including Christopher Columbus, Vasco da Gama, and Bartolomeu Dias to find new trade routes to exchange their finished products for the raw materials and luxuries that they could not produce for themselves. Once industrialization took hold in Europe, the challenge was to find the natural resources and raw materials sorely needed to produce finished goods. Cotton and silk were needed for the British textile mills, gold and silver for the production of coin, and wood to fuel ships transporting finished products into foreign markets. The problem was how to establish both exclusive trade partners and sources of extractive raw materials. The colonial possessions of Great Britain, Spain, Portugal, France, the Netherlands, and the United States were readily available markets for "manufacturers, sources of raw materials and investment opportunities, strategic locations and sources of manpower for national defenses, and as symbols of prestige and great power status."[57] In the United States, the rising economic boost of industrialization compelled it to follow the same pattern by first establishing trade routes and agreements and then acquiring strategically and economically feasible colonial possessions. In 1784, the United States government sent the *Empress of China* to Canton, China, for ginseng, a highly prized herb used for medicinal purposes, tea, and silk. By 1854, the United States annexed Hawaii prized for its sandalwood and the Islands' strategic location as a fuel station for American cargo ships heading to the Far Eastern markets of India, China and Japan. The United States negotiated the **Treaty of New Granada** in 1846 to protect Panama from being seized by Great Britain. Because of its strategic location and sugar plantations, Cuba was eyed by the French, Great Britain, and the United States. Eventually, the United States would take possession of Cuba and the Philippines by winning the Spanish American War and eventually acquiring the Marianas, Marshalls, Virgin Islands and Alaska.

Today the international community gages the strength of their individual economies on the **balance of trade,** which is "a nation's annual net trade surplus or deficit, based on the difference in the value of its total imports and exports."[58] All nation states want a favorable balance of trade whereby they export more goods and services than they import. The United States continues to have an unfavorable balance of trade. An analysis of imports (products entering into the United States) and exports (products leaving the country for foreign markets) indicates that as of November 2020, the United States exported $184.2 billion in goods and services but imported $252.3 billion in goods and services resulting in an unfavorable trade balance or trade deficit of $68.1 billion.[59] All nation states strive for a favorable balance of trade whereby they are exporting more goods and services than they are importing. If an unfavorable balance occurs, then governing bodies will take strides to ensure that domestically made products are cheaper to the consumer than those produced in foreign countries. To ensure this, all nation states have at one time of another turned to a protectionist policy. **Protectionism** is "the theory and practice of utilizing governmental regulation to control or limit the volume or types of imports entering a state."[60] Protectionist trade agreements include tariffs, quotas, exchange controls, and any other options designed to reduce or eliminate competitive imports from entering into a country. During the Great Depression, the United States enacted the **Smoot-Hawley Tariff Act,** imposing high tariffs on agricultural and industrial imports. By making imported products more expensive, the Roosevelt administration wanted American consumers to buy cheaper American-made products and food items. In addition, trade embargos can be used to punish or to compel a nation to reevaluate its course of action. When Fidel Castro assumed power in Cuba in 1956, the United States believed that he would build a government based on democracy. Instead, he opted for a socialist system. In retaliation, the United States government put a trade embargo on the two products that made Cuba famous—sugar and tobacco products, particularly cigars.

To expand its markets, the United States employs a variety of options. Inserting a **most-favored-nation clause** into a trade agreement and extending tariff concessions to participating nations to prevent trade discrimination practices help to reverse an unfavorable trade deficit with another country. With the global economy, an economic downturn in one country can have a domino effect on the international economic community. Consequently, the United States has joined several international organizations to include the **General Agreement on Tariffs and Trade (GATT)**. With a membership representing approximately 4/5's of the world's trade, the major purposes of the organization include: "1) negotiating the reduction of tariffs and other impediments to trade; 2) developing new trade policies; 3) adjusting trade disputes; and 4) establishing rules to govern the trade policies of its members."[61] To develop third-, fourth-, and some fifth-power nation states into potential trade partners, the industrial nation states have formed organizations such as the **International Development Association (IDA)** and the **International Monetary Fund (IMF)** to provide economic assistance and expertise to these nations. One of the contributing factors leading to Great Britain's exit from the **European Union (EU)** was the economic domino effect among the Union's members caused by the economic crisis in Greece.

THE DEVELOPMENT OF AMERICAN FOREIGN POLICY

Constitutional Authority—Is foreign affairs the exclusive prerogative of the president?

Whenever this nation is embroiled in an international incident, the American citizenry naturally turn to their president rather than to Congress for guidance and reassurance that the federal government will indeed do whatever is necessary to fulfill its obligation to "provide for the common defense." The perception is that as the commander-in-chief of the military, the president is completely in charge. But, is he? Did the Framers envision that the executive branch would bear the sole responsibility for foreign affairs? The answer is a resounding no!

The Framers never intended to place the sole responsibility of securing this nation into the hands of the president. "Any latent fears were quickly arrested by assurances from [James] Madison and [James] Wilson that the power of peace and war was not an executive, but legislative function. Given the Framers' conception of the chief executive as little more than an institution to effectuate 'the will of the legislature,' that is, to execute laws and to appoint officers, there was little about the office to fear."[62] The Framers envisioned a shared role between the executive and legislative branches that separated the authority between the two and provided a system of checks and balances to prevent one branch from overstepping its assigned role. A closer look at the president's authority to negotiate treaties, commit American forces to combat situations, and to serve as the nation's commander-in-chief clearly indicates that the president's authority is indeed limited. However, shared governance does not mean that the relationship between the president and Congress is a congenial one.

Commander-in-Chief and Warmaking

Article II, Section 2 of the United States Constitution names the president as the nation's commander-in-chief of the "army, and navy of the United States, and of the militia of the several states, when called into actual service of the United States." Although the Constitution specifically grants the title to the president, it does not specifically delineate the specific duties and responsibilities associated with it. Is it an advisory role? Is it merely a ceremonial role? Or, can the president actually lead American forces into combat situations?

The term commander-in-chief was first used by Charles I of England in 1639 during the First Bishops War. During the civil war between the Royalists Cavaliers under Charles I's command and the Parliamentarian Roundheads under Thomas Cromwell, both designated their lead generals as commanders-in-chief. "In 1645, Sir Thomas Fairfax was appointed commander in chief of all of Parliament's forces, 'subject to such orders and directions as he shall receive from both Houses or the committee of Both Kingdoms.'"[63] Basically, the bearer of this lofty title could exercise no independent authority whatsoever and received his orders from within the British government, primarily from the Secretary of War. Holder of the title, the Duke of Wellington once commented "the commander in chief cannot move a Corporal's Guard from one station to another, without a Route countersigned by the Secretary War."[64] At the beginning of the American Revolution, the Continental Congress named George Washington as the commander-in-chief with the clear understanding "that he was to be 'its creature . . . in and every respect. . . .' Instructions drafted by John Adams, R. H. Lee, and Edward Rutledge told Washington 'punctually to observe and follow such orders and directions . . . as you shall receive from this or a future Congress.'"[65] At the Constitutional Convention, the Framers envisioned a similar role for the newly crafted office of the presidency. At the Virginia Ratifying Convention, Framer George Mason pointed out that he had concerns at first about the evolving role of the president as the nation's commander-in-chief:

The propriety of his being commander in chief, so far as to give orders and have a general superintendency; but he thought it would be dangerous to let him command in person, without any restraint, as he might make bad use of it. He was, then, clearly of opinion that the consent of a majority of both houses of Congress should be required before he could take command in person.[66]

In *Federalist #69*, Alexander Hamilton clarified the role of commander-in-chief by comparing it to the authority granted to both the British monarch and the governor of New York:

> First. The president will have only the occasional command of such part of the militia of the nation as by legislative provision may be called into actual service of the Union. The king of Great Britain and the governor of New York have at all times the entire command of all the militia within their several jurisdictions. In this article, therefore, the power of the President would be inferior to that of either the monarch or the governor. Secondly. The President is to be commander-in-chief of the army and navy of the United States. In this respect his authority would be nominally the same with that of the king of Great Britain, but in substance much inferior to it. It would amount to nothing more than supreme command and direction of the military and naval forces, as first general and admiral of the Confederacy; while that of the British king extends to the declaring of war and to the raising and regulating of fleets and armies,—all which, by the Constitution under consideration, would appertain to the legislature.[67]

Furthermore, the **War Clause of Article I, Section 8** clearly states that only the Congress shall have the power to "declare war [and] grant Letters of Marque and Reprisal and Make Rules concerning captures on Land and Water." Although there was general agreement on vesting executive authority with one person, the Framers debated whether the executive should be given the exclusive authority to declare war. Particularly in Europe, the prerogative of the monarchs to frequently declare war on each other embroiled the entire continent into decades of continuous warfare resulting in severe loss of human life, devastating property damage, and untold misery for noncombatants. The Framers simply did not want their executive to become a divine monarch. However, they also realized that the president in his role as commander-in-chief needed the constitutional footing to immediately call upon the military to repel an invading foreign combatant or to respond to a national emergency without first obtaining congressional approval. Consequently, the compromise was that an official declaration of war could only be declared by a joint session of Congress. However, the president would be empowered to act on his own to repel any internal (insurrection) and external (invasive) sudden attack against the United States. At the Pennsylvania Ratifying Convention, Framer James Wilson defended the Framer's decision:

> This system will not hurry us into war; it is calculated to guard against it. It will not be in the power of a single man, or a single body of men, to include us in such distress; for the important power of declaring war is vested in the legislature at large: this declaration must be made with the concurrence of the House of Representatives: from this circumstance we may draw a certain conclusion that nothing but our interest can draw us into war.[68]

The fine line is the difference between declaring and making war. Congress has officially declared war five times: the War of 1812, the Mexican War, the Spanish-American War, World War I and

World War II. Congress has authorized the president to make war, without an official declaration of war, on numerous occasions to include Vietnam, Korea, Gulf War I, Gulf War II, etc. Also, Congress has enabled the president to use extraordinary means of protecting this nation from harm such as Franklin Roosevelt's **Executive Order 9066**, mandating that more than 100,000 Americans of Japanese descent be held in relocation centers for the duration of World War II, and Abraham Lincoln's suspension of the *writ of habeas corpus* during the American Civil War. In 1964, President Lyndon Johnson asked and received extraordinary authority to repel attacks from North Vietnam levied at American troops stationed in South Vietnam. With overwhelming congressional support, the **Gulf of Tokin Resolution** empowered the president "as Commander in Chief, to take all necessary measures to repel any armed attack against the forces of the United States and to prevent further aggression."[69] In other words, this resolution gave Johnson the authority to make war without an official congressional declaration of war. However, it was not a blank check. The resolution clearly stated in Section 3 "this resolution shall expire when the President shall determine that the peace and security of the area is reasonably assured by international conditions created by the action of the United Nations or otherwise, except that it may be terminated earlier by concurrent resolution of the Congress."[70]

For Lyndon Johnson, Vietnam was his Achilles' heel. Confronted with a rapidly growing hostile anti-war movement at home, Johnson simply could not find a path to victory. He opted not to seek a second term of office. The Nixon administration inherited the failures of Vietnam. For the Nixon administration, the ultimate goal was to find a peaceful honorable means of ending the war without severely damaging America's prestige in the international community. His **Vietnamization**

President Lyndon B. Johnson signs the "Gulf of Tonkin" resolution.
East Room, White House, Washington, D.C.
August 10, 1964
Photo Credit: LBJ Library photo by Cecil Stoughton

Plan called for the gradual withdrawal of American forces by replacing them with a well-trained and equipped South Vietnamese military. Supposedly intelligence reports revealed that the Cambodian government was aiding the cause of the North Vietnamese by launching air strikes against the South Vietnamese and, of course, American military personnel. Consequently, Nixon used the power granted to the president through the Gulf of Tonkin Resolution to order bombing raids of Cambodian military installations and runways. Inflamed by the growing anti-war movement, an angry Congress struck back in 1970 by repealing the resolution, mandating the end to the bombing raids, and scaling back appropriations for the war effort. In retaliation, Nixon continued the bombing raids in "secret" even as he was withdrawing American troops from South Vietnam.

Congress opted to reign in the presidency with the passage of the 1973 **War Powers Resolution**. "The purpose of the War Powers Resolution was to 'fulfill the intent of the framers of the Constitution' (section 2) by reintroducing a balancing role for Congress."[71] The legislation "does not prohibit the president from sending troops into combat, but it does require the president to notify Congress of the reason for committing combat troops within forty-eight hours of their deployment. The act also specifies that hostilities must end within sixty days unless Congress extends the period; gives the president an additional thirty days to withdraw the troops from hostile territory, although Congress can shorten this period; and requires the president to consult with Congress whenever feasible before sending troops into a hostile situation.[72] Congress can opt to support the president's action by extending the period of the deployment or officially declaring war. If Congress disagrees with the president it can issue "a decision not to support the president during the 60 to 90 days, or passage of a concurrent resolution at any time to direct the president to remove forces engaged in hostilities."[73]

As anticipated, Nixon vetoed it, "calling it 'unconstitutional and dangerous to the best interest of the nation', because it would 'attempt to take away, by a mere legislative act, authorities which the President had properly exercised under the Constitution for almost 200 years.' He particularly objected to the 60-day cutoff provisions and the ability of Congress to force a withdrawal by concurrent resolution."[74] Although Congress overrode his veto, a defiant Nixon vowed he would not follow it. He set the trend, because not one president since Nixon has consistently adhered to the act's provisions. In 2011, President Obama called for a no-fly zone over Libya to protect rebel forces trying to overthrow the Gaddafi government. This was a NATO-backed operation with the United States taking the leading role. A handful of Republicans filed a federal lawsuit challenging Obama's initiative on the grounds that it violated the War Powers Act. The administration filed its response by noting that "U.S. operations do not involve sustained fighting or active exchanges of fire with hostile forces, nor do they involve U.S. ground troops. . . . [They] argued that Obama could initiate the intervention on his own authority as commander in chief because its anticipated nature, scope and duration fell short of a "war" in the constitutional sense."[75] The federal court agreed with President Obama. Basically, the War Powers Resolution is a failure because "first, it does not give Congress any substantial powers to check the president or any substantial new opportunities to participate in foreign policy that it did not already have or could not exercise without the resolution. Second, presidents since 1974 have not regarded themselves as bound by the resolution, at least not in the sense Congress seems to have intended. Indeed, they are able to disregard the provisions with impunity, and they seem to have every incentive to do so."[76]

The Power to Make Treaties

Article II, Section 2 of the United States Constitution states "he [the president] shall have the power, by and with the Advice and Consent of the Senate, to make Treaties, provided two-thirds of the Senators present concur." Of equal importance, **Article I, Section 10** prohibits the individual states from entering into any treaty, alliance or confederation. Consequently, the Framers wanted the treaty making responsibility to rest exclusively with the national government under the guidance of both the executive and legislative branches. Framer Charles Pinckney responded to those wanting the president to have exclusive treaty making authority that "surely there is greater security in vesting these powers as the present Constitution has vested it, than in any other body. Would the gentleman vest it in the President alone? If he would, his assertion that the power we have granted was as dangerous as the power vested by Parliament in the proclamations of Henry VIII, might have been, perhaps, warranted. . . . [The Senate] joined with the president . . . form together a body in which can be best and most safely vested the diplomatic power of the union."[77] In *Federalist #75*, Alexander Hamilton underscored the need for legislative input:

> [Treaties] are contracts with foreign nations, which have the force of law, but derive it from the obligations of good faith. They are not rules prescribed by the sovereign to the subject, but agreements between sovereign and sovereign. . . .the vast importance of the trust, and the operation of treaties as laws, plead strongly for the participation of the whole or a portion of the legislative body in the office of making them. It would be utterly unsafe and improper to entrust that power to an elective magistrate of four years' duration. . . . It must indeed be clear to a demonstration that the joint possession of the power in question, by the President and Senate, would afford a greater prospect of security, than the separate possession of it by either of them."[78]

While on one hand calling for a shared role between the president and the Senate, the Framers failed to clearly indicate the extent of and the timing of the Senate's responsibility of "advice and consent." President George Washington took the position that the Senate should advise the executive branch on the matters to be addressed in a treaty prior to initiating the treaty negotiation process. He requested to meet with the entire Senate to discuss the conditions of a pending treaty between the United States and several of the southern Indian tribes. Denying the president access to the Senate chamber, the Senate referred the matter to a committee. Washington met with the committee only to sit "through hours of debate and in the end got what he came for, with minor changes."[79] Washington never again went to the Senate for advice for a pending treaty negotiation. By 1794, the process of seeking senatorial advice waned as the Jay Treaty became the first treaty negotiated without prior senatorial involvement.

What is particularly irksome to presidents, the Senate far too often uses its advice role after the treaty has been negotiated and signed by the president or his appointed representative. The executive branch charges that treaties are subjected to unwarranted and numerous amendments initiated by the Senate that oftentimes change the entire focus of a document that took months to negotiate with foreign delegations. In 1901, the Senate added so many amendments to the Hay-Pauncefote Treaty that the British rejected the treaty after initially agreeing to and officially signing it. Also, presidents must face the rare chance that the Senate will reject the entire treaty. President Woodrow Wilson personally headed the American delegation to Paris to negotiate the Treaty of Versailles. Realizing the final document would face intense Senate scrutiny and, perhaps, a few amendments he was totally surprised when the Senate failed to approve it. President Jimmy Carter faced a similar situation when the Senate rejected his original Panama Canal Treaty and the Strategic Arms Limitation II Treaty. Presidents claim that they are subject to embarrassment in front of the international community. Secretary of State Richard Olney commented that "the treaty in getting itself made by the sole act of the executive, without leave of the Senate first hand obtained, had committed the unpardonable sin. It must be either altogether defeated or so altered as to bear an unmistakable Senate stamp. . . . and thus be the means both of humiliating the executive and of showing to the world the greatness of the Senate."[80] Consequently, presidents opt to avoid the Senate's treaty making role by using the executive agreement.

An **executive agreement** is "an international agreement, reached by the president with foreign heads of state that does not require senatorial approval."[81] Initially, presidents were not required to even submit a copy of the agreement to Congress. Executive agreements fall into four categories: "1) those concluded pursuant to a treaty; 2) those concluded to carry out the intention of an act of Congress; 3) those concluded by the president under his constitutional authority and supported or confirmed by Congressional action such as a declaration of war or a joint resolution passed by majority vote; and 4) those concluded by the president according to his constitutional authority and not submitted to or confirmed by the Senate."[82] Category four agreements are commonly known as **pure executive agreements**.

The first executive agreement was the Rush-Bagot Agreement signed by President James Monroe in 1817. Although he subsequently received Senate approval, the agreement provided for the withdrawal of British and American naval forces on the Great Lakes. The propensity of presidents to use the executive agreement over the treaty option is alarming. Thomas Jefferson used an executive agreement to purchase the Louisiana Territory from France in 1803. In 1940, Franklin Roosevelt used an executive agreement to give Great Britain fifty mothballed destroyers. Since Great Britain had already declared war with Germany, this action could have been used by Germany to declare war against the United States for aiding its enemy. In 1963, John Kennedy pledged to Francisco Franco through an executive agreement to provide aid and military support if Spain were to be attacked. This was controversial since Spain had been excluded from NATO because Franco had started a civil war with Hitler's army and openly demonstrated his sympathy for Nazi Germany. The Korean War was initiated and concluded through executive agreements. A steady stream of executive agreements led to the Vietnam War. A frequent user of pure executive agreements, Richard Nixon stated "in short, there have been, and will be in the future, circumstances in which presidents may lawfully authorize actions in the interest of the security of this country, which if undertaken by other persons, or even by the president under different circumstances, would be illegal."[83] The frequent use of and the sensitivity of their content moved a member of the Senate Foreign Relations Committee to remark that "while many crucially important commitments, including base agreements, have been made by executive agreement, trivial agreements [such as] governing the status of three uninhabited coral reefs in the Caribbean; regulating shrimp fishing off the coast of Brazil; and setting rules to prevent collisions at sea, have been transmitted to the Senate as treaties."[84]

The legality of the executive agreement was affirmed by the U.S. Supreme Court in *United States v Belmont* (1937). They "unanimously held an executive agreement to be a valid international compact. . . The Court said in part: In respect to all international negotiations and compacts, and in respect to our foreign relations generally, state lines disappear."[85] Yet, Congress does have the authority to once again reign in the presidency.

The first congressional act to challenge the use of pure executive agreements, the **Case-Zablocki Act (1972)**, requires that the Secretary of State transmit to Congress the text of any international agreement with the exception of treaties, no later than sixty days after the agreement has been made. However, the president has the option to withhold any agreements he judges would jeopardize national security. Of course, Congress can use its ultimate power of the purse to block the funding for any initiative they believe to be unjustified to include provisions in executive agreements and treaties.

The President's Foreign Policy Team

Basically, the president's foreign policy team is a two-headed structure with the Secretary of State heading the diplomatic front and the Secretary of War, now Defense, charged with the task of militarily defending the country and protecting its vital security interests. Created in 1789, both positions are presidential appointees subject to Senate confirmation. In 2002, President George W. Bush created the Department of Homeland Security, a cabinet-level position, overseeing the merging of various intelligence agencies. The State Department oversees all diplomatic initiatives as well as overseeing all United States embassies and consulates. Working with its international partners, the State Department also provides assistance for victims of natural disasters and crimes of conflict and persecution as well as efforts to support development investments in the poorest and most unstable nations. The State Department also works closely with the United Nations and numerous **nongovernmental bodies (NGOs)** in promotion of humanitarian, health-based, education, and economic development programs. Created in 1947 by the National Security Act, the National Security Council (NSC) advises the president on matters of national security to include domestic, foreign, and military. The nation's largest employer, the Department of Defense has 1,363,816 men and women on active duty as 774,000 civilian employees.[86] The Department of Homeland Security includes the inspector general's office, the U.S. Customs and Border Protection, U.S. Immigration and Customs Enforcement, Transportation Security Administration, the U.S. Coast Guard, U.S. Secret Service, Federal Emergency Management Agency (FEMA), and U.S. Citizenship and Immigration Services. The various agencies grouped under the Intelligence Community include the Central Intelligence Agency (CIA), the Federal Bureau of Investigation (FBI), Army and Air Force Intelligence, National Security Agency (NSA), Defense Intelligence Agency (DIA), Drug Enforcement Administration (DEA), and so on. In the aftermath of September 11, 2001, congressional investigations pointed to lack of cooperation between the CIA and the FBI. Apparently, each agency had minute pieces of a larger puzzle, indicating that a terrorist attack on American soil was in the planning stages. Since the CIA traditionally handles foreign-related issues and the FBI focuses more on domestic criminal activities, they simply did not share their information with each other. Not that the piecing together of this puzzle would have prevented the attacks on the World Trade Center; but it surely would have given the Bush administration a fair warning. Consequently, the Bush administration opted direct oversight of the two agencies through the Department of Homeland Security.

As previously discussed in Chapter 14, the president's foreign policy team will frame their decisions into one of three policy options. The **crisis policy response** calls upon the president to exercise his emergency powers to act quickly to address a perceived or actual threat to national security. A **strategic defense policy** calls upon the deployment of military personnel; whereas, the **structural defense policy** option involves decisions about procurement and the allocation of resources to include manpower and equipment. It is the responsibility of the president's team to present to him the best viable options to include actual and potential costs, possibility of loss of life, and the advantages and disadvantages of each option in reaching the intended goal of the policy decision. For example, President Johnson met with Pentagon officials and members of his team to include Secretary of Defense Robert McNamara, Secretary of State Dean Rusk, and Chairman of the Joint Chiefs of Staff General Earle Wheeler on the best course of action to follow in Vietnam. The president summarized the options presented to him:

> The options open to us are: one, leave the country, with as little loss as possible; two, maintain present force and lose slowly; three, add 100,000 men, recognizing that may not be enough and adding more next year. The disadvantages of number three option are the risk of escalation, casualties high, and the prospect of a long war without victory. . . . Are we starting something that in two or three years we simply can't finish?[87]

Johnson selected option three. He sent more troops to Vietnam. And as he predicted, the war escalated; the number of casualties dramatically increased; and both the White House and Capitol Hill realized that there was no victory in sight! Unfortunately, these dicey policy decisions are not made with a crystal ball in hand. Particularly in dealing with foreign policy issues, the cost of hasty

Jimmy Carter and Giscard d'Estaing at a memorial ceremony for World War II GI's. January 5, 1978. Photo credit: Jimmy Carter Library

(L-R) **President Lyndon B. Johnson, Sec. Robert McNamara, and Sec. Dean Rusk. National Security meeting in the Cabinet Room, White House, Washington, D.C. Photo Credit: LBJ Library photo by Yoichi R. Okamoto**

decisions can be irreversibly damaging to the entire nation. When all is said and done, it is the president that selects the option and bears either the joy of victory or the bitter disappoint of defeat!

Brief Overview of American Foreign Policy

During the nation's formative years, American foreign policy followed an isolationist approach with sporadic and marginal involvement in international affairs. The conflict between Great Britain and France lingered after the end of the American Revolutionary War. Fearful of being entangled into the fray because of France's support to America during the revolution, George Washington issued a **Proclamation of Neutrality** on April 22, 1793. Basically, it was just a statement declaring that "the duty and interest of the United States require that they should . . . pursue a conduct friendly and impartial toward the belligerent powers."[88] By 1794, Congress passed the nation's first neutrality law. "It enjoined American citizens within the United States in four different ways: from accepting commissions to serve a foreign power, from securing the enlistment of others into the armed forces of a belligerent, from launching attacks against a nation with whom their country was at peace, and from arming or equipping private ships for operations against a nation with whom the United States was at peace."[89] Basically, America's foreign policy excursions were more defensive rather than aggressive in nature. For example, Thomas Jefferson received an official declaration of war against the pasha of Tripoli in response to the Barbary pirates attacking American ships in the Mediterranean. The War of 1812 was a defensive measure against the British invasion of the United States. Basically, the nation's focus was on the expansion of the nation's boundary from the Eastern shore of the Atlantic to the Western shore of the Pacific. Jefferson's purchase of the Louisiana territory from France only furthered the zeal of **manifest destiny**.

The only truly bold venture into international affairs was the **Monroe Doctrine** of 1823. Actually written by John Q. Adams, Monroe's secretary of state, the brief statement warns the members of the Quadruple Alliance (France, Austria, Prussia and Russia) that:

we should consider any attempt on their part to extend their system to any portion of this hemisphere as dangerous to our peace and safety. With the existing colonies or dependencies of any European power we have not interfered with and shall not interfere. But with the governments who have declared their independence and maintained it . . . we could not view any interposition for the purpose of oppressing them, or controlling them in any other manner their destiny, by any European power in any other light than as the manifestation of an unfriendly disposition toward the United States. . . Our only policy in Europe remains the same, which is, not to interfere in the internal concerns of any of its powers . . .[90]

Basically, the Monroe administration warned the European powers not to try to colonize or invade any of the Western Hemisphere nations, and, in return, the United States would not interfere into European affairs.

The ensuring American Civil War, Reconstruction, and the transformation of the United States from a semi-agricultural/industrial economy to an industrial giant kept the United States out of the international arena. However, the growth of industry compelled the nation to seek new markets in foreign waters, natural resources needed to fuel industry's smelting pots, and strategic locations to refuel American cargo ships heading for the seaport cities of the Far East. From necessity, American foreign policy shifted from isolationism to colonialism/imperialism and quasi-interventionism. The United States eventually purchased Alaska from the Russians in 1867 and acquired Midway Island in 1867, the Philippine Islands, Johnston Island and Hawaiian Islands in 1898, and Wake Island and American Samoa in 1899. From 1898 to 1915, the United States militarily occupied Cuba, Haiti, the Dominican Republic, and Nicaragua and sent an army expedition into Mexico. In 1903, the United States government gave aid to revolutionaries in Panama in hopes that a victory for them would result in the United States gaining the Isthmus of Panama for a canal.

While the Americans were busy acquiring colonies, Europe was on the brink of war. On June 28, 1914, the Archduke of Austria and his wife were murdered by a Slavic nationalist. In retaliation, Austria-Hungary mobilized to punish Serbia, which was rumored to be the architect of the assassination plot. With the largest army in Europe, Russia called upon France to come to the aid of Serbia. By August 4, 1914, the lines of battle were drawn with the **Triple Entente** of England, France and Russia at war with the **Triple Alliance** of Germany, Austria-Hungary and Italy. In hopes of avoiding the conflict, President Wilson publically announced America's neutrality. As a neutral non-combatant, American merchants carried goods and services to both sides until the British government implemented an unofficial blockade by forcing American vessels into British ports and confiscating their cargo. To halt the continuous flow of American goods into Britain, the Germans freed their submarines to attack and sink any ship near the British Isles. The sinking of the British passenger ship, *The Lusitania*, as well as American ships prompted Congress to approve a formal declaration of war against the Triple Alliance. As a whole, the American public was not solidly behind the war effort. Wilson gained support with his pledge that with the addition of America's military might, a victory would mean the end of all wars. Even before its entry into World War I, the stability of both the Russian monarchy and its government was fragile. After a series of bloody worker and peasant revolts offset by repressive actions on the part of the government, Tsar Nicholas II abdicated and a provisional government was formed. By November 1917, the weak provisional government was overthrown by the Bolsheviks, or the Communists, under the leadership of V. I. Lenin. On March 3, 1918, the Russian government signed the Brest-Litovsk Treaty with Germany, officially withdrawing Russia from the war. After its major offensive into France failed, the Germans surrendered on October 6, 1918. The defeated Germans and her allies agreed to the terms of the **Treaty of Versailles** and Woodrow Wilson's fourteen points, advocating open relations for all nations, freedom of the seas in peace and war, reductions in armaments, and the formation of an international organization known as the **League of Nations** whereby delegates of all member nation states would settle their disputes without warfare.

Germany felt that the punishment levied against them through the treaty was exceptionally harsh. They were "particularly unhappy with Article 231, the so-called **War Guilt Clause**, which declared Germany (and Austria) responsible for starting the war and ordered Germany to pay reparations for all the damage to which the Allied governments and their people were subjected to as a result of the war 'imposed upon them by the aggression of Germany and her allies.'"[91] Germany was forced to reduce its army and navy and completely eliminate its air force. Also, the Germans had to return the Alsace and Lorraine back to France. Germany's humiliating defeat and the subsequent collapse of its economy aided the cause of the rising Nazi movement under Adolph Hitler and, in some respects, set the stage for World War II.

For most Americans the euphoria of going "over there" was short lived. World War I was the first time American soldiers fought on European soil. The United States entered the war eighteen months before it officially ended. "Of the 2 million Americans who had served in France, 50,000 had died in combat and 230,000 had been wounded. By comparison, the war claimed 1.8 million Germans, 1.7 million Russians, 1.4 million French, 1.2 million Austro-Hungarians, and nearly 1 million Britons."[92] Consequently, Americans were war weary and wished to isolate themselves from the international community. With the collapse of the stock market in 1929, the nation's attention had to be directed inward as Americans dealt with the harshness of the Great Depression.

President Franklin Roosevelt was well aware of the mounting tensions in Europe with the rise of totalitarian-based **Nazism** in Germany and authoritarian-based **Fascism** in Italy. With the annexation of Austria in 1938, Adolph Hitler began his quest to establish German control over Europe. Meanwhile, the nationalistic aspirations of the Japanese military gradually took over the reins of government from the emperor, rendering the once divine monarch into a puppet. Once the Japanese seized Manchuria in 1931 and made in-roads into China, the command staff of the Japanese army launched a full-scale aggressive plan to dominate the Far East and Asia. By November 1936, the Japanese and the Germans formed an alliance under the terms of the **Anti-Comintern Pact**. Wanting to forestall a German invasion, the Russians signed a nonaggression pact with Hitler in 1939, only to see the Germans eventually invade their country. On September 3, 1939, France and Great Britain declared war on Germany. Roosevelt was caught in a policy quandary. The American people simply did not want to become involved in another war. Therefore, Roosevelt opted to give the French and the British everything short of manpower through his lend-lease program. With the 1941 Japanese attack on Pearl Harbor, Roosevelt had no option left but to ask for an official declaration of war against Japan and its allies Germany and Italy.

Once the United States entered World War II, there was no turning back to the days of neutrality and isolationism. The waning months of the war laid the foundation for the growing tensions between the Socialist Soviet Union and the democratic-capitalistic nations, particularly the United

States. Once the gunfire stopped, the ideological warfare with its potential outcome of a nuclear confrontation began. The Soviet Union enclosed the Eastern bloc countries to include the eastern portion of Germany, behind an iron curtain under the control of first Lenin then Joseph Stalin. With the horrific destructiveness of the war, both France and Britain were unable to assume the leadership role of confronting the Soviet presence. It was left up to the United States to fill the leadership void. In 1947, President Harry Truman pledged economic and possible military support to protect Greece and Turkey from Soviet intrusion. The **Truman Doctrine** stated "the United States would support free peoples who are resisting attempted subjugation by armed minorities or by outside pressures."[93] The **Marshall Plan** provided economic aid to help those European countries favorable to the United States recover from World War II. In 1949, Truman pledged economic assistance to third world nations. The Russians retaliated by closing off their sector of Berlin to American assistance. Truman responded with the famous **Berlin Lift** whereby American aircraft dropped much needed food and supplies to the "other side." The United States pledged both economic and military support to Latin American countries under the **Rio Pact**. Similar support was guaranteed to Britain, France, Belgium, Netherlands, and Luxembourg through the **Brussels Pact**. The North Atlantic Treaty Organization (NATO) was signed in 1949. These **collective security agreements** were the cornerstone of Truman's **containment policy** of preventing the Soviet Union from expanding its influence over other countries. Every president since has honored and even extended the collective security agreements initiated by the Truman administration.

Today, the Soviet or Eastern bloc no longer exists. The massive country known as the Soviet Union no longer exists as individual states under the strong arm of Moscow are now independent nation states. The Berlin Wall was dismantled during the Reagan administration. East and West Germany have been reunited as one country. The Russian economy has become more capitalistic and a viable free market partner. However, the White House will continue to be watchful of Russia's actions and policy directives. With a sigh of relief on both sides, the Cold War has ended without the predicted nuclear showdown.

CURRENT FOREIGN POLICY ISSUES AND CHALLENGES AHEAD

The incoming Biden administration's foreign policy agenda is focused on re-establishing the United States' role in the international scene by reversing the Trump's administration semi-isolationist policies. While Russia can be a useful international partner, Biden must keep a watchful eye on their desires to interfere in the American political scene. Afterall, it was Russia and not Ukraine that was targeted for interfering in the 2016 presidential election. He must keep an equally watchful eye on North Korea. It was Trump who became the first American president to visit North Korea. The nation's relationships with Central and Latin American are both a foreign and domestic problem for the Biden administration. What does he do about Trump's partially built wall along the shared border between Mexico and the United States? Peace has not been established in the conflict between Israel and Palestine. Biden does indeed have a full plate before him. A closer look at these areas helps us to understand the challenges he faces.

The Far East: North Korea

Initially a tributary of China, Korea fell under the influence of the Japanese and Russians as a result of the Sino-Japanese War in 1894-1895. When the Japanese defeated the Russians in 1905, Korea became part of the Japanese empire until Japan's defeat in World War II. In August 1945, the United States and the Soviet Union decided to create two separate occupation zones at the **38th parallel**. Both sides agreed to hold national elections with the aim of reunifying the country. The fate of Korea and other Asian countries was tied directly to developments in China. The father of modern China, Dr. Sun Yat-sen, led a successful revolution in 1911 that ended the centuries-old monarchial rule of the emperors. However, the newly formed Republic of China was unable to unite the country. While anti-Communist and Nationalist leader Chiang Kai-shek was trying to hold the fragile government together and at the same time fight off Japanese aggression in the southern areas leading to and during World War II, Mao Zedong was gaining support of the peasants in northern China. By 1949, Mao's Communist-inspired peasant army overthrew the Chiang Kai-shek government. China was the beginning of the **domino theory** feared by the Truman administration. The concept holds that if one country in a particular region falls under the influence of socialism/communism, the other weaker nations will fall into line, just like falling dominos. The Cold War dichotomy in Europe was now in Asia.

Cold War politics created two separate Koreas with North Korea as a socialist/communist nation and South Korea as an anti-socialist/communist country. On June 25, 1950, North Korea invaded South Korea. Truman ordered United States naval and air force support for South Korea as his administration sought and received U.N. resolutions condemning North Korea and pledging U.N. forces under the command of General Douglas MacArthur for South Korea. Unfortunately, the Korean War ended with a cease-fire agreement signed in July 1953. Since the cease-fire, the United States has stationed military forces along the 38th parallel to help the South Koreans prevent another invasion from North Korea. Today, North Korea is a socialist/communist ideological state governed by a quasi-militaristic government headed by their president.

The major issue for the international community is the rapid development of North Korea's nuclear program. The North Koreans contend that it is their right, just like any other nation, to use nuclear power for energy-generation purposes. However, the firing of low- and medium-range nuclear missiles for test purposes has the international community on the edge, fearing that North Korea's possession of nuclear weapons in hands of an unstable leadership could lead to war. On June 12, 2009, the United Nations Security Council voted unanimously to sanction North Korea's actions. The resolution mandates that:

- North Korea not conduct any further nuclear test or any launch using ballistic missile technology.
- North Korea suspend all activities related to its ballistic missile program and re-establish a moratorium on missile launches.
- North Korea return immediately to the six-party talks without precondition.[94]

In addition, North Korea cannot export or receive imports of any arms and weapon-related materials with the exception of small arms and light weapons. The U.N. calls for the inspection of all ships entering and exiting North Korean waters. Of course, the North Korean government defied the United Nations sanctions and continues to occasionally launch missiles and stage large state-sponsored parades showcasing its growing weapon arsenal. Obviously, the North Koreans will not abandon their nuclear ambitions without receiving something in return. In the past, North Korea has asked for and received large-scale food shipments from the United States and other nations. North Korea is confronted with a severely sagging economy and agricultural failures. The United States must also take into account China's concerns that while North Korea's actions are unacceptable, the international community simply cannot punish them so severely that the North Korean government feels that the only choice they have to maintain their popularity at home and prestige abroad is to launch a limited war against South Korea.

Far East: China

The United States' relationship with China continues to be dicey particularly when the topics focus on the economic relationship between the two nations and human rights violations charged against the Chinese government. During the 2012 presidential election, Mitt Romney continuously voiced concerns over trade with China and whether the Chinese government was purposely manipulating its currency values to continue its lop-sided balance of trade with the United States. Basically, "a weaker yuan [China's currency] makes Chinese goods cheaper for American consumers and U.S. goods more expensive in China."[95] This is not the first time the Chinese have been accused of illegal and unfair trade tactics. In 1994, the Clinton administration officially labeled China as a currency manipulator. In 1989, the repressive policies of the Chinese government drove thousands of student protestors to Tiananmen Square. After weeks of protesting and international news exposure, the Chinese government launched a bloody crackdown resulting in hundreds killed and many more injured and arrested. Since then, the international community has become more aware of and more vocal about China's government-sanctioned human rights violations. As a candidate, Trump decried the unfavorable balance of trade the United States had with China. Once in the White House, Trump's response was a trade war with the Chinese. "Trump argued that unilateral tariffs would shrike the U.S. trade deficit with China and cause companies to bring manufacturing jobs back to the United States."[96] The Chinese of course, expressed their disdain and fought back with their own tariffs on American-made goods. "Between July 2018 and August 2019, the United States announced plans to impose tariffs on more than $550 billion of Chinese products, and China retaliated with tariffs on more than $185 billion of U.S. goods."[97] Since both China and the United States were hard hit by the coronavirus pandemic, the economies of both nations have been seriously jeopardized. Basically, "U.S. economic growth slowed, business investment froze, and companies didn't hire as many people. Across the nation, a lot of farmers went bankrupt, and the manufacturing and freight transportation sectors have hit lows not seen since the last recession. Trump's actions amounted to one of the largest tax increases in years."[98] Trump's tariff war with China increased "consumer costs by roughly $57 billion annually."[99] The dilemma confronting the Biden administration is whether to continue the tariffs and if ending them, how to reign-in China's abusive economic and trade practices.

Central and Latin America – Mexico and Cuba

When President George H. W. Bush joined Mexican officials in San Antonio, Texas, to sign the North American Free Trade Agreement, Mexico believed it had finally established itself as a viable trade partner with the United States. The agreement pledged seamless international boundaries between the United States, Mexico and Canada. While Canada and the United States have seamless borders, the border between the United States and Mexico is anything but transparent. From the very beginning, the Teamsters Union and the trucking industry in the United States fought to block Mexican trucks from shipping goods into the United States. The arguments against the Mexican trucking industry have ranged from the quality of the trucks, the qualifications of the drivers, and the concern that the Mexican government would use NAFTA to smuggle in illegal drugs and Mexican nationals. Basically, NAFTA had never been fully implemented. Calling it the worst trade deal the United States government had ever made, the Trump administration renegotiated it. Signed in July 2020, the new NAFTA agreement does offer more protections for American automobile manufacturing and requires that "40 to 45 percent of automobile parts must be made by workers who earn at least $16 an hour by 2023."[100] This pushed the Mexican government to agree to increase their workers' minimum wage standards.

Illegal immigration from Mexico into the United States has always been a sore spot. When the American economy is sound, there is a need for Mexican workers in primarily agriculture and in some industries. However, immigrant workers, whether legal or illegal, are not wanted when the American economy sours. Initially, the Bush administration wanted to build a fence between the shared border of Mexico and the United States. The Obama administration canceled the project. On the day he announced his candidacy for the presidency, Donald Trump made several disparaging remarks about Mexican nationals coming into the United States and how he, as president, would rid the nation of their unsavory presence by building a wall between Mexico and the United States. When pressed about the cost of the wall, Trump vowed that he would force Mexico to pay for it. Both the current and former presidents of Mexico replied with a resounding no! After taking office, President Trump vowed to hire additional border guards and called for the deportation of illegals.

The George W. Bush administration wanted to implement a guest worker program similar to the Bracero program following World War II, and an amnesty plan to assist illegal workers who have been in this country for years to become citizens. Mexico is the gateway for the majority of those citizens of Central and Latin American countries who want to enter into the United States. Both the Obama and Trump administrations wanted to curb illegal immigration from Mexico. The Obama administration tighten the requirements for asylum seekers and initiated deportation proceedings for those whose petitions for asylum were denied. However, the Obama administration did want to protect the Dreamers, those who as young children were brought illegally to the United States by their parents but are now themselves, adults. The Trump administration, however, took a more punitive approach by sealing the border with Mexico, requiring asylum seekers to remain in Mexico pending the judicial decision from American courts of their asylum requests, and deporting illegals back to their native countries. The most controversial part of his policy focused on the children of illegal immigrants. The parents were deported, but the children remained in the United States. The children were placed into detention centers with little to no supervision. Many of the children were so young that they could not provide information about their parents nor where any official records kept as to what country their parents were deported to. The Biden administration has already vowed that one of their first tasks is to relocate these children with their parents.

The Obama administration began the process of normalizing diplomatic relationships with Cuba particularly after an ailing President Fidel Castro turned the reigns of the government over to his brother Raul Castro. Less illogically bound to socialist theory, Raul Castro takes a more pragmatic approach to capitalism, free markets, and democracy than his brother did. The Obama administration lifted the barriers for family members in the states to visit their Cuban family members, allowed Cuban Americans to send money back home, and lifted some of the trade barriers between the two nations. After the death of Fidel Castro, the American embassy in Cuba was reopened for business. However, the Trump administration backed off from establishing normalizing relations with Cuba.

The Middle East

The Bush administration focused the majority of its attention on invading Iraq and ending Saddam Hussein's rule over the Iraqi people. On the whole, the invasion was successful particularly with the capture, conviction and execution of Hussein. However, the Bush administration did not have a viable "Plan B" for occupying, stabilizing, and, ultimately, governing Iraq. The Bush team's approach to handling the sectarian differences between the Kurds, Sunnis, and Shiites was simply to try to control the violence without really addressing the root causes of the violence. President Obama fulfilled his election promise of withdrawing all active military personnel from Iraq. The on-going challenge for the Biden administration and, more importantly the American people, is to allow the people of Iraq to select their own governing philosophy and structure without undo interference from the United States. The Iraqi people should have the same opportunity as the international community afforded to our Framers, as they transitioned from a confederative to a federal form of government. Unfortunately, it will not be a peaceful quick process simply because of the centuries old mistrust between the three factions. And, the final governing structure will not mirror the representative democracy of the United States crafted under the principle of separation of church and state. What will emerge is a governing partnership closely tied to the Muslim religion.

Coined as the Arab Spring, it began in 2010 in Tunisia, a former French protectorate that gained its independence in 1956. After weeks of persistent protests, the government collapsed, sending its ruler fleeing from the country. The pro-democratic spirit spilled over as massive oftentimes heated, protests hit Jordan, Egypt, and other Middle Eastern countries. What began as non-violent protests resulted in bloody repressive actions from traditional autocratic governments unwilling to listen to the protesters' concerns and willing to relax their repressive ways. In Libya, the protests of a few turned into a civil war as an angry mob captured, killed and mutilated Gaddafi. In Egypt, massive protests resulted in the toppling of Mubarak. The massive protests of angry Egyptians with their cries of freedom, democracy and jobs overthrew the incumbent Egyptian government. In 1956, Nasser penned his hope for the Middle East in his *Philosophy of Revolution*. He believed that the key to peace in the region was solidarity, both internal and external. Internally, he advocated that regardless of the form of a national government, the survival of that government hinged on internal sovereignty. When he took office, Egyptians were still holding their allegiance to their tribes and clans, not the national government. If he were standing in the square in Cairo during the celebration of Mubarak's departure, he would have been pleased to hear the crowd chant that they were proud to be Egyptians! Finally, nationalism has come to Egypt and perhaps to the entire Middle East region.

The future relationship between the Palestinians and the Israelis is dependent upon the possibility of an internationally recognized independent state of Palestine. The Obama administration supported the "two state concept" believing that the United States could be supportive of Israel while at the same time, recognizing the need for the Palestinian people to exercise their rights to self-determination and have their own country. Then Secretary of State John Kerry spearheaded a series of high-level talks between the Israeli and Palestinian governments. Meanwhile, Israel's Prime Minister Binyamin Netanyahu gave the green light to continuing building settlements further into the land the Palestinians claim historical title to. The Trump administration signaled its opposition to the "two-state" solution when the United States officially recognized Jerusalem as Israel's capital and became relocating the American embassy from Tel Aviv to Jerusalem.

International Terrorism and Afghanistan

American intelligence has laid the responsibility for the attacks on the World Trade Center definitively and accurately on the Al Qaeda terrorist organization founded by Osama bin Laden. Unfortunately, Al Qaeda is a worldwide organization composed of ideologically joined but operationally separate independent cells located throughout the world to include first-world power nation states. The hunt for bin Laden focused in the mountainous region between Afghanistan and Pakistan. On May 2, 2011, a special attachment of Navy Seals successfully entered into Pakistan and killed bin Laden. When the news broke, many Americans celebrated his demise across the country particularly at the gates of the White House.

Just eliminating bin Laden has not eliminated Al Qaeda. The rebels trying to oust the Assad government in Syria welcomed anyone who crossed the border into Syria to join their cause. Originating in 1999 in support of Al Qaeda, the **Islamic State of Iraq and the Levant** (ISIL) also known as **ISIS, Islamic State** (IS) and **Daesh** (the official Arabic name), ISIS became an international household name as it successfully ousted Iraqi forces from key cities in Western Iraq, captured the city of Mosul, and spearheaded the Sinjar massacre. ISIS is now designated a terrorist organization by the United Nations and condemned by international human rights organizations for its brutality and violations of basic human rights. In Syria, ISIS has conducted groups attacks on both government forces and opposition factions butting heads in the Syria civil war as well as captured territory in Western Iraq. Syrian rebel forces have and will continue to request assistance from the United States. Al Qaeda has surfaced in Iraq, particularly in Fallujah and Anbar Providence, Libya, and Iran. Whenever ISIS captures a city, it holds civilians as hostages, brutally kills its military enemies, destroys ancient temples and buildings, and sells ancient relics through the black market to fund its organization. Today's defeat of ISIS could very well be tomorrow's victory and vice versa. It takes a coalition of forces to battle ISIS. For example, the Syrian city of Palmyra was "liberated" from ISIS through the efforts of the Lebanese Hezbollah, Russian and Syrian ground forces, and United States airstrikes. ISIS took Palmyra in December 2016, after eighteen months of constant warfare with Syrian-backed allied forces. "This is the fourth time that Palmyra has changed hands in less than two years, and each time its renowned ruins have been further damaged. "[101] The question now is how long the Syrian government can hold onto the city before ISIS strikes again.

The situation in Afghanistan is further complicated by the struggles between the government and the Taliban. Guided by the traditional Muslim philosophy, the Taliban once ruled over Afghanistan but was ousted. The Taliban has continued their attacks, keeping the ill-equipped Afghanistan military along with American troop support fighting village to village without an end in sight. When he first took office, Obama supported a military surge to oust the Taliban. Yet, every military victory was offset by a defeat. Some have coined the American effort in Afghanistan Obama's Vietnam. As long as bin Laden was alive, Americans supported, although reluctantly so, the commitment of American military forces in Afghanistan. However, the support evaporated once bin Laden was dead. Frustrated by the inept Afghan military, Obama decided to completely withdraw American forces. However, the Obama administration along with NATO officials wanted the Karzai government to sign a security agreement giving the United States an opening to send armed troops into Afghanistan if the security of the nation is compromised by either an invasion or an internal insurgency, particularly from the Taliban. Karzai has refused to sign the agreement. American military forces were scheduled to depart by the end of 2014. The situation became even more complicated when Karzai was defeated in his re-election bid. The Biden foreign policy team must now deal with President Ashraf Ghani Ahjadzai.

CONCLUSIONS

Unlike domestic policy issues, foreign policy decisions impact not only the people back home but also the entire international community. Foreign policy is not benevolent. Every nation state develops its foreign policy responses around its own vital interests. International agreements, compacts, treaties and even wars are geared towards the pursuit of an individual nation state's vital interests.

CHAPTER NOTES

[1] *Treasury of Presidential Quotations*, Caroline Thomas Harnsberger, ed., (Chicago, Illinois: Follett Publishing Company, 1964), 96.

[2] Ibid., 104.

[3] *The International Relations Dictionary,* Jack C. Plano and Roy Olton, eds., (New York, New York: Holt, Reinhart and Winston, Inc., 1969), 127.

[4] Ibid., 313.

[5] Ibid., 120.

[6] Ibid., 58.

[7] Ibid., 45.

[8] Ibid., 128.

[9] Ibid., 121.

[10] Gabriel A. Almond, G. Bingham Powell, Jr., Kaare Strom, and Russell J. Dalton, *Comparative Politics Today: A World View,* 8th ed., (New York, New York: Pearson, Longman, 2004), 12.

[11] Ibid.

[12]Harnsberger, 96.

[13]Susan Welch, JohnGruhl, Michael Steinman, John Comer, and Susan M. Rigdon, *American Government*, 5th ed., (Minneapolis/St. Paul, Wisconsin: West Publishing Co., 1994) 631-632.

[14]*The International Relations Dictionary*, 262.

[15]*The HarperCollins Dictionary of American Government and Politics*, Jay M. Shafritz, ed., (New York, New York: HarperCollins Publishers, Inc., 1992) 305.

[16]Oona Hathaway, "Reengaging on Treaties and Other International Agreements (Part 1: President Donald Trump's Rejection of International Law," *https://www.justsecurity.org*

[17]Ibid.

[18]*The International Relations Dictionary*, 49.

[19]Robert Ergang, *Europe Since Waterloo*, 3rd ed., (Lexington, Massachusetts: D. C. Heath and Company, 1967), 38.

[20]Ibid., 39

[21]*The International Relations Dictionary*, 124.

[22]Ibid.

[23]Ibid., 292.

[24]Fred W. Wellborn, *Diplomatic History of the United States,* 2nd ed., (Totowa, New Jersey: Littlefield, Adams & Co., 1962), 367.

[25]Richard W. Leopold, *The Growth of American Foreign Policy: A History,* (New York, New York: Alfred A. Knopf, 1962), 374.

[26]*Treasury of Presidential Quotations*, 172.

[27]Ibid.

[28]Ibid. 221.

[29]Leopold, 629.

[30]*Treasury of Presidential Quotations*, 154.

[31]Ibid.

[32]Ibid., 104

[33]*The International Relations Dictionary*, 216.

[34]Ibid., 62.

[35]Ibid.

[36]*The HarperCollins Dictionary of American Government and Politics*, 289.

[37]*The International Relations Dictionary*, 114.

[38]Stephen Kinzer, "When Titans Tangled," *American History*, Vol. 52, No. 4, October, 2017, 42.

[39]*The HarperCollins Dictionary of American Government and Politics*, 177.

[40]*The American Political Dictionary,* Jack C. Plano and Milton Greenberg, eds., 10th ed., (Fort Worth, Texas: Harcourt Brace College Publishers, 1997), 583.

[41]Henry j. Hendrix, II, "T.R.'s Virtuous Performance," *American History*, Vol. 38, No. 6, February, 2004, 46.

[42]*The International Relations Dictionary*, 62.

[43]"Congressional Budget Justification: Department of State, Foreign Operations, and Related Programs-Fiscal Year 2017," Department of State, February 9, 2016, 1 (https://www.usaid.gov)

[44]Ibid.

[45]Zachary B. Wolf and JoElla Carman, "Here Are All the Treaties and Agreements Trump Has Abandoned," *CNN Politics*, *https://www/cnn.com/2019/02/21*

[46]*The International Relations Dictionary*, 77.

[47]Ibid.

[48]Ibid., 49.

[49]Ibid., 64.

[50]Ibid., 77.

[51]Ibid., 73.

[52]Guillermo Contrereas, "Bataan Death March Survivors Hear Apology," *San Antonio Express-News,* (Sunday, May 31, 2009), 1A.

[53]The International Criminal Court; The Mandate of the International Criminal Court, *https://www.hrw.org*

[54]Ibid.

55 *The International Relations Dictionary*, 68.

56 Ibid., 57.

57 Ibid., 115.

58 Ibid., 15.

59 U.S. Census Bureau, "Trade in Goods with World, Seasonally Adjusted," *https://www/census.gov*

60 *The International Relations Dictionary*, 39.

61 Ibid., 30.

62 David Adler, "The Constitution and Presidential Warmaking: The Enduring Debate," *Political Science Quarterly*, Vol. 103, Spring, 1988, 15.

63 Ibid., 9.

64 Ibid.

65 Louis Fisher, *Constitutional Conflicts Between the Congress and the President*, 5th ed., revised, (Lawrence, Kansas: University of Kansas Press, 2007), 250.

66 Adler, "The Constitution and Presidential Warmaking: The Enduring Debate," 12.

67 "The Federalist No. 69", Alexander Hamilton, John Jay and James Madison, *The Federalist,* (New York, New York: The Modern Library, 1937), 448.

68 Adler, "The Constitution and Presidential Warmaking: The Enduring Debate," 5.

69 Virginia Stowitts, Chrstine Schultz, Theresia Stewart, and Karen Sunshine, *The Study Guide and Reader for American Government and Politics in the New Millennium*, 6th ed., (Wheaton, Illinois: Abigail Press, 2007), 279.

70 Ibid., 280.

71 Theodore J. Lowi, "Presidential Power: Restoring the Balance," *Political Science Quarterly*, Vol. 100, No. 2, Summer, 1985, 191.

72 Thomas E. Patterson, *We The People: A Concise Introduction to American Politics,* 8th ed., (New York, New York: McGraw Kill, 2009), 450-451.

73 Fisher, 274.

74 Richard M. Pious, *The Presidency,* (Boston, Massachusetts: Allyn and Bacon, 1996) 459.

75 Charlie Savage and Mark Landler, "White House Stands Firm on Libya Action," *San Antonio Express-News* (Thursday, June 16, 2011), 11A.

76 Lowi, "Presidential Power: Restoring the Balance," 192.

77 Raoul Berger, *Executive Privilege: A Constitutional Myth,* (Boston, Massachusetts: Harvard University Press, 1974), 146.

78 *The Enduring Federalist*, Charles A. Beard, ed., 2nd ed., (New York, New York: Frederick Ungar Publishing Co., 1964), 318-319.

79 Michael Kernan, "In 1789, A Farmer Went to New York to Become President," *Smithsonian*, Vol.20, No. 3, June, 1989, 103.

80 Arthur Schlisinger, *The Imperial Presidency*, (Boston, Massachusetts: Houghton Mifflin Co., 1973), 90.

81 *American Political Dictionary*, 190.

82 Amy Gilbert, *Executive Agreements and Treaties, 1946-1973: Framework of the Foreign Policy Period,* (New York: New York: Thomas-Newell, 1973), 3.

83 Loch K. Johnson, *The Making of International Agreements: Congress Confronts the Executive*, (New York, New York: New York University Press, 1984), 24.

84 Thomas M. Franck and Edward Weisband, *Foreign Policy By Congress*, (New York, New York: Oxford University Press, 1970), 145.

85 *The HarperCollins Dictionary of American Government and Politics*, 214.

86 *The World Almanac and Book of Facts 2021*, Brainerd Minnesota: Bang Printing, 2020, 134 and 137.

87 "Conference of July 22 with Pentagon Officials on Committing Large Number of Troops to Vietnam," *Lyndon Johnson and American Liberalism: A Brief Biography with Documents*, Bruce J. Schulman, ed., 2nd ed., (Boston, Massachusetts: Bedford/St. Martins, 2007), 253-255.

88 Leopold, 36.

89 Ibid.

90 Wayne S. Cole, "Myths Surrounding the Monroe Doctrine," *Myth and the American Experience,* Vol. 1, Nicholas

Cords and Patrick Gerster, eds., 2nd ed., (Encino, California: Glencoe Publishing Co., Inc., 1978), 218-219.

[91]William J. Duiker and Jackson J. Spielvogel, *World History,* 3rd ed., (Belmont, California: Wadsworth, 2001), 734.

[92]James West Davidson, William E. Gienapp, Christine Leigh Heyrman, Mark II.Lytle, and Michael B. Stoff, *Nations of Nations: A Narrative History of the American Republic,* (New York, N. Y.: McGraw Hill Publishing Company, 1990), 889.

[93]Wellborn, 364.

[94]Neil MacFarquhar, "N. Korea Faces New Sanctions," *San Antonio Express-News,* (Saturday, June 13, 2009), 1A.

[95]"U.S. Stops Short of Calling China a Currency Manipulator," *San Antonio Express-News* (Wednesday, November 28, 2012), A7.

[96]Ryan Hass and Abraham Denmark, "More Pain Than Gain: How the U.S.-China Trade War Hurts America," *https://www.brookings.edu*

[97]Ibid.

[98]Ibid.

[99]Tom Lee and Jacqueline Varas, "The Total Cost of Trump's Tariffs," *https://www.americanactionforum.org*

[100]Jen Kirby, "USMCA, Trump's New NAFTA Deal, Explained in 600 Words," *https://www/vox.com*

[101]"Syria's Palmyra Again in Hands of the Government." *San Antonio Express-News,* (Friday, March, 3, 2017), A13.

SUGGESTED READINGS

Charles W. Kegley, Jr., and Eugene R. Wittkopf, *American Foreign Policy: Pattern and Process,* 3rd ed., New York, New York: St. Martins Press, 1987.

Charles W. Kegley, Jr., and Eugene R. Wittkopf, *The Future of American Foreign Policy,* New York, New York: St. Martins Press, 1992.

Frederick H. Hartmann, *American's Foreign Policy in a Changing World,* New York, New York: HarperCollins College Publishers, 2004.

G. John Ikenberry, *American Foreign Policy: Theoretical Essays,* Glenview, Illinois: Scott, Foresman and Company, 1989.

Hans J. Morgenthau, *Politics Among Nations: The Struggle for Power and Peace,* 7th ed., Boston, Massachusetts: McGraw Hill High Education, 2006.

John T. Rourke, *International Politics on the World Stage,* 4th ed., Guilford, Connecticut: Dushkin Publishing Group, Inc., 1993.

Joshua S. Goldstein, *International Relations,* New York, New York: HarperCollings College Publishers, 1994.

Louis Fisher, *Constitutional Conflicts Between Congress and the President,* 5th ed., Lawrence, Kansas: University Press of Kansas, 2007.

Web Sites:

www.archives.gov/presidential-libraries/visit/ - Presidential Libraries
www.Realhistoryarchives.com/collections/conspiracies/irancontra.htm - Iran/Contra
www.library.umass/edu/subject/iraqwar - Iraq War 2003 Links
www.nytimes.com
www.cnn.com
www.fsmitha.com/h2/ch26.htm - Vietnam War
www.pbs.org/wgbh/amex/china/ - Détente
www.gwu.edu/~nsarchiv/nsa/publications/DOC_readers/kissinger/nixzhou/ - Détente

Declaration of Independence

Congress, July 4, 1776

When, in the course of human events, it becomes necessary for one people to dissolve the political bonds which have connected them with another, and to assume, among the powers of the earth, the separate and equal station to which the laws of nature and of nature's God entitle them, a decent respect to the opinions of mankind requires that they should declare the causes which impel them to the separation.

We hold these truths to be self-evident: That all men are created equal; that they are endowed by their Creator with certain unalienable rights; that among these are life, liberty and the pursuit of happiness; that, to secure these rights, governments are instituted among men, deriving their just powers from the consent of the governed; that whenever any form of government becomes destructive of these ends, it is the right of the people to alter or to abolish it, and to institute new government, laying its foundation on such principles, and organizing its powers in such form, as to them shall seem most likely to effect their safety and happiness. Prudence, indeed, will dictate that governments long established should not be changed for light and transient causes; and accordingly all experience hath shown that mankind are more disposed to suffer, while evils are sufferable, than to right themselves by abolishing the forms to which they are accustomed. But when a long train of abuses and usurpations, pursuing invariably the same object, evinces a design to reduce them under absolute despotism, it is their right, it is their duty, to throw off such government, and to provide new guards for their future security. Such has been the patient sufferance of these colonies; and such is now the necessity which constrains them to alter their former systems of government. The history of the present King of Great Britain is a history of repeated injuries and usurpations, all having in direct object the establishment of an absolute tyranny over these states. To prove this, let facts be submitted to a candid world.

He has refused his assent to laws, the most wholesome and necessary for the public good.

He has forbidden his governors to pass laws of immediate and pressing importance, unless suspended in their operation till his assent should be obtained; and, when so suspended, he has utterly neglected to attend to them.

He has refused to pass other laws for the accommodation of large districts of people, unless those people would relinquish the right of representation in the legislature, a right inestimable to them, and for-midable to tyrants only.

He has called together legislative bodies at places unusual, uncomfortable, and distant from the depository of their public records, for the sole purpose of fatiguing them into compliance with his measures.

He has dissolved representative houses repeatedly, for opposing, with many firmness, his invasions on the rights of the people.

He has refused for a long time, after such dissolutions, to cause others to be elected; whereby the legislative powers, incapable of annihilation, have returned to the people at large for their exercise; the state remaining, in the mean time, exposed to all the dangers of invasions from without and convulsions within.

He has endeavored to prevent the population of these states; for that purpose obstructing the laws for naturalization of foreigners; refusing to pass others to encourage their migrations hither, and raising the conditions of new appropriations of lands.

He has obstructed the administration of justice, by refusing his assent to laws establishing judiciary powers.

He has made judges dependent on his will alone, for the tenure of their offices, and the amount and payment of their salaries.

He has erected a multitude of new offices, and sent hither swarms of officers to harass our people and eat out their substance.

He has kept among us, in times of peace, standing armies, without the consent of our legislatures.

He has affected to render the military independent of, and superior to, the civil power.

He has combined with others to subject us to jurisdiction foreign to our constitution, and unacknowledged by our laws, giving his assent to their acts of pretended legislation:

For quartering large bodies of armed troops among us;

For protecting them, by a mock trial, from punishment for any murder which they should commit on the inhabitants of these states;

For cutting off our trade with all parts of the world;

For imposing taxes on us without our consent;

For depriving us, in many cases, of the benefits of trial by jury;

For transporting us beyond seas, to be tried for pretended offenses;

For abolishing the free system of English laws in a neighboring province, establishing therein an arbitrary government, and enlarging its boundaries, so as to render it at once an example and fit instrument for introducing the same absolute rule into these colonies;

For taking away our charters, abolishing our most valuable laws, and altering fundamentally the forms of our governments;

For suspending our own legislatures, and declaring themselves invested with power to legislate for us in all cases whatsoever.

He has abdicated government here, by declaring us out of his protection and waging war against us.

He has plundered our seas, ravaged our coasts, burned our towns, and destroyed the lives of our people.

He is at this time transporting large armies of foreign mercenaries to complete the works of death, desolation and tyranny already begun with circumstances of cruelty and perfidy scarcely paralleled in the most barbarous ages, and totally unworthy the head of a civilized nation.

He has constrained our fellow-citizens, taken captive on the high seas, to bear arms against their country, to become the executioners of their friends and brethren, or to fall themselves by their hands.

He has excited domestic insurrections among us, and has endeavored to bring on the inhabitants of our frontiers the merciless Indian savages, whose known rule of warfare is an undistinguished destruction of all ages, sexes, and conditions.

In every stage of these oppressions we have petitioned for redress in the most humble terms; our repeated petitions have been answered only by repeated injury. A prince, whose character is thus marked by every act which may define a tyrant, is unfit to be the ruler of a free people.

Nor have we been wanting in our attentions to our British brethren. We have warned them, from time to time, of attempts by their legislature to extend an unwarrantable jurisdiction over us. We have reminded them of the circumstances of our emigration and settlement here. We have appealed to their native justice and magnanimity, and we have conjured them, by the ties of our common kindred, to disavow these usurpations, which would inevitably interrupt our connections and correspondence. They, too, have been deaf to the voice of justice and of consanguinity. We must, therefore, acquiesce in the necessity which denounces our separation, and hold them, as we hold the rest of mankind, enemies in war, in peace friends.

We, therefore, the representatives of the United States of America, in General Congress assembled, appealing to the Supreme Judge of the world for the rectitude of our intentions, do, in the name and by authority of the good people of these colonies, solemnly publish and declare, that these United Colonies are, and of right ought to be, FREE AND INDEPENDENT STATES; that they are absolved from all allegiance to the British crown, and that all political connection between them and the state of Great Britain is, and ought to be, totally dissolved; and that, as free and independent states, they have full power to levy war, conclude peace, contract alliances, establish commerce, and do all other acts and things which independent states may of right do. And for the support of this declaration, with a firm reliance on the protection of Divine Providence, we mutually pledge to each other our lives, our fortunes, and our sacred honor.

JOHN HANCOCK

BUTTON GWINNETT
LYMAN HALL
GEO. WALTON
WM. HOOPER
JOSEPH HEWES
JOHN PENN
EDWARD RUTLEDGE
THOS. HEYWARD, JUNR.
THOMAS LYNCH, JUNR.
ARTHUR MIDDLETON
SAMUEL CHASE
WM. PACA
THOS. STONE
CHARLES CARROLL OF CARROLLTON
GEORGE WYTHE
RICHARD HENRY LEE
TH. JEFFERSON
BENJ. HARRISON

THOS. NELSON, JR.
FRANCIS LIGHTFOOT LEE
CARTER BRAXTON
ROBT. MORRIS
BENJAMIN RUSH
BENJA. FRANKLIN
JOHN MORTON
GEO. CLYMER
JAS. SMITH
GEO. TAYLOR
JAMES WILSON
GEO. ROSS
CAESAR RODNEY
GEO READ
THO. M'KEAN
WM. FLOYD
PHIL. LIVINGSTON
FRANS. LEWIS
LEWIS MORRIS

RICHD. STOCKTON
JNO. WITHERSPOON
FRAS. HOPKINSON
JOHN HART
ABRA. CLARK
JOSIAH BARTLETT
WM. WHIPPLE
SAML. ADAMS
JOHN ADAMS
ROBT. TREAT PAINE
ELBRIDGE GERRY
STEP. HOPKINS
WILLIAM ELLERY
ROGER SHERMAN
SAM'EL HUNTINGTON
WM. WILLIAMS
OLIVER WOLCOTT
MATTHEW THORNTON

APPENDIX B

The Constitution of the United States of America

PREAMBLE

We the people of the United States, in order to form a more perfect union, establish justice, insure domestic tranquility, provide for the common defense, promote the general welfare, and secure the blessings of liberty to ourselves and our posterity, do ordain and establish this Constitution for the United States of America.

ARTICLE I.—THE LEGISLATIVE ARTICLE

Section 1. All legislative powers herein granted shall be vested in a Congress of the United States, which shall consist of a Senate and a House of Representatives.

House of Representatives: Composition, Qualification, Apportionment, Impeachment Power

Section 2. The House of Representatives shall be composed of members chosen every second year by the people of the several States, and the electors in each State shall have the qualifications requisite for electors of the most numerous branch of the State Legislature.

No person shall be a Representative who shall not have attained to the age of twenty-five years, and been seven years a citizen of the United States, and who shall not, when elected, be an inhabitant of that State in which he shall be chosen.

Representatives and direct taxes shall be apportioned among the several States which may be included within this Union, according to their respective numbers, *which shall be determined by adding to the whole number of free persons, including those bound to service for a term of years and excluding Indians not taxed, three-fifths of all other persons.* The actual enumeration shall be made within three years after the first meeting of the Congress of the United States, and within every subsequent term of ten years, in such manner as they shall by law direct. The number of Representatives shall not exceed one for every thirty thousand, but each State shall have at least one Representative; *and until each enumeration shall be made, the State of New Hampshire shall be entitled to choose three, Massachusetts eight, Rhode Island and Providence Plantations one, Connecticut five, New York six, New Jersey four, Pennsylvania eight, Delaware one, Maryland six, Virginia ten, North Carolina five, South Carolina five, and Georgia three.*

When vacancies happen in the representation from any State, the Executive authority thereof shall issue writs of election to fill such vacancies.

The House of Representatives shall choose their Speaker and other officers; and shall have the sole power of impeachment.

Senate Composition: Qualifications, Impeachment Trials

Section 3. The Senate of the United States shall be composed of two Senators from each State, *chosen by the legislature thereof,* for six years; and each Senator shall have one vote.

Passages no longer in effect are printed in italic type.

Immediately after they shall be assembled in consequence of the first election, they shall be divided as equally as may be into three classes. The seats of the Senators of the first class shall be vacated at the expiration of the second year, of the second class at the expiration of the fourth year, and of the third class at the expiration of the sixth year, so that one-third may be chosen every second year; and if vacancies happen by resignation or otherwise, during the recess of the legislature of any State, the Executive thereof may make temporary appointments until the next meeting of the legislature, which shall then fill such vacancies.

No person shall be a Senator who shall not have attained to the age of thirty years, and been nine years a citizen of the United States, and who shall not, when elected, be an inhabitant of that State for which he shall be chosen.

The Vice President of the United States shall be President of the Senate, but shall have no vote, unless they be equally divided.

The Senate shall choose their other officers, and also a President *pro tempore*, in the absence of the Vice President, or when he shall exercise the office of President of the United States.

The Senate shall have the sole power to try all impeachments. When sitting for that purpose, they shall be on oath or affirmation. When the President of the United States is tried, the Chief Justice shall preside: and no person shall be convicted without the concurrence of two-thirds of the members present.

Judgment in cases of impeachment shall not extend further than to removal from the office, and disqualification to hold and enjoy any office of honor, trust or profit under the United States; but the party convicted shall nevertheless be liable and subject to indictment, trial, judgment and punishment, according to law.

Congressional Elections: Time, Place, Manner

Section 4. The times, places and manner of holding elections for Senators and Representatives shall be prescribed in each State by the legislature thereof; but the Congress may at any time by law make or alter such regulations, except as to the places of choosing Senators.

The Congress shall assemble at least once in every year, and such meeting *shall be on the first Monday in December, unless they shall by law appoint a different day.*

Powers and Duties of the Houses

Section 5. Each house shall be the judge of the elections, returns and qualifications of its own members, and a majority of each shall constitute a quorum to do business; but a smaller number may adjourn from day to day, and may be authorized to compel the attendance of absent members, in such manner, and under such penalties, as each house may provide.

Each house may determine the rules of its proceedings, punish its members for disorderly behavior, and with the concurrence of two-thirds, expel a member.

Each house shall keep a journal of its proceedings, and from time to time publish the same, excepting such parts as may in their judgment require secrecy; and the yeas and nays of the members of either house on any question shall, at the desire of one-fifth of those present, be entered on the journal.

Neither house, during the session of Congress, shall, without the consent of the other, adjourn for more than three days, nor to any other place than that in which the two houses shall be sitting.

Rights of Members

Section 6. The Senators and Representatives shall receive a compensation for their services, to be ascertained by law and paid out of the treasury of the United States. They shall in all cases except treason, felony and breach of the peace, be privileged from arrest during their attendance at the session of their respective houses, and in going to and returning from the same; and for any speech or debate in either house, they shall not be questioned in any other place.

No Senator or Representative shall, during the time for which he was elected, be appointed to any civil office under the authority of the United States, which shall have been created, or the emoluments whereof shall have been increased, during such time; and no person holding any office under the United States shall be a member of either house during his continuance in office.

Legislative Powers: Bills and Resolutions

Section 7. All bills for raising revenue shall originate in the House of Representatives; but the Senate may propose or concur with amendments as on other bills.

Every bill which shall have passed the House of Representatives and the Senate, shall, before it become a law, be presented to the President of the United States; if he approve he shall sign it, but if not he shall return it with objections to that house in which it originated, who shall enter the objections at large on their journal, and proceed to reconsider it. If after such reconsideration two-thirds of that house shall agree to pass the bill, it shall be sent, together with the objections, to the other house, by which it shall likewise be reconsidered, and if approved by two-thirds of that house, it shall become a law. But in all such cases the votes of both houses shall be determined by yeas and nays, and the names of the persons voting for and against the bill shall be entered on the journal of each house respectively. If any bill shall not be returned by the President within ten days (Sundays excepted) after it shall have been presented to him, the same shall be a law, in like manner as if he had signed it, unless the Congress by their adjournment prevent its return, in which case it shall not be a law.

Every order, resolution, or vote to which the concurrence of the Senate and House of Representatives may be necessary (except on a question of adjournment) shall be presented to the President of the United States; and before the same shall take effect, shall be approved by him, or being disapproved by him, shall be repassed by two-thirds of the Senate and House of Representatives, according to the rules and limitations prescribed in the case of a bill.

Powers of Congress

Section 8. The Congress shall have power

To lay and collect taxes, duties, imposts and excises, to pay the debts and provide for the common defense and general welfare of the United States; but all duties, imposts and excises shall be uniform throughout the United States;

To borrow money on the credit of the United States;

To regulate commerce with foreign nations, and among the several States, and with the Indian tribes;

To establish an uniform rule of naturalization, and uniform laws on the subject of bankruptcies throughout the United States;

To coin money, regulate the value thereof, and of foreign coin, and fix the standard of weights and measures;

To provide for the punishment of counterfeiting the securities and current coin of the United States;

To establish post offices and post roads;

To promote the progress of science and useful arts by securing for limited times to authors and inventors the exclusive right to their respective writings and discoveries;

To constitute tribunals inferior to the Supreme Court;

To define and punish piracies and felonies committed on the high seas and offenses against the law of nations;

To declare war, grant letters of marque and reprisal, and make rules concerning captures on land and water;

To raise and support armies, but no appropriation of money to that use shall be for a longer term than two years;

To provide and maintain a navy;

To make rules for the government and regulation of the land and naval forces;

To provide for calling forth the militia to execute the laws of the Union, suppress insurrections, and repel invasions;

To provide for organizing, arming, and disciplining the militia, and for governing such part of them as may be employed in the service of the United States, reserving to the States respectively the appointment of the officers, and the authority of training the militia according to the discipline prescribed by Congress;

To exercise exclusive legislation in all cases whatsoever, over such district (not exceeding ten miles square) as may, by cession of particular States, and the acceptance of Congress, become the seat of the government of the United States, and to exercise like authority over all places purchased by the consent of the legislature of the State, in which the same shall be, for erection of forts, magazines, arsenals, dock-yards, and other needful buildings;—and

To make all laws which shall be necessary and proper for carrying into execution the foregoing powers, and all other powers vested by this Constitution in the government of the United States, or in any department or officer thereof.

Powers Denied to Congress

Section 9. *The migration or importation of such persons as any of the States now existing shall think proper to admit shall not be prohibited by the Congress prior to the year 1808; but a tax or duty may be imposed on such importation, not exceeding $10 for each person.*

The privilege of the writ of habeas corpus shall not be suspended, unless when in cases of rebellion or invasion the public safety may require it.

No bill of attainder or ex post facto law shall be passed.

No capitation, or other direct, tax shall be laid, unless in proportion to the census or enumeration herein before directed to be taken.

No tax or duty shall be laid on articles exported from any State.

No preference shall be given by any regulation of commerce or revenue to the ports of one State over those of another; nor shall vessels bound to, or from, one State, be obliged to enter, clear, or pay duties in another.

No money shall be drawn from the treasury, but in consequence of appropriations made by law; and a regular statement and account of the receipts and expenditures of all public money shall be published from time to time.

No title of nobility shall be granted by the United States; and no person holding any office of profit or trust under them, shall, without the consent of the Congress, accept of any present, emolument, office, or title, of any kind whatever, from any king, prince, or foreign state.

Powers Denied to the States

Section 10. No State shall enter into any treaty, alliance, or confederation; grant letters of marque and reprisal; coin money; emit bills of credit; make anything but gold and silver coin a tender in payment of debts; pass any bill of attainder, ex post facto law, or law impairing the obligation of contracts, or grant any title of nobility.

No State shall, without the consent of the Congress, lay any imposts or duties on imports or exports, except what may be absolutely necessary for executing its inspection laws: and the net produce of all duties and imposts, laid by any State on imports or exports, shall be for the use of the treasury of the United States; and all such laws shall be subject to the revision and control of the Congress.

No State shall, without the consent of Congress, lay any duty of tonnage, keep troops or ships of war in time of peace, enter into any agreement or compact with another State, or with a foreign power, or engage in war, unless actually invaded, or in such imminent danger as will not admit of delay.

ARTICLE II.—THE EXECUTIVE ARTICLE

Nature and Scope of Presidential Power

Section 1. The executive power shall be vested in a President of the United States of America. He shall hold his office during the term of four years, and, together with the Vice President, chosen for the same term, be elected, as follows:

Each State shall appoint, in such manner as the legislature thereof may direct, a number of electors, equal to the whole number of Senators and Representatives to which the State may be entitled in the Congress; but no Senator or Representative, or person holding an office of trust or profit under the United States, shall be appointed an elector.

The electors shall meet in their respective States, and vote by ballot for two persons, of whom one at least shall not be an inhabitant of the same State with themselves. And they shall make a list of all the persons voted for, and of the number of votes for each; which list they shall sign and certify, and transmit sealed to the seat of government of the United States, directed to the President of the Senate. The President of the Senate shall, in the presence of the Senate and House of Representatives, open all the certificates, and the votes shall then be counted. The person having the greatest number of votes shall be the President, if such number be a majority of the whole number of electors appointed; and if there be more than one who have such majority, and have an equal number of votes, then the House of Representatives shall immediately choose by ballot one of them for President; and if no person have a majority, then from the five highest on the list said house shall in like manner choose the President. But in choosing the President the votes shall be taken by States, the representation from each State having one vote; a quorum for this purpose shall consist of a member or members from two-thirds of the States, and a majority of all the States shall be necessary to a choice. In every case, after the choice of the President, the person having the greatest number of votes of the electors shall be the Vice President. But if there should remain two or more who have equal votes, the Senate shall choose from them by ballot the Vice President.

The Congress may determine the time of choosing the electors, and the day on which they shall give their votes; which day shall be the same throughout the United States.

No person except a natural-born citizen, *or a citizen of the United States at the time of the adoption of this Constitution*, shall be eligible to the office of President; neither shall any person be eligible to that office who shall not have attained to the age of thirty-five years, and been fourteen years a resident within the United States.

In case of the removal of the President from office or of his death, resignation, or inability to discharge the powers and duties of the said office, the same shall devolve on the Vice President, and the Congress may by law provide for the case of removal, death, resignation, or inability, both of the President and Vice President, declaring what officer shall then act as President, and such officer shall act accordingly, until the disability be removed, or a President shall be elected.

The President shall, at stated times, receive for his services a compensation, which shall neither be increased nor diminished during the period for which he shall have been elected, and he shall not receive within that period any other emolument from the United States, or any of them.

Before he enter on the execution of his office, he shall take the following oath or affirmation: —"I do solemnly swear (or affirm) that I will faithfully execute the office of President of the United States, and will to the best of my ability preserve, protect, and defend the Constitution of the United States."

Powers and Duties of the President

Section 2. The President shall be the commander in chief of the army and navy of the United States, and of the militia of the several States, when called into the actual service of the United States; he may require the opinion, in writing, of the principal officer in each of the executive departments, upon any subject relating to the duties of their respective offices, and he shall have power to grant reprieves and pardons for offenses against the United States, except in cases of impeachment.

He shall have power, by and with the advice and consent of the Senate, to make treaties, provided two-thirds of the Senators present concur; and he shall nominate, and by and with the advice and consent of the Senate, shall appoint ambassadors, other public ministers and consuls, judges of the Supreme Court, and all other officers of the United States, whose appointments are not herein otherwise provided for, and which shall be established by law: but the Congress may by law vest the appointment of such inferior officers, as they think proper, in the President alone, in the courts of law, or in the heads of departments.

The President shall have power to fill up all vacancies that may happen during the recess of the Senate, by granting commissions which shall expire at the end of their next session.

Section 3. He shall from time to time give to the Congress information of the state of the Union, and recommend to their consideration such measures as he shall judge necessary and expedient; he may, on extraordinary occasions, convene both houses, or either of them, and in case of disagreement between them, with respect to the time of adjournment, he may adjourn them to such time as he shall think proper; he shall receive ambassadors and other public ministers; he shall take care that the laws be faithfully executed, and shall commission all the officers of the United States.

Section 4. The President, Vice President and all civil officers of the United States shall be removed from office on impeachment for, and on conviction of, treason, bribery, or other high crimes and misdemeanor.

ARTICLE III.—THE JUDICIAL ARTICLE

Section 1. The judicial power of the United States shall be vested in one Supreme Court, and in such inferior courts as the Congress may from time to time ordain and establish. The judges, both of the Supreme and inferior courts, shall hold their offices during good behavior, and shall, at stated times, receive for their services a compensation which shall not be diminished during their continuance in office.

Jurisdiction

Section 2. The judicial power shall extend to all cases, in law and equity, arising under this Constitution, the laws of the United States, and treaties made, or which shall be made, under their authority;—to all cases affecting ambassadors, other public ministers and consuls;—to all cases of admiralty and maritime jurisdiction;—to controversies to which the United States shall be a party;—to controversies between two or more States;—*between a state and citizens of another state*;—between citizens of different States;—between citizens of the same State claiming lands under grants of different States, and between a State, or the citizens thereof, and foreign states, citizens or subjects.

In all cases affecting ambassadors, other public ministers and consuls, and those in which a State shall be party, the Supreme Court shall have original jurisdiction. In all the other cases before mentioned, the Supreme Court shall have appellate jurisdiction, both as to law and fact, with such exceptions, and under such regulations, as the Congress shall make.

The trial of all crimes, except in cases of impeachment, shall be by jury; and such trial shall be held in the State where said crimes shall have been committed; but when not committed within any State, the trial shall be at such place or places as the Congress may by law have directed.

Treason

Section 3. Treason against the United States shall consist only in levying war against them, or in adhering to their enemies, giving them aid and comfort. No person shall be convicted of treason unless on the testimony of two witnesses to the same overt act, or on confession in open court.

The Congress shall have power to declare the punishment of treason, but no attainder of treason shall work corruption of blood, or forfeiture except during the life of the person attained.

ARTICLE IV.—INTERSTATE RELATIONS

Full Faith and Credit Clause

Section 1. Full Faith and credit shall be given in each State to the public acts, records, and judicial proceedings of every other State. And the Congress may by general laws prescribe the manner in which such acts, records and proceedings shall be proved, and the effect thereof.

Privileges and Immunities; Interstate Extradition

Section 2. The citizens of each State shall be entitled to all privileges and immunities of citizens in the several States.

A person charged in any State with treason, felony or other crime, who shall flee from justice, and be found in another State, shall on demand of the executive authority of the State from which he fled, be delivered up, to be removed to the State having jurisdiction of the crime.

No person held to service or labor in one State, under the laws thereof, escaping into another, shall, in consequence of any law or regulation therein, be discharged from such service or labor, but shall be delivered up on claim of the party to whom such service or labor may be due.

Admission of States

Section 3. New States may be admitted by the Congress into this Union; but no new State shall be formed or erected within the jurisdiction of any other State; nor any State be formed by the junc-
tion of two or more States, or parts of States, without the consent of the legislatures of the States concerned as well as of the Congress.

The Congress shall have power to dispose of and make all needful rules and regulations respecting the territory or other property belonging to the United States; and nothing in this Constitution shall be so construed as to prejudice any claims of the United States, or of any particular State.

Republican Form of Government

Section 4. The United States shall guarantee to every State in this Union a republican form of government, and shall protect each of them against invasion; and on application of the legislature, or of the executive (when the legislature cannot be convened) against domestic violence.

ARTICLE V.—THE AMENDING POWER

The Congress, whenever two-thirds of both houses shall deem it necessary, shall propose amendments to this Constitution, or, on the application of the legislatures of two-thirds of the several States, shall call a convention for proposing amendments, which, in either case, shall be valid to all intents and purposes, as part of this Constitution, when ratified by the legislatures of three-fourths of the several States, or by conventions in three-fourths thereof, as the one or the other mode of ratification may be proposed by the Congress; *provided that no amendment which may be made prior to the year one thousand eight hundred and eight shall in any manner affect the first and fourth clauses in the ninth section of the first article*; and that no State, without its consent, shall be deprived of its equal suffrage in the Senate.

ARTICLE VI.—THE SUPREMACY ACT

All debts contracted and engagements entered into, before the adoption of this Constitution, shall be as valid against the United States under this Constitution, as under the Confederation.

This Constitution, and the laws of the United States which shall be made in pursuance thereof; and all treaties made, or which shall be made, under the authority of the United States, shall be the supreme law of the land; and the judges in every State shall be bound thereby, anything in the Constitution or laws of any State to the contrary notwithstanding.

The Senators and Representatives before mentioned, and the members of the several State legislatures, and all executive and judicial officers, both of the United States and of the several States, shall be bound by oath or affirmation to support this Constitution; but no religious test shall ever be required as a qualification to any office or public trust under the United States.

ARTICLE VII.—RATIFICATION

The ratification of the conventions of nine States shall be sufficient for the establishment of this Constitution between States so ratifying the same.

Done in Convention by the unanimous consent of the States present, the seventeenth day of September in the year of our Lord one thousand seven hundred and eighty-seven and of the Independence of the United States of America the twelfth. In witness whereof we have hereunto subscribed our names.

GEORGE WASHINGTON
President and Deputy from Virginia

New Hampshire
JOHN LANGDON
NICHOLAS GILMAN

Massachusetts
NATHANIEL GORHAM
RUFUS KING

Connecticut
WILLIAM S. JOHNSON
ROGER SHERMAN

Virginia
JOHN BLAIR
JAMES MADISON, JR

South Carolina
J. RUTLEDGE
CHARLES G. PINCKNEY
PIERCE BUTLER

New York
ALEXANDER HAMILTON

New Jersey
WILLIAM LIVINGSTON
DAVID BREARLEY
WILLIAM PATERSON
JONATHAN DAYTON

Pennsylvania
BENJAMIN FRANKLIN
THOMAS MIFFLIN
ROBERT MORRIS
GEORGE CLYMER
THOMAS FITZSIMONS
JARED INGERSOLL
JAMES WILSON
GOUVERNEUR MORRIS

Delaware
GEORGE READ
GUNNING BEDFORD, JR.
JOHN DICKINSON
RICHARD BASSETT
JACOB BROOM

Maryland
JAMES MCHENRY
DANIEL OF ST. THOMAS JENIFER
DANIEL CARROLL

North Carolina
WILLIAM BLOUNT
RICHARD DOBBS SPRAIGHT
HU WILLIAMSON

Georgia
WILLIAM FEW
ABRAHAM BALDWIN

THE BILL OF RIGHTS

The first ten Amendments (the Bill of Rights) were adopted in 1791.

AMENDMENT I.—RELIGION, SPEECH ASSEMBLY, AND PETITION

Congress shall make no law respecting an establishment of religion, or prohibiting the free exercise thereof; or abridging the freedom of speech, or of the press; or the right of the people peaceably to assemble, and to petition the government for a redress of grievances.

AMENDMENT II.—MILITIA AND THE RIGHT TO BEAR ARMS

A well-regulated militia being necessary to the security of a free State, the right of the people to keep and bear arms shall not be infringed.

AMENDMENT III.—QUARTERING OF SOLDIERS

No soldier shall, in time of peace, be quartered in any house without the consent of the owner, nor in time of war, but in a manner to be prescribed by law.

AMENDMENT IV.—SEARCHES AND SEIZURES

The right of the people to be secure in their persons, houses, papers, and effects, against unreasonable searches and seizures, shall not be violated, and no warrants shall issue but upon probable cause, supported by oath or affirmation, and particularly describing the place to be searched, and the persons or things to be seized.

AMENDMENT V.—GRAND JURIES, SELF-INCRIMINATION, DOUBLE JEOPARDY, DUE PROCESS, AND EMINENT DOMAIN

No person shall be held to answer for a capital, or otherwise infamous crime, unless on a presentment or indictment of a grand jury, except in cases arising in the land or naval forces, or in the militia, when in actual service in time of war or public danger; nor shall any person be subject for the same offense to be twice put in jeopardy of life or limb; nor shall be compelled in any criminal case to be a witness against himself, nor be deprived of life, liberty, or property, without due process of law; nor shall private property be taken for public use without just compensation.

AMENDMENT VI.—CRIMINAL COURT PROCEDURES

In all criminal prosecutions, the accused shall enjoy the right to a speedy and public trial, by an impartial jury of the State and district wherein the crime shall have been committed, which district shall have been previously ascertained by law, and to be informed of the nature and cause of the accusation; to be confronted with the witnesses against him; to have compulsory process for obtaining witnesses in his favor, and to have the assistance of counsel for his defense.

AMENDMENT VII.—TRIAL BY JURY IN COMMON LAW CASES

In suits at common law, where the value in controversy shall exceed twenty dollars, the right of trial by jury shall be preserved, and no fact tried by a jury shall be otherwise reexamined in any court of the United States, than according to the rules of the common law.

AMENDMENT VIII.—BAIL, CRUEL AND UNUSUAL PUNISHMENT

Excessive bail shall not be required, nor excessive fines imposed, nor cruel and unusual punishments inflicted.

AMENDMENT IX.—RIGHTS RETAINED BY THE PEOPLE

The enumeration in the Constitution, of certain rights, shall not be construed to deny or disparage others retained by the people.

AMENDMENT X.—RESERVED POWERS OF THE STATES

The powers not delegated to the United States by the Constitution, nor prohibited by it to the States, are reserved to the States respectively, or to the people.

PRE-CIVIL WAR AMENDMENTS

AMENDMENT XI.—SUITS AGAINST THE STATES
[Adopted 1798]

The judicial power of the United States shall not be construed to extend to any suit in law or equity, commenced or prosecuted against one of the United States by citizens of another State, or by citizens or subjects of any foreign state.

AMENDMENT XII.—ELECTION OF THE PRESIDENT
[Adopted 1804]

The electors shall meet in their respective *States*, and vote by ballot for President and Vice President, one of whom, at least, shall not be an inhabitant of the same State with themselves; they shall name in their ballots the person voted for as President, and in distinct ballots the person voted for as Vice President, and they shall make distinct lists of all persons voted for as President, and of all persons voted for as Vice President, and of the number of votes for each, which lists they shall sign and certify, and transmit sealed to the seat of the government of the United States, directed to the President of the Senate;—the President of the Senate shall, in the presence of the Senate and House of Representatives, open all the certificates and the votes shall then be counted;—the person having the greatest number of votes for President shall be the President, if such number be a majority of the whole number of electors appointed; and if no person have such majority, then from the persons having the highest numbers not exceeding three on the list of those voted for as President, the House of Representatives shall choose immediately, by ballot, the President. But in choosing the President, the votes shall be taken by States, the representation from each State having one vote; a quorum for this purpose shall consist of a member or members from two-thirds of the States, and a majority of all the States shall be necessary to a choice. And if the House of Representatives shall not choose a President whenever the right of choice shall devolve upon them, before *the fourth day of March* next following, then the Vice President shall act as President, as in the case of the death or other constitutional disability of the President.

 The person having the greatest number of votes as Vice President shall be the Vice President, if such a number be a majority of the whole number of electors appointed; and if no person have a majority, then from the two highest numbers on the list the Senate shall choose the Vice President; a quorum for the purpose shall consist of two-thirds of the whole number of Senators, and a majority of the whole number shall be necessary to a choice. But no person constitutionally ineligible to the office of President shall be eligible to that of Vice President of the United States.

CIVIL WAR AMENDMENTS

AMENDMENT XIII.—PROHIBITION OF SLAVERY
[Adopted 1865]

Section 1. Neither slavery nor involuntary servitude, except as a punishment for crime whereof the party shall have been duly convicted, shall exist within the United States, or any place subject to their jurisdiction.

Section 2. Congress shall have power to enforce this article by appropriate legislation.

AMENDMENT XIV.—CITIZENSHIP, DUE PROCESS, AND EQUAL PROTECTION OF THE LAWS
[Adopted 1868]

Section 1. All persons born or naturalized in the United States, and subject to the jurisdiction thereof, are citizens of the United States and of the State wherein they reside. No State shall make or enforce any law which shall abridge **the privileges or immunities** of citizens of the United States; nor shall any State deprive any person of life, liberty, or property, without **due process of law**; nor deny to any person within its jurisdiction the **equal protection of the laws**.

Section 2. Representatives shall be apportioned among the several States according to their respective numbers, counting the whole number of persons in each State, excluding Indians not taxed. But when the right to vote at any election for the choice of Electors for President and Vice President of the United States, Representatives in Congress, the executive and judicial officers of a State, or the members of the legislature thereof, is denied to any of the male inhabitants of such State, being twenty-one years of age and citizens of the United States, or in any way abridged, except for participation in rebellion, or other crime, the basis of representation therein shall be reduced in the proportion which the number of such male citizens shall bear to the whole number of male citizens twenty-one years of age in such State.

Section 3. No person shall be a Senator or Representative in Congress, or Elector of President and Vice President, or hold any office, civil or military, under the United States, or under any State, who, having previously taken an oath, as a member of Congress, or as an officer of the United States, or as a member of any State legislature, or as an executive or judicial officer of any State, to support the Constitution of the United States, shall have engaged in insurrection or rebellion against the same, or given aid or comfort to the enemies thereof. Congress may, by a vote of two-thirds of each house, remove such disability.

Section 4. The validity of the public debt of the United States, authorized by law, including debts incurred for payment of pensions and bounties for services in suppressing insurrection or rebellion, shall not be questioned. But neither the United States nor any State shall assume or pay any debt or obligation incurred in aid of insurrection or rebellion against the United States, or any claim for the loss or emancipation of any slave; but all such debts, obligations and claims shall be held illegal and void.

Section 5. The Congress shall have power to enforce, by appropriate legislation, the provisions of this article.

AMENDMENT XV.—THE RIGHT TO VOTE
[Adopted 1870]

Section 1. The right of citizens of the United State to vote shall not be denied or abridged by the United States or by any State on account of race, color, or previous condition of servitude.

Section 2. The Congress shall have power to enforce this article by appropriate legislation.

AMENDMENT XVI.—INCOME TAXES
[Adopted 1913]

The Congress shall have power to lay and collect taxes on incomes, from whatever source derived, without apportionment among the several States, and without regard to any census or enumeration.

AMENDMENT XVII.—DIRECT ELECTION OF SENATORS
[Adopted 1913]

Section 1. The Senate of the United States shall be composed of two Senators from each State, elected by the people thereof, for six years; and each Senator shall have one vote. The electors in each State shall have the qualifications requisite for electors of (voters for) the most numerous branch of the State legislatures.

Section 2. When vacancies happen in the representation of any State in the Senate, the executive authority of such State shall issue writs of election to fill such vacancies: Provided, that the Legislature of any State may empower the executive thereof to make temporary appointments until the people fill the vacancies by election as the Legislature may direct.

Section 3. This amendment shall not be so construed as to affect the election or term of any Senator chosen before it becomes valid as part of the Constitution.

AMENDMENT XVIII.—PROHIBITION
[Adopted 1919; Repealed 1933]

Section 1. *After one year from the ratification of this article the manufacture, sale, or transportation of intoxicating liquors within, the importation thereof into, or the exportation thereof from the United State and all territory subject to the jurisdiction thereof, for beverage purposes, is hereby prohibited.*

Section 2. *The Congress and the several States shall have concurrent power to enforce this article by appropriate legislation.*

Section 3. *This article shall be inoperative unless it shall have been ratified as an amendment to the Constitution by the legislatures of the several States, as provided by the Constitution, within seven years from the date of the submission thereof to the States by the Congress.*

AMENDMENT XIX.—FOR WOMEN'S SUFFRAGE
[Adopted 1920]

Section 1. The right of citizens of the United States to vote shall not be denied or abridged by the United States or by any State on account of sex.

Section 2. The Congress shall have power to enforce this article by appropriate legislation.

AMENDMENT XX.—THE LAME DUCK AMENDMENT
[Adopted 1933]

Section 1. The terms of the President and Vice President shall end at noon on the 20th day of January, and the terms of the Senators and Representatives at noon on the 3rd day of January, of the years in which such terms would have ended if this article had not been ratified; and the terms of their successors shall then begin.

Section 2. The Congress shall assemble at least once in every year, and such meeting shall begin at noon on the 3rd day of January, unless they shall by law appoint a different day.

Section 3. If, at the time fixed for the beginning of the term of the President, the President-elect shall have died, the Vice President-elect shall become President. If a President shall not have been chosen before the time fixed for the beginning of his term, or if the President-elect shall have failed to qualify, then the Vice President-elect shall act as President until a President shall have qualified; and the Congress may by law provide for the case wherein neither a President-elect nor a Vice President-elect shall have qualified, declaring who shall then act as President, or the manner in which one who is to act shall be selected, and such persons shall act accordingly until a President or Vice President shall have qualified.

Section 4. The Congress may by law provide for the case of the death of any of the persons from whom the House of Representatives may choose a President whenever the right of choice shall have devolved upon them, and for the case of the death of any of the persons from whom the Senate may choose a Vice President whenever the right of choice shall have devolved upon them.

Section 5. Section 1 and 2 shall take effect on the 15th day of October following the ratification of this article.

Section 6. This article shall be inoperative unless it shall have been ratified as an amendment to the Constitution by the Legislatures of three-fourths of the several States within seven years from the date of its submission.

AMENDMENT XXI.—REPEAL OF PROHIBITION
[Adopted 1933]

Section 1. The eighteenth article of amendment to the Constitution of the United States is hereby repealed.

Section 2. The transportation or importation into any State, Territory, or Possession of the United States for delivery of use therein of intoxicating liquors, in violation of the laws thereof, is hereby prohibited.

Section 3. This article shall be inoperative unless it shall have been ratified as an amendment to the Constitution by conventions in the several States, as provided in the Constitution, within seven years from the date of submission thereof to the States by the Congress.

AMENDMENT XXII.—NUMBER OF PRESIDENTIAL TERMS
[Adopted 1951]

Section 1. No person shall be elected to the office of President more than twice, and no person who has held the office of President, or acted as President, for more than two years of a term to which some other person was elected President shall be elected to the office of President more than once. But this article shall not apply to any person holding the office of President when this article was proposed by the Congress, and shall not prevent any person who may be holding the office of President, or acting as President, during the term within which this article becomes operative from holding the office of President or acting as President during the remainder of such term.

Section 2. This article shall be inoperative unless it shall have been ratified as an amendment to the Constitution by the legislatures of three-fourths of the several States within seven years from the date of its submission to the States by the Congress.

AMENDMENT XXIII.—PRESIDENTIAL ELECTORS FOR THE
DISTRICT OF COLUMBIA [Adopted 1961]

Section 1. The District constituting the seat of Government of the United States shall appoint in such manner as the Congress may direct:

A number of electors of President and Vice President equal to the whole number of Senators and Representatives in Congress to which the District would be entitled if it were a State, but in no event more than the least populous State; they shall be in addition to those appointed by the States, but they shall be considered for the purposes of the election of President and Vice President, to be electors appointed by a State; and they shall meet in the District and perform such duties as provided by the twelfth article of amendment.

Section 2. The Congress shall have power to enforce this article by appropriate legislation.

AMENDMENT XXIV.—THE ANTI-POLL TAX AMENDMENT
[Adopted 1964]

Section 1. The right of citizens of the United States to vote in any primary or other election for President or Vice President, for electors for President or Vice President, or for Senator or Representative in Congress, shall not be denied or abridged by the United States or any State by reason of failure to pay any poll tax or other tax.

Section 2. The Congress shall have power to enforce this article by appropriate legislation.

AMENDMENT XXV.—PRESIDENTIAL DISABILITY, VICE-PRESIDENTIAL VACANCIES
[Adopted 1967]

Section 1. In case of the removal of the President from office or his death or resignation, the Vice President shall become President.

Section 2. Whenever there is a vacancy in the office of the Vice President, the President shall nominate a Vice President who shall take office upon confirmation by a majority vote of both Houses of Congress.

Section 3. Whenever the President transmits to the President pro tempore of the Senate and the Speaker of the House of Representatives his written declaration that he is unable to discharge the powers and duties of his office, and until he transmits to them a written declaration to the contrary, such powers and duties shall be discharged by the Vice President as Acting President.

Section 4. Whenever the Vice President and a majority of either the principal officers of the executive departments or of such other body as Congress may by law provide, transmit to the President pro tempore of the Senate and the Speaker of the House of Representatives their written declaration that the President is unable to discharge the powers and duties of his office, the Vice President shall immediately assume the powers and duties of the office as Acting President.

Thereafter, when the President transmits to the President pro tempore of the Senate and the Speaker of the House of Representatives his written declaration that no inability exists, he shall resume the powers and duties of his office unless the Vice President and a majority of either the principal officers of the executive department{s} or of such other body as Congress may by law provide, transmit within four days to the President pro tempore of the Senate and the Speaker of the House of Representatives their written declaration that the President is unable to discharge the powers and duties of his office. Thereupon Congress shall decide the issue, assembling within forty-eight hours for that purpose if not in session. If the Congress, within twenty-one days after receipt of the latter written declaration, or, if Congress is not in session, within twenty-one days after Congress is required to assemble, determines by two-thirds vote of both Houses that the President is unable to discharge the powers and duties of his office, the Vice President shall continue to discharge the same as Acting President; otherwise, the President shall resume the powers and duties of his office.

AMENDMENT XXVI.—EIGHTEEN-YEAR-OLD VOTE
[Adopted 1971]

Section 1. The right of citizens of the United States, who are eighteen years of age or older, to vote shall not be denied or abridged by the United States or by any State on account of age.

Section 2. The Congress shall have power to enforce this article by appropriate legislation.

AMENDMENT XXVII.—VARYING CONGRESSIONAL COMPENSATION
[Adopted 1992]

No law varying the compensation for the service of the Senators and Representatives shall take effect until an election of Representatives shall have intervened.

APPENDIX C

PRESIDENTIAL ELECTIONS

Year	Name	Party Vote	Popular Vote	Electoral CollegeVote
1789	George Washington	Federalist		69
1792	George Washington	Federalist		132
1796	John Adams	Federalist		71
	Thomas Jefferson	Democratic-Republican		68
1800	Thomas Jefferson	Democratic-Republican		73
	John Adams	Federalist		65
1804	Thomas Jefferson	Democratic-Republican		162
	Charles C. Pinckney	Federalist		14
1808	James Madison	Democratic-Republican		122
	Charles C. Pinckney	Federalist		47
1812	James Madison	Democratic-Republican		128
	George Clinton	Federalist		89
1816	James Monroe	Dmocratic-Republican		183
	Rufus King	Federalist		34
1820	James Monroe	Democratic-Republican		231
	John Quincy Adams	Democratic-Republican		1
1824	John Quincy Adams	Democratic-Republican	108,740	84
	Andrew Jackson	Democratic-Republican	153,544	99
	William Crawford	Democratic-Republican	46,618	41
	Henry Clay	Democratic-Republican	47,136	37
1828	Andrew Jackson	Democrat	647,286	178
	John Quincy Adams	National Republican	508,064	83
1832	Andrew Jackson	Democrat	687,502	219
	Henry Clay	National Republican	530,189	49
	Electoral votes not cast		2	
1836	Martin Van Buren	Democrat	765,483	170
	William Henry Harrison	Whig	550,816	73
	Hugh White	Whig	146,107	26
	Daniel Webster	Whig	41,201	14
	Total for the 3 Whigs		739,795	113
1840	William Henry Harrison	Whig	1,274,624	234
	Martin Van Buren	Democrat	1,127,781	60
1844	James K. Polk	Democrat	1,338,464	170
	Henry Clay	Whig	1,300,097	105
1848	Zachary Taylor	Whig	1,360,967	163
	Lewis Cass	Democrat	1,222,342	127
	Martin Van Buren	Free-Soil	291,263	
1852	Franklin Pierce	Democrat	1,601,117	254
	Winfield Scott	Whig	1,385,453	42
	John P. Hale	Free-Soil	155,825	
1856	James Buchanan	Democrat	1,832,955	174
	John Fremont	Republican	1,339,932	114
	Millard Fillmore	Whig-American	871,731	8

1860	Abraham Lincoln	Republican	1,865,593	180
	John C. Breckinridge	Democratic	848,356	72
	Stephen Douglas	Democrat	1,382,713	12
	John Bell	Constitutional Union	592,906	39
1864	Abraham Lincon	Unionist (Republican)	2,206,938	212
	George McClellan	Democrat	1,803,787	21
	Electoral votes not cast			81
1868	Ulysses S. Grant	Republican	3,013,421	214
	Horatio Seymour	Democrat	2,706,829	80
	Electoral votes not cast			23
1872	Ulysses S. Grant	Republican	3,596,745	286
	Horace Greeley	Democrat	2,843,446	
	Thomas Hendricks	Democrat		42
	Benjamin Browns	Democrat		18
	Charles Jenkins	Democrat		2
	David Davis	Democrat		1
1876	Rutherford B. Hays	Republican	4,036,572	185
	Samuel Tilden	Democrat	4,284,020	184
	Peter Cooper	Greenback	81,737	
1880	James A. Garfield	Republican	4,453,295	214
	Winfield S. Hancock	Democrat	4,414,082	155
	James B. Weaver	Greenback-Labor	308,578	
1884	Grover Cleveland	Democrat	4,879,507	219
	James G. Blaine	Republican	4,850,293	182
	Benjamin Butler	Greenback-Labor	175,370	
	John St. John	Prohibition	150,369	
1888	Benjamin Harrison	Republican	5,447,129	233
	Grover Cleveland	Democrat	5,537,857	168
	Clinton Fisk	Prohibition	249,506	
	Anson Streeter	Union Labor	146,935	
1892	Grover Cleveland	Democrat	5,555,426	277
	Benjamin Harrison	Republican	5,182,690	145
	James B. Weaver	People's	1.029,846	22
	John Bidwell	Prohibition	264,133	
1896	William McKinley	Republican	7,102,246	271
	William J. Bryan	Democrat	6,492,559	176
	John Palmer	National Democratic	133,148	
	Joshua Levering	Prohibition	132,007	
1900	William McKinley	Republican	7,218,491	292
	William J. Bryan	Democrat	6,356,734	155
	John C. Wooley	Prohibition	208,914	
	Eugene V. Debs	Socialist	87,814	
1904	Theodore Roosevelt	Republican	7,628,461	336
	Alton B. Parker	Democrat	5,084,223	140
	Eugene V. Debs	Socialist	402,283	
	Silas Swallow	Prohibition	258,536	
	Thomas Watson	People's	117,183	

1908	William Howard Taft	Republican	7,675,320	321
	William J. Bryan	Democrat	6,412,294	162
	Eugene V. Debs	Socialist	420,793	
	Eugene Chafin	Prohibition	253,840	
1912	Woodrow Wilson	Democrat	6,296,547	435
	William Howard Taft	Republican	3,486,720	8
	Theodore Roosevelt	Progressive	4,118,571	86
	Eugene V. Debs	Socialist	900,672	
	Eugene Chafin	Prohibition	206,275	
1916	Woodrow Wilson	Democrat	9,127,695	277
	Charles E. Hughes	Republicn	8,533,507	254
	A.L. Benson	Socialist	585,113	
	J. Frank Hanly	Prohibition	220,506	
1920	Warren Harding	Republican	16,143,407	404
	James M. Cox	Democrat	9,130,328	127
	Eugene V. Debs	Socialist	919,799	
	P.P. Christensen	Farmer-Labor	265,411	
	Aaron Watkins	Prohibiton	189,408	
1924	Calvin Coolidge	Republican	15,718,211	382
	John W. Davis	Democrat	8,385,283	136
	Robert La Follette	Progressive	4,831,289	13
1928	Herbert Hoover	Republican	21,391,993	444
	Alfred E. Smith	Democrat	15,016,169	87
	Norman Thomas	Socialist	267,835	
1932	Franklin D. Roosevelt	Democrat	22,809,638	472
	Herbert C. Hoover	Republican	15,758,901	59
	Norman Thomas	Socialist	881,951	
	William Foster	Communist	102,785	
1936	Franklin D. Roosevelt	Democrat	27,752,869	523
	Alfred M. Landon	Republican	16,674,665	8
	William Lemke	Union	882,479	
	Norman Thomas	Socialist	187,720	
1940	Franklin D. Roosevelt	Democrat	27,307,819	449
	Wendell Willkie	Republican	22,321,018	82
1944	Franklin D. Roosevelt	Democrat	25,606,585	432
	Thomas E. Dewey	Republican	22,014,745	99
1948	Harry S. Truman	Democrat	24,179,345	303
	Thomas E. Dewey	Republican	21,991,291	189
	Strom Thurmond	Dixiecrat	1,176,125	39
	Henry Wallace	Progressive	1,157,326	
	Norman Thomas	Socialist	139,572	
	Claude A. Watson	Prohibition	103,900	
1952	Dwight D. Eisenhower	Republican	33,936,234	442
	Adlai Stevenson II	Democrat	27,314,992	89
	Vincent Hallinan	Progressive	140,023	
1956	Dwight D. Eisenhower	Republican	35,590,472	457
	Adlai Stevenson II	Democrat	26,022,752	73
	T. Coleman Andrews	States' Rights	111,178	
	Walter B. Jones	Democrat		1

1960	John F. Kennedy	Democrat	34,226,731	303
	Richard M. Nixon	Republican	34,108,157	219
	Harry Byrd	Democrat		15
1964	Lyndon B. Johnson	Democrat	43,129,566	486
	Barry Goldwater	Republican	27,178,188	52
1968	Richard M. Nixon	Republican	31,785,480	301
	Hubert H. Humphrey	Democrat	31,275,166	191
	George Wallace	American Independent	9,906,473	46
1972	Richard M. Nixon	Republican	47,170,179	520
	George McGovern	Democrat	29,171,791	17
	John Hospers	Libertarian		1
1976	Jimmy Carter	Democrat	40,830,763	297
	Gerald R. Ford	Republican	39,147,793	240
	Ronald Reagan	Republican		1
1980	Ronald Reagan	Republican	43,904,153	489
	Jimmy Carter	Democrat	35,483,883	49
	John Anderson	Independent candidacy	5,719,437	
1984	Ronald Reagan	Republican	54,455,074	525
	Walter F. Mondale	Democrat	37,577,137	13
1988	George Bush	Republican	48,881,278	426
	Michael Dukakis	Democrat	41,805,374	111
	Lloyd Bentsen	Democrat		1
1992	Bill Clinton	Democrat	43,727,625	370
	George Bush	Republican	38,165,180	168
	Ross Perot	Independent catdidacy	19,236,411	0
1996	Bill Clinton	Democrat	45,628,667	379
	Bob Dole	Republican	37,869,435	159
	Ross Perot	Independent catdidacy	7,874,283	0
2000	George W. Bush	Republican	49,820,518	271
	Albert Gore Jr.	Democrat	50,158,094	267
	Ralph Nader	Green Party	7,866,284	
2004	George W. Bush	Republican	62,040,610	286
	John Kerry	Democrat	59,028,439	251
	Ralph Nader	Green Party	463,653	
2008	Barack Obama	Democrat	66,882,230	365
	John McCain	Republican	58,343,671	173
2012	Barack Obama	Democrat	60,459,974	332
	Mitt Romney	Republican	57,653,982	206
2016	Hillary Clinton	Democrat	64,418,125	232
	Donald Trump	Republican	62,314,184	306
2020	Joe Biden	Democrat	81,268,924	306
	Donald Trump	Republican	74,216,154	232

APPENDIX D

Members of the Supreme Court of the United States

Chief Justices	State App't From	Appointed by President	Service
Jay, John	New York	Washington	1789-1795
Rutledge, John*	South Carolina	Washington	1795-1795
Ellsworth, Oliver	Connecticut	Washington	1796-1799
Marshall, John	Virginia	Adams, John	1801-1835
Taney, Roger Brooke	Maryland	Jackson	1836-1864
Chase, Salmon Portland	Ohio	Lincoln	1864-1873
Waite, Morrison Remick	Ohio	Grant	1874-1888
Fuller, Melville Weston	Illinois	Cleveland	1888-1910
White, Edward Douglass	Louisiana	Taft	1910-1921
Taft, William Howard	Connecticut	Harding	1921-1930
Hughes, Charles Evans	New York	Hoover	1930-1941
Stone, Harlan Fiske	New York	Roosevelt F.	1941-1946
Vinson, Fred Moore	Kentucky	Truman	1946-1953
Warren, Earl	California	Eisenhower	1953-1969
Burger, Warren Earl	Virginia	Nixon	1969-1986
Rehnquist, William H.	Virginia	Reagan	1986-2005
Roberts, John G., Jr.	Maryland	Bush, G. W.	2005-

Associate Justices			
Rutledge, John	South Carolina	Washington	1790-1791
Cushing, William	Massachusetts	Washington	1790-1810
Wilson, James	Pennsylvania	Washington	1789-1798
Blair, John	Virginia	Washington	1789-1796
Iredell, James	North Carolina	Washington	1790-1799
Johnson, Thomas	Maryland	Washington	1791-1793
Paterson, William	New Jersey	Washington	1793-1806
Chase, Samuel	Maryland	Washington	1796-1811
Washington, Bushrod	Virginia	Adams, John	1798-1829
Moore, Alfred	North Carolina	Adams, John	1799-1804
Johnson, William	South Carolina	Jefferson	1804-1834
Livingston, Henry Brockholst	New York	Jefferson	1806-1823
Todd, Thomas	Kentucky	Jefferson	1807-1826
Duvall, Gabriel	Maryland	Madison	1811-1836
Story, Joseph	Massachusetts	Madison	1811-1845
Thompson, Smith	New York	Monroe	1823-1843
Trimble, Robert	Kentucky	Adams, J. Q.	1826-1828

*Acting Chief Justice; Senate refused to confirm appointment.

McLean, John	Ohio	Jackson	1829-1861
Baldwin, Henry	Pennsylvania	Jackson	1830-1844
Wayne, James Moore	Georgia	Jackson	1835-1867
Barbour, Philip Pendleton	Virginia	Jackson	1836-1841
Catron, John	Tennessee	Jackson	1837-1865
McKinley, John	Alabama	Van Buren	1837-1852
Daniel, Peter Vivian	Virginia	Van Buren	1841-1860
Nelson, Samuel	New York	Tyler	1845-1872
Woodbury, Levi	New Hampshire	Polk	1845-1851
Grier, Robert Cooper	Pennsylvania	Polk	1846-1870
Curtis, Benjamin Robbins	Massachusetts	Fillmore	1851-1857
Campbell, John Archibald	Alabama	Pierce	1853-1861
Clifford, Nathan	Maine	Buchanan	1858-1881
Swayne, Noah Haynes	Ohio	Lincoln	1862-1881
Miller, Samuel Freeman	Iowa	Lincoln	1862-1890
Davis, David	Illinois	Lincoln	1862-1877
Field, Stephen Johnson	California	Lincoln	1863-1897
Strong, William	Pennsylvania	Grant	1870-1880
Bradley, Joseph P.	New Jersey	Grant	1870-1892
Hunt, Ward	New York	Grant	1873-1882
Harlan, John Marshall	Kentucky	Hayes	1877-1911
Woods, William Burnham	Georgia	Hayes	1880-1887
Matthews, Stanley	Ohio	Garfield	1881-1889
Gray, Horace	Massachusetts	Arthur	1882-1902
Blatchford, Samuel	New York	Arthur	1882-1893
Lamar, Lucius Quintus C.	Mississippi	Cleveland	1888-1893
Brewer, David Josiah	Kansas	Harrison	1889-1910
Brown, Henry Billings	Michigan	Harrison	1890-1906
Shiras, George, Jr.	Pennsylvania	Harrison	1892-1903
Jackson, Howell Edmunds	Tennessee	Harrison	1893-1895
White, Edward Douglass	Louisiana	Cleveland	1894-1910
Peckham, Rufus Wheeler	New York	Cleveland	1896-1909
McKenna, Joseph	California	McKinley	1898-1925
Holmes, Oliver Wendell	Massachusetts	Roosevelt T.	1902-1932
Day, William Rufus	Ohio	Roosevelt T.	1903-1922
Moody, William Henry	Massachusetts	Roosevelt T.	1906-1910
Lurton, Horace Harmon	Tennessee	Taft	1910-1914
Hughes, Charles Evans	New York	Taft	1910-1916
Van Devanter, Willis	Wyoming	Taft	1910-1937
Lamar, Joseph Rucker	Georgia	Taft	1911-1916
Pitney, Mahlon	New Jersey	Taft	1912-1922
McReynolds, James Clark	Tennessee	Wilson	1914-1941
Brandeis, Louis Dembitz	Massachusetts	Wilson	1916-1939
Clarke, John Hessin	Ohio	Wilson	1916-1922
Sutherland, George	Utah	Harding	1922-1938
Butler, Pierce	Minnesota	Harding	1923-1939

Sanford, Edward Terry	Tennessee	Harding	1923-1930
Stone, Harlan Fiske	New York	Coolidge	1925-1941
Roberts, Owen Josephus	Pennsylvania	Hoover	1930-1945
Cardozo, Benjamin Nathan	New York	Hoover	1932-1938
Black, Hugo Lafayette	Alabama	Roosevelt F.	1937-1971
Reed, Stanley Forman	Kentucky	Roosevelt F.	1938-1957
Frankfurter, Felix	Massachusetts	Roosevelt F.	1939-1962
Douglas, William Orville	Connecticut	Roosevelt F.	1939-1975
Murphy, Frank	Michigan	Roosevelt F.	1940-1949
Byrnes, James Francis	South Carolina	Roosevelt F.	1941-1942
Jackson, Robert Houghwout	New York	Roosevelt F.	1941-1954
Rutledge, Wiley Blount	Iowa	Roosevelt F.	1943-1949
Burton, Harold Hitz	Ohio	Truman	1945-1958
Clark, Tom Campbell	Texas	Truman	1949-1967
Minton, Sherman	Indiana	Truman	1949-1956
Harlan, John Marshall	New York	Eisenhower	1955-1971
Brennan, William J., Jr.	New Jersey	Eisenhower	1956-1990
Whittaker, Charles Evans	Missouri	Eisenhower	1957-1962
Stewart, Potter	Ohio	Eisenhower	1958-1981
White, Byron Raymond	Colorado	Kennedy	1962-1993
Goldberg, Arthur Joseph	Illinois	Kennedy	1962-1965
Fortas, Abe	Tennessee	Johnson L.	1965-1969
Marshall, Thurgood	New York	Johnson L.	1967-1991
Blackmun, Harry A.	Minnesota	Nixon	1970-1994
Powell, Lewis F., Jr.	Virginia	Nixon	1972-1988
Rehnquist, William H.	Arizona	Nixon	1972-1986
Stevens, John Paul	Illinois	Ford	1975-2010
O'Connor, Sandra Day	Arizona	Reagan	1981-2006
Scalia, Antonin	Virginia	Reagan	1986-2016
Kennedy, Anthony M.	California	Reagan	1988-2018
Souter, David H.	New Hampshire	Bush, G. H. W.	1990-2009
Thomas, Clarence	Georgia	Bush, G. H. W.	1991-
Ginsburg, Ruth Bader	New York	Clinton	1993-2020
Breyer, Stephen G.	Massachusetts	Clinton	1994-
Alito, Samuel A., Jr.	New Jersey	Bush, G. W.	2006-
Sonia Sotomayor	New York	Obama	2009-
Elena Kagan	New York	Obama	2010-
Neil M. Gorsuch	Colorado	Trump	2017
Brett M. Kavanaugh	Washington, D.C.	Trump	2018
Amy Coney Barrett	Louisiana	Trump	2020

GLOSSARY

Absolute Poverty - The minimum subsistence income needed to survive deprivation.

Acid Rain - Complex chemical and atmospheric phenomenon that occurs when emissions of sulfur and nitrogen compounds and other substances are transformed by chemical processes in the atmosphere, often far from the original source, and then deposited on earth in either a wet or dry form.

Ad Hoc Committee - A temporary special legislative committee formed to perform a specific task.

Ad Valorum Tax System - Property tax assessment based on the fair market value of the property.

Administrative Law – that branch of law that creates administrative agencies, establishes their methods of procedures, and determines the scope of judicial review of agency practices and actions.

Adversary System - The judicial principle that one is innocent of a criminal act until proven guilty.

Affective Orientations – feelings of attachment, involvement, rejection, and life about political objects.

Affirmative Action - The formalized effort on the part of government to remedy previous incidences of past discrimination particularly in the employment and political processes.

Aid to the Blind - A financial assistance program created through the New Deal to provided assistance to the nation's blind citizens.

Aid to Dependent Children - A New Deal program designed to provide financial assistance to parents of children whose incomes fall below the poverty level. This program became the primary plan for the welfare system. Its name was changed to **Aid to Families With Dependent Children.**

Air - A mixture of nitrogen, oxygen, argon, carbon dioxide with traces of neon, helium, krypton, hydrogen, xenon, methane, and vitreous oxide.

Air Pollution - A group of chemical compounds that are in the wrong place or in the wrong concentration at the wrong time.

Alien and Sedition Acts - A series of four laws passed during John Adams's administration restricting freedom of press and speech and the rights of immigrants.

Alleviative Approach - A public policy option that seeks to relieve the suffering caused by the policy problem without adequately addressing the problem itself.

Alliance - an agreement by nation states to support each other militarily in the event of an attack against any member, or to advance their mutual interests.

Almshouse - Another term for poorhouse.

Americans with Disabilities Act (1990) - Federal legislation mandating equal opportunities in employment, housing, and accommodations to disabled persons.

Annexation - The process by which cities incorporate adjacent land into their municipal boundaries.

Appeal – formal request to a higher court that it review the actions of a lower court.

Appellant – the party, usually the losing one, that seeks to overturn the decision of a lower court by appealing to a higher court.

Appellate Jurisdiction – authority of a court to review decisions of an inferior court.

Appointment Powers – authority of the president to appoint with Senate confirmation individuals to the executive branch, federal judicial benches and heads of bureaucratic agencies.

Apportionment - The process by which the total number of seats in a legislative body is distributed within a state's boundary.

Architectural Barriers Act (1970) - Federal legislation mandating that newly constructed public buildings must be accessible to handicapped persons.

Arraignment – a hearing before a court having jurisdiction in a criminal case in which the identity of the defendant is established, the defendant is informed of his/her rights, and the defendant enters a plea.

Arrest Warrant – document issued by a judicial officer directing a law enforcement officer to arrest an identified person who has been accused of a specific crime.

Article VI - An Article of the United States Constitution mandating that the constitution is the supreme law of the land. See Supremacy Clause.

Articles of Confederation - The first constitution of the United States adopted in 1777.

Association of Southern Women for the Prevention of Lynching - A woman's organization that led the battle to end mob-rule dominated lynchings.

At-Large Election - A city- or county-wide election.

Baker v Carr (1962) - The United States Supreme Court decision mandating that reapportionment of state legislative houses must guarantee the principal of "one man, one vote."

Balanced Budget - Budgetary strategy whereby anticipated revenues equal anticipated expenses.

Balance of Terror - the equilibrium of power among nuclear states stemming from common fear of annihilation in a nuclear war.

Balance of Trade - a nation's annual net trade surplus or deficit, based on the difference in the value of its imports and exports.

Barron v Baltimore (1833) - United States Supreme Court ruled that the Bill of Rights was enforceable only upon the actions of the national government.

Bellwether District – a town or district that is a microcosm of the whole population that has been found to be a good predictor of electoral outcomes.

Benefit Principle System - Based on the principle that those who reap more benefits from government services should shoulder more of the tax burden than people who do not avail themselves of service opportunities to the same degree.

Beyond a Reasonable Doubt - The criteria for determining guilt or innocence in a criminal case.

Bicameral - A two-house legislature.

Biennial Session - A legislative sessions that meets once every two years.

Bilateral Agreements - agreements signed between two nation states.

Bill - A legislative proposal formally introduced for consideration.

Biochemical Oxygen Demand - The amount of oxygen needed by bacteria to breakdown a specific amount of organic matter.

Bipolarity – a rigid balance of power system in which decisive power is polarized into two rival power centers.

Block Grants – federal grant programs given for prescribed broader activities ranging from health care to education with fewer federal regulations attached.

Blue Laws – state legislative acts banning commercial and related activities on particular days usually Sunday for religious reasons or a law against anything a community considers immoral.

Boyd v United States (1886) - The United States Supreme Court tied the Fourth Amendment's protection against unreasonable searches to the Fifth Amendment's protection against self-incrimination.

Bracero Program - A federal government sponsored agreement between the United States and Mexico to hire Mexican nationals as agricultural workers.

Brady Bill - A congressional law mandating that state law enforcement agencies conduct criminal background checks prior to allowing an individual to purchase a handgun.

Branching Question – a question that places respondents into subgroups and directs those subgroups to different parts of the questionnaire.

Bricker Amendment – a failed attempt by Senator Bricker to amend the Constitution forbidding a president from making executive agreements without the prior consent of the Senate.

Brief – a document prepared by an attorney for presentation to the court containing arguments and data in support of a case.

Brown v Board of Education - A 1954 Supreme Court decision that reversed the 1896 *Plessy v Ferguson* decision. The Court, in a unanimous decision, ruled that segregation in public schools was inherently unequal and violated the Fourteenth Amendment and equal protection.

Budget - Technical document in the form of a detailed balance sheet identifying expenditures and revenues.

Bureaucracy - The collective term for government agencies.

Cabinet - The attorney general and the thirteen principle officers of the executive departments that advise the president upon his request.

California v Trombetta (1984) - The United States Supreme Court ruled breathalyzer tests constitute a legal search and are not a violation of protected privacy rights.

Cannon Law – Church or ecclesiastical law.

Capital Expenses - Multi-year or amortized expenses.

Capitalism – an economic system where there is a combination of private property, a generally unrestricted marketplace of goods and services, and a general assumption that the bulk of the workforce will be engaged in producing goods to sell at a profit.

Case-Zablocki Act – Congressional act limiting the president's use of pure executive agreements and requiring the president to submit all executive agreements not deemed a threat to national security to the Senate sixty days after their implementation.

Casework - A collective term for the services performed by legislators and congresspersons and their staffs at the request of and on behalf of their constituents.

Cash Transfers - Direct payments to program recipients.

Categorical Grants – federal payments to state or local governments for a specified purpose.

Central Business District (CBO) - The core of a city.

Centrist – an individual or political group advocating a moderate approach to political decision-making and to the solution of social problem.

Cert Conference - Conference at which the Supreme Court justices decide whether to hear a case. Four of the nine justices must agree to hear a case.

Change of Venue - The right of a judge to change the location of a trial to afford the defendant a fair and impartial trial.

Checks and Balances – the notion that constitutional devises can prevent any power within a nation from becoming absolute by being balanced against, or checked by, another source of power within that same nation.

Child Benefit Theory - The notion that public funding can be provided to students who attend private, public and parochial schools as long as it is the child, rather than the school, that benefits from the funding.

Children's Health Insurance Program (CHIP) - A federally funded health-care plan for children whose parents cannot afford health care even though their incomes are above the poverty level.

***Church of the Lukumi Babbalu Aye v Hialeah* (1985)** - The United States Supreme Court ruled that the church's practice of animal sacrifice was constitutionally protected under the First Amendment's guarantee to religious freedom.

***City of Trenton v State of New Jersey* (1913)** - United States Supreme Court decision upholding Dillon's Rule.

Civil Law – deals with disagreements between individuals.

Civil Rights - Acts of government intended to protect disadvantaged classes of persons or minority groups from arbitrary, unreasonable, or discriminatory treatment.

Civil Rights Acts (1866) - Federal legislation granting former slaves the rights to own property, file lawsuits and make contractual agreements.

Civil Rights Act (1875) - Federal legislation prohibiting private discrimination in accommodations, transportation, and public places of amusement. This law was declared unconstitutional by the United States Supreme Court's ruling in ***Plessy v Ferguson.***

Civil Rights Act (1957) - Federal legislation establishing the United States Commission on Civil Rights and the Civil Rights Section of the United States Justice Department.

Civil Rights Act (1960) - Federal legislation authorizing the use of federal voter referees to conduct voter registration drives and to monitor federal elections in areas with historical patterns of voting problems.

Civil Rights Act (1964) - Federal legislation prohibiting discrimination in public accommodations and employment practices. The law also established a sixth grade education as meeting voter literacy and testing requirements.

Civil Rights Act (1968) - Federal legislation prohibiting discrimination in housing practices.

Civilian Conservation Corps. (CCC) - A New Deal program designed to hire the unemployed to work rural areas.

Clear and Present Danger - The criteria established by the United States Supreme Court in *Schenck v United States* (1919) to determine whether or not spoken words or symbolic displays violate the First Amendment's guarantee of freedom of speech.

Closed-End Question – a survey question that provides the respondent with alternative answers.

Coates v Cincinnati (1971) - United States Supreme Court ruling that a city ordinance denying three or more individuals to gather in a public place was an unconstitutional violation of the First Amendment's guarantee to freedom of assembly and association.

Cognitive Orientations – knowledge, accurate or otherwise, of political objects and beliefs.

Cohen v California (1971) - The United States Supreme Court ruled that the wearing of a jacket bearing an inappropriate word against the draft was a constitutionally protected right to freedom of speech.

Colonialism - the ownership of another territory or state for the sole purpose of exploitation of its people or natural resources.

Common Law – law developed in England by judges who made legal decisions in absence of written law.

Communism – a political theory that espouses the doctrines of historical inevitability, economic determinism, labor value, and the inner contradictions of capitalism, class conflict, capitalist colonialism and imperialism, world wars resulting from competition for markets, and the destruction of the bourgeoisie, the dictatorship of the proletariat, the socialist revolution and the final withering away of the state.

Compensino - A farm laborer.

Concurrent Majority -Calhoun's belief that democratic decisions should be made only with the concurrence of all major segments of a society, i.e., national referendum elections.

Concurrent powers - Constitutional powers that are simultaneously shared by the national and state governments, for example, the power to tax. However, in the process of implementing concurrent powers the state does not have the right to thwart national policy.

Concurrent Resolution - A legislative action passed by a simple majority in both Houses that requires the approval of the president or governor.

Confederation - a loose collection of states in which principal power lies at the level of the individual states rather than at the level of the central or national government.

Conference Committee - A special joint legislative committee composed of members from both Houses to reconcile differences over similar pieces of legislation.

Conflictual Party System – a legislature dominated by parties that are far apart on issues or highly antagonistic toward each other and the political system.

Connecticut Compromise - It is also known as the Great Compromise. It was a compromise reached at the constitutional convention between the New Jersey Plan and Virginia Plan. It established a bicameral legislature, the House of Representatives and the Senate. The House of Representatives was based on population; the Senate on equal representation of states.

Consensual Party System – a political party relationship whereby the parties commanding most of the legislative seats are not too far apart on policies and have a reasonable amount of trust in each other and in the political system.

Conservatism – the political outlook which springs from a desire to conserve existing things, held to be either good in themselves, are at least safe, familiar and objects of trust and affection.

Constitution – a fundamental or organic law that establishes the framework of government of a state, assigns the powers and duties of government agencies, and establishes the relationship between the people and their government.

Constitutional Law – compilation of all court rulings on the meaning of the various words, phrases and clauses in the United States Constitution.

Constitutionalism – the political principle of limited government under a written contract.

Containment - U.S. foreign policy designed to physically restrain the Soviet Union in Europe and the ideology of communism throughout the world.

Contractual Theory – view of presidential power holding that the president is limited by specific grants of power authorized in the Constitution and by statute.

Cooperative Federalism – known as Marble Cake Federalism in which national, state and local governments work together to solve common problems.

Court of Appeal - These courts are the second of the three tiers of the national court system and are designed to hear cases on appeal from the district court.

Cousins v Wigoda (1975) – U.S. Supreme Court ruled that only the credentials committee of a national political party has the authority to settle credential disputes between rival state delegations.

Court of Last Resort – the United States Supreme Court for all appeals.

Creative Federalism – format of intergovernmental relationship characterized by joint planning and decision making among all levels of government as well as the private sector in the management public programs.

Crimes Against Humanity - those acts committed as part of a widespread if systematic attacks directed against any civilian population.

Criminal Law - The code that regulates the conduct of individuals, defines crimes and provides punishment for violators.

Crisis Policy Response - A foreign policy option used when the perception of a threat to national security cuts across normal channels of decisions.

Cultural Conservatism – support for traditional western Judeo-Christian values not just as a matter of comfort and faith, but out of a firm belief that the secular, the economic, and the political success of the western world is rooted in this value.

Curative Approach - A public policy option designed to solve an identified problem.

Dayton Accords - (Dayton, Ohio, 1996.) U. S. brokered peace agreement that attempted to end hostilities between the warring factions in the former Yugoslavia.

Dealignment - Traditional constituents defect from two national political parties.

Decision-making - The choice of an alternative from among a series of alternatives.

Dedicated Revenues - Constitutionally mandated budgetary allocations to a particular budget line item.

De Facto Discrimination - An undeliberate action adversely impacting one group over another group.

De Jure Discrimination - A purposeful action that adversely impacts one group over another group.

Deduction – a type of reasoning in which if the premises of an argument are true, the conclusion is necessarily true.

Defendant – the person accused of causing harm to either the person of or to the property of the plaintiff.

Democracy – a system of government in which the ultimate political authority is vested in the people.

Democratic Party v Lafollette (1891) – U.S. Supreme Court ruled that a state's party leadership could not force the DNC Credentials Committee to accept a delegation that was selected in clear violation of DNC rules.

Détente - French word meaning the easing of strained relations.

Determinate Sentence – a term of imprisonment that has a specific number of years.

Deterrence - the concept of discouraging other states from pursuing policies unwanted by the deterring state or states.

Direct Democracy - A type of democracy, sometimes referred to as a participatory democracy, in which the people make the political decisions and laws by which they are governed.

Direct Order – a congressional law or regulation that must be enforce or grant recipients can be held accountable to civil and criminal penalties.

Discrimination - Unfavorable action towards people because they are members of a particular racial or ethnic group.

Disparate Impact - Standards used in employment practices that have the effect of excluding people with disabilities on the basis of tests or standards that are not directly related to the skills or experience required to perform the job.

Disparate Treatment - Actions in which employers treat people with disabilities differently from others.

Distributive Policies - Governmental actions that convey tangible benefits to individuals, groups, or corporations.

District Court - They are the first of three tiers of the national court system, and they are designed to function as the trial court.

Districting - The process of drawing boundaries on a map that delineate the geographic areas-the districts-from which representatives will be elected.

Divine Right Theory of Kings - The concept of kingship based on the notion that monarchs rule by the will of, indeed, in place, of God.

Dred Scott v Sanford (1857) - United States Supreme Court decision nullifying the Missouri Compromise of 1821 and stipulating that slaves were not citizens of the United States and therefore, could not sue the government in a court of law.

Dual Court System - Network of national and state courts.

Dual Federalism – also known as Layered Cake Federalism – an arrangement whereby autonomous national, subnational, and local governments all pursue their own interests independently of each other.

Due Process - The procedural safeguards guaranteed to those who would be deprived of life, liberty, or property because they are accused of criminal wrongdoing.

Earmarked - Another term for dedicated revenues.

Economic Opportunity Act (1965) - Federal legislation establishing the Office of Economic Opportunity as the coordinator for all federal anti-poverty initiatives with state and local governments.

Elasticity - An economic criterion applied to a tax that refers to the tax's ability to generate increased revenue as economic growth or inflation increases.

Elector - An individual who casts a ballot for the president and the vice president according to the wishes of the majority of state voters. (See "Faithless Elector.")

Elite Theory of Democracy - One of several explanations of who has power in a political community. It holds that power resides primarily with the relatively few people who have the most of one or more of the fundamental values such as wealth, prestige, education, etc.

Emergency Power - An inherent power given to the president to facilitate his ability to act swiftly in times when a national crisis, particularly in the area of foreign affairs, may necessitate an immediate decision or response.

Emergency Relief Administration - A New Deal agency designed to provide food, shelter and clothing to the nation's unemployed during the Great Depression.

Eminent Domain – the authority of government to take private lands for public use as long as the property lower is justifiably compensation for the loss of the property.

Empirical Research – research based on actual 'objective' observation of phenomena.

Empirical Verification – characteristic of scientific knowledge, a demonstration by means of objective observation that a statement is true.

Endangered Species - One in danger of becoming extinct throughout all or a significant part of its natural range.

Engle v Vitale (1962) - United States Supreme Court decision mandating that involuntary prayer in the public schools was an unconstitutional violation of the First Amendment's guarantee to religious freedom.

Entitlements - Benefits provided by government to which recipients have a legally enforceable right.

Enumerated Powers – also known as delegated powers – those rights and responsibilities of the U.S. government specifically provide for and listed in the Constitution.

Equity Law – judicial preventive orders in form of a writ such as an injunction or restraining order designed to afford a remedy that otherwise obtainable, and traditionally given upon a showing of peril.

Escobedo v Illinois (1964) - The United States Supreme Court ruled that an individual can request legal counsel when the interrogation process turns from exploratory to accusatory.

Establishment Clause - The First Amendment to the United States Constitution granting religious freedoms and separating church related matters from state or governmental matters.

Ethnocentrism - belief that one's own culture is far superior to any other culture.

Evaluative Orientations – judgements and opinions about political objects which usually involving applying the value standards to political objects and events.

Everson v Board of Education of the Township of Ewing (1947) - The United States Supreme Court ruled that giving public tax dollars to low-income parents to offset the cost of children's transportation to and from public and parochial schools was not a violation of the separation of church and state doctrine.

Exclusionary Rule - Evidence that is otherwise admissible may not be used in a criminal trial if it is a product of illegal police conduct.

Exclusive Governing Party Format – recognizes no legitimate interest aggregation by groups within the party nor does it permit any free activity by social groups, citizens or other government agencies.

Executive Agreement - an international agreement, reached by the President of the United States with foreign heads of state that does not require senatorial approval.

Executive Office of the President (EOP) - The numerous offices, agencies, organizations, departments, and councils that provide administrative assistance to the president.

Executive Order – a rule or regulation issued by the president, a governor, or some administrative authority, that has the effect of a law.

Executive Order 9981 – issued by President Truman, mandates racial integration of the military to include officer training opportunities and promotion guidelines for minorities.

Executive Privilege – right of executive officials to refuse to appear before or to withhold information for a legislative committee or a court.

Exercise Clause - Another term for Establishment Clause.

External Sovereignty - the right to conclude binding agreements such as treaties with a state or states without interference from other nation states.

Faction – a political group or clique that functions within a larger group, such as a government, party or organization.

Faithless Elector - An individual who follows personal choice, rather than the wishes of state voters, in casting a ballot for the president and the vice president. (See "Elector.")

Federalism - the mode of political organization that unites separate polities within an overarching political system by distributing power among general and constituent governments in a manner designed to protect the existence and authority of both.

Felony - A serious crime punishable by death or imprisonment in a penitentiary for a year or more.

Feminization of Poverty - The increased number of single-parent families headed by a female whose income falls below the poverty level.

Fighting Words - Words that by their very nature inflict injury upon those to whom they are addressed.

Filter Question – a question sued to screen respondents so that the subsequent questions will be asked of only certain respondents for whom the questions are appropriate.

Fiscal Policy - Public policy concerning taxes, government spending, public debt, and management of government money.

Food Stamp Program - A federally funded program in the 1960s providing coupons to those whose incomes were below the poverty level to purchase food items.

Foreign Policy - a strategy or planned course of action developed by the decision makers of a state vis a vis other states or international entities aimed at achieving specific goals defined in terms of national interests.

Free Enterprise – the freedom of private businesses to operate competitively for profit with minimal government regulation.

Full Faith and Credit Clause – Article IV of the U.S. Constitution by mandating that "the citizen of each state shall be entitled to all the privileges and immunities of citizens of the several states."

***Fullilove v Klutznik* (1980)** – Supreme Court ruled that Congress has the authority to use quotas to remedy past discrimination in government public works programs.

Furman v Georgia **(1972)** - The United States Supreme Court ruled that the death penalty was a violation of the Fourteenth Amendment's guarantee of due process and equal protection of the law.

Gag Order – a judge's order that lawyers and witnesses not discuss the trial with outsiders.

Game Theory - A behavioral approach to the study of politics that focuses on the decision-making process.

Gannett v DePasquale **(1979)** - The United States Supreme Court upheld a lower court ruling barring members of the press and the public from pretrial hearings.

Garcia v San Antonio Metropolitan Transit Authority **(1985)** – Supreme Court ruled constitution a federal mandate requiring state public employees must be paid at least the minimum wage and be granted overtime pay as detailed in the Fair Labor Standards Act; overturned Usery decision.

Gatekeeper - An individual or institution who is in a position to control the flow of information.

Genocide – acts committed with the intent to destroy, in whole or part, a national, ethnical, racial or religious group.

Gentrification - The process whereby upper-middle income whites (Anglos) move into inner-city neighborhoods and rehabilitate the properties.

Gerrymandering - The purposeful drawing of legislative districts to favor one group or one political party over other groups or political parties.

Gibbons v Ogden - Supreme Court ruling empowering the national government's use of the interstate commerce clause over the states.

Gideon v Wainwright **(1963)** - The United States Supreme Court ruled that all persons accused of committing a crime have a constitutional right to legal counsel.

Gitlow v New York **(1925)** - The Supreme Court was not involved in First Amendment cases until fairly recent times. In 1925, *Gitlow v. New York,* the Court stated that the Fourteenth Amendment made the First Amendment applicable to the states. This was the beginning of the incorporation doctrine of the Supreme Court.

Glass Ceiling - The practice of denying women accessibility to upper management positions.

Global Warming (greenhouse effect) - The effect of increasing amounts of methane, carbon dioxide, and certain air pollutants resulting in trapping heat in the earth's atmosphere and gradually warming it.

Goesaert v Cleary **(1948)** – Supreme Court ruled unconstitutional any state laws denying women the right to practice certain occupations usually held by men.

Government – the formal institutional structure and processes of a society by which policies are developed and implemented in the form of law binding on all.

Grand Jury - A panel charged with reviewing evidence in a case to determine whether or not a case should be forwarded for trial.

Grandfather Clause - A Jim Crow law requiring that individuals whose grandfathers could not vote before 1860 to pass a literacy test as a requirement for voting; ruled unconstitutional by the United States Supreme Court in *Guinn v United States* (1915).

Grant – a form of gift that entails certain obligations on the part of the grantee and expectations on the part of the grantor.

Grants-in-Aid – federal payments to states or federal or state payments to local governments for specified purposes.

Group Theory of Democracy - One of several explanations of who has power in a political community. It holds that power resides primarily with interest groups.

Guinn v United States 1915) - The United States Supreme Court ruled that Oklahoma's use of the grandfather clause to preclude African Americans from voting was an unconstitutional violation of the Fifteenth Amendment of the United States Constitution.

Haze - Wide-scale, low-level pollution that obstructs visibility.

Hegemony - the extension by one state of preponderant influence or control over another state or region.

Health Maintenance Organizations (HMOs) - Prepaid health-care systems emphasizing preventive medical services.

Homeless - A term used to describe those individuals who lack permanent shelter.

Horizontal Federalism - state-to-state interactions and relations.

Housing Act (1937) - Congressional legislation providing for federal funding for the construction of low-income apartments in inner-city areas.

Hyperpoor - A term used to describe those individuals whose annual incomes are less than half of the official poverty level.

Hypothesis – a tentative or provisional or unconfirmed statement that can in principle be verified.

Illusion of Central Tendency – assumption that opinions are 'normally distributed' – that responses to opinion questions are heavily distributed toward the center, as in a bell-shaped curve.

Illusion of Saliency – the impressions conveyed by polls that something is important to the public when it is not.

Impact Statement - A report detailing any potential harm a project might cause to the environment, the possible solutions to prevent undo environmental damage, and potential efforts on the part of the project sponsors to maintain and hopefully enhance the productivity of the environment.

Impaired Rivers - A waterway that cannot support aquatic life.

Impeachment – a formal accusation, rendered by the lower house of a legislative body, that commits an accused civil official for trial in the upper house.

Imperialism - the domination of one state by another, usually for exploitative purposes.

Implied Powers - also known as the Necessary and Proper Clause or the Elastic Clause – as detailed in Article I, Section 8 of the Constitution, Congress shall have the power "to make all laws necessary and proper for carrying into execution the foregoing powers vested by the Constitution in the government of the United States, or in any department or office thereof."

Impoundment - The refusal of a president to release or spend money that has been appropriated by Congress in the federal budget.

Incorporation Doctrine - The Fourteenth Amendment nationalized the Bill of Rights. The Supreme Court began to incorporate the first ten amendments into the Fourteenth so that whatever the national government was forbidden to do, the states could not do either.

Incrementalism – a doctrine holding that change in a political system occurs only by small steps, each of which should be carefully evaluated before proceeding to the next step.

Indian Removal Act (1830) - Federal legislation mandating the forced relocation of Native American tribes from east to west of the Mississippi River.

Indirect Democracy - A type of democracy, sometimes referred to as a representative democracy, in which the people elect others to make political decisions and laws for them. (See "Republic.")

Individualism – the political, economic and social concept that places primary emphasis on the worth, freedom and well-being of the individual rather than on the group, society or nation.

Inelastic Tax - A tax program that does not generate increased revenues in proportion to economic growth.

Infrastructure - The collective term for roads, buildings, sewers, water supply systems, and similar structures essential for a municipality to operate.

Inherited Powers - These are powers the national government inherited from tradition including the British Parliament and early state legislatures.

Initiative - A set of procedures through which residents in a state or local community may propose new legislation or an amendment to the constitution.

In-Kind Programs - Means-tested services providing assistance that has a cash value even though it is not received in cash.

Injunction – an order issued by a court in an equity proceeding to compel or restrain the performance of an act by an individual or government official.

Integration - The practice of desegregating public schools, public accommodations, residential areas, and so on.

Intergovernmental Relations – the complex network of interrelationships among governments, i.e., political, fiscal, programmatic and administrative processes by which higher units of government share revenues and other resources with lower units of government, generally accompanied by special conditions that lower units must satisfy as prerequisites to receiving the assistance.

Interim Appointments – Presidents also have the option of using temporary or interim appointments to cover the death or resignation of an incumbent. Yet, these individuals can only be employed for 210 days.

Interim Committee - A standing committee of a state legislative house that continues to meet when the legislature is not in session.

Intermestic Issues - Those issues such as trade, finance, pollution, energy, terrorism, human rights, etc., which overlap foreign and domestic policy boundaries.

Internal Sovereignty - the right, without external intervention to determine matters having to do with one's own citizens.

Internationalism - belief that the course of international events demands that a power nation assume an active and to a large degree a leadership role in determining the outcome of those events.

Interposition – Calhoun's concept of placing a state as a buffer zone between its citizens and the national government as to prevent the enforcement of national law upon its citizens deemed to be detrimental to the citizens.

Interstate Compact – an agreement between two or more states requiring congressional approval to settle a common interest or concern.

Interstate Rendition – the return of a fugitive from justice by a state upon the demand of the executive authority of the state in which the crime was committed.

Interventionism - the coercive interference in the affairs of a state by another group of states to affect the internal and external policies of that state.

Iron Law of Oligarchy – in every organization, whether it be a political party, a professional union, or any other association of the kind, the aristocratic tendency manifests itself very clearly. The mechanism of the organization, while conferring a solidity of structure, induces serious changes in the organized mass, completely inverting the respective position of the leaders and the led. As a result of organization, every party or processional union becomes divided into a minority of directors and a majority of the directed.

Isolationism - the policy of curtailing as much as possible a nation's international relations so one's country can exist in peace and harmony by itself in the world.

Issue Network - A set of organizations that share expertise in a policy area and interact with each other over time as relevant issues are debated.

Jim Crow - A series of economic, political, and social laws enacted in the southern states to deny African Americans access to employment, social activities, and political rights including voting privileges.

Joint Committee - A legislative committee composed of members from both legislative Houses.

Joint Resolution - A legislative action passed by a majority in both Houses of Congress or a state legislature requiring the president's or governor's signature for approval.

Judicial Court - Article III inferior courts.

Judicial Activism – the making of new public policies through the decision of judges.

Judicial Self-Restraint – a self-imposed limitation on judicial decision making. The tendency of judges to favor a narrow interpretation of the laws and the defer to the policy judgment of the legislative and executive branches.

Judicial Review - The power of the courts to hold unconstitutional and unenforceable any law, any official action based upon a law, any other action by a public official it deems (upon careful reflection and in line with the taught tradition of the law and judicial restraint) to be in conflict with the Constitution.

Judiciary Act of 1789 - First congressional act passed that specifically dealt with its power to create inferior courts.

Jurisdiction – the authority vested in a court to hear and decide cases.

Just Desserts – the punishment for criminal-wrong doing should be proportionate to the severity of the defense.

Katz v United States (1967) - The United States Supreme Court ruled that wiretapping a public phone is a violation of the constitution's guarantee to privacy.

La Raza Unida - A third political party movement dedicated to the concerns of the Hispanic community.

Law – a body of rules enacted by public officials in a legitimate manner and backed by the force of the state.

Leadership - The ability to make others feel safe and secure by providing them with direction and guidance.

Leading Question – (also known as reactive question) a question that encourages the respondent to choose a particular response.

Lee v Weisman (1992) - The United States Supreme Court ruled that public schools could use a clergy-led prayer at graduation ceremonies only if the prayer was non-sectarian and non-proselytizing.

Legislative Courts - Article I inferior courts.

Lemon Test - The criteria established by the United States Supreme Court to determine governmental violations of the separation of church and state doctrine.

Lemon v Kurtzman (1971) - The United States Supreme Court established the criteria for judging whether or not government actions or legislative acts violated the separation of church and state doctrine.

Libel - Defamation of character in print or by other visual presentations.

Liberalism – a political doctrine that espouses freedom of the individual from interference by the state, toleration by the state in matters of morality and religion, laissez-faire economic policies, and a belief in natural rights that exist independent of government.

Libertarians – political movement that believes in freeing people not merely from the constraints of traditional political institutions, but also from the inner constraints imposed by their mistaken attribution of power to ineffectual things.

Liberty – in a state, that is, in a society where there are laws, liberty can consist only in having the power to do what one should want to do and in no way being constrained to do what one should not want to do.

License - A privilege granted by government to do something that it otherwise considers to be illegal.

Lieutenant Governor - In forty-two states, the second highest ranking state executive officer.

Likert Scale – a five-point scale that uses both words and numbers which respondents are asked to rate an issue, person, or concept.

Limited War - an armed conflict fought for objectives less than the total destruction of the enemy and its unconditional surrender.

Line-item Veto – enables the executive to line out an appropriate budget amount in a bill without actually vetoing the bill. This authority is granted to governors but not presidents.

Literacy Test - A written or oral examination to determine whether or not an individual possessed the required intelligence to vote.

Magna Carta - A document written in 1215 by English noblemen placing restrictions upon the authority of their king.

Majoritarian Theory of Democracy - One of several explanations of who has power in a political community. It holds that power resides primarily with the people or citizens who take the majority position on a given issue.

Malapportionment - A districting plan whereby legislators from some districts represent more people than legislators from other districts.

Mandates - Legislative orders arising from statutes, court decisions, and administrative orders that demand action from a subordinate government.

Manifest Destiny - The concept that the United States was destined because of its innate superiority to govern the North American continent.

Mapp v Ohio (1961) - The United States Supreme Court established the exclusionary rule whereby evidence obtain in an illegal search is inadmissible in court.

Marbury v Madison - An 1803 Supreme Court decision that established the concept of judicial review.

Matrix - A rectangular array of information.

McCulloch v Maryland (**1819**) - A landmark Supreme Court decision in 1819 that established both the concepts of national supremacy and implied powers. The Court maintained that the national government had the "implied power" to establish a national bank and that the state governments did not have the right to thwart national policy.

McLaurin v Oklahoma State Regents (1950) - The United States Supreme Court ruled that segregated facilities at public universities was an unconstitutional violation of the Fourteenth Amendment of the United States Constitution.

Mean Distribution – a measure of central tendency found by summing the values of the variable and dividing the total by the number of observations.

Means-tested Programs - Eligibility based upon the applicant's documented inability to provide for his/herself the desired benefit because of depressed income levels.

Measurement Error – the failure to identify the true distribution of opinion within a population because of errors or poorly worded questions.

Median Distribution – the category of values above or below which one-half of the observations lie.

Medicaid - Government-sponsored health-care program for individuals whose incomes fall below the poverty level.

Medicare - Government-sponsored health-care program for individuals over 65 years of age regardless of income level.

Medigap Insurance - Supplemental health-care coverage.

Miller v California (1973) - The United States Supreme Court established the criteria for obscenity.

Minor v Happersat (1875) - The United States Supreme Court ruled that the Fourteenth Amendment to the United States Constitution did not give women the right to vote.

Minority Vote Dilution - The process of dividing large minority populations into several legislative districts to prevent them from electing candidates from their own minority group.

Minority Vote Packing - The purposeful drawing of legislative districts whereby large minority population groups are placed into one or two legislative districts.

Misdemeanor - A minor criminal offense.

Mitchell v Helms (2000) - The United States Supreme Court ruled that a Louisiana state law providing public funding for instructional equipment to public and private schools was not a violation of the separation of church and state doctrine.

Model Cities Program - A federal program created in the 1960s to encourage urban areas to provide low-income housing units.

Multi-lateral Agreements - agreements signed by three or more nation states.

Municipal Bonds - A bond program used by governments to fund major capital improvement programs to include roads, drainage, convention facilities, and so on.

Municipal Courts - City courts with limited jurisdiction over traffic-related cases; also known as traffic courts.

Municipal Solid Waste - Solid waste resulting from or incidental to municipal, community, commercial, institutional, and recreational activities including garbage, rubbish, ashes, street cleanings, dead animals, abandoned automobiles, and all other solid waste other than industrial waste.

Multiparty System – an electoral system based on proportional representation that often requires a coalition of several parties to form a majority to run the government.

Nation State - a state organized for the government of a nation whose territory is determined by national customs and expectations.

National Ambient Air Quality Standards (NAAQS) - The attainment levels established by the Environmental Protection Agency for air quality standards.

National Association for the Advancement of Colored Persons (NAACP) - A predominately African-American group founded by W. E. B. Dubois to address social, economic, and political discrimination against African Americans.

National Interests – the fundamental objective and ultimate determinant that guides the decision makers of a state in making foreign policy.

***National League of Cities v Usery* (1976)** – Supreme Court ruled that the Tenth Amendment prohibited the national government from setting wages and maximum working hour requirements for state employees.

National Youth Core - A federally fund New Deal program to put unemployed youths to work during the Depression Era.

National Supremacy - It is the concept that the Constitution is supreme to the national government and the national government is supreme to the states. The foundations for national supremacy are found in Article IV of the Constitution in the national supremacy clause.

Nationalism - the spirit of belonging together or the corporate will that seeks to preserve the identity of the group by institutionalizing it in the form of a state.

Nativism - The belief that only those born on their country's soil should reap the benefits of their birthrights.

***Near v Minnesota* (1931)** - The United States Supreme Court established the rule of "no prior restraint" regarding the freedom of the print media to publish news items.

***Nebraska Press Association v Stuart* (1976)** - The United States Supreme Court overturned a gag order issued by a district court as a violation of First Amendment's guarantee to freedom of the press.

Negative Liberty – that tranquility of spirit which comes from the opinion each one has of his security, and in order for him to have this liberty, the government must be such that one citizen cannot fear another citizen.

Negligence – carelessness or the failure to use ordinary care, under the particular circumstances reveled by the evidence in the lawsuit.

Neutrality - the legal status wherein a state takes no part in a war and which establishes certain rights vis a vis the belligerents.

***New York Times v Sullivan* (1964)** - The United States Supreme Court ruled that the *New York Times* was exercising its constitutionally protected right to freedom of the press when it printed a story about a Montgomery, Alabama police commissioner.

***New York Times v United States* (1971)** - The United States Supreme Court ruled that the *New York Times* and the *Washington Post* were constitutionally protected by the First Amendment's guarantee to freedom of the press when they published sensitive data concerning the United States' involvement in Vietnam.

***Nixon v Fitsgerald* (1982)** – Supreme Court held that presidents are entitled to absolute immunity in civil suits regarding all of his/her official acts.

Nixon v Herndon (1927) - The United States Supreme Court ruled that the Texas White Primary Law of 1924 was unconstitutional.

No Prior Restraint - The ability of the print media to publish without government interference.

Nominal Definition - A description that indicates how a concept is to be used.

Non-Working Poor - A term used to describe unemployed individuals whose incomes fall at or below the poverty level.

Nullification – Calhoun's theory that a state or states could declare their association with the social contract as null and void if the national government failed to fulfill its obligations to the state(s) and establish their own independent governments.

Old Age Assistance Program - A New Deal program designed to assist the nation's elderly during the Depression Era.

Old Age Insurance - A program created by the Social Security Act of 1935 providing a self-funded insurance for the nation's elderly and disabled.

Olmstead v United States (1928) - The United States Supreme Court ruled that wiretapping was not a violation of the Fourth Amendment's protection against unreasonable searches and seizures.

Open-Ended Question – a question asking the respondent to give their own opinion without prompting them to a particular anticipated response.

Operating Expenses - Yearly expenses needed to run government such as salaries, benefits, equipment, rent, utilities, supplies, etc.

Original Jurisdiction - the authority of a court to hear a case in the first instance.

Outputs - Tangible manifestations of public policies, the things actually done in pursuance of policy decisions and statements.

Ozone - A primary ingredient of smog.

Palko v Connecticut (1937) - United States Supreme Court ruling distinguishing fundamental rights from non-fundamental rights.

Pardon - an executive grant of a release from the punishment or legal consequences of a crime before or after conviction.

Participatory Democracy – the direct involvement of individuals and groups in the decision-making processes of government.

Paternalistic Attitude - The belief of male superiority over women.

Pay Equity - The term used to recognize that women earn less than their male counterparts employed in comparable positions.

Personal Responsibility and Work Opportunity Act (1996) - Federal legislation initiating reform of the welfare system.

Pink Collar Job - Collective term applied to secretarial and clerical jobs usually held by women.

Plaintiff - the initiator of a grievance in a legal suit.

Platform – statement of principles and objectives espoused by a party or candidate that is used during a campaign to win support from voters.

Plea Bargaining – process through which a defendant pleads guilty to a criminal charge with the expectation of receiving some consideration from the state.

Plessy v Ferguson - An 1896 Supreme Court decision that provided the constitutional foundations for apartheid in the United States. The Court validated the Jim Crow laws that had been passed after Reconstruction and the concept of "separate but equal" facilities for whites and blacks when it upheld a Louisiana statute that required railroads to provide "equal but separate accommodations for the white and colored races."

Plintz v United States (1997) – Supreme Court declared unconstitutional provision of the federal Brady Bill requiring local law enforcement officials to conduct background checks on individuals wishing to purchase handguns as a unfunded mandate.

Pluralism - The view that competition and subsequent negotiation and bargaining among multiple centers of power is the key to understanding how decisions are made.

Pocket Veto - Upon receiving a bill from Congress the president takes no action and, if Congress adjourns within the following ten working days, the bill is automatically killed.

Point of Service (POS) - A health care program charging members a higher premium and co-payments for using non-HMO approved physicians and health services.

Point-Source Pollution - a pollution source that has a precise, identifiable location, such as a pipe or a smokestack.

Police Power – the authority to promote and safeguard the health, morals, safety and welfare of the people.

Policy - A proposed course of action of a person, group or government within a given environment providing obstacles and opportunities which the policy was supposed to utilize and overcome in an effort to reach a goal or realize an objective or purpose.

Policy Making - A pattern of action, extending over time and involving many decisions, some routine, and some not so routine.

Policy Outcomes - The consequences for society, intended or unintended, that flow from the action or inaction by government.

Political Culture – the pattern of individual attitudes and orientations towards politics among members of a political system.

Political Efficacy – a citizen's belief (1) that he or she can understand and participate in political affairs and (2) that the political system will be responsive.

Political Party - an organization whose members are sufficiently homogeneous to band together for the overt purpose of winning elections which entitles them to exercise government power, in order to enjoy the influence, prerequisites, and advantages of authority.

Political Question – a doctrine enunciated by the Supreme Court holding that certain constitutional issues cannot be decided by the courts but are to be decided by the executive or legislative branches.

Political Patronage - The hiring and firing of individuals for governmental jobs based on party loyalty and electoral support.

Political Socialization – the transition from generation to generation of the ethos of a political system by the conscious and unconscious instilling of the values of a political culture.

Politics - Anything related to the making of governmental decisions: the authoritative allocation of values for a society (Easton) or who gets, what, when, how (Lasswell).

Poll Tax - A voting fee; overturned with the passage of the Twentieth Amendment to the United States Constitution.

Porkbarrel Politics - The use of political influence by members of Congress to secure government funds and projects for their constituents.

Poverty - The state or condition of being poor by lacking the means of providing material needs or comforts.

Poverty Level - Based on the assumption that poor families spend one third of their income needed to eat according to a modest food plan.

Powell v Alabama (1932) - The United States Supreme Court ruled that those accused of a crime must be guaranteed their rights of due process and equal protection as guaranteed by the Fourteenth Amendment to the United States Constitution.

Precedent - a case previously decided that serves as a legal guide for the resolution of subsequent cases.

Precinct - Local electoral units.

Preemptive Strike - a first-strike nuclear attack undertaken on the assumption that an enemy state is planning an imminent nuclear attack.

Preferred Provider Organization (PPO) - A health care system where plan members select from a pre-approved list of doctors providing medical services at predetermined fees.

Prejudice - Feeling or act of any individual or any group in which a prejudgment about someone else or another group is made on the basis of emotion rather than reason.

Preponderance of the Evidence – the standard of proof required to prevail a trial.

Prescription – the action of laying down authoritative rules or directions.

Presidential Types - Presidents that share the same personal qualities and are categorized according to these common attributes.

Preventive Approach - A public policy option designed to prevent future damage without adequately solving the problem that caused the damage.

Preventive War - a limited but powerful military maneuver designed to scare the other nation state or states away from a hostile action.

Primary Election - Intraparty election used by political parties to select a candidate to run in the general election.

Privatization - General effort to relieving the disincentives toward efficiency in public organizations by subjecting them to incentives of the private market.

Probability Sampling - a method used by pollsters to select a sample in which every individual has an equal probability of being selected as a respondent so that the correct weight can be given to all segments of the population.

Probable Cause - A reasonable assumption that a crime has or will be committed.

Problem - Condition or situation that produces a human need, deprivation, or dissatisfaction, self identified or identified by others, for which relief is sought.

Procedural Due Process - The manner in which a law, ordinance, an administrative practice, or judicial task is carried out.

Prerogative Theory – view of presidential powers holding that the chief executive can exercise extraordinary power if needed to protect and preserve the nation.

Progressive Tax - A tax that increases the tax burden for upper-income people while reducing it for lower-income people.

Proprietary Function – a governmental activity involving business-type operations ordinarily carried on by private companies to include such activities as supply electricity and gas, recreational facilities, garbage collection, etc.

Proportional Representation - Representatives are not necessarily selected from specific geographic regions or districts. Rather, each political party receives representation in proportion to the amount of votes cast. In contrast to the single-member district, this is not a winner-take-all system.

Proportional Taxes - Tax programs that impose equal tax burdens regardless of one's income level.

Protectionism - the theory and practice of utilizing governmental regulation to control or limit the volume or types of imports entering a state.

Public Opinion – the aggregate of the individual feelings of a political community on a given issue; a force of such intangible power that it sets limits on what a government can do.

Public Opinion Polls – scientific instruments for measuring public opinion.

Public Policy - An officially expressed intention backed by a sanction, which can be a reward or punishment.

Punitive Approach - A public policy option designed to punish the recipients of the benefit by placing stiff eligibility requirements and sanctions for abuse.

Pure Speech - Speech without any conduct.

Quota Sampling Survey – a sampling of respondents whose characteristics closely match those of the general population along several signification dimensions, such as geographic region, sex, age and race.

Racial Profiling - the practice of law enforcement using stereotypes of the criminal element to determine if individuals should be subjected to searches, seizures, and if necessary, arrests.

Random Sampling – a sampling of respondents chosen mathematically, at random, with every effort made to avoid bias in the construction of the sample.

Realignment - Shift in constituent base of two national political parties.

Reasonable Restrictions – The logical and rational curtailments enacted by government upon the absolute unrestrained pursuit of unalienable rights to guarantee the protection of those rights to all members of a civil society

Recall - A set of procedures through which residents in a state or local community may remove an elected official from office.

Recess Appointment – an appointment of a federal official made by the president to fell a vacancy while the Senate is not in session

Redistributive Policies - Conscious attempts by government to manipulate the allocation of wealth, property, rights, or some other value among broad classes or groups in society.

Redlining - Practice used by financial institutions to deny loans to individuals desiring to purchase properties located in racially changing neighborhoods.

Referendum - A set of procedures through which residents in a state or local community may indicate their approval or disapproval of existing or proposed legislation and/or changes to their constitution

Regressive Tax - A tax that increases the burden for lower-income people while reducing it for upper-income people.

Regulatory Actions - Government actions that extend government control over particular behavior of private individuals or businesses.

Rehabilitation - the notion that punishment is intended to restore offenders to a constructive role in society; based on the assumption that criminal behavior is a treatable disorder caused by social or psychological ailments.

Relative Poverty - Measurement of the poverty level by comparing an individual's income to the nation's overall standard of living

Representative Democracy (also known as indirect democracy) - form of governance in which the citizens rule through representatives, who are periodically elected in order to keep them accountable.

Republic - a form of government in which sovereign power resides in the electorate and is exercised by elected representatives who are responsible to the people.

Reserved powers - The Tenth Amendment to the Constitution explicitly states that powers not explicitly granted to the national government are reserved to the states.

Resolution - A congressional or legislative action that deals entirely within the prerogatives of one house or the other.

Restrictive Covenant - A provision in a mortgage loan contract forbidding the buyer of a home from eventually selling the house to a minority.

Reynolds v Sims (1964) - United States Supreme Court ruling that redistricting plans for state Senates must guarantee the principle of "one man, one vote".

Reynolds v United States (1879) - The United States Supreme Court upheld a federal law outlawing the practice of polygamy.

Rider - An extraneous amendment attached to a bill by Congress.

Roe v Wade (1973) - The United States Supreme Court ruled that a woman's choice to have an abortion is a protected Constitutional right.

Roth v United States (1957) - The United States Supreme Court ruled that obscenity is not constitutionally protected by the First Amendment's guarantee to freedom of speech.

Ruiz v Estelle (1980) - United States Supreme Court decision ruling that triple bunking in state prisons was an unconstitutional act.

Russell Amendment – Congressional act preventing presidents from using appropriated funds to finance agencies created by executive order unless Congress specially allocated funding for the agency.

Sample – a small group selected by researchers to represent the most important characteristics of an entire population.

Sampling Bias – occurs whenever some elements of the population are systematically excluded from a sample.

Sanctions - The penalties meted out as consequences of illegal conduct.

Schenck v United States (1919) - The United States Supreme Court decision to apply the term "clear and present danger" to differentiate constitutionally protected from unconstitutionally protected speech.

School District of Abington Township v Schempp (1963) - The United States Supreme Court ruled that the reading of the Bible in a public school constituted an unconstitutional sponsorship of one religious practice over other practices.

Search Warrant – a written document signed by a judge or magistrate, authorizing a law enforcement officer to conduct a search.

Selective Incorporation - The process used by the United States Supreme Court to apply certain rights guaranteed in the Bill of Rights to state actions.

Selective Polling Sample – a sample drawn deliberately to reconstruct meaningful distributions of an entire consistency.

Self-Determination - the right of a group of people who consider themselves separate and distinct from others to determine for themselves the state in which they will live and the form of government it will have.

Senatorial Courtesy - The practice in which a president yields the choice of an agency head or federal judge to a senator in his party.

Separate But Equal - The practice used to segregate public schools, public accommodations, housing, etc., initially upheld by the Supreme Court in *Plessy v Ferguson* (1896); overturned by the United States Supreme Court in *Brown v Board of Education* (1954).

Separate Car Act (1890) – A Louisiana state law mandating that railroads had to provide separate rail cars for Anglos and African-American passengers.

Separation – the belief that each racial or cultural group should live in isolation of other racial and cultural groups.

Separation of Church and State Doctrine - As outlined in the First Amendment, the practice of separating religious issues from governmental control or sponsorship.

Separation of Powers – governing power is distributed among the three branches of government.

Settlement Houses - Community centers located in the poor districts of major cities designed in the 1880s to address the needs of urban poor.

***Shaw v Reno* (1993)** - United States Supreme Court decision ruling that racial gerrymandering is unconstitutional.

Signing Statements – the official pronouncement issued by the president contemporaneously to the signing of a bill into law that, in addition to commenting on the law generally, have been used to forward the presidents interpretation of the statutory language.

***Silverman v United States* (1961)** - The United States Supreme Court ruled that law enforcement violated Silverman's Fourth Amendment rights when they used the pipes of his heating system to eavesdrop on his conversations.

Single-member district - The political system is divided into districts and the people of that district will select one person to represent them. It is a winner-take-all system.

Slander - Verbal malicious attacks against another person.

Smith Act (1940) - A federal law outlawing the right to organize or associate with any member belonging to any organization advocating the overthrow of any agency or branch of the United States government.

***Smith v Allwright* (1944)** - The United States Supreme Court ruled that political parties were agents of state government and therefore, could not deny voting or membership privileges to any qualified voter for any election.

Smog - An air quality problem occurring when nitrogen oxides produced by burning fuels and volatile organic compounds escape into the atmosphere.

Social Security Act (1935) - Federal legislation creating a income support program for the nation's retired citizens funded through payroll taxes.

Socialism – a doctrine that advocates economic collectivism through governmental or industrial group ownership of the means of production and distribution of goods.

Solid Waste - Any garbage, refuse, sludge from a waste treatment plant, water supply, treatment plant or air pollution control facility, and other discarded materials, including solid liquid, semisolid, or contained gaseous material resulting from industrial, municipal, commercial, mining, and agricultural operations.

Sovereignty - the independent legal authority over a population in a particular territory, based on the recognized right to self-determination.

Special Supplemental Program for Women, Infants and Children (WIC) - A federally funded program providing nutritional food staples to pregnant women, breastfeeding mothers, mothers up to six months after giving birth and children under the age of five whose individual or family incomes are at or below the designated poverty level.

Spin Doctor - Serving as a politician and the head of a political party, a president attempts to give the media favorable interpretations (spin) of his own, and his party's actions. This role is also played by his political campaign advisor.

Sprawl - The outward extension of a new low-density residential and commercial development from the core of the city.

Standing Committees - Permanent committees within a legislative house, i.e., Budget Committee, Foreign Relations Committee, and so on.

Standing to sue - A legal reason to be before a court.

State of War - exists in the legal sense when two or more national states officially declare that a condition of hostilities exists between them.

Stare Decisis – let the decision stand.

States' Rights – opposition to increasing the national government's power at the expense of the states.

Statistics - A mathematical method used by some political scientists to analyze data.

Status Quo - Present public policy. What is right now.

Steering - The practice of showing real estate properties to minorities located only in minority neighborhoods thus steering them away from more affluent neighborhoods.

Stewardship Theory – view of presidential powers holding that the president has not only the right but also the duty to do anything needed to safeguard the nation and to protect the American people.

Strategic Defense Policy - Policy response oriented toward foreign policy and international politics involving the use of military force.

Straw Poll – an unscientific attempt to measure public sentiment or opinions on a given issue or political candidate.

Street v New York **(1969)** - The United States Supreme Court ruled that the burning of the American flag was a constitutionally protected right under the First Amendment's guarantee to freedom of speech.

Structural Defense Policy - Policy response oriented toward foreign policy and international politics involving decisions of procurement, allocation, and organization of military forces.

Subsidies - Government grants of cash or other commodities.

Substantive Due Process - The content or subject matter of a law.

Superior/Inferior Theory of Racism – The concept that one group or culture is genetically, intellectually, and culturally more superior than any other group.

Supplemental Security Income (SSI) – A federally funded program providing cash payments to lower income elderly, the blind, and disable adults and children.

Supremacy Clause - Article VI of the United States Constitution mandating that the Constitution is the supreme law of the land.

Supreme Court - The Supreme Court is the only national court that is guaranteed under Article III of the Constitution. Although it serves as a court of original jurisdiction, it is most often the last court of appeal.

Survey - A method used by some political scientists to collect data about the attitudes and beliefs held by a sample of the population.

Sweatt v Painter **(1950)** - The United States Supreme Court ruled that the practice of allowing African Americans to attend racially separated inferior schools was an unconstitutional violation of the Fourteenth Amendment.

Symbolic Speech - Use of symbols, rather than words, to convey ideas.

Tax - A compulsory contribution for a public purpose rather than for the personal benefit of an individual.

Tax Equity - Fairness of tax application.

Temperance Movement - The organized effort to forbid the production, sale, and consumption of alcohol.

Terry v Ohio **(1968)** - The United States Supreme Court ruled that testing for drugs or alcohol by penetrating the skin is not a violation of the Fourth Amendment's protection against unreasonable searches.

Texas v White **(1869)** – Supreme Court ruled that states cannot secede from the union.

Third Party – composed of independents and dissidents from the major parties in a two-arty system that typically is based on a protest movement and that may rally sufficient voter support to affect the outcome of a state or national election.

Threatened Species - A species that is likely to become endangered in the foreseeable future.

Tinker v Des Moines School District **(1969)** - The United States Supreme Court ruled that the wearing of arm bands in protest of the Vietnam War was a protected right to freedom of speech.

Tort Law – the law of civil wrongs.

Total War - an armed conflict involving the participation of the entire population of the combatants with the ultimate aim of total destruction of the enemy with an unconditional surrender.

Trail of Tears - the 1829 forced relocation sponsored by the United States government of the Cherokees, Choctaws, Creeks, Chickasaws and Seminoles from their traditional lands east of the Mississippi to new lands west of the Mississippi.

Transitional Immunity – absolute protection against prosecution for any event or transaction about which a witness is compelled to give testimony or furnish evidence.

Treaty - a formal agreement entered into between two or more countries. The treaty process includes negotiation, signing, ratification, exchange of ratifications, publishing and proclamation, and treaty execution.

True Bill – an indictment made and endorsed by a grand jury when it finds that there is sufficient evidence to bring a person to trial.

Unalienable Rights - Fundamental rights derived from natural law which all people have and which cannot be taken away or transferred.

Unemployment Insurance – A federally funded program providing financial assistance to unemployed workers.

Unfunded Mandate – An order from a higher level of government upon a subordinate level of government to perform a particular task without receiving the additional revenue or resources needed to perform the task.

Unicameral - A one-house legislature.

Unilateral - a foreign policy decision or decree issued by one nation state.

United Farm Workers Union - A labor organization founded by the late César Chávez to address the concerns of migrant farm workers.

Unitary System - one I which principal power within the political system lies at the level of a national or central government rather than at the level of some smaller unit, such as a state or province.

United States v Curtiss-Wright Export Corp. (1936) – Supreme Court upheld President Roosevelt's right to ban Curtiss-Wright from selling arms and ammunition directly to foreign governments.

United States v O'Brien **(1968)** - The United States Supreme Court ruled that the burning of draft cards was an unconstitutional act in violation of the First Amendment's guarantee to freedom of speech.

United States v Lopez **(1995)** – Supreme Court struck down a federal law making it a crime to carry a gun within 1,000 of a school.

United States v Nixon – Supreme Court ruled that only the president had the right of executive privilege and not appointees or employees under his/her supervision.

United States v Pink (1942) – Supreme Court's ruling elevated the executive agreement to same status as a treaty under Article VI of the Constitution.

Urban Renewal Program - A federally financed program designed to clear blighted inner city areas and redevelop them with a mixture of commercial and residential properties.

Vertical Federalism - the governing authority that flows up and down between the national and state governments.

Veto - The return of a bill to Congress without a presidential signature and with his stated objections. (See "Pocket Veto.")

Village of Skokie v National Socialist Party **(1978)** - The United States Supreme Court ruled that the denial of a parade permit to the American Nazi Party violated the organization's constitutionally protected right to assemble.

Vocational Rehabilitation Act (1920) - Federal legislation providing financial assistance to disabled Americans.

Voting Rights Act (1965) - Federal legislation suspending the use of literacy tests to determine voting qualifications.

Wallace v Jaffree (1985) - The United States Supreme Court ruled that Alabama's law requiring a moment for voluntary prayer violated the First Amendment's guarantee to freedom of religious beliefs.

War Clause – as stated in the Constitution, only Congress has the power to declare war.

War Labor Disputes Act (1943) – authorizes the president to nationalize key war-related industries in time of national crisis.

War on Poverty - The collective term used for President Lyndon Johnson's programs to address poverty-related issues during the 1960s designed to create a **Great Society**.

West Virginia State Board of Education v Barnette (1943) - The United States Supreme Court ruled that the school district's mandatory flag salute violated the religious rights of school children belonging to the Jehovah Witnesses.

Westbury v Sanders (1964) - United States Supreme Court decision mandating that the United States House of Representatives implement the concept of "one man, one vote: in its redistricting plans.

White Fear - Feeling of becoming a member of a new minority as the existing minority becomes a majority within the social community.

White Flight - The movement of white (Anglo) residents from central cities to the suburbs.

White House Office (WHO) - The people who run the White House and assist the chief executive in a variety of functions including speech writing and secretarial services.

White Only Primary - A tactic used by the Democratic Party in southern states to deny African Americans the right to vote in primary elections; overturned by the United States Supreme Court in *Smith v Allwright* (1944) and *Nixon v Hernon* (1924).

Wilderness - An area where the earth and its community of life are untrammeled by man, and where man himself is a visitor who does not remain.

Woman's Party - A third party movement founded by Alice Paul to address the concerns of women.

Working Poor - The term used to describe those individuals who are employed at jobs paying at or below the poverty level.

Works Project Administration (WPA) - A federally funded Depression Era New Deal program providing jobs to the nation's unemployed.

Writ – an order in writing issued by a court ordering the performance of an act or prohibiting some act.

Writ of *Certiorari* - Order by the Supreme Court requiring a lower court to send the records of a case for it to review.

Writ of *Habeas Corpus* - A direct order to the person detaining another and commanding him to produce a body of the person or persons detained.

Writ of Mandamus - a court order directing a public official to fulfill his/her duties or otherwise be in contempt of court

Youngstown Sheet and Tube Company v Sawyer (1952) – Supreme Court declared unconstitutional President Truman's executive order nationalizing the steel industry..

Index

A

Abington School District v. Schempp (1963), 377
Abolitionist movement, 427
Absentee voting, 127
Absolute poverty, 514
Acid rain, 559
Adams, Abigail, 453
Adams, John, 11, 106, 140, 453
Adams, John Q., 612
Addams, Jane, 527, 528
Adelson, Sheldon, 149
Adelson, Sheldon and Miriam, 143
Adidas, 202
Administration discretion, 279
Administrative law, 336
Administrative Procedures Act (APA) (1946), 285
Adversary system, 393
Advertisements, 186
  political, 191
Advocacy group, 527
  501c, 147
Affective orientations, 67
Affirmative action, 413
Affordable Care Act (ACA), 47, 208, 215, 270, 501, 535
Afghanistan, 589, 590, 620
African Americans, 426
Agnew, Spiro, 325
Agriculturalist tribes, 420
Aid to Families with Dependent Children (AFDC), 529, 537
Aid to the Blind, 529
Air Pollution Control Act (1955), 559
Air Quality Act (1967), 560
Alaska, 613
Alienable rights, 368
Alien Act (1798), 380
Alito, Samuel, 300
Alleviative approach, 494
Alliance, 592
Almshouse, 527
Al Qaeda, 620
Altman and Company v United States (1912), 311
Amendment,
  Eighteenth, , 456
  Eighth, 64, 372, 399
  Fifteenth, 157, 428
  Fifth, 340, 373, 396
  First, 64, 145, 146, 173, 372, 388, 389, 223
  Fourteenth, 42, 64, 349, 372, 389, 415, 428, 431, 436
  Fourth, 64, 397

Nineteenth, 158, 373, 453, 456
Ninth, 40, 369
Second, 392
Seventeenth, 21
Sixth, 398, 401
Tenth, 40, 46, 52, 548
Thirteenth, 64, 373, 428, 431
Twenty-fifth, 317, 327
Twenty-fourth, 435
Twenty-second, 295
Twenty-sixth, 158
American Association of Retired Persons (AARP), 208, 210, 525
American Bar Association (ABA), 206
American Colonization Society, 427
American Farm Bureau Federation, 206
American Federalism: A View from the States (Elazar), 65
American Forestry Association (AFA), 549
American Hospital Association (AHA), 525
American Medical Association (AMA), 206, 212, 215, 525
American Nazi Party, 388, 389
American Recovery and Reinvestment Act, 487
Americans with Disabilities Act (1990), 462, 485
American Woman Suffrage Association, 455
Amicus curiae, 224
Anarchist, 104
Anthony, Susan B., 116, 455
Anti-Comintern Pact, 614
Antiquities Act (1906), 550
Appointment powers, 298
Appropriations, 257
Approval voting, 137
Arab Spring, 619
Archbald, Richard, 351
Architectural Barriers Act (1970), 462
Arctic National Wildlife Refuge, 562
Arraignment, 340
Arthur, Chester, 293
Article II, Section 2, 293
Article I, Section 10, 402
Article of Confederation, 12–14, 37
Ashcroft, John, 209
AT&T, 218
Attorney General, United States, 342–343
Audubon Societies, 550
Aura, 264
Australian ballot, 158
Avants, Ernest, 411

B

Bagger, Rich, 220
Baker v. Carr (1962), 240
Balance of power, 592
Balance of trade, 602

Barenblatt v United States (1959), 315
Barnett, Ross, 47
Barron v. Baltimore (1833), 372
Barr, William, 343
Bataan Death March, 601
Begin, Menachem, 596
Bell, John, 108
Bellwether district, 83
Berlin Lift, 615
Bernoulli, Jacko, 81
Bicameral, 233
Biden, Joe, 96, 151, 188, 304
  abortion, 294
  election of 2020, 153
  inauguration, 291
  money raised from donors, 142
  nominee, 127
  Pro-choice Catholic, 71
  tele-town hall, 127
Big Pharma, 152
Bilateral agreements, 596
Bill of Rights, 64, 369
bin Laden, Osama, 620
Biochemical oxygen demand (BOD), 566
Biomedical Advanced Research and Development Authority, 264
Bipartisan Campaign Reform Act (BCRA), 144, 150, 192
Bipolarity, 592
Birthers, 293
Black Caucus, 251
Black, Hugo, 347, 375
Black Lives Matter Movement, 78, 390, 411, 437
Blanket primary, 130
Bloomberg, Michael, 149, 152
  Advertising, 154
Blue laws,
  Texas, 71
Boehner, John, 111
Bond, Steven Dewayne, 397
Bonilla, Henry, 116
Booth, John Wilke, 322
Borda, Jean-Charles, 137
Bork, Robert, 347
Bosnia, 496
Bourbon Caucus, 251
Bowers, Sam, 411
Boyd v. United States (1886), 396, 402, 403
Bracero program, 444
Brady Bill, 392
Branching question, 83
Brandeis, Louis, 347
Brandenburg v. Ohio (1969), 389
Brandies, Louis D., 19
Breckenridge, John C., 108
Brest-Litovsk Treaty, 614
Bribery, 225
Brigham City v Stuart (2006), 397
British Petroleum (BP), 35

Brookings Institution, 270
Brooks, Preston, 476
Brown, Michael, 391, 437
Brown v the Board of Education of Topeka, Kansas (1954), 349, 363, 413, 436, 483
Brussels Pact, 615
Buchanan, Patrick, 191
Buchanan v Warley (1917), 432
Buckley v. Valeo (1976), 144, 145, 151, 218, 380
Bundling, 148
Bunting v Oregon (1917), 46
Bureaucracy,
   benefits of, 286
   composition of, 276
   decision-making,
      incremental model of, 281
      rational-comprehensive model of, 281
   development of, 265
   federal,
      organization of, 273
   functions of, 272
   political resources of, 279
   presidential control over, 282
   rule administration of, 277
   size of, 270
Bureaucrats,
   role in policy making, 483
Bureau of Alcohol, Tobacco, Firearms and Explosives (ATF), 345, 392
Bureau of Prisons, 342, 362
Burger, Warren, 376
Burke, Edmund, 1, 10, 95, 100, 236
Burr, Aaron, 106
Burwell v Hobby Lobby (2014), 379
Bush, George H. W.,
   Gulf War, 501
   North American Free Trade Agreement, 618
Bush, George W., 47, 53
   Afghanistan, 79
   civil liberties, 368
   education reforms, 519
   environmental issues, 553
   tax refunds, 502
Business Roundtable, 204
Butler, Andrew, 476
Buttigieg, Pete,
   Iowa Caucus, 129
Byrd, James, 409, 492

C

Cabinet, 273
California Institute of Technology, 269
California v. Trombetta (1984), 403
Campaigns,
   congressional nominations, 133
   effects of financing, 142
   historical background, 128

   nominating candidates, 128
   nominations for state offices, 133
   strategies, 153
Campbell, John, 179
Camp David Accords, 596
Campesino, 442
Canon law, 335
Capitalism, 64
Capitalism: The Unknown Ideal (Rand), 102
Carson, Rachel, 549, 551
Carter, Jimmy, 596
   Iran hostage crisis, 501
   Panama Canal Treaty, 609
   Soviet grain embargo, 489
Casework, 239
Case-Zablocki Act (1972), 311, 610
Castro, Fidel, 485, 603, 619
Castro, Julian, 118, 452
Castro, Raul, 619
Catanzaro, Michael, 220
Catholics, 162
Catt, Carrie Chapman, 456
Caucus, 111, 129, 130
Census, 240
Center for Democracy and Technology, 209
Center for Substance Abuse and Prevention (CSAP), 217
Center for Voting and Democracy, 137
Centers for Disease Control and Prevention, 264
Central Intelligence Agency (CIA), 267, 273
Centrist, 101
Chamber of Commerce, 204
Chaney, James, 411
Change of venue, 401
Charging document, 340
Chase, Samuel, 350
Chávez, César, 213, 442
Chicago,
   convention in, 130
China, 616
Chlorofluorocarbons, 555
Christian Coalition, 71
Church of the Lukumi Babbalu Aye v Hialeah (1993), 379
Ciccone, Christine, 220
Circuit judges, 336
Citizen journalism, 183
Citizens United v Federal Elections Commission (2010), 145, 380
Civil Aeronautics Board (CAB), 268
Civilian Conservation Corps (CCC), 528
Civility Caucus, 251
Civil law, 337
Civil liberties, 368
Civil rights, 412
Civil Rights Act (1875), 431
Civil Rights Act (1957), 434
Civil Rights Act (1960), 434

Civil Rights Act (1964), 246, 434, 435
Civil Rights Act (1968), 390, 434
Civil Service Reform Act (1978), 276
Civil service system, 275
Claiborne, Harry, 351
Clay, Henry, 427
Clean Air Act (1963), 552, 559
Clean Air Act (1970), 278, 552, 560
Clean Air Act (1990), 561
Clean Water Act (1972), 566
"Clear and present danger," 372
Cleveland, Grover, 141
Clientele,
   groups, 215
   services, 272
   support, 280
Clinton, Bill, 53, 320, 549
   welfare reform of, 473, 534
Clinton, Hillary, 120, 457
   campaign of 2008, 134
   e-mails, 155, 173
   popular vote of, 141
Clinton v City of New York (1998), 309
Closed primary, 130
Cloture, 253
Cluster zones, 65
Coates v. Cincinnati (1971), 374
Cognitive orientations, 67
Cohen v. California (1971), 382
Cohen v Virginia (1821), 44
Cold War, 590, 592, 598, 615
Colonialism, 595
Committee on Fair Employment Practices, 313
Common Cause, 152
Communications Decency Act (1997), 388
Communism, 104
Communist Manifest (Marx and Engles), 104, 372
Community Right-to-Know-More Act (1991), 572
Compact theory, 47
Concurrent majority, 48
Confederation, 36
Conference committees, 254
Conglomerate ownership, 182
Congress,
   campaign financing, 243
   caucuses of, 251
   committee system of, 246
      membership of, 249
      types of, 248
   expressed powers of, 233
   formal leadership of, 244
   legislative process of, 251
   organizational structure of, 244
   origin of, 232
   powers of, 232
   representation in, 236
      quality of, 237

staff system of, 250
Congressional Bike Caucus, 251
Congressional Black Caucus, 238
Congressional Budget Office, 250
Congressional Future Caucus, 251
Congressional Hispanic Caucus, 238
Congressional Kidney Caucus, 251
Congressional Oversight Committee, 257
Congressional Research Service, 250
Congressional Soccer Caucus, 251
Congressional Union, 456
Congress of Racial Equality (CORE), 433
Connally, John, 323
Connecticut Plan, 20
Conrad, Jim, 416
Conservatism, 99–100
Constitution,
    Article I, 38
    Article VI, 38
    elastic clause, 39
    Full Faith and Credit Clause, 42
    implied powers doctrine, 39
    necessary and proper, 39
Constitutional law, 336
Constitutional Union Party, 108
Constrained Empathetic Federalism, 53
Containment policy, 615
Continental Congress, 11
Contract clause, 402
Contractual Theory, 296
"Contract with America," 56
Contras, 600
Controlled Substance Act, 451, 343
Cooperative federalism, 51
Cooper v. Harris (2017), 241
Coronavirus Aid, Relief, and Economic
    Security Act, 201, 232
Coronavirus (Covid-19), 33, 77-78, 201,
    263, 469-470, 510
Council on Environmental Quality, 552
Court packing scheme, 350
Cousins v Wigoda (1975), 119
Coyle v Smith (1911), 49
Cranston, Alan, 219
Creative federalism, 51
Credentials committee, 119
Criminal law, 338
Crossroads GPS, 150
Cruz, Ted, 293, 111
    Iowa Caucus, 129
Cuba, 618
Cuban Missile Crisis, 496
Cultural assimilation and separation, 422
Cultural conservatism, 100
Cumulative voting, 137
Cuomo, Andrew, 35
Cuomo, Mario, 118
Curbelo, Carlos, 246
Currency Act, 10
Czolgosz, Leon, 322

D

Dakota Access Pipeline, 563
Daley, Richard, 117
Dawes Severalty Act (1887), 423
Deal, Nathan, 33
Dean, Howard, 155
Dean, John, 321
Death penalty, 372
Debs, Eugene V., 103
Declaration of Independence, 11
Declaration of Paris, 601
Declaration of Sentiments and Resolutions,
    454-455
DeConcini, Dennis, 219
Deduction, 80
De facto discrimination, 413
Defendant, 337
Defenders of Wildlife, 208
Defense of Marriage Act (DOMA), 461
Deferred Action for Childhood Arrivals
    (DACA), 333, 415, 488, 618
Deferred Action for Parents of Americans
    and Lawful Permanent Residents
    (DAPA), 451
De jure discrimination, 413
Delahay, Mark, 351
Delgado, Antonio, 452
Democracy, 5
Democratic Conference (caucus), 245
Democratic National Committee (DNC),
    115
Democratic Party v La Follette (1891), 119
Democratic socialism, 103
Department of Health and Human Ser-
    vices, 217, 267
Department of Homeland Security, 474,
    391, 388, 215, 273
Deregulation, 268
DeVos, Betsy, 150
Dewey, Thomas,
    Polling results, 62
Diaz, President Profirio, 444
Dickinson, John, 12
Digital Due, 209
Disabled Americans, 462
Discharge petition, 246
Disparate treatment, 462
Distributive policies, 495
Domestic surveillance, 247
Domino theory, 616
Donor contributions, 143
"Don't Ask, Don't Tell," 207
Douglass, Frederick, 419, 426
Douglas, Stephen A., 108, 476
Dream Act, 451, 488
Dred Scott v Sandford (1857), 373
Dual federalism, 50
Due process, 373

E

Eagleton, Thomas, 325
Early voting, 128
Earth Day, 554
Economic Opportunity Act (1965), 529
Economic stimulus package, 486
Education, 71
Edwards Recharge Zone, 79
Egypt, 596
Eisenhower, Dwight, 108
Elastic clause, 234
Elasticity, 498
Elderly, poverty of, 520
Elections,
    campaigning in, 142
    candidate image in, 163
    issues of, 162
    political participation in, 157
    presidential, 138
        electoral college, 138
    senatorial, 138
    turn-out, 159
    voter party identification, 161
Electoral College, 21, 141
    allocation of votes, 140
Electronic Frontier Foundation, 209
Ellsberg, Daniel, 387
Ellsworth, Oliver, 354
Emergency Relief Administration, 528
EMILY's List, 206
Eminent domain, 41
Emolument clause, 25
Empirical research, 80
Empowerment zones, 53
Empresario system, 441
Endangered Species Act (ESA) (1973),
    552, 574
Enforcement Act of 1871, 432
Engagious Swing Voter Project, 153
Engles, Friedrich, 104
Engle v. Vitale (1962), 377
Enron, 152, 269
Entitlements, 531
Enumerated powers, 233
Environmental Defense Fund, 208, 578
Environmental groups, 208
Environmental laws, 556
Environmental Protection Act (1970), 575
Environmental Protection Agency (EPA),
    35, 47, 215, 273, 277, 337, 552,
    560, 576
Equal Employment Opportunity Act, 485
Equal Employment Opportunity *Com-
    mission v Abercrombie and Fitch*
    (2015), 379
Equal Rights Amendment (ERA), 246
Equal Rights Party, 453
Equity law, 336
Escobedo v. Illinois (1964), 398
Espionage Act (1917), 381

Essay Concerning Human Understanding (Locke), 369
Establishment clause, 374
Ethics Act, 300
Ethics in Government Act, 225
Ethnocentrism, 595
European Union (EU), 603
Evaluative orientations, 67
Evangelical Protestants, 207
Evers, Medgar, 437
Everson v Board of Education of the Township of Ewing (1947), 359
Exclusionary rule, 339
Executive agreement, 310, 609, 609–610
Executive order, 312
Executive Order 8802, 313
Executive Order 9066, 606
Executive Order 9981, 313
Executive Order 12612, 53
Executive Order 13891, 282
Executive privilege, 315
ExxonMobil, 276
Exxon Valdez, 569

F

Facebook, 170
Factions, 110
    Tea Party Movement, 111
Fair Labor Standards Act, 104
Faithless electors, 139, 141
Faith Spotted Eagle, 139
Family environment, 70
Fascism, 614
Fauci, Anthony, 263
Federal Activities Inventory Reform Act (1998), 270
Federal Advisory Committee Act, 285
Federal Appellate Courts, 352
Federal Aviation Agency (FAA), 274
Federal Bureau of Investigation (FBI), 343, 409
Federal Communications Commission (FCC), 174, 274, 282, 388
Federal Court System,
    Constitutional courts, 346–356
    Federal Appellate Courts, 352-353
    Federal District Courts, 351
    jurisdiction, 351
    selection of judges, 346–347
    Supreme Court, 353–354
Federal Deposit Insurance Corporation (FDIC), 275
Federal District Courts, 351
Federal Election Campaign Act (FECA) (1971), 144, 218
Federal Election Commission (FEC), 144, 145, 152
Federal Election Commission v. Wisconsin Right to Life, Inc., 192
Federal Fair Labor Standards Act, 46

Federal grants, 53–55
    block grants, 54
    categorical grant, 54
    formula grants, 54
    mandates, 55
    project grants, 54
    revenue sharing, 54
Federalism, 37
Federalist #48, 296
Federalist Papers, The, 180
Federal justice system,
    attorney general, 342–343
    Department of Justice, 343–345
    Federal Bureau of Investigation (FBI), 343
Federal Radio Act (1927), 174
Federal Register Act, 312
Federal Regulation of Lobbying Act (1946), 223
Federal system, 36
Federal Trade Commission (FTC) (1914), 266
Federal Water Pollution Control Act of 1972, 552
Felony, 338
Fenno, John, 180
Ferguson, Mike, 220
Fiduciary trust, 5
Fight for the Future, 210
Fighting words, 381
Filibuster, 253
Fish and Wildlife Service, 574
Flemming v Nestor (1960), 531
Floyd, George, 73, 159, 390, 411, 437
Floyd, William, 11
Food and Drug Administration (FDA), 264, 266, 278
Food Stamp Program, 532
Ford, Christine, 348
Ford, Gerald,
    pardon of Nixon, 306
Foreign Operations Bill, 239
Foreign policy,
    definition of, 588
    terminology, 588–590
Fortas, Abe, 382
Fourteen Points, 310
Fracking, 562
Franco, Francisco, 609
Franklin, James, 386
Freedom of Information Act (FOIA) (1967), 285
Freedoms,
    assemble and association, 388
    of religion, 374
    of speech, 379
    of the press, 386
Free enterprise, 64
Free Press, 210
Frémont, John C., 108
Freneau, Philip, 180

Fugitive Slave Laws, 427
Fullilove v Klutznik (1980), 42
Furman v Georgia (1972), 399

G

Gabbard, Tulsi, 251
Gag order, 341
Gallup, George, 63
Gans, Herbert, 184
Garcia v San Antonio Metropolitan Transit Authority (1985), 46
Garfield, James, 275
Garland, Merrick B., 300, 348
Gay and lesbian rights, 207
General Agreement on Tariffs and Trade (GATT), 603
General Revenue Fund, 54
General Revision Act (1891), 550
Geneva Conventions, 601
Genocide, 601
Georgia v Randolph (2006), 397
Gerrymandering, 136, 240
Gibbons v Ogden (1824), 38, 45
Gideon v. Wainwright (1963), 353, 398
Gilman, Francis Perkins, 455
Gingrich, Newt, 56
Ginsburg, Ruth Bader, 399
Gitlow v. New York (1925), 372
Glass ceiling, 457
Glenn, John, 219
Global pandemic of 2020, 127
Global warming, 564
Goesaert v Cleary (1948), 42
Gonzales, Alberto, 247, 452
Gorbachev, Mikhail, 595
Gore, Al, 549, 553
    environmental policies, 553
Gorsuch, Neil, 347
Government contracts, 484
Government corporations, 275
Gradual Abolition Act, 427
Grandfather clause, 429
Grand jury, federal, 340
Grant, 53
Grants-in-aid, 54
Grant, Ulysses S., 117
Grassroots, 108
Grassroots lobbying, 224
Great Britain, 598
Great Compromise, 20, 232
Great Society, 51, 267, 481
Green Book, The (Green), 73
Greenfield, Jeff, 188
Green Party, 110
Greenpeace, 216, 578
Grenada, 176
Gridlock, 231–232
Grimke, Sarah, 454
Grisham, Michelle Lujan, 452
Guest worker program, 618

Guinn v. United States (1915), 435
Guiteau, Charles J., 302
Gulf of Tokin Resolution, 606
Gulf war, 485
Gun Control Act, 392
Gutierrez, Jose Angel, 451

H

Habeas Corpus, Writ of, 42
Hagel, Chuck, 300, 457
Hague Convention of 1907, 601
Hamilton, Alexander, 22, 24, 26, 105,
    106, 180, 293
Hammurabi, King, 335
Hanseatic League, 592
Harris, Fred, 119
Harris, Kamala, 293, 299
Harrison, Benjamin, 141
Hart, John, 11
Hastings, Alecee, 351
Hatch Act (1939), 143
Hate crimes, 418
Hayes, Rutherford, 141
Hay-Herran Treaty, 597
Hay-Pauncefote Treaty, 608
Haze, 555
Health-care package, 535–540
Health-care reform, 525
Health Care Reform Law, 278
Hearst, William Randolph, 181
Hegemony, 595
Hemings, Sally, 107
Highway Traffic Safety Administration,
    267
Hill, Anita, 347
Hinckley, John Jr., 323
History of the Crown (Hale), 395
Hitler, Adolph, 614
Holder, Eric, 342
Holmes, Oliver Wendell, 346
Holt, Rick, 220
Holy Alliance, 592
*Home Building and Loan Association v
    Blaisdell* (1934), 402
Homes, Oliver Wendell, 336
Homosexual Community, 461
Hoover, J. Edgar, 343
Horizontal federalism, 42
Host culture, 414
House Financial Services Committee, 248
House of Burgess, 9
House Oversight and Reform Committe,
    248, 283
House Permanent Select Committee on
    Intelligence, 248
House Rules Committee, 249, 253
Huanan Seafood Wholesale Market, 469
Hudson v Michigan (2006), 397
Hull House, 528
Human Home, The (Walker), 548

Hume, David, 61
Humphrey, Hubert, 131
Humphreys, West, 351
Hurricane Katrina, 511
Hussein, Saddam, 619
Hypothesis, 80

I

Ideology, 99
Illegal immigration, 618
Illinois v Krull (1967), 339
Illusion of central tendency, 79
Illusion of saliency, 79
Impeachment, 233
Inalienable rights, 368, 404
Incompatibility Clause, 299
Incremental process, 500
Independent agencies, 273
Independent delegates, 119
Independent groups-527s, 146
Indian Removal Act (1830), 421
Indian Self-Determination and Education
    Assistance Act, 422
Indirect democracy, 6
Individualistic approach, 66
Ineligibility Clause, 299
Injunction, 336
Integration, 434
Interest groups,
    biases in, 211
    citizen groups, 206
    common features of, 210
    defining, 202
    economic, 204
    government groups, 210
    litigating of, 224
    lobbying, 220
    methods and strategies, 217
    overcoming obstacles of, 212
    political parties versus, 202
    proliferation of, 214
    reform prospects, 226
    roles of, 203
    sources of proliferation, 215
Intergovernmental relations (IGR), 31
Interim appointments, 301
Intermediate-Range Nuclear Forces Treaty,
    599
Intermestic issues, 489
Internal Revenue Service, 279, 498
International Criminal Court (ICC), 601
International Development Association
    (IDA), 603
International Monetary Fund (IMF), 603
International Trade Commission (ITC),
    274
Internet,
    campaigning on the, 155
    mass media of the, 172
Internet surveys, 86

Interposition, 48
Interstate Commerce Commission (ICC),
    45
Interstate compact, 56
Interstate rendition, 43
Interviewer bias, 84
Intrastate commerce, 45
Iowa caucuses, 129
Iran, 590
Iran/Contra Conflict, 600
Iraq, 485
Iron Law of Oligarchy, 116
Iron Triangle, 221-222, 280
Isolationism, 591
Israel, 596
Issa, Darrell, 247

J

Jackson, Andrew, 140, 275
Jackson, Jesse, 158
Japan, 598
Japanese-American Security Treaty, 598
Japanese internments, 418
Jay, John, 14, 26
Jay Treaty, 608
Jefferson, Thomas, 11, 19, 22, 24, 35, 106,
    373, 426
    religious tolerance, 375
    use of executive agreement, 609
Jet Propulsion Laboratory, 269
Jim Crow laws, 417, 429
Jindal, Bobby, 34, 293
John Birch Society, 100
Johnson, Andrew, 25, 319
Johnson, Gary, 112
Johnson, Lyndon, 51, 231, 588
    Great Society, 267
    presidential campaign, 131
    State of the Union, 1964, 509
    War on Poverty program, 215, 493, 529
Joint committees, 249
Judicial activism, 349
Judicial review, 354–355, 372, 483
Judicial self-restraint, 349
Judiciary Act of 1789, 342, 354, 372
Jurisdiction, 351

K

Kagan, Elena, 347
Kai-shek, Chiang, 616
Katrina hurricane, 32
Katz v. United States (1967), 403
Kavanaugh, Brett, 223, 284, 348
Keating, Charles, 219
Keating Five, 219
Kelo v New London (2005), 41
Kennedy, Edward,
    immigration, 448
Kennedy, John, 323
    Cuban Missile crisis, 496

media coverage, 181
    presidential campaign, 131
    use of executive agreement, 609
Kennedy, Robert, 131
Kent, Samuel, 351
Kerry, John, 71, 598
Keynote address, 118
Keystone Pipeline, 554, 563
Kim Jong-un, 586
King, Martin Luther, Jr., 433
Kisor v. Wilkie (2019), 284
Kissinger, Henry, 595
Know-Nothings, 415
Knox, Henry, 22
Korean War, 609
Korematsu v United States (1944), 418
KORUS, 599
Ku Klux Klan (KKK), 388, 389, 409, 431
Kurds, 588
Kuwait, 485
Kyoto Protocol, 565

L

Laissez-faire, 103, 265, 267
Landon, Alf, 62
La Raza Unida (LRU), 451
Law,
    codification of, 334–335
    terminology of, 337–339
Layered cake federalism, 50
League of Nations, 310, 593, 614
League of United Latin American Citizens
        (LULAC), 452
Lee v Weisman (1992), 378
Legislative veto, 283
Lemon test, 376
Lemon v. Kurtzman (1971), 376
Lend-lease, 614
Lenin, Vladimir, 104, 614
Levant (ISIL), 620
Lewinsky, Monica, 320
LGBTQ Victory Fund, 207
Liberalism, 101
Libertarians, 102
Library of Congress, 250
License, 485
Light, Paul, 270
Likert Scale, 83
Limbaugh, Rush, 154, 172
Lincoln, Abraham, 42, 108, 321
    civil liberties, 368
Line-item veto, 255, 309
Literacy test, 429
Little Lenin Library, The (Lenin), 104
Lobbying, 220
    grassroots, 224
Lobbying Transparency and Accountability
        Act, 223
Locke, John, 102, 368
Logan Act, 311

London Protocol of 1936, 601
L'Oréal, 202
Loyalists, 10
Lynch, Loretta E., 342

M

MacArthur, Douglas, 302, 616
Maddox, Lester, 47
Madison, James, 20, 24, 26, 105, 214, 226
Magna Carta, 7, 368
Mainstream, 101
Majority,
    floor leader, 245
Malcolm X, 437
Manifest destiny, 421
Mapp v. Ohio (1961), 396
Marble cake federalism, 51
Marbury v Madison (1803), 359
Marketplace Fairness Act, 210
Mark-up, 246, 252
Marshall, John, 43, 45, 106, 346
Marshall Plan, 615
Marshall, Thurgood, 224, 432
Marshall Trilogy, 421
Marsh, George, 549
Martin, Trayvon, 390, 411, 437
Marxism-Leninism, 104
Marx, Karl, 104
Matthew Shepard and James Byrd, Jr., Hate
        Crime Prevention Act, 418
McCain-Feingold, 132
McCain, John, 219
    campaign financing, 146
    immigration, 448
    public financing, 151
McCarthy, Eugene, 131
McConnell, Mitch, 202, 300, 524
McCullough v Maryland (1819), 43, 50
McGovern-Fraser Commission, 117, 120
McGovern, George, 120, 325
McKinley, William, 322
McKinney, Cynthia, 137
McLaurin v. Oklahoma State Regents
        (1950), 436
McMahon, Linda, 150
McNamara, Robert, 611
Mean distribution, 80
Measurement error, 80
Media, 76
    behavior alteration, 194
    biases, 186
        negativity, 187
    campaign coverage, 188
        gaffes, 188
        horserace, 188
        incumbent, 188
    congressional coverage, 189
    effects of, 193
    government regulation of, 173
    importance of, 178

news gathering process, 184
    personal backgrounds, 184
political functions of, 176
politician management, 189
presidential coverage, 189
setting the political agenda, 193
structure of mass, 170
Median distribution, 80
Medicaid, 525, 537–538
Medicare, 525, 538–541
Medicare Prescription Drug Improvement
        and Modernization Act, 538
Medigap insurance, 539
Meredith, James, 47, 430
Mestizos, 441
Mexican-American Legal Defense and Edu-
        cational Fund (MALDF), 452
Mexico, 618
Microsoft, 224
Middle East, 619
Miers, Harriet, 247, 300
Militia Act of 1862, 428
Militia Act of 1792, 390
Miller v. California (1973), 385
Minimum wage, 516
Minnick v Mississippi (1990), 339
Minority,
    floor leader, 245
Minor v Happersat (1875), 454
Miranda, Ernesto, 394
Miranda v Arizona (1966), 394
Misdemeanor, 338
Mississippi Freedom Democratic Party,
        130
Mississippi v Johnson (1857), 316
Missouri Compromise (1820), 427
Mitchell v Helms (2000), 376
Model Cities, 529
Moderna Therapeutics, 265
"Moment of silence," 378
Monaco v Mississippi (1934), 311
Monroe Doctrine, 612
Montreal Protocol, 555
Moralistic perspective, 65
Morgan v Virginia (1946), 434
Mothers Against Drunk Driver (MADD),
        216, 252
Mott, Lucretia, 455
Moyer, Bill, 188
Muir, John, 549
Mulinix, David, 139
Multiculturalism, 414
Multi-lateral agreements, 596
Muskie, Edmund, 552
Muslim religion, 619
Myers v United States (1926), 19

N

N95 respirator masks, 264
NAACP 433

Nader, Ralph, 110, 133, 191, 267
NASA (National Aeronautics and Space Administrati 273
National Alliance to End Homelessness, 520
National ambient air quality standards (NAAQS), 560
National American Women Suffrage Association, 455
National Association of Counties, 210
National Association of Manufacturers (NAM), 204
National Association of Realtors, 218
National Audubon Society, 208
National Beer Wholesalers Association, 218
National Defense Act, 305
National Environmental Policy Act of 1970, 552
National Farmers Organization, 206
National Firearms Act, 392
National Governors' Association, 210
National Health Act, 536
National Institutes of Health, 263, 265
National interests, 588, 589
National League of Cities, 210
National League of Cities v Usery (1976), 46
National Network for Election Reform, 195
National Organization for Women (NOW), 206
National Origins Act, 450
National Pollution Discharge Elimination System (NPDES), 566
National Resources Defense Council, 578
National Rifle Association (NRA), 209, 212, 392
National Safety Agency (1966), 267
National Security Agency (NSA), 388
National Security Council (NSC), 263, 610
National Wildlife Federation, 208
National Women's Caucus, 206
Native Americans, 420
Nativism, 414
Nazism, 614
Near v. Minnesota (1931), 386
Negligence, 337
Neighborhood Guild, 528
Nelson, Bill, 242
Net neutrality, 175, 209
Neutrality, 591
New Deal, 51, 266
New Federalism, 52
New Hampshire primary, 134
New Jersey Plan, 20, 233
New Left, 102
"New Politics" movement, 216
New Right, 100
New York Times v. Sullivan (1971), 384

New York Times v United States (1971), 386
New York Women's Trade Union, 455
Nixon, Richard, 52, 321, 481, 552
    environmental action by, 560
    environmental leadership, 552
    pardon, 306
    use of executive agreement, 609
Nixon v Fitzgerald (1982), 315
Nixon v. Hernon (1927), 434
Nixon, Walter, 351
No Child Left Behind, 520
Nomadic tribes, 420
Nongovernmental bodies (NGOs), 610
Nonworking poor, 514
North American Free Trade Agreement (NAFTA), 599, 618
North Atlantic Treaty Organization (NATO), 592, 615
North Korea, 590, 616, 616–617
Northrop, 218
Northwest Land Ordinance Act, 53
Nullification, 48
Nutrition Labeling and Education Act, 278

O

Obama, Barack, 190, 191, 270, 379, 391, 511
    Election of 2008, 437
    environment, 549
    health care, 535–540
    natural born status, 293
    net neutrality, 175
    on racial equality, 409
    on sexual discrimination, 461
    public funding rejected, 151
Obergefell v Hodges (2015), 352, 462
Ocasio-Cortez, Alexandria, 452
Occupational Safety and Health Act, 485
Occupational Safety and Health Administration (OSH), 274
O'Connor, Sandra Day, 346
Office of Public Liaison, 220
Office of Special Counsel, 285
Ogden, Aaron, 45
Ohio's Criminal Syndicalism Act, 389
Old Age Assistance, 529
Olmstead, Ray, 403
Olmstead v. United States (1928), 403
Olney, Richard, 609
Olson, Mancur, 211
Omnibus Crime Control and Safe Streets Act (1968), 403
Open primary, 130
Oral arguments, 353
Oswald, Lee Harvey, 33, 323
Outputs, 477
Ozone, 555

P

Paine, Thomas, 10
Pakistan, 620
Palatucci, William, 220
Palin, Sarah, 325
Palko v. Connecticut (1937), 393
Panama Canal Treaty, 609
Pandemic, 470
Pardon, 305
Parenti, Michael, 186
Parent-Teacher Associations, 210
Paris Agreement, 599
Park Protection Act, 550
Parks, Rosa, 433
Participatory democracy, 61
Paternalistic attitude, 453
Patient Protection and Affordable Care Act, 488
Patriot Act, 247, 391, 474
Patriots, 12
Patronage, 239
Patterson, William, 20
Paul, Alice, 456
Paycheck Protection Program, 232
Peace Corp, 313
Peace of Westphalia of 1648, 591
Pearl Harbor, 614
Peck, James, 351
Peer groups, 74
Pelican Island, 550
Pelosi, Nancy, 245, 307, 478
Pence, Mike, 318
Pendleton Act (1883), 275
Penny press, 180
People for the American Way, 206
Peremptory challenges, 341
Perez, Tom, 127
Perkins, Frances, 104
Perot, Ross, 110, 133, 141
Perry, Rick, 110, 276
Personal Responsibility and Work Opportunity Act, 534
Pfizer, 41
Pickering, John, 350
Pinckney, Charles, 608
Pinckney, Clementa C., 410
Pinckney, Thomas, 106
Pink collar, 457
Pitt, William, 395
Plaintiff, 337
Plea bargaining, 339
Pledged delegates, 119
Plintz v United States (1997), 46
Pluralism, 214
Pocket veto, 308, 255
Police power, 40
Policy Committee, 245
Political Action Committees (PACs), 144, 218
    effects of, 219

Political culture, 63
Political efficacy, 69
Political parties,
  anatomy of, 95–98
  caucuses within, 111
  factions in, 110–111
  historical Development of, 96
  multiparty system, 97
  national conventions of, 116
  National Party Organization, 115–117
  platform of, 117
  political spectrum, 99
  role in policy making, 480
  stratarchy of, 115
  two-party system, 98
Political socialization, 68
  Education, 71
  Family environment, 70
  Major events, 77
  Peer groups, 74
  Race/Ethnic orientation, 73
  Religious affiliations, 71
  Social class, 74
Politics Among Nations: The Struggle for Power and Peace (Morgenthau), 600
Polling, 153
Poll tax, 429
Pollution, 555
Pollution Prevention Act (1990), 572
Poll watchers, 157
Pork-barrel legislation, 138, 239, 498
Porteous, Thomas Jr., 351
Postal service system, 275-276
Poverty,
  feminization of, 515
  levels of, 513
  philosophy of, 522
  politics of, 522
  profile of, 516
Powell, Colin, 482
Powell v. Alabama (1932), 398
Pragmatic federalism, 53
Precinct, 121
Preemptive strike, 601
Prerogative Theory, 297
Presidente Rivera, 569
Presidential Succession Act of 1947, 244
President pro tempore, 245
Preventive strategy, 494
Primary system, 129
Private bill, 239
Probability sampling, 81
Probable cause, 396
Procedural problems, 490
Pro-choice abortion position, 71
Proclamation of 1763, 421
Proclamation of Neutrality, 612
Progressive movement, 265
Progressive tax, 499
Project Safe Neighborhoods, 345

Prometheus v. FCC, 185
Promoting the Rule of Law Through Improved Agency Guidance Documents, 282
Proportional tax, 499
Proprietary function, 41
Public assistance programs, 532
Public opinion, 78–81
  measuring, 79
    sample, 81
  role in policy making, 478
Public opinion polls, 80
  Formulating the questions, 82
Public policy,
  agenda building, 492
  budgeting of, 497
  definition of, 476
  evaluation of, 504
  implementation of, 503
  political implications of, 500
  process of, 488
  who makes, 478
Pulitzer, Joseph, 181
Punitive approach, 493
Pure Food and Drug Act, 552

Q

Qatar, 209
Quadruple Alliance, 592, 612
Quartering Act, 10
Quasi-judicial authority, 337
Quasi-legislative authority, 337
Quayle, Dan, 163
Quota sampling, 81

R

Race/Ethnic orientation, 73
Racial profiling, 419
Racism,
  of African Americans, 426
  of Native Americans, 420
  theories of, 414
Radical Republicans, 429
Radical Right, 100
Railroad Retirement Act (1934), 266
Randolph, Edmund, 21, 22, 342
Random sampling, 81
Ratification, 26
Reagan, Ronald, 46, 52, 323
  deregulation viewpoint of, 267
  election of 1980, 267
  immigration, 445
  privatization, 270
Reapportionment, 135
Recess appointment, 301
Reconstruction Acts, 319
Redistributive policy, 495
Redistricting, 240
Redlining, 432
Reed, Kasim, 33

Reed v Town of Gilbert, Arizona (2015), 380
Reflections on the Revolution in France (Burke), 5
Reform,
  health-care, 535
  welfare, 535
Reform Party, 110
Refuse Act (1899), 550
Regressive tax, 499
Regulatory actions, 496
Rehabilitation Act (1973), 462
Relative poverty, 514
Religious affiliations, 71
Religious Right, 100
Renaissance Technologies, 204
Reno, Janet, 458
Representative democracy, 6
Representative Government, in Utilitarianism, Liberty and Representative Government (Mill), 61
Republican National Committee (RNC), 115
Reserved powers, 40, 548
Resource Conservation and Recovery Act, 571
Restoring Internet Freedom Order, 175
Restrictive covenant, 432
Rice, Thomas Dartmouth, 429
Ricketts, Todd, 150
Riegle, Donald, 219
Rights of Man, The (Paine), 8
Rio Pact, 615
Riot Acts, 390
Ritter, Halsted, 351
Robb, Chuck, 588
Roberts, John, 47, 137, 241
Robertson, Pat, 71
Roberts, Owen, 350
Robot journalism, 183
Rockefeller, Nelson, 327
Rodriguez, Ciro, 116
Roe v. Wade (1973), 215, 457-458, 483
Roof, Dylann, 410
Roosevelt, Franklin, 51, 105, 108, 350, 266, 473
  civil liberties, 368
  re-election of 1936, 62
  use of executive agreements, 609
Roosevelt, Theodore, 549
Rotary Club, 210
Roth v United States (1957), 385
Rousseau, Jean Jacques, 368
Rove, Karl, 150, 247
Rubio, Marco, 293, 451-452
Ruby, Jack, 323
Rule adjudication, 278
Rush-Bagot Agreement, 312, 609
Rush, Benjamin, 11
Rusk, Dean, 611
Russell Amendment, 313

Russia, 591
Russian hacking, 156
Rutledge, John, 24

S

Sadat, Anwar, 596
Safety net, 531
Safe Water Drinking Act (1974), 567
Saliency, 78
Sample, 81
Sampling bias, 82
Sanders, Bernie, 118, 120
   campaign of 2020, 127
   Democrat, 133
Scalia, Antonin, 46
Schenck v. United States (1919), 372, 381
Schock, Aaron, 251
Schrank, John Flammang, 323
Schumer, Chuck, 202
Scott, Dred, 428
Scott, Rick, 242
Search warrant, 339
Second-strike capability, 600
Secret Service, 324
Sectionalism, 64
Sedition Acts (1798), 380
Select committees, 248
Selective incorporation, 372
Selective polling, 81
Senate Bill 1070, 419
Senatorial courtesy, 300
Senior Executive Service (SES), 276
Seniority system, 250
Separate but equal, 430, 435
Separate Car Act (1890), 430
Separation of powers doctrine, 19
Serrano, Jose, 452
Sessions, Jeff, 343
Settlement house, 527
Seymour, Horatio, 117
Shaw, Anna Howard, 456
Shays, Daniel, 15
Shelley v Kraemer (1944), 433
Shepard, Matthew, 410
Sherman, Robert, 20
Shiites, 588
Shriver, Sargent, 325
Sierra Club, 94, 216, 549, 578
Signing statements, 314
Silverman v. United States (1961), 403
Skinhead groups, 388
Skinner v. Railway Labor Executives Association (1989), 403
Slaughterhouse Cases (1873), 393
Small Business Administration, 273
Smith Act, 392
Smith, Adam, 103
Smith, Al, 294
Smith, Howard "Judge," 246
Smith v. Allwright (1944), 434

Smog, 555
Smoot-Hawley Tariff Act, 603
Snowden, Eric, 388
Social class, 74
Social contract, 5
Social contract theory, 102
Socialism, 103
Social liberalism, 103
Social Media, 173–174
Social Security, 266, 272, 530
Social Security Act (1935), 266, 489, 528
Social Security Administration, 513
Society of Friends, 427
Soft money, 132, 144, 145, 146
Solicitor General of the United States, 345
Solis, Brian, 187
Soros, George, 149
Sotomayor, Sonia, 347
Souter, David, 348
South Carolina v Baker (1988), 46
Southern Baptist/Methodist Bible Belt, 71
Southern Christian Leadership Conference (SCLC), 433
South Korea, 616
Sovereigntist approach, 592
Speaker of the House, 244
Special interest groups, 132
Special sessions of Congress, 307
Spin doctor, 190
Spirit of the Laws (Montesquieu), 7
Stalin, Joseph, 615
Stamp Act (1765), 10, 180
Standing committees, 248
Stanton, Edwin M., 320
Stanton, Elizabeth Cady, 455
Starr, Kenneth, 320
State of the Union address, 306
States' rights, 47
Steering, 432
Steering Committee, 245
Stephanopoules, George, 188
Stevenson, Adlai, 131
Stevens, Ted, 225
Stevens, Thaddeus, 427
Stewardship Theory, 297
Stimulus packages, 510
Stockton, Richard, 11
Stone, Lucy, 455
Strategic Arms Limitation Treaty (SALT II), 310
Strategic National Stockpile, 264
Straw polling, 62, 84
Strayhorn, Carole Keeton, 110
Street v. New York (1969), 382
Subgovernments, 285
Subpoena, 341
Subsidies, 495
Substantive Due Process, 373
Substantive problems, 490
Sugar Act, 10
Sumner, Charles, 476

Sunni, 588
Sunoco Logistics Partners, 276
Sunshine Act, 285
Superfund programs, 572
Super PACs, 149, 219
Supplemental Nutrition Assistance Program, 532
Supplemental Security Insurance (SSI), 537
Supremacy clause, 34, 369, 483
Supreme Court, 353
Surface Transportation Board, 46
Survey instruments,
   internet surveys, 85
   mail-in questionnaire, 85
   phone or personal interview, 84
   straw poll, 83
Suspended particulates, 555
Swayne, Charles, 351
Sweatt v. Painter (1950), 435
Switzerland, 591
Symbolic speech, 381
Systematic racism, 411

T

Taftian, 296
Taliban, 590
Talkwalker, 194
Tax accuracy, 498
Tax equity, 499
Taxpayer Advocate Service, 279
Tax rebate program, 502
Teamsters Union, 618
Tea Party,
   election of 2016, 111
Tea Party Movement, 49, 479, 111
TechFreedom, 209
Telecommunications Act (1966), 388
Telecommunications Act of 1996, 182
Temperance Movement, 455
Tennessee Valley Authority (TVA), 225, 275
Tenure of Office Act, 320
Terrorism, 368
Terry v. Ohio (1968), 403
Texas Rangers, 73
Texas v California (2020), 537
Texas v Johnson, 383
Texas v White (1869), 48
The Harbour Group, 209
Third parties, 110, 133
Thomas, Clarence, 46, 347, 432
Tildon, Samuel, 141
Tillerson, Rex, 276
Tinker v Des Moines School District (1969), 381
Tories, 10
Tort law, 337
Tory Party, 96
Toxic Substance Control Act (1976), 571

Toxic wastes, 569
Traditionalistic approach, 66
Trail of Tears, 421
Transitional immunity, 341
Trans Mountain Pipeline, 563
Trans-Pacific Partnership, 599
Treaties, 309
Treaty of Guadalupe Hidalgo, 444
Treaty of New Granada, 602
Treaty of Paris, 597
Treaty of Versailles, 310, 593, 609, 614
Triple Alliance, 613
Triple Entente, 613
Tripoli, 375
TriWest Healthcare Alliance Corp., 269
Truman Doctrine, 615
Truman, Harry S.,
    desegregate military branches, 482
    Polling results, 62
Trump, Donald,
    bureaucracy and, 286
    challenged Obama's citizenship, 293
    election of 2016, 50, 53
    emolument violation, 25
    environmental agencies, 474
    global warming and, 578
    impeachment, 320
    leadership team, 96
    lobbyists transition team, 220
    media coverage, 178
    personal wealth, 151
    popular vote of, 141-142
    soundbite, 153
    Twitter use of, 155-156, 173, 190
Trump-Ukraine Impeachment, 248
Trustee, 236
Tunisia, 619
Turing Pharmaceuticals, 152
Tuskegee Institute, 435
TVA v. Hill, 225
Tweed, Boss, 116
Two Treaties on Government (Locke), 368
Tyler, John, 27

U

Ueland, Eric, 220
Ukrainian aid, 286
Ultraconservatives, 100
Underground railroad, 427
Unemployment Insurance, 529
Unfunded mandate, 56
Unitary system, 36
United Arab Emirates, 209
United Farm Workers Union, 213, 443
United Nations, 593
United States Drug Enforcement Administration (DEA), 343

United States Forest Service, 550, 573
United States Marshals Service, 343
United States v Belmont (1937), 610
United States v Curtiss-Wright Export Corp.
    (1936), 311
United States v. Harriss (1954), 223
United States v Lopez (1995), 46
United States v. Nixon (1974), 315
United States v. O'Brien (1968), 382
United States v Pink (1942), 311
United States v Texas (2016), 451
United States v Wong Kim Ark (1898), 293
Urban Institute, 208
U.S. Treasury Inspector General for Tax
    Administration (TIGTA), 279
U.S. Treasury IRS Oversight Board, 279

V

Vacancies Reform Act, 301
Valeo, Buckley V., 152
Velasquez, Nydia, 452
Ventilators, 264
Veto, 308, 254
Vice President, 324
Vietnam War, 78
Village of Skokie v National Socialist Party
    (1978 389
Virginia Plan, 20, 233
Vocational Rehabilitation Act (1920), 462
Voter fraud, 158
Voter-identification laws, 159
Voting Rights Act (1965), 158, 435
Voucher programs, 376

W

Wald, Lillian, 528
Walker, Scott, 210
Walker v Texas Division of the Sons of Con-
    federate Veterans (2015), 380
Wallace, George, 141
Wallace v Jaffree (1985), 378
Walter Reed Army Medical Center, 247
War chest, 243
War clause, 303
War Labor Disputes Act, 313
War on Poverty, 51, 537, 215, 529, 493
War Powers Act (1973), 496
Warrantless search, 339
Warren, Earl, 100, 359, 394
Warsaw Pact, 592
Washington, George, 22, 105, 106
    religious tolerance, 375
Wasserman Schultz, Debbie, 120
Watergate, 144, 182, 235
Waxman-Markey legislation, 226
Ways and Means Committee, 248
Wealth of Nations, The (Smith), 64, 103

Welfare reform, 535
Welfare state,
    historical development of, 526
    programs of, 530
Wesberry v Sanders (1964), 240
Westboro Baptist Church, 381
West Virginia State Board of Education v
    Barnette (1943), 379
Wetlands conservation, 572
Wetlands Reserve Program, 573
Wet markets, 469
WhatsApp, 170
Wheeler, Earle, 611
Whig Party, 97
Whistle-Blower Protection Act (1989),
    285
White, Ben Chester, 410
White House, 189
White only primary, 429
Whitewater, 235
WikiLeaks, 156
Wilderness Bill (1964), 552
Wildlife Federation, 578
Will, George, 188
Wilson, Pete, 163
Wilson, Woodrow, 8, 99, 108, 609
Witness protection program, 340
Woman's Party, 455-456
Women's March Foundation, 224
Women's suffrage, 158
Woods, Robert A., 528
Working poor, 514
Works Progress Administration (WPA),
    528
World Health Organization (WHO), 312,
    469
World Prodigy, 569
World Trade Center, 610
World War II, 266
Wounded Knee, 422
Writ, 336
Writ of *certiorari*, 353
Writ of *habeas corpus*, 394
Wuhan, China, 469

Y

Yalta Agreement, 596
Yat-sen, Sun, 616
Yellow journalism, 181
Youngstown Sheet and Tube Company v
    Sawyer (1952), 313

Z

Zedong, Mao, 616
Zero-based budgeting, 500
Zimmerman, George, 390, 411